Oklahoma Music Guide
Biographies, Big Hits, and Annual Events

by

George O. Carney

&

Hugh W. Foley, Jr.

New Forums Press, Stillwater, Okla., U.S.A.   2003

NEW FORUMS PRESS INC.

Published in the United States of America
by New Forums Press, Inc.
1018 S. Lewis St.
Stillwater, OK 74074
www.newforums.com

Library of Congress Cataloging-in-Publication Data

Carney, George O.
  Oklahoma music guide : biographies, big hits, and annual events / by
George O. Carney & Hugh W. Foley, Jr.
      p. cm. -- (New Forums Oklahoma centennial series)
Includes bibliographical references (p.   ) and index.
  ISBN 1-58107-104-3 (alk. paper)
  1. Music--Oklahoma--History and criticism. 2. Popular
music--Oklahoma--History and criticism. I. Foley, Hugh W. II. Title.
III. Series.
  ML200.7.O5C41 2003
  780'.9766--dc22

                                        2003019831

This book may be ordered in bulk quantities at discount from New
Forums Press, Inc., P.O. Box 876, Stillwater, OK 74076 [Federal I.D. No.
73 1123239]. Printed in the United States of America.

International Standard Book Number: 1-58107-079-9

Cover design by Mac Crank.

To Janie – The one I love
from George

To Nokose - For all the time this has taken away from us
from Papa (HF)

Contents

Foreword

The background of the *Oklahoma Music Guide* emerges from a vision of its authors to assemble as much information possible about Oklahoma music and share it with the public. As teachers who include the material in our classes, we are both passionate about the rich musical diversity of the forty–sixth state and the often-overlooked contribution of its people to American and world music.

Oklahoma State Regents Professor George Carney, known to his colleagues around the world as the Dean of Music Geography, began researching and collating information on Oklahoma music in the 1970s. His writings on Oklahoma folk music, country, blues, jazz, Western swing, and the contributions of Oklahoma women to popular and country music are primary readings on the state's musical legacy.

Perhaps a little homesick, or just interested in materials pertaining to the state where I spent all but a few of my formative years, and to which my great-grandparents arrived in a covered wagon in 1899, I began collecting printed material and recordings related to Oklahoma music in the 1980s while attending New York University. My ultimate hope at that time was to someday write a book about the vast array of Oklahoma musicians who have made significant contributions to world music history.

Upon arrival at the graduate program in English at Oklahoma State University in 1993 with such a project in mind, my advisor, Peter C. Rollins, also a Regents Professor, told me to narrow my focus and to contact George Carney in the geography department. Upon doing so, I met the mentor who guided me through my dissertation work on the origins, development, and significance of jazz in Muskogee, Oklahoma, and also a man who would become my good friend, colleague, and neighbor. George continually inspired me by his work ethic of constantly writing, reading, and collecting information, as well as brainstorming new projects all the time.

While working with him as a graduate student, George suggested we should write a book together about Oklahoma music. I did not think a lot about it at the time as I was mired in the usual hoops through which every Ph.D. candidate must jump. After my graduation, we kept in contact via our mutual work for Friends of Oklahoma Music and the Oklahoma Music Hall of Fame. We also worked on a map of Oklahoma-born musicians, and I contributed a chapter on the contemporary status of American Indian music in Oklahoma to his cultural geography textbook, now in its fourth edition, *The Sounds of People and Places*.

In the spring of 2002, George found us a publisher for the *Oklahoma Music Guide*, New Forums Press, headed up by Doug Dollar who took an immediate interest in our project. Doug told us he would print the book as soon as it was ready, a concept that both surprised and energized us. The more we worked on the book, however, the more we found out we did not know about Oklahoma music, and the more the book grew.

Getting close to completion at the end of 2002, fate dealt us a blow for which we had not planned when George had a stroke that knocked him out of action for a few months, and from which he is still recovering at the time of this writing. While a totally unexpected event because of his good health, George had worked so hard on his part of the book that all I had to do was complete my entries, work on acquiring images and permission to use them, and update his entries with recent occurrences. While the production delay pushed back our completion

Guitarist Terry "Buffalo" Ware (left) discusses Oklahoma music with George Carney (right) backstage at a 2002 James Talley concert in Tulsa.

date, the project is better and more thorough for the extra time, even though the reason is still a source of some melancholy for both George and his family, as well as all of us who know and care for him. Go on we have though, and we have now completed the goal we have both pursued so diligently for the past three decades.

Any book that includes popular music information is out of date the day it hits the shelves. Almost daily, we learn about a new accomplishment by an Oklahoma musician, or a new group starting up. However, we feel this text has enough historical information in it to make it a handy reference, enjoyable return read, and a bright testimonial to the state's music history. Invariably, readers will disagree with some exclusions and inclusions, and we hope those readers will write to us with suggestions, revisions, and additions. We also encourage musicians or their representatives to send us press kits, music, or memorabilia for inclusion in future editions of the *Oklahoma Music Guide*. Contact us either through our website, www.oklahomamusicguide.com, or at New Forums Press, 1018 S. Lewis St., Stillwater, OK, 74074.

We do plan on the continued growth of the *Guide,* and readers can expect the updated centennial edition of the book in 2007 (commemorating Oklahoma's statehood in 1907) to have revisions of entries, additions of new ones, and updates on the lists in the back of the book where we have compiled #1 hits performed and written by musicians with strong Oklahoma ties, a database of Oklahoma place-based songs, a calendar of annual Oklahoma musical events, and an extensive "people's list" of as many people and groups we could find who have or have had musical connections to Oklahoma.

Whenever possible, we sent the biographical and historical entries in the *Oklahoma Music Guide* to the respective subjects of the mini-biographies, or experts on the topics. Occasionally, we received no responses to requests for corrections, nor for images to accompany the entries, but for the most part people felt honored to be included, and helped out however they could. We have tried to thank as many people as possible in the acknowledgements section, and credit all images to their sources of permission or access. We apologize for any omissions, misinterpretations, or misappropriations. Mistakes in the text are the responsibility of the writers, and every effort will be made to correct them the next time around.

More than anything, we hope this book will inspire Oklahomans to be proud of their state's diverse and historic musical and cultural heritage, demonstrate to the world how a place that is often thought to be remote and backward has had so much impact on popular and world culture, and encourage more students to explore the contributions of Oklahomans to the world's multi-colored musical canvas.

Hugh Foley
Stillwater, Oklahoma
September, 2003

Introduction

In her colorful history entitled *Oklahoma: Foot-Loose and Fancy-Free*, Angie Debo writes, "When it comes to music, Oklahomans are like mocking-birds—more interested in getting it out of their systems than in a finished performance."[1] Oklahoma-born musicians prove Debo both right and wrong. Right because Oklahomans sang, performed, and wrote music whenever and wherever they could. Wrong because Oklahomans, amateur and professional, have provided a multitude of finished performances to help form the musical mosaic of our state, nation, and world.

Oklahoma possesses a rich and variegated musical heritage and music has proven to be one of its most important cultural resources. The state has produced performers, composers, institutions, and songs that have significantly shaped the entire realm of American music. One need only to mention performers like Woody Guthrie, Patti Page, Reba McEntire, Vince Gill, and Garth Brooks as well as composers Albert E. Brumley, Jimmy Webb, "Sis" Cunningham, and Hoyt Axton, to demonstrate the profound role that Oklahoma has played in American music. The state has spawned influential institutions including ballrooms such as Cain's in Tulsa and Diamond in Oklahoma City, radio stations like KVOO in Tulsa and WKY in Oklahoma City, and nurtured bands such as the Texas Playboys and the Blue Devils. It has also produced some of the most respected producers in the music industry, including Lucky Moeller, Tim Dubois, and Scott Hendricks. Noted instrumentalists, such as Eldon Shamblin, Barney Kessel, Oscar Pettiford, and Jesse Ed Davis, were born in Oklahoma. Finally, songs such as "Oklahoma!," "Oklahoma Hills," "You're the Reason God Made Oklahoma," "Okie From Muskogee," and "Take Me Back to Tulsa" not only evoke images of Oklahoma, but are a significant part of the American music legacy.

With such a vast array of artists, instruments, historical periods, genres, and levels of success, selecting only two hundred entries for this book was not without its debates. While we have tried to cover some of the more significant American Indian music in the state, important tribal music traditions of the Pawnee, Comanche, Shawnee, Seneca-Cayuga, Euchee and other tribes will be covered in the second edition. Young local groups like Ester Drang, Starlight Mints, and Fanzine, as well as country singer Katrina Elam also appear to be on the brink of national recognition, but have not yet turned that corner. Rock groups who made a splash but have broken up, such as Zeabra, Still Breathing, The Pistol Arrows (now The Candles) and the Chainsaw Kittens, will be given their historical due the next time around, but we leaned in favor of active groups or living elders who have achieved a significant measure of national success. Obvious exceptions come into play when posthumous entries of important figures such as Gene Autry, Chet Baker, Lowell Fulson, The Wills Brothers, and Roger Miller are necessary to paint the major picture of Oklahoma's diverse and bountiful musical output. Musicians who have made substantial contributions as session or studio players will also be given more attention in the second edition of this book, due out as a centennial edition in 2007, in commemoration of Oklahoma's statehood in 1907. For examle, drummer Jim Keltner, a native Tulsan, is widely known as one of the world's best drummers and his list of session work spans from 1969 to the present day. A very short list of his staggering studio credits include recordings with John Lennon, George Harrison, Leon Russell, Barbara Streisand, Steve Miller, Arlo Guthrie, the Bee Gees, Bob Dylan, James Taylor, Dolly Parton, Leonard Cohen, Steely Dan, J.J. Cale, Charlie Watts, Neil Diamond, Earl Scruggs, and Roy Orbison, just an "nth" of his total work.

The question remains, however, why Oklahoma is such a fertile ground for the production of music artists, composers, and institutions when compared with other states?

One must first consider the settlement patterns of Oklahoma because they reflect the cultural diversity of the state. Charles N. Gould, an early twentieth century travel writer and geographer, emphasizes Oklahoma's multicultural traditions: "Oklahoma is a meeting place of many different peoples. Nowhere else is there such a mingling of types. Practically every state in the Union and every civilized nation on the globe is represented among the state's inhabitants."[2] Many different cultural groups brought music in their "cultural baggage" that resulted in the development of a myriad of vibrant musical subcultures. This vast array of people and their music includes the songs and dance music of the American Indian from the southeastern United States and western plains, northeastern woodlands, Great Lakes, and Ohio Valley; Anglo-Celtic ballads from the upland South, country blues from the Mississippi Delta, black and white spirituals from the lowland South, European immigrant music from Italy, Germany, and Czechoslovakia; polka music from the upper Midwest, and Mexican *mariachi* from the Rio Grande Valley. This musical mixture is further reflected in the *WPA Guide to 1930s Oklahoma*: ". . . each successive immigrant to the state brought the dust of another locale on his feet and the lilt of another people's song on his lips."[3]

This cultural confluence of different genres of American music allowed Oklahomans to experiment, innovate, and improvise—traits necessary in the formulation of various forms of American music. Within this Oklahoma cultural mosaic, music knew no color. Black, white, and red musicians borrowed freely from each other, exchanged repertoires and musical ideas, and adopted new techniques and styles. These cross-cultural experiences favored the development of music in Oklahoma. Noted folklorist Alan Lomax's statement that "the map sings" is a fitting description for the music of Oklahoma.[4]

A second factor is Oklahoma's population characteristics and economic history. Oklahoma is home for thirty-eight federally recognized North American Indian tribes, nations, bands, and tribal towns. This diversity of indigenous musical influences provides the state with roots and foundations of the twentieth century powwow world with home grown groups such as Bad Moon Rising, Thunderhorse, Rose Hill, Young Bird, Yellow Hammer, Southern Thunder, Poor Boys, and Grayhorse, as well as a cornucopia of tribal ceremonial musics. From the Kiowa Gourd Dance songs and Caddo Turkey Dance songs, to Ponca war dance songs, Cheyenne-Arapaho Sun Dance songs, Wichita Friendship Songs, and Pawnee hand game songs,

Thunderhorse singers, 2003

Oklahoma's indigenous music is deep and ancient. In future editions of this guide, we will continue to work with tribes to present the very best account of their musical traditions that is appropriate for public consumption. Furthering the unique story of the tribes in Oklahoma is the connection between the Southeastern tribes and the slaves of African descent who were removed with the tribes beginning in the 1820s. As the Cherokee, Choctaw, Muscogee (Creek), Seminole, and Chickasaw were forced to migrate to Indian Territory beginning in the 1820s, several tribal members brought slaves who endured the same "trail of tears" as the owners they accompanied. Thus, a plantation culture emerged in Oklahoma where the spirituals, work songs, and blues of the African-American developed much as they did in other parts of the rural South.

For example, three African-American spirituals are believed to have been first documented in the 1840s via "Uncle" Wallace and "Aunt" Minerva Willis, slaves on a large plantation near Doaksville in the Choctaw Nation. The authenticity and origin of spirituals are seldom credited to individuals, however, it is recorded that the Willis family sang "Swing Low, Sweet Chariot," "Steal Away to Jesus," and "I'm A Rollin'" in the cotton fields of Reverend Alexander Reid, superintendent of a Choctaw boarding school. Reid wrote the words and music and forwarded the transcriptions to the Jubilee Singers at Fisk University in Nashville. Subsequently, the group sang the numbers on a tour of the United States and Europe.[5]

Evolving from African-American work songs and spirituals, with additional musical developments due to the connection between slave-holding Southeastern tribes, the country blues established itself in Indian Territory and Oklahoma via the same plantation and sharecropping milieu that existed in the South. The first-known, commercially printed blues in music history, "Dallas Blues," was published by Oklahoma City's Hart Wand in 1912, three months before W.C. Handy's "Memphis Blues," which is generally thought of, however inaccurately, as the first published blues. Additionally, because of the large African-American population in the state, significant musicians such as ragtime pianist Scott Joplin are known to have played in Indian Territory, and the great Mississippi blues man Robert Johnson is documented as having played in the all-black town of Taft. Traveling territory bands such as the Oklahoma City Blue Devils brought the hot swinging music of the Southwest to black audiences in Oklahoma, a style that may have found its summit in Kansas City, but many of its primary musicians came from Oklahoma, such as Jimmy Rushing, Walter Page, and Don Byas, just a fraction of the jazz musicians from Oklahoma. Popular rhythm and blues eventually flourished in the personages of such noted Oklahoma-born artists as Jay McShann, Lowell Fulson, Robert Jeffrey, Roy Milton, and Joe Liggins, not to mention the "father of funk guitar," Jimmy Nolen, who made his fame as James Brown's guitarist. Eventually, many Tulsa musicians embraced the blues with tremendous success, to include Elvin Bishop, J.J. Cale, Leon Russell, and Junior Markham, as well as other Oklahomans such as Steve Gaines and Jesse Ed Davis.

Alongside the American Indian and African-American music traditions, the oldest Anglo-American music forms migrated into the state when tribal lands opened for settlement with the five land runs beginning in 1889. With this additional layer of music came the fiddle dance tunes, such as the reels, jigs, schottisches, and strathspeys,[6] while other Oklahomans worshipped to the melodies of Old Time and Southern Gospel music. Albert E. Brumley, born in rural LeFlore County, composed three of the best-known gospel songs in American music history: "I'll Fly Away," "Turn Your Radio On," and "Jesus Hold My Hand." Okemah's Woody Guthrie is internationally recognized as composer of more than 1,400 folk songs, including "This Land Is Your Land," which has become the national folk anthem. Woody Guthrie's children songs also represent a strong tradition of children's music in the American folk music tradi-

Mural in downtown Okemah, Oklahoma

tion, currently represented by several Oklahoma artists. Three Stillwater residents, Kel Pickens, and Carolyn Meyer, and Monty Harper have made significant contributions to the children's music field, while former Bristow resident, Tom Paxton, received a GRAMMY nomination in 2003 for his album *Your Shoes, My Shoes* (Red House, 2002).

Oklahoma's population is small town and rural-oriented, both in terms of composition and aesthetics. Moreover, the rural and small town residents have experienced considerable poverty throughout the state's history. Both the rural nature of the state and the poverty challenges confronted by its residents favored the development of various genres of American music, particularly country. Oklahoma's high percentage of tenant farmers and sharecroppers in the past forced many to seek music as an avenue for leaving poverty. Several musicians were children of Great Depression parents who had survived the hard times and dust—parents who longed for their children to realize a better life, such as Merle Haggard, Chet Baker, Bonnie Owens, and Jean Shepard. Therefore, they encouraged their sons and daughters to practice their musical talents and promoted them at any venue available within Oklahoma. A number of Oklahoma-based musicians helped turn music into a profession, including Otto Gray and the Oklahoma Cowboys, Gene Autry, Bob Wills, and Hank Thompson. Many of those young children in rural areas and small towns sought a more secure economic lifestyle. When they listened to the radio broadcasts of Otto Gray over KFRU (Bristow), Johnny Bond on WKY (Oklahoma City), and Gene Autry and Bob Wills on KVOO (Tulsa) during the first half of the twentieth century, it helped inspire them to become professional musicians. Virtually every sub-genre of country music can attribute substantial elements of its growth to Oklahomans or musicians commonly associated with Oklahoma, including singing cowboys (Gene Autry) and cowboy bands (Otto Gray), Western swing (Spade Cooley and Bob Wills), honky tonk (Willis Brothers), country pop (Roger Miller), progressive, or "outlaw" (Ray Wylie Hubbard), "Bakersfield Sound" (Tommy Collins and Bonnie Owens), "Nashville Sound" (Vince Gill, Reba McEntire, and Ronnie Dunn), and alternative country (Cross Canadian Ragweed and The Great Divide). As a result, the Anglo-American tradition of country music may be the most recognized musical export from the state, validated by Country Music Television's 2003 list of the "40 Greatest Men of Country Music," a list that includes ten names, or 25% of that group, that are strongly associated with Oklahoma. Four of the men were born in the state (Toby Keith, Garth Brooks, Vince Gill, and Roger Miller). Gene Autry moved to Oklahoma as an infant, Merle Haggard was born to Okie migrants who left during the Great Depression, and the other four came to Oklahoma for extended performance opportunities (Bob Wills, Buck Owens, Conway Twitty, and Ronnie Dunn). Native-born Oklahoma women who made the 2003 CMT "Top 40 Women of Country Music" included Reba McEntire and Wanda Jackson.

As a neutral gauge of Oklahoma's impact on country music, the 2003 CMT "100 Greatest Songs of Country Music" included nineteen songs with connections to the state. Included in the top ten are Merle Kilgore's "Ring of Fire" (#4), Garth Brooks' performance of "Friends in Low Places" (#6), "Galveston" (#8) written by Jimmy Webb, and "Behind Closed Doors" (#9) written by Kenny O'Dell. Other songs with Oklahoma connections making the list include Garth Brooks' "The Dance" (#14), Conway Twitty's "Hello Darlin'" (#17), Merle Haggard's "Okie From Muskogee" (#21), Reba McEntire's "Fancy" (#27), Roger Miller's "King of the Road" (#37), Vince Gills' "When I Call Your Name" (#44), Brooks and Dunn's "Boot Scootin' Boogie" (#48), Vince Gills' "Go Rest High On That Mountain" (#60), Patti Page's "Tennessee Waltz" (#63), Reba McEntire's "Is There Life Out There?" (#79), Toby Keith's "Should've Been a

Cowboy" (#82), Gene Autry's "Have I Told You Lately That I Love You" (#88), Bob Wills' "Faded Love" (#98), and Gene Autry's "Back in the Saddle Again" (#99). And that does not even include "Take Me Home Country Roads" (#18) by John Denver who spent his teen summers on his grandfather's wheat farm in Bessie, Oklahoma.

Therefore, almost one fifth of the 100 greatest songs of country music, according to CMT, have connections to Oklahoma.

A third factor in Oklahoma's historic music growth focuses on the availability of performance venues. As young Oklahoma musicians honed their musical skills at county fairs, churches, school assemblies, nightclubs, and music contests and festivals throughout the state, many were eventually given the opportunity to perform on the live music radio shows in the state, such as KLPR in Oklahoma City and KTUL in Tulsa. Moreover, public dance halls and ballrooms, virtually nonexistent before the 1920s, proliferated in great numbers to accommodate the new wave of dance styles, e.g., fox trot, sweeping the country. The Ritz and Trianon Ballrooms in Oklahoma City, Casa Loma and Louvre Ballrooms in Tulsa, and the Bluebird Ballroom in Shawnee provided important outlets for amateur musicians to perform for these dances. Finally, Oklahoma music festivals, such as Grant's Old Time and Bluegrass Festival in Hugo, the oldest festival of its type west of the Mississippi, showcased such budding artists as Vince Gill, Joe Diffie, and Jimmy Henley. As a result, these local experiences helped Oklahomans launch their professional careers in music and simultaneously inspired younger musicians in Oklahoma to seek music as a profession.

A fourth and final factor in the state's vast musical output is the numerous local musicians who were influential in the early development of many musical careers. Music teachers, such as Zelia N. Page Breaux, Evelyn Sheffield, and Cornelius Pittman at Douglas High School in Oklahoma City, Ashley Alexander, Sr. at Edison High School in Tulsa, George Bright at Sapulpa High School, and the Manual Training High School in Muskogee, provided sound formal training for aspiring jazz musicians. Local Oklahoma bandleaders, such as Ernie Fields, Eddie Christian, Merl Lindsay, and Hank Thompson, offered opportunities such as singing or playing instruments in bands and performing on live radio shows, and assisted hopeful musicians in securing recording contracts.

Music is one of the cultural traits that make Oklahoma a unique place, distinguishing the state from other places and giving special meaning to its residents—a feeling of pride in place. Psychologists call it "shared ego," while cultural geographers refer to it as "place consciousness." Place itself embodies meaning dependent upon the personal history that one brings to it. It is through these people-place interactions that one develops a deep psychological attachment with a specific place, such as Oklahoma. Recognition and appreciation of the contributions and innovations of Oklahomans in American music can help create a sense of local awareness and, translated correctly can become a source of state pride.

The Oklahoma Jazz Hall of Fame in Tulsa and the Oklahoma Music Hall of Fame in Muskogee are positive steps in this direction.

Oklahomans are awakening to a seemingly neglected segment of the state's cultural history and are now paying tribute to those who participated in its development. When the names of Jimmy Rushing, Lowell Fulson, Nokie

The Greeenwood Cultural Center in downtown Tulsa houses the Oklahoma Jazz Hall of Fame.

Edwards, Kay Starr, and Wanda Jackson are mentioned to Oklahomans, few are knowledgeable of the significance of these musicians to American music or even realize they are Oklahomans. In contrast, political, religious, and sports figures native to Oklahoma, such as Carl Albert, Oral Roberts, and Mickey Mantle, are easily recognized. Therefore, cultural historians, educators, and state arts organizations have a responsibility to teach the citizens of the state the multifaceted aspects of their culture including the role Oklahomans have played in world music.

Twentieth century popular music from Oklahoma is just another example of the state's significant contributions to the national music scene. Among the notable pop composers are Elk City's Jimmy Webb ("Up, Up and Away," "By the Time I Get to Phoenix," "Galveston," "Wichita Lineman," and "MacArthur Park") and Duncan's Hoyt Axton ("Joy to the World," "Greenback Dollar," "The Pusher," and "Boney Fingers"). Known musicians who have landed in the pop mainstream since the 1960s include a host of Tulsa Sound veterans, David Gates, Leon Russell, J.J. Cale, Elvin Bishop, and The GAP Band. Late twentieth century #1 pop successes include Color Me Badd and Hanson, and the critically lauded Flaming Lips won a GRAMMY award in 2003 for Best Instrumental Rock Song. Several groups and individuals with Oklahoma roots are starting to gain national stature in the pop *milieu*, such as Admiral Twin, Ultrafix, Toni Estes, Tony Romanello, and the All-American Rejects. Additionally, the roster of red dirt music artists from Oklahoma includes its elders, Bob Childers, Tom Skinner, and Jimmy LaFave; its workhorse ambassadors, The Red Dirt Rangers; and its young guns, Jason Boland, Stoney LaRue, and Amanda Cunningham. While one

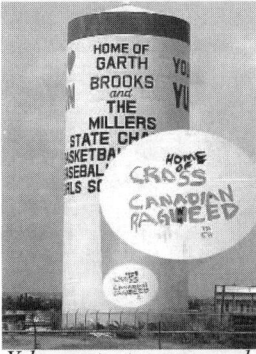

Yukon water tower as modified by Cross Canadian Ragweed fans in 2002

red dirt band, The Great Divide, rode the major label train and decided to get off, Cross Canadian Ragweed had its major label ticket punched in 2001 and has since enjoyed national video and radio airplay, international distribution, and a rabid following regionally and nationally.

Musicologists agree that music is one of the most important indicators of the cultural *milieu* of an area. With the culture of Oklahoma facing increased homogeneity, music remains an enduring characteristic of its changing lifestyle. Historically, Oklahomans have always reacted against cultural conformity. Perhaps the rebellious attitude of a youthful state encourages this demeanor; the unique mixture of the people who settled here may also explain such an ethos. Music is a direct form of expression. One can examine in depth the role of Oklahomans in music—their way of life, value systems, aspirations, and misery. Thus, music is a key to understanding the cultural history of the state. As H. Wayne and Anne Hodges Morgan write in the state's bicentennial history:

"A sense of the past delineates the shape of things to come, since all change is rooted in history. It also reveals tasks that must be fulfilled to secure the state's proper future. A general desire for cultural activities is the state's greatest present lack and future need. . . .Oklahoma must emphasize her native cultural qualities and encourage outlets for cultural ambition designed from national models."[7]

Oklahoma's economy is no longer provincial; her culture cannot remain so. Oklahoma's performers, composers, music institutions, and songs are a significant part of the rich and diversified musical heritage of the state, but, more importantly, this state-based perspective provides us with a fuller and deeper appreciation of the American

The Cain's Ballroom in Tulsa is on the National Register of Historic Places

music landscape. As the scholarship associated with American music continues to increase, so does the need for more in-depth research into regional studies of music. When completed, fuller documentation of music at the state level will become a vital part of American music history.[8] This book is a starting point for that documentation with hopes that students, teachers, fans, and scholars will use it to continue appreciating, researching, and writing about the great array of Oklahoma music and its contributions to world culture.

George Carney and Hugh Foley
September, 2003
Stillwater, Oklahoma

Built around 1916, the historic Frisco Depot in Muskogee is the new home of The Oklahoma Music Hall of Fame. Renovation of the building began in September, 2003.

Endnotes

1. Angie Debo. 1949. *Oklahoma: Foot-Loose and Fancy-Free* (Norman: University of Oklahoma Press), 212.

2. Charles N. Gould. *Travels Through Oklahoma* (Oklahoma City: Harlow Publishing Company, 1928), 157. See also Michael Frank Doran, "The Origins of Culture Areas in Oklahoma, 1893-1900," Unpublished Ph.D. dissertation, Department of Geography, University of Oregon, 1974, and Michael Roark, "Searching for the Hearth: Culture Areas of Oklahoma," *The Chronicles of Oklahoma* 70 (Winter 1992-93), 416-31.

3. Writers' Program of the Works Progress Administration. 1986. *The WPA Guide to 1930s Oklahoma.* (Lawrence: University Press of Kansas, rev. ed.), 104.

4. Alan Lomax. 1960. *The Folks Songs of North America* (Garden City, NY: Doubleday), xv.

5. *The WPA Guide to 1930s Oklahoma,* 105-06.

6. James Hubert Renner. 1974. "Geographic Implications of the Fiddling Tradition in Oklahoma," Unpublished Master's thesis, Department of Geography, Oklahoma State University.

7. H. Wayne Morgan and Anne Hodges Morgan. 1977. *Oklahoma: A Bicentennial History* (New York: W. W. Norton), 176.

8. Along these lines, Burton W. Peretti in his review essay "The Jazz Studies Renaissance" has called for more regional studies of jazz. See Burton W. Peretti. "The Jazz Studies Renaissance," *American Studies* 34 (1993), 139-49.

Acknowledgements

The authors wish to thank the following people and organizations for their gracious assistance in the completion of this text:

Michael Agostino for Sam Harris; Jack Anquoe, Jr. and Jim Anquoe for help understanding Kiowa musical traditions; Anthony Arkeketa and Louis Headman for insight into Ponca musical traditions; Larry Austin; Chet Baker's estate; Elvin Bishop; Kathrean and Clarence Cagle; George Carney's Fall 2002 OSU Geography of Music (GEO 4223) students: Shane Brown, Tracy Strawmyer, Monica Lee Hooten, and Zhila Shariat, who contributed to the place-based songs list and the master list of additional musicians and groups in the back of this book.

Joe Cinocca for help with the current Tulsa music scene; Thomas Conner of the *Tulsa World*; George Coser for leads on Leo Feathers and Jesse Ed Davis; Pete and Joanna Coser for their friendship and guidance; Mac Crank for his expert leadership in laying out this book; the people of the Department of Communications and Fine Arts at Rogers State University for their friendship, collegiality, and the administrative support of Shelly Borgstrom; Sandi Davis and Gene Triplett at *The Daily Oklahoman* for covering Oklahoma City's music scene; Doug Dollar at New Forums Press for the confidence in this project when other presses turned it down because it was too "local" in its appeal; Nola and Howard Downs for collecting research materials; Jack Dunham for sharing his images and knowledge of the Tulsa Sound; Judy and Nokie Edwards; Kenneth Edwards for help with Stoney Edwards' entry; Billy Estes for Toni Estes;

Hugh's Rogers State University music appreciation students for alerting us to several important educators, young musicians, and family members who have played and continue to play a role in Oklahoma's musical history; Sean Foley for help with Zeabra; Friends of Oklahoma Music and the Oklahoma Music Hall of Fame; Jennifer Garrison of www.theminor.com; Matt Gleason of the *Tulsa World* for picking up the torch in T-Town; Chris Greenert for repeated searches of his databases for Hugh; Curtis Hamilton-Youngbird and June and Donnie Hamilton for sorting out Young Bird's entry, help with Oklahoma Music Hall of Fame in 2002, and the star blanket; Bena Harper for her help with information about Oklahoma's children's music scene; Rodger Harris and Mary Jane Warde of the Oklahoma Historical Society; Hellfire Management for The Flaming Lips; Hot Schatz Public Relations for Patti Page.

Hvtce Cvpv Este Cate Mekosvpkv Cuko for Hugh's spiritual sustenance and continued musical inspiration; Jimmy Karstein; Sean Kelly from 1600 AM - KUSH in Cushing; Barney and Phyllis Kessel; Ramona and Mollie King; Alan Lambert and the staff of KRSC-FM in Claremore; Ruth (Hedges) Ipsen for Michael Hedges; the Kiowa Gourd Clan in Carnegie for their permissions and hospitality; Guy Logsdon for sharing his vast expertise on Western swing and Woody Guthrie, and reading this manuscript for the Oklahoma Centennial Commission; Gary Lucas for help with members of Captain Beefheart's Magic

Band who are from Oklahoma; Leigh Lust for help with the Willis Brothers entry; Mary Ann and Jay McShann; Doug Martin and Blaine Greteman of the Delicious Militia; Reed Mathis of Jacob Fred Jazz Odyssey; Debi Miley for help on the Tulsa Sound; Mary Miller for Roger Miller; DC and Selby Minner; Dr. Cornel Pewewardy; Mike Pierce for help with Bob Dunn and sorting out the McEntire legacy.

Mekko David Proctor and Heles Hayv Sam Proctor of the Tullahassee (Wvkokye) Ceremonial Grounds of the Muscogee (Creek) Nation for their friendship, spiritual insight and nourishment, and explanations of Muscogee ceremonial traditions; Mike Rabon for the help with the Five Americans entry; Ron Raper of the Muscogee (Creek) Nation; Teresa Gaines Rapp for help with the Steve and Cassie Gaines entry; Charlene and Steve Ripley; Tyson Ritter of the All-American Rejects; Rogers State University's library staff for the interlibrary loans, special acquisitions and all-around helpfulness and professionalism; John Rosenfelder of Island Records for help with Universal's artist roster; Holly Rosser-Miller at the Oklahoma Music Hall of Fame for scanning images, answering questions, and just generally being very efficient and helpful; John Russell of Admiral Twin; Chad "Charlie 7" Sevigny for contributing his database of current Oklahoma music; Don Tolle for his friendship, courtesy, and sharing his vast knowledge of Western swing; Evan Tonsing for insight into Stillwater's local music scene in the 1970s and '80s; Hugh Tudor-Foley for the jazz books in his garage in Rye Brook; Andrew Vasquez for his thoughtful encouragement;

Mike Ward for his continued musical advice and expertise; Nan Warshaw of Bloodshot Records; Victor Wildcat for sharing his knowledge of Cherokee and Muscogee life, language, and music; Claude and Blanche Williams; Stratford Williams for helping Hugh understand why not everyone understands or embraces American Indian music, and providing continued motivation for the pursuit of its acceptance as a significant world music contribution; Rosetta Wills for offering helpful corrections and additions to the Wills Brothers entry; John Wilson for his knowledge of Scott Joplin's time in Indian Territory; Gerald Wofford of *Muscogee (Creek) Nation News* for interviewing John Riley; John Wooley at *The Tulsa World* for his long and valuable chronicle of articles on Oklahoma music and musicians – especially relating to Western swing, red dirt music, and the Tulsa Sound.

Finally, both George and Hugh want to thank the many additional friends, colleagues, and family members who have encouraged and jovially endured our passion for Oklahoma's rich music heritage and contemporary status.

Key to Abbreviations in The Guide

ACM (Academy of Country Music)

A & R (artist and repertoire, referring to record company talent scouts)

ASCAP (American Society of Composers, Authors, and Publishers)

BBC (British Broadcasting Corporation)

BMI (Broadcast Music Incorporated)

BPA (Bonneville Power Administration)

CCM (Contemporary Christian Music)

CD (compact disc)

CMA (Country Music Association)

CMT (Country Music Television)

DJ (disc jockey)

DVD (Digital Video Disc)

EP (extended play release, usually 3 to 6 tracks)

GC (indicates entries written by George Carney)

GC/HF (indicates entries written by George Carney and Hugh Foley)

GRAMMY (National Academy of Recording Arts and Sciences Award)

HBO (Home Box Office)

HF (indicates entries written by Hugh Foley)

LP (long play album, usually considered vinyl)

Mp3 (digital audio file)

MTV (Music Television)

NAMMY (Native American Music Award)

NEO A & M (Northeastern Oklahoma A & M at Miami)

NEOSU (Northeastern Oklahoma State University at Tahlequah)

NPR (National Public Radio)

OSU (Oklahoma State University at Stillwater)

OU (University of Oklahoma at Norman)

PBS (Public Broadcasting System)

PSA (public service announcement)

R & B (rhythm and blues)

TNN (The Nashville Network)

TU (Tulsa University)

UCO (University of Central Oklahoma at Edmond)

VFW (Veterans of Foreign Wars)

VH1 (cable music network)

WPA (Works Progress Administration)

bold words are cross-references to other entries in the *Guide*

Oklahoma Music Guide

Biographies

200 Noteworthy Musicians, Groups, Tribes, and Musical Movements That Have Made Significant Contributions to Oklahoma's Musical Heritage

A

1. Admiral Twin
2. All-American Rejects
3. Tommy Allsup
4. Buddy Anderson
5. Keith Anderson
6. Tuck Andress
7. Larry Austin
8. Gene Autry
9. Hoyt Axton
10. Mae Boren Axton

B

11. Chet Baker
12. Mark Baker
13. Louis Ballard
14. Glenn Barber
15. Bobby Barnett
16. Bob Beckham
17. Molly Bee
18. Carl Belew
19. Byron Berline
20. Elvin Bishop
21. Ralph Blane
22. Noel Boggs
23. Bob Bogle
24. Jason Boland and the Stragglers
25. Johnny Bond
26. Charles Brackeen
27. Mike Brewer
28. Garth Brooks
29. Albert Brumley, Sr.
30. Anita Bryant
31. Don Byas

C

32. Caddo
33. J.J. Cale
34. Hank Card
35. Henson Cargill
36. Jeff Carson

37. Caroline's Spine
38. Kristin Chenoweth
39. Don Cherry
40. Cherokee
41. Charlie Christian
42. Roy Clark
43. Al Clauser
44. Kellie Coffey
45. Collins Kids
46. Tommy Collins
47. Color Me Badd
48. Spade Cooley
49. Cross Canadian Ragweed
50. Alvin Crow
51. Agnes "Sis" Cunningham

D

52. Gail Davies
53. Jesse Ed Davis
54. Yvonne DeVaney
55. Joe Diffie
56. Dinning Sisters
57. Mark Dinning
58. Big Al Downing
59. Jack Dunham
60. Bob Dunn
61. Ronnie Dunn

E

62. Nokie Edwards
63. Stoney Edwards
64. Tyler England
65. Toni Estes

F

66. Shug Fisher
67. Five Americans
68. Flaming Lips
69. Flash Terry
70. Dallas Frazier
71. Lowell Fulson

G

72. Steve and Cassie Gaines
73. GAP Band
74. Garcia, Benny, Sr.
75. David Gates
76. Vince Gill
77. Bill Grant
78. George Grantham
79. Otto Gray
80. Wardell Gray
81. Great Divide
82. Jack Guthrie
83. Woody Guthrie

H

84. Merle Haggard
85. David Halley
86. Hanson
87. Gus Hardin
88. Sam Harris
89. Roy Harris
90. Wade Hayes
91. Lee Hazlewood
92. Michael Hedges
93. Sam Hinton
94. Becky Hobbs
95. Doyle Holly
96. Ray Wylie Hubbard
97. Billy Hughes

J

98. Wanda Jackson
99. Jacob Fred Jazz Odyssey
100. William Johns
101. Claude Jones

K

102. Toby Keith
103. Wayne Kemp

104. Barney Kessel
105. Merle Kilgore
106. Kiowa
107. Gail Kubik

L

108. Jimmy LaFave
109. Don Lamond
110. Ed Lewis
111. Jimmy and Joe Liggins
112. Susie Luchsinger

M

113. Moon Martin
114. Frank and Johnny Marvin
115. Tony Matthews
116. Cecil McBee
117. Laura Lee McBride
118. Mel McDaniel
119. Reba McEntire
120. Howard McGhee
121. Barry McGuire
122. Jay McShann
123. Chris Merritt
124. Eddie Miller
125. Roger Miller
126. Roy Milton
127. DC Minner
128. Leona Mitchell
129. Lucky Moeller
130. Ralph Mooney
131. Marilyn Moore
132. Sonny Murray
133. Muscogee (Creek)

N

134. "Doc" Tate Nevaquaya
135. Jimmy Nolen
136. Norma Jean
137. Gary P. Nunn

O

138. Kenny O'Dell
139. Oklahoma City Blue Devils
140. Tommy Overstreet
141. Bonnie Owens

P

142. Patti Page
143. Andy Parker
144. Billy Parker
145. Sandi Patty
146. Tom Paxton
147. Oscar Pettiford
148. Cornel Pewewardy
149. Mary Kay Place
150. Ponca

R

151. Red Dirt Music
152. Red Dirt Rangers
153. Dick Reinhart
154. Restless Heart
155. Jimmie Revard
156. Ricochet
157. Steve Ripley
158. Sam Rivers
159. Tony Romanello
160. Joe Don Rooney
161. Marshall Royal
162. Mark Rubin
163. Jimmy Rushing
164. Tim Rushlow
165. Leon Russell
166. Tom Russell

S

167. Lynn Seaton
168. Ronnie Sessions
169. Mike Settle
170. Blake Shelton

171. Jean Shepard
172. John Simmons
173. Cal Smith
174. Tim Spencer
175. Terry Stafford
176. Kay Starr

T

177. James Talley
178. B.J. Thomas
179. Hank Thompson
180. Floyd Tillman
181. Wayman Tisdale
182. Tulsa Sound
183. Dwight Twilley

V

184. Andrew Vasquez

W

185. Jimmy Wakely
186. Wayne Walker
187. Billy Wallace
188. Lily Fern Weatherford
189. Jimmy Webb
190. Kevin Welch
191. Bryan White
192. Wiley and Gene
193. Lee Wiley
194. Claude "Fiddler" Williams
195. Willis Brothers
196. Kelly Willis
197. Wills Brothers
198. Joe Lee Wilson
199. Sheb Wooley

Y

200. Young Bird

Admiral Twin
(Formed 1990, Tulsa, OK)

Self-proclaimed influences ranging from The Cars, Elvis Costello, The Police, Led Zeppelin, and The Beatles, with some classical music and even a bit of honky-tonk thrown in, Admiral Twin is known for up-tempo power pop, the occasional contextually ironic number with dark lyrics and vibrant music, and kooky live shows. The group has brought in marching bands and magicians for their shows, and recruited legendary Tulsa TV kiddie show host Uncle Zeb to play harmonica with them on stage. Named after a landmark Tulsa drive-in theater, Admiral Twin originally formed around guitarist and vocalist John Russell (b. May 12, 1968, Tulsa, OK), bassist and vocalist Mark Carr (b. June 23, 1968, Sapulpa, OK), drummer and vocalist Jarrod Gollihare (b. October 27, 1966, San Jose, CA), and guitarist, keyboardist, and vocalist Brad Becker (b. February 17, 1969, West Palm Beach, FL).

Not every group gets their first national touring opportunity with a band that has a number-one hit, but it happened to Admiral Twin when **Hanson** asked them to open for the Tulsa pop group's 1998 national tour in the wake of the previous year's smash single, "MMMBop." Admiral Twin had only just recorded their first independent CD, *Unlucky*, in their home studio in Tulsa, when Hanson asked the group to hit the road with them in the summer of 1998. The choice was no surprise to Tulsa local music fans due to Admiral Twin's exuberant live shows that had already created a loyal and fervent following. Not only did the Hanson tour take the band from playing in Tulsa clubs to playing in front of 20,000 people on stages across the U.S. and Canada, Admiral Twin also played performed for a myriad of music industry executives and critics who came out to see what all the Hanson buzz was about. This landed the *Unlucky* CD in some influential ears and the group signed a deal with Mojo Records on Halloween of 1998. Subsequently, Admiral Twin their first release on Mojo, *Mock Heroic*

(2000), which collected all of the group's individual tastes and collective abilities for songs that run the gamut from the high-energy pop celebrated in their live shows, to the occasional twangy tune with melancholy lyrics. *Mock Heroic* was recorded in the historic Church Studio in Tulsa, now operated by **Steve Ripley** of Tractors fame.

Admiral Twin had one song featured in the Warner Brothers film, *The In Crowd* (2000), and another song featured in the Universal television program, *Blind Date*. The group released a four-song Christmas EP in 2001, and a collection of previously recorded material in 2002, *Odds and Ends: Demos and Rarities 1996-2000*. *Odds and Ends* is made up of songs that did not make previous records, sometimes against their own wishes, demos of songs that did make it out, or songs that never made any album at all. In June of 2002, the band began recording their third album of original material, and continued playing shows in the Midwest and Tulsa, with old friend Isaac Hanson sitting in with them at one show in Tulsa where Isaac debuted two new Hanson songs. By August 2002, original guitarist and vocalist Brad Becker decided to take a job opportunity in San Francisco at a computer software company, and left the group. Playing as a trio was not unknown to Carr, Russell, and Gollihare, however, as they had already played around Tulsa as a cover band without Becker called the Unlucky Ones in the late 1990s.

In 2002, The Becker-less Admiral Twin soldiered on as a trio, recording some backup vocals for Steve Ripley's solo album, *Ripley*, and the group began work on their next album for New Pop Revival Records in their own studio. One of the album's songs includes local musicians like the Hanson Brothers and Brian Parton, as well as fans, friends, and the barroom public on backing vocals that were recorded at Barkley's Uptown Dive in Tulsa's Brookside district. The group released *Creatures of Bread and Wine* in May, 2003, garnering the group a fifth *Tulsa World Spot* magazine's nomination for the year's Best Local Pop Artist (their fifth time being nominated, having won the award in 2000, 2001, and 2002), as well receiving a nod for Best Local Album. The group continues playing locally in Tulsa and regionally throughout the Midwest, with national tour plans in the works for the fall and winter of 2003. (HF)
www.admiraltwin.com

All-American Rejects
(Formed 1999 in Stillwater, OK)

THE ALL-
AMERICAN
REJECTS

Led by Stillwater natives Nick Wheeler (b. April 24, 1984) on guitars and vocals, and Tyson Ritter (b. March 20, 1982), the All-American Rejects have parlayed their catchy, power pop sound, reminiscent of groups such as Blink 182, The Ramones, and MxPx, into a national recording contract with Doghouse Records that led to a major label deal with Dreamworks. Released in the fall of 2002, the group's first album reached the top 50 of *Billboard*'s album charts in 2003, the video ran constantly on MTV during the first half of 2003, and the group performed coast to coast through May of 2003, ending their spring tour with a performance in the Cain's Ballroom's parking lot in Tulsa and show at Bricktown in Oklahoma City. During the summer of 2003, the group toured the United Kingdom and the United States on the Warped Tour, a noted traveling music and information extravaganza aimed at 14 to 24-year-olds, the primary audience for the band at this stage of their young career.

Nick started playing guitar at age seven, played percussion in the Stillwater school band program, and made extra money by teaching guitar lessons at Daddy-O's music store in Stillwater. Tyson played violin four years in the school orchestra, which led him to playing the bass with Nick in their first group whose name shall remain out of print here. Nick tried a semester at Oklahoma State University, which did not work out, and the two formed the All- American Rejects in 1999. After playing a local Stillwater music festival, they began playing multi-band shows such as the Garden O' Punk in Stillwater, and Playhouse Punk Party in Tulsa, as well as gigs at bars in Stillwater, Tulsa, and Norman, and a Rescue Dog Benefit Show on the OSU campus.

In the spring of 2001, the duo recorded and released an independent CD called *Same Girl, New Songs* which they sold as "five songs for five bucks." This CD and their growing fan base induced Toledo, Ohio-based Doghouse Records to offer them a contract, through which the Rejects recorded their first "proper" album in New York at Mission Sound and Headgear Studio in December, 2001. Produced by Tim O'Heir, who has also worked with Superdrag and Sebadoh, the self-titled release was delayed throughout 2002 by tremendous interest from major labels offering various types of distribution and recording deals for the young band. After signing with Dreamworks, The Rejects made a video for the album's first single, "Swing, Swing," and major advertising pushes at the commercial and music industry level were in the works throughout the fall of 2002. While the duo recorded all instruments and vocals on the album, they enlisted fel-

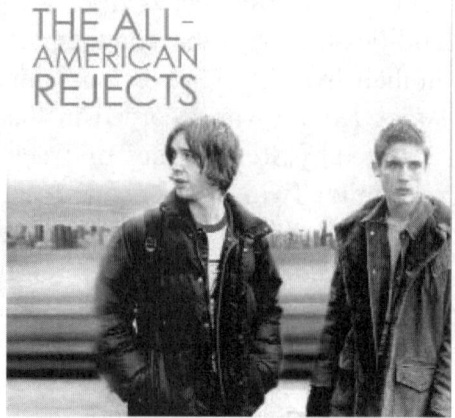

low Oklahomans Mike Kennerty (guitar) and Chris Gaylor (drums) for the touring version of the Rejects. Both Kennerty and Gaylor had been playing with the Edmond-based Euclid Crash, a group the Rejects met while playing local gigs in Stillwater and Oklahoma City.

In January of 2003, the single, "Swing, Swing" received critical acclaim through *Rolling Stone*'s "Hot List," was picked by the magazine's editors as a favorite single, and landed in the Top 10 of *Billboard*'s Modern Rock chart, an indicator of national commercial airplay. Coinciding with the airplay, the album was a top independent national seller in early 2003, eventually raising it to #25 on Billboard's Top 200 Albums in the country as of March, 2003. Their popularity led to performances on *Late Late with Craig Kilborn* and *The Tonight Show with Jay Leno*. Furthering their connection to teen pop culture, "Swing, Swing" was used as the theme song for EA Sports' new baseball simulation game, *MVP Baseball 2003*. Firmly in the groundswell of commercial success and rabid fan interest, through August, 2003 the group had been featured on the cover of *Alternative Press*, and enjoyed press coverage from such teen magazines as *Seventeen*, *YM* (where Tyson was chosen as one of the 20 hottest guys), *Teen People*, *Tiger Beat*, and *Bop*, as well as several feature articles in daily newspapers from New York to Seattle. In September 2003, the group received an MTV Video Music Award nomination for Best New Artist in a Video, but lost out to rapper 50 Cent, and released *Live from Oklahoma . . . The Too Bad for Hell DVD*, a live concert recorded at Tulsa's Brady Theater in May, 2003.

The All-American Rejects play catchy power punk in the vein of the bands mentioned earlier, equally at home in all-ages emo clubs and on modern rock stages. Their youthful angst subject matter provides a logical palate for this brand of very commercial music that is connecting with thousands of teenagers who are experiencing the same thing as the Rejects. As with all groups driven by the teen dollar, however, the proof in their longevity will be based in how well The Rejects and their audience mature together. By early 2003 the young musicians were quoted as saying they would be staying in Oklahoma, most likely to take advantage of being equidistant between the two coasts and within a day's drive or bus ride to most major American Midwest cities, a fact that's been exploited by the state's musicians since the heyday of Oklahoma jazz and Western swing. Like the **Flaming Lips** before them, the All-American Rejects have found that by keeping costs down while living in Oklahoma, a group can pursue independent artistic visions that might be less plausible in bigger cities where paying the rent often influences how much time musicians can spend pursuing their goals. (HF)
www.theall-americanrejects.com

Allsup, Tommy
(b. November 24, 1931)

Born in Owasso, but raised in Claremore, only 16 miles from Tulsa, Tommy Allsup is best known as one of the original Buddy Holly's Crickets, veteran producer of such groups as **Bob Wills** and the Texas Playboys, Asleep at the Wheel, **Hank Thompson**, and Willie Nelson, Grammy Award winner, and instrumentalist on more than 6,500 recordings. He is also recognized as a guitarist, arranger, and percussionist. As a teenager, he would hitchhike from Claremore to Tulsa, where he listened to the noon broadcasts of Bob Wills and the Texas Playboys over radio station KVOO. He began his musical career in Claremore, where he performed with the Oklahoma Swingbillies in 1949, the same year he graduated from Claremore High School. A year later, he played with Art Davis in Miami, Oklahoma, and then moved to Wichita, Kansas, where he performed at the Cowboy Inn with singer and fiddle player Jimmy Hall.

Tommy returned to Tulsa in the early 1950s, and joined **Johnnie Lee Wills'** band, which performed at Cain's Ballroom and over KVOO. Later in the 1950s, he formed his own band, The Southernaires, which played at the Southern Club in Lawton, Oklahoma. On a recording trip to Norman Petty's studio in Clovis, New Mexico, he met Buddy Holly, who asked him to play lead guitar with The Crickets. From 1958 until the ill-fated plane crash in January of 1959 that killed Holly, the Big Bopper, and Ritchie Valens, Tommy was a member of Holly's band. Tommy flipped a coin with Valens for a seat on the Beechcraft Bonanza that resulted in "the day that rock and roll died," while Tommy rode the bus. Tommy's guitar work is heard on the Holly recordings of "Wishing," "It's So Easy," "Love's Made a Fool of You," "Lonesome Tears," and "Come Back Baby."

After Holly's death in 1959, Allsup moved to California where he became the artist and repertoire director for Liberty Records' country music division. In this capacity, he produced Bob Wills and the Texas Playboys from 1960, when he coordinated Wills' *Bob Wills Sings and Plays* album, until 1973, when the *For the Last Time* album was recorded in Dallas on December 2-3. As organizer of the session, Tommy assembled several of the original Texas Playboys, including Leon McAuliffe, Eldon Shamblin, Smokey Dacus, and Al Stricklin. While at Liberty, Tommy produced such well-known artists as Tex Williams, Willie Nelson, and Billy Mize. In 1962 Tommy recorded his first album, *Twistin' the Country Classics*, for Liberty, which was followed in 1968 with *The Buddy Holly Songbook* recorded in the legendary Norman Petty Clovis, New Mexico, studios and released on the Reprise label.

In 1968 Allsup headed for Nashville to assume management of Metromedia Records. Four years later, he met Ray Benson, manager of Asleep at the Wheel, and produced the group's first album for the United Artists label, and continued that relationship when the band recorded four more albums for Capitol Records.

Tommy spent more than thirty years as one of Nashville's top session men, playing guitar, bass guitar, and percussion, and logging more than 10,000 sessions with such notables as Johnny Cash, The Everly Brothers, Janie Fricke, Billy "Crash" Craddock, John Anderson, Jerry Lee Lewis, **Reba McEntire**, Melba Montgomery, Johnny Paycheck, Marty Robbins, Kenny Rogers, and Ernest Tubb.

Following Wills' death in 1973, McAuliffe chose several of the ex-Playboys to tour under the name Bob Wills' Original Texas Playboys, which was sanctioned by the Wills family. After the death of Al Stricklin, the McAuliffe-led group dissolved in about 1990, but Tommy and Leon Rausch, former vocalist with Wills, assumed the Playboys mantle, and have continued to perform as the Original Texas Playboys, again blessed by the Wills family. Former Playboys who have off and on played with the reconstituted group include Tommy Perkins (drums), Curly Lewis (fiddle), Jimmy Young (fiddle), Curly Hollingsworth (piano), and Bobby Boatright (fiddle). The group performed a tribute to the Wills Family at the 2001 induction of the **Wills Family** (Bob, Johnnie Lee, Luke, and Billy Jack) into the Oklahoma Music Hall of Fame in Muskogee, Oklahoma.

Along with Leon Rausch, Allsup has recorded several tribute albums to the late Bob Wills, including *A 50 Song Tribute to the Music of Bob Wills* (1997) on the Sims label, and *Bob Wills Texas Playboys Band Featuring Leon Rausch and Tommy Allsup*, a live recording at Southern Junction in Rockwall, Texas, released by Southland Records in 2000. Tommy has also released two Southland recordings, *True Love Ways* and *Tommy Allsup's Gospel Guitar*.

The Allsup-Rausch Original Texas Playboys performed for the induction of the Wills Family into the Oklahoma Music Hall of Fame in 2001, as well as the Bob Wills Birthday Tribute at Cain's Ballroom in Tulsa in 2002, and continue an extensive tour schedule with appearances in Oklahoma and Texas at such venues as **Byron Berline**'s Double Stop Fiddle Shop in Guthrie. Tommy currently resides in Snyder, Texas. (GC)
www.southlandrecords.com/allsuptommy.htm

Anderson, Bernard Hartwell "Step-Buddy"
(b. October 14, 1919 – d. late 1990s)

A native of Oklahoma City, Anderson was born into a musical family. His older brother played alto sax and was a jazz record fan. Anderson was introduced to various brass instruments, especially the bugle, while a member of the Boy Scouts. He began taking violin lessons at the age of seven. Zelia N. Page Breaux, noted Oklahoma City music teacher, was an inspiration for Anderson. Anderson was a member of the Douglass High School marching and jazz bands under the leadership of Ms. Breaux. One of Anderson's first professional opportunities was with the Ted Armstrong band in Clinton, Oklahoma, in 1934. While a student at Xavier University in New Orleans in the late 1930s, he was a member of the university jazz band.

In 1939, Anderson returned to Oklahoma City and joined the Leslie Sheffield band that included **Charlie Christian** and Hank Bridges. The next year, he left Oklahoma for the Kansas City jazz scene where he became trumpeter for the **Jay McShann** band. McShann's band had become nationally known by 1942 because it included several widely known instrumentalists, such as Charlie Parker on alto saxophone. According to Ross Russell, "Anderson was the most advanced musician in the band after Parker and a perfect brass countervoice for Charlie's alto improvisations." Anderson remained with McShann until the band was decimated by the World War II draft. He then moved from one band to another before joining the Billy Eckstine Orchestra in 1944. Shortly thereafter, Anderson contacted tuberculosis and returned to Oklahoma City for medical assistance and to be among family. After recovery from the disease, he was medically advised to abandon the trumpet and switched to piano for a short time.

By 1992, Buddy, then in his seventies, was frequently seen playing his trumpet on street corners in Westport, the historic district in Kansas City, where young people visited to hear him. The handouts he received helped pay his rent. A 1992 article in the *Kansas City Star* by Art Brisbane retold Buddy's jazz legacy, which spawned an organization, The Musicians Emergency Assistance Fund, overseen by the Kansas City Jazz Ambassadors. The first fundraiser, held in 1992 at Obsessions, a club in Westport, honored Buddy. Anderson remained active by entertaining young crowds in Westport, writing plays and poetry, and jamming at the Mutual Musicians Foundation in downtown Kansas City, where he died in the late 1990s.

Buddy "Step-Buddy" Anderson influenced numerous jazz trumpeters, including Dizzy Gillispie and Fats Navarro. Like many Oklahoma-born jazz artists, Buddy Anderson is another of the obscure but important figures in the evolution of modern jazz styles. (GC)

Anderson, Keith
(b. January 12, 1968)

Best known as co-composer of "Beer Run," the 2002 duet featuring George Jones and **Garth Brooks**, Keith Anderson was born in Miami, Oklahoma, a town of about 13,000 residents in extreme northeastern Oklahoma. He began writing songs in junior high, primarily inspired by his brother who taught Keith to play guitar, and who constantly played Willie Nelson's *Greatest Hits* for the younger Anderson. His early musical influences represented a cross-section of the music industry, including **Merle Haggard**, Willie Nelson, Kenny Rogers, The Eagles, **Restless Heart**, John Cougar Mellencamp, and Southern rock such as Lynyrd Skynyrd, whose band members **Steve and Cassie Gaines** were raised in his hometown of Miami. During his high school days, Steve competed in football, baseball, and bodybuilding. He was selected for the all-state team in football, finished second in the Mr. Oklahoma bodybuilding contest, and was drafted by the Kansas City Royals baseball organization. A shoulder injury, however, halted his pursuit of a major league baseball career.

Majoring in construction engineering while playing baseball at Oklahoma State University, Keith graduated in 1990 and landed a job with an engineering company in Dallas, but could not divorce himself from music. After about a year and a half with the engineering company, he left to attend physical therapy school at the

University of Texas Southwestern Medical School, and began performing at the Grapevine Opry where Lee Ann Rimes and Kix Brooks had also had early career experiences. His dedication to music interfered with his studies, however, and he decided to focus on writing and singing country music.

After early co-writing experiences with Nashville veterans such as George Ducas, Jeffrey Steele, Bob Dipiero, Craig Wiseman, Kim Williams, and Victoria Shaw, Keith released his eponymous album in 1998, and since 1999 has been based in Nashville, where he performs at such local venues as the Bluebird Café, Wild Horse Saloon, and The Broken Spoke. Anderson's most successful song thus far, "Beer Run," co-written with Kim Williams, came about when Williams' daughter returned from college and reminded the two songwriters of the old college party saying "B-Double-E-Are-You-In." Williams' connection with Brooks got the song to the mega-star who cut it as a duet with George Jones. "Beer Run (B-double E-double Are You In?)" was nominated as Vocal Event of the Year for a 2002 CMA award, and led to Anderson signing his first songwriting contract with EMI Music Publishing in Nashville. Anderson won the Jim Beam competition for "Best Unsigned Talent in Country Music" in November of 2002, possibly opening more professional doors for him as Montgomery Gentry and Trick Pony were former winners of this title. He continued performing live through the summer of 2003 while considering various recording options. (GC/HF)
www.keithanderson.com

Andress, Tuck [Tuck & Patti]
(b. October 28, 1952)

A guitarist who blends jazz and New Age music into a duet that has recorded six albums, Tuck Andress was born in Tulsa. While growing up in T-Town, he listened to his parents' favorite recordings of big band jazz. His father played piano and had directed a jazz band in college, while his older sister studied classical piano. Both his father and sister often played in the home during Tuck's early years, and he says it provided "tremendous ear training that would serve me for a lifetime," according to his website.

At age seven Tuck learned piano chords from his sister, and he later took formal lessons until age fourteen. In the meantime, his sister was listening to the popular music of the time, and he soon became interested in the Beatles and Rolling

Stones. As a teenager, he and two neighborhood boys formed a "garage" band with Tuck on the piano, a boy down the street on drums, and his next-door neighbor playing electric guitar. During this time Tuck decided to learn the guitar, using a Mel Bay instruction book. The first electric guitar he owned was a Ventures Mosrite with a Vox Pacemaker amp, and his guitar idol was Chuck Berry. His first guitar instructor was Tulsan Tommy Crook, who Chet Atkins described on the *Tonight Show* with Johnny Carson as the "greatest guitar player in the world."

While in high school, Tuck began to listen to jazz guitarists, such as Wes Montgomery and George Benson, although he continued playing in rock bands. His other major guitar influences were Jimi Hendrix, B.B. King, Albert King, and Eric Clapton, as well as several Tulsa blues style guitarists such as Steve Hickerson, Jim Byfield, and Tommy Tripplehorn.

After high school graduation, Tuck entered Stanford University in 1970, but after the first quarter, he moved to Los Angeles, where he rejoined some of the members of his high school band. He soon became a studio musician and eventually landed a job as guitarist on the *Sonny and Cher* television program, however, he decided to return to Stanford to study classical music theory.

For the next four years, Andress alternated between Stanford and Tulsa. At Stanford, he played in rock and jazz bands as well as the Stanford University Big Band. Whenever he returned to Tulsa, he played with the **GAP Band** (Wilson Brothers). While at Stanford, he teamed with Mike Stillman, a jazz saxophonist, and the duo began playing at the Stanford Coffee House. In the meantime, he took weekly classical guitar lessons for two years.

After leaving Stanford in 1974, Tuck played in countless soul, pop, and rock bands in the Bay Area, while practicing from eight to fourteen hours a day. He immersed himself by listening to jazz legends such as Kenny Burrell, Jimmy Smith, Miles Davis, John Coltrane, and Charlie Parker.

In 1978 Tuck met Patti Cathcart in San Francisco, where she auditioned for vocalist in a band of which he was a member. The two soon left the band, and began to perform as a duo in 1981, and were married in 1983. Honing their act on the West Coast, the two declined recording contracts until they had their sound perfected.

In 1987, Tuck & Patti signed with Windham Hill Jazz, and released their debut album in 1988, *Tears of Joy*, a ten-track jazz-oriented collection, including three songs co-written by them, "Tears of Joy," "Everything's Gonna Be All Right," and "Love Is the Key." *Love Warriors*, featuring songs by Lennon-McCartney and a Jimi Hendrix medley, followed in 1989. Tuck did a solo album of jazz standards for Windham Hill in 1990 entitled *Reckless Precision*, and the duo issued *Dream*, a mix of tracks featuring Stevie Wonder, J.B. Lenoir, and Horace Silver songs, in 1991.

Tuck & Patti switched to the Epic label in 1995, and recorded *Learning How to Fly*, featuring Jimi Hendrix' "Up From the Skies," as well as several of Patti's original songs. They returned to Windham Hill in 1998 with *Paradise Found*, a

collection of songs ranging from Lerner and Loewe to Lennon and McCartney, and two years later, released *Taking the Long Way Home*, with all ten tracks written by Patti. Their 2001 album, *As Time Goes By*, is a mixture of Gershwin, Lerner, Rodgers & Hart, and Lennon-McCartney songs. In 2002, the duo self-released *Chocolate Moment* (T&P Records), a laid-back and soulful collection of the deftly, tasteful guitar work and elegant vocals for which Tuck and Patti have become known around the world. In 2002 and 2003 Tuck & Patti continued touring the globe extensively. A partial list of international places where they have performed includes New Zealand, the Netherlands, Austria, Italy, Hungary, Russia, Germany, Switzerland, Singapore, Hong Kong, Indonesia, South Korea, and China. (GC)
www.tuckandpatti.com

Austin, Larry
(b. September 12, 1930)

Co-founder and editor of *Source*, an *avant-garde* music journal, and well known for his use of electronic, theater, and improvisation in his many compositions, such as *Improvisations for Orchestra and Jazz Soloists* performed and recorded by the New York Philharmonic in 1961 under the direction of Leonard Bernstein, composer and music educator Larry Don Austin was born in Duncan, Oklahoma, a community of roughly 22,000 residents in the south central section of the state. He moved to Texas with his parents when he was five-years-old, graduated from Vernon, Texas High School and received his bachelor's degree in music education and his master's in music theory from the University of North Texas (1947 to 1952). He completed further graduate work in composition and musicology at Mills College, University of California-Berkeley, Stanford University, and the Massachusetts Institute of Technology. His academic appointments have included professorships at the University of California-Davis, University of South Florida, and the University of North Texas in Denton. His many professional activities include president of the International Computer Music Association, founder of the Consortium to Distribute Computer Music, and member of the Academy of the International Institute of Electroacoustic Music, Bourges, France.

Since 1964 Austin has composed more than seventy works using electro-acoustic and computer music media. His symphonic works include performances by the Boston, Baltimore, Buffalo, Oakland, and National Symphony Orchestras. His credits include *The Maze* (1967), *Agape* (1970), *Walter* (1971), *Plastic Surgery* (1970), *Phantasmagoria* (1982), *Sinfonia Concertanta: A Mozartean*

Episode (1986), *Concertante Cybernetica* (1987). Several of his compositions, such as *Life Pulse Prelude* (1974-84), for 20-member percussion orchestra, are based on Charles Ives's compositional sketches for Ives's unfinished *Universe Symphony*. Austin's complete realization of Ives's transcendental *Universe Symphony* was presented and recorded in 1994 by the Cincinnati Philharmonia, followed by performances of the work by the National Philharmonic of Warsaw, Poland, and the Saarland Rundfunk Sinfonieorchester in Saarbrucken, Germany.

For his composition *BluesAx* (1995-96), for saxophonist and computer music, and for his influential leadership in electro-acoustic music genres for the more than thirty-five years, Austin received the Magistère (Magisterium) title at the twenty-third International Electro-acoustic Music Competition in 1996, Bourges, France. He was the first American composer to receive the Magistère prize.

In 1997 Austin was Magistère composer-in-residence at the BEAST computer music studios at the University of Birmingham in the U.K., where he completed his octophonic computer music, *Djuro's Tree,* and *Singing! The Music of My Own Time,* commissioned by baritone Thomas Buckner. The following year, he was honored with a composer residency at the Rockefeller Center in Bellagio, Italy, where he completed *Tárogató!,* for tárogató and octophonic computer music. In 2000, as a guest research fellow at the Electroacoustic Music Studios at the University of York in York, U.K., he completed *Ottuplo!,* for real and virtual string quartet. In September, 2000, Austin was awarded a month-long composer residency at the International Institute for Electroacoustic Music, Bourges, France, which commissioned his work, *Williams [re]Mix[ed] (1997-2001*), for octophonic computer music system. Presented on January 30, 2003, in an Interpretations Series Merkin Concert Hall concert in New York City with composer James Dashow, the world premiere of his most recent work, *Threnos*, for bass clarinet(s) and octophonic computer music, commissioned by Michael Lowenstern, was performed in memory of the victims of September 11, 2001. Other Austin works on the program included *Tárogató!, Williams [re]Mix[ed] and Ottup*lo!

Retiring from his 38-year academic career in 1996, Austin resides with his wife Edna at their Robson Ranch home in Denton, Texas. Working in and out of his Denton studio, *gaLarry*, Austin continues his active composing career with commissions, tours, performances, writing, recordings, and lecturing, anticipating future extended composer residencies in North America, Japan, and Europe. (GC)

Autry, Gene
(b. September 29, 1907 - d. October 2, 1998)

Known forever as "Oklahoma's Yodeling Cowboy," Orvon Gene Autry began singing at age five in his grandfather's Tioga, Texas Baptist church choir and rode his smooth vocal chords, handsome visage, and cowboy authenticity through the 20th century as the first major singing cowboy to succeed on records, radio, the

silver screen, and television. Autry enjoyed a second career as a broadcasting entrepreneur and major league baseball owner. Gene Autry's use of western themes in his music had tremendous impact on country's music development in the 1930s as the lyrical emphasis of the genre shifted from the rural south to the developing west, and the musical emphasis shifted from the nasal vocal delivery of old time country to the crooning style of the singing cowboy. Musically, Gene Autry also helped popularize the Hawaiian-style slack-keyed guitar which evolved into the use of the Dobro and pedal-steel guitar in Western swing and honky-tonk music. Additionally, along with other singing cowboys such as Tex Ritter and Roy Rogers, Autry's fashion sense of wearing a white cowboy hat impacted country music singers from non-Western states such as Bill Monroe from Kentucky and Hank Williams from Alabama, and continues to influence contemporary country music fashion so much that new country stars with no rural background are often thought of derisively as "hat acts." The mass marketing of Gene Autry's image and name through the Sears and Roebuck catalogues of the 1930s continues to resonate throughout the entertainment industry as an ultimate example of promoting, and profiting from, star status.

Born to tenant farmers Delbert Autry and Elnora Ozment Autry in the tiny Grayson County, Texas town of Tioga, just about twenty five miles south of the Oklahoma border, the family moved just across the Red River to Achille, Oklahoma, in Bryan County, when Gene was a small child. In Achille, Gene learned to ride horses and his mother began teaching him to play guitar. When Gene was about fifteen, the Autry family moved to Ravia, Oklahoma, a tiny town in the south central part of the state near Tishomingo, where Gene hauled baggage and did other odd jobs the Frisco Railroad depot leading the station master teach the skills of telegraph operator.

After he finished high school, Gene earned fifteen dollars a week as a ballad singer, saxophone player and black-faced comedian with the Fields Brothers Marvelous Medicine Show for a few months before taking a job as a relief telegrapher for regular Frisco operators from St. Louis to Southern Oklahoma. When the wires were not too busy, Gene had an opportunity to practice his guitar and sing in the style of his hero, Jimmie Rodgers. While riding the Frisco rails and filling in where needed, Gene linked up with another musically inclined railroad man, his boss and uncle-in-law, Jimmy Long, in Sapulpa, Oklahoma. The two formed a duo that played at dances and parties around Sapulpa and wrote songs together, most notably "That Silver Haired Daddy of Mine" which would later become the music industry's first gold record in 1931 and launched Autry as an up-and-coming star. Popular legend has it that sometime in 1928 the famous Oklahoma humorist Will Rogers heard Gene singing in the Chelsea, Oklahoma railroad depot and suggested the 21-year-old singing telegraph operator head to New York and try to make it in the big city on radio. Gene thought about it while continuing to play locally for a year and then took advantage of a free Frisco railway pass to New York City where he had only the slightest connections to fellow Oklahomans **Frankie** and **Johnny Marvin.** Having met the Marvin brothers' parents back in Oklahoma, Autry felt connected enough to contact the musicians.

Two of the most popular entertainers in New York, the Marvin Brothers were recording artists and Broadway and vaudeville stars in 1928, giving them ample opportunity to introduce the fresh-faced kid to some industry connections. After auditioning a few tunes for Victor, the talent scout thought Autry had promise but needed more polish and recommended Autry learn some yodeling songs in the manner of Jimmie Rodgers while continuing to practice singing somewhere else than under the big microscope in New York. Autry heeded the advice and returned to Tulsa where he landed a job on KVOO, Tulsa as "Oklahoma's Yodeling Cowboy," and performed at schools, private parties, and schools along with his radio work. After getting a year of experience under his belt, Gene returned to New York and Victor Records where the Marvin Brothers helped him get his first songs cut, "My Dreaming of You" and "My Alabama Home" on October 9, 1929. Unfortunately for Autry, the stock market crashed twenty days later and the recording business felt the shock as much as anyone.

Autry turned to several small labels during the period and continued recording ballads in the manner of his idol, Jimmie Rodgers. Autry's style was becoming practically indistinguishable from Rodgers's, leading to Gene recording some of Rodgers's songs such as "Jimmie the Kid" and "T.B. Blues." Autry's version of "Jimmie the Kid" was such a mirror image of Rodgers's that when RCA reissued some of Rodgers's recordings in the 1970s they mistakenly included Autry's version instead of the Rodgers version. By 1931, Autry was becoming a smooth performer, confident with his guitar playing and starting to diverge from the dominant influence of Rodgers. In October of 1931, Gene and Jimmy Long recorded the song they had written way back in Sapulpa, "That Silver Haired Daddy of Mine." The song hinted at Autry's movement away from the Rodgers "blue yodel" style and closer to the style of singing ballads that would evolve into his western model of warm, sincere songs about the West of many Americans' imaginations, a much better place to think about than the bread lines and broken fields of the Depression.

As a result of the success enjoyed by "That Silver Haired Daddy of Mine," Art Satherly, vice-president of the American Record Corporation (later subsumed by Columbia), sent Autry to Chicago to audition for the National Barn Dance on fifty thousand watt WLS, a clear channel AM station heard throughout the Midwest. Hired as "Oklahoma's Singing Cowboy" on the National Barn Dance, Autry's success garnered him his own radio show, "Conqueror Record Time," where he portrayed a cowboy fresh off the range who sang tales and tunes of the cattle trails. Before long, Sears Roebuck began taking advantage of the singing cowboy's popularity by marketing songbooks, Gene Autry Round Up Guitars retailing for $9.98 "less case," and Autry recordings on the Conqueror label which was the American Record Corporation's custom-made label for the Sears catalogue and where many Autry recordings appeared. By 1934 Autry was one of the most well-known and successful recording artists in America, but his star had really just started rising compared to the success he would have in the motion picture industry.

As with all elements of the economy during the Great Depression of the 1930s, the motion picture business had to offer special deals and lower prices to entice people into the only audio-visual medium available to them at the time. Although the concept of singing cowboys in a Western had been tried as early as 1930, Autry's entrance into the field came by way of a guest appearance in the film *In Old Santa Fe* (1934) which starred the most popular celluloid singing cowboy to that date, Ken Maynard, and whom filmgoers felt Autry upstaged in the film. Critics and film business types knew they had star in their midst and, in 1935, Autry was cast in the strange, late night cult classic serial, *The Phantom Empire*, a science fiction Western series which ran before main features. Autry's true breakthrough film was *Tumbling Tumbleweeds* (1935), and named after a song Gene recorded the previous January in a trio with his old friend and relative Jimmy Long and film sidekick Smiley Burnette. Just a few weeks after the release of Autry's first film, Republic Pictures released *Melody Trail* (1935), where Gene featured his horse, Champion, for the first time to audiences' rave approval. Two more films, *Sagebrush Troubadour* and *Singing Cowboy* brought the total films to four in just four months at the end of 1935 and provided audiences with the beginnings of Gene's "Cowboy's Code," some of which included the concepts of never shooting first, never hitting a man smaller than yourself, never going back on your word, and never advocating racially or religiously intolerant ideas.

Autry's films were set on a Western landscape and each was an hour long film which gave him the opportunity to break into a song an average of six times per movie which generated a tremendous amount of cross promotion for his records. Over the next eighteen years Autry would star in ninety-one feature films that defined the "B" Western concept, and in 1940, theater exhibitors of America voted Autry the fourth biggest box office attraction behind Mickey Rooney, Clark Gable, and Spencer Tracy. His major records during the 1930s and early 1940s, "Tumblin' Tumbleweeds" (1935), "Mexicali Rose" (1935), "Back in the Saddle Again" (1939), and "(I've Got Spurs That) Jingle, Jangle, Jingle" (1942), sold in the millions.

While Gene's early records such as "Tumblin' Tumbleweeds" and "The Yellow Rose of Texas" featured the simple instrumentation and vocals of his hero Jimmie

Rodgers and other cowboy duos of the early 1930s, in 1937 Gene hired a swing fiddle player from Indiana named Carl Cotner to augment the Autry sound. Cotner played in a popular country swing band and was comfortable with everything from orchestrated arrangements popular with the big bands of the time to gutsier and dance-oriented fiddle tunes. Cotner soon began arranging Autry's recordings and originated the sound for which Autry is so famous and which had such an impact on mainstream country music. By adding smooth strings, subtle steel guitar, occasionally a muted horn section, and featuring the two-beat rhythm famous in cowboy songs to replicate a loping horse, Autry's music was appealing to both rural and urban audiences. In 1939, this crossover success landed Autry the CBS national network radio show, *Melody Ranch*, sponsored by Wrigley's Doublemint Gum, which aired on Sunday afternoons until 1956 and which provided Autry with perhaps the one song most associated with him, "Back in the Saddle Again" (1939), the theme song of *Melody Ranch*. Autry built a working Melody Ranch on sixty acres in Newhall, California to provide the backdrop for numerous films, radio shows, and television programs, starring actors such as John Wayne, The Cisco Kid, Ronald Reagan, Hopalong Cassidy, fellow Oklahoman **Johnny Bond,** and a native Arkansan, **Jimmy Wakely**, whom Autry met in Oklahoma in 1938 when he appeared on Wakely's WKY Oklahoma City radio program; ultimately, Autry signed the Jimmy Wakely Trio to become part of the CBS Radio *Melody Ranch Show* in 1940.

Alongside the films, recordings, and radio shows, Autry had a traveling stage show that would often tout the release of a new film and play in the same theaters as the film. Some of his best-known movies are based on his hit records, including *South of the Border* (1939), *Mexicali Rose* (1939), and *Back in the Saddle* (1941). In the fall of 1941, Gene bought a 1,200 acre ranch west of Berwyn, Oklahoma, about 16 miles west of his high school hometown of Ravia. He intended to make the ranch a showplace and headquarters of his traveling rodeo that sold out such venues as Madison Square Garden in New York City. A Berwyn lawman, Cecil Crosby, suggested to residents they change the town's name to honor their famous new neighbor. The Santa Fe Railroad, postal authorities, and residents all agreed and a celebration took place on November 16th, 1941, the 34th anniversary of Oklahoma's statehood. A crowd of 35,000 people, including Oklahoma governor Frank Phillips, assembled to watch the parade and feast on buffalo meat while a movie camera documented the event to include in newsreels throughout the nation's theaters. Gene recorded an episode of *Melody Ranch* that was aired across the country and then replaced the Berwyn town sign with the new Gene Autry sign. Three weeks later, however, U.S. involvement in World War II threw Autry's career, then at its absolute zenith, into uncertainty.

While Autry had a reported income of $600,000 for 1941, he only made $125 per month as a flight officer with the Air Transport Command from 1943 to 1945 flying large cargo planes in the China-Burma-India theater. For those financial reasons, Autry kept his stock at the ranch outside the Oklahoma town bearing his name, but he sold the property in 1944. When the war ended, Autry was assigned to Special Services, where he toured with a USO troupe in the South Pacific before resuming his movie career with features such as *The Last Round-Up* (1947) and *Strawberry Roan* (1948). His recording career also took off again with multi-million selling songs "Here Comes Santa Claus" (1947), "Rudolph the Red Nosed Reindeer" (1948), and "Peter Cottontail" (1949). In 1950 Gene became one of the first major movie stars to move into television. For the next five years, he produced and starred in ninety-one half-hour episodes of *The Gene Autry Show* as well as producing popular TV series such as *Annie Oakley*, *The Range Rider*, *Buffalo Bill, Jr.*, *The Adventures of Champion*, and the first thirty-nine episodes of *Death Valley Days*.

With such a strong foundation in popular electronic media, Autry's forays into broadcast ownership were not surprising. Through his company Golden West Broadcasters, Gene owned award-winning stations such as KMPC radio and KTLA television in Los Angeles as well as other stations around the country. Gene also lived out a boyhood dream of being involved with professional baseball when he bought the American League's California (now Anaheim) Angels in 1961. Active in Major League Baseball, Autry held the title of Vice-President of the American League until his death, unfortunately before his Angels won the World Series in 2002. Gene continued his television success in the 1980s when he and his former movie sidekick Pat Buttram hosted the highly rated 90-minute Nashville Network program, *Melody Ranch Theatre*, for ninety-three episodes in which they highlighted his old Republic and Columbia movies. At the end of the 1980s, Autry fulfilled another longstanding dream by completing the Autry Museum of Western Heritage which houses a fine collection of Western art, artifacts, and memorabilia such as an 1870s-era steam engine from Nevada, guns owned by Annie Oakley and Wyatt Earp, and costumes of TV's Lone Ranger and Tonto.

In 1990, when the school closed in Gene Autry, Oklahoma, citizens converted it into the Gene Autry, Oklahoma History Museum. The museum celebrates singing cowboys of the "B" western movies, especially Autry, and contains hundreds of collectibles to include photographs, clothing, movie posters, musical instruments, and other items associated with the singing cowboys. The museum also sponsors the Gene Autry, Oklahoma Film and Music Festival each year on Autry's birthday. Autry's birthplace of Tioga, Texas also celebrates the anniversary of his birth when 10,000 people arrive annual to enjoy live entertainment, Gene Autry movies, cowboy games, and chuckwagon breakfasts. In 1996, the most notable contemporary singing cowboys, Riders in the Sky, recorded a tribute album, *Public Cowboy #1: The Music of Gene Autry* (Rounder), including many of the songs for which Autry became famous such as "Back in the Saddle Again," "That Silver Haired Daddy of Mine," and "South of the Border."

Among the hundreds of honors and awards Gene Autry received in his lifetime, a short list must include induction into the Country Music Hall of Fame, the

Nashville Songwriters Hall of Fame, the National Cowboy Hall of Fame, the National Association of Broadcasters Hall of Fame, and the Oklahoma Music Hall of Fame. He received the Songwriters' Guild Life Achievement Award, the American Academy of Achievement Award, the Los Angeles Area Governor's Emmy from the Academy of Television Arts and Sciences, the Hubert Humphrey Humanitarian of the Year Award, a Lifetime Achievement Award by the songwriters' organization ASCAP. Gene Autry was not only the first country musician to get a star on the Hollywood Walk of Fame, but the only person to five stars along the walk.

Autry was a 33rd Degree Mason, and for many years ranked on *Forbes* list of the 400 richest Americans, before he fell to the magazine's "near miss" category in 1995 with an estimated net worth of "only" $320 million. In his biography, Autry credited his music's success to its simplicity and straightforwardness. He also described the fickleness of the music business by saying, "It occurs to me that music, with the possible exception of riding a bull, is the most uncertain way to make a living I know. In either case, you get bucked off, thrown, stepped on, and trampled, if you get on at all. At best, it is a short bumpy ride." Autry's career of 635 recordings, including more than 300 songs written or co-written by him, and 100 million records sold, was more like one long, glorious ride into the sunset of American popular culture for *the* singing cowboy of the 1930s, '40s, and '50s. (HF) www.autry.com

Axton, Hoyt
(b. March 25, 1938 - d. October 26, 1999)

Best known for his compositions "The Pusher," "Joy to the World," "Della and the Dealer," and "Jeremiah the Bullfrog," Hoyt Axton was born in Duncan, a community of about 22,000 residents in south central Oklahoma. Hoyt was the oldest son (younger brother named Johnny) of **Mae Boren Axton**, co-writer of Elvis Presley's "Heartbreak Hotel." His father, John T. Axton, was a teacher and high school coach. Both parents were influential in developing Hoyt's musical talents as his mother required him to take piano lessons and his father taught him the finer points of singing, especially the rich baritone voice. Hoyt earned All-State honors in football at Robert E. Lee High School in Jacksonville, Florida, and received a football scholarship to

attend Oklahoma State University. Before completion of a degree, he joined the Navy in the late 1950s, where he continued his athletic endeavors through boxing.

After leaving the Navy in 1961, Hoyt turned to the music business—writing and performing folk music. Following a brief period in Nashville, he headed to California, where he played the coffee house circuit in San Francisco in 1962. He recorded his first album in 1962 on the Horizon label. Entitled *The Balladeer*, it was recorded live at The Troubadour in Hollywood, and included such songs as "John Henry," "500 Miles," and "Walkin' to Georgia." During the next decade, Axton performed as a folk music artist and co-wrote with Ken Ramsey, "Greenback Dollar," recorded by the Kingston Trio in 1963. It became a Top 20 hit on the *Billboard* charts, however, Hoyt made a grand sum of $800 from the song due to some unfortunate circumstances with his publisher. Other albums, also on the Horizon label, included *Greenback Dollar* (1963), *Thunder 'n' Lightnin,'* (1963), and *Saturday's Child* (1963). He switched record companies in the mid-1960s, and recorded *Hoyt Axton Explodes* (1964) on Vee Jay, The Beatles' first label in the U.S., and *Mr. Greenback Dollar Man* (1965) on the Surrey label.

During the late 1960s, Hoyt composed several major hits, including "The Pusher" and "Snowblind Friend." Recorded by Steppenwolf, "The Pusher" was featured in the 1969 film, *Easy Rider*. During the 1960s, he released *Hoyt Axton Sings Bessie Smith* (1965), reflecting his appreciation for other genres of music, including the blues. Two of his early albums in the 1970s were released by Capitol, including *Country Anthem* (1971) and *Joy to the World* (1971). In the 1970s, two of Axton's compositions, "Joy to the World" and "Never Been to Spain," were recorded by Three Dog Night, and his "No No Song" was recorded by Ringo Starr, formerly of the Beatles. Axton recorded more than thirty albums, primarily in the 1970s. Among these were *Less Than a Song* (1973), *Life Machine* (1974), *Southbound* (1975), *Fearless* (1976), *Road Songs* (1977), *Snowblind Friend* (1977), *Free Sailin'* (1978), and *A Rusty Old Halo* (1979). The latter produced "Della and the Dealer" and "Rusty Old Halo," both of which made the Top 20 charts as singles. Several of his later albums were released by his own recording label, Jeremiah, named after the bullfrog in "Joy to the World," including *Where Did the Money Go* (1980), *Hoyt Axton Live* (1981), and *Pistol Packin' Mama* (1982).

Hoyt's most recent albums were *Spin of the Wheel* (1991), *Jeremiah Was a Bullfrog* (1998), and *Gold* (2001). The title song of the *Jeremiah Was a Bullfrog* album became one of his most requested compositions. Additional noteworthy compositions include "When the Mornin' Comes," "Boney Fingers," Viva Pancho Villa," "Wild Bull Rider," and "Evangelina." His songs were covered by a variety of artists, including Waylon Jennings, Glen Campbell, Tanya Tucker, John Denver, and Commander Cody.

Hoyt also appeared in several movies and on television, including *We're No*

Angels, The Black Stallion, and *Gremlins*, sang the "Head to the Mountains" jingle used in the Busch beer commercial in the 1980s, and was in the hit TV series, *Bonanza*, in 1965. Singer, guitarist, pianist, and songwriter, Hoyt died of a heart attack at his Victor, Montana, ranch in 1999, after suffering a major stroke in 1995, which had left him confined to a wheel chair. Survived by his third wife, Deborah Hawkins, Hoyt had five children. Hoyt had moved to the Bitterroot Valley in Montana after playing a sheriff in the movie, *Disorganized Crime*, filmed there in 1988. He was the nephew of former Governor of Oklahoma and U.S. Senator from Oklahoma, and current President of the University of Oklahoma, David Boren. Hoyt Axton is best remembered by Oklahomans for one of the lines from "Never Been to Spain," "Well, I've never been to heaven, but I've been to Oklahoma." Hoyt once said, "I believe in music—it's the food I feed my soul." (GC)
www.sixcats.com/axton/hoyt.htm

Axton, Mae Boren
(b. September 14, 1914 - d. April 9, 1997)

As co-composer of "Heartbreak Hotel," one of Elvis Presley's major hits, Mae Boren Axton was born in Bardwell, Texas, although she was reared in Oklahoma and attended the University of Oklahoma where she earned a journalism degree. She was the sister of David Boren, one of Oklahoma's most celebrated politicians as he served as state senator, governor, and U.S. Senator from the state, as well as serving as current president of the University of Oklahoma. After college, she worked as a reporter for *Life* magazine. She married John T. Axton, a teacher and coach, and they had two sons, Hoyt and Johnny, both born in Duncan, Oklahoma. **Hoyt Axton** was a well-known singer, songwriter, and actor.

Mae's family moved to Jacksonville, Florida, where she and her husband continued their teaching careers. Moreover, Mae began writing songs with local songwriters Glen Reeves and Tommy Durden, as well as serving as publicist for country singer Hank Snow. It was while working for Snow that she first heard Elvis Presley in May of 1955.

While flipping through the *Miami Herald* newspaper one day in 1955, Durden and Mae came across an article about a man who had committed suicide in a local hotel. The suicide victim left a note with the line, "I walk a lonely street." Within less than a half hour, Mae and Durden had scribbled out the lyrics and recorded a demo of "Heartbreak Hotel." Some sources say that Mae played the demo tape for Elvis at a radio convention in Nashville, while others say they took it to Colonel Tom Parker, Presley's manager. Elvis liked the song, but hated the title. Elvis mandated that he be listed as co-composer, and received one-third of the royalties. As Elvis' first single for RCA Victor and his first #1 hit on the *Billboard* charts, the song was the biggest selling hit on the *Billboard* charts in 1956 and eventually won a Grammy Hall of Fame award in 1995. Presley, however, never recorded any other Axton songs, although he did record Hoyt's (her son) "Never Been to Spain."

Mae's further success as a songwriter was limited. She did write material for several other artists, such as Patsy Cline ("Pick Me Up On Your Way Down"), **Wanda Jackson** ("Honey Bop"), and Hank Snow ("What Do I Know Today"). In addition, her songs have been recorded by a vast array of artists, including The Animals, **J. J. Cale**, Little Jimmy Dickens, Albert King, Jerry Lee Lewis, **Roger Miller**, Tanya Tucker, Conway Twitty, Faron Young, and Doc Watson. She also wrote the sleeve notes to the Elvis tribute album, *The King Is Gone*, by Ronnie McDowell. In 1973, Mae published her memoirs, *Country Singers As I Know'em*. She also started a record label called DPJ Records for which Hoyt recorded. Finally, Mae was noted for helping boost the careers of such legends as Dolly Parton and Willie Nelson, as well as newcomer **Blake Shelton**.

Garth Brooks recently donated $1 million to the city of Nashville to establish a children's zoo, named in honor of Mae Boren Axton. Mae died at her home in Hendersonville, Tennessee, on April 9, 1997.

Baker, Chet
(b. December 23, 1929 - d. May 13, 1988)

Known as the West Coast cool jazz trumpeter who most intensely represented the ethos of 1950s California jazz with his intimate, hushed vocal style and the clear, warm, subdued tone of his horn, Chesney Henry Baker also endured the rugged lifestyle of a habitual narcotics user which resulted in an uneven, although certainly celebrated and distinctive, international musical career. His sharp, photogenic features led some fans to think of him as the jazz James Dean, while others preferred Chet as an urbane, musically sophisticated antithesis to the grease and leather image popular among 1950s rock icons. To many jazz fans, Chet's musical significance is unquestioned, but biographers, critics, and jazz historians all agree his drug habit limited his career, led to several mediocre recordings in the mid-1960s, and caused too many grisly run-ins with the law and other drug addicts. Chet's father, Chesney Baker, Sr., was a semi-professional country guitar player, who met Vera Ruth (Moser) Baker at a barn dance where he was playing near Yale, Oklahoma, a small farm town in north central Oklahoma. Chet remembers Vera in his 1997 unfinished memoir, *If I Had Wings*: "[she was] a sweet and gentle woman, a country girl who'd been born in Yale,

Oklahoma, just as I had." Born two days before Christmas in the first winter of the Great Depression, Chet and the Bakers lived on a small farm his grandfather had acquired in the Oklahoma Territory land runs of 1889. While in Oklahoma his mother took him around to amateur contests where he sang ballads, but never won any contests, and kept him going to church where he sang in the choir. Chet describes his rural childhood bucolically in his memoir, but one has to imagine bleak conditions for supporting a family on the dry prairie land smack in the middle of the dust bowl proper. With jobs limited for his parents around Yale, the Bakers moved to Oklahoma City when he was one-year-old to stay with his father's sister, Agnes, who basically raised Chet until he was eight while his mother worked at an ice cream factory and his father as a timekeeper for the WPA. Chet returned to Yale over the summers to visit his grandparents and the farm where he remembers walking dirt roads while picking wild raspberries and eating fresh watermelons out of the fields. If one is looking for reasons for the melancholy elements of Chet Baker's music and life, or even the lonesome, breathy blowings of his trumpet and the near whisper of his singing and scatting, a good place to begin in the imagination is those peaceful ruminations of his rural childhood which were shattered in 1940 when the family moved to Glendale, California, a suburb just north of Los Angeles. Of course, many Oklahomans had to leave the state after being blown out of work by the drought, dust storms, corporate and government led farm takeovers, and the Bakers certainly symbolize that difficult period in state history when the term "Okie" was not one of positive origin.

After living in Glendale for a couple of years, Chet's father, a Jack Teagarden fan, brought home a trombone for thirteen-year-old Chet, but the instrument proved too unwieldy and after a couple of weeks the trombone vanished and a trumpet appeared. Chet started taking lessons at Glendale Jr. High, but given his inclination toward playing by ear he was not successful in band until his high school year when he marched with the high school band, learned all the Sousa marches by ear, and played in the school dance band in the evenings. After one year of high school, his parents moved again to Redondo Beach to stay with some friends from Oklahoma, further indication of the Baker family's travails during the World War II era. Disenchanted with school at Redondo High and distracted by the beach, Chet quit at 16, and joined the U.S. Army.

After basic training at Fort Lewis, Washington in 1946, the Army dubbed Chet a clerk typist who would spend his time filling out forms, and sent him to Berlin, Germany, just after World War II when the city was still in rubble. After arriving in Germany and gaining an audition for the first trumpet player of the 298th Army band, Chet received a transfer from his intended desk chair to playing on freezing tarmacs for high-ranking officials and politicians as they exited planes. At night, he listened closely to the Victory Discs by Dizzy Gillespie and Stan Kenton being played on the Armed Forces Network. Discharged in 1948, Chet returned to Southern California where his parents had finally been able to purchase a home just north of Redondo Beach in Hermosa Beach, and from which he began attending El Camino Junior College on his GI benefits as a music major and English minor. Chet studied theory and harmony at El Camino, but also started developing music contacts in the area. He met Jimmy Rowles, who at the time was pianist for Peggy Lee on Sunset Boulevard in Los Angeles, and Chet immediately befriended Jimmy to the point of showing up at Rowles's house often and asking the pianist to play songs for him. Chet credits Rowles with the inspiration to keep things simple and not get too busy on the trumpet. Many musicians recognized Chet frequently stayed within one octave in his playing, known musically as *mezzo-forte*, which contributes to his perceived subtlety and economic style. Nineteen forty-eight also marked the release of Miles Davis's *Birth of Cool*. The album had an irrevocable impact on Chet's playing as he confirmed in 1978 when he said he "still listens to [*Birth of Cool*] thirty years later." While many critics feel Chet's horn playing is clearly a descendant of Davis's, thus creating one of Baker's critical sobriquets, "The West Coast Miles Davis," Baker also has a distinct subtlety of tone and pace instantly recognizable apart from Davis's to those who listen closely. In a 1996 interview, Muskogee-born jazz guitar giant **Barney Kessel** remembered Chet's trumpet playing as "him and nobody else."

During 1948 and 1949, Chet followed the session trail around Los Angeles almost every night and learned from artists such as Dexter Gordon, Shelly Manne, Shorty Rogers, Art Pepper, and others, but also traveled to the suburban spots where he would play with more great players like Russ Freeman, with whom he would play later in the 1950s, and another great Oklahoma-born jazz man, bassist **Oscar Pettiford**. By 1950 Chet dropped out of El Camino because his music teacher told him he would never make it playing by ear all the time, and Chet turned completely toward the valuable sessions cooking all around the Los Angeles metro area. Although he was sitting in occasionally at area clubs clubs, Chet was unable to find consistent work as a musician. Knowing one band where he could make some money, Chet re-enlisted in the U.S. Army to join the Presidio Army band in San Francisco. At Presidio he played for the Army during the day, what he called his "day gig," slept until about 1 a.m., then sat in as a regular at clubs like Bop City which did not open until 2 a.m. On off nights he sat in with Cal Tjader at Fack's, or Dave Brubeck and Paul Desmond at the Blackhawk until 5:30 a.m. when he had just enough time to get back to the Presidio for reveille. This routine continued for about a year until he tired of the Army part of the musical equation and proceeded to strategize his way out, which he was successful in doing with not a little difficulty by 1952 when a general discharge declared him unadaptable to Army life.

Freed from the confines of wearing the same color clothes every day, Chet went back to Southern California where he found work with Vido Musso and then Stan Getz before learning of an audition to play some West Coast dates with Charlie "Bird" Parker. For many, Parker was *the* architect of bebop who got his first national exposure with a Kansas City based big band led by Muskogee, Oklahoma native **Jay McShann**. After being moved to the front of the audition and playing only two tunes with Bird, "The Song is You" and "Cheryl" in the key of G, Chet got the job and played a series of gigs in California, Washington, and Canada. The twenty-two-year-old Chet and Parker only split when a club manager fired Parker for obliging the club manager to a charity contribution unbeknownst to the manager. Baker went back to L.A. where he played a few nights with Dixieland specialist Freddie "Schnicklefritz" Fisher, and also was recorded for the first time commercially in jam sessions for *Live at the Trade Winds* (1952). By the summer of 1952, Chet met and formed a critically acclaimed quartet with the great jazz baritone saxophonist, Gerry Mulligan, who had arranged the music and written compositions for Miles Davis's *Birth of Cool*. Leaving out the piano, then a standard instrument of almost any jazz combo, the partnership with Chet and Mulligan as the frontline quartet players became known as the archetype for the breezy, laid-back West Coast cool jazz sound. The group proved to be a success commercially and critically, and the band's first recordings as the Gerry Mulligan quartet included Baker's understated, romantic vocals on "My Funny Valentine," recorded for the newly formed Pacific Jazz Records label. While Chet was enjoying his first tastes of national success as a result of the lyrical wispiness of his trumpet and vocals, he also was arrested for the first time on a drug count, a harbinger of the continued peaks and valleys of his career as a musician and his life as an addict. In June of 1953, Gerry Mulligan had time to do himself for a drug charge, and, therefore, Chet's solo career began. He called his old friend Russ Freeman to play piano, and Baker made his first recordings as a bandleader for the Pacific Jazz label. These recordings led to Chet being voted top trumpet player by the readers of *Metronome* and *Downbeat* magazines in 1953 and 1954.

When Mulligan returned to the streets and suggested the idea of getting back together, Baker disagreed with him over salary ($300 per week), and when Mulligan balked, Chet walked on to rejoin Charlie Parker briefly, then to gigs around the country with his own groups in the latter half of 1954. That year, Pacific Jazz released *Chet Baker Sings* (1954), enhancing Chet's popularity and cementing his status as a vocalist for the rest of his career, albeit at the expense of estranging some more traditional jazz fans. Eager to exploit his good looks and youth appeal, Hollywood featured Chet in the 1955 film, *Hell's Horizon*. Chet declined the subsequent seven-year contract offered by Columbia Pictures, in favor of playing dates such as the Newport Jazz Festival in July, and touring and recording in Europe from September, 1955 to April, 1956. During these peak years of Chet Baker's early career, he scored the *Metronome* and *Melody Maker* "best trumpet" awards in 1955, and second place in the *Downbeat* poll for that same year. The German publication, *Jazz Echo*, named him the top trumpeter in 1956. The European experience was marred by the untimely heroin overdose of his good friend and pianist, Dick Twardzik, in 1955, which caused Chet to take on the additional challenge of assembling musicians for his group, which he abandoned in April 1956. He returned to the U.S., formed a new quartet and recorded

Chet Baker and Crew (1956), which leaned more toward the up tempo bop stylings he demonstrated at Newport the year before, as opposed the cool jazz sound for which he was famous. Although still well known and critically lauded through the end of the 1950s, receiving multiple recognitions from *Playboy*'s jazz polls, Chet called the next two years, 1958 and 1959, "difficult" as he both recorded prolifically, if unevenly, and was arrested for drugs repeatedly. Chet left for Europe to stay in 1959, settling in Italy. Chet's *1959 Milano Sessions* (GMG Music, 2003) are an excellent document of this period when Chet played both with a full orchestra and a sextet. Hollywood maintained his rebellious image as

a jazz outsider in the 1960 fictionalized film biography of his life, *All the Fine Young Cannibals*, with Robert Wagner starring in the role of Chad Bixby. 1959 was also the year Chet met his third wife, Carol (Jackson) Baker, an English fashion model and show dancer, to whom he was married until his death. In many ways Carol has been responsible for keeping Chet's memory alive through the Chet Baker estate by cooperating with documentary makers, releasing rare recordings, making *The Lost Memoir* available, and maintaining the Chet Baker website.

Heroin began to seriously interrupt Chet Baker's career in 1960, when he was arrested on a drug charge in Italy and spent nearly eighteen months in jail. Upon release from prison, Chet celebrated with an RCA release *Chet Is Back* (1962), since reissued as *Somewhere Over the Rainbow*. Chet also portrayed himself in the film *The Stolen Hours* (1963), before he endured a series of drug-related deportations in Germany, Switzerland, France, and England. Ironically, Chet remembers the period as "a very good year" in his memoir when he worked with various European musicians and began playing flugelhorn after his trumpet was stolen in Paris, and which can be best heard on *Baby Breeze* (1965). After another bust in then West Germany, he was deported back to the U.S. in March, 1964, where the Beatles and rock music were anchoring into American music consciousness and jazz's forefront was dominated by the far-reaching, free-jazz master, John Coltrane.

The first fourteen months Chet was back in the states he recorded a number of fine albums: *Lonely Star* (1965), *Stairway to the Stars* (1965), and *On a Misty Night* (1965). Chet also recorded some mediocre albums in 1966 while trying to cash in on the movement in popular instrumental music toward the Tijuana Brass sound of Herb Alpert. The albums were not received well critically but they did help him support his growing family, then with two sons, Dean and Paul. The period is better represented by the album released by Carol Baker known as *Live at Gaetano's* (1966); the recording showcases Chet in a small club in Pueblo, Colorado, with just a few people clapping after some extended jams featuring Chet and his friend Phil Urso, along with some trademark wistful singing by Chet.

As Chet slipped steadily into the reclusive world of the addict, a cataclysmic event occurred in Sausalito, California on the same day his daughter, Melissa, was born back in Oklahoma, July 22, 1966. Many accounts exist for what happened that night, but Carol Baker remembers the end result as her arriving home with a new baby and shortly thereafter receiving a phone call from Chet explaining he had been beaten badly by some thugs who damaged his mouth significantly. One marginal recording exists for 1967, and 1968 is the only year in Chet's profession-al life when no obvious recording was released. The event forced Chet on welfare for two years when he learned to start playing through the side of his mouth instead of with his embouchure, the point of the upper lip that is pivotal to a brass instrument player's musical dexterity. However, Chet's teeth were bad anyway, and one could argue that the imperfect resonation cavity his jaws formed provid-ed an element of his particular tone. But this injury was also aimed at his lip, and the handicap is immediately apparent on the critically derided *Albert's House* (1969), with Chet barely blowing eleven tunes by Steve Allen, the 1950s and 1960s talk show host and would-be jazz pianist. *Blood, Chet, & Tears* (1970), Baker's final release of the period, was no better with maudlin versions of pop hits such as "Spinning Wheel," "And When I Die," "Something," and "You've Made Me So Very Happy." Chet Baker, who many critics, and certainly his fans, con-sider *the* jazz trumpeter of the 1950s, was broke, and resorted to working in a gas station as he tried to figure out how to get his life back. He began picking up small club dates where he could still play on his legendary name.

When Dizzy Gillespie heard Chet was working again, Dizzy helped get Chet a gig in New York at the Half Note in 1973, and Chet began a very slow return to jazz circles, starting with a live reunion at Carnegie Hall with Gerry Mulligan, recorded and released in 1974, followed by several 1970s albums that received better and better reviews such as his "come back" album, *She Is Too Good to You* (1974), and three albums in 1977. Out of financial necessity, during this period Chet returned to Italy as he was better known to European jazz fans, and could still get enough gigs to support himself there. He remained in Europe for the rest of his professional life between intermittent trips to Japan, and the U.S., where he would occasionally visit Carol, their children, and his mother who was in a nurs-ing home in Yale. Nineteen seventy-seven continued a slow, but important, climb back into the music industry's consciousness and the ears of international jazz fans who remembered Baker's significance. Although Chet did not regain his crit-ical acclaim in the U.S., his elevated status in Europe, Japan, and among American jazz collectors provided a market in the 1980s for new releases, and reissues, some of which were done without his knowledge and for which he was never paid. A good example of Chet's ability and state of mind in this period is a recording made on Christmas Eve, 1982 when Baker played the Nine of Cups

Club in Tulsa, Oklahoma. Baker was in the state visiting his family, borrowed a trumpet (which he never returned) from a local music store, and played the date which emerged as *Out of Nowhere* in 1991 on Fantasy. As of 2003, Chet's discography now totals some 180 individual albums, with another seventy some-odd repackaged box sets available, not even including unreleased material yet to be made available by Carol Baker and the Chet Baker estate. This legacy provided ample substance for Bruce Weber's 1987 documentary on Chet's life, *Let's Get Lost*, which premiered in September, 1988, to vast critical acclaim and garnered an Academy Award nomination. However, Chet never enjoyed the success of the film.

On May 13, 1988, at about 3 a.m., he appears to have fallen out of his hotel window in Amsterdam under circumstances never fully explained. While narcotics were certainly involved in the incident, he was fifty-eight-years-old and many critics felt he had not only re-attained his earlier abilities, but was beginning to surpass them with his extensive experience behind the trumpet and microphone as a vocalist. Written a year after Chet's death, J. De Valk's biography/oral history, *Chet Baker: his life and music* (translation by Berkeley Books, 2000), is an excellent overview of Chet's career that uses many interviews and a personal passion for the subject by the author to pursue Chet Baker for a 1987 interview which is fully transcribed in the text. Of particular interest is De Valk's European insight into Chet's career there, especially chapters about his final years through his final moments. The book is well researched and a must read for Baker enthusiasts. Another Baker biographer, James Gavin, did not portray Chet as a flattering character in 2002's *Deep in A Dream: The Long Night of Chet Baker* (Knopf), focusing strongly on Chet's drug abuse, undependability, and selfishness. Also in 2002, six new releases featured Chet Baker's music, to include two sparkling compilations on Blue Note, *Deep in a Dream: The Ultimate Chet Baker*, and *The Definitive Chet Baker*. Like other musicians whose substance abuse problems develop early in their careers, and who subsequently produce a jagged body of work, Chet alternately inspired and disappointed fans, critics, friends and family members who were always willing to give him another chance to match the musical brilliance he brandished from 1954 to 1959 when he was one of the world's best jazz trumpeters. Jazz historians will be discussing his significance for generations to come, but the best confirmation of his self-concept of who he was and where he came from is indicated by the final time he signed into a hotel registry, as Chet Baker of Yale, Oklahoma. (HF) www.chetbaker.net

Baker, Mark
(b. February 28, 1953)

Winner of the 1986 Metropolitan Opera National Council Auditions and performer in more than twenty different Met productions, tenor Mark Baker was born in Tulsa, but reared in Florida. He is a graduate of the University of Indiana with a bachelor's degree in vocal performance and a master's degree in counseling.

Mark made his Met debut during the 1986-87 season in Gounod's *Roméo et Juliette* in the Outdoor in the Parks season as Tibald. Later in the same season, he appeared in the "House" in a number of small roles in such operas as Mussorgsky's *Boris Godunov*, Wagner's *Parsifal*, and a repeat of Tibald in *Roméo et Juliette*. In addition to the Met, he is a regular performer with such U.S. companies as the Lyric Opera of Chicago, Santa Fe Opera, San Francisco Opera, Cincinnati Opera, and Dallas Opera. Overseas, he has performed with the Netherlands Opera; Opera de Lyon, Opera de Nantes, and Bastille in Paris (France); Spoleto Opera and Teatro Bellini in Catania (Italy); Berlin and Bonn Operas (Germany); Santiago Opera (Chile); and Teatro Colon in Buenos Aires (Argentina).

Baker's U.S. credits include Froh in *Das Rheingold*, Grigory/Dimitri in *Boris Godunov*, Narraboth in *Salome*, Vladimir Igorevich in *Prince Igor*, Don Jose in *Carmen*, Siegmund in *Die Walküre*, Florestan in *Fidelio*, and Samson in *Samson et Dalila*. His extensive overseas credits include roles in *Der Fliegende Holländer*, *Salome*, *Wozzeck*, *Peter Grimes*, *Parsifal*, *Die Walküre*, *Katya Kabanova*, *Leonore*, *Jenufa*, and *Samson et Dalila*. He has made recordings of Wagner's *Das Rheingold* and Berg's *Wozzeck*, and has appeared on European telecasts of Janácek's *Jenufa* from Glyndebourne and *Wozzeck* from the Berlin State Opera. (GC)

Ballard, Louis Wayne
(Honganózhe) (b. July 8, 1931)

As a wide-ranging composer who has written many types of music for all instruments and voices, Oklahoma's most successful and prolific classical composer is Louis W. Ballard, a Quapaw-**Cherokee** born at Devil's Promenade in the northeastern corner of Oklahoma near Quapaw. Honganózhe is Ballard's Quapaw name that means "Grand Eagle." His credits include major premiers at Lincoln Center, John F. Kennedy Center, the Smithsonian Institution, Carnegie Hall, the Hollywood Bowl and other major venues around the world. He has received many prestigious awards, such as the National Indian Achievement Award (1972, 1973, 1976), an honorary doctorate from the College of Santa Fe (1973), and the first MacDowell Award for American Chamber Music (1969). He has been awarded grants from the Rockefeller Foundation, Ford Foundation, and National Endowment for the Arts, and, in 1989, he was the first American composer to present an entire program of his music in the Beethoven-House Chamber Music Hall adjoining Beethoven's birthplace. In 1997 he was presented a Lifetime Achievement Award from the First Americans in the Arts.

With a mother of pure Quapaw ancestry (Leona Mae (Perry) Ballard) and a father of Cherokee-French-Scot ancestry (Charles Guthrie Ballard), a diverse array of cultural influences surrounded Louis during his youth in northeastern Oklahoma. As a child, he attended the annual Quapaw powwows where he became familiar with Quapaw and intertribal American Indian musical traditions. His mother played piano at Spring River Indian Mission, and also wrote fox trots and ballads. Encouraged by his Quapaw grandmother, Newakis Hampton, to play the piano she had in her home, he began taking lessons with his mother at the mission.

After attending Bacone College's secondary school, Ballard began his undergraduate education at the University of Oklahoma in 1949 where he sang in the men's glee club, took piano lessons, and studied Latin, harmony, counterpoint, and other rudiments of college music curriculum as well as military science. He also went out for the football team under Bud Wilkinson, but his music suffered and he gave up sports. Financial difficulties caused him to leave OU and he returned home where he attended Northeastern Oklahoma A & M in Miami for his sophomore year.

In 1952, Ballard received a loan from the Mayes County Indian Credit Association for his tuition at Tulsa University. He finished his Bachelor of Music Education and Bachelor of Fine Arts at TU and became a music teacher. His first job was in Nelagony, Oklahoma, near Pawhuska, where he taught for two years, and then Ballard taught for two years at Tulsa Webster High School. He left musical teaching due to the low salary and attended Tulsa Technical College to become a mechanical draftsman, after which he designed oil field equipment, huge offshore well platforms, and pressure wells for the National Tank Company. Unsatisfied by the work, Ballard returned to Tulsa University where completed his Masters of Music in composition 1962.

During graduate school, Louis gravitated to the music and philosophy of Bela Bartok (1881-1945), the Hungarian composer whose compositions set the stage

for 20th century post-modernism by incorporating traditional folk melodies into his formal classical music. Through this exposure, Ballard came to understand the best way of incorporating exotic music into his compositional techniques was to learn as much as possible about the culture, learn as many of the songs as possible, and try to compose music which reflects the quintessence of that culture. Subsequently, Ballard developed his own classical style for which he has become known. Initially, Ballard's compositions sought to generate a greater appreciation for American Indian music, but as his career developed he was determined to shepherd the music into mainstream musical expression. As he writes on his website, Ballard believes, "It is not enough to acknowledge that American Indian music is different from other music. What is needed in America is an awakening and reorienting of our total spiritual and cultural perspective to embrace, understand and learn from the Aboriginal American what motivated his musical and artistic impulses." Ballard's ideas and works at TU brought him to the attention of the Institute of American Indian Arts where he served as director of music and performing arts from 1962 to 1969. While at the school, Ballard developed a new music curriculum in which American Indian tribal music was brought into the classroom and was used to teach the primary elements of music by using tribal songs as examples. As a result, Ballard became the music program director for all the Bureau of Indian Affairs schools throughout the United States from 1969 to 1979. Simultaneously to all of this educational activity, Ballard was writing music at night and on the weekends.

Through a commission from the Harkness Ballet in New York, Ballard wrote music for the ballet *Koshare*, based on the ancient Hopi Creation Story. The ballet premiered in Barcelona, Spain in 1966 and subsequently toured the United States. He continued studying during the summers with the likes of Castelnuovo-Tedesco who taught Andre Previn and Henry Mancini. In 1967 Ballard wrote the ballet *The Four Moons*, inspired by the resilient spirit of the Cherokee, Choctaw, Shawnee, and Osage tribes, and composed in commemoration of Oklahoma's sixtieth anniversary of statehood. Louis's 1968 composition for woodwind quartet, *Ritmo Indio*, impressed German critics as being "ahead of its time," and his *Desert Trilogy* (1969) was nominated for a Pulitzer Prize.   In 1969 his instrumental composition, *Mid-Winter of Fire*, was performed at the White House Conference on Children of Youth, and again at the University of Colorado Conference on American Indian Music in 1971. In 1972, he became the first professional musician to be awarded the Indian Achievement Award created by the Indian Council Fire. Nineteen seventy-two was also the year of one Ballard's most popular compositions, *Portrait of Will Rogers [Tribute to a Great American]*, a choral cantata with a libretto by Ballard and quotations by Will Rogers that has been used by many high school, university, and professional choirs. Also in 1972, Murbo Records released Ballard's *Oklahoma Indian Chants for the Classroom*, an album including instructions for singing and dancing to songs from the Quapaw, Shawnee, Kiowa, Creek-Seminole, Cherokee, and

Choctaw. In 1974, Ballard composed what many consider one of his most important works for orchestra, *Incident at Wounded Knee* (1974). The piece memorialized the tragedies of the Oglala Sioux in 1890 at Wounded Knee, South Dakota, and resonated with the American Indian Movement's conflict with the U.S. government at Wounded Knee in 1973. Although Ballard hoped the music would remain associated with the events of Wounded Knee, he has also written he hoped it would "rise above all political emotions of this epoch." Although premiered in its entirety during a 1974 performance sponsored by the U.S. State Department in Warsaw, Poland, the state department would not sponsor Ballard on the tour because of the subject matter of *Incident at Wounded Knee*. Apparently, the state department feared the communists would use Ballard to embarrass the U.S. However, Gulf Oil Company paid for Ballard's trip to Poland, and the governor of New Mexico declared Louis Ballard Week because of his achievement. Knowledgeable observers recognized having an American Indian in front of an all-white orchestra said more about democracy than any words could ever express. *Incident at Wounded Knee* received a more recent performance in 1999 at Carnegie Hall as part of the American Composers Orchestra millennium themed concerts, where it received positive comments from listeners such as "most attractive piece in the program," and "Louis Ballard's piece effectively reflected its theme, but also went beyond the theme."

Throughout the 1970s Ballard wrote a number of choral pieces, instrumental pieces, and compositions for orchestra. He also continued his development of educational curriculum materials for classrooms, and served as consultant on the widely distributed film *Discovering American Indian Music*. This film depicts the social and ceremonial functions of American Indian music, and also includes Ballard with a percussion ensemble combining indigenous instruments of various tribes. His use of pine branches brushing across a kettledrum in the ensemble has since appeared in other composers' works. In 1981, Ballard composed *A City of Silver*, a concert fantasy for piano inspired by the composer's visit to Buenos Aires, Argentina, which was featured in 1984 at Carnegie Hall in New York City. Ballard wrote *A City of Fire* in 1983, a concert fantasy for piano inspired by Los Alamos, New Mexico, the birthplace of the atomic era, which was also performed at Carnegie Hall and in Taiwan, China. Ballard continued developing his city theme in 1984 with *City of Light*, inspired by Paris, France, and performed in Austria and in Germany at the Beethoven-House Chamber Music Hall in 1989. His series of fantasies based on American Indian oral history, such as *Fantasy Aborigine No. 5: Naniwaya*, based on the Choctaw creation mound, furthered the explorations of Ballard's primary style of fusing European and American Indian cultural resources. Exhibiting more of the range and diversity of Ballard's compositional skills is *Quetzalcoatl's Coattails* (1992), a solo for classical guitar, inspired by Aztec mythology and written to commemorate the sesquicentennial of the arrival in the Americas by Europeans (1492-1992). Other compositions from the 1990s include art songs for soprano and piano in the Lakota dialect inspired

by a Lakota mother's expression of grief, a string quartet composition entitled *The Fire Moon* (1998), and praise songs for American Indian congregational singing that draw their texts from Chippewa, Ojibwa, and Lakota languages. Ballard began the new century with a song called "Thusnelda Louise" (2001) composed for voice and piano and inspired by a 19th century tombstone. In 2002, the composer's *Incident at Wounded Knee* was released with *Cacega Ayuwipi (Decorative Drums)*, and *Music for the Earth and Sky* on Wakan Records. Along with preparing some recordings of his orchestral compositions for commercial release, in 2002 Ballard was working on a string quartet, a piano sonata, a concerto, and an opera. In October of 2002, The Cherokee Honor Society presented Ballard with the Cherokee Medal of Honor for his outstanding contributions to music. Along with the *Marquis* series of *Who's Who in America, Who's Who in Entertainment,* and *Who's Who in the World*, Louis Ballard's biography has been published in *Baker's Biographical Dictionary of 20th Century Musicians, Grove's Dictionary of American Music, The New Grove Dictionary of Music and Musicians, 2nd Edition,* and *Reference Encyclopedia of the American Indian*. The complete catalogue of Louis Ballard's available instructional materials, compositions for performance, and existing recordings may be viewed on his website. (HF)
http://www.nswmp.com/

Barber, Glenn
(b. February 2, 1935)

One of the most multi-talented country music artists of the 1970s with twenty-one hits on the country charts from 1964 to 1980, Martin Glenn Barber was born in Hollis, Oklahoma, a town of roughly 2,500 population located in extreme southwestern Oklahoma near the Texas border. Raised in Pasadena, Texas, Glenn started on the guitar at about age six, but later learned to play the banjo, mandolin, steel guitar, dobro, bass, and drums. As a child he won numerous talent contests, started his own band in high school, and made his first recording at age sixteen ("Ring Around the Moon") on the Stampede label owned by "Pappy" Dailey. Daily later founded Starday Records, one of the most successful independent labels in Texas, and became Glenn's manager for the next decade. Glenn was a disc jockey and featured performer on radio station KIKK in Houston from 1962 to 1968. He and his band, the Western Swingmasters, performed five times per week during that period.

After leaving Houston, Glenn settled in Nashville, where he made his first recordings on the Sims ("How Can I Forget You") and Starday labels ("If Anyone Can Show Cause"/ "Stronger Than Dirt," a double-sided hit). He remained with Starday until 1966 and then recorded a couple of minor hits, including "Most Beautiful, Most Popular, Most Likely to Succeed" and "You Can't Get Here from There." In addition to recording, Glenn signed a contract with Acuff-Rose

Publishing, and wrote songs for Roy Orbison, Don Gibson, and Roy Acuff.

In 1968, Barber signed with Hickory Records and remained with them through 1974, during which time he produced five recordings that made the Top 30, including "Don't Worry 'Bout the Mule" (1968), "Kissed by the Rain, Warmed by the Sun" (1969), "She Cheats on Me" (1970), "I'm the Man on Susie's Mind" (1972), and "Unexpected Goodbye" (1972). *Greatest Hits of Hickory Records, Vol. 2*, released in 1993, features Glenn on two songs, "Unexpected Goodbye" and "She Cheats On Me." He made his debut on the Grand Ole Opry in 1969, and appeared several times thereafter, however, he was never named as a member. One of Glenn's talents is to have someone in the audience suggest a theme for a song and he spontaneously makes one up on an impromptu basis.

After leaving Hickory in 1974, Glenn recorded for several independent labels over the next decade, such as Groovy, Century 21, MMI, Sunbird, Tudor, and Brylen. During this period he produced several low-level entries on the country charts, such as "Yes Ma'am, He Found Me in a Honky Tonk," "Poison Red Berries," "What's the Name of That Song," "Love Songs Just for You," and "Everybody Wants to Disco."

Although Barber never became a major country music star, he has demonstrated creativity in other areas of his life, such as carpentry, a skill he learned from his father and with which he built the Orbit recording studio in the 1970s with the help of his son. He has also enjoyed success as a portrait and mural painter, having sold several of his canvases, and had limited success as screenwriter. (GC)

Barnett, Bobby
(b. February 15, 1936)

Known for his country music albums on Oklahoma heritage and heroes, Bobby Glen Barnett was born in Cushing, Oklahoma, an oil field community of approximately 7,000 folks located west of Tulsa. Born to George and Berls Barnett, he had twelve siblings. Following graduation from Cushing High School in 1953, he moved to El Paso, Texas, where he worked for the El Paso Natural Gas Company as an engineer. After seven years in El Paso, Bobby decided to enter the country music field. Recording for a local Oklahoma label, Razorback, he cut **Eddie Miller**'s "This Old Heart" in 1960, and it reached #24 on the country charts. The single was picked up by the Republic label, which released his next single, "Please Come Home/It Makes No Difference," in 1961, however, it failed to chart.

In 1962, Barnett moved to Reprise Records, only the second country artist on that label. He released two singles, "Crazy Little Lover"/"Last of the Angels" and "Same Old Love"/"Temptation's Calling," neither of which were successful. He then switched to Sims Records in 1963 where he had a #6 hit, "She Looks Good to the Crowd," followed by a Top 50 song, "Worst of Luck" (1964), and a Top 30 number, "Mismatch" (1964). After three years, he returned to the charts with

"Down, Down Came My World"/"Moaning the Blues" on the K-Ark label.

Bobby moved to Columbia Records in 1968, based primarily on his friendship with George Richey, then the new A & R director for the label. Bobby's first single release on Columbia was "Love Me, Love," a Top 15 hit, taken from his album, *Lyin', Lovin' & Leavin'*. It was followed with two more low- level chart singles, "Your Sweet Love Lifted Me" and "Drink Canada Dry." Another decade passed before Bobby scored any hits on the country charts. In 1978, he released "Burn Atlanta Down" followed by "Born in Country Music (Raised on Dixieland)" (1981).

Bobby has cut two albums related to Oklahoma: *Heroes, History and Heritage of Oklahoma, Vol. 1* (1974) and *Vol. 2* (1985), both on the Heritage label. In 1997, Bear Family Records (a German company) released *American Heroes and Western Legends* that includes twenty-seven tracks all written or co-written by Bobby, featuring songs about historical Oklahomans, such as Captain David L. Payne, Pretty Boy Floyd, Pawnee Bill, Bill Pickett, Will Rogers, Sequoyah, Tom Mix, Jim Thorpe, and **Woody Guthrie**. (GC)

Beckham, Bob
(b. July 8, 1927)

A child prodigy in the entertainment world and president of Combine Music, where he helped mold the careers of such country notables as Dolly Parton, Kris Kristofferson, Ray Stevens, Jerry Reed, and Tony Joe White, Robert Joseph Beckham was born in Stratford, Oklahoma, a community of roughly 1,500 residents located southeast of Oklahoma City.

Beckham began a career in the entertainment field at age eight, when he joined a traveling medicine show. He moved to California and entered the motion picture arena as a child actor, appearing in such movies as *The Starmaker* (1939) and *Junior G-Men* (1940). At age thirteen, he returned to Oklahoma and attended high school, before joining the army at seventeen to fight in World War II. Following discharge as an army paratrooper, he became an electrician for a short period, and then worked in radio with the legendary Arthur Godfrey. Because of his Oklahoma roots, he entered the country music field with two Top 40 hits as a singer, "Just As Much As Ever" and "Crazy Arms," the latter remaining a karaoke favorite to this day.

After a short stint touring with Brenda Lee, Bob settled in 1959 in Nashville, where he joined the Shelby Singleton music-publishing firm. He then moved to Combine Music in 1964, and became its president in 1966. Through his diligence and business acumen, including the use of country songs in commercials, he built Combine into one of the major publishing companies in Nashville. Over a twenty-year period, he shaped the careers of Parton, Stevens, Reed, Kristofferson, and White, as well as others. Combine Music was sold in 1986 to SBK music publishers. After a four-year hiatus in the music publishing business, he established HoriPro Entertainment Group in Nashville, a division of Taiyo Music, Japan's largest publisher, and has operated it since 1990. Bob's work as a producer was primarily with Mickey Newbury on six albums, including *Looks Like Rain* (1969), *Frisco Mabel Joy* (1971), *Heaven Help the Child* (1973), *Live at Montezuma Hall* (1973), *Mickey Newbury Collection* (1998), and *Lulled By the Moonlight* (2000). (GC)

Bee, Molly
(b. August 18, 1939)

A childhood star on such television shows as the *Hometown Jamboree, Pinky Lee Show*, and *Tennessee Ernie Ford Show*, singer, dancer, and actress Molly Beachboard was born in Oklahoma City, and earned significant recognition as a yodeler. Her early years were spent singing on a farm near Beltbuckle, Tennessee, but her family moved to Tucson, Arizona, where she began her professional career at the age of ten. Her mother encouraged Molly to audition for singing cowboy Rex Allen at one of his concerts, and the blond-haired, blue-eyed youngster responded with her rendition of Hank Williams' "Lovesick Blues." Shortly thereafter, she debuted on Allen's radio show.

At age eleven, Molly's family moved to Hollywood, where she became a regular on the *Hometown Jamboree*, a Los Angeles television show, hosted by Cliffie Stone. She remained with the show throughout her teenage years, while also appearing as a cast member on the NBC *Pinky Lee Show* from 1954 to 1956.

At the age of thirteen, Molly signed with Capitol Records and debuted with her single entitled "Tennessee Tango." Released in late 1952, "I Saw Mommy Kissing Santa Claus" was her first hit. It was followed by a duet with Tennessee Ernie Ford, "Don't Start Courtin' in a Hot Rod Ford" in 1953. A year later, she joined the *Tennessee Ernie Ford* daytime television show, and began to develop a large following with her live shows drawing record-breaking crowds.

During the late 1950s, Molly's career began to blossom with such hit singles as "Young Romance," "Don't Look Back," and "5 Points of a Star." During the late 1960s, she joined **Roy Clark**'s *Swingin' Country* nationally televised show, and became a major performer on the Las Vegas showroom circuit.

During the 1960s, Molly also added acting to her career, debuting in the musical *The Boy Friend* in San Francisco. This was followed with *Finian's Rainbow* and *Paint Your Wagon* in which she starred with such notable actors as Alan Young and Buddy Ebsen. She also appeared in several films, including *Summer Love* (1958), *Going Steady* (1958), *Chartreuse Caboose* (1960), *The Young Swingers* (1963), and *Hillbillies in a Haunted House* (1967).

In 1965, Molly signed with MGM Records and cut two albums, *It's Great, It's Molly Bee* (1965) and *Swingin' Country* (1967). A string of singles during the

1960s included "Keep It a Secret"/ "Single Girl Again," "I'm Gonna Change Everything"/ "Together Again," "Losing You"/ "Miserable Me," "How's the World Treating You"/ "It Keeps Right on a Hurtin'," "A World I Can't Live In," "Almost Persuaded," "Heartbreak USA," "I Hate to See Me Go," "You Win Again," and "Fresh Out of Tryin'," the latter was her final MGM release. In 1966, she was nominated for Female Vocalist of the Year by the ACM.

By the late 1960s, Molly's personal life began to take a turn for the worse as she was plagued with a drug addiction problem and her third marriage began to crumble. Thus, she took some time off to rebuild her life, save her marriage, and spend time with her two daughters, Bobbi Jo and Malia. After this critical period in her life, Molly re-emerged in 1975 with a new album on Cliffie Stone's Granite label, *Good Golly Ms. Molly*, and released four singles on Granite, including "She Kept on Talkin'," "Right or Left at Oak Street," "California Country," and "I Can't Live in the Dark Anymore." Her last album, *Sounds Fine to Me*, was released on the Accord label in 1982. Capitol Nashville released *Christmas on the Range: Singing Cowboy Classics* in 1995, which featured one of Molly's best-known songs, "I Saw Mommy Kissing Santa Claus."

In 1998, Molly performed "Lonesome Me" for the Cliffie Stone Memorial Reunion in Santa Clarita, California. A graduate of the Hollywood Professional School, she also performed for their reunion in 2000. (GC)

Belew, Carl
(b. April 21, 1931 – d. October 31, 1990)

Best known for his songwriting skills, including such songs as "Am I That Easy to Forget," "Lonely Street," "Stop the World (And Let Me Off)," and "What's He Doing in My World," Carl Robert Belew was born on a farm near Salina, Oklahoma, a town boasting 1,000 people located in the northeastern part of the state. As a pastime on the farm, he began playing guitar, and left school at age fifteen to become a plumber, but decided on a music career.

In 1955, Marvin Rainwater set

up a recording session for Carl with Four Star Records, but he soon worked his way to California, where he appeared on the Cliffie Stone Show and Town Hall Party in 1956. He then moved to the Louisiana Hayride in 1957. A year later, he co-penned with W. S. Stephenson, Johnnie and Jack's Top 10 single, "Stop the World (And Let Me Off)."

In 1958, Andy Williams scored a Top 5 hit on the pop charts with "Lonely Street," which would become Carl's signature song because of subsequent recordings by such artists as Patsy Cline, Rex Allen, Jr., Gene Vincent, and Elvis Presley. It received a BMI Award in 1959. A year later Carl's marriage dissolved which resulted in co-writing with William A. McCall, "Am I That Easy to Forget?" It was recorded by Debbie Reynolds as a Top 40 pop hit, and later covered by such artists as Engelbert Humperdinck, Skeeter Davis, Gene Vincent, Don Gibson, Jim Reeves, and **Leon Russell**. Carl also recorded it in 1959 as his first Top 10 hit. It was also recipient of the BMI One-Million Performance Award.

In 1960, Carl released his eponymous album on the Decca label, which resulted in a Top 20 single, "Too Much to Lose." His first album with RCA in 1964, *Hello Out There*, produced a Top 10 hit, the title track of the LP, which surprisingly he did not write, as was the case with another one of his Top 20 hits, "Crystal Chandelier" (1965). His follow-up album with RCA in 1965 was *Am I That Easy to Forget?* He then reeled off a series of albums beginning with *Country Songs* (1967) and *Lonely Street* (1967) on the Vocalion label, *Twelve Shades of Belew* (1968) on RCA, and *When My Baby Sings His Song* (1972), a record of duets with Betty Jean Robinson, on Decca. The latter LP yielded another hit single, "All I Need Is You." His last charted single, "Welcome Back to My World," was released in 1974.

Additional songwriting successes included "What's He Doing in My World," a #1 hit for Eddy Arnold in 1965, the Jim Reeves hit in 1968, "That's When I See the Blues (In Your Pretty Brown Eyes)," and "Look at Us," which received the *Music City News* Award for Best Song of the Year in 1992. Other songs he penned included "Here's to the Girls," "Wind Me Up," "Working Like the Devil," "Even the Bad Times Are Good," "Don't Squeeze My Sharmon," and "Help Stamp Out Loneliness."

The list of artists who have recorded Carl's songs is impressive and includes such notables not previously mentioned as Waylon Jennings, Bobby Bare, The Browns, Bobby Darin, Everly Brothers, Emmylou Harris, Clarence "Frogman" Henry, **Wanda Jackson**, Dean Martin, George Jones, Willie Nelson, **Patti Page**, Carl Perkins, Esther Phillips, **B. J. Thomas**, Ernest Tubb, Conway Twitty, Tammy Wynette, and Faron Young.

Carl was inducted into the Nashville Songwriters Hall of Fame in 1976. At his induction ceremony, Carl stated: "I'm just thankful that the Lord has given me some talent, and I feel that I can still go on and write good songs . . . but it's cost me a fortune to learn how to read a contract. I think I could WRITE one now . . . and put a melody to it!" He died of cancer in 1990 at the age of fifty-nine. (GC)

Berline, Byron
(b. July 6, 1944)

Former three time national fiddle champion and acknowledged as the only bluegrass musician who has performed with the likes of the Rolling Stones, The Byrds, The Eagles, Elton John, and Bob Dylan, Byron Berline was born near Caldwell, Kansas, just north of the Oklahoma-Kansas border, but raised on a farm in Oklahoma with four older brothers and sisters with his mother, Elizabeth, and father, Lue. Lue, was an old-time fiddler, and Byron began playing the fiddle at age five. After high school graduation, Byron was awarded a football scholarship to the University of Oklahoma, and planned to coach with his physical education degree. While attending the University of Oklahoma, he formed his first band, Cleveland County Ramblers, which performed at campus functions, and also performed on an Oklahoma City television program sponsored by Garrett Household Furniture on which he became acquainted with and performed for **Wiley** (Walker) **and Gene** (Sullivan), who wrote "Live and Let Live" and "When My Blue Moon Turns to Gold Again." In 1963, he was auditioned by the Dillards, who were in concert on campus, and they invited him to play a number. A year later, he joined the Dillards on their *Pickin' and Fiddlin'* album, and won the National Old-Time Fiddling Championship in Missoula, Montana, a feat he would repeat two more times.

In 1965, Berline performed at the Newport Folk Festival, where he met Bill Monroe, who asked him to join the Blue Grass Boys when he completed his degree. After graduating from OU in 1967, Byron decided to fulfill Monroe's request, and his first performance with the band was on the Grand Ole Opry, as well as recording three songs with Monroe. After six months with the Blue Grass Boys, Byron was drafted into the U.S. Army and assigned to the special services unit. Stationed at Fort Polk, Louisiana, Byron performed with a bluegrass band at the officers' club for two years.

Following his discharge, Berline joined the Dillards for a short time, and then followed Doug Dillard when he teamed up with Gene Clark to form Dillard and Clark (1969-70). During this time, he played sessions for several other artists, including the Flying Burrito Brothers' debut album, *The Gilded Palace of Sin*. Dillard and Clark disbanded in 1970, and Byron again followed Doug Dillard to the Dillard Expedition (1970-71). In 1970, Berline scored the ABC television movie, *Run Simon Run*. During the 1970s, Byron scored several films, including

Stay Hungry (his first in 1975), *Bound for Glory* (story of **Woody Guthrie**), *White Lightning*, *The Longest Yard*, *Pat Garrett and Billy the Kid* (featured Bob Dylan), and *Stay Hungry* (Arnold Schwarzenegger's first film). When legendary Henry Mancini scored the film, *Sometimes a Great Notion*, he asked Berline to provide the fiddle music. Byron also scored the music for *Northern Exposure*, the 1990s hit television show.

After the break up of the Dillard Expedition, Byron, bassist Roger Bush, and banjoist Billy Ray Latham formed The Country Gazette in 1971, which later included Oklahoman Alan Munde. The Gazette recorded several albums, including their debut release, *A Traitor in Our Midst* (1972) and *Don't Give Up Your Day Job* (1973), both with United Artists; and *Bluegrass Special* (1973) on the Ariola label, a European recording company.

Byron left The Gazette in 1975 for a permanent move to Los Angeles to concentrate on songwriting, session work, and scoring films. Later that year, he organized Sundance, a group that included John Hickman, Dan Crary, Jack Skinner, Allen Wald, and Skip Conover, and later **Vince Gill** and Mark Cohen. The band remained together until 1985, releasing one album, *Byron Berline and Sundance*, cut in 1976. In 1977, Byron cut the album, *Dad's Favorites*, a tribute to his father, Lue. It included such well-known instrumentalists as Doug Dillard, Alan Munde, Vince Gill, Dan Crary, John Hartford, and Byron's wife, Bette on piano.

From 1978 to 1990, Byron led a trio consisting of himself, Crary, and Hickman. The threesome toured Japan and recorded three albums for Sugar Hill. Concurrently, Berline formed the L.A. Fiddle Band (1979-93) comprised of three fiddles, dobro, banjo, guitar, and bass. This group released one album on the Sugar Hill label, *Byron Berline & The L.A. Fiddle Band* (1980). After adding bassist Steven Spurgin, Berline, Crary, and Hickman, changed their name to simply BCH (first initials of their last names) in 1988, and in 1990 when they added mandolinist-guitarist John Moore, the band renamed itself California (1990-96).

In 1995, Byron released the critically acclaimed, two-time Grammy nominated album, *Fiddle & A Song* (Sugar Hill), which included Vince Gill singing the Bill Monroe classic, "My Rose of Old Kentucky," and a reunification of Bill Monroe and Earl Scruggs on "Sally Goodin'" with backup from their sons, James Monroe and Randy Scruggs.

After twenty-six years in California, Byron and his wife, Bette, returned to Oklahoma in 1996 and immediately launched three new projects: the Byron Berline Band with old friend John Hickman on banjo; the Double Stop Fiddle Shop and Music Hall in historic Guthrie, Oklahoma; and the First International Bluegrass Festival, also held in Guthrie the first weekend of October each year since 1997. Recent albums include *Live at the Music Hall* (1997), *One-Eyed Jack* (1999), and *Tribute to Gene Clark and Gram Parsons* (2000). His latest fiddle album, *Flat-broke Fiddler*, was released in 2002 by his own label, Double Stop Music. By 2003, the Byron Berline Band consisted of banjoist Hickman, bassist

Richard Sharpe, drummer Steve Short, and guitarist Brad Benge who replaced the previous guitarist, Jim Fish. The group plays about thirty to forty shows a year, having performed in California, Nashville, and on the East Coast in 2002 and 2003.

Byron has not only toured the United States, but also Europe, China, Japan, Australia, North Africa, and the South Pacific. As a result, he was named an Oklahoma Ambassador of Good Will since his return to the state. Byron was inducted into the Oklahoma Music Hall of Fame in 1999, and has served on the Oklahoma Music Hall of Fame Board since 2000. (GC)
www.doublestop.com

Bishop, Elvin
(b. October 21, 1942)

As the lead guitarist in the revolutionary earliest incarnation of The Butterfield Blues Band in 1961, a Top 10 hit to his credit in 1976, and five decades of playing and recording his own saucy mix of rowdy, good-time blues, Elvin Bishop helped usher in the resurgence of American interest in blues masters in the 1960s with his personal style of soulful lead guitar. Known for the sense of humor he expresses through his music, his slide guitar work, and fusing several American roots forms in his music, as of 2003 Bishop remains one of America's great blues guitarists, and continues to embody the sound of one who made a conscious effort to learn from the masters of the genre when he had the opportunity.

Elvin's parents, Elvin Bishop, Sr. and Mylda (Kleege) Bishop, were farmers from Iowa and Nebraska. Elvin's father was in the service and stationed in Glendale, California where Bishop was born. After Elvin Sr.'s service time, the Bishops moved back to Iowa where they continued to farm. In 1952, during an Oklahoma drought, Elvin Sr. brought down a load of hay to Oklahoma and took the opportunity to apply at Douglas Aviation in Tulsa where he was hired. Subsequently, at ten-years-old, Elvin moved with his family to Tulsa where he attended John Ross Grade School, Bell Jr. High, and Will Rogers High School. As a child, he would hear **Johnnie Lee Wills and His Boys** on the radio in the morning as he ate his cereal. "The country music influence is free in Oklahoma," Elvin remembered in a 2002 interview.

Since Tulsa was still very segregated in the 1950s, Elvin first became exposed to the blues by listening to Lightnin' Hopkins, John Lee Hooker, and Howlin' Wolf on radio stations from Nashville (WLAC), Shreveport, and Mexico. He tried playing guitar for a while but it hurt his fingers so he gave up until he saw all the

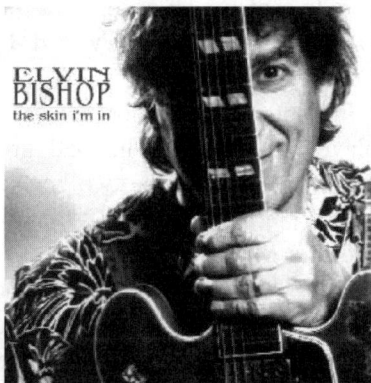

girls hanging around the guitar players from another local band. About that time, in 1959 Elvin Bishop rode a National Merit Scholarship from Will Rogers High to the University of Chicago to be closer to the blues mecca of the South Side of Chicago where blues men like Muddy Waters, Little Walter, and Howlin' Wolf were playing regularly in clubs. "The first thing I did when I got there," Elvin remembers, "was to make friends with the black dudes working in the cafeteria. Within fifteen minutes I was into the blues scene."

Acquaintances included Little Smokey Smothers and who taught Bishop a lot about playing the guitar, as did Sammy Lawhorn, Otis Rush, and Luther Tucker, during hours and hours of lessons in the blues as an art form and as an occupation. Elvin also served an apprenticeship as a sideman with Chicago legends Magic Sam and Junior Wells, and, became an accomplished player. He remembers two of his favorite blues men of the time were artists he had not seen from Oklahoma, **Flash Terry** and **Lowell Fulson**, whose records he collected in Chicago.

In 1960, when Bishop met fellow U of C student Paul Butterfield, a harmonica player and singer who had grown up in Chicago and gotten his start from Smothers as well, the two began frequenting South Side blues clubs where they would jam with Buddy Guy and Otis Rush, or pay two dollars to watch Howlin' Wolf, or Muddy Waters. Soon, they formed a duo and started playing college parties as The Buttercups. Upon the invitation to play a North Side Chicago club, Bishop and Butterfield hired the rhythm section from Howlin' Wolf's group, Sam Lay and Jerome Arnold, and became what was more than likely Chicago's only integrated blues group at the time, The Butterfield Blues Band. The group's popularity among Chicago's white audiences led to gigs at colleges outside of the Chicago area and the music took off.

In 1963, the group added another significant lead guitarist, Michael Bloomfield, as well as organist Mark Naftalin, and the hard-driving, attitude-laden band subsequently popularized the electric Chicago blues sound in America that was already being embraced by British blues enthusiasts John Mayall and the Rolling Stones; however, while the Brits were learning their licks from records, Elvin and company were emerging from the very wellspring of the form. The first recordings made by the group in 1964 became the album *The Paul Butterfield Blues Band* (1965), and were reissued in 1997 as a double CD package with songs not released on the original album. Popular music historians also note the group fueled their sound with the extended jams of the Bishop/Bloomfield twin-guitar attack, such as on 1966's thirteen-plus minute "East West" based on jazz and East Indian raga concepts. These kinds of jams would be the standard by which other late 1960s rock bands, such as the Grateful Dead and the Allman Brothers, based their own multi-lead instrumental techniques.

The group also played a minor part in the shifting tastes of American music listeners. After doing their own set at the 1965 Newport Folk Festival, the group backed Bob Dylan for his controversial electric folk set which sounded the death knell of the acoustic folk resurgence of the late 1950s and early 1960s. Contrary to several published reports, however, Elvin did not play during the set since he was backstage sharing a half pint with Mance Lipscomb and Mississippi John Hurt. Also during this period Bishop adopted the pseudonym of Pigboy Crabshaw to showcase his country material and the band took that name for its 1967 release, *The Resurrection of Pigboy Crabshaw,* which featured a horn section and only Bishop on lead guitar when Bloomfield left to form Electric Flag.

After the group's 1968 album, *In My Own Dream,* Elvin left for good and traveled to New York where he jammed with Jimi Hendrix, whom he called "quiet and humble," and Eric Clapton. Heading to the West coast in 1968, his solid reputation led to releasing three albums on Fillmore Records, a subsidiary of Epic, and two on One Way to include 1975's *Juke Joint Jump.* The latter enjoyed some moderate radio success with "Travelin' Shoes," peaking at #61 on the pop chart, and "Sure Feels Good," registering modestly at #83. Signed by Capricorn Records in 1975 at the urging of Dickey Betts, guitarist for the Allman Brothers who were also on Capricorn, Elvin reevaluated his strategy for commercial success. Lacking the mainstream appeal of his guitar work, Elvin's vocals seemed to be holding back the records, which prompted him to enlist pre-Jefferson Starship singer Mickey Thomas for the vocals to "Fooled Around and Fell in Love," a massive radio hit that landed at #3 on the pop chart and propelled the single's album, *Struttin My Stuff,* to number #68 on the album chart. Bishop's next album, *Hometown Boy Makes* Good (1976), failed to capitalize on his previous hit, even with another vocal by Thomas, however, and prompted critics to wonder if Bishop could ever capture his infectious live spirit on vinyl. Elvin confronted this critique by releasing a 1977 live album, *Raisin' Hell,* which bettered his earlier success on the album charts by reaching #38.

By 1978 Bishop pulled out all the stops and mixed nearly every one of his influences – gospel, R & B, blues, country, funk, and rock – on his final studio album for Capricorn, *Hog Heaven,* the cover art for which shows Elvin pouring beer into

a hog's mouth. After a seven-year recording drought, Alligator Records, one of America's most prominent contemporary blues labels, signed Elvin where he has been releasing critically acclaimed recordings and supporting them through touring ever since. His 1991 release, *Don't Let the Bossman Get You Down,* earned a four star review in *Rolling Stone,* and landed him on *Late Night with David Letterman.* In 1992, he toured the U.S. as part of Alligator Records 20th anniversary, and performs on the Grammy-nominated album recorded during that tour. Bishop was also interviewed for the documentary *Pride and Joy: The Story of Alligator Records.*

In 1998, the Oklahoma Jazz Hall of Fame's inducted Bishop in its blues category. In 2000, Bishop joined his former mentor Little Smokey Smothers for three sold out shows in San Francisco which were culled for the album *That's My Partner*, and a best of collection was released as part of Mercury Records' 20th Century Master series.

As of 2003, Bishop is writing songs about some "difficult subjects" and does not feel pressured to get out the next album. He performs throughout the United States at festivals, club dates, and concerts. However, of the musician's road life he says, "The romance of travel has worn off. More than anything, I just like to go out on the weekends and play like hell." Elvin currently lives with his wife, Cara, in the San Francisco Bay area where he is an avid gardener, and cans jars of tomatoes, green beans, fruit, corn, garlic, and a variety of Japanese vegetables.

"Growing up in Oklahoma," Elvin says, "gives you a soulful background for whatever you want to do." (HF)
www.alligatorrecords.com

Blane, Ralph
(b. July 26, 1914 – d. November 13, 1995)

Co-composer of "Meet Me in St. Louis," "Have Yourself a Merry Little Christmas," and "The Trolley Song," singer, arranger, and lyricist Ralph Blane was born Ralph Uriah Hunsecker on a farm near Broken Arrow, a suburb of Tulsa, to Tracy Mark and Florence Hazel Wilborn Hunsecker. The Hunseckers also had a second son, Tracy Mark, born in 1921. Ralph's father was a businessman, owning three dry goods stores in Broken Arrow and Coweta. Ralph attended elementary school in Broken Arrow and graduated from Central High School in Tulsa. While at Central, he was active as a singer and dancer, often participating in high school talent shows. At age seventeen, Ralph and his parents attended a Broadway show in New York, and, following that visit, he realized that music was his forté.

After studying at Northwestern University in Evanston, Illinois, Ralph moved to New York City, where he studied music under Estell Liebling. He made his Broadway stage debut as a vocalist in *New Faces* in 1936, followed in 1937 by another Broadway musical, *Hooray for What*? Responsible for auditions for the latter production was actress Kay Thompson, star of the show, assisted by pianist Hugh Martin, who suggested Blane for a part because of his rich strong voice. In 1941, Blane teamed with Martin to organize a vocal quartet known as The Martins, who performed in New York City nightclubs and made a guest appearance on *The Fred Allen Show* on radio. Sometime while in New York, Ralph began using Blane because his original last name did not fit theater marquees.

In the 1930s, Blane was co-vocal arranger for such Broadway musicals as *Pal Joey*, *DuBarry Was a Lady*, *Cabin in the Sky*, *Too Many Girls*, *Louisiana Purchase*, *Very Warm for May*, and *Stars in Your Eyes*. During the 1940s, the Blane and Martin team contributed songs for the 1941 Broadway hit, *Best Foot Forward* (326 performances), produced and directed by George Abbott and choreographed by Gene Kelly. Blane and Martin helped MGM convert it into the 1943 Vincinte Minnelli movie musical of the same title, starring Lucille Ball. The most celebrated songs from the musical were "Ev'ry Time" and "Buckle Down, Winsocki," a college fight song for the fictitious Winsocki University ("buckle down, Winsocki, buckle down/you can win Winscocki, if you knuckle down"). It was later recorded by such artists as Glenn Miller, Benny Goodman, and Liza Minnelli. Henry Wallace, third party candidate for President in 1948, used the tune for his campaign song, "We Can Win With Wallace," and the National Safety Council in the 1960s and 1970s used the melody for its "Buckle Up for Safety" commercial. While in Hollywood, the Blane-Martin partnership contributed "The Joint is Really Jumpin' (In Carnegie Hall)" for the movie, *Thousands Cheer* in 1943, and reunited in 1954 to score the film *Anthea*, followed by *The Girl Rush* in 1955.

During this era, the Blane-Martin duo wrote musical scores for several other films, including *Best Foot Forward* (1943), *Meet Me in St. Louis* (1944) which was their most successful soundtrack, *One Sunday Afternoon* (1948), *My Dream Is Yours* (1949), *My Blue Heaven* (1950), *The French Line* (1954), *The Girl Most Likely* (1957). Star of *Meet Me in St. Louis*, Judy Garland sang several of their best-known compositions, such as "Have Yourself a Merry Little Christmas, "The Boy Next Door," and "The Trolley Song" ("clang, clang, clang went the trolley/ding, ding, ding went the bell"). The latter was nominated for an Academy Award for Best Song in 1945. "Have Yourself a Merry Little Christmas" became a holiday favorite, especially after Perry Como and Tony Bennett's recordings in the late 1960s. It later appeared on seasonal albums by such luminaries as Andy Williams, Barbara Streisand, James Taylor, Peabo Bryson, The Jackson 5, and **Garth Brooks**. "Pass That Piece Pipe," a collaboration of Blane, Martin, and Roger Edens, was written as a duet for Gene Kelly and Fred Astaire in the MGM film, *Ziegfield Follies*, but it never made it into the movie. It did resurface in the 1947 movie *Good News*, starring June Allyson and Peter Lawford, and was nominated for an Oscar as Best Song of the Year in 1948. On October 5, 1947, Blane married Emajo Jo Stage at his brother's home in Broken Arrow, and their marriage resulted in one son, George, who currently lives in Broken Arrow.

Returning to Broadway in the 1950s, Blane wrote the music and lyrics for the musical, *Three Wishes for Jamie* (1952), starring John Raitt. He and Martin wrote the score for *Sugar Babies*, another Broadway hit in 1979, starring Mickey Rooney, and the team composed several new songs for a stage adaptation of *Meet Me in St. Louis* in 1960, adding more new material for a 1989 revival on Broadway. It was nominated for four Tony Awards, including Best Adapted Score for a Musical.

Additional highlights from the Blane-Martin catalog include "Shady Lady Bird," "Everytime," "The Three B's," "That's How I Love the Blues," "What Do You Think I Am," "Love" (recorded by native Oklahoman **Chet Baker** in 1954), "Just a Little Joint With a Jukebox," "Brazilian Boogie," "Connecticut (Is the

Place For Me)," "Venezia," "I Don't Know What I Want," and "You Are For Loving." Blane also collaborated with other composers including Harry Warren ("The Stanley Steamer," Someone Like You," and "My Dream Is Yours") and Harold Arlen ("My Blue Heaven"). He also wrote "Duty, Honor, Country," the musical background for General Douglas MacArthur's famous speech to the Corps of Cadets at the U.S. Military Academy at West Point in 1962. His lone television score was for *Quillow and the Giant*.

During the early 1990s, Blane retired to his native Broken Arrow, where he died November 13, 1995. He is credited with more than 500 songs in the ASCAP directory, and was inducted into the Songwriters Hall of Fame in 1983 by the National Academy of Popular Music. He also received the Richard Rodgers Award, a prestigious honor given by the Richard and Dorothy Rodgers Foundation and ASCAP to recognize the achievements of lyricists and composers historically associated with American music.

In 2001 The Ralph Sharon Quartet recorded *The Ralph Blane Songbook*, a fifteen-track tribute to Blane, on the DRG label. The CD included "Buckle Down, Winsocki," " The Trolley Song," and "Have Yourself a Merry Little Christmas," but also featured some of Blane's lesser known songs, such as "An Occasional Man," "At Last We're Alone," and "I Love a New Yorker." In 2003, Rhino Records released the Original Motion Picture Soundtrack of *Best Foot Forward*. In addition to the entire soundtrack recording, much of which had never been released, also included on the *Best Foot Forward* compact disc are four previously unissued Martin and Songs written for *Abbot and Costello in Hollywood* (1945). (GC/HF)

Boggs, Noel
(b. November 14, 1917 – d. August 31, 1974)

Considered one of the finest steel guitarists in the history of the instrument, an inductee into the Steel Guitar Hall of Fame, and appearances on more than 2,000 recordings as a sideman, Noel Edwin Boggs was born in Oklahoma City. He learned to play the steel guitar during junior high after taking a twelve-lesson course in the fundamentals of music at twenty-five cents per lesson. While in high school, he worked for three radio stations in Oklahoma City (WKY, KOMA, and KEXR). His first steel guitar was a Rickenbacker. While in Oklahoma City, Noel befriended the legendary jazz guitarist **Charlie Christian**, who worked on Northeast Second Street ("Deep Deuce"). Noel learned many of the Christian guitar solos, such as "Flying Home" and "Good Enough to Keep."

In 1936, Noel joined Hank Penny's Radio Cowboys and the band toured the southern and eastern regions of the U.S., as well as recording with the group on Vocalion in 1939. He gained further experience working as a staff musician on radio stations WWL in New Orleans and WAPI and WBRC in Birmingham before returning to Oklahoma City in 1937. Working with **Wiley and Gene** on both their recordings and at radio station WKY for the next four years, Noel launched his own band in 1941 with the encouragement of Leon McAuliffe, steel guitarist with **Bob Wills** and the Texas Playboys. After working at the Rainbow Room in Oklahoma City for the next three years with such musicians as **Jimmy Wakely**, Noel joined the Texas Playboys as steel guitarist when McAuliffe left in 1944 to form his own band, the Cimarron Boys. While with the Playboys, he met guitarists Jimmy Wyble and Cameron Hill, and created jazz-like arrangements for three guitars that gave western swing one of its distinctive sounds.

Noel played on some of Wills' Tiffany Transcriptions and Columbia recordings, including "New Spanish Two Step," "Texas Playboy Rag," "Roly Poly," and "Stay a Little Longer." In 1946, he left Wills and reformed a group for an extended engagement at the Hollywood Palladium, but returned to Wills for a brief time before joining another western swing band, the **Spade Cooley** Orchestra in 1947. During this time, he met the famed guitar maker, Leo Fender, while the Cooley band performed at the Santa Monica Ballroom. Fender presented Noel with his first steel guitar, and thereafter Noel became a promoter for Fender's equipment. A friendship between the two ensued and Fender became godfather of Noel's daughter, Sandy. He remained off and on with Cooley until 1954, recording his trademark classics, "Boggs Boogie" (1947) and "Steelin' Home" (1954).

Noel then suffered the first of several heart attacks that curtailed his playing until 1956. After partial recovery from the heart condition, Noel formed his own quintet and toured several western states, and played many of the nightclubs in Las Vegas, Reno, and Lake Tahoe. Along with performances on USO tours, including one to Alaska and the Orient, Noel recorded several albums on the Shasta and Repeat labels, including *Magic Steel Guitar* (1960), *Western Swing* (1965), and *Any Time* (1968), and also owned the Delphine Marina on Redondo Beach, California.

Inducted into the Steel Guitar Hall of Fame in 1981, Noel is recognized as a recording artist who "stylized the 'mellow tone' using multiple, non-pedal tunings for his patented 'neck-hopping' technique." He was noted for his smooth, complex, and full chord expression.

During his career, Noel appeared in several films, including *Rhythm Roundup* (1945), *Blazing the Western Trail* (1945), *Lawless Empire* (1946), and *Everybody's Dancin'* (1950). He also worked on radio with a number of the singing cowboys, such as **Gene Autry**, Roy Rogers, Rex Allen, and the Sons of the Pioneers.

During his final days, he was estranged from his children and wife and plagued with alcoholism. But he overcame his sadness with humor and practical jokes, including a story where Noel returned home from a tour in a hearse and every time the vehicle stopped, he would sit up in the coffin and look around. It is also reported that he left specific instructions for his funeral music—he wanted only lively steel guitar and not sad organ music. His family, therefore, played some of his own recordings for his funeral when he died at Granada Hills, California, in 1974. (GC)

Bogle, Bob
(b. January 16, 1934)

As the original and all-time bassist/guitarist for the best and most significant instrumental guitar group of the early 1960s, The Ventures, Bob Bogle is one of Oklahoma's least-known native musicians who has enjoyed popular success on a massive scale. Bob Bogle and another native Oklahoman, lead guitarist **Nokie Edwards**, were half of the original Ventures that redefined and re-popularized the electric guitar combo in the midst of the late 1950s and early 1960s pop music era of homogenized and watered-down rock and roll. With Top 5 hits like "Walk Don't Run" and "Hawaii Five-0," their drum-driven, fast dance music featuring speedy electric guitars inspired countless 1960s surf music groups and garage rock bands from the U.S., the U.K., and Japan. Called by the *New York Times* "the archetypal 1960s American surf band," their heavy influence tumbled into punk rock era of the 1970s, and the alternative country music of the 1980s through the 2000s. Musicians who are on record as being inspired by the group include Jimmy Page, Stanley Clarke, Steve Miller, George Harrison, The Ramones, Jeff "Skunk" Baxter of Steely Dan, and Larry Carlton.

While The Ventures had admirable success on the single charts in the 1960s with fourteen Top 100 singles, The Ventures' thematic LP collections drove their notoriety. They rank sixth among all 1960s artists on the album charts, behind The Beatles, Frank Sinatra, Elvis Presley, Ray Conniff and Ray Charles. According to the band's website, all totaled, Bob Bogle has recorded more than 3,000 songs with The Ventures, had a hand in writing co-writing many of their more than 1,000 original songs, and appeared on over 250 albums with the group, including compilations. Thirty-seven of the albums made the US charts, more than 150 albums have been released in Japan alone, and their 1960s-era *Play Guitar with The Ventures* series was the first and only set of musical instruction records to ever make the album charts. The group had five gold albums, was named *Billboard's* Most Promising Instrumental Group of 1960, sold an unprecedented one million albums per year from 1961 to 1966, and have ultimately sold over one hundred million albums through 2003.

Robert Lenard "Bob" Bogle was born at the rural residence of his family near Wagoner, Oklahoma, a town founded in 1886 where the Arkansas Valley and Kansas Valley Railroad met the developing Missouri, Kansas, and Texas railway that ran north to south through Indian Territory. The thoroughfare was then known as the Texas Road, and is now U.S. Highway 69, still a major transportation artery through northeastern Oklahoma. According to The Ventures' 2003 website in the "Ask a Venture" section, Bob remembers mainly listening to the radio since TV did not yet exist, and "most of the music at that time in that area was Western music," undoubtedly referring to the prominence of **Bob Wills and His Texas Playboys** on Oklahoma radio. He also remembers listening to the Grand Ole Opry "quite a bit" before moving west when he was six-years-old.

The 1930s Depression-era travails suffered by many of the state's residents led Bogle's father, a native of Siloam Springs, Arkansas who moved near Locust Grove when he was age seven, to sell what few animals and basic farm equipment the family had on a small leased farm, and move west to California. Not only was that the classic Okie thing to do at the time, but they ran into the classic Okie problem in California, no work. The family migrated up and down the West Coast following the various harvests, and Bob, the second of four boys, worked in the fields doing any kind of farm work available. During school months, they worked in the mornings before school and again in the evenings. After a few years, the family finally settled in Portland where his father found work in a sawmill when Bob was in his early teens.

Bogle's earliest musical experiences came when he was twelve and his brother, Clarence, brought home an acoustic lap steel guitar, allowing Bob to learn chords immediately. Because of its open tuning that allows a player to hold a steel bar in a one position on the instrument's neck and make a perfect chord by striking all the strings, Bob was soon accompanying himself on simple, three-chord songs that make up much of country music's core repertoire. He continued playing the instrument for a couple of years, but left home at age fifteen (and halfway through the 9th grade) to begin working in construction. At eighteen in 1952, Bogle became a journeyman brick mason and a member of the Bricklayers Union in Portland. That year his younger brother, Dennis, bought a regular acoustic guitar, showed Bob a few chords, and eventually gave him the guitar when Dennis left for the Air Force. Bob kept learning chords, accompanying himself, and started figuring out lead guitar lines while getting into "all that Top 40 stuff." That stuff would have been the beginning of the 1950s rock and roll movement about the time Bill Haley hit with "Rock Around the Clock" in 1954. For a precursor to the lickety split guitar work that became a hall mark of Ventures' recordings, check out Haley's solo on that landmark single, commonly acknowledged as the first significant popular rock and roll hit.

In 1959, Bob began working at a construction company in Seattle, Washington.

After meeting future Ventures partner Don Wilson (b. February 10, 1937, Tacoma, Washington), who was selling used cars at the time, Wilson expressed interest in getting work in construction and soon the two were working together as mortar removers (or tuckpointers), where they had plenty of time to discuss their mutual interest in guitars. Before long they started practicing together on weekends with guitars and amps purchased from local pawnshops, and began playing as The Versatones at local dances in 1959. With more experience and some acceptance by crowds locally, Bogle and Wilson decided to upgrade their equipment and think about a career in music which couldn't be any worse than a bricklaying career, and might even be a ticket out of that type of work that musicians have been trying to avoid since the time of Orpheus.

Bob's first new guitar was a Fender Stratocaster that came with six lessons, a half-hour a week, for six weeks. Telling the instructor to teach him chords, Bob picked up most of the formal training he would need to play at a rock level that would find national chart success within a year. He began listening to his big three inspirations, Chet Atkins, Duane Eddy, and Les Paul, trying to pick out their songs and key into their primary stylistic aesthetics of playing and tone. While listening to a Chet Atkins album, *Hi-Fi in Focus* (RCA-Victor, 1959), Bob and Don heard "Walk, Don't Run" and decided to record it with a rhythm section they had brought into the group that included bassist **Nokie Edwards** (just out of Buck Owens' band), and drummer Skip Moore (who had played with Edwards in Owens' band). Moore was a local drummer who was given the choice of $25 or ¼ of the song's proceeds, and mistakenly chose the former. Primary drummer Howie Johnson (b. WA, 1938 - d. 1988) was added within a year. While Edwards initially joined the group as a bassist, and soon became the lead guitarist of the band, Bob Bogle played guitar on "Walk, Don't Run," a song that was kept out of the #1 spot in 1960 by Brian Hyland's "Itsy Bittsy Teeny Weeny Yellow Polka Dot Bikini" and Elvis Presley's "It's Now or Never," but forever defined the classic Ventures sound. Bogle also played guitar on the first several Ventures LP releases before switching primarily to bass for concerts and recordings when it became obvious Nokie's stratospheric guitar abilities could be showcased to everyone's advantage.

The Ventures are not only widely known for their instrumental prowess, but also for their important innovations in guitar sound and technique, and widely divergent stylistic abilities. Experimenting with such technical innovations like the "fuzzbox" for a guitar that would distort the sound to give a band a unique aural signature, The Ventures are credited with being the first band to record with it on 1962's "2000 Pound Bee." Additionally, not only did their success "formalize" the standard rock combo of lead and rhythm guitars, electric bass, and drums for countless rock bands from the 1960s through the present in the U.S. and U.K., the Ventures appealing guitar sound also inspired thousands of Japanese youngsters to buy guitars and generally create the same sort of general social nuisance that rock and roll had aroused in 1950s U.S. popular culture.

Incidentally, many of the guitars sold by virtue of The Ventures popularity were made by two Oklahoma natives, Semie Moseley (b. Durant, 1935), and his brother, Andy (b. Durant, 1933), who had moved as children with their parents in the Okie migration west during the Great Depression. After a stint building instruments for Rickenbacker in Los Angeles in the early 1950s, Semie started his own line of guitars, Mosrites, which were first picked up by Bakersfield Sound country musicians such as Joe Maphis, and traveling Grand Ole Opry stars always on the lookout for a performance gimmick. Semie's triple-necked guitar with the longest neck strung as a standard guitar, the second-longest neck tuned an octave higher, and the shortest neck an eight-stringed mandolin provided a versatile and visual instrument. After Nokie Edwards met Moseley in 1962 and enjoyed playing a Mosrite, The Ventures played and marketed the custom guitars by Moseley under an exclusive licensing deal that kept the guitars on their album covers from 1963 to 1968 when the company went bankrupt. At their peak in 1968, Semie and his brother averaged production of 1,000 guitars per month, to include acoustics, standard electrics, double-necks, triple-necks, basses, dobros, and mandolins, but the company's success was largely fueled by The Ventures large following.

The Ventures's fruitful 1960s period was certainly enhanced by recording instrumental collections based on contemporary musical trends in the rapidly changing pop culture world of that decade. According to a 2003 interview posted on his website, Nokie remembers the band members looking at songs bubbling under the various trade charts, listening to those songs, and then picking ones out they thought might be hits about the time the album was ready. Recordings of this type included The Animals "House of the Rising Son," The Surfaris "Wipe Out," Henry Mancini's "Pink Panther Theme," Leiber and Stoller's "Love Potion #9," and Lennon and McCartney's "I Feel Fine," among many others. Not limited by popular music, however, The Ventures also arranged classical music so that it sounded pop, such as "Rap City," based on Brahms' "Hungarian Dance #5," and

Bob Bogle, 2003

"Bumble Bee Twist," based on Rimsky-Korsakov's "The Flight of the Bumblebee." Just a sampling of Ventures album titles traces pop culture trends of the period: *Twist with the Ventures* (Dolton, 1962), *The Ventures Surfing* (Dolton, 1963), *The Ventures in Space* (Dolton, 1964), *The Ventures A-Go-Go* (Dolton, 1965), *Wild Things* (Dolton, 1966), *Guitar Freakout* (Dolton, 1967), *Super Psychedelics* (Liberty, 1967), *Underground Fire* (Liberty, 1968), and *Hawaii Five-0* (Liberty, 1969).

After Nokie Edwards left the band in 1968, The Ventures had their last major U.S. hit in 1969, "Hawaii- Five-O," the theme song for the popular television detective drama set in Hawaii that aired on from 1968 to 1980. Not only did the song reach #4 on the U.S. pop charts, the weekly television show kept The Ventures' sound in front of the public and kept them touring the world, especially in Japan where in 1970 and 1971 the Ventures were that country's #1 composers. Five songs during those years reached the top of the Japanese charts when the band's Japanese label would release a Japanese vocal version of the song, known in Japan as "Kayo-kyoku," or a "ballad song," at the same time as The Ventures' original instrumental hit the market and, subsequently, the charts.

After a three-year hiatus (1968-1971) during which Edwards pursued his passion for horses, Gerry McGee played lead guitar for The Ventures while native Oklahoman John Durrill (**The Five Americans**) played keyboards for the band. Nokie returned to play lead guitar in 1972 and The Ventures' 1970s releases again chronicle some of the decade's popular culture musical trends, as well as the group's ability to capitalize on them: *Theme from Shaft* (United Artists, 1971), *Rock 'N' Roll Forever* (1972), *The Jim Croce Songbook* (1974), *Ventures Play the Carpenters* (1974), *TV Themes* (1977), and the *Latin Album* (1978) that surfaced when the disco era and its heavy Latin influences were a prominent part of mainstream pop music. The Ventures continued recording new material with the original lineup through 1983, touring the U.S. and, especially, Japan where they remain hugely popular. Nokie again left in 1984 to pursue his own music and a steady stream of solo engagements, but repeatedly performed and recorded with The Ventures on select occasions through the beginning of the twenty-first century. No less than seventy re-issues of albums have been produced on various labels both in the states and abroad since 1990, and the group has continued touring through 2003 with a constant demand for their performances at festivals, on cruise lines, and their own headlining concerts, sometimes with Nokie Edwards on lead guitar, and sometimes with old friend Gerry McGee taking the lead spot. Bob wrote in a 2003 e-mail: "Our lengthy summer tours here have sort of become one of Japan's traditions. We started doing concerts here in 1962, and the last few years we have started doing a winter tour also. Since I was the original guitarist, I am featured on lead on a few songs while Gerry or Nokie plays bass, and for the rest of the show I play bass."

Historically, The Ventures are considered one of rock's all-time greatest bands. It seems ironic then they have not yet been inducted into the Rock and Roll Hall of Fame. Given their extremely influential sound, the longevity and magnitude of their commercial success, and their acknowledged impact on younger musicians who are already in the Rock Hall, The Ventures would seem to be a "no-brainer" for enshrinement in Cleveland, and with two of its primary members being native Oklahomans (not to mention Oklahoman John Durrill who played keybs for a spell), honors from home can't be too far off either. Like Nokie Edwards, Bob Bogle, did not begin playing music as a child when he lived in Oklahoma. However, the state's musical vibe of the 1930s, to include the simultaneous radio presence of Western swing and Grand Ole Opry broadcasts, not to mention his

parents accents, must have planted a little twang in his ear that has never really left The Ventures, and by way of their music has found its way across the world. Bogle's story is just one of Oklahoma's many well- kept music history secrets, until now. So, go tell someone. (HF)
www.theventures.com

Boland, Jason and the Stragglers
(Formed 1998 in Stillwater, OK)

Playing a rowdy brand of **Red Dirt Music** that leans toward the heavily bowed fiddle, whiney steel guitar, and the bittersweet lyrical topics of honky-tonk country music, Jason Boland and the Stragglers are one of the most successful young country groups playing on the well-worn stages of Oklahoma, Kansas, Arkansas, Louisiana, and Texas. Led by Oklahoma native and primary songwriter Jason Boland, who began playing professionally with **Cross Canadian Ragweed**'s Cody Canada in Stillwater in 1997, the Stragglers consist of lead singer and rhythm guitarist Boland (b. Harrah), lead guitarist, steel, and dobro player Roger Ray (from Vian), drummer Brad Rice (from Edmond), and bassist Tracy Grant (from Vian). More recently, the group has added fiddler Jeremy Watkins (from Midland-Odessa, TX) who claims **Bob Wills** and

Jason Boland

Merle Haggard as his biggest influences.

Born in Harrah, a farming community of about 4,000 people thirty miles east of Oklahoma City, Jason Boland started playing guitar in the sixth grade after seeing *Crossroads* with his father, a movie about legendary blues man Robert Johnson who is known to have played in Taft, Oklahoma in the 1930s. Inspired by the film, Boland mentioned to his father he would like to play guitar and the elder Boland pulled an old one down from the attic and showed Jason a few blues licks. Boland was in a few bands, and listened to his older sister's rock records as a teenager that turned him onto Ozzy Osbourne's great guitarist, Randy Rhodes. After moving to Stillwater in 1993 to attend Oklahoma State University, Jason discovered Steve Earle, heard Jimmy Buffett in a new light, and started writing songs. Soon, the **Great Divide**'s Mike McClure pointed Boland in the direction

of red dirt music godfathers, Tom Skinner and Bob Childers, as well as toward Cody Canada of Cross Canadian Ragweed. By 1997, Boland met Canada at one of Cross Canadian Ragweed's shows in Stillwater, and the two struck up a musical friendship that evolved into Boland filling the break space between sets in Canada's local solo gigs.

Enter jazz and fusion drummer Brad Rice, who met Boland the same year at OSU, guitarist and steel player Roger Ray who connected with Boland at "The Farm," a rural meeting place for Stillwater musicians in the 1990s, and, finally, bassist and banjo player Tracy Grant who brought jam-band influences of Phish and the Grateful Dead to the Stragglers' rocking alter ego

Brad Rice

that surfaces periodically in the midst of all the honk. With a group in place by 1998, the Stragglers headed to Larry Joe Taylor's annual Texas music festival in Meridian where they played campfire jams, by virtue of which they were invited

Tracy Grant

back the next year to play the new artist showcase at the festival. In 1999, the Stragglers released *Pearl Snaps*, an album produced by Texas music legend Lloyd Maines, and a record Jason has said is suited for a "partyin', drinkin', cryin' in your beer type mood." Quickly becoming one of the biggest selling roots country records in Texas for that year, the songs' party mood and sing-along ethos ("Pearl Snaps" and "Drinking Song") is the opposite of the road stories and marginalized-human studies present on *Truckstop Diaries* (2001), an album full of the Stragglers' multiple musical influences, as well as the characters and the experiences of their continued existence on the road.

With songs such as "Truckstop Diaries," a wry observation of the eccentric personalities of travel plazas, and "Falling with Style," a description of the rough and tumble world of rodeo cowboys, Boland carries the bulk of the band's songwriting load. While he wrote or co-wrote eight of the album's songs, he also brought in tunes written or co-written by fellow red dirt luminaries such as Stoney LaRue, Mike McClure, Cody Canada, Bob Childers, and Randy Crouch to fill out the collection. Eagerly anticipated by fans in 2001, *Truckstop Diaries* hit the shelves in late July, and a few days afterwards, Boland and fiddler Dana Hazzard were involved in a one-car accident that broke Jason's hip and shelved him for about three months. The August 1st date earmarked for the album's release party evolved into a benefit concert and auction for Boland's medical expenses, which led to a series of benefits in Texas and Oklahoma that raised almost thirty thousand dollars for the injured singer. Within a few months, and after extensive rehab on the part of Boland, the Stragglers were back on the road in support of *Truckstop Diaries* and have not stopped since. In their short existence, the band has been able to exploit their popularity into opening slots for Merle Haggard, Asleep at the Wheel, Robert Earl Keen, and Willie Nelson, as well as continuing their own schedule of headlining opportunities throughout the five-state area mentioned earlier, along with newly opened markets in Nebraska, New Mexico, Colorado and Alabama.

In 2002, the group released *Live and Lit at Billy Bob's Texas* as part of a series of live albums recorded in the "The World's Largest Honky Tonk." *Live and Lit*, with lead and

Roger Ray

rhythm guitarist Travis Linville complementing the band's performance, exemplifies the spirit of the group with many of their best songs from the first two albums, as well as new numbers like the Tex-Mex-influenced, lost love song, "Mexico or Crazy," a Top 20 song by March, 2003 in The Texas Music Chart; one that would make Waylon Jennings proud, "When I'm Stoned"; and "Mary," a desperate song about the lonelier side of life.

The group can also be found on compilations of both red dirt musicians and like-minded Texas artists. "Armor" appears on the spiritually influenced compilation, *Dirt and Spirit*, and "Travelin' Jones" appears on *Texas Road Trip*, an album of "Texas" musicians (even though Boland and Cross Canadian Ragweed, also on the album, are from Oklahoma). Boland also added half of a duet performance with Texas honky-tonker Kevin Fowler on Merle Haggard's "I Think I'll Just Stay Here and Drink," included on an album of drinking songs, *Brewed in Texas* (Compadre).

The powerful Texas magnet proved too much for the band to keep its Oklahoma home. By late 2002, the band had relocated to Austin, a logical move given the Stragglers' success in the lone star state. Before going south of the Red River, however, The Stragglers backed their old Stillwater friend, Kyle Everett, a young,

Oklahoma City-based country singer, on his solo album, *Water for My Horses.* According to their website, by August of 2003 the Stragglers had a full slate of performances scheduled through the rest of the year and their third next studio album was being recorded in Austin for a 2004 release. (HF)
www.thestragglers.com

Bond, Johnny
(b. June 1, 1915 - d. June 22, 1978)

Known for writing the western classic "Cimarron (Roll On)" and the bluegrass standard "I Wonder Where You Are Tonight," as well as being one of the first inductees into the Nashville Songwriter's Hall of Fame in 1970 and an inductee into the Country Music Hall of Fame in 1999, Cyrus Whitfield Bond was born near Enville, Oklahoma, a tiny hamlet located near the Oklahoma-Texas border that closed its post office in 1935, and no longer is included on the most recent Oklahoma highway map.

Johnny was raised in a poor farm family who listened to Jimmie Rodgers recordings. As a young boy, he wanted to become a songwriter and guitarist like Rodgers. Once he had earned enough money, he ordered a 98-cent ukulele from the Montgomery Ward catalogue. Although he played trumpet in the Marietta (Oklahoma) High School band, his first love was the guitar because of the Rodgers influence. He also listened to the recordings of Milton Brown and the Light Crust Doughboys, one of the first western swing bands in Fort Worth. Johnny's first professional experience was in 1933 playing in a local string band where he played ukulele, guitar, and banjo.

After graduating from high school in 1934, Bond headed to Oklahoma City, where he auditioned for local radio shows. It was there he met **Jimmy Wakely**, who was to become a life long friend. In 1937, the two formed a trio patterning their sound after the popular cowboy singing group, the Sons of the Pioneers, which included as one of its original members Oklahoman **Tim Spencer** from Picher. The third member of the trio alternated between Scotty Harrell and former Light Crust Doughboy, **Dick Reinhart**, a native Oklahoman from Tishomingo. At the outset, the trio called themselves The Singing Cowboy Trio, but later changed their name to The Bell Boys because of sponsorship by the Bell Clothing Company on radio station WKY in Oklahoma City, where they played on a daily show. In addition, the trio cut transcription discs at radio station KVOO in Tulsa.

During these first years of his career, Johnny used several pseudonyms, such as Cyrus Whitfield, Johnny Whitfield, and finally Johnny Bond. He also attended the University of Oklahoma for a brief time in 1937.

During this Oklahoma City period, Johnny started writing songs, and in 1938, he completed his first classic, "Cimarron (Roll On)," which was used as a theme song for the *Bell Boys* radio show. **Gene Autry** came through Oklahoma City on tour in the late 1930s and heard the trio. Impressed by their repertoire, which included some of his songs, Autry suggested he could use the trio on his *Melody Ranch* radio show should they ever decide to make a move to California.

In 1939, the group was invited to appear as the Jimmy Wakely Trio in the Hollywood Republic Pictures production of *The Saga of Death Valley*, starring Roy Rogers. This taste of Western movies and Autry's offer set the trio to thinking about a move to Hollywood. Therefore, in May of 1940, Bond, Wakely, and Reinhart and their families left in Wakely's Dodge automobile for California, where in September, Autry hired them to become regulars on the CBS *Melody Ranch* radio show, where Johnny remained for sixteen years until the show was canceled in 1956. The trio appeared as Jimmy Wakely and His Rough Riders in a second movie, *The Tulsa Kid* (1940), starring "Red" Barry, and a third in the Universal studio film, *Pony Post* (1940), starring Johnny Mack Brown. Johnny continued his work with the original trio members, along with Scotty Harrell, who moved to Hollywood later. They performed at various concerts, ballrooms, and clubs throughout southern California. But by 1941, the Wakely Trio had ceased to exist and Johnny began to look for other opportunities in furthering his career in the Los Angeles area.

While remaining on the *Melody Ranch* show, Bond also appeared in thirty-eight motion pictures through 1947, primarily as a supporting musician to such legendary singing cowboys as Autry, Tex Ritter, and Wakely, who eventually became a star in his own films at Monogram. Some sources indicate that Wakely was the first trio member recorded on Decca in 1940, while others state that Johnny was the first member to record on Okeh, a subsidiary of Columbia Records in 1941. Regardless of this debate, Art Satherly of Okeh did sign Johnny to a contract in 1941, a deal which spanned sixteen years. Satherly knew talent as he had previously signed Gene Autry, Tex Ritter, Leadbelly, and a host of other music legends. Because of his association with Autry, Satherly was familiar with Johnny's work as acoustic guitarist on all of Autry's recordings. The most memorable was the famous Martin guitar introduction to "Back in the Saddle Again," as well as the first song they recorded together, "You Are My Sunshine." Johnny and Gene also co-wrote a number of songs, including "Don't Live a Lie" and "Funny Little Bunny with the Powder Puff Tail."

Bond's first recording sessions were in August of 1941, and resulted in one notable recording, "Those Gone and Left Me Blues." In April of 1942, Johnny cut three songs, including "Turkey in the Straw," "Mussolini's Letter to Hitler," and "Hitler's Reply to Mussolini," but the company decided not to release them due to a conflict with Carson Robison's then popular recording of "Turkey in the Straw."

Johnny had continued his songwriting talents, and began to have some of his songs published, including "I Wonder Where You Are Tonight" and "Cimarron." In July of 1942, he recorded four songs, including "I'm a Pris'ner of War," and "Der Fuhrer's Face," as well as two of his originals, "You Let Me Down" and "Love Gone Cold," backed by a band that included **Spade Cooley**, another Oklahoman, on fiddle. In addition to his regular work on the Melody Ranch show, Johnny was the hayseed comedian on *Hollywood Barn Dance* radio show from 1943-47.

Although Johnny's career in the movies ended in 1947, his songwriting and recording flourished in the 1950s. Bond had become leader of Tex Ritter's studio band, The Red River Valley Boys, and was involved in playing as a session member on many other West Coast country stars. In terms of recording, Bond scored with three Top 5 country hits in 1947, including "So Round, So Firm, So Full Packed" (the Merle Travis big seller), "Divorce Me C.O.D." and "The Daughter of Jole Blon." The next year, he went Top 10 with "Oklahoma Waltz," and in 1949 charted with "Till the End of the World" and "Tennessee Saturday Night." On most of these numbers, he was backed by the Red River Valley Boys. He charted a Top 10 hit in 1950 with "Love Song in 32 Bars," and in 1951, another Top 10 hit, "Sick, Sober and Sorry." During this period, Johnny made his first guest appearance on the *Grand Ole Opry* in 1948.

By the end of 1957, Bond had written 123 songs. His most significant included "Cimarron," covered by such well-known artists as Sons of the Pioneers, **Bob Wills**, Jimmy Dean, Les Paul and Mary Ford, Harry James, Neal Hefti, and Billy Vaughn. "I Wonder Where You Are Tonight," recorded by such luminaries as Johnny Rodriguez, Porter Waggoner, Bobby Bare, **Roy Clark**, Jerry Lee Lewis, **Norma Jean**, Louvin Brothers, Carl Smith, Hank Snow, and Hank Williams, Jr., became a bluegrass standard as a result of recordings by Flatt & Scruggs, Bill Monroe, and Red Allen & the Kentuckians. Bond's "Tomorrow Never Comes," co-written with Ernest Tubb in 1945, was a hit for Glen Campbell in 1967 as well as being covered by such artists as Elvis Presley, Loretta Lynn, Statler Brothers, Little Jimmy Dickens, **B. J. Thomas**, and Lynn Anderson, "I'll Step Aside," written in 1947, was covered by three more country legends, **Hank Thompson**, Ernest Tubb, and Marty Robbins. Kitty Wells, Faron Young, Billy Jo Spears, Jim Reeves, Jeannie C. Riley, **Patti Page**, and Ricky Skaggs recorded "Your Old Love Letters," and "Glad Rags" was covered by Jimmy Dean, Tennessee Ernie Ford, and Mac Wiseman. Finally, Tex Ritter and Marty Robbins recorded "Conversations with A Gun."

In 1952, Johnny, Tex Ritter, and William Wagnon, Jr., a booking agent, organized a show called *Town Hall Party* in Compton, California, a combination of the *Grand Ole Opry* and *National Barn Dance*. Johnny wrote the script and insisted that all songs performed on the show had to be danceable. Filmed by the Armed

Forces Network and Screen Gems, the Friday/Saturday night shows were aired on local television until the program ended in 1961.

In 1955 Bond launched a music publishing business called Red River Songs. After his solo effort, Ritter and Wagnon joined him to form Vidor Publications, which signed songs written by **Tommy Collins**, a native Oklahoman, Freddie Hart, Lefty Frizzell, Harlan Howard, ("King of Nashville Songwriters"), and Larry and Lorrie Collins (**The Collins Kids**, which often appeared on the *Town Hall Party* shows).

When the rock and roll phenomenon swept the U.S. in the mid-1950s, Johnny adapted his sound to the new genre, and was one of the first to recognize that it had roots in country music. Despite this adjustment, Columbia Records decided not to renew Johnny's contract in 1957. He moved to Gene Autry's Republic Records for a brief period in 1960 during which time he recorded the Charlie Ryan tune, "Hot Rod Lincoln," which became a rock and roll classic made even more popular by Commander Cody and His Lost Planet Airmen in 1977.

Bond signed in 1960 with the Starday label with which he remained until 1971. His first single, "Ten Little Bottles," was previously recorded with Columbia in 1951. This new version of the novelty drinking song proved to be the biggest hit of his career. The follow-up single, "Morning After," did not sell as well. Johnny's first album release with Starday was *The Wild, Wicked But Wonderful West* (1961), which he had written between label deals. It was the first of fourteen albums he would record with Starday, and probably the strongest according to most critics. It included "Carry Me Back to the Lone Prairie," "Dusty Skies," and "High Noon," Johnny's own version of the original Tex Ritter recording on which Johnny played guitar. Unfortunately, most of the later albums focused on drinking songs, such as *Ten Little Bottles* (1965), *Bottled in Bond* (1967), *Bottles Up* (1968), *Ten Nights in a Barroom* (1970), and *Drink Up and Go Home* (1970). These collections appeared to make him a one-theme performer and songwriter, and his contract with Starday ended in 1969. He immediately signed with Capitol and joined Merle Travis in a tribute album to the Delmore Brothers, however, the album sold poorly, and both Johnny and Travis were released by Capitol. He resigned with Starday and recorded five more albums before leaving after two years. After one album on the Lion & Lamb label, he recorded two albums with Shasta Records, his old friend Jimmy Wakely's label. The most notable of these was *Johnny Bond Rides Again* (1975) that included "I Wonder Where You Are Tonight," "Hot Rod Lincoln," "Cimarron," and Johnny's version of "Oklahoma Hills," co-written by **Jack** and **Woody Guthrie**. An album entitled *The Singing Cowboy Rides Again*, made in 1976 by Johnny and the **Willis Brothers**, also native Oklahomans, was released in 1992 by CMH. The 18-track release included a host of singing cowboy songs, such as "Riders in the Sky," "The Last Roundup," "Cool Water," and "Take Me Back to Tulsa," Johnny's version of the **Bob Wills** hit.

From 1964 to 1970, Autry revived the *Melody Ranch* weekly series on his own television station, KTTV in Los Angeles, and Johnny reunited with Gene as performer and scriptwriter. In 1965, Johnny was elected to the Board of Directors of the Country Music Association, and also served two terms as president of the Academy of Country Music. He was reunited with Tex Ritter for a *Grand Ole Opry* appearance in 1973. Finally, Johnny toured England and Italy in 1976.

Bond was recipient of several awards throughout his career, including the BMI Award for "Your Old Love Letters" (1961), and two more BMI Awards in 1965 ("Ten Little Bottles") and 1971 ("Tomorrow Never Comes"). In 1974, he received the John Edwards Memorial Foundation Art Satherley Annual Award and the ACM Pioneer Award.

During his latter years, Johnny became an author, writing his autobiography published in 1976, *Reflections*, for the John Edwards Memorial Foundation at U.C.L.A., a biography of his friend, Tex Ritter, and had begun a book on the history of western music before his death from a heart attack on June 12, 1978 in Burbank, California.

Several scholars and journalists dubbed Bond as the person who helped created the hyphenated title singer-songwriter. In addition to his cowboy and bluegrass songs, he wrote and recorded in several other musical genres, including rockabilly ("The Little Rock Roll"), boogie woogie ("Mean Mama Boogie"), patriotic ("Under the Red, White and Blue"), western swing ("We Might As Well Forget It"), and religious ("Rock My Cradle Once Again").

The most recent CD compilations of Johnny's music include *Country Music Hall of Fame 1999*, a 2000 release by King Records, which features "Ten Little Bottles"; *Country & Western*, a 2001 collection from Bloodshot Records, a variety of cowboy songs such as "Red River Valley" and "Tumbling Tumbleweeds"; and Varese Sarabande's 2002 *Home Recordings*, a twenty track set, including "Oklahoma Waltz," "I Wonder Where You Are Tonight," and "Cherokee Waltz." (GC) www.johnnybond.com

Brackeen, Charles
(b. March 12, 1940)

Regarded as an excellent *avant-garde* jazz tenor, alto, and soprano saxophonist, pianist, and composer, Charles Brackeen was born in Eufaula, Oklahoma, a community of approximately 2,700 residents, located on Lake Eufaula in the southeastern section of the state. He originally studied violin and piano, but settled on reed instruments. He moved to Los Angeles in 1956, where he met and married pianist Joanne Brackeen.

Charles and Joanne moved in 1966 to New York City, where Charles recorded his first album, *Rhythm X* (1968) on the Strata-East label. It featured three former members of the Ornette Coleman Quartet, including fellow Oklahoman **Don**

Cherry, Charlie Haden, and Ed Blackwell. After playing with Melodic Art-tet, peforming regularly on the New York *avant garde* loft scene in the early 1970s, he contributed alto and tenor sax as well as vocals on Cherry's *Relativity Suite* album on the JCOA label in 1973. He was featured on tenor sax on Leroy Jenkins' *For Players Only* album, released in 1975 by JCOA, and reappeared on William Parker's *Through Acceptance of the Mystery Peace* in 1979 on the Centering label, and Ronald Shannon Jackson's *Eye on You* in 1980 on the About Time label. His tenor solos with drummer Paul Motian's trio, heard on the *Dance* (1977) and *Le Voyage* (1979) albums, both released on the ECM label, are noteworthy.

After a period of obscurity, during which time some sources say he worked for a railroad company in Texas, Brackeen resurfaced in Los Angeles in 1987, and was contacted by trumpeter Dennis Gonzalez and Silkheart Records owner Keith Knox to record for their label. With his own quartet, he recorded *Bannar*, a 1987 Silkheart label release, a four-track album all written by Charles. It was followed by two more Silkheart releases, *Worshippers Come Nigh* (1987) and *Attainment* (1987), both of which contained Charles' own compositions.

Brackeen can also be heard on DIW's 1999 release, *Live from Soundscape: Hell's Kitchen*, which features him on "Improvisations No. 3 and 4." Oklahoman Cherry rounds out the album with "Improvisations No. 5 and 6." Brackeen also appears, along with native Oklahomans **Sam Rivers** and **Sunny Murray**, on *Wildflowers: The New York Loft Jazz Sessions*, a three CD set, released in 2000 on the Knitting Factory label. Finally, Brackeen is also included in Silkheart Records release, *Silkheart Sampler: The Spirit of New Jazz*, released in 1990. (GC)

Brewer, Michael
(b. April 14, 1944)

As part of the 1970s duo, Brewer and Shipley, singer, guitarist, songwriter Michael Brewer is best known for the 1971 hit, "One Toke Over the Line," which was banned on numerous radio stations because of its drug overtones. Born in Oklahoma City, his mother was a music teacher and encouraged young Michael to sing which he did at age four on local radio. His father, a postal worker, was an artist and strongly encouraged the development of Michael's musical talent. Michael was first child in the Brewer family, followed

Michael Brewer and Tom Shipley

in order of birth by Keith, Charla, and Timothy. During high school, he played drums in a rock and roll band along with **Jesse Ed Davis**, a fellow Oklahoman and guitarist for Eric Clapton. Shortly thereafter, he sold his drums to purchase his first guitar, a Martin D-18. Following graduation from Northeast High School in Oklahoma City in 1962, Brewer hit the road and performed on the coffee house circuit throughout the country.

In 1964, Brewer met Tom Shipley at the Blind Owl Coffeehouse in Kent, Ohio, a friendship that would develop into a musical relationship later in the decade. He moved to California in 1965, first to San Francisco and later Los Angeles. It was here that Michael began working with Tom Mastin. The duet soon began touring with The Byrds and Buffalo Springfield, and they signed a contract with Columbia Records. The record deal was an unsuccessful venture and the duo soon left Columbia. Brewer then signed on as a songwriter for Good Sam Music Publishing, a subsidiary of A & M Records founded by Herb Alpert in Los Angeles. Shipley moved to Los Angeles and lived in a house around the corner from Brewer, and they soon began to collaborate on songwriting. Shipley joined Brewer as a staff writer for A & M Records. They soon recorded their debut album in 1968, *Down in L.A.*, which featured all original compositions. Their second album, *Weeds*, featured an array of talented musicians, including Mike Bloomfield, Chicago blues guitarist par excellence, along with former members of The Electric Flag. Other notable talents who have performed on Brewer and Shipley recordings include **Leon Russell**, Jerry Garcia, who later enjoyed success in The Grateful Dead, Nicky Hopkins, pianist for the Rolling Stones and the Beatles, Al Kooper, keyboard and organ specialist with Bob Dylan and Blood,

Sweat, and Tears, and Jim Messina, half of the noted 1970s duo, Loggins & Messina, as well as guitarist and bassist for such artists as **Hoyt Axton**, Buffalo Springfield, and Poco. But it was their third album, *Tarkio Road*, released in 1970 that included the track that became a 1970s counterculture hit, "One Toke Over the Line." Despite the controversy over the marijuana-related lyrics, the song reached Top 10 status. Later in 1971, Brewer and Shipley recorded a fourth album, *Shake off the Demon*, which they co-produced. Their fifth and final album on the Kama Sutra label was *Rural Space* (1973), which included fine renditions of "Blue Highway," "Black Sky," and "Yankee Lady." Following the demise of Kama Sutra, the duo signed with Capitol and recorded two albums, *ST-11261* (1974) and *Welcome to Riddle Bridge* (1976), although neither was particularly successful commercially.

In 1980, Brewer and Shipley parted for various reasons. Brewer then recorded a solo album, *Beauty Lies*, in 1983 with backup contributions from Linda Ronstadt, J. D. Souther, and Dan Fogelberg, who also produced the album. In 1986, Brewer and Shipley reunited in the Ozark Mountains of southern Missouri. Prompted by Kansas City rock radio station KCFX, Brewer and Shipley presented in 1989 their first live show in seven years. The duo released their first CD in 1995, *Shanghai*, on their own label, One Toke Productions. It was their first album in almost twenty years. The same year, they joined a national tour, "California Dreamin'," that included Maria Maldaur, New Riders of the Purple Sage, The Mamas and Papas, and a revised version of Canned Heat. Only Maldaur and Brewer and Shipley were the same because the other groups had reformulated due to deaths or members leaving the original ensemble. In 1997, they recorded the *Heartland* album again on their own label, One Toke Productions. *One Toke Over the Line: The Best of Brewer and Shipley* was released on the Buddha label in 2001.

Brewer's songwriting talents are noteworthy. He has composed such songs as "Hearts Overflowing," "Food on the Table," "Bound to Fall," and "Truly Right," recorded by such luminaries as Stephen Stills, Don McLean, The Nitty Gritty Dirt Band, Jonathan Edwards, The Dillards, and The Seldom Scene. When McLean recorded "Food on the Table," he changed the title to "Love in My Heart," in his 1988 Capitol Records *Love Tracks* album. It reappeared on the *Very Best of Don McLean* album in 1989, as well as on the 1989 *And I Love You So* collection, released only in the U.K. The Brewer penned song cracked the Top 10 pop charts in Australia. Throughout their career, Brewer and Shipley have performed at such well-known venues as Carnegie Hall, The Bottom Line, The Troubadour, The Roxy, and Keil Opera House.

In 2003, Brewer and Shipley are still performing at various venues all over the U.S., including Alaska, and remain superb instrumental and vocal technicians as well as performing music in an easy going manner that reflect uplifting lyrics. Their One Toke Productions is based in Rolla, Missouri. (GC)
www.brewerandshipley.com

Brooks, Garth
(b. February 7, 1962)

A relatively unknown singer, songwriter, and guitarist from Oklahoma who changed the course of American country and pop music in the 1990s with total sales of more than 120 million to become the all-time biggest-selling solo artist in pop music history, the only solo artist to have four albums top the ten million mark, and the only artist to take twenty singles to the #1 position on the country charts, Troyal Garth Brooks was born in Tulsa, Oklahoma. The name Troyal is derived from his father and grandfather, and the name Garth came from his great great grandfather, who was a Civil War general. Colleen Carroll and Troyal Raymond Brooks were previously married; she had three children and he had one. Garth and Kelly were born to Troyal and Colleen with Garth the youngest of the six children. Garth learned his first chords on guitar from his father, who was a guitar and mandolin picker. His father, a former U.S. Marine, was a draftsman for Union Oil. Colleen, born in Kansas City, Missouri, but raised in Arkansas, was a country singer who had a short-lived contract with Cardinal and Camark Records, and performed with Red Foley on the Ozark Jubilee in the 1950s. Garth was raised on country music via his parents' record collection, but he also listened to the Beatles and the Rolling Stones. As songwriter models he admired not only **Merle Haggard** and Hank Williams, but also James Taylor and Dan Fogelberg. And it was the wild and "shock rock" Kiss and Queen concerts of the 1970s, not a Johnny Cash performance, that led him in the direction he wanted to take his stage performance.

In 1966, Garth's family moved to Yukon, Oklahoma, where he took part in a number of sports including football, basketball, baseball, and track. He was vice-president of his ninth grade class and received a banjo on his sixteenth birthday. After graduation from Yukon High School in 1980, Garth attended Oklahoma State University on a partial athletic scholarship where he threw the javelin. During his OSU days, Garth enjoyed listening to George Strait, and began to perform in public, representing Iba Hall, the athletic dormitory, when he won a talent show sponsored by the Residence Halls Association. One of Garth's roommates while in college was **Ty England**, who became his singing partner and acoustic guitarist once Garth hit the big time in Nashville. The two had made a pact while in college that if either of them were successful they would call the other, and the first call Garth made when he signed with Capitol was to England. On weekends, Garth performed at local clubs on "The Strip" (South Washington Street) in Stillwater, most notably "Willie's," owned and operated by Bill Bloodworth. Here Brooks performed a repertoire largely from the songs by James Taylor, Billy Joel, and Bob Seger with an occasional country song by George Strait. He also worked at Dupree's Sporting Goods on South Washington Street (across the street from Willie's) where he later had his T-shirts printed for concerts. While working at Dupree's, he would have T-shirts printed for his friends saying "Garth Brooks World Tour." After graduating from OSU in December, 1984 with a B.S. degree in advertising, he spent about a year living in Stillwater perfecting his musical act, making some demo tapes for a possible visit to Nashville, and working as a bouncer at Tumbleweed's, a country music nightclub, where he met his future wife, nineteen year old Sandy Mahl, also an OSU student, rodeo barrel rider, and amateur dancer in campus modern dance functions. It is reported that Garth met Sandy in an incident at "The Weed" where she bashed her fist in the women's restroom wall and was escorted back to her dormitory by Garth during which time he asked her for a date.

In 1985, Garth headed for Nashville where he visited all the major record labels and left demo tapes. After twenty-three hours of negative responses, he left Music City as a discouraged young musician and returned to Oklahoma where he continued to perform at "Willie's," made additional demo tapes, and toured Oklahoma. On May 24, 1986, he married Sandy in her hometown of Owasso, Oklahoma.

In May 1987 Garth applied to become a member of ASCAP and was accepted. The next month, he and Sandy and his band (Santa Fe) returned to Nashville, where he and Sandy worked at Cowtown, a boot store in north Nashville, and Santa Fe was disbanded. Garth found additional work in the advertising sector (his college major) by doing voice-overs on Lone Star Beer commercials. Throughout 1987, he continued to write songs, including "Not Counting You," and was signed by Major Bob Publishing, headed by Bob Doyle, as one of its first two songwriters in 1988. Shortly thereafter, Doyle and publicist Pam Lewis formed Doyle-Lewis Management with Garth as a client. Doyle soon made an appointment with Capitol Records' Jim Foglesong and Lynn Shults for them to listen to Garth in the Nashville office. Shults later attended a Garth performance at the Bluebird Café in Nashville, and made a handshake agreement for a Capitol Nashville (later renamed Liberty Records) contract, which was officially signed on June 18, 1988.

Garth recorded his first album with producer Allen Reynolds at the end of 1988, and the eponymous album was released in early 1989. The album release was supported by an extensive tour by Garth and his newly formed band "Stillwater," named after the town where he attended college. The first single "Much Too Young (Too Feel This Damn Old)" climbed to Top 10 by July 1989. The album produced three more hit singles, including "If Tomorrow Never Comes" (Garth's first #1 single), "The Dance" (#1), and "Not Counting You" (#2). All except "The Dance" was either written or co-written by Garth. He also made his Grand Ole Opry debut in June 1989, and in 1990 became the sixty-fifth member of the Opry roster.

Garth's second album, *No Fences*, released in the fall of 1990, established him as a megastar as it sold 700,000 copies within the first ten days of its release, and has eventually sold more than sixteen million, the biggest selling album in his career. A string of #1 hits were produced from the album, including "Friends in Low Places" (which also was a hit video), "Unanswered Prayers," "Two of a Kind, Workin' on a Full House," and "The Thunder Rolls" (also a hit video). Garth's songwriting abilities on "Unanswered Prayers" and "The Thunder Rolls" were recognized by the Nashville Songwriters Association's Artist of the Year for 1992 as he tied with Alan Jackson for the award. He wrote or co-wrote more than half of the hits on ensuing albums.

Garth's album successes were matched by his concert appearances. By the end of 1990, he was selling out stadiums, for example, 50,000 at the Dallas State Fair, throughout the country, patterning his show after 1970s rock extravaganzas with cordless microphone so he could move around on stage, bust guitars, douse himself and his band in water, use a flying harness to swing out over the audience while he sang, and feature an explosive laser and pyrotechnics show to dazzle the crowd. It would mark the first time a country artist would incorporate such rock techniques into live concerts. His three 1993 concerts in the 65,000 seat Texas Stadium in Dallas broke the attendance record set by former Beatle Paul McCartney.

By the end of 1990, Garth was nominated for every conceivable country music award possible, including the CMA's Single and Song of the Year ("If Tomorrow Never Comes"), Male Vocalist of the Year, Music Video of the Year (*The Dance*), and the Horizon Award; winning the Horizon and Music Video categories. In addition, the ACM nominations included New Male Vocalist of the Year, Top Song, and Top Single, however, he failed to win any of these three awards. For the first time, Garth performed at Nashville's Fan Fair, and was presented with his first gold album (*Garth Brooks*) by Capitol Records' president Jimmy Bowen.

In 1991 the CMA nominated Garth in five categories, including Entertainer of the Year, Single of the Year ("Friends in Low Places"), Album of the Year (*No Fences*), Male Vocalist of the Year, and Music Video of the Year (*The Thunder Rolls*). He captured three of these awards: Entertainer, Music Video, and Album. "The Thunder Rolls" (song and video) was somewhat controversial because of its domestic violence content, but it paved the way for similarly themed songs like Martina McBride's "Independence Day" and the Dixie Chicks' "Goodbye Earl." His third album, *Ropin' the Wind*, was released in September 1991, and quickly entered the country and pop charts at the #1 position. It was the first country record to debut at the top of the pop charts. The album spawned four #1 singles, including "Shameless" (a rework of the Billy Joel song), "Rodeo," "What She's

Doing Now," and "The River," the latter two co-written by Garth, as well as "Papa Loved Mama," which reached #2 on the country charts.

By the end of 1991, Garth had become an American popular music icon. Even his seasonal album, *Beyond the Season*, went multi-platinum. His hometown of Yukon, Oklahoma, proclaimed a "Garth Brooks Day," and officially dedicated one of the town's water towers with a sign reading "Home of Garth Brooks," with Garth on hand for the ceremonies. Garth was a major winner in the *Billboard* Music Awards in 1991 with top honors in five categories. Moreover, he captured his first Grammy in 1991 for Best Country Performance Male for the *Ropin' the Wind* album. Finally in 1991, Garth swept the ACM Awards with honors as Entertainer of the Year, Male Vocalist of the Year, Album of the Year (*No Fences*), Single of the Year ("Friends in Low Places"), and Song and Video of the Year ("The Dance").

Garth's first major television special, *This is Garth Brooks*, received critical acclaim in 1992, and was the highest rated Friday night program on NBC in two years. Filmed at two sold out concerts in Reunion Arena in Dallas, Trisha Yearwood and Chris LeDoux were the opening acts. According to survey data, the special attracted some sixteen million households with ninety percent of the viewers between eighteen and forty-nine.

In April 1992 Garth appeared on the ACM telecast and captured first place honors in two of his five nominations: Entertainer of the Year and Male Vocalist of the Year. In October 1992 Garth swept the CMA awards show with top honors for Entertainer of the Year and Album of the Year (*Ropin' the Wind*), and was nominated for Male Vocalist of the Year. Garth was also recipient of the first ASCAP "Voice of Music" award presented in 1992 at the grand opening ceremonies of ASCAP's new Nashville offices. On July 8, 1992, Garth and Sandy's first child, Taylor Mayne Pearl Brooks, was born in Nashville, named after James Taylor and Minnie Pearl, two of Garth's favorite personalities. To conclude 1992, Garth's hometown of Yukon, Oklahoma, designated a stretch of Highway 92 from the Interstate 40 exit to Main Street as "Garth Brooks Boulevard."

Garth's fourth album, *The Chase*, was also released in 1992 and became the second one to enter both the pop and country charts at #1. Although somewhat controversial, the disc generated four more hit singles beginning with "We Shall Be Free," which featured a strong gospel component and peaked at #12. The song was written as a result of Garth's presence in Los Angeles during the 1992 riots with the video featuring such luminaries as Paula Abdul, Burt Bacharach, Harry Belafonte, Michael Bolton, Whoopi Goldbert, Julio Iglesias, Eddie Murphy, Colin Powell, Elizabeth Taylor, and **Reba McEntire**. It was followed by three #1 hits in 1993, including "Somewhere Other Than the Night," "Learning to Live Again," and "That Summer." The eclectic nature of the album was reflected in such diverse numbers as the Patsy Cline classic "Walkin' After Midnight" and a rousing version of the Little Feat rock number "Dixie Chicken." By the end of 1992, the album was certified platinum and by the end of 1993 had sold more than six million copies.

In Pieces, Garth's fifth album, was released in 1993 and debuted at #1 on the *Billboard* country charts. It yielded several hits, including "Ain't Goin' Down (Til the Sun Comes Up)," the debut single which rose to #1 on the *Radio & Records* chart, "American Honky-Tonk Bar Association," "Standing Outside the Fire," "One Night a Day," and "Callin' Baton Rouge." Garth performed the National Anthem during pre-game festivities at the 1993 Super Bowl to an estimated viewing audience of more than one billion. His award-winning video, *We Shall Be Free*, premiered during the telecast. Finally in 1993, he was nominated for CMA awards in three categories: Entertainer of the Year, Male Vocalist of the Year, and Album of the Year (*The Chase*), however, he failed to win any of these, but was one of the artists who collaborated on the winning Vocal Event of the Year, "I Don't Need Your Rockin' Chair," teaming with George Jones, **Vince Gill**, and **Joe Diffie**, among others.

In 1994 Brooks was nominated for the CMA Entertainer of the Year and Music Video of the Year ("Standing Outside the Fire"), but failed to win either. By 1995, Garth had earned additional honors both at home and abroad, including five American Music Awards, a Juno Award from Canada, two German-American Country Music Federation Awards, a Dutch Country Award, top award from England's *Country Music Round-Up* publication, and two nominations by the CMA for Entertainer of the Year and Music Video of the Year ("The Red Strokes"). Furthermore, he was named Favorite Country Artist by *Rolling Stone* magazine for the first half of the 1990s, Country Performer of the Year for 1991 through 1993 by *Radio & Records* readers, garnered some eleven *Billboard* awards during this productive era, and received a star in the Hollywood Walk of Fame, under which was buried *The Hits*, a limited edition of eighteen singles spanning his career from 1989 to 1994. In addition to these many laurels, Sandy gave birth to their second daughter, August Anna, in May of 1994.

Released in 1994, *The Hits* was a collection of Garth's greatest hits and eventually sold more than eight million copies. In late 1995, *Fresh Horses*, Garth's first album of original material in two years, debuted at #1 on *Billboard*'s country list and #2 on the pop charts, achieving first week sales of an estimated 500,000 copies, and sales of more than three million copies within six months of its release. Eight tracks from the album, six of which were co-written by Garth, received national radio airplay, including "She's Every Woman" (#1), "The Fever" (a rework of The Aerosmith number), "The Change," "The Old Stuff," "The Beaches of Cheyenne" (#1 chart buster), "It's Midnight Cinderella," "Rollin'," and "That Ol' Wind." He was again a finalist for Entertainer of the Year by the CMA in 1996.

Garth's seventh album, *Sevens*, was released in late 1997, after a management shake-up at Capitol Records and a massive publicity campaign including a concert at New York City's Central Park on August 7, which drew am estimated 250,000, the largest crowd ever to attend a concert there. The concert was also

broadcast on HBO. The album quickly catapulted to #1 upon its release and went multi-platinum by the end of the year. Only six of the fourteen tracks were co-written by Garth, but several of them received considerable radio airplay, including "She's Gonna Make It," "Cowboy Cadillac," and "In Another's Eyes." Additional tracks of note were "Longneck Bottle," "You Move Me," and "Two Piña Coladas." The latter also garnered the #1 spot on the country charts, and earned him Entertainer of the Year by the CMA in 1997.

Garth's 1996-98 concert tour was an overwhelming success, but a grueling schedule as he played 350 shows in more than 100 cities totaling 5.3 million tickets sold. One of the major events of the tour was a sold-out show at the Hollywood Bowl with the Hollywood Bowl Orchestra. The concert sold out in twenty-one minutes as "Garthmania" continued to sweep the nation. He captured top honors from the CMA in 1998 for Entertainer of the Year, and was nominated for Album of the Year (*Sevens*) and Vocal Event of the Year, "In Another's Eyes" with Trisha Yearwood.

Perhaps the most crucial move in Garth's career was the decision to try something new in the late 1990s, and it centered on a new persona—Chris Gaines, a brooding, leather-clad rock star. Associated with Garth's interest in film, he won the fictional role of Chris Gaines in a proposed movie, *The Lamb*, a thriller about a tortured rock star. The film featured a collection of Gaines' "greatest hits," which was released in 1999 as an album entitled *In the Life of Chris Gaines*, a set of thirteen pop songs ranging from "Lost in You," a smooth ballad, to "Maybe," a self-conscious Beatles tribute. Garth's fans were unforgiving and some thought he had gone off the deep end. It proved to be a commercial disaster, left Garth's fans bewildered, and release of the film was delayed. Moreover, it dealt a severe blow to Garth's second seasonal album, *Garth Brooks and the Magic of Christmas*, released in late 1999, but he was still a finalist for Entertainer of the Year in 1999 by the CMA.

Garth kept a low profile through most of 2000 because of several factors, including the Chris Gaines experiment that only someone with the resources of Garth could survive, divorce from Sandy, and possible retirement from music. He and Jenny Yates (co-writer) did earn a Golden Globe nomination in 2001 for Best Original Song in a Motion Picture for "When You Come Back to Me Again" from the film *Frequency*. Never to rest on his laurels, Garth returned in 2001 with *Scarecrow*, his strongest album since *Fresh Horses* and one in which he returned to his country roots. It debuted at #1 on both the *Billboard* pop and country charts, the seventh time one of Garth's albums had accomplished this feat and more times than any other artist. The twelve-tracks featured the George Jones duet "Beer Run," co-written by fellow Oklahoman, **Keith Anderson**; "Pushing Up Daisies," another song co-written by Oklahoman **Kevin Welch**; "Squeeze Me In," a duet with his long-time singing partner Trisha Yearwood; and "When You Come Back to Me Again," "Why Ain't I Running," "The Storm," and "Rodeo or Mexico," all of which were co-written by Garth. "Thicker Than Blood," another track co-written by Garth, is a family-oriented song that features a tribute to his mother and father, and cracked the Top 10 in the fall of 2002, and was the forty-seventh Top 20 hit for Garth. *Scarecrow* was certified triple platinum in early 2002, making it the best selling album of 2001, and signifying sales of three million. It also garnered the best selling album in Canada in 2002 with an award from the Canadian Country Music Association.

In March of 2002, Brooks was presented with ASCAP's prestigious Golden Note Award, recognizing his achievements to American music. The ceremony was highlighted by musical tributes to Garth, including vocals by two other Oklahomans, **David Gates** and **Jimmy Webb**. Also in 2002, Garth received the Hitmaker Award from the Nashville Songwriters Hall of Fame, and his *Double Live* album was certified by the R.I.A.A. for shipping more than fifteen million units, making it the best selling live album in American music history. He also accepted in person the People's Choice Award for Favorite Male Musical Performer in 2002. Moreover, he received two CMT Flameworthy Awards in 2002 for Male Video of the Year for "Wrapped Up In You" and Video Collaboration of the Year for "Squeeze Me In," his duet with Trisha Yearwood which also gained him a 2003 GRAMMY nomination for Country Collaboration with Vocals. Finally, Garth's duet with George Jones on Capitol's "Beer Run (B-double E-double Are You In?)" was nominated by the CMA for Vocal Event of the Year in 2002. "Squeeze Me In" was also nominated for a GRAMMY. Seemingly, just for fun, Garth contributed vocals to a song, "Night Birds," on the 2003 album *A Dyin' Breed* (Wondermint) by old friend and songwriting collaborator Royal Wade Kimes.

Following the divorce, Garth and Sandy have both moved back to Oklahoma with Garth purchasing land northeast of Tulsa to be near his three daughters (Taylor, August, and Allie). Garth celebrated his 40th birthday on February 7, 2002. From the outset of his career, he has been active in charitable causes, including benefit work to raise money for the Oklahoma City bombing victims, donation of funds for the Feed the Children program, and his latest effort as chair of the Read Across America campaign, an effort to improve literacy among children.

To reiterate a few vital statistics indicative of the powerful influence Garth has had on American music: total sales of more than 120 million making him the all-time biggest selling solo artist (ahead of Elvis Presley - and behind only the Beatles and Led Zeppelin on the all-time list), only solo artist to have four albums top the ten million mark, more time at #1 on the album sales charts than in other artist, and twenty #1 singles on the country charts. During his career, Garth has garnered eleven CMA awards, including Entertainer of the Year four times, two Grammy awards, seventeen American Music Awards, eighteen ACM Awards, twelve People's Choice Awards, five World Music Awards, and twenty-four *Billboard* Music Awards. The latter achievement is unparalleled in the history of the *Billboard* awards. He was also named as Artist of the Decade (1990s) by the ACM and received the prestigious ACM Jim Reeves Memorial Award in 1994 for promoting international acceptance of country music. In June of 2003, Garth received the Hitmaker Award from the Songwriters Hall of Fame in New York City while "If Tomorrow Never Comes" enjoyed new #1 status when it reached the top spot on the UK charts by former Boyzone frontman Ronan Keating. (GC) www.garthbrooks.com

Brumley, Albert Edward
(b. October 29, 1905 - d. November 15, 1977)

Composer of more than 800 songs and hymns, including such favorites as "I'll Fly Away," "Turn Your Radio On," "Jesus Hold My Hand," and "I'd Rather Be An Old-Time Christian," Albert Edward Brumley was born on a cotton farm near Spiro, Oklahoma, a town of about 2,000 residents in far eastern Oklahoma near the Arkansas border. Albert became interested in music after attending a singing school in around 1921 or 1922 in the Rock Island community near Spiro. Prior to his songwriting career, Albert had learned to play the organ and at age nineteen left his farm near Spiro and attended the Hartford Musical Institute in nearby Hartford, Arkansas, where he sang with the Hartford Quartet, but his shyness for solo work hampered his career as a vocalist. The Hartford Music Company was also a gospel music publishing house that produced the new gospel songs in seven-shape notation systems in the same vein as the James D. Vaughan and Stamps-Baxter publishers (shape-note singing books). Some of Albert's first songs were printed in 1927 in a "convention book" (books designed for all-day singing events) called the *Gates of Glory* published by Hartford. The first song accepted by Hartford was "I Can Hear Them Singing Over There."

Brumley actually composed "I'll Fly Away" in 1929 before he left Oklahoma. His recollection is while picking cotton and singing the popular song, "If I Had the Wings of an Angel," he thought about flying away. Brumley was quoted: "actually, I was dreaming of flying away from that cotton field when I wrote 'I'll Fly Away.'" Many of his songs were developed along these lines because of his deep spiritual convictions.

Albert spent considerable time studying and learning from the veteran songwriters at the Hartford Institute, including Eugene M. Bartlett, original owner of the company and composer of such songs as "Victory in Jesus" and "I Heard My Mother Call My Name in Prayer." After leaving Hartford, Albert traveled the Ozarks of Missouri and Arkansas teaching singing schools. Singing schools were an institution based on an itinerant singer who would move from church to church and teach the local congregations how to use the shape-note method in the published songbooks. Fortuitously, Albert met his future wife, Goldie Edith Schell, at one of these schools, and they were married in 1931 and settled in Powell, Missouri, the home of Goldie's parents. Albert and Goldie raised six children: Bill, Bob, Betty, Al, Tom, and Jackson.

Albert continued to write songs while traveling the singing school circuit, and Goldie encouraged him to publish them. Perhaps the biggest song he submitted was "I'll Fly Away," mailed to the Hartford Music Company in 1932. Hartford agreed to publish his song and it appeared in one of their hymnals, *The Wonderful Message*. At the time this song was published, Albert was working in his father-in-law's general store in Powell for a dollar a day. Hartford Music Company invited him to join their staff for $12.50 per month, and he spent the next thirty-four years writing songs for the Hartford and Stamps-Baxter music publishing companies.

In addition to "I'll Fly Away," Albert wrote and published his best known works from 1932 to 1945, including "Jesus Hold My Hand," "I'd Rather Be an Old-Time Christian," "I'll Meet You in the Morning," "Camping in Canaan's Land," "There's a Little Pine Log Cabin," "Turn Your Radio On," "Did You Ever Go Sailing? (River of Memories)," "I've Found a Hiding Place," "Rank Stranger to Me," "By the Side of the Road," "Nobody Answered Me," "God's Gentle People," "The Prettiest Flowers Will Be Blooming," and "If We Never Meet Again."

After his career with Hartford and Stamps-Baxter, Brumley formed the Albert E. Brumley & Sons Music Company, Country Gentlemen Music, and eventually purchased Hartford Music Company in 1948 in order to retain copyright control over his classic gospel numbers. Brumley began to publish his own songbooks, while serving as postmaster, in the late 1930s from his base in Powell, Missouri, including his best known, *Albert E. Brumley's Book of Radio Favorites*, and founded in 1969 the annual Albert E. Brumley Sundown to Sunup Sing, now the Albert E. Brumley Memorial Gospel Sing, reported to be the largest outdoor gospel sing in the nation.

Based on his illustrious career, accolades and honors began to recognize Brumley's musical significance. He was inducted into the Nashville Songwriters Hall of Fame, one of the first inductees (1970), Gospel Music Hall of Fame (1972), and the Oklahoma Music Hall of Fame (1998). The Gospel Music Association named him as one of only five persons in the U.S. whose compositions directly affected twentieth century gospel music, while the Smithsonian Institution in Washington, D.C., described Brumley as "the greatest white gospel songwriter before World War II." Two of his songs have received national and international attention. "Turn Your Radio On" received a Citation of Achievement from BMI in 1972, while "I'll Fly Away" has been recorded more than 500 times, including the Grammy award winning 2000 soundtrack for the film, *O Brother, Where Art Thou?* performed by Gillian Welch and Alison Krauss.

Brumley's songs have been recorded by a broad spectrum of artists, including Elvis Presley, Ray Charles, Bob Marley, The Supremes, Statler Brothers, Bellamy Brothers, Chet Atkins, Larry Gatlin, Blackwood Brothers, Florida Boys, Aretha Franklin, Loretta Lynn, Oak Ridge Boys, Burl Ives, Roy Rogers, Wynonna, Bill Monroe and the Bluegrass Boys, Chuck Wagon Gang, Red Foley, Stanley

Brothers, and even the Boston Pops Orchestra.

Many stories are associated with the use of Brumley's songs, including how "Rank Stranger" was made into a bluegrass standard in the late 1950s by Ralph Stanley, or how Hank Williams "borrowed" the melody and lyric pattern for "I Saw the Light" from Brumley's 1939 "He Set Me Free," and finally, how Elvis Presley conveyed that "If We Never Meet Again" was his mother's favorite song, and how it was sung at her funeral.

Although Albert E. Brumley died in 1977, his legacy lives on. His family continues to run the publishing house and sponsor the festival. Bob, Bill, and Betty still operate the company offices built by his father in the 1940s, as well as promote and direct the gospel festival now in its 32nd year in 2002. Brumley's songbooks as they were originally printed and published can still be purchased through company offices. As for his other sons, Tom is a well-known steel guitarist in the country field and manages a show in Branson, Missouri, while Al is a gospel singer with several albums to his credit, and Jackson works as a publisher and manager. (GC)

www.brumleymusic.com

Bryant, Anita
(b. March 25, 1940)

Recognized for her million selling single of "Paper Roses," Miss America runner-up Anita Bryant was born in her grandparent's house in Barnsdall, Oklahoma, a town of roughly 1,300 residents located northwest of Tulsa. The doctor declared her dead at childbirth, but her Grandpa Berry splashed her with a pan of cold water and she revived. After her sister was born, Anita's parents divorced, but her Grandfather John Berry encouraged her to sing at family gatherings and in church and school activities. Every Saturday night, she listened to the Grand Old Opry on radio. With the encouragement of her Grandpa Berry, she first sang in public at the age of two in a Southern Baptist church in Barnsdall, where her selection was "Jesus Loves Me," a song learned from her grandpa. By the age of eight, Anita made her singing debut on radio, and at nine, had won her first talent contest.

After moving to Velma-Alma and then Midwest City, Oklahoma, Anita broke into television at age twelve with her own show on WKY-TV in Oklahoma City, where she sang primarily country songs. Her mother remarried and they moved to Tulsa, where Anita attended Will Rogers High School, and captured the lead as a sophomore in the musical, *South Pacific*. She became known as "Oklahoma's Red Feather Girl," and as a high school junior soon drew the attention of Arthur Godfrey Talent Scout Show, where she competed and won first place. Her first recording was "Sinful to Flirt," released in 1956.

In 1958, Anita won the Miss Tulsa and Miss Oklahoma crown and sang as part of the talent competition in the Miss America contest, in which she was second runner-up. This national attention opened new opportunities for Anita. She became a regular on the Don McNeill Breakfast Club show in Chicago and was given a scholarship to Northwestern University. She left Northwestern to sign with Carlton Records in 1958, and her second single, "Till There Was You," from the musical *The Music Man* (1959), reached #30 on the pop charts. It eventually became a million seller and Anita's first gold record. As a result, *Cash Box* magazine named her Most Promising Female Vocalist. Other singles to follow included "Six Boys and Seven Girls" (1959), "Promise Me a Rose" (1959), and "Do-Re-Mi" (1959).

In 1960, Anita produced three major pop hits on the Carlton label, including "In My Little Corner of the World," which charted at #10 and later revived by Marie Osmond in 1974; "Wonderland By Night," which reached #18 as the vocal version of Bert Kaempfert's #1 instrumental hit; and "Paper Roses," which was her most successful hit at #5 on the charts, garnered her another gold record, and was also later covered by Marie Osmond in 1973. Additional singles on the Carlton label included "One of the Lucky Ones," "A Texan and a Girl from Mexico," and "I Can't Do It By Myself."

In 1962, Anita moved to Columbia Records where she recorded several albums, including *In A Velvet Mood* (1962), *Mine Eyes Have Seen the Glory* (1967), *Christmas with Anita Bryant/Do You Hear What I Hear?* (1967), and *Abide With Me* (1970s). Her singles with Columbia included "The World of Lonely People," "Welcome, Welcome Home," and the popular "Step By Step, Little By Little." She later released a children's album, *Orange Bird*, on the Disney label.

From 1960 to 1967, Anita was vocalist with the Billy Graham Crusades after 1965, a regular performer on Bob Hope's Christmas tours of Vietnam, performed at the White House from 1964 to 1967, sang her signature song "The Battle Hymn of the Republic" at both the Democratic and Republican conventions in 1968, as well as half time of the Super Bowl in 1976, and at President Lyndon Johnson's funeral in 1973. Bryant cut seventy-six ads for the Florida Citrus Commission from 1968 through 1980, and served as television spokesperson for Coca-Cola, Kraft Foods, and Holiday Inns during the 1980s. Toward the end of the 1960s, Anita focused more on religious songs and recorded several albums on the Myrrh and Word labels. In addition, she began a series of books in 1970, including *Mine*

Eyes Have Seen the Glory (1970), *Amazing Grace* (1971), *Bless This House* (1972), *Fishers of Men* (1973), *Light My Candle* (1974), *Running a Good Race* (1976), *Raising God's Children* (1977), *The Anita Bryant Story* (1977), *At Any Cost* (1978), and *A New Day* (1992).

In the 1980s and 1990s, Anita became an outspoken advocate against gay liberation and traveled around the country as a motivational speaker from her base in Miami, Florida, where she had organized the Anita Bryant Ministries. After ten years of single life (she and Bob Green divorced in 1980), she remarried astronaut test crewman Charlie Dry, a childhood sweetheart, and they moved from Nashville to Berryville, Arkansas, where they opened a music theater in nearby Eureka Springs, Arkansas, in 1991. She then moved to Branson, Missouri, in 1993, and assumed ownership of the John Davidson Theater in 1995, renaming it the Anita Bryant Theater. In 1998, Anita and Charley purchased the Music Mansion Theater in Pigeon Forge, Tennessee, where she stars in the "Anita, With Love" show. The couple resides in Sevierville, Tennessee. (GC)

Byas, Don
(b. October 21, 1912 - d. August 24, 1972)

Born in the regional hotbed of Southwestern jazz, Muskogee, Oklahoma, Carlos Wesley "Don" Byas is considered one of the few musicians with enough musical abilities to cross the bridge from the swing era of the 1920s and 30s to the bebop period of the 1940s, before moving to Europe in the 1950s where he remained for the rest of his life. Although certainly a part of the Kansas City blues-based "riff"

style, itself imbedded in Oklahoma territory band traditions, Don Byas also negotiated the flurried notes of bebop with a full-bodied tone that ranks him with his closest critical comparisons, Coleman Hawkins and Charlie Parker, as one of the more important tenor saxophone players of 20th-century jazz.

Don Byas began his career gigging out of his hometown of Muskogee, Oklahoma, a jazz rich city founded out of wilderness hunted by the Osage when **Muscogee (Creek)** Indians were removed to the area in 1828. Many Muscogee people, having based their "civilized society" on European models of the South, kept slaves of African descent but allowed them relatively more freedoms than non-Indian slave owners. Subsequent to the Civil War when freed slaves were incorporated into the tribe and given allotments in Indian Territory, Muskogee developed a thriving African-American business district, school system where students learned music and Shakespeare, and an entertainment center that served as a social and economic center for the all-Black towns around Muskogee. The town that produced Byas, **Claude "Fiddler" Williams, Jay McShann, Barney Kessel,** and several other notable jazz figures also served as a railroad nexus for the entire Southwest, which kept new musicians coming to town all the time. This environment provided many performance and learning opportunities for young musicians. For example, Don Byas recruited Jay McShann on his first gigs when McShann was not even a very good piano player.

After playing as a teenager with the most influential territory bands of the Southwest, i.e., Walter Pages's Blue Devils from Oklahoma City, Bennie Moten out of Kansas City, and a group led by transplanted Muskogeeite Terrence Holder call the Dark Clouds of Joy, Byas formed his own group, The Collegiate Ramblers, while in college at Langston University, the historically African-American university in Langston, Oklahoma. In the 1930s, Byas played with some of the West Coast's biggest orchestras, to include Lionel Hampton (1935) and Buck Clayton (1936) before heading to Kansas City to join up with Andy Kirk and his Mighty Clouds of Joy (1939-40).

In Kansas City, Byas became part of the now legendary jam session scene that went all night long and, ultimately, is where Byas's style developed in relation to Coleman Hawkins. Gutarist Eddie Durham remembers a night when Ben Webster, Coleman Hawkins and Byas had a battle of the tenor saxophones: "They started at eight o'clock and they finished at eight o'clock the next morning." Jazz critics often explain Don Byas in the context of Hawkins, who was eleven years older than Byas and had been playing professionally since age 16 in Kansas City. Hawkins was obviously a mentor for Byas, and the experience explains one of the reasons Byas was able to fit in with the new generation of beboppers who felt the basic big band formulas in which they had been forced to operate were stifling and bereft of creative allowances. Since Byas could play fast *and* melodically, Byas once told the story about Charlie Parker getting him out of bed to jam because "I was the only one who could play fast enough." By 1941 Byas moved to New York City to play in the Count Basie Orchestra as Lester Young's replacement. It was then Byas recorded "Harvard Blues" with the Basie band, the song most widely used in demonstrating Byas's input on Basie's sound and the changing style of jazz at that time. Byas's solo on "Harvard Blues" practically set the standard for smooth saxophonists of the 1940s with its lilting flow and and warm, round tone. Gunther Schuller, the classical composer and noted jazz scholar, is so enamored with the Byas solo that opens the record, Schuller calls the playing "flawless," and believes the recording to be one of the early Basie band's best.

Another noted aspect of Don's ability is his capacity for spanning the styles between slow ballads and the breakneck speed of bop. Byas is indebted to Hawkins for his big sound, but Byas also added flutter-phrasing and harmonic scale experiments, the sound most commonly associated with bop via Charlie Parker. While he was in New York City with Jay McShann's orchestra, Parker checked on the burgeoning bop scene at Clark Monroe's Uptown House, one of the two Harlem clubs generally acknowledged as the birthplaces of bop, and recalled, "Don Byas was there, playing everything there was to be played." Oklahoma trumpeter **Howard McGhee**, a player Miles Davis praised as a major influence, remembered telling trumpeter Roy Eldridge, "You're staying too traditional. You ought to come and hang out with Don Byas and learn to play." Subsequently, Eldridge went from playing in the Louis Armstrong style to exploring a rapid fire delivery of harmonic phrases.

Instead of being locked into past jazz styles, Byas moved forward stylistically in the 1940s. An excellent early example of this fluttering, fast-paced phrasing mixed with smooth, soulful melodies, is available on record and CD as *The Harlem Jazz Scene-1941*, featuring Dizzy Gillespie on trumpet, Thelonious Monk on piano, Oklahoma-raised **Charlie Christian** on guitar, and Don Byas on tenor saxophone. Leonard Feather wrote the liner notes for the album and says it is a representative session showing the genesis of bop. Feather, however, focuses on the interchange between Christian and Gillespie, whereas, other critics claim Byas is already a confident player in the idiom while Gillespie is still feeling his way into an identity within the bop movement. From a distance of sixty years hence, Don Byas appears to have been influencing not only one of jazz's and bebop's great trumpeters in Gillespie, but also bop's most monumental saxophonist, Charlie Parker. Even one of Parker's biographers, Ross Russell in *Bird Lives!* (Charterhouse, 1973), describes Parker's style as "a variation of Don Byas out of Coleman Hawkins." Between 1941 and 1944, Byas recorded a number of sessions with Basie, some tracks with Billie Holiday, others with Buck Clayton, did several sessions with other small jazz groups (yet to be seen or heard as a result of the World War II vinyl ban and musicians union strike), and was part of the Coleman Hawkins Sax Ensemble, which recorded for Keynote Records.

In 1944, Dizzy Gillespie hired Byas, Oklahoma bassist **Oscar Pettiford**, drummer Max Roach, and pianist George Wallington for a job that opened up on 52nd Street in New York City. The group is known variously as the first modern jazz group or the first working bebop group in jazz. Their music, with its halting rhythmic regularity and exploration of the unfamiliar dissonance and chromatics of bebop, soon became the talk of the jazz world. The music was controversial and for some time was just known 52nd Street Jazz. As jazz's next evolution developed, Don Byas blew on the front lines and left the interpretation of his true "bopness" up to the critics, some of whom always felt that Byas was more lyrical than Coleman Hawkins, Dexter Gordon, or Charlie Parker which often kept Don from fully representing the often frenetic jazz subgenre. However, Gordon was not even into the style until he came to New York and heard Hawkins and Byas. On the 1944 recordings with Gillespie, Byas seems the most comfortable with adapting his fluid, full-toned sound developed in the swing era to the faster and more musically complicated aspects of bop. By remaining with his blues and ballad roots, and still adapting to the new style, Byas was able to maintain his individuality and creative progression. Other strong evidence suggesting Byas should certainly be classified as a modern jazz artist comes from Benny Goodman's biographer, musician James Collier, who says in 1989's *Benny Goodman and the Swing Era* (Oxford): "To my mind, the only swing musician who managed to cross the line [to bop] was Don Byas." Quite often, Don Byas is classified as both swing and bebop in any number of jazz reference materials. During the period of 1944 to 1946, Byas recorded a number of titles for Savoy which demonstrate the trademark style of his big-toned, beautiful ballad style: "Sweet and Lovely" (1944), "September in the Rain" (1945), and "They Say It's Wonderful" (1946). Don's influence on the bop era is more than evident when the music migrated to Los Angeles. By 1947, when Oklahoman **Wardell Gray** and Dexter Gordon picked another song besides "The Hunt" for a live recording session at Billy Berg's, they chose Don's "Byas-A-Drink," which not only featured a Gray/Gordon sax duel, but an extended bop guitar solo by Muskogee, Oklahoma native, **Barney Kessel**.

In 1946, Byas reached his critical apex when he recorded again with Dizzy Gillespie on "Anthropology," "52nd Street Theme," "Ol' Man Bebop," and the now standard jazz classic "Night in Tunisia." The album on which the songs were released also included four songs by a Coleman Hawkins-led group and was an immediate success and sold very well that year. Byas left Gillespie for a short job with Duke Ellington that did not work out, but the misfire did not discourage Ellington from hiring Byas on a 1950 tour of Europe, or saying in his memoirs Byas "definitely influenced the avant-garde." Byas left the U.S. for Europe in 1946 with the Don Redman band and took up residence there, finding European audiences more appreciative of his work than those back in United States. Byas toured intermittently with American jazz titans such as Dizzy Gillespie, Stan Getz, Art Blakey, and Ben Webster on their tours throughout Europe where Don was widely known. As a result of being in Europe, however, Don never regained the status he held in the U. S during the 1940s. Nonetheless, Byas recorded and released several critically acclaimed albums in the 1950s and early 1960s, *Don Byas [Inner City]* (1953), *A Tribute to* Cannonball (1961), and *A Night in Tunisia* (1963), but he was not recorded often through the late 1960s. He returned to the United States only once in 1970 when he appeared at the Newport Jazz Festival largely because of a Dutch documentary being made about him. Byas died of lung cancer August 24, 1972 in Amsterdam, leaving his wife, Jopie, to care for their four young children: Dotty Mae, Ellie Mae, Carlotta, and Carlos, Jr.

In retrospect, Don Byas's most prolific and influential period of playing happened between 1940 and 1946 when he was making the transition from his solid background in the earthy blues of the Southwest and the smooth swing of the big band era into the oncoming bebop era. Although nearly forgotten in the late 1900s by popular jazz history, with the exception of living contemporaries, or modern saxophonist Stanley Turrentine who credits Byas as a precursor to Turrentine's own fame that resulted from the ability to play sensuous ballads. By the beginning of the 21st century jazz critics and historians, such as Jeroen de Valk in his 2001 biography of Ben Webster (Berkeley Books), began to realize and write that Don Byas's tenor saxophone was a vital bridge between the swing and bebop eras, and Don's huge tone grew out of the foundation set by Coleman Hawkins into a lulling, romantic flow rarely matched in jazz. (HF)

Caddo Nation of Oklahoma
(in the region that became Oklahoma since at least 5,000 B.C.)

As one of thirty-eight federally recognized American Indian tribes, bands, tribal towns, or nations in Oklahoma, the Caddo are one of the first known tribes to have called the state home, along with their historic and current neighbors, the Wichita and their affiliated tribes. While Caddo people sing in Native American Church services with specific Caddo songs, and others are members of Christian churches where hymns are sung in Caddo, the tribe's annual observation of their traditional Turkey Dance, with all of its associated social and ceremonial songs and dances, is the tribe's most significant and unique contribution to world music.

Ancient Caddo people left only a few paths in history. General agreement seems to exist among archaeologists that the Caddo were direct descendants of nomadic hunters who gathered wild seeds and berries for food before they began growing domesticated plants such as corn, squash, and beans thousands of years ago in the general region of what is now Oklahoma. Along with the Wichita, the Caddo are also considered the modern descendants of the people who built the Spiro Mounds temple and occupied the town center from about 800 A.D. to roughly 1450 A.D. in eastern Oklahoma along the Arkansas River near present-day Spiro. For many possible reasons, but most likely due to climate change or war, the Caddo ultimately settled in the region of southeastern Oklahoma that borders Arkansas, Louisiana, and Texas. Clusters of villages were built near, around, or on both sides of waterways by the friendly and peaceful affiliated Caddo tribes. The Red River Valley was the main center for the Caddo Nation and this area was considered organized and neutral territory by neighboring tribes and, eventually, European explorers.

As late as the 1700s, the Caddo maintained villages in and around the area known as Three Forks, where the Arkansas, Grand, and Verdigris Rivers meet, near modern Muskogee. Eventually, explorers and American immigrants to the Caddo country laid claim to the "four-corners" area of southeastern Oklahoma and the Caddo began a history of removal that ultimately placed them in general area of Fort Cobb and Binger, Oklahoma, where their tribal headquarters is now located.

The annual Turkey Dance is held each year where the Caddo perform many ceremonial and social dances such as the Swing Dance, the Bell Dance, the Cherokee dance, the Bear Dance, the Drum Dance, the Duck Dance, and the Fish Dance. The music of the Turkey Dance, and its accompanying social and ceremonial songs, has been preserved by Canyon Records on the compact disc re-release of recordings made in 1975 at the Hasinai Cultural Center near Hinton, Oklahoma. *Songs of the Caddo: Ceremonial and Social Dance Music* (Canyon, 1999) provides a stellar recording of Caddo songs that are still being performed each year by the tribe at their annual dances. Along with the "Turkey Dance Songs," the album features the "Caddo Flag Song," "Bell Dance Songs," "Duck Dance Songs," "Fish Dance Songs," "Bear Dance Songs," and "Morning Songs." Long-time powwow attendees also remember the Caddo hosted some of the very first intertribal powwows in Oklahoma at Murrow's Dance Ground near Binger in southwestern Oklahoma around the time of World War I. The Caddo also have a strong Native American Church musical tradition because of their proximity to its late 19th century development in southwestern Oklahoma, largely instigated by Quanah Parker, the noted Comanche spiritual and political leader.

In 1989, Caddo singer Randlett Edmonds recorded four songs for The State Arts Council of Oklahoma's *Songs of Indian Territory* project. Three of the songs are Caddo Ghost Dance songs with Randlett accompanied by Wimpy Edmonds, one of which can be translated into English as "In the end the Caddos will go to the land above." Also on the cassette release of the project is a Bell Dance song on which Randlett Edmonds is accompanied by Margie Deer, Geneva Edmonds, and Donna Edmonds Williams. As a result of intermarriage and cultural exchange with Seminoles and **Muscogee**, the Caddo also host stomp dances at their tribal facilities.

Currently, two organizations, the Caddo Culture Club and the Hasinai Cultural Preservation Organization actively maintain Caddo traditional life ways. In 2001, Friends of Oklahoma Music inducted the Caddo Nation into the Oklahoma Music Hall of Fame for the tribe's persistence in keeping their musical traditions alive under the overwhelming odds of several relocations, the boarding school movement of the 20th century that suppressed the practice of traditional activities, and the general social pressures of integrating into mainstream American society. In 2002, Chairperson LaRue Parker led the Caddo Nation of roughly 5,000 people.

When she accepted the induction award for the Caddo into the Oklahoma Music Hall of Fame, Parker thanked Friends of Oklahoma Music and said the award was "for all the singers we left behind, and the wonderful singers who carry on our traditions today."

Contemporarily, the tribe maintains a number of programs for its citizens, operates its own art gallery and cultural center, and has its own fire brigade. While many Caddo people have entered the intertribal powwow world, Caddo singers such as Thurman Parton continue ancient musical traditions such as the Turkey Dance that occur no where else in the world of music. (HF)

Cale, Johnny "J. J."
(b. December 5, 1938)

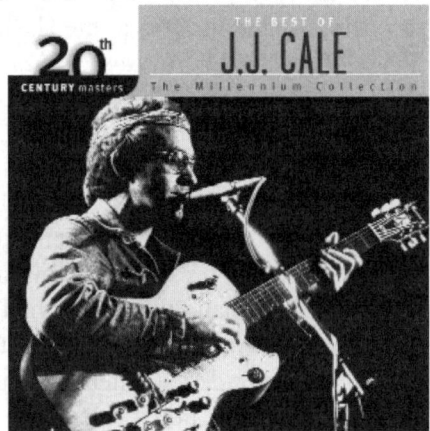

Sounding like he's sitting on his porch, casually playing the guitar on just another song filled with the fusion of country, blues, and rockabilly for which he has become critically revered, J. J. Cale is a widely popular singer, guitarist, and songwriter in Europe, and lesser known by name in the U.S.. Nonetheless, his songs receive regular airplay in the states as done by such notable artists as Eric Clapton, Lynyrd Skynyrd, Deep Purple, Johnny Cash, Santana, the Allman Brothers and Widespread Panic. Exhibiting his broad appeal to musicians of many genres, a wide-ranging and partial list of additional artists who have covered Cale's material include Chet Atkins, Kansas, Dr. John, Nazareth, Larry Carlton, Captain Beefheart, Freddie King, Deep Purple, and Waylon Jennings.

Born in Oklahoma City, but reared in Tulsa, he began playing a friend's guitar in the pre-rock era when **Bob** and **Johnnie Lee Wills** still held sway over Oklahoma's popular music scene. After scraping together enough money to get his own guitar, Cale's earliest musical influences included the Elvis Presley Sun rockabilly records with Scotty Moore on guitar, Clarence "Gatemouth Brown, Chuck Berry, and Chet Atkins, along with other 1950s rock icons such as Buddy Holly, Chuck Little Richard, and Fats Domino. In trying to play like those musicians, J.J. (a stage name he created that has been wrongly interpreted by French writers as Jean Jacque) remembered in a 1990s interview, "I missed it and came up with my own kind of thing."

As a teenager in Tulsa whose age collided perfectly with the first wave of classic rock and roll in the 1950s, he formed his own group, Johnny Cale and the Valentines, and played in clubs for "ten dollars a night and all the beer you could drink," alongside Russell Bridges (aka **Leon Russell)**, Leo Feathers, Carl Radle, Jimmy Karstein, **David Gates** (who would later form Bread), and **Jack Dunham.** Cale moved to Nashville in 1959 and was hired by the Grand Ole Opry's touring compan, but he returned to Tulsa after a few years, reunited with Leon Russell, and in 1964 moved to Los Angeles with Russell and Radle. Once in Los Angeles, Cale played club gigs at night, and fulfilled engineering duties for Leon Russell at Leon's home studio where he met Snuff Garrett who signed Cale to Viva Records in 1965. Cale's Viva album, *Take a Trip Down Sunset Strip* (1966), released in collaboration with fellow Oklahoman Roger Tillison under the group name The Leathercoated Minds, is primarily a collector's album, long out of print, but still a representative statement of the period in which Cale was working behind the controls. One "audition record" single was sent out to radio stations featuring a Cale-Russell composition, "It's a Go-Go Place," and a cover of a novelty tune about the comic book detective, "Dick Tracy." The most important song that came out of the sessions was "After Midnight," later Eric Clapton's first solo hit in 1970. Nothing much was happening for Cale in L.A, so he returned to Tulsa and started working the same club circuit where he had cut his musician's teeth.

After a trip to Nashville where he worked as a recording engineer, Cale signed with Leon Russell's Shelter Records in 1969. Cale was still putting his solo career together when he heard Clapton's version of "After Midnight" on a Tulsa radio station. The song was Cale's first hit as a songwriter and provided him with some much needed exposure and income from royalties. Encouraged by the success of "After Midnight," J.J. released his first album, *Naturally* (1971) which provided the Top 40 hit "Crazy Mama," as well as his own version of "After Midnight," and "Call Me the Breeze," later covered in a five- minute-plus version on Lynyrd Skynyrd's mega-platinum *Second Helping* (MCA, 1974). Skynyrd's version of "Call Me the Breeze" appeared again in 2002 on the *Sunshine State* soundtrack. A particularly interesting element of "Crazy Mama" and "Call Me the Breeze" is J.J.'s use of an Acetone drum machine he had obtained by trading an old banjo for it. Continuing to experiment with recording, Cale ran the drum machine through an old Fender amplifier, turned it up and recorded it, which may be one of the first uses of a drum machine on a pop record, now considered standard practice for many of the manufactured artists of the contemporary era. Cale followed *Naturally* with *Really* (1972) which furthered his recording style of letting the soloing instruments be equal to his vocals on the tracks, produced the minor hit "Lies," and offered a low-key, two-minute song named after his home state, "If You're Ever in Oklahoma."

Cale continued his Oklahoma theme by naming his third album *Okie* (1974), and also persisted in his lo-fi recording techniques by recording the title track on the back porch of his house in Tulsa, and laying down other tracks for the album, such as "Anyway the Wind Blows," inside the house. *Okie* also provided more inspiration for Lynyrd Skynyrd who recorded "I Got the Same Old Blues Again" on *Gimme Back My Bullets* (MCA, 1976). With more royalties coming in from other people's versions of his songs, in 1975 Cale moved to Tennessee and bought a home in Hermitage which was far enough outside of town so people "would not just drop by all the time." In 1976, Cale released *Troubadour* featuring his last chart hit, "Hey Baby," but more significantly included the would-be drug anthem, "Cocaine," covered by Clapton on his 1977 album, *Slowhand* (Polydor). The entire album *Slowhand* is a nod to J.J. Cale and the influence of his trademark bluesy-shuffle on Clapton. Clapton once said the album *Lay Down Sally* was as close as an Englishman could get to being J.J. Cale. On the strength of the single "Cocaine," Cale could have gone back out on the road in support of new album. Instead, he headed back to Nashville where he barely stayed busy, playing on an album by a French singer, Eddy Mitchell, and working on Neil Young's *Comes a Time* (1978).

Cale's next album, *5* (1979), with appearances by old friends Carl Radle and Jimmy Karstein, who has played on practically every J.J. Cale session and show since the early 1970s, as well as his guitarist wife Christine Lakeland on vocals and various instruments. Lakeland, originally from Kalamazoo, Michigan, met J.J. at a prison benefit show in Nashville after she had just come off the road playing with **Merle Haggard**. Cale hired her for his band and Lakeland has been with him since. *5*'s sound reaffirmed the source of Dire Straits' style, who had a hit the year before with "Sultans of Swing" from their self-titled album of Cale clone songs. While radio ignored *5*'s single, "The Sensitive Kind," Santana "got it" and took the tune to the middle of the Top 100. In 1980 Cale left Nashville and returned to California where he promptly sold what he did not want, and packed

the rest into a gleaming Airstream trailer and moved into an Anaheim trailer park where he was notoriously reclusive. Cale released his final Shelter album, *Shades*, in 1981 to very little fanfare although it had songs with his subtle humor, "I Wish I Had Not Said That," and his penchant for straight ahead back porch jams on "Mama Don't." 1982's album, *Grasshopper*, found success in Europe, but not in the U.S., and 1983's album, *#8*, became his first not to chart at all. Following that lack of notice after more than twenty-five years of playing and recording music, Cale went into a

Hugh Foley (left) with J. J. Cale (right) in New York City in 1989.

lengthy seclusion where he recorded songs that finally emerged in 1989 on *Travel-Log*, an album that featured **Hoyt Axton** on backing vocals, James Burton (Elvis Presley's touring guitarist from the 1970s) on one track, and long-time drummer and fellow Oklahoman, Jim Karstein. When he started to tour for the album, Cale told one interviewer he had spent the previous six years mowing the lawn, cycling, and listening to rap and Van Halen.

J.J. released his tenth album, *Number 10*, in 1992 to his fans' delight, but not many others, and in 1994 released *Closer to You*, an album featuring his wry take on the music industry, "Sho-Biz Blues." *Closer to You* garnered the same cultish admiration from long-time Cale devotees, as did his 1996 release, *Guitar Man* that contained solemn, dire predictions of general environmental and cultural disaster in "Death in the Wilderness," as well as the usual misfit and social outsider characters that fill Cale's songs. Mercury released two "Best of" compilations in 1997 and 1998, *Anyway the Wind Blows: Anthology*, and *The Very Best of J.J. Cale*. In 2001, Cale released his first live album, *Live*, recorded at Carnegie Hall and other venues around the U.S. and Germany. Again, the CD featured stalwart Cale sidemen Bill Raffensperger, Rocky Frisco, and Jim Karstein, with "newer" additions to his comfort zone of players, Christine Lakeland and Jim Cruce, who began playing with him in the 1980s. Cale also joined Eric Clapton in 2001 to perform on an album by the Crickets, Buddy Holly's band. Clapton's admiration for Cale has existed since he first heard "After Midnight." When a recent interviewer asked Clapton which musician he would want to be other than himself, Clapton named J.J. Cale. "I like his philosophy, writing skills, and musicianship," Clapton explained, "He's a fine, superior musician, one of the masters of the last three decades of music." Those comments explain why Clapton covered another Cale tune, "Travelin' Light," on his 2001 *Reptile* CD. Also re-surfacing in 2001 was Cale's "Long Way Home" from *Closer to You*, which appeared in the film *Bandits*, starring Billy Bob Thornton and Bruce Willis.

In 2002, Mercury Records released another *Best of J.J. Cale* as part of its *20th Century Masters* collection, and Classic Pictures released a DVD of a 1979 Cale performance as *J.J. Cale: the Lost Session*. Along with filling a niche in American popular culture reserved for rustic musical sages, J.J. Cale's lazy rock songs and minimalist sound have been embraced and popularized by several artists since 1970. His larger relationship to Oklahoma's music history is his particular representation of the state's place as a musical crossroads where country, rock, and blues have coexisted and nourished each other since the 19th century.

Cale toured in 2002 with a host of Oklahoma musicians with whom he has long been comfortable, to include Tulsa-based pianist Rocky Frisco and bassist Bill Raffensperger as well as musicians long known for their association with the **Tulsa Sound**, David Teegarden (drums), Don White (guitar/vocals), and Walt Richmond (keyboards). In June of 2003, Cale returned to Tulsa to record with those same musicians for a new album, along with other veteran Tulsa music luminaries such as Tom Tripplehorn, Tommy Crook, Jimmy Byfield, and Mike

Bruce on guitars, **Steve Ripley** on guitar and backing vocals, Jimmy Markham on harmonica, Larry Bell on Hammond B3 organ, Jimmy Karstein and Chuck Browning on drums, and Chuck Blackwell on drums and percussion. The album "might" be released in 2004. (HF)
www.jjcale.com

Card, Hank
(b. March 31, 1955)

As rhythm guitarist, songwriter, and one of the founding members of the Austin Lounge Lizards, a neo-traditionalist and bluegrass band, formed in Austin, Texas, in 1980, Hank Card was born to William L. and Alva M. Card in Caldwell, Kansas, because his hometown of Medford, Oklahoma, lacked hospital facilities. He, however, lived in Medford, the county seat of Grant County, located in the north central part of the state, until six years old. Hank has one brother, Lee A. Card, who is associate district judge in Ardmore. His father was raised in Medford, and was an attorney there until the Card family, when Hank was about six, moved to Oklahoma City. Hank's father died in 1961. Hank's mother was raised in southeastern Oklahoma, taught high school and college English for many years, and obtained her doctorate at age sixty, and passed away in 2002.

Upon graduation from Putnam City High School in Oklahoma City in 1973, Hank decided to attend Princeton, the prestigious Ivy League university, which had always appealed to him, and, as Hank said in a recent interview, he was fortunate to be admitted and his mother somehow managed to pay the expenses. Graduating with a history degree from Princeton University, Hank headed to Austin, where he completed his law degree at the University of Texas, and became an administrative law judge for the state of Texas, a position he currently retains.

While at Princeton, Hank met Conrad Deisler, and the two combined their folk and country music interests to perform in numerous folk-oriented bands, including Canyon City Limits. Prior to college, Hank had little interest in guitar and songwriting. When both moved to Austin in 1980 to attend law school at the University of Texas, they met Tom Pittman, a philosophy graduate student from Georgia, who played banjo and steel guitar, and the Austin Lounge Lizards were born. Soon they added a bass player (Tom Ellis and then Mike Stevens) and mandolinist (Tim Wilson then Paul Sweeney). After playing bluegrass in local venues, the band took Best Band honors at the 1983 Kerrville Folk Festival. Rather than cover country and folk tunes, the group discovered they had the ability to write political and social theme songs tinged with humor, irony, and satire, a feat accomplished over the past twenty-two years. Hank, along with Deisler, became the primary songwriter for the eight albums released over that time period. Deisler once described their commentary as "guerilla warfare on the conventions of country music." According to Card, his influences in writing satirical songs came from Frank Zappa, Homer & Jethro, and Brave Combo.

The Austin Lounge Lizards cut their first album, *Creatures from the Black Saloon*, in 1984 on Watermelon Records, which features Hank's songs, "Swingin' From Your Crystal Chandeliers," "Didn't Go to College," and "The Golden Triangle." It was followed by *The Highway Café of the Damned*, released in 1988 on the Watermelon label. Hank's songwriting is highlighted with the title track, as well as "Ballad of Ronald Reagan," "Acid Rain," and "Cornhusker Refugee." Their third album, *Lizard Vision*, was recorded live at the Waterloo Ice House in Austin. Released in 1991 on the Flying Fish label, it includes several of Hank's songs, such as "A Case of Coors Beer," "Bust the High School Students," "Pizza on the Ground," and "George Jones is Playin' in the City." In 1993, their fourth album, *Paint Me on Velvet*, was also on Flying Fish. Two years later, the group cut their *Small Minds* album again with Watermelon Records. Hank is at his songwriting finest as he writes or co-writes eight of the eleven tracks on *Small Minds*. His best numbers are "Gingrich the Newt" and "Mourning Edition," poking fun at the politician from Georgia and the NPR broadcast. The *Live Bait* EP album, including some of the group's favorites, such as Hank's "The Highway Café of the Damned," was released in 1996 by Watermelon and re-released in 1998 by Sugar Hill.

In 1998, the group produced *Employee of the Month* on the Sugar Hill label. Nine of the thirteen tracks are written or co-written by Hank, including "Stupid Little Texas Song," "Hey, Little Minivan," "The Dogs, They Really Miss You," "Love in a Refrigerator Box," and "Leonard Cohen's Day Job." To promote the album, the band traveled to Great Britain, their first overseas tour, and was warmly received by 3,000 fans at the Ironbridge Bluegrass and Roots Festival in Shropshire. They also performed a live two-hour show in London, broadcast via satellite to thirty-one countries.

Their latest album, released in 2000, entitled *Never an Adult Moment* (Sugar Hill) features Card's songwriting on seven of the twelve tracks, including "Forty Years Old and I'm Living in My Mom's House," "Big Rio Grande River," "The Me I Used To Be," "Waitin' on a Call from Don," "The Illusion Travels by Stock Car," and "Ashville/Crashville"; the latter two are parodies on stock car racing.

Described on their website as "The Most Laughable Band in Show Business," the Austin Lounge Lizards were the focus of an article in a 1998 *Country Music International* issue, in which Steve Tyler stated: "If the Austin Lounge Lizards have heard of political correctness, they don't acknowledge it, as their song titles may suggest." They garnered the *Austin Chronicle*'s Best None of the Above Band and Kerrville's Band of the Year in 1994.

Card, described by one journalist as "the plummy-voiced chanteur who's written or co-written many of the band's most irreverent and poignant tunes," has recovered from prostate surgery, and he and the boys (only Card, Deisler, and

Pittman remain as original members with recent additions of Boo Resnick and Eamon McLoughlin to the group) performed at various festivals and concerts in 2002, taking them to British Columbia, Alberta, Oregon, Washington, Nevada, Ohio, Minnesota, Virginia, and Maryland, and will perform at the prestigious Wolf Trap venue in Vienna, Virginia, in 2003. (GC)
www.austinloungelizards.com

Cargill, Henson
(b. February 5, 1941)

Known for his 1968 No. 1 hit, "Skip a Rope," singer and songwriter Henson Cargill was born in Oklahoma City. Although he learned to play the guitar as a youngster, Henson's career plans focused on ranching. His family background, however, was in law and politics as his father was a well-known trial lawyer and his grandfather was a former mayor of Oklahoma City. He attended Colorado State University in Fort Collins, where he studied animal husbandry, and married his final year. Following graduation, he returned to the family ranch in Oklahoma, but began playing music at local clubs in the Oklahoma City area, as well as serving as a deputy sheriff in Oklahoma County.

When a country music group, The Kimberlys, came through Oklahoma City, their leader Harold Gay convinced Henson to join them. After touring the Pacific Northwest and playing the Las Vegas nightclub circuit, Henson moved to Nashville in 1966. Here he met producer Don Law who helped him sign a record deal with the Monument label in 1967.

Cargill's debut single, "Skip a Rope," written by blind songwriter Jack Moran, reached #1 on the country charts and remained there for five weeks, as well as crossed over to the Top 30 pop charts. The lyrics of this song raised a few eyebrows in country music circles because of its protest nature. It condemned parents who set a bad example for their children by evading income tax and practicing racial discrimination. The song was later recorded by soul singer Joe Tex.

For the next two years, Henson scored with "Row, Row, Row, a Top 15 hit, and "None of My Business," a Top 10 success. In 1968, he became host of Avco Broadcasting's Midwestern Hayride on WLWT-TV in Cincinnati, which was syndicated as Country Hayride. After a two year hiatus, Henson recorded a 1971 album, *The Uncomplicated Henson Cargill* with "The Most Uncomplicated Goodbye I've Ever Heard" single from the album charting in the Top 20.

In 1972, Henson moved to Mega Records with little success, and then moved again to the Atlantic Records in 1973 and remained with the label until 1975 when they closed their country music operations in Nashville. With Atlantic, he produced two Top 30 hits, "Same Old California Memory" and "Stop and Smell the Roses," a Mac Davis song. He also cut his first album with the new label, *This is*

Henson Cargill Country, in 1974, probably the best album during his recording career.

Henson did not record again until 1979 when he scored with "Silence on the Line" on the independent label, Copper Mountain. His last recording was "Have a Good Day" in 1980. Henson retired from recording and has returned to his Oklahoma ranch, but does commute between Nashville and Oklahoma, performing an occasional show. (GC)

Caroline's Spine
(Formed 1993 in San Diego, CA)

Caroline's Spine, left to right: Jimmy Newquist, Jason Gilardi, Scott Jones, and Mark Haugh.

Scrolling out a moody and meditative pop metal to appreciative audiences throughout North America and Europe, Caroline's Spine has always considered Oklahoma "home" since two of its primary musicians are from Tulsa and the band has based its operations there since 1995. Guitarist and vocalist Mark Haugh, a 1988 Tulsa Bishop Kelly graduate, moved to California where he attended Loyola Marymount University and met singer and guitarist Jimmy Newquist. Newquist, born in Framingham, MA, and reared in Phoenix, AZ, was going to film school at Loyola Marymount and had already signed with an independent label, ANZA Records. Mark Haugh recorded some guitar tracks on the singer's first recordings, called *Caroline's Spine* (ANZA, 1993) after the band name on which Newquist had already decided. With some success on college stations, the two musicians quit their day jobs, acquired a rusty old van, a drummer - native Californian, Jason Gilardi (b. October 21, 1974, Los Angeles) – and began picking up gigs. In the spring of 1994, Jason, Mark, and Jimmy recorded their second album, *So Good Afternoon* (ANZA). The album won the group "Top 5 Unsigned" status in a Yamaha Music Showcase that year, and the band continued touring until the final piece of the band's plan came together when they came through Tulsa in 1995 to recruit Bishop Kelly graduate and Tulsa native, Scott Jones (b. July 30, 1970), to play bass.

Jones had known Haugh since high school when the two had an ill-fated band that got booed off the stage in Tulsa; that and the usual "creative differences" split the group. After graduating high school, Jones attended St. Mary's University in Texas before transferring to Oklahoma State University in Stillwater where he graduated with a degree in psychology. Jones had not heard from Haugh for five years until receiving a phone call from the guitarist who asked Jones to book a show in Tulsa for Caroline's Spine. After the show, the group asked Jones to play bass, knowing he had never played bass, but Scott agreed and the band solidified to what it remains in 2003. With a solid lineup in place, the group began breaking as an independent act in Oklahoma, Utah, and Arizona when they recorded their third independent album, *Ignore the Ants* (ANZA, 1995), where the cult favorite and college radio standard, "Hippie Boy," made its first appearance. The song's appeal to Caroline Spine fans owed to its sentimental interpretation of the relationship between a conservative father and his rock musician son. In the fall of 1995, the group recorded some acoustic tracks that later surfaced on their final ANZA CD *Huge*, an album that sold well enough to get the attention of Hollywood Records who signed the band to a four-album deal.

The band's first release on Hollywood, *Monsoon* (1997), is really a re-mixed greatest hits record taken from the band's four previous independent albums, plus the addition of one new song, "You and Me." The group's next releases came in the form of a single on the soundtrack to *An American Werewolf in Paris* (Hollywood, 1997), "Turned Blue," really a preview of their formal Hollywood Records debut, and first formal studio production, *Attention Please* (1999). According to Mark Haugh, "No other record had utilized the kind of time and measures we did with this one. For this undertaking, the pre-production, recording, post-production, and artwork took all of eight months to complete, about seven and a half months longer than we were used to spending on any other project." For help throughout the recording process, they worked with well-known producer Roy Thomas Baker (Queen, The Cars, Ozzy Osbourne, et. al.), and enlisted engineer Nick Didia, who amped up their material for *Monsoon* and who has worked with Pearl Jam, Rage Against the Machine, and Stone Temple Pilots, to mix the album. The influences of both rock professionals is obvious throughout the album's careful song construction, and big, pop metal sound that relies on a prominent kick-drum-snare drive, just-this-side-of metal guitar riffs, and dramatic, at times soaring, vocals. The album took so long to work out, Hollywood released "Wallflower" as a single, previously included on *Monsoon*, but dating back to 1994's independently released *So Good Afternoon*. The time was worth the wait for the band, however, as the album produced four Top 40 hits on the nationwide active rock radio format charts, and Caroline's Spine toured North America with everyone from KISS and Aerosmith to Bush and New Model Army.

Even with the beginning success that many bands never even reach, the group came to loggerheads with Hollywood Records, and the two parted ways, freeing the band to tour and record on its own. Like many artists who have been less than pleased with their corporate contracts that sometimes deliver as little as eleven cents per CD sold, after production and promotional costs of an album have been paid back, Caroline's Spine turned to their own website and fans to embrace their 2000 self-released and produced album, *Like It or Not*. The album contains new songs, re-mastered tracks from the four out-of-print ANZA CDs, live recordings,

and demos, but is only available from the website and considered by the band to be an "extra" for the fans. Continuing to perform regularly throughout the U.S. during 2001 and 2002, the band released two more independent albums in 2002, *Live,* a collection of concert recordings, and *Overlooked,* their first proper studio album since *Attention Please.* The group played a well-received show New Year's Eve in Rockford, Illinois to close out 2002, and Jimmy Newquist performed an acoustic show in early January, a harbinger of his 2003 solo release. While the band took a break from touring during Newquist's solo effort, Gilardi and Jones worked on a side project they titled New Science. (HF)
www.carolinespine.com

Carson, Jeff
(b. December 16, 1963)

Charting a No. 1 country hit on his first album, "Not On Your Love," and also known as **Merle Haggard**'s duct partner on "Today I Started Loving You Again" in 1997, singer, songwriter, and bass/harmonica player, Jeff Carson was born in Tulsa, Oklahoma. Raised in the small Arkansas town of Gravette, he began his musical career singing in church and playing guitar and harmonica. Jeff came from a musical family with his sister playing piano, his brother a bass, and his grandfather Ernest, who taught Jeff to play the harmonica. His musical influences as a youngster included Vern Gosdin, Merle Haggard (first concert he attended), George Jones, and James Taylor. During high school, Jeff formed a band that won second place in a talent show performing the Eagles' "Seven Bridges Road." This convinced Jeff that he wanted to pursue a career in music. After high school, he entered another talent contest held at the Ozark Mountain Music complex in Rogers, Arkansas. Jeff failed to win, but was invited to join the house band in which he played bass for the next four years.

Jeff then moved to Branson, Missouri, where he played in several local bands while beginning to write songs. He met and married Kim Cooper, who persuaded him 1989 to move to Nashville, where he played bass at the Opryland Hotel. About the same time, Jeff signed a songwriting deal with Little Big Town music and began singing demo tapes for various companies.

In 1994 Carson signed with Curb Records, and released his eponymous album in 1995, which included his first single, "Yeah Buddy," which failed to reach the charts, however, his second single off the album, "Not On Your Love," skyrocketed to #1 on the country charts. It was followed by "The Car," which hit the Top 10.

Since the #1 hit, Jeff has released three more albums on the Curb label, including *Butterfly Kisses* (1997), *Shine On* (1998), and *Real Life* (2001). The latest album includes several excellent love ballads, such as "My One and Only Love,

"Where Did I Go So Right," and "Until We Fall Back in Love Again," the latter was released as a single in 2002.

Carson was recently named national spokesperson for the National Association of Slain Officers, an organization devoted to providing support for the family of slain police officers. He recorded a series of radio PSAs for national distribution and performed at a 2001 fundraiser for NASO in Portland, Oregon. In 2001, Jeff, Rhett Atkins, and Daryle Singletary launched the Honky Tonk Tailgate Party Tour that included ninety concerts around the country.

Jeff was injured in a sledding accident in February of 2002 in which he broke a vertebra in his back, but recovered in time for the March Carnegie Hall benefit concert, "A Night of Encouragement," for victims of the September 11, 2001 tragedy in New York City. Jeff has made numerous appearances on the Grand Ole Opry with April 19-20, 2002 his most recent. (GC)

Chenoweth, Kristin
(b. July 24, 1972)

A multi-award winner in 1999 for her role as Sally Brown in the Broadway production of *You're a Good Man, Charlie Brown*, vocalist, dancer, and actress Kristin Chenoweth was born in Broken Arrow, Oklahoma, the fastest growing suburb of Tulsa. Starting out by performing Judy Garland numbers for her family at age 9, Kristin graduated Broken Arrow High School, and earned a bachelor's degree in musical theater and a master's degree in opera performance from Oklahoma City University. She garnered the "Most Talented Up-and-Coming Singer" award in the Metropolitan Opera National Council auditions, and received a full scholarship to the Academy of Vocal Arts in Philadelphia. Before beginning her studies in Philadelphia, she auditioned for an off-Broadway production of *Animal Crackers*, and when awarded the leading role, decided to turn professional. The *Animal Crackers* role was followed by a stint in the off-Broadway musical, *The Fantasticks*.

Kristin garnered several major awards in 1999 for her role as Sally Brown in the first revival Broadway production of *You're a Good Man, Charlie Brown*, including a Tony Award for Best Featured Actress in a Musical, Drama Desk and Outer Critics Awards for Outstanding Featured Actress in a Musical, Antoinette Perry Award for Best Featured Actress in a Musical, and the Clarence Derwent Award for Most Promising Female Performer. At the time, she was offered a part in *Annie Get Your Gun*, starring Bernadette Peters, but opted for the Charlie Brown role, in which she essentially created the character of Sally, Charlie's sister. She was sent all the *Peanuts* cartoons, in which Sally appeared, by creator of the comic strip, Charles Schulz. Additional Broadway productions in which she has appeared include her Broadway debut in Moliere's *Scapin* (1996), Kander and Ebb's musical *Steel Pier* (1997), and starred in the comedy *Epic Proportions* (1999). In the *Steel Pier* production, she captured a Theatre World Award. Off-Broadway productions include *A New Brain* (1998), *Strike Up the Band* (1998), and *On a Clear Day You Can See Forever* (2000).

Kristin released her first album, *Let Yourself Go*, in 2001 on the Sony Classical label. It includes several pop classics, such as "My Funny Valentine," "I'll Tell the Man in the Street"(both by Rodgers and Hart), "How Long Has This Been Going On?" and "Hangin' Around With You" (both by the Gershwins), as well as the title track number by Irving Berlin. Also in 2001, she starred in her own NBC television sitcom, *Kristin*, a story about a Manhattan newcomer named Kristin Yancey, a conservative girl who left her Oklahoma home with dreams of Broadway stardom. However, the show was cancelled after seven episodes.

Kristin has appeared in several television productions, including *Frasier*, *Another World*, *Lateline*, *Paramour*, *Blind Men*, and the Emmy and Peabody Award winning Disney/ABC television revival of *Annie*. Her regional theater credits include *Strike Up the Band* (Goodspeed Opera House), *Babes in Arms* (Pollard Theatre in Guthrie, Oklahoma), *Sugar* (Lyric Theater in Oklahoma City), *Phantom of the Opera* (North Shore Music Theater), and *Animal Crackers* (Paper Mill Playhouse). Finally, Jerome Robbins selected Kristin as the guest soloist in his *West Side Story Suite of Dances* at the New York City Ballet.

In 2001 Kristin launched her first national tour (accompanied by the Seattle Men's Chorus) in Seattle with follow-up concerts at the Hollywood Bowl and in New York's Central Park accompanied by the New York Philharmonic. Her 2002 tour schedule included appearances with the Virginia Symphony, Kansas City Symphony, Washington, D.C. National Symphony, as well as performances at such venues as Wolf Trap, Hollywood Bowl, and the New Amsterdam Theatre. She was also one of the featured native Oklahoma performers who participated in the grand opening of the newly renovated Civic Center Music Hall in Oklahoma City.

Chenoweth was featured in 2002 on the A & E television special, *Richard Rodgers: Falling in Love*, a celebration of the 100th anniversary of one of the greatest American songwriters. She performed her rendition of "My Funny Valentine" accompanied by violinist Joshua Bell. She was part of a star-studded lineup for the *Richard Rodgers: A Centennial Celebration* held at the Kennedy

Center for the Performing Arts in Washington, D.C. in 2002. As one of the head-liners of the Worth Street Theater Company's Tribeca Playhouse Stage-Door Canteen, she performed for personnel who worked at Ground Zero following the September 11, 2001 Twin Towers tragedy in New York City.

Kristin's active schedule in 2003 included her return to Broadway in *Wicked: The Life and Times of the Wicked Witch of the West*, in which she played the role of Glenda the Good, and which opened appropriately on Halloween; a starring role in the ABC film version of Meredith Wilson's *The Music Man*; and six per-formances in London as part of the "Divas at the Donmar" series at the Donmar Warehouse Theater. She returned to Tulsa for two performances with the Signature Symphony at Tulsa Community College in February, 2003, and had a planned concert version of Leonard Bernstein's *Candide* which was to be per-formed with the New York Philharmonic for later broadcast on PBS.

In a 2002 television interview for the program *Oklahomans*, Kristin credits her professional career to four personal attributes, including a unique speaking voice, dancing skills, small stature, and ability to sing opera. The *New York Times* has described Kristin's voice as "sharp enough to etch monograms into Baccarat crys-tal." (GC)
www.kristinchenoweth.com

Cherokee
(Cherokees began arriving in Indian Territory in 1828)

Cherokee history extends to the philosophical beginning of time. In a 2001 ses-sion of the Cherokee Nation History Course offered to Oklahoma educators by the Cherokee Nation of Oklahoma, cultural preservationist and then deputy chief Hastings Shade explained, "The Milky Way is the footprint of our ancestors." Talking about Cherokee history just depends on how far back a person is willing to go in their visionary abilities. Beginning with the Cherokee word for "creator" that translates roughly into "the one who made it possible," Shade relayed the oral tradition of the tribe began when "Star woman fell, broken open, and man stepped out." Subsequently, according to Shade's oral tradition, the tribe lived on an island surrounded by undrinkable water when a volcano started. After twelve traveling parties loaded into boats with their corn and sacred possessions, they started toward the cold air of the north. Because of the dangerous journey, five boats were lost in transit. The seven parties that arrived in "Amayethla," as the Cherokee have always called the "land in the middle of all the waters" that is North America, represent the contemporary seven clans of the Cherokee. The people continued north until the "water turned to white," either referring to the snow or the rampaging rivers of the north, then turned south where Shade says, "[they] kept traveling over fertile lands, crossed the long river, and found the mound builders, the Natchez, known to us as the red-eyed people, and we became one with the mound builders."

While contradictions will always be present when matching traditional American Indian oral history with the Western scholarship model based on existence of empirical evidence, a basic examination of the mound building periods in North America indicates the Cherokee could have been in their southeastern homelands for a thousand years before DeSoto and his Choctaw guides noted them on 1540 maps as "Chalaqui," the Choctaw word to describe "the people who lived in the caves" of rocky, western North Carolina, and throughout modern Kentucky, Tennessee, and parts of Alabama, Georgia, South Carolina, and the Virginias. As a result, the word "Cherokee" is a rough Anglicized mispronunciation of a Choctaw word for the people who call themselves "Ah Ni-Keetoowah" a name given to the ancient Cherokee by the creator.

Dave Whitekiller, a United Keetoowah Band traditionalist, historian, and fluent Cherokee speaker, explained in a 2001 interview, "the best way to explain it is to make an analogy. It's just like a fowl, a mother chicken or turkey, that will spread its wings during a hailstorm and cover its chicks. So, it means those that are protected, maybe not protected necessarily in a religious sense from rain or hail or anything, but protected as a people by God." Whitekiller also emphasized the name does not mean "chosen people," as that concept became part of Cherokee thought due to Biblical influences, but was given by God to the tribe in the beginning of time. The shortened version, "Keetoowah," has remained due to its ease of use for non-Indians and members of other tribes, in addition to its contemporary use by the Tahlequah-based United Keetoowah Band of Cherokee Indians. Without submerging into the multiple levels of strong feelings on the issue from many angles, Cherokee traditionalist Benny Smith noted simply and emphatically in the 2001 Cherokee Nation History Course that Keetoowah is a religion and a way of life, not a political organization. Nonetheless, the name Cherokee is the primary name by which the tribe and its people are known, resulting from the very first European maps of what became the southeastern United States.

Following DeSoto on the colonization trail through Cherokee country, comprised in the 18th century of at least sixty-four towns and villages throughout forty thousand square miles of the southeastern United States, the British arrived and made the first treaty with the Cherokee in 1721, establishing for international history and legal purposes the "nation" status of the Cherokee. Fast forward through several wars, treaties, court cases, hoodwinking by the developing populace of Georgia and government officials of the United States, not to mention treasonous and debilitating acts by their own people, and the Cherokee found their property being destroyed ("not a chicken shack was left standing"). The final insult came when the Cherokee were rounded up and moved en masse to Indian Territory via the well-chronicled 1838 "trail of tears" or "road where they cried."

Upon arrival in the Indian Territory, the Cherokee went about re-establishing the schools, government, churches and businesses that had qualified them as a "civilized" tribe in the eyes of Anglos in the old country. Cherokee sovereignty remained strong in Indian Territory until the Civil War when a faction of the tribe sided with the South in violation of treaties the Cherokee signed with the U.S. government. A subsequent set of land cessions, the Dawes Allotment Act of 1887, Oklahoma statehood in 1907, and several twentieth century federal laws that terminated and then empowered the Cherokee round out an extremely brief version of the tribe's history and delivers some twenty-first century perspective on the current state of affairs of the Cherokee people, now consisting primarily of three major groups.

With approximately 220,000 enrolled members and its headquarters in Tahlequah, the Cherokee Nation of Oklahoma is the biggest collective group of Cherokees in the country, and the second largest American Indian tribe in the United States. The contemporary Cherokee Nation is comprised geographically of thirteen counties or parts of counties in northeastern Oklahoma, still less than one tenth of one percent of their former homelands in the southeastern U.S. Two other groups of Cherokees are federally recognized tribal entities. The United Keetoowah Band of Cherokee Indians (UKB) is a smaller group of Cherokees with an enrollment of approximately 10,000, and is also located in Tahlequah with additional offices in Waldron, Arkansas. The UKB are descended from Cherokee traditionalists, known as the "old settlers," who realized things were only going to get worse in the old Cherokee country and began moving west as early as the 1790s. After a dispersal by Cherokee people into Tennessee, western Kentucky, southern Illinois, and the St. Francis area of Missouri, the treaty of 1817 granted lands for the Cherokee old settlers (and presumably the rest of the tribe) west of the Mississippi in Arkansas Territory. About two to three thousand people took the U.S. up on its offer and moved to an area along the Arkansas River in present-day Pope County, Arkansas. Unfortunately for the settlers, the Osage considered it Osage property and fought regularly with the Cherokee until the treaty of 1828 set aside land in Indian Territory for the old settlers, and the remainder of the people still in the east. The 1828 treaty guaranteed the Cherokees a "permanent home" that would "under the most solemn guarantee of the United States, be, and remain, theirs forever."

The 1828 treaty also defined the Cherokee Outlet, which gives a pathway to the west over the panhandle of Texas by creating the Oklahoma panhandle, and gave further incentives for Cherokee people to leave Georgia by offering each individual a rifle, a kettle, a blanket, five pounds of tobacco, and the cost of the trip. Subsequently, the old settlers moved out of Arkansas Territory and into Indian Territory a full ten years before the large group began arriving in 1838, and it is those old settlers, according to the official UKB website, who formed the nucleus of what became the United Keetoowah Band of Cherokee Indians. As noted earlier, Cherokee Nation traditionalist feelings about the political use of the word is just one unresolved ideological issue between the UKB and the Cherokee Nation of Oklahoma that illustrates a complicated relationship that is certainly beyond the scope of this musical essay. Official websites for both entities are the best place for students and researchers to begin finding out about individual UKB and Cherokee Nation of Oklahoma histories, bibliographies, and current state of affairs.

With an enrollment of approximately 12,500, the third federally recognized Cherokee group is the Eastern Band of Cherokee Indians, generally descended from Cherokee who avoided removal to Indian Territory by tracing their origin to an 1819 treaty that gave them U.S. citizenship and land allotments not belonging to the Cherokee Nation; therefore, they claimed the 1835 removal treaty did not apply to them since they were not living on Cherokee lands. Persevering on cultural tourism and gaming, the Eastern Band is presently located in Cherokee, North Carolina, in the western part of the state near the Great Smoky Mountains.

In the same way the tribe has fragmented during the continued transitional period all American Indians encountered in the twentieth century, Cherokee musical styles have both eroded and grown in the same way the tribe has over the last 200 years, with some traditions dying out completely, some preserved in very small pockets, and some musical traditions evolving with Christianity, technology, and the interaction with other tribes and U.S. popular culture. As a result, the most prominent contemporary Cherokee musical styles include the traditional stomp dances that are part of the original ceremonial traditions of the Cherokee still being practiced in the Cherokee Nation; river cane flute music; and the Christian-influenced harmonized Cherokee hymns that embrace enough hybrid musicological cross-fertilization to keep graduate students and scholars in that area writing for years. Cherokee people are also active in the intertribal powwow traditions of Oklahoma and have ranged successfully into every musical sphere of American popular and classical music.

Ancient as the tribe itself, the Cherokee stomp dance is sung in the "original language of God," according to UKB elder Dave Whitekiller, and persists as part of Cherokee social dancing and ceremonial activities. The stomp dances were one of the first activities missionaries found southeastern tribes doing that ran contrary to the concept of fire as a

Demonstration Stomp Dance, 2002.

symbol of the Biblical destination of sinners. Missionaries found the Cherokee, and neighboring tribes such as the **Muscogee**, dancing in a counter-clockwise circle around a fire, men singing and women shaking leg rattles made out of turtles for a syncopated rhythm not unlike the swinging eighth notes of African-American jazz, the connections of which have still not been fully explored by scholars and musicologists. While this dance appeared to be worshipping the devil by missionaries, Whitekiller explains the fire at the center of the dance is a symbol for not only for cooking and for heating, but also a symbol for God and used as a focal point for the religion to worship by: "that is to say that the heat rises [from the fire], and as you sing the songs of merriment, or you sing the songs of thanks, or whatever with regards to religion, the sound of your voice carries over the fire and is spiraled up into the beyond to the giver of all things." One can currently find (if you know where to go) at least five active Cherokee ceremonial grounds. Redbird Smith Grounds near Sallisaw is the oldest Cherokee ceremonial grounds in Oklahoma and the source of Stoke's Grounds that broke away from

Dave Whitekiller

Redbird Smith's grounds due to philosophical differences, again beyond the scope of this essay. Stoke's is currently the most highly attended with large crowds each year during the Cherokee Nation Labor Day celebration. Smaller active Cherokee dance grounds include Wolf Grounds near Stillwell, Oklahoma; Rocky Ford Grounds south of Oaks, Oklahoma which some consider a "practice ground"; Long Valley Kituwah Grounds near Chewey, Oklahoma died out in the 1950s, but has been revived in tandem with a Christian church; and Sugar Mountain Ground near Welling, Oklahoma has also held one meeting per year for many years.

Acquiring recordings of Cherokee traditional dance music is problematic, but not impossible. Recorded and produced by Willard Rhodes, the vinyl-only *Delaware, Cherokee, Choctaw, Creek* (AFS L-37) features Cherokee stomp dance songs as well as a Cherokee lullaby, a Christian hymn, the "Horse Dance Song," "Quail Dance Song," and "Pumpkin Dance Song," all performed by Tom Handle in Jay, Oklahoma. While these appear to be the only commercially released songs by the federal Archive of Folk Song, other recordings do exist in the collection, to include 1951 recordings of Christian hymns sung by the Ross Quartet, led by Field Ross in Pryor, Oklahoma, a reading of the Cherokee alphabet by Ross, and his recitation of the Lord's Prayer in Cherokee. Additional Cherokee field recordings housed in the Franz Olbrechts Collection at the Library of Congress, originally from the Frances Densmore/Smithsonian Institution collection of wax cylinders, include a medicine song for protection, a speech in the Cherokee about the allotment of Cherokee lands, a "Mask Dance," "Bear dance," war cry, and "Ball Game Dance." Also from the set of original cylinder recordings are the "Ground Hog Dance," "Eagle Dance," "Pipe Dance," "Bear Hunting Song," "Hymn in Honor of the Rising Sun," "Medicine Song to Cure Wounds," "Medicine Song Against Witchcraft Diseases," and hunting songs for the bear and for the turkey.

The national archive's Artur Moses Collection also holds several 1946 recordings made in North Carolina at the Eastern Cherokee's reservation. Will Weste Long performs several Cherokee dance tunes, although they are not enumerated, along with Christian hymns "The Son of God," and "Meeting of Christians." In 1949, the Smithsonian recorded more traditional dances in North Carolina such as the "Victory Dance," "Friendship Dance," "Snake Dance," "Corn Dance," and "Bear Dance." While these are recordings are well documented, one set of recordings has yet to be explicated. Titled simply "Cherokee Indian Recordings," two reels of sound originating from discs in the Smithsonian's Bureau of American Ethnology have yet to be translated or determined as the collector and contents are unidentified. Interested researchers should consult the widely published work of Dr. Charlotte Heth, a noted Cherokee ethnomusicologist, who recorded sixteen reels of Cherokee music for her dissertation, "The Stomp Dance of the Oklahoma Cherokee: A Study of Contemporary Practice with Special Reference to the Illinois District Ground" (1975), the audio and video field recordings of which are now located in the Museum of the Cherokee Indian in Cherokee, North Carolina.

Contemporary recordings include Kevin Lewis's *Ceremonial Songs and Dances of the Cherokee, Vol. 1 and 2*, and *Cherokee Stomp Dance*, recorded and produced by American Indian rapper Litefoot, and led by Tom Wildcat, Tommy Wildcat, Lucas Wildcat, and Ladney Keener. While all of these recordings are representative of the Cherokee stomp dance tradition, one can only truly appreciate the dance live in its intended environment, as part of a ceremonials that are often remote and hard to find for the person who has no close association with the traditional Cherokee community. However, opportunities do exist to see and participate in the dances at the increasing number of public, social dances that are being performed in gymnasiums and community centers in and around Tahlequah throughout the year, and the previously mentioned Cherokee National Holiday, held over Labor Day Weekend in Tahlequah, provides ample opportunity for learning more.

Perry Urmeteskee (right) demonstrates Cherokee flute making at Rogers State University in 2002.

Another Cherokee traditional music form currently experiencing a renaissance of interest is the Cherokee cane flute. Victor Wildcat, a public school educator in Fort Gibson, and a cultural preservationist of traditional Cherokee arts and crafts who has taught hundreds of school children and adults in northeastern Oklahoma how to make and play the river can flute since 1998, explains the instruments were used traditionally as courting instruments to impress would-be lovers and gain their hearts. The historical record also reflects the flutes being used by Cherokees to greet visitors comming into a village, perhaps, to soothe any would-be attacker. Made from river cane abundant in the Illinois River area of the contemporary Cherokee Nation, Wildcat also notes the flutes are also played "just for the enjoyment of music." He regularly demonstrates Cherokee and Muscogee hymns, traditional songs, and Anglo-Christmas music on the flute for school functions, educational workshops, and other public demonstrations, but has not made an official recording.

National recognition for the Cherokee cane flute came in 2002 when the annual Native American Music Awards voted Cherokee Tommy Wildcat "Flutist of the Year" for his album *Pow-Wow Flutes* (2001). Wildcat, only distantly related to

Victor Wildcat, has released a number of albums through Warrior Spirit productions, a company organized by Wildcat and his twin sister, Tammy, to include *Warrior's Spirit* (Cherokee River Cane Flute), *Cherokee Flute Songs and Voices*, *GWY* (Stomp Dances), and *Cherokee Songs and Flute* (featuring "Amazing Grace"). Both Tammy and Tommy have become well-known performers with their dance troupe, Dancers of Fire, appearing in the Discovery Channel's *How the West Was Lost* series and several other video productions. Tommy, who also appeared in TNT's *Tecumseh: The Last Warrior*, completed two European tours in 1995 and 1997, performs yearly at powwows in Hawaii, and travels extensively across mainland America each year performing at cultural festivals, powwows, historic museum sites, and colleges as a featured artist.

Gospel music and Christian-influenced hymns continue to play an important part of contemporary Cherokee cultural and religious activities. The songs mix tribal history, often relating to the removal of the Cherokee from their homelands in North Carolina, Protestant Christian elements of harmony and lyrical content, and sometimes scales more related to American Indian music than the European musical system. The first major name in contemporary Cherokee gospel music is J.B. Dreadfulwater (b. January 12, 1932 – d. March 9, 2002), who performed for more than fifty

J. B. Dreadfulwater

years with a gospel group, the Osceola Trio. Dreadfulwater was also the director of the Cherokee Choir that traveled the United States for many years under his direction. Collectors can still find vinyl copies of his music on albums such as *Squan-ti-ni-se-sti Ye-ho-wah* (*Guide Me Jehovah*), a representative collection of piano and organ-heavy gospel music. Dreadfulwater also led the Cherokee Indian Baptist Choir on two Cherokee Hymns for the State Arts Council of Oklahoma's 1989 Songs of Indian Territory project, available on cassette. In 2002, the Native American Music Awards nominated his album with the Cherokee Choir, *A Wonderful Place*, as "Best Gospel/Christian Recording," but the album lost out to the Cherokee National Children's Choir which probably would not have disappointed the elder Cherokee singer.

Sponsored by the Cherokee Nation of Oklahoma, the Cherokee National Children's Choir has surfaced on three excellent recordings since 2000, the first of which was *Cherokee Gospel Music* (CNRC, 2000). Recorded at Jeffrey Parker's Cimmaron Labs near Tahlequah, and featuring the Cherokee National Children's Choir singing in the Cherokee language, *Cherokee Gospel Music* is a collection of traditional Cherokee hymns such as "Orphan Child" which has its sources in the Cherokee "Trail of Tears" when many children became orphans as

a result of their parents' deaths on the journey. Young singers on *Cherokee Gospel Music* include Holly Backwater (Kenwood), Keith Brickey (Ft. Gibson), Alese Christie (Stilwell), Rebecca Cook (Owasso), Heather Crittenden (Stilwell), Kayla Davis (Salina), Amanda Gibe (Jay), Leslie Ketcher (Stilwell), Tawni Keys (Tahlequah), Devon Kirby (Eucha), Kandra Liles (Stilwell), Lora Keeter Miller (Stilwell), Haley Noe (Oaks), Holly Noe (Oaks), Ashley Proctor (Salina), Kayla Sharp (Jay), Chris Smith (Tulsa), Samantha Spiker (Salina), and Amie Watkins (Bunch). Choir conductors for the recording included Janis Ross Ballou and Jamie Geneva. In 2001, the Cherokee Cultural Resource Center made its second gospel CD, *Voices of the Creator's Children*, again featuring the children's choir with the additional voice of noted Cherokee pop and country singer Rita Coolidge, whose own group, Walela (after the word in Cherokee for butterfly), also has recorded contemporary versions of traditional Cherokee songs. The makeup of the 2001 choir is essentially the same as the first CD, with the addition of Jon Ross and minus a few of the original voices.

Voted the Best Gospel/Christian Recording in the 2002 Native American Music Awards, *Voices of the Creator's Children* has both traditional Southern gospel songs such as "Amazing Grace" and "What a Friend We Have in Jesus" as well as songs related to the specific experiences of the Cherokee: "On the Road Where They Cried," "One Drop of Blood," "North Wind," and "Evening Song." In 2002, the Cherokee Nation released a third album of the Cherokee National Youth Choir, *Building One Fire*, featuring Gil Silverbird. The album again follows the formula of the first two collections by featuring the Cherokee Youth Choir singing hymns in the Cherokee language. Along with the traditional hymns, the group also recorded native-Oklahoman **Albert E. Brumley**'s "I'll Fly Away," featuring **Red Dirt Music** luminary, and the album's producer, Jeffrey Gray Parker on guitar, mandolin, and bass. The album also includes two live performances by the choir at the Museum of the American Indian in New York City and the Department of Interior in Washington D.C. to commemorate the events of September 11, 2001 in those two cities; sung in the Cherokee language, the choir performs "America" and "The Star Spangled Banner." Singers joining original members of the group include Caroline and Walter Buffalomeat, Christina Catron, Pawnee Crabtree, Delilah Davis, Paige Haines, Christina Hanvey, Vanessa John,

Tracy Pickup, Megan Ross, Kinsey Shade, and Ryan Sierra.

Also in 2001, the Cherokee Nation Cultural Resource Center released, *Children's Songs in the Cherokee Language* (CNCR 002). The CD includes several well-known children's songs, "I'm a Little Terrapin," "Twinkle, Twinkle, Little Star," "Baa Baa Black Sheep," sung Cherokee with instrumental accompaniment. The disc was designed to help young Cherokee school children learn their language in a familiar musical environment. The 2002 Native American Music Awards nominated *Children's Songs in the Cherokee Language* as "Best Historical Recording" in 2002.

Like many of their tribal counterparts throughout the United States, the Cherokee have embraced the "pan-Indian" tradition of the intertribal powwow for social, commemorative, and fund-raising purposes. Both the United Keetoowah Band and the Cherokee Nation sponsor powwows throughout the year at tribal facilities, the Tahlequah Community Center, and other locations in the Tahlequah area. The Cherokee Gourd Society, a dance based largely on **Kiowa** traditions, has organized an annual Christmas powwow since 1992, and a full-blown competition powwow is part of the annual Cherokee National Holiday held since 1952. Additionally, each year a number of smaller competition, benefit, and honor dances are held throughout the Cherokee Nation at public schools, colleges, community centers, fairgrounds, and just about any other place big enough where a dance can be held. While some Cherokees have adopted the intertribal powwow traditions based largely on plains tribes' celebrations, several Cherokees from Oklahoma have also made and continue to make substantial contributions outside of the traditional music realm.

Cherokee-Quapaw **Louis W. Ballard**, a Pulitzer Prize nominee for music, is a versatile composer who has written music for ballet and choral arrangements as well as chamber and orchestral works. Another successful classical music artist is Cherokee mezzo-soprano Barbara McAlister, born in Muskogee, who has performed with prominent opera companies around the globe.

In the popular music genre, pioneering electric guitarist **Nokie Edwards** of the Ventures is Cherokee, and Leo Feathers, born in Stilwell, played guitar for Leon Russell, Jerry Lee Lewis, Bonnie Raitt, Willie Nelson, and Dickie Betts. According to Elvis Presley's official website, his maternal great-great-grandmother, Morning Dove White (b. 1800 – d. 1835), was a full-blooded Cherokee. **Tulsa Sound** luminary **Jack Dunham** is an enrolled Cherokee, and the well-known Cherokee actor Wes Studi plays bass and rhythm guitar with Firecat of Discord who released a self-titled album in 1998. Cherokee blues

Leo Feathers

guitarist James "Ace" Moreland (b. Miami, OK, d. Feb. 8, 2003) recorded four searing albums of blues for Ichiban, Wild Dog, and King Snake Records, and worked as a sideman for notable blues artists such as Sonny Rhodes. Included in Moreland's catalogue is the Cherokee history based song "Indian Giver" on the CD *Give It To Get It* (King Snake, 2000), an album title taken from a **Steve Gaines** song. Increasingly significant, Tahlequah-based Jeffrey Gray Parker, a composer, musician, and studio engineer also associated with **Red Dirt Music**, has released three albums as Coyote Zen and received worldwide airplay and critical praise for his ambient blend of traditional and contemporary instruments.

Hopefully, many more Oklahoma musicians with Cherokee heritage, such as Western swing guitarist Jimmie Rivers, born in Hockerville, will come to light. However, particular difficulties come into play when differentiating between enrolled and non-enrolled Cherokee citizens, also beyond the range of this discussion, but any publicly acknowledged claim of Cherokee heritage, such as that of Presley, rock guitarist Jimi Hendrix, country singers Hank Williams, Willie Nelson, and Loretta Lynn, exemplifies the deep, intertwined connections between Cherokee history and the developing music of American mainstream popular culture. While scholars have been primarily concerned with the music of "the old ones," as Dave Whitekiller called the ancient Keetoowah people, more work should be done on both the evolving Cherokee Christian music and popular music created by both enrolled and non-enrolled Cherokee people, along with the elusive Cherokee fiddle whose minor key tunings exhibit a unique Cherokee take on traditional Anglo fiddle music of the South. Nonetheless, ancient songs expressing the deepest connections between the Cherokee people and their creator are still being sung in a worshipful manner each

Cherokee Fiddler Sam O'Field

year at Cherokee ceremonial grounds, children are singing Christian hymns in the Cherokee language for appreciative audiences nationwide, and the Cherokee flute tradition is active and being cared for by dedicated individuals, all of which bodes well for the continued preservation of Cherokee heritage, language, and music. (HF) www.cherokee.org www.keetoowah.org www.cherokee-nc.com

Cherry, Donald Eugene
b. November 18, 1936 – d. October 19, 1995)

Most often declared a leader of the free jazz movement for his work with Ornette Coleman, Don Cherry was also the first to use the pocket trumpet in jazz, and spent his later years exploring, composing, and learning the instruments of non-Western, world music. In terms of his significance to Oklahoma music and history, Don's family serves the same symbolic purpose as that of many Oklahomans who left the economically depressed state in the 1930s and 40s, as well representing the significance of making music for oneself prior to the television era.

Born into a musical family in Oklahoma City, Don's grandfather played piano, his grandmother played piano for silent movies, and his father owned the 1920s-era Cherry Blossom Club in Tulsa. Don's mother, a parlor piano player, was reportedly half-Choctaw, the same tribe as the mothers of both Charlie Parker and Oklahoma blues man **Lowell Fulson.** When Don was four-years-old, the family's movement to the West Coast in 1940 coincided with the general migration of Oklahomans who went to California to find work during The Depression and World War II. In Los Angeles, Don played trumpet in junior high band, and trumpet in both the Jefferson High marching and dance band. The band director at the time, Samuel Brown, who also taught jazz musicians **Wardell Gray** and Art Farmer, was a significant inspiration.

While Cherry began his professional career as a teen, playing piano in an R & B group led by Billy Higgins, jazz critics and fans began to notice Don playing pocket trumpet as a regular member of Ornette Coleman's L.A. groups from 1957 through Coleman's most influential recording period of the 1960s. The smaller, pocket cornet which Cherry called a pocket trumpet provided a distinctive tone which differentiated him from other jazz trumpeters. Cherry moved to New York with Coleman in 1959 and played with him on many of the seminal albums of free jazz: *Something Else!!!!* (1958); *Change of the Century* (1959); *Free Jazz* (1960). The free jazz movement drew as many detractors as the twentieth century classical music of Stravinsky did from classical purists in the early 1900s. Free jazz was frenetic, with whirling, improvised solos intertwining with one another, a hyperdrive Dixieland band for the turbulent era of the civil rights movement of the 1950s and 1960s. In fact, the music was a conscious effort by Coleman, John Coltrane, and Don Cherry to expand the stylistic elements of jazz when hard bop, with its aim of making jazz palatable to mainstream audiences, did not appeal to the free jazz players specifically because of the style's commercial intent. Free jazz embodied the essential elements of jazz: improvisation, rhythmic vibrancy, knowledge of standard tunes, and a virtuoso's command of an instrument.

Cherry left Coleman in the early 1960s, played with Sonny Rollins and Albert Ayler, and co-led The New York Contemporary Five in 1963-4. Afterwards, like many other American jazz men who were left with little work during the early rock era, Cherry went to Europe where he recorded his first albums as a band leader, two of which became his most highly praised albums, *Complete Communion* (1965) and *Symphony for Improvisers* (1966). The albums were one of the earliest recorded appearances for the Argentinian tenor saxophonist Gato Barbieri, who Cherry discovered in Italy. During this period Cherry switched to a traditional-sized cornet. Cherry taught at Dartmouth College in 1970, moved to Sweden where he was based until 1974, and recorded with the Jazz Composer's Orchestra Association in 1973. During the 1970s, Cherry became increasingly interested in non-Western, world music and traveled extensively through Europe and the Middle East studying ethnic instruments, melodies, and musical contexts. In the late 1970s, Cherry worked with rock singer Lou Reed, and into the early 1980s he led a cooperative trio, Codona, through three albums of jazz incorporating African, East Indian, Asian, and other ethnic music forms. Cherry also acquired another pocket trumpet in 1983 and began to reincorporate it into his repertoire. After Codona ceased as a unit, Cherry formed the group Nu which toured Europe in 1987. Cherry recorded *Art Deco* in 1988, which served as a reunion of sorts from the early Ornette Coleman Quartet. The session reunites Cherry with bassist Charlie Haden and drummer Billy Higgins from the early Coleman group, and provides new opportunities for saxophonist James Clay who had been in obscurity for many years. "Body and Soul," three Ornette Coleman tunes, and some originals make this a fitting representation of mature and experienced musicians who ushered in the free jazz era.

Until the time of his death in Malaga, Spain in 1995, Cherry continued learning new instruments from around the world such as sitar, gamelan, conch, trumpet, and wood flutes, and composing music for them. These multi-ethnic musical elements are apparent on 1990's *Multi Kulti*. While critics report Cherry had an uneven live career, none disagree that he was a major force in the free jazz movement which was the form's final evolution before merging with rock in the fusion period of the 1960s. Cherry even fulfilled that role by playing his pocket trumpet on a recording by the very underground New York group, Bongwater, released on their 1998 collection, *Box of Bongwater*.

Throughout his career, Cherry attempted to stretch the boundaries of jazz and learn as much as he could about the music of the world. Cherry's musical legacy is primarily that of a free jazz originator, and a unique and unpredictable improviser who can be placed at the very top of the list of innovative jazz artists. He is survived in the music industry by son, Eagle Eye Cherry, who has recorded three albums of alternative pop, and his step-daughter, dance music artist Neneh Cherry. A serious man with deep philosophical resonance in his interviews, Don Cherry once warned that "if you start taking music for granted, or take *playing* music for granted, you take away from yourself. It's like they say in India, 'A life is not long enough to learn music.'" (HF)

Christian, Charlie
(b. July 29, 1916 - d. March 2, 1942)

The first significant soloist on the electric guitar in any music genre and one of the major role models for all jazz guitarists from 1940 onward, including **Barney Kessel,** Herb Ellis, Wes Montgomery, and George Benson, Charles Henry Christian was born in Bonham, Texas, but the family moved when Charlie was age two to Oklahoma City, where he was raised in an atmosphere of Kansas City style jazz and country music.

Charlie's first love was baseball, taught to him by his father. During his early childhood, Charlie was "off to hit the stick," as he would say. He had aspirations of playing in the Negro baseball league, and the sport remained one of his greatest passions throughout his life. However, he came from a musical family. His blind father, Clarence "Henry" Christian, was an itinerant trumpeter-guitarist-vocalist, while his mother was a pianist and his brothers were also musicians, including Clarence, who played violin and mandolin, and Edward, a string bass player. The three sons would often accompany their father into the wealthy white neighborhoods of Oklahoma City and serenade residents in return for cash, clothing, or food.

Charlie's first instrument was the trumpet, which he learned in elementary school under the tutelage of Ms. Zelia Page Breaux, noted Oklahoma City music educator. However, he switched to the guitar at about age twelve, and began studying the instrument under local musicians, guitarist Ralph "Bigfoot Chuck" Hamilton and trumpeter James Simpson, who taught Charlie three songs: "Rose Room," "Tea for Two," and "Sweet Georgia Brown." Because the family was poor, Charlie constructed his first guitar out of cigar boxes in a manual training class. By the time Charlie was thirteen, his father had died and older brother, Edward, ten years his senior, had organized his own band, the Jolly Harmony Boys.

After graduating from Douglass High School in Oklahoma City, Charlie toured as a bass player with several territorial bands, including Anna Mae Winburn, Nat Towles, and Alphonso Trent. Eddie Durham, a trombonist and guitarist in Jimmy Lunceford's band, is credited with influencing Charlie's renewed interest in the guitar, and he began performing in Trent's sextet on his $77.50 Gibson ES-150 guitar with magnetic pickup and electric amplifier.

By 1937 Christian was leading his own combo in Oklahoma City and continuing to experiment with electrical amplification on his guitar. Two years later, it is reported that Mary Lou Williams, eminent jazz pianist and member of Andy Kirk's Clouds of Joy, suggested to jazz promoter John Hammond that he come by to hear Charlie who was playing at the Ritz Ballroom in downtown Oklahoma City. Hammond liked what he heard and contacted Benny Goodman about an audition for Charlie in Los Angeles, where Goodman was recording his first sessions for Columbia Records. Christian and Hammond traveled to the West Coast, but Goodman was turned off by Charlie's attire and concept of an electric guitar. One source states that for the audition, Charlie wore a ten-gallon cowboy hat, pointed yellow shoes, a green suit over a purple shirt, and a string bow tie. Despite Goodman's attitude, Hammond persisted and helped Charlie set up his amplifiers on the stage of the Victor Hugo Restaurant in Beverly Hills, where Goodman was performing. With the instigation of Goodman, his band began jamming on "Rose Room," a piece that the leader figured Charlie would not know, but it was one of the first tunes he learned in Oklahoma City. When it was Charlie's turn to solo, he played some twenty-five impressive choruses to the excitement of Goodman, his band, and the audience. That night Goodman hired Charlie to become a member of his entourage, and for the next two years, was featured soloist with the Benny Goodman Sextet. In October of 1939, Goodman played Carnegie Hall, where he introduced Charlie on a sextet number "Flying Home" saying "with Charlie Christian on the electric guitar. I really think he is one of the most terrific musicians that has been produced in years."

CHARLIE CHRISTIAN
RADIOLAND 1939-1941

While in New York with the Goodman ensemble, Christian became interested in the new developments in jazz taking place on 52nd Street. He began jamming with leaders in the bebop movement, such as Dizzy Gillespie and Thelonious Monk, at such venues as The Savoy and Minton's Playhouse, and became a fellow pioneer in the development of this subgenre of jazz. The late night sessions proved to be part of his undoing, however, as the late nights (sometimes until daybreak) and bouts with alcoholism affected Charlie's health. March 13, 1941, would turn out to be Christian's last record date with the Goodman Sextet. Three months later, on a tour of the Midwest in June, he collapsed onstage. He was rushed back to New York, where doctors at Bellevue Hospital determined that his TB had returned. By July, he had been transferred to the Seaview sanatorium in Staten Island to get his health back. Rumors persist that he was smuggled out to Minton's on occasion, or that friends smuggled in female company and marijuana, hastening his demise. At age twenty-five, younger than Robert Johnson or Jimi Hendrix, the founding father and primary architect of the modern jazz guitar style died at Seaview Sanatorium on Staten Island. He is buried in Gates Hill Cemetery in Bonham, Texas.

Native Oklahoman Barney Kessel, one of the major figures in jazz guitar during the twentieth century, paid tribute to Charlie in 1975 at the Concord Jazz Festival: "I would venture to say that there is not a guitarist alive today, whether he knows it or not, who is playing jazz, amplified or unamplified, who doesn't owe something to and have some of Charlie Christian in his playing."

Christian was one of the first inductees into the Oklahoma Jazz Hall of Fame in 1989, was inducted into the Rock and Roll Hall of Fame in 1990 in the category of "Early Influences," and inducted into the Oklahoma Music Hall of Fame in October of 2002. In November of 2002, he was the subject of a NRP story, "Revisiting the Sound of Guitar Pioneer Charlie Christian" by Tom Vitale.

In 2002, Columbia/Legacy Jazz released *Charlie Christian: The Genius of the Electric Guitar*, a four-CD boxed set that is the first comprehensive of the Columbia Recordings with the Benny Goodman Sextet and Orchestra (1939-41), plus the Metronome All Star Nine. The set includes 98 tracks – 17 of which are previously unreleased in the United States, and encompasses master and alternate takes, breakdowns, false starts and rehearsal sequences, and an uncut twenty-minute jam session. A new essay by British biographer Peter Broadbent is included, and it is complemented by an in-depth, track-by-track sessionography researched by Loren Schoenberg. Also in the liner notes is a memoir from close friend Les Paul that tops list of testimonials from B.B. King, George Benson, Jimmie Vaughan, John Scofield, T-Bone Walker, Wes Montgomery, Brian Setzer, Joe Satriani, Barney Kessel, Herb Ellis, Tal Farlow, Bill Frisell, and more.

Vernon Reid, the lead guitarist for Living Colour, says, "It all starts with him: Charlie Christian is The Father. In his all-too-brief time, Charlie changed the world of jazz, blues, and everything else besides. It is literally impossible to overstate the importance of his contribution to the development of jazz. His limitless stream of melodic ideas; the many blue shades of his pungently sad, sweet tone; and his irrepressible swing all continue to influence generations of guitarists. From Wes Montgomery to James Blood Ulmer, from Tal Farlow to Charlie Hunter: It all began with the first master of the electric guitar, Mr. Charlie Christian."

According to a Columbia/Legacy jazz press release to promote the collection in 2002, *Genius* tracks Christian's 14 extant Columbia studio dates spanning 17 months through March 1941 (one year before his death), when he recorded "Solo Flight" with the orchestra, the signature by which the famed Gibson ES150 guitarist would be known forever. The first Goodman feature actually built around Christian (though not issued until nearly two years after his death), "Solo Flight" found him in transition to the nascent Bebop movement, upon which fellow conspirator Thelonious Monk and others considered him a primal force.

54 tracks on *Genius* were first issued on Columbia Records in the U.S. between

1939 and 1989, during the 78 rpm, LP and CD eras. One track, the alternate of "Flying Home," was issued (for the first time) as a 1948 Armed Forces V-Disc. Another number, 1939's "I'm Confessin'," was issued (for the first time) by Time-Life in 1978. The five tracks recorded in 1940 by Goodman and Christian in the company of Count Basie and five of his key band members (including Lester Young, whose long tenor saxophone solo lines were a primary influence on Christian) were secreted away by Hammond and didn't surface until 1972, when they were issued by Jazz Archives.

"[Christian's] name is ranked alongside those of Louis Armstrong, Earl Hines, Lester Young, and Charlie Parker," Broadbent concludes in the boxed set's liner notes. "Each elevated music to a new level of achievement, whilst establishing a new vocabulary that made them the premier voice on their chosen instrument."

Musicologist Loren Schoenberg has contributed invaluable in-depth interpolations of every individual recording session on *Genius*, incorporating track-by-track analysis that carefully traces the evolution of Christian's music and the development of the Sextet. "Hearing these recordings in such superb fidelity is like seeing a newly minted print of a classic film," Schoenberg writes. "All sorts of details appear that were lost in the poorly copied transfers that comprised the great majority of LP and CD issues available until now."

A saxophonist, conductor and educator who played in Goodman's big band, Schoenberg is the executive director of the Jazz Museum in Harlem and the author of The NPR Curious Listener's Guide To Jazz. "[Christian] learned from Eddie Durham and Django Reinhardt and others who brought something new to the guitar," he notes, "but in Christian's hands it became an altogether new instrument. With just a few exceptions, he eschewed the chorded solos that were such a large part of the guitar's legacy. It was all about the line and about how rhythm could extend the line and give it all sorts of new and unexpected shapes."

Genius is rounded out by a series of testimonials from various practitioners of the guitar spanning more than six decades, spearheaded by "My Friend Charlie Christian," an evocative reminiscence by Les Paul. The Gibson guitar legend, already a star on radio in 1938, recalls an odyssey that brought him from New York to a gig in Tulsa starring **Bob Wills & His Texas Playboys**. That is where Les Paul met Christian, and one can only imagine the jam session onstage that night. Paul's story segues to befriending Christian sometime later on his first trip to New York when Les ordered matching blond Gibson electric guitars and custom-made tube amplifiers for the two of them from Eddie Bell's 46th Street store — but the rigs proved too heavy for either of them to schlep down the street, so they returned them.

In his testimonial, Les Paul writes, *"What I'm doing was so much harder than what he's doing* — that's what I thought back then. But over time, through being with Charlie, I realized how tough it is to come down on that one note in the right place, and how much more of a *drive* he had. He had that ability, like Lionel Hampton, to take a note, to take one 'A' and just pound it into your head until it was the greatest note you'd ever heard. He didn't play beyond himself. He didn't think, 'What the hell, no one's listening. Why don't I try this? Charlie wasn't one to go out over his head. The beat came first. He locked himself into that driving sound."

Among the numerous guitarists whose thoughts are included in the booklet are (alphabetically, not in order of appearance): Walter Becker (Steely Dan), George Benson, Herb Ellis, Tal Farlow, Bill Frisell, Warren Haynes (Allman Brothers Band, Government Mule), Barney Kessel, B.B. King, Russell Malone, Wes Montgomery, Vernon Reid (Living Colour), Duke Robillard, Joe Satriani, John Scofield, Brian Setzer, Derek Trucks (Allman Brothers Band, Derek Trucks Band), Jimmie Vaughan, and T-Bone Walker.

An innovative form of sequencing has been employed over the course of discs one, two and three, in which all the sextet master takes for a certain period are followed by the alternate takes for that same period. For example, on disc one the first 17 tracks comprise the Master Takes recorded at sessions between October 2, 1939 ("Flying Home," "Rose Room," "Star Dust") and June 11, 1940 ("These Foolish Things"); these are immediately followed on tracks 18 through 26 by the Alternate Takes covering the same dates.

In that series of dates, February 7, 1940 stands out as a red letter day. After the obligatory annual recording of Metronome All Star winners ("All Star Strut"), featuring Goodman and Christian in the presence of Jack Teagarden, Benny Carter, Gene Krupa et al, the Sextet (with guest Count Basie on piano) then convened for a couple of sides

Disc two picks up the format, from the balance of the June 1940 session ("Six Appeal" *aka* "My Daddy Rocks Me" and "Good Enough To Keep" *aka* "Air Mail Special") through the first number at the December date ("Gilly"). At the November date, Cootie Williams (on trumpet), whom Goodman had lured away from Duke Ellington, effectively changed the combo from the Benny Goodman Sextet (six men) to Benny Goodman & His Sextet (seven men). Conspicuous on disc two are the five October tracks — "Ad Lib Blues," "Wholly Cats," "Charlie's Dream," "I Never Knew," "Lester's Dream" — on which Goodman and Christian recorded with Count Basie on piano and five of his key band members: rhythm guitarist Freddie Green, bassist Walter Page, drummer Jo Jones, trumpeter Buck Clayton, and tenor saxophonist Lester Young.

Likewise disc three follows the format, starting with the balance of the December 1940 sessions, including the five controversial "Breakfast Feud" takes, followed by four more takes of the tune recorded January 1941. Goodman collectors were never positive which takes were spliced together for the infamous 1955 LP version or the equally infamous (but different) 1972 LP version. For the first time, no spliced composites are now heard. Disc three wraps up on March 13, 1941, Christian's last date with Goodman on "A Smo-o-o-oth One" and "Air Mail Special," aka "Good Enough To Keep." Similarly, the latter tune and its alternate take became the subject of infamous spliced versions on the same 1955 and 1972

LPs, but are heard here in their original forms.

A wealth of material is recapped on disc four spanning 1940-41. Its five sections begin with the master takes of Charlie Christian in his one and only date with the Metronome All Star Nine, a combo that boasted Goodman, Harry James on trumpet, Benny Carter on alto sax, and Gene Krupa on drums. Then come the master takes of the only numbers on the boxed set featuring Charlie Christian with Benny Goodman & His Orchestra in 1939 ("Honeysuckle Rose"), 1940 ("Li'l Boy Love"), and 1941 (the historic "Solo Flight"). As before, these are followed by the alternate takes of the All Star Nine and the latter two orchestra dates.

Disc four then proceeds methodically to collect a series of breakdowns and false starts by the Sextet and the All Star Nine, from just a few seconds in length to a minute and a half. The disc moves on to two extended-length rehearsal sequences from the "Benny's Bugle" session of November 1940. The final 21 minutes of the boxed set are devoted to a jam session that took place on March 13, 1941, while the band (without Goodman and bassist Artie Bernstein) were warming up in the studio. As Schoenberg explains, the jam session preceded the formal session (described earlier) which yielded "A Smo-o-o-oth One" and "Air Mail Special," aka "Good Enough To Keep."

Meanwhile, uptown on West 118th Street in Harlem, Christian had become a regular at Minton's Playhouse, ground zero for the new bebop movement ever since October 1940, when Teddy Hill had been put in charge of the music by Mr. Minton. Christian joined the Monday night jam session crew that included Thelonious Monk, Kenny Clarke, Don Byas, Joe Guy, and others. As John Scofield testifies, "Miles Davis told me that he thought Charlie Christian was the original instigator of the bebop movement, Bird and Diz's main influence. When you listen to his playing today, it's still inspiring, fresh, harmonically and rhythmically advanced. I love the fact that the modern jazz movement seems to have been started by an electric guitarist!" (GC/HF)
www.charlie-christian.com or http://home.elp.rr.com/valdes/index.html

Clark, Roy
(b. April 15, 1933)

One of the most multi-talented entertainers in American music and inductee into the Oklahoma Hall of Fame, Oklahoma Music Hall of Fame, and Gibson Guitar Hall of Fame, singer, songwriter, guitarist, banjoist, fiddler, trombonist, pianist, trumpeter, actor, and comedian, Roy Linwood Clark was born in Meherrin, Virginia, although he has resided for the past twenty years in Tulsa, where an elementary school and airport bears his name. His father, Hester, worked at various jobs including cotton picker, tobacco grower, and sawmill worker before the family moved to Washington, D.C., where his father worked as a computer programmer for the Department of Health, Education, and Welfare. Both his father and mother, Lillian, were amateur musicians with father competent on banjo, fiddle, and guitar; and his mother on piano. Roy's first instrument was a cigar box with a ukulele neck and four strings crafted by his father for a school band at Meherrin Elementary. Both parents took an interest in Roy's music, especially his father who tutored him on the banjo. He made his first public appearance in 1948 at a military service club with his father's square dance band. Roy won back-to-back National Music Banjo Championships in 1949-50, garnering his first appearance on the Grand Ole Opry, and later was guest on Arthur Godrey's Talent Scouts Show.

In addition to music, Roy excelled in sports, especially baseball and boxing. At age sixteen, he was offered a tryout with the St. Louis Browns baseball team, but could not afford the fare to the workout. When he was seventeen, he boxed in the light-heavyweight division in and around Washington, D.C., and won fifteen consecutive bouts before opting for a career in music.

Clark's first break came in 1955 when he became a regular on the Jimmy Dean television show, *Country Style*. After Dean left for New York, Clark was given the show, and during the next five years, established himself as a versatile entertainer through his musicianship and comedy. In 1960, he joined **Wanda Jackson** as lead guitarist and front man during which time she recorded one of her biggest hits, "Let's Have a Party," as well as playing concerts with her in Las Vegas. Although Jackson dissolved her band about a year later, Roy continued to play Las Vegas, including the Frontier Hotel. During this time, Jim Halsey, Jackson's former manager, became Roy's manager and landed him a role on the popular television show, *The Beverly Hillbillies*, where he played the dual roles of Cousin Roy and Big Mama Halsey.

In 1963, Roy debuted on *The Tonight Show* and later became the first country artist to host the show. Although he had recorded singles for Four Star, Coral and Debbie, Roy's first contract with a major label, Capitol, was signed in 1962. His first Capitol album was *The Lightning Fingers of Roy Clark*, and his fourth single, "Tips of My Fingers," reached Top 10 on the country charts and achieved Top 50 on the pop charts; his first crossover recording. After recording "Through the Eyes of a Fool" (1964) and "When the Blows in Chicago" (1965) for Capitol, he switched to the Dot label in 1967. In 1969, he scored with Charles Aznavour's "Yesterday, When I Was Young" and "September Song." The former was Roy's second crossover hit; charting Top 10 in country and Top 20 in popular.

In 1969, CBS invited Roy and Bakersfield country star Buck Owens to co-host a new country music and comedy show *Hee Haw*, a country version of *Laugh In*. For the next two years, it became one of the highest rated shows television shows in the U.S. But CBS decided to drop the program because it created an unfavorable image for the network, however, the show's producers syndicated it and began reaching some thirty million viewers weekly on some 200 stations. Roy co-hosted the show for more than twenty-five years.

The decade of the 1970s proved productive for Clark. He continued headlining at Las Vegas' Caesar's Palace with Petula Clark; launched a twenty-one day tour to Russia in 1976 with eighteen sold out concerts in Moscow, Leningrad, and Riga, which resulted in the CMA's "Friendship Ambassador" award (he returned to Russia in 1988 to sold out venues); performed in 1976 with Arthur Fiedler and the Boston Pops Orchestra; appeared at Carnegie Hall in 1977; and recorded several hits, including "Thank God for Greyhound" (1970), "I Never Picked Cotton" (1970), "The Lawrence Welk-Hee Haw Counter-Revolution Polka" (1972), "Come Live With Me" (1973), a #1 hit, "Riders in the Sky" (1973), one of his first instrumental hits, "Somewhere Between Love and Goodbye" (1973), "Honeymoon Feelin'" (1974), "The Great Divide" (1974), "Heart to Heart" (1975), and "If I Had to Do It All Over Again" (1976), the song most identified with him.

By the end of the 1970s, Clark's recording career began to slow. He left ABC/Dot for MCA, and had one hit, "Chain Gang of Love." In 1981, he recorded an inspirational album for Songbird, *The Last Word in Jesus is Us*. By 1982, he had switched to Churchill Records, long time manager Jim Halsey's label. Roy, Grandpa Jones, Buck Owens, and Kenny Price formed the Hee Haw Gospel Quartet in 1984, and recorded an eponymous album on the Hee Haw label.

Roy's career was rejuvenated in 1983 when he was the first nationally recognized artist to build a theater in Branson, Missouri, The Roy Clark Celebrity Theater. His name recognition was responsible for attracting guest appearances by several Nashville stars, including **Roger Miller**, Johnny Cash, **Merle Haggard**, Oak Ridge Boys, Willie Nelson, and a host of others, and to make Branson a new "mecca" for country music performers.

The list of honors, awards, and accolades for Clark are overwhelming, including many firsts. He was the first star to take an act to the Soviet Union, first country artist to headline a night at the Montreaux International Jazz Festival, first country performer to headline at MIDEM, the music industry fair at Cannes, first country artist to receive a five star rating in the jazz periodical *Downbeat*, first national ambassador for UNICEF, and the first country performer to appear as a guest on the *Tom Jones Show* in London.

Roy's awards include ACM Comedy Act of the Year (1969, 1970, and 1971),

ACM Entertainer of the Year (1972 and 1973), CMA Comedian of the Year and Entertainer of the Year (1970 and 1973, respectively), CMA Instrumental Group of the Year with Buck Trent (1975 and 1976), CMA Instrumentalist of the Year (1977, 1978, and 1980), and *Guitar Player* magazine's Best Country Guitarist (1976 through 1980). He was also a finalist for the CMA for Entertainer of the Year (1969, 1970, and 1974) and Instrumentalist of the Year for the years 1967 through 1976, and again in 1979 and 1984.

Clark is an inductee in the Oklahoma Hall of Fame (1982), Gibson Guitar Hall of Fame (1982), and the Oklahoma Music Hall of Fame (2000). In 1987, he was belatedly made a member of the Grand Ole Opry.

His humanitarian efforts are noteworthy. He has received the Minnie Pearl Award from the CMA, donated millions of dollars to the Children's Medical Center in Tulsa and St. Jude's Children's Hospital in Memphis, and sponsors the Roy Clark Celebrity Golf Tournament that annually raises funds for charities.

Roy and his wife, Barbara of more than 45 years, currently reside in Tulsa and own a ranch in northeastern Oklahoma where he raises cattle and horses. He has invested in a wide spectrum of projects, including the Tulsa Drillers, a minor league baseball team affiliated with the Colorado Rockies. (GC)
www.roy-clark.com

Clauser, Al
(b. 1911 – d. March 3, 1989)

Leader of one of the most popular western swing bands in the 1940s and 1950s and one of the first bandleaders to use the term "western swing" in the 1920s, Henry Alfred "Al" Clauser was born in Manitoba, Illinois. He began his musical career in his native state of Illinois, where he played in local clubs in the Peoria area while in high school. Starting first with a trio, Al expanded his band to six pieces, and the group performed over radio station WMBD.

Although none of the band members had ever visited Oklahoma, Al needed a "western" name for the group, when they began appearing on radio station WHO in Des Moines, Iowa, in 1934. While on WHO, Al's group was heard by **Gene Autry**, and hired them to perform in one of Autry's movies, *Rootin' Tootin' Rhythm*. During their time in Hollywood, the band recorded twelve sides for the ARA label in Los Angeles.

By 1938, the band had signed with radio station WCKY in Cincinnati, Ohio, however, after about a year, they returned to KHBF in Rock Island, Illinois, where the Mutual Broadcasting Network began carrying their show to some 272 stations in the Midwest.

During World War II, Al and the band, sometimes referred to as the Oklahoma Outlaws or Oklahoma Cowboys, when they played western swing, or The

Serenaders, when they played pop music, relocated to Tulsa, where the band members worked in the air defense factories.

By the end of World War II, Al had expanded his band to nine members, and they gained regular daily broadcasts on radio station KTUL in Tulsa. Al's band competed with other western swing bands in Oklahoma, such as **Johnnie Lee Wills** and Leon McAuliffe. Later, during the 1950s, the group also performed on KTUL-TV. It is reported that Clara Ann Fowler (**Patti Page**) received her first major break on the Al Clauser show on KTUL-TV when she was twelve years old, and cut her first record with Al's Oklahoma Outlaws.

Al and the Oklahoma Outlaws disbanded in the late 1950s, but Al continued to work on KTUL-TV on his popular children's show in which he starred as "Uncle Zeke." He also built a recording studio west of Tulsa in the Lake Keystone area. Al died in Tulsa on March 3, 1989.

A 2000 compilation entitled *The Golden Age of Al Clauser and his Oklahoma Outlaws*, was issued by Binge Discs, a German company. It consisted of twenty-two tracks, including several pop tunes ("Little Brown Jug" and "Bill Bailey"), traditional western and cowboy tunes ("Little Old Sod Shanty on the Claim" and "Sweet Betsy From Pike"), and three songs co-written by Al ("The Little Black Bronc," "Lonesome Cowboy Song," and "Tired Little Wrangler"). Al and the group also appear on two other recent overseas company releases: Varese's *Gene Autry With the Legendary Singing Groups of the West (1936-1949)*, on which they perform "The Old Home Place," and Bear Family's eight CD box set entitled *A Shot in the Dark-Tennessee Jive: Country Music on Nashville's Independent Labels (1945-1955)*, on which the group sings "Move It Over Rover (Doghouse Blues)." (GC)

Coffey, Kellie
(b. April 22, 1971)

Back-up singer for Barbara Streisand on her *Millennium* album and the Las Vegas New Year's 2000 show before embarking on a Nashville career, singer and songwriter Kellie Coffey hails from Moore, Oklahoma, a suburb of Oklahoma City and the hometown of **Toby Keith**. Her first single "When You Lie Next to Me," released in December of 2001 on the BNA label, cracked the Top 10 of the country charts, and the video was seen on CMT. Her eponymous compact disc with the same title as her hit song was released in May of 2002. She made her Grand Ole Opry debut on April 19, 2002, and received a standing ovation.

Kellie, born on one of the Oklahoma land run days of April 22, came into the world at the Baylor University Hospital in Waco, Texas, because her father was in dental school at that time. After completion of dental school, the family, headed by Bob and Roseann who are native Oklahomans, returned to Oklahoma in

1974 when Kellie was about three years old. She recalls that singing has been a part of her life since childhood, although her immediate family was not especially musical. Her father, a dentist in Moore, occasionally played by ear an upright piano, located in the den of their home, her grandfather played the clarinet, and her two brothers (Rob and John) sang. Her first public singing took place in church, and she took piano and voice lessons from Barbara Ramsey, a local music teacher in Moore.

Kelly's first professional performance came at the age of nine, when her parents encouraged her to participate in the Oklahoma Opry, where she sang "Pecos Promenade," the Tanya Tucker hit, and "Dancing Your Memory Away," a Charley McClain recording. She graduated from Westmoore High School and then enrolled at the University of Oklahoma in Norman. The entire Coffee family graduated from OU. At OU, Kellie majored in vocal performance and participated in such campus activities as Sooner Scandals, an annual musical, in which she sang "Save the Best for Last." It was during this event that Kellie realized she wanted to become a professional vocalist.

Following graduation from OU, Kellie headed for Los Angeles, where she roomed with a friend from college. She began to search for entertainment jobs while working as a singing waitress, writing songs, and taking lessons in a singing/performance class. After making several demo tapes and obtaining work as a demo singer, Kellie met Geoff Koch, who wrote songs for television shows, including "Walker Texas Ranger." Through this contact, she was hired to sing and write songs for the hit show, and began to garner additional jobs in radio, television, and film. The friendship between Kellie and Koch blossomed and they were married. While in Los Angeles, Kellie secured a job singing at Disneyland in Anaheim that resulted in further work at Disney World in Orlando, as well as vocalizing, "Sharing a Dream Come True," which is the corporation's new theme song for its worldwide marketing campaign.

Kellie continued her songwriting endeavors and began to make trips from Los Angeles to Nashville because her songs were primarily country oriented. Through the efforts of Judy Stakee, she signed a contract with Warner-Chappell in Nashville to write country songs for herself and others. By 1998, she had written

or co-written five songs suitable for a demo tape to pitch to the A&R personnel in Nashville, and soon signed a recording contract with Joe Galante, head of the RCA label.

Kellie's debut album includes eleven tracks, of which she co-wrote seven. Brett James, an Oklahoma Citian and family friend, co-wrote two of the songs, one with Kellie. During its first week of release, Kellie's CD sales broke Leann Rimes' country music record held since 1996. During the summer of 2002, she opened for the Kenny Chesney tour, headlined her own show at the Oklahoma State Fair, and released her latest single, "At the End of the Day," which reached the Top 30 on the country charts in the fall of 2002. In October of 2002, Kellie was one of the five nominees for Best New Artist in the ABC Radio's *Country Coast to Coast* Best Country Around-Fan's Choice Awards. Finally, Kellie made her first appearance on the CMA Awards show in November of 2002, singing "When You Lie Next to Me," before a national television audience.

In May, 2003, Kellie was named Top New Female Country Artist by the ACM. In her emotional acceptance speech, she told the audience she remembered watching Reba McEntire winning ACM awards which made the young Oklahoman think she might have a future in country music, a foresight that has proven more true than she could have imagined. (GC)
www.kelliecoffey.com

The Collins Kids
(Larry and Lorrie)
Lawrence Albert Collins
[b. October 4, 1944]
Lawrencine May Collins
[b. May 7, 1942]

Reared on a dairy farm and attending a one-room school (Pretty Water community) near Tahlequah, Oklahoma, Larry and Lorrie Collins were among the most influential rockabilly acts of the 1950s. Their father farmed and later worked in a steel mill, while their mother encouraged their singing as she was an aspiring country and gospel singer. At the age of eight, Lorrie won a talent contest in Tulsa hosted by western swing steel guitarist Leon McAuliffe. McAuliffe encouraged Lorrie's parents to relocate to California to develop her talents, which they did in 1953. In the meantime, Larry had received a guitar as his Christmas present in 1952.

After winning a *Town Hall Party* talent contest in February of 1954, the Collins Kids landed a spot on the Los Angeles television show and performed the next day. *Town Hall Party* was broadcast over KFI radio and KTTV-TV, and later carried by a network of NBC radio stations. Televised every Saturday night from Compton, California, it was hosted by Tex Ritter. This breakthrough gave the

Collins Kids major television and radio exposure before they were teenagers, and they appeared in every episode of the show following their first appearance. Larry often jammed on the show with guitarist Joe Maphis, known as "King of the Double-Necked Mosrite," and who became his mentor. Maphis, who played a sunburst double neck electric guitar designed and constructed by Oklahoman Semie Moseley, arranged for Moseley to build a similar model for Larry with his name inlaid on one neck. Thereafter on the show, Larry and Joe, playing their twin-necked Mosrites, would lay down some exciting instrumentals, such as "Hurricane," "Fire on the Strings," and "The Rockin' Gypsy." The Maphis-Collins synergy was so solid that the pair recorded four instrumentals in 1957. As a guitarist, Larry in turn influenced Dick Dale, the "king of surfer guitarists."

On Larry's eleventh birthday in 1955, the Collins Kids recorded their first releases for Columbia—"Hush Money" and "Beetle Bug Bop." During their tenure with Columbia and Epic Records, they were showcased in their "hopped-up hillbilly" style with such releases as "Whistle Bait," "Hot Rod," "Soda Poppin' Around," "In My Teens," "Hop, Skip, and Jump," "Rock Boppin' Baby," "Hoy Hoy," "Mercy," and their version of **Wanda Jackson's** "Let's Have a Party," all of which spoke directly to the teen generation of the fifties. Generally, Lorrie sang lead and Larry contributed the high harmony vocals and breath-taking guitar licks, and Maphis worked on most of their recording sessions.

Lorrie and teen heartthrob Ricky Nelson dated during the 1950s, after meeting on the *Town Hall Party* show. Lorrie appeared on *The Adventures of Ozzie and Harriet* as Ricky's girlfriend, and the couple sang the Collins Kids' version of "Just Because" on one episode. The romance, however, cooled and Lorrie eventually eloped in 1959 and married Stu Carnall, road manager for Johnny Cash, with whom the Collins Kids toured.

The Collins Kids popularity resulted in appearances on the *Steve Allen Show*, *Ed Sullivan Show*, *Jackie Gleason Show*, *Dinah Shore Show*, *Art Linkletter's House Party*, *Merv Griffin Show*, Ozark Jubilee, and Grand Ole Opry, and in the 1960 Universal Pictures movie, *Music Around the World*, where they were noted for their colorful costumes. The duo won the Best New Instrumental Group Award from the Country Music Disc Jockey's Poll, presented at one of their appearances on the Grand Ole Opry stage in the mid-1950s.

Dissolving their act in 1961 after the birth of Lorrie's first child, Larry continued to write music and is best known as co-composer of "Pecos Promenade" (1980), "Delta Dawn" (1972), and "You're the Reason God Made Oklahoma" (1981), the latter two nominated for Grammy awards. "You're the Reason God Made Oklahoma" was the ACM and Nashville Songwriters Association Song of the Year in 1982, and was nominated for the same award by the CMA. Artists who have recorded Larry's songs include Helen Reddy, Bette Midler, Waylon Jennings, Mac Davis, Three Dog Night, Willie Nelson, Lacy J. Dalton, Lou Rawls, Sonny James, Nancy Sinatra, **Merle Haggard**, and Ann Margaret. Larry also recorded his sister singing duets with longtime associates like Haggard and

Nelson. The latter teamed with Lorrie on the unreleased sequel to Larry's hit, "Daughter of Delta Dawn."

Although Lorrie retired, Larry continued to record as a solo artist for Columbia Records, primarily in Nashville. In later years, he earned his living as a golf pro. Lorrie became an at home mother and raised thoroughbred horses. In 1993, Larry and Lorrie reunited for the Hemsby-on-Thames Rockabilly Festival in the U.K., drawing some 3,000 avid followers. Following the success of the Hemsby festival, they returned to the U.S., and played sold out dates at Bimbo's in San Francisco and the Palamino nightclub in Hollywood. The duo returned to the U.K. festival again in 1995 and 1998, both of which attracted sell-out crowds, and they remain intensely popular in Europe. Larry and Lorrie were inducted into the Rockabilly Hall of Fame in 1997 as the 43rd and 44th members.

Several of their recordings have been reissued in the United States and Europe, especially by Bear Family Records, a German company. The best are the 1991 *Hop, Skip & Jump*, a 2-CD box set with 59 tracks, including several songs the two co-wrote, such as "Mercy," "Whistle Bait," "Hot Rod," "I'm in My Teens," "Heart Beat," "My First Love," and "What About Tomorrow," and the 1998 *Rockin'est*, a 22-track collection containing all their favorites. They are also featured on two other Bear Family compilations—*Ain't I'm A Dog: CBS Rockabilly* and *Whistle Bait: CBS Rockabilly, Vol. 2*. On the former, Larry and Lorrie perform "Hop, Skip & Jump" and "Party." On the same recording, Larry and Joe Maphis present their fancy guitar licks on "Hurricane." Larry's guitar work is highlighted in the title track ("Whistle Bait") of the second compilation. Lorrie was featured as one of the four pioneers of rockabilly in the "Welcome to the Club of Women of Rockabilly," telecast in 2002 on PBS. (GC)

Collins, Tommy
(b. September 28, 1930 – d. March 14, 2000)

One of the pioneers of the Bakersfield Sound in country music, composer of some twenty songs for **Merle Haggard**, including "The Roots of My Raising," "Hello Hag," and "Carolyn," featured in Buck Owens' album entitled *Sings Tommy Collins*, and a 1999 inductee into the Nashville Songwriters Hall of Fame, Leonard Raymond Sipes was born the youngest of six childen to Leslie Raymond and Willie Etta Sipes on a farm near Bethany, Oklahoma, a northwestern suburb of Oklahoma City. During his childhood, Collins listened to Jimmie Rodgers and Ernest Tubb recordings, and learned to play the guitar and sing with encouragement from his mother.

Leonard attended Carson Elementary School, graduated from Putnam City High School in Oklahoma City in 1948, and spent two years at Central State (now University of Central Oklahoma) in Edmond (1949-51). During his stint in college, Collins entered talent contests, worked as a disc jockey, and appeared on Cousin Jay Davis' radio program on station KLPR in Oklahoma City. He won his first talent contest in 1951 on KLPR, which resulted in his own regular show on the station, accompanied by his first band called the Rhythm Okies, consisting of Collins on rhythm guitar and vocals, Billy Porter on lead guitar, Johnny Gilchrist on steel guitar, Russell O'Neill on fiddle, and R.M. Bradshaw on bass. While in Oklahoma City, the Morgan Brothers, a Fresno, California, based group, heard Tommy on radio, and assisted him in obtaining a recording contract. Four songs, three of which were composed by Collins ("Campus Boogie," "Smooth Sailin'," and "Fool's Gold"), were recorded in an Oklahoma City studio, and issued on the Morgan Brothers record label in 1951.

During the Korean War conflict, Tommy enlisted in the Marine Corps, but was discharged due to an injury he suffered during his college days. He, therefore, headed back to Oklahoma to resume his musical career. He met **Wanda Jackson** in Oklahoma City and they started dating, and when the Jackson family visited friends in Bakersfield, California, in 1952, Tommy accompanied them. Although the Jacksons returned to Oklahoma, Tommy decided to remain in Bakersfield.

Tommy soon began making contacts in Bakersfield and became friends and eventual roommates with a young recording artist and disc jockey named Terry Preston, whose given name was Ferlin Husky. Husky recorded some of Leonard's songs for his record company, Capitol, and helped him obtain a recording contract with Capitol in 1953. It was during one of these recording sessions that Husky named Leonard, "Tommy Collins," when one of the musicians ordered a Tom Collins cocktail, and thereafter became Leonard's stage name. Also in 1953, Tommy signed with Cliffie Stone's Central Songs publishing firm as a songwriter, and performed on Stone's Town Hall Party show.

Husky played lead guitar in the back-up band on Tommy's first recording session with Capitol on June 25, 1953, but was replaced with a then unknown Buck Owens, who continued with Tommy through 1957. Four of Tommy's songs were cut during that first session, "You Gotta Have a License," "Let Me Love You," "There Will Be No Other," and "I Love You More and More Each Day." The second session on September 8, 1953, included five songs, all written by Tommy, including "Boob-I-Lak," "I Always Get a Souvenir," "High on a Hill Top," and "You Better Not Do That." The latter became Tommy's first successful single, a 1954 release that remained on the country charts for seven weeks and peaked at #2. He made his first appearance on the Grand Ole Opry in 1954, one of the first West Coast artists to grace the stage of the "mother lode" of country music. He performed two of his self-penned songs, "You Gotta Have a License" and "You Better Not Do That," accompanied by the young Buck Owens. During the mid-1950s, Tommy recorded three Top 10 hits ("What'cha Gonna Do Now," "Untied," and "It Tickles") and two Top 15 cuts ("I Guess I'm Crazy" and "You Oughta See Pickles Now"), all of which possessed a light-hearted narrative, but significantly influenced the Bakersfield Sound. One of Tommy's songs "If You Ain't Lovin'

(You Ain't Livin')," was a major hit for Faron Young in 1954, and was included on seven of Young's subsequent albums.

In 1956, Tommy's life changed as he underwent a religious conversion and began to devote his songwriting to sacred music. Some the songs he wrote were recorded as duets with his wife, Wanda Lucille Shahan. During the late 1950s and early 1960s, he attended Golden Gate Baptist Seminary, served as an ordained Southern Baptist minister for about five years, and spent two years at Sacramento State College taking courses. His contract with Capitol Records expired in 1960 because Tommy had not produced any hits.

In 1963, Tommy missed writing songs and recording country music, and decided to reenter the secular side of the music business. Capitol was willing to resign him to a contract, but he charted only one more song with the label, "I Can Do That," a duet with his wife Wanda.

Following his Marine duty in Vietnam in the early 1960s, Tommy was assisted in 1965 by Johnny Cash. The latter was instrumental in Tommy's switch to the Columbia label. He reentered the Top 10 in 1966 with "If You Can't Bite, Don't Growl." He also recorded several minor hits over the next few years, including "I Made the Prison Band." He soon sought out Merle Haggard after hearing his "Sing a Sad Song" on the radio. Tommy and Merle became instant friends and were soon fishing in the Kern River, when not on tour or in the recording studio. Haggard recorded Tommy's "Sam Hill" in 1964. In addition to Haggard, Tommy also toured as an opening act with old time friend Buck Owens during the late 1960s.

In 1971, Wanda filed for divorce because of Tommy's increasing dependency on alcohol and drugs, and he suffered from severe depression for about a year, although he continued writing songs, especially for Haggard. In 1972, Tommy's song, "Carolyn," was recorded by Haggard and became a #1 hit, although Haggard had reservations about recording it because he felt it was not country. The lyrics of the song were a coded message to his former wife, Wanda.

In 1976, Collins headed for Nashville and signed a recording contract with the Starday label, which released an album of Tommy's compositions that he had written for other artists entitled *Tommy Collins Callin'* (1976). Thereafter, he devoted the remainder of his career to songwriting after signing a contract with Sawgrass Music. After Tommy wrote "Hello Hag," Haggard responded with his hit single, "Leonard," a 1980 song that immortalized Tommy. In 1984, Tommy's "New Patches" was recorded by Mel Tillis and became a Top 10 hit.

Throughout the 1980s and up to the mid-1990s, Tommy continued to write songs, and in 1993, signed a contract with Ricky Skaggs Music. In 1988, he performed at the Wembley Country Music Festival in England based on reissues of several of his songs by the German label, Bear Family.

Honors over the years were showered upon Tommy, including BMI Awards in 1954 ("You Better Not Do That"), 1955 ("What'cha Gonna Do Now"), 1972 ("Carolyn"), and 1977 ("The Roots of My Raising"), one of Haggard's hits in

1976. In addition to the Opry, he also performed on the Ozark Jubilee and the Louisiana Hayride.

Tommy's songs have been recorded and rerecorded by a host of varied artists ranging from Faron Young ("If You Ain't Lovin' (You Ain't Livin'")) to BR5-49 ("You're a Hum-Dinger"), including Bobby Bare and the **Collins Kids** ("What'cha You Gonna Do Now"), Tommy Cash ("Roll Truck Roll"), Jimmy Dean ("Sam Hill"), Little Jimmy Dickens and Dion and the Belmonts ("You Better Not Do That"), George Jones ("New Patches"), Rose Maddox ("Let Me Love You" and "Down, Down, Down"), Johnny Duncan ("All of the Monkeys Ain't in the Zoo"), Johnny Paycheck ("Carolyn"), Jim Reeves ("Just Married"), **Jean Shepard** ("It Tickles," "Just Give Me Love," "I Learned It All From You," and "Did I Turn Down a Better Deal"), Skeets McDonald ("You Talk About Me, I'll Talk About You," "You're Too Late," and "But I Do"), Conway Twitty ("The Roots of My Raising"), The Farmer Boys ("Oh! How It Hurts"), Charley Pride ("After All This Time"), Osborne Brothers and Seldom Scene ("High on a Hilltop"), Hot Rize ("If You Ain't Lovin' (You Ain't Livin'")), Mark Chesnutt ("Goodbye Comes Hard For Me"), Rick Trevino ("Poor, Broke, Mixed Up Mess of a Heart"), and George Strait's No. 1 hit in 1988, "If You Ain't Lovin' (You Ain't Livin')," which is included on five of Strait's albums.

Perhaps the greatest tribute to Tommy's songwriting came in 1963 when Buck Owens recorded an entire album (twelve tracks) entitled *Buck Owens Sings Tommy Collins*, including "If You Ain't Lovin' (You Ain't Livin')," "But I Do," "It Tickles," "I Always Get a Souvenir," "My Last Chance With You," "Smooth Sailing," "You Gotta Have a License," "High on a Hilltop," "There'll Be No Other," "What'cha Gonna Do Now," "No Love Have I," and "Down, Down, Down." Collins is included in the 1996 *Heroes of Country Music, Vol. 4: Legends of the West Coast* (Rhino) with "You Better Not Do That."

Collins died at his home in Ashland, Tennessee, on March 14, 2000. Tommy's humorous and intelligent songwriting style, his impact on the development of the Bakersfield Sound, and his influence on other songwriters were his most significant contributions to the field of country music. His song, "The Roots of My Raising," reflect his roots in Oklahoma, and is included in the five-box CD set, *Leonard*, issued by Bear Family in 1992. **Roger Miller**, another Oklahoman who wrote many songs in the Tommy Collins style, once told Tommy: "I got my *attitude* for songwriting from you." (GC)
www.nashvillesongwritersfoundation.com/fame/collins.html

Color Me Badd
(Formed 1987, Oklahoma City, OK)

Combining tight vocal harmonies with origins in doo-wop and 1960s R & B, and the thumping bass lines and beats of 1980s hip hop, Color Me Badd emerged in the early 1990s during a revival of pop vocal groups such as Boyz II Men and En Vogue. The group's catchy, romantic ballads and made-for-video dance moves foretold the "boy band" trend of American popular music in the late 1990s exemplified by N'Sync and Backstreet Boys. Before disbanding, the group won two American Music Awards and two *Soul Train* awards, as well as earning a pair of Grammy nominations. All four members, Bryan Adams (b. November 16, 1969, Oklahoma City), Mark Calderon (b. September 27, 1970, Oklahoma City), Sam Watters (b. July 23, 1970, Oklahoma City), and Kevin "KT" Thornton (b. June 17, 1969, Amarillo, Texas), attended Northwest Classen High School in Oklahoma City. The four school friends harmonized in the hallways between classes, formed a quartet called Take One, and made their debut at a high school talent show singing a song from a Levi's 501 commercial.

When Kevin Thornton saw Jon Bon Jovi walk into a movie theater where Thornton worked, "KT" assembled the group and convinced Bon Jovi to listen to them for sixty seconds. The pop rocker liked what he heard and gave the group an opening slot in front of the band slated to open for Bon Jovi that night, Skid Row, and the group performed in front of 15,000 people in Oklahoma City. In 1987, Robert "Kool" Bell of Kool and the Gang heard the group and persuaded them to move to New York City and helped them find a manager. The group landed a deal with Giant Records in 1990, and their performance of "I Wanna Sex You Up" was featured on the *New Jack City* soundtrack. The song helped the soundtrack rack up double platinum sales, and then, to everyone's surprise, went Top 5. The complete album was not even finished when the group hit with "I Wanna Sex You Up," so the group worked overtime to produce the full-length collection. Still lacking a complete album, the group released a follow-up single, "I Adore Mi Amor," which became a crossover #1 hit on both the pop and R & B charts in 1991. The song illustrates the group's multi-cultural background when they sing in both English and Spanish which certainly contributed to its international success. This good fortune set the stage for the group's first album, *C.M.B.* (1991), which sold over three million copies. *C.M.B.* also included another number one hit, "All 4 Love," and two more Top 20 hits, "Thinkin' Back" and "Slow Motion" in 1992. Color Me Badd's next single, "Forever Love," was released on the *Mo'*

Money film soundtrack and was their sixth consecutive single to reach the Top 20. In 1992, they finished second only to Boyz II Men as the top pop singles act of the year. At the height of their popularity, the group was recruited by Billy Joel and Jermaine Jackson as a backing vocal group, and appeared on such top-rated television programs as *The Tonight Show*, *Saturday Night Live*, *Live with Regis and Cathy Lee*, *In Living Color*, *Beverly Hills 90210*, and *Oprah*.

After releasing a collection of remixes of their hit singles, *Young, Gifted, and Badd – The Remixes* (1992), Color Me Badd released their sophomore effort, *Time and Chance* (1993). The album sported two Top 20 pop singles, "Time and Chance," and "Choose," and sold more than 500,000 copies, but those numbers did not impress record company executives who had been spoiled by the success of the first album. The third Color Me Badd album, *Now and Forever* (1996), provided their final showing in the Top 20 with "The Earth, the Sun, and the Rain." Having completed their contractual obligations with Giant Records, Color Me Badd signed with Sony for their final album, *Awakening* (1998). The group reworked one song, "Remember When," from the album to benefit the victims of the 1995 Oklahoma City bombing of the Alfred P. Murrah Federal Building. The Oklahoma City Philharmonic Orchestra and the Oklahoma Public Schools Honor Choir appeared on the song, but the album did not sell well and the group decided to call it quits. In 2000, Giant Records released *Best of Color Me Badd* that included the group's biggest hits, as well as two previously unreleased tracks, "Got 2 Have U" and "Where the Lovers Go," both recorded during the *Time and Chance* sessions.

Color Me Badd lasted over ten years as a group, foretold the oncoming late 1990s pop movement with their tight harmonies, coordinated dance moves, and hip hop beats, and experienced success at the very top of the music industry. Subsequently, some of the members of the group continued in the music business and some left for good. Sam Watters has worked as a producer and arranger for Anastacia and 98 Degrees, written and produced songs for Jessica Simpson, and provided background vocals for Paula Abdul, and Patti Austin. Since 2000, Watters has also produced several greatest hits packages, such as *UK More Wicked Hits* (2001), and *Funky Divas Vol. 2* (2002), a compilation of dance-pop songs featuring female vocalists. In 2002, Watters co-wrote and sang background vocals on Celine Dion's "I Surrender," from the album *A New Day Has Gone*, a song made even more famous when covered by *American Idol*'s 2002 winner, Kelly Clarkson. Bryan Abrams most recently released an independent solo album, *Welcome to Me* (2002). Kevin Thornton and Marc Calderon have both taken hiatuses from the music industry. Friends of Oklahoma Music inducted Color Me Badd into the The Oklahoma Music Hall of Fame in 2000. (HF)

Cooley, Spade

(b. December 17, 1910 -
d. November 23, 1969)

Often referred to as the "King of Western Swing" and the first to popularize the phrase, "Western swing," fiddler-bandleader Clyde Donnell Cooley was born in a storm cellar near Pack Saddle Creek near Grand, one of the "best known ghost towns in western Oklahoma," according to author John W. Morris. Born to parents, Emma and John, Donnell was raised in an impoverished home. As Cooley once said, "I was born poor and raised poor." According to most sources, he attended American Indian schools because of **Cherokee** ancestry, reported as around one-quarter.

Spade's first exposure to music was through his father and grandfather who enjoyed playing the fiddle, and, according to several sources, was playing fiddle for dances at eight years old. After moves to Oregon and California, young Donnell was given violin lessons by one of this father's friends. Classically trained, Spade later played violin and cello in his school orchestra. Not caring much for farm labor, Spade began playing fiddle at local dances in the Modesto, California area c. 1930. He then jumped a freight train "with nothing but my fiddle and three cents in my pocket" to Los Angeles, where he met Roy Rogers, who needed a stand-in for his motion pictures at Republic studios and because several of his friends thought he resembled Rogers. This work allowed him to make a reasonable living during the day so he could play his fiddle at night in various clubs around town, including jobs with Stuart Hamblen and **Jimmy Wakely**. Donnell's poker playing skills soon earned him the nickname ("Spade") that was to stick with him the remainder of his life.

Because of his reputation as an excellent fiddler, Spade was hired by promoter Foreman Phillips in 1942 to play with bands at the Venice Pier Ballroom in Venice, California. Management suggested he form his own swing band that included such notables as guitarist **Noel Boggs**, another native Oklahoman; guitarist Smokey Rogers; and crooner Tex Williams. His popularity soared and Cooley's band was soon packing them in by the hundreds at the Pier, Riverside Rancho, and Santa Monica Ballroom, and rivaling **Bob Wills'** outfit that had just moved to southern California.

Spade soon landed a recording contract with Okeh Records (a subsidiary of Columbia) in 1943. The next year, Spade and his band recorded "Shame, Shame on You," which hit #1 on the country charts and was adopted as his theme song. Two years later, another Okeh recording, "Detour," was also a major hit in 1946. By this time, Spade's band had reached headliner status at the prestigious Santa Monica Ballroom, and he and the band were invited to appear in their film debut, *The Singing Sheriff*, a 1944 Bob Crosby movie. They later performed in several films, including *Chatterbox*, *The Singing Bandit*, *Outlaws of the Rockies*, and *Texas Panhandle*. In 1946, Spade and his band left Okeh and signed with RCA in 1947, recording such favorites as "Spanish Fandango," "Hillbilly Fever," and "Wagon Wheels."

In 1947 Spade was poised to enter the new medium—television. He headed his own show on station KTLA, the first commercially licensed television station in Los Angeles. Called the "Hoffman Hayride" (named after the sponsor who was a television manufacturer), it quickly attracted an audience and became the top-rated program in the area in the late 1940s, however, ratings declined and the show was cancelled in the early 1950s, even though Spade attempted several innovations, such as replacing his old band with an all-female ensemble. The stress of remaining a top performer began to tell on Spade as he was sidelined in the early 1950s with a series of heart attacks.

Still popular in southern California, Spade recovered from his heart problems, and toured the region during the mid-and-late 1950s, performing at various venues. Plagued by alcohol and marital problems, Spade was faced with separation from his second wife, Ella Mae. He wavered between divorce and reconciliation that continued for several years, until 1961 when he was living in the Mojave area where he has purchased some land for an amusement park. On April 3, thinking his estranged wife was having an affair with Roy Rogers, he beat and kicked her to death with their fourteen year old daughter, Melody, watching. After a sensational trial at the Kern County Courthouse in Bakersfield during which his daughter testified, Spade was convicted of murder and sentenced to life in prison. During the trial he suffered another heart attack and afterward was sent to a medical detention center at Vacaville rather a high-security prison. While confined, Spade was a model prisoner by teaching inmates the rudiments of fiddle playing, as well as performing for them. His record of good behavior for more than eight years was due for review by the California Parole Board in 1970, but in 1969, Spade was granted leave from Vacaville to participate in a police benefit concert in Oakland. After a well-received performance of three songs before a crowd of some 3,000, he went backstage and suffered a fatal heart attack at the age of fifty-nine.

Recent CD releases of Cooley's material include *Spadella: The Essential Spade Cooley* (1994-Sony), a collection of Spade's singles, including all his hits in its twenty-nine tracks; *Heroes of Country Music, Vol. 4: Legends of the West Coast* (Rhino-1996), presenting Spade on "Shame on You"; *Spade Cooley Big Band, 1950-1952* (1999), a thirty-three track album from Harlequin Records; *Shame on You*, a Bloodshot Records release in 1999, including twenty-five tracks of previous unreleased radio transcriptions; *Spade Cooley, 1941-1947* (2000), released by the Country Routes label and featuring Oklahoman **Noel Boggs**; and *A Western Swing Dance Date with Spade & Tex* (Spade Cooley and Tex Williams), twenty-seven tracks released in 2000 by Jasmine Music. (GC)

Cross Canadian Ragweed
(formed in Yukon, 1994)

Emerging from the often over-generalized **Red Dirt Music** scene of Stillwater, home of Oklahoma State University and regularly referred to as West Nashville or North Austin by alternative and contemporary country insiders, Cross Canadian Ragweed (CCR) has parlayed five of its rootsy and rocking poetic albums into the elevated status of major label recording artists, country music television regulars by way of their video, "17," and fan favorites at clubs and concert venues throughout the southwestern U.S. The group has become so popular south of the Red River they were featured on a 2003 cover of *Best in Texas*, a regional music newspaper that chronicles lone star hit makers with its Texas music chart on which "17" landed at the top spot in January, 2003. Comprised of front man and lead guitarist Cody Canada (b. Pampa, TX, May 25, 1976), drummer Randy Ragsdale (b. Enid, June 27, 1977), rhythm guitarist Grady Cross (b. St. Louis, MO, August 4, 1975), and bassist Jeremy Plato (b. Oklahoma City, February 13, 1976), the group calls itself Cross Canadian Ragweed by combining band members' names, and has played together since they were in Yukon's middle and high schools. The latter is where Canada and Cross met drummer Ragsdale, two years younger than the rest of the band, but also the son of Johnny C. Ragsdale (b. 1951-d. 1997) who had played guitar with **Bob Wills** and **Reba McEntire.** The elder Ragsdale elevated the group's professionalism through discipline and practice, and its musicianship by passing on his lead guitar skills to Canada. Before leaving Yukon for Stillwater, the group played anywhere and everywhere they could get a show in the Yukon area.

After Cross, Canada, and Ragsdale graduated Yukon High School in 1993, '94, and '96 respectively, and Plato graduated from Calumet in 1994, each moved to Stillwater ostensibly to attend Oklahoma State University, but more importantly to regroup. By the middle 1990s, Stillwater's music scene teemed with young bands like **The Great Divide**, Medicine Show, **Jason Boland**, and the **Red Dirt Rangers**, among others, who played local Stillwater outlets such as the Tumbleweed, Willie's Saloon, where **Garth Brooks** started playing on open mic nights, and the Wormy Dog Saloon, a college bar with saddles for barstools. Before long, the band was filling or partially filling Stillwater, Tulsa, and Norman bars and clubs for four years before getting their first Texas gigs in Amarillo and Lubbock, followed by shows in Fort Worth, Dallas, and Austin. CCR's successful shows began developing a fan base that resulted in tens of thousands of independent albums sold, no mean feat for a young band with little to no commercial airplay.

Released on the band's independent label, Underground Sounds, the first Cross Canadian Ragweed album, *Carney* (1998), features a who's who of red dirt musicians as players and co-songwriters. Recorded and mastered by Jeffrey Parker at his Cimarron Sound Lab in Tahlequah, *Carney* is both the perfect introduction to Cross Canadian Ragweed and a further example of red dirt music's hybrid combination of country, folk, blues, and rock. The album is full of acoustic strumming, electric leads, twangy steel accents, and introspective lyrics written or co-written by Cody Canada and a full of cadre of red dirt singer/songwriters such as Jason Boland, Mike McClure of The Great Divide, Bob Childers, and Tom Skinner. Additionally, keyboardist Corey Mauser (Big Head Todd and the Monster) and drummer Jimmy Karstein (**Leon Russell**, Eric Clapton, **J.J. Cale**, et. al.) flesh out the expert musicians prominent throughout the disc. CCR's second disc, *Live and Loud at the Wormy Dog Saloon* (Underground Sounds, 1999), was recorded in the club where the band enjoyed their first big crowds in Stillwater, and is a window into CCR's multiple influences and live show. While not a sonic masterpiece, the album is an excellent illustration of red dirt music's ethos of country, rock, and folk by including Jerry Reed's "Amos Moses," a Bob Childers and Tom Skinner collaboration, "Headed South," that appeared on *Carney*, Neil Young's "Hey, Hey, My, My," Mike McClure's "Down at the Harbor," and Bob Dylan's "Rainy Day Women." *Live and Loud at the Wormy Dog* is also a witness to Canada's developing songwriting skills and guitar abilities ("Bang My Head" and "Workin' on OK"), some everyman political leanings ("The President Song"), and the very popular Gene Collier song, "Boys from Oklahoma," that takes a particularly strong swipe at Stillwater's rivals to the south in Norman.

With a couple of years to play a plethora of shows, practice, and write more songs, CCR released *Highway 377*, an album that really brings out the rock side of the band with power chords ("Back Around" and "Time to Move On"), choogling Grateful Dead riffs ("42 Miles"), and plenty of gritty lead guitar work. The album also represents a spiritual rejuvenation of sorts for Canada as a result of a near disastrous wreck Canada and two friends experienced driving down Highway 377 while working in the oil fields near Wolf, Oklahoma.

Driving a company truck depicted on the album's cover (post-crash), the old '82 Chevy suddenly veered off the road and fell sixty feet down a drainage ditch, but Canada and his two friends walked away with only minor injuries. While Jesus appears regularly in the band's liner notes, *Highway 377* marks the first appearance of the chosen one as the subject of a song. The collection is full of outcast characters ("Look at Me"), broken dreamers ("Back Around"), Vietnam vets ("Long Way Home"), and, of course, Jesus ("Highway 377"). Early hints of commercial potential also resulted from the disc when Dodge picked up "Long Way Home" for a nationwide Dodge truck commercial, and subsequently used "42 Miles" for another nationwide spot in 2003.

Given the relatively lo-fi but fun filled *Live and Loud at the Wormy Dog*, fans have eagerly embraced 2002's *Live at Billy Bob's Texas* (Smith Music). Recorded at the famous honky tonk in Fort Worth that boasts over 15 million visitors and a monthly electric bill of more than $15,000.00, *Live at Billy Bob's Texas* finds the band slinging through their best known songs to that point, a new one co-written by Canada and Mike McClure ("Hey, Hey"), and a few covers ("Crazy Eddie's Last Hurrah," and "Mexican Sky"), along with a toned down "Boys from Oklahoma" in front of a very vocal and obviously appreciative crowd. With an accelerating fan base and selling thousands of records without the assistance of a major, or even minor, record label, the group soon found themselves at the forefront of the rowdy country music coming out of Texas (by way of Oklahoma), and major labels started to notice the band's popularity growing like, ahem, weeds.

Having heard about the band from people as diverse as Radney Foster, Dallas Cowboys' then special teams coach Joe Avezzano, Texas club owners and other bands' managers, Oklahoma native and Universal-South executive Tim Dubois, one of Nashville's most important music industry types, and his business partner Tony Brown, began courting the group with the old "We don't want to change a thing about you" line that often predates haircuts, fashion advice, and hottie-laden videos that have little or nothing to do with a band's original vision of themselves. Universal-South was true to its word, however, and the band delivered the self-titled album known as *Purple* or *The Purple Album* (2002). Dedicated to Randy Ragsdale's younger sister Mandi, who died at age nine on the way home from a CCR show in 2001 and whose favorite color was purple, the album is a mature work of songwriting and musicianship.

As opposed to the band's first album on which they received a mountain of help from red dirt mentors, *Purple* features only two songs co-written by old friend and co-producer Mike McClure, who also adds some guitars and piano to the album. Nodding more toward rock than country, the album is a coming of age collection for many reasons, as Cody Canada's songwriting voice is getting stronger and more reflective with maturity. His usual cast of downtrodden, marginalized and lovelorn characters is present in "Brooklyn Kid," "Don't Need You," "Walls of Huntsville," "Broken," and "Suicide Blues." However, a deeper, more metaphysical side is emerging from Canada's pen with "On a Cloud," an homage to the ten men associated with OSU's basketball program who died in a plane crash on the way back from a game with the University of Colorado January 27, 2001, and "Carry You Home," an extremely personal take on the contemporary relevance of Jesus in the singer's life. The song that has gained the group national attention,

"17," is a watershed moment in the band's career, earning a #1 spot on The Texas Music Chart in January of 2003 (and further illustrating Oklahoma's significance in Texas music).

While steady work for CCR is implied by its growing tour circuit, ranging from coast to coast in the United States in 2003, CMT's regular rotation of "17," a video shot completely in Stillwater and around Payne County, has lifted the band to national familiarity. The song's classic line, "You're always 17 in your hometown," rings with experience of small town life and how one never really gets away from the image they cut as a high school senior in their hometown. Either the town wonders what ever happened to you since then because you've never taken the time to go back, or knows everything that's happened because you never left.

With the single and its accompanying video's success, the group rose to a level where they could even have their own festival in June, 2003, officially called the "CCR Sand Blast on the Lake." Staged at Lake Travis not far from Austin, Texas, acts included old friend Mike McClure and the band he has put together after leaving The Great Divide. Further illustrating their appeal beyond country music, the group hooked up with the Lynyrd Skynyrd/Sammy Hagar tour in July of 2003, playing to large and appreciative crowds in the northeast, Midwest, and South. In Septemeber, 2003, Cody Canada spearheaded a tribute to Waylon Jennings to benefit diabetes prevention programs. Canada called the thirty-act concert "Waylon Jennings: The Red River Tribute," named for the river that separates Oklahoma and Texas. Regarding the purpose for the concert, Canada said in an August, 2003, press release, "Diabetes is what took Waylon from us, so let's give all the proceeds to diabetes [programs], from the ticket sales to the shirt sales, to the food and to the CD itself." The concert was to be recorded and released nationally on compact disc.

With bookings throughout the fall of 2003 in Texas and Oklahoma, as well as taking into account the creative growth and brotherly togetherness of the group,

Cross Canadian Ragweed appears poised for a long career of loading in and out of U.S. stage doors, playing for a rapidly growing fan base, and if Cody Canada's muse holds up, enjoying the always elusive golden egg of art and music: commercial success. (HF)
www.crosscanadianragweed.com

Crow, Alvin
(b. September 29, 1950)

One of the first artists to make Austin a center for live music, played a role in the "outlaw country" movement, participated in development of the "Austin Sound," and helped revive western swing, fiddler, guitarist, and bandleader Alvin Crow was born in Oklahoma City. At the age of four, Alvin learned to play the fiddle on his grandfather's lap, and started playing in country bands when he was seven. He took classical violin lessons for fifteen years before advancing to a seat as the youngest violinist with the Oklahoma City Symphony. His interest in the fiddle was stimulated by growing up in a family of musicians who lived in the Sweetwater community near the Oklahoma-Texas border. His absorption of fiddle music from his family exposed him to a variety of fiddle tunes, including waltzes, polkas, and breakdowns. Crow continued his love for other genres of music, including Cajun, rock-and-roll, and country, which expanded his musical repertoire before leaving Oklahoma.

In 1968 Alvin moved to Amarillo, Texas, where for the next three years, he experimented with combinations of various styles of music, such as blues, jazz, and western swing, all that allow improvisation on the fiddle. He organized the Pleasant Valley Boys in 1969, and moved in 1971 to Austin, where the band became an integral part of the "progressive country" movement during the 1970s. For more than twenty-five years, Alvin has been based in Austin. In addition to the Pleasant Valley Boys, Alvin has fronted other Austin-based bands, such as The Broken Spoke Cowboys, The Neon Angels, and the Route 66 Playboys.

Alvin's touring circuit includes all of Texas and Oklahoma, as well as other neighboring states. His music has taken him to other American venues in New York City, where he played Carnegie Hall, and Washington, D.C. and European countries such as England, France, and Germany. He also performed for President Jimmy Carter at the White House during the late 1970s.

Crow has recorded several albums, primarily with Polydor Records and the independent label, Broken Spoke. The first Polydor recording, *High Riding*, was produced in 1977, and received an award from *Country Music* magazine as the Best Album by a New Artist. The magazine also named Alvin as Best New Male Vocalist in 1978. Additional albums include *Cowboy*, *Honky Tonk Trail*, *Alvin Crow Sings Pure Country*, *Alvin Crow with the Pleasant Valley Boys*, and *Texas*

Classics. He has played session fiddle with a number of artists and bands, including Ed Burleson, Doug Sahm, Sir Douglas Quintet, and the **Red Dirt Rangers**.

Alvin's chart singles include "Yes She Do, No She Don't," "Crazy Little Mama at My Front Door," and "Nyquil Blues." The latter song performed by Alvin and the Pleasant Valley Boys was featured on a compilation album of *Texas Music, Vol. 2: Western Swing and Honky Tonk*, released in 1994. Alvin and his band were selected for another compilation of artists who appeared at the Kerrville Folk Festival (*Early Years 1972-1981*) where he performed "Take Me Back to Tulsa" and "Milk Cow Blues." It was released in 1998. Finally, Alvin is included in *Willie Nelson's Fourth of July Picnic* album released in 1998.

An active participant in artist residency programs, Crow currently works with the Texas Commission on the Arts and the Texas Folklife Resources program in which he performs and teaches K-12 students throughout the state, and makes regular appearances at The Broken Spoke in Austin. (GC)

Cunningham, Agnes "Sis"
(b. February 19, 1909)

A founding member of Oklahoma's Red Dust Players, singer and accordionist with The Almanac Singers, and co-founder and editor of *Broadside: The Topical Folk Song Magazine*, Agnes "Sis" Cunningham was born on a farm near Watonga, Oklahoma, about thirty miles northeast of Weatherford, where her future husband lived and where she would attend college. Agnes' parents had homesteaded on the former Cheyenne-Arapaho Indian Reservation and began farming on the banks of the North Canadian River, however, the soil was sandy, and they moved to another farm with better land closer to Watonga. The middle of five children (two older brothers and a younger brother and sister), Agnes helped her mother raise chickens, tend the vegetable garden, and clean house. When Agnes was six, her father, William "Chick" Cunningham, taught her to play chords on the piano, and she would stop at her grandmother's house after school in Watonga to practice. Her father was an old-time fiddler and claimed to know more than 500 fiddle tunes. Politically, he was a Debs Socialist. One of her brothers, William, a 1925 journalism graduate of the University of Oklahoma, became state director of the Oklahoma's Writers Project in 1935.

While in high school, Agnes joined the debate team and started a school newspaper, *The Shotgun*, which gave her some journalistic experience that served her well later as an editor. She was a voracious reader in high school, including such authors as Dickens (*Tale of Two* Cities), Dreiser (*Sister Carrie*), and Sinclair (*The Jungle*). Her mother had taught school for eight years, so when Agnes graduated from high school, she enrolled at Weatherford Teachers' College (later Southwestern Oklahoma State University) in 1927 to become a teacher. She completed two years, and began teaching music at age twenty.

In the summer of 1931 Agnes attended the Commonwealth College near Mena, Arkansas, an unaccredited labor college with socialist tendencies. Her brother Bill was director of the college and his wife was on the faculty. It was here that Agnes began writing songs, such as "Sundown" and "There are Strange Things Happening in This Land," which her father helped compose. Following Commonwealth, Agnes became an organizer for the Southern Tenant Farmers' Union, and served as a delegate to its convention in Muskogee, Oklahoma, in 1937. She then left Oklahoma for the next two years, and taught music and directed the singing of labor songs at the Southern Labor School for Women near Asheville, North Carolina.

In 1939 Cunningham returned to her native state to help organize the Red Dust Players, a musical and acting troupe formed to present topical skits and songs for sharecroppers and union workers around Oklahoma. She continued to write songs during her two years with the Red Dust Players, such as "The Oil Derrick Out by West Tulsa," reflecting the oil workers strike at the Mid-Continent Refinery of the DX Oil Company near Tulsa. It was during her two-year tenure with the Red Dust Players that she met **Woody Guthrie** and Pete Seeger when they came through Oklahoma City to visit Woody's wife and children. While at a union meeting in Oklahoma City, Woody wrote "Union Maid."

Sis met Gordon Friesen, a Weatherford boy, in March of 1941 through their association with the Communist Party, and married on July 23. Fearing repercussions from their Communist activities, Sis and Gordon moved to New York City the following November.

Pete Seeger invited them to move into the Almanac House at 130 West Tenth Street. A year earlier, Seeger, Lee Hays, and Millard Lampell had formed the Almanac Singers, the first urban folk singing group in America, and invited Sis to join. The Almanac Singers consisted of several musicians, including at various times, Woody Guthrie, Bess Lomax, Peter Hawes, Cisco Houston, Arthur Stern, Josh White, and Burl Ives. Sis appeared on the Almanac Singers 1942 album *Dear Mr. President* released by Keynote Records. Her contribution was "Belt Line Girls," a song she had written urging women to help in the war effort. Several of the Almanac Singers either enlisted or were drafted into the military services as the U.S. entered World War II.

In late 1942 Sis and Gordon moved to Detroit to assist Bess Lomax and others to organize another branch of the Almanac Singers, but the attempt failed, and Sis went to work in a war plant and Gordon became a reporter for the *Detroit Times*. In 1944 they returned to New York, where daughters Agnes and Jane were born in 1945 and 1949, respectively. By this time Gordon was blacklisted and could find no steady employment. He and Sis took turns taking care of the girls and working part time jobs. During this tough period, Sis wrote two of her most remembered songs, "Mister Congressman" and "Fayette County."

In 1961 Pete Seeger returned from a tour of England where he had witnessed a renewed interest in writing songs dealing with the political and social issues of the day. He visited with West Coast folksinger Malvina Reynolds about starting a publication that would print new folks songs concerned with current topics. When Reynolds decided to concentrate on her own singing and writing career, Seeger turned to Sis and Gordon, and in 1962 the first mimeographed issue of *Broadside* was printed. The first edition contained six songs, including "Talking John Birch Society," by a yet unknown Bob Dylan. It was the first Dylan song to appear in print. *Broadside* continued to showcase the work of Dylan. "Blowin' in the Wind," for example, appeared in the magazine nearly a year before Peter, Paul, and Mary recorded it. Other young folk songwriters followed, including Phil Ochs, Janis Ian, **Tom Paxton**, Buffy Ste. Marie, and Peter LaFarge. *Broadside* published not only the songs of the new generation of songwriters, but also those of the older writers, such as Pete Seeger and Malvina Reynolds. With financial assistance from Pete and Toshi Seeger, *Broadside* continued until 1988, sometimes publishing irregularly, either monthly, bimonthly, or quarterly, but for twenty-six years it provided an opportunity for folk music enthusiasts to learn the songs of both new and old songwriters. Throughout those years, it was Sis who transcribed the music in order to print the music notations into the magazine. It was Sis who took part in hootenannies to help support the magazine. Finally, she recorded a full album of her songs, *Sundown,* released by Folkways Records in 1976 as *Broadside Ballads, Volume 9* that has been re-mastered by Smithsonian Folkways Recordings as *Agnes "Sis" Cunningham Sings Her Own Songs and A Few Old Favorites. The Original Talking Union with the Almanac Singers* was released by Folkways Records in 1955 and has been digitally re-mastered in CD format by Smithsonian Folkways Records.

Sis contributed three tracks ("Sundown," "My Oklahoma Home (It Blowed Away)," and "But If I Ask Them") to the *Best of Broadside, 1962-1988* album released in 2000. In 1999, Ronald Cohen, historian and folk music scholar, edited *Red Dust and Broadsides: A Joint Autobiography* of Agnes "Sis" Cunningham and Gordon Friesen. Gordon died in 1996, but Agnes, now in her 90s, lives in a senior citizens home in Modina, New York. Daughter Jane lives in New Paltz, New York, near Agnes, and daughter Agnes lives in Berkeley, California. (GC)

Gail Davies
(b. June 5, 1948)

One of the most influential singer/songwriters in the past twenty-five years, Gail Davies was the first woman to produce her own records and opened many closed doors for women on Music Row in Nashville. Born in Broken Bow in the Ouachita Mountains of southeastern Oklahoma known as "Little Dixie" because of its Southern cultural traditions, Patricia Gail Dickerson was the daughter of William "Tex" Dickerson, a pioneer performer on the Louisiana Hayride. Gail

and her mother and two brothers migrated to the Point Orchard, Washington (near Seattle) area following the divorce of her parents caused by domestic violence in the home due to her father's alcoholism. By the age of nine she was already singing harmony with her brother Ron, patterning themselves after the Everly Brothers. The sibling duo recorded an album, but it was never released. Her mother remarried and the children were adopted by their stepfather, Darby Alan Davies.

Following graduation form South Kitsap High School in 1966, Gail moved to Los Angeles and married jazz musician Robert Hubener, and gave jazz a try, but her marriage dissolved and she became a session singer at A & M Records studio. During her career in Los Angeles, Gail recorded with such artists as Neil Young and **Hoyt Axton**, another Oklahoman. She also met singer-songwriter Joni Mitchell and her producer, who spent many hours instructing Gail on the finer points of producing her own music. While on the L. A. music scene, Gail met Paul Williams, composer of "Rainy Days and Mondays," and would have recorded the song had it not been for The Carpenters making it a giant success. Frank Zappa, who heard Gail sing at The Troubadour, a folk music club in Los Angeles, invited her to join his European tour, but Gail declined because of an opportunity to duet with **Roger Miller** on the *Merv Griffin Show*, her television debut. Troubled by throat problems and advised by physicians to give her voice a rest, Gail purchased a guitar in a pawnshop and began writing songs. She signed with EMI Publishing in 1975 and moved to Nashville, where she met her second husband, Richard Allen, a staff writer for Screen Gems Music. Her first composition, "Bucket to the South," was a hit single for Ava Barber in 1978, and later recorded by Lynn Anderson and Mitzi Gaynor. Because of this writing success, Gail was signed in 1979 to a recording contract with CBS/Lifesong. Her first album was *Gail Davies*, and resulted in two Top 30 singles, "No Love Have I" and "Poison Love." A follow-up single, "Someone is Looking for Someone Like You," one of her own compositions, reached #11 and remained on the country charts for more than four months, and was eventually translated into seven languages. In 1979, Davies moved to Warner Brothers where she began producing her own albums, including *The Game*, her first such effort that was applauded by critics.

During the 1980s, Gail amassed a string of successful singles and LPs, includ-ing "I'll Be There (If You Ever Want Me)" (from the 1980 album of the same name), "It's a Lovely, Lovely World" (which featured a duet with Emmylou Harris), "Grandma's Song," "Are You Teasing Me," "Singing the Blues," and "Blue Heartache," which was her first venture into bluegrass and hit #7 on the country charts. Gail also produced her 1982 album, *Givin' Herself Away*, a "fem-inist oriented collection," according to Robert K. Ocrmann, co-author of *Finding Her Voice: The Saga of Women in Country Music*. It included such songs as "Round the Clock Lovin'" and "You Turn Me On I'm a Radio," both of which charted in the Top 10.

In 1983, Gail gave birth out of wedlock to Christopher Alan Scruggs, son of songwriter and instrumentalist Gary Scruggs and grandson of the legendary blue-grass banjoist Earl Scruggs. When Christopher was five months old, she began preparation for her last album with Warner Brothers, *What Can I Say*. It produced two singles, "Boys Like You" and "You're a Hard Dog to Keep Under the Porch." Her move to RCA in 1984 led to the *Where Is A Woman to Go* album featuring a number of notable singles, such as "Break Away," "It's You Alone" (written by her brother Ron and featuring Ricky Skaggs on the mandolin and singing harmo-ny with Gail), "Jagged Edge of a Broken Heart," and "Unwed Fathers," a song that stirred controversy over the Gary Scruggs' affair with Gail and received lit-tle airplay on country music radio. By 1984, she had garnered ten Top 20 country hits. Gail was invited in 1985 to perform at The Wembley Festival of Country Music in London, and upon her return, she formed Wild Choir, a country rock group. The band released in 1986 a self-titled album on RCA that included two moderately successful singles, "Next Time" and "Heart to Heart." One of the other tracks on the album was "Safe in the Arms of Love," which became a #1 hit for Martina McBride a decade later. The same year, Davies, feeling a need to pro-mote and recognize women composers, organized "Writers in the Round" which aired on *Austin City Limits*, the long-running PBS show. Among the women writ-ers to participate were Emmylou Harris, Rosanne Cash, and Lacy J. Dalton. In 1989, Gail again switched labels to MCA, and released *Pretty Words*, an album that failed to produce any hit singles. One year later, she moved to Capitol/EMI and produced *The Other Side of Love* and *The Best of Gail Davies*. When Capitol became Liberty, Gail was hired by Liberty Records to become the first female staff producer in country music. From 1990 to 1993, she worked with several new country music talents, such as The Kinnleys and Mandy Barnett. After leaving Liberty, Gail toured Europe as a member of the songwriting group Nashville Unplugged. In the mid-1990s, Davies formed her own label, Little Chickadee Productions, which resulted in several albums, including *Eclectic* (an album she wrote), *Gail Davies Greatest Hits* (an album assisted by her new husband Rob Price), and *Live and Unplugged at the Station Inn*, a bluegrass-oriented album released in 2001. The *Greatest Hits* album includes twenty of her hits, such as "Someone Is Looking for Someone Like You" (1970s) to "Unwed Fathers," a duet with Dolly Parton (1980s). Guest appearances on the album include Emmylou Harris, Ricky Skaggs, **Kevin Welch**, Mandy Barnett, and Kathy Mattea.

Gail's recent work includes a duet with bluegrass notable Ralph Stanley on his 2001 Grammy nominated album, *Clinch Mountain Sweethearts*, and her own 2002 production in honor of the legendary Webb Pierce, *Caught in the Webb*, featuring such traditional artists as Billy Walker, Willie Nelson, George Jones, Charley Pride, Del McCoury, Dwight Yoakum, and Pam Tillis, as well as younger acts like BR549, Mandy Barnett, Allison Moorer, and Robbie Fulks. (GC) www.gaildavies.com

Davis, Jesse Edwin III
(b. September 21, 1944 – d. June 22, 1988)

Gifted enough to be mentioned in the same breath as John Lennon, Eric Clapton, and B.B. King, Jesse Ed Davis was one of rock and pop's primary session guitarists from 1966 to 1977. His career and recordings with major rock figures testify to his abilities and status as a multifaceted guitarist known for his fluidity in the idioms of classic rock and roll and the blues, especially on slide guitar.

According to the Kiowa Tribe of Oklahoma's enrollment office, Davis was an enrolled Kiowa, but also had Comanche and **Muscogee** (Creek) heritage. He is often misrepresented as a full-blood Kiowa. Born in Norman at the U.S. Naval Hospital, Davis's mother, Vivian Saunkeah Davis, started Jesse Ed on the piano, but his father, Jesse Edwin Davis II, soon brought home an old Stella guitar for the budding musician who played it along with Jimmy Reed and Elvis Presley records. Davis took lessons from a local guitar instructor, practiced long hours, and exhausted the teacher's knowledge. Soon after, at sixteen-years-old, Davis toured with Conway Twitty on a 30-city Dick Clark American Bandstand tour. Also backing up Conway at the time were Ronnie Hawkins and the Hawks with Levon Helm who befriended the young guitarist. After doing time as a literature major at the University of Oklahoma, and as a guitar teacher at a music store in Norman, where **Moon Martin** also taught, Davis left school and moved to Los Angeles in 1964. Once on the West Coast, Davis contacted Levon Helm who introduced Jesse to fellow Oklahoman **Leon Russell**. Russell was then at the center of studio session work in Los Angeles and was able to get Davis his first ses-

sion work with Gary Lewis and the Playboys. In demand as a session player, Davis made studio work his "bread and butter," eventually playing guitar on the Monkees' 1966 #1 hit, "Last Train to Clarksville."

In 1967, Davis recorded live for the first time with John Lee Hooker for an album released under Hooker's name as *Live at Café Au Go Go*. During the same year, Jesse Ed started his four-album association with blues man Taj Majal, during which time Davis contributed lead electric and acoustic guitar, bass guitar, piano and organ to Majal's recordings from 1967 to 1971. The impact of Jesse Ed's playing during this period cannot be underestimated as it established him as "the" slide guitar player of American popular music. Not only did the Taj Majal recordings endear Davis to his British contemporaries and the L.A. studio scene, Duane Allman appears to have gleaned his interest in, and ability to play, slide guitar from Jesse Ed's recording of "Statesboro Blues" with Majal. Stories vary as to how Duane Allman heard Davis. Some say it was via a Taj Mahal's album given to Duane by brother Greg Allman while Duane was recuperating from a horse riding injury, and others say it was when Duane saw Davis with Majal in an L.A. club. Nonetheless, the fact remains the Allman Brothers' version of "Statesboro Blues," appearing on the landmark 1971 live album, *At Fillmore East*, features a near carbon copy of Jesse Ed's slide work on Taj Majal's version of the song released in 1968.

Also in 1968 Jesse Ed traveled to England with Majal and performed in the Rolling Stones' *Rock and Roll Circus* film. Playing a purple paisley Fender Telecaster, Davis is featured prominently in the song "Ain't That a Lot of Love," also including Tulsa's Chuck Blackwell on drums. During the sessions for the film, Jesse Ed was warming up backstage on Gene Vincent's "Be-Bop-A-Lula" when John Lennon, the former Beatle and avid 1950s rock fan who was also in the film, noticed Davis and spontaneously joined in with him on the tune. The two musicians became friends, and Lennon later featured Davis heavily on the Lennon solo albums *Walls and Bridges* (1974) and *Rock and Roll* (1975), after which the two remained friends until Lennon's death in 1980. Additional indicators of Davis's prowess as a blues player are his inclusion on Michael Bloomfield's *Live at Fillmore West* (1969), and another album with John Lee Hooker, *Endless Boogie*, in 1970.

Also in 1970, after the Taj Majal band broke up in England, Jesse Ed recorded his first solo album at the urging of Eric Clapton in London at Olympic Sound Studio. On the self-titled release featuring a cover painting by Davis of an American Indian smoking a pipe in the artistic style of the well-known group of Kiowa painters, the Kiowa Six, Jesse Ed used many Oklahoma images and place names on the album, such as "Reno Street Incident," "Tulsa County," and "Washita Love Child," a song that may best describe Jesse Ed's perspective of his youth and turn to rock and roll. Davis sings, "I was born on the bank of the Washita River in a Kiowa-Comanche tipi. Daddy had a hard time, mama made his eyes shine. Lord, it was just us three. . . . I did that powwow thing, Daddy showed up with a standard guitar and I knew right then I'd leave. Mama said, 'Son, what about your schoolbooks? . . . What about the draft?' Dad said, 'Honey, don't worry about the boy. (He's) got a guitar and a pen to write.'"

Available in 2003 only as a Japanese import, Jesse Ed's first album exhibits his distinctive, ringing telecaster guitar work, strong sense of blues and boogie, and the party-all-the-time attitude that ultimately served to be his demise. In "Every Night is Saturday Night" Davis sings, "Every night is Saturday night for me, boogie time for me and all my friends. Rock-n-roll and lovin' one another, never gonna let the party end." Among other stalwart players on the album, Jesse Ed enlisted Eric Clapton and Leon Russell. Having finished his own album, Jesse Ed played a variety of session dates in 1971, to include work on Albert King's *Lovejoy*, Leon Russell's *And the Shelter People*, and American Indian folksinger Buffy Saint-Marie's *She Used to Wanna Be a Ballerina*. He also replaced an ailing Eric Clapton during part of the *Concert for Bangladesh*, a benefit concert in New York City organized by another ex-Beatle, George Harrison, to whom Davis had been introduced by Lennon. Davis and Clapton had obvious simpatico and respect for one another in the usually uptight and highly competitive world of lead guitarists.

The next year, 1972, followed the same hectic pace Davis had established the year before. He recorded another solo album, *Ululu*, named after the vocal cry some Plains tribe women will make as an acknowledgement of a special occasion, or as a celebratory complement to a traditional American Indian song. Long before the **Red Dirt Music** movement of the 1980s and '90s centered in Stillwater, Jesse Ed recorded "Red Dirt Boogie, Brother" for *Ululu*, as well as songs by the Band, George Harrison, Leon Russell, and **Merle Haggard**. "Red Dirt Boogie Brother" also gives an indication of Davis's opinion of his place in the pantheon of the rock stars with whom he was associating, as well as the perceived clichés that went along with him being from Oklahoma. As the "Red Dirt Boogie Brother" begins, Davis sings, "Ain't no Beatle, ain't no Rolling Stone, ain't but just one thing. Can't get next to jazz, just plain old rock 'n' roll, ain't got no such dream." Later in the song he emphasizes he is not an Okie from Muskogee, but "just a red dirt boogie, brother, all the time." Also of interest on the album is his cover of Leon Russell's "Alcatraz," largely about the American Indian occupation of Alcatraz Island in San Francisco Bay in late 1960s and early 1970s. To hear the most visible (or, at least, audible) American Indian in American popular music during that time period sing a song critical of the U.S. government's policies toward American Indians places Jesse Ed in a more political context, and a deeper one than the constant partying mode he espouses much of the time. Overall, *Ululu*, also available only as a Japanese import CD, may be his most contemplative album with "Farther On Down the Road" and "Make a Joyful Noise" exploring his philosophical side about life and its purposes. Studio musicians on the album include bassist Donald "Duck" Dunn, of Booker T. and the MG's fame, and Tulsa's Jim Keltner, along with Leon Russell on keyboards.

Also in 1972, Jesse Ed played on the million-selling, first official Jackson Browne album, *Jackson Browne*, and can be heard on the album's hit single, "Doctor My Eyes." Davis also appeared on B.B. King's *L.A. Midnight,* Arlo Guthrie's self-titled album that included many of **Woody Guthrie**'s songs, and the Steve Miller Band's *Recall the Beginning*, all released in 1972. In 1973, Jesse Ed recorded again with Arlo Guthrie on *Last of the Brooklyn Cowboys*, Roxy Music front man Bryan Ferry on *These Foolish Things*, and released a third and final solo album *Keep Me Comin'*.

Jesse Ed's last solo album, *Keep Me Comin'*, opens with the instrumental "Big Dipper," and features the Albert King-style lead blues guitar Davis favored so often. *Keep Me Comin'* continues with his usual slide guitar work ("She's a Pain") and funky blues ("Natural Anthem" and "Bacon Fat"). The album also features a number of oblique references to Davis's consumption with drug use ("Keep Me Comin'," "Bacon Fat," "No Diga Mas," and "She's a Pain," a song co-written partly by John Lennon). The usual all-star suspects are present on the record (Jim Keltner, Leon Russell), and some less clear appearances by "Bonnie, Mick, Rod, and El Mysterioso" which are only indicated by those names in the liner notes. Overall the album is a long party in a studio full of musicians who like funky grooves, sharp horn riffs, and are all enamored with Jesse Ed's world weary Oklahoma-accented vocals, and attitude-laden guitar work, often more convincing because of his confident authority than the originality of the licks.

A less than stellar, but obviously interesting, live performance by Jesse Ed Davis in the Santa Monica Civic Center in 1973 has surfaced on the Internet as *Sue Me Sue You Blues* and is obtainable by those diligent enough to pursue it. Made in Spain, and having sold for as much as $140.00 through the online auction site, E-Bay, the album is a very uneven performance in which Jesse Ed loses his voice after only a couple of songs, to which he credits the flu. He plays through seven songs from his three solo albums, and closes with a cover of Chuck Berry's "Roll Over Beethoven," none of which adds much to his overall legend. Of particular interest on the disc are four studio sessions demo tracks with John Lennon where the two are working out the songs that will be on Lennon's *Walls and Bridges*, to include "Going Down on Love," "Surprise Surprise," "Whatever Gets You Through the Night," and "Nobody Loves You When You Are Down and Out."

Whatever ideas Jesse Ed had for more of his own music, he was subsumed by the work other people wanted him to do for them. In 1974, he recorded with **Brewer** and Shipley on their self-titled album of that year, Harry Nilsson on *Pussy Cats*, the Pointer Sisters on *There's a Plenty,* Ringo Starr on *Goodnight Vienna*, and John Lennon on *Walls and Bridges*. Davis's guitar is featured throughout *Walls and Bridges*, to include slide guitar on "No. 9 Dream" and "Nobody Loves You (When You're Down and Out)," and lead guitar on the instrumental "Beef Jerky." The American Indian presence through Davis is obvious on the album from the "Little Big Horns" horn section, to "Scared," a song that begins with two wolf cries and proceeds with a mock-Hollywood western musical motif while Davis solos. Davis continued working with rock royalty in 1975 when he recorded with The Who's Keith Moon on *Two Sides of Moon*, George Harrison on *Extra Texture*, and John Lennon's "contractual fulfillment" record of 1950s and 1960s standards, *Rock and Roll*. Also that same year, Davis recorded again with Arlo Guthrie (*Together in Concert*) and Harry Nilsson *(Duit On Mon Dei)*, David Bromberg (*Midnight on the Water*), Rod Stewart (*Atlantic Crossing*), the 5th Dimension (*Earth Bound*), and Mac Davis (*Burnin' Thing*).

The significance of Jesse Ed playing on albums by rock artists, R & B artists, and country artists all in the same year serves as further proof of his overall talent which seems to have known no boundaries in popular music. Davis's last prolific year as a sideman was 1976. Along with repeat customers Ringo Starr (*Ringo's Rotogravure*) and Harry Nilsson (*Sandman*), Davis recorded with Neil Diamond (*Beautiful Noise*), and Eric Clapton on *No Reason to Cry* and Clapton's 1976 birthday sessions that have only been released as the bootleg *Happy, Happy Birthday Eric* (Dandelion, 1998). Davis also added his guitar to recordings by several other lesser, second-tier artists such as David Cassidy, Van Dyke Parks, and Geoff Muldaur. Disenchanted with the session scene in Los Angeles, Davis moved to Hawaii in 1977. During that year, he only did two sessions, one for Long John Baldry (*Welcome to the Club*), and one for Leonard Cohen (*Death of a Ladies Man*). At the end of the 1970s, as popular music tastes shifted toward disco and the more youth-oriented punk and new wave scene, Jesse Ed's blues rock expertise was less and less in demand. His own personal demons of alcohol and drug abuse also led to his seclusion and lack of activity. According to his obituary in the *Los Angeles Times*, he returned to Los Angeles from Hawaii in 1981 broke and ravaged by drug addiction.

By 1985, Davis formed the Graffiti Man band with American Indian activist and poet, John Trudell. The duo recorded *a.k.a. Grafitti Man*, first released as an independent cassette available only by mail order. When a copy reached Bob Dylan, he called it the "album of the year" and played it over the public address system before his concerts. Trudell openly credits Davis with the encouragement he needed to put his poetry to music, and Jesse Ed explained to an interviewer in 1986 that the opportunity to play with John Trudell was a saving grace at a time in his career when he had nowhere to play and nothing more than his addictions to keep him busy. Trudell also has connections to Tulsa where he met his wife, Tina Manning, who was pregnant with their fourth child when she and their three children were killed in an arsonist's fire on the Duck Valley Reservation in Nevada. The event largely ended Trudell's activism in the American Indian Movement, in which he served as chairman from 1973 to 1979, and for which he felt his family was targeted. The event also turned him to writing poetry for therapeutic purposes. Ultimately, writing became Trudell's primary artistic activity and led him to the collaboration with Jesse Ed Davis that would become Davis's last creative effort as a musician.

As a final attempt at reconciling his substance abuse problems, Davis checked into a chemical treatment program, and served as an alcohol and drug counselor at the American Indian Free Clinic in Long Beach, California. He also began appearing at club dates on the West Coast with John Trudell and the Grafitti Man Band. When the group appeared in Los Angeles in 1987, George Harrison, Bob Dylan, and John Fogerty joined them on-stage. Davis was not able to overcome his personal issues, however, and only a few days before a scheduled appearance at the Palomino Club in North Hollywood, Davis died of an apparent drug overdose in Venice, California on June 22, 1988. Ironically, Davis's work resurfaced that year on Eric Clapton's *Crossroads*, a boxed set retrospective. Since then, Davis's playing has emerged on several re-issues by artists such as Neil Diamond, Emmylou Harris, Jackson Browne, Lightnin' Hopkins, John Lennon, Taj Mahal, Harry Nilsson, The Rolling Stones, and Ringo Starr. His work has also appeared on film soundtracks such as *Blue Collar* (1995) and *Kent State* (1995), as well as on Sony's *Story of the Blues* and *Guitar Player Presents Rock*, a compilation of significant rock tracks assembled by *Guitar Player* magazine that included Taj Majal's "Six Days on the Road," on which Davis is featured. His first three albums were re-issued in Japan in 1998, and in 2002 the Oklahoma Jazz Hall of Fame inducted Davis in the blues category. At the ceremony, attended by Jesse Ed's widow, Kelly Brady Davis, and his mother, Vivian Davis, Taj Mahal performed in Jesse Ed's honor, and said, "It's about time people started paying attention to what Davis played and how he played it. He was a great player." (HF)

DeVaney, Yvonne McGowan
(b. December 25, 1925)

With a lush voice that recalls Patsy Cline at her finest, and having recorded for several labels (Capitol, Columbia, Decca, et al.) under various stage names, i.e., Yvonne O'Day, Vonnie Taylor, Vonnie Mack, Jean Dee, Yvonne DeVaney's professional music career spans more than sixty years with her best-known song, "A Million and One," a Top 10 hit for Dean Martin in 1968, and also recorded by Pat Boone, David Allan Coe, and Hank Snow. Artists such as Dottie West, **Wanda Jackson**, The Wilburn Brothers, and the U.K. based Cheltenham Singers have also recorded songs by Yvonne. Born as one of six children in Retrop, a tiny crossroads community eighteen miles south of Elk City in southwestern Oklahoma, Yvonne McGowan began singing at age two, won a

classical piano contest at age eleven, and by age fifteen played guitar in a song and tap dance duet act with her accordion-toting sister, Mary Nell. First billed as The McGowan Sisters, and then known as The Oklahoma Sweethearts, the duo had their own show on Elk City's KASA radio after winning an amateur talent contest, and made an appearance with Roy Rogers and Trigger in 1943. After high school, Yvonne and Mary Nell joined an all-girl Western troupe, Billye Gale and the Hollywood Cowgirls, touring the Orpheum Theater Circuit and the Fox Intermountain Circuit in 1944. Ending her professional partnership with Mary who left the duo for marriage and a family, Yvonne began appearing with Art Perry and His All Girl Band in Kansas City, Missouri in 1945, as well as with the Cumberland Mountain Folks on KWFT Radio in Wichita Falls, Texas in 1947.

Returning to Oklahoma in 1948, Yvonne became a featured vocalist with Merl Lindsay's popular Western swing dance band in 1951. In '52 she was invited to join WKY-TV as a featured vocalist with the Chuck Wagon Gang in Oklahoma City on WKY-TV's *Chuckwagon Show*, and a featured singing spot on the station's *Sooner Shindig*. During her stint on the *Chuckwagon Show*, she met honky tonk singer Webb Pierce who urged her to send him some recordings so he could play them for record company executives. In 1953, unknown to Yvonne, Capitol Records A&R executive Ken Nelson flew into Oklahoma City to watch Yvonne perform on the *Chuckwagon Show*. Nelson had come to offer a contract to Yvonne, and immediately after the show signed Yvonne to Capitol Records, one of the first female country singers to receive an individual contract, largely due to the success of pioneering female honky tonker, Kitty Wells, and pop crossover artist **Kay Starr**.

After signing Yvonne, Capitol changed her name to Yvonne O'Day under which she recorded her first minor country hit, "Snowflakes," along with several other country singles, "I Just Want to Be With You," "Kisses on Paper," and "Baby I Go For You." Given **Patti Page**'s massive multi-format success, Capitol decided to move Yvonne into the pop field, changing her name to Vonnie Taylor and recording her with the Van Alexander Orchestra in Hollywood in 1954. Singles released under her new show business moniker included "Love Is a Gamble," "This Is the Thanks I Get," "When You're Making Love to Me," and "Does It Hurt You to Remember." In 1955, as Vonnie, she joined Red Foley on *The ABC-TV Ozark Jubilee* broadcasts out of Springfield, MO, a program that was one of the foundation commercial music successes in Missouri that led to the development of Branson as a country music tourist mecca.

In 1956 Yvonne moved to Columbia Records where her name was again changed, this time to Vonnie Mack, and she made several recordings with backing by the Jordanaires and the Anita Kerr Singers, including "I Live For You," "Please Forgive Me," "Blue Mountain Waltz," and "Slowly I'm Losing You." In 1960, Columbia tried a different approach by again creating a new persona for Yvonne, Jean Dee, under which she recorded "Open Arms," "If You Don't Somebody Else Will," "Hey Punkin'," and "You Don't Have to Tell Me." With some strong name recognition as Jean Dee, Yvonne moved to Decca Records that same year where she again recorded with the Jordanaires on "Sweethearts on Parade" and "Day By Day Your Love Grows Sweeter." During this period she also toured with **Bob Wills and His Texas Playboys** with whom she performed during Wills' first engagement at the Golden Nugget in Las Vegas in 1962. Yvonne continued recording throughout the 1960s as Jean Dee for Phillips ("My Greatest Hurt" and "Nothing Down"), and for King Records as Jean Dee ("Dim the Car Lights" and "You're the Only Thing That Really Matters to Me." She also recorded as Yvonne DeVaney for Spar ("Rome Wasn't Built in a Day, "Step into My World," "We'll Make It This Time," and "You'll Come Home to Mama"), Chart Records, and, eventually, her own label, Compo Records. In 1967, Yvonne received a BMI Citation of Achievement for her songwriting, notably "A Million and One."

Given her lengthy songwriting, recording, and performing background, Yvonne formed her own recording and publishing companies in 1972, to include The YMD Music Group, Sunny Lane Music Publishing (ASCAP), Country Classics Music Publishing (BMI), Compo! Publishing (BMI), and Compo Records. Her first release on Compo, "Sitting in the Amen Seat" (1973) was a hit in Canada, and began a series of chart songs for Country Music Publishing Company with Billy Walker, Hank Snow, Dottie West, Wanda Jackson, Bonnie Guitar, Gary McCray, and Yvonne. DeVaney's "Wine from My Table" reached #1 in Ireland, England, France, and Germany. Her BMI catalogue lists over 75 songs written by Yvonne.

Yvonne DeVaney continued releasing her music through 2003, notably *A Good Thing* (Compo, 2001), featuring ten songs written by Yvonne. While the album was released in 2001, by 2003 it had received airplay worldwide on radio stations in the U.S., Australia, Denmark, France, Kenya, Malta, Poland, Russia, Switzerland, and Wales, just to name a few of the twenty-seven known countries where Yvonne's music has been broadcast. The 2001 Sabre Records release, *Texas Country Winners #3*, features Yvonne performing a duet with Wes Onley, and Charlie Shaw singing "A Million and Two," a follow-up to her biggest hit. (HF) www.ymdmusic.homestead.com

Diffie, Joe
(b. December 28, 1958)

Recognized as one of the 1990s hottest country music stars (songs have been played on radio 25 million times since 1994 and sales of albums have exceeded five million) and once described by Tammy Wynette as all her favorite vocalists rolled into one, singer and songwriter, Joe Logan Diffie was born at St. John's

Hospital in Tulsa, Oklahoma, the son of Joe R. and Flora (Lowrance) Diffie. His first music instrument was a guitar, his father's F-hole Airline from Sears & Roebuck, on which his father taught him to play. Joe recalls his father playing not only guitar, but also banjo and piano. His dad was also a major influence in Joe's listening habits, primarily the songs of George Jones, Lefty Frizzell, **Merle Haggard**, and Johnny Cash. The family often sang country and gospel songs while riding in the family pickup, and Joe harmonized on such songs as "Peace in the Valley" and "Amazing Grace." He made his public debut at age four, singing "You Are My Sunshine," accompanied by his Aunt Dawn Anita's country band in Duncan, Oklahoma. Joe also sang in church with his mother and sisters Meg and Monica. Meg recently graduated from Oklahoma City University School of Law.

Although Joe was based in Oklahoma during his youth, the family did relocate to various other places, including San Antonio, Texas (1st grade); Washington state (4th and 5th grade); and Wisconsin (6th though sophomore year of high school). Joe liked sports, and in high school, lettered in football, baseball, golf, and track; and was named Best All-Around Male Athlete his senior year at Velma-Alma High School in Oklahoma. Both his mother and father and two sisters were also graduates of the same high school

After high school graduation, Joe attended Cameron University in Lawton, Oklahoma, with the intention of pursuing sports and working toward earning credits for medical school. Competition was keen on Cameron's football team, and he decided against following his athletic dreams. He fell in love with a girl who became his first wife in 1977, and abandoned ambitions of medical school (thought he wanted to become a chiropractor). Faced with supporting a family, Joe left college and began work in the Oklahoma oil fields, and later drove a truck in Alice, Texas, used to pump cement into oil wells. Finding the long hours and hard work associated with this job too much, Joe returned to Oklahoma and began work in an iron foundry (Westran) in Duncan, Oklahoma, and started playing music on the side. His music activities during the 1970s and 1980s included participation in two gospel groups, Genesis II and Higher Purpose; a rock band, Blitz; and a bluegrass band, The Special Edition. But it was the bluegrass group that proved most satisfying to Joe as he played clubs and festivals in Oklahoma and surrounding states, including **Bill Grant**'s bluegrass festival in Hugo. Joe began to write music that resulted in setting up an eight-track studio in Duncan to produce demos for him and other musicians in the area.

Joe's lifestyle was dealt a severe blow in 1986 when he lost his job at the foundry, forced to close his studio because of a lack of money, and went through a divorce. After recovering from these personal hardships, Joe borrowed money from his parents, and decided to move to a different environment, namely Nashville, in hopes of making it as a songwriter. Before he left for Nashville, Joe had forwarded some demos to "Music Row," where **Hank Thompson** had recorded one of his songs, "Love on the Rocks," one that his mother had sent Thompson, while Randy Travis almost recorded another, "Love's a Hurtin' Game."

In Nashville, Joe secured a job with Gibson Guitars through one of his bluegrass friends, Charlie Derington, and began making contacts in the country music arena, including Johnny Neel, his next-door neighbor and songwriter with Forest Hills Music. The two began composing when Joe provided transportation for the sight impaired Neel. Soon Joe was given a staff songwriter position with Forest Hills, where his demo tapes attracted the attention of the Nashville crowd, one of which ("There Goes My Heart Again") was recorded by Holly Dunn (Joe sang back-up vocal harmonies) in 1989 and reached No. 4 on the country charts. Joe had co-written the song with Wayne Perry and Lonnie Wilson, who is now Joe's producer and drummer. He recalls his first royalty check for $16,000, and that figure prompted him to compose more songs. By now, he had remarried.

Diffie's demos eventually resulted in a recording contract with Epic Records in 1990. His debut album, *A Thousand Winding Roads*, produced four #1 hit singles, including his first, "Home," as well as "If You Want Me To," "If the Devil Danced (In Empty Pockets)," and "New Way (To Light Up an Old Flame)." The latter was his first composition released as a single. He also debuted on the Grand Ole Opry in 1990 backed by his seven-piece band, Heartbreak Highway, was nominated for the CMA Horizon Award in 1991, ACM nomination for Best New Male Artist in 1992, CMA nomination for Best Male Vocalist in 1992, and *Music City News* Star of Tomorrow nomination in 1992.

Diffie's second album, *Regular Joe*, was released in 1992, and contained several hit singles, such as "Is It Cold in Here," "Ships That Don't Come In," and "Next Thing Smokin.'" In 1993, a third album, *Honky Tonk Attitude*," yielded two major hits, "Prop Me Up Beside the Jukebox" and "John Deere Green." A year later, his *Third Rock from the Sun* album produced two additional hit singles, "Third Rock from the Sun" and "Pickup Man," followed in 1995 with two more Top 10 singles, "So Help Me Girl" and "I'm in Love with a Capital 'U'." Joe also earned several awards and honors in the early 1990s, including the CMA Award in 1993 for Best Vocal collaboration with George Jones, **Vince Gill**, and **Garth Brooks** (among others) on "I Don't Need Your Rockin' Chair;" Grammy, ACM, and *Music City News* nominations for duet with Mary Chapin-Carpenter, "Not

Too Much To Ask;" became the seventy-first member of the Grand Ole Opry cast in 1993; was inducted into the Country Music Hall of Fame Walkway of Stars in 1995; and nominated for Best Male Vocalist and Best Single of the Year for "Third Rock From the Sun" from the ACM in 1995. In 1999 Joe captured his first Grammy Award as one of several country music stars, including **Merle Haggard**, who collaborated on the "Same Old Train" song written by Marty Stuart for the *Tribute to Tradition* album. It was also nominated by the CMA for Vocal Event of the Year in 1999.

Acknowledged as a major country music star, Joe experienced more personal setbacks in the 1990s. His second son, Tyler, was diagnosed with Down's Syndrome. Joe helped establish First Steps, Inc., an organization to raise funds for the physically and mentally handicapped, and Tyler attended the First Steps school until he was three. Diffie has held many fund raising events for First Steps, including Country Steps In for First Steps and the Joe Diffie Charity Golf Classic. The Country Steps In For First Steps concert in 2003 will mark its tenth anniversary, and feature performances by Wynona, Ricky Skaggs, and Cyndi Thompson at the Ryman Auditorium in Nashville. For these charitable causes, Joe received the first Honorary Unsung Hero Award presented by the Nashville Council of Community Services and the Country Radio Broadcasters' Artist Humanitarian Award in 1997.

Joe continued to make waves in Nashville. In 1995, he released two successful albums, *Mr. Christmas* and *Life's So Funny*. The latter included "Bigger Than the Beatles," a #1 hit in 1996. The *Twice Upon a Time* album followed in 1997, the *Greatest Hits* album produced another hit single, "Texas Size Heartache" in 1998, and *A Night to Remember* was released in 1999. *In Another World*, a 2001 album on the Monument label, has produced yet another Top 10 hit, the title song of the album.

In 2002, Joe was joined by Mark Chesnutt and Tracy Lawrence for their Rockin' Roadhouse tour that included stops in seventy-five cities, including Stillwater, Oklahoma. More than 350,000 country music fans attended shows on the tour. The tour won the 2002 International Entertainment Buyers Association All Access Award in the category of "Festival, Fair or Special Event of the Year."

Overall, the "Pickup Man," as Joe is affectionately called in Nashville, has charted numerous Top 10 hits, twelve of which have reached #1. His *A Thousand Winding Roads*, *Life's So Funny*, and *Regular Joe* albums were certified gold, while *Honky Tonk Attitude* was platinum and *Third Rock From the Sun* reached double platinum status. Joe's latest release in 2002 was *Super Hits*, including all his #1 hits, on the Sony/Monument label. He recently shifted to a new label, C4, which is a partnership between The Consortium and Broken Bow Records. Friends of Oklahoma Music inducted Joe Diffie into the Oklahoma Music Hall of Fame in 2002, and Diffie continued touring with Tracy Lawrence and Mark Chesnutt on the Rockin' Roadhouse Tour in 2003. (GC)
www.joediffie.com

Dinning Sisters

Ginger and Jean (b. March 29, 1924)
Lou (b. September 29, 1922)

Known for their Oscar-winning recording of "Buttons and Bows," and as a popular vocal trio in the 1940s and 1950s that rivaled the Andrews Sisters and the Boswell Sisters, the Dinning Sisters were born in Oklahoma (some sources say Grant and others say Wichita). Their father, John Dinning, was a farmer, but musical director in the local church, and their mother played the organ. The Dinning family consisted of nine children (Don, Vern [Ace], Wade, Marvis, Lucille [Lou], twins Eugenia [Jean] and Virginia [Ginger], Dolores [Tootsie], and Mark), all of whom except one brother, pursued careers in music because they were blessed with perfect pitch. They all sang in the their father's church choir at an early age. Ace and Vern, two of the four brothers, formed a band, and the twins (Jean and Ginger) and older sister (Lou) began to sing with the band and won amateur singing contests prior to their teenage years. By their mid-teens, they had progressed to their own fifteen-minute show on local radio, and had performed with older brother Ace's Orchestra in Illinois. By 1935, the trio was touring clubs and theatres in the Midwest with the Herbie Holmes Orchestra.

In the late 1930s, the Dinning trio headed for Chicago to audition for the NBC radio network, which was so impressed that the company signed them to a five-year contract. During the early 1940s, the Dinning Sisters were regulars on such programs as the *Bowman Musical Milkwagon*, Gary Moore's *Club Matinee*, and the WLS *National Barn Dance*, where they appeared with stars like Perry Como and Kate Smith. They also performed at many of Chicago's famous venues, such as the Chez Paree, Chicago Theatre, and the Latin Quarter. Remaining in Chicago for seven years, it is reported they were the highest paid radio act in the Windy City. During this period, they were signed to a Hollywood movie contract to sing with Ozzie Nelson's Orchestra in the film, *Strictly in the Groove*. They later provided vocals for two Walt Disney films, *Fun and Fancy* and *Melody Time*. In the latter, they sang "Blame It on the Samba," accompanied by organist Ethel Smith.

While on the West Coast, the Dinning Sisters auditioned for Capitol Records, which resulted in a seven-year contract with the label. Their debut with Capitol was not a single, but a complete album of songs, *Songs by the Dinning Sisters*, including such titles as "Where or When," "The Way You Look Tonight," "I Get Along Without You Very Well," "I Wonder Wwith the label. Their debut with Capitol was not a single, but a complete album of songs, seven years, it is reported they were the highTimes New Roman titlTimes New Romantitlles as "Where or When," "The Way You Look Tonight," "I Get Along Without You Very Well," "I Wonder Wwith the label. Their debut with Capitol was not a single, but a complete album of songs, seven years, it is reported they were the highTimes New Romanitlles as "Where or When," "The Way You Look Tonight," "I Get Along Without You Very Well," "I Wonder Wwith the label. Their debut with Capitol was not a single, but a complete album   Released in 1948, the Dinning Sisters' biggest hit was the million seller, "Buttons and Bows," from the Bob Hope and Jane Russell movie, *Paleface*. On this song, they were accompanied by Art Van Damme's Quintet. This was the first Dinning Sisters record released in Great Britain, and many requests for it were received on the BBC. During the early 1950s, the sisters recorded several albums with such luminaries as Tennessee Ernie Ford, Tex Ritter, and Bob Crosby.

By the mid-1950s, the Dinning Sisters disbanded because of family responsibilities and interest in their style had declined, but each retained an interest in music. Lou, already a solo act, recorded several more songs not previously mentioned, including "The Little White Cloud That Cried," "Trust in Me," "Just Friends," and "Nobody Else But Me," all with the Paul Weston Orchestra. Jean recorded a few solos with the Essex label, and devoted more time to songwriting, including "Teen Angel," a #1 hit for her younger brother, **Mark Dinning**, in 1960. Tootsie spent twenty-five years singing with the Nashville Edition on such shows as *Hee-Haw*, while Ginger continued to sing with her hometown New Jersey barbershop quartet.

In 1998, the Capitol Record archives released the *Best of the Dinning Sisters*, a 25- track set of songs, including "Love on a Greyhound Bus," "I Don't Stand a Ghost of a Chance With You," and "Sentimental Gentleman from Georgia." In 2001, Jasmine Records issued fifty-two tracks on a two CD set entitled *Almost Sweet and Gentle*, which included material not previously released such as "I Love My Love," "Harlem Sandman," "Brazil," and "I Get the Blues When It Rains." Jasmine then followed in 2002 with the *Back in the Country* album that included some of their best country material, such as **Bob Wills'** "San Antonio Rose," "You Are My Sunshine," and **Albert E. Brumley**'s "Turn Your Radio On." Finally, in 2002, Gold Rhyme Records released *Rhinestone Christian*, a combination of gospel standards and original songs by the Dinning Sisters and the Jordanaires with six of the tracks composed by Jean Dinning. In 2003, the Dinning Sisters remained active in various musical, theatrical, and television productions. (GC)

www.singers.com/jazz/vintage/dinning.html

Dinning, Mark

(b. August 17, 1933 – d. March 22, 1986)

Remembered most for his 1960 #1 pop hit, "Teen Angel," Mark Dinning was born in Grant, Oklahoma, a tiny hamlet with less than 100 residents located in southern Choctaw County. One of nine children (Don, Vern, Wade, Marvis, Lucille, twins Eugenia and Virginia, and Dolores), who all pursued a musical career except one of his brothers, Mark was surrounded by music during his youth. His father was a farmer, but musical director in the local church, his baby sitter was Clara Ann Fowler (later known as **Patti Page**), and three of his sisters formed a vocal group in the 1940s, the **Dinning Sisters**, who had Top 10 single in 1948 with "Buttons and Bows," which won an Oscar. Mark raised turkeys as a child and won first prize in a local 4H club contest.

At seventeen, Mark learned the electric guitar and began performing in local clubs with his brother Ace. After high school, he was drafted and while in the army, he decided to seek a recording contract after his discharge in 1957. He headed to Nashville and auditioned for publisher Wesley Rose, who liked what he heard. Rose phoned Mitch Miller, his friend in New York, who was with Columbia Records. But Miller had just signed a new artist (Johnny Mathis) and rejected Rose's proposition. Rose within six weeks had signed Mark to MGM Records. His early country music career is almost forgotten, however, Binge (German record outlet) has released a CD entitled *I'm Just a Country Boy*, which includes such songs as "Ramblin' Man," "The Streets of Laredo," "Lost Highway," and "The Black-Eyed Gypsy." Millie Kirkham and Dolores Dinning, Mark's sister, provided the backup vocals.

In 1959, Jean, Mark's sister, was reading a magazine article related to juvenile delinquency. The author of the article offered a new name for good teenagers, and suggested "teen angels." As a songwriter, Jean took the phrase and began writing lyrics that evening, and then woke up in the middle of the night and completed the song. At a family dinner shortly thereafter, Jean played several demos for Mark while he was eating, and one of them was "Teen Angel." He liked it so much that before the dinner was concluded, a microphone and tape recorder was set up on the dinner table and he recorded it.

Jean made some 45s of the recording and mailed one to Mark. She did not hear from him for about a month and then called him to find out what had happened to the record. According to Mark, he had not opened the package because he did not have a record player. Jean encouraged Mark to take it to the nearest record shop and play it. He complied with Jean's request and a crowd gathered around the listening booth and asked where they could buy the record. This convinced Mark to take the song to Rose, who was immediately enthralled with it. A change was made from "are you flying up above" to "are you somewhere up above." Rose called Jean, now Jean Surrey, after her marriage to Red Surrey, and invited her to the recording session to sing backup vocals, but she declined as she had just given birth to a daughter and could not make the trip.

The teenage death ballad rose to the top of the pop charts in the U.S. and cracked the Top 40 in the U.K, despite the fact that many radio stations in both the U.S. and U.K. banned it because of its morbid nature. Some rock historians have labeled it as one of the first "Death Rock" songs. One British trade paper ran a headline concerning the song, which read "Blood Runs in the Grooves."

In terms of writing credits, Jean made an agreement with her husband, Red Surrey, that both names would go on any songs either one of them wrote. When

Jean and Red were divorced, "Teen Angel" was turned back to her as part of the divorce settlement.

Mark continued performing throughout the 1960s, but felt his lack of success was because as he said, "groups were in and singles were out," once the British Invasion took America by storm. Mark died from a heart attack in 1986 after returning home from a club appearance in Jefferson City, Missouri. The Dinning music tradition continued into the 1980s and 1990s as Mark's nephew, Dean, played bass for the alternative rock group, Toad the Wet Sprocket.

At last count, "Teen Angel" appears on more than thirty CDs, including the *American Graffiti* movie soundtrack (1993), *Billboard Top Pop Hits: 1960* (1994), *Please Don't Take the Girl* (1996), *Rock N Roll Relix 1954-1959* (1997), *Music That Changed Our Lives: 50s, 60s, and 70s* (1998), *Last Kiss* (2000), *Rock Revival* (2000), and *Teenagers in Love* (2001). (GC)

Downing, Big Al
(b. January 9, 1940)

One of the few African-American artists to span the musical spectrum from country to disco, Downing is best remembered for his compositions, "Mr. Jones," "Touch Me (I'll Be Your Fool Once More)," and "Bring It on Home;" all Top 20 country chart hits, as well as playing piano for such legendary country artists as **Wanda Jackson** and Marty Robbins in some of the first bi-racial American rock and roll bands.

Born in the small Craig County community of Centralia, northwest of Vinita, Downing was one of a dozen children. When Al was eight, the family moved fifteen miles west to Lenapah where most of his early childhood was devoted to such farm work as tending horses and cattle. As a young man while driving truckloads of hay and alfalfa from Oklahoma to Texas, Downing listened to country music radio stations. In a 1992 interview, Downing said, "All they played all day long was country and I just grew to love it." His first musical experience was at age ten when he joined his father and eleven siblings to sing in a gospel choir. He was strongly influenced by a wide array of music genres, including gospel, country, and rhythm and blues. By age ten, Al taught himself to play the piano on an instrument with only forty working keys he found in a trash dump while returning home from cutting hay. The Downing boys loaded the piano onto the back of a hay truck and took it home to use for firewood, only to find it was still playable. "I was about 13 when we brought that piano home," Al laughed in a 2003 interview, "For awhile it was just a stand for the radio. But eventually, I started picking out Fats Domino tunes. Before you knew it, the kids in school were asking if I could play tunes at recess. I never dreamed that it would take me to the places I've been." Domino later recorded two of Downing's compositions, "Mary, Oh Mary" and "Heartbreak Hill."

During his teenage years, he began to perform at community functions and high school proms, and won a talent contest sponsored by radio station KGGF in Coffeyville, Kansas, at age fourteen playing and singing Domino's hit, "Blueberry Hill." Downing's performance impressed Bobby Poe, a Vinita, Oklahoma-born rockabilly bandleader who was in the audience that night, and asked him to join his all-white group, the Poe Kats. Of course, during the 1950s race mixing was still largely unheard of outside of major urban centers on the coasts and in Midwest music towns such as Chicago and Kansas City. However, Poe believed the group could attract more dates if Al would play piano and sing Fats Domino, Little Richard, Chuck Berry, and B.B. King songs, while Bobby and the Poe Cats would cover Elvis, Jerry Lee Lewis and Buddy Holly. After turning down a basketball scholarship offer from Kansas State University, Downing accepted Poe's offer and at age sixteen left Oklahoma for his first tour. The group landed a regular gig in Boston, Massachusetts playing seven nights a week where Al was paid $90.00 weekly.

From 1957 to 1964, Big Al played piano with the group, which recorded several singles on the Dallas-based White Rock label promoted by Lelan Rogers, Kenny Rogers' brother. At a January, 1958 session, the band recorded "Oh Babe" "Rock 'n' Roll Boogie," "Rock 'n' Roll Record Girl," and "Down on the Farm." The latter was picked up by Challenge Records and narrowly missed the charts, but has become a rock and roll classic and deserves recognition as one of the shortest rock and roll records at one minute and thirty-one seconds. The Poe Kats also toured Kansas and Oklahoma playing in V.F.W. halls and honky tonks performing the entire gamut of rock and roll. It was during these tours that Big Al first experienced racial segregation by hiding under a blanket while the band booked hotel rooms and eating in a separate dining area in restaurants. Jim Halsey, a native of Independence, Kansas, and booking agent for the emerging rockabilly queen **Wanda Jackson**, also from Oklahoma, noticed the group and signed them as her back-up band. While touring with Jackson, the Poe Kats opened shows for such country luminaries as Marty Robbins, Bobby Bare, Red Sovine, Dottie West, and Don Gibson. But the most memorable time for Downing was when he backed Jackson on her Capitol Record sessions in Hollywood, including "Let's Have a Party," her biggest hit, released as a single in 1960. In 2003, Capitol-Nashville re-issued both of Wanda Jackson's albums that feature the Poe Kats, the self-titled first album from 1958, and *Rockin' with Wanda* (1960). In the liner notes of Jackson's recordings, she recalled that the group would have to smuggle Downing into a motel room in a bass fiddle body bag. In the meantime, another session for the Poe Kats at White Rock resulted in interest from several larger record firms, including Carlton and Atlantic. Carlton's Jack Scott released Big Al's "Miss Lucy" and "Just Around the Corner" for national distribution, while "Piano Nellie" was sold to the Atlantic subsidiary, East West.

As a solo recording artist in the late 1960s, Downing found modest success with his recording of the Marty Robbins song, "Story of My Life," however, he scored in the early 1970s with his first rhythm and blues chart single, "I'll Be Holdin' On," which made the disco charts in the United States and Europe. During the decade of the 1970's, he toured the world, including concerts in England, Spain, Holland, Germany, Italy, France, Greece, Philippines, Japan, Singapore, and Thailand, where he played for the king. In 1973, he signed with Lenox Records which resulted in a minor hit, "You'll Never Miss the Water (Till the Well Runs Dry)," a duet with Little Esther Phillips. In the late 1970s, Downing signed with the Warner Brothers label and released several Top 100 singles, including the aforementioned "Mr. Jones," "I'll Be Your Fool Once More," "Bring It on Home," "Midnight Lace," "I Ain't No Fool," and "The Story Behind the Story," leading to Downing receiving *Billboard* magazine's New Artist of the Year and Single of the Year Awards in 1979.

After Warner Brothers would not sponsor a complete album of his songs, Downing moved from one "indie" to another in the 1980s, including Team, Vine Street, Jumble, Door Knob, and Rollercoaster. Other minor hits for these labels included "Darlene," "Let's Sing About Love," "The Best of Families," "There'll Never Be a Better Night for Being Wrong," "Oh How Beautiful You Are To Me," "Just One Night Won't Do It," and "I Guess By Now." After 1994's *Back to My Roots*, Magnum, a U.K. label, released *Magnum Rockabilly* in 1999, which includes Big Al performing "Down on the Farm." Still playing rock and roll and country shows, Downing remains active and is a frequent guest at music festivals in Europe, where he discovered J. Ryan Beretti, the French country and rockabilly star. After Beretti recently toured the U.S. with Downing as opening act, Big Al produced Beretti's first CD entitled *Runaway Heart*, on which seven tracks of the thirteen tracks are either written or co-written by Downing, including the title track, "Gator Man," "It Takes a Honky Tonk Woman to Satisfy Me," and "You Are the Love of My Life."

In 2003, the Cayman Islands' based Platinum Express Records released *One of a Kind*, an album that exhibits Downing's multiple influences, running the gamut from country to R&B. On *One of Kind*, Big Al salutes truckers in "Joe's Truck Stop," goes country all the way in "A Cigarette, a Bottle, and a Jukebox," throws down some of his piano pounding roots on "Boogie Woogie Roll," gets as honky-tonk as one can on "I'm Raisin' Hell," and rolls out some gritty urban blues on "Rock Me Baby." Also in 2003, Big Al crossed over into the digital broadcasting age with a national live broadcast from the XMSatellite Studios in Washington, D.C., and appeared on the Grand Ole Opry in August (GC/HF) www.platinumexpressrecords.com

Dunham, Jack
(b. August 31, 1939)

Known in the music industry as a talented songwriter who penned Conway Twitty's 1979 #1 single, "Your Love Has Taken Me That High," Jack Dunham was the first of the 1950s-era Tulsa musicians to migrate to Los Angeles, where he recorded for Imperial Records in the early 1960s. Dunham is also thought of as the man who introduced rhythm and blues to many young Oklahoma musicians who apprenticed in his Tulsa-based bands in the late 1950s, thereby helping to spawn the combination of rockabilly, blues, and rock and roll that has come to be known as the **Tulsa Sound**. An enrolled **Cherokee** whose Grandmother Dunham was a full blood Cherokee and Grandmother Shoemake was ¾ Cherokee, Jack Dunham was born in Albuquerque, New Mexico, to Blanche and Ray Dunham. He moved to Tulsa with his parents when he was one-year-old where he attended Longfellow and Emerson Elementary Schools, Roosevelt and Wilson Junior High Schools, and Tulsa Central High School. His first musical memories in Tulsa are of riding his bicycle to the Cain's Ballroom and peering through the windows at **Johnnie Lee Wills** and his Western swing bands in 1949. In 1951 his mother gave young Jack a record player and cardboard box full of old 78 rpm records, from which Jack promptly learned all the words to songs by artists such as **Bob Wills** and Nat King Cole, among others. While at Central High School from 1955 to 1957, during the peak of the classic period of rock and roll with Elvis Presley as its anointed king, Jack performed with Chuck Fourneir, Bill Ragan, and Bill Miller as the Tri-Lads at various school dances and parties around Tulsa. After graduating high school, Jack enrolled at Oklahoma State University for a year, and then returned to Tulsa in 1959, ostensibly to attend Tulsa University, but a desire to create the music that was electrifying the 1950s quickly overwhelmed his studies.

Leaping into the 1958 Tulsa music scene already roiling with vocal talents such as Bobby Taylor, Gene Crose, **David Gates** and **Flash Terry,** Jack

assembled the now legendary Upsetters, named after Little Richard's band. The flamboyant 1950s front man provided a model for outrageous "Jumpin' Jack" Dunham who walked on tables during shows while screaming out rock and roll and R & B. Jack's first band in 1958 featured **John "J.J." Cale** (guitar), George "Valentine" Metzel (upright bass), and Jimmy Turley (drums). Also during that year, the band evolved into Jackie Dunham and the Upsetters, to include **Russell "Leon"** Bridges (piano), **Cherokee** Leo Feathers (guitar), Chuck Blackwell (drums), Ron Ryle (electric bass), and Johnny Williams (saxophone). At various gigs throughout the '59 and early 1960, practically every musician who is noted for participating in the Tulsa Sound made their way through The Upsetters. Guitarists included Lee Weir, Tommy Rush, and Tommy Crook; bassists were Bill Raffensberger, Jack Cox, Gerald Goodwin, Carl Radle, and Ralph Brumett; Bill Boatman and Sammy Dodge played saxophone; Jimmy Karstein, Buddy Jones, Chuck Farmer, and C.B. Glasby were drummers for the group at various times; and pianists Jimmy Manry, Eddie Spraker, Rocky Frisco, and Doug Cunningham also saw playing time.

The rotating group of musicians performed regularly throughout Tulsa on the stages of the Pla-mor Ballroom, Casa-Del, Cain's Ballroom, Cimarron Ballroom, the Sheridan Club, the Tropicana Club, Danceland, and the Paradise Club. It was during these shows that Jack acquired his stage name, "Jumpin' Jack" Dunham, due to his tendency to bound from the tops of pianos and tables, as well as from the stage into the audience, no doubt founded in his admiration for the crowd pleasing antics of Little Richard, Jerry Lee Lewis, and Elvis Presley. According to Jack Dunham in a 2003 interview, the group was just one of many Tulsa groups playing rock and R & B for Tulsa crowds whose tastes were changing during the period just after the classic rock and roll era and just prior to the surf music and Motown successes of the early 1960s. Their set list featured covers by Little Richard, Chuck Berry, Jackie Wilson, the Del Vikings, and occasionally one of Jack's own songs.

Dunham made his first recordings in 1959 while working at KVOO radio and television. Setting up Johnny Cale on guitar, Bill Boatman on bass, Jim Turley on drums, and (Leon) Russell Bridges on organ, Jack provided vocals for "Lonely Girl," written by Dunham and Boatman, and "You Don't Need a Man Like Me," a bluesy love ballad. With the experience of getting their music down on an acetate master, the group headed down to Oklahoma City to record at Gene Sullivan's studio, then just about *the* primary non-radio station recording studio in the state. They re-did "Lonely Girl," and a new blues tune penned by Dunham, "I'll Leave It Up To You," both of which were released in 1959 on a 45rpm single by a vanity label out of Shawnee, Dixie Records, but the single generated little interest outside of their hometown. Continuing to perform and get tighter as they played on a regular basis in early 1959 at the Tropicana Club in south Tulsa, the band featured Feathers on guitar, Williams on sax, Russell on piano, Ryle on bass, Blackwell on drums, and Jack on vocals. In early '60, Dunham booked the group back into Sullivan's studio with Cale sitting in for an ailing Leo Feathers. The group recorded Cecil McNeely's "Something on Your Mind" and Titus Turner's "All Around the World," not released until Jack moved to California in May of 1960 and struck a deal with Dondee Records.

Inspired by life-long buddy Bill Miller, who had moved to Los Angeles in 1959 to work in the film industry, and who called Jack in 1960 to offer a low-level job at KTLA-TV, Jack loaded up wife Bobbie and Jack Jr. into a 1950 Ford and headed west on Route 66, making him the first of his generation of Tulsa musicians to migrate to the West Coast. At work by the following Monday via Miller's connections, Jack watched job postings on the KTLA mailroom bulletin board and soon took a job in the mailroom at Paramount Pictures. While running mail during the bulk of the day, Jack switched his lunch hours to be able to try to bend the ears of record industry executives, finally getting "Something On Your Mind" and "All Around the World" out on Dondee Records under the name "Jackie Dunham and the Hollywood Weekends." The song received some moderate West Coast airplay, but more importantly proved his abilities and potential as a vocalist to the public and the Hollywood music industry. While working in Paramount's purchasing department, Jack parlayed an acquaintance with Bobby Darin into a meeting with movie star and radio personality, Pat Buttram, largely known as **Gene Autry**'s movie sidekick and Mr. Haney on television's *Green Acres*. Buttram introduced Dunham to Al Joslow, who had managed Tommy and Jimmy Dorsey, and Joslow landed Jack an audition at Imperial Records, then featuring Fats Domino, Ricky Nelson, and Slim Whitman. By the following week he signed with Imperial as "Jackie Dunham" and within two months had recorded four songs.

Jack Dunham's 1961 Imperial Sessions sit at the crossroads of the 1950s rock and roll sound that by then had been completely commercialized by singers such as Frankie Avalon, Fabian, and Bobby Rydell, and prior to the oncoming British invasion that served up grittier American R&B back to the land of its origin. Dunham recorded two of his own songs at the sessions, "Slow Down Your Life," and "My Yearbook," both of which have a decided 1950s flair musically and lyrically. Of particular interest is his recording of "Early in the Morning," previously recorded by Buddy Holly and co-written by Bobby Darin. Jack's vocal style on the record is very reminiscent of what becomes Mick Jagger's early style: the scratchy blues shout, the mix of a soulful croon, and the deliberate swagger of Elvis Presley. Since the Rolling Stones did not begin recording until 1963, one has to wonder if Jagger's extensive R & B record collection would have included Dunham's "Early in the Morning" since it would have been on a label made instantly recognizable by Fats Domino's releases. The further irony and/or coincidence of Jagger and Keith Richards writing "Jumpin' Jack Flash" in 1968 begs for at least a little more research (somebody ask Mick!). Also of note on the recording is **Barney Kessel** as the guitarist on the session, kicking off "Early in the Morning" with a blues riff that further illustrates Kessel's own musical diversity as a session player, and how Oklahomans had already infiltrated the Southern California studio scene by the time the young Tulsa musicians started arriving in the 1960s. Dunham's first Imperial session closed out with Fats Domino's "I Think of You," on which Jack shows influences of Domino and Jerry Lee Lewis, but exhibits a gutsier vocal style than any of the prominent East Coast singers of the early 1960s were able to achieve convincingly.

On the strength of his Imperial singles and their success in the western and southwestern United States, Jack assembled a band and began touring those regions, as well as making TV appearances on the Wink Martindale Show, Steve Allen Show, and Lloyd Thaxton Show in Hollywood. After strain on his family urged Jack to come off the road, he met Bob Keane, founder of Del-Fi Records, and the man who discovered, produced, and recorded Ritchie Valens. Keane introduced Jack to Gene Autry and Joe Johnson, respectively the principal owner and operator of Autry's 4-Star Music Publishing Company, and they signed Jack to a one-year songwriting contract. While writing songs for 4-Star he met another young vocalist and songwriter, Glenn Campbell, who recorded five of Jack's songs as demonstration recordings. One of the songs, "Hurry Up Sundown," was recorded by Ricky Nelson for Imperial, but never saw the light of day after Nelson's death. Also at 4-Star, Jack met Glen Kastner with whom he co-wrote songs for Lonzo and Oscar, who were the opening comedy act at the time for country singer Eddy Arnold, as well as a song recorded by Hank Snow, "Listen." With limited success and his contract up at Imperial, Dunham began looking back across the country for opportunities, and found them in Clovis, New Mexico.

While also visiting family in Clovis in 1964, Jack checked out the Norman Petty Recording Studios where Petty happened to be recording Jimmy Gilmer and the Fireballs. After introducing himself to Petty, Jack was invited to stay around for the sessions, and on the second day met Ray (Ruffin) Ruff, then playing with his own band, the Checkmates, but who had also played with Buddy Holly's Crickets in the 1950s. Ruff operated a studio and booking agency in Amarillo, Checkmate Productions, and after an invitation from Ruff, in 1964 the Dunham family took up residence in Amarillo so Jack could write songs and work in Ruff's studio. In 1965, Jack's second son, Damon Ray Mills, was born, and over the next two years, twenty of Jack's songs appeared on the Checkmate label, to include recordings by Red Steagall, Buddy Knox, the Checkmates, and J. Frank Wilson, known for his million seller, "Last Kiss." Jack wrote Wilson's follow-up, "Unmarked and Covered with Sand." In 1966, Jack wrote "Rebound to Tulsa," a song that garnered him significant enough attention from Capitol Records for them to release it through their Tower Records label. Subsequently, Jack and Ray Ruff put a band together to support the single and toured through Texas, Colorado, Arizona, and Louisiana. The most fortuitous product of the tour was not the single's success, but Jack's meeting with Conway Twitty at a tour stop in Dallas.

When Dunham met the then-successful rocker, Twitty indicated he was changing from rock to country and was aware of Jack's songwriting through "Big" Joe

Lewis, then the bassist for Twitty's band and a friend of Ray Ruff's. Twitty encouraged Jack to call if he ever made it out to Nashville. After a move back to Tulsa to unsuccessfully try and save his marriage in 1967, Dunham took Twitty up on the offer, and by 1968 Dunham was writing for Conway's Twitty Bird Music in Nashville. After two years of songwriting and attempting to manage single parenthood, however, Jack had yet to have any of his songs recorded or released. In a major decision, Jack moved with his two boys to Atlanta, Georgia, supporting himself outside of show business for the first time since 1959 by learning to install wallpaper, and later marrying an old Tulsa girlfriend with whom he had his third son, Derek. He didn't stop writing, however, and sent "The Memory of Your Sweet Love" to Conway, which he recorded in 1971 for his album, *How Much More Can She Stand* (Decca), and began a decade-long relationship between Jack and Conway wherein the country crooner recorded over thirty of Dunham's songs, eighteen of which still remain unissued after Twitty's death.

In 1972 Conway recorded "Back When Judy Loved Me," Jack's song about his first wife, Diane. Twitty recorded two more of Jack's songs in 1973, "When the Final Change is Made," included on Conway's album, *You've Never Been This Far Before* (MCA), and "Lead Us Back to Love," which surfaced on Twitty's only gospel album, *Clinging to a Saving Hand* (MCA). Using memories of his first wife, Diane, and his second wife, Bobbie, Jack wrote "On My Way to Losing You," manifesting on Conway's 1975 Top 10 album, *This Time I've Hurt Her More* (MCA). In 1976, *Music City News* awarded Jack its "Horizon Award" for being one of country music's most promising "new country songwriters," even though he had been writing songs for almost twenty years by that point. Also that same year, he wrote "At Least One Time," recorded by Conway for his album *Now and Then* (MCA), and recorded by a Texas country singer, Nat Stuckey, for his album, *Independence* (MCA).

By 1977, Central Songs Publishing offered Jack a job as staff writer and head of their writing department in Los Angeles, but Dunham did not want to uproot his sons from their schools in Atlanta, so he stayed at home and kept writing, a choice that proved to be the right move when he churned out "Your Love Had Taken Me That High," a song that Conway recorded and took to #1 on *Billboard*'s country singles chart. The album containing the song, *Conway* (1978), reached #13 on the *Billboard* country albums chart. "Your Love Had Taken Me That

High" also received a nomination as CMA Single of the Year, but lost out to Kenny Rogers' "The Gambler."

Marking his career in the music industry, Dunham has received several BMI songwriting awards, two CMA awards, and a BMI #1 song award for "Your Love Had Taken Me That High." With this success, Dunham focused more on family and his commercial wallpaper business than songwriting throughout the 1980s, and returned to Tulsa with his wife, Ginger, permanently in the 1990s. As of 2003, he serves on the board of directors of Friends of Oklahoma Music, the Muskogee-based group that organizes and produces the yearly induction ceremonies and concert for the Oklahoma Music Hall of Fame, of which Dunham will obviously someday be a member. Starting his career with inspirations from the ebullient rock and roll of the 1950s, Jack Dunham evolved into an R & B showman by 1959 along with some of Tulsa's most prominent musicians as his supporting group, and flirted with regional pop stardom on the West Coast in the early 1960s. Turning to country music songwriting to achieve his greatest professional success, much of which was based lyrically on his real life experiences of trying to keep a family together while providing for them via show business, he experienced the extreme highs and lows of following one's dreams of a music career and living to tell the story through his songs.

Jack Dunham's life in music also amply illustrates the multi-genre background that was nurtured in his hometown of Tulsa, and represents the cross-cultural elements of what is commonly referred to as the Tulsa Sound, but whose roots also are intertwined with the **Wills Brothers** multi-faceted "Okie Jazz," the country boogie of **Jack Guthrie** prominent throughout Oklahoma in the late 1940s and early 1950s, and the popular rock and roll of the middle and late 1950s. Jackie Dunham and the Upsetters were a significant catalyst for the musical mélange of blues, rock, and country elements known as the **Tulsa Sound** that echoed through popular music well into the 1970s via Eric Clapton, and into the 1980s by way of Dire Straits, but had its beginnings on the local stages of Tulsa's music scene in 1959 and 1960 with "Jumpin' Jack" Dunham right on the point. (HF)

Dunn, Robert Lee "Bob"
(b. February 8, 1908 – d. May 27, 1971)

Known as *the* number one western swing electric steel guitar player, Bob Dunn was a top-flight musician who serves as the model for all steel guitar players after him in western swing, and other sub-genres of country music that feature the instrument. Although he may not have been the very first to use the amplified electric guitar, music historians do credit him with being the father of the electric steel guitar in country music. He is known for his jazz-tinged, single string ad-libs in the pioneering western swing outfit, Milton Brown and his Musical Brownies, in the 1930s. Born into poverty either in the rural farm town of Braggs,

Oklahoma, just south of Muskogee, or in Fort Gibson which is just twelve miles north of Braggs, Bob Dunn, like many musicians of the early twentieth century, found his ticket out of those dire circumstances by turning to music and excelling. Bob's first musical experiences came by accompanying his father, Silas B. Dunn, on fiddle breakdowns in the old time country tradition. One of four brothers born by Iva (Pruitt) Dunn, Bob was the only one who aspired to be a musician. As a child he heard a group of musicians traveling through and became entranced by their use of the steel guitar. He eventually came into possession of one and began to take lessons through correspondence with a Hawaiian native, Walter Kolomoku, who lived in Oklahoma City. Listening to his early recordings, one can hear the influence this training had on Bob's playing. However, many other influences existed in the area where Bob grew up. The family is known to have lived in Fort Gibson during Bob's youth, the town that also produced jazz singer **Lee Wiley**. Known as Three Forks, where the Verdigris, Grand, and Arkansas Rivers meet, Bob's geographic location placed him just across the river from the music rich town of Muskogee, a regional entertainment center which also produced jazz musicians such as **Barney Kessel**, **Jay McShann**, **Don Byas**, and **Claude "Fiddler" Williams**.

Along with being exposed to all the potential live sources of musical influence, Bob also came of age during the 1920s when phonograph recordings and radio made learning about new styles and players more convenient. Quitting school in the eighth grade, Bob was playing professionally in his early teens during the early to mid 1920s. The first known bands Bob played with were the Panhandle Cowboys and Indians and California Curley and his Cowboy Band. By 1930, Bob was working in Paul Perkins's band at KFKB in Milford, Kansas, voted the most popular radio station in America the previous year. The band played for a quack doctor, J.R. Brinkley, famous for selling "goat gland" to cure all kinds of ailments. During Bob's time in Kansas, he met his wife, and when Brinkley had trouble with the Kansas authorities, the show moved to Texas. To avoid the same troubles he had in Kansas, Brinkley constructed the 75,000 watt station XER in Mexico, just across the Rio Grande River where he was outside the influence of U.S. authorities. After a while with Brinkley, Bob worked and traveled with several western bands, vaudeville tours, and jazz bands. During those years, the early 1930s, Bob began playing trombone, and recorded a few sides with Jimmie Davis. With its slide action, the brass instrument's musical elements found their way into Bob's steel guitar playing technique. Many of his famous ad-libs derived from moving the slide-bar on the steel up and down one string, similar to the way in which a trombone works with its slide. Also about the same time, while Dunn was in New York working wherever he could find jobs on Coney Island, he saw an African-American man playing a slide guitar that had been rigged with a home-made pickup and became inspired to learn more about the instrument.

Many people were experimenting with electric guitars in the early to mid-1930s. During this time, Adolph Rickenbacker and George Beauchamp created one of the first electric guitars, known as the "frying pan," because it looked a frying pan with a long handle, but the instrument did not catch on commercially. Bob Dunn created his own version of the electric steel guitar when he began playing with Milton Brown and & his Musical Brownies. A vaudeville tour landed Bob in Fort Worth in 1934, then the epicenter of the western swing movement, where he went to the studios of KTAT to visit the Brownies who featured a Hawaiian steel number in each one of their broadcasts. After demonstrating his style, Dunn became a Musical Brownie and told Milton Brown what he wanted to do with the instrument. Brown procured an amplifier and Dunn attached a homemade pickup, perhaps modeled after the one he had seen in Coney Island, onto a big guitar he bought in Mexico. An admirer of jazz trombonist Jack Teagarden, Dunn began experimenting with the instrument in order to replicate the sounds of brass instruments played in a jazz style. This technique gave him his unique tone and attack. Dunn's addition to the Musical Brownies substantiated the strong foundation of the first western swing group to gain prominence in the Southwest, even before **Bob Wills and his Texas Playboys**.

In 1935, the Musical Brownies' popularity led to their first recording sessions for Decca in Chicago. At these sessions, Dunn recorded "Taking Off," his signature tune and country music's first important steel guitar number, available on Rhino Records' *History of Country Music, Vol.1: Legends of Western Swing*. Dunn also recorded important solos on "Cheesy Breeze," "You're Tired of Me," and others during the sessions which had wide ranging implications by virtue of the records being sold by the thousands as a result of the Brownies' fame. Dunn's sound became emulated throughout the Southwest and had influence on everyone from other steel players like Leon McAuliffe, to Texas-born, but Oklahoma raised, jazz guitarist **Charlie Christian**, both of whom would have certainly heard Dunn at least on radio. Don Tolle, a guitar player who recorded with **Johnnie Lee Wills** in the 1950s and had a short stint with Bob Wills, remembered listening to Dunn as a child on the radio, and said, "Dunn played some things nobody ever got, but the man who came closest to replicating his style was Paul Mattingly."

Mattingly, born in Sand Springs, Oklahoma on January 12, 1921, was a career military man who had bands in Colorado and Wyoming, and played with The Alabama Boys in Muskogee, Oklahoma, after his retirement from the Army in 1975. Although Mattingly was only recorded informally, he is recognized as an excellent imitator of Bob Dunn. Because Mattingly would have been at the very impressionable age of fifteen or sixteen when Dunn's recordings with Decca were released, he is a good indication of their impact on young musicians of the era. Additional indications of the popularity of the electric steel guitar included the Gibson guitar company's rush to commercialize the instrument, which they did when the first one shipped from their factory in May of 1936.

In 1936, the Brownies recorded again in a New Orleans hotel room with Dunn turning in more spectacular performances on good time tunes such as

"Somebody's Been Using That Thing," blues like "Fan It," and the ballad "An Old Water Mill by a Waterfall." About a month after the New Orleans sessions, Milton Brown suffered fatal injuries in an automobile accident and the band broke up not long after. By 1937, Dunn joined former Brownie Cecil Brower in a western swing band led by Roy Newman on WRR radio in Dallas. Dunn did record with Newman for Vocalion Records in June of 1937, but left soon thereafter to join another ex-Brownie, Cliff Bruner, who had moved his Texas Wanderers to the new home base of Beaumont, Texas. Already recording for Decca, Dunn joined the band of future stars such as Moon Mullican on piano and vocals, and pioneering amplified mandolin player, Leo Raley. Due to internal strife that often afflicts musical groups, Dunn left the Wanderers and returned to Del Rio and spent the winter of 1937-38 playing over another high-powered border radio station, XEPN. By the spring of 1938, Dunn was in Houston playing on radio shows and joined back up with the Texas Wanderers who had returned to their original base of Houston, and reformed with many of their original stars such as Mullican and Bruner. In September of 1937, the group recorded an excellent session of songs that again demonstrated Bob Dunn's high flying, jazz-tinged solos, but the band broke up again over the winter of 1938-39. Most of the highlights of Dunn's recordings with Bruner were reissued by Texas Rose Records under Bruner's name in 1983 and are still in print.

After leaving Bruner, Dunn formed a short-lived group, Bob Dunn's Vagabonds and recorded a solid session for Decca wherein Dunn even sang one song, "When Night Falls." Soon after the sessions, Dunn broke up the Vagabonds and traveled extensively throughout the Southwest and Southeast, to include a stop in Nashville at the Grand Ole Opry that he did not care for at all. Distinctions have long existed between the schooled Western swing musicians who could read music, and the less formally trained old time country musicians of the Southeast who the Western swing musicians considered mountain musicians cut of a lesser musical cloth. Dunn returned to Houston, reformed the Vagabonds for one lackluster recording session for Decca in 1940, recorded another less-than-stellar set with Bruner, and traveled to Dallas where he recorded with Bill Mounce. The second of these sessions with Mounce is significant because Dunn played with Jimmy Wyble, a nineteen-year-old electric guitarist, who played with Bob Wills and **Spade Cooley** before moving gaining prominent jazz status with Benny Goodman, and who has stated Dunn was a significant early influence on his playing. Also during this time, Bob's alcohol consumption, legendary among his peers who often felt he played better after a few belts, began to take its toll on his patience and playing. He did not like having to play commercial melodies that were essentially lesser versions of his original, unique style.

With the arrival of World War II, Dunn served three years in the Navy and returned a somewhat changed person. His drinking problem appears to have abated during the war, and when he returned to Houston he took advantage of the GI Bill by successfully completing his high school equivalency requirements, and enrolling in the Southern College of Fine Arts. Eventually, he earned a master's degree in music. He continued playing in the Houston area and formed the Blue Serenaders, a pop and jazz band, with some of the horn players at the college, and, interestingly, Bob played a lot of trombone with the band. Dunn also joined a couple of Western swing bands in 1948 and 1949, but country music was changing and honky style was becoming more prominent in Texas. Dunn sat in on a few more recordings in 1949 and 1950, but by the fall of 1950 Dunn had opened a music store and focused primarily on his business and teaching. Dunn's sister-in-law, Nina, remembered 1950 as the year Dunn stopped drinking for good and became "the kindest person you would ever want to meet."

Bob Dunn's story has gone largely unnoticed in the last fifty years, but some of country music's leading scholars, such as Bill Malone and Nick Tosches, have been partly responsible for keeping Dunn's name in the forefront of record collectors and country music aficionados. In 1995, Kevin Coffey wrote Dunn's life story in *The Journal of Country Music*, as a result of interviews with many of Dunn's relatives and contemporaries. Subsequently, Dunn's legacy is being recognized more and more for his innovation and contributions to country music, such as his induction into The Steel Guitar Hall of Fame for being "The first steel guitarist to introduce jazz licks into country and western music." On the larger scale of Oklahoma music history, Dunn's ability to combine elements of jazz, blues, and country is a testament to the multiple influences to which he was exposed as a youth in the realm of the state's multi-cultural brew of people and their wide-ranging musical identities and influences. (HF)

Dunn, Ronnie
(b. June 1, 1953)

With their duo harmonies on up-tempo dance hall country and honky tonk rock songs aimed at the high-pocketed jeans set still boot scootin' and two-steppin across the well-worn dance floors of country music-oriented clubs and venues of Oklahoma, Kix Brooks and Ronnie Dunn are members of contemporary pop country's superstar elite. With twenty-four million albums sold, twenty-three #1 country hits, and a score of music industry awards since their first album, *Brand New Man* (ARIST), debuted on the *Billboard* charts in August of 1991 and stayed there three years straight, Brooks and Dunn entered

the twenty-first century with a dynamic and raucous live tour, *The Neon Circus and Wild West Show*, and a decade of hits of behind them to keep their buses and equipment trucks on the road until they decide otherwise. While neither musician is an Oklahoma native, Ronnie Dunn lived in Tulsa and Grove for most of the period between the early 1970s and the early 1990 when he moved to Nashville. During that time he experienced **Leon Russell**'s Shelter Records milieu of the '70s, led the house band at two popular urban Tulsa honky tonks during the 1970s and 1980s, had two records with Jim Halsey's Tulsa-based Churchill label in the early '80s, and won one first place in national talent contest in 1988 while still based in Oklahoma. The prize for winning included $30,000 and a $25,000 recording session with producer and Oklahoma native Scott Hendricks, who ultimately alerted Arista Records' head Tim Dubois, also an Oklahoman (see a trend here?), to Ronnie Dunn's material. It was also Dubois who introduced Dunn to Brooks and then signed them as a duo to Arista's Nashville label. The rest, as they say, is a long story written over a short amount of time.

While Kix Brooks was born in Shreveport, Louisiana (b. May 12, 1955), and started playing guitar as a child, Ronnie Gene Dunn was born in Coleman, Texas, where his pipefitting and truck-driving father, Jessie Dunn, also a hopeful country music artist, played guitar and sang in a country band called the Fox Four Five. The traditional country music Ronnie's dad played did not have enough appeal for the younger Dunn, however, as he indicates on the Brooks and Dunn website: "My mother [Gladys] and father listened to hillbilly music all the time," Dunn remembers, "[but] the music just didn't rock hard enough for me. If the music had been as hard as the feelings, it'd've been perfect. So, when it was our turn, I was intent on making country *rock*." Before getting to rock, however, Ronnie spent a few years learning the lessons of one of country music's primary themes: traveling. Both through their moves and the elder Dunn's work as long haul truck driver, the Dunns accepted geographical transitions as an economic necessity.

Ronnie's first brush with Oklahoma was when the elder Dunn's work brought them to Tulsa and Ronnie attended Skiatook High School for a year, but the family moved back to south Texas, where Ronnie attended Port Isabel High, and started playing bass in bands around local nightspots. After high school he majored in psychiatry at Abilene Christian College, which he attended with the goal of becoming a Baptist minister, but couldn't stop playing the honky tonks. Before long Ronnie had to decide between Bible college and country music, and helping him to make the choice was Ronnie's mother, then living in Tulsa since his father started working for Arrow Trucking, the largest state-based trucking operation in Oklahoma. Gladys sent Ronnie a newspaper clipping about Tulsa-based music promoter and entrepreneur Jim Halsey, thinking the young musician could find opportunities in the early 1970s Tulsa music scene of which Halsey was part. After making the move from Texas, Dunn found a Tulsa music community swirling around the Church Studio. Dunn remembers the years around the Shelter Records on the Brooks and Dunn website: "The Shelter crowd was the *most* soulful. You get around those kinds of people and it makes you think because you've witnessed the difference. It certainly set the bar for me – and you can't clear it every time, but it sure sets a standard you can feel good about."

While working a string of odd jobs during the 1970s, Ronnie Dunn led the house band at Duke's Country, then Tulsa's top-notch live music country nightclub. Later, Ronnie and his band opened for touring headliners at Tulsa City Limits, the popular urban honky tonk open from 1985 to 2000 that inspired Brooks and Dunn's first major hit, "Boot Scootin' Boogie." On the band's website in 2002, Dunn remembered how playing in those clubs inspired his overall understanding of how a group succeeds at the club level: "From playing in bands and watching the patterns of what people would like to dance to – because in Oklahoma and Texas, if they don't dance, you're dead... it's like a honky tonk education. You have to stand and deliver just to get in."

After records in 1983 and 1984 with Churchill records failed to boost his career beyond regional status, Dunn continued to work outside of the music business during the week, while playing on the weekends. Around the time he had moved to Grove by 1988, where he was working in a liquor store, Ronnie's friend and **Tulsa Sound** veteran, Jamie Oldaker, who has played drums for Eric Clapton, entered Dunn's name in the 1988 Marlboro Talent Roundup. With a demo tape featuring the musicians that essentially became The Tractors, minus **Steve Ripley,** who was then working as the band's recording engineer since he owned the Church Studio in which they rehearsed and made the demo, Dunn's band won the Tulsa regional competition and earned the right to compete in Nashville at the finals, which they also won. Along with the prize money the group split, they also received $25,000 worth of studio time with Oklahoma native Scott Hendricks who recorded three songs: "Boot Scootin' Boogie," "You Don't Know Me," and "The Dean Dillon Song." Hendricks passed the songs along to another Oklahoman, Tim Dubois, who had just cranked up ARISTA's Nashville label, and who liked the songs so much he flew to Tulsa to see the band play at Joey's Bar, after which Dubois advised Ronnie to move to Nashville. Unsure of relocating, Dunn had still not moved to Music City in 1990 when Dubois called to get per-mission to include "Boot Scootin' Boogie" on Asleep at the Wheel's *Keepin' Me Up Nights* (ARISTA, 1990). Dunn finally signed with Dubois in 1990. However, Ronnie had not yet moved to Tennessee and preferred to commute back and forth from Oklahoma while seeing how things would turn out in Nashville.

With Alan Jackson as the lead act on ARISTA at the time, Dubois did not want to introduce another solo performer through the label too soon, so Dubois sug-gested Ronnie work out some songs with another young guitarist, singer, and songwriter, Kix Brooks. When the two started working on demos together, Dubois recognized the easy chemistry between the two singers, and suggested they work as a duo. Both blanched at first, sure they could have careers on their own, but Dubois offered them a contract and they signed to ARISTA as a "two-show." Within a year, *Brand New Man* (ARISTA, 1991) hit the shelves and set the course for the musical brand of Brooks and Dunn. Dunn's memories of the era were on the Brooks and Dunn website in 2002: "I remember driving back and forth from Tulsa to Nashville all the time. We had a Ford Explorer and I put 100,000 miles on it that year. In 1991, I heard "Brand New Man" for the first time on the radio when I was coming into Nashville. That was one of the last trips."

Certified in 2002 for sales of six million units, with three million of those coming between 1991 and 1993, *Brand New Man* set a steady course for Brooks and Dunn that continued unabated throughout the 1990s and into the 2000s. The album's title track opens the disc and features the two singers' now instantly recognizable harmonies, along with lyrics that speak of a character's conversion from a disposition of "a wild side a coun-

Kix Brooks and Ronnie Dunn

try mile wide" into a brand new man who can settle down and love a woman right. The song was the first of four from the album to reach #1 on the country charts (a feat never accomplished by a duo or group in successive fashion), also to include "My Next Broken Heart," a fatalistic weeper about not being able to stay in love, and "Neon Moon," a perennial slow dance favorite when the hour gets late and last minute intimate deals are being struck in the glow of beer joint neon signs.

While those three songs were hits, none had more cultural impact than "Boot Scootin' Boogie" that remained at the #1 spot on the country charts for four weeks and crossed over into the pop Top 50 while spawning a national resurgence in country line dancing. Written by Dunn to both commemorate and provide a tune for the country line dancing at Oklahoma and Texas honky tonks, the song does not mention the Tulsa City Limits club specifically, but the opening line gives plenty of references for those who frequented the place "Out in the country past the city limits sign," while making the song generic enough for dance halls throughout the region. Traceable to the pop culture group dancing of the 1970s disco period known as the Bus Stop, then filtered through the urban cowboy flash of the early 1980s, line dancing is still one of the most popular group activities in Oklahoma honky-tonks. While some dancers participate nonchalantly, others concentrate hard to keep up, and others, buoyed by their choice of adult beverages, laugh through the whole process. More often than not, however, Brooks and Dunn's "Boot Scootin' Boogie" is still the song of choice for the dance that doesn't leave anyone in the house out, except the bartenders and bouncers. The duo magnified the whole trend by releasing a six-and-a-half-minute club mix of the song on their second album, *Hard Workin' Man* (ARISTA, 1993).

Before *Hard Workin' Man* really got underway, Brooks and Dunn started receiving what would be steady string of awards for their recordings and live performances. They were named CMA's Vocal Duo of the Year in 1992 and 1993, and started headlining shows in 1993 as *Hard Workin' Man* produced more hit singles to bolster their already hit-filled set. The Top 5 title track featured Ronnie belting out a sympathetic tune for the hard working men and women who like to let it loose on the weekends. The single also earned the pair their first GRAMMY in 1993 for Best Country Performance By a Duo or Group. Also taken from *Hard Workin' Man*, "We'll Burn That Bridge When We Get There," a song about rebound love, made it to #2 in *Billboard*, and a slow ballad lamenting a lost love, "She Used To Be Mine," crested the top of the *Radio and Records* country charts in 1993. Still pulling singles from the album, Brooks and Dunn hit the Top 5 again in 1994 with Kix singing "Rock My World (Little Country Girl), and had another #1 country hit via "That Ain't No Way to Go," both from *Hard Workin' Man*, an album that sold more than four million copies. Not surprisingly, Brooks and Dunn were named CMA's "Vocal Duo of the Year" in 1994 (and again in 1995, 1996, 1997, 1998, 1999, 2001, and 2002).

The third Brooks and Dunn album, *Waitin' on Sundown* (ARISTA, 1994) continued their formula for success: lovelorn characters and general social desolation that has long been a prominent country music theme ("She's Not the Cheatin' Kind," "You're Gonna Miss Me When I'm Gone," and "A Few Good Rides Away); tight harmonies between the two men on almost every song, and at least a few of tunes about embracing the rowdier side of Saturday night ("Whiskey Under the Bridge," "She's the Kind of Trouble I Don't Mind," and "My Kind of Crazy"). The up-tempo "Whiskey Under the Bridge" landed the group another Top 5 hit in 1995, and "If That's the Way You Want It" recalled the easy crooning style of Western swing, emphasized by Dunn's imitation of a **Bob Wills** call during the guitar solo. Major awards followed their career's success with Brooks and Dunn being the ACM Entertainer of the Year in 1995 and 1996, along with holding the ACM's title of Best Vocal Duo from 1991 to 1997.

A month after Brooks and Dunn released their fourth album, *Borderline* (ARISTA, 1996), CMA awarded the duo Entertainer of the Year and they promptly scored a number one hit from *Borderline*, "My Maria," a cover of B.W. Stevenson's 1972 pop hit that earned them a GRAMMY Award for Best Country Performance by a Duo or Group in 1996. The remainder of the album often sounds like a lesser imitation of the duo's stellar earlier material, with the exception of Ronnie's obvious homage to his trucker dad, "White Line Casanova," that starts out with the line "I'm dead headin' down from Tulsa." One has to wonder if the constant grind of the music business caused Brooks and Dunn to rely more on formula than inspiration for *Borderline*, but hardcore fans didn't seem to mind as the album sold over two million copies. With enough scores to justify it, the duo released a *Greatest Hits* (ARISTA) package collection in 1997 that sold more than three million copies and included three new songs, one of which was a hit,

"Honky Tonk Truth," that relied on their trademark danceable twang-rock. With no reason to rush, they took two years to release their next album, 1998's double platinum *If You See Her* (ARISTA), featuring an ace cover by Dunn of **Roger Miller**'s "Husbands and Wives," and a nice vocal collaboration between Brooks, Dunn, and Reba McEntire on "If You See Him/If You See Her." The duo updated their sound somewhat on *Tight Rope* (ARISTA, 1999) by enlisting the talents of producer Byron Gallimore (Faith Hill, Tim McGraw), but dug back for another familiar pop hit for perhaps the album's strongest track, John Waite's 1984 pop hit, "Missing You." While most artists would be satisfied with a gold record, 500,000 copies sold of *Tight Rope* seemed like the group's fan base was holding strong, but the casual country listener and more youthful spender that makes up a lot of the music industry's purchasing element was not embracing the group.

"Bouncing back" in 2001 with *Steers & Stripes* (ARISTA) that debuted at #1 on the *Billboard* country album charts and has been certified gold with 500,000 discs sold as of 2003, Brooks and Dunn sounded familiar and professional, if a little bit too safe on the smooth country side for traditional honky tonk rockers. The album also marked the first one by the duo that did not feature songs mostly written by themselves, with Ronnie only contributing to one, "Good Girls Go to Heaven," that either borrows, or consciously exhibits, a guitar riff from the Kinks' "(Wish I Could Fly Like) Superman," a lyrical motif from the Rolling Stones' "Some Girls," and a vocal delivery from Dire Straits "Money for Nothing." Dunn acknowledges an inspirational drought of sorts when he thanks producer Mark Wright on CD's liner notes for "bringing a whirlwind of much needed creativity and energy to the table."

While *Steers and Stripes* often coasts on the massive production qualities for which Nashville country music has come to be known, the album still produced three #1 singles in the national emotionally and psychologically draining time after September 11th, 2001: "The Long Goodbye," a heartbreaking ballad about the end of a love affair; "Only in America," a pluralistic song by Brooks about diversity in the United States; and "There Ain't Nothing 'Bout You" which became *Billboard*'s "Most Played Country Song of 2001," and stayed at the #1 spot for six consecutive weeks. While their own songwriting may have slowed to some extent, Brooks and Dunn's ability to pick hits aimed at their working class fan-base, and songs tailor-made for the duo's familiar, and one would have to say, comforting, voices has jettisoned them into the twenty-first century as top-of-the-line country superstars.

Confirmation of this fact came in 2001 and 2002 when they were named CMA's Entertainer of the Year both years. By the end of 2002 the duo released their first holiday album, *It Won't Be Christmas Without You* (ARISTA), and had been awarded the Country Radio Board's Humanitarian of the Year award in recognition of their public work for the Monroe Harding Children's Home, Ronald McDonald House, St. Jude Children's Hospital, and the Women's Hospital at St. Thomas Moor where they financed breast cancer imagine machines. Additionally in 2002, Brooks and Dunn won the American Music Award as Favorite Country Duo or Group, the CMT Flameworthy Award for Duo of the Year, and the CMA's Duo of the Year for the 10th time. In February, 2003, Brooks and Dunn received the inaugural Elvis Presley Patriotic Song Award for "Only in America," the video for which won CMT'S Duo Video of the Year Award. Also in 2003, they kept touring with their highly successful *Neon Circus and Wild West Show* that continued to elevate their status as dominant live showmen. The show gained such a reputation for rowdy, hard country that *USA Today* did a photo essay on the tour in 2002, and CBS Television's *Sunday Morning* chronicled the fervent fans that follow the tour across the country in the manner of the Grateful Dead's "Deadheads." By spring, 2003 Brooks and Dunn again found themselves winning Duo of the Year at the 38th Academy of Country Music Awards.

Released in July 2003, *Red Dirt Road* (ARISTA) provided the group with yet another #1 country hit. Appealing to nationwide country music audiences with its chiming mandolin and instantly familiar, sing-along chorus, the album's title track is about learning life's lessons out on the red dirt back roads of the rural south. While the album is much rootsier than their recent outings with a prevalence of dobros courtesy of Jerry Douglas ("Caroline" and "That's What She Gets for Loving Me"), acoustic guitars ("When We Were Kings"), mandolins ("Red Dirt Roads"), fiddles ("My Baby's Everything I Love"), and harmonicas ("That's What She Gets for Loving Me"), the collection also ranges into softer ballads ("I Used to Know This Song By Heart," and "Memory Town"). Surely one of the future singles will be the Brooks and Dunn composition "My Baby's Everything I Love." Pulling out every stop, the honky tonk stomper features most of the previously mentioned instruments taking a solo on a song that seems guaranteed to be a two-stepping favorite. Much of the album centers on the concept of redemption through trial, especially the up tempo gospel-tinged "hidden" track at the end of the collection. Overall, the album sees Brooks and Dunn foregoing much of their more polished latter 90s sound for a grittier approach that befits their origins in the dance halls of Oklahoma, Texas, and Louisiana, and is rowdy enough for thousands to bounce around to in stadiums and arenas throughout North America.

In August, 2003, Brooks and Dunn's cover version of Waylon Jenings' "I Ain't Living Long Like This" appeared on RCA's *I've Always Been Crazy: A Tribute to Waylon Jenings*, and, in November of that year, Friends of Oklahoma Music inducted Ronnie Dunn into the Oklahoma Music Hall of Fame. "Had it not been for Oklahoma," Dunn said in a press release acknowledging the induction, "and the abundance of places to play. . . well, it's where I honed everything I do for the most part. The lion's share of what I know, I learned in Oklahoma and the clubs around there, because it was such a rich musical environment. From **Bob Wills** to **Leon Russell**, the **GAP Band**… the spectrum was so broad, it really gave you an appreciation of what music could be. And nobody worried about what it was, beyond good, so you picked stuff up from every kind of music being played and brought it to what you did." About Tulsa, Ronnie Dunn explained, "Tulsa is also a huge part of who I am musically. We'd play clubs and end up at the Caravan Ballroom, with a lot of the original Bob Wills players – people like Eldon Shamblin. They never lose sight of their musical heritage there – the music always moves forward from the roots, and I carry it with me to this day." (HF) www.brooks-dunn.com

Edwards, Nokie
(b. May 9th, 1935)

While lead guitarist for the most significant instrumental combo in the history of rock music, The Ventures, Nokie Edwards established himself as a fleet soloist and important stylist during The Ventures' peak of popularity in the 1960s and '70s. Playing with fellow Oklahoman and co-founding member of The Ventures, bassist **Bob Bogle**, and the other two Ventures, co-founder and rhythm guitarist Don Wilson (b. February 10, 1937, Tacoma, Washington), and primary drummer Howie Johnson (b. WA, 1938 - d. 1988), Edwards helped redefine and re-popularize the electric guitar combo in the midst of the late 1950s and early 1960s pop music era with its homogenized and watered-down rock and roll. Their drum-driven, fast dance music, featuring Nokie's speedy electric guitar work, inspired countless surf music groups and garage bands from the 1960s, not the least of which were several major British Invasion bands like the Beatles and Kinks. The

Ventures' influence continued into the punk rock movement of the 1970s, and the alternative country music of the 1980s through the 2000s. Musicians who are on record as being inspired by the group include Jimmy Page, Stanley Clarke, Steve Miller, George Harrison, The Ramones, Jeff "Skunk" Baxter of Steely Dan, and all-world guitarist Larry Carlton. Additionally, their success in Japan opened up the American music market in that country.

While the group had admirable success on the single charts in the 1960s with fourteen Top 100 singles, The Ventures' thematic LP collections drove their notoriety. According to The Ventures' website, thirty-seven of their albums made the US charts. More than 150 albums have been released in Japan alone, and their 1960s-era *Play Guitar with The Ventures* series was the first and only set of musical instructional records ever to make the album charts. The group had five gold albums, was named *Billboard's* Most Promising Instrumental Group of 1960, sold an unprecedented one million albums per year from 1961 to 1966, and have sold over one hundred million albums through 2003. While Bob Bogle and Don Wilson started the band under the name of The Versatones, the addition of Nokie Edwards in 1959 ensured the group would be exalted be forever in popular music's Valhalla, although the earthly version of that reverent center for celebrated rocking souls, the Rock and Roll Hall of Fame in Cleveland, has not yet inducted The Ventures.

Born in the tiny western Oklahoma agricultural community of Lahoma, smack in the middle of Oklahoma's famous dustbowl, Nole ("Nokie" is a combination of Nole and Okie) Floyd Edwards joined a musical brood where his father played violin and guitar, and most of his twelve brothers and sisters were also musically inclined. His brothers, uncles, and father spun out bluegrass, country and western, "Everything," as Nokie said in a 2003 telephone interview. Like many other Oklahomans did in the 1930s due to drought and the Depression, the Edwards were forced into moving west when Nokie was not even a year old. Surrounded by music and musicians, by the time he was five, Nokie began teaching himself the guitar, and when he was eleven he could play all string instruments, but decided to concentrate on just guitar. Also at eleven, Nokie made his first radio performance in Idaho, and by the middle 1950s he played with the Grand Ole Opry when they toured the Northwest. Eventually he played with well-known country artists such as Lefty Frizzell, **Cal Smith**, Ferlin Husky, and Buck Owens, with whom Bob Bogle and Don Wilson first saw Edwards play lead guitar.

In a 2002 interview posted on his website, Nokie remembered how he came to be with The Ventures: "It started with Don Wilson and Bob Bogle performing in Washington. Bob came into a club where he heard me playing with Buck Owens in 1959. The next night Don joined Bob and returned to hear me perform on lead with Buck. Don and Bob talked to me about playing with them. Skip Moore was performing on drums where I was playing and I introduced Skip to Bob and Don. As a result they asked Skip to work on some jobs with them. We played around the Tacoma, Washington area in a few clubs, and then went into the studio to record 'Walk, Don't Run' in 1959." By the next year "Walk Don't Run," produced by Don's mother, Josie, on her own Blue Horizon label when the demo was turned down by various labels. The song surged regionally on radio and was picked up by Dolton Records for distribution where it peaked at #2 on the national pop charts, kept off the top spot by Elvis Presley, Chubby Checker, and Bryan Hyland's "Itsy Bittsy Teeny Weeny Yellow Polka Dot Bikini."

Nokie Edwards played lead guitar with The Ventures from 1959 to 1968. While he is often thought of as the early bassist of the group, Nokie explained to an interviewer in 2003, "When we first started recording, I played bass on about five songs, and I was holding the bass when the picture was taken, so everybody assumed I was the bass player. When we did shows, Bob would start playing [guitar] on "Walk Don't Run," "Perfidia," and some of those, then I would change off and finish the evening." During the 1960s Nokie played on nearly fifty albums, usually as the lead guitarist, on all The Ventures' best-known songs: "2000 Pound Bee" (the first song to use a fuzz box effect on a guitar), "Hawaii Five-O," "Fugitive," "Surf Rider," "Lullaby of the Leaves," "Yellow Jacket," "Walk Don't Run '64," "Sleep Walk," "Pedal Pusher," "Ghost Riders in the Sky," "Wipe Out" by the Surfaris, "Pipeline" by Spickard and Carmen, and "Driving Guitars," just to name a few.

Along with Nokie's impact on The Ventures, his guitar playing inspired numerous young people in the United States, Europe, and, especially Japan to take up electric guitar. The demand created a market for Ventures guitar-related products, to include their 1960s-era *Play Guitar with The Ventures* series in which the albums featured Ventures songs with out the respective musical parts. That four-album series was the first and only set of musical instruction records to ever make the pop album charts. Additionally, from 1962 to 1968, Nokie and The Ventures popularized Mosrite guitars designed and made by native Oklahomans whose parents were also part of the great Okie migration west, Semie Moseley (b. Durant, 1935), and his brother Andy Moseley (b. Durant, 1933). The Ventures signed an exclusive distribution agreement with Moseley, and featured the guitar on their album covers. The publicity spurred orders from around the world, especially Japan, for the Mosrites, many of which are now considered collector's items by guitar enthusiasts.

Edwards left The Ventures in 1968, replaced by Gerry McGee who has continued an amicable off-again, on-again musical relationship with the group. Ironically, The Ventures had their last major hit, the theme to the TV series *Hawaii Five-0*, on which McGee plays, after Nokie left the group. Legend holds that a Hawaiian disc-jockey decided to use the Ventures recording of the theme song to back ads for the program on local radio stations, and listeners kept calling to see who was playing the theme on the ad. Released as a single in 1969 and reaching #4 on the pop charts, the song practically pulling the TV show into popularity with it. While the song was the biggest instrumental hit of the year, it could not be nominated for a GRAMMY because it had actually been released in the year previous to its commercial success. Nonetheless, *Hawaii Five-0* and its theme song kept The Ventures sound in front of the American public until 1980 when just about anyone who watched television could sing at least the first few measures of the song's melody, and instantly visualize the Hawaiian natives rowing through the surf when the song played over the show's title credits.

After a four-year hiatus in which he recorded three solo albums, Nokie re-entered the fold from 1972 to 1984 when The Ventures recorded another twenty-plus albums both in the states and in Japan. After 1984, Edwards left for a steady career of solo engagements, but still joined The Ventures for occasional shows (and recordings) in the U.S. and Japan. Aside from his work with The Ventures, Nokie has performed as a guest on twenty-one CDs, and recorded thirteen solo CDs. His solo album in 2002, *Hitchhiker*, available through his website, is a lovely, lyrical album of instrumentals demonstrating Nokie's elegant control of the guitar. Also in 2002, Nokie made his first tour of Europe where The Ventures never traveled, even though they recorded several albums specifically for the European market. By 2003 The Ventures had sold more than 100 million albums worldwide. Additional honors the band received include two gold singles for "Walk, Don't Run," the only time a cover of a song by the same band has ever achieved that status (1960 and 1964); *Billboard*'s Favorite Single Instrumental Record for "Walk, Don't Run" in 1960; the First Gold Eight Track Award from Japan; and the only foreign group to ever receive the prestigious Japanese Grand Prix Award. Nokie received individual recognition in 1994 when his composition, "Ginza Lights," was voted the All-Time #1 Song in Japan, and he has also received a Platinum Sales Award for his "Surf Rider (a.k.a. Spudnick)" that appeared on the million-selling soundtrack for the film *Pulp Fiction* in 1994.

Also in early 2003, Nokie and The Ventures enjoyed a successful Caribbean cruise especially dedicated to Ventures fans, and he returned to Japan for another successful series of solo shows in March. He also had one solo CD in the can for a summer release, and plans to record another one over the summer built around a "nice arrangement of 'Both Sides Now'." Nokie and his wife, Judy, also planned to stage his annual "Nokiefest," properly billed as Nokie's Music, Car, and Bike Festival for July of 2003 in Harrisburg, Oregon. For those fans interested in Nokie Edwards' complete career, according to 2003 telephone interview, he has plans for an autobiography, and would be touring Japan with The Ventures in November, '03. Overall, Nokie shows little sign of slowing his performing and recording pace since the world's pop music audiences are always eager to see and hear one of rock and roll's true guitar legends. Like Bob Bogle who moved away from Oklahoma at a young age, the state's influence on Nokie may have been minimal, but like Merle Haggard whose parents also moved from Oklahoma during the 1930s, Nokie grew up around Okies and their music which imprinted a permanent twang on just about everything he has ever played. (HF)
www.nokie-edwards.com

Edwards, Frenchy "Stoney"

(b. December 24, 1929 - d. April 5, 1997)

With his strong baritone and obvious country accent, Stoney Edwards was one of a handful African-Americans, along with DeFord Bailey, Charley Pride, O.B. McClinton, and **Big Al Downing**, who made significant contributions to the country music field as a singer, songwriter, instrumentalist, and honky tonk stylist in the tradition of Lefty Frizzell. Born on a farm near Seminole, Oklahoma, Stoney was raised on bootlegging and country music. Of mixed ethnic background which he felt made him a perennial outsider, his father's ancestors were African-American, American Indian, and Irish, while his mother's background was African-American and American Indian. When Stoney was young, his father left home leaving Stoney's mother to raise the seven children. As a teenager, he became interested in country music, especially **Bob Wills** via radio station KVOO in nearby Tulsa, and by listening to the Grand Old Opry. His dream was to perform on the Opry, therefore, he taught himself to play the guitar and fiddle while in high school, mentored by his uncles who played in a local string band, and began experimenting with songwriting.

For a short period he was reunited with his father in Oklahoma City, where Stoney worked as a dishwasher. He later moved to California to live with an uncle and was employed at various jobs, including janitor, truck driver, and cowboy, which resulted in several moves around the country. In the early 1950s, he met Rosemary in California and they were married and settled in the San Francisco Bay area. With a family to support, Edwards retained only part-time interest in music as he worked for the next fifteen years as a blue-collar laborer. An accident in 1969 in Richmond, California, forced Stoney to change occupations. Because of severe carbon dioxide poisoning and a broken back, he turned exclusively to singing and songwriting. His first song, "A Two Dollar Toy," based on his little daughter's windup toy, became his first charted single reaching #68 on *Billboard*'s country charts in 1971. This convinced Stoney to become a serious musician, both in terms of writing and playing the guitar.

The next major turn of events included an invitation to open a concert in Oakland for his childhood idol, Bob Wills. An attorney in the audience heard Edwards' version of "Mama's Hungry Eyes," and suggested he contact Capitol Records and provide them a demo. Within a week, he had signed with Capitol, a recording company he remained with for six years, using the then unknown Asleep at the Wheel as one of his backup bands. He released six albums on Capitol, including *Stoney Edwards, A Country Singer*; *She's My Rock*, which produced a 1973 hit by the same title as the album and remained on the Top 20 country charts for nearly four months; *Down Home in the Country*; *Mississippi You're On My Mind*, from which the title track yielded another Top 20 single; *Blackbird*, and *Hank and Lefty Raised My Country Soul*. The latter album produced a single by the same name that became only a Top 40 hit, but over the years has become a country music classic. Additional Top 20 hits included "Don't Be Angry" and "I Bought the Shoes That Just Walked Out on Me."

The 1976 "Blackbird (Hold Your Head Up High)" song created enough controversy that Stoney was banned from some country music radio stations in the United States because of its racial connotations. In 1977, Capitol released Edwards because his albums were unprofitable, and he signed on in 1978 with JMI Records for whom he had a minor hit, "If I Had to Do it All Over Again," a major hit for **Roy Clark** in 1976. In 1981, he recorded *No Way to Drown a Memory* on the Music America/MCA label that produced a single of the same name that reached #53 on *Billboard*'s Hot 100.

During the 1980s, Edwards' health deteriorated because of diabetes and one source states that he lost a leg in a shooting accident, while another source says it was amputated
due to the diabetes. In 1986, he collaborated with several country stars to produce an album that featured Johnny Gimble, Ray Benson, Leon Rausch, and **Ralph Mooney**, another Oklahoman. *Just for Old Time's Sake*, recorded in 1991, was Edwards' first solo album in a decade, and featured several notable country artists, such as Johnny Gimble, Leon Rausch, and Ray Benson. Finally, in 1998, *Poor Folks Stick Together: The Best of Stoney Edwards* was released by the Razor and Tie label, and included a number of his best-known recordings, including "She's My Rock," "Hank and Lefty Raised My Country Soul," as well as "Head Bootlegger Man," a tribute to his early days in Oklahoma, and "I Bought the Shoes That Just Walked Out on Me," one of his personal favorites. Stoney's son, Kenneth, related a story about Stoney finding Lefty Frizzell sitting in a Nashville bar crying while listening to "Hank and Lefty Raised My Country Soul." Frizzell explained he didn't think anyone remembered or cared about him, and it took a black man to remind everyone. "It was a kind of off," the younger Edwards wrote in a 2003 e-mail, but still "a great compliment." Edwards died from stomach cancer on April 5, 1997 at the age of 67. (GC)

England, Tyler
(b. December 5, 1963)

Recognized as one of the fast rising country music stars of the 1990s, Gary Tyrone England was born in Oklahoma City. His grandfather, who played the harmonica, first introduced Tyler to country music by giving him his first guitar and teaching him the basic chords. Whenever Tyler and his grandfather would get together, Tyler would play the guitar and his grandfather,

the harmonica. While growing up, he immersed himself in the country classics by Roy Acuff, Hank Williams, and Lefty Frizzell, as well as contemporary artists, such as Don Williams, **Merle Haggard**, and Keith Whitley. During high school, he sang with the high school chorus (encouraged by his instructor, Winifred Rose), continued to learn the guitar, and played with a number of local bands. His first public performance was in a junior high talent show. While growing up in Oklahoma City, he worked at a variety of jobs, including restaurant busboy, grocery sacker, and an automotive paint plant.

After high school graduation, he attended Oklahoma State University in Stillwater, where he began playing sets at Aunt Molly's, a coffeehouse in the basement of the OSU Student Union. One night, Ted Larkin, a student, approached Ty and told him he should meet another musician attending OSU, **Garth Brooks**. He joined Garth in 1982, and the two began making music while rooming together. The two made a pact that if one of them found success, he would help the other. Apparently more interested in music than grades, Tyler's parents withdrew him from college and assisted him in finding a job back home in Oklahoma City. Tyler eventually completed his marketing degree through courses at night, while working a day job back with the automotive paint plant.

In 1988 England received a call from Garth Brooks, who had just signed with Capitol Records. Garth invited Tyler to join him in Nashville, where he became Garth's guitarist and backup vocalist on such albums as *No Fences*, *Ropin' the Wind*, and *The Chase*. For six years, he toured and recorded with Garth, and soon became a fan favorite. He nearly signed a contract with Liberty Records as a solo artist, but decided to go with RCA in 1995 with the assistance of Garth Fundis, one of RCA's producers.

Tyler's debut album in 1995 was self-titled, and from it came his first single, "Should've Asked Her Faster," which peaked at #3 on the country charts. His second single, "Smoke in Her Eyes," was less successful. His second album for RCA, *Two Ways to Fall*, was released in 1996.

After leaving RCA, Tyler returned to Oklahoma, where he decided to spend more time with his family, wife Shanna and four children, Aspen, Tyler, Levi, and Mattie. After four years, he was ready to record again, signing with Capitol for a 2000 release, *Highways & Dancehalls*, produced by his old friend Garth Brooks. He recently appeared on Garth's video, "Wrapped Up In You," made Oklahoma concert appearances in 2002 at Tumbleweeds (Stillwater), Simmons Theatre (Duncan), and the Oklahoma State Fair (Oklahoma City), continued touring through 2003. (GC)
www.tylerengland.com

Estes, Toni
(b. February 8, 1978)

Tulsa native Toni Estes is the brightest Oklahoma star on the R & B horizon with her soaring and sultry vocal skills. With a Grammy nomination for co-writing Whitney Houston's million selling single, "It's Not Right, but It's OK," and her tough, hybrid R & B meets rap album, *211*, released in 2000 on Priority Records, Toni is poised for a high profile career as a vocalist and songwriter. Growing up in a house filled with music, Toni's father, Billy, is long time session drummer who has worked primarily on commercials and industrial recordings in Tulsa. Her mother, Lachelle (Owens) Estes, reportedly has a fine singing voice, and her brother is a budding record producer. Estes began appearing in television commercials at six as a result of her father's work in that industry, opened for Natalie Cole and Gladys Knight when she was only fourteen, and was in chorus both at Tulsa Booker T. Washington and Tulsa Central High Schools. Through a friend in Tulsa, Toni met producer Jon-John, known for his work with Kenneth "Babyface" Nelson. After hearing her tape, Nelson encouraged Toni to move to Los Angeles after graduating from Tulsa Central High School to begin singing demos and support vocals. This process got her noticed in the highly competitive L.A. music scene and, at seventeen-years-old, she was signed to a major label.

In 1997, Toni provided backup vocals for R & B artists Jon B., Immature, and Laurneá. Although an album was not released through the major label contract, she did connect with Rodney Jerkins who was writing songs and producing for Whitney Houston. The professional relationship grew when Jerkins invited Toni to write songs for a new Whitney Houston album. Estes wrote eight songs, "It's Not Right, but It's Ok" being one of them, and the producers used Toni to record the songs because her voice sounds similar to Houston's. Along with "It's Not Right," Houston picked two more of Toni's songs, "Get It Back," and "If I Told You That" for her 1998 album *My Love Is Your Love*. Not only did Estes get co-writing credits, she also sang background vocals on the three songs. When an album still did not materialize for Estes, she gained a release from her contract and began looking for a new deal that she ultimately found at Priority Records, a label known primarily for rap artists. This led to the inclusion of her song "Hot" on the *Next Friday* soundtrack in 1999, and her subsequent album, *211*, named after the address of the north Tulsa home where she grew up.

Toni Estes describes her sound as "hard core R & B with some real singing on top." Listing influences such as old school artists like Maze and Bobby Womack, the album features several slow jams such as "I Adore," "Let Me Know," and "She's Already," which exhibit Toni's powerful R & B ballad abilities. She co-wrote eight of the songs on the album and collaborated on the album with a number of well-known producers such as Teddy Riley, Warryn Campbell, and Teddy

Bishop. Her brother Angelo, then seventeen, produced two of the songs on *211*.

In 2002, Estes was nominated as Tulsa's "Best R&B" act by the *Tulsa World*'s annual Spot Awards. As of 2003, she lived in Tulsa where she was writing songs for her next album in collaboration with Warryn Campbell, Jaccspade, and rapper Heavy D. In the fall of 2003, Toni performed regularly (with her father on drums) at the Tulsa night club, Suede. Her next album, on an as-yet-to-be-named record label, was due in spring, 2004.
www.toniestes.com

Fisher, Shug
(b. September 26, 1907 – d. March 16, 1984)

A member of the Sons of the Pioneers on three different occasions, cast member of two of the earliest country music radio shows (*WWVA Wheeling Jamboree* and *WLW Boone County Jamboree*), and one of the first to use a stand up bass in country music, George Clinton Fisher was born in Tabler, Oklahoma, a tiny hamlet east of Chickasha. He received his nickname "Shug" from his mother, who considered him such a sweet baby. His father was Scotch-Irish, whereas his mother was one-quarter Choctaw. At age ten, the family moved to Pittsburgh County, Oklahoma, in a covered wagon.

Shug became a talented instrumentalist, learning the mandolin, fiddle, and guitar while still a teenager. His first instrument was the mandolin, for which he traded a saddle blanket, but, by age sixteen, he traded it for a fiddle that he carried around in a pillowcase because he could not afford a case. Shug discovered that his father could play fiddle, therefore, he learned the guitar to back his father at local square dances.

In 1924, Shug attended a medicine show and was excited about the "Toby Show" in which a comedian with red wig and blacked-out tooth performed. Thereafter, he was certain that comedy and music went well together, and decided to make the two his career.

Shug and his father moved to California in 1925, and he worked various jobs in the oil fields, while landing a job on radio station KMS in Fresno. He then appeared on the Hollywood Breakfast Club show, where he was approached by Tom Murray to join his group, the Hollywood Hillbillies. He later joined another group, the Beverly Hill Billies, which were performing in San Francisco.

In 1935, Fisher teamed with Roy Faulkner, "The Lonesome Cowboy," broadcasting from the first of the X-Border stations (XERA) in Del Rio, Texas, owned and operated by Dr. J. R. Brinkley, who advertised his various medical remedies. While on tour in Iowa, he met Hugh Cross, composer of "Back to the Old Smokey Mountains," and the two formed a duet called Hugh and Shug's Radio Pals. The duet became regulars on the *WWVA Wheeling Jamboree* and the *WLW Boone County Jamboree* during the 1930s.

At the outbreak of World War II, Shug returned to Los Angeles, where he worked for the Lockheed Aircraft plant in Burbank, and entertained defense workers for the Victory Committee. Upon the invitation of Pat Brady, Shug joined the Sons of the Pioneers in 1943 as bass player and comedian, appearing on their Lucky U Ranch radio program until 1946. For the next three years, he played with Stuart Hamblen, but returned to the Sons of the Pioneers when Brady left the group to join Roy Rogers for movie and television work. During this stint with the Sons of the Pioneers, Shug and the group performed at Carnegie Hall in 1951. A year later, he was back with Hamblen.

In 1953, Shug met Ken Curtis, best known for his role as Festus on the *Gunsmoke* television series, and worked with him in movies, television, and radio for the next two years. Two years later, he rejoined the Sons of the Pioneers for the third time and stayed with them until 1959, during which he appeared on several of their RCA recordings, including *Western Classics*. He then joined Red Foley's Ozark Jubilee cast for a brief period in the early 1960s.

In addition to his music, Shug appeared in sixteen movies with Roy Rogers, played the role of Shorty Kellums in nineteen episodes of *The Beverly Hillbillies* television series, and performed on several *Gunsmoke* shows with his old friend, Ken Curtis, who was at his side when Shug died in March of 1984, after a long illness. (GC)

The Five Americans
John Durrill (b. 1940), **Norman Ezell** (b. 1943), **Jim Grant** (b. 1943)
Mike Rabon (b. 1943), **Jimmy Wright** (b. 1950)

Originally formed in Durant at Southeastern Oklahoma State University in 1962 as The Mutineers, The Five Americans became nationally known in the 1960s for their Top 40 hits, "I See the Light," "Zip Code," "Sound of Love," "Evol-Not Love," and "Western Union." The latter reached #6 on the *Billboard* charts and #3 on the *Cash Box* list. Rabon, lead guitarist, vocalist, and leader of the group, was born in Port Arthur, Texas, but moved to Hugo at one month of age, while Grant (bassist) was born in Hugo, Wright (drums) in Durant, and Durrill (keyboards) in Bartlesville. The only non-Oklahoman was Ezell (guitar), who was born in Albuquerque, New Mexico.

After playing local venues in and around Durant until the summer of 1964, Rabon proposed the band play some gigs in Dallas in order to pay for tuition the next college semester. In Dallas, the group developed a local following in such nightspots as the Pirate's Nook, where they were noticed by John Abdnor, president of a local record label. Abdnor began to support the group, allowing them to write songs and providing space for them to practice. In the summer of 1965, Abdnor Records released one of the group's original songs, "I See the Light," which reached Top 20 on the *Billboard* charts. This was followed by their biggest hit, "Western Union," co-written by Rabon, Ezell, and Durrill and based on a Western Union telegram sign. The success of "Western Union" prompted invitations to appear twice on *American Bandstand,* four times on *Where the Action Is,* and as guests on *The Steve Allen Show.* The song was recently featured in the Tom Cruise film, *Vanilla Sky,* remains a favorite on classic oldies radio, and reached the one million air play status as certified by BMI in 1998.

After cracking the Top 40 with "Sound of Love" and "Zip Code," the group disbanded in 1969 after their release of "7:30 Guided Tour" barely reached *Billboard*'s Top 100. Rabon later released an album and single on the UNI label, but the company's attention was devoted to its only other signee, Elton John. Rabon organized a later band called Michael Rabon and Choctaw, which successfully toured the Southwest in the mid-1970s, but returned to college for his Master's degree and currently teaches music in Hugo, his hometown. Grant launched his own logo company in Dallas, while Ezell is a teacher and preacher in northern California and Wright plays on commercial jingles, working out of his hometown of Durant. Durrill went on to play organ and write songs for The Ventures, led by Oklahoman **Nokie Edwards**, born in Lahoma. Durrill's most successful songs were "Dark Lady" recorded by Cher, "Misery and Gin" recorded by Merle Haggard, and "Charlotte's Web," recorded by the Statler Brothers.

The Five Americans recorded four albums in the 1960s, including *I See the Light* (1966), *Western Union/Sound of Love* (1967), *Progressions* (1967), and *Now and Then* (1969). The *I See the Light* compilation consisted of twelve tracks with ten original songs written by Rabon, Durrill, and Ezell, including "The Train" and "Good Times." The *Western Union* album featured twelve tracks with nine co-written by Durrill, Rabon, and Ezell. Eight of the ten tracks on *Progressions* were co-written by Rabon, Durrill, and Ezell, including "Zip Code," "Stop Light", and "Con Man." Finally, *Now and Then* was a nineteen track album with fourteen of the contributions co-written by members of the group. According to their website, the latter album was sold in 1985 to Sundazed, an overseas company, without knowledge of the group and the original members have received no royalties on the sales. Not only that, but due to a bad management contract the group when signed when they were young and naïve about the music industry the group could not even call itself the Five Americans if they got back together.

Once all of the management legalities were sorted out, all five original members reunited in 2002 to rerecord all of their 1960s hits. The motivation behind the re-recordings, according to Rabon, was based on the use of "Western Union" in the *Vanilla Sky* movie. Paramount Studios bought the right to use the song from Sundazed Records, which owns the original masters. By rerecording their songs in the same studio with all original members and the same engineer, the group now owns a second original master of all their hits. Rabon states that one cannot tell the difference between the 1967 and 2002 masters, and planned a 2003 release of those re-recorded songs as well as some lost masters that were never released. In 2003, the group performed at a sold out show for the annual Southeastern

Oklahoma State University Arts Gala scholarship benefit (minus drummer Jim Wright who had a scheduling conflict), their first public appearance since 1988. Several gigs were planned throughout 2003 at Six Flags amusement parks across the country, and ocean cruises with a rock music theme.

Known for Rabon's lead vocal work, the group's clear vocal harmonies, and Durrill's outstanding keyboard work, The Five Americans' pop rock sounds, sometimes bordering on bubblegum, presaged the garage band era of the 1990s with ex-rockabilly star Dale Hawkins producing much of their better work. (GC)

Flaming Lips
(Formed in 1983, Oklahoma City, OK)

Having flourished under the leadership of Wayne M. Coyne (b. March 17, 1965, Pittsburgh, PA) for almost twenty years of sonic experiments, rambling extended tracks of mythical and mystical musings, and occasional bouts with commercial success, The Flaming Lips are Oklahoma's most important contemporary rock group. Born in Pennsylvania but raised in northwest Oklahoma City, Wayne Coyne grew up in a large family of

The Flaming Lips, left to right: Steven Drozd, Wayne Coyne, and Michael Ivins

"four brothers, a sister, a dog, two cats, and a snake," according to the band's website. Along with nurturing his ample artistic talents as a painter in high school, Wayne began working as a fry-cook at the local Long John Silver's, a job he kept for several years until signing with Warner Brothers records in 1990. After buying his first guitar at age fifteen, he allegedly stole a collection of musical instruments from an area church hall and convinced his brother Mark and bassist Michael Ivins (b. Omaha, Nebraska, March 17, 1963) to start the band (or so goes one of the legends about the group). The group began their career with an intentionally nonsensical name that refers to either a porn film, an obscure drug reference, or a dream in which a fiery Virgin Mary kissed Wayne in the backseat of his car, all depending on the origin of the story (see a pattern of near mythic yarn-spinning proportions developing here?). After wearing out (or frustrating) a long line of drummers, percussionist Richard English agreed to take on the task of keeping time for the group's initial outings locally in Norman and Oklahoma City. The group released their self-titled debut, a five-song EP on green vinyl, through their own label, Lovely Sorts of Death, in 1985. The album is an earnest first rock album that brought them to the attention of college radio nationwide as a result of its reissue on Pink Dust Records, and sounds like a punk rock group playing Pink Floyd songs as the group wrestled with what kind identity they would have.

Soon after the EP was released, Mark Coyne left the group to get married and Wayne took over the lead vocal role. As a trio, the group released *Hear It Is* in 1986, which hinted at the band's stylistic future on songs that featured Wayne Coyne's sincerely off key vocals and personal lyrics, fairly straight ahead garage rock songs founded in The Who and Stooges, and the occasional noisy ramble by the whole group. Fans can certainly discern Coyne's penchant for musical drama in the album's songs, as well as the early signals of his interest in layering echo-laden vocals and esoteric sounds on multi-tracks for an ethereal effect. In 1987, the group released *Oh My Gawd...The Flaming Lips*, featuring more refined developments of the style on *Hear It Is*, as well as examples of Coyne's interest in sound effects and "noise" as part of his sonic soundscape. The influence of classic rock such as the Beatles and The Who is also readily apparent on songs such as "Everything's Exploding." The band's upbringing in Oklahoma City where mainstream rock has long dominated rock radio might be a partial explanation for this element of their sound. Additionally, close listeners to songs like "One Million Billionth of a Millisecond" can hear riffs and vocals that are eerie harbingers of the future sounds of Seattle groups like Nirvana. While touring in support of the album as an opening act for the Butthole Surfers, the Lips met Jonathan Donahue in Buffalo, New York. After a jam session with Donahue, he and Coyne became friends and Donahue joined the group as their sound technician.

After recording 1988's *Telepathic Surgery*, a continuation of the studio experimentation with multi-tracking and further development of Coyne as a singer and songwriter, English left the band leaving Coyne and Ivins. The group added drummer Nathan Roberts, and Donahue became a full-time member of the group under the pseudonym Dingus. The new lineup recorded 1990's *In a Priest Driven Ambulance*, marking the band's evolution into a very competent rock band with more to offer than studio experiments, musical kookiness, and classic rock references. The album also continued Coyne's long interest in religious imagery and plenty of guitar mania. After *In A Priest Driven Ambulance*, which bolstered the Lips' solidly entrenched cult status on college radio, the band signed a major label deal with Warner Brothers, and released *Hit to Death in the Future Head* that outsold all the Lips' albums before it with the backing of the corporate music industry. The contract also allowed Wayne to purchase the first fireproof house in Oklahoma City that became the Flaming Lips Compound where Coyne still lives. After *Hit to Death*, Donahue left to focus on his group, Mercury Rev, and drummer Roberts left shortly after that.

In 1993, the Lips released *Transmissions from the Satellite Heart* with new guitarist Ronald Jones and drummer Steven Drozd (b. Houston, TX, June 11, 1969). The group supported the album by playing the second stage on the Lollapalooza tour, but the album did not sell well until the single "Don't Use Jelly" surprisingly found its way on to the pop charts after becoming a nationwide college radio favorite. As a result of the unlikely success of their album selling beyond their (and Warner Brothers') wildest expectations, the group appeared everywhere from an arena tour opening for Candlebox to a lip-synched performance of the hit on *Beverly Hills 90210*. Creating new found pop expectations for the band, the Lips pursued their own vision with the eight-song compilation, *Providing Needles for Your Balloons* (Warner Bros., 1994), consisting of live recordings, four-track demos, a Christmas song, and a radio broadcast on KJ-103 in Oklahoma City. Then, baring the process behind their hit, the band released a three-song EP, *Turn It On*, in 1995 that included the demo version of the successful single.

In spite of the success of *Transmissions*, the Lips did not try to replicate the album with another hit, but continued their exploration of the studio with multi-layered pop on *Clouds Taste Metallic* that is roundly felt by critics as the band's most mature and important work up until 1995. Elevated comparisons to the epic Beach Boys' album *Pet Sounds* started to roll forth from the rock press, and song titles on the album such as "This Here Giraffe" and "Christmas at the Zoo" do not hinder the analogies at all. In 1996, the band frayed at the ends when Jones vanished on a spiritual journey from which he did not return, Drozd's hand was rendered inoperative for a time when he was bitten by a spider (later memorialized in "The Spiderbite Song"), and Ivins was the victim of a strange hit-and-run accident when another vehicle's wheel came loose and hit Ivins' car, trapping him inside (mentioned in the same song). Also in '96, Coyne started his famous "parking lot experiments" in Oklahoma City where he produced about forty tapes and invited various people to bring their cars to the lot where they would all play the tapes simultaneously in the cavernous confines of the parking garage. This led to similar displays with multiple boom boxes around the country where Wayne passed out cassette players of all types and had audience members start tapes on cue. Subsequently, Coyne talked Warner Brothers into letting him try one of the most experimental audio projects since John Lennon convinced George Martin to include Revolution #9 on the Beatles' so-called *White Album*.

Zaireeka (Warner Bros., 1997) is a four CD set designed to be played in four different CD players at the same time, individually, and/or in any combination thereof, and was overwhelmingly approved of by rock critics who were probably more stunned by the whole thing than able to dissect it with any relevance whatsoever. At the same time they had been working on *Zaireeka*, the band had been developing songs for their 1999 release, *The Soft Bulletin*, a peaceful and lush album sounding like Neil Young backed by the Salsoul Orchestra. Coyne's vocals continue as a warble, his lyrics are introspectively deep without losing their sense of humor, and the heavy use of synthesized strings often make the record sound like a soul or disco album of the 1970s. On *The Soft Bulletin*, the group also continues to borrow riffs, consciously or unconsciously, from all the rock and pop that has drifted through their ears since their childhood. Beach Boys critical comparisons abounded as Coyne somehow builds up to almost replicating the delicacy of Brian Wilson's most inspired moments while maintaining the Lips' own powerful originality in a song like "Buggin'." Following *The Soft Bulletin*, the group worked on soundtrack music for a documentary on Oklahomans who catch giant flathead catfish using their arms for bait. The film, *Okie Noodling*, produced an entire album for The Lips called *The Southern Oklahoma Cosmic Trigger Contest*, consisted of music Wayne terms "epic country and western," further adding the album features primarily, "harmonica, banjo, upright bass, strings, and occasional hiccups." At the same time, the group also worked on songs for a holiday score called *Christmas on Mars*, which Wayne dubbed "cosmic and religious," and began working on their 2002 release, *Yoshimi Battles the Pink Robots*, which he says was influenced by both of the other projects.

According to Coyne, *Yoshimi's* "theme of sunshine funerals will render its listeners powerless to study or analyze it, and enable them to sit back and –hopefully for a couple of minutes at a time – just simply be ... entertained." While the album is not a concept album per se, it does have several "sound story" compositions connected throughout the record and loosely based on the fictional character of a singer, Yoshimi, who fights robots that are programmed with synthetic emotions. Other songs on the album further Coyne's examination of life's intricacies and dichotomies in songs such as "All We Have is Now" and "Do You Realize??" To derive one's happiness only from specific moments in time is "to miss out on the cosmic accident that is all of life's moments," according to Coyne, and the inspiration for "Ego Tripping at the Gates of Hell." While early Lips material seemed to always be some derivative of what had gone before it, *Yoshimi* is much more of an original and mature artistic production than it is an obvious result of its musical forebears.

The Flaming Lips have also become well known for their elaborate stage shows that exhibit Wayne Coyne's enduring influence of the Butthole Surfers who also provided over-the-top, multi-media stage shows during the 1980s and early 1990s. In their 2002 *Yoshimi* tour, the Lips used the standard rock format of bass, drums, and guitar, but also added several sequencers and other machines. On stage Wayne and other band members have at their disposal several bags of glitter, a dry ice machine, four huge disco balls in the back of the stage, another disco ball hanging from the ceiling, a dozen beach-ball-sized balloons they throw to the audience, and three people standing on stage in stuffed animal costumes resembling public television's Teletubbies. In the tradition of both the Surfers and 1960s psychedelic rock concerts, the Flaming Lips project bizarre combinations of videos on the screen behind them, to include Shannon

Doherty introducing the band on their *90210* appearance, a short film featuring Yoshimi of the Boredoms fighting Japanese girls in school-girl outfits, and a sequence of a naked woman playing Frisbee at a nudist colony. Along with their new songs, the group continues to pull out old favorites such as "Waiting for Superman," and the hit casual fans expect, "She Don't Use Jelly." In August of 2002, the group worked with noted video director Mark Pellington on the video for "Do You Realize??" in which Coyne, clad in all white, strums a white guitar while tutu-wearing dancing girls and two giant rabbits hover about him in Las Vegas. In the fall of 2002, along with their own live performances, the Lips toured as the backing band for alternative folk rock hero Beck. Also in the fall of 2002, *Yoshimi* found its way to the top of the college radio charts, and was a finalist in the second annual Shortlist Prize for Achievement in Music, an award given to an album of artistic merit that has sold less than 500,000 copies.

In September of 2002, Restless and Rykodisc records released two deluxe, multi-disc packages providing a comprehensive look at Flaming Lips material from 1983 to 1991, *The Shambolic Birth* and *Early Life of the Flaming Lips.* Comprised of the band's debut EP, first four full-length albums, and a wealth of previously unreleased or hard-to-find material, *Finally the Punk Rockers are Taking Acid 1983-1988*, and *The Day They Shot a Hole in the Jesus Egg 1989-1991*, are essential releases for Flaming Lips completists. All previously issued material was re-mastered by the Lips' long-time producer Dave Fridmann, while the band's bassist, Michael Ivins, and Wayne Coyne wrote extensive liner notes for each release. In October of 2002, the group recorded the video for "Yoshimi Battles the Pink Robots, Pt. 1" in the Samurai Japanese Restaurant and Saki House in Oklahoma City. The group also appeared on national television several times in the fall and winter of 2002, to include NBC television's *Late Night with Conan O'Brien*, the WB Network's *Charmed*, CBS television's *Late Late Show with Craig Kilborn*, and PBS's *Austin City Limits.*

Through the winter of 2002 and 2003, the group played a series of dates in Spain, Scotland, and England, with a New Year's Eve show sandwiched in between at Chicago's Metro. To coincide with the British appearances, the group released two different CDs of Lips music, plus a DVD. British CD 1 included the *Yoshimi* album and a couple of remixes, British CD 2 contained the *Yoshimi* album and two different versions of songs from the CD, and the DVD included the *Yoshimi* album's audio, the video for the single, a tune from the *Okie Noodling* soundtrack, and a track from the *Christmas on Mars* soundtrack. By the time of its release in Britain, the album had garnered the following accolades: *Uncut* magazine's #1 album of the year, *Mirror* magazine's #1 album of the year, *Mojo* magazine's #2 album of the year, *Esquire* magazine's top 6 albums of the year, *Record Collector* albums of the year, *Time Out* critics' album of the year, *Time Out* readers' album of the year, *GQ* albums of the year, and several other top ten and best of lists from around the world. The recognition crested in February when the group won a Grammy Award for Best Rock Instrumental Performance via

Yoshimi's "Approaching Pavonis Mons by Balloon (Utopia Planitia)." When all-everything rock group Coldplay performed in Oklahoma City that same month, singer Chris Martin changed the lyrics of the band's "Everything's Not Lost" to "because you live in the same town as the Flaming Lips, the greatest band in the world."

Through March of 2003, the Lips toured Europe, playing Austria, Germany, Sweden, Holland, France, Italy, and Greece, among other countries, and followed that up with a steady stream of performances across the U.S. and Canada in major markets. In May, 2003, the group released the *Fight Test* EP CD, and a "Fight Test" 7" vinyl picture disc. The EP covers Beck and Kylie Minogue songs, and includes two new songs. The CD version includes two videos, one for "Fight Test," and the other a trailer for the band's feature length film, *Christmas on Mars*, scheduled for a Christmas 2003 release.

The Lips' website is one of the most interesting band sites on the Internet by featuring Flaming Lips videos, live performances dating back to 1983, and extensive press clippings, interviews, hard-to-tell-if-they-are-tongue-in-cheek bios, and authorial musings by Wayne Coyne. With nearly twenty years of a music career behind them, and nothing but critical raves surrounding their every move contemporarily, The Flaming Lips are more proof that Oklahoma's supposedly isolated environment can produce innovative and enduring music for the world, and the musicians do not have to leave the state to create it. (HF)
www.flaminglips.com

Flash Terry
(b. June 17, 1934)

Born into a musical family in the small country town of Inola, Oklahoma, about 15 miles east of Tulsa, Flash Terry started playing guitar professionally at age seventeen. His first gig was with Jimmy "Cry Cry" Hawkins and the Teardrops in Tulsa. After several years as a back up musician in the 1950s, Flash began recording with Tulsa recording pioneer, Hugh Whitlow, in 1958. The collaboration produced Terry's first and most well known recording, "Her Name is Lou," which was an R & B chart hit for Indigo/Lavendar Records.

Contemporarily, Flash Terry represents the 1940s heyday sound of horn pumped R&B that presaged the rock and roll movement of the 1950s. He has supported blues stalwarts Aaron "T-Bone" Walker and Little Johnny Taylor, as well as R&B vocal groups such as The Impressions. His music has been released on a number of specialty and collector labels such as Relic, Wheel, Indigo, and Lavendar. Flash's songs have also been included on retrospectives of 1950s and 1960s R&B recordings, to include *All Night Long They Play the Blues* (Specialty), *West Coast Modern Blues: The 60s* (P-Vine), *West Coast Winners* (Moonshine), and *Cruisin' the Drag* (Wheel).

In 1966, Flash began a thirty-year career as a bus driver for the Tulsa Metropolitan Transit Authority while continuing to play locally in Tulsa and regionally with his group, the Uptown Blues Band. In 1972, he toured nationally to support Bobby "Blue" Bland. In 1974, Flash recorded an album for **Leon Russell**'s Shelter Records, at the Church Studio in Tulsa, which was finally released by Visionary Records as *Enough Troubles of My Own* in 1986. Visionary also released *A Night on the Town* in 1988, and the independent *Live at the El' Ray with Flash Terry and Sam Franklin* was available by 1992. In 1994, the Oklahoma Jazz Hall of Fame inducted Flash in the blues category and has placed his early records on permanent display in the Greenwood Cultural Center and Jazz Hall of Fame in downtown Tulsa.

In the late 1990s, Flash released two solo albums on his own JFT label: *Backdoor Man* (1996) and *Mr. Bluesman* (1998). *Mr. Bluesman* features some tracks featuring **Bob Wills**' steel guitarist Leon McAuliffe, and features appearances by **Tulsa Sound** veteran Carl Radle. The album included recordings from the Shelter Studio in Tulsa, now known as **Steve Ripley**'s Church Studio, the Rogers State College (now Rogers State University) studios in the defunct **Hank Thompson** School of Country Music, and the Lodestone Studio in Broken Arrow. Highlights on the album include the funky "Open Your Heart," and several songs that exhibit Flash's fine guitar work ("Enough Troubles of My Own" and "Call Me Anything"). An extra bonus is "Milk Cow Blues" featuring McAuliffe on steel guitar. In 1998, Flash Terry and the Uptown Blues Band received a "State of Excellence" award as "Oklahoma's Favorite Blues Band" from then Oklahoma governor Henry Bellmon. Flash Terry has also been actively involved in charitable community causes throughout his career, often playing for benefits and fundraisers for organizations like Special Olympics of Tulsa, Junior League of Tulsa, Women's Business League, the Helena Blues Society, and Fire, Accident, and Trauma Victims in Need of Assistance. Major feature articles about his career have appeared in *Living Blues, Juke Blues, Blues Gazette*, and *Real Blues Magazine*. He continued playing regionally with the Uptown Horns at many concerts, club dates, and several festivals, and was an annual part of the Dusk 'til Dawn Blues Festival in Rentiesville from 1990 to 2003 where his group often backed up the headliner of the show, after Flash played a complete set earlier in the evening. Recorded in 1997 and released commercially in 2002 on **DC**

Minner's Texas Road Recordings, *Guitar Showdown at Dusk 'til Dawn Blues Festival* features Flash on Willie Dixon's "Back Door Man," and a song written by and featuring the guitar style Flash learned from his father, "More and More." Until announcing his retirement in 2002, Flash and his full-throttled horn section were probably the only group in Oklahoma that could really bring back the brass and reed bolstered R & B of **Lowell Fulson** and **Roy Milton**. That group, included Kevin Pharris on rhythm guitar, Ron Martin on bass, Harry Williams on drums, Daryl McGee on trombone and horns, and Mike Sanders on trumpet and horns. In 2003, Friends of Oklahoma Music inducted Flash Terry into the Oklahoma Music Hall of Fame. (HF)
www.flashterry.com

Frazier, Dallas
(b. October 27, 1939)

One of the most prolific songwriters in the 1960s and 1970s, including such songs as "Alley Oop," "Mohair Sam," "There Goes My Everything," and "Elvira," singer and songwriter Dallas Frazier was born in Spiro, Oklahoma, a community of around 2,000 people located in far eastern Oklahoma near the Arkansas border. Dallas' family moved to California when he was about four years old, and settled on a ranch near Bakersfield, a hotbed of country music. One of Dallas' songs, "California Cottonfields," recorded by **Merle Haggard**, realistically portrays the family move to California. He attended elementary school in East Bakersfield and graduated from McFarland High School in 1957. In 1988, Dallas received a bachelor's degree in Christian education from Emmanuel Bible College, and a graduate degree in theology from the same institution in 1989.

By age twelve, Dallas had become proficient on several instruments, including the guitar, trumpet, and piano. He won a children's talent contest in 1952 hosted by Ferlin Husky, then a Bakersfield disc jockey. Held at Bakersfield's Rainbow Gardens dance hall, Dallas sang a Little Jimmy Dickens song that so impressed Husky that he signed him to sing in his traveling band, the Termites. Husky said that Dallas was "something special" and was as "cute as a bug and clear as a bell." Dallas moved in with the Husky family and roomed with another Oklahoman, **Tommy Collins**. It was Collins who taught Dallas his first chords on a $10 guitar.

Husky introduced Frazier to Capitol Records executive Ken Nelson in 1953, but it was not until 1954 that Nelson signed him to a recording contract. At age fourteen, he published his first song and recorded his first Capitol single, "Ain't You Had No Bringin' Up at All." It was followed by another one of his songs, "Love Life at 14." At about the same time, he started singing off and on with Cousin Herb Henson on a local television show.

At age fifteen, Dallas joined Cliffie Stone's *Hometown Jamboree*, a Los Angeles-based television show, often teaming up for duets with another native Oklahoman, **Molly Bee**. Stone, who headed the country music operations for Capitol Records, had been impressed with Dallas and made him a regular cast member on the show. After four years the show folded, and Dallas married his girlfriend, Sharon Carpani.

During his early singing career, Frazier was writing songs, and in 1960, his pop novelty tune, "Alley Oop," recorded by the Hollywood Argyles, hit #1 on the pop charts and eventually sold more than a million copies. He wrote the song while working at a cotton gin in Pond, California. Gary Paxton, member of the Hollywood Argyles, met Dallas at a filling station at two in the morning when he had stopped to ask for directions to Hollywood. The story goes that Dallas, after getting off work, led Gary into Hollywood, and the two of them hit it off. The song was covered by such diverse groups as the Beach Boys, Dante and the Evergreens, Brian Poole and the Tremeloes, Bonzo Dog Doo-Dah Band, and the Dynasores. Following this major hit, Dallas was concerned that the music business was a negative influence, and he and Sharon moved in the late 1950s and early 1960s to various locales, including Phoenix, then back to McFarland, California (where Dallas' family lived), and on to Portland, Oregon, where he decided to renew his songwriting career when Husky came through town on a concert tour.

In 1963, Dallas and Sharon moved to Nashville, where he began to work for Husky's publishing house, continued to perform on radio and television, and expanded his songwriting list. He had a minor hit with Husky in 1964, "Timber I'm Falling," and then scored in 1965 when Charlie Rich and Peggy Lee recorded his "Mohair Sam," who he had penned for Jim Reeves' Acclaim Music.

After moving to Blue Crest Music publishing, Frazier wrote three of the best-selling songs in 1966: Jack Greene's "There Goes My Everything" (#1), which also captured the CMA Song of the Year Award in 1967, Connie Smith's "Ain't Had No Lovin'" (# 3), and George Jones' "I'm a People" (Top 10), all on the country charts. Finally, he penned and recorded "Elvira," which would become a #1 hit for the Oak Ridge Boys in 1981, and also recorded by Kenny Rogers and Rodney Crowell. The Oak Ridge Boys recording sold a million copies and was nominated for the CMA Song of the Year in 1981 and 1982. As an aside, a street named Elvira in east Nashville gave Dallas the idea for the song.

In 1967, George Jones scored with two more of Dallas' songs, including "I Can't Get There from Here" and "If My Heart Had Windows," later recorded by Patty Loveless. Moreover, Engelbert Humperdinck had a huge hit with his recording of Dallas' "There Goes My Everything." Other artists to record this song included Elvis Presley and Jack Greene. As a result, Dallas received in 1967 a host of awards, including the BMI Certificate of Achievement for "There Goes My Everything" in both pop and country categories, Songwriter of the Year by the Nashville Songwriters Association, CMA and *Music City News* awards for Song of the Year, and Grammy Award for Best Country Song. According to Dallas, "There Goes My Everything" was inspired by the divorce of a close friend.

Success for Dallas' songwriting talents continued in 1968 with George Jones recording "Say It's Not You" (Top 10), Connie Smith's "Run Away Little Tears" (Top 10), and O.C. Smith's "Son of Hickory Holler's Tramp" (Top 40 on the pop charts), which was also made a country hit by Johnny Darrell. Moreover, George Jones paid tribute to Dallas' songwriting talents with his *Sings the Songs of Dallas Frazier* in 1968. Finally, Merle Haggard used three of Dallas' songs on his *The Legend of Bonnie and Clyde* album, and Willie Nelson and Brenda Lee both recorded "Johnnie One-Time."

The next year also proved productive for Dallas with two Charley Pride hits, "All I Have to Offer You (Is Me)" and "I'm So Afraid of Loving You Again," as well as another hit for Jack Greene, "Back in the Arms of Love." In 1969, he won the CMA Triple Play Award for the three hits. By the end of the decade, Dallas had written more than 300 songs.

During the 1970s, songs continued to flow from Dallas' pen, including Charley Pride's "I Can't Believe That You've Stopped Lovin' Me," Jack Greene's "Lord Is That Me," Diana Trask's "Beneath Still Waters," Connie Smith's "If It Ain't Love (Let's Leave It Alone), Jerry Lee Lewis' "Touching Home," Elvis Presley's "Where Did They Go Lord," Johnny Russell's "Baptism of Jesse Taylor," **Carl Smith's** "The Way I Lose My Mind," and Tanya Tucker's first #1 hit, "What's Your Mama's Name." This string of songs earned Dallas' induction into the Nashville Songwriters Association International Hall of Fame in 1976. By this time, he had signed as a writer with Acuff-Rose publishing house.

By the 1980s, Dallas' songwriting credits begin to decline, although Emmylou Harris scored a #1 hit with "Beneath Still Waters," Gene Watson topped the charts with "Fourteen Carat Mind," and the aforementioned success of "Elvira" by the Oak Ridge Boys which also crossed over as a Top 5 pop hit. Several of the new country artists also began recording Dallas' songs, including George Strait's "Honky Tonk Down Stairs," Patty Loveless' "If My Heart Had Windows," a song Dallas wrote for his wife Sharon, and Randy Travis' "When Your World Was Turning for Me." In 1982, Dallas was again honored as *Music City News* Songwriter of the Year, and won the Robert J. Burton BMI Award for "Elvira." Frazier is one of several Mercury Records recording artists who is featured on *50 Years of Country Music From Mercury*, a 1995 collection of seventy-three tracks, on which he performs "Shooby Dooby Sue."

In 1988, Dallas retired from songwriting and decided to pursue a career in the ministry, although he has publicly stated that he may write again: "I know I have some things left to say. I feel a stirring in me." (GC)

Fulson, Lowell
(b. March 31, 1921 – d. March 6, 1999)

As the author of classic blues songs such as "Everyday I Have the Blues," "Three O'Clock Blues," and "Reconsider Baby," Lowell Fulson's brand of post-war urban blues helped define the West Coast blues style in the late 1940s with the addition of a horn section to the standard electric blues combo of bass, guitar, and drums. Born in Tulsa, Oklahoma, to parents of Choctaw and African-American descent, Fulson grew up around Ada, Oklahoma in south central Oklahoma. Lowell's grandfather played violin, and two of his uncles played guitar. He listened to Blind Lemon Jefferson records as a child and started playing guitar in the Pentecostal Holiness Church in one key, "G." The first blues he learned to play was in the key of "A." By 1938, Fulson was playing around little clubs in Ada singing everything he had to, such as "Beer Barrel Polka," "Silvery Moon," and other songs whites liked at the time. Given his relatively rural location in southeastern Oklahoma, he was not exposed to the more urban jazz developments in Oklahoma City, Muskogee, and Tulsa.

Around 1939, Fulson played with Dan Wright in a twelve to fifteen piece string band at picnics and other social gatherings. Fulson remembered, "There was a place they called the Bottom where black people gathered together to drink, gamble, play the blues, whatever, and I'd go don there afterward and pick me up some change picking my guitar." That is where Lowell met Algernon "Texas" Alexander, who had recorded as early as 1927, and started playing with him throughout Texas in 1940. Fulson modeled his vocal style after Alexander who had a rambling, low-key vocal technique that played heavily on his rural drawl. Fulson's vocals exhibit this technique throughout his career even though he tried different styles at different times, often at the behest of producers trying to update his sound and image. Fulson played with Alexander for a summer throughout Texas and Oklahoma, but left the elder blues man in 1941 when Lowell moved with his first wife and son to Gainesville, Texas, where he worked as a cook and played mostly in church. In 1943, he was drafted into the Navy, as a cook, but also entertained troops in the U.S. and Guam until the war's end. After being discharged from the military in 1945, he returned to Oklahoma where he worked as cook at the Wade Hotel in Duncan, Oklahoma, but wanted to go to the West Coast to try to find a musical career. As a result of the migration of many African-Americans to the San Francisco Bay area in World War II to work in the shipping and munitions industry, Oakland had a thriving blues scene of nightclubs, bars, and independent record labels. Since Fulson had been stationed in Oakland during part of his Navy stint, Lowell knew about the scene there and decided to make it his home in 1946 when he made his first recordings for a hundred dollars.

Fulson's first release was "Cryin' Blues"/"You're Going to Miss Me When I'm Gone" with his brother Martin Fulson backing him up on guitar. In 1947, Fulson established a solid backing band of bass, drums, and piano and recorded several

more songs for various labels in Oakland where he had an R & B hit with "Three O'Clock Blues," later covered by B.B. King. Playing primarily around San Francisco and Oakland, Fulson moved to Los Angeles in 1949 where he recorded with fellow Oklahoman **Jay McShann** on the Swing Time label. Because McShann was more advanced musically than Fulson, Lowell preferred pianist Lloyd Glenn who had played with T-Bone Walker. Fulson and Glenn decided to add horns to their sound to fatten it up and the hits started to follow, as well as the moniker of uptown blues, sometimes called West Coast blues, or California blues.

Uptown blues is a hybrid form of blues that combines the riffing horn section elements of jazz with the electric blues combo of drums, bass, and guitar. In 1950, Lowell had solid success on the Swing Time label with "Everyday I Have the Blues," an R & B hit that reached #5 on the charts, and became B.B. King's theme song for many years. Fulson followed up with "Blue Shadows" (#1 R & B) and "Lonesome Christmas" (#7 R & B) in 1950. With several children in school, pianist Glenn did not want to tour behind Fulson's growing popularity, but continued playing on the recording sessions. Fulson then teamed up with Ray Charles who played with Fulson's rocking big band until 1953, as did saxophonist Stanley Turrentine. In October of 1950, the group's show at the Elks hall in Los Angeles broke a ten-year standing attendance record for the hall. Once Swing Time folded, Lowell's music was released through the Aladdin Record label that had purchased the masters from Swing Time in order to sell the records throughout the Midwest and South. Aladdin had particular success with Fulson's "I'm a Night Owl."

In 1952, Fulson played a packed Apollo Theater in New York, then toured with Ruth Brown and Joe Turner. In 1953, with Aladdin still releasing his music, Fulson toured with T-Bone Walker when Swing Time officially went bankrupt. Wasting little time, however, Lowell signed with Chess's Checker label in Chicago where he had a major hit with "Reconsider Baby" in 1954. The single reached #3 on the R & B charts and became a blues standard, covered by artists such as Elvis Presley, Ray Charles, and, eventually, Eric Clapton. However, Fulson did not fit in with the Chicago studio environment where his horn section made him stand out from Chess stable of Howlin' Wolf and Muddy Waters. Subsequently, uptown blues became a somewhat snide commentary by Chicago musicians about Fulson's music, which prompted him to move back to the West Coast and mail in all his studio recordings to Chess. The strained relationship did not prove fruitful overall, and Lowell left the label in 1962.

After continuously playing one-nighters and assorted club dates in the early 1960s, Fulson signed with the Kent label and had a minor R & B hit with "Black Nights" in 1965. In 1967, he had two more R & B hits with "Make a Little Love" and "Tramp," which almost broke into the Top 50 on the pop charts. Otis Redding and Carla Thomas also recorded "Tramp" and their version sold much better than Fulson's. During the 1970s, Fulson moved from the Kent label to Jewel Records, owned by Stan Lewis and based in Shreveport, Louisiana, but Lowell's commercial success was relegated to American popular music history. In the 1980s, Fulson "laid low," in his own words, while his classic recordings were reissued to demanding blues collectors. His 1988 recording for Rounder Records, *It's a Good Day*, was well received critically, but garnered only modest sales. In the 1990s, Fulson recorded for Bullseye Records in the same style for which he had become famous, and continued to tour when he was healthy. In 1993 he received five W.C. Handy Awards, was inducted into the Rhythm and Blues Hall of Fame, and the Blues Hall of Fame both for his career and his song, "Reconsider Baby." Fulson's 1996 album, *Them Update Blues* (Rounder), was nominated for Grammy in the "Best Traditional Blues" category. By the time of his death in an assisted care facility near Seal Beach, California, Fulson symbolized yet another Oklahoman who had absorbed the deep musical influences of his youth, and subsequently made major innovative contributions to his art form which came to be known as uptown or West Coast blues, still the most prominent form of blues in popular culture at the turn of the 21st century. (HF)

Gaines, Cassie LaRue (b. January 9, 1948 – d. October 20, 1977)
Gaines, Steve Earl (b. September 14, 1949 – d. October 20, 1977)

As members of southern rock group Lynyrd Skynyrd, guitarist Steve and vocalist Cassie Gaines contributed significantly to the group's live concerts and recordings from 1976 to their tragic demise in 1977 when the band's plane crashed outside Gillsburg, Mississippi, on the way to a concert in Baton Rouge, Louisiana.

*Back row, left to right: Leon Wilkeson, Artimus Pyle, Allen Collins, Leslie Hawkins, Gary Rossington, Ronnie VanZant, **Steve Gaines**, Jo Billingsley*
*Front row, left to right: Billy Powell, **Cassie Gaines***

Both Cassie and Steve were born in the northeastern corner of Oklahoma, in Miami, to Bud and LaRue Gaines. Even though she attended NEO A & M in Miami for two years, Cassie did not start singing professionally until she went to Memphis State University where she graduated with a degree in physical education in 1975. Steve began playing guitar at fifteen, inspired after his father took him to see a 1965 performance by the Beatles in Kansas City. Upon returning to Miami, Steve's father bought him a guitar and Steve started his first group, the Ravens, in 1966, while still in high school. That group consisted of Steve on guitar and vocals, Archie Osborn (bass and vocals), Jerry Sanders (drums and vocals), and Johnny Burrows (guitar and vocals).

After high school, Steve majored in art, first at Northeastern Oklahoma A & M, and then at Pittsburgh State College in Kansas. During this period, Steve joined Pink Peach Mob, a psychedelic outfit, in 1967, with Don Malchi (guitar), John Moss (drums), Jerry Carpenter (bass), Dee Poole (lead vocals), Mike Rivers (keyboards), and Jim Poole (organ). Next, in 1968 Steve formed Manalive that recorded one single, "Boogie," in the Memphis Sun Studios made famous by Elvis Presley and many other blues and country artists in the 1950s. In 1970 Steve joined RIO Smokehouse, then featuring the three-guitar attack for which Lynyrd Skynyrd would later become famous when Gaines joined that group, but also performed and recorded again with Manalive, notably in Memphis where Jerry Phillips, son of Sun Records impresario Sam Phillips, signed the group to Hot Water Records, a subsidiary of the famous soul label, Stax Records.

In early 1972, Steve joined Detroit, essentially the Detroit Wheels without Mitch Ryder, which followed in the same blues rock mold popular among groups of the period, i.e., the Allman Brothers, the Marshall Tucker Band, and Skynyrd. After leaving the band Detroit, Steve and his wife, Teresa, moved to a farm in Seneca, Missouri, just across the Oklahoma border and not far from their home base of Miami, where they had their only child Corrina, named after a Taj Majal version of the song on which Oklahoma native **Jesse Ed Davis** played guitar.

In 1973 Steve formed Crawdad with John Seaburg (bass guitar and vocals), John Moss (guitar and vocals), Terry Emery (keyboards), and Ron Brooks (drums), performing everywhere from high school dances to the clubs and honky tonks in Oklahoma, Kansas, Arkansas, and Missouri. Steve's widow, now Teresa Gaines Rapp, has released two very insightful posthumous recordings from this period, *Okie Special* and *I Know A Little – Live*, both available though the Steve Gaines's website. *Okie Special* demonstrates Steve's varied influences, from Motown (Jr. Walker's "Road Runner") and funky fusion (Billy Cobham's "Crosswinds"), to grooving blues (Chuck Willis's "Snatch it Back and Hold It") and classic rock and roll (Chuck Berry's "No Money Down"). Two songs are also included on *Okie Special* from the Detroit group. Gaines's original composition, "Ain't No Good Life," later found on Skynyrd's *Street Survivors*, is also on *Okie Special*.

Another family-released disc indicating Steve Gaines's ultimate impact on Lynyrd Skynyrd can be found on *I Know a Little-Live*, recordings made by Gaines's groups Crawdad and Manalive in the early-to-mid-1970s. No dates are included on the compact disc, so determining their place in Gaines's development is difficult. However, the group's sound is so rooted in the popular southern rock of the time that Gaines's composition "I Know a Little" appears to have been written for Lynyrd Skynyrd even before they knew who he was. Again, Gaines's influences are prominent on the disc with cover versions of songs by Freddie King, Big Joe Turner, Curtis Mayfield, and Bob Dylan. Cassie also makes a vocal appearance on one of Steve's songs, "People Comin' At Me."

In 1975 one of Cassie's friends from Memphis State, Jo Jo Billingsley, was a backup singer for Skynyrd. When the group told Billingsley they were looking for another singer, she asked Cassie to audition for the gig and she got it. Once on the job, Cassie found out Skynyrd also wanted to hire another guitarist to fatten up their sound after the relatively disappointing sales of their 1976 album, *Gimme Back My Bullets* (MCA). She suggested her younger brother, and when the group

was playing in Kansas City, Cassie convinced them to let Steve sit in for one song. Singer Ronnie Van Zant agreed and instructed the soundman to cut Steve out of the mix if he could not keep up well enough. Gaines played slide on Jimmie Rodgers "T for Texas," impressed the whole band, and was invited to join the group.

The first Skynyrd recording to feature both Steve and Cassie Gaines is the Top 10 live album *One More for the Road* (MCA, 1976), which includes the famous fourteen-minute jamathon version of "Free Bird." Back in the studio with a renewed sense of purpose and a fresh injection from Steve Gaines's guitar work and compositions, Skynyrd recorded *Street Survivors* (MCA, 1977). Two of Steve's songs he had been playing for years with his other groups, "Ain't No Good Life" and "I Know a Little," appear on the album, and he co-wrote two new songs with vocalist Van Zant, "You Got That Right" and "I Never Dreamed." Steve's trademark "popping Stratocaster" style can be heard on the band's cover of **Merle Haggard**'s "Honky Tonk Night Time Man," and Cassie's backup vocals are also prominent on the best-selling Lynyrd Skynyrd album. While *Street Survivors* returned the group to the international stardom, three days after the album's release, the band's plane crashed due to a seemingly negligent decision by the pilot to have enough fuel in the aircraft, killing Cassie, Steve, Ronnie Van Zant, and the band's manager, Dean Kilpatrick. Ironically, the album cover for *Street Survivors* included a picture of the group engulfed in flames, and the record was taken off the market in the U.S. to have the cover photo replaced, however, European releases maintained the original cover.

Periodically, more material from Gaines's career has been made available. In 1988, MCA Records released a Steve Gaines solo album, *One in the Sun*, culled from tapes he had recorded with producer John Ryan at the Capricorn Studio in Macon, Georgia, and **Leon Russell**'s Church Studio in Tulsa. Enlisting his old band mates from Crawdad to back him up, the out-of-print album is clearly a work in progress with the Capricorn tracks recorded "live," and the Church tracks pieced together track-by-track. Steve's promise as a guitarist and vocalist in the southern rock boogie blues genre is obvious on the album's lead-off track, "Give It to Get It," a song later covered by **Cherokee** guitarist Ace Moreland (also from Miami) and used as the title for Moreland's 2000 album on Icehouse Records. Released in 2003, the Manalive recordings made at the Sun Studios in Memphis are available only through the Steve Gaines website. Also in 2003, the Rock and Roll Hall of Fame in Cleveland, Ohio exhibited Steve's Fender Stratocaster guitar as part of the Lynyrd Skynyrd exhibit. (HF)
www.stevegaines.com

The GAP Band

(Formed in 1967, Tulsa, OK)

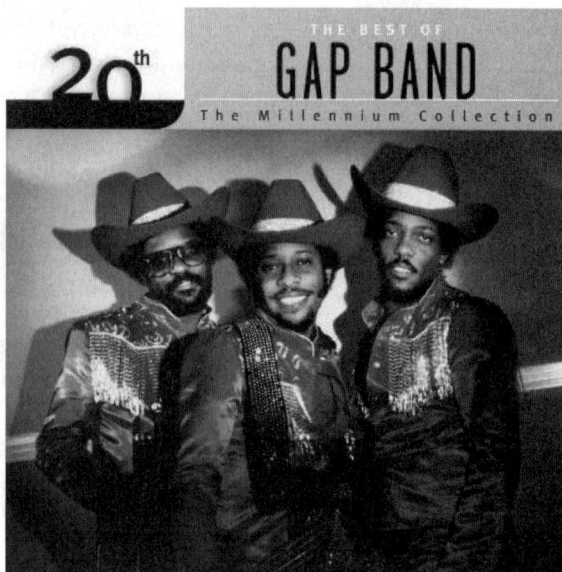

Leaning on influences ranging from Parliament-Funkadelic to Sly and the Family Stone and Earth, Wind, and Fire, The GAP Band, comprised of multi-instrumentalist brothers Ronnie, Charlie, and Robert Wilson (all Tulsa natives), surfaced as one of the most popular R & B groups of the 1980s. With fifteen Top 10 R & B hits, the group has become a perennial favorite of sample-happy hip hop and R & B artists looking for a fat bass lines, smooth vocal hooks, and funky beats. The brothers grew up performing in their father's Pentecostal church in Tulsa where their mother was a pianist, and where they sang every Sunday before their father's sermon. All three brothers took piano lessons, and their parents demanded they practice at home. Ronnie, the oldest, started a group when he was fourteen and eventually recruited his younger brothers to play in the band they named after streets in the heart of Tulsa's historic African-American business district — Greenwood, Archer and Pine. After a typographical error changed their name from the G.A.P. Street Band to The GAP Band, the name stuck. The group played various clubs around Tulsa and got their break in 1974 when they provided bass, horns, and vocals to **Leon Russell**'s album, *All That Jazz* (Shelter/MCA). Subsequently, Russell signed the band to record their first album for his Shelter label, *Magician's Holiday* (1974). The group moved to Los Angeles shortly thereafter and recorded a gospel single for A & M, "This Place Called Heaven," and a slightly noticed self-titled album for Tattoo in 1977.

The GAP Band's success really took flight in 1979 via *The Gap Band II* (Mercury), now a gold album, from which the group scored a Top 5 R & B hit "Shake," followed by other 1980 R & B Top 10 hits, "Steppin' Out" and "I Don't Believe You Want to Get Up and Dance (Oops, Up Side Your Head)." Their 1980 platinum-selling album, *The Gap Band III* (Mercury), sported more R&B hits, including the #1 "Burn Rubber (Why You Wanna Hurt Me)" and 1981's #5 R&B hit, "Yearning for Your Love," which sealed their status top recording stars. Their 1982 album, *Gap Band IV* (Total Experience), provided their biggest pop hit, "You Dropped a Bomb On Me," exhibiting their trademark bass-heavy style and the silky smooth vocals of Charlie Wilson. The song is still played at Allie P. Reynolds Stadium in Stillwater when an Oklahoma State baseball player hits a home run. The group continued a string of R&B hits through the 1980s, including "Party Train" (1983), "Jam the Motha" (1983), "Beep a Freak" (1984), "Big Fun" (1986), "I'm Gonna Git You Sucka" (1988), "All of My Love" (#1 R&B, 1989), and "We Can Make it Alright" (1990).

While Ronnie Wilson became a born-again Christian and began pastoring in 1984, Charlie Wilson is one of the most in-demand vocalists in the R & B, urban contemporary, and rap music industry. His vocals have appeared on albums by Ray Charles, Snoop Dogg ("Snoops Upside Ya Head," et al.), Zapp, Quincy Jones, Master P, Mia X, and Mystikal. Charlie also continues working with some of the top producers and young performers in the music industry: Steve Huff, Terry Lewis, Shekspeare, Tricky, D.J. Quik, Dr. Dre, D.J. Pooh, and Daz Dilinger. Through his publicist, Charlie Wilson says, "I feel very fortunate to be able to return musically to somewhere I never really left, and it's flattering to know that the younger generation of musicians still fill their tracks with the sounds my brothers and I created years ago."

Numerous compilations have documented The GAP Band's career, from *Gap Gold: The Best of the Gap Band* (Mercury, 1985), to a best-of collection through Mercury's *20th Century Masters Series* (2000). In 2001 Hip-O released *Ultimate Collection*, a thorough collection of their greatest hits with extensive liner notes, while Ark 21 released *Love at Your Fingertips*, featuring a few new tunes, live recordings, and several remixes of "You Dropped a Bomb On Me." The group does make occasional concert appearances, and periodic performances for nationally syndicated urban radio host Tom Joyner on his cruises or benefit shows for charities such as the United Negro College Fund. (HF)

Garcia, Benny, Sr.
(b. March 20, 1926)

One of Oklahoma's elder statesmen guitarists, Benny Garcia is highly regarded by jazz fans and Western swing musicians for his vibrant melodic ability and full-bodied sound that derives from his idols, **Charlie Christian** and **Barney Kessel**. While Garcia may not have garnered the same critical acclaim as those two Oklahomans, his performances and/or recordings with bandleaders such as **Bob** and **Johnnie Lee**

Wills, Benny Goodman, and singing cowboy Tex Williams, as well as playing with Merl Lindsay, **Jimmy Wakely**, **Johnny Bond**, and Patsy Cline, cement his stature as an important Oklahoma musician.

Born in Oklahoma City of Mexican-American ancestry, Benny started taking guitar lessons at age fourteen. He listened intently to Benny Goodman records with Charlie Christian playing lead guitar, trying to pick out the melody lines. Later, Garcia met Christian's mother who became fond of the young guitarist, and let Benny play Charlie's amp and guitar. Benny still owns one of Charlie's tortoise shell picks given to him by Mrs. Christian. As a teenager he played live broadcasts on WKY radio with local buddies, tenor saxophonist Fred Beatty, pianist Al Good, singer/guitarist Jimmy Wakely, and singer/guitarist Johnny Bond. By his early 20s, Benny played regular gigs with Merl Lindsay and the Oklahoma Night Riders at Oklahoma City's Elmwood Ballroom and the Warner Theater. Later, he joined the staff band at KOMA radio in the Biltmore Hotel that was right across the street a movie theater where singing cowboy star Tex Williams, then at the height of his fame with the million-selling hit, "Smoke, Smoke, Smoke That Cigarette," stopped to play and promote one of his movies in 1948. Tex also took in the KOMA broadcast and offered Benny a job in his traveling Caravan of three long, black Packards and an equipment truck. Garcia accepted and was officially a touring musician in Williams' ten-piece Western swing band, alongside the great pedal-steel player, Earl "Joaquin" Murphey, traveling across the U.S. and Canada for three years before settling in Burbank, California.

Once in California, Benny recorded on several sessions for Capitol and Columbia Records, and in 1950 joined the Hank Penny jazz band. He also took guitar lessons from jazz guitar giant, and heir to Charlie Christian's throne, Oklahoma native Barney Kessel who was also living in the Los Angeles area at the time. Before Benny became too immersed in the L.A. music scene, however, he was drafted during the Korean War and wound up at the Camp Desert Rock atomic bomb test site in Nevada. Once out of the Army, Benny headed back to Oklahoma where Johnnie Lee Wills hired him for regular performances at Cain's Ballroom and on KVOO radio in Tulsa through 1957. Garcia also toured with Bob Wills in 1958, traveling throughout the United States, again, and then picked up work with Patsy Cline for several of her live performances. Returning to Oklahoma City in the early 1960s, Benny played regularly with the Al Tell Quartet and Wayne Nichols Orchestra until getting a call from Benny Goodman who recruited Garcia to record on *Hello Benny* (Capitol, 1968). Subsequently, he joined the Benny Goodman band and hit the road for several U.S. and Canadian tours into the 1970s.

Settling down in Oklahoma City, Benny has been a fixture on the jazz club, lounge, and restaurant circuit for the last 30 years. He has also been featured in a German concert video, *Legends of Western Swing Guitar* where he duets with Eldon Shamblin on "Stay a Little Longer." In 1999, Benny was asked by Barney Kessel to represent the ailing Kessel who was unable to play for his induction into the Oklahoma Music Hall of Fame. Garcia has also been a regular at reunion gigs of remaining members of Bob and Johnnie Lee Wills' bands, most recently in March, 2003 at the Cain's Ballroom. Playing with a Latin-tinged jazz group, Los Locos, Benny recorded a self-titled album on Lunacy Records in 2001, sound samples of which are available on MP3.com.

In 2002, Benny played on a Western swing-styled album by Oklahoma vocalist and fiddler Harvey "Preacher" Davis, *Harvey Davis and Friends* (Lunacy), on which former Wills drummer Tommy Perkins also appears. In 2003, Friends of Oklahoma Music inducted Garcia into the Oklahoma Music Hall of Fame. Continuing the family tradition of fine guitar playing, Benny Garcia, Jr. has performed with **Vince Gill,** as well as served as Gill's guitar technician, and also played with the Dixie Chicks. (HF)
www.lunacyrecords.com

Gates, David
(b. December 11, 1940)

Best known for his work with Bread, and as a songwriter whose songs have been hits around the world, David Gates helped define the genre of "soft rock" in the 1970s with Bread hits such as "Make it With You," "If," and "Guitar Man," as well as his solo single "Goodbye Girl." At last count, Bread and Gates have sold more than 17 million records. Born to a band teacher and band director in Tulsa, Oklahoma, Gates was surrounded by the classical music of his parents and the big band sounds of his older siblings. Encouraged and instructed by his father, Gates could read music by age five, and was proficient on bass, guitar, and piano by his high school years at Tulsa Rogers. He formed his first rock band in 1957 and backed Chuck Berry. In 1958, he wrote, recorded and released his first single, "Jo-Baby," named after his high school sweetheart, Jo Rita. An indication of his romantic hits to follow, "Jo-Baby" was recorded to sway Jo Rita away from another boy. Gates paid to press 500 copies of the single and it became a local hit, as well as winning over Jo Rita whom he married and started family with while enrolled at Oklahoma University.

Eager to continue his musical career, Gates loaded his wife and two children into a ten-year-old Cadillac, and moved the family to Los Angeles in 1961. Soon thereafter, in early 1962, Chuck Blackwell and Gates's Tulsa Rogers classmate **Leon Russell** arrived and the three formed a trio, worked clubs at night, and did some session work during the day. One of the clubs was called the Crossroads in the San Fernando Valley. Jam sessions there included a young Glen Campbell, Russell, Elvis Presley's future guitarist James Burton, and future super session men Hal Blaine and Jim Horn. What set Gates apart from the rest, however, was his classical music background, which provided opportunities for him to write arrangements for other artists. Gates remembers, "I had an advantage. I knew rock and roll, country, and rhythm and blues. I could read and write music. I could do arrangements. I could produce. I could play bass. I could do a lot of different things to make a living." By 1963, Gates had his first hit as a songwriter, "Popsicles and Icicles," a #3 pop hit for The Murmaids. Throughout the 1960s, Gates arranged music for Elvis Presley, Duane Eddy, The Nitty Gritty Dirt Band, **Merle Haggard**, **Hoyt Axton**, Buck Owens, Captain Beefheart, Ann-Margret, and Bobby Darin. Gates also produced the movie theme to *Baby the Rain Must Fall* in 1965 that became a Grammy-nominated top ten hit for Glenn Yarbrough.

By the late 1960s, Gates decided he wanted to record his own songs and founded the group Bread in 1968. Released in 1969, the group's first album, *Bread*, featured strong songs such as "Dismal Day," "London Bridge," and "It Don't Matter to Me" which became a hit later when the group's second album was released. The album *Bread* was not an overwhelming success, as the group had not yet established their signature sound of soft, acoustic guitar based songs with a supporting string section that would surface on 1970's *On the Waters*. By adding an occasional electric guitar solo, *On the Waters* established the sound known as "soft rock" and in many ways launched the adult contemporary radio format. The album featured the #1 hit, "Make It with You," and caused enough interest in the band to bring back "It Don't Matter to Me," from the first album, which went to #10 on the pop charts. *Manna* (1971) continued the group's smooth studio pop sound and produced more hits, "Let Your Love Go" (#28), and the mega-hit, "If" (#1). *Baby I'm-a Want You* (1972) followed up on the group's string of chart hits with the album's title track (#3), "Mother Freedom" (#37) which was the closest the group really ever got to rocking out, "Everything I Own" (#5), and "Diary" (#15). The band followed up this success with another 1972 album, *Guitar Man*, with three more Gates-penned hits, "Sweet Surrender" (#15), "Aubrey" (#15), and "Guitar Man" (#11). 1972 also saw the albums *Manna, Baby I'm-a Want You,* and *Guitar Man* go gold (500,000 in sales), and *Baby I'm a Want You* was nominated for a Grammy.

With a tremendous amount of success under their belts, but a less than perfect working relationship, the group decided to call it quits in 1973. In 1974, Ken Boothe had a British hit with a reggae cover of "If" (#1), and *The Best of Bread Vol. 2* went gold. Bread reunited briefly in 1977, and produced another hit written by Gates, "Lost Without Your Love," the title track of an album that became the group's seventh consecutive gold record, and final project as a group. David Gates released a series of solo albums throughout the 1970s that produced consistent hits in the adult contemporary format, the biggest of which was the theme song to the Oscar-winning film *Goodbye Girl* (1977). Also in 1977, Joe Stampley had hit on the country charts with his version of "Everything I Own." Later, in 1987, Boy George had #1 one international hit with his own rendition of the song.

After 1981's modestly selling solo album, *Take Me Now*, Gates withdrew from the music industry to spend more time with his family on a Northern California ranch he purchased in 1974 just after the height of Bread's success. Even though Gates went into semi-retirement, his song "If" was recorded by Julio Iglesias in 1984 and became a worldwide hit in a bilingual version of the song. In 1992, Gates built his own studio at the ranch and collaborated with country artist Billy Dean in 1993. In 1994, the Warner Brothers subsidiary, Discovery Records, released a Gates solo album, *Love Is Always Seventeen*, and in 1996 Gates joined a world tour with three original members of Bread to play their hits in South Africa, Australia, Southeast Asia, England, and various other countries.

In 1998, Gates also began a trend of playing with symphony orchestras, an idea based on the heavy string arrangements in Bread's hit material, when he played with Tulsa Symphony and debuted an original song, "Tulsa, My Hometown." Also in 1998, Friends of Oklahoma Music inducted him into the Oklahoma Music Hall of Fame. In 2002, Gates performed with the Tulsa Community College Signature Symphony for a benefit concert and returned to perform for a celebration of the 50th anniversary party for the Utica Square Shopping Center. Further indicating David's widespread appeal, his composition "If," now covered by more than one hundred artists, was included on Dolly Parton's 2002 traditional country album, *Halos and Horns* (Sanctuary). To support the release of the retrospective *David Gates Songbook* (Zomba/Jive) in 2002, which included five new songs, Gates performed on a successful 2003 spring tour of England. (HF)

Gill, Vince
(b. April 12, 1957)

As one of the most multi-talented and highly regarded country music artists on the Nashville scene in the 1980s, 1990s and 2000s, Vince Gill has hosted the CMA Awards on CBS for eleven consecutive years, tied for the most Grammy Awards by a country artist (15), and won more CMA Awards than any artist in the history of the organization (18). Singer, songwriter, guitarist, fiddler, mandolinist, and dobroist Vincent Grant Gill was born to Stan and Jerene Gill, the youngest of three children, in Norman, Oklahoma, home of the University of Oklahoma and now a southern suburb of Oklahoma City. Vince was raised around music as his father, Stan, a lawyer and judge, played banjo part time in a country band, and encouraged his son to consider a career in country music. His brother Bob was a blues fan, while his sister Gina followed folk music. Early on, Vince learned the banjo from his father, but a neighbor, Bobby Clark, introduced Vince to acoustic guitar, which became his instrument of choice. Vince and Clark formed a teenage bluegrass group called The Bluegrass Review that later became Mountain Smoke, both of which played at **Bill Grant's** Old-Time Country and Bluegrass Festival in Hugo, and Mountain Smoke once opened for Pure Prairie League as well as KISS, the heavy metal group, at The Myriad in Oklahoma City.

Following graduation from Northwest Classen High School in Oklahoma City in 1975, Gill headed to Louisville to join the Bluegrass Alliance that featured Dan Crary and Sam Bush. Following the Bluegrass Alliance stint, he was a member of Ricky Skaggs' Boone Creek bluegrass band. Perhaps his biggest break was in 1976 when **Byron Berline** contacted Vince to become a member of Sundance, based in Los Angeles. After two years with Berline, he auditioned for Pure Prairie League, who remembered him from their previous encounter. Some fifty guitarists were auditioned, but Vince was hired in 1979 because of his versatility on other instruments, such as the banjo and fiddle, as well as his vocal talents. He became their lead singer for the next three years and appeared on their albums *Can't Hold Back*, *Something in the Night*, and *Firin' Up*, the latter included six of Vince's compositions, one of which became a Top 40 single in 1980, "I'm Almost Ready."

Gill left Pure Prairie League to spend time with his new wife, Janis, a member of Sweethearts of the Rodeo, a West Coast all female bluegrass duo consisting of Janis and her sister, Kristine. Vince and Janis were married in 1980 and soon had daughter Jenny. He then joined Rodney Crowell's Cherry Bombs as a harmony singer and guitarist, often backing Rosanne Cash. Tony Brown, former keyboard player for the Cherry Bombs and then A & R man for RCA, signed Vince to a contract in 1984, and the Gills moved to Nashville. Later that year, Vince recorded a mini-album, *Turn Me Loose*, including six of the eight tracks written or co-written by him, two of which reached the Top 40, "Victim of Life's Circumstances" and "Oh Carolina." He was named ACM's Top New Male Vocalist for 1984.

In 1984, Vince switched record companies and recorded two albums for the Buddha label, *The Things That Matter* (1985) and *The Way Back Home* (1987) with a majority of the tracks written by him. The 1985 album included "True Love" (Top 40), "Oklahoma Borderline" (Top 10), and "If It Weren't for Him" (Top 10). The latter single featured Rosanne Cash singing harmonies with Vince. The 1987 album produced a Top 5 hit, "Cinderella," and a Top 20 hit, "Let's Do Something." During this time, Vince also concentrated on vocal harmonies and playing guitar on more than 120 records, primarily with Emmylou Harris, as well as focusing on songwriting, especially with Rosanne Cash.

Gill's career began to take off in 1989 when he joined the MCA-Nashville roster. He was reunited with Tony Brown, who had originally signed him. The first album for MCA, *When I Call Your Name*, yielded two important singles that launched Vince to stardom, the title track with Patty Loveless singing harmonies, and "Oklahoma Swing," featuring a duet with fellow Oklahoman, **Reba McEntire**. These two songs also highlighted Vince's talents as a songwriter, both of which he collaborated on with another Oklahoman, Tim Dubois. "When I Call Your Name" won the CMA Single and Song of the Year for 1990, a Grammy for Best Country Vocal Performance by a Male in 1990, and *TNN/Music City News* Award for Single of the Year for 1991. The album was later certified double platinum.

Vince continued his successes in 1991 with the release of *Pocket Full of Gold*, a bluegrass-oriented album that went double platinum a year later, and featured three important singles, "Lisa Jane," "Look at Us," and the title track. The 1991 release was followed with two highly acclaimed 1992 albums, *I Never Knew Lonely* and *I Still Believe in You*. The latter album produced two #1 hits, "Don't Let Our Love Start Slippin' Away" and the title track, both co-written by Vince, and reached double-platinum status in 1993.

Honors and awards were showered on Vince during the 1990s, beginning with his invitation to become a Grand Ole Opry member (1991); CMA Entertainer of the Year (1993/1994); CMA Male Vocalist of the Year (1991, 1992, 1993, 1994, 1995); CMA Songs of the Year for "When I Call Your Name" (1991), "Look At Us" (1992), and "I Still Believe in You" (1993); CMA Album of the Year-*I Still Believe In You* (1993) and *Common Threads: The Songs of the Eagles* (1994); CMA Vocal Events of the Year with Mark O'Conner and the New Nashville Cats for *Restless* (1991), George Jones and two other Oklahomans **Garth Brooks** and **Joe Diffie** for "I Don't Need Your Rockin' Chair, *TNN-Music City News* Award for Instrumentalist of the Year (1991, 1992, 1993, 1994), as well as their awards for Album of the Year-*I Still Believe In You* and Single of the Year –"I Still Believe In You" (1993), and Best Vocal Collaboration for "Go Rest On That Mountain" with Patty Loveless and Ricky Skaggs, Grammy Awards for Best Country Vocal Performance by Male (1990, 1992, 1994, 1996, 1997, 1998), Best Country Song for "I Still Believe in You" (1992), Best Country Instrumental Performance Collaboration with Asleep at the Wheel for "Red Wing" (1993), Best Country Vocal Collaboration for "Restless" (1991), Top Male Vocalist Award from the ACM (1992/1993), and the Minnie Pearl Award for Humanitarian Efforts from *TNN/Music City News* (1993).

In 1993, Vince released *Let There Be Peace on Earth*, a platinum seasonal album, s followed by two albums in 1994, *Vince Gill & Friends* and *When Love Finds You*, which later went triple platinum. The *Friends* tracks included vocals by such notables as Emmylou Harris, Bonnie Rait, and the Sweethearts of the Rodeo with Janis, Vince's wife. In 1994, the *When Love Finds You* production soared to the Top 3 country album and crossed over to become Top 10 in the pop charts. The album garnered Grammies for Vince for Best Country Vocal Performance Male for "Go Rest High on That Mountain" and Best Country Song for "Go Rest High on That Mountain" (1995), and CMA top honors for Song of the Year in 1996. Vince had written the song in memory of his half-brother, Bob, who had died of a heart attack in 1993. Gill appeared on television with Gladys Knight at the American Music Awards in inaugurate promotion of an ambitious project teaming the legends of R & B with the legends of country in an MCA album that offered an innovating blend of these two American music subgenres.

In 1996, Gill released *High Lonesome Sound*, a platinum album that featured his high tenor vocals and bluegrass instrumentation. The album soon went platinum and earned Vince three more Grammy Awards, including Best Male Country Vocal Performance for "World's Apart" (1996), Best Male Country Vocal Performance for "Pretty Little Adriana" (1997), and Best Country Collaboration with Vocals for "High Lonesome Sound" featuring Alison Krauss and Union Station (1996). In addition, he was given the Vocal Event of the Year by the CMA for his duet with Dolly Parton on "I Will Always Love You," and Song of the Year for 1996, "Go Rest High on That Mountain." Finally, 1996 was capped off with the *TNN-Music City News* Award for Best Vocal Collaboration with Patty Loveless and Ricky Skaggs for "Go Rest High on That Mountain."

In 1998, Vince released *The Key*, a highly acclaimed gold album with ten of the thirteen tracks written by him, including "My Kind of Woman/My Kind of Man," a duet with Patty Loveless, which captured the 1999 CMA Vocal Event of the Year, "Hills of Caroline," featuring Alison Krauss; "The Key to Life," a tribute to his late father; "Kindly Keep It Country," a duet with Lee Ann Womack; and "What They All Call Love," with harmony sung by Faith Hill. The album highlights Vince's talents on the guitar and mandolin with instrumental contributions by such legendary Nashville session artists as guitarist Randy Scruggs, pianist Hargus "Pig" Robbins, and fiddler Stuart Duncan. "If You Ever Have Forever in Mind," the second track on the album, won Vince a Grammy Award for Best Country Vocal Performance by Male in 1998. Vince's instrumental greatness was showcased on "A Soldier's Joy" in the Randy Scruggs' album *Crown of Jewels*, and won him a 1998 Grammy for Best Country Instrumental Performance. *Breath of Heaven: A Christmas Collection*, a seasonal album, was released in 1998. Finally Vince's most recent contribution is "All Prayed Up," one of the tracks on the *Will the Circle Be Unbroken, Vol. III*, released in 2002 by Capitol Records.

In addition Vince was a finalist for several other CMA Awards, including Song of the Year ("When I Call Your Name') and Vocal Event of the Year ("The Heart Won't Lie") with **Reba McEntire** (1990), Entertainer of the Year (1991/1992/1995/1996/1997/1998), Album and Single of the Year for *Pocket Full of Gold* (1991), Single of the Year ("Look at Us") in 1992, Single and Music Video of the Year ("Don't Let Our Love Start Slippin' Away") in 1993, Single and Video of the Year ("Look At Us") in 1992, Singles of the Year for ("Don't Let Our Love Start Slippin' Away") in 1993, ("When Love Finds You") in 1995, and ("Go

Rest High On That Mountain") in 1996, Albums of the Year for (*Rhythm, Country & Blues*-1994), (*When Love Finds You*-1995), (*High Lonesome Sound*-1996), and (*The Key*-1999), Male Vocalist of the Year (1997/1998/1999/2000), Song of the Year ("If You Ever Have Forever in Mind") and Vocal Event of the Year for "No Place That Far" with Sara Evans, both in 1999. He has also garnered twenty BMI Songwriter Awards and nine *Music City News* Songwriter Awards for such compositions as "Pretty Little Adriana," God Rest High on That Mountain," "I Still Believe in You," and "When I Call Your Name."

In 2000, Vince released *Let's Make Sure We Kiss Goodbye*, a thirteen-track album with twelve written or co-written by him. It was recorded just months before his marriage to CCM artist Amy Grant on March 10, 2000, and contains several romantic songs, such as "When I Look Into Your Heart," a duet with Grant; "The Luckiest Guy in the World," and "Little Things." It also features Vince's daughter, Jenny, on harmony vocals for "That Friend of Mine." Also in 2000, Vince released a children's album, *The Emperor's New Clothes*, and received a Grammy for his instrumental performance on "Foggy Mountain Breakdown," a collaboration with Earl Scruggs, Randy Scruggs, **Leon Russell**, Steve Martin, and several others. Vince and Amy were made proud parents on March 12, 2001, when Corrina Grant Gill was born. Finally, Vince teamed with pop diva Barbara Streisand on her latest album, *Duets* (Columbia, 2002) on which they perform "If You Ever Leave Me."

Vince Gill, Barney Kessel, and Byron Berline at their induction into the Oklahoma Music Hall of Fame in 1999.

After recent inductions into the Oklahoma Hall of Fame, National Cowboy Hall of Fame, and Oklahoma Music Hall of Fame, Vince was elected president of the Country Music Hall of Fame and Museum in Nashville in 2002. Vince last appeared in Oklahoma was on November 16, 2002 when he served as master of ceremonies for the dedication of the new Capitol building dome in Oklahoma City. He opened the ceremonies by singing "Oklahoma Hills" co-written by **Woody** and **Jack Guthrie**.

Gill's self-produced his 2003 release, *The Next Big Thing* (MCA), reached #4 on the country album charts, #14 on the *Billboard* Top 200 album charts, and the album's title track made the Top 20 of the country singles charts. The follow up single, "Someday," was a Top 40 country track, and Vince played more than sixty

dates in 2003 to support the album. Also in 2003, two of Gill's songs, "When I Call Your Name," and "Go Rest High on That Mountain," landed at 44 and 66 respectively on CMT's 100 Greatest Country Songs of All Time. In August, 2003, Gill accepted the PGA of America's Distinguished Service Award as a result of his Vinny Pro-Celebrity Golf Invitational raising more than three million dollars to benefit junior golf programs. Without picking or singing another note, Vince Gill has created an incredible legacy matched by few other artists in country music history. His website is a thorough documentation of his total accomplishments and current happenings. (GC)
www.vincegill.com

Grant, Bill
(b. May 9, 1929)

As part of the perfect bluegrass duo and a bluegrass festival promoter for almost thirty-five years, singer, songwriter, and mandolinist Billy Joe Grant was born in Hugo, Oklahoma, a community of about 6,000 residents, county seat of Choctaw County, and site for the first outdoor bluegrass festival west of the Mississippi. Bill was born, raised, and still resides on the 360-acre ranch that has been in his family for more than a century. Growing up as a Grand Ole Opry listener (Grant family purchased their first radio in 1937 and Bill began tuning in to WSM-Nashville), Bill considers Bill Monroe and the Stanley Brothers as his bluegrass idols. While listening to the Opry in the 1940s, Bill began singing some of the songs broadcast over the airwaves. A friend loaned Bill a guitar, and he began learning a few chords on his mother's piano. Those were the beginnings of Bill's interest in music.

After high school, Bill devoted more time to his cattle business, and his music hobby occupied less of his time. But in 1959, Bill met Delia Bell, a native Texan, whose husband was a friend of Bill's. They discovered their voices blended well together, and they began to sing at local functions, and decided to form a musical act, "Bill Grant and Delia Bell." In about 1960, Bill and Delia began singing on the *Little Dixie Hayride* broadcast on local radio (KIHN in Hugo) and television stations (KTEN in Ada). Bill and his new singing partner, Delia, formed the Kiamichi Mountain Boys in 1969.

After a visit in 1969 to Bill Monroe's bluegrass festival in Beanblossom, Indiana, where Bill and Delia were invited to sing a number with the "father of bluegrass," Bill and his wife, Juarez, decided to establish an outdoor bluegrass festival site on his ranch (about two miles east of Hugo) in 1969 calling it the Salt Creek Park Old-Time Country and Bluegrass Festival. The first festival line-up was a virtual "Who's Who in Bluegrass," including Bill Monroe and the Bluegrass Boys, Ralph Stanley and the Clinch Mountain Boys, The Country

Gentlemen, and Mac Wiseman. Following the first festival, bluegrass fans in Oklahoma launched the first bluegrass club in the state, Oklahoma Bluegrass Club, based in Oklahoma City. Because of Grant's festival and formation of the Oklahoma Bluegrass Club, Governor David Hall proclaimed a "Bluegrass Week in Oklahoma" in 1973.

Since its inception, Grant's festival has added a variety of amateur contests, including those that focus on old-time fiddling, mandolin, banjo, guitar, dobro, and bands. Notable winners in the amateur contests who have achieved national and international stature include **Vince Gill** and **Joe Diffie**. In 1997 the Oklahoma state legislature recognized Grant's festival as the "oldest bluegrass festival in the world under original management and name."

In 1971, Bill launched his own Kiamichi Records and released several albums, including *My Kiamichi Mountain Home* (1972), eight of the twelve tracks were penned by Bill, *Kiamichi Country* (1973), *There Is a Fountain* (1973), *The Last Christmas Tree* (1976), *My Pathway Leads to Oklahoma* (1978), *The Blues-Mountain Style* (1979), and *The Man in the Middle* (1979). Many of the above out of print albums have been re-released on the Old Homestead label.

Bill's songwriting talents have focused on his home area, the Kiamichi Mountains of southeastern Oklahoma, and include such compositions as "Stairway to Heaven," "Cheer of the Home Fires," "A Few Dollars More," "My Kiamichi Mountain Home," "Where the Old Kiamichi Flows," "Beneath the Old Pine Tree," "When the Angels Come For Me," "Bluer Than Midnight," "I Know the Time Has Come For Me," and "Kiamichi Moon." He and Delia are internationally recognized for their vocal harmonies in the old-time mountain style.

In 1979, Bill and Delia toured the U.K., where they recorded *Bill Grant and Delia Bell in England* on the U.K. label, Kama. The Kiamichi Mountain Boys, consisting of the Bonham Family, Delia, and Bill, disbanded in 1980 because the Bonhams did not want to travel. Since then, Bill and Delia have cut four albums for Rounder, including *The Cheer of the Home Fires* (1983), *A Few Dollars More* (1985), and *Following a Feeling* (1988), backed by the Johnson Mountain Boys. Released in 1997, the duo's *Dreaming* was a fourteen-track album featuring several cuts from the three albums completed for Rounder in the 1980s.

Bill and Delia also recorded for Old Homestead, a label that specializes in old-time country and bluegrass, and released *Dreaming of the Times*, *Kiamichi Moon*, *Classic Bluegrass Today and Yesterday*, *Sacred Favorites Through the Years*, *Forty Years of Memories*, *I'll Get By*, and *The Good Woman Blues*. Bill's songs have been recorded by Ralph Stanley ("Stairway to Heaven") and the duo appeared on the 1992 *Stained Glass Hour: Bluegrass & Old-Timey Gospel Songs* with Ricky Skaggs, as well as *Rebel Records: 35 Years of the Best in Bluegrass (1960-1995)* released in 1996.

In addition to managing the festival and recording, Bill and Delia maintain an active tour schedule, having performed in 2002 and 2003 in several states, including Oklahoma, Texas, Alabama, Florida, and Mississippi. (GC)

Grantham, George
(b. January 20, 1947)

An original member of Poco, the country rock group, from 1969 to 1977, George Edwin Grantham was born in Cordell, Oklahoma, a community of roughly 3,000 residents located in southwestern Oklahoma. Poco was formed in Los Angeles by two former members of Buffalo Springfield, Richie Furay and Jim Messina as well as Rusty Young. Along with the Byrds, Flying Burrito Brothers, and Dillard & Clark, the group helped pioneer the synthesis of country and rock, but it is Poco that is considered the most "countrified" of the country rock groups. Its whiney steel guitar and mountain-style banjo picking anticipated the coming of the neo-traditionalist movement in the 1990s. One of their most popular singles was a satirical version of native Oklahoman **Dallas Frazier's** "Honky-Tonk Downstairs."

Young, steel guitarist with Poco, had known George since he was sixteen because they had performed together in a band called Boenzee Cryque in Colorado. When Poco was organized, Young contacted George for his percussion and vocal skills. George played on twelve albums with Poco, including *Pickin' Up the Pieces* (1969), their first album on the Epic label, *Crazy Eyes* (1973), and *Seven* (1974), in which George's drum solo on "Drivin' Wheel," is a highlight. Poco's most notable singles on which George played and sang include "You Better Think Twice," "C'mon," and "Rose of Cimarron." George again performed with Poco in 1984 on the *Inamorta* album. In 1989, Poco reunited (Messina, Furay, Meisner, Young, and Grantham) on the 20th anniversary of the founding of Poco to record an album with RCA called *Legacy*, which charted two pop singles, "Call It Love" and "Nothin' To Hide."

Three collections featuring the best of Poco, with George on drums and vocals, are MCA's *Crazy Loving: The Best of Poco 1975-1982* (1989), Sony/Columbia's *Forgotten Trail (1969-1974)*, released in 1990, and *Best of Poco: 20th Century* (MCA-2000).

After leaving Poco, Grantham joined a band called Secrets, and has recorded backup vocals and played drums with the Flying Burrito Brothers, The Gaithers, Rick Roberts, Ricky Skaggs, Sylvia, Steve Wariner, and Ronnie McDowell, with whom he played for four years. In the late 1990s, he joined Scotty Moore and DJ Fontana on a tribute to Elvis Presley, "All the King's Men," which was nominated for a Grammy.

Grantham formed a new band in 1998 called Hoopla and the group released an album entitled *It's Always Something* on the Spoon label. (GC)

Gray, Otto

(b. March 2, 1844 - d. November 8, 1967)

Leader of the first nationally known band to perform western music, to appear on radio and stage, to tour the U.S., to wear cowboy attire, to appear on the cover of *Billboard* magazine, to present the first female singer in country music, and to become a model for other cowboy and western music ensembles, Otto Gray was born in Lincoln County, South Dakota. Although born in South Dakota, Gray's parents homesteaded in Payne County, Oklahoma, in 1889 during the first land run into Oklahoma Territory. Gray was raised on a farm near Ripley, Oklahoma, where he became adept at roping skills, and eventually joined "Wild West" shows in Wyoming, Oklahoma, and other western states. He married Florence Opal Powell, a native Kansan, in 1905, and the marriage resulted in one son, Owen. Otto never became a musician (he tried his hand at the fiddle on occasion), but both "Mommie" (Florence's nickname) and Owen both sang, and their son played several musical instruments and wrote songs.

The Billy McGinty Cowboy Band (1925). Back row, left to right: Henry Hackney, Frank Sherrill, Roy Munday, Guy Messecar, and Paul Harrison. Front row, left to right: Marie Mitchell, Norma (last name unknown), Molly McGinty, Paul Sharum, and Ulyss Moore. Sitting in front: Ernest Bevins.

In 1926, Gray assumed management of Billy McGinty's Cowboy Band, a Ripley, Oklahoma-based outfit that had appeared on radio station KFRU in Bristow, Oklahoma, perhaps the first ever appearance of a Western band on radio in the United States. KFRU eventually became KVOO, and later moved its studio and transmitter to Tulsa. The cowboy band, under Gray, continued to broadcast over radio, and gained sponsorship from an Oklahoma hosiery company, the first instance of a country music band's commercial success. The band traveled in Gray's $20,000 customized Cadillac, equipped with a two-way radio transmitter, could accommodate all the band members, and featured a set of longhorns on the hood. The band soon began touring the Midwest, traveling some 2,000 miles to cities, such as Kansas City, Jefferson City, and St. Louis, Missouri, where they performed on radio station KMOX.

In 1928, Gray apparently changed the name of the band from its original name to Otto Gray and his Oklahoma Cowboys, and moved operations of the band from Ripley to Stillwater, home of Oklahoma A & M College, some fifteen miles to the northwest. During the next two years, Gray led the band on tour again through the Midwest and on to the East. Gray's group began to gain national attention, especially when *Billboard* magazine carried an article on them in 1929, and they broadcast over the Columbia Broadcasting System later that year. This network included the largest stations in the Midwest, such as WBBM (Chicago), WCCO (Minneapolis-St. Paul), MKBC (Kansas City, KMOX (St. Louis), KOIL (Omaha), and KFH (Wichita). Reports indicated that Gray and the Oklahoma Cowboys performed in such cities as Schenectady, Buffalo, and Binghamton, New York; Pittsburgh, Pennsylvania; and Cincinnati, Ohio, traveling the RKO and Orpheum vaudeville theater circuit. While traveling the East Coast, Gray signed a contract with the National Broadcasting Company in New York, and in 1930, *Billboard* again carried feature articles on the band, raving about their shows.

But the major breakthrough for the band was in 1931 when Otto Gray and his Oklahoma Cowboys were featured on the front cover of *Billboard*, the first country or western band to appear on the magazine's cover. Gray himself appeared on the front cover again in 1934, and would later use the magazine to advertise the act. After seeing the Oklahoma Cowboys in *Billboard*, other acts around the country began to emulate their western fashion, which included ten-gallon hats, chaps, and boots, as well as playing western music.

Between 1926 and 1931, Gray's band recorded on such labels as Gennett, Champion, Savoy, Superior, Fast, Bell, Okeh, Supertone, Vocalion, Meltone, Polk, and Pana. The band's repertoire included old-time fiddle tunes, ballads, novelty songs, and original pieces, such as "She'll Be Comin' Round the Mountain," "Suckin' Cider Through a Straw," "Plant a Watermelon on My Grave," "I Had But Fifty Cents," "The Cowboy's Lament," "Pistol Pete's Midnight Special," "Who Stole the Lock from the Hen House Door?" "Cowboy's Dream," and "Where Is My Wandering Boy Tonight." In 1931 Otto and Mommie were signed by Film Exchange, a New York-based company, to appear in several short films.

Over the years, the Oklahoma Cowboys Band personnel changed. The lineup generally consisted of Otto (emcee), Mommie (vocals), Owen, their son, who assumed the moniker "Zeb" in the act, played banjo, Wade "Hy" Allen (cello), "Zeke" Clements (vocals and guitar) and Chief Sanders (fiddle). Other members at one or another included Whitey Ford, vocalist and banjo player, who later appeared on the Grand Ole Opry as the "Duke of Paducah." The act also included Rex, a dog who barked when Otto entered or departed the stage, rope tricks performed by Otto and Mommie, and Owen singing his signature song, "It Can't Be Done," a novelty number that included lyrics such as "you can't hit a ball with a bat of your eye" and "you can't raise a cow from the calf of your leg." Only Otto, Mommie, and Owen remained with the band from its inception. It should be noted that Gray's band was the first country music act to use a cello in its ensemble.

After their last tour in 1935, the band disbanded with Otto Gray's retirement from music. He returned to his ranch near Stillwater and later became a real estate

Otto Gray and His Oklahoma Cowboys (early 1930s). From left to right: Otto Gray, Florence "Mommie" Gray, Lee Allen, Wade Allen, Owen Gray, and "Chief" Sanders. Rex, "The Bark of the Air," sits on the floor.

entrepreneur. Owen Gray prematurely died in 1947, reportedly brought on by alcoholism. Otto died in Springdale, Arkansas, where his second wife resided, while Mommie died on November 14, 1950 in Stillwater. Both Otto and Mommie Gray are buried in Fairlawn Cemetery in Stillwater. (GC)

Gray, Wardell
(b. February 13, 1921 - d. May 25, 1955)

Considered an important figure in Benny Goodman's first experimentation with the bebop style of jazz, and playing tenor saxophone on Dexter Gordon's jazz classics, "The Chase" and "The Hunt," Wardell Gray was born in Oklahoma City, but left the state at an early age. The youngest of four children, Gray's family moved in 1929 to Detroit, where his first music lessons were on the clarinet which he played when he entered high school at Northeastern High School. After transferring to Cass Technical High School in 1935, he left school in 1936, realizing that jazz was his favorite subject. His brother-in-law and noted Detroit musician, Junior Warren, advised him to stay with the clarinet, but once Wardell heard Lester Young on record, he switched to tenor saxophone. His first job was with Isaac Goodwin's small band, a part-time ensemble that played local dances. Thereafter, he played with the Dorothy Patton combo in Flint, Jimmy Raschel's band in Detroit, and Benny Carew's group in Grand Rapids. At about this time, he met Jeanne Goings and they had one daughter, Anita, born in 1941.

In 1940, Wardell took a tenor chair at the Congo Club, a popular nightspot in Detroit's black entertainment area. At one time or another, the club featured such well-known jazz artists, such as **Howard McGhee** and Teddy Edwards. He and Jeanne were separated and he met Jeri Walker, a young dancer in the chorus line at the Three Sixes, a club near the Congo. Jeri, who he eventually married in 1945, knew Earl "Fatha" Hines, and when he came to Detroit in 1943, she persuaded Hines to hire Wardell. He doubled on tenor and clarinet with Hines until 1945. He then joined Billy Eckstine's big band for a short period before working with Benny Carter in 1946.

In 1947, Gray relocated with Carter's band to the West Coast where he was active in the growing bebop revolution, playing with Dexter Gordon in the South Central Los Angeles jazz clubs, such as The Bird in the Basket, Lovejoy's, and Club Alabam. His success in these sessions resulted in Ross Russell inviting him to participate in a studio session he was organizing for his Dial label. The session was designed to showcase Charlie "The Bird" Parker, but Wardell held his own.

Wardell and Dexter Gordon continued their tenor battles, and Ross Russell managed to arrange a simulation of one of their competitions on *The Chase*, which became Wardell's first nationally recognized recording. With his newly gained national fame, Wardell was invited to join the Just Jazz series for which he recorded "Just You, Just Me" and "Sweet Georgia Brown," some of his best work. Another break for Gray occurred when Benny Goodman heard him in a concert in 1947. Goodman was so impressed that he hired Wardell, and Gray played his first gig with Goodman at the Click Club in Philadelphia in 1948. Financially unsuccessful, Goodman eventually dissolved the group, but by then Wardell was firmly established on the East Coast jazz circuit, working with Tadd Dameron and Count Basie's band.

In 1949, Gray returned to Goodman, this time in Benny's big band, but life with Goodman was an unhappy one for Wardell with the constant traveling and his marriage to Jeri breaking up. On leaving Goodman, he rejoined Count Basie c. 1950, however, it was now a septet, including Clark Terry and Buddy DeFranco, rather than the big band. He played with Basie, both with the septet and big band, intermittently until 1951 when he decided to return to the West Coast and remarried after divorcing Jeri. By this time, jobs in the Los Angeles area were scarce and recording sessions were few. Although his home life was going well, he seemed disillusioned with the music business, although in 1952, another live recording session with Dexter Gordon proved that he was still capable of playing superbly, as did the recordings with Wardell's septet in Los Angeles that same year. Around this time, he appears to have become involved in the drug scene, which affected his playing and was reflected in his last studio session in 1955. When Benny Carter opened the Moulin Rouge in Las Vegas in 1955, he called upon Wardell to join his band, but when the show opened on May 25, Wardell was absent. The next day he was found with a broken neck on a stretch of desert on the outskirts of Las Vegas. Wardell Gray was mysteriously dead at age thirty-four. Gray's solo work on such numbers as "Twisted" (1949), "Farmer's Market," (1952) and "Little Pony" (1950) have become classics, and his *Memorial Albums, Vols. 1 and 2* are among the best collections of his work. A biographical film, *The Forgotten Tenor*, was made in 1994 by Abraham Ravett, and in 2002 the U.K. label Proper Records released a four-CD set of Gray's music, *Blue Lou*, featuring a retrospective of Gray's work from 1947 to 1952. (GC)

The Great Divide
(formed in 1992, Stillwater, OK)

Green, Kelley (b. January 22, 1968)
Lester, J.J. (b. July 16, 1968)
Lester, Scott (January 1, 1964)
McClure, Mike (b. July 7, 1971)

Surfacing in the college town of Stillwater, Oklahoma, The Great Divide are one of a few groups categorized loosely as **red dirt** musicians, and were the first musicians classified solidly as such to have been signed to a major label. The Great Divide's brand of music, sometimes categorized as y'allternative or

Americana, combines classic country tropes and instrumental styles that weave in and out of traditional honky tonk music and Southern rock. Starting out with practices in an old Quonset hut south of Stillwater in 1992, and fronted by vocalist, guitarist, and primary songwriter Mike McClure (b. Shawnee), The Great Divide's sound is rounded out by brothers Scotte (b. Stillwater) and J.J. Lester (b. Stillwater), on guitar and drums respectively, and bassist Kelley Green (b. Little Rock, AR).

Raised in Tecumseh where he began playing guitar at age ten and writing songs in high school, Mike McClure attended Seminole Junior College in 1989, and after two years transferred to Oklahoma State University in Stillwater where he met Scotte Lester, a former bull rider and firefighter, J.J., also a former bull rider, and Kelley, an agricultural economics major at the time. McClure learned a lot of his songwriting skills by hanging out "The Farm," a house rented by John Cooper of the **Red Dirt Dangers** outside Stillwater, where a lot of local musicians and songwriters would gather and jam from 1989 to 1999. The Great Divide's first gig was in 1992 on the back of flat bed trailer at a steer-roping event in Perry, Oklahoma. The group played often at the Wormy Dog Saloon near the Oklahoma State University campus and released their first CD, *Goin' for Broke*, independently in 1994 which went on to sell more than 10,000 copies.

With repeated trips to Texas where they developed a strong fan base, the band's status elevated quickly as they began opening for artists like Willie Nelson, Tracy Lawrence, the Dixie Chicks, the Charlie Daniels Band, and Chris LeDoux. The band signed over their second album, *Break in the Storm*, to Atlantic Records who released the album in 1998. The album was produced by Lloyd "praise the Lloyd" Maines, the Texas steel guitar player and father of Dixie Chick Natalie Maines, who has produced projects for Jerry Jeff Walker, Robert Earl Keen, Red Dirt Rangers, Charlie Robison, and others. The result was a national coming out party for red dirt music in which The Great Divide acknowledged all those musicians who had in many ways created the style, such as Bob Childers, Tom Skinner, and **Jimmy LaFave**. LaFave does a guest vocal on the Tom Skinner song, "Used To Be." Atlantic Records had difficulty in marketing the album, however, and after further trouble understanding 1999's *Revolutions*, The Great Divide left the corporate music industry machine to go back to their independent ways.

Subsequent to leaving Atlantic, the group released a compilation of previously mentioned red dirt artists on their own Broken Records label, *Dirt and Spirit,* and in 2000, the group loaded up their gear into the historic Will Rogers Theatre in Oklahoma City where they recorded *Afterglow: The Will Rogers Sessions.* In 2001, the band re-released *Dirt and Spirit*, and released *Remain* independently in September of 2002.

Recorded in Nashville and featuring vocalist and songwriter McClure for the final time as he made the decision to go solo in 2003, *Remain* features more of the introspective songs with the hybrid country rock sound for which many of the red dirt groups are known. The album enjoyed success on the Texas Music Chart, reaching #3 south of the Red River while the group toured heavily throughout the Southwest during the fall. Over the winter months of 2002 and '03, Mike McClure did a string of solo acoustic shows through Texas and Oklahoma, and released his first solo CD, *Twelve Pieces* (Compadre). The album features acoustic songs McClure felt were not appropriate for the band, and also enlisted guest vocalists Cody Canada of **Cross Canadian Ragweed,** and Susan Gibson, known for writing the Dixie Chicks' hit, "Wide Open Spaces." The album's release and McClure's solo performances led fans to speculate that he would leave the group. Those rumors were confirmed when The Great Divide announced they would perform their last show with McClure on March 28th at the The Tumbleweed outside of Stillwater, a performance that was recorded for release as *The Great Divide Absolutely Live at Tumbleweed Vol. 1.* With his compositions having been recorded by **Cross Canadian Ragweed**, **Jason Boland and the Stragglers**, and **Tyler England,** and having produced albums for Ragweed and Boland, McClure seems content to work things out on his own. Given his lyrical gift and further abilities as a singer and producer, McClure's musical path appears secure.

The post-McClure Great Divide continue on since they do have a recognizable name and strong fan base through the Southwest and Midwest. While J.J. Lester took time out in the spring of 2003 to produce another new Stillwater act, No Justice, by summer's end the group added singer and lead guitarist Micah Aills to front the band, and debuted the new lineup at, where else, The Tumbleweed. www.thegreatdivide.com   www.mikemccluremusic.com

Guthrie, Jack
(b. November 13, 1915 - d. January 15, 1948)

Best known as co-composer of "Oklahoma Hills," cousin of famed folksinger **Woody Guthrie,** and producer a distinctive style of singing and yodeling based on his idol, Jimmie Rodgers, Jack Guthrie was born Leon Jerry Guthrie in Olive, Oklahoma, a tiny hamlet southwest of Tulsa in Creek County. Jack disliked the names of Leon and Jerry and assumed "Jack" when he cut his first record. When he moved to California, he was also known as "Oklahoma" or "Oke," monikers given to him by folks in that state because of his roots in Oklahoma. His father was John Camel Guthrie, younger brother of Charley Guthrie, the father of the noted folksinger Woody Guthrie.

Jack was influenced by his father, a blacksmith by trade, but also an old-time fiddler, as well as by several of his relatives, such as Woody, who were musicians. As a result, Jack learned several instruments, including the guitar, fiddle, and bass fiddle. Jack's family moved to Amarillo, Texas, when he was eight, but returned to Oklahoma City in 1929. They then relocated to Texas once again, but returned to Sapulpa, Oklahoma when Jack was fifteen. According to Guy Logsdon's liner notes to *Oklahoma Hills*, Wava, Jack's sister, reports that he learned some guitar chords from **Gene Autry** while Autry was working as a telegraph operator in Sapulpa. Wava also relates in the Logsdon notes that Jack was not infatuated with schoolwork, and would enter the front door of school and then head out the back door. Apparently, the last school Jack attended was seventh grade in tiny Midlothian, Oklahoma, located in Lincoln County.

The family moved to California in the mid-1930s finally settling in Sacramento. Prior to their residence in Sacramento, Jack worked several jobs in the Los Angeles area, including a laborer for construction companies, driving a truck, and working for the WPA and U.S. Forest Service. Following a rodeo accident in which he broke his back, Jack began serious pursuit of a career in music.

At age nineteen, Jack married Ruth Henderson in 1934, resulting in a chaotic marriage in which they often were separated. Shortly after they were married, Jack developed a rodeo act that included trick roping and bullwhip performances during which Ruth assisted him. During the act, Jack would always sing and play several songs.

In 1937, Woody, his cousin, moved to Los Angeles, and he and Jack soon formed a musical team. Because their singing styles varied, the two rarely sang together with Jack playing the guitar or fiddle when Woody sang, while Woody would pick the guitar and play the harmonica when Jack sang. After several successful performances, they auditioned for radio station KFVD in Hollywood, and on July 19, 1937, made their debut as the *Oke & Woody Show*. Shortly thereafter in 1937, Woody penned "Oklahoma Hills," which they used during their shows. But after two months of the show, Jack left because of family responsibilities, including a new baby son, and the program became the Woody and Lefty Lou Show. Maxine "Lefty Lou" Crissman was introduced to Woody through Jack, and Woody soon discovered the two harmonized well; hence, she became his new singing partner on the KFVD show. In 1939, Woody left the West Coast for New York City, but Jack remained as construction worker, rodeo performer, and playing music at beer joints and nightclubs, where he was dubbed "Oklahoma's Yodeling Cowboy."

In 1944, Jack recorded "Oklahoma Hills" for Capitol Records, his first for the recording company, after meeting several musicians who worked as session personnel for the company and assistance provided by Ruth Crissman, a friend who had joined his rodeo act and provided funding for his venture into the recording field. The famed song was released by Capitol in 1945, and soon became a #1 country music hit across the nation. When Woody heard the recording over a jukebox, he contacted Capitol and declared it was his composition. After negotiations between Jack and Woody, the two compromised and decided to share the copyright.

In 1945-46, Jack served a short period in the US Army. When "Oklahoma Hills' was released, he was stationed in the Pacific. After discharge, Jack formed a band called the "Oklahomans," and the group played dances along the West Coast and did some touring with Ernest Tubb. His health began to decline and it was suggested by his family that he check into a sanitarium because his sister had suffered with tuberculosis, however, Jack refused and kept writing songs, performing with his band, and recording for Capitol, including eight sessions between 1944 and 1947 that included thirty-three songs. Among these sessions were two more of Jack's compositions, "Oklahoma's Calling" and "For Oklahoma, I'm Yearning," the latter he co-wrote with his sister, Wava.

In 1947, Tubb arranged for Jack to appear in the film, *Hollywood Barn Dance*, in which he sang another one of his hit songs, "Oakie Boogie," a song that is particularly important for its representation of the hybrid style of music known as country boogie, itself an outgrowth of Western swing and a musical forebear to the rockabilly movement of the 1950s. His last recording session was similar to the last Jimmie Rodgers session. A cot was set up in the studio on which he could rest between songs. He died a few weeks later at the Livermore Veteran's Hospital, located near Sacramento, shortly after his 32nd birthday. Buried in Memorial Cemetery in Sacramento, Jack Guthrie is often overlooked in the popularization of such songs as "Oklahoma Hills" and "Oakie Boogie."

In 1996 Rhino Records released *Heroes of Country Music, Vol. 4: Legends of the West Coast*, which featured Jack and His Oklahomans performing "Oklahoma Hills." Bear Family, a German company, released a thirty-track CD entitled *Milk Cow Blues* in 2001, which features Jack singing some of his Jimmy Rodgers' favorites like "Muleskinner Blues" and "Peach Pickin' Time in Georgia." Additionally, Bear Family has released *Oklahoma Hills*, which features most of Guthrie's better known tunes, and *When the World Has Turned You Down,* that includes the remainder of Guthrie's Capitol session recordings, as well as the remainder of his transcriptions. Exhibiting his wide-ranging interests, *When the World Has Turned You Down* finds Guthrie performing Roy Acuff's "Low and Lonely," Ernest Tubb's "You Nearly Lose Your Mind," Red Foley's "Freight Train Blues," and **Bob Wills**'s "Time Changes Everything" and "Take Me Back to Tulsa," and several traditional blues numbers. All discs feature extensive notes from Tulsa's Guy Logsdon, who has carried out more than 40 years of research into the hard-to-track Jack Guthrie, and is also one of the absolute foremost experts on Woody Guthrie. (GC/HF)

Guthrie, Woodrow Wilson "Woody"
(July 14, 1912 – October 3, 1967)

Because of the volume and historical significance of his work, Woody Guthrie is the single most important Anglo-American folk singer of the twentieth century. His most enduring song in the popular consciousness is "This Land is Your Land," however, his songs about the dust bowl and Great Depression in the 1930s, and the union movement of the 1940s, are important documents of life and politics in those times. By writing and singing about current events from his perspective, Guthrie recast the folk ballad into medium for social protest, observation, and contemplation of political activism. Born in Okemah, Oklahoma and named after President Woodrow Wilson, Guthrie's enduring music continues to influence countless musicians and singer songwriters to the present day. Of the thousands of songs he wrote but never recorded, new interpretations by contemporary artists are constantly reviving Woody, and his children's songs are still valuable and fun experiences for young people, parents, and teachers.

Woody Guthrie's family first came to Indian Territory sometime in the early 1890s when his maternal grandfather moved with his schoolteacher wife and five daughters to a farm outside Welty, a speck of a town now in Okfuskee County, but then in the **Muscogee (Creek)** Nation. Around the same time, Woody's paternal grandfather, Jeremiah Guthrie, came in from Texas to start a cattle ranch on the Deep Fork of the Canadian River. Guthrie's father, Charles Edward Guthrie, met Woody's mother, Nora Belle Tanner, in the rural society of northeastern Okfuskee County, and the two were married in 1904. Born five years after Oklahoma's statehood, Woody heard old-time ballads his mother sang to him as a child, and

started playing a harmonica as a young boy by imitating an African-American man who shined shoes in a barber shop and also played the mouth organ. Woody wrote in his autobiography that his father played guitar and banjo, and sang, "Negro and Indian square dances and blueses." Guthrie also remembered hearing black men making up songs every day as they built his grandparents' new house, and Indians, most likely Creeks, singing and chanting as they walked the back-trails in the woods. Woody's tragedy-filled family life is an important part of his story and is covered thoroughly in Joe Klein's authorized 1980 biography, *Woody Guthrie: A Life* (Delta). His sister died in a fire accident, and his mother wound up in a state asylum as a result of the socially and medically misunderstood Huntington's Disease that Woody also later developed. With little supervision at home, Woody lived on the fringes of Okemah's rough and tumble social elements in his early teens. However, he also continued going to high school where he started drawing cartoons, and was on the high school newspaper and yearbook staff. His classmates thought him entertaining enough to put him on the back of flatbed truck for a show on Main Street in hopes of raising money for the junior prom.

After the family with whom he had been staying moved to Arizona in 1928, Woody quit school and traveled to Texas where he worked odd jobs of all types. He picked grapes, helped carpenters, drilled water and oil wells, and hauled wood, all the while carrying his harmonica and playing with everyone he could wherever he could. After making it as far south as the Gulf of Mexico in the summer of 1929, he tired of the migrant farm lifestyle and headed back to Okemah. When he arrived, a letter from his father was waiting that asked Woody to head west to the oil-boom town of Pampa in the Texas panhandle. Seventeen when he arrived in Pampa, Woody worked at various odd jobs before getting a job at a drugstore across the street from his father's rooming house. In the back of the drugstore, he found an old guitar and started to learn some chords from his father's brother, Jeff. Next to the store, an African-American shoe shine man knew how to play the blues, and showed Woody the rudiments of the form on guitar which would influence many of his greatest songs with blues in the titles. Although Woody did not finish high school in Pampa, he attended for a short while and during that time met Matt Jennings who had purchased a pawn shop fiddle but did not really know how to play it. The two struck up a friendship, learn to play together, and before long met another boy, Cluster Baker, who played guitar, and they formed the Corncob Trio. Matt also connected Woody to his first wife, Mary (Jennings) Guthrie, with whom Guthrie had three children – Gwen, Sue, and Bill.

The group got their first taste of being paid musicians at a dance at the local skating rink, and continued playing mostly at people's houses and local functions. By 1934, the Corncob Trio started getting better gigs and Woody started writing his own songs. Then, the event that would shape Woody's identity as a musician and folksinger occurred on April 14, 1935. As a result of a long drought, thousands of tons of topsoil roared through the Oklahoma and Texas panhandles and covered Pampa in a heavy dirt blanket. Following the dust were migrants, fliers in their hands that promised work in the verdant fields and valleys in California. The stories they told and the experiences of living through the dust storm and the Great Depression caused Woody to start writing the first of his dust bowl songs. Woody began to ramble from Pampa and his young wife more and more in 1936. He wrote and sang about what he saw on the roads and highways of the Southwest. He sang to the dispossessed, repossessed, and depressed. He sang songs about their lives in songs he was making up as he traveled, songs from their past lives he remembered from his mother's old time ballads, and the cowboy and country songs that were popular on the radio.

After a lot of traveling around the Midwest, Southwest, West, and back to Pampa, Woody decided to go to California in 1936. He arrived in Glendale,

California, a gathering place for migrant Okies, a negative term in the national jargon at that time. Several other Guthries had made their way to Glendale, including Woody's cousin, Jack Guthrie, who would later have a hit with "Oklahoma Hills," written by Woody but made popular by Jack. Already working as a would-be cowboy singer, Jack found work for them in a cowboy vaudeville show that led to the *Oke and Woody* radio show on KFVD, a Los Angeles station. Due to financial difficulties (they were not being paid for the show), Jack left, and Woody continued on the show with Maxine "Lefty Lou" Crissman. The homespun show appealed to the thousands of former farm dwellers who inhabited Los Angeles in the late 1930s, and in late 1937 Woody and Maxine signed a one-year contract with Standard Broadcasting. In 1938, Woody took an offer to assemble a hillbilly musical troupe to perform on powerful Mexican radio station XELO, but it did not work out and he and Maxine wound up back in Los Angeles on KFVD. Exhausted, Maxine's interest and ability in performing faded and the show ended in June of 1938. Woody began traveling through California and seeing the destitution of the people who lived in the farm camps, under bridges, and on the streets. His songs started to become more political and even more of a document of the people's hard lives he was witnessing. Guthrie became an active supporter of worker's rights and labor unions. Songs like "Vigilante Man," "Do-Re-Mi," and "Dust Bowl Refugee" entertained thousands of people at labor rallies, communist related meetings, and organized meetings touting unions, good wages, and government assistance for the economically disadvantaged, also known as "the poor." This status led to his interaction with Ed Robbin, a reporter for the *People's World*, the West Coast's Communist newspaper, and began a long misunderstood musical and authorial connection between Woody and the Communist Party detailed fully in the previously mentioned Klein biography.

In 1940, Guthrie moved to New York where he met and sang with Pete Seeger, Burl Ives, and **Agnes "Sis" Cunningham**. He traveled the East Coast performing widely for both folk music fans and gatherings of workers who were trying to upgrade their rights. During this time he also wrote his first version of "This Land Is Your Land" under a working title of "God Blessed America," and made an important connection with noted folklorist Alan Lomax who recorded Woody in Washington D.C. in March of 1940. During these sessions, Woody recorded some of his best known songs: "Talking Dust Bowl Blues," "Do-Re-Mi," Hard Times," "Pretty Boy Floyd," "They Laid Jesus Christ in His Grave," and "I'm Going Down the Road Feeling Bad," among others. In addition to singing on the Library of Congress sessions, Guthrie talked a lot. Tracks such as "Monologue on the Youth of Woody Guthrie" and "Dialogue on the Dust Bowl" serve as very informative oral histories of both Guthrie's life to that point and of his time in Oklahoma and California. Subsequent to the sessions, Lomax convinced RCA to record Woody's dust bowl songs in their studios, which they did in April, 1940, and released them on Victor as *Dust Bowl Ballads Volume 1 and 2* in sets of 78 rpm 10" records, again in 1950 as *Talking Dust Bowl* (Folkways), and in 1964 as *Dust*

Bowl Ballads. Critics often cite these recordings as his most important works and are primary listening for students of Guthrie. Songs from *Dust Bowl Ballads* include "Talking Dust Storm Blues," "Dust Bowl Refugee," "Dust Cain't Kill Me," and "So Long, It's Been Good to Know You." The songs are not only important documents of Woody's style in his strong Oklahoma accent, they are also novellas of the rough life many people endured in the 1930s. His knowledge of the realities in the Depression-era dust bowl are as important as any history book on the period. Collectors should note that all the *Dust Bowl Ballad* releases have subtle track differences, which is why Guy Logsdon's discography in *Hard Travelin': The Life and Legacy of Woody Guthrie* (Wesleyan University Press, 1999) is a primary source for understanding the complexities and details of Woody Guthrie's recording career.

Woody's New York years in the early 1940s were busy with performances on radio, concerts, and recordings. In 1941, Guthrie began touring the United States with Lee Hays, Pete Seeger, and Millard Lampell in a group called the Almanac Singers whose core members went onto form The Weavers, sans Woody, that became the most commercially successful folk group of the late 1940s and early 1950s. They appeared alternately at concerts, charity affairs, radical meetings, and union gatherings. In addition to traditional folk songs, the group performed topical Guthrie compositions such as "Union Maid," "Talking Union," and "Union Train a Comin'." Woody's period with the Almanac Singers is explored in some detail by Richard A. Reuss with JoAnne C. Reuss in *American Folk Music & Left Wing Politics: 1927 to 1957* (Scarecrow Press, 2000). Between stints with the Almanac Singers, Woody was commissioned by the U.S. Interior Department to travel to Oregon and write songs in support of the Bonneville Dam's construction in Oregon, which he did by writing twenty-eight songs in twenty-eight days for the Bonneville Power Authority. The end product of the project culminated as *The Columbia River Songs*, to include "Roll on Columbia" and "Grand Coulee Dam." In 1942, he divorced Mary, and began a relationship with Marjorie Mazia, a dancer in the Martha Graham troupe, whom he married in 1946 and with whom he had four children – Cathy, Arlo, Joady, and Nora. In 1943, his novel, the semi-autobiographical, sometimes philosophical, and all Woodysized *Bound For Glory* was published. With World War II in full swing, and Woody all of thirty-one-years old, he joined the U.S. Merchant Marine and traveled from the British Isles to Russia, a journey that provided the lyrics for several anti-fascist songs. After the war ended, Guthrie returned to New York where he settled in New York with Marjorie and continued writing songs of all types, especially children's songs that manifested on the album *Songs to Grown On* (1946). Tragically, their first child was killed in a fire. Their other children included Arlo, who is a noted folk singer in his own right, Joady, and Nora.

In the years after 1946, Guthrie performed as a soloist and in concerts with other well-known folk singers of those years, such as Ramblin' Jack Elliot, Leadbelly, Pete Seeger and the Weavers. He also began to experience the first symptoms of the Huntington's disease that plagued his mother many years before in Oklahoma. Recordings followed for Moses Asch's Folkways Records that provided material for many albums throughout the late 1940s. Smithsonian Folkways Records made previously unreleased recordings from this period (1944-1949) available in 1994 on *Long Ways to Travel* which included the whole diversity of Woody's repertoire. The collection contains union songs, tragic ballads, nonsensical fun songs for children, and talking blues. By 1950, however, Woody's life started to unravel due to his illness, and his recordings of the early 1950s are not indicative of his genius. He did marry again in 1952, to Anneke Van Kirk, but his condition and the age difference between the two doomed the union. His health deteriorated to such a point in the 1950s he could not play guitar, type, nor hold a pen anymore.

In 1954, Guthrie entered Greystone Hospital in New Jersey by his own choice, the first of thirteen hospitals in which he would stay until his death. During the 1960s, Guthrie only degenerated slowly due to Huntington's, a disease of the muscles that leaves the mind active but slowly robs the body of its ability to move, and for which no known cure exists. Ironically, Guthrie was not able to participate in the resurgent folk music scene of the 1960s when artists such as Bob Dylan modeled themselves after his iconoclastic ideals. Dylan made repeated visits to Guthrie's hospital room in the years before Guthrie died, and did much to maintain Guthrie's songs and style before the public. In 1965, a collection of Woody's stories, drawings, poems, new songs, articles, and reminiscences were published as *Born to Win*. After his death in 1967 at the Creedmoor State Hospital in Queens, New York, Guthrie was honored by many memorial concerts to raise money and awareness for Huntington's disease. Woody Guthrie's legacy has not gone unnoticed nationally, nor locally in Oklahoma. In 1971 Woody was inducted into the Songwriters Hall of Fame, and the Nashville Songwriters Hall of Fame followed suit in 1977. In 1988, Guthrie was inducted into the national Rock and Roll Hall of Fame for his pioneering work in using the folk song as an agent for social change.

In 1990, *Pastures of Plenty: A Self-Portrait*, edited by Dave Marsh, provided the public with many excellent photos of Guthrie, and also printed drawings and other unpublished writings by him. In 1996, the year he was awarded a posthumous Lifetime Achievement Award by the Folk Alliance, Woody's daughter, Nora Guthrie, opened the Woody Guthrie Archives in New York City. The collection of Guthrie's personal papers, to include letters, notebooks, diaries, photographs, drawings, and thousands of songs, is open to the public by appointment. As a benefit to the archives, in 1996 a live concert was organized in honor of Woody at the Rock and Roll Hall of Fame and Museum that became the CD, *'Til We Outnumber Them*, released on Ani Difranco's Righteous Babe Records in 2000. On the album, Arlo Guthrie, Billy Bragg, the Indigo Girls, Bruce Springsteen, Ramblin' Jack Elliot, and Dave Pirner of Soul Asylum play Woody's songs. The Woody Guthrie Archives also served as the foundation for alternative folk rockers Billy Bragg and Wilco to collaborate on songs for which Woody left lyrics but only the slightest musical notation. The result of the project became two albums, Mermaid Avenue (1998) and Mermaid Avenue Volume II (2000). In 1997, Rounder Records released *This Land Is Your Land*, a collection of Woody's children's songs performed by Woody and Arlo to accompany the video *This Land Is Your Land: The Animated Kids' Songs of Woody Guthrie* (LIVE Enterntainment). In 1999, the aforementioned *Hard Travelin': The Life and Legacy of Woody Guthrie*, edited by Rock and Roll Hall of Fame staffers Robert Santelli and Emily Davidson, brought together friends, family, and scholars to celebrate the life and achievements of America's foremost folk singer, to include the excellent discography and bibliography by Oklahoma writer and music historian, Guy Logsdon.

While Oklahoma has had a somewhat uneven love affair with its celebrated son, Woody is becoming more and more revered in his home state. In 1997, the newly founded Oklahoma Music Hall of Fame made Woody its first inductee, and in 1998, Woody's hometown of Okemah became the site for the annual Woody Guthrie Free Folk Festival. Singer-songwriters come from around the country to play in Woody's memory, scholars assemble to talk about his legacy, and seminars raise awareness about Huntington's disease. While the city of Okemah regularly celebrates the event with banners along the street, and businesses welcome Guthrie fans from around the world, some people have still not gotten beyond their deeply set opinions of Guthrie. As late as 2002, an enlarged article appeared in one Okemah business window during festival week titled "Woody Was No Hero," wherein the author speaks negatively of Woody, and one local church greeted festival goers with the maxim, "Words without deeds is like a garden with weeds," perhaps referring to Guthrie's incredible volume of writing but perceived lack of moral character. Further examples of the tension still existing in the state over Guthrie occurred in 2000, when the Smithsonian Institution, in conjunction with the Woody Guthrie Archives, developed a traveling exhibit, *This Land is Your Land: The Life and Legacy of Woody Guthrie*, to illustrate Woody's important life and career. Due to mostly unexplained or vague reasons, the exhibit almost never made it to Oklahoma when the Smithsonian could not find a museum host in the state. Finally, the Oklahoma Historical Society and the Oklahoma Arts Council joined forces to put the exhibit in the Oklahoma Historical Society's building at the tour's end. In 2001, The Friends of Libraries in Oklahoma, a local extension of the national organization, made Woody's birthplace of Okemah the state's first Literary Landmark, and placed a plaque by the statue of Woody in his hometown.

New books by and about Woody's include those targeted toward preschoolers, *Howdi Do* and *My Dolly*, while *Bling Blang* and *Woody Guthrie: Poet for the People* are for ages 4-8. Two documentary film projects are also in the planning stages, one for cable television and one looking into the true story behind Woody's song, "1913 Massacre." A number of potential CDs are in the works: a klezmer album of Woody's Jewish songs; a set of songs performed by Oklahoma and Texas musicians; a jazzy, improvisational album headed by Rob Wasserman and based on Woody's diary entries. Vocalists who are contributing to this project include Ani Difranco, Studs Terkel, and Dj Logic, and Lou Reed. In 2002, five-time Grammy nominees, Cathy Fink and Marcy Marxer covered the Guthrie/Billy Bragg song "Birds and Ships," gleaned from *Mermaid Avenue, Volume I*, and released it on their CD, *Postcards* (Community Music). In 2003, the National Folk Alliance's Nashville Local Committee helped sponsor The Woody Guthrie 90th Year Celebration in Music City. A concert featured Arlo Guthrie, Nanci Griffith, Gillian Welch and David Rawlings, **James Talley**, Jimmy LaFave, Ramblin' Jack Elliott, Slaid Cleaves, Ellis Paul, Janis Ian, Corey Harris, and others, and the month-long celebration also included a photo exhibit from the Woody Guthrie Archives, a Woody Guthrie film festival, and outreach into the Nashville schools with Woody's music. As part of the celebration, the Country Music Hall of Fame sponsored an exhibit of Woody Guthrie-themed paintings by renowned folk artist Kathy Jakobsen, and presented a panel discussion led by pop music journalist and historian Dave Marsh. The panel, entitled "Can You Get from the Dust Bowl to Music Row?", discussed how Guthrie's songs relate to the great populist tradition of country music in the manner of Jimmie Rodgers, Merle Haggard, and Steve Earle. The hall of fame's museum also displayed Guthrie's 1930s model Slingerland guitar.

While a multitude of musical albums, exhibits, books, films, articles, and experts continue to tell the story of Woody Guthrie, the best place to learn about his legacy is through the music he produced and the books he wrote or were compiled from his writing. While historical context and critical explanation can help one gain deeper insight into the complicated and rich life of Woody Guthrie, no one tells his story better than he has through his songs and words. The Woody Guthrie Archives has put together an excellent website that directs students, teachers, scholars, musicians, and fans to multiple resources for further study and appreciation of Woody Guthrie's life, legacy, and music. (HF) www.woodyguthrie.org

Haggard, Merle
(b. April 6, 1937)

Having written and recorded several country music standards, such
as "Okie From Muskogee," "The
Bottle Let Me Down," and
"Workingman's Blues," Merle
Haggard is one of the great songwriters and singing voices of
country music. He has won
numerous music industry awards,
garnered thirty-nine #1 country
hits, and is the only country performer to ever be featured on the
cover of the historic jazz magazine, Downbeat. His mother,
Flossie (Harp) Haggard, and his
father, James Haggard, lived in
Checotah, Oklahoma, about fifteen miles south of Muskogee,
until 1934. On land that is now
under Lake Eufala, the Haggards
were surviving as tenant farmers
in the 1930s until their barn
caught fire and they lost all of their livestock and farm tools. As a result, they followed the stream of unfortunates heading west in the great Okie migration to
California, where Merle was born in their converted boxcar house in Bakersfield.
Haggard's father played fiddle, but his mother was the inspiration behind him to
taking violin lessons at an early age. The death of his father, when he was nine-
years-old, began an unruly childhood that led to rocky adult life and landed
Haggard a stint in San Quentin prison in 1957. While in San Quentin, Haggard
not only had a chance to reflect on his life, but he continued picking a guitar as
he had since high school, and started writing songs in the vein of his heroes
Jimmie Rodgers and Jimmie Davis. He also saw Johnny Cash perform twice at
the prison, which inspired Haggard to think he could make music a career once
he was released in 1960.

Helped by Buck Owens and his wife Bonnie Owens (whom Haggard eventually married in 1965, divorced in 1978, and featured as a vocalist through the 1990s
and 2000s), Merle formed his own backing group, the Strangers. The Strangers
began playing a diverse array of country songs founded in western swing, blues,
jazz, and folk with Fuzzy Owen in the oil field bars and honky tonks around
Bakersfield. Owen helped Haggard get his first recording date with Tally Records

in 1962, beginning a career that continues through 2003. Haggard first broke into the country charts with "Sing a Sad Song" in 1963, and followed with an impressive string of honky tonk hits throughout the 1960s: "All My Friends Are Going to Be Strangers" (1965); "I'm a Lonesome Fugitive" (1966); "The Bottle Let Me Down" (1966); "Branded Man" (1967); "Mama Tried" (1968); "The Ballad of Bonnie and Clyde," "Hungry Eyes," "Silver Wings," and "Workin' Man Blues" (1969). Two songs from 1969 and 1970, "Okie from Muskogee" and "The Fightin' Side of Me" respectively, cemented Haggard's re-connection to Oklahoma for all time and made him an unwitting spokesperson for the conservative faction of Vietnam-era America, and won him CMA's Entertainer of the Year, Male Vocalist of the Year, Album of the Year, and Single of the Year in 1970. "Okie from Muskogee" is a tongue-in-cheek espousing of red, white, and blue values that was antithetical to the counterculture that evolved in the 1960s. However, right-wing conservatives, who felt their country's ideals were being unfairly assailed by the anti-war and anti-establishment elements of the United States, took the song very seriously and catapulted it to the top of the pop and country charts. "Fightin' Side of Me" is a similarly strong statement aimed at those who would disparage the United States. The song was heartily embraced by the same fans and it also jetted to #1.

Haggard opened the 1970s with a monster country hit, "Today I Started Loving You Again" (1970), now considered a country standard and has been covered by more than 400 artists. The 1970s witnessed a further string of hits, "Think I'll Just Stay Here and Drink" and "Rainbow Stew," and also saw Haggard experiment with dixieland jazz and western swing. Haggard won the CMA's Album of the Year Award in 1972 for Let Me Tell You About a Song (Capitol). His album A Tribute to the Best Damn Fiddle Player in the World teamed original members of the Bob Wills band, such as Eldon Shamblin, with his own Strangers. Since he grew up with Western swing as a strong influence, Haggard happily contributed to Wills' final recording project, For the Last Time.

In 1982, Haggard released a duet album with George Jones, A Taste of Yesterday's Wine, providing another #1 single, "Yesterday's Wine." In 1983, he released another duet album, Pancho and Lefty, with Willie Nelson, whom he had met in a poker game in 1963. Pancho and Lefty garnered Nelson and Haggard the CMA's Vocal Duo of the Year in 1983. More hits followed throughout the 1980s: "That's the Way Love Goes" (1983), "Natural High" (1984), "Kern River" (1985) and "I Had a Beautiful Time" (1986).

Haggard toured incessantly through the late 1980s and early 1990s although his commercial recording success dwindled as pre-packaged "hat acts" (young guys with cowboy hats) began to monopolize the country charts and record companies' promotional dollars. As a result, Merle restricted his touring and spent more time on his ranch near Lake Shasta, California, releasing Merle Haggard 1994 to limited commercial success. The Country Music Hall of Fame inducted Merle in 1994, and his 1997 induction into the Oklahoma Music Hall of Fame coincided with a resurgence of interest in his work. Foregoing the traditional major label track he had been on for almost thirty years, Merle's 2000 album, If I Could Only Fly, was released by the independent label Anti, a subsidiary of Epitaph, known primarily for punk rock recordings. The album is a stripped-down, back-to-basics country music effort that put Haggard back on the road to accolades from both old and new fans. He explained in a 2000 interview, "I feel at home with these young punk rebels." In 2001, Haggard started self-releasing projects, such as the gospel album, Cabin in the Hills, and Two Old Friends, an album of duets with Albert Brumley, Jr., son of the famous gospel composer from Spiro, Oklahoma, Albert Brumley, Sr. Also in 2001, Merle released Roots, Volume 1, an album of traditional country music by Hank Williams, Hank Thompson, and Lefty Frizzell, along with four of his own songs. The album was recorded live in the studio without any overdubs as an attempt to recapture the spontaneity of the earlier era in recording music that inspired the project.

In 2002, Audium Records released *The Peer Sessions*, an album featuring a duet with Jimmie Davis, piano work by Nashville legend Owen Bradley, and covers of songs by Jimmie Rogers, Floyd Tillman's famous "It Makes No Difference Now," and Tommy Duncan's "Time Changes Everything," made famous by Bob Wills and his Texas Playboys. In 2003, Haggard donated some of his family's heirlooms to the Smithsonian Institution, and continued to tour extensively throughout the United States, to include appearances in Norman at the Lloyd Noble Center, at the First Annual Merle Haggard UFO Concert in Roswell, New Mexico, and as part of the Electric Barnyard Tour with Marty Stuart and Connie Smith. In September, 2003, Merle released *Haggard Like Never Before* on his on label, Hag Records. The album's first single, "That's the News," generated significant national interest as a result of the song's critique of American media for focusing on sensational domestic news instead of international events of significance to U.S. foreign policy, enough publicity to land Merle on *Late Night with David Letterman* in October, 2003. (HF)   www.merlehaggard.com

Halley, David
(b. 1950)

Most associated with the west Texas sounds of Jimmie Dale Gilmore, Joe Ely, and Butch Hancock and the Austin progressive country scene in the 1990s, songwriter and guitarist David Halley was born in Oklahoma City, although he was raised in Lubbock, Texas. He first became interested in music when he saw Elvis Presley on the Ed Sullivan Show in 1958 or '59. With music surrounding him in the home where his mother played piano, and the family stereo had stacks of records around it, Halley began writing songs while attending Coronado High School. As one of the new generation of country and Americana songwriters, David has composed songs for such artists as Stacy Dean Campbell, Katy Moffatt, Jerry Jeff Walker,

Joe Ely, Jimmie Dale Gilmore, Mickey Newbury, and Keith Whitley. His most notable song is "Hard Livin'," recorded by Whitley on several of his albums, and was a Top 10 hit for Whitley in 1987. David wrote "Fair and Square," which was the title of Gilmore's 1988 release. Additional songs of note include "Rain Just Falls," recorded by Campbell on his 1999 album, *Ashes of Old Love*, and "Further" on her *Cowboy Girl* album of 2001. David has played session guitar for several artists, including Gilmore, Hancock, Dick Hamilton, Jo Carol Pierce, and Darden Smith. He appeared with Gilmore, Ely, and Hancock on an *Austin City Limits* special in 1983 entitled West Texas Songwriters.

Halley's first album, *Stray Dog Talk*, released in 1990 by Elvis Costello's Demon Records, included eleven tracks all written by him, and featured a duet with Syd Straw on "Dreamlife." It also included "Hard Livin'," "Rain Just Falls," and "Further." His second album, *Broken Spell*, released in 1994 on the now defunct DOS label, included eleven tracks all composed by David with such songs as "Hometown," "Close to Your Heart," and "Man of Steel." His recent recorded appearances include albums such as, *Horse Songs*, in which he is featured on one track with his composition, "Further," and *Frisco Mabel Joy Revisited*, the 2000 tribute album to Mickey Newbury, in which he performs "Swiss Cottage Place."

Halley continues to perform in Austin clubs, including a 2001 appearance in which he teamed with Syd Straw at the Cactus Café, and has had multiple record deal offers to be the primary singer and face on country music industry projects, but has turned them down in order to do his own work. He has also appeared at the Blue Door in Oklahoma City, his hometown.

Hanson

Hanson, Clarke Isaac (b. November 17, 1980)
Hanson, Jordan Taylor (b. March 14, 1983)
Hanson, Zachary Walker (b. October 22, 1985)

Riding their tight harmonies and sugar grooves inspired by Motown and 1960s R & B, Hanson became Oklahoma's biggest pop stars of the 1990s, **Garth Brooks** not included. While Isaac and Taylor were born in Tulsa to musical parents, Walker and Diana, who met when they attended Nathan Hale High School, Zach was born in Arlington, Virginia. The group rocketed to the top of the international pop music charts in 1997 with their single, "MMMBop," and have since racked up sales in excess of eight million worldwide for the single's Grammy nominated album *Middle of Nowhere*. Originally, the group's sound was based in the feel-good pop of the 1950s and 1960s with well-blended harmonies and strong sense of melody, while their "later" releases have matured into a soulful rock. Whether they will ever recapture the dynamism and frenzy achieved when they were the same age as the majority of record buyers remains to be seen.

Left to right: Taylor, Zach, and Isaac Hanson

The Hanson brothers' parents performed together in high school musicals and continued to pursue their musical interests at the University of Oklahoma. While Diana majored in music, they both sang with a Christian group called The Horizons that performed across the United States. After college, the two went back to their hometown of Tulsa, started a family, and Walker began working for Helmerich & Payne Inc., an international oil drilling and gas exploration company. As they Hanson family grew in the 1980s, Walker progressed through management at the company and in 1989 began a series of transfers that led the Hansons to Ecuador, Venezuela, and Trinidad-Tobago. Eager to give their kids a taste of home, the parents ordered a *Time/Life* collection of classic rock roll from 1957-1969. The boys started listening to the music and singing along with it, which became their primary musical influence. The family returned to Tulsa in 1990 and settled in a rural section of West Tulsa where they were home-schooled by Diana. After hearing the boys harmonize on songs they had learned from the *Time/Life* set, Walker and Diana taught them to sing "Amen" after saying a prayer at the dinner table. From there, the boys took piano lessons and decided to form a group called the Hanson Brothers, which they changed to The Hansons, and, finally, Hanson.

In 1990, the boys began singing *a capella* (without instruments) at private parties, local events, clubs, and made their first major appearance at Tulsa's Mayfest in 1992. That performance led to many others and for the next few years the group traveled throughout the Midwest doing shows, with Walker as their roadie, and Diana as their publicist and t-shirt vendor. In 1995, the group picked up a manager, Christopher Sabec, as a result of an impromptu performance on the street at the South by Southwest Music Conference in Austin, Texas. Then, in 1995, the boys decided to add instruments to the group. Although all three had already been taking piano lessons, Taylor stayed on keyboards, Isaac picked up a Gibson Les Paul guitar at a Tulsa pawnshop and began learning how to play the instrument, and Zac borrowed a set of Ludwig drums from a friend who had them in the attic, later replaced by a set of Pearl drums (both the Les Paul and the Pearl drum set are on loan to the Rock and Roll Hall of Fame in Cleveland, Ohio). Later that year, as the group became more proficient, Diana and Walker put together the resources necessary to record and release Hanson's debut CD, *Boomerang*. In addition to five songs they wrote, they also included covers by the Jackson 5, to whom they have been compared vocally, and the rhythm and blues standard, "Poison Ivy."

Hanson released their second independent CD in May of 1996 with the first public version of "MMMBop." Not long after, Hanson's manager, Christopher Sabec, sent a copy of the album to Steve Greenberg of Mercury Records. Greenberg made a trip out to Coffeyville, Kansas, where the group was playing, and immediately signed them. Greenberg wanted to get Hanson into the studio immediately, but felt the group's sound needed fattening, and their songs needed tightening, so he enlisted studio remix kings the Dust Brothers who had produced Beck's multi-platinum album, *Odelay*, as well as Steve Lironi who had worked with Black Grape, and Mark Hudson who had some pop success with his own family act, The Hudson Brothers, in the 1970s. After six months in a Los Angeles studio, the group finished the album, *Middle of Nowhere*, in January 1997.

While the album was being scheduled for a March release, the group made the video for "MMMBop" with noted video director Tamra Davis, and the promotion machine was set to make whatever it could out of the group's debut major label release. With the album due to hit stores in May, "MMMBop" was released to radio nationwide in late March and the song caused an immediate stir on the charts, entering at #16. With this success, the Mercury promotions department went into hyperdrive and began setting up interviews, performances, photo shoots, CD signings at record stores, and mall performances. Within days of the album's release, Hanson appeared on the *Rosie O'Donnell Show*, *The Late Show with David Letterman*, *CBS This Morning*, *The Today Show*, and *Live with Regis and Kathy Lee*. With all of this exposure, and the upbeat sound of "MMMBop" that was totally antithetical to the grunge rock that had dominated popular music since the arrival Nirvana, the single went to #1 on the *Billboard* pop charts and the album entered the album charts at #9.

Acclaim back home soon followed when Oklahoma governor Frank Keating declared May 26, 1997 Hanson Day in the state. In June, Hanson presented an award at the MTV Movie Awards, performed live in Oklahoma City to a frenzied audience, appeared on Jay Leno's *Tonight Show*, and their video for "MMMBop" was in heavy rotation on MTV. In July, the group had a cover story in *Entertainment Weekly*, and continued making promotional appearances in the U.S., Europe, Canada, Asia, Australia, and Indonesia throughout the year. If any doubt existed about Hanson's significance beyond pop, *SPIN* magazine, which typically focuses on music outside of the mainstream, featured the group in a September article. By the time the swell of Hansonmania crested, "MMMBop," the infectious single that introduced the band to the world, went #1 in twenty-seven countries.

Critical accolades coincided with the song's success. New York's *Village Voice* named "MMMBop" best single of 1997. *Rolling Stone* named *Middle of Nowhere* one of the "Essential Albums" of the decade, and *SPIN* noted, "Hanson [is] perhaps the only band in recent history beloved by both hormonally crazed 12-year-olds and their Motown loving parents, by both *Tiger Beat* and the *New York Times*." In October of 1997, the group sang the National Anthem at the opening game of the World Series. After building up so much momentum, what could Hanson possibly do for an encore? Other singles followed from *Middle of Nowhere*, "Where Is the Love?" and "I Will Come to You," both of which made the Top 40, but failed to achieve the success of the debut single. Wanting to satisfy the clamoring for more material by Hanson fans, Mercury rushed out a Christmas album, *Snowed In*, just in time for the 1997 holiday season. The group debuted songs from the album on a Saturday morning Fox broadcast of *Hanson's Jingle Bell Jam*, directly targeted toward the cartoon-aged audience. They also played the Jingle Ball at Madison Square Garden on the same bill as Aerosmith, The Wallflowers, and Fiona Apple, among others. Hanson's Christmas spirit was so infectious they performed "Merry Christmas Baby" for President Clinton and millions of television viewers.

By the end of 1997, *Oklahoma Today* magazine name Hanson its Oklahomans of the Year, and they were awarded Best Song and Best Breakthrough Act by the MTV Europe Music Awards. The frenetic pace of Hanson's life and the way in which their fans reacted to them is well documented in the *Tulsa, Tokyo and The Middle of Nowhere* video, released in 1997 by Polygram Video. In 1998, Hanson was nominated for three Grammy awards, to include Record of the Year, Pop Performance by Duo or Group with Vocal, and Best New Artist. In February of 1998, they taped an episode of VH-1's *Storytellers* concert series, and in May of 1998, Mercury released the group's earlier independent recordings as *3 Car Garage: The Indie Recordings '95-'96*. The album included the earlier version of "MMMBop" that ultimately got the band signed. Also in 1998, the group went on a three-month North American tour and took along Tulsa pop group **Admiral Twin** as their opening act. As a result of the tour, Mercury released a concert recording, *Live from Albertane*, which had limited sales impact on the record-buying public, but does provide a document of the group's progression as performing musicians in 1998.

With such a tremendous amount of success in such a short amount of time, the group returned to their Tulsa home, continued their home schooling, and started writing songs for their next album. 2000's *This Time Around* retains the undeniably catchy melodies and exuberant singing that distinguished *Middle of Nowhere*, and finds the boys exploring new sonic avenues, however, it did not achieve the momentous success of their previous studio outing. "Our songwriting and musical style have developed in a lot of ways," observed Isaac in a Mercury press release. "The guitar sound is heavier in points than before. But there are also more soft moments, more piano- and keyboard-driven material than on the last record. There's been an overall evolution within the band." Taylor added, "We just felt that song best represented where the music was going, and the genre we want to be associated with. It's a little more rock and roll, the chord structure is more complex." Musical guests on the album included such notables as Beck cohort DJ Swamp and John Popper (of Blues Traveler) on harmonica. Guitar prodigy Jonny Lang lends a hand on three tracks, including "This Time Around," and "Dying to Be Alive" augments its inspirational message about living life to the fullest with backing vocals from a gospel choir led by Rose Stone of Sly & the Family Stone fame.

After *This Time Around* did not measure up to the group's previous critical and sales success, Isaac explained he and his brothers were not worried. "Getting to make the music, and having a good time doing it, is the most important thing to us," he said in a 2000 interview. In 2001, another concert recording, *At the Fillmore*, was released, and the group contributed their voices to a recording of John Lennon's "Imagine" to benefit children who lost parents in the September 11 terrorist attacks. Throughout 2001 and 2002, local Tulsa music fans were treated to unscheduled, impromptu appearances around town when different members of the group tried out new material, or appeared with their friends in Admiral Twin. In 2002, Hanson appeared on an episode of *Sabrina, the Teenage Witch*, wherein the group debuted "Strong Enough to Break," from their expected 2003 release, *Underneath*, and were featured in a documentary by VH1, *Bubblegum Babylon*, that discussed the darker sides of the teen pop industry. They have also produced a self-made documentary about their meteoric climb to pop stardom, scheduled for a 2003 release, planned to release *Underneath,* a collection of acoustic versions of seven songs from their forthcoming album, in August of 2003, and scheduled an 13-city acoustic tour for the fall of 2003 to support that album's release. Their third studio album, *Underneath*, was scheduled for a spring, 2004 release on their own 3CG Records. (HF)
www.hansononline.com

Hardin, Gus
(b. April 9, 1945 – d. February 17, 1996)

Named as Top New Female Vocalist in 1983 by the ACM, Carolyn Ann Blankenship was born in Tulsa, Oklahoma. Nicknamed "Gus" as a teenager, she was also called "Red" and "Cookie" because of her red hair. Gus was the daughter of Mikey O'Malley, who she never knew, and was raised by her mother, Hopie, a **Cherokee** photographer. She began singing in church as a child, and sang in talent contests while in junior high. Gus graduated from Will Rogers High School in Tulsa, which produced such well-known artists as **J. J. Cale**, **David Gates**, **Elvin Bishop**, Gary Busey, Gailard Sartain, and **Leon Russell**.

Gus' first public performance was at age twenty-three with her husband Steve Hardin's band. For this public debut, she sang Aretha Franklin's hit, "(You Make Me Feel Like) A Natural Woman." Shortly thereafter, she cut three albums, including one at Leon Russell's Shelter studio in Tulsa. In 1974, Gus was plagued with cataracts on her eyes after taking steroids and cortisone derivatives for her allergies, and for five years was legally blind (1979-84) having to take atrophine eye drops to see anything.

After performing in Tulsa nightclubs for fifteen years, Gus became the project of GPC (Giant Petroleum Company) Entertainment (an agency primarily consisting of oilmen from Tulsa, including Fred Williams, Rick Loewenherz, and Mike Kimbrel) who formed in 1979 with the intention of making her a star. She opened for several big name country acts, including Johnny Paycheck and the Oak Ridge Boys, during the next three years.

In 1982, Gus signed with RCA Records and began working under the tutelage under Rick Hall of Fame Studios in Muscle Shoals, Alabama, where she cut her debut album, *Gus Hardin*, in 1983. Her first single to make the Top 10 was "After the Last Goodbye," which was followed with several low-level singles, "If I Didn't Love You" (#26), "My Mind Is On You," "What We Gonna Do," "Just as Long as I Have You," and "Loving You Hurts" (#32). She was recognized in 1983 by the ACM as Top New Female Vocalist, and by *Billboard* and *Cashbox* as New Country Artist of the Year.

In 1984, Gus underwent two intraocular lens transplant operations in Tulsa, which provided full sight. The same year, she released her second album, *Fallen Angel*, which spawned three chart singles, including the title track, as well as "I Pass," and "How Are you Spending My Nights," all of which made the Top 50. Her third album, *Wall of Tears*, was released in 1985, and yielded her most successful single, a duet with Earl Thomas Conley, "All Tangled Up in Love," which became a Top 10 hit, remained on the country charts for thirteen weeks, and earned her nominations for Best Performance by a Duet from CMA, ACM, and *Music City News*. Her 1985 video for "I Pass" garnered an American Music Awards nomination for

Favorite Country Music Female Vocalist Video.

Because of her perceived "abrasive" manner, Gus was dropped by RCA, and she returned to Tulsa in the late 1980s to perform in clubs there. She appeared on the 1993 compilation, *Sounds of Tulsa*, produced by radio station KMOD, and a 1995 holiday album, *Classic Tulsa Christmas*. Divorced six times, she became known as the "Elizabeth Taylor of Country Music," and publicists often made that fact part of her image. Described as having a voice that was "whiskey-soaked," Gus never achieved the great potential that many people saw in her, including fellow Oklahoman Leon Russell, who said she "sounds like a combination of Tammy Wynette, Otis Redding, and a truck driver." Tragically, Gus Hardin died in an automobile accident in 1996. (GC/HF)
www.gushardin.com

Harris, Roy
(b. February 12, 1898 – d. October 1, 1979)

One of the most important figures in the establishment of American symphonic music including thirteen symphonies, such as *Farewell to Pioneers*, *Symphony No. 3*, and *Folksong Symphony*, as well as composer of more than 200 works in a variety of genres and media, Leroy Ellsworth Harris was born near Chandler in Lincoln County, Oklahoma, where his family had claimed land during one of the Oklahoma land rushes. Roy's father, a farmer, took his family to the San Gabriel Valley in California. His first music instruction was from his mother who gave him piano lessons, although he later learned the clarinet.

As a teenager, he shortened his name to Roy. He enlisted in the U.S. armed services in 1916 to fight in World War I. Following his discharge, Roy enrolled at U.C.L.A. in 1917 and continued his music studies at the University of California-Berkeley from 1918 to 1921. As a student, he earned his tuition by driving a dairy cart.

During 1924-25, Roy studied with Arthur Farwell, who introduced him to Walt Whitman's poetry, which became one of his inspirations for musical composition, including the *Whitman Suite*. Among his other early teachers and advisers were Clifford Demorest, Ernest Douglas, Alec Anderson, Fannie Charles Dillon, Henry Schoenfeld, Modeste Altschuler, and Arthur Bliss.

In 1926 Roy traveled to the East Coast for the premier of his "Andante for Orchestra" by the New York Philharmonic. While staying at the MacDowell Colony, he met Aaron Copeland, who encouraged Roy to study under Nadia Boulanger in Paris. With financial assistance from Alma Wertheim and two Guggenheim fellowships, he spent 1927 through 1929 under Boulanger's tutelage. During this time, he wrote the "Concerto for Piano, Clarinet, and String Quartet," which premiered in Paris. This established him as one of the promising young American composers.

In 1929 Harris returned to the U.S. only to injure his spine in a fall that immobilized him following surgery. During this time of convalescence, he learned to compose on the piano and devoted his recovery period to refinement of his concepts of melody, harmony, and texture. Following his recuperation, he joined the Julliard School of Music summer faculty in 1934, and married Beula Duffey in 1936, his fourth marriage. Roy renamed his bride Johana, after J.S. Bach, and the couple had five children. Johana was an integral part of Roy's musical career thereafter, and served as consultant on many of his piano compositions, including "American Ballads" and the "Fantasy for Organ, Brass, and Timpani."

Roy's first national recognition came through Serge Koussevitzky, for whom he wrote his first symphony, *Symphony 1933*. His most successful work was *Symphony No. 3*, which premiered under Koussevitsky in Boston in 1939. Additional works for which he is noted include *Chorale* and *Prelude and Fugue* for string orchestra, *Song for Occupation, Story of Noah, Symphony for Voices, Three Symphonic Essays, Memories of a Child's Sunday, Variations on a Theme* for flute and string quartet, and *4 Minutes 20 Seconds* for flute and string quartet, and *Children's Suite*.

Roy's teaching positions included Mills College in Oakland, California (1933), Westminister Choir College of Rider University in Princeton, New Jersey (1934-38), Juilliard School of Music in New York City (summers only from 1934-38), Cornell University in Ithaca, New York (1941-43), Colorado College in Colorado Springs (1943-48), Utah State Agricultural College (1948-49), Peabody College for Teachers in Nashville (1949-50), Chatham College in Pittsburgh (1951-56), Southern Illinois University (1956-57), Indiana University (1957-60), *Universidad Interamerican de Puerto Rico* in San German (1960-61), and California State University-Los Angeles (1970-76). His best-known pupils were William Schuman, who later was president of the Juilliard School of Music and director of the Chamber Music Society of Lincoln Center, Peter Schickele, one of the most versatile composers in American music, and George Lynn, who became director of the Westminister Choir College.

Roy's other accomplishments include the organization of numerous music festivals, such as the Pittsburgh International Festival of Contemporary Music. Moreover, he founded the International Congress of Strings (1959), served as chief of music programming for the overseas branch of the Office of War Information (1945-48), elected to the American Institute and Academy of Arts and Letters, received the title of Composer Laureate of the State of California, awarded the Elizabeth Sprague Coolidge Medal, given the Naumburg Award for his *Symphony No. 7*, and visited the U.S.S.R in a delegation of American composers sponsored by the U.S. State Department (1958).

During the 1970s, several tributes were established for Harris, including the Roy Harris Archive at California State University-Los Angeles (1973) and the Roy Harris Society (1979). The latter organization was formed to promote performances, recordings, and research dealing with Roy's career. Roy Harris died in Santa Monica, California on October 1, 1979. (GC)

Harris, Samuel "Sam" Kent

(b. June 4, 1961)

Along with having gained substantial attention for his acting, songwriting, producing, screen writing, photography and directing, Sam Harris is one of the most successful singing stars to ascend from Oklahoma to a fixed place among the brightest lights of Broadway in New York City. His full singing range, his showmanship, and his choreographic expertise make him an in-demand concert performer and hot ticket in contemporary musical theater, as well as a respected director and performance consultant. Born in Cushing, Oklahoma, but raised in Sand Springs just west of Tulsa, Sam's earliest musical performance was at two-years-old singing "The Star Spangled Banner" at a football game in Oklahoma. Exposed to gospel music at an early age and musical theater before he moved from Oklahoma at fifteen, Sam's first national exposure was on the television talent program, *Star Search* in 1983. After winning his first competition on the program by singing "Somewhere Over the Rainbow," Sam continued as "Grand Champion" on the show for sixteen weeks during its inaugural season.

The success on *Star Search* led to a two-record deal with Motown, producing *Sam Harris* (1984) and *Sam-I-Am* (1986), both now out of print. His only minor R & B hit, "Sugar Don't Bite," came from the first album and peaked at #36. Sam's limited chart success was not reflected in album sales, however, as *Sam Harris* went on to be a million-selling album. The album included his version of

Sam Harris, 2003

"Somewhere Over the Rainbow," now a signature piece of his live performances. *Sam-I-Am* featured several original songs co-authored by Sam and his brother, Matt Harris. Even though the album had no hit to speak of, and was released only on vinyl and cassette as the CD revolution was taking place, *Sam-I-Am* also sold over a million copies. After having sales success with his two albums, Sam turned to other show business challenges of writing and directing for television and Broadway. Harris wrote the TBS sitcom, *Down to*

Earth, that lasted four years, the Los Angeles produced musical *Hurry! Hurry! Hollywood!*, and the stage production of *Hard Copy*.

In addition to touring the country in concert, Harris has played to sold-out audiences at Carnegie Hall, Los Angeles's Universal Amphitheatre, and London's West End. On Broadway in New York, Sam received strong critical notices and a Drama Desk nomination for his work in *Grease*. He received a Drama League award for his performance in *The Life,* in addition to Tony, Outer Critic's Circle and Drama Desk nominations for the role. Off Broadway and regionally, Sam starred as Al Jolson in *The Jazz Singer*, played the lead role in the Broadway musical revue *Revival*, which he wrote, performed in *Jesus Christ Superstar*, *Different Hats, Hair, Cabaret,* and toured nationally in Andrew Lloyd Weber's *Joseph and the Amazing Technicolor Dreamcoat*. Harris has also appeared on numerous television shows and specials, working with Stevie Wonder, George Michael, Liza Minnelli, Madonna, Elizabeth Taylor, Whitney Houston, Roberta Flack, and Elton John. After working with Sam, Liza Minnelli waxed rhapsodic about his work: "When Sam sings, I'm perfectly all right, except for the fact that I can't breathe! I find myself crying and laughing and applauding and knowing why I went into this business." He has also made guest appearances on major talk shows such as *The Tonight Show* with Jay Leno, *Oprah, Rosie, Arsenio, Geraldo,* and others.

Sam has continued releasing albums, mostly of standards and songs he has written, to include *Different Stages* (1994), *Standard Time* (1997), *Revival* (1999), and the popular Christmas collection, *On This Night* (2000). Some highlights from his Motown career were released on *The Best of the Motown Sessions* in 1994, and various compilations have included his music, such as *Being Out Rocks*, *Tap Your Troubles Away: Words and Music of Jerry Herman*, and *George and Ira Gershwin: A Musical Celebration*. Along with his recordings throughout the 1990s, he also ranged into the realm of photographer, shooting cover images for Eagle-Eye Cherry, D*Note, and Beth Orton. In 2001, Sam worked behind the scenes at the Michael Jackson anniversary concert where he supervised Liza Minnelli's segment by arranging her songs with a 400-person gospel choir, and directed and arranged songs for Deborah Cox and Missy Elliot on the show. In late September of 2001, Sam appeared on Oprah Winfrey's *Music to Heal Our Hearts*, a show to comfort those affected by the events of September 11th of that year. In December of 2001, he returned to Tulsa for sold out Christmas shows at the Van Trease Performing Arts Center for Education, and his solo cabaret show in New York City garnered him a Manhattan Association of Cabaret and Clubs Award (MAC) as Major Male Vocalist of 2002.

By the fall of 2002, Sam gained rave critical reviews for his starring role of Carmen Ghia in the Mel Brooks Broadway production of *The Producers* that extended through December 15th of the year. In early 2003, Harris began performing his one-man show, *Sam*, to rave reviews from the *Los Angeles Time, Variety,* and several other West Coast publications. Harris brought the show to Tulsa in

April, 2003 when he performed at the VanTrease Performing Arts Center and delighted the crowd with his eclectic repertoire of songs ranging from pop standards to Broadway songs and his own music. Along with **Kristin Chenowith**, and Muskogee-born pianist and arranger Linda Twine, Sam Harris is not only one of the brightest lights on Broadway, his multi-faceted impact on the entertainment industry guarantees his name will remain on marquees, liner notes, and end credits for many years to come. (HF)

www.samharris.com

Hayes, Wade
(b. April 20, 1969)

One of the first young country music artists to have his first album reach gold record level, singer, songwriter, and guitarist Tony Wade Hayes was born in Bethel Acres, Oklahoma, a community of about 2,500 residents southeast of Oklahoma City. Growing up in a country music atmosphere, Wade's grandfather was a fiddle player and his instrument was passed on to Wade by his father, Don. Don was a professional country musician, who also moon lighted as a carpenter, while his mother, Trisha, was a hairdresser. The Hayes household listened to a variety of country music from the "outlaw country" of Waylon Jennings and Willie Nelson to the "Bakersfield Sound" of **Merle Haggard** and Buck Owens to the honky tonk style of Lefty Frizzell. Wade's first instrument was mandolin, perhaps influenced by another one of his idols, Ricky Skaggs, but by the time he was a teenager, he was playing lead guitar with his father's band, Country Heritage, in honky tonks around Oklahoma. Around the same time, Wade's father signed a contract with an independent record company in Nashville, where he took the family for about a year. The Nashville label folded, leaving the Hayes family broke. Upon returning to Oklahoma, Wade continued to play in his father's band during high school. After high school Wade attended three different colleges, including the University of Central Oklahoma in Edmond, where he declared business as his major, but left college after about a year.

In 1991, while watching Ricky Skaggs emotional speech at the CMA awards suggesting young artists should follow their dreams, Wade decided to make the

move to Nashville. With about $450 in his billfold and all that he could pack in his truck, he arrived in "Music City" in the fall of 1992. Working construction in the daytime, primarily roofing houses, he performed at amateur nights on Music Row, primarily Gilley's nightclub, where he was offered a regular job singing at night. In 1993, country artist Johnny Lee heard Wade at Gilley's, and was impressed enough to hire him as lead guitarist for his backup band. While in Nashville, Wade had begun to cutting demo tapes, as well as honing his songwriting skills. Chuck Rains, a veteran songwriter and vice-president for Sony/Tree publishing house who had written hits for **Reba McEntire** and Mark Collie, invited Wade to write some songs and eventually arranged an audition with record producer Don Cook, who had produced among others Brooks and **Dunn**. Within a 72-hour period in 1994, Wade had landed a deal to write songs for Tree and a seven-album recording contract with Columbia.

Wade's debut album, *Old Enough to Know Better*, was released in 1995, and generated two singles, "Old Enough to Know Better" and "I'm Still Dancin' With You." The former climbed to #1 on the charts, while the latter reached #4. Wade was co-writer on both singles. The album was certified gold, a rare accomplishment for a first recording, and succeeded in making it the best selling debut record of the year. Wade was named *Billboard* magazine's Top New Country Artist and was an ACM nominee for Top New Male Vocalist of the Year for 1995. His second album, *On a Good Night*, released in 1996, was followed with *When the Wrong One Loves You Right* (produced by Don Cook) in 1998. The title track of his second album, "On a Good Night," climbed to the Top 5 of the country charts, and his second album was also certified gold. He was a 1996 Horizon nominee by the CMA. Additional Top 10 hits on the *Billboard* charts included "Don't Stop Me," "What I Meant to Say," "She's Actin' Single (I'm Drinkin' Doubles)" and "The Day She Left Tulsa (In a Chevy)." The "Don't Stop" video was controversial, and CMT originally threatened to ban it, however, three months later fan support had pushed it to #1.

Honors and awards continued for Wade in the late 1990s. At the TNN/*Music City News* Country Awards show, Wade was presented with the Male Star of Tomorrow honor, followed by the Blockbuster Entertainment Award for Favorite New Country Artist, and *Entertainment Tonight* named him the "Hottest Face to Watch" in country music.

In 1999 Hayes moved to Monument Records and recorded his fourth album, *Highways and Heartaches*, in 2000. It was co-produced by **Ronnie Dunn**, Terry McBride, and Don Cook, and includes two hit singles, "Up North (Down South, Back East, Out West)" and "That's What Honky Tonks Are For." He continues to tour as one of country music's most eligible bachelors. Wade's 1952 reissue of Fender Telecaster guitar that he still plays on stage bears the signatures of his three country music idols—Merle Haggard, Willie Nelson, and Waylon Jennings. The latter, who died in 2002, was one of Wade's vocal influences. He was able to meet Waylon when he played lead guitar for him on the NASCAR album,

Mark McClurg

Columbia's *Hotter Than Asphalt* collection released in 1996. In describing Wade, *Country Music* magazine stated: "He's got the sort of guts, attitude, and instincts that you just can't fake. At time he sounds like he sort of sprang full-blown from the Oklahoma dirt." As far as his devotion to country music, Wade recently said, "Music is about the only way I feel comfortable expressing things. . . .A lot of the other kids when I was growing up were into mainstream pop, but country always moved me."

In 2003, Wade teamed up for a duo act with Claremore native Mark McClurg, a twelve-year veteran of Alan Jackson's band, the Strayhorns, as well the long-standing country group out of Claremore, Stonehorse. The two are known as McHayes and were signed to Universal South. McHayes released their first single, "It Doesn't Mean I Don't Love You," in the spring of 2003, and their debut full-length, *Lessons in Lonely*, was due out by the end of summer, 2003. (GC)
www.2steppin.com/WadeHayes/

Hazlewood, Lee
(b. July 9, 1929)

Best remembered for his compositions "These Boots Are Made for Walking" and "Jackson," major hits for Nancy Sinatra in the 1960s, Barton Lee Hazlewood was born in Mannford, Oklahoma, a community of roughly 2,000 inhabitants west of Tulsa. He was the first child of Gabe and Eva Lee Hazlewood. His father was a wildcatter in the Oklahoma oil fields and occasionally promoted dances as a part-time booking agent. One of Lee's fondest memories is being lifted onto the shoulders of **Bob Wills** at a show booked by his father. Oil field wildcatters travel wherever the new oil strikes occur and, when Lee was twelve, the family moved to McClain, Texas; Ft. Smith, Arkansas; Paris, Arkansas; and eventually to Port Neches, Texas. Lee attended high school in Huntsville, Texas, where he met Naomi Shackleford, his future wife. But Naomi stayed in Huntsville to attend Sam Houston State, while Lee enrolled at Southern Methodist University in Dallas to study medicine. He was soon called to the armed services; receiving his basic training at Colleen, Texas, stationed at Ft. Hood, Texas, and played drums in Alaska for the 4th Army Division band. After his discharge, he married Naomi and they had two children, Debbie (1954) and Mark (1955).

Lee was again called into military duty during the Korean War, and served as a disc jockey for the AFRS radio in Korea and Japan. After this stint in the service, Lee decided not to return to college and moved to Los Angeles, where he attended Spears Broadcasting School to develop his skills at deejaying. He was hired as country DJ at KCKY radio in Coolidge, Arizona, where he earned $40 a week. A newly arrived young New Yorker by the name of Duane Eddy began to visit Lee at the station, and they soon struck up a friendship. They would drive to Phoenix for country music shows and met 17-year-old Al Casey. By 1953 Lee was honing his songwriting skills and registered his first song with BMI, "Four Bell Love Alarm." Lee's first record production came in mid-1955 when he took Duane Eddy and Al Casey to Phoenix to cut "I Want Some Lovin' Baby" and "Soda Fountain Girl," two of Lee's songs.

In 1955, Lee was fired at KCKY and took another DJ job on KRUX in Phoenix, where he also organized his own Viv Record label and Debra Publishing House. He penned several songs for **Sanford Clark**, another Oklahoman, including "Run Boy Run," "Son of a Gun," and "The Fool." Lee asked Clark to record "The Fool" on a Phoenix-based label, MCI. Some 500 promotional copies were distributed throughout the U.S., and a Cleveland DJ sent it to Dot Records, who immediately signed Clark and released it on the Dot label. "The Fool" hit #7 on the *Billboard* charts and sold more than 800,000 copies.

Because of his success with "The Fool," Lee was offered a producer position with Dot Records, and the family moved to Los Angeles. It was here that Lee met publisher Lester Sill and Dick Clark, television host, and they formed Jamie Records. Another break came for Lee when he began writing songs with his old Coolidge friend, Duane Eddy. Lee is also credited with the "twangy guitar" sound of Eddy, and they collaborated on "Rebel Rouser," "Cannon Ball," "Shazam," and "Dance with the Guitar Man," all released on the Jamie label. Much of Eddy's success stemmed from his regular appearances on Clark's *American Bandstand*.

Moving to the Reprise label in 1965, Lee wrote and produced U.S. hits by Dean Martin ("Houston") and Dino, Desi, and Billy ("I'm A Fool"). Lee was introduced to Nancy Sinatra, who had recorded several unsuccessful singles with Reprise. He charged Nancy with developing a new sound that would appeal to truck drivers, and nicknamed her "Nasty Jones." Lee's "These Boots Are Made for Walkin'" made Nancy an international star, and she followed with more of Lee's songs, including "How Does That Grab You, Darlin'," "Sugartown," and "Lightning's Girl." Lee and Nancy cut the following duets, "Jackson," "Some Velvet Morning," and "Lady Bird," all released on the *Nancy and Lee* album (1968). The pair recorded a follow-up album in 1972, *Nancy and Lee Again*. The partnership ended because Nancy grew tired of singing Lee's songs, although her career plummeted thereafter.

Lee's own recordings in the 1960s, which appeared on various labels, included *Trouble Is A Lonesome Town* (1963), *The N.S.V.I.P. [Not So Very Important People]* (1965), *Friday's Child* (1966), *The Very Special World of Lee Hazlewood*

(1966), which featured his own version of "Boots", *Love and Other Crimes* (1968), and *The Cowboy and the Lady*, a duet with Ann Margaret (1969). Lee's only album in the 1970s, *Poet, Fool, or Bum* (1973), was panned by critics and included one track, "The Performer," which expressed his disillusionment with the music business.

Hazlewood moved to Sweden and continued making records for the Scandinavian market, although remained in relative obscurity in the U.S. during the late 1970s and 1980s. He resurfaced in the U.S. in 1995, touring with Sinatra after her comeback album, *One More Time*, was released. Lee contributed two vocal tracks to his old friend Al Casey's *Sidewinder* album, released by the German Bear Family label in 1999, and the same year, released his first album in twenty-five years, *Farmisht, Flatulence, Origami, ARF!!! and me*, a collection of standard pop tunes, such as "Honeysuckle Rose," "It Had To Be You," and "Don't Get Around Much Anymore," despite its title. It was well received by critics because Lee's voice has remained strong.

In the late 1990s, Sonic Youth drummer Steve Shelly and his Smells Like Records began to release a series of Lee's classic albums, including *Cowboy in Sweden*, *Requiem for an Almost Lady*, and *The Cowboy and the Lady*. In 2002, German label, City Slang, released *Total Lee! The Songs of Lee Hazlewood* with a host of college radio types, i.e., Lambchop, St. Etienne, Jarvis Cocker, Tindersticks, and Evan Dando, covering some of Hazlewood's most famous material. (GC)
www.leehazlewood.net

Hedges, Michael
(b. December 31, 1953 – d. December 1, 1997)

Regarded by critics and musicians as one of the 20th century's most technically complicated and stylistically advanced acoustic guitarists, Michael Hedges combined several unusual guitar techniques, such as personal tunings, fret board tapping, and percussive plucking styles, to achieve a musically dense and harmonically rich texture in his playing and compositions which he called "violent acoustic," "heavy mental," and "acoustic thrash." Although born in Sacramento, California, Hedges grew up in Enid, Oklahoma, a town of 45,000 people in

north central Oklahoma. His mother, Ruth, who was from Marshall, Oklahoma and a cornet player, and his father, Thayne, a piccolo player from Enid, met in the band at Phillips University in Enid.

After a series of moves for academic reasons, the family wound up back in Enid in 1955 at 1323 W. Broadway. Michael had his own record player from the time he could turn it on, and his musically oriented parents started him with piano lessons at age five. However, they discontinued the lessons after a couple of years because Michael would not practice once he had a piece of music committed to memory. When Hedges was in the fifth grade, he came home from the YMCA and told his mother that one could rent a guitar and have lessons for $5 a month at the Y, and the Hedges agreed to the lessons. Also while in grade school, Michael began playing cello in the school orchestra. During his junior high years, his parents gave him the red electric guitar he asked for on Christmas and he began playing it in the Enid High School Stage Band. However, in order to be in the band he had to play something else besides guitar, so he started playing flute and took lessons from Dr. Milburn Carey.

The Hedges family spent one year at Humboldt State in Arcata, California, where Michael spent his junior year playing flute and guitar in the high school band. The Hedges returned to Enid for Michael's senior year, where he was graduated in 1972. He continued in the band, and, after high school, Hedges enrolled at Phillips University where his father was a director of the Community Speech and Hearing Center. At Phillips he studied flute and classical guitar, as well as composition and music theory under Dr. Eugene Ulrich, whom Hedges repeatedly cited as an important mentor. According to his mother Ruth, during his time at Phillips he also formed various trios and dance bands, and spent countless hours in the university practice rooms. Not able to get any significant guitar instruction in Enid, Michael drove to St. Louis periodically for lessons. After his third year at Phillips, Hedges transferred to the Peabody Conservatory in Baltimore, Maryland, where he earned his degree in composition. He started Peabody as a guitar major, but switched to composition, and then continued at Stanford University's Center for Computer Research and Musical Acoustics. While enrolled at both universities, Michael would study and practice during the day and play area clubs, bars, and cafes at night.

During a gig at the Varsity Theater in Palo Alto, California in 1980, Windham Hill Records founder Will Ackerman discovered Hedges and offered him a recording contract on the spot. Ackerman later recalled about the night, "Michael tore my head off. It was like watching the guitar being reinvented." Just before meeting Ackerman, Michael had already started playing with bassist Michael Manring and, subsequently, Hedges and Manring began their recording careers on Hedges' first Windham Hill release, *Breakfast in the Field* (1981). The album established Hedges as a unique force in the acoustic guitar world and began his journey to significant notoriety for his innovative style of sounding like several guitars playing at once, what he called his "man-band." The technique was produced by his left hand tapping notes while his right hand picked the remaining strings. 1984's Grammy-nominated *Aerial Boundaries* manifested the diverse array of Hedges' performance and compositional developments, as well as the technical innovations in acoustic amplification for which he also gained his elevated reputation. According to Windham Hill press materials, *Aerial Boundaries* is considered one of the most important acoustic guitar albums ever.

In 1985, Hedges increasingly became known as a new age artist, primarily because of his association with Windham Hill, which had essentially created the genre and received substantial credibility by Hedges' success. Realizing the "new age" tag did not totally describe Hedges' eclectic musical inspirations, Windham Hill created a new subsidiary label, Open Air, to release Michael's 1986 album, *Watching My Life Go By*, featuring Michael's vocals for the first time, chanting by Bobby McFerrin, and music played on wine glasses. Also released in 1986 was a holiday album, *Santa Bear's First Christmas*, containing background music performed, arranged, and composed by Hedges. *Santa Bear* also marked the first appearance of the rare harp guitar Michael favored for several recordings and performances throughout the remainder of his career. Displaying both his incredible abilities to sound like an accompanying and a solo guitar at the same time, as well as his improving vocal style, 1987's *Live on the Double Planet* was recorded at various concerts across the U.S. and Canada. The album also features two compositions for the harp-guitar, covers of Bob Dylan's "All Along the Watchtower" and the Beatles' "Come Together," and several more original compositions recorded live.

In 1988, Hedges released *Strings of Steel,* furthering the style for which he has become praised by such jazz and rock notables as Steve Vai, Crosby, Stills, and Nash, Pat Martino, and Pete Townshend. Rock virtuoso Vai said about Michael, "The first time I heard him play, I was stunned into silence." The Who's guitarist, Pete Townshend, explained, "Michael will never by forgotten as one of those who respected, absorbed, and yet rose above all trends to create accessible and commercial music for a new age."

In 1990, Michael released the Grammy-nominated *Taproot*, featuring instrumental pieces and one vocal composition set to the lyrics of poet e.e. cummings. The album was Michael's first recording in his Northern California recording studio, The Speech and Hearing Clinic, and furthered his interest in the metaphorical and symbolic potential of instrumental compositions by basing some of the music on writings by poet Robert Bly and mythologist Joseph Campbell. Hedges also experimented with more varied sound textures by including woodwinds, drum programs, synthesizers and percussion on the album, as well as harmony vocals by David Crosby and Graham Nash. In addition, on *Taproot* Michael started creating his own labels for his playing, such as "savage myth guitar" and "transterm guitar." In the years following the release of *Taproot*, Hedges received accolades such as *Guitar Player*'s readers' poll awards for "best acoustic guitarist" five years in a row, and was also named by the same magazine as one of

"25 Guitarists Who Shook the World." In 1992, Michael wrote and played all the music for the children's animated video, *Princess Scargo and the Birth Day Pumpkin* (BMG Kidz). Eager to remain outside of the standard categories of New Age and solo guitarist, Hedges released 1994's *The Road to Return*, featuring more of his vocals, and an astonishing array of instruments played by Hedges on the album, to include drums, flutes, synthesizers, harmonica, and electric guitar.

The only other musician on the album is Janeen Rae Heller who plays musical saw. In 1995, Michael wrote an autobiography of sorts, *Michael Hedges: Rhythm, Sonority, Silence* (Stropes Editions), which included an introduction by him about his life, some of his more famous tunings, and tablatures of popular Hedges tunes such as "Aerial Boundaries" and "Rickover's Dream." That year he also went back out on the road with Michael Manring in support of *The Road to Return*, and then began performing solo as he developed new material that would become the Grammy Award-winning *Oracle* album in 1996.

Oracle featured the return of a guitar to him that had been stolen back in 1982 when he was opening for Jerry Garcia in Palo Alto, California in support of *Breakfast in the Field*, on which he had played the same custom-built guitar. The guitar reenergized Michael, and also signaled his return to purely instrumental music. Along with another Beatles cover, "Tomorrow Never Knows," and a solo guitar interpretation of Frank Zappa's "Sofa #1," Michael ranges expertly through his dramatic fingerings and unique tunings on *Oracle*. The album won a Grammy for "Best New Age Album" in 1998. Sadly, it would be his last full-fledged release as Michael Hedges was killed in an automobile accident over Thanksgiving weekend in 1997 near Medocino, California. Subsequently, in 1998 Phillips University renamed its music building in honor of Hedges, and in 1999 Windham Hill released material recorded shortly before his death on *Torched.* The album included six original instrumentals, eight vocal tracks, and a live track from 1994. Intended as "sketches" for the album *Torched*, the label left them just as they were recorded and mixed by Michael. Included on the CD is his only song that is directly titled after the state in which he grew up, "Rough Wind in Oklahoma." In 2000, Windham

Hill released a *Best of Michael Hedges* CD that contains many of the highlights of his career, and in 2001 duplicated much of that set with some additional live tracks on *Beyond Boundaries: Guitar Solos*. (HF)

Hinton, Sam
(b. March 21, 1917)

One of the first professional musicians to use the term *folk music* in describing his performances and claimed to know more than a 1,000 songs, singer, guitarist, accordionist, and dulcimer player Samuel Duffie Hinton was born in Tulsa, Oklahoma. His mother, Nell Duffie Hinton, was a talented musician and taught both ragtime and classical piano, while encouraging Sam to pursue music. When Sam was five years old, she took him to Jenkins Music Store in Tulsa and purchased a harmonica for him. According to Sam's mother, he was playing "Turkey in the Straw" before they left the store, and, when he was eight or nine years old, won an amateur contest on the harmonica at the Strand Theater in Tulsa, receiving two dollars for first prize. His grandfather presented Sam with a push-button diatonic accordion for his eighth birthday. During his youth Sam often sang for pleasure, usually for family and friends. He learned many folk songs from his mother who had learned them from Sam's great-grandfather, and from the time she spent as a child in Texas, where she learned several cowboy songs. Sam's father, Allan F. Hinton was interested in art, but his parents discouraged this avenue, and he became a civil engineer.

Sam was also interested in nature and devoted many hours exploring the natural environment around him, especially snakes. When Sam was about twelve years old, his family moved to Crockett, an east Texas community rich in wildlife and folklore, and from where he graduated from high school. One of the graduation gifts he received in 1929 was a copy of Carl Sandburg's *American Songbag*, a gift from his older sister Mary Jo, which was to have a tremendous influence on his musical direction as he read it from cover to cover while in college.

In 1934 Sam enrolled at Texas A& M University as a zoology major. While in college, he learned the guitar and continued to sing the songs that he had learned as a boy, what he discovered people called folk music. He supported himself during the two years at College Station working as a musician, calligrapher, scientific illustrator, sign painter, and selling snake venom to Sharp and Dohm pharmaceutical company in Pennsylvania. The venom came from sixty water moccasins that he raised as a hobby.

During his sophomore year at A&M, Sam made friends with Professor J. Frank Dobie at the University of Texas-Austin, a noted folk scholar. Dr. Dobie invited Sam to do a lecture-recital of East Texas folk songs, his first professional performance, for the Texas Folklore Society.

After two years at A&M, Sam traveled to the East coast to join his family in 1935, when his brother and sister-in-law were killed in an auto accident, which also seriously injured his mother who never fully recovered from the accident. His father had identified a better paying civil service job in the Washington, D.C. area (Riverdale, Maryland) and went to work for the U.S. Department of Interior.

During the summer of 1935, Sam and his two teenage sisters, Nell and Ann, formed a group called the Texas Trio, which performed in and around the D.C. area. Sam's father promoted the trio, acting as chauffeur and was able to get them on local radio. In early 1937, he also drove them to New York City, where they auditioned for the Major Bowes Original Amateur Hour, a popular radio program during the late 1930s. Sam was also working part time as a window decorator and sign painter for a department store, as well as scientific illustrator in the Department of Herpetology at the National Museum.

On January 18, 1937 the Texas Trio won The Major Bowes Amateur Hour. The winners were expected to travel with one of the Bowes units around the country. His sisters were too young, but Sam fulfilled the requirement and toured for the next two years with various troupes under the names of Major Bowes and Ted Mack, playing in forty-six states and Canada. When the troupe completed its visit to Los Angeles, Sam dropped out and went back to U.C.L.A. as the Department of Interior had relocated his father to Los Angeles.

Hinton graduated with a degree in zoology from U.C.L.A. in 1941. During the last two years of college, Sam continued to sing as a part-time job to help pay for his tuition. One of those jobs (1939-40) was a part in the musical comedy *Meet the People*, in which he worked alongside such budding stars as Nanette Fabray, Virginia O'Brien, and Doodles Weaver. While at U.C.L.A. he met and married Leslie Forster, a violinist and soloist with the university's *a capella* choir, who taught Sam the more classical side of music.

After gaining his degree, Sam worked for three years as director of the Desert Museum in nearby Palm Springs, California. In 1944 he served as editor-illustrator for the University of California Division of War Research in San Diego, and worked there through the end of World War II. He then took a position as curator with the famed Scripps Institution of Oceanography at the University of California in San Diego. While there, he taught courses in music, folklore, geography, and biology for the University of California extension service. He was also a lecturer in folklore in the University of California-San Diego Department of Literature. In 1965 he was appointed as assistant director of Relations With Schools at U.C.S.D. Two years later, he became associate director, and remained in that position until his retirement in 1980.

While in the D.C. area in the mid-1930s, Sam visited the Library of Congress and met Dr. John Lomax and his son Alan. Alan suggested at the time that Sam record some of his East Texas folk songs, but it was not until some ten years later, while Sam was in Washington on business that he approached Dr. Duncan Enrich, who had become the curator of the Archive of Folk Song at the Library of

Congress. Thus, in 1947 Sam made his first recording for the Library of Congress Archive of American Folk Song, *Buffalo Boy and the Barnyard Song*, an album of Anglo-Irish songs and ballads. On the recordings Sam played a steel stringed Washburn guitar.

Three years later, Hinton made his first commercial recording, a 78-rpm single, "Old Man Atom" (later known as "Talking Atomic Blues") for Columbia Records. It became his most requested number and was later covered by The Weavers and several other folk groups. He also sang it at the Newport Folk Festival on many occasions. In 1952, he teamed with Ben Cruz, a singer of Spanish and Mexican folk songs, to record an album on the Bowmar label, *Folk Songs of California and the Old West*.

Sam moved to the Decca label in the early 1950s to record several children's folk songs in their "Children's Series," including "The Barnyard Song," "Country Critters," "The Frog Song," and "The Greatest Sound Around." He participated in a two-record album, *How the West Was Won*, in which he helped Alan Lomax and Si Rady select the songs, write the liner notes, and sang nine of the songs. Other luminaries to record on this RCA album included Bing Crosby, Rosemary Clooney, Jimmy Driftwood, and the Salt Lake City Mormon Tabernacle Choir. Continuing his relationship with Decca, Sam recorded three more albums in the 1950s, including *Singing Across the Land* (1955), *A Family Tree of Folk Songs* (1956), and *The Real McCoy* (1957).

In the 1960s Sam was featured on several albums, including *American Folk Songs and Balladeers* (1964), *Newport Folk Festival, 1963* (performed "Barnyard Song" and "Arkansas Traveler"), *The Songs of Men: All Sorts and Kinds* (1961), *Whoever Shall Have Some Peanuts* (1961), *The Wandering Folksong* (1966), and *I'll Sing You a Story: Folk Ballads for the Young* (1972). The latter four collections appeared on Folkways Records in association with his good friend, Moe Asch. The Folkways recordings have all been reissued under the Smithsonian/Folkways series of compact discs. Finally, in 1976, Sam recorded *Cowboy Songs* for the National Geographic Society.

After his retirement in 1980, Sam devoted full time to performing, particularly to schoolchildren in the San Diego area. His programs, such as "Old Songs for Young Folks" and "Singing Through History," were presented to more than one million children over a sixty-year span. He continued active in folk music circles, including performances at the Newport Folk Festival, Berkeley Folk Festival, and Topanga Folk Festival, service on the Board of Directors of *Sing Out: The Topical Folk Song Magazine*, founding member of the San Diego Folk Song Society, anchorperson for National Public Radio's coverage of the Smithsonian Festival of American Folklife in Washington, D.C., and host of a thirteen-part series on folk music for the National Education Television network.

The 2002 Sam Hinton Folk Heritage Festival, held in La Jolla, California, featured Sam at age eighty-five as one of its performers.

During the decline of the folk song movement, Sam persisted with this statement, "The *Variety* headline 'Folk Music is Dead' made no sense to me. In the 1930s, songwriters used themes from Tchaikovsky, Chopin and other classical composers. When that era disappeared, you could just as well have written the headline 'Classics are Dead'."

For a first hand account of Sam's musical career, go to the following website for an oral history interview conducted at his home in La Jolla, California. (GC) www.sandiegohistory.org/audio/hinton

Hobbs, Becky
(b. January 24, 1950)

One of the most prolific songwriters in the country music field, Becky Hobbs has composed hits for such luminaries as Alabama, Emmylou Harris, Moe Bandy, George Jones, Glen Campbell, John Anderson, Janie Fricke, Shelly West, Helen Reddy, and Loretta Lynn. Born Rebecca Ann Hobbs in Bartlesville, Oklahoma, she began writing songs and playing piano before she was ten years old. Bill Hobbs, her father, was a violinist and loved Big Band music, while her mother preferred country music. By fourteen, Becky was playing the guitar and writing protest songs, influenced by Bob Dylan, and formed a folk duo with her friend, Beth Morrison. While in high school, she formed her first all-female band, The Four Faces of Eve, as age fifteen. As a student at the University of Tulsa, she performed in miniskirts and go-go boots in her second all-female band, The Sir Prize Package.

By 1971, Becky had moved to Baton Rouge, Louisiana, where she was performing with a bar band called Swamp Fox. The band then settled in Los Angeles and Becky remained with the group until 1973, when she began to write songs on a serious basis. Signing with MCA Records, she released her first album, *Becky Hobbs*, in 1974. Canadian vocalist Helen Reddy heard the album and recorded four of Becky's compositions, "I'll Be Your Audience," "I Don't Know Why I

Love that Guy," "I Can't Say Goodbye to You," and "Long Distance Love."

Hobbs then moved to Nashville and recorded two albums for the Tatoo label, *From the Heartland* (1975) and *Everyday* (1977). While in "Music City," she began to write songs for Al Gallico, who was considered one of the top country music independent song publishers in Nashville. Gallico introduced Becky to Jerry Kennedy, who signed her to a Mercury Records contract. In 1978, she recorded "The More I Get the More I Want," which reached the Top 100 and gave her first feel of recording success. She followed with a second single, "I Can't Say Goodbye to You," which made the Top 50, and won the American Song Festival Award. She then cut three more singles with limited success. During the 1980s, Becky continued to write with her songs recorded by Lacy J. Dalton ("Feedin' the Fire"), John Anderson ("Look What Followed Me Home"), and the Tennessee Valley Boys ("Lo and Behold").

In 1983, Becky teamed with Moe Bandy for a Top 10 hit, "Let's Get Over Them Together," on the Columbia label. During the next two years, she had two hit singles for Liberty/EMI-America, "Oklahoma Heart" and "Hottest 'Ex' in Texas." In 1984, Becky's "We Sure Made Good Love," was recorded by Loretta Lynn and George Jones and was included on Jones' *Ladies Choice* album.

Perhaps 1985 was one of the most important years in Becky's career. It started with Alabama recording "I Want to Know You Before We Make Love," and was included on the group's quadruple-platinum album, *Forty Hour Week*. Co-written with Candy Parton, the song had already gone #1 with Conway Twitty. Alabama also recorded Becky's "Christmas Memories" for their Christmas album, which was certified double platinum. Moe Bandy and Joe Stampley recorded Becky's "Still on a Roll," and Shelly West released two more of Becky's compositions, "I'll Dance the Two Step" and "How It All Went Wrong." Finally, Becky was invited to join the Grand Ole Opry cast.

Two years later, Becky's songs were picked up by several more country music celebrities, including Glen Campbell and Emmylou Harris ("You Are") and Moe Bandy ("Rodeo Song"). The Campbell-Harris duet was nominated for a Grammy.

In 1988, Becky released one of her best albums, *All Keyed Up,* originally on the MTM label, but her contract and album were picked up by RCA after MTM's demise. It
included three hit singles, "Jones on the Jukebox," one of the best tributes to George Jones, "Are There Any More Like You," and "Do You Feel the Same Way Too." Two years later, she released "Talk Back Tremblin' Lips," an old Ernest Ashworth hit, on the Curb label, however, it was unsuccessful as a single, but the video was well-received.

In 1992, "The Beckaroo," a nickname bestowed upon her by friends, and her band, The Heartthrobs, toured Africa as part of the U.S. Government Arts America, performing in nine countries. Returning to the studio in 1994, Becky released *The Boots I Came to Town In* album on Intersound, which included "Pale Moon," "Mama's Green Eyes (And Daddy's Wild Hair)," and her own version of

"Angels Among Us," previously recorded by Alabama. The latter song received considerable television exposure when Patty Duke hosted the show, *Angels, The Mysterious Messengers*, and TNN recently aired a show called *Angels*, featuring Becky singing "Angels Among Us." She was named *Cashbox* magazine's Independent Country Music Female Artist of the Year for 1994. Additional honors include a BMI Performance Award for "I Want to Know You Before We Make Love," a Gold Album for Helen Reddy's *Live at the Palladium* recording, Most Promising Act of 1989 by the British Academy of Country Music, and earned the title in her Switzerland appearances as "Das Energie Bundel."

In 1996, Becky married Duane Sciacqua, guitarist who played with Glenn Frey, formerly of The Eagles. Duane produced Becky's 1998 album, *From Oklahoma With Love* with all tracks written by Becky, including "Yellow Pages Under Blue," "God's Gift to This Woman," and "Rockin' and Rollin' and Raisin' Hell." It was also on Becky's record label, Beckaroo. Often referred to as the "female Jerry Lewis," Becky's style has been described as a fusion of hard-hitting honky-tonk songs with an electrifying rockabilly sound. An enrolled **Cherokee** and great grand-daughter of the Cherokee woman leader, Mary Ward, Becky has also recorded a three-song EP, *Let There Be Peace: Tribute to Mary Ward, Beloved Woman of the **Cherokee**.

Currently based in Nashville, she continues writing and recording, and has an active personal appearance schedule with performances for troops in Sarajevo, Bosnia, in 2001; Americana International Music Festival in Newark, New Jersey, in 2001; Hodag Country Festival in Rhinelander, Wisconsin, in 2002; the WildWood Songwriter's Retreat in 2002; and performances scheduled in the U.S. and Switzerland in 2003. (GC)
www.beckyhobbs.com

Holly, Doyle
(b. June 30, 1936)

As bass guitarist, harmony singer, comedian, and soloist for Buck Owens' Buckaroos from 1963 to 1970, Doyle Floyd Hendricks was born in Perkins, Oklahoma, a community of around 2,000 residents located south of Stillwater. Doyle learned the bass guitar at an early age, and formed a band with his older brothers, which performed at rodeos. As a child, his musical influences included **Bob Wills**, Tommy

Duncan, and Ernest Tubb, and considered the Texas Playboys the best band ever assembled. As a teenager, he worked in the Kansas, Oklahoma, and California oil fields. Following high school graduation, he joined the U.S. Army and was stationed in Okinawa and Japan. After his four-year stint in the armed services, he returned to the oilfields around Bakersfield, California, where he performed on a part time basis with Johnny Burnette's band, alongside Fuzzy Owen and **Merle Haggard**, played bass for **Jimmy Wakely**, and worked for Joe and Rosalee Maphis.

Doyle joined Buck Owens and the Buckaroos in 1963. During his seven-year career with the group, he played bass guitar and sang on some nine albums with Owens, including *I've Got a Tiger by the Tail* (1965) and *Carnegie Hall Live Concert* (1966). On the former album, Doyle sings an excellent rendition of "Streets of Laredo," and on the latter, track thirteen features "Fun 'N' Games with Don (Rich) and Doyle." He also toured the U.S., Canada and Europe with the group, performing at such venues as the White House and the Palladium in London. After leaving the Buckaroos in 1970, Doyle formed his own band, the Vanishing Breed. Two years later, he signed a recording contract with the Barnaby label for which he cut two albums, *Doyle Holly* (1973) and *Just Another Cowboy Song* (1974). In 1972, Doyle was named Bass Player of the Year by the ACM. He was also considered one of the top session men in Nashville.

During the 1970s, Holly released several singles, including "My Heart Cries for You," "Queen of the Silver Dollar" (Top 30), "Lila" (Top 20), "Lord How Long Has This Been Going On," "A Rainbow in My Hand," "Just Another Cowboy Song," "Cinderella," "Woman Truck Drivin' Fool," "Gatherin' Dust," "I'll Be All Right Tomorrow," and "Richard and the Cadillac Kings," for which he received an ASCAP award.

Holly has appeared on the Grand Ole Opry and the Opry Gospel Show. In addition, he has performed on several televisions shows, including *Dean Martin Presents*, *Music Country USA*, *Hee Haw*, and *Nashville Now*. Doyle and his band have opened for numerous artists, such as Conway Twitty, The Whites, Gene Watson, and Randy Travis. Doyle also served on the Board of Directors of R.O.P.E. (Reunion of Professional Entertainers), an organization devoted to artists who have remained in the music business for more than twenty-five years. He was also honored in 1980 with induction into the Walkway of Stars at the Country Music Hall of Fame in Nashville.

In the early 1990s, Doyle left country music, and opened Doyle Holly's Music Store in Hendersonville, Tennessee. More recently, has driven a customized entertainers bus, most recently for Shania Twain. Several Buck Owens and the Buckaroos albums were released in the 1990s, including *The Buck Owens Collection* (1992) and *The Very Best of Buck Owens, Vols. 1 and 2* (1994), which include Holly playing the bass guitar. In 2002, OMS Records released *Together Again*, a bluegrass-oriented tribute to Buck Owens that features all the living Buckaroos, including Tom Brumley, Willy Cantu, and Holly. (GC)

Hubbard, Ray Wylie
(b. November 13, 1946)

Hubbard is best known for his early classic "Up Against the Wall, Redneck Mother," which became the impromptu rallying call for the "outlaw country" rebellion against the Nashville Sound of the 1970s. Born in Soper, Oklahoma, a small town of about 500 residents west of Hugo in Choctaw County, singer-songwriter-guitarist Hubbard and his family moved during the mid-1950s to Oak Cliff near Dallas where his father served as high school principal. During high school years at Adamson High School, which also produced such future stars as B.W. Stephenson ("My Maria") and Steve Fromholz ("Hondo's Song"), he learned the guitar and became acquainted with Michael Martin Murphey. The two formed a folk duo that performed in a coffee house, The Rubaiyat, where he met the legendary Ramblin' Jack Elliott and "folkie" newcomer Jerry Jeff Walker. Following high school, he attended the University of Texas-Arlington and North Texas State University, where he was an English major. After leaving college, he assembled several folk groups, including The Coachmen, Three Faces West, and Texas Fever. While traveling the folk music circuit, Hubbard performed at such venues as The Bottom Line in New York City and Freight and Salvage in Berkeley.

Hubbard then moved to Red River, New Mexico, and performed in his own club, The Outpost, where he renewed friendships with Walker, who sold him a 1938 Roy Smeck Stage Deluxe guitar complete with an angel painted on the side. He performed at the first Kerrville Folk Festival in 1972, as well as other noted folk music festivals held in Napa Valley, Mariposa, Newport, and Philadelphia. Upon his return to the Dallas area in the early 1970s, Hubbard spent most of his time writing and performing with Walker, and in 1973 Walker recorded Hubbard's notable anthem for the progressive country music movement in Austin, "Up Against the Wall, Redneck Mother," on his highly acclaimed *Viva Terlingua* album. The album was a phenomenal success and brought Hubbard instant cult status within the progressive country community. About the same time, Hubbard formed a back-up band he dubbed The Cowboy Twinkies, considered by many the first "cowpunk" band, which included fellow Oklahoman Terry "Buffalo"

Ware, guitarist who played with Hubbard from 1972 to 1978 and again from 1986 to 1997.

The Cowboy Twinkies' repertoire included an array of music forms ranging from **Merle Haggard** to Led Zeppelin. In 1975, Hubbard's band released a self-titled debut album, *Ray Wylie Hubbard and the Cowboy Twinkies*, for Warner Brothers' Reprise label. The album sold poorly and resulted in the break up of the band. Hubbard did not reappear again until 1978 when he recorded his debut solo album, *Off the Wall*, on the Willie Nelson short-lived label, Lone Star, which included his own rendition of "Redneck Mother" as well as "Bittersweet Funky Tuesday" and "Freeway Church of Christ." A year later, Hubbard began performing with Jerry Jeff Walker's old back-up band (Lost Gonzo Band), which he renamed the Ray Wylie Hubbard Band. During the early 1980s, Hubbard released two live albums, *Caught in the Act* (Waterloo), recorded at the Soap Creek Saloon in Austin, and *Something About the Night* (Renegade), which featured Walker and a different back-up band, Bugs Henderson Trio.

Although Hubbard made news headlines in 1987 when his 1954 Martin guitar was stolen from a pawn shop in Dallas, he did not record again until 1992 when

Lost Train of Thought was released by his own record label, Misery Loves Company. The 1992 release included a duet with Willie Nelson on "These Eyes" as well as several other Hubbard songs such as "When She Sang Amazing Grace." *Loco Gringo's Lament* (Dejadisc) followed in 1995. Produced by the veteran Lloyd Maines, father of the Dixie Chicks' Natalie Maines, it received rave reviews from such publications as *Rolling Stone* magazine. Two years later, Hubbard recorded *Dangerous Spirits* (Philo), which included guest artists Lucinda Williams and Tony Joe White. Hubbard returned with *Crusades of the Restless Nights* in 1999, *Live at Cibelo Creek Country Club* in 2000, and *Eternal and Lowdown* in 2001, all on the Philo label. These albums reflect Hubbard's turbulent lifestyle and flair for storytelling. After a period of substance abuse in his early career, Hubbard has remained sober, and is a strong supporter of charities, including benefit performances for Vietnam Veterans and Clown Ministry, an agency that provides clowns for terminally ill children.

In 2003, Hubbard's album, *Growl*, displayed a return to roots, of sorts. Aside from the classic, experienced take on the music industry on "Rock and Roll is a Vicious Game," the album is heavy on blues constructs, themes, and instrumentations, and includes what may be Ray Wylie's next anthem for musicians south of the Red River, "Screw You, We're From Texas," which Ray Wylie points out in the liner notes of the album, "is not screw you, Oklahoma or Arkanasas or any other state. It's screw you, people who don't appreciate cool music, because we're from Texas, and this is the kind of music we do." (GC)
www.raywylie.com

Hughes, Billy
(b. September 14, 1908 – d. May 6, 1995)

Composer of "Tennessee Saturday Night," a #1 hit for Red Foley, as well as songwriter for such notables as Eddy Arnold, Ernest Tubb, and **Spade Cooley**, singer, fiddler, and songwriter Everette Ishmael "Billy" Hughes was born in Sallisaw, Oklahoma, an eastern Oklahoma community of roughly 7,000 population, near the Arkansas border. He was first noticed as a fiddler and singer with "Pop" Moore in Oklahoma City, and later performed with **Johnny Bond** in the same city.

In 1938, Hughes moved to southern California, where he performed at a Los Angeles club called Murphy's with his band, the Pals of the Pecos. To record his band, he formed his own label, Fargo Records. He also recorded for several labels, including Four Star, King, Mutual, in which he displayed an exceptional voice for western swing and blues music.

In addition to "Tennessee Saturday Night," Billy composed such songs as "Rose of the Alamo," "Take Your Hands Off of It," "Atomic Sermon," and "Stop That Stuff." While in California, Billy played fiddle and wrote songs for **Jack Guthrie** and sang on some of **Luke Will's** recordings.

Additional recording artists who used Hughes' songs include a wide range of vocalists such as Rosalie Allen, Tex Williams, Jerry Lee Lewis, Hank Locklin, Ella Mae Morse, and Pat Boone. Finally, his talents as a fiddler and vocalist were demonstrated on two of pop singer Barry Manilow's recordings in the early 1990s, just before Hughes died in 1995. (GC)

Jackson, Wanda
(b. October 20, 1937)

Widely recognized as the "Queen of Rockabilly" in the 1950s and one of the first women to break the male barrier in country music, Wanda Lavonne Jackson was born in Maud, Oklahoma, a community of roughly 1,000 residents located southeast of Oklahoma City, as the only child of Tom and Nellie Jackson. One of her early mentors was Betty Lou Ledbetter, an older cousin, who taught Wanda how to yodel when she was nine years old. After working in a bakery during the day and pumping gas at night, Tom Jackson headed for California in 1942 looking for more steady work. Leaving Nellie and Wanda at Nellie's parents' house in Roff, Oklahoma, Tom found work for North American Aviation in Los Angeles and moved the family to the West coast. Following World War II, Tom left the aviation company and completed schooling to become a barber. Nellie became homesick and the Jackson family returned to Oklahoma in 1948 in their 1946 Pontiac.

Renting an apartment in the Capitol Hill neighborhood in Oklahoma City, Tom began driving a taxicab. He was something of a musician and made certain Wanda knew guitar and piano chords, and bought her small Stella guitar to practice and purchased an upright piano so Wanda could take lessons. It was at about this time that Wanda heard the first record that made an indelible impression upon her: Hank Williams' *Lovesick Blues*. Soon after the Jacksons returned to Oklahoma, Nellie entered Wanda in local talent contests and her rendition of Jimmie Rodgers' "Blue Yodel #6," won her a fifteen-minute slot on radio station KLPR in March of 1953. While a student at Capitol Hill High School, Wanda performed over KLPR only a few blocks from the school. Demonstrating her resourcefulness as a teenager, Wanda gained her own sponsors and wrote her own ad copy. Carrying her guitar from home to school to the studio each day, she was eventually given a slot on two of the station's local broadcasts, Cousin Jay's Mountain Jamboree and Uncle Willie's Country Show. During her teenage years, she wrote her first songs: "If You Knew What I Know" and "You'd Be the First One to Know."

One of the most fortuitous times in Wanda's career was when she met the country music legend—**Hank Thompson**. Thompson was holding down the stage at the Trianon Ballroom as well as performing over WKY-TV between 1952 and 1954. Having heard Wanda's KLPR program, Thompson invited Wanda to perform at the Trianon Ballroom with the Brazos Valley Boys. Another break in her career was when KWTV television station in Oklahoma City invited her to perform each week before a live audience. Soon thereafter, Wanda cut a demo tape at Thompson's studio on North May and it was sent to Capitol Records that passed on Wanda because her voice was too immature. Undaunted, Thompson forwarded the tape to Decca which signed her in 1954. Thus, Wanda was a Decca recording artist before she left high school. The five songs that Wanda first recorded with Decca included "If You Knew What I Know," one of her own com-

positions, "The Heart You Could Have Had," "The Right to Love," and "Lovin' Country Style." She recorded fifteen country tracks for Decca, one of which, "You Can't Have My Love," a duet with Billy Gray, made the country Top 10. This success prompted a call from the Grand Ole Opry for a guest performance that ended on a negative note—she was asked to cover her shoulder less dress that her mother had made especially for the Opry. Wanda did not return to the Opry stage for forty years. Her mother, despite the Opry experience, continued to design Wanda's dresses throughout her career.

After high school graduation in 1955, Wanda joined the *Ozark Jubilee*, an ABC television network show based in Springfield, Missouri, and hosted by the venerable Red Foley. While performing on the Jubilee from 1955 to 1957, she also hit the tour circuit with Tom serving as her manager. Another opportune time for Wanda was when she met Elvis Presley on tour in 1955-56. A friendship developed between the two and Elvis advised Wanda to consider changing her style to the new rock and roll. The two-year relationship between Wanda and Elvis resulted in the gift of a ring from the legend of rock and roll, a ring that she possesses today.

With the help of Jim Halsey, Wanda signed a contract with Capitol Records, a company she would remain with for the next eighteen years. Her first single was "I Gotta Know," backed by Joe Maphis and Buck Owens. Her second release was "Hot Dog! That Made Him Mad," which portended her switch to the rock and roll idiom. In 1956, *Cash Box* magazine voted her "Most Promising Female Vocalist." In 1958, Wanda recorded "Fujiyama Mama." It was not a rousing success in the United States, but the Armed Forces Radio network picked it up and it became a monumental hit in Japan. This resulted in a sensational tour of Japan in 1959 with thousands of fans greeting her at every stop in the two-month tour. Shortly before she departed for Japan, Wanda and Halsey decided to hire her own band. Previously known as Bobby Poe, a Vinita native, and the Poe Kats, it was an integrated band with **Big Al Downing**, a fellow Oklahoman as pianist.

After her return from Japan, Wanda and the Poe Kats traveled to Los Angeles to cut an album entitled simply, *Wanda Jackson*. The twelfth track on the album was "Let's Have a Party" that remained in obscurity for another two years. Based on the "Fujiyama Mama" recording, *Disc Jockey* magazine named her as "Best New Female Singer" in 1958. Wanda returned to the recording studio in late 1958, but had dropped the Poe Cats as her back-up band. She did not record in 1959, but in 1960 decided to assemble another band and entered the recording studio. Two of the interesting cuts on this session were "In the Middle of a Heartache" and her own composition, "My Destiny," a reflection of the current status of her life.

In early 1960, Wanda began receiving overtures from Las Vegas where country music had been introduced by Hank Thompson and **Bob Wills**. After seeing **Roy Clark**, near Washington, D.C., Wanda and Tom asked Clark to front her band in Vegas and he consented. Another unusual break came for Wanda in 1960 and it was in the unlikely place of Des Moines, Iowa. A local disc jockey began using "Let's Have a Party" as his theme song and, after many requests, contacted Capitol Records. It was issued as a single and by August of 1960, it was a Top 40 hit on the rock and roll charts. Because of its success, Wanda named her newly formed band, The Partytimers, when they opened at the Golden Nugget in Las Vegas in late 1960. From that time until the early 1970s, Wanda was a favorite on the Las Vegas nightclub scene with appearances at the Golden Nugget, Silver Nugget, and Show Boat.

In 1961, Jackson recorded two singles, one of which was "Right or Wrong," a composition she penned in Oklahoma at an earlier date. It peaked at #9 in the country charts and #29 in the pop charts, and eventually became her second biggest hit after "In the Middle of a Heartache" that also reached Top 10 country in 1961 after Wanda rewrote the words and re-cut it as a single. Overall, she charted thirty country hits from 1954 to 1974 and was twice nominated for a Grammy Award for Best Country Vocal Performance by a Female. Also in 1961, Wanda married Wendell Goodman, and they were blessed with two children, Gina and Greg.

One of the overlooked anecdotes concerning Wanda's music is its influence on an international scale. She was truly an "ambassador of American music." Not only was she highly popular in Japan, but was a member of the Capitol Caravan that toured Europe in 1970, voted Favorite Female Country Music Singer in the Scandinavian countries in the early 1970s, and was Capitol Records' biggest selling female in the German language. Many more accolades and honors associated with Wanda Jackson are worthy of mention, but perhaps the most noteworthy achievement of her career is that she influenced an entire generation of women singers and will influence a generation more. Wanda's home state has honored her with induction into the Oklahoma Music Hall of Fame in 2000, as well as presented her with the Oklahoma Native Daughter Award. In addition, she was inducted into the Rockabilly Hall of Fame and the International Gospel Music Hall of Fame.

Wanda's recent activities include a performance at the 2000 Rockabilly Fest held at the International Rockabilly Hall of Fame and Museum in Jackson, Tennessee, and she was featured as one the four rockabilly pioneers, along with Oklahoman **Lorrie Collins**, on the PBS special, *Welcome to the Club of Women of Rockabilly* telecast in 2002. Her 2002 tour schedule included dates in Germany, Austria, and Sweden, and in August of 2002, she performed at the "Red Hot Rockabilly Party," an outdoor concert at Damrosch Park at Lincoln Center in New York City.

Several labels have found a ready market for Wanda's catalogue and newer material. In 2000, the Ace label released *Queen of Rockabilly* containing thirty tracks of her major rockabilly hits. In December, 2002 Wanda's performance at the Village Underground in New York City was recorded for a live album on DCN Records, *Live and Still Kickin'*. On the album covers several of her biggest hits, throws in some of her old favorites by Hank Williams and Elvis, and even adds her take on Bob Seger's "Old Time Rock and Roll." Perhaps equally as interesting are the monologues she gives in between tracks, often telling the audience the source of songs, or her memories associated with them. In 2003, Capitol Nashville re-released her first two Capitol LPs, *Wanda* (1958) and *Rockin' with Wanda* (1960). *Wanda* features her hit "Let's Have a Party," several country numbers, and rocking cover versions of "Money, Honey" and "Long Tall Sally." *Rockin' with Wanda* includes her compositions "Mean, Mean Man" and "Fujiyama Mama," as well as Buck Owens adding some sizzling guitar, and an appearance by her band, the Poe Cats, with rockabilly pianist **Big Al Downing**. As of the fall of 2003, Wanda had several shows lined up in the U.S., as well as a September appearance at the Eddie Cochran Festival in England. She and her husband, Wendell, reside in Edmond, Oklahoma. (GC)
www.wandajackson.com

Jacob Fred Jazz Odyssey
(Formed in 1994 in Tulsa, OK)

Keyboardist, Brian Haas

Named after a combination of pianist Brian Haas's life long infatuation with the name Fred, and a scene in the rock satire film *Spinal Tap* when the fake band members talk about performing a "free form jazz odyssey," Jacob Fred Jazz Odyssey (JFJO) is Oklahoma's most significant jazz group since the heyday of the state's jazz heritage in the 1920s and 1930s. Their extended improvisational jams meld funk, rock, hip hop, jazz and tribal polyrhythms into a distinctive fusion that is both rooted in and flowers from their collective influences. JFJO has gained a strong enough following to play 200 to 300 shows a year since 1999, and have been featured in *Down Beat*, the nation's premier jazz magazine, although the writer was unaware of Tulsa's jazz legacy and made it seem like the group emerged from a cultural and musical wasteland. While the *Oklahoma Music Guide* is an attempt to inform the general public about the diversity of Oklahoma's music legacy and current activity of its musical artists, music historians as a whole have overlooked Tulsa and the rest of Oklahoma as a fertile jazz scene that provided a training ground, performance opportunity, and milieu for the development of twentieth century jazz and some of its great practitioners. "T-Town" is where Count Basie joined up with the **Oklahoma City Blue Devils**, the birthplace of trumpeter **Howard McGhee**, **Earl Bostic**, **Cecil McBee**, and **Waymon Tisdale,** and the city where **Bob** and **Johnnie Lee Wills** popularized the hybrid western swing known as "Okie Jazz" in the 1930s, 40s, and 50s.

Very good jazz musicians were still around town in the 1990s and some of them were playing in jazz ensembles at the University of Tulsa, where Brian Haas was studying classical piano on a full music scholarship. Needing a break from his extensive solitary practices, he began scouting out musicians he felt matched his own zeal for music and started calling them. The first version of JFJO formed around very talented trombonist Matt Leland, guitarist Dove McHargue, drummer Sean Layton, who served as mentor for many young musicians in the Tulsa scene at the time, and Haas playing bass lines on the piano. After playing around Tulsa at small clubs and restaurants, the group recruited percussionist Matt Edwards (b. June 6, 1976, Norman, OK), and seventeen-year-old Reed Mathis (b. September 27, 1976, Saginaw, Michigan). As of 2003, Mathis and Haas are the only two remaining original members of the group, paired down from a seven-piece band to a trio that is consistently touring and selling out major venues across the United States.

Bassist, Reed Mathis

Born to parents who were choir directors and voice teachers, Reed Mathis started singing in church choirs at four-years-old in Menlo Park, California and then the First Presbyterian Church in Tulsa when the family moved to Oklahoma. He started playing cello when he was seven-years-old, and then began playing bass when he was twelve. Since Mathis never took bass lessons, he attributes his playing style to those roots in vocal training and uses the bass to "sing" through JFJO's extended jams. Mathis played in the Tulsa Youth Symphony and the World Youth Symphony, and made several one-time performances with the Tulsa Philharmonic, including a performance of Vivaldi's *Mandolin Concerto in D* with the Tulsa Philharmonic's string section and Mathis as the mandolin soloist. Reed won the National Association of Music Educators first place award in composition for his nine-minute piece for piano, string quartet, and classical guitar. He attended Interlochen Arts Academy in Michigan for a semester in 1993, and played in the jazz band at Tulsa Booker T. Washington High School for three years. Reed met Haas because the two had musician friends in common at TU and those friends told Haas he needed to check out the young bass player from Booker T., then only a junior who agreed to be part of the band. Once assembled, JFJO started as an eight-piece, free form group with a full horn section, and immediately started drawing large crowds around Tulsa with their combination of hip hop beats and melodic anchors of Prince, Thelonious Monk, Wayne Shorter, and John Zorn. Based on the success of their energetic live shows, the group recorded and released two live albums that are now out of print: *Live at the Lincoln Continental* (1995), released while Mathis was still a senior in high school, and *Live in Tokyo* (1996). Both album titles are jokes and early indications of the band's whimsical sense of humor, as no Lincoln Continental Club exists, and the group recorded *Live in Tokyo* at the Tulsa punk/rock club, Eclipse.

On the strength of the second disc, JFJO started getting gigs around the United States. After a couple of well-received shows in Boston, Accurate

Drummer, Matt Edwards

Records, the label that launched other new-jazz experimentalists such as Medeski, Martin, and Wood, Morphine, and Jazz Mandolin Project, offered the group a deal to release another album. The resulting disc, *Welcome Home*, was recorded during two sold out shows at Club One in Tulsa in September of 1998, and also included two studio tracks from April of 1998. While the album received rave critical reviews, it also opened doors for more gigs around the U.S. outside of their primarily Midwestern base. With a heavy touring schedule getting more and more intense with every passing month, JFJO started showing the haggard signs of an independent band touring the country in a van. First, ace trombonist Matt Leland left the group in the spring of 1999, and original JFJO drummer Sean Layton was replaced with Matt Edwards who had already been playing percussion with the group. Under similar circumstances of touring duress, guitarist Dove McHargue and trumpeter Kyle Wright played their last show with JFJO in July of 1999. Pared to a trio formally, as they had already been experimenting with the three-man format, Haas, Mathis, and Edwards began an intense touring schedule of more than 500 shows over the next two years, selling out venues in Boston, San Francisco, Atlanta, Washington, D.C., and Austin, Texas. The primary document from this period as a trio with Matt Edwards on drums is the very independently produced CD, *The Jacob Fred Trio: Live at Your Mama's House Volume I*, recorded on two dates in January 2000 at the Bowery in Tulsa. Given the relative lo-fi quality of *Live at Your Mama's House* and being eager to get something else out the group could sell at its shows, JFJO also released *Bloom 1996 to 1998* in 2000. According to the JFJO website, *"Bloom* is a retrospective release covering Spring '96 to Spring '98. [It] includes some live material from the opening for Medeski, Martin, and Wood days of '96, and JFJO's first time in the studio without an audience later that summer (including the hauntingly beautiful 'Hymn 1008'); also some 1997 live recordings from San Francisco's Elbo Room, and two never before heard Sean Layton vocal tunes from '98 that represent Fred's only venture into the land of multiple overdubs... Some of the material was originally released on 1996's *Live in Tokyo* and is back, re-mastered and all polished up."

JFJO spent the latter half of 2000 and the early part of 2001 recording, mixing, and mastering *Self Is Gone*, named after a *Tulsa World* headline about then TU basketball coach Bill Self leaving the university. Recorded in Los Angeles and Chicago, *Self Is Gone* contains ten, first-take, improvised songs in the spirit of jazz's spontaneous recording history prior to the 1970s. Interested fans can gain tremendous insight into the album's recording history and sources of inspiration for all songs on the group's website.

Having pretty much worn out drummer Edwards by 2001, Bryan Haas's younger brother Richard joined the group and added a decidedly African tribal influence to the group's sound that can be heard and seen online via the band's website at a concert recorded live at Tipitina's in New Orleans. Since the two brothers had played together since grade school, the interplay between the two was a natural symbiosis, however, the constant touring took its toll on the younger

Haas, and Richard only lasted until October of 2001. Subsequently, JFJO replaced him with Jason Smart, a drummer from Cincinnati who had been working at a Tulsa music store, and who is featured on JFJO's most recent recording, 2002's *All Is One: Live in New York City*. *All Is One*. *All is One* was recorded live in New York City at the well-known experimental music venue, the Knitting Factory, and for the label that has grown out of the club's extensive history with avant-garde music. The group also released two limited edition live discs on their own, one recorded at the High Sierra Music Festival in July of 2002, and one recorded at the Telluride Acoustic Festival. Still to be released is an album recorded live for the New York independent label, Phoenix Presents, which specializes in improvisational music.

In the spring of 2003, Jacob Fred Jazz Odyssey had scheduled residencies at jazz clubs in New York and Boston, and returned to Oklahoma where they played a few select shows in Tulsa and Stillwater. In the summer of 2003, JFJO was honored by the Oklahoma Jazz Hall of Fame with the Legacy Tribute Award, and Bryan Haas linked up with former JFJO drummer Matt Edwards as The Void, a vehicle for long form improvisation, and called their show "Lab One featuring Return of the Void." Reed Mathis has also performed with Matt Edwards and other friends outside of JFJO, most recently in December, 2002 where he was able to play other instruments on which specializes: cello, sitar, and acoustic guitar. With a steady string of shows planned nationally throughout the fall of 2003, and with critical and consumer enthusiasm bolstering their every move, JFJO is poised to be a lasting and dominant force on the American jazz scene, the latest of many musicians with Oklahoma roots to ascend to that status. (HF)
www.jfjo.com

Johns, William
(b. October 2, 1936)

An operatic tenor who has performed throughout Europe and the United States, especially in roles developed by Richard Wagner, William Johns was born in Tulsa, the second largest urban area in Oklahoma. William made his American debut in 1967 at the Lake George Opera in Saratoga Springs, New York, in the role of Rodolfo in Puccini's *La Boheme*. His European debut in the early 1970s was with the Bremen Opera (Germany), followed by the Welsh National Opera (Cardiff, Wales) in the roles of Radames in Verdi's *Aida* and Calaf in Puccini's *Turandot*.

Johns' Royal Opera House (Covent Garden in London) debut was in 1987 as Bacchus in Strauss' *Ariadne auf naxos*. This was followed by the role of Florestan in Beethoven's only opera, *Fidelio*, in Philadelphia in 1988, and the role of Tristan in Wagner's *Tristan und Isolde* in San Francisco in 1991. Additional roles played by William include Siegfried in Wagner's *Siegfried*, Lohengrin in Wagner's *Lohengrin*, Tannhauser in Wagner's *Tannhauser*, and the Emperor in Strauss' *Die Frau ohne Schatten*. Additional performances were with the Hamburg Opera, Vienna Opera, Houston Opera, Dallas Opera, and New York Metropolitan Opera. (GC)

Jones, Claude
(b. February 11, 1901 – d. January 17, 1962)

One of the jazz trombonists who helped free the instrument from its traditional role as a rhythm instrument by providing melodic improvisation and mobility, Claude B. Jones was born in Boley, Oklahoma, one of the states's last remaining all-black towns boasting a population of around 1,000 and declared one of Oklahoma's National Historic Landmarks. Claude attended Langston High School in Langston, Oklahoma, another one of the all-black communities in the state and home of Langston University. During his high school musical career, he played drums and trumpet in the band, but was influenced by a carnival parade with a trombonist leading the band. At around twelve years of age, Claude's parents gave him a Wurlitzer trombone, took lessons on the instrument from a local teacher, and eventually played trombone in the community band.

Following high school, Claude served a two-year stint with the U.S. Army band, in which he played bass horn, trumpet, and trombone. After discharge from the armed services in 1922, he attended Wilberforce College in Wilberforce, Ohio, where he played in the Wilberforce College Band, but soon dropped out and joined the Synco Jazz Band, a forerunner of McKinney's Cotton Pickers, based in Springfield, Ohio, but later performed at the Greystone Ballroom in Detroit and various nightclubs in Harlem. He played and recorded intermittently with the band from 1923 through 1929, during which time he was known for the melodic flexibility of his solos.

Jones gained attention for his work with Fletcher Henderson during the late 1920s and early 1930s, and then played off and on in the 1930s with such big bands as Don Redman, Chick Webb, Alex Hill, Jelly Roll Morton, and Cab Callaway. In the decade of the 1940s, his longest stint was with Duke Ellington from 1944 to 1948. Additional bands for which he played included Coleman Hawkins (Golden Gate Ballrooom in New York City), Zutty Singleton, Joe Sullivan, Benny Carter, Louis Armstrong, and second periods with Callaway and Redman. During the 1940s, he left full-time music to manage his own sausage manufacturing company.

In the early 1950s Claude was back with the Fletcher Henderson Sextet and again with Ellington for about six months. In 1952, he became a mess steward aboard the S.S. United States upon which he died at sea on January 17, 1962.

Claude's best-known solo work was on "Sugar Foot Stomp" recorded with Fletcher Henderson in 1931 on the Victor label. It is now in CD format in Henderson's *The Crown King of Swing* album issued by Savoy Jazz in 1996. Another piece on which Claude is featured is "Down in Honky Tonk Town" with Louis Armstrong in 1940 on the Decca label. It can be found in CD format as *Louis Armstrong 1940-1942* by Melodie Jazz Classics in 1996. He also recorded with such luminaries as Henry "Red" Allen, Sidney Bechet, Lionel Hampton, and Ben Webster. (GC)

Keith, Toby
(b. July 8, 1961)

With his debut single "Should've Been a Cowboy" that reached #1 on the country charts and was adopted as an anthem by the Dallas Cowboys as well as college teams, such as the Oklahoma State University Cowboys, singer, songwriter, and guitarist Toby Keith Covel was born and raised on a farm near Clinton, Oklahoma, a community of about 10,000 residents west of Oklahoma City on Interstate 40. Born to H.K. and Joan Covel, Toby possessed varied interests while growing up in western Oklahoma, such as rodeo, football, and music. His early musical influences included a wide array of artists, including Alabama and **Merle Haggard** (country), John Prine and Steve Goodman (folk), and Elton John, Jimmy Buffett, Billy Joel and Lionel Ritchie (pop).

While in high school, Toby worked for a rodeo company (test rode bulls and broncos for rodeos) adjacent to his parent's farm, but was too tall (6' 4") to become a professional rodeo rider and inept with a rope. He had aspirations of playing professional football because of his size (some 235 lbs.) and football letters playing defensive end in high school, and did join the Oklahoma City Drillers (defensive end) for two seasons in the short-lived United States Football League. He was an avid Oklahoma Sooners football fan, and during his youth, worked as a vendor for Saturday games in Norman, and eventually passed up a football scholarship to work in the oil fields where he thought the money was better.

As to music, Toby learned to play the guitar when he was about eight years old (later some mandolin), began writing songs when he was in the sixth grade, and occasionally sat in on bands playing at his grandmother's supper club in Arkansas. His father worked in the oil fields, therefore, after high school Toby decided that was the career for him. For about four years, he toiled in the Oklahoma oil patch as a roughneck, moving his way up to become operational manager, often working seventy hour weeks (ran steel casing pipe into wells) before losing his job due to the oil bust. Throughout this time, he was playing in country bands, and for seven years, was lead singer for an Oklahoma City-based band called Easy Money (still the name of his band) that played local honky tonks and nightclubs in and around Oklahoma City, primarily for tips and beer. Any surplus money, Toby reinvested in equipment for his band. One of Toby's first paying gigs was at a stock car track and, according to Toby, not one note could be heard over the noise the stock cars made.

By 1988, Keith and his band, Easy Money, had purchased a Silver Eagle bus, and hit the road, playing the major dance halls, especially Dallas' Top Rail. Keith and the band recorded several of his original songs on an independent label. After placing second for Oklahoma in the Dodge-Wrangler band competition, the band made a series of demo tapes that Keith peddled in Nashville, but was rejected by the major companies, including Capital.

One of Toby's fans, an airline stewardess, had given Harold Shedd, Mercury Records/Nashville president and former Alabama producer, a demo tape on one of his flights, and, after he had listened to the tape, flew to Oklahoma City to see Toby and the band perform. Toby signed with Shedd in 1991, and his self-titled debut album, released in 1993, eventually went platinum. Eight of the ten tracks on the album were written by Toby, and included "Should've Been a Cowboy," (#1 on *Billboard* chart) "He Ain't Worth Missing," (#5 on *Radio & Records* chart) "A Little Less Talk and a Lot More Action," (#2 on *Billboard*) and "Wish I Didn't Know Now," (#1 on *Radio & Records*). To promote his first album, Toby went on a "Triple Play Tour" with two then relatively unknowns Jon Brannen and Shania Twain. Finally, *Billboard* magazine named Toby as Top New Country Artist for 1993, and reported that "Should've Been a Cowboy" received the most airplay of any song in the 1990s. According to reports, "Should've Been a Cowboy" was written by Toby after an attractive woman at a dance hall spurned one of his band members for a dance, but later accepted a dance proposal from a man dressed in cowboy attire. Someone in the club who was watching yelled, "Should've Been a Cowboy." Even though Keith's debut album sold more than a million copies and was certified gold, he received little recognition from the CMA in 1994-95 for any of its awards.

In early 1996, Shedd left Mercury to become president of Polydor, Mercury's sister label. He took Toby with him to become the flagship artist of the new label, and they released the same year, Toby's second album *Boomtown* with seven of the ten tracks, primarily working-class type songs, written or co-written by Toby, including four hit singles, "Who's That Man," "You Ain't Much Fun," "Big Ol' Truck," and "Upstairs Downtown." "Who's That Man" was also made into a video in 1994. The *Boomtown* album was spawned by Toby's experiences in the western Oklahoma oil patch, where he watched several towns, including Elk City, realize overnight growth with 1,500 oil rigs pumping crude. Following the *Boomtown* success, Toby recorded a seasonal album in 1995, *Christmas to Christmas*, featuring songs from the top Nashville songwriters.

In 1995, Keith received the CMA Triple Play Award recognized for composers who had attained three #1 songs during the past year in *Billboard, Radio & Records,* or *The Gavin Report*. He also made his film debut in 1996 when he appeared in *Burning Bridges* with Tanya Tucker and Vanessa Williams. By the time Toby had recorded his third album, Polydor had merged with A & M Records/Nashville. *Blue Moon*, released in 1996, was a more romantic-oriented production with "Does That Blue Moon Ever Shine on You" reaching #1. Toby was writer or co-writer of eight of the ten tracks. A & M closed its Nashville division and Toby moved back in 1997 to Mercury, where he released his fifth album, *Dream Walkin'*. It featured a #1 hit "We Were In Love" and the Grammy-nominated collaboration with Sting, "I'm So Happy That I Can't Stop Crying." In 1998, he released his *Greatest Hits: Volume I* album, which went platinum, and produced a Top 20 single, "Getcha Some." Toby was honored by the Country Music Hall of Fame in 1996 with his induction into the Walkway of Stars.

By 1997, Toby was frustrated with the music industry and wrote a poignant ballad entitled "Tired," reflecting his dissatisfaction with all the corporate shuffles and label changes. In 1999 he approached the new president of Mercury, Luke Lewis, a New York City business executive, concerning an album project which included "How Do You Like Me Now" as one of its tracks. Lewis was concerned about the "political correctness" of the lyrics and dropped Toby from the label in 1999. Toby then purchased the album tracks from Mercury for a six figure sum and took the concept to a new record label, Dreamworks Nashville, headed by James Stroud, who was to eventually give Keith more artistic freedom.

Signed by Stroud in 1999, Keith released *How Do You Like Me Now?* his *tour de force* album with nine of the twelve tracks written or co-written by him. It included the title song and "You Shouldn't Kiss Me Like This," both of which scored #1 on the charts. This seventh album was his most successful, capturing a number of awards, including CMT's #1 Video of the Year ("How Do You Like Me Now?") and Male Video Artist of the Year, ACM's Male Vocalist and Album of the Year honors for *How Do You Like Me Now?* (2000), CMA's Male Vocalist of the Year (2001), nominations for CMA's Single, Song, and Music Video of the Year, and American Music Award nominee for Favorite Country Album.

A repeat of the highly acclaimed 1999 release was a difficult task for Toby, but the *Pull My Chain* album, which Dreamworks released in 2001, was equal to or better with nine of the thirteen tracks co-written by him, including "I'm Just Talkin' About Tonight," (#1 on the *Billboard* charts), "I Wanna Talk About Me," one of the first rap-like singles in country music (#1 on the *Billboard* charts), "Pull My Chain," and "My List." The latter became another #1 hit in 2002, Toby's tenth single to reach the top of the charts. It was certified double platinum in 2002, and was the only country vocalist to have three #1 hits during the year. The "My List" video was used by the New York police and fire departments for a training video. Also in 2001, Keith performed at the White House, singing a medley of Stephen Foster songs, such as "Oh! Susanna," which aired on PBS' *In Performance at the White House* the same year.

In 2002 the ACM recognized Toby's accomplishments with six nominations, including Top Male Vocalist, Entertainer of the Year, Video of the Year ("I Wanna Talk About Me"), Album of the Year (*Pull My Chain*), Single Record of the Year ("I Wanna Talk About Me"), and Song of the Year ("I Wanna Talk About Me"). He won the 2002 CMT Flameworthy Award for "Funniest Video," with "I Wanna Talk About Me" gaining top honors.

Keith collected nine nominations in six different categories for CMA awards in 2002, including Entertainer of the Year, Male Vocalist of the Year, Single of the Year as both artist and producer for "Courtesy of the Red, White & Blue (The Angry American)," Album of the Year as both artist and producer with James Stroud for *Pull My Chain*, Song of the Year as both songwriter and primary publisher for "Courtesy of the Red, White & Blue", and Video of the Year for "I Wanna Talk About Me".

Toby's hit "Courtesy of the Red, White and Blue (An Angry American)" soared to the top of both country and pop charts in the summer of 2002, and he performed it at the ACM Awards show in May of 2002. Toby was invited to sing this song by Peter Jennings, ABC news anchorman and host for the network's July 4 special, although the network denies that he was ever booked. According to Toby, Jennings reneged on his invite because one of the song's lines, "You'll be sorry that you messed with the U.S. of A./Cause we'll put a boot in your ass/It's the American way." Controversy ensued between Keith and Jennings, and Toby appeared on a number of talk shows discussing the snub by ABC. Asked how he wrote the song, Toby related that following the September 11 Twin Towers tragedy, he began to think about how his father who had served in the Army in the 1950s, lost an eye in combat, and always flew the flag in the front yard to show his patriotism. His dad had died just six months earlier in an automobile accident, and he dedicated the song to his father. Toby says, "It came from inside me. I never really intended for this to be a single. It was originally called "Angry America."

Keith has sold more than four million albums during the past two years, and his latest album, *Unleashed* (includes "Courtesy of the Red, White and Blue" and a live introduction by Toby of the song), released in the summer of 2002, had more than one million pre-orders, already making it platinum (more than one million units) status. It sold 338,000 units in its first week on the market thereby debuting #1 on the *Billboard*'s Top Ten country albums charts. Moreover, it debuted at #1 on the *Billboard* 200, the magazine's ranking of all albums from all genres of music. It was only the eighth time a country album reached #1 on the *Billboard*'s Top 200, the other seven were **Garth Brooks** albums. The album contains twelve tracks, all of which were written or co-written by Toby. It includes "Beer for My Horses" (a duet with Willie Nelson that went #1 in June, 2003), "Rodeo Moon" (co-written with Chris LeDoux), "Rock You Baby" (co-written with Scott Emerick, one of Toby's background vocalists), and "Who's Your Daddy?" which moved into the Top 5 of the country charts in the fall of 2002, and was Toby's contribution to the televised CMA awards show on November 6, 2002.

In October of 2002, ABC Radio's *Country Coast to Coast* satellite program, broadcast on more than 150 stations to approximately 1.5 million listeners, announced the winners of the 2002 Best Country Around-Fan's Choice Awards. Listeners voted for their favorite artists and songs in six categories. Toby captured both Entertainer of the Year and Male Vocalist honors, competing with George Strait, Alan Jackson, Tim McGraw, and Kenny Chesney, as well as Song of the Year for "Courtesy of the Red, White & Blue (The Angry American)."

Because of his recent successes, Toby realized a lifelong ambition when he established Dream Walkin' Farm, a thoroughbred/quarterhorse breeding and training facility near Oklahoma City. One of his quarter horses ("The Down Side") recently qualified for the prestigious American Futurity at Ruidoso Downs in New Mexico. Though it received little media attention, Toby personally loaded and delivered rescue equipment in his pickup following the 1995 bombing of the Alfred P. Murrah Federal Building in Oklahoma City that killed 168 people. In 1999, he performed a benefit concert for victims following the tornado that devastated Moore, Oklahoma, now his hometown in Oklahoma, where he resides with his wife (Tricia) and three children (Shelley, Krystal, and Stelen), preferring to remain in his native state, rather than live in Nashville.

Keith has starred in several television commercials, appeared in an occasional television series, such as *Touched by an Angel*, and was subject of a CMT Inside Fame segment on August 18, 2002. His tour schedule for 2002 remained active with appearances in Florida, Texas, Colorado, and Wisconsin. Some of the Nashville crowd thought Toby had too much attitude, but he seems to have changed a few attitudes in Music City. Toby says, "I just did my own thing. I am what I am. I wasn't afraid of attitude . . . I'm a big boy, and I can shoulder any criticism I might get for doing things differently. I talk Southern; I sing stone-cold country—my roots are there . . . I see compromise all the time, and in the end, you lose with that. Most successful people are not afraid, and they don't compromise to please whoever." Toby continued, "You have to go do what you do best, and not what somebody else tells you. You've got to fight the system a little bit."

In 2003, Toby's status elevated even more, if that's possible, by a number of awards and recognitions of his contemporary status. In January of 2003, Pollstar named Toby the #1 ticket seller in country music for 2002, the United Stations Radio Networks named Toby the most successful country music artist in the 21st century so far, *Billboard* magazine named him the #1 country artist of 2002, as did *Radio and Records*, the radio industry's primary publication after *Billboard*. Toby received CMT's 2003 Flameworthy Cocky Video of the Year, Male Video of the Year, and Video of the year for "Courtesy of the Red White and Blue (The Angry America)." He returned for a sold-out performance in Oklahoma City in March, 2003, was named as ACM's Entertainer of the Year in 2003, his duet with Willie Nelson, "Beer for My Horses," reached #1 in June, 2003, and his *Greatest Hits Volume I* turned double-platinum with more than two million sold. He expected to release his 10th album, *Shock 'N Y'all*, in November, 2003, and its first single, "I Love This Bar," was released in August, 2003, when he also received seven CMA Award nominations. While Toby's phenomenal success continues to skyrocket, he is also just the latest in a long line of country music artists who have been able to parlay their ordinary roots in Oklahoma to a nationwide connection with people for whom the glitz and glam of contemporary media and multi-national corporations do not reflect the average lifestyle of working class people who have always been the bedrock of country music's fan base. (GC) www.tobykeith.com

Kemp, Wayne
(b. June 1, 1941)

With than thirty-five artists having recorded his songs, ranging from such diverse acts as Elvis Costello and Tom Petty to Patsy Cline and Johnny Cash, Wayne Kemp is considered one of the most prolific songwriters in the country music field. A 1999 inductee into the Nashville Songwriters Hall of Fame, Wayne Kemp was born in Muldrow, Oklahoma, and lived in Greenwood, Arkansas as child where he played mandolin in his family's band at churches, high school, and other local functions until 1953 when his family sold their farm and moved to California. While attending high school in Stockton, Wayne played in a band until his family moved back to Oklahoma in 1956. That year, Wayne hired on with Benny Ketchum as a lead guitar player and toured the Southwest backing up star like Jimmy Dickens, Red Sovine, and **Wanda Jackson**.

Wayne moved back to California in 1961 where he performed in night clubs and on local TV shows with artists such as Glen Campbell and Jeannie Seely. By 1964, he returned to Oklahoma where he settled in the southwestern town of Cache. With nearby Fort Sill as a resource for a party-ready clientele, Kemp played regularly at the Bonanza Club, and had a weekly TV show in Lawton. This visibility translated into a meeting with L.D. Allen who introduced Wayne to George Jones, and the rest, as they say, is history.

In 1965, Jones took Wayne to Nashville and recorded nine of Kemp's songs, to include the classic #1 hit, "Love Bug," and featured Kemp on lead guitar. Kemp also went on to play guitar for Patsy Cline, Red Sovine, and Conway Twitty. In 1967, Wayne recovered from a horrendous automobile accident to play guitar again. A year later, when Conway Twitty recorded Wayne's "The Image of Me," Kemp was signed by Tree Publishing in Nashville. He recorded for a variety of labels, first with Dial in 1963 and later with MCA, United Artists, Mercury, and Door Knob. From the late 1960s through the late 1980s, he charted twenty-four singles, including "Honky Tonk Wine" (Top 20 hit in 1973), "Won't You Come Home," "Don't Send Me No Angels," and "Who'll Turn Out the Lights." His last charted single, "Red Neck and Over Thirty," was a duet with Bobby G. Rice in 1986. Two of Kemp's albums are available, including *Kentucky Sunshine*, a MCA release in 1974, and *The Alcohall of Fame* from Country News, a Swedish company. The latter album contains several of Kemp's lesser known compositions such as the title track as well as "Leavin's Been Comin'," "I'm Gonna Get a Whippin'," "Daddy's Livin' off the Memories of Mama," and "Love Comes Here to Die."

Kemp's songwriting talents earned him legendary status in country music. His song, "Darling, You Know I Wouldn't Lie," was nominated in 1969 for CMA Song of the Year, and Johnny Cash included Kemp's "One Piece at a Time" (a #1 hit in 1976) on more than twenty of his albums, and used it as the title track for a 1976 collection. George Strait has recorded Kemp's songs on more than ten albums, including such compositions as "My Old Flame Burnin' Another Honky Tonk," "She Knows When You're On My Mind," "The Fireman" (Top 5 in 1985), "Won't You Come Home," "I Should Have Watched That First Step," "That's Where My Baby Feels at Home," "Hot Burning Flames," and "Love Bug" (Top Ten in 1994). In addition to "The Image of Me," Twitty scored with such Kemp songs as "Next In Line," "Darling, You Know I Wouldn't Lie," and "That's When She Started to Stop Loving You" (Top 5 in 1970).

George Jones' continued to use Kemp's "Love Bug" on eight of his albums, while Ricky Van Shelton's favorite Kemp songs were "I'll Leave This World Loving You," which reached #1 in 1988, and "Who'll Turn Out the Lights," recorded on six of his albums. "I'm the Only Hell (Mama Ever Raised)" was a Top 10 hit for Johnny Paycheck in 1977, and was included on ten of his albums. Two contemporary country vocalists, Emmylou Harris and Chely Wright, have included the Kemp song, "Feelin' Single, Seein' Double," while another new country artist, Jason Allen, has recorded "Next In Line" and "Cryin' for Their Mamas." More traditional country artists such as the Ernest Tubb and Loretta Lynn duet ("Won't You Come Home"), Hank Williams, Jr. ("Waitin' on the Tables to Turn"), Faron Young ("I Just Came By to Get My Baby"), Ronnie McDowell ("Hot Burning Flames" and "Who'll Turn Out the Lights"), Ronnie Milsap ("Who'll Turn Out the Lights" and "I'll Leave This World Loving You"), Carmol Taylor ("I Really Had a Ball Last Night"), and Darrell McCall ("Here We

Go Again") have featured Kemp's songs. Outside country music, Elvis Costello & the Attractions recorded "Darling, You Know I Wouldn't Lie."

Although "Darling, You Know I Wouldn't Lie" was a CMA nomination, it was Kemp's "The Image of Me" that was recorded the most times and by a vast array of artists, including **Bob Wills** and the Texas Playboys, Charley Pride, Ernest Tubb, Jim Reeves, Conway Twitty, Tom Petty & the Heartbreakers, Flying Burrito Brothers, Doug Sahm, and The Country Rockers. (GC/HF)

Kessel, Barney
(b. 17 October, 1923)

In a 1960s interview, B.B. King recounted seeing and hearing Barney Kessel for the first time at a 1950s after hours session on the West Coast: "I heard Barney Kessel, and he shamed me. It made me want to study hard to better myself as a person and a musician." Not only blues and jazz guitarists respected Kessel, but those players in the country music world were also very aware of Kessel. Don Tolle, recording guitarist for Western swing band leader **Johnnie Lee Wills** in the early 50s, also explained what it was like to be playing in a club when Kessel walked in: "He would come around when we were playing as the Texas Playboys. Hell, he didn't know who we were. He was so damn far above the rest of us we just knew who he was. I always felt humbled when he walked in." Born in Muskogee, a town with a vibrant jazz scene in the first third of the twentieth century that also produced other acclaimed jazz musicians such as **Don Byas**, **Jay McShann**, and **Claude Williams**, Barney Kessel is known and celebrated for his stylistic versatility and improvisational genius on the guitar from the 1940s through the 1980s when health problems curtailed his playing. A revered musician and composer who shaped the sound of jazz guitar for all time, perhaps his best-known tune is the jazz classic, "Swedish Pastry."

Barney spent his early years surrounded by the thriving jazz scene of Muskogee in the 1930s. His Eastern European Jewish father owned a shoe store at 110 S. 2nd across the street from the black theater in Muskogee, right in the heart of the African-American commercial and entertainment district on South 2nd Street in Muskogee. As a result, Barney Kessel was significantly exposed to the deep jazz tradition in Muskogee. Not only was his father's shop on South 2nd Street, a few doors down at 128 S. 2nd was the family residence which doubled as a clothiers, and both were nestled between night clubs, theaters, pool halls, and what the maps of early Muskogee only call "Negro joints." Kessel was literally reared in the shadow of, and eventually took the spotlight in, Muskogee's and Oklahoma's jazz scene in the 1930s. His subsequent success in jazz further emphasizes the importance of Muskogee's jazz scene, because if Barney Kessel could grow up and absorb the music he did in Muskogee, and then become an original, innovative, and highly regarded jazz guitarist, one must say that Muskogee was genuinely a primary development center of American jazz, wherein the traditions of jazz were relayed from one generation to the next.

Barney's first musical memories of Muskogee echo from the box cars and hobos who played Jimmie Rogers songs as they rolled along the tracks just a couple of blocks from South Second Street. He began guitar lessons when he was twelve from a Hawaiian man who taught for the WPA. Barney remembers never having to unlearn the lessons in chords, harmonies, and reading music that he learned in the six months he took lessons from the Hawaiian. At thirteen, Kessel played on the local radio station, KBIX, with his friend Cobal Parker. By fourteen, Barney worked regularly in three bands that played dances at places like Honor Heights park, then a "whites only" social hall. While he played in two primarily white bands, Barney was also the only white player in a group led by Ellis Ezell from 1937 to 1939. Ezell's group required Barney to play horn lines in the manner of **Charlie Christian** who, at the time, was the featured guitarist in the Benny Goodman Orchestra, and is commonly acknowledged by scholars and Kessel alike as his major influence. Other influences drifted into Barney's ears when he worked in Muskogee movie theaters and heard all the Hollywood musicals, the songs of which later became pop standards and foundation melodies for jazz. Kessel has also cited Lester Young, Nat King Cole, Duke Ellington, Charlie Parker, and Bill Evans as influences, but acknowledges the Christian influence is deepest because it is on the guitar.

Barney left Muskogee in the fall of 1939 where he attended high school in Stillwater and played with the Varsitonians, an OSU dance band. In the spring of 1940, he moved to Norman and played with the Varsity Club, but did not graduate from high school. Also that spring Kessel met Charlie Christian in Oklahoma City, and jammed with him on three separate occasions. However, Barney told himself at that time he would not take licks from Christian, but would play his own way and develop his own style. Nonetheless, Kessel's most common stylistic touchstone is found in the work of, and the connection to, Christian, and is an important starting point for any newcomer to Barney Kessel's music. While it is true Christian provided the foundation for Kessel, Barney built a musical structure unique to his own vision on it.

Arriving in Los Angeles with a guitar, an amplifier, a bag of clothes and a nickel, Barney started his career on the West Coast with the Chico Marx big band in 1942 and '43. In 1944, Barney was featured in the award-winning jazz documentary, *Jammin' the Blues*; however, because of racist sensitivities in Hollywood, and Barney being the only white musician in the production, Warner Brothers died his skin black and put him in the film's shadows. Through 1945 and '46 Barney played with Artie Shaw in a group with significant bop leanings as the style had migrated across the country from 52nd Street in New York City. Kessel also stared playing with Charlie Barnet in 1945 and continued through 1947 while picking up significant studio gigs like those with Charlie Parker in '47 that are considered jazz classics. Parker and Kessel jammed that year, and afterwards Parker called Kessel for the now legendary Dial Records session. While some critics are divided on the significance of Kessel's contributions to the Dial sessions, he is clearly making significant bop statements in "Cheers, Cheers," "Barbados," and "Relaxin' at Camarillo." By Kessel's own account, he was also learning a great deal from the acknowledged architect of bebop in Parker. In 1948, Barney purchased two guitars from guitarist George M. Smith, who owned the 1933 Gibson L-5 and 1937 Gibson L-5 since they were made. As a staff musician at the time, Smith played with 20th Century Fox movie studio in Hollywood in the 1930s and '40s. After purchasing the two guitars from Smith, Kessel played them from July 1948 through March 1969 for all his work. This included movies for all the major Hollywood studios, to include four Elvis Presley movie soundtrack sessions, Barbara Streisand's *On A Clear Day You Can See Forever* (1970), two movies with Dean Martin and Jerry Lewis, and another with Jerry Lewis alone. He also played the guitar on numerous recordings, including those with the Righteous Brothers, Sarah Vaughan, Ella Fitzgerald, Billie Holliday, Sonny & Cher, the Beach Boys, and records produced by Phil Spector. Barney also played the guitars for numerous television shows, including *Hollywood Palace*, *The Judy Garland Show*, a Bing Crosby Christmas Special with Paul Weston's orchestra, *The Bob Crosby Show*, and Jack Smith's radio show five days a week for two years.

In 1952, Kessel joined the trio led by Oscar Peterson, one of the most recorded pianists of the 1950s. It was with Kessel when the trio, including Ray Brown on bass, helped usher in both the hard bop movement and the laid back West Coast cool jazz of the 1950s. After Peterson, Kessel's concept of replacing the piano with guitar in a jazz trio set new standards for the guitar as a lead instrument in jazz combos. As a result of his elevating status among musicians, critics, and fans in the 1950s, Barney was a regular winner of critic and fan polls. Along with Ray Brown and drummer Shelly Manne, Kessel recorded the historic *Poll Winners* albums from 1957 to 1960, considered some of his finest and most representative moments. Kessel won numerous awards for his work with Lionel Hampton, Ben Webster, Roy Eldridge, Woody Herman, Lester Young and Billie Holliday, as well as his own solo albums starting with 1953's *Barney Kessel, Volume I* (Contemporary). Among the accolades bestowed on Barney are the *Esquire* Silver Award (1947), Best Guitarist in *Down Beat*'s Readers' Poll (1956-1959), the Jazz Critics' Poll (1953 through 1959), the *Metronome* Readers' Poll (1958 through 1960), and the *Playboy* Readers' Poll (1957 through 1960). Exhibiting his diverse talent, Barney also composed, arranged, and recorded a jazz rendition of the opera *Carmen* in which André Previn played piano.

Kessel did not limit himself to the jazz idiom, however, as he became one of Hollywood's top session for artists from many different genres throughout the 1950s and '60s. Along with recordings for the Elvis Presley films, *Girls, Girls, Girls* (1962) and *Fun In Acapulco* (1963), and two other Presley sessions in July and August of 1965, Kessel played guitar for the Righteous Brothers' 1965 hit "You've Lost That Lovin' Feelin'," and on the Beach Boys' "Good Vibrations" from *Pet Sounds* in 1966. He recorded with a dizzying array of artists, to include Judy Garland, Barbara Streisand, Marlene Dietrich, Gene Autry, Tex Ritter, Ike and Tina Turner, Fred Astaire, The Coasters, Stan Kenton, Sam Cooke, Duane Eddy, Dexter Gordon, Woody Herman, Frank Sinatra, Big Joe Turner, Lester Young, Johnny "Guitar" Watson, T-Bone Walker, Dinah Shore, and Dinah Washington. Kessel's session work could also be heard on television shows such as *Man from UNCLE*, *The Odd Couple*, *Love American Style,* and *I Spy.*

In all, Barney worked for almost forty years in Hollywood as an arranger and freelance musician for radio, hundreds of films, and TV music for many commercials, including Der Wiener Schnitzel and Rice Krispies. Outside of a few pop and rock guitar players, Barney Kessel may be the most heard American guitarist of the 1950s, '60s, and '70s, even if the majority of the listening public did not know his name. Kessel was also a musical ambassador for the U.S. State Department during the Carter administration, touring Europe, Asia, the Balkans, Egypt, and South America. Barney released several guitar and music instruction videos, lesson books, and sheet music through his esteemed career, in addition to a steady stream of solid, and sometimes brilliant, albums until 1988.

A respected and in-demand educator, Barney he gave guitar seminars and workshops throughout the world in conjunction with his performances. He continued touring consistently throughout the world with successful performances in the U.S., Canada, Portugal, Sweden, Italy, Germany, the British Isles, and Japan in 1991. Also in 1991, Kessel was inducted into the Oklahoma Jazz Hall of Fame along with **Chet Baker**. In early 1992, Barney received rave reviews when he played in Australia, New Zealand, and across the U.S. Later in 1992, Barney had his first major health problems when he suffered a massive stroke that incapacitated his right arm, ending his playing career.

Through the 1990s Kessel was feted around the world with honorary concerts and awards. In 1995, Vestapol Videos released a one-hour video, *Barney Kessel: Rare Performances 1962-1991* which includes his acceptance speech at the Oklahoma Jazz Hall of Fame Induction Ceremony. Additional film clips of Kessel are included on Vestapol's *Legends of Jazz Guitar* series. In 1996, the University of Oklahoma awarded Barney an honorary doctorate for his great contributions to the world of jazz. In 1997, *Just Jazz Guitar* dedicated an entire collectors' issue to honor Kessel's work. The magazine, now out of print, features several photos provided by Barney and Phyllis Kessel, interviews with Barney from around the world, and scores of some of his compositions. In 1999, Barney was inducted into the Oklahoma Music Hall of Fame in his hometown of Muskogee. By the end of 1999, in the rush of end of the decade/century/millennium lists, *The Daily Oklahoman* named Barney as one of the top ten musicians from the state in the twentieth century behind **Woody Guthrie, Charlie Christian, The Oklahoma City Blue Devils, Bob Wills,** and **Roger Miller**. Additionally, the Beach Boys' "Good Vibrations," on which Kessel plays, was chosen as one of the top ten rock songs ever by a panel of 700 music industry people in another end-of-century list. Looking back at the twentieth century and the musicians who pioneered jazz as an art form, Barney Kessel stands third in the holy trinity of jazz guitarists, next in line after Django Reinhardt and Charlie Christian. Barney Kessel's playing is intellectual and effortless. While challenging for a musician, a joy for the jazz fan, and a simple pleasure for the casual listener, Barney's music is in many ways the story of jazz told in melody, harmony, rhythm, tone, and texture. If the narrative of jazz is its improvisation, Barney Kessel can be claimed as one the form's master storytellers, and that story is best told through his elegant recordings that will delight fans for generations to come with his fifty-seven years of excellence in harmonic elaboration, superior improvisation on the electric guitar, progressive arrangements, and sparkling original compositions. (HF)

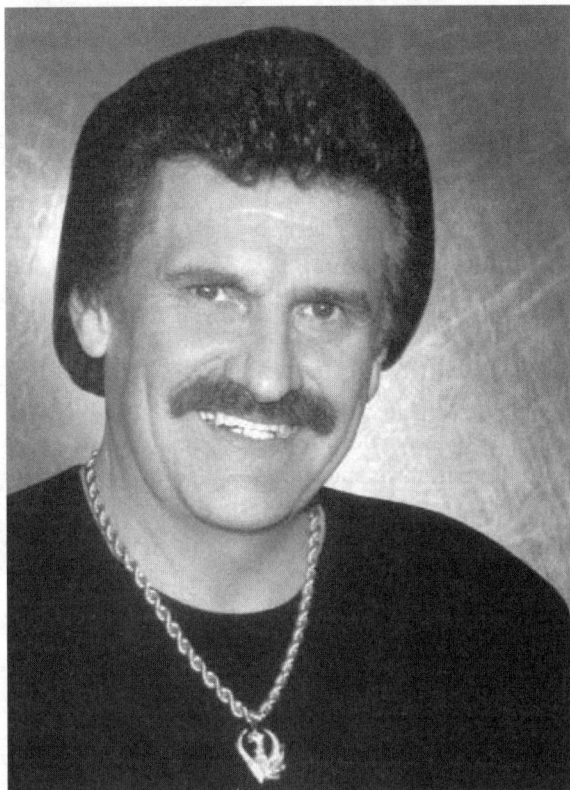

Kilgore, Merle
(b. August 9, 1934)

A member of the Nashville Songwriter's Hall of Fame and composer or co-composer of more than 330 songs, including "More and More," "Wolverton Mountain," and "Ring of Fire," singer, songwriter, guitarist, disc jockey, actor, and talent manager Wyatt Merle Kilgore was born in Chickasha, Oklahoma, a community of about 15,000 residents located southwest of Oklahoma City. Multitalented Merle has also recorded songs for more than twenty-five years. His family moved to Shreveport, Louisiana, when Merle was about four or five, and from 1940 to 1947, he attended Creswell Elementary School. As a fourteen year old, he started carrying Hank Williams, Sr.'s guitar at the Louisiana Hayride, and two years later, was performing on the show as principal guitar accompanist, while still in high school. He was also working for the American Optical Company delivering glasses during his after school hours. He graduated from Byrd High School in Shreveport in 1952, and attended Louisiana Tech University in Ruston for a year.

While in college, Merle gained his first job as a disc jockey at radio station KRUS in Ruston, and a year later was appearing on television shows as "The Tall Texan" (Merle is 6' 4" in height) on KFAZ (Ouachita Valley Jamboree) and KNOE in Monroe. During his late teens, he co-wrote with Webb Pierce, "More and More," which became a No. 1 hit for Pierce for ten weeks and a million seller, and was later recorded by Guy Lombardo, Johnny Duncan, and Charley Pride. Merle also signed his first recording contract with Imperial Records, and his first single was "More and More." For this major hit, Merle was recipient of a BMI award.

From 1955 to 1960, Kilgore worked as a disc jockey for several Louisiana radio stations, including KBSF (Springhill), KCU (Shreveport), KENT (Shreveport), and KZEA (Shreveport). During this time, he penned and recorded his first Top 10 hit, "Dear Mama," on the Starday label, continued to perform on the Louisiana

Hayride, and wrote several more songs, including "I Can't Rain all the Time" and "Seeing Double" (1954); "Funny Feeling" (1955); "I've Got a Good Thing Going," "Tom Dooley, Jr.," and "Hang Doll" (1958); and "Baby Rocked Her Dolly," "I Will Be My First Time," and "Jimmie Bring Sunshine" (1959). To close out the decade, Merle wrote "Johnny Reb," recorded by Johnny Horton, a Top 10 hit, which eventually sold more than fifteen million records.

During the early1960s, Kilgore hosted the Big Ten Jamboree in Eldorado, Arkansas (1960), made his debut on the Grand Ole Opry (1960), received the WSM Nashville "Mr. DJ" award (1960), signed a contract with Mercury Records (1961), moved to Nashville to become manager of Shapiro-Bernstein Music (1961), joined the Johnny Cash road show (1962), performed at Carnegie Hall (1962), and co-wrote with Claude King, the million seller No. 1 country hit, "Wolverton Mountain," recorded by King on Columbia in 1962. Written for Merle's uncle who introduced him to the Arkansas mountain, it also became a Top 10 pop hit.

In 1963, Merle and June Carter wrote "Love's Burning Ring of Fire," first recorded by Anita Carter, and later revived as "Ring of Fire," which became a No. 1 hit on the country charts for Johnny Cash, June's future husband. For his many songs, Merle was named one of *Billboard* magazine's Top 10 Songwriters in 1963.

After performing at the Hollywood Bowl in 1962, Kilgore appeared in his first feature film, *Country Music on Broadway*, in 1963. His other acting credits include *Second Fiddle to a Steel Guitar* (1965), *Sing as Song for Heaven's Sake* (1966), *Nevada Smith* (1966), *Five Card Stud* (1968), *Educated Heart* (1970), *W.W. and the Dixie Dance Kings* (1974), *Nashville* (1975), *Roadie* (1979), *Coal Miner's Daughter* (1980), and played himself in the NBC television movie, *Living Proof*, the story of Hank Williams, Jr. (1981).

Merle released two more albums with Starday, *There's Gold in Them Thar Hills* (1963) and *Merle Kilgore* (1964), before he switched to the Mercury label to record *Merle Kilgore, The Tall Texan* (1966). He signed with Ashley Records in 1968 and released *Ring of Fire*, and then resigned with Starday for one of his last albums, *Big Merle Kilgore* (1973).

In 1969, Kilgore became general manager of Hank Williams, Jr.'s publishing companies, and was Hank, Jr.'s opening act for more than twenty years. In 1986, he was named executive vice-president and head of management of Hank Williams, Jr. Enterprises. He performed on and managed a majority of Hank, Jr.'s biggest albums in the 1970s and 1980s, including *Habits Old and New*, *Rowdy*, *Strong Stuff*, *Man of Steel*, and *Hog Wild*, as well as negotiated the deal for Hank, Jr.'s performance of the ABC Monday Night Football theme song in 1989.

Kilgore was elected to the CMA Board of Directors in 1989, and still serves in that capacity, and in 1990, was elected president of the Nashville Songwriter's Association Board of Directors. The same year, he was voted the first CMA Manager of the Year. In 1998, he was inducted into the Nashville Songwriters

Hall of Fame (Connie Smith and Marty Stuart provided the musical tributes to Merle) and the North American Country Music Association Hall of Fame.

Kilgore's songs have been recorded by a host of artists representing a variety of music genres, including The Animals, George Benson, Brothers Four, Ray Charles, Country Joe McDonald, Country Gentlemen, Bing Crosby, Dick Dale, Lefty Frizzell, Mickey Gilley, Bill Haley and the Comets, Tom Jones, Burl Ives, Jerry Lee Lewis, Rick Nelson, Willie Nelson, Olivia Newton-John, Nitty Gritty Dirt Band, Carl Smith, Blondie, Carlene Carter, Hank Snow, Joe Stampley, Ray Stevens, Ernest Tubb, Tammy Wynette, Dwight Yoakum, Faron Young, Frank Zappa, Van Morrison, and Bob Dylan. In 1995, Bear Family, the German company, released *Teenager's Holiday*, a CD that included all the classics written by Merle.

In 1994, Merle opened Merle Kilgore Management in Nashville, representing Hank, Jr., as well as several other artists. Now in his late sixties, Merle remains active in the management field in 2002, and still oversees Hank, Jr.'s enterprises. www.merlekilgore.com

Kiowa Tribe
(In Oklahoma since at least the late 1700s)

With their tribal administration offices located in Carnegie, Oklahoma, the Kiowa are one of the thirty-eight federally recognized American Indian tribes that maintain their contemporary headquarters in Oklahoma, and one of six tribes currently based in the Southwestern quadrant of the state that was all once known as Indian Territory. Considered a menace to Spaniards, Mexicans,

2003 Kiowa Gourd Clan encampment,and dance arbor, in Carnegie, Oklahoma

and Anglo-Americans traveling the Santa Fe Trail, the Kiowa gave the U.S. Government fits in trying to corral the nomadic Plains tribe with thousands of years of traditions. The Kiowa also provided lively copy for sensationalized western pulp fiction of the 19th century with their constant raiding, or defending, depending which side you were on, and the Kiowa's image of a chief with an eagle feather war bonnet has become one of America's iconic if not stereotypic images of the American Indian. While exact locations differ according to individual oral and scholarly historic perspectives, the Kiowa traditionally trace their origins as a tribe to the mountainous regions of western Montana at the sources of the Yellowstone and Missouri River. Recent linguistic studies have also suggested the tribe may have come from as far south as what became Mexico before arriving in Montana. The Kiowa are the only tribe classed in their linguistic family.

An extremely truncated version of Kiowa history includes the oral history of their entrance into the above world through a hole in the ground, some of the tribe being left behind when a pregnant woman could not get through. Not knowing what glacial period that might have been, modern history begins when the Kiowa are known to have migrated into the Black Hills from Montana after acquiring the horse in the 1600s. Devil's Tower, in eastern Wyoming near Sundance, is still an important identity marker for the Kiowa. Expelled from the Black Hills by the Lakota and the Cheyenne around 1750, the group headed south beyond the Arkansas River where they subsequently fought with the Comanche until about 1790 in the southern plains region of what is now Kansas, Texas, Oklahoma, Colorado and New Mexico. Realizing friends would be important and necessary during the oncoming Plains Indian Wars with the U. S. government, the Kiowa, and their allies the Na-I-Sha Apache, made peace with the Comanche about 1790 and together harassed travelers who were on their way west through Kiowa, Comanche, and Apache (KCA) land, then known as Indian Territory. After the Civil War finished, the U.S. government turned its attention to the "Indian problem," and sent troops out to Indian Territory, what is now Oklahoma, and began to round up Plains tribes. Some Kiowa begrudgingly accepted reservation life in 1865, while others opposed it violently and resisted colonization until the Medicine Lodge Treaty of 1867.

The Medicine Lodge Treaty attempted a peace agreement in return for future paternal care of the Cheyenne, Arapaho, Comanche, Na-I-Sha Apache (then known as the Kiowa-Apache because of historical alliances with the Kiowa), and the Kiowa. The sternest elements of the warrior societies did not give in, however, and maintained combat through the Battle of the Washita (1868-1869) until the U.S. Army forced the Kiowa onto reservations where diseases caused many deaths and ultimate resignation to reservation life. By 1879, the systematic elimination of the buffalo had also been successful by government and commercial enterprises to deprive the Kiowa, and other Plains tribes, of their traditional subsistence lifestyle. The end of the Kiowa reservation period began with the planned allotment of "excess" tribal lands in the 1892, but did not actually happen until 1901 when the remaining land could be opened to homesteaders, or Oklahoma's legendary "boomers." With the complete eradication of their ancient lifestyle in just about fifty years, the 20th century provided many hardships for tribal members as they attempted to adjust to mainstream society all around them, and maintain significant elements of their traditional life. While the Kiowa made significant contributions in the areas of art (the Kiowa Six) and literature (N. Scott Momaday) throughout the 20th century, the maintenance of their tribal musical traditions of the Black Leggins Society, the Oh-Ho-Mah Lodge, the Kiowa Gourd Clan, Peyote songs, and sacred Kiowa hymns are their most significant contributions to world music.

Many of the Kiowa songs and ceremonies are related to warrior societies that provided Kiowa people with both identity and purpose throughout the 20th century. Men and women of the Kiowa, as well as all American Indians, served in greater proportional capacities in the U.S. Armed Services than any other ethnic group through the Vietnam War. This provided another century's worth of music related to war expeditions, coming home, and the remembrance of those who never returned from any wars in which the Kiowa have ever participated.

In a 2002 presentation at the annual American Indian Sovereignty Symposium in Oklahoma City, Jim Anquoe, a Kiowa singer who is also a cultural preservationist and historian with the Oklahoma Historical Society, explained the Omaha gave many Plains tribes the war dance songs that still exist today among tribes such as the Kiowa and Cheyenne. Many tribes have acquired the war dance songs through the Ponca via the Omaha, according to Anquoe, to include the Kiowa who have adopted the songs of many different tribes, such as their flag song from the Arapaho, and their memorial song from the Cheyenne. In fact, the Cheyenne gave Kiowas the dance bustle one sees in the Kiowa O-Ho-Mah Lodge warrior society, representing a long tradition of interconnectedness between Plains tribes.

Kiowa music is one of the most heavily recorded American Indian musical traditions. Due to the foresight of the Smithsonian Institution's concern for American folk life in the 1930s, '40s, and '50s, several recordings exist of Kiowa singers from that period who were still closely related to the 19th century. Indian House Records and Canyon Records took up the Kiowa commercial recording flag from the 1960s forward to 2003 with several excellent releases. Some independent recordings were made for vinyl release throughout the 1960s and 1970s, and have long been out of print, such as *16 Kiowa Songs* (Indian Records) sung by Roland Horse, Bruce Haumpy, and Billy Hunting Horse.

Founded in the 1940s by the late Rev. Linn D. Pauahty, a Kiowa Methodist minister from Carnegie, Oklahoma, Soundchief recorded and released extensive recordings of the best singers throughout the northern and southern plains. The American Soundchief label introduced the popular in-depth approach to recording American Indian

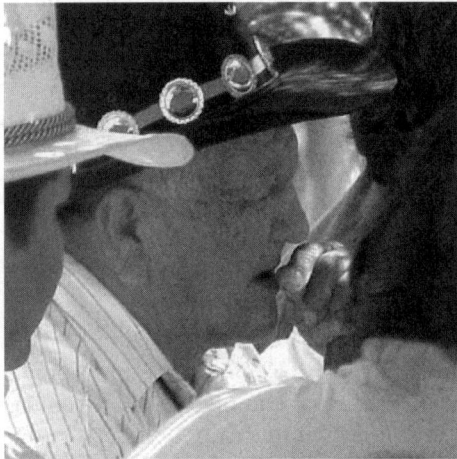

Kiowa singer, Billy Evans Horse

music. Whereas early albums of Indian music often presented several tribal groups and types of songs on one album, Rev. Pauahty was the first to publish albums where one tribal group sang one set of songs such as war dance, grass dance, peyote, or round dance songs. The format was more enjoyable for the experienced listener of American Indian music. While most of the original vinyl releases are now out of print, Indian House Records in Taos has made the recordings available through cassette reissues. Kiowa recordings on the Soundchief label include war dance songs, war expedition songs, circle songs, two-step songs, several recordings of peyote songs, and Kiowa Black Leggings Warriors Society songs.

Along with Indian House Records, Canyon Records is one of the longest-standing companies devoted to releasing American Indian music. Canyon's albums of significance to the Kiowa include 1972's *Kiowa: Forty-Nine and Round Dance Songs* sung by Mr. and Mrs. Vincent Bointy, Raymond White Buffalo, Mr. and Mrs. Bruce Haumpy, Mr. and Mrs. Bill Botone, Herschel Kaulaity, Mr and Mrs. John Emhoolah, Jr., and Ted Creeping Bear. Several stories exist for the origin of "49" songs, to include the story of fifty men who went to war and only 49 returned, or a second version with only one returning. The songs might also be connected to a famous Sioux war expedition of 1849, or dances that were held by Plains Indians to disrupt the Army's sleep during the gold rush year of 1849. A story on the back of the *Kiowa: Forty-Nine and Round Dance Songs* recounts the appearance at a 1920s Oklahoma county fair of a dancing-girl-show themed after the California Gold Rush of '49. Later that night, Kiowas and other Indians went off to a social dance where they started making fun of the barker from the show, including English lyrics, and the imitation became a standing joke and name for Kiowa social dances. Whichever history one chooses to believe, a commonly known story also has the songs deriving from Kiowa round dances in the late 1940s to accompany the social gatherings of returning soldiers from World War II. As many American Indian veterans had difficulty in adjusting to second class life back in the states after they had just enjoyed full status as important men in extremely difficult combat situations, 49 dances also developed a reputation for alcohol consumption. The songs and term "49," or now just "the nine," have since evolved into a standard term for songs that are sung "after the powwow" in a field or someone's backyard to wind down from a day and night's dancing in the rule-laden powwow arena where alcohol is almost always forbidden. Jim Anquoe says Bill Koomsa, Jr. is the undisputed best singer of "49" songs. A spirited set of 49 songs were released as *"49" at Hog Creek* by Millard Clark on his Indian Sound label in 2002. The album has no titles, a few English lyrics relating to beer and the pizza delivery man, and includes many singers whose names are mentioned on other Kiowa albums. Clark has released at least three other volumes of "Round Dance Songs with English Lyrics," or "49" songs, with Millard and Tom Ware as lead singers.

In 1975, Canyon released *Kiowa Scalp and Victory Dance Songs* sung by Bill Koomsa, Sr., Billy Hunting Horse, Wilbur Kodaseet, Bill Koomsa, Jr., and Lonnie Tsotaddle. Women singers on the album are Georgia Dupoint, Ann Koomsa, Martha Koomsa Perez, and Pearl Woodard. Bill Koomsa, Sr. remembers in the album's liner notes that the scalp dance songs were sung when a war party returned from its destination, as were victory songs. He also explained that victory dances are danced in a circle like a round dance except in the opposite direction – counter clockwise. Koomsa's father, Bob Koomsa, was a prominent Kiowa singer who was on the committee that adopted the Kiowa Flag song after World War I. Some of the material from *Kiowa Scalp and Victory Songs* was reissued on Canyon's 1998 CD, *Traditional Kiowa Songs*. Serious scholars, enthusiasts, and preservationists will want to research the Library of Congress Music Division in Washington, D.C. where many recordings remain unissued, and the Oklahoma Historical Society where the important collections of Jim Anquoe and Edwin Chapabitty, Sr. are housed.

The Smithsonian released an important early album under the title of *Folk Music for the United States: Kiowa* (AAFS L35). The songs were recorded from 1936 to 1951 and included sun dance songs, death songs, ghost dance songs, legend songs, peyote songs, Christian hymns, round dances, two steps, war dance songs, rabbit society songs, and a flag song. Singers include George Hunt, Matthew Whitehorse (leader), and Kiowa Singers at the Big Tent on the Christian Hymns. In 1964, Folkways Records, now part of the Smithsonian Institution, released *Kiowa Songs* (FE 4393) featuring brothers Kenneth Anquoe and Jack Anquoe, Sr. on gourd dance songs, war dance songs, round dance songs, trot dance songs, buffalo dance songs, and a flag song. Also singing on *Kiowa Songs* were Nick Webster (Arapaho), Oscar Tahlo, Adam Kaulaity, Laura Tahlo, and 71-year-old chorus leader Sally Kaulaity.

Kenneth Anquoe is also significant for starting one of the first urban powwows in the U.S. in Tulsa in 1946. As a family, to include Jim Anquoe (b. Mountain View), Mary Ann Anquoe (b. Mountain View, OK, July 19, 1930 –d. 2002, Tulsa, OK), and Jack Anquoe Jr. (b. Claremore, OK, September 17, 1956), who have also been featured on several recordings, the Anquoes have also released important independent recordings such as 1985's *Original Kiowa War Mother Songs Volume 1* on cassette, and Jack Anquoe, Sr. has recorded albums with his drum group under the name Grayhorse, such as *Spirits Who Dance* (1996), on Sound of America Records. All totaled, the Anquoes have at least nineteen recordings, six of which are cassette releases, the rest on vinyl and CD. The Anquoe family itself is one of the Kiowa's original singing families, according to Jim Anquoe, which has been documented by the family back to the 19th century when the drum was only a flat hide on the ground. Mary Ann Anquoe's "War Mothers Song" is featured on the 1995 Smithsonian Folkways release, *Heartbeat 2:More Voices of First Nations Women*.

War Mother songs are an important part of 20th century Kiowa musical heritage. The songs emerged from the clubs formed by Kiowa mothers who had sons in the service during World War II. Forty seven known war mother songs exist, according to Jim Anquoe, and were composed by his father James Anquoe and Louis Toyebo. The family now maintains those songs with a different family member able to sing a group of them. A few these songs were released on a 1997 Rykodisc album, *American Warriors: Songs for Indian Veterans*. The recordings were made on the World War II era radio program, *Indians for Indians Hour,* on the University of Oklahoma's radio station, WNAD, in Norman.

Another series of songs called hand game songs go along with the "hide and guess" games that many Plains tribes play. The team that is "hiding" the bones or sticks in their hands will sing songs and generally cause confusion for the team who is guessing where the marked bones or sticks are. Two albums of hand game songs were recorded in 1968 by Indian House Records and subsequently released as *Handgame of the Kiowa, Kiowa Apache, and Comanche – Volume 1 and 2: Carnegie Roadrunners vs. Billy Goat Hill*. A few of these songs resurfaced on a 1996 compilation CD released by Indian House called *Proud Heritage: A Celebration of Traditional American Indian Music*. Indian House also recorded war journey songs in 1969 and released them as *Kiowa 49 – War Expedition Songs*, which featured singers Gregory Haumpy, Billy Hunting Horse, Ralph Kotay, Bill Koomsa, Jr., Barbara Ahaitty, Pearl Kerche, Angeline Koomsa, Nan B. Koomsa, and Wilda Koomsa. The uptempo war expedition, or war journey, songs were sung to get warriors up before going off to battle and date to the Plains period. While some Kiowa songs may be borrowed or part of larger Plains singing traditions, Jim Anquoe made clear in his 2002 presentation that songs the Kiowa "own" are the songs that go along with the war dance society known as the Black Leggins Ceremonies, sometimes called "Black Legs," to indicate the black leggings members of the war dance society wear in the ceremonies. Pronounced "Tone Kone Go" in roughly Anglicized Kiowa, the ceremonies are conducted each year in May at Lone Bear's Dance Ground in Carnegie. Two accessible recordings exist of the Black Leggings Society: one is available on the Indian Soundchief reissues through Indian House Records, the second is by Bill Kaulaity, James Cozad, and Daniel Cozad: *Kiowa Black Leggings Society Songs* (Canyon).

Music is highly personal in Kiowa society and ceremonies. Many families and individuals have songs that are restricted in their use by that family or individual. In a 2000 oral history interview with Dr. Mary Jane Warde and Jim Anquoe of the Oklahoma Historical Society, Parker Emhoola provides a good example of how the Kiowa feel about their individual songs. As a member of the O-Ho-Mah Lodge, a Kiowa war dance society centered around a pipe dance ceremonial held until the mid-20th century at the Whitehorse family dance grounds, Emhoola was given a song he liked by the leader of the O-Ho-Mah Lodge at the time, Charlie "Old Man" Whitehorse. According to Jim Anquoe, Parker's song is one of the few remaining individual songs in the O-Ho-Mah lodge. Parker Emhoolah explained in his oral history, "The song came from the north, as did other songs in the O-Ho-Mah. It's a special occasion song and is not meant to be sung just as a pow wow song." This distinction between commercial popular music, or even intertribal pow wow music, and the intensely personal and often spiritual nature of American Indian music is further detailed by Emhoolah in the interview: "We have a song called the 'tagging song.' This is when we are taking new members and recruits into the organization. We only sing it once a year, and that song is being used by other tribes as a regular intertribal song and it is not. It is an O-Ho-Mah song. You are not supposed to use that song. It is a ceremonial song. One day is set aside during the ceremonial to use that song. It is forbidden to use the song outside of the Oh-Ho-Mah ceremony. There are special songs for special reasons and special occasions and some of those songs are restricted. If you want to use a song, you go through the family and ask before you sing anything that is not yours."

Two excellent sets of Oh-Ho-Mah Lodge recordings exist thanks to Indian House Records and members of the Oh-Ho-Mah Lodge who permitted the preservation enterprises to take place. The first two volumes were accomplished in Anadarko, Oklahoma in 1975 and are titled *War Dance Songs of the Kiowa: O-Ho-Mah Lodge Singers*. These recordings include singers Ralph Kotay, Dixon Palmer, Rusty Wahkinney, Bill Ware, Tom Ware, Truman Ware, Mac Whitehorse, Mildred Kotay, Maxine Wahkinney, Florene Whitehorse, and Lucille Whitehorse. The second set were made in 1994 at Stecker, Oklahoma, and subsequently released by Indian House Records as *Songs of the O-Ho-Mah Lodge: Kiowa War Dance Society Volume 1 and 2*. Singers on these releases included Parker Emhoolah, Ralph Kotay, Bill Ware, Mac Whitehorse, Roland Whitehorse, and Florene Whitehorse Taylor. *Songs of the O-Ho-Mah Lodge: Kiowa War Dance Society Volume 3 and 4* feature different singers than the first two volumes and were recorded October 2000. Released in 2001, Volumes 3 and 4 include singers Joe Fish Dupoint, Bill Ware, Stony Ware, and Mac Whitehorse. "Oh-Ho-Mah songs were sung for warriors who were going away," according to 2001 Oklahoma Historical Society interview with full-blood Kiowa, Alice Jones Littleman, "so they would come back in a good way." In World War II –era Oh-Ho-Mah ceremonials, Littleman remembers, "They prayed for all the soldiers, not only the Indians. They prayed for all the young people."

Another example of Kiowa musical traditions that has influenced intertribal powwows throughout the U.S., Canada, and Europe is the music of the Kiowa Gourd Clan (Tia-Pah), or "Tdiepeigah" as it is known in Kiowa. Pronounced roughly as "Thigh-a-pay-go" in English, and now usually shortened to just "Thia-pay," the Kiowa Gourd Clan is a primary identity marker for the Kiowa and major source of traditional music and language preservation. According to Jim Anquoe, Tia-pah is also the Kiowa word for the dialect of Kiowa spoken east of Fort Cobb, whereas, Tone-kon-go (Black Leggins) is the Kiowa word for the Kiowa dialect west of Fort Cobb. Two accessible recordings exist of Kiowa Gourd Dance Songs: one set was released by Canyon Records as *Gourd Dance Songs of the Kiowa* (CR-6148), and Tony Isaacs and Indian House Records recorded a 1974 set entitled *Kiowa Gourd Dance Volume 1 and 2*, featuring singers Daniel Cozad, Joe Cozad, Larry Cozad, Leonard Cozad, Sr., Billy Hunting Horse, Adam Kaulaity, Vincent Spotted Bird, Yale Spotted Bird, Velma Cozad, Barbara Ahhaitty Monoessy, Dobbin Monoessy, and Naomi Svitak. The Gourd Dance songs' origins are traced by the Kiowa to the red wolf that gave them the songs, which is why one will hear what sounds like "yelps" at the end of some Gourd Dance songs, in honor of that red wolf. These yelps are an excellent example of how the uninitiated listener of American Indian music might consider elements of Indian songs as just vocables, or sounds with no meaning, whereas, the so-called vocables in these Kiowa songs are directly related to the oral history behind their origin.

According to the liner notes by Tony Isaacs in *Kiowa Gourd Dance Volume I,* the meaning of "Tia-pah-go" refers remotely to the words meaning skunkberry and brave, the translation of which has become obscure, and now is specifically the name of the war dance society known as the Kiowa Gourd Clan. The English name of "gourd dance" comes from the rattles used by the dancers, which at one time were made out of gourd or rawhide, but now consist of baking powder cans or metal saltshakers. Even though these rattles have been used since the revival of the dance in the 1950s, they are still called gourds when speaking in English. The origin of the dance itself is imbedded in the Kiowa ceremonial traditions of the sun dance, shut down in the latter 19th century by the U.S. Government out of fear and ignorance of American Indian rituals and religion. The sun dance was "put away" by the tribe in exchange for badly needed rations and clothing from the government, and a buffalo hunting party could no longer be held which eliminated an important part of the ceremony. Jim Anquoe pointed out in his presentation that gourd dance songs grew out of the Kiowa's sun dance and brush dance songs, and the Kiowa Gourd Dance is the traditional dance of Thia-pah-go warrior society.

Leonard Cozad, Sr., who is generally considered *the* Kiowa elder singer in 2003, told Tony Isaacs his memories of the gourd dance's origins in a 1974 interview

Cozad Family Singers

included on *Kiowa Gourd Dance Volume 1*: "The Kiowas had bands or societies, I don't know how far back. From what I got from a few of my elders, they had these dances only once a year in the summertime. In those days we had a sun dance – a bigger place to go for all the societies and organizations; and these sun dances were put on by different societies, such as the Young Colts, the Mustangs, the Gourd Society, the Black Leggins, and the Elite Warriors. Each of these societies had their own songs. When they are going to put up a sun dance lodge, each society has a brush dance, from gourd dance and Black Leggins on down, except for the Elite Warriors, we never heard anything about that. But these others are the ones, the people who have work to do to put up the lodge. When it's done, that's when the sun dance begins. In the meantime, all these different societies have their own places in the circle – a big circle with the lodge in the center, and they put on dances as time goes on."

After the last Kiowa sun dance was held in 1887 at Oak Creek, members of the original "Gourd Clan," or Tia-pah-go, continued dances until 1927 when the last dance was held a few miles south of Carnegie. The Gourd Dance was not held again until Armistice Day of 1946 when it was again performed in Carnegie. In 1956, some of the descendants of the original members began working out the songs for the Kiowa Gourd Clan. A recent treasure trove of reel-to-reel tapes, donated to the Oklahoma Historical Society by the Edwin Chapabitty, Sr. family, document the singings when the gourd dance songs were formed, as well as many other Kiowa songs and songs from surrounding tribes such as the Cheyenne, Arapaho, and

Kiowa Gourd Dancers, Carnegie, Oklahoma, 2003

Comanche. The cataloguing of these significant recordings, and other important work on the American Indian music of Oklahoma, is ongoing through the Oklahoma Historical Society and its Oklahoma Folklife Council's Tribal Songs Project. As for the Kiowa Gourd Dance, those who revived the dance in the 1950s and formed the Kiowa Gourd Clan have now essentially split into three different organizations, discussed in detail by Luke E. Lassiter in his 1998 book, *The Power of Kiowa Song*. Regardless of factionalism, the public is welcome to attend the annual Kiowa Gourd Clan Ceremonies held in Carnegie Park next to the rodeo grounds every year on July 4th. While the event does not feature the usual trappings and vendors of intertribal powwows, the event is one of tremendous depth and significance for both the Kiowa and American culture in general. As Leonard Cozad, Sr., the original drum keeper of the revived Kiowa Gourd Clan, explained to Tony Isaacs, "It's just like prayers songs, it just makes you happy, and makes people feel good. . . . When they hear the drum and the song, then they want to live – they want to go on to hear these good things among the homes and their children." Many singers have been recorded throughout the years, but even more have not. The Kiowa Gourd Clan's 1996 program mentions some of the common family names known around the Gourd Clan drum: Whitefox, Daugomah, Ahhaitty, Koomsa, Tenedooah, Kaulaity, Lone Bear, Doyeto, Cozad, Toyebo, Lone Wolf, Anquoe, Bointy, Botone, Emhoolah, Red Bird, Tsoodle, Satepauhoodle, Horse, Gayton, and Tenequoot.

In addition to the Gourd Dance itself, The Little Rabbit Society is a Kiowa children's organization and has its own set of songs that are sung during morning ceremonies on the last two days of the encampment. An added element of bittersweet fun and irony has also been present for several years in the presence of a bugler dressed in authentic 19th century U.S. cavalry regalia. The bugler, most recently Bill Bartee of Bethany who married into the Tsoodle family, plays cavalry calls during some of the Gourd Clan's songs. The history behind the bugler lies with Kiowa chief Standing Bear's military strategy. During the Plains Indian Wars, the Kiowa captured a bugler. Chief Satanta, pronounced roughly "Sate-I-tay," or White Bear, who was obviously a military genius,

Kiowa Gourd Clan bugler, Bill Bartee

learned how to play the cavalry's bugle calls. When the cavalry played charge or retreat on the battlefield, White Bear would play the opposite call and confuse the mounted troops. During one portion of the Kiowa Gourd Clan Ceremonies, a bugle and other war trophies are mounted on staffs in the center of the arena. While humorous, the Kiowa do not forget White Bear refused life under U.S. government rule, and continued raiding off the reservation because of meager rations and the intrusion of the railroad into traditional buffalo country. Taken to a Texas prison, he committed suicide rather than conforming. This episode in Kiowa history only adds to the reverence of the annual and open-to-the-public Kiowa Gourd Clan proceedings.

Sacred singing is not limited to the warrior societies in Kiowa life. Kiowa singers have made significant contributions to both the peyote religion's music, and the sacred hymn singing of the Kiowa Christian church. Bill Kaulaity and Daniel Cozad, as well as Joe Fish Dupoint and Dewayne Tofpi have each recorded sets of Kiowa peyote songs for Canyon Records, and Indian House Records has released several sets of Kiowa peyote songs, each one different from the other. The first set on Indian House, recorded and released in 1997 and 1998, is called *Kiowa Spiritual Peyote Songs Volume 1, 2, and 3.* Volumes 1 and 2 feature Kiowa, Apache, and Comanche peyote songs sung by Nelson Big Bow and

Kenneth L. Cozad. Volume 3 of *Kiowa Spiritual Peyote Songs* consists of 28 Kiowa and Comanche peyote songs sung by Nelson Big Bow, and assisted by Howard Cozad. In 1998, Indian House recorded and released *Faith, Hope, and Charity: Kiowa Native American Church Prayer Songs, Volume 1 and 2*, recorded at Medicine Park, Oklahoma. Both volumes of *Faith, Hope, and Charity* contain 32 Kiowa and Comanche peyote songs sung by Daniel K. Cozad, Sr., Joe Fish Dupoint, Kenneth L. Cozad, and Howard Cozad. Finally, Indian House released the first of a four-volume set of *Kiowa Peyote Songs* in 2002 recorded at Hog Creek, Oklahoma, and featuring singers Joe Fish Dupoint, Howard and Kenneth Cozad, Lonnie Emhoolah, and Herbert Redbird, with Volumes 2 and 3 being released in the summer of 2003.

On the Christian side of Kiowa music, Indian House also recorded two volumes of sacred hymns in 1971, *Kiowa Church Songs – Volume 1 and 2*. Singers on the albums of church songs, both available on cassette, include David Apekaum, Ray Cozad, Harry Domebo, Walter Geionety, Tom Tointigh, Ruby Beaver, Kathleen Redbone, Joyce Robinson, and Nancy Tointich. Fred Tsoodle, a Kiowa sacred hymn singer, won a 2001 National Heritage Fellowship award from the National Endowment for the Arts for his preservation of Kiowa hymns. As of 2003, Tsoodle was the song leader at the Rainy Mountain Kiowa Indian Baptist Church in southwestern Oklahoma. Another public source of Kiowa hymns is the *Songs of Indian Territory* cassette produced by the State Arts Council of Oklahoma in 1989. Ralph and Mildred Kotay and Vivian Komartly sang two hymns for that project to preserve the Native American music traditions of Oklahoma. Also on the cassette are Kiowa Gourd Dance, Round Dance, and War Dance songs by Ernest "Iron" Toppah, Tommy Ware, Joe Fish Dupont, and Stoney Ware.

The Kiowa have also played an important role in the development and preservation of the Plains flute tradition. Also part of the Smithsonian's Folk Music Series of American Indian music, Belo Cozad (1864-1950), seventy-seven at the time of the 1941 recording by Willard Rhodes in Anadarko, explained the story of the Kiowa flute which is included on *Plains: Comanche, Cheyenne, Kiowa, Caddo, Wichita, Pawnee* (AAFS L39), later released on *A Treasury of Library of Congress Field Recordings* (Rounder, 1997). Belo said he got the music from "way back in Montana," when a poor boy went up on a mountain for four nights, and learned this music from "some kind of spirit" who told the boy to "make good music this way, keep it as long as you live, and it will give you a good living." The boy got the flute from a great cedar tree on the mountain, and with the music he became well off, had a good home, good wives, and good children. Belo considered himself one of those children. Cozad then plays a short rendition of the song that can be considered at the root of the Kiowa flute tradition. Also on the album, Cozad sings and plays a Kiowa love song on the flute.

Contemporarily, artists such as Tom Mauchahty-Ware and **Cornel Pewewardy** maintain the Kiowa flute tradition. Both Ware and Pewewardy are of Kiowa and Comanche descent, and both tribes' music influences the musical output of both artists. One of Mauchahty-Ware's several recordings includes *Flute Songs of the Kiowa and Comanche* (Indian House, 1978). The album includes the "Kiowa Flag Song," love songs, and Comanche hymns. Additionally Ware has also recorded on albums of previously discussed Oh-Ho-Mah recordings from 1975, "49" songs with Millard Clark, and is also a vocalist and guitarist with the American Indian blues group, Blues Nation. Furthering the obvious connection between blues and "49" songs, Blues Nation records and performs electric blues with lyrics reflecting Indian themes and subjects like "Empty Tipi Blues," and "Can't See the Signs" on their 1999 self-titled album. Other Kiowas in the group include Terry Tsotigh on drums and harmonica, and bassist Sonny Klinekole who is of Kiowa, Comanche, and Apache descent. Along with Comanche guitarist Dusty Miller and Muscogee (Creek) keyboardist Obie Sullivan, Blues Nation is part of a substantial blues tradition among the Kiowa spearheaded by Kiowa/Comanche/Muscogee guitarist **Jesse Ed Davis** who made significant contributions to rock, pop, and blues music in the 1960s and 1970s. Another recognized Kiowa guitarist is Cecil Gray who plays with the all-Native group, the Blackhawk Blues Band, nominated for a Native American Music Award in 2002 for "Debut Group of the Year," even though they have been playing together since 1990.

Phillip "Yogie" Bread, also Comanche and Kiowa, has been recognized for both his musi-

Kiowa Gourd Clan singers, left to right: Cletus Gayton, Sidney Toppah, and Earnest "Iron" Toppah

cal abilities on the traditional flute and as a blues harmonica player. He has been playing harmonica since he was ten, and travels the country playing festivals, tribal affairs, and other special occasions. Bread toured Europe and was featured at the Budapest Hungary Blues Festival in 1994 and 1995. Bread has also contributed music to a video documentary, *Oklahoma*, and in 1997 released an independent CD, *Thon-Gya!*, Kiowa for "This is what they say." *Thon-Gya* is a spoken word and traditional-meets-contemporary music release that explores various aspects of Kiowa and lifestyle and tradition.

While Kiowa musicians have ranged into the realm of popular music and blues, the majority of Kiowa singers carry on ancient traditions of which they are the contemporary representatives and conservators. While tremendously important work is being done by scholar/singers such as Jim Anquoe, some singers have not been recorded professionally who are well known and highly respected, such as Evans Ray Satepauhoodle and Billy Evans Horse. While many tribes throughout the United States have lost their musical traditions and converted to either Anglo-influenced Christian music or the intertribal powwow tradition, the Kiowa continue to preserve and practice music that existed before the Europeans ever arrived in North America. (HF)
www.indianhouse.com or www.canyonrecords.com

Kubik, Gail
(b. September 5, 1914 – d. July 20, 1984)

One of the youngest American composers to garner a Pulitzer Prize, for his *Symphony Concertante* in 1952, and awarded a full scholarship to study at the Eastman School of Music at age fifteen, composer and violinist Gail Thompson Kubik was born in South Coffeyville, Oklahoma, a community of approximately 800 residents, located near the Oklahoma-Kansas border in the northeastern part of the state. At Eastman from 1930 to 1934, Gail studied violin with Samuel Belov and composition with Bernard Rogers and Edward Royce. He continued compositional study with Leo Sowerby at the American Conservatory in Chicago in 1935 and with Walter Piston and Nadia Boulanger at Harvard University in 1937-38.

During the early 1940s, Kubik served as staff composer and program adviser for NBC radio in New York City, music consultant for the Office of War Information Film Bureau, and coordinator of the First Motion Picture Unit of the U.S. Army Air Corps. During the mid-1940s, he was considered one of the best composers for wartime documentaries.

Following World War II, Gail spent considerable time in Europe after capturing in 1950 the Rome Prize, a coveted fellowship that provides residency in Italy for gifted American artists and scholars. He was in Europe from 1950 to 1955 and again from 1959 to 1967. From 1970 until his retirement in 1980, he was composer-in-residence at Scripps College in Claremont, California.

Kubik's honors include two Guggenheim Fellowships in 1944 and 1965, and the Pulitzer Prize for his *Symphony Concertante* in 1952. At that time, he was the youngest recipient to win that award. His second and third symphonies were commissioned, respectively, by the Louisville Orchestra and the New York Philharmonic.

Gail's varied works include *Frankie and Johnnie*, composed in 1946 for dance band and folksong; *In Praise of Johnny Appleseed*, originally written in 1938, but revised in 1961, for chorus and orchestra; *Trivialities* for flute, horn, and string quartet (1934-36) *Variations on a Thirteenth Century Troubadour Song* (1935-37); *Folk Song Suite* (1941-44) for orchestra; *Memphis Belle* (1944) for orchestra; *Thunderbolt Overture* (1953) for orchestra; *Pastorale and Spring Valley Overture* (1947) for orchestra; *Boston Baked Beans: A New England Fable* (1950) for chorus and orchestra; *Magic, Magic, Magic!* (1973-76) for chorus and chamber orchestra; *A Christmas Set* (1968) for chorus and chamber orchestra; *A Record of our Time* (1970) for chorus and orchestra; *Litany and Prayer* (1943-45) for male chorus; *Prayer and Toccata* (1969) for chamber orchestra; *Fables in Song* (1950-69) for voice; *Stewball* (1942) for band; *Fanfare and March* (1945) for band; and *Fanfare for One World* (1947) for band.

Gail also completed numerous radio, television, and film scores, including *Puck: A Legend of Bethlehem* (1940) for radio; *Thunderbolt* (1945) for film; *C-*

Man (1949) for film; *Gerald McBoing-Boing* (1950) for film; *The Miner's Daughter* (1950) for film; *The Desperate Hours* (1955) for film; and *The Silent Sentinel* (1958) for television.

Finally, Kubik worked as an arranger with a number of chorale groups, including the Robert Shaw Chorale (*Amazing Grace*), Atlanta Singers (*American Sampler*), Dale Warland Singers (*Blue Wheat*), and Westminister Abbey Choir (*Folk Songs*). A CD entitled *Gail Kubik*, recorded in 1960, is available on the Contemporary label.

He died at his home in West Covina, California, on July 20, 1984. (GC)

LaFave, Jimmy
(b. 1955)

Considered a protégé of **Woody Guthrie** and one of the founders of the "**red dirt music**" sound, Jimmy LaFave was born in Wills Point, Texas (about thirty miles east of Dallas), but moved to Stillwater, Oklahoma, as a teenager. He began school in Mesquite, Texas, where he started his musical career playing on a Sears & Roebuck drum set. Shortly thereafter, his mother cashed in some green stamps for Jimmy's first guitar, and he wrote his first song in junior high school, which was "something about traveling around and being a hobo." Jimmy's mother was a devout country music fan, listening to such artists as Hank Williams, **Merle Haggard**, and Sonny James. Thus, Jimmy was exposed to almost exclusive country music during his childhood days. He started listening to other sounds, such as Bob Dylan and Jackson Browne, during his teenage years. In a recent interview with *Best in Texas: Texas Music for the Country*, Jimmy states that his music is comprised of four basic genres: rock, folk, country, and blues, all of which are intrinsic to the red dirt music sound.

When Jimmy was about fifteen, his family moved to Stillwater, where he graduated from Stillwater High School. During this time, Jimmy came of age musically while living in Oklahoma. Jimmy recalled in the *Texas Music* interview, "there is such a vein of great music from up around the Stillwater and Tulsa area." Jimmy relates in the interview, "we call it Red Dirt music because that's the color of the dirt around there and it symbolizes a good fertile music scene."

During his time in Stillwater, Jimmy became well acquainted with **Garth Brooks**, a student at Oklahoma State University. The two shared band members and played at Willie's, a college hangout on "The Strip" (area of shops and bars south of the campus on Washington Street). According to Jimmy, Garth was the Wednesday night "happy hour" performer and he played the Friday and Saturday night gigs. Jimmy says that Garth was performing a lot of cover songs, mostly George Strait and Dan Fogelburg material. His favorite story on Garth was when the OSU Cowboys played the Nebraska Cornhuskers in a home football game, he cut his version of "Devil Went Down to Georgia" replacing the original lyrics with "when the Cornhuskers come down to Stillwater." Garth sold out the tape in front of the football stadium reflecting his promotional talents.

LaFave was strongly influenced by the music of Oklahoma. In an interview with *Twangin'* magazine, he stated: "There's so much music that's come from Oklahoma, such as **Woody Guthrie, J.J. Cale, Chet Baker, Garth Brooks, Vince Gill, Reba, and Leon Russell**. There's a cool music scene around Tulsa and Stillwater that has its own sound." While in Oklahoma, Jimmy began to define his sound which, he states, was based on a "combination of his experiences there among authentic songwriters from the tradition of Woody Guthrie." Before leaving the state, Jimmy toured the Southwest with Night Tribe, his original band.

In 1986 LaFave moved to Austin, Texas, in order to find a larger audience, locate a recording studio, and rub elbows with singer-songwriters like Joe Ely, Butch Hancock, and Guy Clark. He soon identified a new venue, Chicago House, an Austin coffeehouse. For the next eight years, he devoted his time to songwriting, improving his performance skills as a solo artist, working in other Austin clubs, and assembling a new version of Night Tribe.

In 1992 Jimmy released a self-produced compact disc, *Austin Skyline*, a sixteen-track album containing thirteen of his own songs. His songwriting talents were recognized which resulted in a publishing agreement with Polygram Music. A second album, *Highway Trance*, was released in 1994 with fifteen of the sixteen tracks composed by Jimmy, five or six of which, he says were written during his Stillwater days. A third album, *Buffalo Return to the Plains*, was recorded in 1995 with all fourteen tracks written by Jimmy.

In 1996 LaFave was invited to perform on the PBS *Austin City Limits* series. The highlight of the year was when Nora Guthrie, Woody's daughter, requested that Jimmy represent Woody Guthrie's music when he performed the "Tribute to Woody Guthrie," for the induction ceremonies when Woody was inducted into the Rock and Roll Hall of Fame in Cleveland. Finally, he was awarded for the second consecutive year, The Austin Music Awards' Best Singer-Songwriter of the Year.

LaFave's fourth album on the Bohemia Beat label was a 1997 release, *Road Novel*, which included fifteen tracks, such as "Home Sweet Oklahoma," all penned by Jimmy. His interest in road songs is reflected in two albums on which he appears: *Songs of Route 66: All-American Highway* (1998) and *More Songs of Route 66: Roadside Attractions* (2001). On the former, he sings "Route 66 Revisited," and on the latter, "Oklahoma Hills." Also in 1997 he was again asked by Nora Guthrie to speak and perform at the induction of Woody Guthrie into the Oklahoma Music Hall of Fame in Muskogee. To cap off the year, Jimmy toured Europe twice as well as stops in the U.S. and Canada.

In 1999, Jimmy recorded a two-CD set, *Trail*, which featured extensive material by Bob Dylan. Its thirty-one tracks, including twelve Dylan songs, were recorded live in Texas and other parts of the world. Two years later, he released the critically acclaimed *Texoma*, a sixteen-track collection that featured one of the best recent tributes to his idol Woody Guthrie simply titled "Woody Guthrie," as well as "The Moon is a Harsh Mistress," written by Oklahoman **Jimmy Webb,** and more of his unique brand of observationally astute American music. He is attracted to Guthrie's music because he says "it's music for the common man," and reflects "bits and pieces of the landscape," but also "the people around the country. I like that sense of rambling in his music."

LaFave has appeared three times on NPR's Mountain Stage, was featured performer at the first Woody Guthrie Festival in Okemah, Oklahoma in 1998, and has performed numerous times at the Kerrville Folk Festival, including the 1995 festival that was made into a *Kerrville Folk Festival: 1995 Highlights* album, on which Jimmy sings "When the Tears Fall Down." He has produced and hosted a benefit for the American Indian College Fund in Austin, which featured twenty of Austin's best singers and songwriters. Moreover, he has sung back-up vocals for such artists as **Ray Wylie Hubbard, Tom Russell**, and Bob Childers.

During his 2002 tour, Jimmy stopped at the Woody Guthrie Foundation in New York City, where Nora Guthrie presented him with a set of Woody's unpublished lyrics that will be converted into an upcoming LaFave album. Also in 2002, Jimmy was again a headliner at the Fifth Annual Woody Guthrie Folk Festival in Okemah, Oklahoma. In 2003, he spearheaded a Woody Guthrie tribute tour entitled "A Ribbon of Highway – Endless Skyway Tour," along with Ellis Paul, Slaid Cleaves, and Eliza Gilkyson. Stops on the tour included Old Town School of Folk Music (Chicago), Ryman Auditorium (Nashville), The Ark (Ann Arbor, MI), Westport Arts Center (Westport, CT), Sommerville Theater (Sommerville, MASS), and the Palladium Theater (St. Petersburg, FL). LaFave's tour schedule had him booked solid across the country through the end of 2003, and in January of 2004 he was scheduled to perform in the Endless Skyway Tour in New York City and California. (GC)
www.jimmylafave.com

Lamond, Don
(b. August 18, 1920)

Best known as drummer for Woody Herman's Herd and George Wein's Newport Festival All-Stars, jazz percussionist Donald Douglas Lamond was born in Oklahoma City, although he was raised in Washington, D.C. His lawyer father took an interest in Don's early grade school music by renovating the home basement so Don could practice his drums downstairs. In high school Don took percussion lessons from Horace Butterworth. Upon completion of high school, he studied all percussion instruments at the Peabody Institute in Baltimore.

Lamond made his professional debut with Sonny Dunham in 1943, and then worked with Boyd Raeburn in 1944. He joined Woody Herman's First Herd in 1945 and remained until it disbanded in 1946. Thereafter, he freelanced in 1947, including studio work with the famed bop jazz artist Charlie Parker, including the well known "Relaxin' at Camarillo," which included three other Oklahomans in the session (**Wardell Gray**, **Barney Kessel**, and **Howard McGhee**). He also recorded with other noted bop artists such as Coleman Hawkins and Dizzy Gillispie. He rejoined Herman's Second Herd and stayed with the band for two years until it dissolved in 1949. Terry Gibbs, vocalist with Herman's band, stated: "We must have had six or seven of the greatest drummers, but they didn't fit like Don. It was Don's band." Overall, he appeared on more than a dozen recordings with Herman's ensembles.

Around 1953 Don settled in New York, and for the next two decades vacillated between big bands and small combos. He worked primarily as a television show and studio drummer. He played on several television shows, such as Steve Allen, Gary Moore, and Ed Sullivan, and recorded with such bands as Stan Getz (five albums), Benny Goodman (six albums), Sonny Stitt, Jack Teagarden, Quincy Jones, Eddie Condon, Al Cohn, Miles Davis, Duke Ellington, Bud Freeman, Maynard Ferguson, Stan Kenton, and Bob Crosby. He also recorded with such popular vocalists as Billie Holiday (five albums), Perry Como,

1947 Slingerland Drum advertisement.

Lena Horne, June Christy, Anita O'Day, Harry Belafonte, Carmen McCrae, and another Oklahoman **Lee Wiley** on her *Back Home Again* album in 1971. In the late 1960s he was drummer for George Wein's Newport Jazz Festival All-Stars, and toured Europe with the group.

By the late 1970s Lamond was leading his own ensemble, Big Swing Band, in Florida, as well as working with Harry Wuest's Top of the World Band at Disney World. By this time Don had become a resident of Florida, where he helped young musicians by giving them an opportunity to play in his big band.

Don's discography as bandleader includes a 1962 Command Records album *Off Beat Percussion* featuring Doc Severinsen on trumpet, and *Extraordinary*, a LP on the Statiras label that includes both his big band and quartet. It was reissued in cd format in 1996 on the Circle label. Buddy Rich, the notable drummer, once said, "Don Lamond is one of the greatest jazz drummers I have ever heard, in every respect." (GC)

Lewis, Ed
(b. January 22, 1909 – d. September 18, 1985)

Trumpeter with such jazz bands as Bennie Moten, **Jay McShann**, and Count Basie, trumpeter, bandleader, and composer Edward ("Big Ed") Lewis was born in Eagle City, Oklahoma, a tiny hamlet northwest of Oklahoma City in Blaine County. Prior to starting school, Ed's family moved to Kansas City, Missouri, where he learned baritone horn from his father, trumpeter Oscar Lewis, and marched alongside him in Shelly Bradford's Brass Band. It is recorded that Ed was involved in his high school marching band and completed music classes during his high school days.

Lewis made his professional debut with Jerry Westbrook's ensemble in 1924, playing baritone horn, but soon switched to trumpet. After brief stints with groups led by Paul Banks and Oklahoman Laura Rucker, he was hired by Bennie Moten, for whom he played lead trumpet from 1926 to 1931. Following a short stay with the Thamon Hayes band, Ed joined Harlan Leonard's Kansas City Rockets from 1934 to 1936, and then became lead trumpeter with Jay "Hootie" McShann's Orchestra in 1937.

In 1937 Ed joined the Count Basie Orchestra and was a member of the ensemble until 1948. Coincidentally, Ed auditioned for Basie on the same day as Billie Holiday. During his tenure with Basie, he appeared on more than a dozen albums Basie recorded in the 1930s and 1940s, although was never a major soloist with the band. He was a member of the Basie ensemble at the same time as several other Oklahomans, such as **Jimmy Rushing** and **Ted Donnelly**. During this time, Ed composed several songs, including "Justrite" and "It's Sand, Man!" The latter was recorded by such notables as Natalie Cole, Bud Shank, Cullen Offer, and Lambert, Hendricks, and Ross.

Following the Basie years, Lewis retired from music and drove a taxicab in New York City, however, he returned in the mid-1950s to lead his own band in the "Big Apple," playing local club dates. A year before his death, Ed toured Europe with The Countsmen.

Although Ed never cut an album of his own, his recording credits, in addition to the Basie albums, included trumpet work for such diverse artists as Chuck Berry, **Charlie Christian**, Dave Brubeck, Buck Clayton, Coleman Hawkins, Billie Holiday, Jimmy Rushing, Lester Young, and Johnny Otis. Ed died in Blooming Grove, New York, on September 18, 1985. (GC)

Liggins, Joe
(b. July 9, 1915 - d. August 1, 1987)

Liggins, Jimmy
(b. October 14, 1922 - d. July 18, 1983)

These Oklahoma brothers were among the top rhythm and blues artists in the late 1940s and early 1950s, and totaled more than fifteen Top 10 hits in various *Billboard* charts. Pianist, vocalist, songwriter, and bandleader Joe, the oldest was born in Guthrie, located north of Oklahoma City and the first state capital of Oklahoma. Guitarist, vocalist, and bandleader Jimmy was born in Newby, Oklahoma, a tiny hamlet southwest of Tulsa.

Before he turned twenty, Joe had become an accomplished pianist and arranger. In 1932 he moved first to San Diego, and later in 1939 to Los Angeles, where he performed with various groups, including Sammy Franklin's California Rhythm Rascals. Franklin rejected Joe's rolling boogie tune, "The Honeydripper," therefore, Joe organized his own combo dubbed The Honeydrippers, and recorded it on the Exclusive label. It charted at No. 1 in 1945 (remained for eighteen weeks), and eventually became the first million selling instrumental in R & B history. The Honeydrippers, a sextet that included saxophonists Willie Jackson and James Jackson, Jr., developed a sound based on a mixture of pop, big band swing, and blues, featuring Joe's rhythmic piano and smooth vocals. Joe and the group registered nine more hits with Exclusive from 1945 to 1948, including "I Got a Right to Cry," "Roll'em," "Dripper's Boogie," and "Dripper's Blues." In 1949 the Exclusive label folded because of financial difficulties and Joe sought a new recording home.

Art Rupe at Specialty Records had already signed Jimmy, thus Joe joined his younger brother at that label in 1950. Joe's debut with Specialty was his version of "Rag Mop," followed by the No. 1 rhythm and blues hit in 1950, " Pink Champagne," voted R & B record of the year by *Billboard* magazine. Because of the national success of their recordings, The Honeydrippers toured the Midwest and East Coast, including Chicago (Pershing Ballroom) and New York City

(Apollo Theater). Joe returned to California and teamed with Amos Milburn to draw more than 6,000 fans in Oakland. To conclude 1950, Joe recorded "Little Joe's Boogie" and "Daddy on My Mind," his first 45 rpm.

In 1951, Joe signed a three-year contract with Specialty, and recorded "Frankie Lee," "I Just Can't Help Myself," "This One's For Me," "Bob Is My Guy," "That's the One for Me," and "Whiskey, Gin, and Wine," with vocals by Candy Rivers, an ex-gospel singer from Indianapolis. The first all-black radio network developed by Mutual Broadcasting Company went on the air in 1951, and Joe and his Honeydrippers were featured.

Joe continued to tour in 1952-53 with stops in Chicago, Cincinnati, St. Louis, Kansas City, and Denver, playing at such venues as Wrigley Field. He recorded several more sides for Specialty in the early 1950s, including "Tanya," "The Big Dipper," and "Boogie Woogie Lou," but the rock and roll era was launched and Specialty dropped Joe from its roster in 1954.

In 1954, Joe moved to the Mercury label, then to Aladdin, then back to Mercury in 1962, but never matched the success he had with Specialty or Exclusive. "The Honeydripper" continued to play dates on the West Coast through the mid-1980s, always promoting the jump blues sound that bridged the gap between swing and rock and roll.

Jimmy's entry into the rhythm and blues field was attributed primarily to older brother Joe's success. He moved from Oklahoma to San Diego in 1932, was a professional boxer having trained with Archie Moore, and worked as a radio disc jockey, before serving as Joe's chauffeur and right hand man for more than a year (1945-46), while teaching himself guitar chords.

Jimmy dubbed his octet ensemble with three reeds (Harold Land, Charlie "Little Jazz" Ferguson, and Maxwell Davis) and himself on guitar as The Drops of Joy, after Joe's Honeydrippers. They signed with Specialty Records in 1947 recording "I Can't Stop It" and "Troubles." This first release was unsuccessful, however, in 1948, "Teardrop Blues" and "Cadillac Boogie" signaled that another member of the Liggins family was ready to make some noise. The blues number cracked the Top 10 of the R & B charts and "Cadillac Boogie" was to become one of the major precursors to rock and roll. According to some musicologists, it was the first rock and roll record.

In 1949, Jimmy scored with "Careful Love" and "Don't Put Me Down," both of which cracked the Top 10 on the R & B charts. The Drops of Joy toured the Southwest, primarily Oklahoma and Texas, and remained a favorite in their southern California base. While on tour, Jimmy was shot in the face in Jackson, Mississippi. The bullet broke his jaw and severed his tongue, however, he recovered and resumed his career. Jimmy's last hit recording for Specialty was "Drunk," a one-chord up-tempo tune.

By 1954, Specialty's emphasis was on other artists, such as Guitar Slim, and the Jimmy's seven-year association with the label ended. He moved to a rival Los Angeles company, Aladdin, where he recorded an answer tune to "Drunk" entitled "I Ain't Drunk," a classic later covered by bluesman Albert Collins. His last hit with Aladdin was "Boogie Woogie King," a solid jump blues number.

In 1958, Jimmy formed his own record label, Duplex, which he retained until 1978. His recording popularity was beginning to wane, and the handful of sides he recorded for his own label never achieved the success of his work with Specialty and Aladdin. In the mid-1970s, Jimmy moved from Los Angeles to Durham, North Carolina, where he opened a music school, and the "Boogie King" died there in 1983. (GC)

Luchsinger, Susie
(b. November 8, 1957)

Winner of several awards in the 1990s from the Country Gospel Music Association and the Christian Country Music Association, Martha Susan McEntire Luchsinger was born in McAlester, Oklahoma, but raised on a ranch near Chockie, some thirty miles south of McAlester and fifteen miles north of Atoka. As the younger sister of country music megastar **Reba McEntire**, she was born to Clark Vincent and Jacqueline Smith McEntire. She has an older brother, Del Stanley, or "Pake," and another older sister, Alice Lynn Foran. Her father was a professional rodeo rider and rancher, who taught Susie how to ride, while her mother taught her music. Her first public performance was at a second grade Thanksgiving program. She graduated from Kiowa High School in Kiowa, Oklahoma, where Susie, Reba, and Pake performed as The Singing McEntires, and recorded a local hit in 1971 entitled "The Ballad of John McEntire," a tribute to their grandfather. She received a bachelor's degree in personnel management (accounting minor) in 1980 from Oklahoma State University in Stillwater, and began work at J. D. Simmons in Oklahoma City.

Susie soon began to tour behind Reba as a back-up vocalist, and appeared on Reba's 1981 album *Heart to Heart* and its 1982 follow-up *Unlimited*. During this time, she met Paul Luchsinger, a rodeo champion, and they were married in 1981 in Stringtown. Susie and Paul gave birth to their first child, Eldon Paul, or E.P., in 1983. By 1984, she had discontinued her singing career and started traveling with

Paul on the rodeo circuit. During the National Finals Rodeo, she was invited to sing for the Cowboy Christian Fellowship. Because her music was so well received by the group, Susie decided to launch a solo career, and released her debut album, *No Limit* (1985), produced by Palm Ministries, an organization founded by Susie and Paul, which focused on ministering to rodeo people. In 1986, a second album was recorded, and for the next ten years, she would record an album per year. Based on these recordings, she was named Female Vocalist of the Year and Video of the Year for "So It Goes (With Everything But Love)" by the International Country Gospel Association and Country Gospel Artist of the Year by *Gospel Voice Magazine* Reader's Award. Her eighth album in 1993, *Real Love*, on the Integrity label, produced four #1 hits on the Positive Country charts, including "There is a Candle," "For Pete's Sake," "I Don't Love You Like I Used To," a duet with her husband Paul, and "I Saw Him in Your Eyes." As a result, Susie captured more honors in 1993 with Entertainer of the Year from the International Country GMA, Christian Country Female Artist of the Year from *Cashbox Magazine*, and Favorite Female Artist of the Year and Favorite Album of the Year based on reader's poll of the *Christian Country Research Bulletin*. During these years, Susie gave birth to their second and third children, daughter Lucchese (1986) and son Samuel (1989).

Susie's next album, *Come As You Are*, was also successful in reaching the #1 spot on the Positive Country charts with three singles, including "Two in the Saddle," "Take It to the Rock," and "You're It." In 1994, she garnered top honors as Female Vocalist of the Year and received the Vanguard Award from the Christian CMA, Christian Country Artist of the Year and Performance Excellence Album of the Year from *Gospel Voice* magazine, and was nominated for New Artist of the Year, Country Song of the Year, and Country Album of the Year for the GMA Dove Awards, and Christian Country Artist of the Year by *TNN/Music City News*.

A Tender Road Home was released in 1997 on the New Haven label, and an accompanying book of the same title was co-authored by Paul and Susie. The single from the album, "Holy Heart," reached #1 on the Christian Country charts. In 1995, she was given the *Gospel Voice* Diamond Award as Christian Country Artist of the Year and captured Female Vocalist of the Year from the Christian CMA, as well as nominations for Country Song of the Year ("For Pete's Sake') for the GMA Dove Award and Christian Country Artist of the Year by the *TNN/Music City News*. The next year, she was honored with another Diamond Award as Christian Country Artist of the Year, and was nominated for Christian Country Album of the Year (*Come As You Are*) for the GMA Dove Award and Christian Country Artist of the Year by *TNN/Music City News*. In 1997, she was nominated as Christian Country Artist of the Year for the *TNN/Music City News* Award, and the next year received a nomination for Christian Country Artist of the Year for the GMA Dove Award.

In 1999, Susie released the *Raised on Faith* album, which yielded two important singles, "My Kind of People," a #1 hit on the Christian Country charts, and "You Are the One," a #1 hit on the European Country Gospel charts. She was nominated for three more awards in 1999: Female Vocalist of the Year and Pioneer Award from the Christian CMA, and Christian Country Recorded Song of the Year ("Whispers in My Heart") by the GMA.

Susie's 2001 album, *My Gospel Hymnal*, was nominated as Christian Country Album of the Year for the GMA Dove Award, and in 2003 she released *You've Got a Friend*, a thirteen-song album of contemporary Christian music and pop classics such as Bill Withers' "Lean On Me," James Taylor's "How Sweet It Is," and Carole King's "You've Got a Friend." In the fall of 2003, she had performances scheduled across the country through the end of the year at churches, rodeos, carnivals, fish fries, and private parties. Susie maintains her Psalms Ministries in Atoka, Oklahoma, with her three children and Paul, her husband of twenty-one years. Her website reflects her personal ethos: "The music is country, the message is Christ." (GC)
www.susieluchsinger.com

Martin, John David "Moon"
(b. October 31, 1945)

Not nearly as popular in his home country as he is in Europe, with notable exceptions among musicians, quirky rock music fans, and smiling Oklahoma music historians, Moon Martin is a talented multi-instrumentalist, vocalist, and songwriter whose own rockabilly-tinged power pop, usually linked to the 1970s new wave era, has gained him cult-like status in Europe, much like another power popper from Oklahoma, **Dwight Twilley**, with whom Moon shared a manager. Martin also has broad respect throughout the music industry from artists such as B.B. King, Linda Ronstadt, and **Steve Ripley** who have featured him on their recordings, and Moon is a prolific songwriter. Robert Palmer had a hit with Martin's "Bad Case of Love You (Doctor, Doctor)" in 1979, and other singers who picked his songs to record include Bette Midler, the Mamas and the Papas, the Association, Nick Lowe, Mink DeVille, Koko Taylor, and Paul Rodgers of Bad Company. Martin's music exhibits many stylistic elements of late 1970s new wave rock, but the constant presence of the blues, and the ease with which twang seeps into some of his songs, also displays common elements of Oklahoma's influence on his generation of musicians, such as **Steve Gaines** and **Jesse Ed Davis**. Additionally, his nods to 1950s rock conventions he learned from second-hand records, and his propensity for Beatles covers all indicate the broader context of his teenage years and musical influences in the United States during the 1960s.

Nicknamed "Moon" as an adult because of his tendency to put the moon in song lyrics, John David Martin was born in extreme southwestern Oklahoma in Altus where he spent his childhood and teen years in Altus, the home of Altus Air Force Base, and just fourteen miles north of the Red River and the Texas border. Being so close to Texas and Mexico had its advantages, namely blues blasting out of the radio from Big Joe Turner, Bo Diddley, and Louis Prima, all coming from Texas and Mexico border stations (mega-watt stations that didn't have to adhere to U.S. broadcast power regulations). In Altus, a friend's father was a jukebox distributor, and Moon would go to the warehouse where stacks and stacks of worn-out 45's and 78's sat after coming out of jukeboxes. He was able to buy a lot of the records cheaply, and began to play his guitar along with them, the first being Buddy Holly's "Peggy Sue" and then several Chuck Berry records. After taking some lessons from a local musician, Lou Vargas, to whom all his records are dedicated, Moon first joined a country outfit in the mid-60s, Cece Wilson and the Panhandle Ramblers. Then, caught up in the general excitement of the British Bands Invasion, he formed a Beatles tribute group with some high school friends to earn money by playing at school dances.

After high school graduation in 1963, and that means the night of graduation, Martin had his car loaded with his clothes and a hotel room reserved in Duncan, Oklahoma where he had a job lined up to play in a band with bassist David Dickey, who went on to be the bass player for the country rock group, America. The band's first gig was in Lawton, where Ft. Sill supported a number of bars and the necessary musicians to entertain in them. Unfortunately, when the club was raided authorities discovered Martin was underage, and that put him out of a job.

Re-strategizing, Moon headed north for Norman to enroll at the University of Oklahoma, and joined a band with Paul Blaylock who needed a bass player. In the fall of '63, he started teaching guitar alongside **Jesse Ed Davis** at a music store owned by the booking agent for a local rockabilly band, The Disciples, who regularly toured the Midwest and Gulf South. When The Disciples' guitar player left, the group auditioned both Martin and Davis, and Martin got the gig, a point of ribbing between Davis and Martin for years.

During the years between 1963 and 1967, The Disciples toured colleges as far south as Louisiana and Mississippi and as far north as Illinois and Michigan. In 1967, at a club in Detroit, The Disciples played with another group in which Bob Seger played keyboards, and Fontaine Brown, a strong-voiced blues singer, was on vocals. Before long, Brown moved to California and was working as a producer at Blue Thumb Records when he called Martin and suggested he bring out The Disciples to make a recording. Fifteen credits short of a degree from the pharmacy school at OU, Martin decided to give it a whirl. The experiment did not really work out as the group was not really able to get their dynamic live sound down on tape. So, Fontaine Brown joined the band as a singer and the group changed their name to Southwind. Under that moniker, and as the only white band on the label, they recorded two fairly obscure country-rock albums: a self-titled one, *Ready to Ride* (Blue Thumb, 1969), and *What a Place to Land* (Blue Thumb, 1973). As an opening act, the group shared stages with Jimi Hendrix, Janis Joplin, Creedence Clearwater Revival, Spirit, Sly Stone, Tower of Power, Chicago Transit Authority, Jethro Tull, Canned Heat, John Lee Hooker, David Lindley, and Linda Ronstadt, but Southwind's recordings received little attention from radio or the buying public. While Martin had been splitting his time between Oklahoma and California, when the group split in 1972 Moon moved to Los Angeles permanently where he worked as a truck driver, wrote songs in his spare time, and continued doing studio work.

Along with session work for Linda Ronstadt on her third solo album in 1971, during which Moon turned down an offer from Glenn Frey to try out for the just-forming Eagles, Martin also recorded with Gram Parsons, blues giant B.B. King, and Michelle Phillips of the Mamas & the Papas. Also during the '70s, while plans for a solo album never materialized, his songs were being covered by the wide array of artists. Mink DeVille's cover of Martin's "Cadillac Walk" on the punky soul crooner's 1977 LP, *Cabretta* (Capitol), finally brought Moon to the attention of Capitol executives as a potential solo artist. Like every other label trying to catch up with the British punk movement, the label needed artists it could market as new wave, a more palatable term for the new music coming out of New York, Boston, Los Angeles, and Great Britain. Sire Records had the Ramones and Talking Heads, Chrysalis had Blondie, Epic had the Clash, A&M had the Police, Columbia had Billy Burnette, Elektra had the Cars, Warner Brothers had to deal with the Sex Pistols, and Capitol had The Knack, The Motels, and Moon Martin. While Martin didn't exactly fit the mold musically with his Oklahoma country-rock background, he looked the part in horn-rimmed glasses, foofy Sgt. Pepper-period Beatles hair, and seemingly sullen disposition. Also, his songs were smart enough, and catchy enough, for his music to garner frequent critical comparisons to Elvis Costello when Moon's first two albums produced radio friendly pop songs about desperate subjects of the human condition.

Eager to get his music out, Moon released a five-song-EP, *Victim of Romance* (Capitol, 1978), containing his studio version of "Victim of Romance" that had been recorded and released by Michelle Phillips in 1977 on her A&M Records release by the same name. The EP also had four live songs, recorded at the El Mocambo in Toronto: Moon's own version of "Cadillac Walk"; a Lennon and McCartney cover, "I Saw Her Standing There," indicating his Beatles tribute days still weren't over; and the song that would become his signature piece, "Bad Case of Loving You (Doctor, Doctor)." Another fan favorite, "Hot Nite in Dallas," also made its first appearance on the EP. With exception of the Beatles cover (which he changed to Lennon and McCartney's "All I've Got to Do") the other four songs became the core of his debut solo album, *Shots From a Cold Nightmare* (Capitol, 1979). While the record did not generate much commercial or radio interest, it did energize music critics in the U.K and in the U.S. who admired Martin's holistic perspective of rock, able to incorporate his rootsy Oklahoma background with the smarty pants pop of new wave L.A. and beyond. As Moon described it in an interview on his official website, "Being from that part of the country, all the players were more blues-oriented. My hero was Freddie King."

In the same year Robert Palmer's version of "Bad Case of Loving You" reached #14 on the pop charts, Moon Martin's second album of 1979, *Escape from Domination* (Capitol), proved to be his greatest commercial success as a solo artist. Produced by Craig Leon, who produced the first Ramones album, *Escape from Domination* provided Moon with his biggest hit single, "Rolene," that landed at #30 on the pop singles charts and spurred enough interest to have commercial sheet music published for it. During this period, he toured internationally as an opening act for Blondie, Joe Jackson, The Kinks, The Police and Rockpile. A second single, "No Chance," made the Top 50, and the album apexed at a modest #80 on the album charts. Also, Rachel Sweet was inspired enough by "I've Got a Reason" to include it on her 1980 album for Stiff Records, *Protect the Innocent*.

Martin's third album, *Street Fever* (Capitol, 1980), did not produce a hit single, and made it to a humble #138 on the U.S. album charts, but splashed the Top 20 in both Sweden and France. Subsequently, according to Martin, he "made some bad decisions" with his next outing. While recording the album *Mystery Ticket*, with Robert Palmer producing, or overproducing, Martin had to return from the recording studio in Nassau to do promotion for his first album. That left Palmer to create what he felt was the first American techno record by using Gary Numan and people from Tangerine Dream on the recording. With its heavy synthesizer sound, Capitol Records was eager to capitalize on the success of the first record, and released *Mystery Ticket* with all of its warts. While the album gave Moon his last American chart success when "X-Ray Vision" made the dance club charts, and the album again hit the Top 20 in Sweden, it confounded fans, radio, and critics in the U.S. Perhaps, the record was just too much of a stylistic shift too soon, as the Human League hit ninth months later with the same sound to receptive ears throughout the music media and commercial market.

Having played professionally for almost twenty years, and being lucky enough to have a major hit as well as income from other people recording his songs, Martin put together a Los Angeles studio in the mid-1980s where he recorded *Mixed Emotions*, but Capitol did not want to promote the album that was almost completely created on a sampler and sequencer. Moon turned to his enthusiastic European fan base for its primary acceptance, and *Mixed Emotions*, released on vinyl only in France, gained little notice in the U.S.

Moon popped back up in the early 1990s with two albums on small, independent labels, *Dreams on File* (FNAC, 1992), which not only saw his return to roots rock guitar, but also marked Moon's public appearance in a cowboy hat (an Oklahoma birthright). *Bad News Live* (1993), recorded over three nights in Paris, preceded two compilations of older songs, *Cement Monkey* (Core), and *Lunar Samples* (Core).

In 1995, the British label, Eidsel, repackaged Martin's first four albums as double CD packages: *Shots from a Cold Nightmare/Escape from Domination* and *Street Fever/Mystery Ticket*. Also in '95, Moon settled in a Nashville-area log cabin and built Ponyboy Studio, where he recorded and engineered a solo album in 1999, *Louisiana Jukebox* (Eagle), recorded without the use of any "music machines." The album's rowdy brew exhibits some of Nashville's best session players on new songs like "Get Hot or Go Home," "Pictures of Pain," and "Good Mornin' Policeman." Martin enjoyed working with session players in Nashville. He said in a 2002 interview, "In Nashville it was the first time that guys came up with musical ideas that weren't clichés." Additionally, the album also served as the impetus for several tours of France, Germany, Holland, and Belgium.

Also in 1999, EMI released a twenty-two track compilation, *The Very Best of Moon Martin*, and Moon again toured Europe, where he could be seen on tour in France wearing a flannel shirt with cut off sleeves and an OU baseball cap. He returned to France again in the spring of 2000 for more enthusiastically received shows. In 2002, Moon sold his Nashville house and studio (without the gear) to Steve Earle and moved back to L.A. where he has recorded 15 songs that are "all over the place – ballads, blues, nice songs." He planned on recording the album in French and English to satisfy both fan bases, and as of 2003 thought he would move to France where he could find work and record steadily. For excellent examples of both how fans react to him in Europe and to get a free sampling of his high-octane rockabilly, visit his site at www.mp3.com. Asked what Oklahoma gave him musically, Moon replied, "experience in live music situations, an understanding of the mixture of country and Black music that is rock and roll, and the fact that a lot of good musicians came from the state challenged me to be better. At this stage, I realize the only satisfaction I'm going to get out of music is to get better, and I think I have." (HF)
www.moonmartin.com

Marvin, Frankie and Johnny

Frankie (b. January 17, 1904 – d. January 1985)
Johnny (b. July 11, 1897 – d. December 20, 1944)

Long associated with the origin and evolution of **Gene Autry's** career, Frankie and Johnny Marvin were born in Butler, Oklahoma, a tiny hamlet of about 300 people in the western part of the state. John Senator Marvin, adept on both banjo and guitar, ran away from home when he was around twelve years old to join a circus, and later joined a traveling show called the Royal Hawaiians. During this stint, he learned to play the steel guitar and ukulele. After service in the U.S. Navy during World War I, Johnny developed an act called Honey Duke and His Uke, performing in vaudeville shows. Johnny eventually landed in New York City, where he began writing songs and worked on NBC radio for five years as The

Lonesome Singer of the Air, a daily show. He cut a several   records and also appeared in the musical *Honeymoon Lane* on Broadway. Frankie, his younger brother, joined him in the late 1920s in New York, and found work as a steel guitarist, ukulele player, and comedian.

With the encouragement of Oklahomans Will Rogers and Jimmy Long, Autry decided to visit New York in the late 1920s. The Marvin Brothers, who were living in New York, took the young Autry under their wings. They arranged for Autry to audition and make some test records for the Edison and Victor companies. Although Autry was unsuccessful, he never forgot the Marvin Brothers had assisted him and made him feel at home in the big city.

When the Depression hit and work slowed for the Marvin Brothers, Autry brought them to Hollywood in 1934. For almost twenty years, steel guitarist Frankie was a unique component of the Autry sound on all his recordings and radio shows, especially the *Melody Ranch Show* on CBS radio. He also appeared in Autry's films, both as an actor and stuntman. Johnny was a songwriter and producer for the *Melody Ranch Show*, during which time he wrote approximately eighty songs for Autry's films.

Johnny toured the South Pacific during World War II and entertained the troops. While there in 1943, he contacted dengue fever, which eventually resulted in a heart attack that led to his death in 1945.

Frankie continued to work on the *Melody Ranch Show* on radio until it was dropped in 1956, and then became something of a recluse. When the television version of the *Melody Ranch Show* was launched in the 1960s, sponsored by Autry's own station KTLA in Los Angeles, Frankie resurfaced in the 1960s to work both on and off camera. After a seven year run, the show ended and Frankie retired to Frazier Park, California, to devote more time to his favorite hobby of fishing. After undergoing open-heart surgery, he died in 1985. Although not as prolific in songwriting as his brother, Frankie did co-write with Autry the well-known "Cowboy's Heaven." The German company, Binge, has released a CD of Frankie Marvin selections under the title, *The Golden Age of Frankie Marvin*. (GC)

Mathews, Arthur "Tony"
(b. November 4, 1941)

Born into a family of gospel singers in Checotah, Oklahoma, Tony Mathews toured the world and recorded with Ray Charles and Little Richard, released a highly praised solo album of his own on Alligator Records in 1981, *Condition: Blue*, and continues playing in Los Angeles at clubs, private parties, and various recording sessions. Inspired by gospel groups such as the Soul Stirrers with RH Harris, his own family of multi-racial (African/**Muscogee**/Choctaw/Cherokee/Anglo) gospel singers, and by local guitarist Herbie Welch, Mathews started playing guitar at age 14, and served an apprenticeship with a self-destructive blues man from Rentiesville, Oklahoma, Tim Gilkey. He also sang with gospel quartets on local radio shows in Muskogee, and during the 1950s, Mathews made several recordings with his uncle, vocalist Robert Love, for Chess Records in Chicago, to include "Good Morning Little School Girl," "Shy Guy," and "Another Night Alone."

At 17, Mathews traveled to Dallas where he backed up musicians like Joe Turner, the Five Royals, and the Upsetters, but returned to Checotah to finish high school at the urging of his parents. In 1962, Arthur left Checotah for California, changed his name on arrival to avoid confusion with another Arthur Mathews, and wound up touring with the Simms Twins, forerunners of Sam and Dave, with whom he appeared on the *Jackie Wilson Show* in 1963. From 1964 to 1966, Tony toured with Little Johnny Taylor during Taylor's hit period with "Part Time Love," did studio work for Motown in L.A. on tapes that were sent to Detroit where vocals were added, and recorded for Convoy Records. In 1966 he landed a job with Ray Charles who picked out Matthews because of his "gospel feel." In 1967, Tony left Ray Charles and started touring with Little Richard, staying on the road with the 1950s rocker until 1970, with an intermittent gig supporting shows by Billy Preston.

After starting a family and staying close to home until 1972, Tony hit the road again with Ray Charles from 1973 until 1976. He played sessions and live dates around Los Angeles through the late 1970s, and recorded with Louisiana blues man Lonesome Down in 1977. The next year he played guitar on Chicago blues man Louis Myer's *I'm a Southern Man*, and on Rudy Love's disco album, *This Song Is for You*. Tony spent 1980 through 1982 touring again with Ray Charles, taking a break in 1981 to record *Condition: Blue*, originally released on Alligator in 1981, and subsequently released through Hightone where it is currently available. An album that has not received the credit it deserves for predicting the development of smooth, studio blues that became popular via Robert Cray in the 1980s, the album features Tony's unmistakably gospel-influenced vocals and his guitar work that is deeply rooted in Oklahoma's rural blues traditions. In 1983, Tony sang background vocals for one of Robert Cray's finest early albums, *Bad Influence*, and while Tony went back out with Ray Charles briefly in 1988, he primarily continued playing private parties, occasional club dates, and various sessions as a sideman.

In 1994, Tony played guitar for Bobby McClure's *Younger Man Blues*, and added some work to a comedy album, *Outrageous Radio*. Matthews was one of the featured guitarists on *Guitar Showdown at the Dusk 'til Dawn Blues Fetival*, recorded in 1997 at **DC Minner**'s festival just a couple of miles from Tony's childhood home, and where he is an annual performer. Hear him at his most relaxed and easy going in this recording of Elmore James' "Dust My Blues" and Jimmy Rogers' "You Told Me Baby." In 2000, he played on the Broadway sound-track for a revue of African-American musical styles that traced the evolution of blues from Africa and slavery through the end of the 20th century, *It Ain't Nothin but the Blues*. Tony has also had some minor roles on television, such as in *Matlock* and *Mannix*, and played in the film *Lost Highway*, a movie about Hank Williams learning his trade from black musicians. In 2001, he produced an album by saxophonist Hollis Gilmore. As of 2003, Tony Mathews continued playing around Los Angeles and began setting up a home studio where he would have control over his recording, with plans to release a new album by 2004. (HF) www.hightone.com

McBee, Cecil
(b. May 19, 1935)

One of the most significant bass sidemen in jazz having played with such lumi-naries as Paul Winter, Freddie Hubbard, Miles Davis, Sonny Rollins, and Chico Freeman, as well as one of the most respected composers of the post-bop era, Oklahoma Jazz Hall of Fame 1991 inductee Cecil McBee was born in Tulsa. He performed clarinet duets with his sister while in high school and played the same instrument in his high school marching band at Booker T. Washington in Tulsa, but switched to bass at age seventeen. During the early 1950s, Cecil performed at local nightclubs in Tulsa.

Cecil studied bass and jazz composition at Central State University in Wilberforce, Ohio, and began his professional career with Dinah Washington in 1959. His college studies were interrupted for a two-year stint (1959-61) in the U.S. Army where he conducted and played clarinet in the "158th Band" at Fort Knox, Kentucky. After discharge, Cecil completed his bachelor's degree in clar-inet and music education at CSU.

After training to become a music educator, McBee decided to give performance a try and moved to Detroit's jazz community in 1962. Within the next year, he joined the Paul Winter Sextet, and relocated to New York City with the group. During the 1960s and 1970s, he played bass with Grachan Moncur III, Jackie McLean, Wayne Shorter, Freddie Hubbard, Miles Davis, Charles Lloyd, Yusef Lateef, **Sam Rivers**, Bobby Hutcherson, Pharoah Sanders, Alice Coltrane, Charles Tolliver, Lonnie Liston Smith, Sonny Rollins, Abdullah Ibrahim, Michael White, Jorace Tapscott, Anthony Braxton, Buddy Tate, Harry "Sweets" Edison, Wayne Shorter, **Chet Baker**, and Chico Freeman. His longest stint was with fel-low Oklahoman Rivers from 1967 to 1973 during which he was bassist on such Rivers recordings as *Involution*, *Dimensions and Extensions*, *Hues*, *Streams: Live at Montreux*, and *Sam Rivers Trio Live*. His only recording with Chet Baker was

Blues for a Reason in 1984. He also freelanced with several other artists during the two decades, including Art Pepper, McCoy Tyner, Mal Waldron, James Newton, and Joanne Brackeen.

During the 1980s, McBee was bassist with the *avant-garde* The Leaders that included trumpeter Lester Bowie, alto saxophonist Arthur Blythe, tenor saxophonist Chico Freeman, pianist Kirt Lightsey, and drummer Famoudou Don Moye. Cecil may be heard on The Leaders' albums, *Mudfoot* (1986), *Out Here Like This* (1986), *Heaven Dance* (1988), and *Unforeseen Blessings* (1988).

As bandleader, McBee has produced six albums, including *Mutima* on the Strata East label in 1974; *Music from the Source*, a live recording at New York's Sweet Basil Club in 1977, featuring Chico Freeman; *Alternate Spaces* on the India Navigation label, also in 1977, which featured five of Cecil's original compositions ("Alternate Spaces," "Consequence," "Come Sunrise," "Sorta, Kinda Blues," and "Expression"); *Flying Out*, a chamber jazz collaboration with a mix of instruments such as piano, bass, cello, cornet, violin, and drums, on the India Navigation label in 1982; *Compassion* on the Enja label in 1983; and his first CD, *Unspoken* on the Palmetto label, featuring eight McBee works, including "Pantamime," "Unspoken," "Catfish," "Sleeping Giant," "Lucia," "Inside Out," "Slippin' and Slidin'," and "Tight Squeeze." In addition to the above works, Cecil was composer or co-composer of "Song of Her," "Close to You Alone," "Wilpan's," "Morning Change," "All the World Moved," "Moments: Generation/Regeneration/Reprise," "Peacemaker," "Cecil to Cecil," "Little Big John," "Portraits," "Felicite," "Love," "Cary Paul and Louisa," "Paradox," "D Bass-IC Blues," and "Tulsa Black." From 1996 through 1998, Cecil fronted his own quintet that toured Europe. Overall, McBee has appeared on more than 200 recordings over the past forty years.

Among McBee's other notable achievements are two NEA composition grants, Grammy award for his 1989 performance of *Blues for John Coltrane*, and faculty member of the New School in New York City.

As of 2003, Cecil serves as a member of the Improvisation and Jazz Studies faculty at the New England Conservatory of Music, and is currently working on a book related to techniques for string bass improvisation. (GC)
www.cecil-mcbee.com

McBride, Laura Lee
(b. May 20, 1920 – d. January 25, 1989)

Known as the "Queen of Western Swing" because she was the first female vocalist with a western swing group, **Bob Wills** and the Texas Playboys, Laura Frances Owens was born in Bridgeport, Oklahoma, a small town of just over 100 people located west of Oklahoma City on the Canadian River. Laura was the daughter of

Maude and D. H. "Tex" Owens, composer of the country classic, "Cattle Call." Her father gave up his occupation as a mechanic to devote his career to music, and the family moved to Kansas City, Missouri, where "Tex" launched his own radio show on KMBC. Laura Lee's first public performance was at age ten with her sister, teaming as "Joy and Jane" on their father's radio program.

Following high school graduation in 1938, Laura Lee organized her own band, the Prairie Pioneers, and the next year married Herb Kratoska, her father's guitarist. The band migrated to California, where they made thirteen movies with the legendary cowboy singer-actor, **Gene Autry**. She soon divorced Herb and returned to her native state of Oklahoma, where she began to perform with a reformulated band, Sons of the Range, on radio station KVOO in Tulsa. Influenced by her aunt, Texas Ruby Owens, who sang with W. Lee "Pappy" O'Daniel's Hillbilly Boys, Laura Lee was soon noticed by Wills, who was now based in Tulsa and also performing on KVOO. Because of her dynamic vocals, and because Wills needed a female vocalist, Wills hired her. She traveled with the Playboys to California, where they toured the West Coast and made several B-grade western films. She also married Cameron Hill, a guitarist with Wills.

In 1943 and 1944, Laura Lee recorded two programs with Wills on the Armed Forces Radio Transcriptions, including "I Betcha My Heart I Love You," which became her trademark song. During this period, she briefly toured with Tex Ritter.

In 1945, Hill, her second husband, joined Dickie McBride's Village Boy's band in Houston, where Laura Lee sang with the band over radio station KTRH. This led to a divorce from Hill and she soon married McBride, who was known for his work with **Floyd Tillman**, Moon Mullican, and Cliff Bruner's Texas Wanderers, for whom he sang the first recording of "It Makes No Difference Now," a country standard. Dickie and Laura Lee developed a loyal following throughout Texas, Oklahoma, and Louisiana.

In 1950, Laura Lee returned to Bob Wills and rerecorded her signature song, "I Betcha My Heart I Love You," on the Kapp label. During the 1950s, she continued singing with McBride, did some disc jockey work, managed a restaurant, sold real estate in Bryan, Texas, and briefly worked with the legendary Hank Williams.

When Dickie died in 1971, Laura Lee joined Ernest Tubb and toured with him for the next eight years. During the 1970s, she recorded *The Queen of Western Swing*, an album of western swing classics, on the Delta label, and participated in several Texas Playboys reunions following Wills' death in 1975.

In the 1980s, Laura Lee disc jockeyed in Farmington, New Mexico, and managed Grandpa and Ramona Jones' dinner theater in Mountain View, Arkansas. During this decade, she received several honors, including the Texas State Ambassador award and induction into the Western Swing Hall of Fame. She died of cancer in Bryan in 1989. (GC)

McDaniel, Mel
(b. September 9, 1942)

A member of the Grand Ole Opry cast since 1986 and best known for his "Baby's Got Her Blue Jeans On," singer and songwriter Mel McDaniel was born in Checotah, a town of about 3,000 population located south of Muskogee, but was raised in other Oklahoma communities such as Okmulgee and Tulsa. Mel's parents divorced when he was a child and this event affected him deeply as he became estranged from his father. His first interest in music was when he learned the trumpet in the fourth grade, but soon learned the guitar. After seeing Elvis Presley on television, he decided to become a singer. He made his professional debut at age fifteen performing in a talent contest at Okmulgee High School. While in high school, Mel played in several local bands, and after graduation, began working as a musician in Tulsa clubs, as well as married his childhood sweetheart, Mary. While in Tulsa, he recorded several singles for local labels (**J.J. Cale** wrote and produced his first single, "Lazy Me"), but decided to leave Oklahoma and try his luck in other locations, first in Ohio and then in Nashville.

Mel's goal in Nashville was to develop his skills as a songwriter. Working at a gas station to earn a living, he tried to gain the attention of music publishers and performers, which failed. He and Mary moved to Alaska, and he became a favorite performer in Anchorage, where he performed at the Club King X, a job lined up by his brother. During this time, he developed a new relationship with his father, who was working in pipeline construction in Alaska, and began to polish his act for Nashville.

In 1973, McDaniel returned to Nashville and signed a contract with Combine Music as a demo singer and songwriter, while also performing at the Holiday Inn for almost a year. His acquaintance with the Wilburn Brothers and record producer Johnny MacRae led to a recording contract with Capitol in 1976. During the next two years, he recorded several low level hits, such as "Have a Dream on Me," "I Thank God She Isn't Mine," "All the Sweet," "Soul of a Honky Tonk Woman," and "Gentle on Your Senses (Easy on Your Mind)," which became the title track of his first album. During this time, he was on tour with his newly formed band, A Little More Country, and made several television appearances. Based on this early success, Mel was nominated in 1977 as Most Promising Male Vocalist by the ACM.

In 1978-79, Mel reached the Top 15 with "God Made Love," and hit the charts with such singles as "Border Town Woman," "Play Her Back to Yesterday,"

"Loved Lies," and "Lovin' Starts Where Friendship Ends." He also released his second album, *Mello*, in 1978.

Mel's third album, *I'm Countrified*, produced the title track single that reached the Top 20 in 1981. This was followed by his most successful releases to date, "Louisiana Saturday Night" and "Right in the Palm of Your Hand," both of which hit the Top 10. To round out the year, "Preaching Up a Storm, reached the Top 20.

In 1982-83 McDaniel released his fourth and fifth albums, *Take Me to the Country* and *Naturally Country* with the title track of the former hitting the Top 10. It was followed by several other Top 20 singles, including "Big Ole Brew," "I Wish I Was in Nashville," "Old Man River (I've Come to Talk Again)," and "I Call It Love." After a one-year hiatus, Mel recorded a fifth album, *Mel McDaniel with Oklahoma Wind*, which received little success.

McDaniel finally achieved a #1 hit in 1984 with "Baby's Got Her Blue Jeans On" from his *Let It Roll* album. The song stayed on the charts for twenty-eight weeks and garnered Mel several honors, including nominations for CMA Horizon Award and Single of the Year (1985), as well as a Grammy for Best Country Vocal Performance-Male. His 1985 output included the singles, "Let It Roll (Let It Rock)" and "Stand Up," both of which charted in the Top 10.

During the late 1980s, McDaniel's chart success began to decline, but did score with such hits as "Shoe String," "Stand on It" (his version of the Bruce Springsteen hit), "Real Good Feel Good Song," "Ride This Train," Henrietta," "You Can't Play the Blues (In an Air-Conditioned Room)," and "Walk That Way." Capitol Nashville released *Rock-A-Billy Boy* (1989), a ten track CD, including "Blue Suede Shoes" and "Oklahoma Shines."

By the 1990s, Mel was still on the road with his six-piece band, Oklahoma Wind, completing some 200 dates a year. As with many country stars in their later years, he began performing at theaters in Branson, Missouri, and, after his break with Capitol Records in 1990, he signed with Intersound's new label, Branson Entertainment, which released *Baby's Got Her Blue Jeans On* in 1993.

McDaniel's songwriting career is worthy of note. Fellow Oklahoman **Hoyt Axton** was the first to record one of his songs with "Roll Your Own," a hippie anthem later recorded by Commander Cody, Arlo Guthrie, and the Poodles. Recorded by Conway Twitty, Mel's "Grandest Lady of Them All" was used for the Grand Finale on the Grand Ole Opry's nationally televised 60th anniversary special. Additional songs and those who recorded them include "Goodbye Marie" (Kenny Rogers and Johnny Rodriguez), "I Could Sure Use This Feeling" (Earl Scruggs Revue), and "I Just Want to Feel the Magic" (Doug Kershaw). In the mid-1990s, Mel was honored with a star in the Country Music Hall of Fame's Walkway of Stars.

In 2003, Mel lived in the Nashville area with Mary, his wife of more than thirty-five years, occasionally graces the stage of the Grand Ole Opry, performs on selected dates around the country, and enjoys practicing his hobby of fishing. (GC)

McEntire, Reba
(b. March 28, 1955)

The reigning "Queen of Country Music" in the 1980s and 1990s with a total of eighteen #1 singles, singer, songwriter, record producer, and actress Reba Nell McEntire was born and raised on a 7,000 acre ranch near Chockie, Oklahoma, a tiny hamlet of approximately twenty residents, northeast of Atoka in the southeastern section of Oklahoma known as "Little Dixie" because of its Southern cultural traditions, including food, religion, and music. Her mother (Jacqueline, or "Jackie") was an elementary schoolteacher, school secretary, and a gifted singer, who had her own dreams of a career as a country singer. Her father (Clark) was a rancher and champion rodeo steer roper (three time world champion), and her grandfather (John) was also an award winning rodeo steer roper. Her father's rodeo experience later influenced Reba to participate in rodeo competitions as a horseback barrel rider during which she started at age eleven and competed until she was twenty-one. Growing up on cattle ranch, Reba could brand a steer, castrate a calf, or vaccinate a cow. Her siblings consisted of Alice, an older sister; Del Stanley, or "Pake," an older brother; and Martha Susan, "Susie," a younger sister, who eventually developed a stellar career in the field of CCM. Two of Reba's earliest public performances were in the first grade when she sang "Away in a Manger" for a Christmas program, and at age seven when she sang "He" for the Kiowa, Oklahoma, high school commencement. One of her first honors was in the fifth grade when she won a trophy in a local 4-H talent show singing "My Sweet Little Alice Blue Gown." She also sang at the Kiowa Baptist Church after joining at age twelve. During her high school days at Kiowa High School (Kiowa is located northeast of Chockie and southwest of McAlester on U.S. Highway 69), Reba was a member of the Kiowa High School Cowboy Band led by Clark Rhyne, one of her teachers. While in high school, Reba and brother Pake and sister Susie formed "The Singing McEntires." The trio was often booked into rodeos, clubs, and community centers by their mother. The group recorded in 1971 "The Ballad of John

McEntire," a song dedicated to their grandfather and distributed on a local label, Boss. Reba eventually included it on one of her albums.

In making future plans, Reba thought of following her mother in the teaching profession and enrolled as an elementary education major and music minor at Southeastern Oklahoma State University in Durant. While in college she was a member of a singing group known as the Chorvettes. During her college career, Reba was invited by rodeo announcer and Oklahoma politician Clem McSpadden to sing the national anthem at the National Finals Rodeo in Oklahoma City in 1974, televised on ABC's *Wide World of Sports*. Red Steagall, veteran cowboy and western music star, heard her sing the anthem and invited her to appear with him at a rodeo event for Justin Boots. Reba accepted the invitation and did her rendition of Dolly Parton's "Joshua." Steagall was impressed and arranged for McEntire to make a demo record in Nashville. First rejected by ABC Records because they did not need another girl singer, Reba with assistance from Steagall signed with Mercury Records in 1975. Her first recording session was the 1950s song, "Invitation to the Blues," co-penned by **Roger Miller** and Ray Price.

Reba recorded her first chart song in 1976, "I Don't Want to Be a One Night Stand," which barely cracked the Top 100. The same year, she married Charlie Battles, a three time world steer wrestling champion and bulldogger ten years her senior, who gave up his rodeo career to help manage Reba's career. After their marriage, Reba and Charlie remained in Oklahoma where they operated a cattle business on a 225-acre ranch. After releasing three more unsuccessful singles, none of which charted in the Top 40, Reba completed her teaching degree, in case her musical career floundered. But in 1977, Reba cut her first album for Mercury, a self-titled release, which included Miller/Price composition, "Invitation to the Blues," however, none of the tracks from this first album made much headway. She toured with Steagall's band in 1977, and made a guest appearance on the Grand Ole Opry, where she performed Patsy Cline's "Sweet Dreams." Her recording of the Cline hit rose to #19 on the country charts.

In 1978 Reba cut a double-sided duet with Jacky Ward ("Three Sheets in the Wind"/"I'd Really Love to See You Tonight") that also entered the Top 20 on the country charts. Her second album for Mercury, *Out of a Dream*, released in 1979 produced five singles that cracked the country Top 40 charts, including "Last Night, Ev'ry Night," "Sweet Dreams," "(I Still Long to Hold You) Now and Then," " That Makes Two of Us" (another duet with Jacky Ward), and "Runaway Heart," perhaps the best of the songs.

McEntire's third Mercury album, *Feel the Fire*, released in 1980, spawned her first Top 10 hit, "(You Lift Me) Up to Heaven," reaching #8 on the country charts, and remained on the charts for fifteen weeks. The album also yielded "I Can See Forever in Your Eyes" (Top 20) and "I Don't Think Love Ought to Be That Way" (Top 15). In 1981, she recorded her fourth album with Mercury, *Heart to Heart*, however, it failed to produce any notable singles.

In 1982 Reba released her most successful album to that point—*Unlimited*. It included her first #1 single, "Can't Even Get the Blues" and a second #1 single, "You're the First Time I've Thought About Leaving." In addition, it spawned a #3 hit, "I'm Not That Lonely Yet." Her last Mercury album in 1983 was *Behind the Scene*, which produced "Why Do We Want (What We Know We Can't Have)," which cracked the Top 10, and "There Ain't No Future in This," which charted in the Top 15. For these successes, she received the CMA Horizon Award in 1983, and was a nominee for Female Vocalist of the Year.

One of the momentous occasions in Reba's career took place in 1980 when she added former Prudential insurance agent and steel guitar player Narvel Blackstock to her band. Narvel left his wife and three children at home for the itinerant life on the road. Shortly thereafter, Narvel became her bandleader and important adviser, and then progressed to become her road manager, tour manager, full manager (1988), and second husband in 1989 following the divorce from Charlie in 1987, when she relinquished the 214-acre ranch in Oklahoma, and moved permanently to Nashville. In 1990, Reba gave birth to Shelby Steven McEntire Blackstock.

With Narvel's support, Reba decided to switch labels, leaving Mercury after seven albums to sign with MCA in 1983. It was during this move that Reba began to take more charge of her career. In a step to broaden her audience and gain long-term visibility, she began appearing on the new cable television channel, *The Nashville Network*. During 1983, she made four appearances on the channel's live show, *Nashville Now*, hosted by Ralph Emery, WSM radio personality. These moves resulted in establishing herself as one of the decade's most popular artists, selling more than twenty million albums, winning four Female Vocalist of the Year awards from the CMA (1984-87), and five Female Vocalist of the Year awards from the ACM (1985-87 and 1990-91). Between 1985 and 1992, she had twenty-four straight Top 10 hits, including fourteen #1 singles. During this period, Reba was named *Music City News* Female Artist of the Year for the years 1985 through 1989, was acknowledged by *Rolling Stone* Critic's Choice Poll as one of the Top Five Country Artists, and received CMA's Entertainer of the Year Award for 1986, only the fourth female singer, after Loretta Lynn, Dolly Parton, and Barbara Mandrell, to win this highly coveted award. She also was nominated for the CMA's Entertainer of the Year (1985, 1987-89), Albums of the Year (*My Kind of Country*-1985), (*Whoever's in New England*-1986), and (*What Am I Gonna Do About You*-1987), Music Videos of the Year ("Whoever's in New England-1986) and ("What Am I Gonna Do About You"-1987), and Single of the Year ("Whoever's in New England"-1986). Finally, after making her debut on the Grand Ole Opry in 1977, she became a permanent cast member in 1986. The announcement was made on *Nashville Now*—the first artist to join the Grand Ole Opry during a televised broadcast. To complete the year, she made her first appearance at Carnegie Hall.

Reba's debut album with MCA, *My Kind of Country*, was released in 1984, and produced two #1 hits, "How Blue" and "Somebody Should Leave." The album eventually earned Reba's first gold record award from the Recording Industry Association of America (RIAA).

The mid-1980s saw Reba release of string of noteworthy albums, including *Have I Got a Deal for You* (1985), *Reba Nell McEntire* (1986), *Whoever's in New England* (1986), *What Am I Gonna Do About You* (1986), *Reba McEntire's Greatest Hits* (1987), *The Last One to Know* (1987), and *Merry Christmas To You* (1987). The most successful of these was *Whoever's in New England*, which yielded two #1 hits, "Little Rock" and the title track, as well as *Music City News* and ACM's Video of the Year and a Grammy for Best Country Vocal Performance Female in 1987. "Whoever's in New England," Reba's first video, was filmed in Boston and premiered on the network television show *Entertainment Tonight*. As one of the most influential country collections of the 1980s, *Whoever's in New England* quickly reached platinum status and her *Greatest Hits* album eventually achieved triple platinum honors. *Have I Got a Deal for You* and *What Am I Gonna Do About You* scored as gold albums, and the latter's title track reached #1 on the country charts. *The Last One to Know* album was recorded during the divorce proceedings from Charlie Battles, and is understandably strong on songs about breakups and marital problems. The title track of the album charted at #1 in 1987 as did "Love Will Find Its Way to You" in 1988.

Reba closed out the 1980s with three more hit albums she helped produce: *Reba* (1988), *Sweet Sixteen* (1989), and *Reba Live!* (1989). The *Reba Live!* collection features nineteen of her biggest hits and best known songs, including the single releases "Let the Music (Lift You Up)" (#3), "Sunday Kind of Love" (#5), "I Know How He Feels" (#1), "One Promise Too Late" (#1), and "New Fool at an Old Game" (#1). *Sweet Sixteen*, her sixteenth album, went to the top of the country album chart, where it stayed for thirteen weeks, and the single from the album "Cathy's Clown," Reba's rendition of an Everly Brothers song, reached #1 in 1989. The 1988 Reba album eventually reached platinum level in sales. More honors came Reba's way in the late 1980s in the form of American Music Awards Favorite Female Country Artist (1988/89), TNN Viewer's Choice Favorite Female Vocalist (1988/89), Gallup 1988 Youth Survey selection among the Top 10 Female Vocalists, and *People* magazine inclusion in the Top 3 Female Vocalists.

McEntire began the 1990s with another hit album, *Rumor Has It*, released in 1990, and it eventually reached triple platinum sales. Singles from the album included "Rumor Has It" (Top 5), "Fallin' Out of Love" (Top 3), and "You Lie" (#1). The CMA nominations for 1991 included Entertainer, Female Vocalist, Music Video ("Fancy"), and Album (*Rumor Has It*).

Unfortunately, events took a turn for the worse for Reba in March of 1991 when seven members of her band, her road manager, and the pilot and co-pilot of a chartered private jet were killed in an accident when the plane hit a mountainside during takeoff. Reba, Narvel, and two other band members were booked on other flights. Her 1991 album, *For My Broken Heart*, reflected some of the sorrow and sympathy for this tragic loss. The album quickly reached sales of more than two million, and eventually went quadruple platinum. "If I Had Only Known," a moving tribute to the deceased band members, provided a #1 single. Additional singles from the album that charted well included "Is There Life Out There" (#1) and "The Greatest Man I Ever Knew" (#1), a tribute to her father, who still actively ran his Oklahoma ranch in his mid-sixties.

Reba's 1992 album, *It's Your Call*, eventually reached triple platinum sales, and produced two #1 hits, including "The Heart Won't Lie," a duet with label mate and fellow Oklahoman **Vince Gill**, and the title track. Reba had previously recorded a Top 15 single with Vince entitled "Oklahoma Swing," released in 1990. Her 1993 compilation of *Greatest Hits, Volume 2* reached triple platinum status, and spawned two new cuts, one of them a duet with Linda Davis, long time backup singer for Reba, "Does He Love You," which became a #1 hit. Reba was honored once again in 1992 with the *Music City News* Award for Female Artist of the Year and *People*'s Choice Award for Favorite Female Country Music Performer, a feat she would achieve for the years 1993 through 1998. Her CMA nominations for 1992 included Entertainer, Female Vocalist, Music Video ("Is There Life Out There"), and Album (*For My Broke Heart*).

At the 1993 CMA awards, Reba received three nominations for Entertainer of the Year and Vocal Event of the Year (duet with Gill). She failed to either of these awards, but her duet with Davis from the *Greatest Hits, Volume 2* album was named CMA Vocal Event of the Year in 1994, as well as a 1994 Grammy for Best Country Vocal Collaboration.

In 1994, Reba released her twenty-second album, *Read My Mind*, which reached triple platinum sales, and another 1994 album, *Oklahoma Girl*, included many of earlier singles, such as "I Don't Want to Be a One Night Stand," her first recording, "Invitation to the Blues," and "Runaway Heart." But it was her 1995 release, *Starting Over*, which cemented her 1990s mega-stardom. It peaked at #1 on the *Billboard* country chart and #5 on the pop list. It provided such singles as "On My Own," recorded with Trisha Yearwood, Martina McBride, and Linda Davis; "Ring on My Finger, Time on Her Hands," "You Keep Me Hanging On," and "By the Time I Get to Phoenix," Reba's version of native Oklahoman **Jimmy Webb**'s composition. She was nominated for CMA awards in 1994 in five categories: Entertainer, Female Vocalist, Music Video ("Does He Love You"), Single ("Does He Love You"), and Album (*Rhythm, Country & Blues*). Reba was also nominated by the CMA in 1995 for Entertainer and Female Vocalist of the Year.

Reba's next collection, *What If It's You*, was released in 1996, and contained such singles as "The Fear of Being Alone," "She's Calling it Love," and "I'd Rather Ride Around With You." It attained double platinum sales. Her collaboration with McBride, Davis, and Yearwood ("On My Own") was nominated for the CMA Vocal Event of the Year in 1996. Following in 1998 was the *Out of a Dream*, an album that featured one of her own compositions, "Daddy," another tribute to her father, and a second 1998 release, *If You See Him*. To stimulate inter-

est in this album, Reba recorded a duet with Brooks & **Dunn**, "If You See Him/If You See Her," another #1 hit on the country charts. Reba co-produced this album with Tony Brown, her long time producer, and native Oklahoman Tim DuBois. The album was supported by Reba's tour with Kix Brooks & Ronnie Dunn in 1998, which was the highest grossing tour in the history of country music. It was a finalist for CMA's Vocal Event of the Year in 1998. The 1999 release, *So Good Together,* co-produced by Reba and Tony Brown, was acclaimed as her best album since *Starting Over*. It explored one of Reba's favorite themes—relationships with songs like "We're So Good Together," "What Do You Say," "Where You End and I Begin," "She Wasn't Good Enough for Him," and "Nobody Dies from a Broken Heart."

The year 2001 marked twenty-seven years since Reba was first discovered singing the national anthem in Oklahoma City. Appropriately, Reba released her twenty-seventh album, *Greatest Hits III-I'm a Survivor*. It included fifteen tracks supported by Alison Krauss vocals, and co-produced by Tony Brown, Tim DuBois, and Reba. The title track single, "I'm a Survivor," was one of the top country hits in 2002. She also organized a 2001 24-city tour of "Girls' Night Out," the first all female country tour, starring Reba, Martina McBride, Sara Evans, Jamie O'Neal, and Carolyn Dawn Johnson.

Reba took Broadway by storm in 2001 with a six-month run as Annie Oakley in the revival of Irving Berlin's *Annie Get Your Gun*, and received rave reviews from the New York critics. Although ineligible for a Tony award, her highly acclaimed performance received every other major theater award. In 2001, she took on her first major television sitcom, *Reba*, which focuses on the character Reba Hart and her trials and tribulations as a Texas "soccer mom." Although panned by some critics, fans appreciated the program that led to a #1 position in her time slot for women 18-34. As a result, the half-hour show was renewed for season number three in 2003 and '04. The title track and first single from her *Greatest Hits, Volume III-I'm A Survivor* became the show's theme song. Finally, the *I'll Be* album was released in May of 2001. Co-produced by Reba and Jimmy Bowen, the fifteen tracks include the Lennon-McCartney composition, "If I Fell," and several old favorites such as "Starting Over Again," "Please Come to Boston," and "What Do You Say."

Called country music's "first video superstar," Reba ranked #6 on the CMT "Forty Greatest Women in Country Music" special aired in the summer of 2002. During the program, Carolyn Dawn Johnson, Lee Ann Womack, Trisha Yearwood, Sara Evans, Terri Clark, and Shania Twain all paid tribute to Reba as one of their major influences. In 2003, she received the Country Radio Broadcasters' Career Achievement Award, and hosted the Academy of Country Music Awards where the ACM bestowed upon her the title of Leading Lady of the Academy of Country Music in honor of her all-time leading wins in the Top Female Vocalist category. Also, two of her songs, "Fancy" and "Is There Life Out There," were included on CMT's 100 Greatest Songs of Country Music at #27 and #79, respectively. Reba began recording her next album in the summer of 2003, with a November release date on tap.

One of Reba's greatest accomplishments as a businesswoman is the building of Starstruck Entertainment, a conglomerate that contains her own booking, management (includes another Oklahoman **Joe Diffie** as well as Aaron Tippen), publishing, transportation (jet charter service), recording services, and horse farm. It is housed in a luxurious, 29,000 square foot office building on Music Row and includes a state-of-the-art music studio.

As of 2003, the "grand dame of country music," who has sold more than 50 million records, lived outside Nashville with her husband, Narvel, and their son Shelby in a Civil War era home. Their property is a large working ranch as Reba is also an avid horse breeder and trainer, however, they also purchased a 9,000 square foot, gated home in Beverly Hills that includes a tennis court, pool, spa, library, and wine cellar. (GC)
www.reba.com

McGhee, Howard B. "Maggie"
(b. March 6, 1918 - d. July 17, 1987)

McGhee was one of the most talented instrumentalists, composers, arrangers, and bandleaders in the 1940s jazz scene. Born in Tulsa, his family moved to Detroit in 1921 when Howard was about three years old. Although his father was a physician, Howard learned the basics of music from his half-brother who played the guitar. In Detroit he attended Cass Technical High School, where he learned several instruments, including clarinet, piano, tenor saxophone, and trumpet, the latter being his final instrument of choice at age sixteen, after hearing Louis Armstrong and Roy Eldridge.

At age sixteen, Howard quit high school and headed for the West Coast. After joining Lionel Hampton's band in 1941, he then became principal soloist for two years with Andy Kirk during which he was known for his "McGhee Special" solos. After Kirk, he joined Charlie Barnet (1942-43), returned to Kirk where he sat next to Fats Navarro in the trumpet section. Thereafter, he had brief stints with Georgie Auld and Count Basie, before moving to California with Coleman Hawkins in 1945. During the next two years on the West Coast, he recorded several swing-to-bop transitional numbers with Hawkins, such as "Stuffy," "Rifftide," and "Hollywood Stampede;" recorded "How High the Moon" with Jazz at the Philharmonic; and gigged and recorded with Charlie Parker, including the famous *Lover Man* and *Relaxin' at Camarillo* albums, the latter included fellow Oklahomans **Barney Kessel**, **Wardell Gray**, and Don Lamond.

As one of the pioneers in the bebop movement in the early 1940s, McGhee performed at jam sessions at Minton's Playhouse and Monroe's Uptown House on

42nd Street in New York City. By the end of the 1940s, he was one of the most highly respected musicians in the bebop movement and was named Best Trumpet Player by the *Down Beat* poll in 1949.

Returning to New York in the late 1940s, McGhee's albums with such labels as Dial, Savoy, and Blue Note are among his best, including *Howard McGhee Sextet* (1947), *Maggie*, backed by vibraphonist Milt Jackson and trombonist J. J. Johnson (1948), and *Howard McGhee's All Stars* (1948). Although relatively inactive during the 1950s due to drug addiction, he did complete a U.S.O. tour during the Korean War, and had recorded three albums on the Bethlehem label, including *The Return of Howard McGhee*, including five of his own compositions, "Tweedles," "Oo-Wee But I Do," "Transpicious," "Tahitian Lullaby," and You're Teasing Me."

During his career, McGhee worked as an arranger for such notables as Billy Eckstine, Woody Herman, and Charlie Barnet. His most notable compositions include "McGhee Special," "Night Mist," "Midnight at Mintons," "Dorothy," and "Carvin' the Bird." Many of these compositions were recorded by the likes of Charlie Barnet, Wardell Gray, Freddie Hubbard, and Fats Navarro. He also appeared on sessions as trumpeter with such jazz artists as Gene Ammons, Kenny Clarke, Sonny Criss, and Miles Davis.

McGhee's comeback in the 1960s and 1970s included formation of his own big band and recording dates with the Steeple Chase, Jazzcraft, Zim, Bethlehem, Contemporary, Black Lion, and Storyville labels. The latter label provided the last two recording sessions for Howard, including *Home Run* (1978) and *Wise in Time* (1979). The former included two of his compositions, "Get It On" and "Jonas," while the latter contained a track by fellow Oklahoman **Oscar Pettiford**, "Blues in the Closet." His final activities included touring Europe and Japan with George Wein, performing with Duke Ellington, and participating in jazz services at St. Peter's Lutheran Church in New York City, where he died in 1987. The Oklahoma Jazz Hall of Fame inducted McGhee in 2003. (GC)

McGuire, Barry
(b. October 15, 1935)

Composer or co-composer of three of the biggest hits in the 1960s, "Greenback Dollar," "Green, Green" and "Eve of Destruction," as well as lead singer with the New Christy Minstrels in the 1960s, singer and songwriter Barry McGuire was born in Oklahoma City. Prior to his vocal and songwriting career, Barry was a minor actor in the television series *Route 66*. His first venture into professional singing came with Barry Kane in an act known as Barry and Barry.

In 1962 both Barry Kane and Barry McGuire joined the New Christy Minstrels, and McGuire was the group's lead singer on their fourth album, *Ramblin'*, released in 1963 by Columbia Records. It featured McGuire singing his own song "Green, Green," which became the group's first hit, peaking at #3 in 1963, and later covered by such artists and groups as The Brothers Four, Glen Campbell, and Johnny Rivers.

When Randy Sparks, the group's leader departed in 1963, he appointed McGuire as the new head of the New Christy Minstrels. McGuire was also lead singer on several other Minstrel hits, including "Saturday Night" and "Three Wheels on My Wagon." While still a Minstrel, McGuire wrote "Greenback Dollar," which became a major hit for the Kingston Trio, and recorded his first solo album, *Barry Here and Now*, in 1962 on the Horizon label.

After leaving the Minstrels in the mid-1960s, McGuire signed with Lou Adler's Dunhill Records and was assigned as a staff writer with P.F. Sloan and Steve Barri. During the peak of the "protest song" movement, the trio wrote "Eve of Destruction," which McGuire recorded and topped the U.S. charts in 1965, as well as reaching #3 in the U.K. The anti-establishment nature of the lyrics resulted in it becoming one of the most prominent protest songs during the 1960s as it questioned the Vietnam War and its civil rights connotations. The song was pulled from retail store shelves and banned on radio because of its anti-Vietnam lyrics. It even provoked an answer record, "Dawn of Correction." Ironically, it had been offered to the Byrds and was originally conceived as a flip-side selection. Barry's album, *Eve of Destruction*, was released in 1965 on the Ember label. The song resurfaced in 1998 as part of the soundtrack to Warren Beatty's political comedy film, *Bulworth*.

McGuire played a significant role in bringing the popular million selling quartet Mamas and Papas to the attention of producer Lou Adler at Dunhill Records in the mid-1960s. For that connection, he received a mention in their hit "Creeque Alley" (a hilarious song of how the group was formed), and they later offered their services as his back-up singers.

McGuire was unable to follow-up his worldwide hit, although he released several singles and albums, including the highly acclaimed Sloan song, "Upon a Painted Ocean." He continued to pursue the protest song angle with the 1966 album *This Precious Time*, which featured the Mamas and Papas. It was followed with *World's Private Citizen* in 1967, which included assorted members from the Byrds and the Eagles. Both albums were released on the Dunhill label. The latter album generated such mediocre sales that McGuire stopped recording until 1971, when he returned with former Mamas and Papas sideman Dr. Eric Hord on *Barry McGuire and the Doctor* on the Ode label. The album featured such folk rock artists as the Byrd's Chris Hillman and Michael Clarke. During the 1960s, McGuire did some acting with a Broadway appearance in the musical *Hair*.

On Father's Day in 1971, McGuire was baptized and soon signed a record deal with Myrrh, a Christian music label. He recorded three albums in the mid-1970s associated with the "Jesus Movement," including *Seeds*, *Lighten Up*, *Narnia*, and *To the Bride*, all on Myrrh. The latter was a live recording with the 2nd Chapter of

Acts group. When Billy Ray Hearn left Myrrh to launch Sparrow Records, McGuire followed and recorded three albums with Sparrow in the late 1970s, including *C'mon Along*, *Have You Heard*, and *Cosmic Cowboy*.

In 1984 McGuire and his wife moved to New Zealand, her homeland, and lived there until 1990. While in New Zealand, he became involved in World Vision, a Christian international relief organization. Upon his return to the U.S., McGuire toured with Terry Talbot, doing about thirty-five to forty concerts per year. In 1994 his *Anthology* album was released by One Way Records, and included all of his hit songs, such as "Eve of Destruction." Overall, McGuire has recorded more than fifteen albums of Christian music for such labels as Myrrh, Sparrow, Word, and Maranatha. Steve McGuire (Barry's son) aka Peacemaker has recently released his version of "Eve of Destruction."

In 2002 McGuire participated in a PBS special, "This Land Is Your Land," during which he sang with several of the original New Christy Minstrels and performed "Eve of Destruction." As of January 1, 2003, Barry retired from doing concerts. He was only available for engagements in which he and his son, Brennon, would play a few songs while Barry engaged in "a mixture of theological discourse, storytelling, and music." (GC)
www.barrymcguire.com

McShann, James Columbus "Jay"
(b. January 12, 1916)

Called a prophet of the prime era of Kansas City's jazz scene by music historian Gary Giddins, and "one of the original exponents of big band jazz" by adventurous big band leader Stan Kenton, Jay McShann is perhaps best known by many critics as the bandleader who provided saxophonist Charlie Parker with his first major professional gig and recording opportunities. However, McShann is also recognized as an important transitional pianist whose style rose out of the ragtime and boogie-woogie traditions of the Southwest to foreshadow the oncoming swing and popular R & B eras. Jay McShann was also a progressive bandleader whose keen ear for musical talent encouraged the flourishing of the likes of Parker, Gene Ramey, Jimmy Witherspoon and Lowell Fulson. As an influence on other musicians, his songs have been covered by Count Basie, Chuck Berry, B.B. King, Maceo Parker, The Rolling Stones, and Buddy Tate.

McShann's birthplace of Muskogee, Oklahoma, is now a known a source of tremendous jazz talent, producing more acclaimed musicians than its more populous neighbor Tulsa, fifty miles northwest. Factors included the city's well-educated and economically thriving African-American population at the turn of the 20th century, the city's position as a travel nexus for several railroad lines, and Muskogee's location as the Indian Territory hub of the Black town movement in the late 19th century. This population provided solid music education for those who went to Manual Training High School, like McShann, and also offered multiple employment and mentoring opportunities for musicians. Muskogee's location and entertainment district also made the city a natural stopover for major touring artists such as Count Basie, Cab Calloway, or Louis Armstrong who were between Kansas City and Dallas. Additionally, Muskogee also became a dependable place for groups traveling through to pick up musicians, or for bandleaders like "T" Holder to use as a base for forming his hot blowing and hot swinging territory bands. As Jay told a *Living Blues* interviewer in 2002, "In Muskogee, for the black people, we had two [dance halls] on Second Street and two on Main. We had the Wintergarten and a lot of other dance halls."

Jay's father, Jess McShann, came to Oklahoma from Ratliff, Texas, about twenty miles east of Dallas, because he had an uncle living in the "black friendly" town of Muskogee. His mother, Leona (McBee) McShann, came to Oklahoma from Alabama and settled around Chickasha before making her way to Muskogee in the early 1900s. As many families did as a result of the piano sales boom at the turn of the 20th century, the McShanns had an upright piano in their house on which his mother would play church songs. Devout Christians, McShann's mother took Jay to Central Baptist regularly, and his father took him to choir singing contests in neighboring small towns such as Redbird, Coweta, and Tullahassee where groups would come from various towns and have singing conventions. McShann had some of earliest musical impressions at these conventions, which he liked because of the variety of singing, as he remembered in a 1994 interview: "Sometimes you'd be sitting on a bench with an old guy that sang bass and he could sing those low notes so low that it would almost shake the seat you're sitting on." His grandmother would take him to holiness churches in Muskogee where "They got in the groove," according to Jay.

Jay's first exposure to blues was through his father's job at Ferguson Brothers furniture in Muskogee when the elder McShann brought home a Victrola record player, and continued to bring home old records from the store that were being thrown out. "I remember I picked up a record and it was Bessie Smith and James P. Johnson backing her up," Jay said in 1994. "I put that record on and I really enjoyed it because the blues was good, [he sings],'It thundered and it lightninged and the winds began to blow/And some poor folks didn't have no place to go.' Then she'd moan a little bit about it, making like it was so sad she couldn't sing no more. I knew then I liked that." McShann also began his interest in piano at a young age, picking up tips while his sister took piano lessons from Muskogee bassist Aaron Bell's mother, who was also the pianist at Central Baptist. He listened to Earl Hines secretly at night in the early 1930s on the radio from Chicago, and started sneaking out to see bands that were coming through Muskogee led by Bennie Moten or Muskogee native Clarence Love.

McShann also played in the band at Manual Training High School and first learned to "complement the blues" on piano from Russell when the high school director, a Texan named Kyle Collins, would put together small combos for area gigs. "I remember he took me on a gig with him, and I didn't know nothing," Jay said, "I thought you just played and played, and keep playing. So, he turned around to me and says, 'Complement the blues. Complement the blues.' I didn't what he was talking about, but when he starts doing his hands like this [ripples the fingers on his right hand], then I realized what he meant." Before long, he was playing with local musicians like Ellis Ezell, with whom **Barney Kessel** played, and **Don Byas**.

"How I met Don Byas," Jay remembered in 1994, "was because of this black lawyer in town who played tenor sax, Lawyer Kimble. He'd get together with Don Byas, another guy named Weaver, and Ellis Ezell. They would get that group together and get me to come play piano, but I couldn't. They'd say, 'We got to have somebody, so, come on, you got to play.' I was pretty young then." By age fourteen, Jay had his first paying gigs with Don Byas in Muskogee and nearby Wagoner, and those led to more performances in towns like Taft and Haskell. He also played with a family band out of Haskell called Professor Gray's band in places such as Shawnee, Wewoka, and Okmulgee, or "Dance towns" as McShann called them. The year was 1933, however, and those years were mean for just about everybody involved, so McShann left Muskogee at 17 for Tulsa where he had a stint with Al Denny's band before hooking up with some Kansas bootleggers looking for musicians to play in their south Kansas clubs. When that busted up, McShann headed for Kansas City, met a friend who gave him an apartment key, and within a few days he was working with a drummer named Hop on his first jobs in Kansas City.

As a result of Kansas City, Missouri's wide-open and free-flowing liquor atmosphere of the 1930s prohibition era, musicians from throughout the region went to Kansas City for work in the speakeasies, nightclubs, theaters, ballrooms, and other joints that existed there to support the good time center of the Midwest. Adding to his already formidable blues and jazz influences from Muskogee, Jay began listening to, and jamming with, master boogie woogie player Pete Johnson who played the uptempo and vibrant precursor to rock and roll, and ultimately recorded its primary song, "Roll 'em Pete," with Joe Turner in 1938. Often noted for his percussive piano playing, McShann has been praised critically for his boogie woogie style, and his original solo work that blends blues, boogie, and his major early influence, Earl Hines. Jay is often thought of as an important second generation boogie woogie player who was more refined than the first round of rowdy players who grew out of the ragtime and honky tonk tradition. McShann played variously and regionally throughout Kansas City and the Midwest from 1934 to 1937. In 1937, McShann worked in a Kanas City group led by Buster Smith, of which seventeen-year-old Charlie Parker was also a member. Also in

1937, Jay formed his first group as a leader in Kansas City, which encouraged him to bring in new young players like Parker.

The beginning of this period are well documented on the compact disc *Charlie Parker with Jay McShann: Early Bird*, which features radio transcriptions from 1940 in Wichita, Kansas, and 1942 live performance at the Savoy Ballroom in New York City. The association with Parker became inescapable for McShann, as Jays' name comes up in 20th century jazz history books most often in reference to being the bandleader for Parker's first recordings and eventual debut appearance in New York City. However, more credit is being given to McShann as time has passed for leading one of the most progressive musical bands of the late 1930s and early 1940s. Even though bop was a combo oriented jazz movement, the forebodings of the next era can be heard in McShann's recordings with Parker of 1941 and 42.

Instead of staying in the relatively safe confines of boogie- woogie, Jay explored more range and tonal possibilities within the form on his solos on "Hootie Blues" (1941) and "Vine Street Boogie" (1941). These transformations in his playing were natural developments as the big band era declined into small combo jazz that played more complex harmonic music, and perhaps also from the influence of having Charlie Parker in his band. Parker's first major calling card for his signature butterfly phrasing of bebop is on 1942's "Sepian Bounce" with McShann. For this reason alone, McShann is often regarded as an important leader in the evolution of big band musicians from the swing era into the bebop period.

McShann went to New York on the success of a national hit, "Confessin' the Blues," featuring Walter Brown on vocals and Parker on saxophone. The song was one of the biggest sellers for a black group during the 1940s, even though it was not in the style the band preferred to play. The group's repertoire was largely made up of "riff tunes" on which the band could jam, but when the opportunity arose to record for Decca Records in 1941, the company's producer who had overseen earlier Count Basie Sessions, wanted a blues tune and so the group did it as an afterthought. Eventually, the record sold more than 500,000 copies and lit up the nation's jukeboxes in 1941 and 1942. From then on Jay McShann was considered a blues player, and in not too much more time Charlie Parker would leave the band for his own storied career.

Because so much has been made of Charlie Parker's life and career, the departure from McShann is a source of massive interpretation by Parker biographers and/or jazz historians. At least two critics say it was because of McShann's basic blues format Parker stayed behind in New York when the group planned on returning to Kansas City in 1942, whereas, others believe the McShann band offered Parker the right place to develop his ideas within the framework of a disciplined organization, and it was the McShann blues influence that provided Parker a foundation to progress through his dominant period of the mid 1940s when "Bird" showed a strong allegiance to the blues in his recordings. Without delving too far into the life of Parker, at least one of his biographers, Brian

Priestley, and one very well known critic, Dave Dexter, report Parker's heroin addiction had worsened when he left McShann; so much so, Priestley says, Parker fell asleep on the bandstand and on a trip to Detroit with his next group, Parker overdosed and had to be left behind. Dexter reports more details of Parker's slip into heroin-addled oblivion, even though his most illustrious recordings were yet to be made, and McShann headed back to Kansas City.

Nineteen forty-three was the final year for the Jay McShann Orchestra as a large unit. While Kansas City bands were able to play through the depression, they could not play through World War II. The final blow came when McShann was accosted by federal agents as he came off the bandstand in New York and given his induction papers. Most critics define the demise of the McShann Orchestra as the end of the Kansas City era since so many of the New York bands were downsizing and replacing out-of-town members with New York musicians. On returning from the service, McShann led a number of small groups and record-ed quite frequently throughout the rest of the 1940s and 1950s with small com-bos, and with the blues-jazz singer Jimmy Witherspoon, considered a leading jazz singer in league with Jimmy Rushing and Joe Turner. Witherspoon may have made his finest recordings with McShann in 1957. Also during the 1950s, McShann began working with fellow Muskogeean **Claude "Fiddler" Williams**, a relationship which continued at least through the summer of 2001 when both appeared at the Kansas City Jazz Festival. McShann continued recording in the 1960s for Capitol Records, began touring the United States and Europe, often with only a bassist and a drummer.

The 1966 Capitol LP, *McShann's Piano*, enjoyed solid worldwide success and brought him to the fore as the singer he needed to be in order to play his big hit of 1941 and 1942, "Confessin' the Blues." Jay recorded two albums with Eddy "Cleanhead" Vinson in 1969, and in 1972, and McShann's album *The Man from Muskogee*, not only boosted McShann's already noteworthy career, but also res-urrected the career of Claude "Fiddler" Williams by featuring Williams on the album. Jay recorded two albums with Clarence "Gatemouth" Brown in 1973, recorded once with Helen Humes in 1974, with Ralph Sutton twice in 1979 and 1980, and Slim Gaillard in 1982, all of whom clearly benefited from his presence. In 1986, as a lot of music from the first half of the twentieth century began to be released on compact disc, Jay's music became more and more available through a series of reissues and jazz retrospectives. McShann had major associations with three albums in 1991, five in 1993, "only" one in 1994, five in 1995, eight in 1996, and seven in 1997. Included in the 1997 releases were his first work with Clint Eastwood on *Eastwood After Hours: Live at Carnegie Hall*, and a Stony Plain Records release, *Hootie's Jumpin' Blues*, which contained an oral history, as well as renewed versions of Jay's best-known songs with Duke Robillard's band. Six more albums with major credits for Jay appeared 1998.

McShann is the subject of the 1978 documentary film, *Hootie Blues*, and is also showcased in the TV documentary *Last of the Blue Devils*, even though he was never in the important territory group from Oklahoma after which the program is named. He has recorded for the Capitol, Atlantic, Master Jazz, Sackville, and Stony Plain labels in the United States, and the Black and Blue label in Europe. McShann has received many accolades, to include induction into the Kansas City Hall of Fame, the Jazz Oral History Award from the Rutgers Institute of Jazz Studies, the Jass Master Award from the Afro-American Museum in Philadelphia, the National R & B Foundation Pioneer Award in Los Angeles, the Kansas City Jazz Heritage Award, and the Jazz Era Pioneer Award from the National Association of Jazz Educators. His home state has honored him with induction into the Oklahoma Music Hall of Fame, and the Oklahoma Jazz Hall of Fame, the latter having named its Lifetime Achievement Award in his honor. As a result of consistently touring and recording in Europe from the 1960s through the early 90s when he gave up "going across the big pond," McShann is widely considered a major pianist there with a repertoire that encompasses the first half of the 20th century's popular music traditions of ragtime, boogie woogie, swing, jazz, and R & B. He is still highly regarded and sought after by knowledgeable jazz musicians, fans, and educators in the United States. In 2001 and 2002 Jay traveled to Long Beach University in California, Detroit, Michigan, Atlanta, Georgia, and a jazz festival at Wichita Kansas, only to name a few gigs for the eighty-seven-year old pianist and singer. In 2002, Stony Plain also recorded a forthcoming album by Jay in Kansas City, and, after an admonishment by his cardiologist to take his blood pressure medicine in August of 2002, Jay was healthy and ready for a planned meeting with Clint Eastwood for another project in the fall of 2002.

Jay McShann must be considered an important jazz musician and bandleader who not only fostered the flourishing of Charlie Parker, but is also representative of several American musical piano styles. Additionally, Jay set off musical depth charges under jazz in the late 1930s and early 1940s that helped propel it into its next evolutionary period, known as bebop. With a foundation in Muskogee of African-American gospel music, formal music lessons, instruction in complementing the blues in high school, and having played with accomplished jazz musicians by the time he was eighteen, Jay McShann added boogie woogie to his repertoire in 1930s Kansas City, formed a band with Charlie Parker as a lead saxophonist, and subsequently played and recorded his way to being one of the 20th century's major blues, jazz, and R & B pianists. By the beginning of the the 21st century, he and **Claude "Fiddler" Williams** were the primary living proponents of not only Kansas City jazz, but the respective precursor traditions from which they came in Muskogee. By 2002, Jay McShann was, more often than not, given due credit by jazz historians and fans for his own diverse abilities, techniques, foresight, and longevity. In 2003, he continued playing select dates around the United States. (HF)

Merritt, Chris

(b. September 27, 1952)

A major force in the new generation of operatic tenors, the first American tenor to open the famous La Scala Theater in Milan, Italy, in thirty-nine years, and with more than twenty different Gioachini Rossini roles to his credit (considered by several sources as a world record), Chris Allan Merritt was born in Oklahoma City, the state's capital. He was trained at Oklahoma City University, from which he has received an honorary Doctorate of Music.

Chris apprenticed at the Santa Fe Opera before making his professional debut in Santa Fe in 1975 as Fenton in Verdi's *Falstaff* under the baton of Edo de Waart. He made his European debut in 1978 at the Salzburg Landestheater, where he sang Lindoro (*L'italiana in Algeri*). From 1981 to 1984, he performed in Augsburg, where his repertory included Tamino, Idomeneo, Rodolfo, Julien, Faust, and Rossini's Otello. From the latter, he has developed an international reputation as a Rossini specialist, including Pyrrhus in *Ermione*, Erisso in *Maometto II*, James in *La donna del lago*, Contareno in *Bianca e Fallioero*, Arnoldo in *Guillaume Tell* (a role he has sung at La Scala, Paris, and Covent Garden), Argirio in *Trancredi*, Antenore in *Zelmira*, and Idreno in *Semiramide*. The latter was his debut at the world famous Covent Garden in London in 1985. His La Scala debut was in the role of Count Libenskof in *Il viaggio a Reims* in 1988, and repeated that role in Vienna and Pesaro.

Additional tenor roles for which Chris is noted include Amenophis in *Moise et Pharaon*, Antenore in *Zelmira*, Argirio in *Rancredi*, Aeneas in *Les Troyens*, Admetus in *Alceste*, Leukippos in *Daphne*, Arturo in *I Puritani*, Nemorino in *La Juive*, Arrigo in *Vespri siciliani*, Sobinin in *A Life for the Tsar*, and Percy in *Anna Bolena*. He has portrayed a wide range of operatic heroes, ranging from the Mozartian classics like *Idomeneo, Mitridate, La Clemenza Di Tito, La Finta Giardiniera, Cosi Fan Tutte*, and *Die Zauberflote*, to Berlioz's *Benvenuto Cellini, Les Troyens*, and *The Damnation Faust*, to Puccini's *La Boheme, Madama Butterfly*, and *Il Trovatore*, as well as Meyerbeer's *Roberto le Diable* (Carnegie Hall) and Offenbach's *Les Contes d'Hoffman*.

Chris' illustrious career includes performances in the major operatic centers of the world, including the Metropolitan Opera (New York City), La Scala (Milan), Royal Opera House (London), Lyric Opera (Chicago), State Opera (Vienna), San Francisco Opera, Paris Opera, Teatro Colon (Buenos Aires), as well as on stages in Barcelona, Madrid, Amsterdam, Hamburg, Munich, Rome, Geneva, and Venice.

In addition to those previously mentioned, the high points of Chris' career include opening the Milan opera season for two consecutive years in 1988 and 1989 in Rossini's *William Tell* and Verdi's *I Vespri Siciliani*, opening the 1990 Chicago opera season as Gluck's Admete, and recording several of his roles, including Faust, Arrigo, and Sobinin. (GC)

Miller, Eddie
(b. December 10, 1919 – d. April 11, 1997)

Best known as co-writer for the #1 hit on pop and country charts, "Release Me," and composer of more than 1,000 songs, Edward Monroe Miller was born in Camargo, Oklahoma, a tiny hamlet of about 200 people located in the western part of the state. He attended grade school in Dodson, Texas, and completed high school at Arnett and Hollis, Oklahoma. While still a teenager, Eddie wrote his first song, "I Love You Honey," which became his first published song. Raised on western swing, Eddie formed his own swing band, Eddie Miller and His Oklahomans, but it was disbanded during World War II when he worked as a locomotive engineer for the MK & T Railroad Company.

After World War II, Eddie reorganized the Oklahomans and made some recordings with the Bluebonnet label in Dallas during the late 1940s. He then moved to the West Coast and signed with Four Star as a recording artist and songwriter. According to several sources, Eddie, while in San Francisco playing in a nightclub, overhead a woman tell her male friend, "If you would release me, we'd get along all right." After hearing this statement, he and fellow Oklahoman Clarence Boyd, a Vinita-born and later Kellyville resident, co-wrote "Release Me" in 1946, and Miller later recorded the song on the Four Star label. It was overlooked until 1954 when Jimmy Heap recorded it for Capitol, but was soon covered by Ray Price and Kitty Wells, also in 1954. All three versions charted on the Top 10 in 1954. By 1975, more than 400 versions of the song had been recorded with Little Esther Phillips and Engelbert Humperdinck turning it into a Top 10 hit on the pop charts, and Humperdinck's recording reaching #1 status on the international level. It became the signature song for Eddie as he was soon known as "Mr. Release Me."

Miller's songwriting success continued in the 1950s and 1960s with such numbers as "There She Goes," first recorded by Carl Smith in 1955, but later covered by Patsy Cline and Jerry Wallace, and "Thanks a Lot," co-written with Don Sessions, and a hit for Ernest Tubb in 1963. Tubb also recorded several other Miller songs, including "Rainbow at Midnight" and "Half A Mind." "Thanks A Lot" was later covered by a multitude of artists, including Brenda Lee, Ricky Van Shelton, Hank Williams, Jr., Rick McCready, 3rd Tyme Out, Wallace Brothers, and Two Dollar Pistols. Additional songs included "After Loving You," recorded by Eddy Arnold in 1962, and later covered by Della Reese, Buddy Greco, Little Esther Phillips, Jim Reeves, and Elvis Presley; "Playboy," recorded by **Roger Miller** and Wynn Stewart; and "Burn Me Down," another co-written piece with Sessions, recorded by Marty Stuart in 1992. "I Love You Honey"(his first song), "Hungry For Love," "I Loved and Lost Again," "A Church, a Courtroom & Then Goodbye," and "Three Cigarettes in an Ashtray," were all recorded by Patsy Cline, and the latter was covered by k.d. lang.

In 1967, Miller moved to Nashville and became actively involved in the country music industry. He was co-founder of the Nashville Songwriters Association, serving as first president and two terms on the board of directors, and was later inducted into its Hall of Fame in 1975. He was also co-founder of the ACM in Hollywood. Moreover, he taught songwriting classes at the University of Tennessee and wrote a country opera entitled "The Legend of Johnny Brown," which was performed in The Netherlands.

While in Nashville, Eddie turned to religion and revised his trademark song as "Release Me (From My Sins)," recorded by the Blackwood Brothers, and "Jesus, Let Me Write You a Song," released by James Blackwood. He also wrote a gospel opera entitled "It Was Jesus."

Miller received during his songwriting career a host of awards and honors, including BMI Performance Award for "There She Goes" and "Release Me" (1954), *Disc Jockey's Digest* Achievement Award (1963), BMI Performance Award for "Thanks A Lot" (1964), BMI Citation of Achievement Award for "Burn Me Down" (1992), and the Nashville Songwriters Association Outstanding Achievement Award (1993).

Eddie was recognized in his home state of Oklahoma with such honors as All Time Greatest Songwriters Award, gubernatorial proclamation for Eddie Miller Week in 1968, and named an Honorary Okie in 1971.

When he was inducted into the Nashville Songwriters Hall of Fame, Eddie said, "I write a song backwards. I know what the end is going to be before I start. I don't follow a trend. I go the opposite. I think a writer should set a trend, not follow it . . . I write all the time. Ideas are everywhere. Songs are all around you."

Miller died at his home near Nashville in 1977. (GC)

Miller, Roger Dean
(b. January 2, 1936 – d. October 25, 1992)

The witty Roger Miller will always be known for his ability to bring light-hearted sensibility to heavy life subjects. His skills as a songwriter and singer culminated in the 1960s with major pop and country hits such as "Dang Me," "England Swings," "King of the Road," "Little Green Apples," and "Chug-a-Lug." Born in Fort Worth, Texas, Roger's father, Jean Miller, died at twenty-six when Roger was only a year old. As a result, Roger's mother, Laudene Holt Miller, sent her three boys to live with Jean's brothers, and Roger wound up with Armelia and Elmer Miller on a farm outside the tiny southwestern Oklahoma town of Erick.

Although fifteen years older than Roger, Erick native **Sheb Wooley**, who later had a hit

with "The Purple People Eater," taught Roger his first chords on guitar, bought him his first fiddle, and spent a lot of time listening to the radio that brought them the Grand Ole Opry on Saturday nights and the Light Crust Doughboys from Fort Worth by day. The connection also provided Sheb the opportunity to meet his wife, Melva Miller, Roger's cousin, which probably explains some more of the closeness between the two. Filled with the hopes of youth, and desperate to escape Erick at the end of the Depression-ravaged 1930s, Roger traveled Oklahoma and Texas working where he could find it, and learning what he could in the honky tonks at night. He could not make enough money to buy a needed guitar, so he stole one in Texas and brought it back into Oklahoma. His conscience got the best of him though and he turned himself in to a judge who offered Miller an opportunity to enlist in the U.S. Army. After some hard lessons in Korea in 1952, Miller returned to the states and played fiddle in Special Services group at Fort McPherson, Georgia, called the Circle A Wranglers. After getting his discharge in 1956, Roger took off for Nashville where he had an unsuccessful audition with Chet Atkins and began washing dishes at the Andrew Jackson Hotel smack in the middle of Nashville's country music scene.

Roger's first break came as fiddler in Minnie Pearl's road band, and his second professional opportunity occurred when he met George Jones at WSM radio one night. Roger played George some songs, and Jones then introduced Miller to Don Pierce and Pappy Daily of Mercury-Starday Records. The meeting led to a record deal in which Miller recorded his first single, "My Pillow" b/w "Poor Little John." Although the single had no success, Roger rode to the Texas session with George Jones and the two co-wrote some songs along the way, to include "Tall, Tall Trees," which Jones recorded in 1957, and "Happy Child," which Jimmy Dean also recorded the same year. The lack of significant success urged Miller to move out to Amarillo, only a couple of hours west from Erick, with his wife and first child on the way. He joined the Amarillo Fire Department where he worked during the day, and played Amarillo nightspots to further his dreams. Miller certainly drew from the period for the opening lines of "Dang Me," but the relocation also proved fortuitous when Miller met Ray Price one night at a club in Amarillo. Several months later Price hired Roger to replace singer Van Howard in the Cherokee Cowboys, and the family was back on their way to Nashville. In the meantime, Miller had written "Invitation to the Blues," and the song made its way to singing cowboy Rex Allen, who had a hit with it in 1958. As Allen's version started to succeed, Miller suggested Ray Price cover the song and it became a #3 country hit. Roger also entered his first songwriting deal in 1958 with Tree Publishing and Buddy Killen, a Grand Ole Opry bassist Roger met in a Nashville bar. The two began a life-long friendship that saw Roger Miller rise to the heights of the country and pop music worlds.

With Killen getting his songs to artists, Roger began a string of country hits as a songwriter. Ernest Tubb hit with "Half a Mind" (#8), Faron Young made the Top Ten with "That's the Way I Feel," Jim Reeves took Miller's "Billy Bayou" to #1, and followed it a few months later with "Home" (#2). Even though Miller was having hits vicariously through other artists, he still wanted his own deal and landed one in 1958 on Decca Records for which he recorded an unsuccessful honky tonk single, "A Man Like Me," with Donny Little, later known as Johnny Paycheck, on harmony vocals. After leaving Ray Price's group, Roger joined Faron Young as drummer, and soon thereafter signed with RCA-Nashville, run by the legendary guitarist and architect of the Nashville pop sound, or, depending on one's perspective, the man who genericized country music, Chet Atkins.

In 1960, Miller's first single of that year was "You Don't Want My Love," later known as "In the Summertime," and defined much of what would follow from Roger Miller. The song is uptempo while the subject matter is about a man who has lost the love in his life, and features Roger's ad-libbed, bluesy scatting. The song made it to #14 on the country charts and was covered by pop crooner Andy Williams. "In the Summertime" also established Roger as a solo act. Less than a year later, Roger cracked the country top ten with "When Two Worlds Collide," a slow, weepy lament about what happens when people from different sides of life get together, and a title inspired by the sci-fi "B" film, *When Two Worlds Collide* (1951), a favorite of Miller's. Those two songs were the highlight of Roger's RCA career as he was dropped in 1963 by the label after "Lock, Stock, and Teardrops" failed to gain any chart response, and Atkins reportedly tired of Miller's celebratory lifestyle.

Even though he had some success with his songwriting and performing, Miller did not get remotely wealthy, or even stable, from his work to that point. His next break came from television when his old friend Jimmy Dean, then guest hosting *The Tonight Show*, called Roger whose walk-on performance of "I Walk the Line" with ad-libbed lyrics was an audience favorite. Appearances on other TV shows followed, and Roger decided he might have a better chance at a career in California than in Nashville. Smash Records entered the picture and picked up Roger in 1963. By January of 1964, Miller was ready for a session in which he cut fifteen songs with some of Nashville's top session musicians. Songs that came out of the session include 1964's million-selling Top Ten hit, "Dang Me," and the catchy popular drinking song, "Chug-a-Lug." However, the songs had not yet become hits, so Roger collected his $1,500 for doing the session, moved to California, and landed upstairs from the eccentric country and pop songwriter and producer from Mannford, OK, **Lee Hazlewood.** While Roger was scrounging for gigs in California, "Dang Me" became a #1 country hit, staying on the chart for twenty-five weeks, and peaked on the pop charts at #7. The song changed his fortunes for good and he became an in-demand performer on stage, TV, and in the recording studios. A few months later, "Chug-a-Lug" hit #3 on the country charts and #9 on the pop charts, and by fall Miller was back in the studio for Smash Records, recording "Do-Wacka-Do," a solid #15 hit on the country charts in 1964. Later that year, Miller recorded the song for which he has become most known, "King of the Road."

Known by those close to Miller at the time as "the hobo song," "King of the Road" was released early in 1965 and in March hit #1 on the country charts where it remained for five weeks, made #4 on the pop charts, and by May had sold a million copies. In April 1965, Miller received five Grammy Awards for "Dang Me," to include Best Country Music Album, Single, Song, Vocal Performance, and, ironically, Best New Country and Western Artist. By the summer of 1965, Miller's career had reached its zenith, and he received his first royalty check for $168,000. Picked *Jukebox Magazine*'s Artist of the Year in 1965, Miller's crossover status inspired a number of mainstream press articles. *Life* magazine dubbed him a "cracker barrel philosopher," *Time* called him the "unhokey Okie," and in 1966 the *Saturday Evening Post* put him on the cover to represent a story chronicling the "Big boom in country music." The 1966 Grammy Awards also showered Miller with awards for the previous year's "King of the Road," to include Best Country and Western Album, Single, Song, and three Best Vocal Performance Awards: Country, Contemporary and Rock and Roll. The Academy of Country Music honored also honored him with Songwriter, Man, and Single of the Year Awards for 1965.

Miller continued recording uptempo songs mixing sad topics with humorous lyrics such as "My Uncle Used to Love Me but She Died," tear-in-your beer ballads like "The Last Word in Lonesome is Me" and "Don't We All Have the Right to Be Wrong." Roger also became known for the occasional pop song of pure, if not naïve, happiness as on "Walkin' in the Sunshine." One of his most ironic songs was the postcard view of London in 1965's "England Swings." The song presented a complete opposite view of England from the one being represented by the British Invasion, and appealed to Anglo-Americans from whom the "old country" had become a comfortable stereotype.

By 1966, Roger was everywhere. Starting with his national fame in 1965, Roger made television appearances on the *Andy Williams Show, Dean Martin Show, Hollywood Palace with Bing Crosby, Tonight Show with Johnny Carson,* and *The Glen Campbell Goodtime Hour.* The Roger Miller Special aired in January of 1966, and NBC gave him his own TV show that featured many big names but was not renewed at the end of its thirteen-week run in 1966. On his last show, he blew up the train set used on the program so no one else would use it. Early in 1967, Roger had his last crossover hit as a writer, "Walkin' in the Sunshine," and later in the year he recorded, but did not write, the western soundtrack for the film *Waterhole #3.* Subsequently, as a recognizable country music voice, Miller proved his good ear for commercial tunes and turned to recording other people's songs, to include Bobby Russell's "Little Green Apples" in 1968, his last Top 40 crossover hit as an artist, and Kris Kristofferson's "Me and Bobby McGhee," a Top 20 country hit in 1969.

With his peak success years past, Miller recorded several country standards with honky-tonk arrangements in 1970 called *A Trip in the Country.* The album had no real impact, but "Don't We All Have the Right," which he had written in 1962 and included on the album, turned up on Ricky Van Shelton's first album, *Wild-Eyed Dream* (1987), which indicated Roger's influence on young country singers. Mercury folded the Smash label in 1970, but not before Miller had one more minor chart single with "Hoppy's Song," about the death of singing cowboy Hopalong Cassidy which Roger related to the end of an era in America. Columbia Records signed Miller after Smash folded, and Roger released *Dear Folks: Sorry I Haven't Written Lately*, which did not provide any hits.

In 1973, he wrote and sang songs for the Disney film, *Robin Hood*, and also appeared as the voice of Allan-A-Dale in the movie. That performance opened a new world of opportunities for his recognizable voiceovers and songs in productions aimed at children. He hosted and sang on *The Muppet Show* in the late 70s, and narrated several other youth-oriented features and specials throughout the remainder of his career. He also appeared in episodes of television programs such as *Love American Style*, *Daniel Boone* (as Johnny Appleseed), *Murder She Wrote*, and *Quincy* where he played a singer with a substance abuse problem. Along with operating his King of the Road hotel chain, and making regular concert appearances, Roger continued recording moderate hits for Mercury and Elektra through the 1970s until 1982's *Old Friends*, on which he teamed up with old friends Willie Nelson and Ray Price.

With *Old Friends*, Roger made it back into the country Top Ten with the album's title track, written for his folks back in Oklahoma. Miller also enjoyed a significant resurgence of interest in his work when he was commissioned in 1984 to write songs for a Broadway musical adaptation of Mark Twain's *Adventures of Huckleberry Finn* called *Big River*. Broadway producer and long-time fan had seen Miller at a live appearance at New York City's Lone Star Café, and knew Roger would be perfect to write the music and songs of the musical that opened in 1985 and was huge hit. When actor John Goodman left for a film role, Roger played the part of Pap, based on Miller's uncle in Oklahoma, for a few months on Broadway and in a national tour. Thanks to the show's success, Roger recorded a self-titled album for MCA in 1986, on which he sang several songs from the play, and *Big River* received seven Tony Awards, including Roger's for "Best Score." The extra attention induced the Academy of Country Music to give Roger their Pioneer Award for 1987, and *Big River* turned out to be the crowing achievement of his thirty-year career. The success of *Big River* led him to relax with his family until he was convinced by his manager and long-time friend, Stan Moress, to get back on the road, solo with guitar. The shows were met with enthusiastic response from critics and fans, but in the fall of 1991, Miller was diagnosed with lung cancer. His last performance was during CMA Week in Nashville, and after a year of treatment, with one remission, he died in Nashville at the relatively young age of 56. In 1995, Miller was inducted posthumously into the Country Music Hall of Fame. His third and final wife, Mary Miller, a former singer with Kenny Rogers and the First Edition, and backup vocalist for Roger from the 1970s forward, said the induction "would have been his ultimate dream come

true." He is survived by seven children: Alan, Rhonda, Shari, Dean, Shannon, Taylor, and Adam. Roger's posthumous fame has been significant.

Since 1992, at least forty-four albums have been released devoted fully or in part to Miller's recorded output, The Nashville Network aired a two-hour television special remembering Roger's life and music featuring Reba McEntire, Willie Nelson, Trisha Yearwood and other country stars, and he received Grammy Hall of Fame Awards in 1997 and 1998. In 1999, his song "Husbands and Wives" was nominated as Song of the Year, and in one of the more significant "best of" lists produced in 2000, the Recording Industry of America and the National Endowment for the Arts listed "King of the Road" #84 on their combined "Songs of the Century" list. Roger's career sales included a platinum single (1,000,000 sold), six gold singles (500,000 sold each), and five gold albums (500,000 sold each). In 2003, CMT named "King of the Road" as one of the 100 Greatest Country Songs, placing it at #37 in the somewhat arbitrary list, and the musical, *Big River*, opened again on Broadway in November. Also in 2003, Roger's son, Dean, released an album on Universal South Records, the first single from which was called "The Gun Ain't Loaded." Finally, the people of Roger's hometown of Erick created the Roger Miller Museum Foundation in 2001 with the goal of building a museum to exhibit memorabilia from the life and career of yet another successful singing and songwriting Oklahoman. Miller certainly gained musical sense and his rural identity from the state, but his drive to accomplish goals regardless of the sacrifice produced lyrics that were at times melancholy and poignant, and other times celebratory and just downright silly, all of which parlayed into country and pop hits to which many people could relate. That was Roger Miller. (HF)

www.rogermiller.com

Milton, Roy

(b. July 31, 1907 – d. September 18, 1983)

As jump, jive, and rhythm and blues from the late 1930s to the early 1950s mowed a path for rock and roll in American popular music, bandleader, vocalist, and drummer Roy Milton, along with his contemporaries of Louis Jordan, Wynonie Harris, and **Lowell Fulson**, fronted one of the primary R&B combos that presaged the rock movement. Milton's top 5 R & B hit, "R.M. Blues," met the celebratory stateside mood in immediate post-World War II, and established Roy as an important small combo bandleader. The song's success also established Specialty Records as an important source for R & B, blues, gospel, and nascent rock and roll.

Born in the small, south central Oklahoma oil town of Wynnewood, Milton's father was a gospel singer, and his mother was reportedly American Indian. The family moved to Tulsa when Roy was four and he began singing in the local church choir as a child. By high school he played in his high school brass band, and in 1929 formed his own combo to play various social functions in the Tulsa area. From 1931 to 1933, Milton played with Tulsa bandleader Ernie Fields before moving to California in 1935 where he formed his Solid Senders orchestra. The Solid Senders mixed big band swing with gospel and blues and Milton released his first records independently before joining Hamptone, and then Juke Box Records.

Under the entrepreneurship of Art Rupe, Milton recorded four songs for the newly formed Specialty label in 1945 to include "Groovy Blues," "Milton's Boogie," "Rhythm Cocktail," and the 1946 Top Five R&B hit, "R.M. Blues" which placed Roy on a pedestal next to the king of jump blues, Louis Jordan. The success also allowed Specialty to attract other artists such as **Jimmy Liggins**, develop a reputation for significant recordings by gospel artists like the Soul Stirrers and The Swan Silvertones. The label also released blues such as Guitar Slim's "The Things I Used to Do," and, ultimately, early rock and roll gems such as Lloyd Price's "Lawdy Miss Clawdy," Little Richard's major songs, "Tutti Fruiti," "Long Tall Sally," "Lucille," and "Rip it Up," and Sam Cooke's early gospel recordings. Rupe recorded numerous Roy Milton songs through 1953, and scored 19 Top Ten R&B hits with Roy such as "Thrill Me," "The Hucklebuck," "Information Blues," a cover of Louis Prima's "Oh Babe!" and, finally, "Night and Day" (1952) was Milton's last chart record for Specialty. The Specialty records featured Milton's earthy witticisms, such as "Keep a Dollar in Your Pocket" and "I've Had My Moments," the pianist Camille Howard, and two bold saxophone players, Buddy Floyd and Benny Waters.

After leaving Specialty, Milton recorded for Dootoone and King throughout the 1950s with little success, and had a minor R & B hit for Warwick, "Red Light," in 1961. Milton worked one-nighters with his band throughout the 1950s and 1960s, but did not enjoy as much recognition from the British blues boom as other blues and R & B artists from the 1940s and 50s, primarily because Roy's group was not guitar based. Funky guitarist **Jimmy Nolen**, who provided James Brown's primary guitar licks, remembered seeing Roy's group in Oklahoma in the 1950s, and saxophonist Stanley Turrentine talked about running into Milton's bands in the "blacks only" restaurants of the south during the same period. In 1970, Milton appeared with Johnny Otis at the Monterrey Jazz Festival and experienced a resurgence of sorts as he toured the U.S. and Europe, sometimes with Otis, but retired for all purposes at the end of the 1970s. Roy Milton is another Oklahoma musician who is credited with mixing several styles of music (gospel, swing, and blues) that were part of his primary musical experiences in the state. Subsequently, he not only crafted a sound tailored to his own identity that reached the masses as much as any post-World War II black artist of the late 1940s, but also is one of the forerunners of the multi-influenced hybrid popular music known as rock and roll. (HF)

Minner, DC
(b. January 28, 1935)

No one has done more in Oklahoma to keep the blues alive among young people and adult blues fans in the state by the turn of the 21st century than DC Minner and his bassist and wife, Selby, known collectively as Blues on the Move. A smooth vocalist and fluid blues guitarist with a sharp tone, Minner has written, recorded, and released his own "down home blues" since 1992 after playing through thirty years as a touring musician with only one minor break: when he did not speak for seven months in 1969 as his own form of social protest. The history of Minner's birthplace, Rentiesville, Oklahoma, stems from the collective stories of the **Muscogee (Creek) Nation**, a major Civil War battle at Honey Springs, and the black town movement of late 19th century Indian Territory. Also the birthplace of esteemed African-American historian John Hope Franklin, Minner bases his Texas Road Recording Company and the

Annual Dusk 'til Dawn Blues Festival in the rural Rentiesville nightclub where he entered the world and grew up.

The Dusk 'til Dawn Blues Club, known from the 1930s to the 1960s as the grocery-plus-juke joint, Cozy Corner, where his grandmother sold corn whiskey and a Choctaw brew known as "Chock" beer to support the family, featured the first live music DC heard outside of church where he sang constantly alongside his aunties, mother, and grandmother. Al Freeman, a black man who played slide guitar with a pocketknife, and a white named Slim, played Delta blues and country dance tunes for customers. DC borrowed Al's guitar when the musician would pass out drunk, fool with it until a string popped, and then put it back on the bandstand. His grandmother, Lura Drenna, promoted large gospel sings in Muskogee, just twenty-eight miles to the north, and took DC to see major gospel groups like the Soul Stirrers. The first song DC remembers learning was "Sitting on Top of the World," which his grandfather used to sing working behind the mules, and which **Bob Wills** made popular in Oklahoma. The family listened to Wills on the radio when they came in from the fields at noon, which was the first time DC heard horns with a band.

Minner's first instrument was an old front porch piano that became a pie safe after his family tired of him playing it, and he sang in gospel quartets when he was 14. DC explained the connection between gospel and blues in a 1997 interview: "I don't believe there's ever been any difference between church music and the blues in any area, except instead of saying 'Oh Lord' you say 'Oh baby'." As a teenager, DC listened to R & B via Tennessee radio stations, Wolfman Jack out of Del Rio, Texas, and the X-border station, XERA, from Ciudad Acuna, Mexico. He left Rentiesville in 1953 to join the service where he learned to play flamenco guitar from two Army buddies, and returned to the states carrying a guitar. Not long after returning, he married his high school chorus teacher, and by 1961 was in Oklahoma City playing bass for Little Eddy Taylor. Soon thereafter, he played bass with Larry Johnson and the New Breed, a group that played independently through early 1967, but also made a living out of backing up blues stars like **Lowell Fulson**, Chuck Berry, Bo Diddley, Jimmy Reed, and Eddie Floyd when he had a hit with "Knock on Wood."

O.V. Wright, the gospel singer turned soul vocalist who epitomized the blend of gospel and R & B into 1960s soul music, kept New Breed working as his backup band for two years, and DC also played and led the band for two years with Freddy King, arguably DC's biggest influence on guitar. Minner has long used King's "Hideway" as his break song for starting and/or ending sets, and claims King "the best guitar player I've ever heard." When the group broke up about 1965, DC headed for California and played in a group with **Tony Matthews**. By 1969, DC opted for San Francisco and the Bay Area where he met Selby, his future bass player, wife, and business partner, who had come from Providence, Rhode Island where she was an art student and aspiring singer shocked into musical action by a four-hour Janis Joplin concert.

Traveling in a folk duo with Jim Donovan through Washington, D.C., Chicago, and New Orleans, Selby Minner heard about the blues scene in the Bay Area and headed west in the late 1960s. While working the coffeehouses and clubs as an acoustic blues and folk singer over the next few years, Selby eventually met DC in places where they crossed paths as musicians around 1973, and the two started performing together in 1976. The next year they left Berkeley in a step-van as Blues on the Move and stayed on the road for twelve years. With DC on guitar and vocals, Selby on bass and vocals, and a series of pick up drummers, the group traveled the U.S., frequently in the Southwest and on the West Coast. They stayed in San Francisco for a year in 1984, and then in L.A. during 1986 and 1987 where they played regularly five nights a week throughout the metropolitan area.

Tiring of the road life and urban hassles, DC and Selby returned to Rentiesville in 1988 when they opened the Down Home Blues Club in the same house where he was reared. Saying nobody would ever come that far out in the country to hear music, neighbors and onlookers laughed as he started building the club, determined as Noah, and put the place together. At first, the club served the after hours clientele of the area who would bring beer in coolers, pay a cover, dance, or just listen to DC, Selby, and/or various guests jam until dawn. Given the town's location and history, the club has an easy, relaxed feel of multicultural society where no one is above the blues. In 1991, the ethos escalated into the Dusk 'til Dawn Blues Festival, featuring a wide roster of local, regional, national, and international blues artists, many of whom

Selby and DC Minner

DC and Selby met on their travels throughout the U.S. Claimed by the Blues Foundation in Memphis as a "must-see to say you are in touch with the blues scene in the country today," legendary artists such as Carey Bell, Eddie Kirkland, Magic Slim, and Nappy Brown have stunned blues fans with 4 a.m. sets at the festival, and up-and-coming artists like Indigenous and Rosie Ledet have played before they became national figures. Lesser-known, but extremely authentic artists, such as James Peterson and Drink Small, have been to the festival, and a bevy of Oklahomans are featured each year.

The Minners also released a series of notable recordings in the 1990s on their Texas Road Recording label. Starting with the independent cult-favorite cassette, *Shake Hands & Make Friends with the Blues* (1992), DC and Selby released critically praised albums *Live 1991* (1994) and *Love Lost and Found* (1997), *Morning Train* (1998), *I Can Tell You Got Good Loving* (2001), and *Full Moon Over Rentiesville* (2003). The albums are full of DC's experienced vocals merging soul, blues, and gospel with a rhythm and lead guitar style drenched in Freddy King, but filtered through a lifetime of exposure to R & B, country, and rock and roll. Selby also complements the albums with her own easy rolling bass work and warm singing, now seasoned by many years of playing with DC and backing up Little Johnny Taylor, Albert Collins, Lowell Fulson, Hubert Sumlin, and Smokey Wilson.

Of particular interest from Texas Road Recording is the *Guitar Showdown* CD, recorded at the festival in 1996. The set sears through a battle of Oklahoma blues guitarists to include DC, Tony Matthews (Checotah, OK), Larry Johnson (Muskogee, OK), **Flash Terry**, and Berry Harris (Stringtown, OK). Recorded live and released as an Oklahoma Blues Heritage CD free only to public schools in 1998, the album was reissued commercially by Texas Road in 2002.

DC and Selby have also been active with the Blues in the Schools (BITS) program in which they do residencies with band programs and teach students how to play blues, R & B, and rock, as well as some life lessons. DC began working with BITS on the West Coast in the 1970s, and has continued teaching in the program with Selby from kindergartens to colleges in Rhode Island, Massachusetts, California, and across Oklahoma. One of Minner's students, Garrett Jacobson, already a classically trained pianist in his hometown of Edmond, Oklahoma, started playing with DC at age twelve in 1997 after meeting the elder blues man through BITS. After releasing two critically praised blues albums of his own by the time he was 18, Garrett now fronts his own blues-rock group regionally as "Big G" Jacobson.

DC and Selby have also been on the Oklahoma Arts Council's Touring and Artist in Residence rosters since 1989, and have worked with the Mid America Arts Alliance since 1993 in Kansas, Missouri, Texas, Nebraska, and Arkansas. The Minners' story is not unnoticed on a local nor national level. In 1998, DC was interviewed for *The Oprah Winfrey Show* about growing up in one of Oklahoma's original twenty-eight African-American towns. DC and Selby taped two songs in the club, "Hideaway" and "Shade Tree Mechanic," recorded for the program airing March 6, 1998 on CBS. In 1999, The International Blues Foundation honored them in Memphis with a Keeping the Blues Alive Award, and featured them in a nationally distributed video about Blues in the Schools. In 1999, DC was inducted into the Oklahoma Jazz Hall of Fame in the blues category, and was the only one honored who actually lived in the state at the time of the award. The accolades of 1999 culminated with Rentiesville renaming the dirt road next to the Down Home Blues Club as DC Minner Street. ¼ mile north of the club, the street also borders the Honey Springs Civil War Battlefield where African-Americans, Anglo-Americans, American Indians, and Mexican-Americans fought against and among one another. Now, they celebrate the blues together every Labor Day at the Dusk 'til Dawn Blues Festival.

In 2002, Texas Road Video released a 53-minute video documentary of the festival. Shot in the late 1990s and dedicated by DC to Oklahoma City native and former New Breed member Claude Williams, who led Ike and Tina Turner's band as a trumpeter in the 1970s, the video includes interviews and music with Indigenous, Flash Terry, Blackhawk Blues Band, Michael Burton, Lem Shepard, Hiram Harvel, DC Minner and Selby. Friends of Oklahoma Music inducted DC Minner into the Oklahoma Music Hall of Fame in 2003, a year designated as the "Year of the Blues" by the U.S. Congress. (HF)
www.dcminnerblues.com

Mitchell, Leona
(b. October 13, 1948)

According to folklore, when a mother is carrying a child, she can make a wish for the baby growing inside of her. Pearl Mitchell made a wish that her tenth child would become a singer. Born in Enid, Leona Pearl Mitchell was one of fifteen children, all still living as of 2002. At age four, Leona could sing "The Lord's Prayer" to perfection, and it appeared that her mother's wish was to become a reality. Leona recalls that during her early childhood, she dreamed of becoming a world-class vocalist, a dream that was to become true by all standards of stardom. She received early vocal training in the choir at the Antioch Church of God in Christ in Enid, where her father, Reverend Hulon Mitchell, was the minister. Mitchell sang in her father's church choir from about age ten through high school, and during her teenage years was the choir director. The Mitchell household contained numerous musical instruments, including xylophone, bass violin, clarinet, saxophone, and guitars. Her father played several of these instruments by ear. Her mother, Pearl, was an excellent pianist, and young Leona took lessons from her. Because of the musical influences in the home, Leona's older siblings formed "The Musical Mitchells."

Leona attended Carver Elementary, Emerson Junior High, and Enid High School. During Leona's public school music education, her major influence was Maurine Priebe, director of choirs for the Enid school system. It was Priebe who discovered Leona's vocal talents while singing at Carver Elementary and Emerson Junior High. Mitchell played violin in the Enid High School orchestra, but had to drop it for choir as participation in both was disallowed at the time. Priebe played the Maria Callas and Leontyne Price recordings of *Aida* for Mitchell which inspired her future favorite role. Her most vivid recollection of high school performances under the direction of Priebe was the role of Aida in Verdi's *Aida*.

With encouragement from Priebe, Mitchell auditioned for the music department at Oklahoma City University, and received a full scholarship (the first student to receive such an honor) to study music there following graduation from Enid High School. At OCU, she studied with Inez Silberg and performed several soprano roles in operas produced at the university. Her first was the role of Susanna in Mozart's *The Marriage of Figaro*. She obtained her B. A. in Music in 1971 from OCU.

During her post-college career, Mitchell completed graduate studies at the Julliard School of Music in New York, received the prestigious Kurt Herbert Adler Award of the San Francisco Opera, and was awarded the highly coveted $10,000 Opera America grant that enabled her to study with Ernest St. John Metz in Los Angeles. As a soprano, she debuted with the San Francisco Opera in 1973 as Micaela in Bizet's *Carmen*.

Mitchell's long and illustrious career as one of America's leading lyric-spinto sopranos has featured many extraordinary and riveting performances. Noteworthy among these are her 1975 debut as Micaela in Bizet's *Carmen* with New York City's Metropolitan Opera. She remained on the Met's roster in the 1980s and 1990s. It was an auspicious debut with Placido Domingo as her singing partner. A second highlight was also in 1975 when Mitchell received international acclaim for her selection to sing the role of Bess in the Decca-London complete stereo recording of the George Gershwin classic *Porgy and Bess* with the Cleveland Symphony Orchestra. A third highlight was in 1984 when Mitchell was pregnant with her son, she sang the role of Elvira in Verdi's *Ernani* with Luciano Pavarotti, the greatest lyric tenor of our time. Additional roles for which she has won international recognition include Donna Anna in Mozart's *Don Giovanni*, Mme. Lidoine in Poulenc's *Dialogues of the Carmelites*, Pamina in Mozart's *Die Zauberflote*, Musetta in Puccini's *La Boheme*, Leonora in Verdi's *La Forza del destino*, Elvira in Verdi's *Ernani*, Amelia in Verdi's *Un Ballo in Maschera*, Butterfly in Puccini's *Madama Butterfly*, Leonora in Verdi's *Il Trovatore*, Elisabetta in Verdi's *Don Carlo*, Liu in Puccini's *Turandot*, and her favorite, the title role in Verdi's *Aida*. She has sung nearly 200 performances of this revered opera that has become so lovingly identified with her. Critical acclaim from the London *Daily Telegraph* for Mitchell's unforgettable interpretation of *Aida*: "American Leona Mitchell produced a torrent of beautiful sound from one of world's greatest prima donnas. If Verdi were alive today, he would applaud Ms. Mitchell's performance as generously as did the opening night audience." Her performances with the most prestigious opera companies have virtually spanned the globe with appearances on six of the seven continents, including Rio de Janeiro, Buenos Aires, Mexico City in South America; Paris, Nice, Bordeaux, Marseille, London, Edinburgh, Berlin, Frankfurt, Bonn, Hamburg, Rome, and Madrid in Europe; Tokyo and Hong Kong in Asia; Sydney and Melbourne in Australia; Cairo in Africa; and throughout North America from New York City to San Francisco. Her ravishing vocal opulence and commanding presence have resulted in recitals at some of the most important venues in North America, including Carnegie Hall, Lincoln Center, Kennedy Center, and the White House where she performed for Presidents Gerald Ford, Ronald Reagan, Jimmy Carter, and Bill Clinton. In 1985, Mitchell was honored in a joint session of the Oklahoma legislature where she was recognized for her achievements and named honorary chair of Black Heritage Month. She has also been recognized in her home state with honorary doctorates from OCU and OU. Other honors include grants from the Rockefeller Foundation and the National Opera Institute.

Currently residing in Houston, Mitchell is married to Elmer Bush, her personal manager, and they have one son, Elmer "E.C." Bush IV. She performed in 2001 in her hometown of Enid as a fundraiser for the Martin Luther King, Jr. Scholarship program. In 2002, she performed for the 50th Anniversary of the OCU Musical Theater and Opera Company, sang a benefit concert for the Simon Estes

Foundation in Tulsa, performed at the dedication of the new Capitol dome in Oklahoma City during which she sang the national anthem, and launched a concert tour with stops in her hometown performing with the Enid Symphony, as well as in Oklahoma City, Denver, Miami, St. Louis, and Washington, D.C. Her current project is a forthcoming recording of hymns that will include such selections as "Praise God From Whom All Blessings Flow" and "How Great Thou Art," her father's favorite gospel number. Finally, Mitchell is an inductee into the Oklahoma Hall of Fame and the Oklahoma Music Hall of Fame. (GC)

Moeller, Lucky
(b. February 12, 1912 – d. June 15, 1992)

Booking agent and promoter *par excellence* in the 1960s, especially the career of Webb Pierce, Walter Ernest Moeller was born in Okarche, Oklahoma, a German community of around 1,000 population located on the county line between Kingfisher and Canadian counties. During the mid-1940s, Lucky was a banker and ballroom owner that had booked such acts as **Bob Wills** and the Texas Playboys.

In 1954, Lucky moved to Nashville, where he helped manage Webb Pierce, the "King of Honky Tonk" music. Three years later, he landed at the Ozark Jubilee and managed talent for the Top Talent Agency. This move coincided with Pierce's move to the Ozark Jubilee in the mid-1950s. Lucky returned to Nashville to work for the Jim Denny Artist Bureau, which managed most of the top country stars in the 1950s and 1960s, including Pierce, Carl Smith, Hank Snow, and Minnie Pearl. When Denny died in 1963, Lucky assumed the reins of the agency, changing the name to Denny-Moeller, and two years later, to Moeller Talent. Nashville continued as home base for the agency until 1974, when Lucky suffered a major stroke. He moved the agency back to Okarche, his hometown, and less than a year later, it closed.

Moeller was one of the founding members of the Nashville Association of Talent Directors organized in 1958. (GC)

Mooney, Ralph
(b. September 16, 1928)

A forty-year veteran steel guitarist, who has backed such stars as **Merle Haggard**, Buck Owens, and Waylon Jennings, as well as a noted songwriter, including the much recorded "Crazy Arms," Ralph Mooney was born in Duncan, Oklahoma, a community of about 21,000 residents southwest of Oklahoma City. As a youngster, Ralph learned the fundamentals of guitar, mandolin, and fiddle from his brother-in-law. After hearing Leon McAuliffe, legendary steel guitar player for **Bob Wills** and the Texas Playboys, he chose that instrument and learned to play McAuliffe's "Steel Guitar Rag" employing an old knife to fret his flat top guitar. During his early career, he crafted his own steel guitar composed of birch slabs for the body, coat hangers for pullers, and thick steel rods for legs.

As a teenager, Ralph followed his sisters to California, where they settled in Bell Gardens, a suburb of Los Angeles. It is reported that Ralph did not see his first steel guitar until he was about thirteen years old. After working as a machinist at Douglas Aircraft and Alcoa Aluminum, he finally decided to devote his life to music. Ralph discovered that his neighbor was Merle Lindsay, another native Oklahoman, who gave Ralph his first professional job as a steel guitar player with his band, the Nightriders. Following this break, he began playing on weekends and doing session work for Skeets McDonald, known for his "Don't Let the Stars Get Into Your Eyes" composition. During this time, he refined his style with the help of Jesse Ashlock, fiddler with **Bob Wills' Texas Playboys**.

Around 1950, Mooney became a regular performer on Carl Moore's "Squeakin' Deacon" radio show on KXLA in Los Angeles where he met teenager singer Wynn Stewart, who was winning all the weekly talent contests on the program. This acquaintance developed into a life long friendship, and when Ralph returned to the Los Angeles after a brief stint in Las Vegas, he began to play on a regular basis with Stewart, one of the pioneers in the development of the "Bakersfield Sound" in country music. He played lead guitar on Stewart's first Capitol sessions, and they teamed in 1961 to open the Nashville Nevada Club in Las Vegas.

By the end of the 1950s, Mooney had created his trademark rolling chord steel guitar sound, and had become the premiere steel guitar payer on the West Coast. He was invited to join the recording sessions of such legendaries as Merle Haggard (played on Haggard's first sessions with Talley Records in 1963 and on such Haggard hits as "Sing Me Back Home," "Swinging Doors," and "The Bottle Let Me Down"), Buck Owens (played on the early Owens' hits such as "Foolin' Around" and "Under Your Spell Again"), Johnny Cash, Neil Young, **Wanda Jackson**, Rose Maddox, **Hoyt Axton**, and Waylon Jennings, with whom he was a member of the Waylors, Jennings' band, for twenty years from 1970.

Probably his Mooney's best-known recording is an album titled *Corn Pickin' and Slick Slidin,'* on which he collaborated with guitarist extraordinaire James Burton, known for his Telecaster technique and rock and roll sideman with such as artists as Elvis Presley and Ricky Nelson, as well as country artists such as Merle Haggard and Emmylou Harris. Overall, Ralph played on recording sessions for more than seventy artists. He recorded several instrumentals for Challenge Records, including "Release Me" and "Moonshine," both of which later appeared on 4 Star Records releases, *Country Love* and *Tennessee Pride*, respectively. Mooney may also be heard with the Waylors on the soundtrack album from the 1975 film, *Mackintosh and T.J.*, as well as on *Wail Man Wail! Original Rockabilly & Chicken Bop, Vol. 3*, released by Sundazed Music in 1993. His contribution is

"Moon's Boogie," a previously unreleased number.

Throughout his career as an instrumentalist, Mooney was writing songs, including such standards as "Crazy Arms," "Falling for You," and "Foolin'." Ray Price had his first #1 hit in 1956 with "Crazy Arms," and the song later became a Top 20 hit for Willie Nelson. "Foolin'" was a Top 5 hit for Johnny Rodriguez in 1983. Ralph's compositions were recorded by a wide array of artists, such as Chuck Berry, Andrews Sisters, Patsy Cline, Duane Eddy, Elvis Presley, Stanley Brothers, Bing Crosby, Barbara Mandrell, and Ernest Tubb.

Inducted into the Steel Guitar Hall of Fame in 1983, Mooney was recognized for his innovative tuning (High G Sharp) and creating the "Mooney" take-off and "chicken pickin" before such styles had a name. According to the induction statement, he is described as "so uniquely original that he remains unduplicated." He was also named as Steel Guitar Player of the Year in 1966 by the ACM.

After retirement, Ralph has remained active by attending steel guitar conventions and seminars where he demonstrates his techniques. In 2002, he appeared at the Texas Steel Guitar Jamboree in Dallas. (GC)

Moore, Marilyn
(b. June 6, 1931 – d. March, 1992)

Soloist with the Woody Herman, Ray McKinley, and Charlie Barnet Big Bands and often compared to Billie Holliday of the 1930s, jazz singer Marilyn Moore was born in Oklahoma City. Marilyn's parents were in vaudeville, and she broke into the act at age three singing and dancing in the finale of the family's act. While attending high school in Oklahoma City, she sang with bands in local clubs.

After high school Marilyn moved to Chicago for a short while, singing in clubs in the Windy City, but, after serving as vocalist with Woody Herman and Charlie Ventura in 1949, she eventually landed in New York in the early 1950s. During this time, she was vocalist for Ray McKinley, Boyd Raeburn, and Al Cohn, whom she married in 1953. The couple had two children, Lisa and Joe Cohn. Joe is a talented jazz guitarist who has recorded an album, *Two Funky People*, and is often guitarist for Muskogee's **Claude "Fiddler" Williams**, such as his *Swingin' the Blues* album. He also performed at the March of Jazz Party in 2003 in Clearwater Beach, Florida, to commemorate the 77th birthday of Bucky Pizzarelli.

During the mid-1950s Marilyn concentrated on raising her family, but was invited to record for the Bethlehem label in 1957. The resulting album, *Moody Marilyn Moore*, was critically acclaimed due in part to the backing of such musicians as Al Cohn, Don Abney, Barry Galbraith, and Joe Wilder. It is reported that Marilyn pushed her recording on John Hammond, famed record producer, saying she would personally "kick" him if he did not sign her. The next year she was cast in *Oh Captain!* a jazz musical that was recorded by MGM Records. It also featured such legendary jazz artists as Coleman Hawkins, Art Farmer, Harry "Sweets" Edison, and Okmulgee's **Oscar Pettiford**.

Marilyn and Al were divorced in the late 1950s, and she once again focused on her children's upbringing. Unfortunately, she never returned to professional singing or to the recording studio, despite her interest in doing so. The MGM record was never reissued, however, *Moody Marilyn Moore* was re-mastered into CD format in 1990, and is available from a Japanese outlet. It includes twelve tracks featuring such songs as "I Got Rhythm," "Lover Come Back to Me," "You're Driving Me Crazy," "Is You Is or Is You Ain't My Baby," and "Trouble Is a Man."

Jazz critic Leonard Feather described Marilyn as "one of the few young singers with a natural jazz timbre and sense of phrasing, she has been seriously handicapped by critical resentment of the resemblance to Billie Holiday." Often referred to as the "white" Billie Holiday, Marilyn died in March of 1992. (GC)

Murray, Sunny
(b. September 21, 1937)

One of the most creative *avante-garde* jazz drummers in the 1960s who helped establish the instrument's role in free improvisation, drummer, composer, arranger, and bandleader James Marcellus Arthur "Sunny" Murray was born in Idabel, Oklahoma, a community of roughly 7,000 population located in the southeastern "Little Dixie" region of the state. His family moved to Philadelphia, Pennsylvania, where he began playing drums at age nine, often with his brother, but also learned the trumpet and trombone.

In 1956, Sunny moved to New York City where he worked with diverse artists as Henry "Red" Allen, Willie "The Lion" Smith, Jackie McLean, Rocky Boyd, and Ted Curson. He moved closer to free jazz when he joined Cecil Taylor's group in 1959, and, after hearing John Coltrane's quartet and playing with him informally in 1963. While touring Europe with Taylor and Jimmy Lyons, he met Albert Ayler, and performed off and on with his group from 1965 to 1967. He was a member of the legendary trio that produced *Ghosts* and *Spiritual Unity*, as well as paying on several more Ayler albums, such as *New York Eye and Ear Control*, *Bells*, and *Spirits Rejoice*.

Murray made his first albums as leader in 1965 (*Sunny's Time Now*) and 1966 (*Sunny Murray Quintet*). Ayler was guest performer on Murray's debut album. It was this album that garnered him the *Down Beat's* Criteria Poll for Talent Deserving Wider Recognition in 1966 in the Drums category. From 1968 to 1971, he lived in France, where he played with Archie Shepp. In 1971, he returned to Philadelphia, where he was raised. Here he worked with Philly Joe Jones, an influential hard bop drummer, and fronted his own group, The Untouchable

Factor. His hard bop drumming style resulted in sessions with Ornette Coleman, John Tchicai, and another Oklahoman, **Don Cherry**.

Sunny's additional albums include *Big Chief* (1968) [Pathe-Marconi]; *Hard Cores* (1968) [Philly Jazz] on which **Cecil McBee**, another Oklahoman, plays bass; *Homage to Africa* (1969) [BYG] on which he joined by Shepp; *Sunshine* (1969) [BYG]; *An Even Break (Never Give a Sucker)* (1969) [Affinity]; *In Paris: Big Chief* (1970) [EMI]; *Charred Earth* (1978) [Kharma]; *Applecores* (1978-79) [Philly Jazz]; *Live at Moers Festival* (1979) [Moers Music]; *13 Steps on Glass* (1996) [Enja], which features a trio of tenor saxophonist Odean Pope and bassist Wayne Dockery; *Illuminators* (1996) [Audible Hiss]; and *We Are Not at the Opera* (1998) [Eremite], featuring Sabir Mateen on flute and alto/tenor sax.

Murray's compositions include "R.I.P.," "Suns of Africa, Parts 1 & 2," "Flower Trane," "Real," "Red Cross," "An Even Break," "Giblets, Part 2," Complete Affection," and "Invisible Blues." (GC)

Muscogee (Creek) Nation
(began arriving in Indian Territory in 1828)

With one traditional story explaining their origins in the West when the earth's mouth opened, and a subsequent journey toward the sunrise where they eventually created the highly evolved and structured mound building culture of the Southeastern United States, the tribe now known as the Muscogee (Creek) Nation, with its contemporary headquarters in Okmulgee, began arriving in Indian Territory in 1828 after leaving their pre-historic homelands of Alabama, Georgia, Florida, and South Carolina as a result of the United States government's removal policy of the early 19th century. With several active ceremonial grounds where traditional Muscogee music is very much alive, a deep Christian hymn singing tradition that is more than two-hundred-years-old, and several contemporary musicians who have made significant contributions to the popular music and intertribal powwow music worlds, the Muscogee (Creek) Nation is a musically rich and diverse tribe whose contributions to world music illustrate both the preservation of ancient songs under oppressive circumstances, and more modern music that has evolved due to cross-cultural contact between Muscogee people and Americans of African and European descent.

According to the Muscogee (Creek) Nation's website, the Muscogee people are descendents of a remarkable culture that, before 1500 AD, spanned most of the region known today as the American Southeast. Early ancestors of the Muscogee constructed magnificent earthen pyramids along the rivers of this region as part of their elaborate ceremonial complexes. The historic Muscogee later built expansive towns within these same broad river valleys in the present states of Alabama, Georgia, Florida and South Carolina.

The Muscogee were not one tribe but a union of several. This union evolved into a confederacy that, in the Euro-American described "historic period," was the most sophisticated political organization north of Mexico. Member tribes were called tribal towns. Within this political structure, each tribal town maintained political autonomy and distinct land holdings. At least three contemporary tribal towns, Kialegee, Alabama-Qaussarte, and Thlopthlocco, are federally recognized as independent tribal towns apart from the contemporary Muscogee (Creek) Nation because they all had government-to-government relations with the United States prior to removal. Additionally, Creeks who fought on the side of the United States against Muscogee traditionalists in 1813 and 1814 are now federally recognized as the Poarch Creek Indians, located presently in southern Alabama on land granted to them by the U.S. Government. Bands of Creeks who relocated to Florida in order to escape removal are still seeking federal recognition, with at least one band, the Muscogee Nation of Florida (formerly known The Florida Tribe of Eastern Creek Indians), on active consideration in 2003 by the Bureau of Indian Affairs.

The pre-removal confederacy was dynamic in its capacity to expand. New tribal towns were born of "Mother towns" as populations increased. The confederation was also expanded by the addition of tribes conquered by towns of the confederacy, and, in time, by the incorporation of tribes and fragments of tribes devastated by the European imperial powers. Within this confederacy, the Muscogean language and the culture of the founding tribal towns became dominant. John R. Swanton's *Social Organization and Social Usages of the Indians of the Creek Confederacy* (Washington: GPO, 1928) is particularly helpful in sorting out this period of Muscogee history, as is Swanton's *Aboriginal Culture of the Southeast* (ibid.).

Throughout the period of first contact with Europeans, most of the Muscogee population was concentrated into two geographical areas. The English called the Muscogee peoples occupying the towns on the *Coosa* and the *Tallapoosa* rivers, Upper Creeks, and those to the southeast, on the *Chattahoochee* and *Flint* rivers, the Lower Creeks. The distinction was purely geographical as was the fact that the Muscogee people lived along the creeks and rivers of Alabama, which earned the entire group of towns the term of "Creek" Indians. Also due in part to their proximity to the English, the Lower towns were substantially affected by intermarriage and its consequent impact on their political and social order, including the introduction of Christianity in the late 1700s. The Upper towns remained less effected by European influences and continued to maintain distinctly traditional political and social institutions.

In the early 19th century, the United States Indian policy focused on the removal of the Muscogee and the other Southeastern tribes to areas beyond the Mississippi River. In the removal treaty of 1832, Muscogee leadership exchanged the last of the cherished Muscogee ancestral homelands for new lands in Indian Territory. Many of the Lower Muscogee had settled in the new homeland after the 1827

Treaty of Washington, but for the majority of Muscogee people, the process of severing ties to a land they felt so much a part of proved impossible. As a result, President Andrew Jackson (who many Creeks feel should not be on the U.S. twenty dollar bill) and the U.S. Army enforced the removal of more than 24,000 Muscogee to Indian Territory in 1836 and 1837, and although estimates vary, as much as forty percent of the people did not survive the trip. In 1857, the Bureau of Indian Affairs counted 14,888 Creeks in Oklahoma.

In the new Nation the Lower Muscogees located their farms and plantations on the Arkansas and Verdigris rivers. The Upper Muscogees re-established their ancient towns on the *Canadian River* and its northern branches, therefore, essentially reversing the "Upper" and "Lower" geographical designations of the two major groups, however, several people did cross these artificial boundaries due to family allegiances or intermarriage. The tribal towns of both groups continued to send representatives to the National Council that met near High Springs, and the Muscogee Nation as a whole began to experience a new prosperity until the "war between the white men."

The American Civil War was disastrous for the Muscogee people. The first three battles of the war in Indian Territory occurred when Confederate forces attacked a large group of neutral Muscogee led by Opothle Yahola who was guiding the people to Kansas where they could be free of the conflict. Once there, however, they found desperate conditions and many died. For the majority of the Muscogee people, neutrality proved impossible. Eventually Muscogee citizens fought on both the Union and Confederate sides. The reconstruction treaty of 1866, which implicated the entire tribe with violating previous treaties in which the tribe agreed not to fight the United States, required the cession of 3.2 million acres, approximately half of the Muscogee domain, due to some Creek collusion with the Confederates.

In 1867, the Muscogee people adopted a written constitution that provided for a Principal Chief and a Second Chief, a judicial branch and a bicameral legislature composed of a House of Kings and a House of Warriors. Representation in both houses of this Legislative assembly was determined by tribal town. This "constitutional" period lasted for the remainder of the 19th century. A new capital was established in 1867 on the Deep Fork of the *Canadian* at Okmulgee. In 1878 the Nation constructed a familiar native stone Council House that remains at the center of the modern city of Okmulgee.

In the late 1800s the Dawes Commission began negotiating with the Muscogee Nation for the allotment of the national domain. In 1898, the United States Congress passed the Curtis Act that made the dismantling of the National governments of the Five Civilized Tribes and the allotment of collectively-held tribal domains inevitable. In 1890, the noted Creek statesman Chitto Harjo helped lead organized opposition to the dissolution of Muscogee National government and allotment of collectively-held lands. Harjo epitomized the view of a majority of Muscogee people who believed they possessed an inherent right to govern themselves. For tribal leaders like Chitto Harjo, it was unimaginable that the Nation could be dissolved by the action of a foreign government. This perception proved to be correct. The ultimate end of the Muscogee Nation as envisioned by its architects within the United States Congress did not occur. In the early 20th century, the process of allotment of the national domain to individual citizens was completed. However, the perceived dismantling of the Muscogee government was never fully executed. The nation maintained a Principal Chief throughout this stormy period. For significant insight into many of the governmental processes that affected the Muscogee people, see Angie Debo's *And Still the Waters Run: The Betrayal of the Five Civilized Tribes* (OU Press, 1940), and Debo's *The Road to Disappearance: A History of the Creek Indians* (OU Press, 1941). While imperfect in their description of Muscogee traditional activities, both books are substantive catalogues of the conflict between the Creeks and the U.S. Government from a non-Indian historian's perspective.

In 1971, the Muscogee people, for the first time since the partial dismantling of their national government, freely elected a Principal Chief without Presidential approval. In the 1970s the leadership of the Muscogee (Creek) Nation drafted and adopted a new constitution, revitalized the National Council and began the challenging process of Supreme Court decisions affirmed the Nation's sovereign rights to maintain a national court system and levy taxes. The federal courts have also consistently re-affirmed the Muscogee Nation's freedom from state jurisdiction.

By 2003, a full century after the difficult days of the allotment era, the Muscogee (Creek) people are actively engaged in the process of asserting the rights and responsibilities of a sovereign nation with economic enterprises such as truck stops and gaming centers, a resort hotel, a tribal motor vehicle licensing bureau, and varied programs in housing, elderly and child services, and cultural preservation. The Muscogee also have a full legal system to include district and supreme courts that have modern legal structures but often take traditional values into account when making judgments. As a culturally distinct people via their language and ceremonies, the Muscogee are also aware of the necessity for knowing and understanding their extraordinary historical and cultural inheritance. While much of this culture is maintained locally at rural ceremonial grounds, churches, and community centers, the Muscogee Nation does provide an opportunity each year for tribal members and non-tribal members to experience stomp dances,

Muscogee Council Mound Okmulgee, Oklahoma

Christian hymns, and modern popular music at the Annual Creek Nation Festival and Rodeo.

The most traditional forms of music still practiced by Muscogee people are the stomp dances and songs that go along with the annual Green Corn Ceremonies, or posketv (pronounced "bosketa"), to include the ribbon dance, feather dance, and buffalo dance. All are still a vital part of the active ceremonial life of Creek people. While much has been written on Muscogee traditions by non-Indian anthropologists and historians, a contemporary person interested in traditional Muscogee spiritual values could do no better than seeking out *A Sacred Path: The Way of the Muscogee Creeks* (American Indian Studies Center, 2001). Written by a full-blood Muscogee, Jean (Hill) Chaudhuri, and her husband Joy Chaudhuri, a political science professor, *A Sacred Path* provides a knowledgeable viewpoint of traditional Muscogee history, values, philosophy, theology, and worldview, as well as insight into the Muscogee traditional ceremonial ways. John R. Swanton's *Religious Beliefs and Medical Practices of the Creek Indians* (Washington: GPO, 1928) is also a foundational work in understanding the historical perspective of Muscogee ceremonial traditions, although it is laden with the usual non-Indian anthropological perspectives present in many works of its type. Additionally, the excellent website created through William and Mary by Jack Martin, Margaret Mauldin, and Mary McCarty (www.wm.edu/linguistics/creek/) also provides easily accessible language lessons, music examples, and multiple websites for further studying Muscogee history and culture. From there, one can obtain the context to begin listening to traditional Muscogee music.

The oldest commercially available set of Muscogee songs can be found through the Library of Congress Music Division, which released *Delaware, Cherokee, Choctaw, Creek* (AAFS L37) as part of its series, *Music of the American Indian*, recorded by Willard Rhodes between 1936 and 1951. Included on this vinyl LP are "Creek Ball Game Songs," a "Creek Lullaby" by Amanda Wesley, a "Creek Counting Song" by Victor and Amanda Wesley, "Creek Christian Hymns" led by Marcellus Williams, a "Creek Ribbon Dance Song" by Amanda Wesley, and "Creek Stomp Dance Songs" led by John Mulley. While this out-of-print record may prove difficult to track down, several excellent recordings of stomp dances and Muscogee ceremonial songs are available through Indian House Records.

Although the term "stomp dance" is often less favorable than the term "ceremonial songs" by more traditional Muscogee people, stomp dance is a common term for the dance and songs practiced the Muscogee and their neighbors, the Euchee, Seminole, and Cherokee. Intrinsically linked to the yearly ceremonial dance cycle that reaches its high point during the Green Corn Ceremony, or "Creek New Year," when traditional people fast and perform purification ceremonies to clean out the "nasty things" that have built up over the previous year, the stomp dance is the vehicle by which prayers (included in the songs) are offered through the ceremonial fire that is the center of Muscogee traditional religion and ceremonies. Additionally, the songs and dances help the people who are taking medicine stay awake all night as is required of the ceremony's participants. According to liner notes on *Stomp Dance Songs of the Muscogee Nation* (IH 3009), the Green Corn Ceremony "is a time of coming together, purification, prayers for the people, the animals, all living things, for the world, and spiritual renewal for the coming year. It is a time of good feelings." Sam Proctor, a Muscogee medicine man at the

Tallahassee (Wvkokye) Ceremonial Grounds, adds, "Our ancestors believed in the 'overseer,' or what they called, 'Ofvnkv.' When they built the fire in the circle, they said the smoke goes up to Ofvnkv, and when he smells it, if it smells good, that's when the blessing will come."

Usually taking place during the overnight hours until past sunrise, stomp dances feature a song leader who guides the song in a call-and-response fashion while women shell shakers keep the rhythm of the song by shaking turtle shell rattles attached to their legs. Singers and dancers form a line that becomes several rows of circles around the fire with the leader and elderly people at the center of the dance near the fire, and younger dancers and singers in the outer circles. By singing and dancing around the sacred fire, the prayers are carried up to Ofvnkv (pronounced "Ofúnga") via the smoke twirling out of the fire, similar to the incense practices described in Revelations 5:8 that symbolize "the prayers of saints." As for the primary theology, Sam Proctor continues, "In order for the blessings to come, everyone has to come in unity, with one heart, one mind, and one love. The ceremonial ground is supposed to be built on love, run by love, and all the activities are supposed to be done by love." Proctor adds, that based on his studies, the Bible and the ceremonial grounds have identical teachings where the two forms of worship are founded on the concept of love and humility.

While the traditional ceremonies and their accompanying songs and dances have been performed for thousands of years, when European missionaries first encountered the Muscogee people worshiping through the fire, the symbolism of the fire and its relationship to the Christian hell proved to be an immediate focal point for reducing paganism within the Muscogee people, along with the Christian concept of no one entering the kingdom of heaven but through Jesus. Compounding the problem is the contradictory nature of the Old and New Testaments. Traditional Muscogee people note the Bible itself claims in Ecclesiastes 3:1 "To every thing there is a season" and that includes "a time to dance" in Ecclesiastes 3:4. The Song of Solomon (2:12) also indicates that with the coming of spring "the voice of the turtle is heard in our land," which some traditionalists have interpreted as a reference the turtle shell rattles worn by women during the stomp dance, and provide further ancient connectedness between the two religions.

John Riley, a chairman at Hvtce Cvpv Baptist Church where he grew up, told the *Muscogee Nation News* in 1999: "They used to be like one. The stomp-grounds, they believe in God, they depended on him, just like the churches did. But they used the sacred medicine that was for the health of their bodies and the churches were for the spirit, so it was all one. But in this day and time, even the ministers that we are today, we kick at one another. I remember the older pastor, or minister, of our sister church across the river, Thlewarle. My mother used to tell me that when the pastor, who belonged to a certain stompground, used to fast,

John Riley

he would ask the church and get permission to go over there and use the medicine. They would let him go and he would fast and use the medicine. He didn't dance or anything, just use the medicine. After everything was over, he would report himself back in and they would take him back. He would get up there and lead the church."

Even so, the concept of including "paganism" in stern Christianity did not fit into the 18th and 19th century Christian visions of converting Muscogee people, which began largely in Georgia and Alabama when President George Washington appointed Benjamin Hawkins as the Indian superintendent of the Southeastern U.S. in 1796. Hawkins encouraged Creek leaders to allow Christian missionaries into Creek country. As a result, the missionary teachings and subsequent incorporation into the belief system by Muscogee Christians created divisions among Creek tribal towns, clans, and families that still exist today. Reverend James Wesley, a Kialegee Tribal Town elder and long time Creek minister, explained in a 1998 interview about the difficult transition for Creeks from the traditional religion to Christianity: "All they knew back in those days was God, and that is good, but they did not know Jesus, and Jesus is our savior and Lord. When the Christianity came in, many ceremonial grounds people went into Christianity, and many Indians suffered. My mother told me, that in 1868, or so, when she was a young girl, an old preacher from Alabama Church north of Weleetka, the oldest Creek church, would come and have a meeting at somebody's house, and tell them about the gospel. While they were there sometimes the ceremonial people would come, some drinking, and chase these people off. They didn't do nothing to the women, but they would catch the men and whip them for listening. It was that way because at that time they all believed in the fire, but when Christianity started to take place, the ceremonial ground people said, 'That's not yours. Yours is the ceremonial ground. That's for the white people.' But the Christian people kept meeting and finally overcame some of these things. They established churches through all this persecuting, but they really had to sacrifice to build some of those churches. Many Christian people were beat up pretty bad because they believed in the Lord and were getting away from the ceremonial ground." Given that history, one can easily see why deep-seated divisions still exist. Nonetheless, at least fourteen active Muscogee ceremonial grounds in the contemporary Muscogee (Creek) Nation of Oklahoma continue the stomp dance and ceremonial traditions of the Muscogee people. In addition, at the turn of the turn of the 21st century, the very active Muscogee ceremonial traditions that revolve around the stomp dance are slowly becoming an accepted social dance outside of the ceremonial environment.

Muscogee ministers, left to right: Dorsey Nero, Wilbur Hobia, Kenneth Fixico, Alec Buck, David Mitchell, Franklin Harjo, Sr., John "Wayne" Tulsa, Wallace Gambler, and Eugene Harjo.

Long featured as the concluding element of some powwows in northeastern Oklahoma such as the annual Copan Powwow hosted by the Eastern Delaware, stomp dances are now being held at universities, public schools, community centers, and armories. Diverse reasons for the dances include educational exhibitions, fundraisers for ceremonial grounds or other organizations, or substitute holiday activities for non-Christians or traditional people who do not celebrate "American" holidays. Dances give the people a place to come together to share their own values and traditions. Itself a point of controversy between traditionalists and "transitionalists," or those who are trying to preserve ancient traditions in contemporary times, the public, social stomp dance also provides an alternative to the pan-Indian powwow for descendants of the Southeastern tribes who have not been raised in the powwow world. As a result of the stomp dance's increasingly public nature, Indian House Records, founded in 1966 by Tony Isaacs and his wife, Ida, began releasing Muscogee stomp dances on cassette in 1969, the first of which is *Songs of the Muskogee Creek – Part I* (IH 3001). *Part I*, recorded May 2, 1969 in Seminole, features "Buffalo Dance," "Long Dance," and five stomp dances. Lead singers include Harry Bell, James Deere, Netche Gray, Frank Jackson, Tema Tiger, and David Wind. Shell shakers (women who wear turtle shell or milk can rattles on their legs) are Frances Deere, Stella Deere, Helen Tiger, and Eliza Wind. *Songs of the Muskogee Creek – Part 2* (IH 3002), recorded the same night and featuring the same singers and shell shakers, includes three stomp dances, a "Friendship Dance," "Gar Dance," "Guinea Dance," and "Morning Dance."

In 1978, Indian House released two more cassettes of stomp dances by Muscogee, Seminole, and Euchee singers and shell shakers. *Stomp Dance I: Muskogee, Seminole, Yuchi, Volumes I & II* (IH 3003 & 3004), feature twelve stomp dances between the two recordings made in Okemah, May 5, 1978. Lead singers are Jimmie Skeeter, Oscar Pigeon, Vernon D. Atkins, William M. Beaver, John McNac, and Harry Bell. Shell shakers for the recordings are Linda Alexander, Frances Cosar, Edna Deere, Caroline Harry, and Eliza Wind. New recordings of stomp dances released by Indian House in 1992 were *Stomp Dance – Volume 3 & 4* (IH 3005 & 3006), recorded in Bristow, March 8, 1991. *Volume 3* contains six stomp dances and a traditional introduction by Spencer A. Frank. Lead singers are Eugene Thomas, George McNac, Sam Watson, Tema Tiger, Ralph Gray, and Spencer A. Frank. Shell shakers are Linda Alexander, Wenona Bunny, and Chumona Harjo. Along with detailed liner notes to explain the various dances, *Volume 4* features a "Double-Header Dance" led by Spencer A. Frank and Tema Tiger, a "Garfish Dance" led by Spencer A. Frank, and stomp dances led by Gary Bucktrot, Sonny Bucktrot, Joe Sulphur, and Billy J. Scott. Shell shakers are the same as on *Volume 3.*

In the 1990s, Indian House released two more cassettes of Muscogee stomp dances and ceremonial songs. Recorded October 22, 1994, at the Tallahassee Ceremonial Grounds, then near Wetumka, *Tallahassee Ceremonial Ground of the Mvskoke Nation* (IH 3007) includes a "Peace Dance," an "Old Dance," and six stomp dances. Song leaders are John Proctor, Leon Bell, Jonas Harley, Eddie Lowe, Jimmy Gibson, and Thomas Yahola. By the following cassette's release, an expanded cultural sensitivity appeared on *Ceremonial Songs of the Muscogee* (IH 3008), recorded November 9, 1997 at the Tallahassee Ceremonial Ground. The words "stomp dance" do not appear anywhere but in the liner notes of the cassette: "The dances recorded in this album are often called 'stomp dance' in English, but since this name does not convey the real meaning of these dances, 'ceremonial dance' is preferred to be more accurate." Song leaders are from various ceremonial grounds: John Proctor (Tallahassee), Jimmy Gibson (Duck Creek), Eunice Hill (Nuyaka), Philip Deere (Nuyaka), Leon Bell (Tallahassee), Billy Joe "B.J." Jackson (Gar Creek), and Thomas Yahola (Tallahasee). Additional singers include Daniel Billie, Alfred Harley, Kelly Lowe, and Richard Williams. Shell shakers are Linda Alexander (who has appeared on Indian House stomp dance recordings since 1979), Frankie D'Ann Bell, Pat Bell, Marie BerryHill, Bonnie Gibson, Linda Grammer, Naomi Harjo, Shatota Harjo, Corina Lowe, Vivian Proctor, and Bertha Tilkens.

In 2000, Tony Isaacs and Indian House produced the first compact discs featuring only Muscogee stomp dances, *Stomp Dance Songs of the Muscogee Nation Vol. 1 & 2* (IH 3009 & 4000). Recorded at the Muscogee Nation Omniplex in Okmulgee, July 19, 1999, the two discs feature fourteen stomp dances reproduced beautifully by Isaacs' who by now has thirty years of experience recording stomp dances. Song leaders, with their home ceremonial grounds in parenthesis, include Wayland Gray (New Tulsa), Farron Culley (Okfuskee), Andy Butler (Peach Ground), Jimmy Gibson (Duck Creek), Russell Thompson (Nuyaka), Wendell Reschke (Peach Ground), Chapman Cloud (Nuyaka), Kevin Mack (Fish Pond), Roman Hill (Peach Ground), Vincent Butler (Kialegee), Darren Mack (Fish Pond), James Mosquito (Duck Creek), Joe Sulphur (Thlopthlocco), and Wesley Buter (Peach Ground). Shell shakers include the ageless Linda Alexander (New Tulsa), Alexis Crosley (New Tulsa), Irene Culley (Okfuskee), Lela Culley

(Okfuskee), Bonnie Gibson (New Tulsa), Lee Harjo (Green Leaf), Sharon Harjo (Green Leaf), Sheila Harjo (Green Leaf), Dora Hill (Muddy Waters), Joann Hill (Okfuskee), Ella Mack (Fish Pond), Judy Proctor (Peach Ground), Irene Thompson (Kialegee), and Bertha Tilkens (New Tulsa). One other "Creek Stomp Dance Song" has been released through the Oklahoma State Arts Council's *Songs of Indian Territory*, and includes leader Thomas Yahola and members of the Tulahassee Ceremonial Grounds, the most recorded group of stomp dance singers and dancers.

As a final element of significant interest to American music historians, the stomp dance's influence on the music of 18th and 19th century Muscogee slaves of African descent (or vice-versa) has yet to be fully detailed. For example, the "swinging" eighth notes of jazz are essentially the same rhythm of the Muscogee shell shakers during most of the stomp dances, and the call and response pattern of the dances is analogous to the basic blues and gospel patterns of African-Americans. Upon further study, if too much hasn't been lost in the hazy passing of time, significant alterations may be necessary in the overall story of American music's development in the Southeastern U.S., especially with regard to the African-American traditions of blues and jazz. Given those possibilities, the Muscogee stomp dances are not only important elements of traditional Muscogee lifeways, but may also exemplify deeper connections between American Indian and African-American music, which in turn may lead to reinterpretations of the origins and development of much of American popular music.

Muscogee shell shaker's turtle shell leg rattles.

The second most prominent form of Muscogee (Creek) musical expression is the Christian hymn tradition that has existed since before removal when both intermarriage and convincing missionaries introduced Christianity to Creek people via Superintendent Benjamin Hawkins' encouragement in the late 18th century. Perhaps in order to ease the transition from ceremonial traditions to Christian services, many connections (with multiple exceptions) were allowed and still exist between the more traditional Muscogee Baptist and Methodist churches and the older, traditional ways of the ceremonial grounds. For example, the number four plays prominently in both; "camps" are arranged in a circle around the center arbor or arbors; fasting is an important element for both religions; music is a core activity in both church services and ceremonials; the front church doors and the ceremonial arbor where the mekko (chief) sits both face east; men and women are segregated during services or ceremonies; humility is a primary teaching; and vnokéckv (pronounced roughly. "Uh-no-git-ska"), or "love" in English, is an intrinsic concept at both, as noted earlier by Sam Proctor.

However, most traditional Muscogee Christians forego any overt connections to the traditional ceremonial ways, as that would be contrary to Jesus's admonition in Matthew 6:24, that "no man can serve two masters: for either he will hate the one, and love the other; or else he will hold to the one, and despise the other." Another often quoted scripture by Muscogee preachers is John 14:6, where Jesus declares, "I am the way, the truth, and the life: no man cometh to the father but by me." With that as fuel, the argument has raged for two centuries now about whether or not a person can be traditional Creek and/or Christian, or even whether an Indian ceases to be Indian when they become Christian.

Blown four times, a conch shell or a steer's horn is used to call worshippers into service at some Muscogee Baptist churches. These horns are from Hvtce Cvpv Baptist Church.

Reverend Wesley did acknowledge that positive things do take place during the ceremonies: "At the ceremonial grounds, at the end of the main dance, the spokesman of the grounds would get up and tell people to have love toward one another, tell people to take care of their children and families, and to not commit adultery. There were some good things that came out of the ceremonial grounds and some good things that came out of the church. But years ago, a Christian man would go to the ceremonial ground and it was a sin, because they don't sing hymns, preach, don't pray, and don't know Jesus. The ceremonial ground is for the physical side, because that's where you clean yourself for the next year, but the church is for the spiritual side. For that reason, the Christian people were not allowed to go to the grounds. But today, it seems like there is no sin anymore. A lot of Christians go out there now. They say, 'I'm just going out to there look. I'm going out to observe,' so that kind of gives them an excuse. We don't have what we used to call sin anymore."

As a final note on the conflict between the two Muscogee spiritual ways of life, the complete commitment necessary to one or the other is often one of the primary barriers between maintaining traditional and Christian sensibilities, although some contemporary Muscogee people are trying to balance the two. Additionally, as separate areas of cultural interest, the ceremonial ground activities contain words, theological concepts, and songs that are not part of the Christian services, and vice-versa. For example, Hesáketvmesé (pron. Heesáhgidimeseé), or "Giver of Breath," is the word used for God at the churches, whereas, the previously mentioned Ofvnkv, or "overseer," is used for the creator at the ceremonial grounds. In *Sacred Path*, Chadhuri explains an important relationship exists between the two entities in Muscogee history, with Hesáketvmesé being a helper of sorts to Ofvnkv, which in turn may have made the acceptance of the term easier for early Muscogee Christians since it was already part of the belief system.

Obviously, the connections and differences between the two Muscogee religious perspectives are extensively complicated, and could use more explanation for the benefit of all from a Muscogee point of view, but are ultimately beyond the scope of this essay.

Contemporarily, some of the more rural Muscogee Baptist churches maintain musical traditions linked not only to the 18th century Anglo missionaries, and 19th century rural Southern Baptists, but also to the 18th and 19th centuries when the Muscogee people owned slaves of African descent. When the tribes were removed to Indian Territory the slaves came with them and often the slaves could speak both Muscogee and English. As a result, some slaves became the first interpreters and preachers in Indian Territory and preached to mixed audiences. The first Baptist Church in Oklahoma, established in 1832 by a cooperative congregation of black, white, and Creek people near the north bank of the Arkansas River near Muskogee, illustrates this cross-cultural environment that led to the evolution of Muscogee hymns. As slaves of African descent began to separate from their tribal owners, the Muscogee Christians maintained some of the older styles of singing African-American hymns and spirituals intermingled with common American Indian musical qualities of sliding pitches and the use of microtones. Therefore, today in rural Muscogee Baptist churches one may hear uptempo Baptist hymns in Muscogee and English, middle-tempo Methodist hymns in Muscogee and English, and the very slow and solemn spiritual hymns reflective of 19th century African-American slaves. Interestingly, these hymns are not heard in Oklahoma's African-American rural churches. Therefore, the rural Muscogee Baptists appear to be the contemporary stewards of centuries-old African-hymn styles in the United States, and at the same time exhibit the aforementioned oft-overlooked contributions of Muscogee musical styles to the development of African-American music styles of the Southeastern U.S. Nonetheless, Muscogee hymns can be said to be tri-cultural in the least, as the lyrics display both Christian concepts, the songs exhibit both Anglo and African hymn styles, and they are sung in the Muscogee language. Finally, the Muscogee hymns also include some of the previously mentioned generalized qualities of American Indian music that can waiver in between the accepted tones of Western music, often allowing for several sliding tones on just one syllable of text much like jazz and blues, and are often sung in either B flat or B flat minor, keys that appear frequently in African-American blues and jazz.

Recordings of Muscogee hymns are not as widely available as stomp dances. While sometimes found on compilations, such as the earlier noted Library of Congress recording, and the State Arts Council of Oklahoma's 1989 release, *Songs of Indian Territory*, on which George Bunny leads Thlewarle Indian Baptist Church in "Must This Body Die," Muscogee hymns are best heard in the churches where they are maintained. Tantalizing clues to the form's origin can be found on the Smithsonian Folkways compilation, *Classic Mountain Songs* (SFW CD 40094). Sung by The Indian Bottom Association of the Defeated Creek Church in

Linefork, Kentucky in 1997, "I am a Poor Pilgrim of Sorrow" exhibits the singing style of the Old Regular Baptist denomination that obviously had an impact on Muscogee hymn traditions prior to removal to Indian Territory. The song is a little faster than the Muscogee hymns, which are often slow and mournful, but still uses the "lining out" method of a singer starting individual lines with the congregation following, and has no instrumental accompaniment. A subtle difference exists in Muscogee hymns in that the leader does not sing a whole line with the congregation responding, but the congregation quickly joins in once the line has started. Also "I am a Poor Pilgrim of Sorrow" has strong melodic similarities to the first hymn in all Muscogee hymnals, "Hesáketvméset Likes," or "God, Our Creator and Preserver." Muscogee hymnals have no written music in them, only words. A singer must learn the melodies by the oral tradition and then apply the text, which can be typically found quickly by looking up the first few words of the song introduced by the singer. No song leader in a traditional Creek church says, "Now turn your hymnals to page so and so." People just have to learn the songs and/or learn how to look them up in a hymnal once the song has been introduced.

Some small churches have released their own recordings of Muscogee hymns. In 1972, the Witt Memorial Indian United Methodist Church of Tulsa, founded in 1945, released two albums on vinyl of traditional Indian hymns that are now out-of-print. While not all of the songs or singers are Muscogee, *Volume I* includes two Creek-Seminole hymns, "Song of Hope" and "Help Me to Pray," and *Volume II* includes perhaps the best-known Creek hymn, "Heleluyvn," as well as "Hvlwen Heckvyofvn" (High where I am born"), and "Lord, Dismiss Us." Slightly more accessible are the two cassettes released by Salt Creek Methodist Church, recorded March 20 and 21, 1998. Available through Long and Scott Recordings based in Oklahoma City and Tuscon, *Yvhiketv Vhecicvlke* (The Song Keepers) *Volume 1 & 2* preserves nearly forty Muscogee hymns in the Methodist tradition with some insightful commentary on the recordings of the hymns' history. Singers on *Volume 1* include Harry Long, Kenneth Fixico, Leonard J. Harjo, Amilia Deer, Molly Brown, and Imogene Harjo. Singers on *Volume 2* include Melissa Deer, Lizzie Bruner, Bessie Fixico, Amilia Deer, Imogene Harjo, Bessie Spencer, Molly Brown, Lora Ann Beaver, Semarian Fixico, Juanita Harjo, Harry Long, Leonard Harjo, and Kenneth Fixico. Finally, Canyon Records has released *Hymns in Creek* (CR-611) by the American Indian Hymn Singers.

While the music of Muscogee hymns provides all kinds of fodder for conversation about origins and influences, the texts of the hymns offer ample opportunity for understanding the way in which Creek Christian music records both tribal experience and spiritual expectation. While several hymnals exist in the Muscogee language, *Nakcokv Esyvhiketv* (*Song Book*), a hymnal translated by George Bunny, Woodrow Haney, Rev. James Wesley, and Morina Wildcat, provides non-speakers an interlinear translation of the songs wherein a lot can be learned about Muscogee Christianity, the general spirituality of Muscogee people, and how music provides both a vehicle for memory, celebration, and mourning for Muscogee Christians.

With a clear link and opposition to the Muscogee traditional ceremonial ways that revolve around the taking of medicine for health and spiritual reasons, "Vc oh Vtes, Cv Kicetskes" ("Just as I am, without one plea") alludes to "the spirit's medicine." One can also relate a double meaning to many hymns that refer to a hard journey, or otherwise represent the removal of Creeks to Indian Territory, while at the same time representing the Christian spiritual journey from this world to heaven. "Cesvs em Vhakvn Pohis" ("Christian Triumph") refers to land that has been appointed for the singer, and after wickedness has been overcome, the singer will go and see that land. "Yvmv Estemerketvn" explains that "Here suffering, I pass." When sung, the song slows to a trudge in the repetition of "Tehoyvnvof," or "I pass, I pass," before eventually getting to the "Elkv Hvtcen," or death river, thought of as either the metaphorical river of death and/or the literal Mississippi River or other rivers the Muscogee people crossed or otherwise died on during the removal period. A final example can be found in the Christian dismissal song, "Ce Mekusapeyvte," in which the lyrics plainly explain the thoughts of Christian Creeks on the "Long Walk" to Indian Territory: "Mohmen yvmv ekvnv, En kvpvkakeyofvt, Cen liketvn roricet, Fekvpetvn pu 'yaces" or "Now here land, We leave, Your place when we arrive, Rest we want."

Aside from the ceremonial songs and Christian hymns, Muscogee people have made significant contributions to popular music, jazz, country, and to intertribal powwow singing. Country music star Hank Williams is said to have had Creek blood, and was inducted as such into the Native American Music Awards Hall of Fame. Jim Pepper (Kaw/Muscogee) successfully merged American Indian traditional music with jazz, most notably his "Witchi Tai To" which hit both the Top 40 and jazz charts in 1969. Pepper was born in June 18, 1941 in Portland, Oregon, where he also died February 10, 1992, but he reportedly spent part of his youth in Oklahoma, the extent of which has yet to be determined, as is what impact it may have had on his significant jazz career. A documentary video, *Pepper's Powwow* (Upstream Productions, 1995), shows the Kaw Powwow near Kaw City, and features Pepper explaining his connections to Native American music that apparently lean toward the music of the Kaw and other Plains traditions, not the Muscogee (Creek).

Mostly noted for her award-winning poetry, Joy Harjo (b. Tulsa, 1951) has also released two albums of music with her own spoken word poetry, singing, and alto and soprano saxophone work. Performing with the genre-busting band, Poetic Justice, *Letter from the End of the Twentieth Century* (Silver Wave, 1997), combines rock, jazz, and multiple American Indian tribal music elements with Harjo's powerful poetry delivered with the confidence of someone who has given a thousand public readings of her work. Nominated for eight Native American Music Awards, and given the 1998 Outstanding Musical Achievement Award by the First Americans in the Arts, *Letter from the End of the Century* is an atmospheric, multi-styled musical album whose strength lies in the poems from Harjo's books: *She Had Some Horses* (Thunder's Mouth, 1983); *Secrets from the Center of the World* (University of Arizona, 1989); *In Mad Love and War* (Wesleyan University, 1990); and *The Woman Who Fell from the Sky* (Norton, 1994). While her poetry, and, therefore, the lyrics to her songs on *Letter from the End of the Century*, explores American Indian and world indigenous themes, Harjo only mentions being Muscogee once, in "Fear Poem." She also acknowledges her ceremonial participation in the album's title track, wherein she is haunted by a story she heard from a taxi driver that haunts her "from Tallahassee Grounds to Chicago, to my home near the Rio Grande."

In March, 2003, Joy Harjo received the Arrell Gibson Lifetime Achievement Award at the annual Oklahoma Book Awards, and the poetry award for her book *How We Became Human: New and Selected Poems* (Norton, 2002). Currently a professor at UCLA, Harjo planned to release her second album, *Native Joy*, on her own independent label, Mekko Records, in the summer of 2003. While the CD will feature her alto and soprano saxophone work, she also be sings for the first time on record, whereas, up to this point she has relied on her spoken poetry performance skills. According to Harjo, "I'm incorporating Mvskokean elements in it. My favorite tune is called 'Eagle Song,' and part of it is in the Mvskoke language." Helping Harjo translate some of the lyrics were elder traditionalist, Linda Alexander, and Ted Isham, Mvskoke language specialist and curator of the Creek Council House Museum in Okmulgee.

Joy Harjo

Also gaining popularity fast is Muscogee rapper Julian B! who was born Julian B. Watson, September 26, 1970 in Okmulgee. A member of the Bear Clan, Julian has lived in South America, Colorado, and now Dewar, Oklahoma. He worked with the **GAP Band** in 1990, and has performed at the Apache Nation Unite concert, the American Indian Movement's anniversary celebrations, the Montreux Jazz Festival, the Denver March Powwow, and various universities, festivals, and Native gatherings around the country. Nominated for a Native American Music Award for Best Rap Artist in 1998, Julian B! has two albums, *Once Upon a Genocide* (Warrior, 1994), and

Injunuity (Hot Commodity, 2002), with all songs written, produced, and "injuneered" by Julian B! Both albums feature a rebellious, yet insightful, Native lyrical stance supported by slinky dance beats, and Julian B!'s vocals range closer to soul than most hip hop.

Julian B!'s lyrics are deeply interwoven with the Muscogee identity, mentioning the Muscogee Nation and making "a ritual out of being humble" in "Revolution." Julian also ties his songs back to the previously mentioned concepts of love from both the Muscgoee Christian church and ceremonial grounds when he sings, "Vnokéckv" (love) in "Mother Earth." Additionally, the young rapper's music expresses a lot of things Indian people have been talking about for years, but have never had put to music. "My Moccasins" discusses the Bureau of Indian Affairs, living in a racist society, and otherwise trying to maintain a spiritual outlook in the face of general societal apathy toward American Indians.

Julian B!

Nominated as Best Rap/Hip Hop Recording at the 2002 Native American Music Awards, *Injunuity* as a whole is a much better than average rap album due to its use of additional smooth vocalists, horn riffs, harmonicas, and guest rappers like Shadowyze and Physics. The lyrics will be especially insightful to Muscogee citizens, and others who are generally aware of such insider Indian commentary as "Uncle Tomahawks," the history behind "Free Peltier," and the dangers of embracing non-Indian society ("Don't be Dancin' Wit Wolves in Sheep's Clothing"). By late 2002, Julian worked with Lord Tim Hinkley (The Who, The Rolling Stones, et al.) on new recordings, and in 2003 had made two videos to promote *Injunuity*.

Along with rap and jazz-fusion, several Muscogee musicians have taken the musical direction pointed out by the blues. Of course, guitarist **Jesse Ed Davis** (Kiowa/Comanche/Muscogee) made a strong impact on 1970s popular music specifically due to his ability to play bottleneck blues guitar. Obie Sullivan was a long-time keyboardist for the American Indian blues band, Blues Nation. Lead singer Vic Gutierrez of blues group Smilin' Vic and the Soul Monkeys is Muscogee/Euchee, and guitarist Chebon Tiger has been leading his own blues band since 1998. In the realm of country music, twelve-year-old Muscogee citizen Taylor Osborn won vocalist of the year in her age category at the 2003 North American Country Music Association's international competition at Pigeon Forge, Tennessee. Competing in the traditional country category, she sang "Blue" and "Walkin' After Midnight" to take the top honors. Also, guitarist Katie Thomas Smith from Coweta, ninety-one in 2003, was inducted in the Bluegrass Hall of Fame in 2002.

Finally, Muscogee musicians have also made notable contributions to contemporary music of the powwow arena. Three brothers, Wayne Coser (b. Okmulgee), George Coser, Jr. (b. Tulsa), and Peter G. Coser (b. Okmulgee), have been members of the intertribal Redland Singers since the early 1970s, a drum group noted for being the very first to bring the high-pitched style of northern powwow singing to Oklahoma. Pete joined Redlands in 1973 and his two brothers, who had been singing with the Brave Scout Singers, followed shortly thereafter. Subsequently, Pete Coser's son, Pete "Petey" Robert George Coser, began singing with the Redland Singers as a youngster, and currently is a member of Thunderhorse, a northern style group with two albums on the Arbor label, *Riding the Storm* (AR-113820) and *Native America* (AR-11592). In the southern singing style genre, G.C. Tsouhlarakis (Muscogee/Navajo) and Sam Cook (Muscogee/Pawnee) have recorded for Canyon Records with the Grammy-nominated drum group, **Young Bird**.

Given the extremely diverse history of music in the Muscogee (Creek) Nation and among its people, one can learn a lot in a short amount of time at the Annual Creek Nation Festival and Rodeo held the third weekend of June of each year. Along with the rodeo and softball and track tournaments, the annual festival always features a gospel concert and exhibition stomp dance, but also includes American Indian popular and country music artists of national stature, as well as an intertribal powwow. (HF)

www.muscogeenation-nsn.gov
www.canyonrecords.com   www.arborrecords.com
www.indianhouse.com
w w w . c o w b o y . n e t / n a t i v e / r e d l a n d /
www.joyharjo.com

*Dr. Pete Coser(left) sings with Tony Arkeketa (**Ponca**/Otoe) in the Redland Singers.*

Nevaquaya, "Doc" Tate
(b. July 3, 1932 – d. March 5, 1996)

Widely known as an award-winning artist who depicted many traditional elements of his native Comanche life and heritage, Doc Tate Nevaquaya is also generally credited with reviving the traditional American Indian flute in the 1970s, and inspiring a generation of new players, including **Andrew Vasquez**, R. Carlos Nakai, Kevin Locke, and Tom Mauchahty Ware. Born as Joyce Lee Tate Nevaquaya in Apache, Oklahoma, "Doc" replaced "Joyce" due to his close friendship with Dr. C. W. Joyce. When Doc entered Fort Sill Indian School and was required to have a Christian name, the family arrived at Tate via a friend of Doc's grandfather's. Nevaquaya's parents died eight months apart when he was thirteen, and he moved in with grandparents where he listened to their stories, and began drawing landscapes of the Wichita Mountains.

Self-taught because he did not want to be told what to do in art classes at the Indian school, he began painting professionally in 1958. His paintings have been exhibited extensively throughout the United States, and purchased by Queen Elizabeth II, as well as such important institutional collections as the Smithsonian Institution, San Francisco Museum of Modern Art, the Metropolitan Museum in New York City, the Philbrook Museum of Art in Tulsa, and the Gilcrease Institute of American History and Art in Tulsa. While curious about the flute in his youth, Nevaquaya became increasingly interested in the 1960s when noted American Indian flute expert Richard W. Payne, M.D., of Oklahoma City, gave Doc Tate a traditional plains flute in 1967 as a trade for some artwork. Along with learning a tremendous amount from Dr. Payne, the flute inspired Nevaquaya to pursue remaining elder Comanche and other Plains flute players, and travel to the Smithsonian Institution and Library of Congress to listen to older American Indian flute recordings and study their flute collections. By 1975, he was well known in non-Indian music circles for his playing abilities and shared the stage with Freddy Fender, Mel Tillis, and **Roy Clark** at the Roy Clark Ranch in Tulsa. He also performed with Loretta Lynn, Sammy Davis, Jr., and Wayne Newton. In 1976, he recorded *Indian Flute Songs from Comanche Land*, the first modern commercial recording consisting entirely of American Indian flute music, and *Comanche Flute Music* (1979), now available through Smithsonian Folkways Records.

Perhaps the best-known contemporary American Indian flutist, R. Carlos Nakai, has said on his website, "When I began in the early 1970's the sum total of indigenous native flute players were "Doc" Tate Nevaquaya, Tom Mauchahty Ware, and

Woodrow Haney, Sr. There were no others." Interestingly, all three of those players are native Oklahomans.

With his releases in the 1970s, Doc Tate furthered the repertoire for the American Indian flute by innovative use of melodies borrowed from traditionally vocal genres, such as war dance songs, victory songs, social dance songs, and Christian hymns. His notoriety carried him on tours of Asia in the 1970s, and multiple national television appearances on CBS with Charles Kuralt, and on ABC's *Good Morning America*. In 1982 Doc Tate performed for the "Night of the First Americans" at the Kennedy Center for the Performing Arts in Washington, DC, and in 1986, he became the first American Indian to receive the National Endowment for the Arts Heritage Award, which recognized his contribution to Native American art forms and revival of the American Indian flute. He performed at the United Nations in New York City in 1988, and opened the archery competition at the 1989 U.S. Olympic Festival in Norman, Oklahoma with a flute song.

Named a "Living Legend" along with six other American Indian artists, he performed at Carnegie Hall in New York in 1990, and he composed the song "Flight in Spirit" for the Oklahoma Arts Council in 1991 to honor the five famous American Indian ballerinas from Oklahoma. In 1992, he recorded another definitive album for Riversong Soundworks, *The Master*, including original songs and his trademark adaptations of traditional music. From 1992 through 1995, he served in a variety of advisory and board positions, continued his performance-lectures, and received multiple national and statewide awards for his art and music, culminating in a "National Living Treasure" award in 1995 by the state of Oklahoma. Although he died in 1996, footage of Doc Tate playing the flute and talking about its origins appeared posthumously in *Songkeepers* (1998), a video documentary about the history of the flute in American Indian music. *Songkeepers* also features Doc's eldest son, Sonny Nevaquaya (b. Apache, OK), who began playing and recording flute professionally in 1993 when he released *Spirit of the Flute*. In 1998 the younger Nevaquaya released *Viva Kokopelli!*, which blends contemporary instruments with traditional flute.

In 2000, the Red Earth Festival and Museum in Oklahoma City sponsored a major exhibit designed to interpret Doc Tate's life, *In the Realm of the Thirteen Feathers*, and 2001 saw the release by Sonny Nevaquaya of *Doc Tate Nevaquaya – Legend and Legacy*, with songs from Doc Tate as well as four of his five sons who play and make flutes as they were taught by him. He and his wife, Charlotte, also had four daughters. In 2002, Dr. Paula Conlon, of Norman, Oklahoma, announced on her website she was under contract to produce a biography of Nevaquaya that will focus on his contributions to the flute from the various perspectives of his family, friends, and colleagues. The biography will examine Doc Tate's impact on the history and development of Native American flute in the 20th century. Upon his death in 1996, he was survived by his wife, Charlotte, their nine children, seventeen grandchildren, and one great-granddaughter. (HF)

Nolen, Jimmy
(b. April 3, 1934 – d. December 18, 1983)

Although born in Oklahoma City, the father of funk guitar, Jimmy Nolen, grew up with his nine brothers and sisters on a farm close to Wealaka, Oklahoma, where he began playing violin at age nine. Not getting proficient enough for his satisfaction, Nolen bought an acoustic guitar when he was fourteen and began teaching himself how to play by listening to blues on the radio, especially T-Bone Walker and **Lowell Fulson**. At eighteen, he picked up his first electric guitar while living with a sister in Wichita, Kansas, and began playing with J.D. Nicholson and His Jivin' Five with whom Jimmy first recorded in 1952.

In 1955, blues singer Jimmy Wilson came upon Nolen playing at a club in Tulsa and hired him to go on the road with him nationally, which Nolen did until the group broke up in Los Angeles in 1956. An imposing figure at 6'4", Nolen settled in L.A. where he joined trumpeter Monte Easton's band, recorded some long out-of-print singles with Jimmy Wilson and Ray Agee, and also worked and recorded with Chuck Higgins, a popular R&B saxophonist from southern California. Nolen's first national exposure came in 1957 when he began playing and recording with Johnny Otis, and contributed guitar to Otis's "Willie and the Hand Jive," a major hit in 1958. Nolen also made several recordings under his own name in the late 1950s and early 1960s for Federal, Elko, and Imperial Records, but none surfaced as hits. A good compilation, *Honky Tonk!*, on the UK label Ace, features 24 rare tracks from Federal and King records. All the instrumental R&B tracks were recorded between 1948 and 1964, and Nolen is included with Freddy King, Johnny "Guitar" Watson, and King Curtis.

After leaving Otis in the early 1960s, Nolen formed his own nine-piece group and backed up famous blues men who came to L.A. and needed a band, such as B.B. King. He and his band played constantly throughout the smaller clubs and ballrooms in the African-American communities of California in the early 1960s. In 1965, Nolen accepted James Brown's offer to join the Godfather of Soul on tour. One of Nolen's former sidemen, tenor saxophonist L.D. Williams, recommended Jimmy to James Brown, and Nolen made an instant and eternal impact with his ringing dominant 9th chords, now universally known as funk chords, first on Brown's hit "Papa's Got a Brand New Bag" (1965), but even more dramatically on "I Got You (I Feel Good)" (1966), and "It's a Man's, Man's, Man's World" (1966). While the same chords had long been used in jazz, Nolen's rhythm guitar on songs such as "Cold Sweat" and "I Got the Feelin'" set the standard for all future guitarists who would attempt the funk form. While known as the guitar style known as "chicken scratch" by guitarists, the form became widely accepted as the benchmark example for funk guitar, exemplified by a "chucka-chucka" rhythm, or funky "scratches" followed by chords, or a combination of both.

Nolen and his band mates are also roundly given credit for converting the soul music of the 1960s into funk, but Brown never gave the musicians credit on any album, and rarely in concert. Nevertheless, Nolen's guitar work appears on all of Brown's records of the period, including *Sings Raw Soul* (1967), *Live at the Apollo Vol. 2* (1968), *Say It Loud, I'm Black and I'm Proud* (1969). Brown's stern leadership, to include a full-length set rehearsal before James arrived in the hall for two shows a night, caused Nolen and the group to walk out in 1969. Led by saxophonist Maceo Parker, the musicians formed All The King's Men and played throughout California until 1972, when most of the musicians, including Nolen, returned to Brown's camp as the "J.B.'s." Along with serving as James Brown's backing band for live performances and recording sessions on *Get on the Good Foot* (1972), *Payback* (1973), and *Hell: The Payback* (1974), the J.B.'s recorded five albums under their own name from 1972 to 1975 while Nolen was in the group, to include *Damn Right I'm Somebody* (1974).

Jimmy continued playing his trademark and revolutionary style with Brown until 1983 when the big man from Oklahoma City and Wealaka had a fatal heart attack at home in Atlanta, Georgia. After Nolen's death, his recordings with Brown and as a solo instrumentalist continued resurfacing on compilations through 2003. Along with several James Brown reissues and compilations, Nolen could be found on Ace UK import compilations *Dapper Cats, Groovy Tunes, and Hot Guitars* (1992), and *Dig These Blues: The Legendary Dig Masters* (1992). Credited with popularizing the "chicken scratch" guitar style through James Brown records that sold millions, Jimmy Nolen was inducted into the Oklahoma Jazz Hall of Fame in 1996 for his extremely significant contribution to American popular music. (HF)

Norma Jean
(b. January 30, 1948)

Best remembered as "Pretty Miss Norma Jean," Porter Wagoner's singing partner on his television show from 1960 to 1967, Norma Jean Beasler was born in a little farmhouse to a poor family near Wellston, Oklahoma, a town of roughly 1,000 residents northeast of Oklahoma City. Her family moved to Oklahoma City when Norma Jean was five, and she soon traded her bicycle for a guitar. Taking lessons from her aunt who was a skilled guitarist, Norma Jean debuted on KLPR radio in Oklahoma City at age twelve singing "If Teardrops Were Pennies," which resulted in her own show three times a week, and a long lasting friendship with **Wanda**

Jackson, another future Oklahoma music star, who was also performing on the same station. While in high school she toured with Oklahoma Western swing bands led by Billy Gray, Merl Lindsay, especially at his Lindsay Land Ballroom in Oklahoma City, and Leon McAuliffe. She also performed on the *Jude and Jody Show*, a weekly television program on WKY in Oklahoma City.

With several years of local radio and television experience and the assistance of Wanda Jackson, Norma Jean Beasler was invited in 1958 to join the cast of the *Ozark Jubilee*, an ABC television show broadcast from Springfield, Missouri. Red Foley, host of the series, requested that she shorten her name to "Norma Jean." It was also here in Springfield that she met Porter Wagoner, a regular on the *Ozark Jubilee*. She signed a contract with Columbia in 1959 and recorded ten songs, none of which were hits.

In 1960, Norma Jean left the *Ozark Jubilee* and headed to Nashville where she joined the Porter Wagoner touring group and syndicated television show as his singing partner.

With considerable exposure on television and under the tutelage of Chet Atkins, she signed with RCA Victor for which she made twenty-seven albums during her recording career with them from 1963 to 1973. After performing the song on the Porter Wagoner Show, Norma Jean's "Let's Go All the Way," released in 1964, peaked in the Top 15 of the country charts. She followed with "I'm a Walkin' Advertisement (For the Blues)" and "Put Your Arms Around Her," both Top 40 hits. She joined the rockabilly movement, partially influenced by the success of Wanda Jackson, with "Go Cat Go," released in 1964. It became a Top 10 hit, remaining on the country charts for four months, and crossing-over to the lower echelon of the pop charts. Based on these early recording successes, she was invited to join the Grand Ole Opry cast in 1965. In the same year, she released "I Cried All the Way to the Bank" and "I Wouldn't Buy a Used Car from Him," which became of Top 10 hit. Her most successful singles in 1966 were "The Shirt," "Pursuing Happiness," and "The Game of Triangles." The latter was a trio with Bobby Bare and Liz Anderson and was nominated for a Grammy. It became Norma Jean's biggest selling record and went Top 5 on the country charts.

During her tenure with Porter Wagoner, Norma Jean became romantically involved with him, who at the time was separated from his wife. The romantic affair resulted in Norma Jean's departure from the Porter Wagoner Show in 1967.

The break-up did not affect Norma Jean's career as she continued to perform on the Grand Ole Opry and record with RCA. In early 1967 she scored a Top 25 hit with "Don't Let That Doorknob Hit You," and later that year, released "Heaven Help the Working Girl (In a World That's Run by Men)," a Top 20 hit that made a statement for the emerging feminist movement. Also in 1967 she recorded *Norma Jean Sings: A Tribute to Kitty Wells*, an album dedicated to her life-long role model. In 1968, she recorded "Truck Drivin' Woman," one of the first female-oriented truck driving songs. One of the best albums reflecting her poverty-stricken background was the 1972 *I Guess that Comes From Being Poor*, including such tracks as "Hundred Dollar Funeral," "There Won't Be Any Patches in Heaven," and "The Lord Must Have Loved Poor Folks (He Made So Many of Them)."

Following the Porter Wagoner affair, in the late 1960s she married Jody Taylor of the popular *Jude and Jody Show* on Oklahoma City television, and returned to her Oklahoma roots, while commuting to the Opry and remaining with RCA until 1973. Her last albums for RCA were *Love's A Woman's Job* (1968), *The Best of Norma Jean* (1969), *Another Man Loved Me Last Night* (1970), *It Wasn't God Who Made Honky Tonk Angels* (1971), *Norma Jean Sings: A Tribute to Hank Cochran* (1971), and *It's Time for Norma Jean* (1971). Less active in Oklahoma, Norma Jean released *Norma Jean*, a Bear Family Records album in 1978, but returned to Nashville in 1984 to record *Pretty Miss Norma Jean* for Roma, a label named after her only daughter. In 1999, Collector's Choice music released *The Best of Norma Jean*, the only CD of her music currently in print.

After Norma Jean and Jody Taylor divorced in 1982, she married long-time country music front man George Riddle in 1990. She has remained active in R.O.P.E. (Reunion of Professional Entertainers) organization, and since 2000, has performed with **Jean Shepard**, another native Oklahoman, Jan Howard, Helen Cornelius, Margo Smith, and Leona Williams in The Grand Ladies of Country Show in Branson, while working on her autobiography, *All the Way and Back*. She is currently working on a country/gospel show with The Hortons in Branson, and recently returned to her home state to perform at a Tulsa concert associated with the release of a new book entitled *Distinguished Oklahomans*, which included a chapter on her. In August 2003, she performed with Porter Wagoner for the first time since the early 1980s. (GC)

www.prettymissnormajean.com

Nunn, Gary P.
(b. December 4, 1945)

Composer of "London Homesick Blues" better known as "Home With the Armadillo," the theme song of the long-running PBS show, *Austin City Limits*, for the past two decades, singer, songwriter and guitarist, Gary P. Nunn was born in Okmulgee, a community of roughly 14,000 residents almost due south of Tulsa. Nunn's musical career started in Brownfield, Texas, as member of a garage band. Following high school graduation in Brownfield, where he was an honor student and athlete, he completed courses at Texas Tech University and South Plains College, and played in a 1960s rock band, The Fabulous Sparkles. In 1968 he transferred to the University of Texas to pursue a pharmacy degree, while participating in the vibrant local music scene in Austin.

By the early 1970s, Austin was the center for a new movement in country music, often referred to as "outlaw country," "progressive country," or "redneck rock." Gary was soon involved in this new wave of country by playing bass for the likes of Willie Nelson, Michael Martin Murphey, and Jerry Jeff Walker, three pioneers in the genre. By 1973, Nunn was leading The Lost Gonzo Band, the back-up group for Walker. The high point for Nunn in 1973 was when Walker allowed Nunn to sing lead vocals on the "London Homesick Blues" track for the monumentally successful *Viva Terlingua!* album recorded in the small town of Luckenbach, Texas, which featured **Ray Wylie Hubbard**'s "Up Against the Wall, Redneck Mother." Gary played keyboards and sang back-up vocals on three additional Walker albums, including *Ridin' High* (1975), *It's A Good Night for Singin'* (1976), and *Man Must Carry On* (1977). Gary was also honing his writing skills at this time, and his songs were recorded by several artists, including David Allen Coe, another one of the "outlaw country" leaders, Roseanne Cash, as well as Walker, Murphey, and Nelson.

During this time, Nunn's Lost Gonzo Band also recorded a self-titled album in 1975 followed by *Loose & On My Way* (1975), *Thrills* (1976), and *Signs of Life* (1978); all on the Capitol label. But in 1980, the Lost Gonzo Band called it quits, and Gary went out on his own. He also began writing songs with his singer-songwriter wife, Karen Brooks, and their songs often reflected their relationship, such as "Couldn't Do Nothin' Right," by Karen, and "Kara Lee," by Gary.

A string of albums beginning with two live performances in 1979 and 1980, when Gary was featured on two albums of various artists recorded at the Kerrville Folk Festival in Kerrville, Texas. These were followed by *Nobody But Me* (1980), *Home With the Armadillo* (1984), *Border States* (1987), *For Old Times Sake* (9189), *Live at Poor David's* (1992), *Totally Guacamole* (1993), *Roadtrip* (1994), *Under My Hat* (1996), *What I Like About Texas* (1997), *It's a Texas Thing* (2000), and *Greatest Hits: Live from Mingus, Texas* (2001), several of which were issued by Campfire Records, a independent label out of San Antonio.

In 1985, Nunn was designated by Mark White, governor of Texas, as the state's Official Ambassador to the World. In 1990, he was presented an Award of Appreciation by the San Antonio chapter of the Texas Music Association, followed by his inclusion on the list of Lone Star Greats by the Texas Department of Commerce and Tourism. In 1991, Gary was given a Citation of Recognition by the Oklahoma House of Representatives for his preservation of Southwestern music and, in 1995, was placed in the West Texas Walk of Fame in Lubbock.

According to his official website, Nunn performs throughout Texas and the Southwest with his band, The Sons of the Bunkhouse, almost year round with dates scheduled for 2002 in such venues as the Luckenbach Dancehall in Luckenbach, Texas, White Elephant Saloon in Fort Worth, and Blanco's in Houston. He has returned to Oklahoma and operates an 800-acre cattle ranch (A-O Ranch) near Hanna in eastern Oklahoma (north of McAlester), or the "northern frontier," as Gary calls it. His ranch is the site of the annual Terlingua North Summer Social Maverick Chili Cookoff and Music Festival.

Since returning to Oklahoma, Gary has been instrumental in helping young country music talent, such as the Stillwater-based band **The Great Divide**, find gigs in Oklahoma and Texas. Nunn always invites his audiences to sing along on the "Go Home with the Armadillo" song. Being stranded in 1973 in London, where he wrote "London Homesick Blues," has paid rich dividends for this native Oklahoman. (GC)

www.garypnunn.com

O'Dell, Kenny
(b. early 1940s)

One of the most celebrated composers of the 1970s and 1980s, especially songs such as "Behind Closed Doors" and "Mama He's Crazy," Kenneth Gist, Jr. was born in Oklahoma. He began writing songs as a teenager, and following high school, he formed his own Mar-Kay record label in California. In the early 1960s, he recorded a self-penned song, "Old Time Love." While on the West Coast, he worked briefly with Duane Eddy, and then formed his own group called Guys and Dolls, which toured for about five years.

In 1967, Kenny wrote and recorded "Beautiful People," which was later recorded by Bobby Vee, with both versions cracking the pop chart Top 40. It was the title song of his first album in 1968 on the Vegas label.

Kenny moved to Nashville in 1970 to manage the Bobby Goldsboro publishing company. He continued writing songs, often with Larry Henley. Sandy Posey recorded one of their songs, "Why Don't We Go Somewhere and Love," which cracked the charts and was noticed by record producer Billy Sherrill. Sherrill began to use some of Kenny's songs on Charlie Rich's recordings, such as "I Take It on Home" and "Behind Closed Doors." The latter was a smash hit on both country and pop charts and was showered with awards, including a Grammy for Best Country Song, CMA's Song and Single of the Year, and ACM's Song and Single of the Year; all in 1973. "Behind Closed Doors" earned the BMI Three Million-Air Award and ranked in the Top 50 most performed songs of all time. Interestingly, Kenny played guitar on the Rich recording. During 1973, Kenny also released a self-titled album on the Capricorn label.

O'Dell's recording career continued in 1978 with "Let's Shake Hands and Come Out Lovin'," which was a Top 10 country hit, and title song from his 1978 album on Capricorn. It was followed by "Medicine Woman" in 1979, which was his last charted entry.

Kenny's songwriting ability was again recognized in 1984 when The Judds recorded "Mama He's Crazy," which garnered numerous awards, including BMI Country Song of the Year and Nashville Songwriters Association Song of the Year, and was nominated for Song of the Year by the CMA in 1985. Kenny was also named Songwriter of the Year by NSA in 1984. The song eventually won the BMI Million-Air Award .

In addition to the aforementioned songs, O'Dell penned such numbers as "I've Got Mine," "Lizzie and the Rainman," "Too Much Is Not Enough," and "When It's Just You and Me." His songs have been recorded by a diverse group of artists, including Bobby "Blue" Bland, Glen Campbell, Floyd Cramer, Sammy Davis, Jr., Freddy Fender, Bobby Goldsboro, Tom Jones, Albert King, Little Milton, Loretta Lynn, Boots Randolph, Ray Stevens, **B. J. Thomas**, Bobby Vee, Bobby Womack, Percy Sledge, Billie Jo Spears, Dottie West, Tanya Tucker, **Anthony Armstrong Jones**, Bellamy Brothers, Forrester Sisters, and The Rat Pack (Sinatra/Martin/Davis).

O'Dell served on the Board of Directors of the Nashville Songwriters Association in 2001-02, and runs Kenny O'Dell Music in Nashville. (GC)

Oklahoma City Blue Devils

The Oklahoma City Blue Devils formed around 1923-1924 in Kansas City as Billy King's Road Show, a traveling vaudeville troupe. Titular head of the band was trombonist Ermir "Bucket" Coleman, however, the musical leader was Walter Page, who had studied under both Major N. Clark Smith and Charles Watts, two of the best music teachers in Kansas City during the 1920s. The Billy King Road Show disbanded in 1925 in Oklahoma City, where Page kept the band intact and renamed it—some say it was "Walter Page's Original Blue Devils" and others contend it was the "Oklahoma City Blue Devils." Page expanded the band from its original nine members to as many as thirteen to fifteen members.

When the Blue Devils were reorganized in Oklahoma City, Page persuaded a group of Oklahoma City businessmen to back the venture. The backing consisted of a little cash, a set of uniforms, a supply of meal tickets good at a restaurant owned by one of the sponsors, and the donation of a large hotel room (Littlepage Hotel in the "Deep Deuce" district, or Northeast 2nd Street) that served as a dormitory, mess hall, rehearsal hall, and recruiting office. Most jazz scholars agree that of all the bands figuring in the Kansas City story, none excites the imagination more than the Blue Devils.

From 1925 to 1933, the Blue Devils were among the finest bands in the region and were certainly the most romantically appealing. They epitomized the spirit of the era in many ways—dance halls packed with enthusiastic dancers, long drives between jobs on dusty Southwestern roads, and good friends enjoying their music and each other. The Ritz Ballroom in Oklahoma City was home base for the Blue Devils as the group had a standing contract to play there during the winter months, while playing engagements at nearby Oklahoma towns, including El Reno, Chickasha, Shawnee, Enid, and Tulsa. During the fall and spring, the band traveled the ballroom circuit ranging from Omaha in the north to Houston in the south to El Paso in the west and Little Rock to the east. Occasional forays took them to western states, such as New Mexico and Colorado as well as to such northern states as Iowa and Minnesota.

Early members of the Blue Devils included Oran "Hot Lips" Page, Jimmy Lu Grand, Harry Youngblood, James Simpson (trumpets); Ermir Coleman, Eddie Durham, Druie Bess, and Dan Minor (trombones); Reuben Roddy, Ted Manning, Theodore Ross, and Buster Smith (reeds); Willie Lewis and Turk Thomas (piano); Reuben Lynch (guitar); Edward McNeil and Alvin Burroughs (drums); Walter Page (bass, tuba, and baritone saxophone); Ernie Williams (vocals). Four native Oklahomans, at one time or another, were members of the Blue Devils, including Abe Bolar (bass), Lemuel C. Johnson (clarinet/tenor saxophone), **Jimmy Rushing** (vocals) from Oklahoma City, and **Don Byas** (tenor/alto saxophone) from Muskogee. During their heyday, the Blue Devils added such luminary jazz artists as Lester Young (tenor saxophone) in 1930 and again in 1932-33; and William, later known as "Count," Basie (piano) from 1928 to 1929 (approximately eight months). According to jazz scholars, it was the strongest lineup of that era anywhere in the Midwest and Southwest because the band possessed such extraordinary spirit, enthusiasm, and talent. The personnel included some of the finest musicians produced in two decades of jazz in the Southwest and Midwest. Several of the Blue Devils alumni organization then went on to provide the nucleus of such legendary bands as Bennie Moten and Count Basie, including "Lips" Page, Jimmy Rushing, Eddie Durham, and Walter Page. The single recording session made by the Blue Devils was in Kansas City in 1929 on Vocalion 1463. It produced two three-minute performances: *Squabblin'*, a riff tune taken at medium tempo, and *Blue Devil Blues*, with a Jimmy Rushing vocal. Friends of Oklahoma Music inducted the The Blue Devils band into the Oklahoma Music Hall of Fame in 2000. (GC)

Overstreet, Tommy
(b. September 10, 1937)

Named as the Most Promising New Male Vocalist in country music by the *Music City News* in 1971, appeared as a frequent guest on *Hee Haw* in the 1970s, and honored in 1985 with induction into the Country Music Hall of Fame Walkway of Stars, Thomas Cary Overstreet was born in Oklahoma City, but raised in Houston, Texas. Tommy's parents gave him a guitar when he was about thirteen that led to his first professional appearance on radio station KTHT in Houston for about four months. He then joined a local production called *Hit the Road* as a replacement for pop vocalist Tommy Sands, who was a high school chum. He graduated from Mirabeau B. Lamar High School in Houston in 1955.

Tommy's family moved to Abilene, Texas, after his completion of high school. While in college studying radio and television production, he was featured on local television as "Tommy Dean from Abilene," singing and playing guitar, and toured during summers with cousin Gene Austin, a singer who was well known for his hit records, "My Blue Heaven" and "Ramona."

After a two-year stint in the armed forces, Overstreet moved to Los Angeles, where he worked as a songwriter for Pat Boone's Cooga Music and signed with Dunhill Records, although no records were released. His unsuccessful recording career resulted in a move back to Texas, where he appeared on the Slim Willet tel-

evision show in the mid-1960s, and formed his own band to play club dates in the Houston area.

In 1967, Tommy moved to Nashville, where he used his college degree in radio and television production to gain a position as manager of Dot Records, and signed with the label as a recording artist. His first two singles, "Rocking a Memory (That Won't Go to Sleep" (1969) and "If You're Looking for a Fool" (1971) entered the country charts at the lower echelon. He finally scored his first major hit later in 1971 with "Gwen (Congratulations)," the title track of his first album, which charted at #5, and was followed with "I Don't Know You (Anymore)."

In 1972, Overstreet produced three more chart singles, including "A Seed Before the Rose," "Heaven Is My Woman's Love," and "Ann (Don't Go Runnin')," which reached #2 and became his overall biggest hit. The next two years, he charted with "Send Me No Roses," "I'll Never Break These Chains," "If I Miss You Again Tonight," "I'm a Believer," and "(Jeannie Marie) You Were a Lady," the latter reaching the Top 3.

During the remainder of the 1970s, Tommy scored with several Top 20 hits, such as "That's When My Woman Begins" (1975), "From Woman to Woman" (1975), "Here Comes that Girl Again" (1976), "Young Girl" (1976), "If Love Was a Bottle" (1977), "Don't Go City Girl on Me" (1977), which reached #5 on the charts, "This Time I'm In It for Love" (1977), "Yes Ma'am" (1978), "Better Me" (1978), and "Fadin' In, Fadin' Out" (1978).

After leaving the Dot label in 1979, Tommy moved to Tina Records, and then on to Elektra, where his most successful singles were "I'll Never Let You Down," "What More Could a Man Need," "Fadin' Renegade," "Down in the Quarter," and "Sue." Although he never achieved a #1 hit, Tommy registered twenty-seven *Billboard* entries during the 1970s.

During the 1980s, Overstreet and his band, the Nashville Express, continued to tour nationally and internationally. He was especially popular in Germany, where his "Heaven Is My Woman's Love," sung in German, was a hit, and also performed at the Peterborough Country Festival in England in 1988. He was named Entertainer of the Year by the International Rodeo Association for the years 1979, 1980, and 1981 because of his extensive appearances throughout the U.S. on the rodeo circuit. In 1985, Tommy and his wife, Diane, moved to Branson, Missouri. The next year, his son, Thomas, who was his road manager, was killed in an accident. This tragedy was a major blow to Tommy's career, but he slowly rebuilt his life by opening a restaurant in Branson and signing with Silver Dollar Records, a local Branson label. Tommy still tours on a regular basis and is managed in 2003 by Music City Attractions in Nashville.

Released in 2000 by Classic World Productions in CD format, *Tommy Overstreet: Country's Best, Vol. 1* includes ten of his hits, such as "Gwen," "I Don't Know You (Anymore)," and "I'm A Believer." (GC)

Bonnie Owens
(b. October 1, 1932)

Recognized as the first woman singer-songwriter to emerge from the Bakersfield Sound country music movement in the 1950s, Bonnie Owens was born Bonnie Campbell near Blanchard, Oklahoma, a town of about 2,000 citizens southwest of Oklahoma City. Her father worked for the WPA during the Great Depression of the 1930s, and her mother made all the children's clothes. As a child, she picked cotton on their Oklahoma sharecropper farm before the family, which eventually consisted of six daughters and two sons, moved to Arizona.

As a teenager, Bonnie developed a talent for yodeling and won contests throughout the state. After performing in various clubs, she met Alvis Edgar "Buck" Owens at the Mazona Roller Rink in Mesa. Bonnie immediately liked Buck because he could play the guitar. She soon joined Owens on the Buck and Britt Show on station KTYL in Mesa. Bonnie and Buck then signed up with Mac MacAtee's Skillet Lickers band and toured throughout the western U.S. In 1948, the two were married and within a year, Alan Edgar "Buddy" Owens was born, followed by a second son, Michael Lynn Owens. Buck was picking oranges in the daytime and playing music at night, while Bonnie was a stay at home mom.

By 1951, the marriage was not working, and Bonnie and the two boys left for Bakersfield, where they moved in with Buck's aunt and uncle. Buck soon followed his family to Bakersfield and hooked on with a local band, Bill Woods and the Orange Blossom Playboys. Though legally married, Buck and Bonnie remained separated because neither could afford a divorce. In order to support the children, Bonnie took several jobs as a carhop and cocktail waitress at the Clover Club and The Blackboard, two venues that were to play an important role in her career. At the Clover Club, while serving up drinks, she sang with Fuzzy Owen and Lewis Tally. Her first single was "Dear John Letter," a duet with Fuzzy Owen (1953) on the Tally label. When the Clover Club band in 1953 landed a job as the house band for *The Trading Post Show* on KERO-TV, Bonnie joined Owen and Tally as a singer.

Continuing her career as a cocktail waitress at The Blackboard, Bonnie met **Merle Haggard** one evening in 1961, however, she did not see him again until he was a guest performer on *The Trading Post Show*. He had just finished a 2 ½ year sentence for burglary in San Quentin. By this time, Merle's marriage to Leona Hobbs was in shambles. Merle soon called Bonnie in Alaska where she was on tour and asked her to marry him, and they were hitched on June 28, 1965 in Tijuana, Mexico. Bonnie continued recording for independent labels. Her singles for Mar-Vel and Tally included "I Traded My Heart for His Gold," (1953), "Why Don't Daddy Live Here Anymore," (1963), "Don't Take Advantage of Me" (1964), and a duet with Merle Haggard, "Just Between the Two of Us" (1964), a pairing suggested by her old friend, Fuzzy Owen, who had by then become Merle's manager.

Shortly after their marriage, Bonnie and Merle signed with the Capitol label. She soon released her first two solo albums, *Bonnie Owens* and *Don't Take Advantage of Me*, in 1965. Singles from those albums that produced mid-chart positions, included "Number One Heel," "Consider the Children," and "Lead Me On." In 1966, Bonnie and Merle recorded their first duet album for Capitol, *Just Between the Two of Us*. Bonnie and Merle were becoming major country music stars and were among those bringing the Bakersfield Sound to national attention. Merle and Bonnie were named Best Vocal Group by the ACM in 1965, 1966, and 1967, and Bonnie was selected as Top Female Vocalist by the ACM in 1965. The two were also nominated for the Best Vocal Duo of the Year Award by the CMA in 1970. Solo albums for Capitol during the next five years included *All of Me Belongs to You* (1967), *Your Tender Lovin' Care* (1967), *Somewhere Between* (1968), *Lead Me On* (1969), *A Hi-Fi to Cry By* (1969), and *Mother's Favorite Hymns* (1970), as well as another duet album with Merle in 1971, *The Land of Many Churches*.

By 1974 Bonnie had stopped touring with The Merle Haggard Show after almost ten years to focus on handling Haggard's business affairs. She soon filed for legal separation from Haggard and the marriage was dissolved in 1978. Bonnie and Merle remained good friends and when Merle married Leona Williams in 1978, Bonnie was a bridesmaid. She eventually resumed touring with Merle and The Strangers in the 1980s and remains a part of the tour as of 2001. With her husband of nineteen years, Fred McMillan, she resides in rural Missouri close to Springfield, where she uses the airport to catch up with the next Merle Haggard and the Strangers show. (GC)

Page, Patti
(b. November 8, 1927)

One of the pure superstar voices of 20th century American popular music, Patti Page has sold more than 100 million records. With fifteen certified gold records, Page will always be remembered for her mega-crossover hit of 1950, "Tennessee Waltz," the most successful single in country music history with ten million sold,

and to a lesser extent for her novelty song recorded for a children's album, "The Doggie in the Window." She has charted 111 songs on the pop, country, and R & B charts, and her hit "Confess" is the first song in music history to feature a vocalist performing both lead and backup vocals via overdubbing in the studio.

Born Clara Ann Fowler in Claremore, Oklahoma, a town about fifteen miles northeast of Tulsa that humorist Will Rogers also called home, her father was a section hand for the Midland Valley Railroad and her mother picked cotton to help support the eleven Fowler children, eight of whom were girls, and all of whom sang in church. Since Clara had hoped for a career as an artist, and her family needed financial help at home, she applied for a job in the art department at KTUL radio in Tulsa. She did not stay in the art department long, however, when a KTUL radio executive heard her sing "Frankie and Johnny" at a local high school function. Soon thereafter, she began singing country songs on KTUL, and playing weekend gigs with Al Clauser and his Oklahoma Cowboys. Shortly thereafter, she was selected for KTUL's program *Meet Patti Page*, sponsored by the Page Milk Company, which provided the name she has kept for the rest of her career. Having heard Page sing on the radio in 1946, Jack Rael, a baritone saxophonist and road manager for the Jimmy Joy Band, hired her as a vocalist for the group and began a 40-plus year partnership as her manager. Soon she was appearing as Patti Page in clubs and small theaters throughout the Midwest, and by 1947 had moved to Chicago where she had her own show on the CBS Radio Network, sang with the Benny Goodman Septet, and signed with Mercury Records.

In June of 1948, Patti had her first hit record, "Confess," on which she and Rael collaborated on the idea of adding her own backup vocals to the track to create the impression of a vocal group. While guitarist Les Paul received a lot of credit for popularizing the process of overdubbing, now standard practice in the music industry, Patti made the first multi-track recording with "Confess." In 1949, Patti recorded the first of her 15 million-selling singles, "With My Eyes Wide Open I'm Dreaming," which also furthered the use of multi-tracking via her overdubbed four-part harmony on the song, hence the listing of the Patti Page Quartet as the song's "performers."

The following year, 1950, proved to be a high mark for Patti. She had her first number one hit with "All My Love," and recorded "Tennessee Waltz," initially as a B-Side to a Christmas single, "Boogie Woogie Santa Claus." The song became the first crossover country hit to score #1 status on both the pop and R&B charts, and sold over ten million records, the biggest selling single by a female artist in the 20th century, and second only to Bing Crosby's "White Christmas" in total single sales. The song's appeal to so many different people is a product of its use of a blues melody, Patti's country vocal (with a bit of an Irish brogue on "Darlin'"), and orchestral production that presaged the Nashville Sound of the late 1950s and early 1960s. Establishing her as the "Singing Rage," "Tennessee Waltz" was a hit from Bakersfield to Harlem and led to a string of extremely successful songs through 1965. Countering the rough-tinged rock and roll movement with her lovely voice and urbane production, Page sang to the considerable Tin Pan Alley tastes still part of the American musical mainstream in the 1950s. Some of the era's hits included "Mockin' Bird Hill" (1951), "I Went to Your Wedding" (#1 for two months in 1952), "The Doggie in the Window" (#1 for two months in 1953), "Steam Heat" (1954), "Allegheny Moon" (1956), and "Old Cape Cod" (1957). During the 1950s, Patti repeatedly earned honors as *Billboard* and *Cashbox*'s favorite female vocalist, and was crowned *American Bandstand*'s favorite female vocalist in its first nationwide audience poll of 1957.

Patti was a consistent presence on television, starting in 1952 with CBS-TV's "Scott Music Hall" and proceeding throughout the 1950s as host of several network shows for NBC, CBS and ABC, making her the only singer to ever have shows bearing her name on all three major networks. Patti made several films, including *Elmer Gantry* (1960) with Burt Lancaster, *Dondi* (1961), and *Boys Night Out* (1962). Her solid-selling hits continued through 1965 when she had her last Top Ten single, the Oscar nominated theme song from the film *Hush, Hush, Sweet Charlotte*. She charted minor hits in 1968 with "Gentle on My Mind" and "Little Green Apples" before turning completely to country music in the 1970s with Nashville as her recording base. In 1972, her duet with Tom T. Hall, "Hello We're Lonely," made the country Top 20.

In 1980, Patti received the Pioneer Award from the Academy of Country Music for popularizing country music to the general public, and her hear early use of overdubbing. She responded with "No Aces" in 1981, which dipped into the country Top 40, and earned her the distinction of being the only female vocalist to score a country hit in five consecutive decades (1940s to 1980s). Patti signed with Plantation Records in the 1980s, continued recording, and performing. In 1983 she was inducted into the Oklahoma Hall of Fame. She has a star on the Hollywood Walk of Fame, and her name is on the Country Music Walk of Fame in Nashville. In 1988, she released an album of Lou Stein's music, and garnered strong reviews for performances in New York City. In 1992, she received the Lynn Riggs Award, named after the Claremore author whose play, *Green Grow the Lilacs*, became the inspiration for Rogers and Hammerstein's *Oklahoma!*, and in 1995 Mercury released three "Best of" compilations, complete with stunning cover photos from Patti's early

period.

In 1997, Patti was one of the inaugural inductees into the Oklahoma Music Hall of Fame, along with **Woody Guthrie**, **Merle Haggard**, and **Claude "Fiddler" Williams**. That year, she also celebrated her 50th year in show business with a well-received concert at New York's Carnegie Hall, a 1998 live album of which earned Patti her first Grammy Award in 1999 as "Best Traditional Pop Music Performance." Also in 1998, a public television documentary, *Miss Patti Page: The Singing Rage*, featured classic songs, clips from her TV shows in the 1950s, and concert performances from her long career to that point. In 1999, Verve reissued her 1956 album, *Patti Page in the Land of Hi-Fi*, which finds Patti fronting a big band style orchestra on several jazz standards. In 2001, Patti released *New Tennessee Waltz* through the Gold label, including new renditions of "Tennessee Waltz" and "The Doggie in the Window," as well as guest vocal appearances from admirers Emmy Lou Harris, Trisha Yearwood, Kathy Mattea, and Alison Krauss. In 2002, *Mercury* released an 80-song retrospective of her career, and Patti began doing a two-hour weekly radio show on the Music of Your Life radio network, featuring popular music in her vein from the big band era, the 1950s, and 1960s. Also in 2002, the Oklahoma Jazz Hall of Fame honored Patti with the *Living Legend Award*, and the *Tulsa World* inducted her into their Spot Awards Hall of Fame, and she released a holiday album, *Sweet Sounds of Christmas*.

In 2003, Universal/MCA released a 20th Century Masters Collection of her best known songs, and Patti released her first children's album (although "That Doggie in the Window" has been a hit with children since its release). Available exclusively on her website, *Child of Mine* had its genesis when Patti and her husband, Jerry, began raising two of their 13 grandchildren. The album includes her famous pet store classic, as well as "Rainbow Connection," "Ants in their Pants," and "Somewhere Over the Rainbow." The title track was written by Carole King.

As of 2004, Patti planned to continue touring, hosting her radio show, and maintaining a thriving business in New Hampshire with her husband, through which they market maple syrup and pancake mixes packaged under the name of Patti Page Pure Maple Products. (HF)   www.misspattipage.com

Parker, Andy
(b. March 17, 1913 – d. October 2, 1977)

Best known as the singing cowboy on NBC radio's *Death Valley Days* and leader of one of the early western music bands (The Plainsmen), singer, songwriter, and guitarist Andy Parker was born in Mangum, Oklahoma, a Greer County town of about 3,500 residents located in the southwestern part of the state. According to most sources, Andy made his radio debut on KGMP in Elk City, Oklahoma, when he was a teenager, and later appeared on several radio shows in the Midwest. He then relocated in 1937 to San Francisco, where he began to appear as the singing cowboy in *Death Valley Days* on NBC radio, a run that would last until 1941. He also sang on radio station KGO on Dude Martin's Roundup before moving to the Los Angeles area in 1944.

Andy soon formed The Plainsmen, a trio composed of himself, Charlie Morgan, and Hank Caldwell, and they made their film debut in *Cowboy Blues* with Ken Curtis. By 1946, they had released some recordings on the Coast label, and began to appear regularly on the Hollywood Barn Dance on CBS radio, as well as Sunrise Salute on local radio station KNX in Hollywood. When Caldwell left the trio, he was replaced by Paul "Clem" Smith, who played standup bass, and the act became Andy Parker and the Plainsmen. The Plainsmen also recorded for Capitol Records for which they did more than 200 radio transcription discs. Until 1946, when the group disbanded, several excellent musicians were members of the group, including George Bamby, an accordionist and arranger, who worked with **Spade Cooley** and later played with the Sons of the Pioneers, Charlie Morgan on lead guitar, Deuce Spriggens, who later was a member of the Sons of the Pioneers, and **Noel Boggs**, another Oklahoman, and Joaquin Murphy, two of the finest steel guitar players in the business, both of whom were inducted into the Steel Guitar Hall of Fame. They appeared in eight Eddie Dean western movies and on several television shows. Andy and Charlie Morgan sang the theme song with Marilyn Monroe for the 1954 film, *River of No Return*.

When Morgan left in 1956, Andy dissolved the group. Parker is also noted for his songwriting, including the popular "Trail Dust," which can be found on Rounder Record's *Stampede! Western Music's Late Golden Era 1945-1960*. In his later years, Andy suffered from a heart condition that prevented him from working and touring. He retired in San Francisco and died in 1977. (GC)

Parker, Billy
(b. July 19, 1939)

Recognized as one of the nation's top country music disc jockeys having won Country Music Association and Academy of Country Music honors for Disc Jockey of the Year five times in the 1970s and 1980s and inducted into the Country Music Disc Jockey Hall of Fame in 1992, Billy Parker was born in Okemah, Oklahoma, a town of roughly 3,000 residents located east of

Oklahoma City on Interstate 40, and also the hometown of Woody Guthrie. Although known primarily for his deejaying work, Billy is also a country music performer. He began singing and playing guitar at age eleven, and made his professional debut on the Big Red Jamboree, a local Tulsa radio program. According to one source, he also spent some time later on the Ozark Jubilee. After performing in local clubs, he began his first disc jockey work in 1959 on Tulsa radio station KFMJ.

By 1963, Billy had landed on radio station KFDI in Wichita, Kansas, where he was the daytime disc jockey for this 50,000 country music outlet. The same year, he recorded his first single, "The Line Between Love and Hate," followed by a second single, "I'm Drinking All the Time," released in 1966, both on the Sims label. Also in 1963, in a nationwide poll, he was voted Mr. DJ which resulted in a guest spot on Nashville's WSM, the radio home of the Grand Ole Opry. Two years later, he joined Ernest Tubb and his Troubadours and remained with the group until 1971, when he was hired by Tulsa's **KVOO**, the Voice of Oklahoma, as a country music deejay.

Continuing his recording work as well as deejaying, Billy charted his first hit single in 1976 with "It' Bad When You're Caught (With the Goods)," one of the tracks from his Sunshine label album entitled *Average Man.* This was followed by several singles, such as "Thanks E.T. Thanks a Lot," a tribute to Ernest Tubb, and "Lord If I Make It to Heaven (Can I Bring My Own Angel Along)," one of his most popular recordings. During the late 1970s, his most successful singles were "You Read Between the Lines" and "Until the Next Time."

Billy's music resurfaced in the 1980s with several cuts on Soundwaves, his new recording label, including "I'll Drink to That," "I See an Angel Every Day," "If I Ever Need a Woman," "Who Said Love Was Fair," and "Love Don't Know a Lady (From a Honky Tonk Girl)." He also appeared on an album of duets, *Something Old, Something New*, which featured "Who's Gonna Sing the Last Country Song" (with Darrell McCall) and "Too Many Irons in the Fire" (with **Cal Smith**).

After moving to the Canyon Creek label in 1988, Billy charted several singles, such as "It's Time for Your Dreams to Come True," "You Are My Angel," "She's Sittin' Pretty," and "Who You're Gonna Turn To (duet with Rosemary Sharp). In 1990, he released a gospel album, *I'll Speak Out for You, Jesus*, for which he earned the Country Personality Award from the International Gospel Music Association. Bear Family, the German company, released all his Soundwaves recordings on an album entitled *Billy Parker and Friends* in 1990.

In addition to the aforementioned honors, Billy was inducted into the Western Swing Hall of Fame in 1993, and received the Oklahoma Association of Broadcasters Lifetime Achievement Award in 1995. Overall, Billy had twenty-two *Billboard* chart entries, performed with Ernest Tubb, Bob Wills, and Red Foley, and appeared on the Grand Ole Opry, Hee Haw, and TNN's Nashville Now. (GC)

Patty, Sandi
(b. July 14, 1957)

Winner of thirty-nine Dove Awards and five Grammy Awards, producer of three platinum and five gold albums, and referred to as "The Voice" in the CCM genre, Sandi Patty was born to Ron and Carolyn Patty in Oklahoma City. Her singing debut was at the age of two when she performed "Jesus Loves Me," in her church. Along with two younger brothers, Sandi formed the Ron Patty Family Singers that began performing at small churches throughout the U.S.

Sandi took voice lessons at San Diego State University, and later graduated with a degree in music from Anderson College in Indiana, where she partially supported herself singing commercial jingles. During her college days, she met and married John Helvering, who helped produce her debut album, *For My Friends*. On the album, a printer's mistake changed her name from Patty to Patti, and the name remained for some time.

In 1979, Sandi signed with an independent label and released her second album, *Sandi's Song*, with the title track her own composition. It was later released on the Word label in 1990. Her 1979 album was followed by the 1981 release, *Love Overflowing*. The next year, she won her first two Dove Awards based on her album, *Lift Up the Lord*, followed by *More Than Wonderful* (platinum) and *The Gift Goes On* (gold), both 1983 releases. In 1984, she launched her first major U.S. tour to promote her *Songs From the Heart*, also a gold album.

During the remainder of the 1980s, Sandi recorded five more albums, including *Hymns Just For You* (platinum), *Morning Like This* (platinum), *Make His Praise Glorious* (gold), *Sandi Patty and the Friendship Company*, and *The Finest Moments* (gold), all on the Word label.

In the 1990s, Sandi continued to produce albums at a prolific rate, including *Another Time. . .Another Place* (certified gold and Grammy winner) in 1990, *Open for Business* and *More Than Wonderful* in 1991, *Celebrate Christmas*, a 1992 album which sold more than 1.5 million copies, *Le Voyage* in 1993, *Quiet Reflections* in 1994, *Find It on the Wings* in 1995, *O Holy Night, An American Songbook*, and *It's Christmas!* (1.3 million seller), all in 1996, *Artist of My Soul* and *Libertad Me Das* in 1998 (Dove Award for Best Spanish Language Album), *Together: Sandi Patty and Kathy Troccoli* in 1999, *These Days* in 2000, and *All the Best. . .Live* in 2001. The latter features guest appearances by family members. Worth noting is the collaboration of Sandi and Kathy Troccoli, another CCM

vocalist, on the *Together* album comprised of thirteen tracks of pop tunes with emphasis on Sandi's love for George Gershwin, such as "Summertime," "The Man I Love," and "Embraceable You." *Artist of My Soul* was Sandi's first album of new material since her remarriage and revelation of her extramarital affairs. In 1995, Sandi married Don Peslis, one of her backup singers and with whom she had an extramarital affair during her first marriage, which ended in a 1993 divorce from John Helvering. One of the tracks on the *Artist of My Soul* album, "Breathe on Me," reflected her personal desire to regain her audience after this incident.

Sandi's honors include five Grammy Awards, including Best Gospel Performance-Duo or Group for the song "More Than Wonderful" with Larnelle Harris (1984), Best Gospel Performance-Duo or Group for the song "I've Just Seen Jesus" with Larnelle Harris (1986), Best Gospel Performance-Duo or Group for the song "They Say" with Deniece Williams (1987), Best Gospel Performance-Female for the album *Morning Like This* (1987), and Best Pop Gospel Album for *Another Time. . .Another Place* (1991). Moreover, Sandi's thirty-nine Dove Awards include eleven consecutive Female Vocalist of the Year honors. Finally, she garnered *Billboard Magazine*'s Inspirational Artist of the Year four times.

Among her other talents, Sandi has co-written several inspirational songs, including "Miracles Can Happen," "Masterpiece," "Beautiful Feet," "In the Name of the Lord," "There is a Savior," "Willing to Wait," "Who Will Call Him King of Kings," "Lift Up the Lord," "Doxology," and "All this Time (Anna's Song)," a tribute to one of her daughters.

In 1997, Sandi was lead singer at the Presidential Inaugural Gala of Bill Clinton. She has performed with numerous symphony orchestras including those in Indianapolis, Dallas, Atlanta, Boston Pops, Cincinnati Pops, Houston, Louisville, Nashville, St. Louis, and the two in her home state in Tulsa and Oklahoma City.

In 2001, Sandi released *For God and Country*, a multi-artist production, commemorating the September 11 terrorist attack on the World Trade Center. She contributed three of her most celebrated renditions of "The Star Spangled Banner," "Amazing Grace," and "God Bless America." Her most recent project is *Take Hold of Christ*, a CD released in 2002, the same year she returned to her roots for a concert in Oklahoma City.

With tour dates scheduled through the end of 2003 across the United States, Sandi currently resides in Anderson, Indiana, with her eight children ranging from elementary school age to young adult, including four from her previous marriage and four with Peslis. (GC)
www.sandipatty.com

Paxton, Tom
(b. October 31, 1937)

Emerging in the 1960s as one of the most talented folksingers of the protest era, singer, songwriter, guitarist Tom Paxton was born on the south side of Chicago, Illinois, but raised in Bristow, Oklahoma, where he graduated from high school. His family moved to Bristow when he was nine, but his father died soon after their arrival in Oklahoma. Thus, he was raised by a single parent and had to face the harsh realities of life at an early age. His aunt gave him a guitar at age sixteen, and when Tom entered the University of Oklahoma, he began working up his own repertoire of folk songs (more than 200 songs by the time he graduated) and later performed as a folksinger in a campus variety show. He wrote his first song in an English literature class while avoiding the professor's lecture on Shakespeare—says it was one of the worst songs ever written in the English language. He earned a bachelor's degree in fine arts (drama major) in 1959, and still considers Oklahoma his home state.

Following college, Paxton joined the army and spent six months stationed at New Rochelle, New York and later, Fort Dix, New Jersey. This proximity gave him an opportunity to spend his weekends in Greenwich Village, a hot spot for the beginning of the folk music revival of the 1960s with such newcomers as Bob Dylan, Joan Baez, and Phil Ochs. He was soon trading sets with such noted folk artists as Dave Van Ronk and Paul Stookey of Peter, Paul, and Mary, and eventually settled in Greenwich Village after completion of his active duty. After working the coffeehouse circuit at such venues as The Bitter End and The Gaslight, he auditioned for the Chad Mitchell Trio, but was rejected as the group's director thought Tom was more adept at songwriting.

Beginning in 1962 Tom penned a long list of songs inspired by his idols Burl Ives and **Woody Guthrie**, some of which impressed his folk colleagues who incorporated his songs in their shows, including the Weavers, who performed Paxton's "Ramblin' Boy" in their 1963 Carnegie Hall concert and included on their subsequent album. As his writing abilities increased, Tom thought it was time to try recording an album, and in 1964, Jac Holzman of Elektra Records auditioned him in his living room. His debut album, *Ramblin' Boy*, released in 1964 served notice to the folk music community that Paxton was the real deal. The late 1960s proved to be one of Tom's most prolific songwriting and recording periods, including *Ain't That News* (1965), *Outward Bound, Morning Again* (1967), *The Things I Notice* (1968), *Tom Paxton 6* (1969), and *The Compleat Tom Paxton* (1970; all issued by the end of the decade. Paxton paid homage to one of his idols when in 1972 he performed two songs, "Pastures of Plenty" and "Biggest Thing Man Has Ever Done" for the 1972 *A Tribute to Woody Guthrie* collection.

In 1971, Paxton switched to the Reprise label to record four albums, *How Come the Sun* (1971), *Peace Will Come* (1972), *New Songs for Old Friends* (1973), and *Something in My Life* (1975). By the mid-1970s the folk music revival had waned leading Tom and his family to move England where he was highly regarded as a folk troubadour. But he returned to the U.S. in 1977 and settled in East Hampton on Long Island, New York. Renewed by experiences overseas and rediscovery of his own country, Tom launched a new album, *New Songs from the Briarpatch* (1977), on the Vanguard label, followed by *Heroes* in 1978. He finished the decade with two albums on the Flying Fish label, *Up & Up* (1979) and *The Paxton Report* (1980).

During the 1980s and 1990s, Tom toured throughout the U.S., performing on college campuses and in folk clubs. By 1995, he had recorded thirty-two albums, including several children's albums, such as *The Marvelous Toy and Other Gallimaufry* (1984), *Balloon-alloon-alloon* (1987), *A Child's Christmas* (1992), *Suzy is a Rocker* (1992), and *Peanut Butter Pie* (1992). In addition to his children's works, Tom completed a number of satiric topical albums in the 1980s and 1990s, including *Bulletin* (1983), *One Million Lawyers and Other Disasters* (1986), *Politics* (1988), and *Wearing the Time* (1995), the latter was nominated as Best Folk Album of the Year by the National Association of Independent Record Distributors. The 1995 album included "Getting Up Early," a Paxton original that premiered on NPR's *Prairie Home Companion*.

In 1997, Paxton released two more children's albums, *Goin' to the Zoo* and *I've Got a Yo-Yo*. Two years later, the BBC launched a highly acclaimed radio show dubbed *Paxton's Picks*, later renamed *Tom Paxton's America*, which included special guests such as Pete Seeger, Iris DeMent, and John Prine.

Paxton's songwriting credits include a host of well-known songs that he penned, including "Ramblin' Boy," in which he mentions Tulsa town; "The Last Thing on My Mind" (a major hit for Peter, Paul, and Mary as well as Dolly Parton and Porter Wagoner); "Bottle of Wine" (a Top 10 hit for The Fireballs); and "All Night Long" (a 1968 chronicle of the assassinations of Martin Luther King, Jr. and Robert Kennedy). Additional topical songs reflecting the protest movements of the 1960s and 1970s include "Bring Back the Chair" (capital punishment); "Talking Vietnam Potluck Blues," "Jimmy Newman," and "Lyndon Johnson Told the Nation" (anti-Vietnam War songs); "Talking Watergate" (Nixon tapes); "I'm Changing My Name to Chrysler (an attack on the government bailout of the auto giant); and "Litty Bitty Gun" (a mock of Nancy Reagan). Many of these Paxton classics were assembled for the retrospective *I Can't Help Wonder Where I'm Bound: The Elektra Years*, released by Rhino in 1999. In addition to those afore-mentioned artists who have recorded Paxton's songs, others include Joan Baez, John Denver, Judy Collins, Arlo Guthrie, Nanci Griffith, Chet Atkins, Jose Feliciano, Neil Diamond, Placido Domingo, Willie Nelson, and Tiny Tim. The *Best of Broadside* released in 2000 by Smithsonian Folkways Recordings con-tained four of Tom's original songs, including "Ain't That News," "Train for Auschwitz," "Christine," and "What Did You Lean in School Today?" Tom teamed with Anne Hills for a 2001 release, *Under American Skies*, on the Appleseed label.

Paxton performed a 9/11 tragedy tribute at the Library of Congress in 2002, including his composition "The Bravest," a song written to remember the heroes of the New York City police and fire departments who died on September 11, 2001. Paxton's recent honors include winner of the prestigious Parents' Choice Gold Medal for his album, *Suzy is a Rocker*, and appointment as honorary chair of the World Folk Music Association. In 2003, Paxton earned a Grammy nomina-tion in the category of Best Musical Album for Children for his album, *Your Shoes, My Shoes* (Red House).

Also in 2003, Tom and Midge had celebrated almost forty years of marriage and remain living in their East Hampton home, where he continues to write children's songs for his own label (Pax) and books (Morrow), as well as perform at such venues as the Freight and Salvage in Berkeley and the Old Town School of Folk Music in Chicago. (GC)
www.tompaxton.com

Pettiford, Oscar
(b. September 30, 1922 –
d. September 8, 1960)

Designated by exalted Oklahoma jazz guitarist **Barney Kessel** as **"one of the five best bassists of all time,"** Oscar Pettiford appeared under his own name on more than twenty albums under his own name during his brilliant career as bassist, cellist, and bandleader. All testament one needs for Pettiford's abilities can also be found on his recordings with jazz giants such as Louis Armstrong, **Charlie Christian**, Miles Davis, Duke Ellington, Stan Getz, Dizzy Gillespie, Lionel Hampton, Coleman Hawkins, Billie Holiday, Thelonious Monk, Charlie Parker, Sonny Rollins, and Ben Webster. Born of mixed African and American Indian heritage in Okmulgee, Oklahoma, the capital of the **Muscogee (Creek) Nation** where many slaves of African descent began their post-Civil War freedom, and to which many African-Americans migrated as a result of the large population of blacks in the town, Oscar came into a musical family where his mother was a pianist and music teacher. His father, Harry "Doc" Pettiford, was a practicing veterinarian as well as a guitarist, drummer, and leader of the Doc Pettiford Family Orchestra.

With Doc Pettiford's wife on piano and the six children who preceded Oscar, the group included sisters Leontine and brother Harry on the reed instruments, Marjorie on reeds and flute, Ira on trumpet, Alonzo on various brass, Rose May on guitar, and three younger sisters on vocals. The band toured the Midwest, and when Oscar was three the family moved to Minneapolis, Minnesota. While Pettiford family music history is rooted in the development of music in the early days of Oklahoma's statehood through the 1920s, they also left the state for Minneapolis in 1925 as part of larger migration of African-Americans out of Oklahoma due to increasing racial and economic strife in the state.

Once in Minnesota, Oscar studied guitar, trombone, and piano, sang in front of the orchestra at age ten, and ultimately became designated for the vacant bass chair at fourteen. When he expressed disinterest in that instrument, Harry Sr. conked his son on the head with a pair of drumsticks to convince Oscar otherwise. After Oscar, five more Pettifords followed to re-supply the band until "Doc" Pettiford's death in 1943. Influenced by Duke Ellington's bassist of the 1930s and 1940s, Jimmy Blanton, and Milt Hinton who encouraged Pettiford to not give up music for a secure day job, Oscar started playing bass with Charlie Barnet in 1943. Pettiford parlayed that visibility into an integral role in New York City's formative bebop scene with Dizzy Gillespie and Charlie Parker, a good example of which exists on *Dizzy Gillespie Volume 4: 1943 and 1944* (Masters of Jazz). The recordings mark the early stages of the bebop era with a jam between Parker, Gillespie, and Pettiford on "Sweet Georgia Brown." Oscar was "the" bassist on 52nd Street from 1943 to 1945, whose playing with Coleman Hawkins, Thelonious Monk, Roy Eldridge, Errol Garner, and Max Roach had a permanent influence on the development of bebop as a form and the bass as an instrument in jazz. Fans and critics took notice of his elevated skill and status in 1944 when he won *Esquire*'s "All Star Bassist" award, and in 1945 when he repeated the *Esquire* award and won the *Metronome* poll for best bassist.

As bebop's newness and marketability began to fade, Pettiford left New York for California where he appeared in a murder mystery film set in the world of jazz musicians, *The Crimson Canary* (1945), wherein he performed one song with Coleman Hawkins and fellow Oklahoman **Howard McGhee**, and also joined Duke Ellington with whom he was a featured soloist until 1948. That year he formed a trio that played for a year at The Clique Club in New York City, and in 1949 he joined Woody Herman's band for a nationwide tour. Even though Oscar's job with Herman was cut short when Pettiford broke his arm playing softball with the band team, he did have the opportunity to introduce the cello into jazz, for which he is roundly given credit. As a joke on Herman, Pettiford substituted a cello for his bass solo. Subsequently, audience members convinced Pettiford the instrument had great possibilities for jazz.

After his arm healed, Pettiford led a series of innovative bands through the mid-1950s in which he featured the instrument on several recordings, but had trouble keeping regular musicians due to his combustible personality, a trait no doubt stemming from the "drumsticks-to-the-head" episode with his bandleader father. Nevertheless, he continued earning top recognition for his playing by winning the *Down Beat* Critics Poll as best bassist in 1953, 1955, 1956, and 1957. Excellent recordings still in print from this period include 1953's *The New Oscar Pettiford Sextet* (Debut) and 1954's *Another One* (Bethlehem). In 1958, Pettiford traveled to Europe with the Carnegie Hall Jazz Band. New to Europe's lionization of American jazz stars, Pettiford enjoyed it so much he decided to stay there, picking up gigs with local musicians and with touring American artists like Stan Getz, Bud Powell, and Kenny Clarke. He also began experimenting with an amplified cello, and made his final recordings in 1960, heard on *Montmartre Blues* (1201 Music).

In addition to his instrumental accomplishments, Pettiford composed "Blues in the Closet," "Bohemia After Dark," "Tricrotism," "Black-Eyed Peas and Collard Greens," "Laverne Walk," and "Swingin' Til the Girls Come Home." Musicians who have recorded his compositions include Cannonball Adderly, **Chet Baker**, Herbie Mann, Charlie Mingus, and Oscar Peterson. By his career's end, his list of credits as a side man on various jazz recordings included sessions with Louis Armstrong, Art Blakey, Kenny Burrell, Charlie Parker, **Don Byas**, **Charlie Christian**, John Coltrane, Miles Davis, Billy Eckstine, Lionel Hampton, and Quincy Jones.

Pettiford's surprising death came in Copenhagen, Denmark, at the young age of thirty-eight, but not before he established the double bass as a solo instrument equal to any other horn voice in jazz. He was inducted into the Oklahoma Jazz Hall of Fame in 1995, and in 1998, Topaz records released a wonderful retrospective of Pettiford's career, *Bass Hits*, featuring recordings with Duke Ellington, Dizzy Gillespie, Coleman Hawkins, and Ben Webster, and others. (GC/HF)

Pewewardy, Cornel Derek

(b. January 20, 1952)

Cornel Pewewardy is an assistant professor at the University of Kansas School of Education, an author of many academic papers, essays, and articles, an avid intellectual opponent of American Indian mascots, and a sought after keynote speaker. Pewewardy is also one of the most recorded and widely known Plains Indian singers and flutists throughout world music circles. Pewewardy has recorded acclaimed albums of his own flute music, Southern Plains powwow music, multiple Comanche and **Kiowa** traditional songs, and contemporary hybrid recordings of traditional music and contemporary instrumentation laden with studio effects. His Kiowa hymns have been distributed internationally on compilations of musicians and singers who are the pinnacle performers of their respective international traditions.

Born to a Kiowa mother, Mary Lee Pewewardy, and a Comanche father, "Doc" Pewewardy, in Lawton, Oklahoma, Cornel is an enrolled member of the Comanche Nation and grew up around the collective musical traditions of his extended family and tribes. His first musical memories as a child were hearing his grandfather sing peyote songs as the elder drove around in the family car. While Pewewardy played saxophone in junior high and high school band, Kiowa flutist Woody Bigbow **(Kiowa)** gave Cornel his first flute in 1975 at home in Anadarko, Oklahoma, and his uncle, George "Woogie" Watchetaker,

a noted Comanche dancer and artist, mentored Cornel in flute composition and performance in the Plains traditions, most of which were historically linked to courting. Pewewardy credits his quick progress on the flute to his saxophone training since the fingerings for both instruments were often the same.

Additional music experiences came for Pewewardy from learning Ponca songs from Morris Lookout, and Kiowa hymns from Ralph Kotay. In 1976, Cornel received a B.S. in Education from Northeastern Oklahoma State University in Tahlequah, Oklahoma, and a Master's in Education in 1977 from the same school. That year, Pewewardy moved to New Mexico where he taught for Navajo schools in Crown Point and Cuba, New Mexico until 1984, and earned his Master of Arts in Educational Management and Development from New Mexico State. In 1986, he became director of research and development at Southwestern Indian Polytechnic in Albuquerque, received another degree from New Mexico State in Education Administration, and in 1987 released his first collection of music, *Flute and Prayer Songs* (Tribal Music International). Next, Pewewardy was off to Pennsylvannia State University where he earned his Doctor of Education in 1989, and then spent a year as a post-doctoral fellow at the university in Norman.

In 1991, Cornel moved to Saint Paul, Minnesota and became the founding principal at an American Indian magnet school. Given the amount of relocations he experienced in a relatively short amount of time, no wonder he named his 1992 release *Spirit Journey* (Sound of America Records). Anchored by ancient melodies, *Spirit Journey* explores the sonic possibilities of multi-track recording, studio effects, and contemporary instrumentation that gained Pewewardy notice in some new age music circles for the album's atmospheric and meditative qualities. By 1994, Cornel felt the need to return to southwestern Oklahoma, and became a lecturer at the University of Science and Arts in Chickasha, a thirty-minute drive from his hometown of Lawton. That year, Cornel and the Alliance West Singers also released the first of their highly acclaimed albums, *Dancing Buffalo: Dances and Flute Songs from the Southern Plains* (Sound of the World, 1994). The album is an excellent introduction to the varied musical abilities of Pewewardy and the Alliance West Singers, as well as the music of the Southern Plains, including several songs that accompany Plains dances, *a cappella* Kiowa Hymns, and flute songs by Cornel. While the drum group's songs were recorded in New Mexico, the hymns and flute songs were recorded in McGee Chapel in Broken Bow, Oklahoma. In 1994, Cornel moved to Lawton and taught for two years at Cameron University. In 1995, Narada Records included two songs, "Kiowa Hymn III" and "Love Song," that represent Pewewardy's more contemporary sound, a hybrid of traditional flute and contemporary instruments on *Between Father Sky and Mother Earth*. In 1996, Sound of America Records released Pewewardy and other Comanche singers on *Comanche Hymns from the Prairie*, and Cornel moved to his current home of Lawrence, Kansas where and began teaching for the University of Kansas. Also in 1996, Pewewardy's "Voices from the Sky," originally released on 1992's *Spirit Journey*, was included on

Arctic Refuge: A Gathering of Tribes, an album dedicated to raising awareness of the wilderness and indigenous people of the Arctic.

In 1997, The Wordcraft Circle of Native Writers and Storytellers named Cornel its musician of the year. The following year Pewewardy's "Kiowa Hymn" appeared on *Invocations* (Music of the World), a compilation of international faith-based songs designed to invoke the divine, and on *Native American Music: The Rough Guide* (World Music Network). Also in 1997, the Lawrence, Kansas art commission gave Cornel their "Phoenix Award for Music," and he harmonized with Robbie Robertson on *Contact from the Underworld of Red Boy* (Capitol), an album coordinated by Oklahoma City native Jim Wilson. In 1999, Shortwave Records released *The Warrior's Edge: Songs from the Southern Plains Powwows* by Pewewardy, the Alliance West Singers, and Intertribal Veterans. The album contains intertribal war dance songs, a "**Kiowa O-ho-mah Lodge** song," "Kiowa Round Dances," the "Comanche Little Ponies' Gourd Dance song," "Alvin Tsosie's Gourd Dance Song," a "Comanche Gourd Dance song," and a "Comanche Prisoner of War Song."

In 2000, the compilation *Spirit of the Native American Indians: Songs and Dances of the Kiowa, Comanche, Navajo* featured Cornel both on new compositions and traditional songs with the Alliance West Singers. Along with his recordings, Pewewardy also travels extensively and works with students on developing their traditional music skills. According to a press release for a 2000 North Carolina performance, "Cornel dedicates his music to the memory of those many prominent Southern Plains singers from Oklahoma and the Southwest, and hopes to promote and perpetuate their songs so younger generations will be able to enjoy and learn from them." A widely published author, Pewewardy has written numerous articles on American Indian and multi-cultural education issues, as well as authored essays and articles on the imagery of the American Indian in popular culture, including sports mascots and comic books. In a 2001 essay about American Indian music he wrote, "Our music, in both its longevity and its diversity, is a testimony to our survival as a people. Our drums beat strong, our flutes still sing like birds, and our rattles sound like rain. We still sing in the ancient tongues and perform dances in the prescribed manner."

In 2002, Cornel provided some background vocals for the contemporary new age American Indian group Brulé. While many American Indian musicians are widely recorded and distributed throughout Indian Country, Cornel Pewewardy is one of the few whose music has crossed international boundaries to be considered on par with other leading figures of world music. Along with his distinguished career as a nationally recognized educator, his recordings and performances have placed him in an elite group of recognizable voices and flutists in the traditional and contemporary American Indian music world. (HF)

Place, Mary Kay
(b. August 23, 1947)

Named Top New Female Country & Western Singer by *Record World* in 1977 and her album, *Tonite! At the Capri Lounge Loretta Haggers*, was nominated for a Grammy Award in 1976, singer and actress Mary Kay Place was born in Tulsa, Oklahoma, to Brad and Gwen Place. She had two brothers, Phil and Ken. Her father was an art professor and chair of the art department at the University of Tulsa, while her mother was a public school teacher. She graduated from Tulsa's Nathan Hale High and from the University of Tulsa with a degree in radio and television production. While growing up in the state, Mary Kay enjoyed singing both pop and country songs for school and local events. In a 2002 interview with the *Tulsa World*, Mary Kay fondly recalled her music experiences in and around Tulsa, especially singing for her grandparents at an early age.

After graduation from TU, Mary Kay headed to Hollywood to seek a career in writing and comedy performance. As a temporary receptionist at CBS, she was noticed by Tim Conway, who hired her as an assistant for the short-lived *Tim Conway Comedy Hour* in 1970. This led to a job as secretary to producer/creator Norman Lear on the set of *Maude*. Lear overheard Mary Kay and a co-worker singing one of her quirky songs, and decided to have her sing it for another one of Lear's sitcoms, *All in the Family*. She made her television debut as a friend of Gloria (Sally Struthers) and sang the song, "If Communism Comes Knockin' on Your Door, Don't Answer It," for Archie Bunker.

When Lear created the *Mary Hartman, Mary Hartman* nightly soap opera in 1976, Mary Kay was cast as the country singer Loretta Haggers, who was Mary Hartman's best friend. Mary Kay won an Emmy for her portrayal of Loretta Haggers. During the two-year run of the show, Mary Kay wrote more than seventy-five songs for her character, and as country music scholar Robert K. Oermann stated: "Mary Kay's Tulsa twang was authentic, and so was her country music ability." As a result, Columbia Records signed her to a contract and released in 1976 the Grammy nominated *Tonite! At the Capri Lounge Loretta Hagers* album. Accompanied by Emmylou Harris' Hot Band, including **Byron Berline** on fiddle, with back-up vocals provided by Dolly Parton, Emmylou Harris, and Anne Murray, the album produced a No. 10 hit, "Baby Boy," one of Mary Kay's own songs. It remained on the Top Singles list for thirteen weeks. Additional tracks from this album worth noting include "Vitamin L," one of Mary Kay's compositions, "All I Can Do," a Dolly Parton song, "Settin' the Woods on Fire," a Hank Williams number, and two country gospel songs, "Have a Little Talk with Jesus" and "Good Old Country Baptizin'."

Mary Kay's second album with Columbia in 1977 was *Aimin' to Please*, which included another Top 10 hit, "Something to Brag About," a duet with Willie Nelson. Back-up musicians on this album included fellow Oklahoman **Leon Russell**, as well as James Burton, Emmylou Harris, and Albert Lee. The ten tracks on this album include such favorites as "Don't Make Love to a Country Music Singer," "Marlboro Man," "Cattle Kate," "Dolly's Dive," "Anybody's Darlin' (Anything But Mine)," "Even Cowgirls Get the Blues," and "Paintin' Her Fingernails."

Place has become more involved with her television and movie career during the past twenty-five years. She wrote scripts for such television sitcoms as the *Mary Tyler Moore Show*, *Phyllis*, *The Paul Sand Show*, and *M*A*S*H*, as well as guest appearances in such television series as *The West Wing* and *Law and Order*. In addition, she has appeared in more than thirty films, including *Bound for Glory* (1976), *The Big Chill* (1983), *Captain Ron* (1992), *Manny & Lo* (1996), *The Rainmaker* (1997), *Pecker* (1998), *Being John Malkovich* (1999), *Girl, Interrupted* (1999), *Committed* (2000), *My First Mister* (2001), *Human Nature* (2002), *Sweet Home Alabama* (2002), and as a band singer in Martin Scorsese's *New York, New York* (1977), in which she does a dynamite rendition of "Blue Moon." During this period, she did sing and play bass on John Stewart's *Bombs Away Dream Babies* album, released in 1979.

In 2001, Raven Records, an Australian company, released the *Ahern Sessions: 1976-1977*, an album of twenty tracks from the *Tonite! At the Capri Lounge* and *Aimin' to Please* collections. Named after veteran producer Brian Ahern, the best of Mary Kay Place vocals is once again available, and features contributions by two Oklahomans, **Leon Russell** and **Byron Berline**.

Place returned to Tulsa from her Los Angeles home to serve as keynote speaker for the 2002 Harwelden Awards ceremony, presented by the Tulsa Arts and Humanities Council to recognize supporters of the arts and humanities. (GC)

Ponca Tribe
(Arrived in Oklahoma in 1877)

One of several tribes removed to Indian Territory in the 19th century from their settlements on the Great Plains, and now one of thirty-eight federally recognized American Indian tribes, bands, nations or tribal towns in Oklahoma, the Ponca Tribe is one of the primary musical sources for much of what has become the Southern Plains powwow singing tradition, dispersed in the 20th century through the intertribal, pan-Indian powwow now prominent throughout North America. Their songs and style are derived from ancient times when they were one people with the Omaha, Osage,

Kansa, and Quapaw, all of whom form the Dhegiha group in the Siouan linguistic family. Additionally, the Ponca's powwow tradition and song history produced the first "world champion fancy dancer," Augustus MacDonald, and the Ponca "hethoshka" war dance and tail dance ceremonies are the model for the intertribal men's powwow dance, the straight dance. The hethoshka songs and dances are also the source of the Osage Inlonshka drums and ceremonies in Hominy, Fairfax, and Pawhuska, Oklahoma. Marking their first modern powwow with the year they left Nebraska in 1876, the Ponca Tribe hosted its 127th official powwow in 2003 with Jasper Clark as head singer. The Ponca Powwow is both a homecoming opportunity for tribal members who live outside the area, and a chance for people who live around White Eagle to see their relatives. Before removal, the powwow was a community day of thanks, honor, and recognition. Today, the powwow is based around entertainment and contest dancing where one hears the strong legacy of Ponca war dance singing. Family songs and individual songs may be heard at more private gatherings during the powwow weekend.

Tony Arkeketa

Ponca songs are often credited as deriving from the Omaha, but Ponca singers, such as Anthony Arkeketa (b. March 7, 1943, Pawnee, Oklahoma), who grew up and still lives on his family's allotment land on the Ponca reservation, believe the cultural wellspring was the same for all five Dhegiha tribes before they split in the 1600s. The Omaha language and Ponca languages are the same, but have different dialects. Ponca elder and one of the few remaining fluent speakers of the Ponca language, Louis Headman, explains that Dhegiha means "people on our side."

Ponca songs name places the Dhegiha where the group camped on migrations east to the Atlantic Coast of Virginia and the Carolinas, and then back west to the Mississippi River before dividing. The Quapaw went downstream, and the other four groups traveled to the mouth of the Osage River in Missouri where they divided again. The Osage stayed in Missouri, the Kansa (Kaw) migrated up the Missouri River into Kansas, and the Ponca separated from the Omaha and began traveling toward the Black Hills of South Dakota and southwestern Minnesota's pipestone quarries.

Historical records place the Ponca along the Niobrara River as early as 1673. The Omaha appear to have rejoined the Ponca for a time, but increasing pressure from settlers and the Sioux presaged the Ponca ceding all of their lands in a treaty with the U.S. Government in 1858. Assigned to a reservation in north central Nebraska at the confluence of the Niobrara River and Missouri Rivers, the Ponca began peaceful, agrarian progress toward self-subsistence. Known for their friendliness, the tribe helped a group of Mormons survive a harsh winter near the town of Niobrara, Nebraska. In 1865, the Ponca ceded one-third of their reservation to the U.S. Government in exchange for permanent title of certain land tracts totaling about 96,000 acres. Nonetheless, the year after Nebraska's statehood, an "oversight" included the Ponca reservation on a large tract of land set aside for the Dakota Sioux in the Treaty of Fort Laramie in 1868. While the Laramie Treaty spells out details so minute as to how many yards of calico and cotton would be provided to Dakota reservation girls over the age of twelve for their clothing, the drafters "forgot" the Ponca were living on land given to the Dakota. Since the Poncas were all of a sudden on Sioux lands, the Dakota began raiding the Ponca reservation for eight years and the Government had a major "Indian problem" on their hands.

Without consulting the tribe, Congress claimed the rest of the Ponca lands in 1876 and began removing the tribe to Indian Territory, a journey of nearly 600 miles over muddy roads made worse by spring rains, and on which many people died. In the summer of 1877, 681 Ponca arrived on the wooded Quapaw Reservation in the flint hills of northeastern corner of Indian Territory. After several months, the Ponca and their agent traveled west and located the space for a reservation along the Salt Fork River in north central Oklahoma near present day Ponca City. Meanwhile, more Ponca people died of multiple health problems both in their time with the Quapaw and in their first year staying on the reservation. Ponca Chief Standing Bear's son was one of the dead, and to fulfill a promise to his son, Chief Standing Bear returned the body to the Ponca homelands in Nebraska.

Arriving at the Omaha Agency a few weeks later after traveling through a blizzard in the winter of 1879, the thirty Ponca in Standing Bear's party were promptly arrested by U.S. Troops and imprisoned at Fort Omaha. The subsequent 1879 case of *Standing Bear v. Crook* brought national attention to the Ponca's plight and established Standing Bear as the country's "first civil rights" leader. In the outcome of the case, the federal court decided American Indians are "people" and enjoy the same rights as any other person under the U.S. Constitution. As a result of the trial's publicity, the nation's eyes and sentiment turned to the Ponca and their situation. Standing Bear made a highly publicized speaking tour of East Coast cities, and Congress made special appropriations to help the Ponca with their situation in Indian Territory.

In 1883, a boarding school opened near the Ponca Agency, a Methodist mission began operation in 1890, and the Ponca began their uneasy journey of negotiating the two distinctly different worlds of traditional American Indian life and the American mainstream. According to Tony Arkeketa, Ponca oral tradition says, "The people were lost at that time, no longer a community, and their social structure was in disarray. Alcohol came into the tribe via traders and became prevalent to the extent that there were killings within the tribe." Arkeketa further explains, "The remaining Ponca traditional leaders saw this happening, and picked three men of the tribe to go and find a means of bringing the people back together. The men traveled to Cache, Oklahoma, where they met Quanah Parker, the Comanche who had synthesized Christianity with the Native American Church's peyote religion. From there, they created a Native American Church chapter around 1900 that was openly derided by drunken tribal members outside of the tipi. Since the men of the church only brought back four Comanche Native American Church songs, more songs had to be created."

Tony Arkeketa's grandfather, Ed Roy, was one of the three men, along with Robert Buffalohead, and Roy became the fireman for the church ceremonies. Roy also composed some of the songs that are sung today, which began a spiritual rejuvenation of the tribe. The same people who had been outside of the tipi making noise began to go inside out of curiosity, and a meaningful spiritual change took place in the tribe. These songs are best heard on *Ponca Peyote Songs Vol. 1, 2, & 3* (Indian House, 1972), an album recorded by Tony Isaacs in 1972 in Ponca City, Oklahoma. The songs praise the medicine (peyote) and God's word, ask Jesus for

Sylvester Warrior, Harry Buffalohead, James Clark, Franklin Smith, and Joe H. Rush

help, and celebrate the coming daylight of each service as well just being alive. Singing in the Ponca language are Sylvester Warrior, Harry Buffalohead, James Clark, Franklin Smith, and Joe H. Rush. The songs are typical of other Native American Church songs with vocals, water drum, and rattle all played at a fast pace, but their uniqueness lies in the Ponca language and perspective. While the Peyote songs are a developed element of traditional Ponca life in the last 100 years, the original music of the "hethoshka" may be the most influential Ponca contribution to world music in general, but specifically to the North American powwow singing tradition.

"Hethoshka" songs are derived from Ponca history and tell stories about the tribe's experiences in battle and on the hunt. Although never used in preparation for war, nor for the period after conflict, the "hethoshka" ceremony is called a war dance because the songs refer to experiences warriors had in battle, and were a way of preserving Ponca history. The dance continues unabated today with annual gatherings at White Eagle, and one often sees the traditional "straight dancer" at intertribal powwows in regalia whose roots are settled into Ponca traditions. Additionally, through the Ponca "hethoshka," the Osage derived their "I'n-Lon-Schka" drums from the Ponca via the Otoe-Missouria and the Kansa.

According to Archie Mason, an Osage/Cherokee elder and long-time Tulsa public school and university educator, "When the Poncas first arrived on their reservation in Indian Territory, they did not arrive in time to plant crops and were starving. The Osage were already in place on their reservation across the Arkansas River and had plenty of corn and other crops. At that time, one could ford the Arkansas River in a wagon, and the Osage took a lot of corn over to the Ponca. As a return gesture, the Ponca gave the Osage people at Grayhorse a drum and the ceremonial religion of hethoshka, or war dance, and the Grass Dance, most likely from the Omaha. The Osage translated the words into "I'n-Lon-Shka," meaning "war dance."

Contemporarily, that story explains why many songs the Osage use in the Gray Horse I'n-Lon-Shka are of Ponca Origin. One also finds several Ponca people at the Grayhorse I'n-Lon-Shka, usually the first weekend of June. Subsequently, the Ponca gave the Otoe a drum and permission to perform the ceremonies, however, the Otoe could not fulfill the requirements for the drum and they passed it on to the Osage at Hominy, who still have it today. The Ponca also gave the Kansa (Kaw) a drum and permission to dance the hethoshka, but the Kansa could not fulfill the requirements for keeping the drum and passed it on to the Osage at Pawhuska, Oklahoma where it remains until the present time for the annual Pawhuska I'n-Lon-Shka ceremonies. Many of these songs can be heard on *War Dance Songs of the Ponca, Vol. 1 and 2* (Indian House 1967). The albums are full of ancient Ponca songs recorded at Ponca City in May of 1967, and include singers Lamont Brown, Harry Buffalohead, Joe H. Rush, Russell Rush, Sylvester Warrior, Albert Waters, Louis Yellow Horse, Alice Cook, Lucy C.F. Ribs, and Stella Yellow Horse. A few of the songs were later released on *Proud Heritage: A Celebration of American Indian Music* (Indian House 1996).

One of the Ponca songs on the album recounts the bravado of a warrior during battle with these taunting lyrics: "The enemy, they are coming. There they are. They're coming to seek me out. Enemy, if you're looking for me, here I stand. Come over here!" *Volume 2* includes twenty-two "War Dance Songs" with the same singers but also includes trot songs and charging, or contest, songs.

In addition to the album of Ponca songs released by Canyon Records, *Ponca War Dances* (CR-6143), the historic American Indian Soundchiefs label, founded by Rev. Linn D. Pauahty (**Kiowa**), also produced albums of Ponca tribal songs and Ponca war dance songs in 1967 that are available on reissue cassette through Indian House Records. *Ponca Tribal Songs* (SC119), recorded August, 1967, contains the "Ponca Flag Song," "Veterans' Song," "Memorial Song," "Three Trot

Dance Songs," "Seven War Dance Songs, and "Four Contest Songs," and includes singers Lamont Brown, Sylvester Warrior, Albert Waters, and Henry Snake. *Ponca Warriors Dance Songs and Pawnee Warriors Dance Songs* (SC118) presents ten Ponca "Warrior Dance Songs" sung by Sylvester Warrior, Albert Waters, and Francis Eagle. Finally, the Oklahoma State Arts Council's *Songs of Indian Territory* cassette includes Tony Arkeketa, Edwin Littlecook, and Maynard Hinman singing Ponca War and Scalp Dance Songs.

While the Ponca tried to get back to some semblance of normalcy in the early 20th century, the 101 Wild West Show opened in 1905 just about eight miles south of White Eagle and the Ponca Reservation. The 101 expanded its annual rodeos to include cowboy sports of roping, riding, bulldogging, all sorts of trick riding, and Ponca dancers doing war dances for Eastern tourists who came to Indian territory in hopes of seeing some "wild Indians." Since the stately and reserved "het-hoshka" dances were not quite flashy enough for tourists, the Ponca evolved regalia based on the single bustle they and the Omaha once wore, and started performing athletic dances with a lot of movement to the fast war dance songs as part of the wild West show. The long-term effect of these performances was to popularize Ponca songs outside of their original context to create some of the first "Pan-Indian" music, and to draw interest to the annual Ponca powwows where contemporary fancy dancing was in its infant stages. While the dance was new to the American public and other tribes, the fancy war dance has its roots in both Ponca musical and cultural traditions.

Although various explanations exist for the origin of the fancy dance that has become so emblematic of the contemporary powwow, to include the dancer's replication a champion stallion's footwork, the Ponca have a song about the creation of the dance that has diffused through throughout the powwow world. According to Ponca elder Louis Headman, in the fast war dance songs, one song tells the Ponca story of the origin of the fancy war dance. Headman explains the English translation is, "When I was young, my elder brother

Fancy War Dancers

took me to see them kill the buffalo." The story behind the words is that the elder brother, a chief's son, took the younger brother out to see the Poncas kill the buffalo. In those days the hunters would drive the buffalo off a cliff by waving buckskin in the air in hopes that the buffalo would fall to their death. Sometimes the buffalo would not die, but would just get angry. Headman says, "The Ponca hunters would wave the buckskin and do all kinds of crazy antics in front of the buffalo so the other hunters could creep around behind them and kill them. The boy saw this and when he got back to the camp he began to mimic the hunters, do somersaults, and do a fast dance with his feet." When the song maker saw this, he began to roll the drum and keep time with the boy's impression of the buffalo hunters. Contemporarily, one will see a lot of quick footwork, fast head movements, and whip sticks twirled around in time with the drum in the manner of the previously mentioned hunters' buckskin.

Given the historic musical connection between the fancy dance and the Ponca, it was not surprising for Ponca dancer Augustus MacDonald to win the first fancy dance championship in 1926 at Haskell Indian Nations Institute in Lawrence, Kansas. MacDonald's victory also secured the right for the Ponca to host the annual world fancy dance championship during the annual Ponca Powwow at White Eagle. The Ponca Powwow remained "the" proving ground for champion fancy dancers throughout the 20th century. While mega-powwows may offer more prize money, no first place trophy means more to a fancy dancer than the one they can win at Ponca. Additional information and history of the fancy war dance can be gleaned from the video *Fancy Dance* (Full Circle Productions, 1997).

Contemporary Ponca singers continue to make an impact on the intertribal powwow world. Anthony Arkeketa grew up around the Native American Church, sleeping behind his grandfather in tipi services as a small child. As he matured into a teenager and began to show musical inclinations, Arkeketa's grandparents paid for his place at the Ponca drum so he could develop into a singer in the late 1950s. Once there, he sat and sang with the famous names of Ponca singing, such as Charlie Waters, Albert Waters, Joe Rush, Russell Rush, Sylvester Warrior, Lamont Brown, and Harry Buffalohead. During that period, Arkeketa was tasked with learning the songs through the oral tradition with Harry Buffalohead. After learning the songs through the oral tradition, as opposed to the modern way of learning from an audio recording, Tony maintains many of the songs today. He points out that many Ponca songs exist about the way the Ponca's dress, to include the bustle that is now worn by many contemporary traditional dancer, songs for children, songs for society, famous chiefs like Sioux leader Spotted Tail, and places the Ponca lived along the Niobrara River.

As World War I developed the Ponca sang songs about German Kaiser Wilhelm, and during World War II they created songs with Hitler in them. Older men of the tribe wrote songs for returning service people who returned from World War II, and those songs became individual songs that are only performed when the individual or the family of the individual requests them, unless they are "put back on the drum" so everyone can sing them. Every Ponca song has a story behind in it, and in many cases the origin relates directly to Ponca history. Since Tony's generation was the last to learn the Ponca language from fluent speakers, one of the few places Ponca youth can learn the language and history the tribe are through the songs. Some of the music is so old, however, no one knows what some of the words in the songs mean, and the tribe continues singing the songs with the words in them anyway. While some songs related to family groups still exist, others have been forgotten, such as the Sun Dance Songs that seem to have vanished with the participants of the last Ponca Sun Dance held in 1902, while new ones are written for new events and people.

With regard to contemporary inter-tribal singers, Tony Arkeketa is also generally credited with bringing the higher pitched, northern style of American Indian singing to Oklahoma powwows. In the early

*Redland Singers, left to right: Berwyn Moses (Pawnee/Ft. Sill Apache), Eddie Arkeketa (Ponca/Otoe), George Coser (**Muscogee**), Joe Don Waters (Ponca/**Kiowa**).*

1960s, Tony began traveling on his vacations to the Dakotas, Wyoming, and Montana where he sang with Arikarees, Mandans, Hidatsas, Sioux, all of whom sing in the northern style. Upon returning to Oklahoma, Tony formed a group of intertribal singers to replicate the northern style and started singing in public as the Redland Singers in 1968. Since then, they have served as host drum from Washington D.C. to Los Angeles, and the North Country Fair to Corpus Christi, Texas, but have never been recorded commercially. A group agreement decided not to profit personally from the music, but to provide the music for people and communities, and record only for historic preservation.

However, some Ponca singers have appeared on commercial recordings, most notably Yellowhammer who have recorded three albums for Indian House Records: *Live at Hollywood, Florida* (1995), *Red Rock, Oklahoma* (1995), and *World Champions* (2001). Although some Otoe-Missouria songs are included on the discs representing the current geographic proximity and intermarriage between the Ponca and the Otoe in north central Oklahoma, Yellowhammer is made up primarily of Ponca singers. Singers on the albums have included Perry Lee Botone, Jr., Mike Gawhega, Jim Grant, Wesley J. Hudson, James Kemble, Jim Kemble, Jr. Garland Kent, Jr., Gregory Lieb, Kinsel Lieb, John McIntosh, Patrick T. Moore, Jade Roubedeaux, Stephen Little Cook, Patrick Moore, Oliver

Littlecook, Jr., Tesa Roubedeaux, and Andrea Morning Star Kemble. In 1995, the group won first place in the Southern Plains singing competition at the Schemitzun, Connecticut Powwow, and repeated the feat in 1997, 1998, and 2001. Many of these same singers contributed to the Fort Oakland Ramblers' initial release in 1992 on Indian House Records, *Oklahoma Intertribal and Contest Songs*, recorded at

Yellowhammer Singers

White Eagle. Since then, under the leadership of contemporary Tonkawa tribal President, Donald Patterson, the Fort Oakland Ramblers have focused more on the Tonkawa's language and cultural roots. Nonetheless, these last few recordings represent the intertribal, cross-cultural influences that have taken place throughout the 20th century in Oklahoma, where a shared sense of "Indianness" and a need for commonality in a non-Indian world developed a community of singers who learned from one another and sang together to play a primary role in creating Oklahoma's powwow music, and by extension, a good share of the southern style intertribal powwow music that has now become commonly heard at powwows across North America. (HF)
www.indianhouse.com or www.canyonrecords.com

Red Dirt Music

With Jimmy LaFave, Tom Skinner, Bob Childers, **The Great Divide**, **Red Dirt Rangers**, **Cross Canadian Ragweed**, **Jason Boland and the Stragglers**, and a host of other rootsy singer songwriters and groups leading the way, the multi-influenced music known as red dirt music is varying degrees of blues, country, Tin Pan Alley, rock and roll, folk, and cowboy songs, often delivered with lyrically sardonic humor that is often dry as the red earth around north central Oklahoma, to include Enid, Oklahoma City, and especially Stillwater where its primary musicians met, usually as college students at Oklahoma State University. When humor is not the object of the song's lyrically focused intent, subtle and melancholy appraisals of rural and small town society's decay fill the verses of red dirt music, and, occasionally, a song about love lost or gained creeps or weeps its way into the mix. In 2003, Cross Canadian Ragweed's Cody Canada suggested the term should possibly be transmogrified to Red River music because of the propensity of the Oklahoma bands having equal success in more populated Texas than in the state where they started, but we'll leave that heresy alone for the time being.

The first Oklahoman to hint at the "genre" is Kiowa-Comanche-Muscogee guitarist **Jesse Ed Davis,** whose "Red Dirt Boogie, Brother," a funky, self-defining tune about "plain old rock and roll," appeared on his 1972 album *Ululu* (Atco). Close behind in name, if not definition, is **Steve Ripley** whose early 1970s band, Moses, recorded for Ripley's independent Red Dirt Records. Liner notes by Mike Dougan on the band's self-titled debut in 1974 explains Red Dirt is a record label and "also the color of the earth surrounding Enid and nearby Stillwater, Moses' home base. More important, Red Dirt is a hue of funk, a shade of sound, a basic spirit embodied in Moses' music."

While the genre's anthem is **Jimmy LaFave**'s "Red Dirt Roads at Night," and LaFave recorded his first album in Stillwater in 1978, the first artist to emerge on a national scale from the Stillwater scene was **Garth Brooks** who began singing

Santa Fe, 1987, left to right: Tom Skinner, Jed Lindsey, Garth Brooks, Mike Skinner, Matt O'Melia (not pictured).

at Willie's Saloon on Washington Street in 1985. After a failed attempt that year at breaking through Nashville's long established musical hierarchy, Brooks returned to Stillwater and started a group called Santa Fe in 1986. Filling out Santa Fe were Tom Skinner, roundly considered along with Bob Childers as one of red dirt music's early shapers, as well as Tom's brothers Mike and Craig, on fiddle and guitar respectively, and other Stillwater musicians to include Matt O'Melia (drums), Dale Pierce (steel guitar and dobro), and Jed Lindsey (guitar). A particularly good take on the early Stillwater scene that produced Santa Fe can be gleaned from drummer O'Melia's book about those years, *Garth Brooks: The Road Out of Santa Fe* (University of Oklahoma Press, 1997). After graduating from OSU with a degree in marketing, Garth again headed for Nashville. There, he connected with Bob Childers who introduced the one-time OSU javelin thrower to the manager who ignited Brooks' star in the country music firmament.

Bob Childers was born in West Virginia, studied music at the University of California-Berkeley, and began traveling the country in 1972 when he arrived in Stillwater and discovered Chuck Dunlap, a local Stillwater-based singer songwriter who still reins as the elder statesman of the movement. Childers decided to stay in Stillwater and played locally until 1978 when he met Jimmy LaFave. With LaFave's assistance, Bob recorded his first album, *I Ain't No Jukebox* (1979).

Bob Childers

Childers' second album, 1982's *Singing Trees, Dancing Waters*, gained him enough critical attention for a White House gig in Washington, D.C., and enough confidence to move to Nashville in 1986, followed closely by Tom Skinner and Garth.

Childers released two albums in 1986, *Four Horsemen*, and the all-instrumental *King David's Lament.* Nashville's "smooth" requirements ultimately alienated Childers, and the songwriter moved to Austin where he recorded *Circles Toward the Sun* (1990) that produced a couple of minor regional hits, "Restless Spirits" and "Mexican Mornings." Finally coming full circle, Childers moved back to Stillwater in 1996 and recorded an album that received considerable attention in Europe, *Nothin' More Natural* (Binky Records). Bob's 1999 CD, *Hat Trick*, featured songs co-written by Mike McClure (**The Great Divide**), Brad Piccolo (**Red Dirt Rangers**), and Garth Brooks. Bob also added two tracks to The Great Divide and Friends 1999 gospel album, *Dirt and Spirit*. In 2000, Binky Records released Childers' *La Vita e Bella – Outtakes, Demos and Jams 1980 – 1988*. According to the Binky Records website, Bob's future music industry plans are on hold in 2003 while he "is concentrating on the education of his children." Nonetheless, younger red dirt musicians continue recording his songs, such as the Red Dirt Rangers, Cross Canadian Ragweed, Jason Boland and the Stragglers, and Stoney LaRue. LaRue included Childers' "Dance with the Gypsies" on the 2002 CD, *Downtown* (Lone Star Music). As much as any musician, Childers defines the genre, often known by fans as a "Dylan of the dust," or simply, "the Godfather."

Although Tom Skinner was born in San Francisco, he and his two musically inclined brothers, Mike and Craig, grew up in the Route 66 town of Bristow about thirty miles southwest of Tulsa. Skinner moved to Stillwater in 1972 where a short attempt at Oklahoma State University bore few fruits other than Skinner's first guitar chords. After a stint in the Air Force where he played in his first bands, Tom returned to Oklahoma in 1978 and re-enrolled at Oklahoma State. Soon, his brothers followed and they began performing around town as The Skinner Brothers Band, most notably at Willie's Saloon where Garth Brooks also frequented the open microphone nights. Garth hooked up with the brothers who eventually became the nucleus of his first group, Santa Fe, where the evolving red dirt sound began to take solid commercial shape. Skinner moved to Nashville for a short time in the late 1980s, but returned to Oklahoma for his young son's sake, and then migrated to Louisiana where he began recording for Binky Records, to include *Times Have Changed* (1996), and *Acoustic Skinner* (1998). Skinner continues to perform in Oklahoma at venues such as the Blue Door in Oklahoma City, itself a primary outlet for the sound, and could be heard there in 2003 with his Wednesday Night Science Project.

Greg Jacobs

Along with Bob Childers' albums, Binky has also released two compact discs by Greg Jacobs, the Choctaw, Oklahoma native who found his way to Stillwater in the 1970s for college, and turned into another singer-songwriter now associated with the red dirt sound. After rambling through Kentucky and then taking a shot at the Nashville scene that did not take to his highly personal songs, Jacobs returned to Oklahoma. Working as an opening act for **Kevin Welch** and Jimmy LaFave, Jacobs recorded two independent albums, *Looking at the Moon* (1994), and *Reclining with Age* (1996). Currently a high school history teacher in Checotah, Jacobs' albums, *South of Muskogee Town* (1997) and *Look at Love* (1999), are chock full of stories about Oklahoma's hard rural history in the 20th century - "A Little Rain Will Do," and "Okie Wind," as well as seldom-told stories like that of **Muscogee (Creek)** patriot Chitto Harjo in "South of Muskogee Town," a song about the Green Corn Rebellion of 1918. His 2001 release recycled an earlier album title, *Reclining with Age* (Binky), and continued Jacobs' themes and storytelling style of his earlier collections.

Young bands and singer-songwriters have played local talent nights and open microphones in Stillwater for as long as college students have been drinking beer in the north central Oklahoma town, but a unique environment opened in May of 1989 when John Cooper of the Red Dirt Rangers and recreation specialist major Danny Pierce moved into a rural six-bedroom farmhouse on 149 acres for a hundred bucks a month. Only a few miles west of Stillwater, "The Farm" quickly gained a reputation as a communal jam space, party center, and flophouse for local musicians and college students throughout the 1990s. Roughly 60 roommates moved through The Farm during its ten-year existence, and although the Red Dirt Rangers' Brad Piccolo didn't live there, he was a constant presence and credits his inspiration for seeking a music career to seeing Jimmy LaFave singing a Bob Dylan song on the front porch one night. Also present at various times were Bob Childers, Tom Skinner, Greg Jacobs, and Garth, all of whom headed out to The Farm when Stillwater's bars closed and musicians still had the desire to play. Texas singer-songwriter Robert Earl Keen stopped by at one time or another where bonfires were set and musicians jammed until dawn, as did Brandon Jenkins, Mark Lyons, Curt Nielsen, and Chuck Dunlap. Dunlap recorded a 1980 album called *Daze Gone By* (Snowbound), featuring Kevin Welch on guitar, and

Mike McClure

sporting a jazzy, folk feel with pedal steel, bongos, saxophone, banjo, and plenty of harmony vocals.

In the last year or two of The Farm's existence, before a Methodist church bought the property in 1999, relative newcomers to Stillwater, Cody Canada of Cross Canadian Ragweed, Mike McClure, formerly of the Great Divide who now fronts his own band, and Jason Boland emerged on the scene. Boland had one of the Stragglers' first promo pictures taken on the porch of The Farm, and images of the now legendary homestead have been forever preserved on Mike McClure's website (www.mikemcclure.com). Other bands that played in the garage, the front room, the basement, or the fields throughout the 1990s included the Cimarron Swingsters, the Red Valley Barnstormers, the Flat Mountain Boys, and the Medicine Show, whose 1994 album, *Medicine Show Live at the Tower Theater*, stirs up great clouds of red dirt music, as does their 1997 release, *Midnight Ramble,* recorded live in Fayetville, Arkansas.

While the Delicious Militia did not play at The Farm, their lyrically twisted, if not gifted, 1998 country rock album, *What Ever Happened to the Banjo Girl* (Hog Frost), featured several Stillwater college students, to include OSU Rhodes Scholar and Hydro, Oklahoma native, Blaine Greteman, who went on to be the London entertainment editor for *Time* Magazine, and, as of 2003, was a Ph.D. candidate at the University of California at Berkeley. Other local Stillwater artists who have close connections to the scene include Mitch Cason, Beverly Mayes, and DaddyO's Music owner, songwriter and guitarist, Mike Shannon (b. Tulsa, 1953). Also, Monica Taylor and Patrick Williams, both Cherokee Nation citizens better known as The Farm Couple who currently live in Afton, have been performing together since 1996 when they debuted at the Winfield Bluegrass Festival. Monica was living at The Farm at that time, and Patrick was living near Grove, Oklahoma. Their independent CD, *Songs from the Kitchen Table*, was recorded in "one take per song" in a studio overlooking a lake in Eureka Springs, Arkansas, and features songs about ramblers, Civil War veterans, and other down-and-outers.

Additional musicians who have been placed in the red dirt genre (whether they like it or not) include Tulsa-based Larry Spears, whose CD, *Reflection in the Wishing Well*, featuring songs about Woody Guthrie, Jesus, and better times that have passed. Tom Skinner also adds bass and vocals to the album. The Burtschi Brothers from Norman have also been allied with the sound. The Brothers' band includes Travis Linville (guitar), Mike Phenix (bass), Kevin Webb (guitars), and Chris Foreman (drums). Exhibiting the back-and-forth-from-Oklahoma-to-Texas-nature of red dirt groups, The Burtschi Brothers' debut album, *Uncertain Texas*, was recorded in Linville's Norman bedroom, and after a little success, the group recorded CD number two in Austin, Texas. Next, their most recent effort was recorded live in Tahlequah and exhibits their extended jams where "Jimi Hendrix meets Willie Nelson in outer space."

Another Oklahoma native musician with red dirt tendencies, Brandon Jenkins (b. June 7, 1969, Tulsa), has made his home in Austin after growing up in Tulsa. Jenkins attended Oklahoma State where he graduated with a B.A. in Sociology, tried out Nashville for a while after he had signed with a label in Alabama that tried to market him as a country act, and then returned to Tulsa before heading south across the border to Austin's intensely music friendly environment. Jenkins' 1998 CD, *Faded*, brands his style as "Western Soul, a hybrid of country, blues, and rock-n-roll," which allies it closely with basic tenets of red dirt music. A song Jenkins wrote in Stillwater, "Feet Don't Touch the Ground," was included on a Pete Anderson produced compilation of America's best unsigned artists outside of Nashville called *Country West of Nashville* (2001). In 2003, Jenkins planned to release his next project, *Unmended*, and had tour dates scheduled from Waco and Lubbock to Stillwater and Norman through the summer and fall of that year.

Stoney LaRue

Two of the latest arrivals on the red dirt scene are Amanda Cunningham (b. 1978) and Stoney LaRue and the Organic Boogie Band. Cunningham's independent CD, *Gypsy's Daughter*, mines the red dirt vein well enough to have earned her the *Oklahoma Gazette*'s 2003 Woody Award for Best Singer/Songwriter in Oklahoma. Larue, originally from Texas, but who lived in Chickasha through his teens, guides the Organic Boogie Band through twelve songs on their debut CD, *Downtown*. The album is drenched in red dirt influences, with two songs co-written by LaRue and Jason Boland, and covers of songs by Brandon Jenkins, Bob Childers, and Mike McClure. The Organic Boogie band itself is made up of three Bartlesville natives: bassist Donnie Wood, guitarist Mark Lacy, and drummer Doug Wehmeyer.

A final figure of note is multi-instrumentalist, music teacher, studio artist, and recording engineer Jeffrey Gray Parker who was born in Arkansas City, Kansas in 1956, but raised in Newkirk, Oklahoma. After a short stint in St. Louis, Parker lived in Norman from 1970 to 1989, and moved to Stillwater where he resided from 1989 to 1998. With two albums under his studio alter ego, Coyote Zen, influenced not only by the red dirt sound and his own American Indian (Cherokee) background, *Blood of Many Nations* (1997) and *Medicine Dog* (2002) also fuse multiple world music elements into unique releases that transcend the red dirt genre. As a performer, Parker has traveled widely and played with a myriad of nationally recognized artists (Buck Owens, Kevin Welch, Ricochet, Rita Coolidge, Alice Cooper, **Brewer** and Shipley, **Kevin Welch**, et al.), and has had his music used in various film and television projects, as well as radio and television commercials.

Aside from Jeffrey Parker's individual releases, his Cimarron Sound Lab in Stillwater was the site for the recording of *Red Dirt Sampler, Volume 1: A Stillwater Songwriters' Collective*. The album is a primer for red dirt music fans. Songs by all the first generation of the sound's luminaries, Tom Skinner, Brad James, Mike McClure, Greg Jacobs, Bob Childers are on the CD, as well as songs co-written by Parker with Skinner and Bob Kline. A **Cherokee Nation** citizen, Parker relocated his Cimarron Sound Lab to Cherokee County, near Tahlequah, in 1998.

While DaddyO's is still on Main Street, and two of the Red Dirt Rangers live in rural areas east of Stillwater near the small town of Glencoe, by 2003 many of the musicians who created the scene moved on to Tulsa, Oklahoma City, Austin, Nashville, or back to the small Oklahoma towns they had left behind for college, although Bob Childers can still be seen occasionally in Stillwater grocery stores. Perhaps even the term itself has left the area. In the spring of 2003, country pop act Brooks & Dunn, featuring **Ronnie Dunn,** who has deep Tulsa ties, released *Red Dirt Road* (Arista), featuring a #1 country single by the same name that is a rowdy tribute to the lessons of rural life learned out on the dusty crimson pathways of the country. Of course, it could just as well be Georgia or Texas as north central Oklahoma, but the duplicity serves their marketing goals nicely. While red dirt music may often only be a tag placed on musicians from the Stillwater area (and now much of central Oklahoma) who write their own songs and play in traditional American music veins, the category is also useful for describing music that is at times one person with a guitar and a story to tell, and at other times a gutsy jam band freak-out not afraid of a little twang; all of which draws inspiration from **Woody Guthrie**'s lyrical abilities, **Bob Wills**' wide open approach to popular music, and Will Rogers' plain-spoken humor to create a sound and story unique to Oklahoma. (HF) www.reddirtmusic.com ; www.bobchilders.com ; http://members.aol.com/straycatm/tomskinner.htm ; www.binkyrecords.com ; www.brandonjenkins.net ; www.bluedoorokc.com ; www.amandasmusic.com ; www.coyotezen.com; www.organicboogieband.com

Red Dirt Rangers
(formed loosely in 1981, Stillwater, OK, then Oklahoma City in 1989)

Inspired by **Jimmy LaFave**'s song "Red Dirt Roads" and the red dirt around Oklahoma City where the group took its primary shape in the late 1980s, the Red

Red Dirt Rangers, left to right: Ben Han, Brad Piccolo, and John Cooper

Dirt Rangers are one of the most representative and long-lasting groups who emerged from the hybrid **Red Dirt Music** scene around Stillwater, Oklahoma in the 1980s and early 1990s.

The band formed when Stillwater native Brad Piccolo (b. April 22, 1961), Oklahoma City-born John Cooper, and Bob Wiles (b. Tulsa, OK) all became musically inspired during their college days at Oklahoma State. Piccolo had picked up a guitar when he was fifteen, strumming it alone and learning chords, but never played with anyone until meeting Cooper in college. Cooper's first musical experience was singing in church choirs, and started playing mandolin when he arrived at O.S.U. and met Piccolo who had one and showed Cooper a few chords. With Bob Wiles, they traveled to the Winfield Bluegrass Festival in Winfield, Kansas, known as "the picker's paradise," and gained both confidence and a bluegrass base that would stay with their music for the duration of their playing and recording career.

The first semblance of a gig between future members of the Red Dirt Rangers occurred in 1981 at Aunt Molly's Coffee House, an open microphone setting in the Oklahoma State student union. The group did not play formally until the mid 1980s when Cooper and Piccolo would get together because of the lack of a music scene in Oklahoma City and jam on covers, eventually adding Ben Han (b. Borneo) on lead guitar, and connecting with drummers. **Jimmy LaFave** came by their place one night and invited them to his annual Stillwater reunion show at Willie's Saloon in the late 1980s and early 1990s. As a result of the success of that performance, the Red Dirt Rangers formed and had their official paid debut in May of 1990 at a festival in Oklahoma City. Piccolo lived in Austin at the time where he played in another band and would drive up from Texas to play with the Rangers.

Keeping their day jobs, the Rangers played around once a month experimenting with various musical configurations, one of which involved two accordionists, one on rhythm and one on lead. Gradually, the Rangers began to get better gigs and played in New York City in 1993 because of an old friend, which turned into more dates in upstate New York. Subsequently, Piccolo relocated to Oklahoma City and the band recorded their first album in 1992, a cassette-only release intended as a demo, *Cimarron Soul*, now the name of the Rangers' publishing company. The group recorded and mixed the album in one night at Stillwater's Lamb Studios and its primal rawness still makes it a fan favorite, although it is long out-of-print and circulates primarily by bootlegs. Later in 1992, The Rangers' dropped the accordion players, and added Dale Pierce, who had played in early incarnations of Garth Brooks' band, on dobro, banjo, and Melobar, drummer Scott Buxton, and Dave Clark on guitar. The band recorded their first proper album, *Red Dirt Music*, at Bill Belknap's Long Branch Studio in Tulsa, and called in red dirt luminary Tom Skinner to help with the mixing. Along with a geographic nod to the area around Stillwater in "Cimarron Valley," the man often referred to as the godfather of red dirt music, Bob Childers, wrote two songs and co-wrote another song on the album.

In 1994, the band decided to tour Oklahoma in a school bus and do thirty shows in thirty days across the state. The Rangers played from Black Mesa to Wilburton at clubs, weddings, festivals, and campfire gigs at state parks. They also met multi-instrumentalist Benny Craig in Tahlequah on the tour and he started playing fiddle and steel in the group in time for the 1994 independent recording, *Oklahoma Territory*. The album was a watershed moment for the band as they enlisted legendary producer Lloyd Maines in Lubbock, Texas, and had their first taste of national chart success in the developing Americana radio format. The band spent fourteen hours a day in the studio for a week and recorded songs with a lot of Oklahoma references such as "Cimarron Valley" and "Idabel Blues." Continuing to play regionally, the Rangers' used the disc as a springboard to Europe where they played a trucker festival in Switzerland in 1997.

On returning to the states, the Rangers recorded a one-off track for the Lazy SOB compilation, *The Songs of Route 66*. As a result of "Used to Be," a Bob Childers/Bob Wiles composition about a once active and now lonely stretch of Route 66, the band negotiated a deal with Lazy SOB to record their next album, and continued touring until 1999 when they began laying down *Rangers' Command* in Austin, Texas. Again working with Lloyd Maines, the band added **Alvin Crow** on fiddle and mandocaster for one track, Cindy Cashdollar from

Asleep at the Wheel and Bob Dylan's band on dobro and steel guitar, and rough country sizzler Dale Watson on electric guitar on another. While drawing on major southwestern musical sources for inspiration and players, the lyrics drew a blueprint for red dirt music's literary perspective: original tunes with a sense of humor, two songs with Bob Childers as a co-writer, one song with Tom Skinner as a co-writer (an eerie foreshadowing of Benny Craig's premature death on "The Day the Mandolin Died"), two sets of obscure Woody Guthrie lyrics that had not been put to music before, and a wacky bluegrass cover of Prince's "1999." Partly due to the millennium change in 2000 and the inclusion of the Prince song, *Rangers' Command* made it to #21 on the Americana chart in January of 2000. That success led to constant regional touring, ceasing only in the spring of 2002 to record a new album with the Tractors' **Steve Ripley** at the legendary Church Studio in Tulsa, once owned by Leon Russell, and from 1987 to the present is owned and operated by Ripley.

Released independently by the Rangers, *Starin' Down the Sun* marked a shift in personnel for the group as they recruited a new drummer, Jim Karstein, known for his work with Gary Lewis and the Playboys, Leon Russell, Eric Clapton, J.J. Cale, Joe Cocker, Bobby "Blue" Bland, and Taj Mahal, and lesser known for his work on Cheech and Chong's "Basketball Jones." Rocky Frisco, another J.J. Cale luminary, plays on the record, as does their old friend from the Medicine Show, **Corey Mauser**. Muskogee trombonist and trumpeter Lee Norfleet adds tracks, as does Terry "Buffalo" Ware, Steve Ripley, Bob Childers, and **Byron Berline**. **Dwight Twilley** makes an appearance on vocals as well as being the topic of one song, "Dwight Twilley's Garage Sale." While Piccolo and Cooper wrote several songs on the album, as did Bob Childers and Brandon Jenkins, Bob Wiles also wrote or co-wrote a few tunes on the record as his swan song performance with the band due to carpal tunnel syndrome, as well as just a general need for a change after 13 years with the group. With a new album full of Oklahoma music luminaries, a new bassist in Jamie Kelly, and starting to work with steel/fiddle/guitarist Randy Crouch, the Red Dirt Rangers toured consistently through 2003. They added an additional element to their performance repertoire by releasing a children's album, *Blue Shoe: Music for Kids of All Ages*, which garnered them gigs at elementary schools and other children's activities across the state. (HF) www.reddirtrangers.com

Reinhart, Dick
(b. February 17, 1907 – d. December 3, 1948)

Considered as one of the finest western swing vocalists (especially the blues) and known for his compositions, such as "Fort Worth Jail" and "A Broken Heart for a Souvenir," former Light Crust Doughboy Dick Reinhart was born in

Tishomingo, Oklahoma, the county seat of Johnston County, and home to about 3,000 residents. By the late 1920s, he was living in Dallas, where he learned to sing the blues from African-American musicians in Deep Ellum, a well-known blues district that produced "Blind Lemon" Jefferson.

Dick recorded with the Three Virginians on the Okeh label in 1929, when he displayed a falsetto jazz voice on such songs as "June Tenth Blues." Two years later, Dick formed the Wanderers with Roy Newman and Bert Dodson and they recorded for Bluebird. Later that year, Dick joined the Light Crust Doughboys, in which he played rhythm guitar and shared the vocals with Dodson until the latter departed. Two of his classic performances with the Doughboys were "Ding Dong Daddy" in 1936 and "Sittin' on Top of the World" in 1938.

Reinhart left the Doughboys in 1938 to join the Universal Cowboys and they completed a recording session in Dallas with Vocalion. On June 23, 1939, they recorded "Aloha Means Goodbye" and "Cow Town Swing" with Dick singing the vocals. On April 21, 1940, he recorded four more songs, including "Just a Honky Tonk Girl," "It Won't Do you No Good," "Don't Ever Say Adieu," and "Little Brown Eyed Girl." Before leaving the Dallas area, Dick formed The Lone Star Boys which are featured in a rare recording of "Truck Driver's Coffee Shop" on the new Country Music Hall of Fame and Diesel Only Records collaboration *Truck Driver's Boogie: Big Rig Hits, 1939-1969*. He moved to Oklahoma City where he teamed with **Johnny Bond** and **Jimmy Wakely** to form The Bell Boys who had a daily radio show on WKY in Oklahoma City and on KVOO in Tulsa. After **Gene Autry** had toured Oklahoma and suggested he could use the trio, Dick joined Johnny Bond and Jimmy Wakely and their families for the trek to California in May of 1940. Autry hired the trio as regulars on his CBS Melody Ranch show.

After the move to California, Dick signed with Art Satherly on the Okeh label, a subsidiary of Columbia Records. In the early 1940s, he recorded several sides for Okeh, including "Don't Make Me Wait Too Long," "I Know What You're Thinkin'," "No One to Kiss Me Goodnight," "You're the Red Red Rose of My Heart," "Hey Toots," and "Wooly Booger." It is reported that Bond and Wakely accompanied him on the Okeh sessions.

Reinhart composed several songs including "Fort Worth Jail," which was recorded by such diverse artists as Lonnie Donegan, Woody Herman, Skeets McDonald, and Ernest Tubb. Dick's final recording session for (Okeh) Columbia in 1947 included "Muddy Water," which demonstrated that he had retained a bluesy flavor until his death. Dick returned to Fort Worth, where he suffered a fatal heart attack at age forty-one. Dick is featured in two recently completed CDs, *Night Spot Blues* released by Krazy Kat Records, a U.K. label, and *Hot Rod Baby* by the German label, Binge, as well as on the 2001 Bloodshot release of *Country & Western*, a compilation of Johnny Bond's hits. (GC)

Restless Heart

Gregg, Paul (b. December 3, 1954)
Innis, Dave (b. April 9, 1959)
Jennings, Greg (b. October 2, 1954)

Formed in 1983 as the "Okie Project," Restless Heart included three native Oklahomans (Gregg born in Altus, Innis born in Bartlesville, and Jennings born in Nicoma Park) and were produced by Scott Hendricks, another Oklahoman from Clinton and an Oklahoma State University alumnus, and Tim Dubois, born in Grove, Oklahoma, and holder of a master's degree in accounting from OSU. The original Restless Heart was a quintet with John Dittrich and Larry Stewart as the non-Okies. Some called the group the latter-day Eagles with their soft country rock harmonies and adult contemporary sound.

Stewart, a Kentucky native, moved to Nashville and enrolled at Belmont College, where he met Innis at a recording studio on campus. Innis introduced Stewart to DuBois. The latter and Hendricks needed an outlet for specific compositions because some of their material was "too popular" for Nashville and "too country" for Los Angeles. Thus, the two Oklahomans invited five musicians to cut some demo tapes, and the combination worked as the group scored a streak of fifteen Top 10 country hit singles in a row with six of those topping the country charts, beginning in 1986 and ending in 1990. DuBois and Hendricks were already familiar with the musicianship of keyboard player Innis, who had written the Pointer Sisters hit "Dare Me," while guitarist Jennings had played on several Dan Seals hits.

The group's first single, "Let the Heartache Ride," broke into the Top 40 of the country charts, and they were signed to a RCA recording contract in 1985. Their debut album in 1985, *Restless Heart*, spawned a Top 10 hit single, "I Want Everyone to Cry." However, it was their second album, *Wheels*, released in 1986, that became their most successful with three #1 hits, including "Wheels," "Why Does He Have To Be (Wrong or Right)," and "I'll Still Be Loving You," which has become a wedding classic, entered the Top 40 of the popular charts at #33, and reached #3 on the adult-contemporary charts. The ten-track album also contained four songs penned by DuBois, Jennings, Innis, and Gregg, including "The Boy's on a Roll," "Victim of the Game," "Hummingbird," and "We Owned This Town." As a result of their accomplishments, Restless Heart was nominated for the CMA Horizon Award and Vocal Group of the Year in 1987.

Although the *Big Dreams in a Small Town* (1988) and *Fast Movin' Train* (1989) albums, both RCA releases, did not fare as well as *Wheels*, their 1991 collection, *The Best of Restless Heart*, featured three more of their #1 hit singles, "Bluest Eyes in Texas," "That Rock Won't Roll," and "A Tender Lie." It was followed by the 1992 album, *Big Iron Horses,* which produced one the biggest crossover hits in 1992, "When She Cries." It became a Top 10 country hit, soared to #3 on the adult-contemporary charts, and reached #11 on *Billboard*'s Hot 100 pop singles.

For these successes, it captured the ASCAP Song of the Year award in 1992.

The *Matters of the Heart* (1994) and *Tell Me What You Dream* (1995), both RCA productions, were the last of the early 1990s albums as the group began to disintegrate. Stewart had already departed the group in 1990, whereas Jennings joined **Vince Gill**'s band as guitarist and Gregg took a three-year hiatus from music, managing several family-owned businesses. The group members, however, remained in contact, and, in 1996, produced a tape for an ill fan. This resulted in a reunion album, *Greatest Hits*, released by RCA in 1998. The thirteen-track come back collection included the five #1 hits, as well as "When She Cries." Shortly thereafter, Stewart, Jennings, Gregg, and Dittrich joined Vince Gill on a national tour.

During their history, Restless Heart had five certified gold albums, received a dozen Grammy, CMA, and ACM nominations, and were named ACM's Vocal Group of the Year in 1990. In 2003, Restless Heart regrouped and began touring, with plans to release a new album in 2004. (GC)
www.restless-heart.com

Revard, Jimmie
(b. November 26, 1909 - d. April 12, 1991)

Regarded as leader of one of the most successful western swing bands, the Oklahoma Cowboys, in the 1930s, and one of the top country acts for the Bluebird Record Company in the late 1930s, singer, bass fiddler, guitarist, and clarinetist,

James Osage Revard was born in Pawhuska, Oklahoma, a community of roughly 4,000 residents located northwest of Tulsa in Osage County. At age nine, Jimmie's family moved to the San Antonio area. Jimmie began taking violin lessons at twelve because he came from a long line of fiddlers, however, he switched to guitar and bass fiddle.

Beginning in about 1928, Jimmie worked with small dance bands in various clubs and dance halls in south Texas. Around 1935, he formed the Oklahoma Playboys, a western swing band, which included early recruits Adolph Hofner (guitar), Emil "Bash" Hofner (steel guitar), Ben McKay (fiddle), Eddie Whitley (piano), and Curley Williams (guitar). McKay, Whitley, and Williams were former members of Buster Coward's The Tune Wranglers. Typically numbering around eight to ten members, the vocals were handled by Revard, Williams, and Adolph Hofner. Whitley, a jazz pianist, was shortly replaced by another former Tune Wrangler, George Timberlake.

In San Antonio, the Oklahoma Playboys appeared on smaller radio stations KMAC and KONO, but moved to the 50,000-watt stations KTSA and WOAI by the mid-1930s. The band cut their first Bluebird session in San Antonio in October of 1936, and eventually recorded more than seventy-five masters over the next four years, including such songs as "There's A Picture in My Heart," "You're As Pretty As a Picture," "Bundle of Old Southern Sunshine," "Fox and Hounds," "Thinking," and "Oh! Swing It."

By 1938, McKay was replaced with fiddler-vocalist Leon Seago, drummer Edmond Franke was added, and Jimmie began to feature himself on the clarinet, which solidified the Oklahoma Playboys as one of the most innovative western swing bands of the era. The same year Jimmie moved the band to KOAM in Pittsburg, Kansas, where they were staff musicians as well as played dances in the surrounding area. But the economy suffered in 1938 that created fewer dance opportunities and the six band members became homesick, leading Jimmie to dissolve the band in 1939 after their recording session in October of 1938. Adolph Hofner assumed leadership of the band and continued as Adolph Hofner and His Texans, who later recorded for Okeh and Columbia in the early 1940s.

Jimmie recorded again in 1940 with a pick-up band, but dropped out of music to become a San Antonio policeman. After World War II, he later led or worked in other bands in the San Antonio region, and recorded again for the Everstate label in 1950. He remained active in music through the 1970s, and, in the 1980s, recorded once again—a single on the Shag label. In 1982, Rambler Records, which assembled an extensive western swing series, released *Oh! Swing It*, a collection of the Oklahoma Playboys Bluebird sessions from 1936 to 1938, featuring Jimmie playing the clarinet on one of their most popular selections, "Oh! Swing It."

With a rejuvenation of interest in the western swing genre, Jimmie and the Oklahoma Playboys have appeared on various anthology albums [song name in brackets] including *Wanderer's Swing: Texas Dance Hall Music* (1995) ["Holdin' the Sack"], *Doughboys, Playboys, and Cowboys: The Golden Years of Western Swing* (1999) ["Big Daddy," "Dirty Dog," and "Lose Your Blues and Laugh at Life"], *Vintage Country and Western: A Nostalgic Collection* (2000) ["Fox and Hounds], and *Western Swing Texas: 1928-1944* (2001) ["Blues in the Bottle," "Ride'em Cowboy," and "Oh! Swing It"]. (GC)

Ricochet
(formed Columbia, Missouri in 1984)

Known for their dynamic and twangy stage shows, multi-part *a cappella* harmonies, and renditions of "The Star-Spangled Banner" at major professional sporting events, Ricochet bounced to the top of country music in 1996 with a the #1 country hit, "Daddy's Money," and have been on the road since. While other original

WELCOME TO VIAN
HOME OF
HEATH WRIGHT
&
GREG COOK RICOCHET
Of Columbia Recording Artist

members hail from such diverse places as East Greenbush, New York and Lafayette, Tennessee, Ricochet's Perry Heath Wright (lead vocals/lead guitar/fiddle – b. April 22, 1967) and Greg Cook (bass/vocals – b. January 28, 1965) were both born in the east central Oklahoma town of Vian, ten miles west of Sallisaw, and have been playing together at least since 1988. In 1993, Drummer Jeff Bryant (drums/vocals) first hired Heath Wright into Bryant's group Lariat, already featuring his brother, Junior, who played anything with strings and sings. Lariat disbanded shortly thereafter, and players came and went for a year until Ricochet settled into Teddy Carr (pedal steel), Eddie Kilgallon (keyboards/horns/vocals), and Greg Cook, Wright's childhood friend, in early 1994.

The group played widely for a couple of years in the honky-tonk and dance hall country circuit that extends from coast to coast in the southern half of the United States. The band developed a fan base, practiced, and cut a demo that landed in the hands and ears of a Columbia Records-Nashville talent scout, who then signed the band to a development deal, which provides a little cash for a group under a pre-determined producer. By 1995 the group's vocal and instrumental talent became more and more obvious to record executives through live performances and subsequent crowd reactions, and the deal quickly escalated into an official contract. They recorded their first album, *Ricochet* (Columbia), and toured with **Merle Haggard**, Doug Stone, and Charlie Daniels while the label released their first single, "What Do I Know," that became a Top 5 country hit. Presto, Ricochet was rolling, and since the full album came out in early 1996, the wheels of their tour bus have not stopped rolling around the country.

Behind the #1 country single, "Daddy's Money," and Top 10 hit, "Love Is Stronger Than Pride," *Ricochet* careened through the charts as the best selling group in country music for nineteen weeks that year. The ACM awarded Ricochet Top Vocal Group and Top New Vocal Group honors for 1996, and the radio industry publication, *Radio and Records*, named Ricochet as "Group of the Year" in their 1996 readers' poll, voted on by radio programmers from around the U.S. After being named CMA's Vocal Group of the Year in 1997, their follow-up effort, *Blink of an Eye* (1997), did not keep up the first album's sales figures, but the album did garner three humble country chart singles, "Connected at the Heart," "He Left a Lot to be Desired," and the title track. Continuing to tour through 1998 and 1999, and again named the ACM's Top Vocal Group in 1998, the band had a few more modest charting singles taken from recordings that were never released as an album.

The fast ride and long haul had worn out a couple of members; drummer Jeff Bryant's carpal tunnel syndrome necessitated a replacement (Tim Chewning), and steel guitarist Shannon Farmer took over for Carr who left the road for home, family, and a successful carpet cleaning business. With Farmer's additional vocal abilities, Ricochet began finding further success with specialty *a cappella* (voice only) recordings and performances.

In 2000, the group's third release, *What You Leave Behind* (Columbia), is a transitional collection of unreleased songs from a few years previous, some new tunes written or co-written by the band, a first in itself for Ricochet albums, and a few songs contributed by their producers. The album's first single, "She's Gone," enjoyed subtle chart success, and the song's video received substantial airing on CMT.

The only group to ever chart the National Anthem, Ricochet has become a constant presence at major sporting events with their *a cappella* rendition of "The Star Spangled Banner," which one can hear free on their website. They have also become closely connected to the hugely popular NASCAR racing circuit. They are the first musical act to sponsor a qualifying day for a major NASCAR race, having signed on for the 2000 "Ricochet Qualifying Day" at the Winston 500, and have opened numerous races with their beautifully layered harmonies. Every year since 1995, Ricochet headlines the Annual Green Country Jam in the Vian Football Stadium to benefit St. Jude Children's Research Hospital. Well-known acts the band has met through the years appear as well, such as Steve Wariner, **Bryan White**, and Lila McCann. The band continued touring through 2002, gaining accolades for a July 30th show in which they "wowed country fans" with their sonically powerful vocal harmonies, full force country band, and confidence that only comes with being a #1 group. In 2003, Ricochet was booked solid through the end of the year, and added Marty Mitchell on drums, and Dwayne Dupuy on piano, organ, and baritone vocals. (HF)
www.ricochetonline.com

Ripley, Steve
(b. January 1, 1950)

Recognized as an ace studio engineer, record producer, multi-faceted guitarist, vocalist, and guitar craftsman, Steve Ripley led the Tractors, a roots-rocking country outfit whose aesthetics run from **Bob Wills** and 1950s rock and roll, to the evolving bluesy shuffle of the Tulsa sound of the 1960s and 70s, as well as **Red Dirt Music**'s equally hyphenated descriptions from the 1980s and 1990s, to multi-platinum status with the best selling album in country music for 1994. With its Top 10 country hit, "Baby Likes to Rock It," co-written by Ripley and keyboardist Walt Richmond, the debut, self-titled album sold over two million copies,

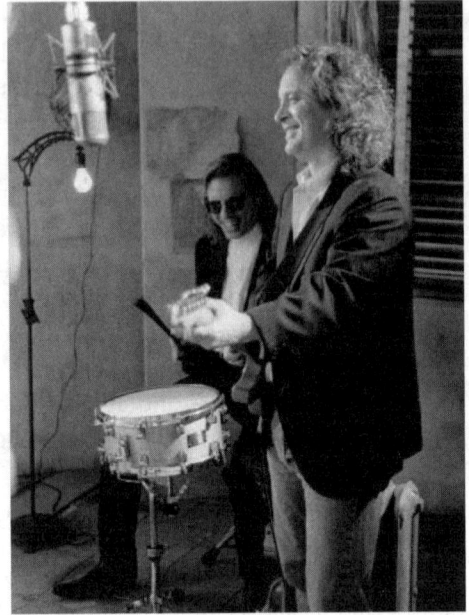

Steve Ripley (right) with Jamie Oldaker

earning double platinum status and a gaggle of accolades. The album earned The Tractors three ACM award nominations (Top Vocal Group, Top New Vocal Group, and Album of the Year), a TNN/*Music City News* Award nomination (Stars of Tomorrow/Vocal Duo or Group), two Grammy nominations (Best Country Performance by a Group for "Baby Likes to Rock It" and "Tryin' to Get to New Orleans"), and won the Country Music Association's Video of the Year Award for "Baby Likes to Rock It." *USA Today* raved about the album, and *Entertainment Weekly* gave it an "A."

Grasping The Tractors comes with understanding Steve Ripley, born in Boise, Idaho to Oklahoma native Robert, then a mid-twenties traveling cookware salesman just out of the Army, and Mary (Bonser) Ripley, whose family came from Oregon. The couple traveled throughout the north and mid-western United States, moving as many as twenty times before buying a farm next to the old Ripley homestead Steve's great grandfather acquired about ten miles southwest of Pawnee in the Cherokee Strip land run of 1893 when "excess" tribal lands were opened to white settlement. His father's cookware business led the family from the farm to Tulsa in 1954, then on to Oklahoma City for three years, a period in which Ripley's first musical experiences came when the family returned to the homestead on Christmas holidays and summers. At the farm his Uncle Elmer, a Bob Wills fan, had a great collection of Bob Wills, **Johnnie Lee Wills**, and Hank Williams 78 rpm singles that became Steve's earliest musical passion. Subsequent musical influences were his older cousins, then teenagers in 1955, who came back from working the west Texas oil fields talking about a guy tearing it up down there named Elvis Presley, at the time still touring the southwest and southeast United States on the strength of his Sun singles.

Ripley's parents gave him his first guitar in 1956, and Presley's domination of shifting American popular music tastes collided with the six-year-old's energy, and there was a match. In a 2002 interview, Ripley remembered being firmly convinced he was Elvis at that age, and could sing the songs banging along on an out-of-tune guitar. In the summer of 1958, the family relocated permanently to the farm near Glencoe, an agricultural and former copper mining community of about 500 people in north central Oklahoma, and within a year Steve learned his first chords on guitar. Ripley's age also put him in line to hear and be influenced by the music of the Ventures in 1962 and '63 with their guitar heavy sound fronted by native Oklahoman **Nokie Edwards**, leading Ripley and early musician buddies to play surf tunes like the Surfaris' "Wipeout," later covered by the Ventures, and several other bands. By 1965, Ripley began playing with various incarnations of rock and roll bands, and made his first recordings with The Verzatiles at age 15 in Gene Sullivan's Oklahoma City studio, then one of the few recording studios in Oklahoma, and most of the primary equipment from which Ripley now owns and has in his Church Studio in Tulsa.

Just as Ripley became confident with the 1950s rock of Elvis and Chuck Berry in various guitar-based bands, the Beatles elevated the American roots music of Berry, Motown, and rockabilly to the next level by writing their own songs and experimenting with developing studio technology. Evolving with the times musically and becoming more aware of the significant lyrical developments in rock through Bob Dylan, Ripley joined his next band, the Stillwater-based In-Keepers, who played teen dances and became regulars on Ronny Kaye's Oklahoma City television show, *The Scene*, an Oklahoma version of *American Bandstand*. Ripley remembered the band "had seven or eight guys and two go-go dancers."

After graduating high school in 1968, and since he had already been playing with the In-Keepers out of Stillwater, Steve enrolled in the state school known for "pigs and plans," Oklahoma State University, just about 10 miles as the crow flies from his home in Glencoe. While at OSU, Ripley continued playing with In-Keepers at frat parties, teen dances, and around the various bars in and around Stillwater. A nucleus of the In-Keepers evolved into the band, Moses, and that group helped put its members through college by playing a steady line of gigs in the area. Graduating in 1972 with a B.S. in Broadcasting and a double major in sociology, Ripley worked steadily with Moses and started his own label, Red Dirt Records, to release an album by Moses. The record became the first release locally of any consequence in the town that would come to be known as the center of **Red Dirt Music**, and also marks the beginning of Ripley's engineering and producing career enhanced by his radio/TV training in college.

While red dirt music is generally associated with Stillwater, *Moses Live* (Red Dirt Records, 1974) was actually recorded in Enid at the Fillin' Station. The liner notes for the album, written by Mike Dougan, imply the geographical inspiration for the music comes from "the color of the earth surrounding Enid and nearby Stillwater, Moses' home base." Recorded live to an Ampex eight-track tape machine Ripley hauled to Enid in a pickup, and mixed at Stillwater Sound, the studio started in 1973 by Ripley with a Small Business Administration loan, *Moses Live* features Ripley on guitar and vocals, Steve Irby on keyboards and vocals, Bruce Hueston on drums and vocals, and Robert Hatfield on bass and vocals. Of particular interest is the early version of Ripley's composition, "Oklahoma Blues," the only original on the album and a clear aural window through which one can hear the infant musical rumblings of Ripley's future success with The Tractors.

After a couple of years trying to run the Stillwater studio as a business, and not getting ahead significantly beyond meeting his wife, Charlene, who came through the studio in 1974 as a trumpeter and keyboardist in the Perkins High School jazz band, Ripley closed the studio in 1975, continued playing in bands, and married Charlene in 1976. The young couple moved to Nashville for a couple of broke months before returning to Oklahoma City that same year where he worked for a couple of weeks at Benson Sound in Oklahoma City as a recording engineer, a job that did not last because of Steve's "hands-on" approach to the recording process that clashed with the owner's production philosophy. Out of work, Ripley called an old friend who was working as an engineer for Leon Russell's Shelter label at the Church Studio, and talked his way into a job running monitors for Leon's live shows through the rest of 1976.

By early 1977 and the end of the tour, Russell decided to relocate his operation back West, and Ripley picked up a side gig driving Leon's motor home filled with various studio and band gear to California, and is when Ripley played some of his demos, recorded at the Church Studio, for Leon. While Russell liked the way they sounded, and subsequently hired Ripley as an engineer in his studio, the gig did not last for similar reasons as Ripley's Benson Sound experience: mainly that Ripley wanted to be involved in the process of the music's creation, an ethos Russell perceived as "too busy," and so Leon let the twenty-eight-year-old engineer go. With his newly acquired free agent status, Ripley and Charlene returned to Tulsa in 1977 where Steve started working for the Oklahoma-based talent impresario, Jim Halsey, who had plans to build a studio in Tulsa and put Ripley in charge of assembling the studio space and equipment.

In April of 1978, Halsey enlisted Ripley's services as a producer and engineer for Johnnie Lee Wills' *Reunion* album for Flying Fish Records, a recording that brought back many of the elder and active Western swing players, and in the fall of the same year Ripley produced and played on a collaboration album by Roy Clark, then managed by Halsey, and Clarence Gatemouth Brown, *Makin' Music* (MCA, 1979). By 1979, Leon Russell called Ripley again since Ripley basically set up the California studio, and was really the only person who knew how it was put together.

Charlene and Steve move back to California in 1979 where Ripley again assumed the engineering duties for Leon, and had the occasion to stick his head into the open Steinway while Russell was playing it. This aural experience began an obsession by Ripley with getting the same full sound out of a guitar that he heard in Leon's piano. With all of Leon's equipment at his disposal, Ripley began experimenting with using a guitar, fabricated by an old steel player out of Steve's favorite Fender Telecaster, to create an output from each string and then run them through six different amplifiers at the same time. "Everybody loved it and people kept coming around to play it," Steve remembers. Just as word started getting around the Los Angeles music scene about Ripley's invention, Russell decided to leave California again, and left Steve wondering what to do next. He would not wait long as fellow-Oklahoman, and all-world drummer, Jim Keltner called and invited Steve to some rehearsals for Bob Dylan who wanted to try out some new material before recording it, and urged Keltner to bring along anybody he wanted to play guitar. Keltner called Ripley, who had long admired Dylan, and whose guitar then had six outputs for six amplifiers. Not wanting to bring in six amps, which were all Leon's anyway, Ripley stopped at a music store on the way to the rehearsals and bought a small mixer to run the six outputs through, and then took a stereo output from that mixer into two amplifiers. Dylan and Steve hit it off, and after five or six weeks of rehearsals, Ripley played guitar on Dylan's "Shot of Love" in 1981, and toured Europe and the states with Dylan throughout the rest of the year.

After getting off the tour, Ripley began working with building a small mixer into the guitar, and everyone he showed it to wanted one, including Ry Cooder and Eddie Van Halen, who introduced Ripley to the Kramer Guitar Company. Ripley started working for Kramer, with his guitars favored by artists such as **J.J. Cale,** John Hiatt, and Jimmy Buffett. Ripley also built a strong friendship with Eddy Van Halen's becoming his guitar man, and business partner from 1982 through 1986 when Steve's mother became ill, and necessitated Ripley's return to Oklahoma, with assistance from Van Halen who funded the expensive move.

After moving back to Tulsa in the fall of 1986, Ripley, along with his friend and partner, Glen Mitchell, bought the building at 304 S. Trenton Avenue in the fall of 1987, known more famously as Leon Russell's Church Studio, and began writing and recording songs. Ripley's first release as The Tractors was a Christmas single in 1988, and he subsequently spent several years creating the Tractors' debut album by putting together an excellent collection of musicians: Walt Richmond (b. McAlester, OK, April 18, 1947), pianist and co-producer for the album, played keyboards for years with Bonnie Raitt and Rick Danko; Ron Getman (b. Fairfax, OK, December 13, 1948) is a guitarist and steel guitarist who has toured with Janis Ian and Leonard Cohen; Casey Van Beek (b. Leiden, Holland, December 1, 1942) anchored Linda Ronstadt and the Righteous Brothers' stage bands with his steady basslines; and Jamie Oldaker (b. Oakland, CA, September 5, 1951) kept time for many years on stage and in the studio as Eric Clapton's drummer.

Taking his time to figure out how the group could embody his vision of "Hank Williams meets Chuck Berry," the Tractors' debut, self-titled album with its persistent nods to the musical heritage of country music, brought down the houses on Music Row when it came out of Oklahoma in 1994 to outsell major acts like Alan Jackson and Brooks & Dunn. With guest shots by Ry Cooder and James Burton, *The Tractors'* success opened up multiple touring opportunities and the group hit the road in 1995 to play a hundred shows to roughly half a million people in the U.S. and Europe. Riding completely unexpected mega-success, the group released a full Christmas album (with plenty to celebrate) in 1995, *Have Yourself a Tractors Christmas* (ARISTA-Nashville), featuring "Baby Likes to Rock It" as "Santa Claus is Comin' (In a Boogie Woogie Choo Choo Train)." Over the next couple of years, the group rarely played out in public, but contributed tracks to well-received tribute compilations. In 1996, the band provided "Think It Over" for *Not Fade Away: (Remembering Buddy Holly)* (MCA), and received a Grammy nomination as Best Country Duo or Group for "Tryin' to Get to New Orleans." In 1997 the group covered "It's All Over Now," on *Stone Country* (Beyond), an album of country artists twanging up Rolling Stones songs.

Given Ripley's penchant for perfection, and following his own schedule of quality over quickness in the Church Studio, The Tractors' second album, *Farmers in a Changing World* (1998), arrived in a pop country world altered by Shania Twain and other country pop icons who enjoyed the cyclical return of Nashville pop that has taken place since Chet Atkins added brush drums and tinkling piano to Elvis Presley's music in 1956. The same retro-**Tulsa Sound** that boosted the first album into the commercial stratosphere hindered the sophomore effort's acceptance in Nashville. The album also arrived on shelves just as ARISTA's Nashville office, bolstered by The Tractors' success in 1994, and headed by Oklahoma State University alum Tim Dubois, closed its doors, effectively shutting off any promotional effort on behalf of the album. Fans loved *Farmers in a Changing World* for exactly what it was not, another hackneyed Nashville studio production geared toward the video market. Bonnie Raitt plays slide on the album, and Ripley shows off James Burton, Scotty Moore, and D.J. Fontana, all of whom made careers with Elvis Presley, among others, and many music historians would say helped make the career of Elvis Presley. Hear the guts of Elvis's greatest musical periods on "The Elvis Thing." Also reaching back to Tulsa's Western swing history, Ripley enlisted **Bob Wills'** long-time fiddler, Curly Lewis, for "Way Too Late," on which the spirit of Wills' guitarist Eldon Shamblin is also invoked via recordings made by Steve before Shamblin's death, and included posthumously on the album. Additionally, as a result of Ripley's long career as an engineer privy to moments the public never hears, a fun element of Tractors' albums includes the various sound clips, musicians' commentary, and hidden tracks from the sessions, all of which are crystalline moments that really encapsulate the recordings, but rarely make it onto commercial country albums. Whatever qualities the album possesses for Tractors fans, it got lost in the Nashville music industry shuffle.

With no record deal, Ripley went back to the business of the studio and preparing material for the next Tractors release. In 2000, he signed with Audium records and in 2001 released *Fast Girl*. The project again brought together great players from all corners of Steve's long career of acquaintances and friendships. "Ready to Cry" was co-written by Leon Russell who played Steinway piano and Hammond organ on the track. Bluegrass mandolin virtuoso Sam Bush is on the recording, as are repeat offenders D.J. Fontana, and James Burton who has played on every Tractor release up to *Fast Girl*. Tulsa-born drummer Jimmy Karstein, who has played with Gary Lewis and the Playboys, Leon Russell, Eric Clapton, J.J. Cale, Joe Cocker, Bobby "Blue" Bland, and Taj Mahal, makes a guest percussion appearance, while Fontana's drums and Burton's guitar fuel the album's primary single, "Can't Get Nowhere," the video for which features shots around various Tulsa locations, to include the Church Studio and Cain's Ballroom, the legendary home of Bob Wills and Johnnie Lee Wills, and includes cameos from Leon's Russell's daughter, Tina Rose, **Zac Hanson**, and various other insiders and musicians who do and don't play on the song.

Fast Girl also contains a spooky reminder of September 11th, 2001. "911" was certainly never intended as such (it was meant as a tribute to New Orleans pianist Huey Piano Smith) but now has a macabre resonance. Ripley laments the digital age in "Computer Controlled," a lazy J.J. Cale-influenced tune drenched in the **Tulsa Sound**, and covers a Moon Mullican Western swing number, "Don't Ever Take My Picture Down." He also reflects on the people of his rural background in Oklahoma on "Higher Ground," with mentions of Pawnee County and Black Bear Creek.

In 2001, "Baby Likes to Rock It" resurfaced on a patriotic country compilation, *This Is Your Country: 20 Contemporary Country Classics* (Universal), a collection that places the song on par with Lee Greenwood's "God Bless the U.S.A." and tracks by Shania Twain and **Vince Gill**. Also in 2001, Steve Ripley began working on his first solo release, spent time at the helm of recording projects for contemporary Oklahoma artists such as the **Red Dirt Rangers**, and contributed two songs to the soundtrack of an independent Oklahoma film, *Round and Round*, the subject of which is the issue of cockfighting in Oklahoma, since banned in the 2002 state election by a narrow vote, but broadly ignored by several county judges. Ripley wrote and performed both the film's title track, "Round and Round," and "Oklahoma Blues," the latter of which can be traced back to Ripley's Stillwater group, Moses. Both songs appear on Steve's 2002 solo album, *Ripley*, released jointly through his own Rocking Boy Records and Audium.

While the J.J. Cale-tinged "Round and Round" was originally written with the cockfighting film in mind, Ripley was also influenced by the events of September 11, 2001 and re-reading of Revelation that hearken back to his days in the Baptist church. For "Gone Away," also from his solo album, Ripley enlisted the advice of ex-ARISTA Nashville executive Tim Dubois and *Tulsa World* music writer John Wooley for help on the song which is a rumination on the many American popular culture icons that have gone by the wayside or into nostalgic status, such as Marilyn Monroe, Elvis, '57 Chevys, and *Leave It To Beaver*. Lyrically, the entire album is a meditation on aging and its inherent loss of connection to popular culture, old friends, and the death of loved ones. Through the first eight tracks on *Ripley*, the singer laments the dissolution of his personal connections to popular culture from the 1930s through the 1960s, faded childhood dreams, and absent adult lovers before finding salvation in an old 1937 Alvin Carter song, "No Depression (In Heaven)." A Southern gospel-influenced song with the Jordanaires on backing vocals, "Crossing Over," is the final cut on the album where the singer's mother waits to welcome him home on the other side of the River Jordan.

The Jordanaires, who backed Elvis Presley on his most significant gospel recordings, further extend Ripley's associations with musicians who worked with Elvis. With sharp guitar solos, shuffling drum beats played mostly by Ripley, and the warm resonance of the antique tube microphones he uses in the studio for vocals, the album represents both the modernity of the Tulsa Sound and the evolution of Ripley as a solo artist who has deeply personal themes to express in his music.

Ripley released a ten-track Christmas CD under The Tractors' name, *The Big Night* (Rocking Boy/Audium, 2002), and planned a 2003 children's album, *Chicken Covers* (Rocking Boy/Audium), the title song for which was co-written by Tulsa-based character Gailard Sartain. Also in 2003, his solo album reached #10 on *Radio and Records* Americana Radio Chart, and *Farmers in a Changing World* was re-released. While future commercial success is unknowable for The Tractors and Steve Ripley, his fixed place as a multi-platinum artist, his always-interesting releases that express the musical aesthetic that matured in Stillwater and Tulsa, and his stewardship of one of America's historic recording studios, all point to continued significance for the man who plowed into Nashville with an Oklahoma tractor and knocked off country music's often unearned cowboy hat. (HF)
www.thetractors.com

Rivers, Sam
(b. September 25, 1930)

As one of the leading *avant-garde* jazz composers, arrangers, and instrumentalists of the 1960s, Samuel Carthorne Rivers was born in El Reno, Oklahoma, a community of approximately 15,000 population located immediately west of Oklahoma City. Sam was immersed with music at an early age as his father and mother, as well as grandparents were musicians, especially in the gospel genre. His father was a graduate of Fisk University and sang with the Fisk Jubilee

Singers and the Silvertone Quartet, while his mother was a pianist who gave him lessons as early as four years old. Sam's grandfather wrote and published in 1882, *A Collection of Revival Hymns and Plantation Melodies*. He was also exposed to other styles of music including jazz (listened with his father to Count Basie and Cab Calloway) and classical, primarily Stravinsky. At age eleven, Sam began working on the trombone and tenor sax, and played soprano sax in school marching band at age twelve.

Sam's family left El Reno and moved first to Chicago and then to Little Rock, where his mother taught music and sociology at Shorter College. While in the U.S. Navy, Sam played his first professional job with Jimmy Witherspoon in Vallejo, California. He completed his bachelor's degree at Jarvis Christian College in Hawkins, Texas, where he took up the tenor sax seriously; and then moved to Boston in 1947 to study violin, viola, and saxophone at the Boston Conservatory and Boston University for the next five years under Alan Hovhauess, the Armenian composer. After leaving school in 1952, Sam played with Herb Pomeroy's small band, which, in the early 1950s, featured such players as Nat Pierce and Quincy Jones. After a short time in Florida, Sam returned to Boston in 1958 and formed his own quartet, and played on his first Blue Note recording session with pianist Tadd Dameron. It was in the late 1950s that Sam became involved in the *avante-garde* jazz movement, approaching jazz from a classical perspective.

In the early 1960s, Sam joined the Jazz Composer's Guild, working with such jazz notables as Archie Shepp and Cecil Taylor. In 1964 he moved to New York, where Miles Davis hired him and they immediately left for Japan where they played three concerts resulting in the *Miles in Tokyo* album (1964). Later that year, Sam's second session with Blue Note produced *Fuchsia Swing Song*, his first sole recording, and four more albums with Blue Note in the 1960s, *Contours* (1965), *Involution* (1966), *A New Conception* (1966), and *Dimensions and Extensions* (1967).

In 1970, Sam and his wife, Bea, opened a studio in Harlem, Studio Rivbea, where he and wife trained young musicians and dancers, as well as becoming known as one of the best venues for jazz performances. Later the Rivbea was relocated to a warehouse in the Soho section of New York City. Sam organized three unique ensembles—Rivbea Orchestra, Sam Rivers Trio, and his Winds of Change woodwind group. Rivers' trio reflected the free improvisation of the new jazz—no written music. Sam's music during this 1970s period was recorded on the Impulse label—*Hues* (1971), *Streams* (1973), *Live* (1973) *Crystals* (1974), and *Sizzle* (1975). In 1975, Sam won the *Down Beat* Critics Poll for Talent Deserving Wider Recognition for Flute, *Streams* album captured the Best Record award from the French *Academie du Disque*, and he was guest soloist with the San Francisco Symphony.

During the late 1970s, Rivers found fewer opportunities to record, but continued to remain active in other areas, such as composer-in-residence for the Harlem

Opera Society, lecturer on African-American music history at Connecticut College, guest soloist with Symphony of the New World, and formation of additional groups, including the Harlem Ensemble and Winds of Manhattan.

In the 1980s, Sam relocated to Orlando, Florida, where he created a new version of his Rivbea Orchestra, composed of local musicians who played in the area's theme parks. On various labels, he and the Rivbea Orchestra recorded in the 1980s and 1990s, such as titles as *Colours* (1982), *Lazuli* (1989), *Tangens* (1997), *Portrait* (1997), *Inspiration* (1999), a Grammy nomination, *Winter Garden* (1999), *Culmination* (2000), another Grammy nominated album on RCA, and in 2001, *Firestorm*, which featured the Sam Rivers Trio. In 2000, Sam and the Rivbea Orchestra premiered his new works at the Alice Tully Hall in the Jazz at Lincoln Center series in New York City. (GC)

Romanello, Tony
(b. March 8, 1977)

Tony Romanello Band, left to right: Paul Cristiano, Josiah Borgos Tony Romanello, Andy Callis

By starting to play guitar at age six in his native Tulsa and forming his first band at age fourteen (YSY), it should be no major surprise Tony Romanello surfaced in 2003 as the latest Oklahoma pop/rock musician to receive national critical recognition, and appears poised to transform his multi-layered, lush arrangements, sensitive lyrics, and pleading vocal style into wider success beyond the national college radio charts.

After taking guitar lessons from Dick Gordon, Sr. from ages six to twelve, and graduating Tulsa Bishop Kelley High School in 1995, Tony attended the University of Oklahoma where he formed the independent rock group, Murmur, and recorded a six-song CD with Matt Vandever (bass) and high school buddy, Ben Marshall (drums). After adding Eric Knox on keyboards, Murmur played regionally with some limited success before disbanding in 1999. After the group dissolved, Romanello went into the studio with Trent Bell, long known for his guitar work in the Chainsaw Kittens and a multitude of production and engineering credits (Chainsaw Kittens, Starlight Mints, Pistol Arrows, **Flaming Lips**). Having all the songwriting credits on Murmur's songs, Romanello added several and converted the lot into his first solo project, *The Mumble Odd* (Engine Shed, 2000), an album that makes many promises of bigger things to come

Full of Romanello's talented guitar work that ranges from simple power chords, flashy leads, and lyrical melody lines ("Fingertips," "Run Away," "Sky"), *The Mumble Odd* also exhibits his more contemplative acoustic guitar ("How to Drop Things," "Can You Feel This"). Vocally, Romanello is often compared to the tragically-fated Jeff Buckley, largely because of a singing style that often soars over the music without dominating it obtrusively ("Everything"), or Brian Wilson of the Beach Boys due to the upper register singing backed by layers of harmonies ("Lo-Fi Dreams in Stereo"). Inner-self lyrics are often written in the first person, making the singer the spokesperson for an introspective life channeled through a sparkling melancholy ("A Red Shade of Somber," "Under the Blue." Pianist Eric Knox also adds some beautiful keyboard work to the album that elevates it beyond the basic drums, bass, guitar rock format. Additionally in 2000, Romanello released an independent collection of out-takes, demos, sketches, and finished works, *Lo-Fi Dreams in Stereo*, an album whose title takes its name from the final track on *The Mumble Odd*, and is available only through his website.

After graduating OU in 2000, Tony returned to Tulsa and formed The Tony Romanello Band (TRB). Assembled with the intention of being able to play *The Mumble Odd* live, the group consisted of Josiah Borgos (drums), Andy Callis (guitar), Brad Hall (bass), and Blaine Nelson (Rhodes piano). TRB played regionally most of the way through 2001 before returning to Tulsa and recording the EP, *Shades of Grey* (Engine Shed, 2001). A three-part suite of his now trademark crushing guitars, stratospheric vocals and ability to assemble musicians who provide just the right musical atmosphere and cohesion, *Shades of Gray* earned the *Tulsa World's* Best Rock Act of 2001 at the annual Spotnik Awards, just one of several he has earned from his hometown's paper (Artist of the Year 2002, Best Local Album 2002, Best Rock Act 2001 and 2002, Rising Star 2000).

Following *Shades of Gray*, Romanello returned to Bell Labs to again record with Trent Bell where they worked together to assemble a massive studio album that is diverse as it is glistening. At times recalling The Beatles' *Magical Mystery Tour* and *Yellow Submarine* period ("An Insomniac's Diary," "Finally Found") and continuing to channel the ghost of Buckley ("The Amazing Disappearing

Man," "The Artist"), *Counting Stars* (Engine Shed, 2003) features a multitude of overdubs, samples, experimental instrumentation (string quartet, horns, tablas), and effects-laden vocals that place it in line with Oklahoma's other pop mad scientists, **The Flaming Lips** (Lips' drummer Steven Drozd plays all drums and percussion on the album) and Starlight Mints. Lyrically, the album continues Romanello's thematic fascination with lonely and misguided characters trying to find the big answers ("Finally Found," "Algiers," "Tell Me Please"). Hook after memorable hook ("Novocain," "De Leon") makes one wonder how long it will be before some major label discovers this talented songwriter and musician who is making epic pop songs for the post-rock & rap world.

Critical raves for *Counting Stars* have come from as far away as France and England, but Romanello's appeal to the American college radio market has cemented his status as an up-and-coming artist in the U.S. While the album did not break the *College Media Journal*'s top fifty, it did receive airplay on at least fifty college stations nationwide from California to New York, by all counts a national success for an independently released album in Tulsa by an artist who is really just starting what could be a career of significant distinction. In July, 2003, Romanello released a four song EP, *Where Are You Tonight*, produced by Brad Mitcho (Glass House, Molly's Yes). The EP includes a song recorded live at Rogers State University's college radio station, KRSC-FM. He had further plans to continue playing live regionally with the goal of branching out to national stages. (HF)

www.tonyromanello.com

Rooney, Joe Don
(b. September 13, 1975)

As a member of the contemporary country trio, Rascal Flatts, winner of the CMA Horizon Award in 2002, talented instrumentalist (plays guitar and mandolin), vocalist, and songwriter Joe Don Rooney was born to Windel and Jo Rooney in Baxter Springs, Kansas, but raised in Picher, Oklahoma, a community of roughly 2,000 residents located in extreme northeastern Oklahoma that is a former lead-and-zinc mining town and still a source of environmental controversy as the U.S.'s oldest Superfund site. Joe Don graduated from Picher-Cardin

High School and attended Northeastern Oklahoma A & M junior college in Miami, for two years.

Joe Don's primary musical influences were his siblings (Robin, Kelly, and Mike), all interested in myriad forms of music. Several Oklahomans were influential in Rooney's early musical training, including **Steve Gaines**, **Merle Haggard**, and **Vince Gill**, who Joe Don lists as his favorite singer. His first musical performance was with his mother, father, and sister Kelly, when they sang for church. "Freight Train," composed by the legendary Elizabeth "Libba" Cotton, was the first song Joe Don learned as a child. As a teenager, Joe Don was an electrical apprentice to his father and worked various janitorial jobs.

Country music became an important professional element in Joe Don's early career when he began working at age nineteen at the Grand Lake Opry in Grove, Oklahoma, located approximately thirty miles south of his hometown. The Grand Lake Opry, modeled after the Grand Ole Opry, sponsored monthly shows featuring country music artists from Nashville and Bakersfield, such as Porter Wagoner, **Billy Parker**, **Wanda Jackson**, Connie Smith, and **Merle Haggard**.

Rooney met the other two members of Rascal Flatts (Jay DeMarcus and Gary LeVox, second cousins and close friends from Columbus, Ohio) when he and Jay were working in Chely Wright's band in 2001. At the same time, the two cousins were playing gigs in Nashville. Lacking a full time guitarist, they invited Joe Don to sit in with them at a weekend show at Printers Alley in Nashville, and the trio was complete. According to Joe Don, his high voice blended well with the other two members and the Rascal Flatts chemistry was born, although the group was originally called Okla-hio, combining the states of origin of the band members. As Joe Don recalled after hearing themselves on stage, "It really, really was magical. We honestly didn't have to work hard at it. It was so natural and so much fun."

The threesome recorded some demo tapes that were sent to producer Dan Huff, who liked the group's strong vocal harmonies and outstanding musicianship. Although not involved in the project, Huff recommended the group to Lyric Street Records Senior Vice-President of A&R, Doug Howard. Within four days, Howard had signed the trio to a contract.

Joe Don believes the group is successful because of the eclectic mix of their musical roots, including bluegrass, gospel, and rhythm-and-blues. Moreover, the trio reports that Lyric Street Records, a division of the Disney Corporation, is taking country music in a new direction with other new groups like SHeDAISY and **Rushlow**, and they wanted to be part of that trend.

Their self-titled album went platinum in 2002, and resulted in four consecutive Top 10 hits, including the first single, "Prayin' for Daylight," followed by "This Everyday Love," "While You Loved Me," and "I'm Movin' On." Rascal Flatts was invited to perform at Nashville's Wild Horse Saloon as part of Country's Class of 2000 during the Country Radio Seminar in March of 2000. Because of their ties with the Disney Corporation, the group recorded a new Sting song

("Walk the Llama Llama") for the movie soundtrack, *The Emperor's New Groove*, released in 2000. They were invited in 2001 to the 74th annual Macy's Thanksgiving Day Parade in New York City, where they rode the Santaland Express float, performing their "Prayin' for Daylight" single.

Rascal Flatts received their first major award in 2000, given by the ACM for Top New Vocal Duo or Group. The video of "I'm Movin' On," the single from their eponymous album that soared to the top of the country charts in 2002, was nominated for the CMT Flameworthy Video Awards in the category of Best Video From an Artist's Debut Album. At the 2002 CMA awards press conference in Nashville, where Rascal Flatts helped with the announcements, the trio was nominated for two honors: Vocal Group of the Year and the Horizon Award. They won the latter at the televised CMA awards show in October of 2002. The group released their next single, "These Days," from their second album, the platinum-plus *Melt*, that hit the record stores in the fall of 2002. "These Days" debuted at #2 on Yahoo's LAUNCH, the highest spot a country group had achieved on the Yahoo chart, and also charted #4 on *Radio & Records*, #1 on *Billboard*, and #4 on Blue Chip Radio Report, in the fall of 2002. In October of 2002, ABC Radio's *Country Coast to Coast*, broadcast on more than 150 stations to some 1.5 million listeners, nominated Rascal Flatts as Best Vocal Group/Duo for 2002 for their Best Country Around-Fan's Choice Awards. Competing with **Brooks and Dunn**, Dixie Chicks, Trick Pony, and Montgomery Gentry, the latter was declared the winner.

Joe Don's songwriting credits include "1/2 That Makes Me Whole," "How Do You Feel," and "Right Now," recorded by Chad Brock, and co-writer on "Like I Am" and "Shine On," both on the *Melt* CD. The latter song is Rooney's tribute to students and faculty at Picher-Cardin High School.

After touring for three years as the opening act for the likes of Alan Jackson and Jo Dee Messina, Rascal Flatts was the opening act for the spring, 2003, leg of Oklahoman **Toby Keith**'s "Unleashed" tour. Also in the spring of 2003, after receiving ACM's Top Vocal Group Award, the group received CMT's Flameworthy Group/Duo Video of the Year Award for "These Days," but their follow up video for "I Melt" received even more attention because it gave viewers a brief glimpse of Rooney's backside.

A sensuous song about sexual attraction, "I Melt" served as the palate for a steamy video that might not be any different than the common fare of network soap operas, but the appearance of Rooney's rear end stuck out like a sore, uh, thumb on Country Music Television, the target audience for which is primarily the conservative leaning, Anglo-American, country-music-loving, segment of the U.S. population. While CMT's website bulletin board showed some fans giving their approval, others questioned the band's moral and religious convictions as if the video were the worst thing since Rhett Butler's final words in *Gone with the Wind*. On another website, FlattDogPound.com, a fan-based Internet site that promotes the band, 90% of the band's fans approved of the video. Nonetheless, the whole affair developed enough public controversy and priceless press attention through the end of the summer to get the group on *The Tonight Show with Jay Leno* at the end of July, as well as a feature interview on *CNN* that aired on the evening news and repeated through an entire weekend in early August. The added worth of an Oklahoman having the most famous posterior in America has yet to be determined, but the single, "I Melt," was the fastest rising single of the group's career, indicating the band (and their management) knows a thing or two about marketing in a crowded marketplace. (GC/HF)

www.rascalflatts.com

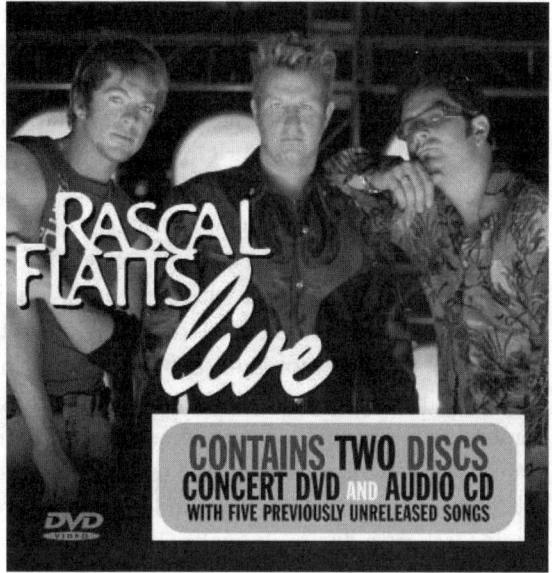

Rascal Flatts live concert DVD/CD was released in September, 2003.

Royal, Marshal Walton
(b. May 12, 1912 - d. May 9, 1995)

As lead alto sax player and music director of the Count Basic Orchestra for almost twenty years (1951-1970), instrumentalist, bandleader, and arranger Marshal Royal was born in Sapulpa, Oklahoma, immediately west of Tulsa. Marshal was raised around music as his father was a bandleader, music teacher, and played all the reeds, strings, and some of the valve instruments, while his mother was a pianist. The family moved to Los Angeles in 1916. Prompted by his father at age four, Marshal studied violin under a graduate of the Paris Conservatory, and while in high school, he was first chair (concert master) in his high school orchestra. His father had organized a family orchestra, known as The Three Royals, and Marshal made his professional debut with the group at age twelve.

Marshal began playing clarinet and saxophone in high school, and became first chair clarinet in the band. While in high school, his music teacher helped him form his own band at age thirteen to play at school functions. Also during high school, he played alto sax with Curtis Mosby's Blue Blowers at the Apex Club in Los Angeles in 1929. Following high school, he joined the Les Hite Orchestra in

1931 and remained with the group until 1939 when he briefly played with Cee Pee Johnson. Among the musicians with the Hite Orchestra were Lionel Hampton and Ernie Royal, his brother who played trumpet. When Hampton formed his own group in 1940, Marshal joined and became the band's mentor for the younger musicians, including Dexter Gordon, who later paid tribute to Marshal for teaching him how to breathe and phrase correctly. He left Hampton in 1942 to complete a four-year stint in the Navy where he led his own band.

After the navy, he worked with Eddie Heywood in 1946 in New York, but returned to the West Coast where he was a studio musician.

In 1951, Royal joined the Count Basie octet following the demise of his big band. When Basie reorganized his big band in 1952, Marshal was his primary assistant in the reorganization process, and served as the band's "unofficial" leader by mentoring the young musicians similar to the duties he performed under Hampton, as well as holding the lead alto sax position. He maintained these dual roles with Basie until 1970, including several world tours. While absent from the Basie Orchestra due to ill health, he was quietly replaced.

After leaving Basie, Royal freelanced with several bands in the Los Angeles area, where he permanently settled. Among these were Bill Berry's big band and the Frankie Capp-Nat Pierce Juggernaut. He recorded as a soloist with Dave Frishberg in 1977, and the next year with Warren Vache. He also played numerous club and festival dates, while recording with a band he co-led with Snooky Young, also under his own name. In 1982, he recorded with Ella Fitzgerald, as well as a 1987 Concord Jazz Festival Basie tribute led by Gene Harris. In 1989, he returned to Europe for several festivals, and the same year, he visited Japan with the Basie-style big band co-led by Frank Wess and Harry Edison, resulting in the *Dear Mr. Basie* album in 1989. Often compared to Benny Carter, Royal's rich alto sax solos with a string of excellent big bands made him popular both nationally and internationally. He died in Los Angeles on May 9, 1995. *Marshal Royal: Jazz Survivor*, an autobiography written with Claire P. Gordon, was released in 2001 by Continuum Press. (GC)

Rubin, Mark
(b. August 8, 1966)

Having anchored country/punk/rock Bad Livers from 1991 to 2000 on string bass, tuba, and band management, as of 2003 Stillwater native Mark Rubin continued rumble-thumping, popping and oomping through an ever-growing musical career of live performances and recordings both in the U.S. and internationally. Born in Stillwater to musically inclined parents who met in the University of Arizona marching band, Mark's father was national secretary of the Kappa Kappa Psi Marching Band Fraternity, announcer for the Oklahoma State University Cowboy marching band, and member of several community orchestras. After a childhood in Stillwater where he would sit in awe of the Oklahoma State tuba players while his father prepared to announce the band's halftime show, Rubin spent his teen years in Norman where his father became director of the University of Oklahoma's Hillel House.

After an unsuccessful attempt at violin as child, he started playing tuba in the Norman High School symphony in 1982 and 1983, just as the national hardcore and alternative rock scene developed around the U.S. Oklahoma City became a primary stopover between larger gigs for Black Flag and other groups who followed their pioneering path that eventually became the alternative music trail for bands from the West Coast, Minneapolis, Austin, Athens, Georgia, and, ultimately, Seattle. After switching to electric bass after high school, and seeing reggae artists like Eek-a-Mouse, Rubin played in the Legendary Streetpeople, a reggae group in which he debuted at the Norman High School cafeteria in 1984. After a couple of years of traveling back and forth to Dallas, making connections, and managing bands from his Norman apartment, Mark moved to Dallas in 1986 where he had his first stage experience, singing "Suspicious Minds" on stage with **The Flaming Lips**. He played bass with a punk rock group, The Bedrockers, and became inspired to take up string bass by Smiling Jack Barton, the Reverend Horton Heat's bassist. Barton guided Rubin in picking up a string bass in a 1988 classified ad for $100, and soon thereafter, Mark joined Killbilly, a Dallas-based roots band with a punk rock attitude. That same aesthetic connected Mark to Killbilly's newly arriving banjo player and musician extraordinaire, Danny Barnes. After a year-and-a-half, the two musicians left Killbilly in simpatico and

Danny Barnes (left) with Mark Rubin (right) formed the Bad Livers

moved to Austin, played as a trio for a year with fiddler Ralph White, and began to form Bad Livers in 1989.

After starting with their first single, a cover of Iggy Pop's "Lust for Life" recorded in the Butthole Surfers' Paul Leary's living room, the Bad Livers partnership produced six albums appreciated both by fans and music critics, but not always by bluegrass or country traditionalists because of the band's eclectic take on Americana. With a raging hybrid of rock, country, and blues played on traditional instruments one usually hears in bluegrass or other American folk styles, Bad Livers released *Delusion of Banjer* (1992), *Horses in the Mines* (1994), a collection of old-time gospel songs, *Dust on the Bible* (1994), and three releases on the Sugar Hill roots-oriented label, *Hogs on the Highway* (1997), *Industry and Thrift* (1998), and *Blood and Mood* (2000). While Rubin humbly admits he has only been the bass and tuba player for Bad Livers and did not write any of the songs, 1998's *Industry and Thrift* bears his most indelible print. From the opening notes of the tuba on "Lumpy, Beanpole, & Dirt," to his rapid-fire bass on "Brand New Hat" or "Cannonball Rag," to his traditional arrangement of "A Yid ist Geboren inz Oklahoma," a nod to his Jewish heritage (he has the ten commandments tattooed on his arm in Hebrew) and love of klezmer music, Rubin's mark is obvious on the album, and clearly demonstrates his influence on the Bad Livers' songwriting. The album not only features their popular "I'm Going Back to Mom and Dad," but a hidden jam track with Mark pulling and popping hard on the string bass while Barnes rolls the banjo.

In 1998, Barnes moved to Washington state and the group really ceased to be a touring group, although more albums could be released from live recordings and yet-to-be-heard studio material. Since then, Rubin has supervised and composed for a film soundtrack, *The Newton Boys* (1998), hosted a music television show, *Breakin' In*, on local access TV in Austin, and a radio show on KUT, the University of Texas' college station. He has also worked consistently with Texas western swing traditionalist, Don Walser, both supporting Walser on bass, and releasing some of Walser's live radio recordings from the early 1960s on a "house label" Rubin has established, LumpyDisc. His interests have also diversified deeper into ethnic music beyond the traditional American styles that first inspired him, to include Tex-Mex, Tex-Polish, and Persian music. In 1999, Mark traveled to France with his Yiddish ensemble, Rubinchik's Orchestra, which mutated into a bluegrass band, a Tex-Mex conjunto, or a Hungarian folk band, depending on the occasion. In 2001, he played tuba on *Brotherhood of Brass*, a release by Frank London's Klezmer Brass Allstars, and contributed bass and tuba to *buttermilk & rifles*, a solo effort by Kevin Russell, well known for leading the Austin favorite roots radicals, the Gourds. He also recorded an album of old-time string band music with the Bing Bang Boys in Port Townsend, Washington, and released in 2002. Also in 2K2, Rubin's Yiddish band accompanied Neil Blumofe on a few of the tracks on *Hazzan Neil Blumofe*, and released an album of all-acoustic old time music with Texas-Polish dance band fiddler, Brian Marshall, called *Texas*

Kapela. As of 2003, Rubin continued his eclectic career of musician, producer, writer, and teacher, most recently joining up with the Ridgetop Syncopators, a "classic Texas Western swing combo." His website is a thorough and constantly updated resource to keep track of this outrageously diverse musician. (HF) www.markrubin.com

Rushing, Jimmy
(b. August 26, 1903 - d. June 8, 1972)

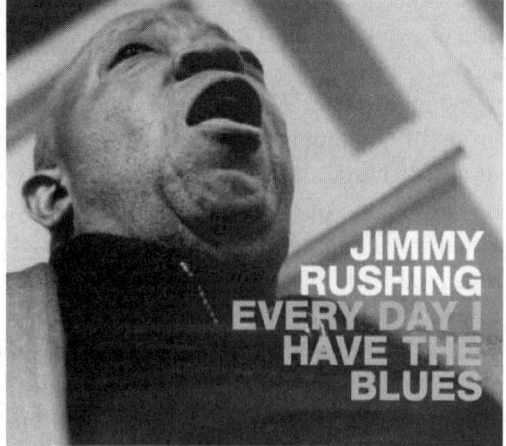

Achieving his greatest fame as the vocalist for the Count Basie band from 1935 to 1950 and solo recording in the 1960s, James Andrew Rushing was born in Oklahoma City. His father, Andrew Rushing, who played the trumpet, ran Rushing's Café on Northeast Second Street in Oklahoma City, an African-American business district that was to become known as "Deep Deuce." His mother, Cora Freeman, played piano and sang in choirs, and at one time was a professional religious singer. His brother was a singer. Thus, Jimmy was around music throughout his early home life, and eventually played piano at his father's café, however, the first instrument he learned was the violin. While at Douglass High School in Oklahoma City, he studied music theory under the tutelage of Zelia Page Breaux, a well-known music teacher who also influenced several other jazz greats to come out of Oklahoma City, including **Buddy Anderson** and Lem Johnson. As a teenager, Jimmy sang at any venue available, including school pageants, glee clubs, church choirs, and opera houses in the Oklahoma City area. His piano and vocal talents were influenced by his Uncle Wesley Manning, who played and sang in a local sporting house. A barrelhouse pianist in Oklahoma City by the name of Gerry Stoner was also an influence on Jimmy's piano talents. During the summers of his high school years, he hoboed from Chicago to Dallas, playing music. As he matured, Jimmy was known as "Mr. Five By Five" because of his physical stature.

After high school Rushing attended Wilberforce University in Wilberforce, Ohio, where he was the "official" pianist at the university dances. After two years of college, he moved to Los Angeles, where he worked several non-music jobs, but occasionally played with Jelly Roll Morton and Paul Howard at private parties and nightclubs, such as the Quality Night Club and the Jump Steady Club.

Around 1926, Jimmy returned to Oklahoma City because he became unhappy with life in Los Angeles. He worked in his father's café for more than a year, but an opportunity arose where Jimmy would reenter music. The Billy King Road

Show disbanded in 1925 in Oklahoma City, where Walter Page kept the band intact and renamed it—some sources say it "Walter Page's Original Blue Devils," while others contend it was the "**Oklahoma City Blue Devils**." Page expanded the band from its original nine members to as many as thirteen to fifteen members, and one of those was Jimmy. In addition to Jimmy, three other native Oklahomans were at one time or another member of the Blue Devils, including Abe Bolar, Lemuel C. Johnson, and **Don Byas**. Rushing also played with several artists who would become legendary, including Lester Young and William "Count" Basie.

When the Blue Devils were reorganized in Oklahoma City, Page persuaded a group of Oklahoma City businessmen to back the venture. The backing consisted of a little cash, a set of uniforms, a supply of meal tickets good at any restaurant owned by one of the sponsors, and the donation of a large hotel room (Littlepage Hotel in the "Deep Deuce District" district) that served as a dormitory, mess hall, rehearsal hall, and recruiting office. The Blue Devils used the Ritz Ballroom in downtown Oklahoma City as their home base while they performed on the Territorial Band circuit from Omaha, Nebraska, to Little Rock, Arkansas. The Blue Devils traveled to Kansas City for a "battle of the bands" competition and recorded their only music on the Vocalion label in 1929, featuring Jimmy on the vocal number, "Blue Devil Blues."

While in Kansas City, Jimmy, as well as Basie and Page, was invited to join the Bennie Moten Orchestra, one of the top bands in the Kansas City jazz scene. The Moten Orchestra had drawn national attention and was on tour around the country. Jimmy was also the vocalist on all the Moten recordings for Victor through 1935, when Moten died. Basie reorganized the Moten ensemble into the Count Basie Orchestra, and Jimmy became the lead vocalist until 1950.

The Basie Orchestra's 1936 recording of "Boogie Woogie" featured Jimmy and marked his presence on the national scene. Rushing appears on all the Basie recordings during this period and can be found on several reissues on Decca, Columbia, and RCA. While with Basie, Jimmy also performed in a number of films, including *Crazy Horse*, *Take Me Back Baby*, *Air Mail Special*, and *Top Man*, as well as the "From Spirituals to Swing" concerts at Carnegie Hall in 1938.

In 1950 Basie dissolved his orchestra due to hard times for big bands, and Rushing briefly retired to South Carolina. But it was not long until Jimmy was again on the music scene with his own combo, as well as doing solo work. Basie and Rushing were reunited in 1954 when they appeared on the *Tonight Show*, hosted by Steve Allen. Jimmy's recording output increased in the 1950s, especially a series of albums with Vanguard, such as *Jimmy Rushing Sings the Blues* and *Listen to the Blues*, both released in 1955.

Jimmy then signed with Columbia Records and released several notable albums, *The Jazz Odyssey of James Rushing, Esq.* (1955), *Cat Meets Chick* (1956), *Little Jimmy Rushing and the Big Brass* (1958), *Rushing Lullabies* (1959), and *Jimmy Rushing and the Smith Girls* (1960). For this work, Jimmy won the *Down Beat*

Critics Poll for Best Male Singer in 1957, 1958, 1959, and 1960; British magazine *Melody Maker* Critics Poll as Best Male Singer for the same years; and the German magazine *Jazz Podium* Critics Award in 1958. The same year, Jimmy and Benny Goodman performed together at the World's Fair in Brussels, which resulted in collaboration on "Brussels Blues." Jimmy also appeared in a CBS film, *The Sound of Jazz*, and reunited with Count Basie at the Newport Jazz Festival; both occurring in 1957.

The 1960s also proved to be a productive period for Jimmy. He toured the world with several jazz greats, including Dave Brubeck, Thelonious Monk, Eddie Condon, Harry James Orchestra, and Joe Newman; won *Jazz & Pop* Critics Award in 1967, completed a singing and acting role in *The Learning Tree* film in 1969, and was guest on the *Mike Douglas Show* on television.

Rushing became ill in 1971, but the awards kept rolling in with *Down Beat* Critics Poll Record of the Year in 1972 for *The You and Me That Used to Be*; *Down Beat* Critics Poll for Best Male Singer in 1972; and the Kansas City Jazz Hall of Fame Award in 1971. Jimmy was considered a first-class jazz singer, but his numbers were always tinged with the blues. In his later years, he favored certain songs, such as "Going to Chicago," "Everyday I Have the Blues," "Exactly Like You," "I Surrender Dear," and "When I Grow Too Old to Dream." On June 8, 1972 "Mr. Five By Five" died with leukemia at the Flower and Fifth Avenue Hospital in New York City. He is buried at the Maple Grove Cemetery, Kew Gardens, in Queens. (GC)

Rushlow, Tim

Tim Rushlow (center, in black)

Born in Midwest City at Tinker Air Force base where his father, Tom, was stationed in the Air Force, Tim Rushlow went on to be the lead singer of the country rock group Little Texas, one of the most popular country acts of the 1990s to the tune of more than six million albums sold. After being discharged from the military, Tom Rushlow moved the family to Arlington, Texas, where he formed the band Moby Dick and the Whalers with three of his brothers-in-law via his wife, and Tim's mom, Patricia. The group toured regionally and released some of their own records, but more importantly they provided the environment in which Tim could learn to play music. Picking up drums, bass, piano, and guitar from his father and uncles, Tim sang along with his parents' record collection, inspired especially by the country group, Alabama. As a teenager, Tim sang in school choirs, formed garage bands around 1984 with vocalist/guitarist Dwayne O'Brien that landed gigs in the north Texas and southern Oklahoma area, and performed in the live music shows at Six Flags Over Texas that led to a job in 1986 imitating country music legends at Opryland in Nashville.

When Rushlow left Arlington, O'Brien attended East Central Oklahoma State University in Ada where he earned a chemistry degree, and then followed Rushlow to Nashville where they formed Little Texas with Rushlow's high school buddies, lead guitarist Porter Howell and bassist Duane Propes who were attending Nashville's Belmont University. Starting to tour in the country by booking themselves and being their own roadies, the band met keyboardist Brady Seals and drummer Del Gray in Massachussetts, who joined the band shortly thereafter. By 1988 the group had been signed to Warner Brothers and named themselves Little Texas, after Little Texas Boulevard where they practiced in Nashville. Buying a 1972 Chevy van for $300 and building a trailer themselves, the group played clubs around the country, appeared on *Star Search* (they didn't win), and by 1990 had developed enough material to record their first album, *First Time for Everything* (Warner Brothers, 1992). The band's debut single, "Some Guys Have All the Love," became a top ten country hit and launched the band on a six-year ride of top ten hits, million-selling albums, and sold out concerts.

Merging glam rock looks (and some music not that far from the genre), earthy lyrics about Daddy, high school football games, hayfields, and plenty of references to Texas, the group continued its meteoric rise in 1994 with *Big Time* (Warner Brothers, 1993). The platinum-selling album provided two, top five country hits, "What Might Have Been" and the line-dancing favorite, "God Blessed Texas," as well as the #1 country hit, "My Love." Little Texas followed up *Big Time* with *Kick a Little* (Warner Brothers, 1993). The album's title track went top ten, as did "Amy's Back in Austin," and the group had another platinum album in its catalogue. In 1995, the band released a greatest hits package with two new songs, to include the foreshadowing "Life Goes On." Once 1997's self–titled album did not produce any hits, the group of old friends who were doing just fine financially, decided to call it quits in 1998.

With a little time and a comfy cash cushion to think about what to do next, Rushlow took time out from the music business, cut his hair, and began writing songs, the fruit of which was his 2001 self-titled solo album on Atlantic Records. A conservative effort with all of the safe studio trappings of Nashville's corporate country establishment, the album can only be looked at as Rushlow stretching out to find out who he was outside of Little Texas. While some of the songs are about inspirational people who make sacrificial choices in life ("In the Meantime"), and love their partners through something so difficult as Alzheimer's disease ("She Misses Him"), which did make the country top ten, the album was so far away from the rowdy rural insights of Little Texas that only the most ardent fans picked it up. The singer-songwriter apparently got the message. By spring of 2002, he had formed a group, Rushlow, with Billy Welch (keyboards, vocals), Kurt Allison (lead guitar), Tully Kennedy (bass guitar, vocals), Rich Redmond (drums), and

Tishomingo native (and Rushlow's cousin) Doni Harris on acoustic guitar and vocals.

Furthering Rushlow's connection to Oklahoma, Doni Harris grew up on Lake Texoma near the Texas border. "Everybody in our family plays or sings," Harris says on the band's website, "and Tim and I grew up singing on the Oklahoma Opry and places like that." Harris played in a local band, Atlantis, and was the president of the Tishomingo High School Marching Band. After a period of commuting from Oklahoma to Nashville to sing demos for songwriters, he settled in Nashville permanently and landed a publishing deal. Before long, he hooked up with his cousin Tim who was putting together Rushlow. In March, 2003, the group signed to Lyric Street Records, the label that has released debut albums by SheDaisy and Rascal Flatts. The band's first single, "I Can't Be Your Friend," reached #29 on the *Billboard* country chart, the album was due September 5, and Rushlow was booked solid through the end of 2003 at venues across the U.S. (HF) www.timrushlow.com

Russell, Leon
(b. April 2, 1941)

As one of pop and rock's most significant artists from the early 1960s through the mid-1970s, Leon Russell's career as a multi-instrumentalist, record producer, arranger, studio owner and stylistic iconoclast is legendary in music circles. His gold albums, pop hits, and continued success as a touring performer as of 2003 are testament to his popularity among legions of worldwide music fans. Born Claude Russell Bridges in the southwestern Oklahoma town of Lawton, home to the massive Fort Sill army base, he studied classical piano from age three to thirteen. Having moved to Tulsa when he was fourteen, he attended Tulsa's Will Rogers High School, played briefly with Ronnie Hawkins and the Hawks, and eventually formed a group called the Starlighters with local musicians Leo Feathers (guitar),

Chuck Blackwell (drums), Jack Dunham (vocals), Lucky Clark (bass), and Johnny Williams (saxophone). The group played locally until Jerry Lee Lewis signed the musicians as his touring band in the late 1950s. They toured the Midwest for two years with the fifties rock and roll icon known for "Great Balls of Fire" and "Whole Lotta Shakin' Goin' On." The Lewis influence on Russell is obvious on Leon's first two singles, "Swanee River" and "All Right," recorded in Tulsa and released on the Chess label in 1959.

In January of 1962, Russell and drummer Chuck Blackwell headed to California where they met up with **David Gates** and formed a group that played country and rock in supper clubs, and began getting session work around Los Angeles. That led to a friendship with Rick Nelson's guitarist, James Burton, who taught Leon how to play guitar. Russell became a member of an elite group of session musicians known as the "Wrecking Crew," and he built and an impressive resumé during the 1960s with his presence on hit recordings such as Herb Albert's "A Taste of Honey," the Righteous Brothers "You've Lost That Loving Feeling" (also featuring Muskogee guitarist **Barney Kessel**), and the Byrds' cover of Dylan's "Mr. Tambourine Man." He also appeared on a dizzying array of sessions with the likes of Glen Campbell, Dorsey Burnette, Frank Sinatra, Bob Dylan, Ike and Tina Turner, Aretha Franklin, The Rolling Stones, Barbara Streisand, The Ventures, Bobby Darin, Wayne Newton, Sam Cooke, Nitty Gritty Dirt Band, Johnny Mathis, and The Byrds. As an arranger, he supervised the musical production Gary Lewis and the Playboys' #1 hit of 1965, "This Diamond Ring." His piano playing is prominent on Jan and Dean's "Surf City," Bobby Doris Pickett's "Monster Mash," the Carpenters' "Superstar," The Byrds' "Mr. Tambourine Man," Herb Alpert's "A Taste of Honey," The Beach Boys' "California Girls" and *Pet Sounds* album, and virtually all of Phil Spector's hit recordings, to include the Crystals' "He's a Rebel," one of the quintessential girl group recordings.

From 1965 to 1967, Russell built his own studio in California where he began experimenting with recording techniques, producing the critically lauded but commercially unsuccessful *Asylum Choir* in 1968. He also recorded and toured with Delaney and Bonnie that year, and enjoyed his first major success as a songwriter with Joe Cocker who had a hit with Russell's "Delta Lady" in 1969, a song originally written for Rita Coolidge. As a result of serving as Joe Cocker's musical director and arranger for *Joe Cocker!* (1969), and the live album that resulted from Cocker's famous Mad Dogs and Englishmen tour in 1970, the 43 member band for which Leon assembled and led, Russell became an important figure in the royal British music scene of Eric Clapton, with whom he wrote "Blues Power," Steve Winwood, the Rolling Stones, and soon-to-be ex-Beatles George Harrison and Ringo Starr.

Russell formed Shelter Records in 1969 and recorded *Asylum Choir II* with Marc Benno, unreleased until 1972 and producing no hits, but clearly indicating Russell's musical directions with its honky-tonk piano-driven blues-rock. *Asylum Choir II* also features usually unexamined strong political statements on some of the most resonant anti-war songs of the Vietnam era, such as "Down on the Base" and "Ballad for a Soldier," which may account for the hesitancy on the part of the label that would not release it. Shelter also provided the forum for such notable artists as Tom Petty, Freddie King, **J.J. Cale**, Phoebe Snow, **The GAP Band**, and **Dwight Twilley**. In 1970, Leon's first album surfaced under his own name and produced one hit single, "Roll Away the Stone," a gospel anti-war anthem, "Give Peace a Chance," and his own version of Cocker's hit, "Delta Lady," as well as now-standard Russell concert pieces, "Shoot Out at the Plantation," and "A Song for You." In 1971, Russell released the Top 20 album, *Leon Russell and the Shelter People*, which featured, among others, George Harrison as a "performer," **Jesse Ed Davis**, and a backup group called the Tulsa Tops on songs such as "Home Sweet Oklahoma," "The Ballad of Mad Dogs and Englishmen," and "Stranger in a Strange Land." Also in 1971, as a result of George Harrison guesting on Russell's first solo album, Leon played for Harrison's Concert for Bangladesh, at New York's Madison Square Garden, and is featured prominently on the resulting album.

In 1972, Russell bought the tapes for *Asylum Choir II* and released it to some success as it reached the top 100 album charts, largely as a result of his significant rock star status at the time. He also released the gold-selling *Carney* in 1972, his best-selling album ever, which produced the Top 20 pop hit "Tightrope," and the song "This Masquerade," later a Grammy winning song for Russell in 1977 via George Benson who had a Top 10 hit with it on the #1 album *Breezin'* (1976) when it became the first song in music history to land at the top spot on the pop, jazz, and R & B charts.

Needing a rest from the constant pressures of touring, recording, writing, and performing, Russell returned to Oklahoma in 1972 when he bought 7 ½ acres on Grand Lake in northeastern Oklahoma and began building a massive spread to include a 3,500-square foot house, studio, swimming pool, and guest apartments that became known as "the hippie place" by locals. In 1973, at the peak of his popularity as a rock artist, Russell surfaced for the first time with his alter ego, Hank Wilson, the country performer Leon uses as a vehicle for traditional country and gospel songs that are an obvious cornerstone of his music. Recorded in Owen Bradley's famous barn studio in Mt. Juliet, Tennessee, which burned not long afterwards, *Hank Wilson's Back* features country standards such as "Rollin' in My Sweet Baby's Arms," "I'm So Lonesome I Could Cry," **Hank Thompson**'s "Six Pack to Go," and "Truck Drivin' Man." Also in 1973, when *Billboard Magazine* reported Leon was the top concert attraction in the world, Russell's *Leon Live*, a triple album recorded in front of 70,000 people at Long Beach Arena and released in late 1972, went gold. Late in 1972, Russell released a Christmas single, "Slipping into Christmas," that rose to #4 on the pop charts.

Given this tremendous success, Russell also began acquiring several properties around Tulsa, to include the First Church of God at Third and Trenton. Russell converted the building into the now famous Church Studio, currently owned and operated by **Steve Ripley** of the Tractors. The Church Studio provided a nexus through which some of rock's biggest performers of the 1970s channeled their recording sessions away from the microscopic pressures of New York or L.A. While musicians such as Bob Dylan and **J.J. Cale** recorded there in the 1970s, Tulsa power popster **Dwight Twilley** recorded his 1975 Top 20 hit, "I'm On Fire," in the studio, and the GAP Band experienced some of their early tastes of recording on Russell's 1974 album, *All That Jazz*, recorded in part at the studio. *All That Jazz* featured Russell's version of Tim Hardin's "If I Were A Carpenter," a humble pop hit at #74, and the album peaked at #34 on the album charts. Leon's 1975 release, the gold-selling *Will O' The Wisp*, provided Russell's last Top 20 hit, "Lady Blue," in the fall of 1974, and "Bluebird" which was a Top 40 hit for Helen Reddy in 1975.

Also in 1975, Leon formed Sheltervision, a video branch of Shelter that began documenting various elements of the music industry milieu swirling about Russell who was the ever-calm eye of the hurricane. While a film has yet to be released, Russell said in a 2001 interview that live performances will surface on DVD. Russell ended his ties with Shelter in 1976 and started a new label, Paradise Records, a formative training ground for members of Concrete Blonde and Steve Ripley. Subsequently, Shelter released the *Best of Leon Russell*, which went gold. Also that year, Russell married Mary McCreary, a vocalist with the Sly and the Family Stone spin-off group, Little Sister. The two recorded *Wedding Album* (Paradise, 1976), which produced Russell's last chart single, "Rainbow in Your Eyes."

Make Love to the Music went practically unnoticed in 1977, and in 1979, his solo album, *Americana*, sold modestly; however, Leon also released a duet album with Willie Nelson in 1979, *One for the Road*, which earned gold status, and peaked at #25 on the pop album chart. *One for the Road* was the CMA's Album of the Year, and the version of "Heartbreak Hotel" included on the album topped the country charts. Leon's association with Willie included doing some overdubs on some of Willie's early 1960s recordings, and later hosting the first of Nelson's 4th of July Picnics, which began a significant mixing of the country and rock audiences around Austin in the 1970s.

In the early 1980s, Russell relocated permanently to Nashville, and toured with the New Grass Revival, a bluegrass band with whom he recorded rock standards on *The Live Album* in 1981. Also during the 1980s, Leon toured with Edgar Winter around the world to include concerts in Russia, Brazil, Mexico, Canada, and throughout the United States. In 1984, Leon released *Hank Wilson Volume II*, another collection of country standards, and in 1989 his initial solo release from 1970 was reissued with additional tracks. In 1992, Bruce Hornsby urged Leon back into the studio for a largely unsuccessful commercial release, *Anything Can Happen*, and in 1995 Leon released a set of traditional Christmas songs, *Hymns of Christmas*, on his own label, Leon Russell Records. In 1996, The Right Stuff label re-released *Leon Live*, a two-CD set that includes all the material from the original three-record set, and also released *Retrospective* (1997), a compilation of Russell's major hits from the Shelter period of 1970 to 1975. In 1998, Ark 21 Records released the third installment of Leon's Hank Wilson series, *Legend in My Time, Hank Wilson Volume III*. Along with covers of **Merle Haggard**'s "Okie from Muskogee," and Willie Nelson's "Crazy," the album features excellent musicians such as Marty Stuart on mandolin, Willie Nelson's harmonica player, Micky Raphael, and background vocals by the Oak Ridge Boys on "Daddy Sang Bass" and Willie Nelson on two songs. An extra bonus is an audio interview with Russell that is included prior to the first track on the album.

Russell released a new collection of his own material in 1999 with *Face in the Crowd*, and a collection of Russell's blues-flavored material, *Blues: Same Old Song*. In 2000, Atlantic Records released a live set recorded at Gilley's, and in 2001 Leon started releasing a series of albums on his Leon Russell Records label, to include a tribute to himself on *Signature Songs*, his greatest hits reinterpreted acoustically just on piano and vocals. Also in 2001, Leon re-released an album of blues songs in which he plays the guitar exclusively, *Guitar Blues*, previously available only in Japan, and in 2002 released a compilation of standards such as "My Funny Valentine," "'Round Midnight," and "As Time Goes By," with Leon accompanied by the Nashville Symphony Orchestra.

Currently, Leon lives in Nashville where he has contributed piano work to sessions for George Jones, Bela Fleck, and the Tractors. He continues to tour throughout the United States and was booked solidly through the end of 2003, at times with Edgar Winter. In an October 2002 show at Oklahoma State University's Seretean Center, Leon traveled with a five-piece group featuring bass, drums, guitar, himself on piano, and his daughter, Sugaree Noel, on African beaded gourd percussion. Russell keeps a personal mixer on his keyboard platform to get the stage monitor sound he wants, and a laptop computer on top of his keyboard to keep track of songs. While playing many of the songs for which he is known such as "Delta Lady," "Hummingbird," and "Tightrope," Russell also showed his range of American musical influences with country songs such as "Sweet Dreams," "16 Tons," and "He Stopped Loving Her Today," rock songs like "Jumping Jack Flash," and the blues of "Kansas City." His website not only chronicles his career and current activities, but also lists a variety of personal items Leon no longer needs such as amp racks, old furniture, a dump truck, and a mobile recording studio. (HF)
www.leonrussellrecords.com

Russell, Tom
(b. February 8, 1955)

With seventeen albums of original songs and a host of compositions recorded by the likes of Johnny Cash, Nanci Griffith, Doug Sahm, Ian Tyson, Suzy Bogguss, and Iris DeMent, Tom Russell was born in Oklahoma City. As a child Tom's family moved to southern California, where he grew up listening to artists such as **Merle Haggard**, Buck Owens, and **Spade Cooley**. In the 1960s, he was influenced by such folk artists as Bob Dylan and Ian & Sylvia, and began to haunt the folk clubs in Los Angeles, hoping one day to become a songwriter.

By 1971 Russell had moved to Vancouver, British Columbia, where he made his first public performances in bars and nightclubs. While playing these venues, he met a variety of characters that would become subjects for his later songs. In 1973 Tom headed for Austin, Texas, the center for the emerging "progressive country" or "outlaw" scene. He teamed with pianist Patricia Harden, and they released two albums (*Ring of Bone* and *Wax Museum*) combining Austin music and Beat poetry, or what Tom called "cosmic folk." This material was reissued on the Philo label in 1994 as *The Early Years (1975-79)*. The duo migrated to San Francisco where they played folks clubs, however, the two parted company in 1979.

Russell decided to pursue a career as a novelist and moved to New York City, where he drove a cab in order to survive. While driving his cab, Tom met The Grateful Dead's Robert Hunter, who was impressed with Tom's songwriting talents and invited him to perform at a Grateful Dead concert in New York. Soon thereafter, he met guitarist Andrew Hardin, and they began to tour Europe (one source states Tom performed as a cowboy singer in a Puerto Rican carnival) and recorded three albums in Norway before returning to the U.S.

Tom's debut solo album was *Heart on a Sleeve*, released in 1984 on the Demon label and reissued by Bear Family in 1995. He reunited with Hardin on the next several albums, including *Road to Bayamon* (1988), *Poor Man's Dream* (1990), and *Hurricane Season* (1991). *Cowboy Real*, released in 1992, is a collection of cowboy songs and includes two duets with folk legend Ian Tyson, "Navajo Rug," which won the 1987 CMA Single of the Year, and "Gallo de Cielo," one of the best songs ever written about a cockfight.

A compilation of Russell's recordings was released in 1992 on the Roundtower label, *Beyond St. Olay's Gate (1979-1992)*, which was followed by two albums with rhythm-and-blues artist Barrence Whitfield, *Hillbilly Voodoo* and *Cowboy Mambo*. The former includes Bob Dylan's "Blind Willie McTell," Jesse Winchester's "Mississippi, You've Been on My Mind," and Jimmy Driftwood's "What is the Color of the Soul of a Man?" *Box of Visions* was also released in 1992 and features Rosie Flores and Katy Moffatt singing back-up vocals. *The Rose of the San Joaquin, Songs of the West*, and *The Long Way Around*, all released on the Hightone label, were released in the mid-1990s. The latter album features duets with Katy Moffatt, Dave Alvin, Jimmie Dale Gilmore, Iris DeMent, and Nanci Griffith.

Tom made a dramatic move in 1997, leaving Brooklyn for a small ranch in Canutillo, Texas (near El Paso). The following year he launched *The Man From God Knows Where*, a folk opera based on the Russell family background. In the album, Tom traces the family ancestry to Ireland and Norway through his father. Recorded and initially released in Norway, the project, which was seven years in the making and currently available from HighTone Records, features several Norwegian musicians as well as Iris DeMent, Dave Van Ronk, and noted Irish singer Dolores Keene. Interestingly, four artists in a group called Imagine That!, all from Lawton, Oklahoma, produced one of the community's Oklahoma Centennial events in 2002. The musical production centers on Tom's *The Man From God Knows Where* music and lyrics with vignettes drawn from the local area's pioneer history.

On Tom's latest album, *Borderline* (2002), he tracks the border between the U.S. and Mexico, but also the distances between men and women. **Jimmy LaFave** sings back-up harmony vocals. Tom has also worked as a producer, and in 1995 was co-producer of one of the best tributes to one of his musical heroes, Merle Haggard, in *Tulare Dust*.

Russell has been described as the "songwriter's songwriter" and "one of the finest folk artists Americans never heard of." His compositions are literate and narrative, often centering on real people, such as "Blue Wing," a story about a man who was once jailed with blues artist Little Willie John; "William Faulkner in Hollywood," traces the novelist's disastrous story of writing screenplays to pay off Southern loan sharks; "Haley's Comet," tracks the downward career of rock-and-roll pioneer Bill Haley; "Chocolate Cigarettes," a story about the famous cabaret diva Edith Piaf; "Jack Johnson," narrative abut the world's first great African-American prize fighter; "Blue Wing," a story about the infamous Inuit Indian who dies on skid row; "The Evangeline Hotel," about a lonely actress; "Somebody's Husband, Somebody's Son," a hobo's waltz; and "Outbound Plane," a story of lost love.

In 2003, Tom appeared on *Late Night with David Letterman* and finished a book documenting his correspondence with Los Angeles underworld poet Charles Bukowski. The tentative title is *California Bloodlines: The Letters of Charles Bukowski and Tom Russell*, with an intro written by Dave Alvin. Russell also released the first CD on his own label, Frontera Records. The album, *In Between Films: The Piano of George Malloy*, features Tom's eighty-three-year-old uncle playing piano on everything from Ira Gershwin standards to the Beatles and "The Streets of Laredo." He also had plans to release a "cowboy record" later in the year, and has another album, *Magnum Opus Western Epic*, scheduled for release on Hightone in 2004. (GC/HF)
www.tomrussell.com

Seaton, Lynn
(b. July 18, 1957)

One of the most in-demand jazz bass players during the last twenty years, Lynn Seaton was born in Tulsa. He started at the age of seven on the guitar, but soon switched to the bass at nine. While studying music at the University of Oklahoma, he performed at various clubs within the state. By 1980, Lynn had relocated to Cincinnati, Ohio, where he joined pianist Steve Schmidt's Trio and John Von Ohlen's big band at the Blue Wisp jazz club. About a year later, he was awarded a NEA Jazz Studies Fellowship to study under Rufus Reid in New York City. In 1984, he joined Woody Herman's Young Thundering Heard, and in July of the following year, he began a two-year stint with the Count Basie Orchestra. Following his time with the Basie ensemble, he worked with Tony Bennett, George Shearing, and Monty Alexander.

In 1993 Seaton turned to freelancing and during the next five years performed in forty-nine of the fifty states as well as more than thirty-five countries abroad, appearing at such prestigious jazz festivals as Concord, Newport, North Sea, and Bern. His freelance work included performances with such notable jazz artists as Clark Terry, Buck Clayton, Herb Ellis, Thad Jones, Mel Lewis, Marian McPartland, and Teddy Wilson. In addition, he appeared on more than 100 albums as side bassist for such artists as Diane Schuur, Kenny Drew, Jr., Nancy Wilson, Joe Williams, Bucky Pizzarelli, Milt Hinton, Hoagy Carmichael, Ernestine Anderson, and Al Cohn. Seaton's only recorded album during this period was *Bassman's Basement*, a 1991 release on the Timeless label, on which he is accompanied by pianist Lee Musiker and drummer Tim Horner. Three of Lynn's compositions are included on the ten tracks, including "Major's Grand Slam," "Marianna's Waltz," and "Naptown Zebras."

By the late 1990s Seaton had become a respected jazz educator, instructing students at Cincinnati's College Conservatory of Music, Long Island University,

State University of New York at New Paulz, William Patterson College, and North Texas University in Denton, where he joined the faculty in 1998. He has also participated in jazz camps and clinics sponsored by Jamey Aebersold and Clark Terry.

In 2000 the OmniTone label released *Solo Flights*, a 12-track collection with seven of the selections written by Seaton. One of the most challenging tasks for any musician is a solo album, especially on the bass, however, Seaton rises to the occasion and runs the gamut of music genres, including "Ode to Jimi," a tribute to the late rock icon Jimi Hendrix, "Liltin' with Milton," dedicated to the late jazz bassist Milt Hinton, two of his compositions. Additional forays into other genres include "Moten Swing" (Big Band jazz), "How High the Moon" (bebop), and "Barcelona" (flamenco). He also appears on the Woody Herman *50ᵗʰ Anniversary Tour* album (Concord 1986) and *Live at the 1990 Concord Jazz Festival* with Frank Wess (Concord 1990).

As of 2003, Seaton resides in Denton, where he is lecturer in the Jazz Studies Division of the College of Music at the University of North Texas. He teaches applied jazz bass lessons, jazz fundamentals and styles, jazz improvisation, and a rhythm section master class. Finally, he continues to perform by leading his own jazz trio with gigs in the Dallas-Fort Worth metroplex. (GC)

Sessions, Ronnie
(b. December 7, 1948)

A childhood prodigy known for recording ten Top 10 hits, singer, guitarist, and songwriter, Ronnie Sessions was born in Henryetta, Oklahoma, a community of roughly 6,000 residents located east of Oklahoma City on Interstate 40. Ronnie's family moved to Bakersfield, California, when he was about nine years old, and he began to take guitar lessons from Andy Moseley, another native Oklahoman and inventor of the Moserite guitar. Ronnie's first recording was made in 1957, a novelty version of Little Richard's "Keep A-Knockin'," made with Little Richard's band. Through a school friend, he learned of Cousin Herb Henson's Trading Post television show, and became a regular on the show form 1958 to 1961.

In 1957, Ronnie signed his first recording contract with the Pike label. The next year, he was invited to sing on stage during a Grand Ole Opry troupe tour at the Bakersfield Civic Center. So impressed with Ronnie's performance, the troupe invited him to continue on the tour.

Sessions signed with **Gene Autry's** Republic label, and broke into the Top 10 in 1968 with **Hoyt Axton's** "Never Been to Spain," which was followed with "I Never Go Around Mirrors," a #6 hit. He also recorded on Republic a revival of the pop song, "Tossin' and Turnin'," as well as several regional hits, such as "The

Life of Riley" and "More Than Satisfied."

In 1969, Ronnie moved to MCA Records, and scored with "Wiggle Wiggle," which reached #4 in 1969, which was followed with a revival of the Bobby Goldsboro song, "Me and Millie (Stompin' Grapes and Getting' Silly)." He recorded two albums with MCA, *Ronnie Sessions* (1969) and *Ronnie Sessions Live* (1970), but was eventually dropped by the label in 1980.

After moving to Nashville, Sessions wrote several songs, most notably "When I Play the Fiddle," which Kenny Rogers recorded on his 1977 album, *Lucille*. His last charted single, "I Bought the Shoes That Just Walked Out on Me," was in 1986. He retired from the music business in 1987. (GC)

Settle, Mike
(b. March 20, 1941)

Composer or co-composer of more than 130 songs, co-founder of The First Edition with Kenny Rogers, and musical director of the New Christy Minstrels, singer, songwriter, instrumentalist (guitar and harmonica), and producer Mike Settle was born in Tulsa, but, in the ninth grade, moved to Muskogee, a city of roughly 38,000 residents located southeast of Tulsa. While in Tulsa, he was a member of the Tulsa Boy Singers (fifth through seventh grade) in which he received much of his early musical training. According to Mike, he considers Muskogee his "hometown" because of the friends and relatives who still live there, as well as the many pleasant memories he recalls from his early years spent in the community.

Upon completion of high school, Mike majored in music at Oklahoma City University. After performing at coffeehouses in Oklahoma, Mike replaced John Montgomery in the Cumberland Three in 1960, including a Carnegie Hall concert with Shelley Berman. The group, which patterned themselves as another Kingston Trio, disbanded in 1961 when John Stewart left to replace Dave Guard in the Kingston Trio. He had also performed at New York City's Bitter End as a solo artist. Settle performed at the 1963 Newport Folk Festival in one of the festival workshops, made several appearances on the ABC television series *Hootenanny*, and toured the coffee house circuit as a soloist before leaving New York City for California as a replacement for one of the last original members in The New Christy Minstrels.

Settle spent 1966-67 with The New Christy Minstrels, serving as musical director while with the group. He left the Minstrels, along with Kenny Rogers, to form The First Edition with Thelma Comacho, Terry Williams, and drummer Mickey Jones. On the group's *The First Edition '69* album for the Reprise label, Mike is credited with writing or co-writing five of the ten tracks, including his signature song, "But You Know I Love You," which became a major hit for Bill Anderson in the 1970s, a #1 hit for Dolly Parton in the 1980s, and logged more than two million performances with BMI. Mike also served as music director for Glenn Yarbrough as well as The New Seekers.

In 1971 Mike released his only solo album, *Mike Settle*, on the Uni label. It included "But You Know I Love You," "Saturday's Only," "The Nights of Your Life," and "Nobody Knows."

Settle's songs have been recorded by myriad artists. In addition to those previously mentioned, they include "But You Know I Love You" (**Henson Cargill**, Buck Owens, Kenny Rogers, and Alison Krauss), "Sing Hallelujah" (Judy Collins, Joe & Eddie, and Stephane Grappelli), "Settle Down [Goin' Down That Highway]" (The Springfields, Peter, Paul, & Mary, and Bobby Darin), "I'd Build a Bridge" (Glen Campbell, Charlie Rich, Wayne Newton, and Johnny Rodriguez), "Lady Lonely" (Wayne Newton), "Morning Star" (Glenn Yarbrough), "Bound for Zion" (Lonnie Donegan), "Nights of Your Life" (Bobby Goldsboro), "Saturday's Only" (Bobby Goldsboro), "Goo Ga Gee" (Kingston Trio), and "Little Boy" (The Highwaymen, Kingston Trio, and Andy Williams). Other artists to record Mike's songs include Harry Belafonte and The Limelighters. Additional songwriting credits to Mike include "Sometimes Love is Better When It's Gone," and three songs for the film *Vanishing Point*, including "Nobody Knows," "Where Do We Go From Here," and "The Girl Done Got It Together." In addition to writing songs, Mike has appeared as a back-up vocalist and instrumentalist for such artists and groups as Kim Carnes, John Stewart, Glenn Yarbrough, and the Kingston Trio.

As of 2003, Settle remains active in the songwriting business and works as a free-lance journalist, while residing in the Nashville area. (GC)

Shelton, Blake
(b. June 18, 1976)

One of the hottest new stars in country music with his "Austin" single reaching #1 on the country charts for five consecutive weeks (which tied a *Billboard* record for an artist's debut album), Blake Tollison Shelton was born to Dick and Dorothy Shelton in Ada, Oklahoma, a college town (East Central University) of approximately 15,000 population southeast of Oklahoma City. His siblings include a sister, Endy, who resides in Oklahoma, and a brother, Richie, who was fatally injured in an automobile accident in the early 1990s.

Blake started singing in his bedroom at a tender age, and his mother was so excited, she entered him in a beauty pageant talent show with fifty little girls when he was eight, singing "Old Time Rock-n-Roll." According to Blake, he was so embarrassed that he vowed never to sing again. Blake retained his interest in country music, primarily because his Uncle Dearl taught him the basic chords of C, F, and G on the guitar. By the time he reached his teens, Blake was singing at local honky tonks in and around Ada, including the Country Music Palace and Legends, became a regular on a local country music show, and wrote his first song, "Once in a Long, Long While," when he was fifteen. Blake began receiving statewide attention when he captured the Denbo Diamond Award for young Oklahoma entertainers. Based on this award and his local singing reputation, Blake was invited to perform at a tribute show in Ada for Mae Boren Axton, the noted Nashville songwriter (co-wrote "Heartbreak Hotel" recorded by Elvis Presley). Ms. Axton was impressed and encouraged him to come to Nashville, where she had built a reputation for assisting young musicians.

Two weeks after graduating from Ada High School in 1994, Blake at age seventeen moved to Nashville where he reunited with Ms. Axton, who provided him with his first paying job in Music City—painting her house. While working for Ms. Axton, Blake met **Hoyt Axton**, Mae's son and influential singer-songwriter who was temporarily living in his tour bus parked in Mae's driveway. Hoyt gave Blake several tips about the music industry and presented him with a long Bowie knife on his eighteenth birthday. Hoyt also introduced Blake to the song "Ol' Red," which was included on his debut album *Austin*, and has become a 2002 Top 20 hit single.

For the next few years, Blake performed at several Nashville venues, such as Douglas Corner and the Bluebird Café, while working for Sony Tree publishing house making tape copies of writers' songs. Unfortunately, Blake spent too much time visiting with the writers and was terminated. During this period, he had several songs published with Naomi Martin Music, Warner/Chappell Music, and Jerry Crutchfield Music. In 1997 Bobby Braddock, veteran songwriter-producer, member of the Nashville Songwriters Hall of Fame, and co-composer of such songs as "D-I-V-O-R-C-E," " Time Marches On," and "He Stopped Loving Her Today" was given a tip on Blake. Braddock secured a contract for Blake with Tree Productions for which they recorded "Ol' Red," the song Hoyt Axton had given him. Braddock then produced the *Austin* album released in 2001 on the Warner Brothers label. It included several of Blake's songs, such as "That's What I Call Home," "Every Time I Look at You," "Problems at Home," and "All Over Me," co-written with Earl Thomas Conley, one of Blake's mentors and idols. "All Over Me" cracked the Top 20 on country charts in 2002. Blake made his debut on the Grand Ole Opry, March 5, 2001.

Shelton was named *Radio & Records'* Breakthrough Artist of the Year in 2001, received the coveted Critics Pick Award from *Music Row Magazine*, and was nominated for Favorite New Artist in Country Music for *Billboard*, American Music, Country Weekly Fan Favorite, and ACM awards in 2001-02. His single, "Ol' Red," cracked the Top 10 of the country charts in the summer of 2002, and the video of the same title was given considerable broadcast time on CMT. It focuses on a love story about a bloodhound set in the context of an escape from prison. The video was shot at the historic Tennessee State Prison. Finally, Shelton recently adopted two puppies that wandered onto his Tennessee farm, and appropriately named them "Austin" and "Ol' Red."

Blake Shelton Day was proclaimed on March 15, 2002 in Blake's hometown of Ada, and he will make a stop with his band, Road Kill, on his 2002 tour at Legends, a country music bar in Ada, where he performed as a teenager. His latest single, "Baby," was the Blue Chip Radio Report Song of the Week for October 28, 2002, debuted on the country charts at #33, and cracked the Top 25 in November of 2002. As Blake recently stated: "It's weird to think people are calling for me now. That's new to me. I've always dealt with begging somebody for a job."

In February 2003, Blake released his sophomore CD, *The Dreamer* (Warner Brothers). The album sold 77,000 copies the first week it was on the shelves, debuting at #2 on *Billboard*'s country album charts, and within three weeks "The Baby" became his second #1 country hit where it stayed at the top of the *Billboard* country charts for three weeks, and also reached #1 at *Radio and Records*. The video also reached #1 on both the Great American Country and Country Music Television video charts. By spring of 2003, Blake was nominated by the ACM as the Top New Male Vocalist, sang on Tracy Byrd's wildly popular "The Truth About Men," had a #1 video hit at GAC with his second single from *The Dreamer*, "Heavy Liftin'," and joined **Toby Keith** on the massively successful Shock'n Y'all tour through September. His third single from the album, "Playboys of the Southwestern World," was released in July. (GC/HF)
www.blakeshelton.com

Shepard, Jean
(b. November 21, 1933)

Paul's Valley native Jean Shepard is noted for several firsts in the field of country music. She was one of the first women to break the country music barrier in the 1950s. Upon the recommendation of **Hank Thompson**, Shepard signed with Capitol Records in 1952. One year later, she scored with a #1 country hit, a Korean War song entitled "A Dear John Letter" with narration from Ferlin Husky, who was appointed as her guardian for tours outside the state as Jean was not yet twenty-one. It topped the country charts for twenty-three weeks and crossed over to the Top 5 pop charts, selling some ten million records in 1953. This success made her California's first major female recording artist since Patsy Montana. Moreover, she was one of the first women to join the Grand Ole Opry in 1955, and is the first woman to hold membership in the "mode lode of country music" for more than forty-seven years. In addition, Jean was the first country music female vocalist to overdub her voice on records. Furthermore, she was the first female in country music to sell a million records. Finally, she was the first woman in country music to record a concept album. Jean's 1956 *Songs of a Love Affair* featured twelve songs, all written by her, from a single woman's point of view on one side, while the other side portrayed the wife's perspective.

Born to parents, Hoit and Alla Mae Shepard, who raised eleven children in rural Oklahoma, Ollie Imogene Shepard was an avid listener to the Grand Ole Opry and **Bob Wills'** radio broadcasts over KVOO in Tulsa. She learned to sing by listening to Jimmie Rodgers records on a wind-up Victrola. After living in Hugo, Jean and her family relocated to Visalia, California, near Bakersfield, at the conclusion of World War II. At the age of fourteen, she and several friends formed The Melody Ranch Girls, an all-female western swing band, named after Noble's Melody Ranch, owned by Noble Fosberg, who managed and booked the band. Jean sang and played upright bass, an instrument that overwhelmed her five feet, one inch height. She recalled her mother and father hocking every stick of furniture in their home to pay for the bass which cost $350, a sum that would have bought a whole house full of furniture at the time. In 1948, the group recorded Hank Thompson's song "Help."

Jean was becoming a well known music personality in the San Jaoquin Valley, while working three nights a week at Pismo Beach, performing on local radio station KNGS, and appearing on Jelly Sanders' radio show on Porterville's KTNV. Through these appearances, she came to the attention of Thompson, who was personally responsible for her first recording contract with Capitol. Her first solo recording was "Crying Steel Guitar Waltz/Twice the Lovin'" in 1953 with Speedy West on steel. The aforementioned "A Dear John Letter" was followed with "Forgive Me John," which charted at #4 on the country lists as well as on the Top 25 pop charts. Her early Capitol recordings were backed by Bill Woods' band out of Bakersfield, which included guitarist Buck Owens. She later formed her own band called The Second Fiddles, after her 1964 hit "Second Fiddle (to an Old Guitar)." With the Capitol and United Artists labels, she produced several Top Five country hits such as "A Satisfied Mind," "Beautiful Lies," "Second Fiddle to a Steel Guitar," "Take Possession," and "Slippin' Away." The latter won her a Grammy Award nomination in 1973 for Best Country Female Vocalist of the Year.

The same year Jean joined the Grand Ole Opry (1955), she helped launch the *Ozark Jubilee* telecast on ABC television as part of Red Foley's cast, where she remained until 1957. She was named Top Female Singer by *Cash Box* magazine in 1959 following such hits as "I Want to Got Where No One Knows Me" and "Have Heart, Will Love." In 1963, her husband Hawkshaw Hawkins was killed in a plane crash near Camden, Tennessee, which also killed Patsy Cline and Cowboy Copas.

Jean's string of medium-sized hits in the 1960s on Capitol included "Many Happy Hangovers to You," "If Teardrops Were Silver," "I'll Take the Dog," "Mr. Do-It-Yourself," "Heart, We did All We Could," "Your Forevers (Don't Last Very Long)," and "Seven Lonely Days." The late Jim Reeves was quoted as saying, "All the girl singers should sound like Jean Shepard. She always hits her notes, holds them and wraps them around an audience like nobody else can."

In 1973, Jean moved to the United Artists and remained with that label until 1977. Her biggest hits with UA included "At the Time," "I'll Do Anything It Takes (To Stay With You)," "Poor Sweet Baby," and "The Tips of My Fingers." Her last hit single was in 1978, "The Real Thing," which peaked at #85. Thereafter, she made fewer and fewer recordings, mostly on small, independent labels. Her greatest successes in the 1970s were with Bill Anderson's songs, such as "Slippin' Away," "The Tips of My Fingers," and "Mercy," all of which were released in an album of Anderson penned songs, *Poor Sweet Baby*. In 1975, Jean recorded a tribute to her late husband Hawkshaw Hawkins, "Two Little Boys," written by their sons, Don Robbins (named after Don Gibson and Marty Robbins) and Harold Franklin Hawkins II after his father.

During the 1980s and 1990s Jean continued to tour, especially the U.K., where she was well received. It was at the Wembley Country Festival in the U.K. in 1977 that she stated to the audience, "John Denver, Glen Campbell, and Mac Davis are not country," reaffirming her viewpoint on the retention of pure country sounds. She helped form the Association of Country Entertainers to "keep it country," after her objections to Olivia Newton-John's award from the Country Music Association. In 1996, two of the best collections of Jean's recordings were released, including the Country Music Foundation's *Honky Tonk Heroine: Classic Capitol Recordings, 1952-1964*, a 24-track compilation of Jean's #1 hits plus such songs as "Twice the Lovin' (In Half the Time)," "Under Your Spell Again," and "The Root of All Evil (Is A Man)," and the Bear Family five-disc box set, *The Melody Ranch Girl*, which included all 151 tracks recorded on Capitol from 1952 to 1964. This Oklahoma "honky tonk heroine" charted forty-five hits from 1953 to 1978.

Since 1968 Jean has been married to bluegrass guitarist Benny Birchfield, who was Roy Orbison's road manager at the time of Orbison's death. Her latest releases are *Jean Shepard, Precious Memories*, a gospel album, and *The Tennessee Waltz*. Shepard's role in the development of the country music on the West Coast is highlighted with one of her selections ("Dear John Letter") on the 1996 *Heroes of Country Music, Vol. 4: Legends of the West Coast* (Rhino).

As of this writing, she continues to perform on the Grand Ole Opry as well as in Branson, Missouri, in "Grand Ladies of Country Music," a show launched in 2000 that includes Jan Howard, Helen Cornelius, Margo Smith, Leona Williams, and **Norma Jean**, another Oklahoman. She also appeared at Dollywood in 2002 in a show called "Grand Ladies of the Grand Ole Opry," which included Jeanie Seely and Jan Howard. Finally, Jean was the Golden Voice Awards winner for 2002 in the Female Golden Voice category, and was a participant in the fourth annual show held in Nashville to "honor the men and women who have given country music her voice." (GC)

Simmons, John Jacob
(b. June 14, 1918 – d. September 19, 1979)

One of the most highly regarded and in demand jazz bassists in the 1940s and 1950s, John Jacob Simmons was born in Haskell, Oklahoma, a community of about 2,000 residents located southeast of Tulsa. John's family relocated to Tulsa, where he attended school until 1936, first playing the trumpet, but forced to switch to the bass after a football injury affected his mouth. While in high school, John's family moved to California, and he played his first gigs in the Los Angeles and San Diego areas.

John's first major work was with Nat "King" Cole in Los Angeles nightclubs, and then recorded with Teddy Wilson in 1937. He then relocated to Chicago and worked brief periods with Johnny Letman, Jimmy Bell, King Kolax, and Floyd Campbell, before joining Roy Eldridge in 1940. After the brief stint in Chicago, he moved to New York City and worked with Benny Goodman (recorded two albums), Louis Armstrong (recorded four albums), and Cootie Williams in the early 1940s. He was a studio musician with the CBS Blue Network Orchestra, briefly with Duke Ellington (1943), Eddie Heywood Sextet (1945), and Illinois Jacquet (1946). He also appeared with Lester Young in the film, *Jammin' the Blues*, in 1944.

During the 1940s and 1950s, Simmons also played with James P. Johnson, Hot Lips Page, Sid Catlett, Ben Webster, Dexter Gordon, Sidney DeParis, Bill DeArango, Al Casey, Charles Thompson, Milt Jordan, Cozy Cole, Benny Carter, Billie Holliday, and the Rolf Ericson-Duke Jordan band in Scandinavia. He performed with both Dixieland and Big Bands, as well as Bebop combos during this period, including sessions with fellow Oklahoman **Don Byas** on 52nd Street in New York City, and other beboppers such as Coleman Hawkins and Thelonious Monk.

John also toured and recorded with Harry "Sweets" Edison, Tadd Dameron, Art Tatum, John Coltrane, Andre Previn, Buddy Rich, and Phineas Newborn, as well as recording with the famed vocalists Billie Holliday, Ella Fitzgerald, and Lena Horne.

Plagued by illness in the 1960s and 1970s, Simmons died in Los Angeles, California, on September 19, 1979. (GC)

Smith, Cal
(b. July 4, 1932)

With three #1 country hits to his credit, including "The Lord Knows I'm Drinking," "Country Bumpkin," and "It's Time to Pay the Fiddler," Calvin Grant Shofner was born in Gans, Oklahoma, a small hamlet of around 200 people located in eastern Oklahoma near the Arkansas border. Cal and his family moved to California when he was a youngster, and they settled in the Oakland area. Prior to his high school days, Cal learned the guitar from rodeo-rider Todd Mason, and began to play local clubs with a San Francisco-based country band called Kitty Dibble and Her Dude Ranch Wranglers, while still a teenager. He recalls that his professional debut was at a diner-beer joint place called "The Remember Me Café," when he was fifteen. He and a friend played for $1.50 a night plus food, according to Cal. Despite his love of country music, Cal had to work during the day and play music at night. He worked at a variety of jobs throughout the 1950s, including truck driver, steel mill worker, and broncobuster. His wife wanted him to give up music and concentrate on making a living, and gave him an ultimatum of choosing between her and his music. Cal opted for the latter.

Cal joined the California Hayride out of Stockton in 1954, and stayed with the show for two years before service in the military. After his discharge, he worked as disc jockey on radio station KEEN in San Jose, and was vocalist with Uncle

Phil Philley's band when it performed at San Quinten Prison along with Johnny Cash in 1958. Cal's first recording on Plaid Records in 1960 was a prison ballad, "Eleven Long Years." Shortly thereafter, he was playing with a group that included Bill White, whose brother was a member of Ernest Tubb's Texas Troubadours. When Tubb came to San Jose for a concert, Cal auditioned for him, and soon became a Troubadour, serving as master of ceremonies, using the name Grant Shofner, and vocalist from 1961 to 1967. During this time, Cal toured and performed on the Grand Ole Opry with Tubb, appeared on Tubb's syndicated television show, and was on one of Tubb's recordings, "The Great Speckled Bird," in 1963.

With assistance from Tubb, Smith signed a recording contract with Kapp in 1966, and cut his first single, "I'll Just Go on Home"/"Silver Dew on the Blue Grass Tonight." He cracked the country charts with his second release, "The Only Thing I Want," and throughout the rest of the decade, had eight more singles that reached the charts, including "Drinking Champagne" (#40 in 1968) and "Heaven Is Just a Touch Away" (#50 in 1969). During that time, Cal released four albums for Kapp, including *All The World Is Lonely Now*, *Goin' to Cal's Place*, *Travelin' Man*, and *Drinking Champagne*.

In 1970, Smith switched to the Decca label for which he had recorded as a member of Ernest Tubb's group. Two years later, he hit the Top 5 with "I've Found Someone of My Own," but his next single, "For My Baby," barely cracked the charts. It took three months to gain momentum, but "The Lord Knows I'm Drinking" became Cal's first #1 hit, which also surfaced on the pop charts, and was nominated by the CMA for Single of the Year in 1973.

After a couple of minor hits, Smith again scored in 1974 with another #1 hit, "Country Bumpkin," which was to become his signature song. The song won numerous awards, including the ACM, *Music City News*, and CMA's Song of the Year and Single of the Year, and his album by the same title was nominated for the CMA Album of the Year in 1974. To cap off 1974, Cal released "Between Lust and Watching TV," a Top 15 hit, and his third #1 hit, "It's Time to Pay the Fiddler." For these successes, he was named Most Promising Male Artist by *Music City News* and was nominated by the CMA for Male Vocalist of the Year.

Smith remained with Decca (by then MCA) until 1979, and charted several hits, including "She Talked a Lot About Texas," "Jason's Farm," and "I Just Came Home to Count the Memories," all of which reached the Top 20. During this time, he recorded six albums for MCA, including *Cal Smith* (1973), *Country Bumpkin* (1974), *It's Time to Pay the Fiddler* (1975), *Cal's Country* (1975), *My Kind of Country* (1975), *Jason's Farm* (1976), and *I Just Came Home to Count the Memories* (1977).

Cal resurfaced in 1982 with "Too Many Irons in the Fire" and "Honky Tonk Girl," two duets with **Billy Parker**. He recorded two more albums in the 1980s, *Stories of Life by Cal Smith* and *A Touch Away*, the former on the Step One label and the latter back again with MCA.

During the 1990s, Cal performed throughout the country and did some guest spots on television shows, such as the *Nashville Network*. As of 2002, he and his wife, Darlene, reside in Branson, where he practices his fishing on one of the area lakes in the Missouri Ozarks.

In 1999 First Generation Records released *Cal Smith*, a ten-track CD collection of Smith's greatest hits, including "Country Bumpkin," "The Lord Knows I'm Drinking," and "It's Time to Pay the Fiddler." (GC)

Spencer, Tim
(b. July 13, 1908 – April 26, 1974)

One of the original members of the Sons of the Pioneers formed in 1934 and an inductee into the Nashville Songwriters Hall of Fame in 1971, Vernon Tim Spencer was born in Webb City, Missouri, but was raised in Picher, Oklahoma, a former lead and zinc mining community of approximately 1,700 residents in extreme northeastern Oklahoma, where he attended grade school. As a teenager, he left home because of an argument with his father over the purchase of a music instrument without parental permission, and began working in the lead and zinc mines of the Tri-State Mining District until a mine accident hospitalized him with a cracked vertebra. Unable to return to the mines, he began singing in local venues, and eventually relocated to his brother Glenn's home in Los Angeles in 1931. During the day Tim worked at a Safeway warehouse, and played and sang music at night, hooking up with short-lived bands, such as the Rocky Mountaineers, International Cowboys, and O-Bar-O Cowboys.

In 1933, Spencer, Leonard Slye (Roy Rogers), and Bob Nolan formed the Pioneer Trio, later to become known as the Sons of the Pioneers, and the trio soon added brothers Hugh (fiddle) and Karl (guitar) Farr. The group was featured on radio station KFWB in Hollywood, where their show captured an immediate audience, and gained enough popularity for invitations to appear with Oklahoman Will Rogers and at the Texas Centennial. The Pioneers featured unique western themes, developed a smooth harmony style later emulated by almost every western singing group in the U.S., and may have been the first western ensemble to feature group yodeling. In 1935, the Pioneers became only the third West Coast unit signed by Decca Records, following Bing Crosby and Stuart Hamblen. Filmmakers soon noticed the group, and they were cast in a 1935 Liberty Studio film, *The Old Homestead*, followed by an appearance in **Gene Autry**'s first feature film, the 1936 *Tumbling Tumbleweeds*. They were then hired by Columbia Studios to provide music for a series of westerns starring Charles Starrett. It should be noted that another Oklahoman, **Shug Fisher**, born in Tabler near Chickasha, was member of The Pioneers (1943-46 and 1949-51) as comedian and bass player.

Spencer, who had not written any songs prior to the group's formulation, soon began to compose, including his first song in 1934, "Will You Love Me (When My Hair Turns to Silver)," later recorded by the Pioneers. Many of the their most successful songs, including "The Everlasting Hills of Oklahoma," "Room Full of Roses," "Cigarettes, Whiskey and Wild, Wild Women," "Over the Santa Fe Trail," and "The Timber Trail," were written by Spencer, while he also co-wrote "Yippi-Yi, Yippi-Yo" and "Roses" with his brother Glenn, "Blue Prairie" with Bob Nolan, and "Ride'em Cowboy" with Roy Rogers. Additional songs credited to Spencer include "Careless Kisses," "Cowboy's Sunday Prayer," "Bunkhouse Bugle Boy," "Go West, Young Man," and "I'm Happy in My Levi Britches." His most successful song was "Room Full of Roses," which soared to the top of the *Billboard* pop charts in 1949, went to #1 on the country charts in 1974 with Mickey Gilley's version, and received a one million performance award from BMI.

Spencer retired from the The Pioneers in 1949 because of vocal problems, finding his own replacement, Ken Curtis, or Festus of *Gunsmoke* fame. He continued to serve as the group's manager until 1955, and added his nephew, Sunny Spencer. After leaving the Pioneers, he headed the religious record division of RCA Victor, and eventually started his own gospel publishing company, Manna Music, where he wrote "We've Got a Great Big Wonderful God," "Open Your Heart," and "Cowboy Campmeetin'." He later handed down the company to his son, Hal, and died in 1974 in Apple Valley, California.

Spencer was recipient of many honors because of his affiliation with The Sons of the Pioneers, such as Walk of Stars on Hollywood Boulevard (1974), Country Music Hall of Fame (1978), and Western Music Hall of Fame (1989). As an individual, he was inducted into the Nashville Songwriters Hall of Fame (1971), Gospel Music Hall of Fame, Cowboy Hall of Fame (Oklahoma City), and Western Music Hall of Fame, all in 1985, primarily because of his songwriting career. (GC)

Stafford, Terry
(b. November 22, 1941 – d. March 17, 1996)

Best known for his Top 10 1964 hit single, "Suspicion" and composer of such country hits as Buck Owens' "Big in Vegas" and George Strait's "Amarillo by Morning," Terry LaVerne Stafford was born in Hollis, a town of about 2,500 residents located in extreme southwestern Oklahoma, but later moved to Amarillo, Texas, where he excelled in athletics, listened to Elvis Presley and Buddy Holly as a teenager, and graduated from Palo Duro High School in 1960. During his senior year, Terry told his classmates that he planned to leave for California to make hit records. With his parents' consent, he moved to Hollywood, and worked for two years as a nightclub entertainer. In one of these performances, he was spotted by John Fisher and Les Worden, who had just launched Crusader Records.

Terry's first single, "Suspicion," with Crusader was released in February of 1964. It soared to #3 in 1964 on the U.S. charts with the Beatles holding down the other four positions of the Top 5. His voice resembled Elvis Presley, who had earlier recorded "Suspicion" on his 1962 album, *Pot Luck*. Following this first success, his second single, "I'll Touch a Star," reached #23 on the charts. Subsequently, none of his singles made the Top 40.

Realizing that he might be destined for the "one hit wonder" status, Stafford turned to professional songwriting in the late 1960s, and composed for the next twenty years. One of his greatest achievements in songwriting was his "Amarillo by Morning," which Terry recorded as a "B" side for Atlantic Records, while the "A" side was a country cover, "Has Anyone Seen My Sweet Gypsy Rose." Atlantic eventually promoted the "B" side because it reached #31 on the country charts in 1973, and received the attention of country artists such as Chris LeDoux, Moe Bandy, and George Strait. LeDoux was the first to include it in his *Life As A Rodeo Man* album (1975), and again in his *American Cowboy* collection (1994). Strait's single shot to the top of the country charts in 1982, and he used it in his *Strait From the Heart* (1982), *Greatest Hits* (1986), and *Strait Out of the Box* (1995) albums. Finally, Bandy included it in his 1987 *Act Naturally* album.

Stafford returned from Nashville to Amarillo in 1995, and died from liver complications on March 17, 1996. He is buried in Llano Cemetery in Amarillo. (GC)

Kay Starr
(b. July 21, 1922)

One of the most celebrated pop singers of the 1950s and recognized for charting numerous hit singles, including "Bonaparte's Retreat," "Side By Side," "Wheel of Fortune," and "Rock and Roll Waltz," Kathryn LaVerne Starks was born in Dougherty, Oklahoma, a hamlet of about 100 residents south of Oklahoma City. Her father Harry was a full-blooded Iroquois Indian and mother Annie was of mixed American Indian and Irish descent. And contrary to some reports, Kay was not born on a reservation. When Kay was three the

family moved to Dallas where her father found work installing sprinkler systems (Automatic Sprinkler Company) in buildings. When the Great Depression hit, Kay's mother raised chickens in a hen house behind their home, and it was here that Kay first began singing concerts each day after school to the chickens at age nine. Although her parents considered the hen house concerts amusing, Kay's Aunt Nora recognized her singing potential and suggested to her parents that she enter a talent contest sponsored by radio station WRR in Dallas. Performing at the Dallas Melba Theatre, she won the contest singing "Now's the Time to Fall in Love." Because of the overwhelming response to her singing, Kay was given her own fifteen-minute radio program broadcast three times per week. Singing primarily pop and country music, she earned three dollars for each appearance, but her family soon moved to Memphis. Here Kay soon landed her own show, *Starr Time* on WREC radio, and was also featured on WMPS radio's popular *Saturday Night Jamboree* program. Dubbed "The Kid" by station management, she was given the opportunity to sing requests whenever someone would call. Around this time, she changed her name to Kay Starr because of continual misspellings received in fan mail.

Starr's first major break was when noted big band leader and jazz violinist Joe Venuti came to Memphis in 1937. Venuti's contract with the Peabody Hotel in Memphis specified that he have a girl singer with his band—a void that he had not been able to fill. Venuti's road manager heard Kay on radio and was so impressed that he and Venuti scheduled a visit to Kay's parents to discuss the possibility of hiring her since she was only a junior in high school. This meeting resulted in a three-week engagement with Venuti at the Peabody and singing with the band for the next two summers (1937-1939), accompanied by her mother since Kay was only fifteen.

In 1939, Venuti assisted Kay in furthering her career by suggesting that Bob Crosby's Orchestra needed a female vocalist. Crosby hired Kay and she appeared on the Camel Caravan radio program in New York, making her network debut singing "Memphis Blues." She was soon replaced with Helen Ward when Crosby determined the program needed a more veteran performer. Within a short time, Kay was offered an opportunity to sing with the Glenn Miller Orchestra to replace the ailing Marion Hutton. During her two week stint with Miller, she made several remote radio broadcasts from the famous Glen Island Casino as well as making her first recordings on the Bluebird label singing "Love With a Capital You" and "Baby Me."

After the Miller job, Kay and her mother returned to Memphis where Kay completed high school. Upon graduation from high school in 1940, she immediately headed to California to work for Venuti once again, however, the band was decimated due to the World War II draft in 1941. She briefly sang with Wingy Manone's New Orleans Jazz Band until Charlie Barnet hired her in 1943 to replace Lena Horne. She recorded five sides with Barnet on the Decca label, including "Share Croppin' Blues," which was received with critical acclaim. Her association with Barnet ended abruptly in 1945 when she collapsed on stage. Apparently, she had caught a cold while entertaining army troops during World War II. The cold developed into pneumonia and Kay spent time in an army hospital. She eventually developed nodes on her vocal chords and required surgery. During her recuperation, she realized her voice was gone, and had to communicate by writing notes. She regained partial use of her voice after about six months, but it was more than a year before she was able to sing with a full band again. After Kay's singing hiatus, she returned with a deeper and huskier voice that has since become her trademark.

Kay settled in Los Angeles and launched her career as a solo performer, singing in several local nightclubs where she was heard by Dave Dexter of Capitol Records. Dexter invited her to contribute two songs for Capitol's Volumes of Jazz series in 1945. In 1946, she recorded several singles of jazz classics for independent labels, such as Lamplighter, Standard, and Jewell.

Kay's next major opportunity came in 1947 when she signed a contract with Capitol Records, a company that was blessed with an exceptional roster of female singers, including Peggy Lee, Jo Stafford, and Margaret Whiting. Her first Capitol recording was "I'm the Lonesomest Gal in Town," but was not released until 1950. Her first Top 10 hit came in 1949 with "So Tired," followed by "Hoop-Dee-Doo," which charted at #2 in 1950. Interestingly, on a hometown visit to Dougherty, Kay heard a fiddle tune being played on a jukebox in the local honky tonk. It was Pee Wee King's "Bonaparte's Retreat." She called Roy Acuff's publishing house in Nashville and received permission from Acuff to record it with lyrics provided by Acuff. It was released by Capitol in 1950 and became Kay's first major hit as it sold almost a million copies. After several successful duets ("I'll Never Be Free" and "You're My Sugar") with country singer, Tennessee Ernie Ford, Kay was called into the Capitol studio on January 17, 1952. Management wanted her to record a rush release of a new song, "Wheel of Fortune," which was also recorded by two competing labels. It is the song that has become historically associated with Starr, and resulted in her first gold record. It remained on the charts at #1 for ten weeks and eventually became the number two selling single in 1952. From 1948 to 1954, Kay charted twenty-seven hits with Capitol, but the studio failed to renew her contract in 1955, and she accepted an offer from RCA.

In 1956, Starr hit both American and British charts with her million selling gold record, "Rock and Roll Waltz." It stayed on the charts at #1 for six weeks, and eventually became the number two selling single in 1956 in the U.S., and the number one single of the year in the U.K. It was the first #1 single by a female singer in the rock era, the first to have "rock and roll" in the title, and the first #1 single for RCA Records.

Kay remained with RCA until 1959 when she returned to Capitol, and recorded several new albums, including *Movin'* (1959) which included "Lazy River," *Losers, Weepers* (1960), *I Cry By Night* (1962), and *Just Plain Country* (1962), which included Patsy Cline's "Crazy" and Buck Owens' "Foolin' Around."

By the mid-1960s, rock and roll had changed American music tastes that led to Kay's second departure from Capitol. She continued to perform at major concert venues in the U.S. and England, including the Riveria, Sands, and Fremont Hotels in Las Vegas, and Harrah's in Reno. Recording with several independent jazz and country labels, she teamed with Count Basie in 1968 for an album of classic jazz, *Back to the Roots* (1975). In the 1980s, she teamed with Helen O'Connell and Margaret Whiting for a 3 Girls 3 revue and later with Kaye Ballard as 4 Girls 4. In 1993, she joined Pat Boone on The April Love tour of the U.K.

Starr is also remembered as one of the first recording artists to "overdub" her own voice in her recording of "Side by Side." Along with Jo Stafford, Rosemary Clooney, and **Patti Page**, Kay Starr was one of the most influential women in American music during the early 1950s. Author Leonard Feather and jazz critic said this of Starr: "Steeped in the tradition of Bessie Smith and the big-voiced blues singers of the past, she retained some of their jazz qualities in her work despite its increasingly pop-aimed emphasis in later years." "Kay Starr is a brassy fusion of urban swing and country twang," according to jazz historian Gary Giddens. In 2001, Kay was featured on Tony Bennett's new album for Capitol to commemorate his 75th birthday, *Playin' With My Friends: Tony Bennett Sings the Blues*, in which she duetted with Tony on "Blue and Sentimental." Starr was inducted into the Oklahoma Jazz Hall of Fame in 2000 and into the Oklahoma Music Hall of Fame in 2002. (GC)

Talley, James
(b. November 9, 1943)

Considered by some critics as the modern-day **Woody Guthrie** and recognized by former President Jimmy Carter's wife, Rosalyn, as her favorite singer, James Talley was born in a Tulsa hospital, but never lived there. His parents were living in Pryor and went to Tulsa to have James delivered. Both parents were from Oklahoma with his father's family from Welch in the northeastern part, while his mother's parents (Ogden and Mary) were farmers near Mehan, where they resided in a pyramidal house with a well for water and no indoor plumbing. It was here that James spent much of childhood learning about Oklahoma, such as his great grandfather participating in two land rushes into Oklahoma (1889 and 1893). While working near Pryor, Oklahoma, his parents met while making munitions and gunpowder at the Oklahoma Ordinance. One of the venues where his parents courted was Cain's Ballroom in Tulsa, dancing to the sounds of **Bob Wills and the Texas Playboys**. James' mother, who was raised on a small farm near Glencoe, received a degree in elementary education from Oklahoma A & M (Oklahoma State University) in Stillwater in the 1930s. When James was age three, the family eventually migrated to Washington state where his father worked at the Hanford Works in Richland, and his mother taught school for five years. Wages for teachers and construction workers in the booming town of Richland were good, and when the Talleys left for Albuquerque, New Mexico, they had accumulated $8,000 in their coffers. But his father paid a dear price for the wages at Hanford for a large tumor in one of his lungs was detected shortly after they moved to New Mexico. Half of one of his lungs was removed, but the doctors never fully diagnosed the problem and its causes. During the next few years, his father suffered three heart attacks and died in 1969 at age fifty-seven. James always believed that the plutonium use by his father at Hanford caused his father's death, and wrote a song about the plant entitled "Richland, Washington," included in his 2002 CD, *Touchstones*. James recalls fond memories of his father, such as playing the guitar, singing Jimmie Rodgers songs, and listening to the music of Bob Wills, especially Tommy Duncan, crooner for the Texas Playboys, who his father met in Washington. James paid tribute to the western swing genre on his first album with a song, "W. Lee O'Daniel and the Light Crust Doughboys." One of the stories James relates about his father is when he faced poverty: "It ain't no disgrace to be poor, it's just unhandy as hell."

After graduation from high school in Albuquerque, Talley attended Oklahoma State University the fall semester of 1961. He was a singer with the Student Entertainers, under the leadership of Ashley Alexander, participated in Air Force ROTC, and, according to James, almost memorized Dante's *Inferno* in a humanities course. While visiting James in Stillwater, his father suffered a massive heart attack and was hospitalized in Stillwater until James was able to transport him to Albuquerque. Lacking funds, he enrolled at the University of New Mexico, where he received a degree in fine arts, and then completed two years of graduate study at U.C.L.A. and Univeristy of New Mexico in American Studies, but failed to finish his Ph.D. While in graduate school at U.C.L.A. in 1966, he read Woody Guthrie's book, *Born to Win*, which he says changed his life. He soon discovered his favorite songs were also by Guthrie, and claims to have learned almost all of them before he left campus. In his autobiography, he says Guthrie became his idol probably because of his "Okie" roots. After employment for a year as a caseworker for the New Mexico Department of Public Welfare, he moved to Nashville in 1968, and while continuing as a caseworker, he met his wife, Jan.

In the mid-1970s, Talley recorded four critically acclaimed albums for Capitol

Records, *Got No Bread, No Milk, No Money, But We Sure Got Lots of Love* ((1975), which was originally released on Talley's own Torreon label, but then picked up by Capitol; *Tryin' Like the Devil* (1976), which included the brutally honest track, "Give My Love to Marie," with lyrics describing a coal miner with black lung disease; *Blackjack Choir* (1977), on which B.B. King appeared on James' tribute to King in the track entitled "Bluesman"); and *Ain't It Somethin'* (1978). By 1978, James was dropped from the Capitol label because the recordings received little radio airplay, and James was forced to lay off his band, which included such notable instrumentalists as Josh Graves, Johnny Gimble, and Charlie McCoy. One bright spot for James is when President Jimmy Carter and wife, Rosalynn, informed the media that he was one of their favorite artists and invited him to sing at the 1977 Inauguration Ball, and later performed twice at the Carter White House. Thus, James was forced to enter the real estate business in Nashville in 1983 to support his family because his Capitol albums soon fell out of print.

In 1985, Talley signed with the German label, Bear Family Records, after Richard Weize, head of the label, asked him to perform at the company's tenth anniversary party. Weize reissued the magnificent Capitol albums, as well as releasing several new ones, including *American Originals* (1985), *Lovesongs and the Blues* (1989), and *James Talley: Live* (1994), recorded at The Lone Star Café in New York and The Great Southeast Music Hall in Atlanta. Talley launched an ambitious project in 1992 with the publication and accompanying CD entitled *The Road to Torreon: Love Songs and Other Writings by James Talley*. The contents of the book featured Talley's prose and incredible photographs of New Mexican villages by Cavalliere Ketchum. The book was published by the University of New Mexico Press and the CD was released by Bear Family Records, a German company.

In 1994, Talley went to Santa Fe, where he recorded a tribute album, *Woody Guthrie and Songs of My Oklahoma Home*, one of the best collections to date of Guthrie's classic material from the 1930s and 1940s, including "Dust Bowl Blues," "Do Re Mi," and "Pretty Boy Floyd." After unsuccessful negotiations with Capitol, James released the album on his own Cimarron label, followed by *Nashville City Blues* (2000) and *Touchstones* (2002). The latter contains an eclectic variety of songs in the sixteen tracks, including such cuts as "W. Lee O'Daniel and the Light Crust Doughboys" with some Oklahoma images of Tulsa and Cain's Ballroom. After hearing the Woody tribute album, Nora Guthrie (Woody's daughter) was quoted: "You sound eerily like my father."

Talley was selected as Amazon.com's Folk Artist of the Year in 2000, and recently headlined "ASCAP Presents. . .Up Close" (ASCAP's new emphasis on roots music) held at Manhattan's new West Side venue, Makor. In July, 2003, James Talley performed at the Woody Guthrie Festival in Okemah. (GC) www.jamestalley.com

Thomas, B. J.
(b. August 7, 1942)

A career that has spanned four different genres of American music (pop, country, rock, and gospel) and best known for his "Rain Drops Keep Fallin' on My Head," Billy Joe Thomas was born in Hugo, a southeastern Oklahoma town boasting roughly 5,000 citizens and county seat of Choctaw County. He was raised in Rosenberg, Texas, near Houston, and grew up singing in church. His early influences were both country and rhythm and blues artists, including Hank Williams, Sr., Ernest Tubb, and Jackie Wilson. The first record he purchased was "Miss Ann" by Little Richard. He chose the initials B.J., when he was ten, because there were five Billy's on his Little League baseball team. At fourteen, B.J. joined his church choir and also sang in his high school choral group. While still in high school, he joined The Triumphs, a Houston-based group, who recorded a local hit entitled "Lazy Man." Collaborating with songwriter Mark Charron, a member of The Triumphs, B.J. co-wrote "Billy and Sue," which also failed to gain any attention.

On July 4, 1965, The Triumphs performed at a state park in Houston, where they were noticed by Charles Booth, owner of Pacemaker Records. He signed the group to his label and released their first album, which included as one of the tracks the Hank Williams, Sr. song, "I'm So Lonesome I Could Cry," which B.J. recorded for his father, who had suggested this might be a hit. Backed by his old group The Triumphs, B.J. recorded the number at the Houston studio of Huey P. Meaux. A Houston disc jockey named Bob White thought it was a potential hit and gave it airplay. Pacemaker Records released it as a single and New York-based Scepter Records picked it up for national distribution, and it peaked at #8 on the Hot 100 in 1966.

Based on the success of using Hank Williams material, B.J. recorded "I Can't Help It (If I'm Still in Love With You)," which failed to achieve the same popularity as his first recording, as well as a re-release of "Billy and Sue."

Thomas did not enter the Top 10 list until 1968 when he recorded "Hooked on a Feeling," which charted at #5 and became a million seller. It was Dionne

Warwick, recording colleague at Scepter, who suggested to Burt Bacharach and Hal David that B.J. be given the opportunity to sing "Raindrops Keep Fallin' on My Head," for the motion picture *Butch Cassidy and the Sundance Kid* in 1969. Apparently, Bacharach and David had approached both Bob Dylan and Ray Stevens, but both had conflicts, and B.J. became their next choice. The night before he was to record "Raindrops" B.J. was ordered by his doctor not to use his voice for two weeks because he was suffering from a severe case of laryngitis. B.J. pleaded with the doctor and was given some medication to lubricate his throat. The next day, B.J. did five takes of the song before Bacharach was satisfied. An executive from 20th Century Fox present at the recording session congratulated B.J. on sounding so much like Paul Newman, and inquired how the thought of using such a raspy voice. A few weeks later with his voice healed, B.J. recorded the single version of "Raindrops", and at this session Bacharach added the "da-da-da-da-da" tag. It won an Academy Award, was B.J.'s biggest hit, and was Bacharach and David's first million seller. B.J. sang it on the 1970 Academy Awards telecast before a national audience.

By the late 1960s, Thomas had captured four gold records, including "The Eyes of a New York Woman," "Hooked on a Feeling," "It's Only Love," and "Raindrops." In addition, he had a series of soft rock hits, such as "Everybody's Out of Town," "I Just Can't Help Believing," "No Love at All," "Rock and Roll Shoes" (a duet with Ray Charles), and "Rock and Roll Lullaby." The latter featured guitarist Duane Eddy and the Beach Boys. In 1968, he married Gloria and they raised three daughters—Paige, Erin, and Nora.

Following Scepter Records' demise, B.J. signed with Paramount with little success, and he moved in 1975 to ABC Records to pursue a more country-oriented style. "(Hey Won't You Play) Another Somebody Done Somebody Wrong Song," his first single at ABC, reached #1 in both the pop and country charts, and became his second biggest seller. It also won the 1975 Grammy for Best Country Song and was nominated for the CMA Single of the Year in 1975. It still retains the record for having the longest title for a #1 hit. In his autobiography, B.J. admits he barely remembers the recording session for his second #1 hit. At the time, he was spending up to $3,000 per week to feed a drug habit that included Valium, cocaine, and amphetamines.

Plagued by a series of personal problems, including bankruptcy and drug addiction, B.J. emerged as a born-again Christian in 1976, and recorded on the Christian label, Myrrh, including the platinum *Home Where I Belong* album, as well as penning his autobiography, *Home Where I Belong*. He and his wife, Gloria, also wrote another book, *In Tune*. He received two Dove awards and five Grammys for his gospel recordings, one each year from 1977 to 1981, including the albums *Happy Man* in 1978, *You Gave Me Love (When Nobody Gave Me a Prayer)* in 1979, and *Amazing Grace* in 1981.

Thomas returned to the country field in the 1980s and peaked with such hits as "Whatever Happened to Old Fashioned Love" and "New Looks From an Old

Lover," both of which hit No. 1 on the country charts. These were followed by two Top 10 hits, "The Whole World's in Love When You're Lonely" and "Two Car Garage." On his thirty-ninth birthday in 1981, B.J. became a member of the Grand Ole Opry, its sixtieth member.

In 1985, Thomas released *Throwin' Rocks at the Moon*, which contained "As Long as We've Got Each Other," the theme song for the highly successful ABC-TV sitcom *Growing Pains*. His final album for Columbia was *Night Life*, a collection of country standards produced in Nashville. As of 2002, a live album is in the works as well as a dance mix of some of his classic pop hits.

B.J. and Gloria, his wife of thirty-four years, reside in Arlington, Texas, and he continues to maintain an active tour schedule (approximately 100 dates per year) performing at various venues, including Tulsa's Brady Theater, the Toledo Symphony, and the Hiawassee, Georgia Mountain Fair, and performs on the Grand Ole Opry about four times a year. During his career, Thomas has sold more than fifty million records, and earned two platinum and eleven gold records. (GC) www.bjthomas.com

Thompson, Hank
(b. September 3, 1925)

A musical career spanning more than seven decades and producing some 60 million records, Country Music Hall of Famer Henry William Thompson was born in Waco, Texas, the only child of Ilda and Jule Thompson. Although a native Texan, Thompson is associated with Oklahoma in many ways, including host of a variety show on WKY-TV in Oklahoma City during the mid-1950s; sponsor of and teacher at the Hank Thompson School of Country Music in Claremore in 1973, the first such entity in the U.S.; owner of a radio station in Sand Springs, where he made his home for several years; his recordings of such songs as "Oklahoma Hills" and "Oklahoma Home Brew," his 1969 album, *Hank Thompson Salutes Oklahoma*, and serving as mentor for such Oklahoma country music stars as **Wanda Jackson** and **Norma Jean**.

Growing up in Waco, Hank was influenced by a variety of country music ranging from **Gene Autry** to Jimmie Rodgers. His first choice was the harmonica, an instrument he used to win several local amateur contests. But Gene Autry strummed the guitar and young Hank at age ten was given a $4 model for Christmas by his parents. He devoted hour upon hour to learning chord patterns and guitar runs, as well as ventriloquist skills, and it resulted in a job performing on a Saturday morning program in the early 1940s at a local theater broadcast over radio station WACO. A local flour company liked what they heard, and provided sponsorship for six months for a show dubbed "Hank the Hired Hand," while Hank completed high school.

Following graduation in 1943, Hank enlisted in the U.S. Navy and, while stationed in San Diego, he convinced his superiors to allow him to play in local clubs. While at sea, Hank also entertained on board and broadcast over a small network of stations established by the Navy in the South Pacific. During his tour of duty, he completed several college credits though Southern Methodist University and the University of Texas-Austin. It is also reported that he attended Princeton University after his discharge from the Navy. Studying primarily electrical engineering at these three universities, Hank is one of the most educated of the country music artists, although he never completed a degree.

Returning to Waco, Hank started a noon show on KWTX, and the response was so positive that he formed his own band, the Brazos Valley Boys (named after the river running through Waco), and began to play dances throughout Texas. Hank had tried his hand at writing songs in the Navy, and continued this endeavor after his discharge. He recorded two of his songs, "Whoa Sailor" and "Swing Wide Your Gate of Love," both on the local Globe label, and with the help of Hal Horton, a disc jockey on KRLD, a 50,000 watt station in Dallas, "Whoa Sailor" became a regional hit. After recording four more cuts with the Blue Bonnet label (most notable was "A Lonely Heart Knows"), another independent company in Texas, Hank was given a break by Capitol recording artist, Tex Ritter, who assisted him in obtaining a contract with this major label in 1948, an association that lasted until 1966. During the next two years, Hank justified Ritter's faith in him by releasing four hits, "Humpty Dumpty Heart," "Today," a redo of "Whoa Sailor," and a new composition, "Green Light."

In 1951, Hank began a thirteen-year partnership with the Hollywood record producer, Ken Nelson, who produced his first number one hit and signature song, "Wild Side of Life," in one take. The single remained at the top of the country charts for fifteen weeks in 1952, and Hank earned a gold record, as well as prompting an answer song from Miss Kitty Wells, "It Wasn't God Who Made Honky Tonk Angels." In 1953-54, Hank charted seven Top 10 singles, including "Wake Up Irene," and answer song to "Goodnight, Irene," "No Help Wanted," "Breakin' the Blues," "Honky Tonk Girl," "New Green Light," "We've Gone Too Far," and "You Can't Have My Love," the last five songs written or co-written by him. Hank was also instrumental in helping a future country star on "You Can't Have My Love." Her name was Wanda Jackson.

During the late 1950s and on into the 1960s, Hank and the band averaged about 240 personal appearances annually, taking them to all fifty states, Canada, Far East, and Europe. Moreover, he continued to record at a furious pace with such hits as "Don't Take It Out on Me," "Wildwood Flower," a Carter Family song that Hank learned as a youngster, "I'm Not Mad, Just Hurt," "I've Run Out of Tomorrows," "A Six Pack to Go," "Squaws Along the Yukon," "Oklahoma Hills," "Waitin' in the Lobby of Your Heart," "Rub-A-Dub-Dub," "Rockin' in the Congo," "The Blackboard of My Heart," and "Breakin' in Another Heart," the latter co-written with his wife Dorothy.

Hank left Capitol in 1964, but signed with Warner Brothers in 1966. By the time Hank had left Capitol, he had generated record sales of more than 30 million and had produced roughly 100 singles on the hit charts. His tenure with Warner Brothers lasted only two years, but he did produce the *Where is the Circus* album. He then moved in 1968 to ABC/Dot Records, an association that lasted a decade. While at the new label, Hank celebrated his twenty-fifth year as a recording artist in 1971, and the company issued a two-record set in his honor, *Hank Thompson's 25th Anniversary* album. Additional hits during his period with ABC included "On Tap, in the Can, or in the Bottle," "Smokey the Bar," "Next Time I Fall in Love (I Won't)," "Kindly Keep It Country," "The Older the Violin, the Sweeter the

Music," "Who Left the Door to Heaven Open," "The Mark of a Heel," "Mama Don't 'Low," and "I Hear the South Calling Me."

Over the years, Hank and the Brazos Valley Boys were featured on several television shows, including *The Tonight Show* (Johnny Carson), *Jimmy Dean Show*, and *Swingin' Country*, as well as singing the theme song for the movie *Smoky*, starring Fess Parker and **Hoyt Axton**. He was elected to the Country Music Hall of Fame in 1989, and the Country Music Foundation released a package of hits titled *Hank Thompson Country Music Hall of Fame Series*.

Hank Thompson was a pioneer in country music during the twentieth century, including the first color broadcast of a variety show on television (WKY-TV in Oklahoma City), first act to use a sound and lighting system developed through Hank's engineering skills, first music act to receive corporate tour sponsorship, first "live" country music album recorded at the Golden Nugget in Las Vegas, first act to use drums on the Grand Ole Opry, first country music artist to play Las Vegas, and the Brazos Valley Boys, Hank's group, were voted the number one country band for fifteen consecutive years by *Billboard* magazine.

From Carnegie Hall to Las Vegas to the Hollywood Palladium, Hank's contributions to country music are immeasurable. In 1997, the *Hank Thompson and Friends* album was released on Curb. The thirteen tracks include such notables as Marty Stuart, **Brooks and Dunn**, George Jones, Kitty Wells, and **Vince Gill**. The latter is featured in a duet with Hank on "Six Pack to Go." Thompson's 2000 album on the Hightone label was produced by the veteran Lloyd Maines. *Seven Decades* includes songs ranging from the traditional "Wreck of the Old 97" to Jimmie Rodgers' "In the Jailhouse Now" to the Kingston Trio's "Scotch and Soda." Only one other artist, Frank Sinatra, has achieved the honor of recording for seven decades, a remarkable feat. His latest release in 2001 is *Humpty Dumpty Heart* on the Country Stars label. Hank was inducted into the Nashville Songwriters Hall of Fame in 1997, and the Oklahoma Music Hall of Fame in 2002. As of 2003, Thompson continued performing throughout the U.S. (GC)

Tillman, Floyd
(b. December 8, 1914)

Member of the Country Music Hall of Fame (1984) and Nashville Songwriters Hall of Fame (1970), as well as one of the first to champion the use of the electric guitar in country music (first known country singer to accompany himself with an electric guitar) and the first to define the honky tonk subgenre of country music, Floyd Tillman was born near Ryan, Oklahoma, a community of about 1,000 residents located just north of the Red River boundary between Oklahoma and Texas. Floyd was the youngest of eleven children born into a sharecropper family that moved to Post, Texas, a cotton mill town, when he was only a few months old. He attended grade school in Post from 1923 to 1929, and worked as a messenger boy for Western Union when he was in his early teens.

Floyd started his musical career on the mandolin and banjo, but later changed to the guitar (it is reported he played his first job after two weeks of practice) in order to backup local fiddle players, and in 1931, he and his brothers formed a string band trio. At age nineteen Floyd started writing songs and joined Adolph and Emil Hofner's western swing house band at the Gus' Palm Garden in San Antonio, where he played lead electric guitar and sang with the group, although he admitted that he could not sing and wanted to become a songwriter. He also performed on radio station KABC in San Antonio.

During the mid-1930s, Tillman played banjo, mandolin, and guitar with Mack Clark's dance band in Houston, and then left to join the Blue Ridge Playboys led by Leon "Pappy" Selph, during which time they recorded with Vocalion Records. He departed from the Clark ensemble because members of the band claimed that Floyd's song, "It Makes No Difference Now," was too hillbilly. As personnel changed often during the Depression, Floyd also worked with such western swing and honky tonk notables as Cliff Bruner, Moon Mullican, and **Bob Dunn**.

In 1938, Cliff Bruner and the Texas Wanderers recorded Floyd's first songwriting hit, "It Makes No Difference Now," which has become a country classic and covered by such diverse artists as Eddy Arnold, Bing Crosby, The Supremes, **Gene Autry**, Ray Charles, Willie Nelson and Hank Snow, **Hank Thompson**, Burl Ives, and Jimmie Davis. The latter bought the song from Floyd in 1938 for $300, and both are listed as co-writers. "It Makes No Difference Now," along with "San Antonio Rose," was the first crossover hit when Bing Crosby in 1940 sang both songs on the same record. In 1939, Floyd made his first recording with his own song, "I'll Keep on Loving You" on the Victor label.

During World War II, Tillman served as a radio operator in Army Air Corps, and was stationed near Houston, where he continued his songwriting and recording. His first No. 1 hit as a recording artist came in 1944 with "They Took the Stars Out of Heaven" on the Decca label. It was followed by a string of Top 10 hits for Floyd, including "G.I. Blues," "Drivin' Nails in My Coffin," "Each Night at Nine," "I Love You So Much It Hurts," "I Gotta Have My Baby Back," "Slippin' Around," and "I'll Never Slip Around Again."

From 1945 to 1950, Floyd and his band, Floyd Tillman and All the Gang, performed on radio station KTRH in Houston. In 1945, he signed with Columbia Records where his first major hit was "Drivin' Nails in My Coffin." In 1948, he hit the Top 5 country charts with "I Love You So Much It Hurts Me," which was covered by such pop and country artists as Vic Damone, Red Foley, Ernest Tubb, Ray Charles, Ray Price, Mickey Gilley, Andy Williams, Marie Osmond, Eddy Arnold, and **Jimmy Wakely**.

In 1949, Tillman wrote and released the song that would define his career, "Slippin' Around," regarded by music historians as the first song to deal with cheating and infidelity. It, too, was covered by a wide array of artists, such as

Margaret Whiting and Jimmy Wakely, which made it into a #1 pop hit and a million seller for them in 1949, and Ernest Tubb, who took it to #1 on the country charts and #17 on the pop charts also in 1949. Additional artists to cover the song included Texas Jim Robertson (1950), Marion Worth and George Morgan (1964), Roy Drusky and Priscilla Mitchell (1965), and Mack Abernathy (1988). "Slippin' Around" was also selected by the Smithsonian Institution as one of the tracks of an eight record set titled *The Smithsonian Collection of Classic Country Music* released in 1981.

In the early 1950s, Tillman dissolved his band and discussed retirement. The last song he recorded with his band, "I Don't Care Anymore," perhaps summarized his feelings. Floyd's last charted solo success was in 1960 with "It Just Tears Me Up," however, he made further recordings on minor labels, including an album of his songs with various friends such as **Merle Haggard** and Willie Nelson, both of whom were influenced by his style. Nelson was on hand to celebrate Floyd's 85th birthday bash in Llano, Texas in 1999.

Several other songs written by Tillman not previously mentioned include "I Am Music," recorded by Skeets McDonald, "This Cold War With You," "Some Other World," "Daisy Mae," recorded by Ernest Tubb, "Please Don't Pass Me By," and "I'll Never Slip Around Again," released by Margaret Whiting and Jimmy Wakely. His 1944 hit, "Each Night at Nine," captured the feelings of lonely servicemen so well that both Axis Sally and Tokyo Rose played it heavily to encourage desertion among American troops during World War II.

In addition to the aforementioned honors and accolades, "I Love You So Much It Hurts" earned Tillman a BMI One-Million Performance Award. When he was inducted into the Nashville Songwriters Hall of Fame, Floyd said: "You don't know when it's time to write a song. You just feel the song. It comes through you. . . . Sometimes you get an idea from what somebody said . . . But you don't write it unless you feel like it . . .They're personal songs, but they weren't written during the time they were personal. In other words when you have these problems you don't . . . the last thing you think of is writing a song about a problem. But later on you laugh at it, and then you write a song about it."

One of the best recent CD releases of Tillman's songs is *Country Music Hall of Fame 1984* (King Records-2000) that includes "I Love You So Much, It Hurts," "Drivin' Nails in My Coffin," and "This Cold War With You."

As of 2003, Tillman in his 88th year resided in Marble Falls, Texas. (GC)

Tisdale, Wayman
(June 9, 1964)

Although Wayman Tisdale will always be remembered as a basketball legend in the state of Oklahoma, his notable music career is active and fruitful with five nationally released jazz albums that explore his preferred funky, smooth jazz style, and a collection of gospel songs to his credit. Born in Ft. Worth, Texas but reared in Tulsa, Wayman uses the bass as a lead instrument in the model of his greatest influences, Stanley Clark and Marcus Miller, and his vocals are representative of his upbringing in the gospel choir and its association with American soul music.

Tisdale's father, Reverend Louis Tisdale, bought Wayman a toy guitar and the ten-year-old eventually broke all but the fattest strings, so he began playing bass lines on what was left. He also began playing basketball that year, eventually reaching 6'9". A foot taller than his teen contemporaries, he became the first Oklahoma high school player ever to have his number retired, and he remembered those high school basketball years at Booker T. Washington musically on his 1986 album *In the Zone* (Mo Jazz). Over a bluesy bass line, Tisdale describes the supercharged environment of a meeting between Booker T. and Tulsa McClain in "High School Interlude." One could not be in a more super-charged basketball environment than when the two historically African-American schools met on the court during his era, a milieu that eventually played itself out in the 1990s when a game had to be held in a gym with only players, cheerleaders, referees, and select visitors present.

Known for his massive dunks and his left-handed jumper at the University of Oklahoma, Wayman is roundly considered the greatest player in school history. He is the only three-time, first-team, consensus All-American in college basketball history, and completed his career #3 on the all-time NCAA scoring list. Leaving OU as a junior, he was second overall pick in the 1985 NBA draft, after Patrick Ewing. He was also a member, along with Michael Jordan, of the 1984 Olympic gold-medal team coached by Bob Knight. Tisdale averaged fifteen points-per-game over twelve years in the NBA, four years each with Indiana, Sacramento, and Phoenix, and appeared in twenty-two career playoff games before retiring in 1998.

Throughout his basketball career, Wayman kept playing bass not only out of enjoyment, but to keep his spirits up through the long non-stop NBA road trips and changes in urban locations with trades to new teams. By the time he signed with the Phoenix Suns in 1994, he had also signed with Mo Jazz, an offshoot of Motown Records, and released his first CD, *Power Forward* (Mo Jazz), in 1995. The title and several selections on the disc refer to Tisdale's rough and tumble position in the NBA, to include "Inside Stuff," "After the Game," and the title track. While his musical skills on all fronts matured on *Power Forward*, a Top 10 hit on *Billboard*'s contemporary jazz chart, they coalesce in 1996's *In the Zone*, another Top 10 jazz album of smooth grooves, harmonized vocals, and tastefully played lead bass guitar, as well as some excellent additional session players. When Mo Jazz folded in 1997, semi-retired and forever legendary, Ahmet Ertegun, who helped mold the Atlantic Records R&B stable of artists in the 1950s and 1960s, signed Tisdale. While the first two albums were recorded during off-seasons by Wayman, 1998's *Decisions*, recorded in his home studio, exhibited the total focus of a fully matured musician, and brought in some of the biggest names in contemporary jazz, such as Gerald Albright, Marcus Miller, and Everette Harp. From 1998 to 2001, Wayman toured extensively, spent time with family, and set up a commercial studio.

In 2001, Wayman released *Face to Face* (Atlantic), a slam dunk of a contemporary jazz album with obvious commercial R&B leanings that hit #1 on *Billboard's* jazz chart, but garnered the usual mixed reviews from jazz critics that highly successful crossover albums often receive. Critics do not put money in children's college funds, however, and Tisdale enjoyed continued success with national radio airplay and consistent bookings. In May, 2002, Wayman presented his own shows in Tulsa at the Sager Center, featuring Gerald Albright, the Los Angeles saxophonist with whom Tisdale recorded on *Decisions*, and whose own 2002 album on GRP is highly touted for its full flavor of jazz, funk, soul, and R&B. Also in 2002, the Oklahoma Sports Hall of Fame inducted Waymon, and the Oklahoma Jazz Hall of Fame presented Waymon with its Legacy Tribute Award, given to an Oklahoma musician who has created a level of outstanding musical accomplishment for a given year.

Currently, he and Regina Tisdale, his wife of fifteen years, have four children, and Wayman heads Tisway Productions in Tulsa, from which he manages his musical affairs, and offers complete studio access and production services. In the fall of 2002, Wayman was booked solidly in such diverse settings as a radio promotional cruise line show in New York, music festivals from Detroit to Los Angeles, and further gigs in Seattle, Atlanta, and Fort Worth, Texas. Also in 2002, the Smooth Jazz Awards named him the 2002 Bassist of the Year, and Oklahoma governor Brad Henry appointed him to the state tourism and recreation commission. Through his agent, the Richard De La Font Agency, Tisdale says, "I am very conscious not to take credit for what I do. It is all rooted in family and grounded firmly in God. I had great parents that helped show me the way and I knew everything would turn out all right. From being the #1 basketball player in the nation in high school to a gold medal in the Olympics, and success in both my professional careers, God is smiling on me." His fifth nationally released CD was scheduled for a 2003 release. (HF)

www.tisway.com

Tulsa Sound

Left to right: Leo Feathers (guitar), Chuck Blackwell (drums), Ron Ryle (bass), Johnny Williams (saxophone), Russell Bridges, a.k.a. Leon Russell (piano), Jack Dunham (vocals), and Junior Markham (vocals) perform at the Tropicana Club in Tulsa in 1959.

By all accounts, the Tulsa Sound is a musical mélange of country, blues, rock, and occasionally jazz, that has its sources in the multi-faceted "Okie jazz" of **Bob Wills,** the rich R&B/jazz history of Tulsa, and the teenage musicians of the 1950s, such as **Leon Russell, David Gates, J.J. Cale,** and **Jack Dunham,** who embraced the burgeoning rock and roll movement while infusing a heady dose of R&B into the twangy blues of Elvis Presley. What later becomes known as the Tulsa Sound of the 1970s might best be described as 50s rockers slowing down,

Gene Crose (far right) has led bands in Tulsa since 1956 including Gene Crose and the Rockets, circa 1967.

maturing, starting families and changing priorities, which is reflected in the more relaxed style of music manifested most directly by J.J. Cale and Leon Russell's easy paced recordings of the early 1970s. Eric Clapton's 1974 tribute to Cale, *Slowhand* (MCA), with a rhythm section of Oklahomans Jamie Oldaker and Carl Radle, and then Dire Straits *Sultans of Swing* (Sire, 1978) is just mainstream popular music catching up with Tulsa's hip hybrid of blues, country, and rock. An updated version of the sound ran through American pop culture again in 1985 when Dire Straits' "Money for Nothing," with Mark Knopfler's thinly veiled imitation of J.J. Cale's vocal style, led to high rotations on the nascent video music channel, MTV. In the 1990s, **Steve Ripley**'s Tractors mined the same vein for

Clyde Stacy, 1957

their multi-platinum success, and by 2003, periodic reunions of Tulsa Sound musicians drew appreciative crowds while some of its primary musicians continued active careers in the recording studios and on concert stages around the world.

Aside from the previously mentioned R&B, Western swing, and rockabilly influences, the groundwork for what became known as the Tulsa Sound was laid in the middle 1950s as young Tulsa musicians began to form R&B leaning rock and roll bands while 50s rock and roll had a stranglehold on popular music and culture. According to **Jack Dunham**, more often than not, musicians would play in several bands, which may have led to the similar style they all seemed to develop. Musicians from this era who went on to make significant impact on American popular, country, and rock music include drummers Chuck Blackwell, David Teegarden, and Jimmy Karstein, singer/songwriters J.J. Cale (then Johnny Cale) and David Gates, guitarists Tommy Crook and Leo Feathers, pianist/singer/songwriter Leon Russell (then Russell Bridges), guitarist/pianist Tom Tripplehorn, and singer/songwriter Jack Dunham.

Bobby Taylor (left) led rock and roll bands in Tulsa from 1956 to 1958. He is pictured here with bassist George Metzel in 1957 at an Oklahoma A&M performance in Stillwater.

Additional musicians who played important roles in Tulsa's 1950s music scene were vocalists Gene Crose, Bobby Taylor, Clyde Stacy, Wally Wiggins, Lucky Clark, Jack Thurman, Billy Mecon, and Jimmy ("Jr.") Markham. Bassists of the period include Ron Lyle, Bill Raffensperger, Gerald Goodwin and Ralph Brumett. Saxophonists included Johnny Williams, Bill Boatman, and Sammy Dodge. Primary drummers were Chuck Farmer, Don Kimmel, Gerald Goodwin, Jim Turley, and C.B. Glasby. Pianists of note were Jimmy Manry, Eddie Spraker, Rocky Frisco, and Doug Cunningham. Notable 1950s guitarists included Lee Weir and Tommy Rush.

While Jack Dunham was the first of the 1950s generation of Tulsa musicians to migrate to the Los Angeles area to take advantage of recording and performance opportunities there, several followed close behind. Along with Gates, Russell, and Cale, drummer David Teegarden recorded with Skip "Van Winkle" Knape on "God, Love, and Rock & Roll," a Top 40 hit in 1970, and kept time for Bob Seger's recordings and road shows from 1972-1991. Born in Tulsa, guitarist/pianist Tommy Tripplehorn (b. Feb. 2, 1944) toured and recorded with Gary Lewis and the Playboys in the 1960s, and continued as a session musician for several years before returning to Tulsa where he also played on the Tractors' 1994 smash album. Drummer Jim Karstein, born in 1942 in Tulsa, played on several sessions with Eric Clapton, toured

Rocky Frisco

Tommy Rush

with Gary Lewis and the Playboys, and appeared on J.J. Cale's albums from 1972 to 1992. Karstein has also worked with **Steve Ripley**, and James Burton, and was a member of Eric Clapton's Rainbow Concert Band. Chuck Blackwell, also born in Tulsa, is a drummer and songwriter who recorded with Joe Cocker, **Jesse Ed Davis**, and Freddie King, and whose songs were recorded by Taj Majal, Freddie King, and Ian Moore.

Born in Oklahoma City in 1942, but reared in Tulsa where he played in bands with the other Tulsa Sound titans, Carl Radle was one of the most sought after rock and blues bassists of the 1970s. He played on Delaney & Bonnie's 1969-70 tour, then joined Leon Russell and Joe Cocker for the famous Mad Dogs and Englishmen tour of 1970. After that circus of a road band, Radle formed Derek and the Dominos with Eric Clapton, Bobby Whitlock, and Jim Gordon, all of whom played in Delaney and Bonnie's group. With Derek and the Dominos, Carl plays bass and percussion on the famous album *Layla and Other Assorted Love Songs* (Atco, 1970), the title track of which has long been a classic rock radio standard. In 1971, Radle joined Leon Russell, Ringo Starr, Billy Preston, Bob Dylan, **Jesse Ed Davis**, and several others, in George Harrison's Concert for Bangladesh, a benefit concert to aid victims of a massive flood in India. While playing in Eric Clapton's band throughout the 1970s, during which time the Tulsa Sound became internationally known, Carl Radle also performed with a host of major artists, to include recording with some of the giants of the 1970s rock era: John Lee Hooker, Dave Mason, Buddy Guy, Rita Coolidge, Art Garfunkel, Doctor John, Duane Allman, and J.J. Cale. Radle died in 1980.

Junior Markham

Vocalist, harmonica player, Jimmy "Junior" Markham began playing trumpet in high school where he met up with Leon Russell, J.J. Cale, and Carl Radle. He led his first bands in Tulsa from 1959 to 1969, and found his way to California where many of his friends were already enjoying musical success stories. Along with Bobby Keyes, Junior played in the Flying Burrito Brothers' horn section in the 1960s. He returned to Tulsa in 1970 where he opened a club and began playing harmonica primarily. Since then, he has recorded or performed live with Muddy Waters, John Lee Hooker, Charlie Musselwhite, Sonny Terry and Brownie McGhee, Delbert McClinton, Leon Russell, J.J. Cale, Jerry Lee Lewis, A.C. Reed, Waylon Jennings, and Willie Nelson.

In 1987, Markham relocated to Nashville where he continued performing live regularly on stage and in the recording studio. He released a solo CD, *Wound Up Tight* (King Snake Records), and has appeared on recent recordings by A.C. Reed, The Tractors, Dave Onley, and Bonnie Raitt. His song, "Soul Food," appeared on Leon Russell's *Asylum Choir II*, and had a cut with his band, Junior Markham and the Jukes, on the Taxim Records Import CD, *Even More Good Whiskey Blues*, a compilation CD of Tennessee blues bands.

Although younger than the first wave of Tulsa rock musicians, Jamie Oldaker (b. September 5, 1951) has also made numerous significant recordings that are part of the Tulsa Sound's legacy, most notably with the Bob Seger Band in 1973, on Leon Russell's 1974 album, *Stop All That Jazz*, and with Eric Clapton from 1974 to 1979, and again in 1984. Oldaker also played with Freddie King, Peter Frampton, and ex-Kiss guitarist Ace Frehley, before joining Steve Ripley and The Tractors for the group's 1994 self-titled album that sold more than two million copies.

One musician who has foregone touring the country to remain in Tulsa, where "in-the-know" music enthusiasts recognize him as one of the premier guitarists in the United States, if not the world, is Tommy Crook. While not widely recognized as part of the Tulsa Sound per se, Crook often relies on its multiple elements for his musical inspiration, and played in bands with some of its primary movers and shakers in the early 1960s. With his unique fingerpicking style, and placement of bass strings on the bottom two positions on his guitar, Crook's sound is as unique as it is inspirational.

A native Oklahoman, Tommy Crook started playing guitar at age four when his father, Buck Crook, gave him his first guitar, and taught him to play rhythm and lead.

Tommy Crook

With Chet Atkins and Les Paul as his major influences, by age eleven Crook became a featured solo act on Porter Wagoner's touring show, and was soon a regular on Hank Thompson's live TV show from Oklahoma City, and Leon McAuliffe's TV show in Tulsa. While Tommy attended Tulsa's Central High School in the early 1960s, he played in bands with David Gates, Jimmy Karstein, Carl Radle, Leon Russell, J.J. Cale, Gene Crose, and Jimmy Markham, a blues vocalist and harmonica player who has recorded with .38 Special and A.C. Reed. After graduating Central in 1962, Crook tried pharmacy school for a while at Southwestern Oklahoma State University, but tired of the academic environment and returned to Tulsa where he worked as guitar salesman with Eldon Shamblin at The Guitar House, and later a traveling factory rep for Ampeg Amplifiers. Giving up the retail business after a few years, Tommy turned to playing full time, touring Southeast Asia with the USO, and then taking jobs around Tulsa before landing a 12 ½ year gig at the Tulsa Airport Sheraton where he accompanied himself with a drum machine.

Tommy Crook has played with a cadre of great musicians (Chet Atkins, **Merle Haggard**, Leon Russell, Pat Boone, Lou Rawls, Chuck Berry, Charlie Daniels, and Jerry Lee Lewis). It was Chet Atkins who provided the most regularly repeated praise of Crook when the man who saved (or destroyed) country music in the 1950s answered Johnny Carson's question of whether or not "anyone, anywhere played guitar as well or better" than Atkins. Atkins said, "Yes, Johnny. Tommy Crook in Tulsa, Oklahoma."

In 1989, Tommy Crook recorded an album with David Teegarden that wound up in the hands of Asleep at the Wheel's Ray Benson who has said, "Tommy Crook is the most unique and talented guitar player I have seen in my life." Benson passed the album on to Willie Nelson, who in turn gave the tape to *Guitar Magazine*, and the internationally recognized publication featured Tommy in its March, 1989 issue. Since then, he has continued playing a steady series of gigs at restaurants and clubs in Tulsa, as he does not like to travel and has no desire to tour. In 2002, he recorded a CD, *110 Degrees in the Shade*, available primarily from him or via the Internet, and performed in honor of **Charlie Christian** at the 2002 Oklahoma Music Hall of Fame induction ceremony and concert. As of 2003, Crook could be seen playing every Friday night at Lanna Thai Restaurant on Memorial Boulevard in Tulsa.

Another Tulsa Sound group that had more of cult following in Europe than anywhere else was Rockin' Jimmy and the Brothers of the Night. Led by guitarist and vocalist Jim Byfield, (b. February 7, 1949 in Tulsa) who really came of age a little later than the first generation of Tulsa Sound players, his

Rockin' Jimmy and the Brothers of the Night

music is very similar to both J.J. Cale's career-long style, and Eric Clapton's 1970s derivative of it. In fact, Clapton covered Byfield's "Little Rachel" on *There's One in Every Crowd* (Polydor, 1975). Before leading the Brothers of the Night, Byfield fronted Guava (1977), and then Jim Byfield and His Band (1978). In 1980, Byfield recorded for Pilgrim Records, established by former Joe Cocker roadie Peter Nichols, an engineer for Leon Russell's Shelter Records who became enthusiastic about recording local Tulsa bands. Pilgrim released at least two Tulsa band compilations, *Tulsa Sampler* (1977) and *The Green Album* (1978), as well as Rockin' Jimmy and the Brothers of the Night, *By the Light of the Moon* (1980).

Recorded at George Bingham's Ranch Studio in Glenpool, *By the Light of the Moon* relies on the laid-back, R&B influenced rock with a shuffle that has become the trademark of the Tulsa Sound. Byfield's musicians on the album include many familiar names: bassist Gary Gilmore (J.J. Cale, Taj Majal); keyboardist Walt Richmond (Bonnie Raitt, Rick Danko, The Tractors, et al.); drummer Chuck DeWalt; and guitarist Steve Hickerson. Backup vocalist Debbie Campbell (from Fort Worth, Texas) had fronted the Los Angeles-based group Buckwheat and toured with Bonnie Raitt before moving to Tulsa in the mid-1970s where she worked as a back up singer and opening solo act for multiple artists. Backup vocalist Jim Sweeney had already had his own solo album on Pilgrim in 1979, *Didn't I Blow Your Mind*, supported by the Brothers of the Night, as they did for Campbell's 1982 album, *Two Hearts* (Churchill). The Brothers released a self-titled album in 1983 on Intercord with Gary Cundiff replacing Gilmore on bass, but the record saw little success outside of local music fans and those who kept track of Tulsa's music scene. Bringing the story full circle, Byfield also played guitar on The Tractors' 1994 self-titled hit album which brought the lazy Tulsa shuffle right back to the forefront of the music business, although this time in the country arena.

Don White, born in Tulsa in 1940, is another singer and songwriter whose career has been intertwined with the Tulsa Sound. A singer, songwriter, and guitarist, J.J. Cale played guitar in White's first group and developed a deeper appreciation for country music via White. Artists who have recorded Don White's songs include Roseanne Cash, The Oak Ridge Boys, Suzy Boggus, and Razzy Bailey. His root-sy guitar work has been featured in recording sessions by J.J. Cale, Waylon Jennings, Marty Stuart, The Tractors, Katie Moffitt, and Johnny Rodriguez. While he also verges into straight-ahead country, Don White's 1999 independent CD, *Okie Fiesta*, is an ample illustration of both his guitar skills and songwriting style, both indicative at times of the common touchstones of the Tulsa Sound: relaxed and raspy vocal delivery reminiscent of Cale and Leon Russell, a shuffling rhythm section, and rootsy, blues-leaning guitar solos. Additionally, Tulsa Sound vets and old friends Tommy Tripplehorn and Casey Van Beek make appearances on the album, and White covers two songs by J.J. Cale ("Riverboat Song," "Magnolia") as well as one by Tom Waits ("Blind Love").

While the definitive Tulsa Sound history has yet to be written, many of the people who were there when it started are largely still around Tulsa. Several can be found on Sundays at the Beams of Light Family Tabernacle, pastured by former Tweed front man and guitarist, Jimmy Ray, who has recorded an inspirational CD with the many talented members of the tabernacle congregation. Given the contribution of Tulsa musicians to American pop, rock, and country music from 1960 to the present, a complete account can't be far off. For the time being, researchers can learn a lot from just going to the *Tulsa World's* online archives and putting any one of the names from this essay in the search engine. (HF) www.tulsaworld.com

Tulsa sound, 2003, left to right: J. J. Cale, Rocky Frisco, and Gene Crose

Twilley, Dwight
(b. June 6, 1951)

Equally influenced by Sun rockabilly and Beatlesque songwriting and harmonies, Dwight Twilley and his partner, Tulsa native Phil Seymour (b. May 15, 1952 – d. August 17, 1993), created a tight and punchy pop sound in the mid-1970s that peaked early on a national scale with their Top 20 hit, "I'm on Fire." Since then, Dwight Twilley's recordings with Seymour have become landmarks of the evolving "power

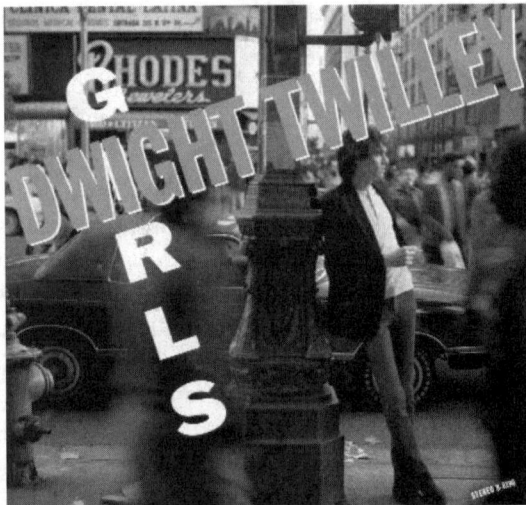

pop" sound that predated both punk in the U.K., and new wave in the United States. The two met at a Tulsa theater where they had both taken their brothers to see the Beatles' *A Hard Day's Night* during a matinee special's "take a friend free" promotion. Inspired by the film, the two teenagers, already accomplished instrumentalists, began writing and recording songs together, taking on the name Oister for their group, and occasionally playing with guitarist Bill Pitcock IV.

After practicing in their home-based studio, "The Shop," and making several recordings, they released two low-budget albums, *Oister Presents Swirling Clouds*, and *Oisters Greatest Hits*. Figuring New York and L.A. were too far to drive, Seymour and Twilley made a trip to Nashville, but never made it after they stopped at the legendary Sun Studios in Memphis, well-known for its recording of early blues artists like Howlin' Wolf and B.B. King, but also for being the epicenter of the rockabilly movement with Elvis Presley as its kingpin. At Sun, they met one of the label's early rockabilly artists, Ray Harris, who later invited the boys down to his Tupelo, Mississippi studios to record, and encouraged them to toughen up their sound. With some demos in hand, the Dwight Twilley Band traveled to Los Angeles and wrangled a deal with Shelter Records, co-owned by **Leon Russell**. Their first single, "I'm On Fire," mined from the same glam boogie as T. Rex's #1 hit, "Bang a Gong (Get It On), created an instant national stir by reaching #16 on the national pop charts in 1975, with practically no promotion from Shelter's haphazard industry management technique. Via the song's success, the band landed an *American Bandstand* appearance, and previewed the song they intended as the follow-up single, "Shark," recorded at Leon's home studio in Tulsa and on which Russell played bass, piano, and percussion. The label thought the group would be perceived as a novelty act trying to capitalize on the shark craze spreading through American pop culture at the time on the fins of the 1975 film *Jaws*, and refused to release the single, which was ultimately dropped from *Sincerely*.

When *Sincerely* (Shelter) finally did hit the shelves in 1976, the band's notoriety had all but faded and the record went virtually unnoticed by anyone but critics noting the change in American pop from rebel Southern rock to a smarter, more polished sound that mirrored the punk pop emanating from England at the time via Elvis Costello and American cult figures Big Star, led by Alex Chilton. After *Sincerely* stalled at #138 on *Billboard*'s pop album charts, the band's second album, virtually all of which had been recorded during the *Sincerely* sessions, languished on the tape shelf while they negotiated a deal with ARISTA to release a new album, *Twilley Don't Mind*, on which their old Shelter label mate, Tom Petty, added backing vocals. In spite of the album's pop potential, the record only reached #70 on the pop album chart, and Seymour left the group, pursuing a solo career that produced on Top 30 hit, "Precious to Me," from his self-titled debut in 1980. After recording backing vocals for Tom Petty's first hits, "American Girl" and "Breakdown," Phil Seymour also worked with Del Shannon, Moon Mullican, and Oklahoma's other power poppers, 20/20, before joining the L.A.-based Textones. Diagnosed with Lymphoma in the middle 1980s, Seymour died in 1993 in Tarazana, California.

Soldiering on as a solo performer, Twilley had another largely unnoticed album for ARISTA, *Twilley* (1979), and an equally received album on EMI, *Scuba Divers* (1982), both of which charted at #113 and #109 respectively on the pop album charts. At least the single from *Scuba Divers*, "Somebody to Love," reached #16 on *Billboard*'s mainstream rock chart. Finally, in 1984, Twilley achieved some more commercial success with "Girls" (#16, 1984) from *Jungle*, which reached #39 on the pop album charts. His final album of the 1980s, *Wild Dogs*, created no buzz for CBS.

Twilley blipped again on the pop culture radar screen in 1992, when his "Why You Wanna Break My Heart" was included on the *Wayne's World* soundtrack. In 1993 he added some backing vocals to the album *Hi-Fi Sci-Fi*, by a young, like-minded group from New Jersey, Dramarama, and in 1994 his book for divorced fathers, *Questions from Dad*, won an award from the Children's Rights Council. Always appreciated by critics and music fans who follow his progression closely, the 1996 best of compilation, *XXI* (The Right Stuff), met with solid enough commercial success in the U.S., but increased his already rabid following in Europe.

When an earthquake destroyed his California home in 1995, Twilley returned to Tulsa and recorded his first new album since 1986, *Tulsa*, recorded entirely in his mid-town Tulsa converted garage studio. Released on the Copper label in 1999, the album ran away with a couple of Tulsa's local Spot Music Awards, sponsored by the *Tulsa World*, including Artist of the Year and National Album of the Year. In 1997, Twilley showed sixty pieces of his graphic art collection in a Tulsa exhibit titled *Out in the Rain*, and began releasing vinyl singles through Pop the Balloon Records in Europe in 1998. As a result of resurgent interest in Twilley's career, Not Lame Records released a compilation of rarities and outtakes from Twilley's thirty-year career, *Between the Cracks* (1998). In 1999, one of the largest European independent labels, Castle, picked up *Tulsa* for distribution there, as well as *Between the Cracks*.

In 2001, sessions from new material recorded in the early 1990s, but never released, found new life as *Luck* on Twilley's own label, Big Oak. His tenth full-length release met with critical and commercial raves in Europe, and behind the new/old album, he headlined the Serie-B pop festival in Spain, playing alongside younger alterna-rockers Mudhoney, Bevis Frond, Cotton Mather, and Death Cab for Cutie. Also in 2001, Dwight Twilley made the magical list of potential Rock and Roll Hall of Fame inductees with other newly eligible artists, Bruce Springsteen, the Sex Pistols, and Blondie. In 2002, Dwight hit the road nationally for the first time since the late 1980s with a group consisting of original Twilley guitarist Bill Pitcock IV, early drummer Jerry Naifeh, and bassist Dave White who played with Dwight for several years. His fall, 2003, tour through the Midwestern U.S. exchanged White for 20/20's Ron Flynt on bass and backing vocals. In a 2003 interview, Twilley said that Capitol-EMI plans to release *Scuba Divers* and *Jungle* on CD for the first time, with bonus tracks. He also planned to return to the studio in late 2003 to lay down another album's worth of his extensive catalogue of songs that have yet to be recorded. An extensive, fan-friendly biography is available on Twilley's website. (HF)
www.dwighttwilley.com

Vasquez, Andrew
(b. November 30, 1957)

An enrolled member of the Apache Tribe of Oklahoma, Andrew Vasquez is one of the nation's leading American Indian flutists whose recordings have enjoyed international success for their blend of sound effects, modern and traditional instruments, occasional philosophical musings from Vasquez, and the soothing, echo-laden Plains Indian flute. Born in Anadarko, the southwestern Oklahoma town so heavily associated with American Indians it bills itself as the capital of Indian Country. Along with Vasquez's own Na-I-Sha people (sometimes known as Kiowa-Apache in the history books) whose musical traditions are thousands of years old, as well as those of the neighboring **Kiowa**, Comanche, and Wichita tribes, traditional and Pan-Indian music surrounded Vasquez in his youth. Participating in the powwow dance culture of that area led to his participation in the New York-based *American Indian Dance Theater* from 1986 through 1991. While on tour, Andrew traded for his first flute, and began to develop his own style on the instrument preserved in the 20th century by Belo Cozad, **"Doc" Tate Nevaquaya**, Tom Ware, and **Cornel Pewewardy**.

Andrew's Na-I-Sha name is "Ditkal Te-Bikas," which means "cedar stalk" in the Apache language and is rooted in the part of the cedar tree from which flutes are made. He has three recordings to date for the North Dakota based Makoché label. His first CD, *Vasquez* (1996), features less percussion and modern instruments than his subsequent albums, *Wind River* (1997) and *V3: An American Indian* (1999). Named 1998's Best Contemporary Native American Album at the New Age Voice Awards *Wind River*'s cover design by his wife, Myra Vasquez, also received the Best Album Cover Award. *Wind River* also garnered Vasquez several notable nominations in 1998 from organizations such as the Association of Independent Music, and the Native American Music Awards (Songwriter of the Year/Flutist of the Year). In 1999, he was nominated as Flutist of the Year and Best Male Artist while his album of that year, *V3: An American Indian*, received a nomination in the Best New Age Recording Category. *V3* features Vasquez's strongest use to date of contemporary instrumentation in his music, mixing in acoustic and electric guitars, more keyboards, and his trademark flute work.

In 2000, Andrew received the Best Male Artist Award from the Native American Music Awards for *V3*. Vasquez has also released an album of Kiowa-Apache music on the Spalax label. As a northern style traditional dancer, Andrew creates his own regalia and beadwork, has performed professionally around the world, and won many powwow dance titles around the United States. He currently resides in Bismarck, North Dakota with his wife, Myra, where he continues composing music, enjoying family life, and preparing his next artistic ventures as one of the country's leading contemporary American Indian musicians. According the Makoché Records website, Andrew says about his music: "Everything I play comes from my heart and stands for what I believe in. I compose my songs for special reasons." (HF)
www.makoche.com

Wakely, Jimmy
(b. February 16, 1914 – d. September 23, 1982)

One of the most revered singing cowboys whose recordings appealed to both country and pop music audiences, and a 1971 inductee into the Nashville Songwriters Hall of Fame, James Clarence Wakely was born in Mineola, Arkansas, but when he was a small child, the Wakely family relocated to Battiest, Oklahoma, a tiny hamlet in McCurtain County in the southeastern part of the state. The family moved several times around the state as struggling sharecroppers, and Jimmy wound up graduating from Cowden High School, located in Washita County southwest of Oklahoma City. He was musically inclined at an early age, learning both the piano and guitar, as well as singing in both country and pop styles. According to his son, Johnny, Jimmy played the piano in church and later directed the church choir. After winning a local radio talent contest, he decided to become a musician.

In 1937, Jimmy married Inez Miser, and they moved to Oklahoma City, where he worked part time in a service station, played piano with Merle Salathiel (better known as Merl Lindsay) and his Barnyard Boys, and traveled the summer with Little Doc Roberts' Medicine Show. He auditioned for local radio shows, where he met **Johnny Bond**, who was to become a life long friend. The two formed a trio patterning their sound after the popular singing cowboy group, the Sons of the Pioneers. The third member of the trio alternated between Scotty Harrell and former Lightcrust Doughboy, **Dick Reinhart**, a native Oklahoman born in Tishomingo. At the outset, the trio called themselves The Singing Cowboy Trio, but later changed their name to The Bell Boys because of sponsorship by Bell Clothiers on radio station WKY in Oklahoma City, where they played on a daily show. In addition, the trio cut transcription discs and also played live on radio station KVOO in Tulsa. On the daily radio broadcasts, the trio used Johnny Bond's "Cimarron (Roll On)," which he had composed in 1938, as their theme song.

According to Wakely's son, Johnny, Jimmy was hitchhiking one night in the rain and a bolt of lightning lighted up a sign reading "**Gene Autry** Now Appearing" at a local fair. Jimmy caught a ride to the fair and met Autry, who discovered that Jimmy was living in Oklahoma. Autry told Jimmy to write him and they began corresponding after Autry's return to California. During this correspondence, Autry encouraged Jimmy to move to Hollywood and, if he became a member of the musician's union, he would try to find a spot on his *Melody Ranch* radio show.

A second source indicates that Gene Autry was on tour promoting his movie *Rancho Grande* in Oklahoma and Kansas in the late 1930s, and the trio traveled to Okemah, Oklahoma, and Lawrence, Kansas, to meet Autry and audition for him. After hearing the trio, Autry was impressed by their repertoire, which included some of his songs. Autry suggested that he could use the trio on his *Melody Ranch* show should they ever decide to move to California.

Whatever the case, Jimmy and Inez and their two daughters, Deanna and Carol, Johnny and Dorothy Bond, and Dick Reinhart packed their belongings in Jimmy's Dodge automobile and left for California on May, 31, 1940, leaving Scotty behind as he wanted to remain in Oklahoma. Autry hired them as the Jimmy Wakely Trio for his CBS *Melody Ranch* radio show. For the next two years, Jimmy worked for Autry, often known as "The Melody Kid." After leaving Autry, Jimmy formed his own band, which off and on included such legendary country artists as Merle Travis, Cliffie Stone, and **Spade Cooley**. He signed a recording contract with Decca in 1942, and over the next five years, released some thirty-four sides, including "I Wonder Where You Are Tonight," "Cimarron (Roll On)," Bond's composition, "There's A Star Spangled Banner Waving Somewhere," a cover of Elton Britt's song, and "I'm Sending You Red Roses," his first record on the country charts, peaking at #3 in 1944.

Wakely's first acting appearance was in 1939 in a B movie western, *Saga of Death Valley*, starring Roy Rogers. He went on to appear in support roles during the next six years, usually with the Jimmy Wakely Trio or Jimmy Wakely's Rough Riders, in western movies starring such legendaries as Johnny Mack Brown, Charles Starrett, and Slim Summerville. He finally starred in his first movie in 1945, *Song of the Range*, which resulted in a series of twenty-eight leading roles for Monogram over the next five years to his last, *Lawless Code*, in 1949. In a poll conducted in 1948, he was voted the #4 cowboy star after Rogers, Autry, and Starrett, and only Autry, Rogers, and Tex Ritter starred in more musical westerns.

In 1948 Wakely decided to devote his career to music, including penning his own song, "Song of the Sierras," and switched to the Capitol label, and returned to the Top 10 with "Signed, Sealed, and Delivered." It was followed by two of the most successful records of the post-World War II decade, "One Has My Name (The Other Has My Heart)," which held the top spot on the country charts for eleven weeks and crossed over to the Top 10 pop charts, and **Floyd Tillman**'s song, "I Love You So Much It Hurts," which held the #1 position on the country charts for five weeks and crossed over to the Top 25 of the pop charts. His final hit for 1948 was "Mine All Mine," which cracked the Top 10 of the country charts.

Wakely's recording success continued in early 1949 with "Forever More" (Top 10), "Till the End of the World" (Top 10), "I Wish I Had Nickel" (Top 5), and "Someday You'll Call My Name" (Top 10). Later the same year, he teamed with Margaret Whiting, celebrated pop singer, to record a cover of another Tillman song, "Slippin' Around," which reached #1 on both country (seventeen weeks) and pop charts and became a million seller for the duet. "Wedding Bells," the flip side, also went Top 10 on the country charts and crossed over to the Top 30 of the pop charts. To round out the year, Jimmy and Whiting released another Tillman song, "I'll Never Slip Around Again," which charted at No. 3 on the country list and crossed over to the Top 10 of the pop charts.

Referred to as the "Bing Crosby of Country Music," Jimmy became so popular that in a nationwide poll in 1948, he was voted America's third most popular singer behind Perry Como and Frankie Laine, edging Bing Crosby into fourth place. His solo successes in 1950 included "Peter Cottontail" and "Mona Lisa." The flourishing partnership with Whiting also continued the same year with the double-sided Top 3 release, "Broken Down Merry-Go-Round"/"The Gods Were Angry With Me," another Top 3 single, "Let's Go to Church (Next Sunday Morning)," and a Top 10 release, "Bushel and a Peck."

Wakely returned the charts in 1951 with his solo hits, "My Heart Cries for You" (Top 10) and "Beautiful Brown Eyes" (Top 5). His final hits with Whiting included "When You and I Were Young Maggie Blues" (Top 10) and "I Don't Want to Be Free" (Top 5). Overall, Jimmy and Whiting had nine total hits during their career as one of the most popular partnerships in American musical history. Jimmy never made the country charts again. During the late 1940s and 1950s, he toured extensively in the U.S., the Pacific, the Far East, including Alaska and Korea, where he often appeared with the Bob Hope Show.

In 1952 Jimmy starred in his own CBS radio network show, *The Jimmy Wakely Show*, which remained on the air until 1958. In 1953 he signed with Coral Records and in 1955 joined Decca, Coral's parent label. Although Jimmy was never able to attain the singles success of the later 1940s, he released several albums on Decca worth noting, including *Santa Fe Trail*, a 1956 production of excellent cowboy songs. With the exception of two albums for Dot in 1966, he remained on the Decca label through 1970.

In the early 1950s, Wakely built a recording studio in his home, where his son Johnny assisted him, and they eventually formed their own record label, Shasta. Jimmy released in 1959, *Merry Christmas*, a seasonal album, and *Country Million Sellers*, both on his label. In addition to his own albums, Shasta released material by other singing cowboy stars, including Rex Allen, Johnny Bond, Tex Ritter, and Eddie Dean.

In 1961, Jimmy co-hosted the ABC television network series *Five Star Jubilee* with another singing cowboy star, Tex Ritter. During the remainder of the 1960s and 1970s, he formed a family act with his children, Johnny and Linda, and they played the nightclub circuit including Reno, Tahoe, Las Vegas, and Elko. He was elected to the Nashville Songwriters Hall of Fame in 1971.

Due to age and emphysema, Jimmy died on September 23, 1982 at his home in Mission Hills, California, with Inez and four children (Johnny, Carol, Linda, and Deanna) at his bedside.

Wakely's songs were recorded by numerous artists, including Gene Autry ("I'll Never Let You Go", co-written with Autry), Spade Cooley ("The Solid South"), Woody Herman ("Too Late"), Louvin Brothers ("Too Late"), Elvis Presley ("It Wouldn't Be the Same Without You"), **Jean Shepard** ("You Can't Break the Chains of Love"), T. Texas Tyler ("Follow Thru"), Slim Whitman ("I'm Casting My Lasso Towards the Sky"), and Leona Williams and **Merle Haggard** ("You Can't Break the Chains of Love"). In 2000, *The Very Best of Jimmy Wakely* was released on Varese Sarabande, the U.K. label, and included such hits as "Beautiful Brown Eyes," "Slippin' Around," "I Love You So Much It Hurts," "One Has My Name (The Other Has My Heart)," and "I'll Never Let You Go, Little Darlin'." *Heroes of Country Music, Vol. 4: Legends of the West Coast* (Rhino-1996) celebrates Wakely's contribution to that region's importance in country music with his "One Has My Name (The Other Has My Heart)." One of the most recent releases of Wakely material is *Jimmy Wakely: The Singing Cowboy* (Varese Sarabande-2002) which contains such songs as "I'm An Old Cowhand," "Tumbling Tumbleweeds," and "The Last Roundup." (GC)

Walker, Wayne
(b. December 13, 1925 – d. January 2, 1979)

Recipient of more than twenty BMI Awards for songwriting and an inductee into the Nashville Songwriters Hall of Fame in 1975, Wayne Paul Walker was born in Quapaw, Oklahoma, a community of roughly 1,000 people located in the northeastern part of the state, but was raised in Kilgore, Texas, and attended Kilgore High School from 1940 to 1942, apparently never graduating. He worked at various jobs throughout his early career, including car and vacuum cleaner salesman and roofing houses.

Wayne performed on the *Louisiana Hayride* and recorded for several companies, including Decca, Columbia, Ric, ABC-Paramount, Everest, and Chess, although he never achieved much success cracking the charts. His recordings included "All I Can Do Is Cry," "It's My Way," "A Teenage Love Affair (Can Cause the Blues)," "Whatever You Desire," "Just A'Walkin' Around," "Sands of Gold," "Bo-Bo Ska Diddle Daddle," "Come Away From His Arms" (1957), "I'm Finally Free," "It's Written in the Stars," (1958), "You've Got Me (Where I Wanna Be)," "What Kind of 'God' Do You Think You Are," and "Little Ole You" (1959).

Walker's greatest achievements were in the field of songwriting, especially after he signed in 1954 with Cedarwood Publishing Company, organized by Webb Pierce and Jim Denny. Cedarwood became one of the most important publishers in Nashville with its roster including such legendary songwriters as John D. Loudermilk, Danny Dill, Mel Tillis, Marijohn Wilkin, and Pierce. Four years after signing with Cedarwood, Wayne married the oldest daughter of Ernest Tubb, Violet Elaine "Scooter Bill" Tubb.

Walker was one of the most prolific songwriters in country music in the 1950s and 1960s. His first major hit in 1957, "I've Got a New Heartache," a song co-written and recorded by Ray Price, reached #2 on the country charts. It was later covered by such notables as Ricky Skaggs, Sarah Vaughan, and the Flying Burrito Brothers. "Are You Sincere" became Wayne's signature song and the one most often recorded by a variety of artists from both country and pop fields such as Elvis Presley, Andy Williams, Marty Robbins, Trini Lopez, Melba Montgomery, Faron Young, Lenny Welch, The Platters, Bobby Vinton, and Bobby Bare. It received a BMI Million Airplay Award.

The list of songs written or co-written by Wayne and recorded by various artists representing genres from country to rock is impressive. It includes "Burning Memories" (Ray Price, Waylon Jennings, Kitty Wells, Jerry Lee Lewis and Mel Tillis), "It's My Way" (Tammy Wynette, Webb Pierce, and Don Gibson), "Pride" (Janie Fricke, Ray Price, and Dean Martin), "Cut Across Shorty" (Carl Smith, Nat Stuckey, Eddie Cochran, and Rod Stewart), "Walk on Boy" (Dion and the Belmonts and Doc Watson), "Leavin' On Your Mind" (Patsy Cline and LeAnn Rimes), "Thoughts of a Fool" (Ernest Tubb and George Strait), "All the Time" (Kitty Wells, Jack Greene, and Anne Murray), which was nominated for Song of the Year by the CMA in 1967, "Little Boy Sad" (Johnny Burnette, Bill Phillips, and James Darren), "Pathway of Teardrops" (Ricky Skaggs and K.T. Oslin), "Holiday for Love" (Webb Pierce), "She's Gone, Gone, Gone" (Lefty Frizzell), "Cajun Queen" (Jimmy Dean), "Why, Why" (Carl Smith), "How Do You Talk to a Baby?" (Webb Pierce), "Fallen Angel" (Webb Pierce), "Sweet Lips" (Webb Pierce), "Hello Out There" (**Carl Belew**), "Unloved, Unwanted" (Kitty Wells), "A Little Heartache" (Eddy Arnold), "I Thank My Lucky Stars" (Eddy Arnold), "Memory No. 1" (Webb Pierce), "Since She Turned Seventeen" (Billy "Crash" Craddock), "Ancient History" (Johnny Cash), "Rock the Bop" (Brenda Lee), "Dream Baby (How Long Must I Dream)" (Jerry Lee Lewis), "I Chased You 'Til I You Caught Me" (Ernest Tubb), "Lonely Island" (Marvin Rainwater), "I'll Be Satisfied With Love" (Faron Young), "(I Wished for an Angel) The Devil Sent Me" (Johnny Horton), "When I Look in the Mirror" (Kalin Twins), "(Is My) Ring on Your Finger" (Hawkshaw Hawkins), "Money Tree" (**Merle Haggard**), "In the Misty Moonlight" (Bobby Bare), "You Don't Know Me" (Elvis Presley), "Honey 'Cause I Love You" (Carl Perkins), "Set Up Two Glasses, Joe" (Ernest Tubb), "Papers and Pens" (Ernest Tubb), "Answer the Phone" (Ernest Tubb), "Forgive

Me" (Ernest Tubb), "Fool, Fool, Fool" (Webb Pierce), "Livin' Alone" (Hank Locklin), and "Foreign Love Affair" (Hank Locklin).

When inducted into the Nashville Songwriters Hall of Fame, Wayne said, "If I write enough songs, some of them will get recorded, and some of these will sell records. You know the law of averages is bound to work out. I figure a good song-writer can write a song anytime he has to. It may not be a good song, but it will be a song. Of course, there are times when I'm in different moods and can write better than at other times, but that is true of any business. This is the business I'm in, and I enjoy it."

Walker died at his home in Nashville on January 2, 1979. (GC)
www.nashvillesongwritersfoundation.com/fame/walkerw.html

Wallace, Billy
(b. March 26, 1917 – d. June 3, 1978)

Composer of the #1 hit in 1952 for Webb Pierce, "Back Street Affair," as well as several other country hits in the 1950s, Cright "Billy" Wallace was born in Oklahoma City, but raised in Alabama. He is reported to have learned guitar from the Delmore Brothers, but cited Ernest Tubb and Roy Acuff as the major influences on his singing style. As a vocalist, he never charted any hits, but recorded for several labels, such as Decca (1952), for which he recorded "Back Street Affair," Blue Hen (1955), Mercury (1956), Deb (1957), Del-Ray (1962), and Acadia, a Canadian label for which he recorded an album in 1963.

Wallace's first radio job was in Decatur, Alabama, and he later worked on WSB in Atlanta and WLAC in Nashville. He joined the cast of the *Louisiana Hayride* in 1951. Webb Pierce heard Billy's recording of "Back Street Affair" and took it to #1 in 1952. It was a song based on Billy's lifestyle experiences, and was later covered by such stars as Loretta Lynn, Billy Walker, and John Prine. Pierce also scored with Billy's "Don't Throw Your Life Away," later covered by the Johnson Mountain Boys, a bluegrass group.

Kitty Wells was the country artist who later recorded most of Billy's songs, including "Whose Shoulder Will You Cry On," which was later covered by two bluegrass groups, Del McCoury and the Dixie Pals and IIIrd Tyme Out, "Cheatin's a Sin," "I'm Paying for That Back Street Affair," and "Honky Tonk Waltz."

Additional songs that Wallace wrote include "We're Steppin' Out Tonight," recorded by David Ball and Bobby Hicks; "I've Just Got to See You Once More," cut by Little Jimmy Dickins, and "Slaves of a Hopeless Love Affair," waxed by Red Foley.

Several of Billy's songs have been compiled into a compact disc by Cattle

Eileen Dale and Billy Wallace perform on stage, 1939

Records, a German company. The album is entitled *Billy Wallace Sings His Hits*, and includes "Ghost of a Honky Tonk Slave," "Honky Tonk Row," "I'm Going Out of Your Arms," "If All Other Girls Were Like You," "Judge of Hearts," "The Sycamore Tree," "Your Kisses and Lies," and "My Heart Needs an Overhaul Job."

Wallace died in 1978 at his home in Huntsville, Alabama. (GC)

Weatherford, Lily Fern
(b. November 25, 1928)

Inducted into the Southern Gospel Music Hall of Fame in 2000 and described as one of the pioneer women in Southern gospel with her trademark recordings of "Tell My Friends" and "What a Precious Friend Is He," Lily Fern Weatherford was born in Bethany, a suburb of Oklahoma City with a population of roughly 20,000. Lily Fern Goble was raised in a strict Church of Nazarene home as her father, Lon, was a minister. He pastored churches in Kingfisher, Yukon, and El Reno prior to Lily Fern's birth. In addition to the ministry, her father was a dairy farmer and worked at the Oklahoma City Ford plant. Although her father did not sing, he loved a variety of music, while her mother, Lillie, sang and played piano. Her family moved to California in the early 1930s so her father could find work

Lily Fern Weatherford and the Weatherforords

as hard times hit Oklahoma. Their first stops were Wilmar and later Compton, where Lily Fern attended elementary school. Lily Fern's first exposure to gospel music was in California churches that used the Vaughan or Stamps/Baxter shape-note songbooks as their regular church hymnals.

At about age sixteen, Lily Fern met Earl Weatherford, another native Oklahoman born in Paul's Valley, at the same church Lily Fern attended. Earl had moved to California during World War II to work in the shipyards and was singing gospel quartet music in 1944 with a group called the Gospel Harmony Boys. He left the group in 1944 to form his own gospel quartet, The Weatherfords. Lily Fern and Earl were married in 1945, a relationship that continued for the next forty-seven years, until his death in 1992. Earl eventually taught her to blend her singing with men, especially the heavier tones, and in 1948, she persuaded Earl to give her a permanent position with his quartet, singing alto. Prior to that she had served as a replacement when-ever one of the quartet members would leave.

Throughout the late 1940s, The Weatherfords worked regular jobs and sang on weekends, but in 1949, they decided to leave California and hit the road as a full-time singing group in their 1948 Buick pulling a one-wheel trailer. So they could be closer to the heart of gospel music and take advantage of a radio contract, the quartet landed at WOWO in Fort Wayne, Indiana, a clear channel 50,000-watt radio station that broadcast nationally.

During the late 1940s, Rex Humbard, noted evangelist, was preaching in Akron, Ohio, where he heard The Weatherfords on radio. Humbard invited them to Akron and work at the Calvary Temple Church as well as appear on his new television show. By 1953, WOWO dropped The Weatherfords and they moved to Akron to join Humbard's new *Cathedral of Tomorrow* television show, which lasted almost a decade. Considered by many as the premier gospel quartet at this time, the "classic" sound of The Weatherfords included Earl, Lily Fern, Henry Slaughter, Armond Morales, and Glen Payne. During this time, Lily Fern and Earl adopted two children, Susan and Steve. Humbard wanted The Weatherfords to become full time staff members and work at The Cathedral each day, however, Earl and Lily May felt their work was singing on the road.

In 1963, The Weatherfords moved to Johnstown, Pennsylvania, which became their base of operations, while they traveled the country singing in some of the largest churches across the U.S. and Canada. During the mid-1960s, The

Weatherfords moved to southern California, where they eventually settled in Sacramento and were members of the Assembly of God staff. In 1967, they moved back to Oklahoma because of family considerations and because it was more centrally located. First in Yukon, they moved to Paoli, just south of Oklahoma City, where they spent the last twenty years of Earl's life, until his death in 1992. Although their daughter was uninterested in music, son Steve joined Lily Fern to carry on The Weatherfords gospel tradition, now in its 58th year as of 2002. Some ninety individuals at one time or another were members of The Weatherfords during this period, and the list reads like a Who's Who of gospel singers. The Weatherfords and the Speer Family rank as the oldest gospel groups still traveling with original members.

Lily Mae has received many honors, including Female Entertainer of the Year in 1993 and 1994, Achievement Award in 1990, and Hall of Fame induction, all from the Great Plains Southern Gospel Association; Living Legend Award from the Grand Ole Gospel Reunion in 1992; and the Living Legacy Award from Women's International Center in California in 1998 for 50 years of providing inspirational music.

As of 2003, Steve served as the manager, lead singer, and emcee, and introduced his mother as the "Grand Lady of Gospel," recognized by her induction into the Southern Gospel Music Hall of Fame in 2000. (GC)
www.geocities.com/Heartland/Prairie/6093

Webb, Jimmy
(b. August 15, 1946)

One of the most prolific song-writers of the twentieth century having composed such hits as "By the Time I Get to Phoenix," "Wichita Lineman," "Up, Up and Away," and "MacArthur Park," and the only artist to ever receive Grammy awards for music, lyrics, and orchestration, song-writer, producer, arranger, singer, and keyboard artist James Layne Webb was born in Elk City, Oklahoma, a community of roughly 10,000 inhabitants west of Oklahoma City. Jimmy learned to play piano at age six, and wrote his first song, "Someone Else," when he was about twelve. Jimmy's father was a Baptist minister in Elk City, where he made his first public appearance, playing organ in his father's church, while rearranging, improvising, and re-harmonizing church hymns. Jimmy also led his own rock and roll band, and began writing songs, primarily religious in nature, although one was a musical.

In 1964 Jimmy and his family moved to California, and he enrolled at San Bernardino Valley College as a music major, but dropped out shortly thereafter when his mother died. While in college, he arranged a single for The Contessas, a girl group, as well as writing another musical, *Dancing Girl*, for his girlfriend. The college drama department rejected it, although it included a song, "Didn't We." In 1965, he headed for Hollywood where he was employed with Jobete Music, the publishing division of Tamla-Motown Records. While here, he wrote "This Time Last Summer" for Brenda Holloway and "My Christmas Tree" for the Supremes, as well as publishing his "Honey Come Back" composition. These reached singer Johnny Rivers, and in 1966, Jimmy signed a contract with Johnny Rivers Music Company and Rivers' new Soul City Records. Rivers recorded the original version of Jimmy's "By the Time I Get to Phoenix" in 1966. It was here that Jimmy met The Fifth Dimension, who recorded his "Up, Up and Away" in 1967. An immediate hit, the song sold one million copies, was eventually used by TWA for a series of commercials, and played in the locker room of the Apollo XI astronauts as they journeyed to the moon. His strong relationship with The Fifth Dimension continued with two albums, *Up, Up and Away* (contributed five of the fourteen tracks) and *The Magic Garden* (wrote all but one of the twelve tracks, including "Carpet Man"), both released in 1967. Jimmy also wrote a majority of the songs for Rivers' 1967 album, *Rewind*. His connection to The Fifth Dimension waned, however, Glen Campbell released "By the Time I Get to Phoenix" in 1967. Jimmy's "Up, Up and Away" and "By the Time I Get to Phoenix" had garnered eight Grammy Awards by 1968. Jimmy formed his own company that provided jingles for such companies as Chevrolet, Doritos, and Hamm's beer, and was a millionaire by age twenty-one.

In 1968, *Jim Webb Sings Jim Webb* was released on the Epic label, an album that Jimmy reportedly disliked, contained none of his hit songs, and released without his consent. An earlier venture into singing resulted in a 1967 single, "Love Years Coming," with an obscure group called the Strawberry Children. Also in 1968, the Brooklyn Bridge scored a hit with Jimmy's "The Worst That Could Happen." Jimmy continued writing songs, one of which was "MacArthur Park," a melodramatic composition some seven minutes in length backed by a rock combo, full orchestra, and choir. First offered to The Association, which rejected it, Jimmy persuaded his friend, Richard Harris, the brilliant Irish actor, to record it. The orchestral part was recorded in Los Angeles, while Harris' voice was added in a Dublin studio. Released in 1968 by Dunhill Records, it reached #2 on the pop charts, and was later covered by Waylon Jennings (won a Grammy in 1969 with it), Donna Summer, and the Four Tops. The accompanying Richard

Harris album, *A Tramp Shining*, was written entirely by Jimmy, and reached #4 in the summer of 1968. It also included one of Jimmy's finest compositions that he had written in college, "Didn't We," later recorded by Frank Sinatra and Barbara Streisand. Jimmy also scored another entire album for Harris, *The Yard Went On Forever*, also released by Dunhill in 1968, but it never sold well, although critics had called it more impressive than the first. A banner year continued for Jimmy as Glen Campbell released "Wichita Lineman," which went to #1 on the country charts, followed by another Campbell hit, "Galveston," in 1969.

In 1969, Webb scored the music for the films, *How Sweet It Is* and *Tell Them Willie Boy Is Here*, began work on a semi-autobiographical Broadway musical, *His Own Dark City*, and was composer-arranger for Thelma Houston's debut album, *Sunshower*.

In 1970, Jimmy decided to launch a solo concert tour kicked off in Los Angeles, as well to record a series of solo albums. His concert tour was largely unsuccessful because of his inexperience as a performer, but his albums were well received, although sales were not.

Jimmy's official debut album, *Words and Music*, included a tribute to P.F. Sloan, a neglected songwriter. It was followed in 1971 with *And So On*, which featured jazz musician Larry Coryell, in 1972 with *Letters*, highlighted by Jimmy's own version of "Galveston" and a cameo appearance by Joni Mitchell, in 1974 with *Land's End*, featuring Art Garfunkel on "Crying in My Sleep" and another cameo appearance from Joni Mitchell, and 1977 with *El Mirage*, produced, conducted, and arranged by George Martin of Beatles fame, and a track entitled "The Highwayman," a title popularized by the noted country group consisting of Johnny Cash, Willie Nelson, Kris Kristofferson, and Waylon Jennings.

The decade of the 1970s also saw Jimmy producing such albums as *The Supremes Produced and Arranged by Jimmy Webb* (1973), Glen Campbell's *Reunion* (1974), The Fifth Dimension's *Earthbound* (1975), Cher's *Stars* (1975), and Art Garfunkel's *Watermark* (1978).

In 1981, Webb moved to New York in hopes of breaking through on Broadway, a dream he never realized. During the 1980s, he scored the animated feature film, *The Last Unicorn*, as well as other film soundtracks such as *Doc*, *Voices*, and *Hanoi Hilton*. He also wrote music for television, including *Amazing Stories*, *Tales From the Crypt*, and *Faerie Tale Theater*. He released only one solo album during the decade, *Angel Heart* (1982), one of his weakest compilations.

In the 1990s, Webb released his highly acclaimed *Suspending Disbelief*, produced by Linda Ronstadt, one of his biggest fans, in 1993, and included his own version of David Crosby's "Too Young to Die." It was followed in 1996 by *Ten Easy Pieces*, a remake of several of his most classic songs accompanying himself on the piano. Two 1993 tribute concerts to Jimmy were held in New York, featuring Glen Campbell, David Crosby, Art Garfunkel, Brooklyn Bridge, Michael Feinstein, and Nanci Griffith. In 1998, Jimmy published his first book, *Tunesmith: Inside the Art of Songwriting*, acclaimed as the "finest book about songwriting of our time," by *Musician* magazine. In the late 1990s, Australia's Raven Records issued two albums, *Richard Harris: The Webb Sessions, 1968-69* and *Reunited*, a collection of Glen Campbell's recordings of Jimmy's songs. A multi-artist tribute to Webb, *Someone Left the Cake Out in the Rain*, was released by Debutante Records in 1999. It featured tracks by Glen Campbell, Linda Ronstadt, Four Tops, Judy Collins, and the Johnny Mann Singers.

Recent activities include his tribute to **Garth Brooks** at the ASCAP Golden Note Awards ceremony in Washington, DC, where he sang "By the Time I Get to Phoenix" and "MacArthur Park," featured vocalist on *An All-Star Tribute to Brian Wilson* DVD release on which he sings "In My Room" with Carly Simon and David Crosby and "Surf's Up" with Crosby and **Vince Gill**, performances at Mountain Stage in Charleston, West Virginia along with **Hank Card** and the Austin Lounge Lizards, a concert with Vince Gill in Oklahoma City, an overseas tour in Australia, and performance at the dedication of the new Capitol dome in Oklahoma City on November 16, 2002, during which he sang and played the piano for two of his memorable songs, "By the Time I Get to Phoenix" and "Wichita Lineman."

Awards and honors bestowed upon Jimmy are impressive, including ACM/Song of the Year for "Wichita Lineman" (1968), induction into the National Academy of Popular Music-Songwriter's Hall of Fame (1986), Nashville Songwriter's Hall of Fame (1990), National Academy of Songwriters-Lifetime Achievement Award (1993), Oklahoma Hall of Fame (1999), two of his songs included in the BMI list of Top 100 Songs of the Century ("By the Time I Get to Phoenix" and "Up, Up and Away"), election to Board of Directors of ASCAP, and recipient of the Johnny Mercer Award in 2003 at the Songwriters Hall of Fame. Also in 2003, Webb released a Jimmy Webb boxed set only available through his website, and planned to release an album with Michael Feinstein on Concord Records in October of that year. (GC)
www.jimmywebb.com

Welch, Kevin
(b. August 17, 1955)

One of the most prominent Americana/alternative country music songwriters and performers to hail from Oklahoma, Kevin Welch was born in Long Beach, California, but raised in Midwest City, Oklahoma, a suburb of Oklahoma City and home of Tinker Air Force Base. He moved throughout the U.S. during his early childhood as the family followed his father's job, but at age seven, finally settled in Oklahoma. Because of his extensive travels as a child, he claims to have learned to read by viewing billboards and highway signs. Following graduation from Midwest City High School, Kevin attended the University of Central

Oklahoma for one semester as a music major. During his time in Oklahoma, he met John Hadley, a songwriter for Tree International, who was an art instructor at the University of Oklahoma in Norman. Hadley criticized Kevin's guitar playing, which made Welch work harder in developing his picking talents. Early examples of his playing can be heard on Stillwater musician Chuck Dunlap's 1980 album, *Daze Gone By* (Snowbound).

After leaving UCO, Kevin traveled the nightclub and honky tonk circuit for five years in a van and a truck dubbed "Phyllis." During this time he first played with a band called New Rodeo and then joined Blue Rose Café, named after a popular restaurant in Tulsa, and including drummer Mike McCarty, keyboardist Gary Johnson, and bassist Steve Grundner.

After life on the road, he married Jennifer Patten and they moved in 1978 to Nashville, where he spent ten years as a staff writer for Sony Tree, and began raising a family of three children, Dustin, Savannah, and Ada. During that decade, he wrote or co-wrote songs for **Roger Miller** ("Everyone Gets Crazy Now and Then"), Ricky Skaggs ("Let It Be You"), Gary Morris ("Plain Brown Wrapper" and "Velvet Chains"), Carlene Carter ("Time's Up"), Moe Bandy ("Too Old to Die Young"), Trisha Yearwood ("That's What I Like About You"), **Garth Brooks** ("Pushing Up Daisies"), Jimmie Dale Gilmore ("Headed for a Fall"), Marie Osmond ("Steppin' Stone"), Randy Travis ("Heart of Hearts"), Del McCoury ("True Love Never Dies"), Charley Pride ("I Came Straight To You"), **Reba McEntire** ("Whoever's Watchin'" and "What Do You Know About a Heartache"), and Fairfield Four ("Life Down Here on Earth"). Other recording artists who used Welch's songs included Pam Tillis, Conway Twitty, The Highwaymen, T. Graham Brown, The Judds, Waylon Jennings, Patty Loveless, Don Williams, The Kendalls, and Sweethearts of the Rodeo. He is in great demand as a session musician and vocalist having performed with Carlene Carter, **Gail Davies**, **Ray Wylie Hubbard**, and **Kelly Willis** during the 1990s.

After playing the club circuit in Nashville with bands like The Roosters, which included Mike Henderson and Harry Stinson, Kevin formed his own band, The Overtones, in about 1988. Several of his colleagues at Tree, including Kieran Kane and Paul Worley, suggested Kevin pursue a recording contract with Warner Brothers/Reprise. His self-titled debut album was released in 1990. It yielded three minor country hits, "Stay November" "Till I See You Again," and "True Love Never Dies," as well as "The Mother Road," Kevin's tribute to Route 66. His second album, *Western Beat*, was released in 1992, also by Reprise. It was critically acclaimed, but produced no hits because mainstream country radio did not buy into Kevin's acoustic sound and Jack Kerouac-type lyrics. Kevin and Warner Brothers mutually agreed to release him.

In 1995, Kevin and cohorts Kieran Kane, Harry Stinson, Mike Henderson, and Tammy Rogers decided to form their own independent recording label they named Dead Reckoning Records. They released more than twenty records over the next seven years, as well as touring as a group called A Night of Reckoning throughout Europe, Canada, and the U.S. Kevin's first album on Dead Reckoning, *Life Down Here on Earth*, was released in 1995 to rave reviews by those who said he defined the new "Americana" sound. His second Dead Reckoning album, *Beneath My Wheels*, also was well received. A collaboration with the The Dead Reckoners, *A Night of Reckoning*, was released in 1997.

In 2000, Kevin and Kieran developed a two-person show (two guitars and two voices), and recorded a live album in Melbourne, Australia, titled *11/12/13: Live in Melbourne*. During the last two years, Kevin recorded *Millionaire*, an album featuring several of his friends from Denmark. It reached the Top 15 of the Americana charts in the summer of 2002. That same year, Welch launched an extensive overseas tour with performances in Sweden, Denmark, Australia, and Canada, although it was interrupted for his appearance at the annual **Woody Guthrie** Festival in Okemah in July. In 2003, Welch continued touring the world and the U.S., with occasional stops in Oklahoma for performances in Norman and Wiley Post Airfield in Oklahoma City. (GC)
www.kevinwelch.com

White, Bryan
(b. February 17, 1974)

One of Nashville's youngest stars to have two #1 hits from his first album, singer, songwriter, guitarist, and drummer, Bryan Shelton White was born in Lawton, Oklahoma, but raised in Oklahoma City, where he graduated from Putnam City West High School. Bryan was the oldest child (younger brother Daniel) of two professional musicians (Bud and Anita), while his great-grandmother was a popular square dance caller in Oklahoma. His grandfather, Wilford White, was an auctioneer, and gave Bryan some early advice: "You've got to have rhythm, a lot of endurance and a strong throat."

At an early age, Bryan began banging on pots and pans, and his parents bought him his first drum set when he was five. His mother directed him

toward country music at about age ten, when she took him to a show she opened for Loretta Lynn. After his parents divorced, Bryan was shuttled between homes, but both encouraged him to pursue music and allowed him to play drums with their respective music groups. While during a sound check, his mother heard him sing "Stand By Me," and she suggested he also try vocals with the drums. While in high school at Putnam West, he switched from drums to guitar, formed a trio, and began writing songs. He decided after high school, he would try his luck in Nashville. According to Bryan, "mowing lawns and fishing were the only two options I had besides music."

Thus, in 1992, after high school graduation, White headed to Nashville. For the first year, his parents had to wire money each month for him to survive. But he soon connected with Billy Joe Walker, Jr., a friend of the family who was a session musician in Music City. Over the next two years, Walker helped Bryan refine his act and assisted him in landing a position as a demo singer, as well as a staff songwriter's job and artist management deal with Glen Campbell Music and GC Management. This relationship eventually resulted in Bryan meeting Kyle Lehning, who had worked with Randy Travis and Dan Seals. Lehning was president of Asylum Records, which signed Bryan to a contract in 1993, with Walker producing his first two singles, "Eugene You Genius" and "Look at Me Now," both of which made Top 40.

Bryan's management team outlined a performance schedule that included opening for such stars as Pam Tillis, Tracy Lawrence, and Diamond Rio. He did not have a backup band, it was just he and his acoustic guitar. He performed some 200 concerts across the U.S. and Canada. Later, he hired members of Pearl River for his band.

His debut album, *Bryan White*, crafted by Lehning and Walker, was released in 1994, and two #1 hit singles ensued, "Someone Else's Star" and "Rebecca Lynn." The eponymous album eventually went platinum, and CMT's poll named him Rising Video Star of the Year. Bryan continued to co-write songs for other artists, including the Top 5 "I Don't Believe in Goodbye" for Sawyer Brown and "Imagine That" for Diamond Rio.

In early 1996 White completed his second album for Asylum, *Between Now and Forever*, which included four songs he had co-written, "Blindhearted," "So Much for Pretending," "On Any Given Night," and the title track. From this album, "I'm Not Supposed to Love You Anymore" and "So Much for Pretending" became his third and fourth #1 hits.

Honors for White include the ACM's Top New Male Vocalist for 1995, followed by the CMA's Horizon Award and Best New Touring Artist for 1996, the *TNN/Music City News* Male Star of Tomorrow Award in 1996, "Up and Coming Artist" for the 1998 Viewpoint Award, and nominations for Male Vocalist of the Year by the CMA in 1996 and 1997.

Following the Oklahoma City bombing in April of 1995, Bryan returned home for a benefit concert to raise scholarship money for children injured or orphaned in the blast, and helped raise funds for the Oklahoma City Bombing Memorial. In 2001, Bryan and Patty Loveless were among several stars to perform for the grand opening of the newly-renovated Oklahoma City Civic Center. He has also participated in benefit concerts for Cerebral Palsy, Cystic Fibrosis Foundation, Native American Clothing Drive, "Country Cares", Boys and Girls Clubs of America, Buddies of Nashville, and St. Jude Children's Research Hospital.

White's recorded output for 1996 included his version of "When You Wish Upon a Star," from the animated Disney film *Pinocchio*, for the *Disney Country* album. In 1997, Bryan released his third album, *The Right Place*, which included "Love Is the Right Place," "Leave My Heart Out of This," "Bad Day to Let You Go," and "One Small Miracle," the latter penned by his good friend, Steve Wariner. He opened for **Vince Gill** on a highly successful tour the same year. Two years later, Bryan recorded the *How Lucky I Am* album, and released his first seasonal album, *Dreaming of Christmas*.

Bryan is in great demand as a backup vocalist and instrumentalist as he has sung vocals on albums for LeAnn Rimes, Lila McCann, Shania Twain, and was a guest drummer on Steve Wariner's *No More Mr. Nice Guy* album.

In 2000, Elektra Records put together four of Bryan's #1 hits and several other Top 20 hits for his *Greatest Hits* album. Also in 2000, he married actress Erika Page, who stars on the television soap opera *One Life to Live*.

Bryan's latest recording project is *Traveling Light: Songs From the 23rd Psalm*, released in 2002 by the Creative Trust Workshop label. It features Bryan and several other CCM, pop, and country artists, such as Amy Grant. His last appearances in Oklahoma were at the Bricktown Ampitheatre in Oklahoma City in June of 2002, and for the dedication of the new Capitol dome in Oklahoma City on November 16, 2002. Looking to change his direction from country teen idol to a more mature artist, Bryan states on his website: "I want to keep making positive music that not only inspires me, but everyone else out there to have hope in what they want to strive for. I want it to be a real light to them and a good influence, to encourage them all I can." (GC)
www.bryanwhite.com

Wiley and Gene

Wiley Walker (b. November 17, 1911 – d. May 17, 1966)
Gene Sullivan (b. November 16, 1914 – d. October 24, 1984)

One of the most successful duets in the 1930s and 1940s and co-writers of two country music classics, "Live and Let Live" and "When My Blue Moon Turns to Gold Again," Winston Lee Moore (Wiley's birth name) was born in Laurel Hill, Florida, while Gene Sullivan was born in Carbon Hill, Alabama. Although born outside of Oklahoma and spent several years of their career in Louisiana and

Texas, Wiley and Gene spent some of their most productive years in Oklahoma from 1941 on when they joined radio station KWXX. Wiley and Gene teamed as a duet in 1939 in Dallas.

After their move to Oklahoma, Wiley and Gene wrote and recorded "Live and Let Live" and "When My Blue Moon Turns to Gold Again" in 1941. Neither song was successful as a record at the outset, but was frequently requested on their radio program. In 1943, Zeke Manners recorded "When My Blue Moon Turns to Gold Again" and it became a hit. Wiley and Gene's record was reissued on a more successful basis. Others who recorded the song were Elvis Presley, who had the biggest hit with it in 1956, Slim Whitman, Cindy Walker, Eddy Arnold, Cliffie Stone, Jim and Jesse, Jerry Lee Lewis, Bashful Brother Oswald, Red Allen and Frank Wakefield, Clarence "Gatemouth" Brown, Bill Monroe, **Leon Russell** and the Newgrass Revival, Tex Ritter, Foy Willing and the Riders of the Purple Sage, and **Merle Haggard**.

Jimmie Davis, Carl Smith, Johnny and Jack, Joe Val and the New England Bluegrass Boys, and Hank Williams, Sr. recorded "Live and Let Live," while another one of their songs, "I Want to Live and Love," became Rose Maddox' theme song. Additional songs they co-wrote were "I Might Have Known," "Kansas City Blues," "Teardrop Waltz," and "Make Room in Your Heart For a Friend." Because of their achievements in songwriting, Wiley and Gene were inducted into the Nashville Songwriters Hall of Fame in 1971.

In the late 1940s, Wiley and Gene entered the new medium of television. For years, they hosted the *Oklahoma Jamboree* on KOCO-TV in Oklahoma City that featured local bands, such as the Bluestem Boys, a bluegrass group that included Bill Caswell, **Byron Berline**, Frank Deramus, and Gary Price. Television gave them an opportunity to expand their talents for comedy and dancing as Wiley was a buck dancer and fiddler and Gene liked to recite humorous poetry, such as "Sleeping at the Foot of the Bed,' which became a popular recording for Little Jimmy Dickens, and "Wash Your Feet Before You Go to Bed."

In 1946, Wiley and Gene recorded for Columbia, "Make Room in Your Heart For a Friend," which reached #3 on the country charts, and was selected for the *Anthology of Country Music, Volume 2: Early Country Harmony 1940's*. By the early 1950s, Wiley and Gene began to fade from prominence on the music scene, but Gene had one more recording that achieved notoriety, "Please Pass the Biscuits," a 1957 novelty song with recitation that cracked the Top 10. He had originally cut a demo of it for Little Jimmy Dickens, however, Columbia Records like Gene's version best.

Wiley and Gene continued to make occasional public appearances in the early 1960s, until Wiley's death in 1966. In addition to his performance career, Gene owned Sullivan's Recording Studio in Oklahoma City where many Tulsa Sound musicians recorded in the 1950s and 1960s, and also operated a music store in Oklahoma City during the 1970s. In 1988, Old Homestead Records released a 24-track album entitled *Radio Favorites*, including all the Wiley and Gene favorites plus several not previously mentioned songs, such as "After I'm Gone," "Don't That Moon Look Lonesome," and "Take Away Those Blues From My Heart." (GC)

Wiley, Lee
(b. October 9, 1915 - d. December 11, 1975)

One of the first jazz singers to organize a set of songs around a common composer or theme known later as the songbook or concept album, as well as one of the first women jazz composers, vocalist and songwriter, Lee Wiley was born in Fort Gibson, Oklahoma, a community of approximately 3,000 residents northeast of Muskogee. She had three siblings, including two brothers (Ted and Floyd) and one sister (Pearl). One of her ancestors, Worcester Willey was a missionary to the Cherokee Indians, and helped found Dwight Mission near Fort Gibson. Believed to have been of Cherokee heritage, she began her jazz career as a run away from home teenager in Tulsa, where she studied music (heavily influenced by the "race" records of Mildred Bailey and Ethel Waters) and sang on local radio. Sometime during her teenage years, Lee's singing career was briefly interrupted when she was temporarily blinded due to a fall while horseback riding.

When Lee was about fifteen, she migrated to New York City and sang on the Paramount Show. By seventeen, she joined the Leo Reisman Orchestra at the Central Park Casino, and remained with Reisman until 1933, during which she made one of her first recordings, "Time on My Hands." Wiley's career peaked in the mid-1930s when she launched a successful radio series on CBS titled *Saturday Night Swing*. From 1936-38, she was the star vocalist. Sometime during her early jazz career, Lee dropped the second "l" in Willey because she thought her original last name sounded unprofessional for a jazz singer.

Lee also began recording her own sides for the Kapp label, backed by the Casa Loma Orchestra and the Dorsey Brothers. Married to swing pianist Jess Stacy from 1943 to 1948, Wiley was vocalist for Stacy's big band jazz ensemble. In addition to Stacy, she was vocalist for several other big bands, including Eddie Condon and Paul Whiteman. Lee also worked with several small combos, including those led by Bud Freeman, Max Kaminsky, Fats Waller, and Bobby Hackett.

During the 1940s, Lee appeared at several New York City jazz clubs, such as Kelly's, Hickory House, Famous Door, and the Stable, and performed a Town Hall concert organized by Condon. In 1947, Lee recorded a duet with Bing Crosby, "It Still Suits Me," reportedly completed in one take. According to Harold Arlen, her manager, "Lee was a divine-looking girl. She was beautiful in a very unsophisticated way and yet she was a very sophisticated singer."

Lee was an exceptional interpreter of such songs as "I've Got a Crush on You," "How Long Has This Been Going On?" "Baby's Awake Now," and "You Took Advantage of Me," primarily with Waller, Freeman, and Condon. Collaborating with composer and arranger Victor Young, she is noted for co-composing as lyricist such hits as "Got the South in My Soul," "Eerie Moan," and "Anytime, Anyday, Anywhere," the latter becoming an R & B hit in the 1950s for Joe Morris and Laurie Tate. With more than fifty recordings to her credit, Wiley was the first jazz vocalist to record albums devoted to one composer's works, including Irving Berlin, Cole Porter, Vincent Youmans, Rodgers & Hart, Harold Arlen, and George Gershwin. Cited in more than forty jazz publications, Wiley was featured in a 1963 television drama based on her life *Something About Lee Wiley*, starring Piper Laurie.

Lee signed with Columbia Records in 1950, recording *Night in Manhattan* with Joe Bushkin and Bobby Hackett and *Lee Wiley Sings Irving Berlin* (1951), her first concept album. She made her television debut in 1951 on the *Once Upon a Tune* show, and later appeared on the *Tonight* show hosted by Steve Allen.

In 1952, Wiley performed a live concert at Carnegie Hall that was recorded on the Audophile label. After recording her Rodgers & Hart album with Storyville in 1954, she moved to RCA Victor where she recorded *West of the Moon* (1956) and *A Touch of the Blues* (1957). The most notable of the two, *West of the Moon*, featured Lee's versions of "Can't Get Out of This Mood," "East of the Sun," and "Who Can I Turn to Now," backed by such fine instrumentalists as trumpeter Billy Butterfield and trombonist Urbie Green.

Lee retired in 1958 after becoming disenchanted with the music business. Her final studio recording in 1971 was *Back Home Again*, but by this time Lee's voice was no longer in its prime and she continued to bemoan the fact she was not a commercial success. She was persuaded by Condon and George Wein, festival organizer, to make a farewell performance at the first Newport in New York Jazz Festival in 1972, and died in New York three years later at the age of sixty-seven from colon cancer.

Several of Lee's recordings have been released in CD format, including *Back Home Again* (1995) and *Lee Wiley at Carnegie Hall-1972* (1996), both on Audiophile, *Hot House Rose* (1996) on Pearl, *Rarities: Thinking of You* (1997) on Jazz Classics, *Lee Wiley: Complete Fifties Studio Masters* (2-CD set) and *Lee Wiley: Manhattan Moods* (2-CD set), both from the Jazz Factory label, *Legendary Lee Wiley* (1999) on Baldwin Street Music, and *Lee Wiley: Manhattan Nights-The Complete Golden Years Studio Sessions* (4-CD set with 92 tracks) available from Collectors Choice distributors.

Wiley was inducted into the Oklahoma Jazz Hall of Fame in 2000 and Oklahoma Music Hall of Fame in 2003. She is survived by a brother in California and a niece in Fort Gibson, and she is buried in Fort Gibson where the family home remains standing. A Lee Wiley documentary by a Japanese filmmaker, part of which was shot in Muskogee and Fort Gibson, was also scheduled for release in 2003. (GC)

Williams, Claude "Fiddler"
(b. February 22, 1908)

Known as one of "the" primary jazz fiddlers in a career that spans nearly the entire history of jazz, Claude "Fiddler" Williams suffered early professional setbacks, such as being replaced by John Hammond in the Count Basie Orchestra on the eve of that band's national success in 1937, but has outlived all of his detractors to enjoy status as one of the premier jazz violinists of the twentieth — and now – twenty-first century. He continues performing and recording actively as of 2003, and well-deserved attention, slowly forthcoming during most of the twentieth century, has mounted impressively in the last few years for this important

musician who is the primary living proponent of the jazz string band tradition. Born in Muskogee, the same jazz hotbed that produced **Jay McShann**, **Don Byas**, and **Barney Kessel**, Williams grew up in a house surrounded by music. He learned piano by ear through playing with his older brother, and at ten, he began playing mandolin and bass with his brother-in-law's string band in the hotels and barber shops in Muskogee and surrounding towns. The group played ragtime standards, blues, and occasional Western songs like "Wagoner" and "Red Wing." Of course, these ingredients form a large part of jazz's nucleus.

Williams switched to violin upon hearing a Joe Venuti concert in Muskogee, and Venuti is often cited as making a giant impression on Williams. An interesting aspect about the concert that is usually left untold in Williams' multitude of interviews about his life is that because he was African-American, he and his family were not allowed into the park where Venuti played. Williams heard the music over and above the bushes, without amplification, which convinced him he wanted to play the ubiquitous instrument of the 19th century American west.

After apprenticing with his brother-in-law's string band, and other traveling groups who would come through town and pick him up for area engagements, Williams played with the Pettiford Family Band, although the great bassist Oscar Pettiford was only an infant at the time, and went on the road with a traveling variety show called Kid Thomas and His Jazz Babies. By the time he was nineteen, in 1927, Williams joined Torrence (sometimes spelled Terrence) "T" Holder's territory band in Muskogee, which became the Clouds of Joy under the leadership of Andy Kirk when "T" Holder ran into money troubles. The Clouds of Joy were one of the leading territory bands of the area, playing in Kansas City in 1929 and recording for the Brunswick label, on which Williams appears on fiddle. After recording, the group began touring the East Coast. Although he played banjo and violin in the Clouds of Joy all the way to New York's Roseland Ballroom and Harlem's Savoy Theater, Kirk wanted Williams to focus more on guitar, which Williams did not want to do. So, when Williams hurt his leg during a string of one-night stands, Kirk left Williams behind, calling Williams' wife to let her know where to send for him. Those years are preserved on two albums, *The Territories, Vol. 1* (Arcadia) and *Loose Ankles* (Brunswick).

Back in Kansas City, Williams worked with Alphonso Trent in 1932 and moved to Chicago where he played fiddle with bassist Eddie Cole, whose brother, Nat, was featured on piano. Williams left the group when jobs started to slow down with the Cole brothers. After leaving the Coles, Williams went back to Chicago where Count Basie sent for him to join that orchestra in 1936. Williams only played on one recording session for Basie in 1937, before John Hammond replaced him with Freddie Green, who would stay with Basie for fifty years. Although different accounts exist as to why Williams was replaced, the end result was the same and Claude moved on. Williams does speak for himself musically on MCA's three-CD late-'30s Basie collection, *The Original MCA Recordings*, as well as *The Count at the Chatterbox: 1937* (Jazz Archives), and *Count Basie: The Complete Decca Recordings 1937-1939* (GRP).

After being released from the Basie orchestra, Williams returned to Kansas City where he started a string band that was a fairly successful live draw, but did not record, so he moved to Flint, Michigan where he stayed until being called up for service during World War II. Afterwards, Williams worked as a guitarist in a WPA band in Michigan, and with The Four Shades of Rhythm in Chicago. In 1951 and 1952, he was a member of the Los Angeles-based R & B band led by Oklahoman **Roy Milton**, then moved back to Kansas City where he had his own combos, one of which featured saxophonist Eddie "Cleanhead" Vinson. From the mid 1950s through the 1960s, Claude toiled in relative obscurity, leading groups in Denver and Las Vegas before returning to Kansas City in 1969. Williams returned to the spotlight when he started playing with Jay McShann in the early 1970s, and was featured prominently on McShann's *The Man from Muskogee* (1972).

While Williams seems to have fought an uphill battle throughout the early and mid-twentieth century to keep his fiddle in the jazz mix, his playing became appreciated more and more throughout the 1970s and 1980s because of his obvious connection to the string band tradition and territory bands, which made him a historic, if not romantic, figure. During that period, he performed at numerous major festivals in the United States and overseas, and began recording again. Steeplechase Records released *Call for the Fiddler* (1976), Classic Jazz released *Fiddler's Dream* (1977), and in 1980, Big Bear Records released *Claude Willliams' Kansas City Giants*. Showing his stylistic range and further demonstrating the multi-musical influences of his Oklahoma background, in 1982 Williams was featured with the **Johnnie Lee Wills** Western swing band at the Smithsonian Folklife Festival in Washington, D.C. Subsequently, Claude played in the Broadway production of *Black and Blue*, along with continuing a constant schedule of touring, performing and recording. He surfaced again on two highly acclaimed discs recorded in New York, *Live at J's Volume 1* and *Volume 2* (Arhoolie, 1989), the same year he was inducted into the Oklahoma Jazz Hall of Fame.

Since 1990, Williams has received more critical attention than he has in his entire life. Williams has been featured on the network television program *CBS News Sunday Morning*, played Carnegie Hall twice, and opened Lincoln Center's *Kansas City Swing and Shout* event with his trio. Williams performed for President Clinton's first inaugural, and toured Australia. The two previously mentioned CDs, *Claude Williams, Live at J's, Volumes 1 & 2*, landed on the Best of 1994 jazz critics' polls in the *Village Voice* and *Pulse!* In 1994 and 1995, his live recordings aired on NPR's *Jazz Set* and he toured twenty-three cities headlining a *Masters of the Folk Violin* tour. In 1994, he earned the first and only **Charlie Christian** Jazz Award from Black Liberated Arts Incorporated in Oklahoma City. Also in 1994, he recorded a highly lauded session released as *Swingtime in New York* on Progressive Records in 1995.

Williams' successes and accolades continued in 1997. He celebrated his 89th birthday in Washington D. C. educating and entertaining students at the Smithsonian by day, and playing with a trio at night to great reviews in the *Washington Post*. Along with his successes around the U. S. and abroad, his home town honored Claude Williams in 1997 by making him one of the first inductees into the newly formed Oklahoma Music Hall of Fame in Muskogee, Oklahoma. Williams was inducted with three other giants of American music, whose roots are in Oklahoma: **Woody Guthrie**, **Patti Page**, and **Merle Haggard**. In 1998, Williams performed at the White House, the recording of which was subsequently featured in a PBS special. In 1999, Williams was the first installment in *Down Beat's* First Person Project, which plans to round up jazz's elder statesmen for a history of the music in their own words. Although only two pages with two photographs, the article signaled the permanent return and historical significance for the man who was written out of jazz history in 1937 when he was given his notice to leave the Count Basie Orchestra. By the end of 1999, the then-91-year-old, toured consistently, stopping at Oklahoma State University on September 16 for a day in classes with students and a concert that night at the Seretean Center.

Critically lauded by *The New York Times* and the *Los Angeles Times*, Claude Williams has come to be one of a handful of contemporary jazz violin masters. Oscar-nominee Mark O'Connor has said there is no doubt Williams is one of the great, original musicians of the twentieth century. For the yearning, sweet sound of Claude Williams' fiddle, listen to his composition "Fiddler's Dream" on *Claude Williams Live at J's Part 2*. The first notes he strikes are long, mournful blue notes. Then, Williams proceeds to establish the head riff, or the guiding theme of the tune, before cascading through improvisations on the blues, which ultimately adds up to jazz. Claude exemplifies many elements of the 19th and 20th century African-American musical tradition with his playing — the haunting and sad melodies of the blues, as well as the spritely nature of the early 20th century string bands that mirrored the evolution of dixieland, and, finally, the harmonic improvisations on a blues theme which is at the foundation of jazz. The violin is not often thought of as a contemporary jazz instrument outside of the legendary Stephane Grappelli or Joe Venuti, however, Claude Williams may be solely responsible for raising the consciousness of it at the end of the twentieth century, and establishing it as a fixture in the twenty-first. His resurrection of the early string band style, of which he has been a player since he was 10-years-old in Muskogee, is testament both to his tremendous abilities and the hotbed of jazz from which he came in Muskogee, Oklahoma. As of 2003, the ninety-five-year-old fiddler was still playing gigs in Kansas City and around the country. (HF)

The Willis Brothers

Willis, James Ylisis "Guy"
(b. July 5, 1915 – d. April 13, 1981)
Willis, Charles Ray "Skeeter"
(b. December 20, 1917 – d. March 5, 1976)
Willis, John Victor "Vic"
(b. May 31, 1922 – d. January 15, 1995)

Known variously as the Oklahoma Wranglers and the Willis Brothers, these multi-instrumentalists were long-time country music stars in the middle of the 20th century, famous for a blend of Western swing, old-time country, cowboy songs, and several tunes about the open road as a truck driver. Their truck driving songs are still a common sight in truck stop budget display cassette and CD cases throughout the United States. The Willis family moved from Alex, Arkansas, where Guy was born, to Coalton, Oklahoma, where Skeeter was born, and finally landed for good in Schulter, Oklahoma, a small town just south of Okmulgee, where "Vic" was born. Trained informally on front porch family singings, all three brothers sang and played various instruments. Their first gig as the Oklahoma Wranglers occurred at KGEF radio in Shawnee, Oklahoma in 1932, and they continued appearing on various radio programs throughout Oklahoma, to include KTUL, Tulsa in 1933 and 1934, and in Gallup, New Mexico in 1935.

In 1940, the brothers moved to Kansas City where they appeared KITE radio, and then on the KMBC weekly radio program, *Brush Street Follies*, before calling it quits due to World War II. They reunited in 1946, moved to Nashville and joined the Grand Ole Opry. Signed to Sterling Records, they recorded four songs one December morning as the Oklahoma Wranglers, and took a lunch break. On returning, they were assigned a backing job for a young hillbilly singer named Hank Williams, and the group became the Country Boys for a session when they recorded eight original songs with Williams, including several sacred, gospel flavored songs, "Calling You," "Wealth Won't Save Your Soul," and "When God Comes and Gathers His Jewels." Additionally, the brothers and Williams recorded four secular songs, the immortal "Honky Tonkin'", and a couple of darker tunes, "I Don't Care (If Tomorrow Never Comes)" and "My Love For You (Has Turned to Hate)." Had the Willis Brothers not done anything else they would still be forever ensconced in the history of American country music via Hank Williams' initial recording session.

The brothers left the Grand Ole Opry in 1949, and toured with Eddy Arnold as his band from 1949 to 1953, appearing in two films with Arnold, *Feuding Rhythm* (1949) and *Hoe Down* (1950). It was Arnold who suggested they change their name to avoid being typecast as only a Western group. Already having recorded in 1948 for MCA and Sterling, the Willis Brothers recorded for RCA in 1950, and Coral in 1954, before moving to Starday where they had major chart successes.

After becoming members of the *Ozark Jubilee* in Springfield, Missouri in 1953, the brothers toured the U.S. extensively and were in high demand as session players. In 1956, they joined the *Midwestern Hayride* television program, and over the next several years enjoyed television stints in Chattanooga, Tennessee and Birmingham, Alabama before rejoining the Grand Ole Opry in 1960 where they remained as regulars until Guy's death in 1981. While Guy wrote most of the songs, such as "I Miss My Old Oklahoma," "My Pillow Talk," and "Drive My Blues Away," the group did not enjoy commercial success until their 1964 Top Ten hit, "Give Me 40 Acres (To Turn This Rig Around)," landed them on the country charts. That began a long series of recordings in which they chronicled the ups and downs of being a truck driver, to include "The Only Shoulder (A Trucker Can Cry On)," "Diesel Drivin' Donut Dunkin' Dan," "Diesel Smoke on Danger Road," and "Soft Shoulders and Dangerous Curves."

The Willis Brothers charted again with a novelty tune in 1965, "A Six Foot Two-by-Four," and revisited the country charts only two more times with "Bob" and "Somebody Knows My Dog," both in 1967. Highlight albums include *Code of the West* (Starday, 1963), *Road Stops – Juke Box Hits* (Starday, 1965), *The Willis Brothers Goin' to Town* (Starday, 1967), and *The Best of the Willis Brothers* (Starday, 1975). Not only were the Willis Brothers known for their instrumental prowess, they could all sing well, which endeared them to fans through the U.S., as well as Europe and Central America where they performed on USO tours. Skeeter died in 1976 from Lymphoma, and Guy and Vic continued as a duo. Guy died in 1981, and Vic became Secretary/Treasurer of the American Federation of Musicians, AFM Local 257, in Nashville. He was killed when his car went out of control late at night on a Mississippi highway in 1995. The group's recordings with Hank Williams resurfaced in 1998 on *The Complete Hank Williams* boxed set, and in 1999, First Generation Records released a self-titled album by the Vic

Willis Trio, although it offered none of the originality, humor, nor traditional country music quality of the early material. (HF)

Willis, Kelly
(b. October 1, 1968)

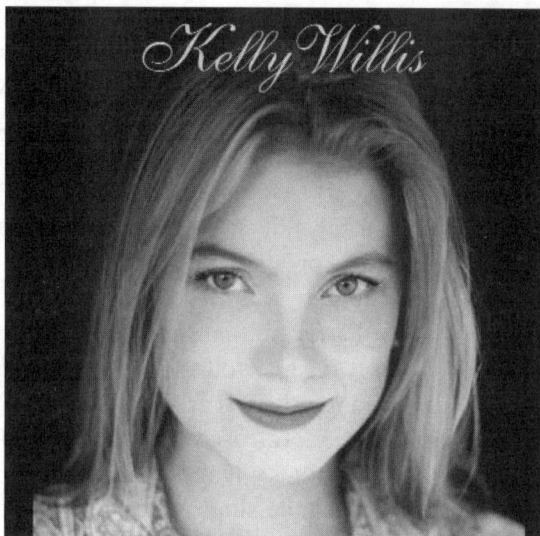

One of the rising stars on the Austin neo-traditionalist country music scene, singer and songwriter Kelly Willis was born in Lawton, Oklahoma, the third largest city in the state and home of Fort Sill military base where her father, a career Army officer, was stationed. As the youngest of three children, she was raised primarily in Virginia and North Carolina, especially in the Washington, D.C. area, but some of her family was from Sentinel, a very small town in southwestern Oklahoma, and she spent many holidays and summer breaks there. According to a *Washington Post* online chat in which she participated in 2003, she considers herself an Okie. While Kelly was a child, her mother was involved in musicals and that influence may have affected her interest in singing. Her singing idols as a child were the likes of **Wanda Jackson** and Patsy Cline. As a teenager Kelly entered a pay recording booth and sang "Teddy Bear," one of Elvis Presley's hits. Using this demo tape at age sixteen, she convinced her boyfriend (and future husband) percussionist Max Polermo to join his rockabilly band.

Kelly's powerhouse vocals attracted a large following in the D.C. area, and Polermo's band renamed itself to Kelly and the Fireballs in 1987. Following Kelly's graduation from high school, the band headed to Austin, Texas, where they dissolved shortly thereafter. Kelly and Palermo launched a new group, Radio Ranch, consisting of Kelly on vocals and rhythm guitar, Polermo on drums, Michael Hardwick on steel guitar, Michael Foreman on bass, and David Murray on lead guitar. The band received great reviews at the 1989 Austin South By Southwest Music Festival. While playing the Austin live music circuit, Kelly was noticed at the Continental Club by singer Nanci Griffith, one of the mainstays of the Austin music scene. Griffith contacted MCA producer Tony Brown, who had signed Griffith, Lyle Lovett, and Steve Earle. Shortly thereafter, a record deal was consummated that resulted in Kelly's debut album, *Well Traveled Love*, released in 1990. The album received critical acclaim, but fared poorly on radio airplay.

In 1991 Kelly recorded her second album, *Bang Bang*, the title track taken from an obscure song from rockabilly artist Janis Martin. Her sophomore album was also not well received by the buying public, but, by this time, she was the opening act for Dwight Yoakum and honing her considerate abilities. A third effort for MCA, a 1993 self-titled production that included the majority of tracks penned by Kelly and performed without a band. One of the highlights of the release was a duet with another Oklahoman, **Kevin Welch**, on "That'll Be Me." The album also failed to generate any improvement in sales over the previous recordings. Thus, MCA dropped Kelly from their roster shortly after its release.

During the early 1990s, Willis contributed songs to the soundtracks of the films *Thelma & Louise* ("I Don't Want to Love You But I Do") and *Boys*, appeared as Clarissa Flan, a folksinger, in Tim Robbins' satirical film *Bob Roberts*, and was featured on television's *P.S. I Love You* program with Dwight Yoakum. Following a couple of inactive years in recording, Kelly resurfaced in 1995 duetting with Son Volt's Jay Farrar on the *Red Hot & Bothered* compilation. A year later, she released *Fading Fast*, a four song EP, on A&M Records. She married fellow Austin singer/songwriter Bruce Robison in 1996, following a divorce from her first husband. Her EP release was followed by *Wrapped*, a 1997 production on the independent label Lucky Dog, and the same year, she joined Sarah McLachlan, Jewel, and other female singers in the Lilith Fair concert tour.

In 1998 Kelly switched labels and recorded for Rykodisc, *What I Deserve*, a 1999 thirteen track album featuring several of her own songs with a portion of the album's sales going to the National Coalition Against Domestic Violence. The album continued to elevate her status as a premier songwriter. She has also now written or co-written (several with Robison) such songs as "Baby Take a Piece of My Heart," a crowd favorite at such Austin venues as the Cactus Club, "Shadows of Love," "World Without You," "Not Long for This World," "Happy With That," "Take Me Down," "What I Desire," "Talk Like That," and "Fading Fast." She took some time off after the 1998 album because of the birth of Kelly and Bruce's first child in 2001, a son they named Deral Otis.

Kelly is featured on the tribute album to Johnny Cash, *Dressed in Black*, released in 2002 on the Dualtone label, and in the summer of 2002 released her latest recording, *Easy*, a ten track album which she co-produced on the Ryko label. Seven of the ten tracks were written or co-written by Kelly, including "Not What I Had in Mind," "If I Left You," "Easy (As Falling Apart)," and "Reason to Believe." The latter cut is dedicated to Deral Otis, her two-year-old son, and spawned a conversational CD titled *Reason to Believe* in 2002. Backgrounds vocals on the *Easy* CD are provided by **Vince Gill**, Alison Krauss, Dan Tyminski, and Robison (her husband). The *Easy* album reached #1 on the Americana Roots chart in the summer of 2002. Kelly's "If I Left You" video reached #2 on the CMT Most Wanted Live's Great Eight in the fall of 2002.

Kelly's 2002 tour included stops in Oregon, Washington, Michigan, Minnesota, West Virginia, and Illinois, where she performed at the Old Town School of Folk Music in Chicago, The Mountain Stage in Charleston, West Virginia, and the

Village Underground in New York City. She also was one of the headliners at the National Americana Festival in Nashville in September of 2002, and also hosted the VH1 tribute to country music in that year. In 2003, the Dwight Yoakam box set, *Reprise Please Baby: The Warner Bros. Years*, contained two previously unreleased duets with Kelly, and she performed a few shows in Texas in the summer of 2003. According to her website, she has taken time off the last couple of years to devote her attention to being a new mother, and lives with her son and husband, Bruce Robison, in Texas. (GC/HF)
www.kellywillis.com

Bob Wills
(b. March 6, 1905 – d. May 13, 1975)
Johnnie Lee Wills
(b. September 2, 1912 – d. October 25, 1984)
Luke Wills
(b. September 20, 1920 – d. October 21, 2000)
Billy Jack Wills
(b. February 26, 1926 – d. March 6, 1991)

Luke, Johnnie Lee, Bob, and Billy Jack

Emerging from the East Texas fiddle and string bands of the 1920s, but gaining their fame in Oklahoma through daily broadcasts on KVOO-Tulsa from 1934 to 1958, Bob Wills and his Texas Playboys, as well the bands of his brothers, Johnnie Lee, and to a lesser extent Billy Jack and Luke, popularized the hybrid country music offshoot, Western swing, in the 1930s and 1940s. Johnnie Lee began leading the radio program in 1942 when Bob left Tulsa for opportunities in film, and it was Johnnie Lee who led the primary Tulsa band on-air until 1958 and until 1964 from his Tulsa base. As a result of the KVOO broadcasts and countless shows within a day's or weekend's drive of Tulsa, along with subsequent recordings that became very popular, the Wills brothers became synonymous with the music that was a direct product of the multi-ethnic population of the southwestern United States, particularly Oklahoma and Texas.

An improvisationally based form, Western swing is the country musician's way of playing jazz. The music turns where it needs to go to fit the audience, shapeshifting square dances into blues, old time fiddle reels into jazz, and mariachi, polkas, and waltzes into danceable pop. With a beat and a riffing horn section influenced by the big band movement of the 1930s, a western sound via steel guitar, and the country comfort of old time fiddles, the Wills bands featured dexterous virtuosos improvising on electric guitar and smooth vocalists to rival any crooner of the swing era. As Western swing guitarist Don Tolle explained in a 2002 interview, the essence of Western swing is related to jazz, and to play it a musician wants to "get as far out as you can, improvising as far away from the melody as possible while staying within the chord structure of the song." Add Bob, a cigar-smoking, charismatic leader, bantering with the band as they played, and urging them on with his "Ah-ha's," and the Wills' brand of cowboy jazz bounded into the grateful ears of Oklahomans being smacked daily by the Depression era.

While Milton Brown, **Spade Cooley**, and Hoyle Nix had bands that may have been equal to the Wills groups in musical caliber, Bob's added gimmicks and reputation as a great bandleader catapulted him and the music to immense popularity. Granted, Western swing surfaced first in Fort Worth, Texas, but the style leapt to the national stage from Tulsa via the clear channel mega-wattage of KVOO. Along with providing the Wills with both a significant live and radio audience, Oklahoma also contributed to Bob and Johnnie Lee's excellent crew of musicians with notables such as Eldon Shamblin (b. April 24, 1916, Weatherford, OK – d. August 5, 1998), Tommy Perkins (r. Oklahoma City – d. June 7, 2003, Oklahoma), Julian "Curly" Lewis (b. Stigler, 1924), Glen "Blub" Rhees (b. Oilton, July 28, 1924 – d. March 28, 1996), "Famous" Amos Headrick (b. Van Buren, AR), Clarence Cagle (b. April 19, 1920, Oklahoma City), Noel Boggs (b. November 14, 1917, Oklahoma City – d. August 31, 1974, California), Tommy Elliot (Ponca City), Jack Rider (Stillwell), **Benny Garcia** (b. March 20, 1926, Oklahoma City), Millard Kelso (b. Cleveland, OK), Keith Coleman (b. Chickasha?), Gene Crownover (b. Cromwell), Don Tolle (b. April 24, 1924, Rushville, IL, reared near Shidler, OK – d. December 5, 2002, Cushing, OK), Robert "Zeb" McNally (Tulsa), Art Haines (Oklahoma City), Gene and Lester "Junior" Bernard (Leonard), William "Smoky" Dacus (Quinton), James Guy "Cotton" Thompson (b. Tulsa – d. June 8, 1953, Muskogee), Buster Magnus

(Tulsa), Gene Crownover (Muskogee), Charles and Ted Adams (Tulsa), Bob and Glen Morris (Tulsa), Tommy Dee (b. April 6, 1928, Wetumka, OK), Jay and Ray DeGeer (Oilton), Ramona Reed (b. November 16, 1930, Talihina), and **Tommy Allsup** (b. November 24, 1931, Owasso).

The often-told Wills story begins with Bob (born James Robert), the eldest of ten children descended from fiddle players on both sides of John Wills' and Emma (Foley) Wills' families. As a child in the east Texas cotton fields near Kosse, about 40 miles southeast of Waco, the inherent musical multiplicity of that area filled Bob's ears: the old time fiddle tunes, reels, and square dances of his family, the field hollers, work songs, and country blues of the African-American cotton pickers, the omnipresent black and white church music traditions, as well as the various styles of dance music styles brought in by Mexican, Czechs, and Germans immigrants. In 1913, the family moved to a farm between Turkey and Memphis in the Texas panhandle, about seventy five miles from the Oklahoma border, where Bob started on mandolin, but switched over to fiddle by necessity and ease since the strings on both instruments are the same, G-D-A-E. He launched his professional career playing square. dances and fiddle contests at age ten, first urged into soloing due to his father's lack of sobriety at a performance. After graduating an Amarillo barber school in 1927, Bob cut hair in Turkey, Texas, until he moved to Fort Worth in 1929 where he joined a medicine show, played on KTAT radio, played house parties, and added Milton and Durwood Brown to his group on fiddle and guitar respectively.

After winning a fiddle contest on KFJZ, Fort Worth in 1930, the Wills fiddle group landed a gig on the hugely popular cross-town station, WBAP, that boosted attendance at dances and elevated their star to the top of the Fort Worth music scene, bubbling with the nascent Western swing style. When the group's popularity as a dance band grew, so did the need for extended versions of familiar tunes. This led Bob to encourage his musicians to take improvisational solos on choruses that swung out and linked the music to the primary creative elements of jazz. The group's heightened notoriety led to another radio program for sponsor Burrus Mill and Elevator Company of Fort Worth. Burris's Light Crust Flour inspired the Light Crust Doughboys, the band's working name during the period. After only a few weeks on the air, Burris Mills' General Manager W. Lee "Pappy" O'Daniel moved the show to noon on WBAP, officially launching the Western swing rocket into the peak listening period of lunch time. Within six months, the program was simulcast in San Antonio and Houston, and eventually aired via the Southwest Quality Network over several more stations in Texas and Oklahoma. The radio programs served not only as entertainment, but also as music lessons for many young people who had acquired an instrument through their family or some other means, and had little else but the radio as a source of information and entertainment during the poverty-stricken 1930s.

The group cut their first two first two records in a Dallas hotel for Victor Records in 1932, "Suebonnet Sue" and "Nancy Jane." While the records were not hits in any sense of the word, Burrus Mills and Pappy O'Daniel envisioned big financial returns from the group and built a studio at the mill where the band was supposed to practice eight hours a day. O'Daniel also required the group to stop playing dances, which caused Milton and Durwood Brown to leave the group and form the most popular Western swing group in Texas, Milton Brown and his Musical Brownies, featuring **Bob Dunn** on steel guitar, and Milton's smooth vocals that served as a benchmark for future crooners of the style. While Wills

Bob Wills Ranch House, 1951, left to right: Bobby Koeffer (steel), Kenny ? (trombone), Wayne Nichols(trumpet), Billy Briggs (sax), Ramona Reed (vocals), Luke Wills (standing), Billy Houck (drums), Bob, Jack, Lloyd (bass), Snuffy Smith (standing), Skeeter Elkin (piano), Eldon Shamblin (guitar), seated on the stool wearing a suit is the announcer, either Dan Valentine or Lynn Bigler

stayed with the Light Crust Doughboys until 1933, having added his brother Johnnie Lee on tenor banjo in 1931, his "artistic differences" with Pappy O'Daniel (and occasional alcoholic lapses in judgement) forced a separation between the two headstrong entities, and Bob moved to Waco, taking several of the Doughboys with him.

Once in Waco, Wills formed Bob Wills and the Playboys and began broadcasting over radio station WACO. Not long after, Bob met future manager O.W. Mayo, who began booking gigs for the group around Waco. Having peaked in Waco, the two drove to Oklahoma City in 1934 to explore the possibilities of getting hired on KOMA, a station familiar with Wills since the Light Crust Doughboy days. Unfortunately, the station was also familiar with O'Daniel and knew the future Texas governor and U.S. Senator would not stand for Wills to be on the same station as O'Daniel's "new" Doughboys. Wills and Mayo then headed for WKY who booked the band and then pulled the rug out due to financial intimidation from O'Daniel. Subsequently, the WKY program director made a call to KTUL in Tulsa where he secured the group an offer to play on the relatively new station with only a small power output.

On the trip to Tulsa, Mayo convinced Bob to stop at the 25,000-watt radio station, KVOO, "the voice of Oklahoma," and the group was hired for a midnight spot February of 1934. During that first broadcast, the band (now called Bob Wills and the Texas Playboys) promised a promotional photo to the listener who sent in a letter from the most distant place, and a woman from Oakland, California won the contest. Convinced of the group's audience appeal, KVOO began broadcasting the Playboys straight from the stage of the Cain's Ballroom on February 9, 1934. Within weeks, the group began receiving piles of mail and multiple offers to play throughout Oklahoma where the Depression hung heavy over many rural communities. While the Wills band offered a moment of sunshine during an otherwise bleak existence for many rural Oklahomans caught up in the Depression, several towns, such as Oilton, Bristow, Cushing, Drumright, and Seminole, were still in the midst of heavy oil production that provided dance gigs where flush oil field workers were ready to dance away the weekends.

Of course, O'Daniel tried to hijack the Playboys again in Tulsa, but KVOO held out and before long the Wills band had a prime lunchtime slot of 12:30 to 1 p.m. that provided the foundation for their ascent to fame which lasted until 1958 between the bands of Bob and Johnnie Lee, all broadcast from the stage of the Cain's Ballroom, a building that began its life in 1924 as a garage for city founder Tate Brady, evolved into the Louvre Ballroom in the late 1920s, and became Cain's Dance Academy in 1930 when Madison W. "Daddy" Cain purchased it and featured the swinging country jazz string ensembles from Texas that became the foundation sounds of Western swing. With KVOO's raised power to 50,000 watts and status as one of America's "clear channel" radio stations, preventing any other station from the AM dial position of 1170, Bob Wills and the Texas Playboys became known throughout much of the United States, Canada, and Mexico as well as any big band leaders of the 1930s.

After shifting personnel through 1935, Wills added Texas-born steel guitarist Leon McAuliffe, who was heavily influenced by **Bob Dunn**, to the group. Wills also brought in more Texans, pianist Al Stricklin, and Everett Stover who began fleshing out choruses with his trumpet. Oklahoma's first contribution came to the band in the form of saxophonist Robert "Zeb" McNally, the son of the apartment manager where the Wills band lived in Tulsa, followed by trombonist Art Haines who filled out a horn section that led to Nashville's derisive term for Wills' music, "Okie Jazz." Another Oklahoman in Wills' pioneering band was drummer William Eschol "Smokey" Dacus (b. Quinton) who had played music on scholarship at the University of Tulsa and was working in a Tulsa hotel orchestra when Bob found him in 1935 and added him to the Playboys. Dacus is thought of as one of the very first drummers of country music. Until Bob added the drum kit to his group in 1935, the instrument was not accepted in the country music genre due to its association with African-American music, specifically jazz. Dacus played drums in the Dixieland style that put a swing in the music that made it premier for dancing and allied it with the big band movement of the 1930s. Set for the moment, the group's popularity landed them a recording contract with Art Satherley and Brunswick Records in Dallas.

At those first Brunswick sessions in September of 1935, Wills recorded several songs with Oklahoma titles and themes in the style that has come to be known as Western swing: "Good Old Oklahoma," "Tulsa Waltz," "Oklahoma Rag," and "Osage Stomp." Other favorites from the session included "Sittin' on Top of the World" and "Get With It," along with a cover of Big Bill Broonzy's "I Can't Be Satisfied." Interestingly, the jazz element in the music, with Dacus on drums, Zeb McNally on sax, and Haines on fiddle and trombone, is provided by Oklahomans, which further exemplifies the strength of Oklahoma's jazz and blues scene from the turn of the 20th century through World War II. The 1935 Wills recordings sold well and Satherly booked the group again, although trombonist Haines left to form the Ragtime Rascals in Shawnee, Oklahoma.

In 1936, Wills recorded several more jazz and blues-tinged numbers in Chicago, none more significant than "Steel Guitar Rag," "Trouble in Mind," and "Bring It On Down To My House," all of which became long-time Wills standards. The group's 1936 recordings on Brunswick's Vocalion label outsold other major artists that year such as Louis Armstrong, **Gene Autry**, Fletcher Henderson, and Bix Beiderbicke. The 1937 recordings in Dallas produced "Tulsa Stomp," and several blues-jazz numbers, including "Oozlin' Daddy Blues," "Old Jelly Roll Blues," "The New St. Louis Blues," as well as a cover of Jimmie Rodgers' "Blue Yodel #1," further exhibiting the group's diverse abilities and foundation in all American roots music forms. By 1937, Eldon Shamblin, born in Weatherford, Oklahoma, joined the group and began providing a completely unique sound on guitar by duplicating bass lines on the bass strings of the guitar while playing chords of tunes on the tenor strings. Shamblin went on to make the guitar a front-line solo instrument in the group and represented the guitar sound evolving nationally in jazz via Oklahoma City's **Charlie Christian** in Benny Goodman's band. One of Wills' best biographers, Charles R. Townsend, in his excellent account of Wills' career, *San Antonio Rose: The Life and Music of Bob Wills*, speculates Christian heard Shamblin in Wills' band over KVOO in 1938 and began emulating some of Shamblin's work. Whatever similarities and cross-fertilization occurred between Shamblin and Christian, the two musicians who matured in Oklahoma were intrinsic to the developing significance of the electric guitar as a frontline instrument in American popular music. Shamblin's significant duet recordings with steel guitarist Leon McAuliffe on "Bob Wills Special" and "Twin Guitar Special" are Western swing standards and benchmarks of the genre. By century's end *Rolling Stone* magazine called Eldon the world's greatest rhythm guitarist, and *Musician* magazine declared him one of the twenty prime movers in guitar history.

In the spring of 1938, the Wills band recorded again in Dallas for Columbia, who had purchased Brunswick, and Wills continued producing music linked more closely to jazz and blues than country, such as "Alexander's Ragtime Band," "Mississippi Delta Blues," "Gambling Polka Dot Blues," by Jimmie Rodgers, and "Empty Bed Blues." However, the group also shifted more toward Tin Pan Alley type numbers such as "Oh You Beautiful Doll" and "I'll See You in My Dreams," and George and Ira Gershwin's, "Oh, Lady Be Good." In November of 1938,

Wills recorded a number of fiddle tunes for Art Satherly and Columbia, to include "San Antonio Rose," "Dreamy Eyes Waltz," "Prosperity Special," and "Drunkard's Blues," as well as "Twinkle, Twinkle Little Star," "Silver Bells," and "Little Girl Go Ask Your Mother." With his rapidly growing popularity and considerable record sales, Bob purchased a large house and piece of land in north Tulsa where his parents moved, and where the group often rehearsed and had dances after home-cooked meals.

The Playboys' career continued skyrocketing in late '30s as they became one of the best-known and best selling bands in the United States, popular as a dance band for thousands of people each week, perennial jukebox favorites, and omnipresent via KVOO radio. Clarence Cagle's wife, Kathrean, remembered in a 2002 interview, "During that time you could walk down the street and never miss a beat of their music because all the windows were open and all the radios were playing the band." By most counts, the band's peak was from 1938 to 1941 until World War II broke up the group. By 1940, however, the group's eighteen members made it one of the biggest orchestras in the country, and the band could alternate between a horn-led swing band and a fiddle-led country group, often combining the two. In the April, 1940 sessions in Saginaw, Texas, the group had three fiddlers, a steel guitarist, a rhythm and lead guitarist (hinting at the oncoming rock movement), a drummer, five saxophonists, two trumpet players, bass, banjo, piano, and a vocalist, with some men having the ability to play two instruments. The group made their definitive recordings in 1940, to include "Corrine Corrina," "Bob Wills Special," "Big Beaver," and a new version of Bob's composition, "San Antonio Rose," which in many ways defines the concept of Western-swing. With a swing beat, a Spanish melody played by horns, Tommy Duncan's crooned vocal, Bob's trademark commentary, and its danceability, the record sold over 500,000 copies in 1940 for Columbia whose only other gold record of the year was Frank Sinatra's "All or Nothing at All." The known Oklahomans who contributed to the recording include Eldon Shamblin (guitar), Smokey Dacus (drums), and Zeb McNally (saxophone). Bing Crosby eventually sold more than 1.5 million copies of his version of "New San Antonio Rose," and the song elevated Bob Wills to genuine pop star status.

With the success of Bob's big band and "New San Antonio Rose," Hollywood came calling to capitalize on Bob's status as a potential musical cowboy star. Bob's first role, along with established singing cowboy Tex Ritter, came in *Take Me Back to Oklahoma* (1940). In 1941, Wills recorded his last sessions with the original Playboys group in Dallas, the products of which included one of his best known songs, "Take Me Back to Tulsa" and the previously mentioned Shamblin/McAuliffe duet, "Twin Guitar Special." After performing in another film, *Go West Young Lady* (1941), and recording tracks such as "Cherokee Maiden" and "Bob Wills Stomp" while in California with the smaller group he had taken out west to be in the film, Bob and his movie band returned from California to Tulsa where the glory days of Bob Wills and the Texas Playboys ended when the Japanese attacked Pearl Harbor, Hawaii on December 7. Vocalist Tommy Duncan Left, as did pianist Al Stricklin. By 1942, all that remained of the original group was Bob, Leon McAuliffe and Eldon Shamblin.

Bob assembled a new group complete with horns, fiddles, steel and electric guitar that recorded in Hollywood in the summer of 1942. Later in the year he performed as part of the broadcasts Johnnie Lee kept going on KVOO, but World War II eventually took most of the band, including Bob who landed in the Army by the end of that year, a few days after Christmas. The life of musician had not prepared the thirty-seven-year-old for the rigors of the Army, and by the summer of 1943 he was discharged. Bob made it back to Tulsa where he put a band together by borrowing some of Johnnie Lee's musicians. By this time, Johnnie Lee had solidly established himself at Cain's and on KVOO after having started his own band when Bob continued going west to make movies, record, and play to the large number of displaced Oklahomans who had sought out California as a respite from the dust bowl in the 1930s. Among the films Bob appeared in, often with various incarnations of his band, include *The Lone Prarie* (1942), *Silver City Raiders* (1943), *Saddles and Sagebrush* (1943), *Riders of the Northwest Mounted* (1943), *The Vigilantes Ride* (1944), *Wyoming Hurricane* (1944), *Bob Wills and His Texas Playboys* (1944), *The Last Horseman* (1944), *Rhythm Roundup* (1945), *Blazing the Western Trail* (1945), *Frontier Frolic* (1946), and *Lawless Empire* (1946).

The musical hits also continued for Bob throughout the 1940s in California, to include the following #1 songs: "Smoke on the Water" (1945), "Stars and Stripes in Iwo Jima" (1945), "Silver Dew on the Bluegrass Tonight" (1945), "White Cross on Okinawa" (1945), "New Spanish Two Step" (1946), and "Sugar Moon" (1947). Along with recording roughly 200 songs for the Tiffany Music Company from mid-1945 through 1947, usually referred to as The Tiffany Transcriptions, the band also recorded several other Western swing standards and favorites during the period: "Roly Poly," "Bob Wills Boogie," "Brain Cloudy Blues," "Might as Well Forget It," "Texas Playboy Rag," "Bob Wills Boogie," and "Bubbles in My Beer." With Bob's movie career in full swing and his brothers leading bands in Sacramento and Tulsa, opportunities were ripe for many musicians who could play the Wills standards, swing out, and take off on their instruments. The process of drafting musicians back and forth between Wills bands was not unlike baseball teams who trade players or bring them up through a farm system. A long line of Oklahoma musicians made their way through the Wills bands of the 1940s, '50s, and '60s with Bob or Johnnie Lee, or eventually in bands led by the other Wills brothers, Billy Jack and Luke. Additionally, the groups provided a professional training ground for musicians who would go on to form their own groups like Leon Rausch, Leon McAuliffe, and Tommy Duncan.

From the time Johnnie Lee started his band in 1940, the younger Wills held sway over the Western swing music scene throughout Oklahoma, Kansas, Missouri, and Arkansas by continuing the broadcasts over KVOO until 1958 when the cosmopolitan Nashville Sound and rock and roll had all but subsumed Western swing as an important musical in popular consciousness. While Johnnie Lee's band did not reach the heights of Bob's triumphs, Johnnie Lee and his boys did have some national success with hits such as "Milk Cow Blues" (1941), "Rag Mop" (1949), and "Peter Cottontail" (1950). Oklahoma musicians who made significant contributions to Johnnie Lee's recordings of the 1940s and early 1950s include pianist Clarence Cagle, who played with **Charlie Christian** in the 1930s, Junior Barnard, whose "country boogie" guitar work is a harbinger of the rockabilly movement of the 1950s, fiddler and vocalist Cotton Thompson, and later, Don Tolle, recommended to Johnnie Lee by Merl Lindsay in whose Oklahoma

Don Tolle

Night Riders Don had been playing. While most of the major players in the Wills bands have had their stories documented, Don Tolle's career has been relegated to footnotes and asides, until now.

Like most of the musicians who played with Bob and Johnnie Lee, Don Tolle was classically trained (on violin) but heard the Playboys on the radio as a child and wanted nothing more than to be a jazz player in the Wills style. While Tolle was born in Rushville, Illinois to tenant farmers, at age one he moved with his family to a rural home between Denoya and Shidler in Osage County where his father worked in the oil fields. Surrounded by musical instruments in the home, he began playing fiddle at the age of five when his father arranged for lessons from a Jewish music teacher, Julian Choates. Tolle

had already begun playing mandolin, and switched to violin for the lessons wherein he became formally trained to read, much like many of the other Western swing players who could read and play from charts the same as most big band musicians. His earliest public musical experiences occurred when he accompanied his father, also an accomplished fiddle player, at various dances and other social events. He attended high school in Wolf, Oklahoma and began his professional career in 1939 playing with bands around Seminole, Oklahoma. After a stint in the service, and performing on radio in Portland, Oregon in 1945, Don played fiddle and guitar in Fresno, California Western swing bands sponsored by Bob Wills in 1946, and moved back to Oklahoma City where he began playing

1978 reunion of Western swing greats, seated left to right: Johnny Gimble, Claude Clemmons (holding drum sticks), Gene Crownover, Don Tolle, and Eldon Shamblin; standing left to right: Roy Ferguson, Curly Lewis, Joe Holley, Ted Adams, Glenn Rhees, Johnnie Lee Wills, Wayne Johnson, Clarence Cagle, John Thomas Wills, Alex Brasheare, and O. W. Mayo.

guitar exclusively with Merl Lindsay and his Oklahoma Night Riders in 1947.

After recording one single with Lindsay, "Grade A Pasteurized Baby," Tolle moved to Nashville to play guitar for Paul Howard and His Arkansas Cotton Pickers with whom he toured the southeastern United States until 1951 when he received a call from Johnnie Lee Wills who needed a "take off man," the term for a hot soloist in Western swing. Don returned to Tulsa and joined Johnnie Lee as lead guitarist in August of 1951, just in time for the group's RCA Victor recording sessions, made in the KVOO studios, that produced three singles, "The Thingamijig," "There Are Just Two I's in Dixie," and a cover of Tennessee Ernie Ford's "Blackberry Boogie," all re-released in 1983 through Bear Family Records as part of their *Rompin' Stompin' Singin' Swingin'* series of American roots music artists. Tolle's leads on these recordings are clear indications of the guitar's evolution in American popular music by way of Junior Bernard's style, which permeated Western swing, and surfaced in many ways through the guitar work of Scotty Moore on the Elvis Presley Sun Sessions (Presley's own awareness of the Wills music sprouts on the 1966 home recording by Elvis of "San Antonio Rose," and later on the recording of "Faded Love" by Elvis in 1970, which appeared on the 1971 gold-selling RCA album, *Elvis Country*). As a guitarist and fiddler, Don Tolle played regularly with Johnnie Lee on KVOO radio, Tulsa television station KVOO (where Don eventually hosted his own Sunday night show), and throughout the region's dance halls with Johnnie Lee and His Boys. When Johnnie Lee needed a break from the rigors of the road life, namely the constant partying, Tolle took to the highways with his own Western All Stars.

After leaving Johnnie Lee and His Boys in 1961, Tolle moved to Big Springs, Texas, and spent four years playing guitar with Hoyle Nix and His West Texas Cowboys from 1962 to 1966, and in 1966 opened the Don Tolle School of Music in Big Springs which he operated until 1988. Don also continued fronting his own Western All-Stars, a rotating lineup he began using in 1957 and continued booking through 1969.

Another one of the Oklahoma native musicians who had an important part of the Wills legacy is Glenn "Blub" Rhees who became a Texas Playboy for Bob in 1957 and played saxophone on all of the Liberty Recordings through 1962 when he returned to Johnnie Lee's band. Glenn began playing sax in the seventh grade in Jennings, Oklahoma, moved on to Oilton High School where he played in the high school band, and finally wound up at Tulsa Webster High School where he performed with **Patti Page** before graduating. Subsequently, he worked in the oil business for a few years in Texas, New Mexico, Wyoming, and Louisiana before returning to Tulsa where he played with Art Davis and the Rhythm Riders from 1946 to 1948 throughout the Oklahoma, Texas, and Arkansas region. While with Art Davis, Lucky Moeller heard Glenn and offered him a job with the Western Okies. When Lucky was hired to be Bob Wills manager, Rhees moved to New Mexico where he found steady work in clubs.

In 1950, Glenn moved back to Oklahoma City where he joined Luke Wills' group, the Rhythm Busters, at the Trianon Ballroom. A year later, he moved to Lawton where he joined the Southernaires where he packed up Nashville stars such as Lefty Frizzel, Hank Williams, Webb Pierce, and others. By 1955, Rhees was back in Tulsa and working for Johnnie Lee, and when Bob was looking for a sax man in 1957, Johnnie Lee suggested "Blub," a nickname given to him because of his expansive waistline. After the Liberty recordings with Bob, Glenn returned to Tulsa where he recorded again with Johnnie Lee where he was featured on two successful singles, "Blub Twist" and "Slush," in 1962. Johnnie Lee kept the band active until 1964, the year of the Beatles' arrival in America, when Wills dissolved the group and opened a western wear store on Memorial Drive in Tulsa.

Johnnie Lee did regroup the surviving and available musicians from the Wills' salad days for two albums. 1978's *Reunion* album, produced by **Steve Ripley** for Flying Fish Records, featured many of the old time Western swing musicians including Tolle, Johnny Gimble, Gene Crownover, Eldon Shamblin, Glen Rhees, Curly Lewis, and Clarence Cagle. Don Tolle plays all the lead guitar parts on *Reunion*, while Shamblin was satisfied to hold down the rhythm on the album. The musicians got together for one more recording session in 1980 for *Dance All Night* (Delta), which followed much the same format of elder Playboys playing Western swing favorites.

While the height of Johnnie Lee's national popularity passed by 1950, Bob Wills

Tommy Perkins

made one of his most memorable hits that year, the eternal Western swing favorite, "Faded Love," an old fiddle tune Bob learned from his father that featured lyrics written by brother Billy Jack. The song became #1 country hit on *Billboard's* country and western chart in the fall of 1950 and is Oklahoma's official state country and western song. One of the players on the session, drummer Tommy Perkins, was only fifteen-years-old at the time.

Tommy Perkins was born in Oklahoma City in 1934. At age three, he performed with his parents' group, The Arkansawyers, and by age fourteen played six nights a week with a three-piece band in Clinton. At fifteen, Perkins joined the Bob Wills band for California tour that started in Oklahoma. Perkins was still in school at the time, and had to get special permission from the Oklahoma Lt. Governor, James E. Berry, to leave school for a month to six weeks to do the California tour. While in California, Perkins was the drummer on the recording of Wills' "Fade Love," a #1 hit in 1950, and now the state country song of Oklahoma.

Returning from California, Perkins went to work with Richard Rozelle's band, when Rozelle had country hits with "Old, Man" and "Mom and Dad's Waltz." He worked with Rozelle for a year, and then played with Little Jimmy Dickens and Hank Thompson. Back in California by 1952, Perkins played with Billy Jack Wills', Bob's youngest brother who was leading a band at Wills Point, also known as the West Coast base for Western swing. Perkins played on Billy Jack's two rockabilly, or country boogie albums, recorded in total from 1952 to 1954. Perkins then returned to Oklahoma where he worked for Leona Culp in Tulsa at the Cimarron Ballroom, off and on for about four years. It was during that stint when Tommy met Western Swing vocalist Leon Rausch, an association that continued into the 1990s when Perkins joined the touring and recording Playboys II group, primarily made up of living Playboys getting together in the 1990s on old favorites from the Western swing's peak period of the late 1930s through the early 1950s.

In 1992, he also recorded an album with jazz guitar giant Herb Ellis, known as *Texas Swings*, and recorded an album called *Life's Like Poetry* with traditional country singer and songwriter Lefty Frizzell.

Modern Drummer magazine featured Perkins in its July, 2000 issue, and he was also a member of the Western Swing Hall of Fame. Demonstrating his diverse ability and longevity, during his sixty-plus career, he also played with the Ink Spots and Arlo Guthrie. Tommy Perkins always kept a basic, steady tempo without all the "butterflying around," as Bob Wills called overactive drummers who like to roll around the tom-toms a lot, instead of just keeping good dance time. Perkins died tragically in an automobile accident in June 7, 2003, returning from the Legends of Western Swing Festival in Wichita Falls, Texas.

Even though financial and health problems plagued Bob Wills throughout the 1950s, he still maintained a steady recording and performance schedule that benefited from his tremendous fame through 1957, although his music did not enjoy the success of his peak period of the 1930s and early 1940s. Bob returned to Tulsa in 1957 to join forces with Johnnie Lee for two years before heading back out west to Las Vegas where he performed regularly through 1962. From 1960 to 1961, he reunited with his old singer, Tommy Duncan, for three albums on Liberty Records containing new recordings of some of their hits and several other selections that exhibited Bob's wide ranging musical tastes of blues, jazz, fiddle tunes, swing and pop. Bob had the first of his heart attacks in 1962, and after recovering in Tulsa, started touring and recording again before settling in Fort Worth, Texas in 1963.

All but worn out, Wills had another heart attack in 1964, ending his days as a bandleader. He sold the management of the band to Missouri-born singer and guitarist Leon Rausch for $10,000, and the Texas Playboys soldiered on under Rausch's direction, sometimes with Bob and sometimes not. While he continued fronting other leaders' bands, he kept recording through 1969, but the music had little impact on the national scene, treasured as the recordings are by Wills enthusiasts. He traveled Texas and Oklahoma by car in the middle 1960s, carrying with him only a vocalist or guitarist, and would play with various local pickup musicians at one-night stands throughout Texas and Oklahoma.

Inducted into the Country Music Hall of Fame in 1968, the plaque commemorating his contributions reads, "Bob Wills – established himself as King of Western Swing – a living legend whose road map has chartered new pathways into the world of American stage, radio, TV, records, and movies." In May of 1969, Bob had a stroke that incapacitated him.

Not willing to let his idol go quietly into the forgetful night of popular culture's memory, **Merle Haggard** supervised a *Tribute to the Best Damn Fiddle Player in the World (Or My Salute to Bob Wills)* from his home studio in 1971 which reunited many of Wills' original Playboys. In 1973, a final session was organized in Dallas where Bob just added voice tracks on recordings released as *For the Last Time* (United Artists). On the second day of the sessions, when Merle Haggard was to play fiddle, Wills had a massive stroke that left him comatose until he died in 1975, after which he was buried in Tulsa's Memorial Park Cemetery in section 15, lot 560, space 2, next to which his wife Betty was buried in 1993.

In 1997, Bob Wills won a posthumous Grammy Hall of Fame Award, and in 1999, the Rock and Roll Hall of Fame inducted Bob Wills and His Texas

Playboys as an early influence on rock. The Wills legacy's latest accolade came in 2001 when Friends of Oklahoma Music inducted Bob, Johnnie Lee, Luke, and Billy Jack, along with special recognition for all those Oklahomans who recorded with any of the brothers, into the Oklahoma Music Hall of Fame.

While Bob Wills' music will be forever associated with the zenith of Western swing's popularity, the music of his brothers, Johnnie Lee and Billy Jack, is now also receiving acclaim through reissues available on Rounder, Rhino, and Bear Family Records. One particularly insightful compilation, *Heroes of Country Music, Volume One: Legends of Western Swing* (Rhino, 1996), has Bob's "Faded Love," Johnnie Lee's "Milk Cow Blues," and Billy Jack's "Troubles (Those Lonesome Kind)," as well as songs by **Hank Thompson**, **Spade Cooley**, and Milton Brown and His Brownies featuring the extremely significant steel player **Bob Dunn** on "Taking Off." As Johnnie Lee is being given more credit as an important Western swing band leader, younger brother Billy Jack is now often cited as leading a significant group that was a pre-cursor to rock and roll by leaning more toward the R&B and jump blues of the 1940s than the Western swing of his brothers. Billy Jack started playing bass with Johnnie Lee's group before relocating to California with Bob and ultimately leading his own band when Bob left California for Oklahoma City. The two representative recordings from Billy Jack's career as a bandleader based in Sacramento, California, include *Crazy Man Crazy* (Western, 1952 – reissued in 1999 on Joaquin Records) and *Billy Jack Wills and his Western Swing Band* (Western, 1952). Harder to find, but worth the search, are Billy Jack's *There's Good Rockin' Tonight* (Bear Family) and *Sacramento 1952-54* (Bear Family). Luke Wills' sole and out-of-print album *High Voltage Gal* features "(Gotta Get To) Oklahoma City," "Cain's Stomp," and "Oklahoma Blues."

While Charles R. Townsend's previously mentioned biography of Bob Wills is the most comprehensive source for information regarding Wills' professional career, discography, and recording sessions, the 1998 biography by Bob's daughter, Rosetta, *The King of Western Swing: Bob Wills Remembered*, is an excellent insider's view into the legendary band leader's life. A more obscure book certainly worth seeking out is John E. Perkins, Jr.'s *Leon Rausch – The Voice of the Playboys* (Swing, 1996), which provides a wealth of anecdotal information about various Wills bands, sidemen, and performances, as well as a thorough document of the life of vocalist and guitarist Leon Rausch, who fronted the Texas Playboys with Bob starting in 1958, but whose musical connections in Tulsa go back to 1955 when he was performing with Don Tolle's Western All Stars, and who lived in Tulsa until 1965. The Hal Leonard music company has also made an important contribution to the preservation of Bob Wills' music with *Bob Wills: King of Western Swing*, a compilation of piano/vocal/guitar sheet music scores.

Demonstrating the continuing impact of Bob Wills on contemporary musicians, a group of alternative-country-tinged musicians, to include Jimmie Dale Gilmore, Robbie Fulks, Jon Langford, Neko Case, Alejandro Escovedo, and The Meat

Purveyors, more known for underground success on the college radio level or in the alt- country Americana radio format, appear on *The Pine Valley Cosmonauts Salute the Majesty of Bob Wills* (Bloodshot 1998). The collection features Wills standards redone with both the reverence and rowdiness one might expect from the artists on the album.

In 1999, the group that is most representative contemporarily of the Western swing tradition, Asleep at the Wheel, released their own tribute to Wills on *Ride with Bob* (Dreamworks), covering the Playboys' best-known songs and featuring Oklahomans such as **Tommy Allsup, Vince Gill** and **Reba McEntire**. Through 2003, former Playboys continued reunion gigs at celebrations such as the annual Bob Wills Day on the Oklahoma capitol's house floor, the annual Bob Wills celebration in Turkey, Texas, and at regular gatherings for fans in Medicine Park and Pawhuska, Oklahoma. The 10th Annual Bob Wills Birthday Bash, held in March of 2003 at the Cain's Ballroom, forever known as the House That Bob Built, featured the remaining active musicians of the Wills bands, fiddlers Curly Lewis and Bob Boatright, guitarist **Benny Garcia**, drummer Tommy Perkins, and vocalist Truitt Cunningham. Additionally, Johnnie Lee's adopted son, John T. Wills, still led his own Western swing group, the Sons of Swing, as of 2003.

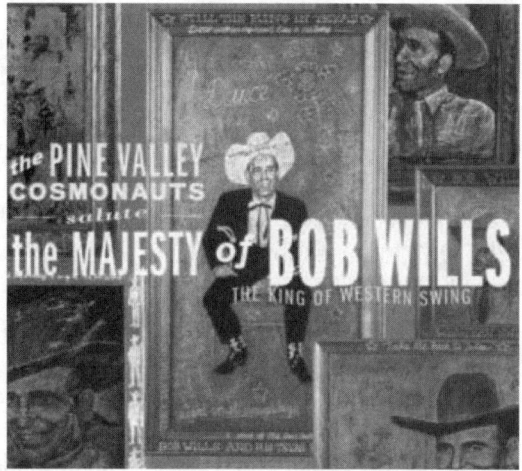

While many recordings exist for the various incarnations of the Playboys, first-time listeners should begin with a standard compilation of Bob Wills' best-known songs, such as *The Essential Bob Wills: 1935-1947* (Columbia Classics, 1992), Rhino's excellent compilation, *Bob Wills & His Texas Playboys: Anthology 1935-1973*, or Bear Family Records eleven-CD boxed set, *San Antonio Rose*, that includes a DVD of *Take Me Back to Oklahoma* and a 168-page book full of photos and copies of movie posters. (HF)

Wilson, Joe Lee
(b. December 22, 1935)

One of the most popular jazz vocal stylists of the 1970s, Joe Lee (Joseph) Wilson was born on a farm near Bristow, Oklahoma, a community of roughly 4,000 population located southwest of Tulsa. Of African-American and American Indian ancestry (maternal grandmother was Creek), Joe Lee, or J. L., spent his early childhood singing while doing farm chores, as well as vocalizing in school and church functions. It is also reported that he took piano lessons for about two years from ages seven to nine.

Although documentation is scarce regarding Joe Lee's schooling in Oklahoma, he apparently relocated to California around 1955. He was a voice major at the Los Angeles Conservatory from 1956 to 1957, and then studied jazz at Los Angeles City College, majoring in music from 1957 to 1958. He began his professional career in Santa Monica, California, in 1958, and then toured the West Coast and spent a year in Mexico.

In 1962 Joe Lee moved to New York City, where he worked with Sonny Rollins, Freddie Hubbard, Lee Morgan, Miles Davis, Roy Haynes, Jackie McLean, Frank Foster, **Sunny Murray**, Pharaoh Sanders, and Archie Shepp, with whom he is lead vocalist on Shepp's notable albums in the early 1970s, *Cry of My People*, *Attica Blues*, and *Things Have Got to Change*. The latter was reissued in 2002 on the Universal International label.

During the 1960s and 1970s, Wilson made New York City his base of operations. Dubbed "The Big Voice," he appeared at the Newport in New York and Live Lofts Jazz Festivals during this time, opened and operated the Lady's Fort Jazz Club, hosted his own jazz radio show, performed on a U.S. State Department tour with his own group, Joy of Jazz, and was one of the innovators of the Loft Movement which gave struggling young jazz musicians performance opportunities. During this time, Joe Lee recorded three solo albums with guitar, including *Livin' High off Nickels and Dimes*, *Secrets from the Sun*, and *Without A Song*, all on independent labels. One of his greatest achievements during this period was winning the *Down Beat* Critics Poll in 1973 in the category of Talent Deserving Wider Recognition-Male Vocalist.

In 1978 Wilson performed at Ronnie Scott's Club in London, and was guest vocalist with Humphrey Lyttelton's Big Band while in the U.K. He thus discovered and liked the European jazz scene, and eventually moved to Europe, living in the U.K. and France from the late 1970s on. The *London Evening Standard* newspaper once described Joe Lee as "the male equivalent of Ella Fitzgerald, Sarah Vaughan, and Carmen McRae."

As of 2002, Wilson is still performing a combination of jazz, blues, and gospel music at age sixty-seven with appearances on three continents and release of two recent albums, *Feelin' Good* (Candid Records) and *What Would It Be Without You* (Knitting Factory Records). He toured the U.K. and Ireland twice in 2001 with his Joy of Jazz group, led a six-week series of gospel workshops at King's School Canterbury, and sang for sold out crowds at the Faith and Light Festival at Lourdes. (GC)

Wooley, Sheb

(b. April 10, 1921 - d. September 16, 2003)

One of the most versatile performers in country music as a songwriter, recording artist, actor, and comedian, Sheb Wooley was born to William Curtis and Ora Wooley on a farm near Erick, Oklahoma, a community of about 1,000 residents just off Interstate 40 near the Texas border. Sheb learned to ride a horse by age four and later competed in rodeos while in high school. Local sources say his father traded a shotgun for Sheb's first guitar, and while in high school, Sheb formed a country music band (The Plainview Melody Boys), playing at neighborhood dances and on local radio in Elk City. Sheb liked music, but realized it would not provide much of a living, therefore, he worked as a welder in the Oklahoma oil fields after graduating from high school. As with many other Oklahomans, Sheb pulled up stakes in the 1930s and headed to California, where he found work in a plant moving orange crates. In the meantime, Sheb had married Melba Laurie Miller, a cousin of **Roger Miller**, whom he had met at Erick, where the Miller family lived. At the outset of World War II, Sheb was declared unfit for military service (4-F) due to injuries suffered during his rodeo days, but he did work in defense plants during the war. Following the war, Wooley headed to Nashville, where he cut his first records for the Bullet label in the studios of WSM, the radio home of the Grand Ole Opry. He also appeared on radio station WLAC as a singer/guitarist, but neither the record deal or radio work proved fruitful, and Sheb relocated to Fort Worth after about a year in Music City.

From 1946 to 1949, Sheb fronted his own show on radio station WBAP in Fort Worth, sponsored by Calumet Baking Powder, and formed his own band, The Calumet Indians. While in the area, he recorded several cuts for the Bluebonnet label in Dallas. Several of these vintage recordings have been reissued by Bear Family as *Country Boogies Wild Wooley*. He then left Texas and returned to California, thinking that movies might fit into his future plans. About the same time, Sheb signed on as a songwriter with Hill & Range publishing company, which resulted in 1950, a recording contract with a new company MGM Records, remaining with the label for more than twenty years. In hopes of some movie work, Sheb took acting lessons at the Jack Koslyn School of Acting in Los Angeles, which led to his first screen role in 1949 as a heavy in the Errol Flynn film *Rocky Mountain*. Three years later, he was cast as Ben Miller, the whiskey-drinking killer in the Gary Cooper film *High Noon*, in which he gained considerable notice.

In the 1950s, Wooley appeared in several other films, including *Little Big Horn*

(1951), *Distant Drums* (1951), *Man Without a Star* (1955), *Giant* (1956), and *Rio Bravo* (1959), but his most memorable work was in television, where he was cast as Pete Nolan in the *Rawhide* series from 1959 to 1967. He also appeared in several other television shows, such as *Lassie, Cheyenne, Range Rider*, and *The Lone Ranger*, as well as writing several scripts for *Rawhide*. During his career in Hollywood from 1950 to 1979, Sheb appeared in more than seventy films.

During his acting career, Sheb continued to write songs and make records. His songs were recorded by such artists as Hank Snow, who had a big hit in 1953 with "When Mexican Joe Met Jole Blon," Theresa Brewer's million seller "Too Young to Tango" in 1954, and Rusty Draper scored a Top 20 hit in 1955 with "Are You Satisfied?" But it was the novelty hit "The Purple People Eater," released in 1958, which turned Sheb into an international star. MGM Records was at first reluctant to release the single, but it became a million seller (in 2002 it had sold more than 100 million copies worldwide), remained atop the U.S. pop charts for six weeks, and became a Top 20 hit in the U.K. His next major hit was in 1962, another novelty number titled "That's My Pa," which reached #1 on the country charts. It is reported that Sheb was in line to record "Don't Go Near the Indians," but because of film obligations, Rex Allen's version was released before he could record it. He jokingly told MGM he would write a sequel that resulted in another comic parody, "Don't Go Near the Eskimos," featuring a new drunken persona to present it—Ben Colder.

As Ben Colder, Sheb recorded several more humorous parodies of popular hits, such as "Almost Persuaded No. 2," "Harper Valley PTA (Later That Same Day)," "Hello Wall No. 2," and "Fifteen Beers (Years) Ago." Under his own name, he recorded a few minor hits, including "Blue Guitar" and "Tie a Tiger Down." He received a *Cash Box* magazine special award in 1964 for his contributions to country and popular music. In 1967, 1968, 1969, and 1979, Ben Colder was nominated as Comedian of the Year by the CMA, and captured top honors in 1968. In 1969 when the popular television show *Hee Haw* went on the air, Sheb was hired to perform as Ben Colder, served as the resident songwriter, and wrote the show's theme music. He appeared in thirteen segments of the show.

In 2002 Bear Family released *Eskimos, Mean Old Queen & Itty Bitty Steers*, a twenty-six track compilation under the Ben Colder name, and includes all the well-known parodies of popular hits, such as "Ballad of a Mean Old Queen" ("Ballad of a Teenage Queen"), "Detroit City #2," and "Make the World Go Away #2."

Album credits for Sheb include his self-titled debut (1956), *Songs from the Days of Rawhide* (1960), *That's My Ma and That's My Pa* (1962), *Tales of How the West Was Won* (1963), *It's a Big Land* (1965), *Warm and Wooley* (1969), and *The Purple People Eater*, released in 1997 by Bear Family, the German label. Wooley's songs have been recorded by a variety of artists, including **Johnny Bond**, Ray Stevens, Frenchie Burke, Flying Burrito Brothers, Johnny Cash, **Bob Wills**, Connie Francis, and even Judy Garland.

As of 2003, Wooley continued to write songs with his entertainment company, Dotson-Wooley, based in Hendersonville, Tennessee, where he makes his home. (GC)

www.ben-colder.com

Young Bird
(formed in Pawnee, OK in 1997)

While other Oklahoma intertribal singing groups may have been in existence longer, such as Southern Thunder, Gray Horse, Cozad, Yellow Hammer, Red Land, and Fort Oakland Ramblers, the Young Bird drum, led by Curtis Hamilton-Young Bird (Cheyenne/Sauk & Fox) has risen to national status as one of the most significant southern style powwow drum groups in the United States. On the strength of their powerful group sound, Young Bird has toured nationally and internationally, released nine albums through Canyon Records, one of which was Grammy nominee in 2001, and has won a host of singing competitions through-out North America.

Curtis Hamilton-Young Bird

Born June 25, 1976 in the north central Oklahoma town of Pawnee, where the Pawnee Nation maintains its headquarters, Curtis Hamilton-Young Bird's first musical experiences were through his attendance of Native American Church peyote meetings with his father, Don Hamilton (Cheyenne/Apache (Na-I-Sha)/Tonkawa), and his mother, June Hamilton-Young Bird (Pawnee/Sauk & Fox/Otoe). Curtis started dancing early in powwows, first as a tiny tot straight dancer, then a junior fancy dancer, and finally as a teen-aged traditional dancer. Growing up around his grandfathers, uncles, and father who sang around the big center drum in the powwow circle, Curtis sat with them for the first time when he was eight years old. When he was twelve and thirteen, Curtis traveled and sang with a northern style group, Blue Hawk, before joining the Rose Hill Singers, led by Lloyd Gwen, in 1989. After singing with Rose Hill for several years at powwows, and a trip to the 1996 summer Olympics in Atlanta where his family's group performed with 112 dancers and singers for four weeks in a fixed venue, Curtis started the Young Bird singers in 1997 with his father, brothers, friends, and other family members.

The group recorded their debut album, *Déjà vu: Pow-Wow Songs from Oklahoma*, in 1998 for Canyon Records, one of the premier outlets for American Indian music since 1951. The album was recorded in the 1st National Bank of Pawnee for its acoustics, and included titles that show the group's affinity for rap and R&B, as in "Getting' Jiggy," "Wu Tan," and "R&B Connection." Not to say the songs mirror those musical genres in any way, other than attitude, but the group has been noted as a favorite by artists such as Busta Rhymes and 'N Sync. In 1998, Young Bird won the United Tribes Singing Contest, and in 1999 released their second album, *Rendezvous*, also recorded in the Pawnee 1st National Bank. Also in 1999, the group toured Italy for a week with six performances at different venues throughout the country.

Word Up (Canyon, 2000) is the group's first live recording, made in Tempe, Arizona at Arizona State University's Powwow, and includes a "Cheyenne Flag and Victory Song," as well as a song dedicated to the northern district of the Sac and Fox Nation, "Skushy Strut," and a tune called "Flipmode," which is the pseudonym the group has used when they get together with singers from other groups at powwows. Also released in 2000, *Down for Life* was recorded live at the annual Shakopee Mdewankanton Sioux Community Pow-Wow, and is one of the first non-compilation albums to feature a Northern plains and a Southern plains style powwow group on the same album. Paired with The Boyz, a championship northern-style drum group from St. Paul, Minnesota, among Young Bird's contributions are "Bling, Bling," "Road Warrior," and "Killing Time."

In 2000, the group was the youngest ever to win the overall world singing competition at Schemitzun Powwow in Connecticut, and their 2001 *Change of Life* album for Canyon Records was nominated for a Grammy as the Best Native American Album of 2001. As a result, the group traveled to Los Angeles where they performed at a pre-Grammy Awards reception in early 2002. Young Bird followed *Change of Life* in 2001 with *Double Platinum* (Canyon) featuring them and another northern style group, *River Cree*, on alternate tracks recorded live at the annual Ermine Skin Band Pow-Wow in Alberta, Canada. In 2002, Young Bird released another live album, *Only the Strong Survive* (Canyon), recorded in Iowa City, Iowa at the University of Iowa's 13th annual powwow. The album featured more of their trademark big drum and strong, soaring vocal stylings for which they have become known through Indian Country.

While the group has had a number of singers from many different tribes in the group since 1997, all of which are listed on their various albums, the lineup for *Only the Strong Survive* included Curtis as lead singer, and additional singers Ron (Ski) James, Sr. (Arapaho/Colville/Pawnee/Otoe), G.C. Tsouhlarakis (**Muscogee**/Navajo), Hah-Tee Delgado (Comanche), Ben Nakai (Navajo/Pawnee), Danita Cornelison (Sauk & Fox), Jeff McClellan (Sauk &

Fox), Sunny Rose Yellowmule (Pawnee/Crow), Anthony Monoessy (Comanche/**Kiowa**), Sam Cook (Muscogee/Kiowa), Rusty Diamond (Pawnee/Otoe), and Curtis's father, Don Hamilton-Young Bird. Additionally, current active members of the group not included on the album are Curtis's mother, June Hamilton-Young Bird, brother Juaquin Hamilton-Young Bird who has also begun serving as head

Young Bird, circa 2000

singer at powwows in Oklahoma, and sister, Rebecca "Tooky" Hamilton-Young Bird. In September of 2002, the group won first place in the southern singing competition at a powwow in Washington, D.C. organized to celebrate the continued progress on construction of the Smithsonian's National Museum of the American Indian.

In October, 2002, the group received the Oklahoma Music Hall of Fame's first Rising Star Award for the outstanding achievements the group has made thus far. By late fall of 2002, the group shifted between three vehicles they owned to crisscross the United States and Canada to perform at the biggest powwows in North America. In 2003, Young Bird's music appeared in *The World of American Indian Dance*, an NBC television special focusing on contemporary powwow dances. Also released in 2003, *Southern and Northern Pow-Wow Songs* (Canyon) featured both Young Bird and a northern-style group, Midnite Express, alternating tracks throughout the disc. Alongside singers from previous albums, new members of the group reflect Curtis's relocation to Albuquerque and include Valerie Tenequer (Navajo), Mario Tenequer (Comanche/Navajo), Sunny Rose Yellowmule (Pawnee/Crow), Ben Nakai (Navajo), Ronald Monoessy (Comanche/Mexican), Charles Walker, Jr. (Washoe/Shoshone), Shawn Yazzie (Navajo), and Freeland Jishie (Navajo). By fall, 2003, the group had another Canyon release, *YB Style*, a collection of Southern style powwow songs recorded live in October of 2002 at the Cabazon Band of Mission Indians Powwow in Indio, California. Along with the members of the group from the previously mentioned disc, G.C. Tsouhlarakis (Muscogee/Navajo), Sunny Rose Yellowmule (Pawnee/Crow), and Danita Cornelison (Sac & Fox) were also part of the *YB Style* recording.

Discussing the group's passion for their music, Curtis Hamilton-Youngbird said in 2002 interview, "Once you start singing around the drum, you want to do it more and more, to celebrate the spirit of the creator, and the songs he gives us." (HF) www.canyonrecords.com

Oklahoma Music Guide

Number One Hits Recorded Or Written By Oklahoma Artists or Groups

Number One Hits Recorded or Written
by Oklahoma Artists or Groups
(Hit Parade/Billboard/Radio & Records/Gavin Report/Cash Box)
N=350

1940s
"They Took the Stars Out of Heaven"—**Floyd Tillman** (1944)
"The Trolley Song"—co-written by **Ralph Blane** & Hugh Martin (1944)
"Shame On You"—**Spade Cooley** (1945)
"At Mail Call Today"—**Gene Autry** (1945)
"Oklahoma Hills"—**Jack Guthrie** (1945)
"Smoke on the Water"—**Bob Wills** (1945)
"Stars and Stripes on Iwo Jima"—**Bob Wills** (1945)
"Silver Dew on the Blue Grass Tonight"—**Bob Wills** (1945)
"White Cross on Okinawa"—**Bob Wills** (1945)
"New Spanish Two Step"—**Bob Wills** (1946)
"Detour"—**Spade Cooley** (1946)
"Drivin' Nails in My Coffin"—**Floyd Tillman** (1946)
"Divorce Me C.O.D."—Merle Travis (1946)
"So Round, So Firm, So Fully Packed"—Merle Travis (1947)
"Sugar Moon"—**Bob Wills** (1947)
"One Has My Name (The Other Has My Heart)"—**Jimmy Wakely** (1948)
"Humpty Dumpty Heart"—**Hank Thompson** (1949)
"I Love You So Much It Hurts"—written by **Floyd Tillman**
    (recorded by **Jimmy Wakely**) (1949)
"Slippin' Around"—written by **Floyd Tillman**
    (recorded **Jimmy Wakely** and Margaret Whiting) (1949)
"Rudolph the Red Nosed Reindeer"—**Gene Autry** (1949)

1950s
"Faded Love" – **Bob Wills** (1950)
"Pink Champagne" – **Joe Liggins** & His Honeydrippers
"All My Love"—**Patti Page** (1950)
"The Tennessee Waltz"—**Patti Page** (1950)
"With My Eyes Wide Open I'm Dreaming"—**Patti Page** (1950)
"Bonaparte's Retreat"—**Kay Starr** (1950)
"I'll Never Be Free"—**Kay Starr** with Tennessee Ernie Ford (1950)
"I Saw Mommy Kissing Santa Claus"—recorded by **Molly Bee** (1952)
"Back Street Affair"—written by **Billy Wallace**
    (recorded by Webb Pierce) (1952)
"I Went to Your Wedding"—**Patti Page** (1952)
"Wheel of Fortune"—**Kay Starr** (1952)
"Wild Side of Life"—**Hank Thompson** (1952)

"Dear John Letter"—**Jean Shepard** with Ferlin Husky (1953)
"How Much is That Doggie in the Window"—**Patti Page** (1953)
"Comes A-Long A-Love"—**Kay Starr** (1953)—#1 in UK
"Rub-A-Dub-Dub"—**Hank Thompson** (1953)
"Wake Up, Irene"—**Hank Thompson** (1953)
"More and More"— written by **Merle Kilgore** (recorded by Webb Pierce) (1954)
"Release Me"—co-written by **Eddie Miller** (#1 for Jimmy Heap in 1954/Little Esther Phillips in 1962/Engelbert Humperdinck in 1965)
"Reconsider Baby"—**Lowell Fulson** (1954)
"You Better Not Do That"—**Tommy Collins** (1954)
"Rock and Roll Waltz"—**Kay Starr** (1955)
"There She Goes"—written by **Eddie Miller** (recorded by Carl Smith) (1955)
"Crazy Arms"—co-written by **Ralph Mooney** (recorded by Ray Price) (1956)
"Heartbreak Hotel"—co-written by **Mae Boren Axton** (recorded by Elvis Presley) (1956)
"Allegheny Moon"—**Patti Page** (1956)
"Old Cape Cod"—**Patti Page** (1957)
"Billy Bayou"—written by **Roger Miller**/recorded by Jim Reeves (1958)
"It's Only Make Believe"—Conway Twitty (1958)
"Purple People Eater"—**Sheb Wooley** (1958)
"Squaws Along the Yukon"—**Hank Thompson** (1958)

1960s
"Alley Oop"—written by **Dallas Frazier** (recorded by Hollywood Argyles) (1960)
"Teen Angel"—recorded by **Mark Dinning**/written by **Jean Denning** of the **Dinning Sisters** (1960)
"That's My Pa"—**Sheb Wooley** (1962)
"Thanks A Lot"—written by **Eddie Miller** (recorded by Ernest Tubb) (1963)
"Ring of Fire"—written by **Merle Kilgore** (recorded by Johnny Cash) (1963)
"Dang Me"—**Roger Miller** (1964)
"King of the Road"—**Roger Miller** (1965)
"England Swings"—**Roger Miller** (1965)
"Engine Engine #9"—**Roger Miller** (1965)
"Eve of Destruction"—**Barry McGuire** (1965)
"These Boots Are Made For Walkin'"— written by **Lee Hazlewood** (recorded by Nancy Sinatra) (1966)
"The Fugitive"—**Merle Haggard** (1966)
"I Threw Away the Rose"—**Merle Haggard** (1967)
"Up, Up and Away"—written by **Jimmy Webb** (recorded by The Fifth Dimension) (1967)
"Branded Man"—**Merle Haggard** (1967)

"MacArthur Park"—written by **Jimmy Webb**
   (recorded by Richard Harris) (1968)
"Wichita Lineman"—written by **Jimmy Webb**
   (recorded by Glen Campbell) (1968)
"Next in Line"—Conway Twitty (1968)
"I Take A Lot of Pride In What I Am"—**Merle Haggard** (1968)
"Hooked on a Feeling"—**B. J. Thomas** (1968)
"Skip a Rope"—**Henson Cargill** (1968)
"The Legend of Bonnie and Clyde"—**Merle Haggard** (1968)
"Today I Started Loving You Again"—written and recorded by **Merle Haggard**
    and **Bonnie Owens** (1968)
"Mama Tried"—**Merle Haggard** (1968)
"Sing Me Back Home"—**Merle Haggard** (1968)
"It's All in the Movies"—**Merle Haggard** (1968)
"I Love You More Today"—Conway Twitty (1969)
"To See My Angel Cry"—Conway Twitty (1969)
"Workin' Man Blues"—**Merle Haggard** (1969)
"Hungry Eyes"—**Merle Haggard** (1969)
"Raindrops Keep Fallin' On My Head"—**B. J. Thomas** (1969)
"Galveston"—written by **Jimmy Webb** (recorded by Glen Campbell) (1969)
"Okie from Muskogee"—**Merle Haggard** (1969)
"All I Have to Offer You (Is Me)"—written by **Dallas Frazier**
   (recorded by Charley Pride) (1969)
"(I'm So) Afraid of Losing You Again"— written by **Dallas Frazier**
   (recorded by Charley Pride) (1969)

1970s

"Make It With You"—**David Gates** and Bread (1970)
"Hello Darlin'"—Conway Twitty (1970)
"Fifteen Years Ago"—Conway Twitty (1970)
"The Fightin' Side of Me"—**Merle Haggard** (1970)
"Help Me Make It Through the Night"—Sammi Smith (1970)
"If"—**David Gates** and Bread (1971)
"Joy to the World"—written by **Hoyt Axton** (recorded by Three Dog Night)
   (1971)
"Carolyn"—**Merle Haggard**-written by **Tommy Collins** (1971)
"After the Fire Is Gone"—Conway Twitty with Loretta Lynn (1971)
"How Much More Can She Stand"—Conway Twitty (1971)
"Lead Me On"—Conway Twitty (1971)
"(Lost Her Love) On Our Last Date"—Conway Twitty (1972)
"I Can't Loving You"—Conway Twitty (1972)
"She Needs Someone to Hold Her (When She Cries)"—Conway Twitty (1972)
"The Lord Knows I'm Drinking"—**Cal Smith** (1972)

"It's Not Love (But It's Not Bad)—**Merle Haggard** (1972)

"Everything I Own"—written by **David Gates** (recorded by Boy George) (1972)

"Grandma Harp"—**Merle Haggard** (1972)

"Delta Dawn"—co-written by **Larry Collins** (recorded by Tanya Tucker) (1972)

"Louisiana Woman, Mississippi Man"—Conway Twitty with Loretta Lynn (1973)

"You've Never Been This Far Before"—Conway Twitty (1973)

"If We Make It Through December"—**Merle Haggard** (1973)

"Everybody's Had the Blues"—**Merle Haggard** (1973)

"What's Your Mama's Name"—written by **Dallas Frazier** (recorded by Tanya Tucker) (1973)

"Come Live With Me"—**Roy Clark** (1973)

"Things Aren't Funny Anymore"—**Merle Haggard** (1974)

"Room Full of Roses"—written by **Tim Spencer** (recorded by Mickey Gilley) (1974)

"Old Man From the Mountain"—**Merle Haggard** (1974)

"There's A Honky Tonk Angel (Who'll Take Me Back In)"—Conway Twitty (1974)

"As Soon As I Hang Up the Phone"—Conway Twitty with Loretta Lynn (1974)

"I See the Want To In Your Eyes"—Conway Twitty (1974)

"Country Bumpkin"—**Cal Smith** (1974)

"It's Time to Pay the Fiddler"—**Cal Smith** (1974)

"Kentucky Gambler"—**Merle Haggard** (1974)

"(Hey Won't You Play) Another Somebody Done Somebody Wrong Song"— **B. J. Thomas** (1975)

"Linda On My Mind"—Conway Twitty (1975)

"Touch the Hand"—Conway Twitty (1975)

"Feelins'"—Conway Twitty with Loretta Lynn (1975)

"This Time I've Hurt Her More Than She Loves Me"—Conway Twitty (1975)

"It's All in the Movies"—**Merle Haggard** (1975)

"Always Wanting You"—**Merle Haggard** (1975)

"The Who Am I"—written by **Dallas Frazier** (recorded by Charley Pride) (1975)

"After All the Good Is Gone"—Conway Twitty (1976)

"The Games That Daddies Play"—Conway Twitty (1976)

"I Can't Believe She Gives It All To Me"—Conway Twitty (1976)

"Movin' On"—**Merle Haggard** (1975)

"Daddy Frank (The Guitar Man)"—**Merle Haggard** (1976)

"Cherokee Maiden"—**Merle Haggard** (1976)

"The Roots of My Raisin'"—**Merle Haggard**-written by **Tommy Collins** (1976)

"One Piece at a Time"—written by **Wayne Kemp** (recorded by Johnny Cash) (1976)

"Ramblin' Fever"—**Merle Haggard** (1977)

"Play, Guitar Play"—Conway Twitty (1977)

"I've Already Loved You In My Mind"—Conway Twitty (1977)

"If We're Not Back in Love By Monday"—**Merle Haggard** (1977)

"I'm Always on a Mountain When I Fall"—**Merle Haggard** (1978)

"It's Been a Great Afternoon"—**Merle Haggard** (1978)

"Heartbreak Hotel"—**Leon Russell** and Willie Nelson (1979)

"Your Love Had Taken Me That High" – written by **Jack Dunham** (recorded by Conway Twitty) (1979)

"Don't Take It Away"—Conway Twitty (1979)

"I May Never Get to Heaven"—Conway Twitty (1979)

"Happy Birthday Darlin'"—Conway Twitty (1979)

1980s

"Beneath Still Waters"— written by **Dallas Frazier** (recorded by Emmylou Harris) (1980)

"I'd Love To Lay You Down"—Conway Twitty (1980)

"Bar Room Buddies"—**Merle Haggard** with Clint Eastwood (1980)

"I Think I'll Just Stay Here and Drink"—**Merle Haggard** (1980)

"All My Love"—**GAP Band** (1980)

"Elvira"—written by **Dallas Frazier** (recorded by Oak Ridge Boys) (1981)

"Blue Shadows"—**Lowell Fulson** (1981)

"Rest Your Love On Me"—Conway Twitty (1981)

"Tight Fittin' Jeans"—Conway Twitty (1981)

"Red Neckin' Love Makin' Night"—Conway Twitty (1981)

"But You Know I Love You"—written by **Mike Settle** (recorded by Dolly Parton) (1981)

"Love in the First Degree"—co-written by Tim DuBois (recorded by Alabama) (1981)

"Midnight Hauler"—written by Tim DuBois (recorded by Razzy Bailey) (1981)

"Big City"—**Merle Haggard** (1981)

"My Favorite Memory"—**Merle Haggard** (1981)

"Rainbow Stew"—**Merle Haggard** (1981)

"Fourteen Carat Mind"—written by **Dallas Frazier** (recorded by Gene Watson) (1981)

"You're the Reason God Made Oklahoma"—written by **Larry Collins** (recorded by Shelly West and David Frizell) (1981)

"Burn Rubber (Why You Wanna Hurt Me)"—**GAP Band** (1981)

"Early in the Morning"—**GAP Band** (1982)

"The Clown"—Conway Twitty (1982)

"Slow Hand"—Conway Twitty (1982)

"The Rose"—Conway Twitty (1982)
"Yesterday's Wine"—**Merle Haggard** with George Jones (1982)
"Are the Good Times Really Over?"—**Merle Haggard** (1982)
"Can't Even Get the Blues"—**Reba McEntire** (1982)
"Going Where the Lonely Go"—**Merle Haggard** (1982)
"You're the First Time I've Thought About Leaving"—**Reba McEntire** (1982)
"You Dropped a Bomb on Me"—**GAP Band** (1982)
"Pancho and Lefty"—**Merle Haggard** with Willie Nelson (1983)
"Outstanding"—**GAP Band** (1983)
"You Take Me for Granted"—**Merle Haggard** (1983)
"That's the Way Love Goes"—**Merle Haggard** (1983)
"New Looks From an Old Lover"—**B. J. Thomas** (1983)
"Whatever Happened to Old Fashioned Love"—**B. J. Thomas** (1983)
"Somebody Should Leave"—**Reba McEntire** (1984)
"Baby's Got Her Blue Jeans On"—**Mel McDaniel** (1984)
"Somebody's Needin' Somebody"—Conway Twitty (1984)
"I Don't Know A Thing About Love (The Moon Song)"—Conway Twitty (1984)
"Ain't She Somethin' Else"—Conway Twitty (1984)
"Let's Chase Each Other Around the Room"—**Merle Haggard** (1984)
"A Place to Fall Apart"—**Merle Haggard** (1984)
"Someday When Things Are Good"—**Merle Haggard** (1984)
"Don't Call Him A Cowboy"—Conway Twitty (1985)
"Natural High"—**Merle Haggard** (1985)
"How Blue"—**Reba McEntire** (1984)
"Somebody Should Leave"—**Reba McEntire** (1985)
"Desperado Love"—Conway Twitty (1986)
"Whoever's in New England"—**Reba McEntire** (1986)
"Little Rock"—**Reba McEntire** (1986)
"That Rock Won't Roll"—**Restless Heart** (1986)
"I'll Still Be Loving You"—**Restless Heart** (1986)
"What Am I Gonna Do About You"—**Reba McEntire** (1986)
"The Last One to Know"—**Reba McEntire** (1987)
"One Promise to Late"—**Reba McEntire** (1987)
"The Last One to Know"—**Reba McEntire** (1987)
"Wheels"—**Restless Heart** (1987)
"Why Does He Have To Be (Wrong or Right)"—**Restless Heart** (1987)
"Twinkle, Twinkle Lucky Star"—**Merle Haggard** (1987)
"I'll Leave This World "Loving You"—written by **Wayne Kemp** (recorded by Ricky Van Shelton) (1988)
"Love Will Find Its Way To You"—**Reba McEntire** (1988)
"Bluest Eyes in Texas"—**Restless Heart** (1988)
"A Tender Lie"—**Restless Heart** (1988)

"I Know How He Feels"—**Reba McEntire** (1988)
"New Fool at an Old Game"—**Reba McEntire** (1988)
"Cathy's Clown"—**Reba McEntire** (1989)
"If Tomorrow Never Comes"—**Garth Brooks** (1989**)**

1990s
"Walk On"—**Reba McEntire** (1990)
"You Lie"—**Reba McEntire** (1990)
"Rumor Has It"—**Reba McEntire** (1990)
"The Dance"—**Garth Brooks** (1990)
"The Heart Won't Lie"—**Reba McEntire** and **Vince Gill** (1990)
"When I Call Your Name"—**Vince Gill**—
    written by **Vince Gill** and Tim DuBois (1990)
"Never Knew Lonely"—**Vince Gill** (1990)
"Home"—**Joe Diffie** (1990)
"If You Want Me To"—**Joe Diffie** (1990)
"If the Devil Danced (In Empty Pockets)"—**Joe Diffie** (1990)
"New Way (To Light Up an Old Flame)"—**Joe Diffie** (1990)
"You Lie"—**Reba McEntire** (1990)
"Rumor Has It'—**Reba McEntire** (1990)
"Not Counting You"—**Garth Brooks** (1990)
"Friends in Low Places"—**Garth Brooks** (1990)
"My Next Broken Heart"—Brooks & **Dunn** (1991)
"Brand New Man"—Brooks & **Dunn** (1991)
"Liza Jane"—**Vince Gill** (1991)
"Unanswered Prayers"—**Garth Brooks** (1991)
"Two of a Kind, Workin' on a Full House"—**Garth Brooks** (1991)
"The Thunder Rolls"—**Garth Brooks** (1991)
"Shameless"—**Garth Brooks** (1991)
"What She's Doing Now"—**Garth Brooks** (1991)
"The River"—**Garth Brooks** (1991)
"Rodeo"—**Garth Brooks** (1991)
"For My Broken Heart"—**Reba McEntire** (1991)
"If I Had Only Known"—**Reba McEntire** (1991)
"The Greatest Man I Ever Knew"—**Reba McEntire** (1991)
"For My Broken Heart"—**Reba McEntire** (1991)
"All 4 Love"—**Color Me Badd** (1991)
"I Adore Mi Amour"—**Color Me Badd** (1991) #1 pop and R & B
"I Wanna Sex You Up"—**Color Me Badd** (1991) #1 R & B and dance
"Boot Scootin' Boogie"—Brooks & **Dunn** (1992)
"I Still Believe In You"—**Vince Gill** (1992)
"Look at Us"—**Vince Gill** (1992)
"Don't Let Our Love Start Slippin' Away"—**Vince Gill** (1992)

"Is There Life Out There"—**Reba McEntire** (1992)

"It's Your Call"—**Reba McEntire** (1992)

"Ships That Don't Come In"—**Joe Diffie** (1992)

"Is It Cold In Here?"—**Joe Diffie** (1992)

"Somewhere Other Than the Night"—**Garth Brooks** (1992)

"Neon Moon"—Brooks & **Dunn** (1992)

"One More Last Chance"—**Vince Gill** (1993)

"The Heart Won' Lie"—**Vince Gill** *and* **Reba McEntire** (1993)

"Honky Tonk Attitude"—**Joe Diffie** (1993)

"John Deere Green"—**Joe Diffie** (1993)

"My Love"—Little Texas (1993)

"What Might Have Been"—Little Texas (**Tim Rushlow**) (1993)

"God Blessed Texas"—Little Texas (**Tim Rushlow**) (1993)

"We'll Burn That Bridge"—Brooks & **Dunn** (1993)

"She Used To Be Mine"—Brooks & **Dunn** (1993)

"Standing Outside the Fire"—**Garth Brooks** (1993)

"That Summer"—**Garth Brooks** (1993)

"Ain't Going Down (til the Sun Comes Up)"—**Garth Brooks** (1993)

"American Honky-Tonk Bar Association"—**Garth Brooks** (1993)

"Learning to Live Again"—**Garth Brooks** (1993)

"Does He Love You"—**Reba McEntire** and Linda Davis (1993)

"Should've Been a Cowboy"—**Toby Keith** (1993)

"Wish I Didn't Know Now"—**Toby Keith** (1993)

"A Little Less Talk and a Lot More Action"—**Toby Keith** (1993)

"Does That Blue Moon Ever Shine on You"—**Toby Keith** (1994)

"Me Too"—**Toby Keith** (1994)

"What the Cowgirls Do"—**Vince Gill** (1994)

"Tryin' to Get Over You"—**Vince Gill** (1994)

"Whenever You Come Around"—**Vince Gill** (1994)

"Third Rock from the Sun"—**Joe Diffie** (1994)

"Pickup Man"—**Joe Diffie** (1994)

"She's Not the Cheatin' Kind"—Brooks & **Dunn** (1994)

"That Ain't No Way To Go"—Brooks & **Dunn** (1994)

"My Love"—Little Texas (**Tim Rushlow**) (1994)

"Till You Love Me"—**Reba McEntire** (1994)

"The Heart is a Lonely Hunter"—**Reba McEntire** (1995)

"And Still"—**Reba McEntire** (1995)

"Rock My World (Little Country Girl)"—Brooks & **Dunn** (1994)

"Someone Else's Star"—**Bryan White** (1995)

"Rebecca Lynn"—**Bryan White** (1995)

"Little Miss Honky Tonk"—Brooks & **Dunn** (1995)

"You're Gonna Miss Me When I'm Gone"—Brooks & **Dunn** (1995)

"Go Rest High on That Mountain"—**Vince Gill** (1995)

"When Love Finds You"—**Vince Gill** (1995)

"You Better Think Twice"—**Vince Gill** (1995)

"She's Every Woman"—**Garth Brooks** (1995)

"Beaches of Cheyenne"—**Garth Brooks** (1995)

"Old Enough to Know Better"—**Wade Hayes** (1995)

"Bigger Than the Beatles"—**Joe Diffie** (1995)

"Who's That Man"—**Toby Keith** (1995)

"You Ain't Much Fun"—**Toby Keith** (1995)

"Not On Your Love"—**Jeff Carson** (1995)

"So Help Me Girl"—**Joe Diffie** (1995)

"So Much For Pretending"—**Bryan White** (1996)

"On a Good Night"—**Wade Hayes** (1996)

"The Fear of Being Alone"—**Reba McEntire** (1996)

"How Was I To Know"—**Reba McEntire** (1996)

"My Maria"—Brooks & **Dunn** (1996)

"A Man This Lonely"—Brooks & **Dunn** (1996)

"I Will Always Love You"—**Vince Gill** and Dolly Parton (1996)

"Pretty Little Adriana"—**Vince Gill** (1996)

"Daddy's Money"—**Richochet** (1996)

"I'd Rather Ride Around With You"—**Reba McEntire** (1997)

"Me Too"—**Toby Keith** (1996)

"Sittin' On Go"—**Bryan White** (1997)

"I'm So Happy I Could Stop Crying"—**Toby Keith** with Sting (1997)

"When We Were In Love—**Toby Keith** (1997)

"Long Neck Bottle"—**Garth Brooks** (1997)

"Two Pina Coladas"—**Garth Brooks** (1997)

"In Another's Eyes"—**Garth Brooks** (1997)

"She's Gonna Make It"—**Garth Brooks** (1997)

"A Little More Love"—**Vince Gill** (1997)

"MMMBop"—**Hanson** (1997)

"It's Not Right, But It's OK"—written by **Toni Estes**
    (recorded by Whitney Houston) (1998)

"How Long Gone"—Brooks & **Dunn** (1998)

"Husbands and Wives"—Brooks & **Dunn** (1998)

"To Make You Feel My Love"—**Garth Brooks** (1998)

"You Moved Me"—**Garth Brooks** (1998)

"If You Ever Have Forever in Mind"—**Vince Gill** (1998)

"If You See Him, If You See Her"—**Reba McEntire** with Brooks & **Dunn**
    (1998)

"How Do You Like Me Now?"—**Toby Keith** (1999)

"You Shouldn't Kiss Me Like This"—**Toby Keith** (1999)

"What Do You Say"—**Reba McEntire** (1999)

"My Kind of Woman/My Kind of Man" - **Vince Gill** with Patty Loveless (1999)

"Don't Come Cryin' To Me"—**Vince Gill** (1999)

"I Wanna Love You Forever" – Jessica Simpson (co-written by Sam Watters) (1999)

<u>2000s</u>

"There Ain't Nothing 'Bout You"—Brooks & **Dunn** (2001)

"I'm Just Talkin' About Tonight"—**Toby Keith** (2001)

"I Wanna Talk About Me"—**Toby Keith** (2001)

"My List"—**Toby Keith** (2001)

"Only in America"—Brooks & **Dunn** (2001)

"The Long Goodbye"—Brooks & **Dunn** (2001)

"Austin"—**Blake Shelton** (2001)

"Courtesy of the Red, White, and Blue (The Angry American)"—**Toby Keith** (2002)

"These Days"—Rascal Flatts/**Joe Don Rooney** (2002)

"Who's Your Daddy" – **Toby Keith** (2002)

"One Day in Your Life" - Anastacia (co-written by Sam Watters of **Color Me Badd**) (2002)

"The Baby" – **Blake Shelton** (2003)

"Beer for My Horses" – Toby Keith (duet with Willie Nelson) (2003)

"Red Dirt Road" – Brooks and Dunn (2003)

Analysis of #1 Hits by Oklahomans

1940s –   20
1950s –   31
1960s –   35
1970s –   61
1980s –   67
1990s – 123
2000s –   13 (As of August, 2003)

   Total=350

Most Popular Oklahoma Musician By Decade
with More Than One #1 Song Composed or Recorded
(**Bold** indicates the artist has an entry in this guide):

<u>1940s</u>

Bob Wills (6 recorded)	6
Floyd Tillman (2 recorded/2 written)	4
Spade Cooley (2 recorded)	2
Gene Autry (2 recorded)	2
Jimmy Wakely (2 recorded)	2
Total	16

<u>1950s</u>

Patti Page (7 recorded)	7
Kay Starr (5 recorded)	5
Hank Thompson (4 recorded)	4
Eddie Miller (2 written)	2
Total	18

<u>1960s</u>

Merle Haggard (11 recorded)	11
Roger Miller (4 written/recorded)	4

Jimmy Webb (4 written)	4
Conway Twitty (3 recorded)	3
Dallas Frazier (3 written)	3
Total	25

1970s

Conway Twitty	24
Merle Haggard	19
David Gates	3
Cal Smith	3
Dallas Frazier (2 written)	2
Total	51

1980s

Merle Haggard	17
Reba McEntire	15
Conway Twitty	11
Restless Heart	6
GAP Band	4
B. J. Thomas	2
Dallas Frazier (2 written)	2
Tim DuBois (2 written)	2
Total	59

1990s

Note: Oklahomans completely dominated the country charts in the 1990s with 10 different artists/groups appearing regularly in top album and singles charts. Artists outside of the country genre with #1 hits in the 1990s were **Color Me Badd**, and former Color Me Badd singer/song-writer, Sam Watters, **Hanson**, and **Toni Estes**.

Garth Brooks	24
Reba McEntire	22
Vince Gill	21

Brooks & **Dunn**	16
Joe Diffie	12
Toby Keith	12
Color Me Badd	5
Little Texas (**Tim Rushlow**)	4
Bryan White	4
Wade Hayes	2
Sam Watters (co-written)	1
Tim Dubois (co-written)	1
Total	124

<u>2000s</u>

Toby Keith	6
Brooks & **Dunn**	4
Sam Watters (co-written)	1
Total	11

<u>Most #1 Hits Recorded by Artist or Group with Oklahoma Connections</u>

Merle Haggard	47
Reba McEntire	37
Conway Twitty	34
Garth Brooks	25
Vince Gill	21
Brooks & **Dunn**	20
Toby Keith	18
Color Me Badd	5

<u>Most #1 Hits Written by Oklahoma Composer</u>

Dallas Frazier	7

(spans three decades of songwriting)
    "Alley Oop"—1960
    "All I Have to Offer You (Is Me)"—1969
    "(I'm So) Afraid of Losing You Again"—1969
    "What's Your Mama's Name"—1973
    "The Who Am I"—1975

"Beneath Still Waters"—1980
"Fourteen Carat Mind"—1981

Color Me Badd and Sam Watters   5

"I Adore Mi Amor" – 1991 (CMB)
"All 4 Love" – 1992 (CMB) #1 Pop and R & B (Counts as 2)
"I Wanna Love You Forever" – 1999 (co-writer Watters)
"One Day in Your Life" - 2001 (co-writer Watters)

Jimmy Webb   4

"Up, Up and Away"—1967
"MacArthur Park"—1968
"Wichita Lineman"—1968
"Galveston"—1969

Oklahoma Music Guide

A
Musical
Postcard
from
Oklahoma

Oklahoma Place-Based
Song Titles,
Lyrics,
and Album Titles

A Musical Postcard from Oklahoma
(*Oklahoma Place-Based Song Titles, Lyrics, and Album Titles*)

Songs With Oklahoma in the Title:
"Oklahoma!" (state song) - recorded more than 100 times

"Oklahoma" - Billy Gilman

"Oklahoma Wind" (state waltz)—Billy Joe Shaver/Waylon Jennings

"Oklahoma Hills"—Jack Guthrie/Woody Guthrie (recorded more than 70 times)

"Oklahoma's Calling"—Jack Guthrie"You're the Reason God Made Oklahoma"-David Frizzell and Shelly West (co-composed by Larry Collins-b. near Tahlequah)

"For Oklahoma, I'm Yearning"—Jack Guthrie

"If I Ever Get Back to Oklahoma" – Jason Boland and the Stragglers

"If You're Ever in Oklahoma"—J.J. Cale

"Home, Sweet Oklahoma"—Tom Paxton/Leon Russell/Jimmy LaFave

"Oklahoma and O.J."-Paul Krassner

"Oklahoma Bill"—Jimmy Dean

"Oklahoma Country"—Stampeders

"Oklahoma Double Shuffle"—Jerry Riopelle

"Oklahoma Dreamer"—Kent Unruh

"Oklahoma Elegy"—G. E. Stinson

"Oklahoma Flats"—Alan Munde

"Oklahoma Front Porch Band"—Terri Lynn

"Oklahoma Gals"—Bob Wills

"Oklahoma Honky Tonk Girl"—Sheb Wooley

"Oklahoma Lou"—Swinging West

"Oklahoma Man Blues"—Lucille Bogan

"Oklahoma Morning"—Charley Pride

"Oklahoma Plain"—Bucket No. Six

"Oklahoma Polka"—Rotondi

"Oklahoma Posse"—Gordon Payne

"Oklahoma Quickstep"—Traditional Fiddle Music

"Oklahoma Redbird"—old time fiddle tune recorded by many

"Oklahoma Rooster"—Young Fogies/Backwoods Banjo

"Oklahoma Roots"—Michael Davis

"Oklahoma Round Dance"—Vintage Native American Music

"Oklahoma Run"—traditional fiddle music/also known as "Old Purcell"

"Oklahoma Shines"—Mel McDaniel

"Oklahoma Song"—Hoyt Axton

"Oklahoma Shuffle"—Ray Drew

"Oklahoma Sunday Morning"—Glen Campbell

"Oklahoma Superstar"—Brenda Lee

"Oklahoma Territory"—Far and Away

"Oklahoma Sunshine"—Waylon Jennings

"Oklahoma Toad"—Richard "Groove" Holmes/Bob Dorough/Dave Fishberg

"Oklahoma Twilight"—Wayne Parker

"Oklahoma Woman"—Roger Miller

"Oklahoma Rodeo Queen"—Dana Cooper

"Oklahoma Dancer"—The Monkees

"Oklahoma Going Home"—Kate Wolf & Wildflower Flower

"Oklahoma Heartaches & California Dreams"—Kris Carpenter

"Oklahoma"—Billy Gillman ("Son we think we found your dad in Oklahoma. . .
   Son it's time to meet your Dad in Oklahoma. . . "Son welcome to your home
   in Oklahoma")

"Oklahoma Joe"—Chris LeDoux

"Oklahoma Man Blues"—Lucille Bogan

"Oklahoma Boy"—Willis Alan Ramsey/Dewayne Boyd and Silver Dollar Band/Lazarus

"My Oklahoma"—Riders in the Sky/Steve Young

"King of Oklahoma"—Michael Franks

"Oklahoma Intertribal Song"—Southern Thunder

"Oklahoma Kid"—Goebel Reeves

"(My) Home in Oklahoma"—Roy Rogers

"Oklahoma Cry Song"—Dean Evenson

"Night in Oklahoma"—Larry McNeely

"Oklahoma Borderline"-Vince Gill/Rodney Crowell/Guy Clark

"Oklahoma Crude"—Henry Mancini

"Oklahoma Home Brew"-Hank Thompson

"Oklahoma Blues"—Patti Page/Western Caravan/Luke Wills/Steve Ripley

"Oklahoma Rag"—Bob Wills

"Oklahoma Stomp"—Duke Ellington/Spade Cooley/Byron Berline

"Oklahoma Stroke"—Albert Lee

"Oklahoma Sweetheart Sally"— Maddox Brothers & Rose

"Oklahoma Sweetheart"—George Thorogood & The Destroyers

"Oklahoma, U.S.A"—The Kinks

"Oklahoma"—Michael Been ("Another hot Oklahoma night")

"The Girl Who Danced Oklahoma"—Terry Allen

"The Headless Samuraii of Oatmogie Oklahoma"—The Scabs

"Rough Wind in Oklahoma"—Michael Hedges

"Take Me Back to Oklahoma"—Tim Rex

"Tokyo, Oklahoma"—John Anderson

"Oklahoma Swing"—Reba McEntire/Vince Gill

"Oklahoma Two-Step"—Songs of Earth, Water, Fire, and Sky

"Oklahoma Waltz"—Johnny Bond/Cavaliers

"Oklahoma Country Girl"—Elvin Bishop

"Oklahoma Baby"—Rockabilly Fever

"Oklahoma Dreamer"—Kent Unruh

"Oklahoma Breakdown"—Flying Burrito Brothers

"My Oklahoma Home (It Blowed Away)"-Agnes "Sis" Cunningham

"Gotta Get to Oklahoma (Cause California's Gettin' To Me)"—The Hagars

"Ballad of Oklahoma"—Bob Duncan

"Happy Oklahoma"—Hank Thompson

Oklahomadejaneiro [album title]—Tattoed Love Dogs

"Big Boat Across Oklahoma"—Hank Thompson

"Oklahoma's Fall"—Alvaro's Brazilian Jazz

"Spring in Oklahoma"-Butterfly Wing

"Oklahoma's OK!"—Bobby Barnett

"Oklahoma, Land of the Sunny West"—Frankie and Joe Marvin
"The Everlasting Hills of Oklahoma"—Sons of the Pioneers
"Boys From Oklahoma"—Red Dirt Rangers/Cross Canadian Ragweed
"The Gal From Oklahoma"—Junior Brown
"My Oklahoma"—Riders in the Sky/Steve Young/Clay Greenburg
"Where the Arkansas River Leaves Oklahoma"—Don Williams
    ("I met her in Stilwell")
"Good Old Oklahoma"—Bob Wills
"Oklahoma Nights"—Jimmy Webb/Arlo Guthrie
"A Yid Iz Geboren Ins Oklahoma"—Bad Livers
    (Mark Rubin was born in Stillwater, OK)
"Boy From Oklahoma"—Willis Alan Ramsey
Southern Oklahoma Cosmic Trigger Contest (album title)—The Flaming Lips
"From Oklahoma With Love"—Becky Hobbs
"Long Way From OK"—Jeff Wood ("This sure don't feel like Oklahoma")
"My Pathway Leads Me to Oklahoma"—Bill Grant
"Bill Doolin (King of the Oklahoma Outlaws)"—Bobby Barnett
"Oklahoma Breeze"—Left of Memphis
"Back to Oklahoma"—Michael Fracasso
"Soft Winds of Oklahoma"—Bill Emerson
"God is Down in Oklahoma"—Mike West
"Oklahoma '41"—Mark Elliott
"Dark Night in Oklahoma"—Mr. Jones
"They Came from Oklahoma"—Bob Schneider
"Oklahoma"—Whiskeytown
"Oklahoma State of Mind"—Christian Kane
"Oklahoma Credit Card"—Kinzel & Hyde
"The Unfriendly Cows of Oklahoma"—Billy Burke
"At Old Bill's Place in Oklahoma"—Peter Power and Ulrich Jonas
"Oklahoma 1912"—Lou Ann Bardash
"Texas & Oklahoma"—Rattlesnake Annie
"Oklahoma Crude"—Bob Corbin
"Oklahoma"—Last Forever
"Oklahoma Bluegrass Blues"—Bill Grant and Delia Bell
"Oklahoma" [not the musical]—Susan Toney
"Oklahoma Suite"—Jeff Dufine (OKC bombing)
"Oklahoma"[not the musical]—Chris Chandler/Dan Bern (OKC bombing)
"Oklahoma"—AteOlf Hitler's Nipples ("I'm comin' back to you, Oklahoma,
    Before my dark and dismal life away is through")
"Oklahoma"—Common Rotation ("There's a skyline in Oklahoma . . .
    Oklahoma's sunset has color")
"Hooray Oklahoma" – composed by Frank Douglas, 1952
"Oklahoma: A Toast"- 1935 Oklahoma state song composed by Harriet Parker Camden
"Out in Oklahoma" – composed by Stephen Shannon, 1911
"The Oklahoma Twirl" – lyrics by William Tracey, music by Lewis F. Muir
    and James McGavisk, 1910
Oklahoma Girl (album title) — Reba McEntire

Songs With Oklahoma in the Lyrics:

"Shirts by the Millions" from the Gershwins' musical *Let' em Eat Cake* [Act I]
("from Maine to Oklahoma")
"Go Pato! All over America"—Pato Banton
(mentions Oklahoma as one of several states)
"Doc McDonald's Indian Medicine Show"—Terence Martin
("Through Texas, Oklahoma, and the Arkansas hills")
"Make Bucks, Get Rich, Be Better Than Anybody, Get Fat and Have a Heart Attack"—
Greg Keeler ("Long ago my granddad had a farm in Oklahoma")
"You Only Leave Your Heart Once"—Jack Hardy ("Left your heart in Oklahoma")
"Rolling Western Union"—music by Elton John/lyrics by Bernie Taupen—1970
[never released] ("She died in Oklahoma")
"My Hat"—Pere Ubu ("Some hats are shaped like Oklahoma")
"Why Wyoming"—Kellie Coffey (Oklahoma blue skies)
"Hide the Beer, the Pastor's Here"—The Swirling Eddies ("let's drive to Oklahoma")
"Get My Fill"—Steve Earle ("I never been out of old Oklahoma")
"The Ballad of Billy the Kid"—Billy Joel
("Well he robbed his way from Utah to Oklahoma")
"J.55"—Becker & Fagen ("I don't know if Oklahoma is a missing secret")
"The Grapes of Wrath"—Terry MacNamara ("Flies for Oklahoma all alone"
"Shoot Out on the Plantation"—Leon Russell (mentions Oklahoma)
"Hot Skin Cold Cash"—Puffball ("Back in Oklahoma")
"Banner Year"—Five Iron Frenzy
("Maps won't hold the melanoma, blurry part of Oklahoma")
"Red River"—Erectrons ("I drive to Oklahoma")
"Millionaire"—Killer Crows ("It all started when daddy struck oil in Oklahoma")
"Home In Your Arms"—Beverly Ellis ("couldn't find a job in Oklahoma")
"Short Skirts"—Baby Beesh ("And Oklahoma love the short skirts")
"The Heart of the Appaloosa"—Fred Small
("They were sent to Oklahoma, malaria ran rife")
"Travelin'"—Spencer Bohren (mentions Oklahoma)
"When You Say Texas"—Red Johnson ("From Oklahoma to the Rio Grande")
"My Guy"—Snackpants ("Been to Oklahoma, too")
"The Unabomber's Last Typed Letter to the New York Times"—Delicious Militia
("I'm going to send the Oklahoma militia")
"World Be Free"—Keith Murray ("on fire in Oklahoma")
"Three Button Hand-Me Down"—The Faces
("I was raised in a clinic down in Oklahoma")
"On the Road"—Tom Waits ("road to Oklahoma")
"Love of a Rolling Stone"—Bonnie Tyler ("On a path right in that Oklahoma sun")
"I've Got a Good Thing Going"—Garth Brooks ("This may be California,
but Oklahoma's in her eyes. . . I guess Oklahoma's more her style of living")
"Homogenized"—4th Blowing of the Great Nose ("Oklahoma bombing")
"The Rite of Spring"—David Dragov ("Oklahoma bombing")
"I-40 at Night"—Nate Borofsky ("I remember Oklahoma dark")
"Kneejerk . . ."—Thieves' Kitchen ("In Oklahoma or Littleton")

"Everybody Rise Again"—Busta Rhymes (mentions Oklahoma)
"The Mountain"—Steve Early & Del McCoury Band
    ("Would have lived in Oklahoma")
"Dallas-Bound Greyhound"—Blake Powers ("Oklahoma's movin' past me")
"Thumbelina"—Pretenders ("Oklahoma sunrise becomes the Amarillo dawn")
"Something's Got a Hold on Me"—Steve Forbert ("Oklahoma looks just fine")
"Little Bit of Heaven"—Jeffrey Rodman ("most of Oklahoma")
"Only God (Could Stop Me Loving You)"—Emerson Drive
    ("Now we struck oil in Oklahoma")
"My Summer Vacation"—Ice Cube (mentions Oklahoma)
"Tommy's Down Home"—Tesla ("Well a hail from Oklahoma")
"Benjamin"—Bobbie Gentry ("Ben and me spent some time in Oklahoma")
"Western Dreams"—Mustang Mesa ("Oklahoma is O.K. with me")
"Gypsy Roadhog"—Slade ("I powdered my nose in Oklahoma")
"Alcatraz"—Nazareth ("I left my home in Oklahoma")
"Texas Moon"—The Church ("I met a bunch of fools in Oklahoma")
"Never Been to Spain"—Hoyt Axton/Three Dog Night
    ("Never been to heaven, but I've been to Oklahoma")
"The Good Die Young"—Tupac Shakur [2Pac] ("Rest in peace [Oklahoma]")
"Saint Judas"—Natalie Merchant
    ("Go on down to Oklahoma" along with several other states)
"Sols of the Departed"—Bruce Springsteen ("Like dark geese into the Oklahoma skies")
"Woof Woof"—69 Boyz (mentions Oklahoma)
"Jim Thorpe"—Bobby Barnett ("born in Oklahoma")
"Road to Alaska"—BeeGees ("I dialed Oklahoma")
"By the Time I Get to Phoenix"—Jimmy Webb/Glen Campbell/Reba McEntire/
    Nashville West ("By the time I make Oklahoma")
"Muswell Hillbilly"—The Kinks ("Never seen New Orleans, Oklahoma, or Tennessee)
"Good to Go to Mexico"—Toby Keith ("cold Oklahoma wind")
"Billy Austin"—Steve Earl ("I was born in Oklahoma . . . Don't remember Oklahoma")
"Next to the Soil"—Jack Guthrie ("Wanna go back to Oklahoma, I'm happy there,
    livin' next to the soil")
"Pretty Boy Floyd"—Woody Guthrie/Bobby Barnett ("Oklahoma knew him well" and
    "Every crime in Oklahoma was added to his name")
"Richland, Washington"—James Talley (mentions "my daddy came from Oklahoma")
"When the Sun Shines Down on Me"—Kevin Welch ("raised in Oklahoma")
"Surprise, AZ"—Richard Buckner
    ("Where they take us back to Oklahoma where we belong")
"Dust of the Chase"—Ray Wylie Hubbard ("I came down from Oklahoma")
"California Cottonfields"—Merle Haggard
    ("This run-down mortgaged Oklahoma farm")
"Case Closed"—Redman ("Bomb n*gg*z like they did in Oklahoma")
"Da Bump"—Redman ("We be the bomb like that Oklahoma blast")
"Swordfishtrombones"—Tom Waits (Oklahoma)
"Gin Soaked Boy"—Tom Waits (Oklahoma)
"Dust Pneumonia Blues"—Woody Guthrie
    ("Down in Oklahoma, the wind blows mighty strong")
"If You Ain't Got the Do Re Mi"—Woody Guthrie (mentions Oklahoma)

"Blowin' Down This Road"—Woody Guthrie ("Lost my farm down in old Oklahoma"

"Tom Joad"—Woody Guthrie ("buried Grandpaw Joad on the Oklahoma road")

"Moonlight and Skies"—Glenn Orhlin ("Back in old Oklahoma")

"I Never Picked Cotton"—Johnny Cash ("When I was big enough to run,
   I'd never stay a single day in that Oklahoma sun")

"Press"—Paul McCartney ("Oklahoma was never like this . . .")

"Sweet Rosie Jones"—Buck Owens (mentions Rosie was from Oklahoma)

"Jools and Jim"—Pete Townshend (Oklahoma)

"Tony's Leaving Friendly's"—St. Huckleberry ("beyond the Oklahoma plains")

"Made in California"—Liquido ("She is the girl living in Oklahoma")

"Only in America"—Brooks & Dunn ("They just might go back to Oklahoma")

"Big Ol' Truck"—Toby Keith ("She's got Oklahoma plates")

"Bill Pickett of the 101"—Bobby Barnett ("back to Oklahoma and the famous 101")

"Somebody Slap Me"—John Anderson ("Runner up to Miss Oklahoma")

"The Year We Tried to Kill the Pain"—Bob Woodruff ("To a trip down to Oklahoma")

"Outlaw Man"—The Eagles ("Headed for Oklahoma")

"I Like Whiskey"—Freddie Krc (mentions Oklahoma)

"Somebody Must Be Prayin' For Me"—Tim McGraw
   ("She left Oklahoma for California sunglasses")

"Everywhere"—Tim McGraw ("Maybe in Oklahoma drivin' 'cross the prairie")

"Only God Could Stop Me Loving You"—Lari White and Toby Keith
   ("Now we struck oil in Oklahoma")

"Good Christian Soldier"—Bobby Bare ("Not so long ago in Oklahoma")

"Tumble Weed"—Bill Miller ("In an Oklahoma cow town where the sky begins to rain.
   . . Back when Indian territory was Oklahoma's name. . . . And you pass through
   Oklahoma and the sky begins to rain.")

"The Beast"—Fugees ("Connie Chung brung the bomb as it comes from Oklahoma")

"Up Against the Wall Redneck Mother"—Kinky Friedman
   ("He was born in Oklahoma")

"Rap Guys"—D12 ("First it was in Oklahoma")

"What the Cowgirls Do"—Vince Gill ("They ain't no different up in Oklahoma")

"Never Met a Man I Didn't Like"—Barry Manilow (mentions Oklahoma)

"W. Lee O'Daniel and the Light Crust Doughboys"—James Talley
   ("down in Oklahome")

"Let the Music Lift You Up"—Reba McEntire
   ("Hey, I'm a country girl, Over Oklahoma way")

"Till It Snows in Mexico"—Reba McEntire ("Riding up in Oklahoma")

"Sleepin' All Alone"—Jeremy Castle
   ("take her far away from our love and our Oklahoma home")

"I Wanna Make Her Mine"—Jeremy Castle
   ("Cause it's the girls from Oklahoma who make livin' in the country so much fun")

"Mister Jones"—Big Al Downing ("Killed a man in Oklahoma")

"Lady America"—"My mind keeps going back to Oklahoma"

"Everybody Rise"—Busta Rhymes (mentions Oklahoma in chorus)

"Blame It on Texas"—Mark Chesnutt ("Met a girl out in eastern Oklahoma")

"Closin' Time at Home"—Toby Keith
   ("If it's midnight in California, must be closin' time in Oklahoma")

"Tulsa Time"— performed by Don Williams and Reba McEntire
Danny Flowers-songwriter ("I left Oklahoma")
"Alkaholik"—Xzibit ("Got the spot blown, BOOM! Oklahoma")
"Captain David L. Payne"—Bobby Barnett ("Led his boomers to Oklahoma
. . . On to Oklahoma the promised land")
"Grandma's Song"—Gail Davies ("Oklahoma in the summertime")
"Bucket to the South"—Gail Davies
("Grandma's back in Oklahoma/Take me back to Oklahoma.")
"Yellow Pages Under Blue"—Becky Hobbs ("And if you're back in Oklahoma")
"Boogie Till the Cows Come Home"—Clay Walker ("The Oklahoma Stomp")
"Nowhere, Texas"—Cross Canadian Ragweed ("Leave Oklahoma far behind")
"Everybody's Got to Grow Up Sometime"—Sons of the Desert
("And owns half of Oklahoma")
"Let Us Begin (What Are We Making Weapons For?)"—John Denver
(I am a son of a grassland farmer . . . Western Oklahoma nineteen forty three")
"Tom Mix"—Bobby Barnett ("He came to Oklahoma")
"Motivators"—A Tribe Called Quest ("ask my peeps from Oklahoma")
"Salute to Will Rogers"—Bobby Barnett ("Oklahoma's favorite son")
"The Cowboy Hall of Fame"—Bobby Barnett ("In the state of Oklahoma")
"Humanesque"—Jeffrey Lee Pierce ("an even Oklahoma calls your name")
"I Got a Feelin'"—Tracy Lawrence ("I'm out here stranded on this Oklahoma road")
"Tumbleweed"—Afroman ("Met this lady in Oklahoma")
"Bill Pickett of the 101"—Bobby Barnett ("He'd head back to Oklahoma")
"Texas Dust"—Echolyn ("we get the dark dust of Oklahoma")
"Ballad of Pretty Boy Floyd"—Bobby Barnett ("In an Oklahoma town")
"Just Out of Reach"—Burtschi Brothers ("in that red Oklahoma clay")
"Walter's Theme"—R.E.M. ("I've got a hat the size of Oklahoma")
"Song for Hogs and Frost"—Delicious Militia ("hogs took over Oklahoma")
"I've Been Telling My Mom I'm Gonna Get a Sex Change"—Delicious Militia
("We can drive 75 miles an hour on the Interstate in Oklahoma" . . .
"if you don't like the weather in Oklahoma")
"Everytime That It Rains"—Garth Brooks ("Back to a rainy day in Oklahoma")
"American Bad Ass"—Kid Rock ("Who knew I'd blow up like Oklahoma")
"100% Texan"—Kevin Fowler ("Now, I don't mind going to Oklahoma")
"Alive and Well"—The Great Divide
("Well, I really hate leaving south Texas, And Oklahoma so far away")
"Bakersfield Bound"—Chris Hillman
("We lived in Oklahoma, the wind whistled through the door")
"State to State"—Black Child and Ja Rule ("On some Oklahoma bombing s_ _ _")
"The Open Book"—Glenn Ohrlin ("boosters from Oklahoma")
"Pawnee Bill"—Bobby Barnett ("His spirit for adventure brought him to Oklahoma")
"Tribute to Woody Guthrie"—Bobby Barnett ("Born in those Oklahoma hills")
"Henry Joseph"—Paul Kamm & Eleanore Macdonald
("Henry Junior was a farmer in the Oklahoma sun")
"The Howdy Song"—Monty Harper ("In Oklahoma we say 'Howdy'")
"Stampede to Read"—Monty Harper (It's a challenge in Oklahoma")
"What Did Delaware, Boys?")—traditional ("She's gone to Oklahoma')

"Brush Arbor Meeting"—Kevin Johnson
("Years ago, when I was just a boy in the Oklahoma hills")
"Swinging Home for Christmas"—The Tractors ("Oklahoma is my home")
"Cherokee Fiddle"—Michael Martin Murphy ("And then he'd go out to Oklahoma")
"Carolina Mountain Dew"—Alabama ("Somewhere in a motel out in Oklahoma")
"Follow Your Heart"—Kyle Shiver ("I was born in Oklahoma in 19 and 18")
"Blue Eyed Cowboy"—Terri Hendrix ("Dreamin' of Texas and south Oklahoma")
"Case of the Empty Stare"—David Hanners ("In a small town in Oklahoma")
"Ballad of the Newton Boys"—Bob Grez ("flauntin' the law in Oklahoma")
"Dance on Vaseline"—Talking Heads ("It started in Oklahoma")
"Frankie the Yankee"—Roots Quartet ("Stuck in Oklahoma, living in a coma")
"Dear Mary of Long Ago"—Scott Endsley
("Left your discontent behind—in Oklahoma way")
"The Little Man"—The Tractors ("You can bet all the wheat in Oklahoma")
"Dizzy"—Throwing Muses
("He said you're the only Indian in Oklahoma . . . The last time I saw Oklahoma")
"Northeast Texas Women"—Willis Alan Ramsey/Luke Olsen ("South of Oklahoma")
"Thinking About You"—Solange Knowles (mentions Oklahoma)
"Outlaw Man"—The Eagles ("Lived in Oklahoma")
"Boomtown Bill"—Woody Guthrie ("I lit in Oklahoma")
"Run of '89"—Bobby Barnett ("It was a clear and sunny day on the Oklahoma plains . .
. In the land called Oklahoma in the Run of '89")
"John 3:16"—D J Muggs ("We got'cha got'cha set up in Oklahoma")
"Post-Modern Blues"—Greg Keeler ("Lady, please drive me back to Oklahoma")
"Dust of the Chase – Ray Wylie Hubbard
("I come down from Oklahoma with a pistol in my boot")
"Back on the Road" – Willie Nelson with Lil' Black
("From Oklahoma, Louisiana, and back to Salt Lake City")
"For Anna Mae Pictou Aquash, Whose Spirit is Present Here and in the Dappled Stars"
Joy Harjo ("I heard about it in Oklahoma or New Mexico")
"Country Haiku" – Ty Hager ("Oklahoma's nice, Sometimes as I remember")
"I'm in Texas" – Ty Hager ("Went to California then back to Oklahoma")
"The Estates" – Chuck Dunlap ("There's a place in Oklahoma for a young man to go")

Songs With "Okie" in the Title or Lyrics:

"Dear Oakie"—Jack Rivers
"Oakie Boogie"—Jack Guthrie
"Dear Okie"—Hank Thompson
"Pour Me"—Trick Pony ("I always though he was a simple minded Okie")
"Here Comes that Rainbow Again"—Kris Kristofferson
("And two Okie kids by the door")
"Miss America's After Blaine"—The Delicious Militia (Okieland)
"Homesick, Lonesome, Hillbilly, Okie"—Hank Thompson
"I Wanna Make Her Mine"—Jeremy Castle

("If the girl you love's an Okie, then you know she's gotta be the one")
"100% Texan"—Kevin Fowler ("Ain't never met an Okie I didn't like")
"Okie's in the Pokie"—Jimmy Patton
"Miss America's After Blaine"—Delicious Militia
("covering Okieland . . . "the sky in Okie land")
"You Okies and Arkies"—Woody Guthrie
"The Ballad of Mad Dogs and Englishmen"—Leon Russell ("Okies")
Okie Special (album title)—Steve Gaines
"Texas Dust"—Echolyn ("they've left and become Okies")
"Okie Fiesta" – Don White ("It was an Okie fiesta, and just a poco loco")

Songs With Tulsa in the Title or Lyrics:

"Tulsa Time" -Don Williams/Eric Clapton/Reba McEntire/Danny Flowers (songwriter)
("Livin' on Tulsa time")
"On Your Own" – Cross Canadian Ragweed ("in a hotel room in Tulsa)
"Oil Derrick by West Tulsa"-Agnes "Sis" Cunningham
"24 Hours From Tulsa"—Burt Bacharach/H. David
"Ridin' into Tulsa"—composed by Ralph Blane (Broken Arrow native)
"Almost of Tulsa"—Red Rhodes
"Big Tulsa Tillie"—Donnie Rohrs
"Last Trip to Tulsa"—Neil Young
"Tulsa Queen"—Emmylou Harris
"Tulsa Turnaround"—Kenny Rogers & The First Edition
"Tulsa (Don't Let the Sun Set On You)" - Waylon Jennings/Dwight Twilley/
Billy Joe Royal
"T-U-L-S-A Straight Ahead"—Asleep at the Wheel/Leon McAuliffe
"Tulsa Style"—Brad Absher
"Passing Through Tulsa"—Tom Paxton
"Ten Miles to Tulsa"—String Cheese Incident
"Tulsa Baby"—Ecco-Fonic
"Tulsa Ballroom"—Dottie West
"Tulsa Black"-Cecil McBee
"The New Tulsa Blues"—Bennie Moten
"Tulsa Chili Bop"-Seldom Scene
"Tulsa Hop"—30 Fiddlers Greatest Hits
"Tulsa Imperative"-Diskothi-Q or The Wandering Jew
"Tulsa Love Affair"-Molly & the Heymakers
"Rebound to Tulsa" – Jack Dunham
"Tulsa, Oklahoma Blues"-Dave Brubeck
"Tulsa Rag"-Stewart Copeland
"Tulsa Shuffle"-Elvin Bishop/The Tractors
"Tulsa Stomp"—Bob Wills
"Tulsa Sunday"-Lee Hazlewood
"Tulsa Tango"-Stewart Copeland

"Tulsa Telephone Book"-Tom T. Hall

"Tulsa Twist"—Speedy West

"Tulsa Waltz"—Bob Wills

"Take Me Back to Tulsa"-Bob Wills & Texas Playboys/Asleep at the Wheel

"Tulsey Waltz"—old time fiddle tune (Marion Thede)

"Don't Make Me Come to Tulsa"—Wade Hayes

"The Day She Left Tulsa (In a Chevy)"—Wade Hayes

"Tell Me Something Bad about Tulsa"—Merle Haggard (1986) George Strait (2003)

"Tulsa Trot"—Tex Williams

"Tulsa County" – The Byrds

"Where I Come From"—Alan Jackson ("Aren't you from out in Tulsa")

"Long Black Road into Tulsa Town"—Dave Carter

"(Don't Let the Sun Set on You In) Tulsa"—Waylon Jennings

"I've Been Everywhere"—Hank Snow (Tulsa, Oklahoma)

"Texas Women (Don't Stay Lonely Long)"—Brooks & Dunn
　　　("by the time she gets to Tulsa")

"Convoy"—C. W. McCall ("By the time we got into Tulsa-Town")

"Rodeo"—Garth Brooks ("She knows his love's in Tulsa")

"Show Me What You Got"—Limpbizkit ("Tulsa")

"Back to Texas"—Tracy Byrd ("Drove all night to Oklahoma . . . I found you in Tulsa")

"Closin' Time at Home"—Toby Keith
　　　("Right now in Tulsa they've turned up the lights.")

"Back to Texas"—Tracy Byrd ("Drove all night to Oklahoma . . . I found you in Tulsa")

"Texas in 1880"—Radney Foster ("Ah, from Phoenix to Tulsa . . .")

"Groupie"—Snoop Dogg ("From Long Beach, California, from Tulsa, Oklahoma")

"With a Suitcase"—Tom Waits ("downtown Tulsa")

"I'm In Love All Over"—Reba McEntire ("Well I'm flying out of Tulsa")

"Prisoner of the Highway"—Ronnie Milsap
　　　("I've got to be hittin' Tulsa by first morning light")

"Blame It on Texas"—Mark Chesnutt ("Her daddy was a Tulsa millionaire.")

"Honky Tonk Saturday Night"—Becky Hobbs ("Well, I've loved'em back in Tulsa")

"White Line Casanova"—Brooks and Dunn ("I'm dead headin' down from Tulsa")

"A Little Place of Our Own"—The Tractors ("But I knew Murphy back in Tulsa")

"Seven Cups of Coffee, Fourteen Cigarettes"—Cornell Hurd Band
　　　("That Greyhound bound for Tulsa")

"W. Lee O'Daniel and the Light Crust Doughboys"—James Talley (mentions Tulsa)

"Till It Snows in Mexico"—Reba McEntire ("We met on a road from Tulsa")

"W*O*L*D*"—Harry Chapin ("So I drifted down to Tulsa, Oklahoma")

"W. Lee O'Daniel and the Light Crust Doughboys"—James Talley (mentions Tulsa)

"Going Nowhere Slow"—Bloodhound Gang (mentions Tulsa)

"Farmer's Luck"—Greg Jacobs (mentions Tulsa)

"Ramblin' Boy"—Tom Paxton (Tulsa town)

"Tulsa, My Hometown"—David Gates

Tulsa (album title)—Dwight Twilley

"200 Miles"—Cowboy Junkies ("Tulsa burns on the desert floor")

"The Heart of Rock and Roll"—Huey Lewis and the News (mentions Tulsa)

"Casey"—Marge Calhoun ("Casey went to Tulsa")

"The Glory Road"—Daniel Amos ("We hit the Metro out in Tulsa")

"From Kabul to Khartoum"—David Rovics ("From Tulsa to El Chorillo")
"Oklahoma Crude"—Bob Corbin ("I left my folks just south of Tulsa")
"Someday"—D.W. Phipps ("That night you came from Tulsa")
"Jack Straw"—The Grateful Dead ("Gotta get to Tulsa")
"Is This Any Way to Run an Airline?"—Tom Paxton
    ("And Tulsa's closed tonight you know")
"Northern Cross"—CryCryCry ("I can take this road all the way to Tulsa")
"14 Hours From Tulsa"—Red Meat
"Little Annie"—Songo ("And the family she left back in Tulsa")
"Tulsa"—Sixty Acres
"Can't Buy Happiness"—Bob Whitelock ("I pulled into Tulsa")
"Rock and Roll Music To The World"—Jimmy LaFave (mentions Tulsa)
"On the Road to Rock and Roll"—Jimmy LaFave ("Tulsa time")
"Tulsa on Saturday Night"—old time fiddle tune
"You're the Reason God Made Oklahoma"—David Frizell and Shelly West
    ("There's a full moon over Tulsa")
"Tampa to Tulsa"–The Jayhawks ("Tampa to Tulsa, just one layover")
"Where I Come From" – Alan Jackson ("Aren't you from out in Tulsa?")
"T-Town Blues" – Ernie Fields Orchestra

Songs with Oklahoma City in Title or Lyrics:

"Oklahoma City"—Elsie Muniz/Captain Janks/Winston Grennan
"Oklahoma City Alarm Clock"-Fixtures/Virus That Would Not Die
"Oklahoma City and Anti-Pol-Fixtures/Virus That Would Not Die
"Oklahoma City"—Dan Bern (OKC bombing)
"Happy All the Time"—Rod MacDonald
    ("Who built the bomb (that blew Oklahoma City down?")
"Cast the First Stone"—7BN (OKC bombing)
"Damnation Alleyway"—Hawkwind ("Oklahoma City, what a pity it's gone")
"The USA Don't Exist"—Solefad ("An' the fire that blew up Oklahoma")
"Heart of Rock and Roll"—Huey Lewis and the News (mentions Oklahoma City)
"Route 66"—Nat "King" Cole and others/composed by Bobby and Cynthia Troup
    (mentions Oklahoma City) "as being mighty pretty"
"For a While"—Jeremy Castle (mentions Oklahoma City)
"Positively Negative"—Xzibit ("By sending birds to Oklahoma City")
"Stockyard Blues"—Jeremy Castle (mentions Oklahoma City)
"Country Comes to Town"—Toby Keith ("As I pass that Oklahoma City limit sign")
"The Great Dust Storm (Dust Storm Disaster)"—Woody Guthrie
    ("From Oklahoma City to the Arizona line")
"Hillbilly Hollywood"—Nitty Gritty Dirt Band
    ("from Oklahoma City down to Tupelo")
"Never Goin' Back"—John Stewart
    ("Oklahoma City, yes, I know that she won't treat me cruel")
"Pretty Boy Floyd"—Woody Guthrie/Bobby Barnett ("Was in Oklahoma City")

"Dodge the Sprinkles"—Mr. Nitro (Oklahoma City streets)
"Radio Waves"—Roger Waters ("Oklahoma City radio waves")
"The Cowboy Hall of Fame"—Bobby Barnett ("In Oklahoma City")
"Okahoma"—Chris Chandler/Dan Bern
   ("In Oklahoma City, on Wednesday nine o'clock") [OKC bombing]
"Happy Death Day"—Gwar
   ("Let's make the world an Oklahoma City" [OKC bombing]
"Dreamweapon Benefit for Oklahoma City"—Angus Maclise [OKC bombing]
Brain Damage in Oklahoma City [album title]—Angus Maclise
"On My Way"—Encanto ("I'm in Oklahoma City")
"Oklahoma City Times"—Bobby Sherman
"Oklahoma City Blues"—Jimmy Wakely/Buddy Jones/Neal Pattman
"(Gotta Get To) Oklahoma City"—Luke Wills
"Hennessey"—Mr. Nitro (Oklahoma City)
"Capital"—Sean Altman (mentions Oklahoma City as one of the state capitals)
"Going Nowhere Slow"—Bloodhound Gang (mentions Oklahoma City)
"So, Virginia, What Do People Look Like There?"—The Delicious Militia
   (mentions Oklahoma City)

Songs With Muskogee in Title or Lyrics:

"Okie From Muskogee"—Merle Haggard "We don't smoke marijuana in Muskogee"
   and "Muskogee, Oklahoma, U.S.A."
"Muskogee"-Tex Roberg
"Muskogee Blue"—Bobby Gordon
"Muskogee Blues"-Mugsy Spanier
"Muskogee Small"-Jacob Fred Jazz Odyssey
"Who's Gonna Fill Their Shoes?"—George Jones ("The Okie from Muskogee")
"Waitin' Round to Die"- ("took me back to Muskogee")
"Leonard"—Merle Haggard ("Hey! Back before Muskogee came along")
"South of Muskogee Town"—Greg Jacobs
The Man From Muskogee—album title/Jay McShann
"Mama's Milk"—Betsy Jones ("Nairobi, Muskogee, or Marakesh")
"Up Against the Wall Redneck Mother" - Ray Wylie Hubbard ("Muskogee, Oklahoma

Song and Lyrics That Mention Additional Oklahoma Cities/Towns:

"Oklahoma on My Mind"—Jeremy Castle
"Wanna Make Her Mine"—Jeremy Castle (mentions Blanchard, OK)
"Yellow Pages Under Blue"—Becky Hobbs ("Got some friends in Chickasha")
"Tom Joad"—Woody Guthrie ("Got out of the old McAlester pen")
"Pretty Boy Floyd"—Woody Guthrie/Bobby Barnett ("Was in the town of Shawnee")
"Trains Don't Run Here No More"—Greg Jacobs (mentions Checotah)
"Farmer's Luck"—Greg Jacobs (mentions Checotah)

"Moffett, Oklahoma"—Charlie Walker
"W. Lee O'Daniel and the Light Crust Doughboys"—James Talley (mentions Pawnee)
"Do the Damn Thing"—Mr. Nitro (mentions Spencer, Oklahoma)
"Idabel Blues"—Red Dirt Rangers
"Bucket to the South"—Gail Davies ("Broken Bow was good to me.")
"Mehan, Oklahoma"—James Talley
"The Ballad of John McEntire"-Reba, Pake, and Susie McEntire
    ("1897 was the year he was born in Loula, Oklahoma, On a small dirt farm")
"I Wish You'd Stay"—Brad Paisley ("Once you reach Sallisaw it's interstate")
"Tribute to Woody Guthrie" —Bobby Barnett
    "From Okemah, Oklahoma, to a small West Texas town"
"Songs for Hogs and Frost"—The Delicious Militia (mentions Stillwater)
"Guthrie"—Hank Thompson
"Tom Mix"—Bobby Barnett ("He was a bartender in Guthrie")
"Matthew Kimes"—Woody Guthrie ("In old Okemah")
"Moonlight and Skies"—Glenn Ohrlin ("not far from Shawnee")
"Ballad of Belle Starr"—Bobby Barnett/James Talley
    (she lived near Wilburton, Porum, and Fanshawe)
"Old Purcell"—traditional fiddle tune
"I've Been Telling My Mom I'm Gonna Get a Sex Change"—Delicious Militia
    ("I've been to Perry")
Red Rock, Oklahoma (album title)—Yellowhammer
"I'm Addicted to the Weather Channel"—Delicious Militia
    ("Lightnin' struck tonight in
    Hydro, Oklahoma")
"I'm Addicted to the Weather Channel"—Delicious Militia
    ("The streets are all so empty now in Stillwater")
"No Woman's Flesh But Hers"—Johnny Dowd ("Paul's Valley, Oklahoma")
"Ballad of Bodacious"—Primus
    ("He's born in Galry, Oklahoma") [not on Oklahoma map]
"Gutra's Garden"—Janis Joplin ("Back in Owens [Owen],Oklahoma")
"Bill Doolin"—Bobby Barnett ("gunfight at Ingalls, Oklahoma")
"Songs for Hogs and Frost"—Delicious Militia ("Stillwater militia")
"I've Been Telling My Mom I'm Gonna Get a Sex Change"
    ("We don't smoke marijuana in Muskogee/We don't roll fat stogies in Okmulgee")
"Don't Leave Me for Frank Sinatra"—Delicious Militia
    ("let me take you to Tishomingo")
"Where the Arkansas River Leaves Oklahoma"—Don Williams ("I met her in Stilwell")
"Ballad of Pretty Boy Floyd"—Bobby Barnett ("bank of Sallisaw")
"Rock and Roll Music To the World"—Jimmy LaFave ("Okemah to Stillwater")
"Gear and Dust"—Jason Boland & the Stragglers ("At a roadside up in Guthrie")
"Cherokee Bill"—Bobby Barnett ("town of Lenapah, Oklahoma")
"Salute to Will Rogers"—Bobby Barnett ("Claremore")
"Boy From Oklahoma"—Willis Alan Ramsey ("Born in Okemah")
"Barnsdall Blues"—traditional fiddle tune
"My Chickashay Gal"—co-written by Spade Cooley-recorded by Roy Rogers
"Broken Bow"—traditional fiddle tune
"The Three Guardsmen"—Bobby Barnett

("He [Chris Madsen] was a U.S. Marshal in the town of Guthrie")
"Rose of Ol' Pawnee"—Roy Rogers & Riders of the Purple Sage
"Spavinaw Bill"—traditional fiddle tune
"Boomtown Bill"—Woody Guthrie ("in that boom town called Seminole")
"The Story of the Dalton Gang"—Bobby Barnett ("And they settled near Kingfisher")
"Old Time Fiddle" – Vince Gill ("It was Piedmont, Oklahoma")
"Red Dirt Roads" - Jimmy LaFave ("Stillwater lights")
"Goin' to Caney" – Rick Reiley
    ("I was 8 miles from Caney when a farmer crossed the road")
"Full Moon Over Rentiesville" – DC Minner
("There's a full moon over Rentiesville when people come out to play")

Song Titles or Lyrics With Oklahoma Counties:

"Greer County"—traditional ballad
"Thirty Bad Days in Tillman County"—Dave Carter
"Higher Ground"—The Tractors ("Pawnee County")
"Tulsa County Blues"—Jesse Ed Davis/The Byrds
"Pontotoc County Line"—Burtschi Brothers
"Ballad of Pretty Boy Floyd"—Bobby Barnett
    ("everybody's his friend in *Sequoyah* County")
"Crusin' Cleveland County"—Terry "Buffalo" Ware
"Cleveland County Cage"—Hosty
"Beaver County Waltz"—old time fiddle tune
"Creek County Waltz"—old time fiddle tune
"Delaware County Blues"—old time fiddle tune
"Osage Stomp"—old time fiddle tune
"You're the Reason God Made Oklahoma"—David Frizell and Shelly West
    ("Nights are getting colder in Cherokee County")
"Red Dirt Roads" - Jimmy LaFave ("Payne County girls look so fine")

Song Titles or Lyrics With Oklahoma Natural Features:

"Verdigris Bottom"—old time fiddle tune
"Deep Fork River Blues"—Tom Paxton
"Farmer's Luck"—Greg Jacobs("Deep Fork River and South Canadian River")
"Cimarron (Roll On)"—Johnny Bond
"I've Been Everywhere"—Hank Snow (mentions Grand Lake)
"Red River Valley"—Woody Guthrie
"Higher Ground"—The Tractors ("Black Bear Creek")
"My Kiamichi Mountain Home"—Bill Grant
"Where the Old Kiamichi Flows"—Bill Grant
"Kiamichi Moon"—Bill Grant

"Kiamichi Country"—Bill Grant
"Kiamichi Morning"—Rusty Hudelson
"Ballad of Belle Starr"—Bobby Barnett/James Talley ("Robber's Cave")
"La Viborron"—Joe Merrick (mentions Antelope Hills)
"Cimarron Valley"—Red Dirt Rangers
"Okie Wind"—Greg Jacobs
"Banks of the Caney"—old time fiddle tune
"On the Road to Rock and Roll"—Jimmy LaFave ("Wewoka hills")
"Battle of the Washita"—composed by Gary Gackstatter
    (battle took place near the Washita River in Oklahoma)
"Red Dirt Song"—Jimmy LaFave ("Let an Okie wind just take my soul away . . .
    Let an Okie rain just take my cares away . . . Let an Okie sunset be my only pay")
"Arbuckle Mountain High"—Ross Chafin
"Ballad of Pretty Boy Floyd"—Woody Guthrie/Bobby Barnett
    ("Cookson Hills"and "On that Canadian River's shore")
"Waltz of the Arbuckles"—old time fiddle tune
"Little River Stomp"—old time fiddle tune
"The Cookson Hills"—words and music by Charles Stacey
"The Cowboy Hall of Fame"—Bobby Barnett ("Persimmon Hill")
"Where I Can See the Wichitas" – Phil Sampson

Song Titles and Lyrics With Oklahoma Highways, Streets, and Miscellaneous Places:

"Letter from the End of the Twentieth Century" – Joy Harjo
    ("from Tallahassee Grounds to Chicago")
"66 Highway Blues"—Woody Guthrie
"Reno Street Incident"—Jesse Ed Davis (street in OKC)
"Washita Love Child"—Jesse Ed Davis (county & river in Oklahoma)
"Stand Watie"—Greg Jacobs (mentions Honey Springs)
Boggy Depot—Jerry Cantrell
    (album title for area where his father, Jerry Cantrell, Sr., was raised)
"Take Me Back to Tulsa"—Bob Wills
    ("Let me off at Archer and I'll walk down to Greenwood") [streets in Tulsa]
"Highway 377" – Cross Canadian Ragweed ("We drove him off that Seminole Bridge")
"No Place Like the Cain's" – Don White
"T-Town Blues" – Ernie Fields
    ("Come on down to Greenwood and I'll sing these blues some more")

Please send corrections or additions to <u>authors@oklahomamusic.com</u>

Analysis of Place-Based Songs

Oklahoma place-based songs titles, album titles, and song lyrics are found in virtually every genre of American music, including American Indian, jazz, blues, folk, country and its various substyles (bluegrass, Western swing, singing cowboys, honky tonk, and alternative country), pop, rock and its myriad subgenres (classic rock, heavy metal, punk, and modern rock), gospel, contemporary Christian music, Broadway musicals, rap/hip-hop, and reggae.

I.   A broad spectrum of artists and groups has included Oklahoma in the titles and lyrics of their songs:

American Indian [1]
Southern Thunder

Contemporary Christian [1]
Daniel Amos

Reggae [2]
Pato Banton
Winston Grennan

Rap/Hip Hop [16]

Afroman	Keith Murray
A Tribe Called Quest	Mr. Nitro
Baby Beesh	Redman
Black Child & Ja Rule	69 Boyz
Busta Rhymes	Snoop Doggy Dogg
D-12	The Fugees
D J Muggs	Tupac Shakur (2Pac)
Ice Cube	Xzibit

Folk [19]

Woody Guthrie	Fred Small
Tom Paxton	Jack Hardy
Dave Carter	Terri Hendrix
Arlo Guthrie	Dana Cooper
Harry Chapin	Steve Forbert
Dan Bern	Kate Wolf
Rod MacDonald	Mike West
John Stewart	Bill Miller
Last Forever	CryCryCry
Agnes "Sis" Cunningham	

Jazz/Blues [21]

Cecil McBee	G.E. Stinson
Elvin Bishop	Lucille Bogan

Jay McShann
Jesse Ed Davis
Bennie Moten
Nat "King" Cole
Dave Brubeck
Duke Ellington
Mugsy Spanier
George Thorogood
Bobby Gordon

Michael Davis
Ray Drew
Bob Dorough
Richard "Groove" Holmes
Dave Frishberg
Mr. Jones
Spencer Bohren
Neal Pattman

Pop/Rock [67]
Bruce Springsteen
Paul McCartney
Eric Clapton
Elton John
Billy Joel
The Grateful Dead
The Eagles
Barry Manilow
Huey Lewis
R.E.M.
Natalie Merchant
Solange Knowles
Kid Rock
Talking Heads
Limpbizkit
Janis Joplin
Three Dog Night
Nazareth
BeeGees
The Byrds
The Kinks
The Monkees
The Scabs
The Faces
Tesla
Jerry Riopelle
Roger Waters
Songo
Puffball
Bonnie Tyler
Greg Keelor
Sixty Acres
Gene Pitney
The Jayhawks

Throwing Muses
Gwar
Stampeders
Henry Mancini
Neil Young
String Cheese Incident
Burt Bacharach
Tattooed Love Dogs
Elsie Muniz
Pere Ubu
Thieves' Kitchen
Jeffrey Lee Pierce
Cowboy Junkies
Common Rotation
Hawkwind
Solefad
The Bloodhound Gang
Nine Days
Liquido
Fixtures
The Church
Five Iron Frenzy
Bucket No. 6
Rotondi
Angus Maclise
Jerry Cantrell
Becker & Fagen
Tom Waits
Stewart Copeland
Echolyn
Bobby Sherman
Mustang Mesa
Slade

Country [72]

Terry Allen
Willis Alan Ramsey
Rodney Crowell
Guy Clark
Junior Brown
Bob Corbin
Marge Calhoun
Gordon Payne
Young Fogies
Red Meat
Flying Burrito Brothers
The Hagers
Rattlesnake Annie
Kinky Friedman
Asleep at the Wheel
Clay Walker
Nitty Gritty Dirt Band
Michael Martin Murphey
Hank Snow
Don Williams
Tom T. Hall
Mark Chesnutt
Alabama
Charley Pride
Dottie West
Tim McGraw
Bobby Bare
Tracy Lawrence
Reba McEntire
Glen Campbell
John Anderson
Tracy Byrd
Ronnie Milsap
Waylon Jennings
Emmylou Harris
Shelly West

Merle Haggard
Toby Keith
Whiskeytown
Christian Kane
C.W. McCall
Jeff Dufine
Goebel Reeves
Bill Emerson
Terri Lynn
Brenda Lee
Bevery Ellis
Albert Lee
Steve Young
Cornell Hurd
Bobbie Gentry
Kevin Fowler
Chris Hillman
Glen Ohrlin
Del McCoury
Garth Brooks
Bob Woodruff
David Hanner
Emerson Drive
Richard Buckner
Alan Jackson
Brooks & Dunn
Buck Owens
Vince Gill
Roy Rogers
Jimmy Dean
Johnny Cash
Brad Paisley
Kenny Rogers
Robert Earl Keen
Steve Earl
David Frizzell

II. More than 220 songs on the Oklahoma place-based songs list were written or recorded by native Oklahoman artists or groups associated with the state during their careers. Each artist or group from the following list has paid musical tribute to their home state in the form of song and album titles or lyrics mentioning various places in the state:

Garth Brooks
Reba McEntire
Vince Gill
Toby Keith

James Talley
Sheb Wooley
Gail Davies
Becky Hobbs

Bob Wills
Johnny Bond
Roger Miller
Spade Cooley
Steve Gaines
Ronnie Dunn
 or Brooks & Dunn
Woody Guthrie
Jack Guthrie
Patti Page
Hank Thompson
Tom Paxton
Hoyt Axton
Dave Carter
Cecil McBee
Jay McShann
Jesse Ed Davis
Elvin Bishop
Leon Russell
J.J. Cale
Ralph Blane
Wade Hayes
Lee Hazlewood
Dwight Twilley
Bobby Barnett
Mel McDaniel
Jimmy Wakely
Johnny Durrill
Larry Collins
David Gates
Mark Rubin
The Great Divide
Mr. Nitro

Jerry Cantrell
Jacob Fred Jazz Odyssey
The Flaming Lips
Brad Absher
Byron Berline
Frankie and Joe Marvin
Michael Hedges
Cross Canadian Ragweed
Delicious Militia
Joe Merrick
Big Al Downing
Jeff Wood
Burtschi Brothers
Hosty
Bill Grant
Ray Wylie Hubbard
Jesse Ed Davis
Greg Jacobs
Red Dirt Rangers
Jeremy Castle
Luke Wills
Southern Thunder
Jimmy LaFave
Agnes "Sis" Cunningham
Kevin Welch
Terry "Buffalo" Ware
Kellie Coffey
Jason Boland & the Stragglers
Clay Greenburg
Jimmy Webb
Cecil McBee
Michael Been
Jack Dunham

III.   In the actual mention of places in the Oklahoma place-based song list, the two major urban centers, Oklahoma City and Tulsa, are not unsurprisingly the most frequently mentioned places in the songs. However, the smaller of the two cities, Tulsa, doubled Oklahoma City (90 to 45) in song titles and lyrics dealing with the two locales. Muskogee is the third city most often mentioned, coming in with a total of 12 mentions, a further indication of the city's unusually prominent place in the musical aesthetic of the state given Muskogee's relatively small population compared to the other two much larger, but younger, urban counterparts.

IV. In addition to Oklahoma City, Tulsa, and Muskogee, 35 other Oklahoma cities and towns were mentioned in song titles or lyrics. Those mentioned more than once included the following municipalities:

Okemah [4]
Stillwater [4]
Guthrie [3]
Sallisaw [2]
Broken Bow [2]
Shawnee [2]
Checotah [2]
Pawnee [2]
Chickasha [2]

The following cities or towns received one mention in the Oklahoma place-based song list:

Ada
Barnsdall
Blanchard
Boggy Depot
Claremore
Fanshawe
Hydro
Idabel
Ingalls
Kingfisher
Lenapah
McAlester
Mehan
Moffett
Okmulgee
Owen
Pauls Valley
Piedmont
Perry
Porum
Red Rock
Seminole [2]
Spavinaw
Spencer
Stilwell
Tishomingo
Wilburton

V.   Twelve Oklahoma counties were given recognition in song titles or lyrics:

Beaver
Cherokee
Cleveland
Creek
Delaware
Greer
Osage
Pawnee
Pontotoc
Sequoyah
Tillman
Tulsa

VI.   In terms of natural features in Oklahoma, 14 were mentioned, with rivers most prominent:

Canadian River [2]
Cimarron River [2]
Deep Fork River
Verdigris River
Red River
Little River
Washita River

The most often mentioned Oklahoma natural feature was the Kiamichi Mountains, all in Bill Grant's songs, but hills, caves and creeks also made appearances:

Cookson Hills [2]
Arbuckle Mountains
Antelope Hills
Wewoka Hills
Black Bear Creek
Robber's Cave

VII.   In terms of positive and negative perceptions of Oklahoma in the 290 mentions of the state in the place-based list of songs, album titles, and lyrics, Oklahoma's varying relationship to the term "Okie" played a dominant role in the list. As most Oklahomans know, historically the term is associated with people who left the state for California in the Depression-heavy 1930s, but came to represent any poor, uneducated, migrant farmer no matter their origin. As the transplanted "Okies" began to better their situation in California, however, the term evolved into one of a pride to represent someone who overcomes adversity in the hardest of times. On the other hand, those people who were born in, or came to, Indian Territory before statehood in 1907 never appreciated the term and felt it derogatory and demeaning to be associated with such a description. Therefore, negative and positive examples of the term's use can be found throughout the lyrics:

Negative Example:

>Lyrics: "I always thought he was simple minded Okie"
>Trick Pony "Pour Me"

>Title: "Okie's in the Pokie"
>Jimmy Patton

Positive Examples:

>Lyrics: "Ain't Never met an Okie I didn't like"
>Kevin Fowler "100% Texan"

>Lyrics: "If the girl you love's an Okie,
>   then you know she's gotta be the one"
>Jeremy Castle "I Wanna Make Her Mine"

>Lyrics: "I'm proud to be an Okie from Muskogee"
>Merle Haggard "Okie from Muskogee"

VIII.   Positive Oklahoma Song Titles
"Oklahoma" (state song)
"Oklahoma Hills"
"Oklahoma's Calling"
"You're the Reason God Made Oklahoma"
"For Oklahoma, I'm Yearning"
"Home, Sweet Oklahoma"
"Gotta Get to Oklahoma (Cause California's Getting to Me)
"Good Old Oklahoma"
"From Oklahoma with Love"
"Long Way from OK"
"Back to Oklahoma"
"God is Down in Oklahoma"
"The Everlasting Hills of Oklahoma"
"Oklahoma, Land of the Sunny West"
"Oklahoma's OK!"
"Oklahoma Shines"

Negative Oklahoma Song Titles
"My Oklahoma Home (It Blowed Away)"

IX.   Positive Oklahoma Lyrics – And The Songs From Which They Derive
"I'm comin' back to you, Oklahoma, before my dark and dismal life away is
    through" – "Oklahoma" (not the state song)
"Would have lived in Oklahoma" – "The Mountain"

"Oklahoma looks just fine" – "Something's Got a Hold On Me"

"Oklahoma is O.K. with Me" – "Western Dreams"

"Never been to heaven, but I've been to Oklahoma" – "Never Been to Spain"

"Like dark geese into the Oklahoma skies" – "Souls of the Departed"

"Where they take us back to Oklahoma, where we belong" – "Surprise, AZ"

"Take her far away from our love and our Oklahoma home" – "Sleepin' All Alone"

"Cause it's the girls from Oklahoma who make livin' in the country so much fun" – "I Wanna Make Her Mine"

"My mind keeps going back to Oklahoma" – "Lady America"

"Grandma's back in Oklahoma . . . Take me back to Oklahoma" – "Bucket to the South"

"Now, I don't mind going to Oklahoma" – "100% Texan"

"Dreamin' of Texas and south Oklahoma" – "Blue Eyed Cowboy"

"Lady, please drive me back to Oklahoma" – "Post-Modern Blues"

"Wanna go back to Oklahoma, I'm happy there, livin' next to the soil" – "Next to the Soil"

"They just might go back to Oklahoma" – "Only in America"

"Hey, I'm a country girl, over Oklahoma way" – "Let the Music Lift You Up"

"This may be California, but Oklahoma's in her eyes . . . I guess Oklahoma's more her style of living" – "I've Got a Good Thing Going"

Negative Oklahoma Lyrics – And The Songs From Which They Derive

"couldn't find a job in Oklahoma" – "Home in Your Arms"

"They'll hold you up for days on end
 Threaten your life and take your money" - "If You're Ever in Oklahoma"

"They were sent to Oklahoma, malaria ran rife" –
    "The Heart of the Appaloosa"

"I met a bunch of fools in Oklahoma" – "Texas Moon"

"Lost my farm down in old Oklahoma" – "Blowin' Down This Road"

"When I was big enough to run,
 I'd never stay a single day in that Oklahoma sun" - "I Never Picked Cotton"

"She left Oklahoma for California sunglasses" – "Somebody Must Be Prayin' For Me"

"Leave Oklahoma far behind" – "Nowhere, Texas"

"I'm out here stranded on this Oklahoma road" – "I Got a Feelin'"

"Stuck here in Oklahoma, living in a coma" – "Frankie the Yankee"

"This run down mortgaged Oklahoma farm" – "California Cottonfields"

"We get the dark dust of Oklahoma" – "Texas Dust"

"We lived in Oklahoma, the wind whistled through the door" –
    "Bakersfield Sound"

Oklahoma Music Guide

Annual Oklahoma Music Festivals, Powwows, and Other Events Featuring Music

Annual Oklahoma Music Festivals, Powwows, and Events

January
Annual Miami Tribe Indian Art Market and Stomp Dance (Miami)/Ottawa-Peoria
Cultural Building (918) 542-1445
Annual New Year's Powwow (Oklahoma City)/State Fair Park
Western Hills Bluegrass Festival (Wagoner)/Western Hills Guest Ranch/(918) 772-2545

February
Bluegrass Festival (Checotah)/Fountainhead Resort/(800) 345-6343
"Circle the State With Song" Festival (Duncan)/Simmons Center Theatre
(580) 351-9729
Fiddlers Festival (Wagoner)/Western Hills Guest Ranch/((918) 772-2545 X7169
Keetoowah Spring Contest Powwow (Tahlequah)/Community Building/(918) 696-3093
Mardi Gras Parade ["unusual music"] (Norman)/Downtown/(405) 329-5108
Northwest Oklahoma Bluegrass Winter Festival (Woodward)/Northwest Inn
(580) 995-3147
Southwestern Oklahoma State Annual Jazz Festival (Weatherford)/SWOSU Fine Arts
Center (580) 774-3063
Tulsa Indian Art Festival (Tulsa)/Greenwood Cultural Center/(918) 838-3875

March
Barbershop Concert (Duncan)/Simmons Center/(580) 591-8048
Bob Wills Birthday Bash & Texas Playboy Reunion (Medicine Park)/Music Hall
(580) 529-2511
Dyson Family Blue Grass Festival
three miles west of the traffic light in Sayre on SH 152/(580) 928-5909
Green Country Jazz Festival (Tahlequah)/NSU Center for Performing Arts
(918) 456-5511 X4602 www.nsuok.edu/jazzlab/history.html
OK Chorale (Alva)/NWOSU Herod Hall Auditorium/(580) 327-8590
Oklahoma City University Spring Powwow
Oklahoma City University Field House/(405) 521-5302
United Scot Clans Scottish Heritage Festival [piping/drumming] (Edmond)
Hafer Park/(405) 767-9598
Wearin' of the Green Irish Festival [Celtic music] (Broken Arrow)/St. Patricks Day
Community Center (918) 252-5241

April
Annual Symposium of the American Indian (Tahlequah)/NSU campus
(918) 456-5511 x4350 www.nsuok.edu/native
Apache Rattlesnake Festival Powwow (Apache)/(580) 588-2880
Brown Bag It Concert Series (Tulsa)/Performing Arts Center/(918) 596-7111
Choctaw Intertribal Powwow (Durant)/Bryan County Fairgrounds (580) 924-9411
www.choctawnation.com
Far West Fiddlers Convention (Elk City)/Holiday Inn/(580) 225-4363

Festival of the Arts [four stages with non-stop music] (Oklahoma City)
Myriad Botanical Gardens (405) 270-4848
Festival of Spirituals (Norman)/First Presbyterian Church/(405) 364-8962
Indian Festival & Powwow (Talihina)/Talihina School Gym/(918) 567-2539
Medieval Fair [period music] (Norman)/Brandt Park/(405) 288-2536
Oklahoma State University Spring Contest Powwow (Stillwater)
OSU campus/(405) 744-5481
Old Fort Days Heritage Festival [music of the 1800s] (Fort Gibson)
Fort Gibson Historic Site (918) 478-4780
Old Time Music Festival (Harrah)/Blackjack Hills Festival Grounds Park
(405) 391-2338
Pawnee Folk & SpringFest [bluegrass and gospel music] (Pawnee)
Pawnee Bill Park (918) 762-2493
Pioneer Day Country Western Festival (Guymon)/Henry C. Hitch Rodeo Arena
(580) 338-3376
Redbud Jazz Festival (Tonkawa)/Northern Oklahoma College Campus
(580) 628-6366 www.north-ok.edu
Run for the Arts Land Run & Music Festival (Stillwater)/Couch Park/(405) 747-8084
Seiling Music Festival (Seiling)/Seiling Schools/(580) 922-7381
Spring Bluegrass Festival (Duncan)/Shady Oaks RV Park/(580) 255-7042

May
'50s Bash [classic rock and roll] (Okmulgee)/Downtown/(918) 756-6172
Adafest [live music] (Ada)/Main Street/(580) 436-3032
Arbuckle Mountain Bluegrass Pasture Pick'n (Wynnewood)
Arbuckle Mountain Bluegrass Park (405) 665-5226
Barnsdall Bigheart Day [live music] (Barnsdall)/(918) 847-2221
Black Gold Days Bluegrass Festival (Glenpool)/(918) 322-3505
Boiling Springs Bluegrass Festival (Woodward)/Boiling Springs State Park
(580) 995-3147
Canterbury Choral Festival (Oklahoma City)/Civic Center Music Hall
(405) 232-7464 May through June
Carney Fireman's Festival [live music] (Carney)/Main Street/(405) 865-2380
Cherokee Square Arts & Crafts Festival [live music] (Tahlequah)
Cherokee Courthouse Square (800) 456-4860
Cinco de Mayo [Hispanic music] (Marietta)/Downtown/(580) 276-4661
Cinco de Mayo [Hispanic music] (Oklahoma City)
Claremore State Powwow (Claremore) RSU campus/(918) 343-7566
Davis Music Festival (Davis)/Davis City Park/(580) 369-2402
Eastern Delaware Powwow (Copan)/Falleaf Dance Grounds/(918) 336-5272
www.delawaretribeofindians.nsn.us
Edmond Blues & Jazz Festival (Edmond)/Stephenson Park/(405) 359-7989 X1
www.ucojazzlab.com/jazzfest.htm
Gospel Fest (Stapp/Zoe Community Center)/(918) 653-2187
Harrah Polish Festival [polka music] (Harrah)/NE 23rd Street & Whites' Meadow Drive
(405) 454-2961

Jazz Banjo Festival (Guthrie)/Downtown/(800) 652-2656 or (405) 282-1948
    www.banjofestival.com/home.asp
Kiowa Black Leggings Ceremonial (Anadarko) Indian City Dance Grounds/
    (580) 654-2351 www.indiancityusa.com
Kolache Festival [polka music] (Prague)/City Park/(405) 567-4866
Oklahoman Steel Guitar Association's Memorial Day Convention/Tulsa
    (918) 587-5197 or 272-1205
Paseo Arts Festival [showcase talent of Oklahoma's best musicians]
    (Oklahoma City)/NW 30th & Dewey (405) 525-2688
Red Earth Festival/State Fair Park, Oklahoma City/(405) 427-5228/www.redearth.org
Skyline Bluegrass Festival (Muldrow)/Rogers Mountain Music Park/(405) 677-1509
Tri-State Music Festival (Enid)/Citywide Venues/(580) 237-4964
Tulsa International Mayfest [live music] (Tulsa)/Downtown
    (888) 737-0966 or (918) 582-6435
Tumbleweed Calf Fry (Stillwater)/Tumbleweed's/(405) 377-0075/www.calffry.com
Vietnam Veterans' Celebration and Powwow (Anadarko)/Wichita Dance Grounds
    (405) 247-2425 X133
Wolf Creek Jamboree [country/big band/western swing/jazz/gospel] (Grove)
    Runs through December/3659 North Highway 59/(918) 786-2014

June

1850s Lawn Social & Heritage Festival [music] (Park Hill)
    Murrell Home/(918) 456-2751
Amadeus Piano Festival (Tulsa)/(918) 745-0743
American Heritage Music Festival (Grove)
    Grove Civic Center and Snider's Camp/(800) 526-2523
Apache Tribe of Oklahoma (Na-I-Sha) Blackfeet Ceremonials (Anadarko)
    (405) 247-9493/no cameras
Bar-B-Que 'n Blues Festival (Cushing)/(918) 225-2400
Brews & Blues Festival (Tulsa)/T. Paul's Beer Company/(918) 855-6842
Cedar Street Blues & Jazz Festival (Wewoka)/Cedar Street/(405) 257-5485
Citizen Potawatomi Powwow (Shawnee)/(405) 275-3121/www.potawatomi.org
Clear Channel Riverfest [music] (Tulsa)/River West Festival Park/(918) 596-2001
Concerts in the Park (Frederick)/Entire month of June/201 North 9th/(580) 335-7300
Funfest [live music] (Pryor)/Whitaker Park/(918) 825-0157
Fun Fest [live music] (Medford)/Medford Municipal Airport/(580) 395-2823
Gilbert and Sullivan Light Opera Festival (Tulsa)/
    Kendall Theatre-University of Tulsa/(918) 583-4267
Grand Lake National Fiddle & Clogging Festival (Grove)/Grove Civic Center
    (918) 786-8996
Grovefest Thunder on the Pond Cruise, Blues & BBQ (Grove)/Citywide/(918) 786-9079
Gusher Day Festival [live music] (Seminole)/Downtown/(405) 382-3640
Iowa Powwow (4 miles south of Perkins on Highway 177)/(405) 547-2402
    www.iowanation.org
Jazz and German Car Festival (Stillwater)/(918) 747-8070
Jazz in June (Norman)/Citywide Venues/(405) 325-3388

Juneteenth on Greenwood Heritage Festival [jazz/blues/gospel] (Tulsa)
  Greenwood District/(918) 596-1001
Kaw Fest [live music] (Ponca City)/Kaw Lake/(580) 762-9494
Love County Frontier Days [bluegrass and gospel] (Marietta)/Downtown
  (580) 276-4601
Muscogee (Creek) Nation Festival (Okmulgee)/(918) 756-8700/www.ocevnet.org/creek
Oklahoma Gourd Dance Club Annual Dance (Medicine Park)
  Whitewolf Ceremonial Grounds (580) 353-1440
OK Mozart International Festival (Bartlesville)/Citywide/(918) 336-9900
  www.okmozart.com
Old Greer County Pioneer Reunion [fiddlers contest] (Mangum)
  Courthouse Lawn/(580) 782-5154
Old Settler's Day Reunion & Centennial Celebration [gospel singing] (Boswell)/
  Downtown & Boswell Lake/(580) 566-2268
Old Settler's Day [live music] (Colcord)/Downtown Square/(918) 326-4811
Peoria Powwow (Miami)/(918) 540-2535/www.peoriatribe.com
Route 66 Blowout Festival [music] (Sapulpa)/Downtown/(918) 224-5709
Sanders Family Bluegrass Festival (McAlester)/Highway 270 West/(918) 423-0450
Santa Fe Trail Daze Celebration [fiddlers contest] (Boise City)/Downtown
  (580) 544-3344
Stigler Reunion Days [gospel singing] (Stigler)/Downtown/(918) 967-8681
Stockyards Stampede Festival [country and western music] (Oklahoma City)
  Stockyards City (405) 235-7267
Sunday Twilight Concerts (Oklahoma City)/June and July/
  Will Rogers Park Amphitheatre, Myriad Botanical Gardens/(405) 270-4848
Tuesdays in Central Park [several music genres] (Broken Arrow)/Entire month of June
  1500 South Main Street/(918) 259-8381
Tulsa Powwow/Tulsa/(918) 747-9232
Tonkawa Powwow (Fort Oakland, 2 miles east of Tonkawa)/(580) 628-2561
  www.tonkawatribe.com
Wildfire Music Festival (Tecumseh)/Jude 'n Jody Ranch Arena/(405) 899-4476

July

Annual Cookson Jubilee (Cookson)/(918) 457-4390
Arts, Crafts, Music, and Cajun Festival (Grove)/(918) 762-786-8896
  www.grandlakefestivals.com
Bluegrass Jam (Duncan)/Shady Oaks Lakeview RV Park/(580) 255-7042
Bluegrass Jamboree (Spiro)/Spiro School Cafetorium/(918) 962-2756
Cajun Music Festival (Grove)/Civic Center/(918) 786-8896
Comanche Homecoming Powwow/Walters, Sultan Park/(580) 492-3751
  www.comanchenation.com
Cookson Jubilee [musical entertainment] (Cookson)/T.A.C.O. Building/(918) 457-5400
Eskimo Joe's Birthday Bash [live bands] (Stillwater)/Eskimo Joe's/(405) 372-8896
Kihekah Steh Powwow/Skiatook/(918) 396-4417
Kiowa Gourd Clan Ceremonials (Carnegie)/Carnegie Park/(405) 793-0958
McLoud Blackberry Festival [live bands] (McLoud)/6th & Park/(405) 964-6566

O-Ho-Mah Lodge Ceremonials (Anadarko)/Indian City USA/(405) 247-3987
  www.indiancityusa.com
Otoe-Missouria Powwow/Red Rock/(580) 723-4466
Pawnee Veterans' Homecoming & Powwow/Pawnee, Memorial Field/(918) 762-3621
  www.pawneenation.org
Praise in the Park [gospel music] (Ardmore)/(580) 226-0231
Quapaw Powwow (Quapaw)/Beaver Springs Park/(918) 542-1853
  http://eighttribes.org/quapaw
Sac & Fox Nation Powwow (5 ½ miles south of Stroud)/(918) 968-1141
  www.cowboy.net/native/sacnfox.html
Stratford Peach Festival [live music] (Stratford)/City Park/(580) 759-3300
Woody Guthrie Folk Music Festival (Okemah)/Pastures of Plenty/(918) 623-2440
  www.woodyguthrie.com

August

American Indian Exposition [exhibition and contest powwow]
  (Anadarko)/Fairgrounds/(405) 262-5708
Annual GCBA Bluegrass Festival (Okmulgee)/Dripping Springs State Park
  (918) 341-4689
Annual "Trail of Tears" Gospel Singing (Westville)/Old Green Church Amphitheater
  (918) 723-5140
Arcadia Festival [gospel singing] (Arcadia)/Municipal Park/(405) 396-2899
Bluegrass Festival (Wilburton)/Robbers Cave State Park Amphitheatre/(918) 754-2790
BOK/Williams Jazz on Greenwood (Tulsa)/Archer & Greenwood/(918) 584-3378
Cornstock [classic rock concerts] (Guymon)/Henry C. Hitch Rodeo Arena
  (580) 338-6974
Fiddlers Festival (Wagoner)/(918) 772-2545/www.oklahomaparks.com
Grant's Bluegrass Festival (Hugo)/Salt Creek Park/(580) 326-5598
Green Country Bluegrass Festival (Langley)/(918) 782-3214
Intertribal Indian Club of Tulsa/Powwow of Champions/Tulsa Fairgrounds
  (918) 836-2183/www.iicot.org
Kansa (Kaw) Powwow/Kaw City, Kaw Lake/(580) 269-2552/www.kawnation.com
Kiwanis Lakeside Music Fest (Wister)/Lake Wister State Park/(918) 655-7886
Konawa Gospel Singing Festival (Konawa)/City Park/(580) 456-7796
Midwest Bluegrass Festival (Shawnee)/Citizen Potawatomi Nation Powwow Grounds
  (405) 391-2338
Oklahoma Indian Nation Powwow/Concho, Football Field/(405) 262-5708
Ponca Powwow/White Eagle Park, 5 miles south of Ponca City/(580) 762-8104
Seminole Gospel Singing (Seminole)/South of City/(405) 382-8351
Summerfest [music] (Vinita)/Downtown/(918) 256-7133
Urban League Family Fun Festival [blues and jazz] (Oklahoma City)/N.E. 4th & Lottie
  (405) 424-5243
Watermelon Day Festival [music] (Valliant)/City Park/(580) 933-5050
Wichita & Affiliated Tribes Annual Dance (Anadarko)/Wichita Dance Grounds/
  (405) 247-2425 www.wichita.nsn.us

Labor Day Weekend

Cherokee National Holiday (Tahlequah)/(918) 456-0671/www.cherokee.org
Cheyenne & Arapaho Labor Day Powwow (Colony)/(405) 262-0345
    www.cheyenne-arapaho.nsn.us
Choctaw Nation Labor Day Festival (Tuskahoma)/(580) 924-8280
    www.choctawnation.com
Dusk 'til Dawn Blues Festival (Rentiesville)/Down Home Blues Club/(918) 473-2411
    www.dcminnerblues.com
International Music Festival and Jana Jae Fiddle Camp (Grove)
    Grove Civic Center & Snider's Camp (918) 786-8896
Ottawa Celebration and Powwow (Miami)/Adawe Park/(918) 540-1536
    http://eighttribes.org/ottawa

September

All-Day Gospel Singing in the Park (Marlow)/Redbud Park/(580) 658-2212
Arbuckle Bluegrass Festival (Wynnewood)/Arbuckle Mountain Park/(405) 665-5226
Backdoor Cajun Music Festival (Tulsa)/Williams Center Green/(918) 583-2617 X11
Bikers and Blues Festival (Stillwater)/Community Center/(405) 624-2921
Bluegrass and Chili Festival (Claremore)/Expo Center/(918) 342-5357
Bob Wills Texas Playboys Reunion Festival (Pawhuska)/Constantine Center/Elks
Lodge/(918) 287-3612
Eastern Shawnee Tribal Powwow (West Seneca) Tribal Complex/(918) 666-2435
    http://eighttribes.org/eastern-shawnee
Enid Intertribal Club Annual Powwow (Enid) Garfield County Fairgrounds
    (580) 234-5261
Fall Bluegrass Festival (Duncan)/September and October
    Shady Oaks Lakeview RV Park/(580) 255-7042
Festival Hispano [Hispanic music] (Tulsa)/Williams on the Green
    Plaza Santa Cecilia/(918) 384-0096
Fort Sill-Chiricahua-Warm Springs Apache Dance (Apache) Tribal Complex
    (580) 588-2298/no cameras
Gene Autry Film & Music Festival (Gene Autry)/Gene Autry Oklahoma Museum
    (580) 294-3047
Indian Summer Festival Art Market and Powwow (Bartlesville)
    Community Center/(918) 337-2787
Jazz on Bell Street Festival (Shawnee)/Main & Bell/(405) 273-1080
Music Under the Stars (Watonga)/T. B. Ferguson Home/(580) 623-5069
Oklahoma Scottish Festival [piping/drumming] (Tulsa)/Chandler Park/(918) 499-2585
Okrafest (Checotah)/(918) 473-4178
Old Germany Octoberfest [polka music] (Choctaw)/Old Germany Restaurant
    15920 Southeast 29th (405) 390-8647
Red Buck Outlaw Days [ragtime music] (Clinton)/Rodeo Grounds/(580) 323-2222
River Rumba Music Festival (Muskogee)/Three Forks Landing-Arkansas River
    (918) 684-6305
Seminole Nation Days (Seminole)/Mekusukey Mission Grounds/(405) 257-6287
Septemberfest [gospel] (Okmulgee)/Okmulgee State Park/(918) 756-5971

Standing Bear Powwow (Ponca)/Standing Bear Park/580-762-1514
    www.north-ok.edu/sb
Tonkawa Hills Blues Festival (Anadarko)/Indian City USA/(405) 247-6665
    www.indiancityusa.com
Wheat Country Festival [music] (Billings)/Main Street/(580) 725-3424
Wyandotte Powwow (Wyandotte)/Wyandotte Powwow Grounds/(918) 678-2297
    www.wyandot.org/oklahoma

October

Annual Intertribal Fall Gourd Dance (Norman) Bryan Country Fairgrounds
    (405) 341-7874
Council House Indian Art Market and Powwow (Okmulgee)/
    Old Muscogee (Creek) Council House (918) 756-2324
Chickasaw Festival (Tishomingo) Pennington Park/(580) 371-2040/www.chickasaw.net
Cross Timbers Music & Heritage Festival (Stillwater Vicinity)
    Washington Irving Museum
    Six miles east of Stillwater on Highway 51-2.6 miles south on Mehan Road
    (405) 624-9130/www.cowboy.net/non-profit/irving
Czech Festival [polka music] (Yukon)/Citywide/(405) 354-3567
Deep Deuce Jazz Festival (Oklahoma City)/N.E. 2nd & Walnut/(405) 524-3800
Jerry Kirk Memorial Fiddlers Convention (Elk City)/Holiday Inn/(580) 225-1391
Kiowa Black Leggings Ceremonial (Anadarko)/Indian City Dance Grounds
    (580) 654-2351 www.indiancityusa.com
Konawa Annual Band Day (Konawa)/Citywide/(580) 925-3244
Lefty Frizell Country Music Festival (Pawnee)/Pawnee Bill Ranch/(918) 762-2108
Master Works Sawdust Dulcimer Festival (Bennington)/Master Works/(888) 752-9243
Octoberfest [polka music] (Ponca City)/Marland Mansion Grounds/(580) 762-1462
Octoberfest [polka music] (Tulsa)/River West Festival Park/(918) 744-9700
Oklahoma International Bluegrass Festival (Guthrie)/First weekend of October/
    Cottonwood Flats Campground/(405) 282-4446/ www.oibf.com
Pawnee Title VII Annual Youth Dance (Pawnee)/high school gym/(918) 762-3564
Puckarama Whistling Festival (Tulsa)/Various Venues/(918) 298-2445
Robbers Cave Fall Festival [bluegrass and gospel] (Wilburton)/Robbers Cave State Park
    (918) 465-3400
Shattuck Heritage Festival [live music] (Shattuck)/Downtown/(580) 938-2818
Sorghum Festival [music] (Wewoka)/Downtown/(405) 257-5484
Yukon Celtic Nations Festival [piping/drumming] (Yukon)
    Kirkpatrick Family Farm/(405) 350-0425

November

Annual Veterans' Day Dance (Pawnee)/Pawnee Nation Reserve
    (918) 762-3621/www.pawneenation.org
Beavers Bend Folk Festival [folk music] (Broken Bow)/Beavers Bend Resort Park
    (580) 494-6497
Oklahoma State University Fall Powwow (Stillwater)/OSU campus/(405) 744-5481
Oklahoma State University Madrigal Concert (Stillwater)/November through December
    OSU student union/(405) 744-6133

Rogers State University Heritage Festival and Stomp Dance (Claremore
    RSU campus/(918) 343-7566
U.S.O. Show [musical variety] (Muskogee)/Civic Center/(918) 684-6363 X21

December

Cherokee Gourd Society Annual Christmas Powwow (Tahlequah)/
    Community building/(918) 456-3637
Good Medicine Society New Year's Eve Sobriety Powwow (Oklahoma City)
    Oklahoma State Fairgrounds Kitchens of America Building/(405) 943-7935
Intertribal Indian Club of Tulsa Christmas Powwow/(918) 836-2183/www.iicot.org
New Year's Eve Gospel Singing (Pawnee)
    Oklahoma Steam Threshers Headquarters Building (918) 762-2493
New Year's Eve Sobriety Powwow (Tulsa)/Convention Center/(918) 402-2568
Opening Night [rock and roll/country/big band] (Oklahoma City)/December/Downtown
    (405) 270-4848
Pawnee New Year's Eve Hand Game and Ghost Dance (Pawnee)
    Pawnee Nation Reserve/(918) 762-4048
Tulsa All-Lutheran "Messiah" Concert (Tulsa)/First Lutheran Church/(918) 827-3869

Monthly Events

Greater Oklahoma Bluegrass Society Concert (Midwest City)/Community Center
    (405) 485-2370
Oklahoma Country Music Association Jubilee (Del City)
    Country Western Museum Hall of Fame (405) 677-6107

For corrections, additions, or deletions, please write the
Oklahoma Music Guide **1018 S. Lewis St., Stillwater, Oklahoma, 74074,**
or write authors@oklahomamusicguide.com

Oklahoma Music Guide

Additional
musical groups,
musicians,
music industry
professionals,
educators, and
tribal entities from
Oklahoma

The following list contains Oklahoma musical groups, musicians, music industry professionals, educators, and tribal entities being considered for individual entries in the centennial edition of the *Oklahoma Music Guide* due in 2007 on New Forums Press.

Format: Individual or Group/Oklahoma Connection/Notability
Code: b=born, r=resided, f=formed, I.T.=Indian Territory, *=unknown at press time,
bold refers to entries in this guide

A

Abandon Style/f. Oklahoma City/rock group
Absentee Shawnee Tribe/based in Shawnee, moved to I.T. in 1868
   Veterans Day dances & powwows
Absher, Brad/r. Tulsa/blues/rock guitarist and singer
Ackmann, Rod/Tulsa University music faculty, 2003/bassoonist
Acoustic Ross/f. Tulsa/singer, songwriter, guitarist
Act Casual/f. Oklahoma City, 1991/blues band
   Ellis, Dorothy "Miss Blues"/b. Texas, r. Oklahoma City/singer
   Ford, Kenneth/b. Tom/vocalist, songwriter, bassist
Adams, Brant/Oklahoma State University music faculty, 2003/music theory
Adams, Frank/r. Tulsa/jazz saxophonist
Adams, Joe/r. Tulsa/opera singer
Adams, Jody/r. Oklahoma/bluegrass fiddler, mandolinist, songwriter
Adams, Ron/r. Tulsa/jazz bassist
Adson, Robert (Pawnee/Diné/Comanche)/r. Pawnee/intertribal powwow head singer,
   sings with Southern Thunder
Agent, Dan/r. Tahlequah/co-managed Randy Crouch and the Flying Horse Opera
A Girl Thang/f. Oklahoma City/rock group
Agony Scene/f. Tulsa/Christian heavy metal on Solid State Records
Ahhaitty, Bill/r. Oklahoma/intertribal powwow head singer
AJ and Why Not/f. Oklahoma/blues group
Aldrich, "Walkin' Talkin'" Charlie/b. Ogawana, 1913/classical guitarist,
   country singer, songwriter
Alexander, Dave/ r. Broken Arrow/Western swing bandleader
Alig, Kelley/East Central Oklahoma University music faculty, 2003/music education
Al-Jibouri, Sean/r. Tulsa/blues rock guitarist
ALLBLAK/f. Tulsa/rap, hip-hop
Allen, Bill/b. OK, 1925, r. Wewoka/Western swing rhythm guitarist, fiddler
Allen, Steve/r. Tulsa/guitarist, vocalist with pop rock group 20/20
Alred, Casi/b. OK, 1988/country singer
Altamont Speedway/f. Norman
Alter Ego/f. Oklahoma City, 1995/blues rock group
Alvaro's Brazilian Jazz/r. Edmond, 2002/Latin jazz group
Amazing Rhythm Chickens/f. Norman, 1973/classic rock and roll group
Ambassador Bill/f. Oklahoma City, 1995/punk rock group
Ambient Music Cartel/f. Oklahoma City, 1998/rock group
Ambrosini, Armand/Oklahoma University music faculty, 2003/music appreciation
American Boyfriends/f. Oklahoma City, 1992/pop rock group

Goad, Matt/r. Oklahoma City/guitarist, vocalist

Harmon, Eric/r. Oklahoma City/drummer

Johnson, Matt/r. Oklahoma City/bassist

York, Richard/r. Oklahoma City/guitarist

American Girlz/f. Broken Arrow/retro pop music singing and dancing group

American Horse/f. Tulsa/rock group

AMF/f. Tulsa/punk metal rock group

Anderson, Jonathan/b. 1990 – d. 2001, r. Enid/rapper and leader of Midwest Hustlaz

Andrews, Jack /b. Oklahoma City, 1930/country music talent scout

Anderson, Kenny/Oklahoma Opry house band guitarist

And There Stands Empires/f. Tulsa/loud rock group

Animation/f. Oklahoma City/rock group

Anita's Anger/f. Weatherford/neo-punk pop rock group

Anonymous/r. Claremore/rap, spoken word performance artist

Another Roadside Attraction/f. Stillwater/acoustic folk

Anquoe, Jack, Sr. (**Kiowa**)/b. Mountain View, 1933/head singer with Grayhorse,

Anquoe, Jack, Jr.(**Kiowa/Cherokee**)/b. Claremore/singer with Grayhorse, Red Land
    intertribal powwow head singer

Anquoe, Jim (**Kiowa**)/b. Mountain View/Kiowa and intertribal powwow back up singer

Anquoe, Kelly (**Kiowa/Cherokee**)/r. Tahlequah/intertribal powwow head singer

Anquoe, Mary Ann (**Kiowa**)/b. Mountain View/singer (War Mothers' songs)

Anquoe, Quentin/r. Oklahoma/intertribal powwow head singer

Anquoe, Rick/r. Oklahoma/intertribal powwow head singer

Anquoe, Ron/r. Oklahoma/intertribal powwow head singer

Antenna Lodge/f. Tulsa/hardcore punk rock group

    Forbis, Jeremy/drummer

    Kendrick, Kelly/singer, guitarist

    Sutliff, Danel/bassist

Apache Tribe of Oklahoma/in state for centuries, now in Anadarko

    Blackfeet Society Ceremonials

Apparitions in Blue/r. Norman/techno dance music

Aqueduct/f. Tulsa/pop rock group

Aranda/f. Oklahoma City/rock group

The Arbuckles/f. Shawnee/bluegrass group

    Talley, Tony/r. Shawnee/dobro player, lead vocalist

    Thomas, Don/b. Cushing/banjo, lead/tenor vocalist

    Thomas, Russell/r. Shawnee/bassist, lead/baritone vocalist

    Thomas, Steve/b. Cushing/guitarist, lead/tenor vocalist

Arkeketa, John (Otoe/Cherokee)/r. Tahlequah/intertribal powwow head singer

Arnold, John/Oklahoma City University music faculty, 2003/violin

ARRAKIS/f. Oklahoma City/rock group

Attebery, Melissa/Oklahoma City University music faculty, 2003/music education

Austin, William, W./b. Lawton, 1920/musicologist

Awake/f. Oklahoma City, 1998/contemporary Christian group

Axolotls/f. Seminole 1999/rock group

Aycock, Scott and Empty Pockets/f. Tulsa, 1999/Americana music group

    Aycolk, Scott/singer, songwriter, guitarist, and KWGS *Folk Salad* radio program host

    Grant, Russell/drummer

Leonard, Tom/bassist
Murphy, J. Pat/guitarist
Parker, Charlie/saxophone
Schad, Carolyn/harmony vocals

B

Baby M/f. Tulsa/modern rock group
Bageyes/f. Tulsa/loud rock group
Baggech, Melody/East Central Oklahoma University music faculty, 2003/choir, opera
Baggot, Edward/r. Oklahoma/traditional fiddler
Bagsby, David/r. Tulsa/keyboardist, electronic music
Bagsby, Steve/r. Tulsa/banjo player
Bahr, Jason/Oklahoma University music faculty, 2003/composition
Bailey, Fred/b. northwest Oklahoma/singer songwriter
Bailey, Robert/Northeastern Oklahoma State University music faculty, 2003/trumpeter,
Baker, Adam/b. Oklahoma City, 1964/graphic artist for album covers
Baker, Andrea/b. Muskogee/jazz singer
Baker, Bobby/r. Clarerore/Western swing steel guitarist, fiddler with Cowjazz
Baker, Danny/b. Tulsa, 1964/blues-rock band leader
Baker, Jimmie/b. Tulsa/big band leader
Baker, Sandra/Northeastern Oklahoma State University adjunct music faculty, 2003/voice
Bakerville/f. Tulsa/country group
Balageur, Jean-Michel/r. Tulsa/guitarist
Ballard, John R.(Ottawa/Cherokee)/r. Oklahoma/stomp dance leader
Ballard, Joyce (Shawnee/Peoria)/r. Oklahoma/shell shaker
Ballenger, William/Oklahoma State University music faculty, 2003/department head
Balletto, Luigi/r. Tulsa/lounge singer, entertainer
Ballista/f. Oklahoma City/rock group
   Almanza, Cesar/b. Harlingen, TX, 1975/guitarist/back-up vocalist
   DuVall, Rick/b. Muskogee, 1974/bassist, lead vocalist
   Martinek, Billy/b. Oklahoma City, 1973/drummer
Ballistic/f. Tulsa/rock group
Banana Seat/f. Tulsa/rock group
Banish Misfortune/r. Oklahoma City/Celtic music group
   Morrow, Dana/pianist
   Reid, Phil/fiddler
   Vanlandingham, Steve/banjo player, mandolinist
Banks, Damen/b. Tulsa/rapper
Banks, Hobart/r. Muskogee/jazz pianist
Barker, Brandy Michelle/r. Moore/country singer
Barker, Rolland/r. Cushing/intertribal powwow head singer
Barnard, Rachel/Oklahoma City University music faculty, 2003/voice
Barnes, Ben/r. Oklahoma/stomp dance leader
Barrett, Celeste/Tulsa University music faculty, 2003/voice, vocal pedagogy
Barrett, Roland/Oklahoma University music faculty, 2003/music theory
Barnett, Jeremy/Kelleyville Ceremonial Grounds/stomp dance leader
Barry, Nancy/Oklahoma University music faculty, 2003/music education

Barton, George/r. Tahlequah/singer, songwriter, guitarist for Barton and Sweeney
Barton, Lorelei/r. Tulsa/harpist
Bass, Sam D./b. Oklahoma/played cello with Tommy Duncan/Tex Ritter/Moon Mullican
The Bastions/f. Oklahoma/Southern gospel
Batcheller, Joe/r. Oklahoma/singer, songwriter
Bates, Jim/Tulsa University music faculty/bassist
Baylor, Helen/r. Tulsa/contemporary gospel
Beams of Light Family Church/Tulsa/contemporary Christian music
   Applegate, Jarod/drummer
   Billie, Nora/vocalist
   Clark, Michael/vocalist
   Cupps, Laura/vocalist
   Dinsmore, Katie/vocalist
   Dinsmore, Margaret/vocalist
   Dinsmore, Mike/electric, acoustic, bass guitarist, keyboardist
   Hooker, Regina/vocalist
   Johnson, Amy/electric bass guitarist, contrabass violinist
   Lovins, Tim/electric bass guitarist
   Peck, Tamra/vocalist
   Ray, Jimmy/pastor, vocalist, electric and acoustic guitarist, **Tulsa Sound,** (Tweed, Cripple Creek)
   Reed, Lindsey/vocalist
   Rhoads, Cindy/vocalist
   Stegner, Diana/vocalist
   Stegner, Leslie/vocalist
   Surrat, Daniel/keyboardist
   Tarpenning, Brian/drummer
Bearpaw, Josh/Kelleyville Ceremonial Grounds/stomp dance leader
Bebb, Martin/Northeastern Oklahoma State University adjunct music faculty, 2003/oboist, bassoonist
Beckham, Bob/b. Stratford, 1926/country music publisher
Beef & Lemons/f. Tulsa/independent rock group
Beefeater Project/   f. Oklahoma City/psychedelic rock band
Been, Michael/b. Oklahoma, 1957/pop rock group The Call
Belanger, Paul/r. Gene Autry/cowboy singer,yodeler
Belken, Jim/b. Dallas, TX, 1931, r. Oklahoma/Western swing fiddler
Belknap, Bill/r. Oklahoma/pop rock group 20/20
Bell, Aaron/b. Muskogee, 1922/jazz bassist
Bell, Ann/r. Oklahoma/rock vocals
Bell, Larry/r. Tulsa/keyboardist, played with Jerry Lee Lewis, recorded with Paul Anka
Bell, Trent/b. Norman/Bell Labs studio engineer, producer, Chainsaw Kittens
Bellvue/f. Norman, 1995/rock group
Belter, Babette/Oklahoma State University music faculty, 2003/clarinetist
Berline, Lue/r. Oklahoma/old time fiddler (**Byron Berline**'s father)
Ben.Ben/f. Tulsa/jazz fusion group
Bennett, Mike/r. Tulsa/trumpet for Johnnie Lee **Wills**/Ray Charles/**Flash Terry**
Bennett, Reid/Tulsa University music faculty, 2003/saxophonist
Bennett, Wayne/b. Sulphur/blues guitarist

Bentley, Rick/r. Oklahoma/banjo player

Bentonelli, Giuseppe Joseph Benton/b. Sayre, 1898/opera singer

Bernard, Gene/b. Leonard/Western swing

Bernard, Lester "Junior"/b. Leonard/Western swing guitar

Bernston, David/r. Tulsa/blues harmonica player

Berryman, Ric/r. Broken Arrow/rock multi-instrumentalist and vocalist

Bibb, Teri/b. Altus/Broadway musical performer

Big Big Brains/f. Broken Arrow/classic rock group

Big Daddy & the Blueskickers/f. Beggs/blues group
   Big Daddy/guitarist, vocalist
   Gallie, John/pianist, organist
   McCallister, Donn/drummer, percussionist
   McDuffie, Doug/bassist, vocalist

Bigelow, Tracy/r. Tiawah/lead guitarist for retro-jazz group Early Swing Now

Bighley, Mark/Northeastern Oklahoma State University music faculty, 2003

BigHorse, Vann/r. Pawhuska/intertribal powwow head singer

Big Ric/r. Tulsa/neo-soul, R & B, owner of Made Records

Bihari, Jules, Joe, Saul and Lester/r. Oklahoma/Modern Records founders

Bill & Bink/recorded for Hobart-based Hu-Se-Co label in the 1950s/country music duo

Billy & Baby Gap (Billy Young and Anthony Walker)/r. Tulsa/R & B vocal duo

Billy Joe Winghead/f. Oklahoma/psychobilly, country, punk rock group

Binge/Purge Society/f. Oklahoma/heavy metal group

Bingham, Ray/r. Tulsa/music promoter, booking agent

Bio Mass/f. Norman/rock group

Bird, Margery/r. Tulsa/music philanthropist benefiting Tulsa University

Birdwell, Florence/Oklahoma City University music faculty, 2003/voice

Bishops Alley/f. Oklahoma City, 2000/rock group

Bita, Gabriel/Southeastern Oklahoma State University adjunct faculty, 2003/pianist

Blackbear Creek/f. Pawnee/intertribal powwow singing group

Blackbird/f. Shawnee and Norman, 1990/intertribal northern style powwow group
   Primeaux, Graham/r. Shawnee/head singer

Blackhawk Blues Band/f. Oklahoma City, 1990/blues group (American Indian)
   Garcia, Al/r. Oklahoma City/drummer
   Gray, Cecil/r. Oklahoma City/guitar/vocalist
   Jones, Batiste/r. Oklahoma City/guitarist, harmonica, vocalist
   Scott, Melvin/r. Oklahoma City/bass/vocalist

Black Out/f. Locust Grove/skater pop group

Blackstone, Tsianina/b. I. T., 1882/opera (Florence Evans)

Blackwell, Chuck/b. Tulsa/drummer with Eric Clapton, Taj Majal, and others

Blair, Greg/b. Claremore/contemporary Christian singer

Blake, Al/r. Oklahoma City/blues guitarist

Blak Kat Bone/f. Hartshorne/blues rock group

Blalock, Jay (Shawnee/Ojibwe)/r. Oklahoma/intertribal powwow head singer

Blane, Ralph/b. Broken Arrow, 1914/wrote "Have Yourself a Merry Little Christmas"

Blazer, Jim/r. Tulsa/pianist

The Blue Cats/f. Oklahoma City/blues/R & B group

The Blue Collars/f. Tulsa/pop rock group
   Abbot, Nick/trombonist

Dalby, Mike/baritone saxophonist
Halka, Charles/keyboardist
Halka, Dan/bassist
Hull, Jojo/drummer
Plumlee, James/drummer
Swain, Todd/tenor saxophonist
VanValkenburgh, Parker/vocalist, guitarist, alto saxophonist
Blue Combo/f. Tulsa/blues group
  Armstrong, Robby/b. Tulsa/drums, vocalist
  Davis, Shannon/b. Tulsa/vocalist
  Elmore, Steve/b. Tulsa/keyboardist
  Miller, Rusty/b. Chattanooga, TN/guitar, vocalist
  Waggoner, "Tex"/b. Wichita Falls, TX/bass
Blued/f. Tulsa/heavy metal group
Blue Diamond/f. Muskogee/classic rock group
The Blue Flame/f. Oklahoma City/blues group
Blue Funke/f. Tulsa/funk rock group
Blues Nation/f. Anadarko, 1980s/American Indian blues band
  Klinekole, Sonny/b. Lawton/bass
  Mauchahty-Ware, Tom/b. Lawton/guitar, vocals, **Kiowa**/Comanche flutist
  Miller, Dusty/b. Lawton/   guitar
  Sullivan, Obie/b. Okmulgee/keyboards
  Tsotigh, Terry/b. Carnegie/drums/harmonica
BMP (Bill Murray's Prostate)/f. Pryor, 1998/rock group
Boe, Dennis/East Central Oklahoma University music faculty, 2003/applied piano
Bocanegra, Cheryl/Tulsa University music faculty, 2003/music theory, recording
Bohannon, Ken/Oklahoma University of Science and Arts music faculty, 2003
Bointy, Joe/r. Oklahoma/powwow singer (**Kiowa**/Comanche)
Bolar, Abe/b. Oklahoma City, 1909/jazz bassist for **Oklahoma City Blue Devils**
Bolen, Chuck/r. Oklahoma/pop, rock vocalist, recorded for Sheridan Records in Tulsa
Bonham, Virgil/b. Talihina/**Bill Grant**'s Kiamichi Mountain Boys, Bonham Review
Bonham, Glen/b. Coalgate/**Bill Grant**'s Kiamichi Mountain Boys, Bonham Review
Boondogs/f. Tulsa/rootsy, Americana group
Boone, Michale/Oklahoma University music faculty, 2003/assistant band director
Bop Cats/f. Tulsa/rock and roll revival group
Bordeaux, Tonya/r. Tulsa/world music guitarist, singer, songwriter
Bostic, Earl/b. Tulsa, 1913/jazz saxophonist/arranger/composer
Bovenschen, Wayne/Oklahoma State University music faculty, 2003/percussionist
Browa, Frank/Duck Creek Ceremonial Grounds/stomp dance leader
Boyd, Clarence/b. Vinita, r. Kellyville/co-wrote "Release Me"
Boyles, Kay/Oklahoma City University music faculty, 2003/accompanist
Brackeen, William/Langston University music faculty, 2003/piano, music theory
Brady, Felicia/r. Oklahoma/folk pop singer, songwriter
Brant, Nathan/r. Tulsa/pop rock singer, songwriter
Bravo Brass Quintet/r. Oklahoma City/chamber music group
Brazille, Emmitt/r. Oklahoma City/jazz pianist, multi-genre/multi-instrumental abilities
Bread, Phillip "Yogie"/r. Oklahoma/ American Indian flutist, **Kiowa**
Breashears, David/Tulsa University music faculty, 2003/percussionist

Breaux, Zelia Page/b. MO, r. Langston and Oklahoma City/educator
Breeden, Harold/b. Guthrie, 1921/jazz reeds and educator
Bryan, Mark/r. Stillwater/pianist
Brick Face Lovely/f. Tulsa/rock group
Bridges, Henry (Hank)/b. Oklahoma City, circa 1908/jazz saxophonist
Bright, Jeff/Northeastern Oklahoma State University music faculty, 2003/band director
British Invasion/f. Oklahoma City/1960s British pop tribute band
Britt, Brian/Oklahoma University music faculty, 2003/associate band director
Brooks, Colleen/b. in Kansas City, r. in OK/country singer, **Garth Brooks**'s mother
Brooks, Joan/r. Edmond/classical music
Brooks, Mary/ Oklahoma University of Science and Arts part-time music faculty, 2003
Brooks, William/b. Ardmore, 1959/singer, songwriter
Broughton, J.C./r. Sapulpa/champion old time fiddler
Brown, Buddy/r. Oklahoma/blues guitarist, led Buddy Brown and the Hound Dogs
Brown, Darrell/r. Oklahoma/gospel producer
Brown, Felix, Jr./Duck Creek Ceremonial Grounds/stomp dance leader
Brown, Joseph/b. Wagoner/JOB Records founder
Brown, Junior/taught at Hank Thompson School of Music, Claremore/guit-steel guitarist
Brown, Tanya Rae/r. Oklahoma/country singer (Mrs. Junior Brown)
Brown, W. Lawson/r. Bethany/gospel singer
Bruce, Buddy/r. Tulsa/recording guitarist with Champs on "Tequila", still active in 2003
Bruner, Mark/r. Tulsa/guitarist
Bryant, Freddie/r. Norman/guitarist
Bryant, Jim/b. Midwest City, r. Del City, Inola/music educator
Bucchianeri, Diane/Tulsa University music faculty, 2003/cellist, chamber musician
Buchanan, Roy/r. Tulsa in 1955/blues guitarist
Buckner, Acee/Tallahassee Wvkokye Ceremonial Grounds/stomp dance leader
Bueker, Glen/Tulsa University music faculty, 2003/saxophonist
Buffalomeat, Lavern/r. Oklahoma/intertribal powwow head singer
Bunds, Monica/Tulsa University student, 2003/singer on jazz CD, *Sophisticated Ladies*
Burford, Annette/b. Oklahoma City/opera singer
Burgstahler, Patrice/Northeastern Oklahoma State University music faculty, 2003
Burkhart, Sara Maybelle/b. Tulsa, 1910/classical composer
Burleigh, Glenn Edward/b. Guthrie/gospel composer, conductor
Burns, William O./b. Calvin, 1921/Texas State Champion old time fiddler
Burris, Chip/r. Tulsa/jazz saxophonist, educator at ORU and TU
Burris, Eddy/r. Tulsa/co-wrote "Okie from Muskogee"
Burrow, Chad/Oklahoma City University music faculty, 2003/clarinetist
Burtschi Brothers/f. Norman/Okie rock, dirt jazz, Americana, roots music group
    Foreman, Chris/drums
    Linville, Travis/guitar
    Phenix, Mike/bass
    Webb, Kevin/guitars
Busey, Gary/b. Goose Creek, TX, 1944, r. Tulsa and Stillwater
    starred in the *Buddy Holly Story*
Butcher, Marlin/b. Oklahoma City, 1951/rock and country bassist
Butler, John (Kaw/Otoe)/r. Oolagah/intertribal powwow head singer
Butler, Kate/Oklahoma State University music faculty, 2003/mezzo-soprano, voice

Butler, Wesley/Peach Ceremonial Grounds/stomp dance leader
Butler, Zachary/r. Oklahoma/stomp dance leader
Byfield, Jim/b. Tulsa, 1949/vocalist, guitarist, **Tulsa Sound**
Byington, Presley/r. Idabel/Choctaw flute maker, flutist

C

Cable, Kelly/r. Oklahoma/intertribal powwow head singer
Cagle, Clarence/b. Oklahoma City, 1920/Western swing pianist for **Bob Wills**
Cain, Cindy/b. April 5, 1959, Carlsbad, N.M., r. Pryor/jazz and blues singer
Cain, Donna/Oklahoma City University music faculty, 2003/violist
Caliman, Hadley/b. Idabel, 1932/jazz saxophonist
Call of the West/r. Strang/cowboy singers
Campbell, Debbie/b. Ft. Worth, r. Tulsa/rock, pop, jazz vocalist
Campbell, Royce/r. Oklahoma/finger picking guitarist
Campbell, Will/Northeastern OSU music faculty, 2003/saxophonist, jazz education
The Candles/f. Norman, 2003/pop rock group, formerly The Pistol Arrows (1999-2003)
　Flato, Chance/b. July 21, 1975, Houston, TX/bassist (w/ The Green Owls 1996-97)
　Sarmiento, Adam/b. April 4, 1976, Rochester, NY/drummer, songwriter
　　(w/ The New Tribe 1993-96)
　Sarmiento, Eric/b. March 20, 1974, Rochester, NY/singer, guitarist, songwriter
　　(w/ The New Tribe 1993-96)
　Williams, Brent/May 25, 1976, Riverdale, GA/violinist
　　also plays with the Oklahoma City Philharmonic
Candy, Stewart/r. Hammond/Cheyenne church song singer
The Canis/f. Tulsa/rap group, recorded for Made Records
Canning, Jessi/r. Tulsa, based in Washington D. C. circa 2002/sparkle pop
The Cannons/r. Oklahoma/country group
Cantrell, Jerry/r. near Boggy Depot/rock guitarist (Alice in Chains)
Cantwell, Wayne/r. Del City/old time musician (fiddle/dulcimer/mandolin/banjo/guitar)
Cardin, Fred/b. Quapaw Reservation, I.T., 1895/classical composer
Carlton, Larry/parents were old time musicians (fiddle/guitar) in southeastern Oklahoma
　　guitarist/jazz guitarist
Carman/b. Trenton, NJ, r. Tulsa/gospel singer
Carnival Groove/f. Oklahoma City/rock group
Carroll, Claudia/Oklahoma City University music faculty, 2003/pianist
Carothers, Dale/r. Cushing/old time fiddler
Carrington, Rodney/b. Texas, r. Tulsa/country singer
Carson, Jeff/b. Tulsa/country singer, songwriter
Carson, Ken/b. Coalgate-Centrahoma vicinity/Sons of the Pioneers
Carter, Dave/b. Oxnard, CA, r. Oklahoma/folk singer
Carter, Karen/University of UCO music faculty, 2003/elementary music education
Carter, Rose/b. Snyder, 1931/Chuck Wagon Gang
Carter, Roy/b. Calumet/Chuck Wagon Gang
Cassity, Marca/r. Oklahoma City/acoustic guitarist, singer, songwriter
Castle, Jeremy/b. Blanchard/country singer

Caswell, Bill/r. Oklahoma City/Bartlesville/country, bluegrass guitarist
Cate, Merry Kay/r. Tulsa/contemporary Christian singer
Catfish String Band/p. KFRU in the 1920s, later on KVOO/old time country group
Cats of the Thin Earth/f. Norman, OK/rock group
Cawley, Jack/r. Stillwater/led Oklahoma Ridge Runners
Cedar Ridge/f. Shawnee/bluegrass group
Certified Fools/f. Stillwater, 1993/blues, funk rock group
  Andrew, Brett/reared in Perkins, r. Stillwater/vocalist
  Hardy, Brad/b. Stillwater/bassist
  Headrick, Adam/b. Stillwater/guitarist
  Labow, Benji/b. Toronto, r. Stillwater/drummer who recorded on CD
  Presley, Jason/b. Stillwater/guitarist
  Suratt, Toby/b. Fremont, CA, r. Stillwater/drummer
  Turner, Travis/r. Stillwater/drummer
Chainsaw Kittens/f. Norman, circa 1989-2001/glam pop rock group
  Bell, Trent/guitarist after Mark Metzger until group's demise
  Bones Edward, Eric/drummer (1996)
  Harmon, Eric/drummer (1993)
  Johnson, Matt/bass guitarist (1993-1996)
  Leader, Ted/drummer (1990)
  McElhaney, Kevin/bassist (1990)
  Meade, Tyson/guitarist, vocalist from beginning to end of the group's existence
  Metzger, Mark/lead guitarist (1990)
Chalapa, Sean/Gar Creek Ceremonial Grounds/stomp dance leader
Chalepah, Alonzo (Apache Tribe of OK – Na-I-Sha)/r. Anadarko
  intertribal powwow head singer
Champagne, Salvatore/Oklahoma University music faculty, 2003/voice
Chanate, Jake (Kiowa)/r. Tahlequah/intertribal powwow head singer
Chapman, Gary/b. Waurika, 1957/gospel singer
Charles, Bobby/r. Oklahoma City/soul singer
Charm Pops/f. Oklahoma City, 1997/pop rock group (Beggar's Banquet)
Charmichael-Everitt, Jane/Tulsa University music faculty, 2003/voice, vocal pedagogy
Cheng, Amy I-lin/Oklahoma State University music faculty, 2003/pianist
Chenoweth, Vida/r. Enid/classical marimbist
Cherry Blossom Clinic/f. Altus/rock group
The Cherry Playground/f. Oklahoma City/modern rock band
Cheyenne-Arapaho/based in Concho/Sun Dance, Native American Church songs,
  powwow
Chickasaw Nation/based in Ada, relocated to state in 1838/Chickasaw Christian hymns
Childer, Lemuel Jennings/b. Tulsa/composed "Pictures from Hiawatha"
Childers, Bob/b. West Virginia, r. Stillwater/singer/songwriter/**Red Dirt Music**
Childers, Lemuel/b. Tulsa or Pawhuska/classical composer
Charoenwongse-Shaw, Chindarat/UCO music faculty, 2003/pianist
Chioldi, Ronald/NEOSU music faculty, 2003/pianist, class piano, theory
Choctaw Nation/based in Durant, moved to I.T. in 1831/Choctaw Christian hymns,
  Southern gospel, intertribal powwows
Chosen/f. Hugo/Southern Gospel group
  Compton, Carol/r. Broken Bow/lead vocalist, harmonies

Grissam, Gary "Butter/r. Duncan/drummer
Harvey, Del/r. Duncan/lead vocalist, harmonies
Leach, B.J./b. Bartlesville/bassist
Tims, Jerry/r. Hugo/keyboardist, vocalist
Tims, Stacy/r. Broken Bow/harmony vocalist
Chozen/f. Tulsa/rock group
Chozen Figgaz/r. Tulsa/rap group
Christie, Chooch/Chewey Ceremonial Grounds/stomp dance leader
Christy, David/SEOSU music faculty, 2003/concert band director
Chuck and Sandy/f. Tulsa/jazz duo
Chunk/f. Oklahoma City, 1995/rock group
Chute 5/f. Oklahoma City/country group
Cinematic Blue/f. Tulsa, 2001/pop rock trio
    Bartee, Brandon/bassist
    Finton, Zane/drums
    Moore, Chris/vocals, guitar
Cinocca, Joe/r. Tulsa/owner, Yawn Records
Cissel, Charles/b. Tulsa, 1948/R & B singer, OK Jazz Hall of Fame executive director
Citizen Potawatomi/based in Shawnee/powwow
City Moon/f. 1988, Oklahoma City/country group
    Blair, Jim P./b. Odessa, TX, r. Clayton,Muskogee/multi-instrumentalist, vocalist
      (also plays with Neverly Brothers, Neverly Hillbillies, and solo)
    Blair, John/b. Odessa, TX, r. Oklahoma City/fiddler
    Bonham, Virgil/b. Talihina/vocalist, guitarist, band leader
    Parret, Clifford/b. Nowata/bassist, banjo player
    Wyatt, Cory/b. Norman/drummer
Claroscuro/f. Oklahoma City/Latino rock, world music group
Clark, Bobby/b. Oklahoma City/bluegrass, Grand Ole Opry
Clark, Earl/b. Tulsa/jazz saxophonist
Clark, Jim/r. Owasso/steel guitar maker, steel guitarist
Clark, John/Drumright High School graduate, 1978/country singer, songwriter,
    played backup for Hank Thompson
Clark, Lucky/r. Tulsa/**Tulsa Sound** vocalist and bandleader from 1958 to 1960
Clark, Millard/r. Moore/intertribal powwow singer, owner of Indian Sounds Records
Clark, Sanford/b. Tulsa, 1935/rockabilly singer
Clear Creek Band/f. Guymon/traditional country group
Cletro, Eddie/b. Coalgate, 1920s/rockabilly singer, bandleader
Cleveland, Ingram/b. Vinita, 1908/classical composer
Clewell, Jeannie/OCU music faculty, 2003/theory, composition, piano
Click, Joey/b. Altus/bassist for Trace Adkins
Clifford, K.C./b. Oklahoma City/folk singer, songwriter
Clour, Deral/recorded for Hobart-based Hu-Se-Co label in the 1950s
    country boogie singer
Clupper, Dave/r. Jenks/spiritual alternative folk
C-Note/r. Tulsa/hip hop artist
Cobb, Bob/r. Wagoner/Western swing bassist
Coburn, Sarah/r. Oklahoma, OCU graduate/opera singer
Cochran, Eddie/b. Albert Lea, MN, various family members from OKC

rockabilly singer

Codynah, Van/r. Oklahoma/Gourd Dance singer, intertribal powwow head singer

Coe, David/r. Oklahoma/traditional fiddler

Coe, Richard/r. Oklahoma/mountain dulcimer

Cogan, Mary and The Sundowners/r. Tulsa/singer, songwriter
  Bruner, Mark/guitarist
  Cogan, Mary/singer
  DeWalt, Chuck/drummer
  Eicher, Shelby/fiddler-mandolinist
  Morgan, Ron/bassist
  Sutton, Spencer/keyboardist

Cole, Darrel and the New Country Revolution/f.Tulsa/country group

Coleman, Keith/b. Chickasha/fiddler for **Bob Wills**

Coleman, William/University of Central Oklahoma music faculty, 2003/accompanist

Collins, Emogene/Oklahoma City University music faculty, 2003/voice

Collins, Henry/r. Oklahoma/intertribal powwow head singer

Collum, Bob/b. Tulsa/folk rock singer, songwriter

Coloton, Diane/Oklahoma University music faculty, 2003/voice

Comanche/based in Lawton, in state for centuries/flutists, Native American Church
  songs, Christian hymns, powwow

Comer, Marilyn/SEOSU adjunct music faculty, 2003/sacred music

Come Together/f. Oklahoma City/Beatles tribute band

Common Tyme/f. Blanchard/bluegrass group

Commonwealthy/f. Tulsa, Bixby/rock group

Composition B/f. Pryor, 2001/rock group

Compston, Don/r. Tulsa/steel guitarist, Oklahoma Steel Guitar Association presdident

Conaway, Shane/b. Tahlequah, r. Muskogee, Edmond, Yukon/guitarist with **Ty England**

Conklin, Roscoe/r. Oklahoma/intertribal powwow head singer

Conlon, Paula/Oklahoma University music faculty, 2003/ethnomusicologist

Connor Raus/f. Tulsa/rock group

Conoscenti, Don/r. Oklahoma City, originally from Atlanta/folk singer

Convertino, John/b. Long Island, r. Stillwater, Tulsa/drummer (Giant Sand/Calexico)

Copas, Cowboy/b. Ohio/country singer, originally from Ohio, who claimed to be from
  Muskogee to enhance his rural credibility, died in plane crash with Patsy Cline

Copenhaver, Dave/staff engineer of Studio Seven in Oklahoma City since 1990
  producer, Lunacy Records, bassist

Council Oak Trio/r. Tulsa/chamber music group

Cowen, Jeffery/Tulsa University music faculty, 2003/principal violinist
  Tulsa Philharmonic, 1990-present

Cowen, Michele/Tulsa University music faculty, 2003/pianist

Cox, Donna/r. Yukon, Oklahoma University music faculty, 2003/jazz vocalist, voice

Cox, Johanna/Oklahoma State University music faculty, 2003/oboist

Cox, Richard/r. Tulsa/cool jazz saxophonist

Cox, Ted/Oklahoma University music faculty, 2003/tuba

Cozad, Daniel (**Kiowa**)/r. Oklahoma/intertribal powwow head singer

Cozad, Kenneth (**Kiowa**)/r. Carnegie/intertribal powwow head singer

Cozad, Larry (**Kiowa**)/r. Hominy/intertribal head powwow singer, Gourd Dance singer

Cozad, Leonard, Sr. (**Kiowa**)/b. Hog Creek/Cozad Family Singers

elder statesman of Kiowa singers
Cozad, Leonard, Jr. (**Kiowa**)/r. Oklahoma City/intertribal powwow head singer
Cozad, Lewis (**Kiowa**)/r. Oklahoma/Gourd Dance singer
   intertribal powwow head singer
Cozad, Vernon (**Kiowa**)/r. Norman/intertribal powwow head singer
Cozad, Rusty (**Kiowa**)/r. Oklahoma/intertribal powwow head singer
CPH (Corporate Puppet Halitosis)/f. Tulsa/Christian rock, pop group
Cradle/f. Mustang, 1998/rock group
Craig, Forrest, H./b. MO, r. OK/four time grand champion fiddler
Craige, Mary Ann/Southeastern Oklahoma State University music faculty, 2003/piano
Crank, M.A. "Mac"/b. Arkansas City, KS, 1948, r. Stillwater/started Stillwater blues festival
Creed, Kay/University of Central Oklahoma music faculty, 2003/opera
Criss, Marie/r. Oklahoma/intertribal powwow singer
Crist, Richard/Oklahoma University music faculty, 2003/voice
Critchlow, Slim/r. Oklahoma as a child/cowboy singer
Crittenden, Melodie/b. Moore, 1969/country singer
Croney, Merle/r. Oklahoma/band leader, multi-instrumentalist/
   Merle Croney Family bluegrass group
   Croney, Danny/fiddle, guitar, mandolin player
   Croney, Frank/banjo, bass, guitar player
   Croney, Karen/bass, mandolin, fiddle, guitar player
   Croney, Mark/mandolin, guitar, fiddle player
Crook, Tommy/b. Oklahoma, 1944/jazz, country guitarist, **Tulsa Sound**
Crosby, Bill/r. Tulsa/jazz bassist
Crose, Gene/r. Tulsa/1950s rock and roll singer, guitarist, band leader, **Tulsa Sound**
Crosset, Steve/b. Oklahoma City/guitarist for Glen Campbell
Crouch, Randy/r. Tahlequah/folk singer
Crownover, Gene/b. Cromwell, buried near Seminole/steel guitarist for **Bob Wills**
Crumbley, Elmer/b. Kingisher, 1908/jazz of the territory band era
Crush Molly Sunshine/r. Moore, 1996/rock group
Crutcher, Joe/*/Oklahoma Jazz Hall of Fame inductee, gospel category
Cruz, Edgar, Manuel, and Mark/r. Oklahoma City/classical guitarists
Cryout Reggae Band/f. Tulsa/"reggae with a funky twist"
   Criner, Jerry/vocals, guitar
   Ewing, Beau/drums
   Heidon, Eric/bass
Cubie, Greta/b. near Stroud, 1933, OU graduate/multi-instrumentalist,
   music teacher at Tulsa Edison High School, 1960-90
Cummings, Boss/Rocky Ford Ceremonial Grounds/stomp dance leader
Cummins, Jon/r. Tulsa/jazz bassist
Cunningham, Amanda/b. Elgin, 1978, r. Oklahoma City/**Red Dirt** singer, songwriter
Curtis Lowe Band/f. Tulsa/rock group
Curtis Moore Band/f. Tulsa/blues-rock group
Curtis, Steven/Oklahoma University music faculty, 2003/chorus, music education
Cynderplay/f. Blackwell/contemporary Christian rock group

D

Daniel, Robert/NEOSU music faculty, 2003/opera singer, vocal pedagogy

Daniel, Sean/Oklahoma University music faculty, 2003/voice

Daniels, Jack/b. Choctaw, 1949/guitars, vocals Highway 101

Daddy D/r. Oklahoma City/rapper

Daisy Strange/f. Tulsa/pop rock group

Damascus Road/f. Sapulpa/Christian rock group

Dane, Matthew/Oklahoma University music faculty, 2003/violinist

Dansby, Brad/r. Valliant/contemporary Christian

Dark, Danny (Danny Croskery)/b. Tulsa/1950s trumpeter, bandleader,

The Darlings/f. Tulsa/independent, Emo rock group

David R/r. Oklahoma/singer-songwriter

Davidson, Michael M./NWOSU music faculty, 2003/trombonist, music education

Davis, Bill/r. Tulsa/blues harmonica player, vocalist

Davis, Dale/born Dale Siegenthaler, Morris, 1928/1950s rock and roll singer, guitarist,

Davis, Elmer, Sr./*/Oklahoma Jazz Hall of Fame Inductee, gospel category

Davis, Harvey "Preacher"/r. Cushing/fiddler, vocalist

Davis, LaVonne "Sister Boogie" Faris/r. Noble/pianist with **Bob Wills** in the 1960s

Davis, Joe/r. Tahlequah (NEOSU professor)/saxophonist

Davis, Kevin/b. Walters/country singer

Davis, Mark/Langston University music faculty, 2003/department chair

Davis, Michael Rees/b. Tulsa/opera tenor

Davis, Ray/r. Lawton and Ada/blues singer

Dawes, Kevin (Ottawa)/r. Baxter Springs, KS/intertribal powwow head singer

Day by Day/f. Tulsa/hard rock group

Dayton, Ronny/b. Tulsa/Ronny and the Daytonas

DDS/f. Tulsa/hard rock group

Deck Sachse/f. Tulsa/independent rock group

Deer, Richard (Iowa/Sac & Fox/Cheyenne)/r. Tulsa/intertribal powwow head singer

Deerinwater, Joe (**Cherokee/Muscogee**)/r. Tahlequah/intertribal powwow head singer

DeGeer, Jay/r. Oilton/multi-instrumentalist, instrument repair

DeGeer, Rae/r. Oilton/saxophonist for Charlie Barnett and **Johnnie Lee Wills**

Dehnert, Lon/UCO music faculty, 2003/choral studies director, choral conducting

Delavan, Mark/b. Tulsa (ORU Graduate)/opera singer

Delaware, Marcella/r. Oklahoma/intertribal powwow singer

Delaware Nation (Western)/based near Anadarko, moved to I.T. in 1859/
    powwow singers

Delaware Tribe of Indians (Eastern)/based in Bartlesville, moved to I.T. in 1867/
    powwow, stomp dance

The Delicious Militia/f. Stillwater, 1997/country rock group, **Red Dirt Music**
    Foley, Nokose/b. Claremore, 1994/singer, 49 drum
    Greteman, Blaine/b. Oklahoma City, 1975/singer, songwriter, guitarist
    Martin, Doug/b. Clinton, IN, r. Stillwater and Claremore/singer, songwriter, guitarist
    McCubbin, Derek/b. Stillwater, 1978/drummer (trap set)
    Phillips, Mark/r. Stillwater/bassist

Dell, Charlene/Oklahoma University music faculty, 2003/music education

Delladova, John/r. Tulsa/jazz drummer

DeNada/f. Tulsa/reggae, jazz, R & B, soul group
  Edwards, Matthew/drummer, percussionist
  Fite, Travis/vocalist, guitarist
  Hebert, Al Ray/bassist
Deng, Lu/University of Central Oklahoma music faculty, 2003/violinist
Denim/recorded in Broken Bow/country group
Denison, Cal/b. Fairfax, 1956/gospel acoustic guitarist
Denizens/f. Oologah, 2002/rock group
Dennie, "Al" George/b. Arcadia, 1903/jazz bandleader
Dennis, James, T./OU graduate, 1951
  invented phonograph and CD changers from 1940s through 2000
Dennis, Jody/r. Oklahoma/banjo player
Dennis, Levi/b. Sapulpa/country fiddler
Denver, John/r. Bessie with his grandparents/country rock singer, songwriter
Dewitt, Scotty/r. Yukon/steel guitar
Dillard, Ernestine/b. Nesbitt, MS, 1941, r. Tulsa 1990/gospel singer
DeRamus, Judy/r. Broken Bow/gospel singer
Dixon, Clarence/*/Oklahoma Jazz Hall of Fame inductee
Dixon, Gabe/b. Guymon/singer with country group Copperhead
Dizmal Failure/f. Hartshorne, 1999/rock group
DJ Dvyne/r. Emond/dance music disc-jockey, mixer
Dobrin, Duilio/Oklahoma University music faculty, 2003/orchestra
Dog Hill/f. Norman/blues band
DOG & LOC/r. Oklahoma City, 2002/rap *(The Okla-Homiez)*
Donnelly, Ted/b. Oklahoma City, 1912/trombonist, trumpeter, alto saxophonist
  for Erskine Hawkins and Count Basie
Dosher, Kennon/r. Tipton/country singer, songwriter
Double Excel/r. Tulsa/R & B vocal group, recorded for Made records
Double Not Spyz/f. Oklahoma/disbanded folk music group now the Hapless Romantics
Dowd, Johnny/b. Fort Worth, TX, r. Pauls Valley/singer, songwriter
Down for Five/f. Tulsa/heavy metal rock group
Downing, Don/b. Lenapah, 1940/dance band singer/pianist, brother of **Big Al Downing**
Downing, Ken/*/Oklahoma Jazz Hall of Fame inductee
Dozier, Billy/r. Oklahoma/Western swing guitarist
Drake, Charly/recorded for Hobart-based Hu-Se-Co in the 1950s/country boogie singer
Dramacyde/f. Tulsa/shock rock group
Dreadfulwater, J.B./b. Oklahoma/**Cherokee** gospel singer, bandleader
Drege, Lance/Oklahoma University music faculty, 2003/percussionist
Drew, Ray/r. Oklahoma City/blues singer
Driscoll, Phil/b. Seattle, r. Tulsa, 1961/gospel singer, trumpeter
Drive by Romeo/f. Tulsa/techno group
Driven/f. Tulsa/rock group
  Autry, Brandon/guitarist
  Campbell, Gary/drummer
  Montgomery, Matt/lead singer
  Nipps, Colt/bassist
Dru, Daniel/b. near Thomas, 1924/Cheyenne drum maker
The Drum Busters/f. Tahlequah/intertribal powwow singing group

DuBois, Tim/b. Grove, 1948/music industry executive, songwriter
Due North/f. Oklahoma City/contemporary Christian duo
Duhon, Olivia/2003 TU music student/sings on TU jazz CD, *Sophisticated Ladies*
Duke, Johnny and Shootout/f. Tulsa/country music group
Dulcinea/f. Tulsa/acoustic duo
   Fort, Andrea/double bassist, harpist, percussionist
   Loman, Kasey/guitarist, vocalist
Dunlap, Chuck/r. Stillwater/**Red Dirt Music**
Dunn, Donald/b. Sallisaw/blues guitarist
Dupoint, Phil "The Fish"/r. Carnegie/intertribal powwow head singer
Duvall, Brad/b. Tulsa/touring lead guitarist for Gus Hardin and Pake McEntire
D.W. Sides/f. Atoka/Christian rock band

E

Eagle, Wilke D., Sr. (Ponca)/r. Marland/intertribal powwow head singer
Earlene, Gayla/r. Tulsa/country-gospel singer
East, Lyndel/b. Oklahoma City/country singer
Eastern Shawnee Tribe/based in Seneca, MO, just across state line, since 1832/powwow
Eaves, Jimmy/b. Eaves City/rockabilly singer
Edgar, Jim/r. Perry/1950s and 60s rock and roll vocalist, bandleader
Eicher, Shelby/r. Tulsa/fiddler, mandolinist
Eighth Day/f Oklahoma City/contemporary Christian rock group
Eisenhauer, Kathy Jean/b. Chelsea, 1979/country singer
Elam, Katrina/b. Bray/country singer, songwriter, signed by Universal South Records
Electric Rag Band/f. 1994, Tulsa/blues band
Element/f. Oklahoma City, 1998/loud rock
Elija's Ride/f. Tulsa/Christian hard rock group
   Brown, Matt/vocalist
   Ballinger, Aaron/drummer
   Cross, Shannon/bassist
   Williamson, Kenny/guitarist
Elling, Hank/b. Lawton, 1948/cowboy singer
Ellis, E.P. "Vep"/ r. Tulsa/gospel singer
Ellis Family/f. Tulsa/Southern gospel group
Ellis, Jimmy/reared in Oklahoma/blues singer
Ellison, Scott/b. Tulsa/blues guitarist, singer
Elms, Enoch/Oklahoma City University music faculty, 2003/accompanist
Emge, Steven/SEOSU music faculty, 2003/opera singer, applied voice
Enevoldsen, Adam/b. Charlottesville, VA/vocals, guitars w/Plastic Jack,
   bassist for Fried Okra Jones
Enevoldsen, Kyle/b. Ponca City/percussionist, drummer with Fried Okra Jones
   and Plastic Jack, also played in Wensell Jazz Trio
The Engine Hearts/f. Tulsa/rock group
   Disney, Andy/drummer
   Foster, Jo/bassist
   Scott, Justin/guitarist, vocalist
   Simmons, Alex/guitarist, vocalist

Enlow/f. Tulsa/Christian hardcore rock group

Enrico, Eugene/Oklahoma University music faculty, 2003/musicologist

Enriquez, Mikaila/b. Edmond, 1987/pop singer

Entry 5/f. Oklahoma City/acoustic singer, songwriter duo

Erotic Suicide/f. Oklahoma City/hard rock band

Estell, Oscar/*/Oklahoma Jazz Hall of Fame inductee

Ester Drang/f. Broken Arrow, 1996/space rock on Jade Tree Records
  Chambers, Bryce/vocalist, keyboardist, guitarist
  McAlister, James/drummer, pianist, samples
  Shoop, Jeff/guitarist, keyboardist
  Winner, Kyle/bass guitarist, bass synth

Estes, Billy/r. Tulsa/session drummer, father of **Toni Estes**

Eternal Decision/f. Oklahoma City, 1997/punk rock group

Etheridge, David/Oklahoma University music faculty, 2003/clarinetist

Euchee Tribe/based in Sapulpa, moved to I.T., 1829/Green Corn ceremonial cycle,
  Euchee Christian hymns

Exit 125/f. Oklahoma City/rock group

Eye/f. Norman/rock group

Ezell, Ellis/b. Tahlequah, 1913, r. Muskogee/jazz saxophonist, bandleader,

F

Facci, Mark/Tulsa University music faculty, 2003/bassist

Factor 9/f. Norman/rock group

Failsafe/f. Tulsa/hard rock group

Faison, George/*/Oklahoma Jazz Hall of Fame inductee

Falcon Five-0/rock group
  Falcon, J./vocalist, guitarist
  King, Wally/guitarist
  Simon, "Sugar Stick"/drummer

Falderal String Band/f. Oklahoma City/folk group

Falkner, Jay, & the South 40 Band/f. Panama/classic rock, country and western group

Fallen Hero/f. Sapulpa/Christian pop group

Fanny Grace/r. Oklahoma City/gypsy soul

Fanzine/f. Tulsa/rock group

Far from Sanity/f. Tulsa/Christian hard rock
  Edens, Christian/b. St. Louis, r. Tulsa/drummer
  Goodnight, Mark/b. Kansas, r. Tulsa area/vocalist, samples
  Laywell, Eddie/   b. Maryland, r. Tulsa/bassist, vocalist
  Melton, Jimmy/   b. Tulsa/guitarist
  Sanchez, Willie/b. Fredericksburg, TX, r. Tulsa/guitarist, vocalist

The Farm Couple/f. outside Stillwater, 1996/folk singers, **Red Dirt Music**
  Taylor, Monica/r. Stillwater/singer, songwriter, guitarist
  Williams, Patrick/r. Grove/singer, songwriter, guitarist

Farmer, Kelly/b. Tulsa, 1977/opera singer (Tulsa Opera)

Farrell, Gail/r. Oklahoma/vocalist with *The Lawrence Welk Show*

Farrier, Marshall/r. Tulsa/leads pop rock group

Fasol, Rober/Oklahoma City University music faculty, 2003/concert choir

Fast, Barbara/Oklahoma University music faculty, 2003/piano pedagogy
Faulconer, James/OU music faculty, 2003/music theory, composition, technology
Faulconer, Sally/Oklahoma University music faculty, 2003/oboe
Feathers, Leo/b. Stilwell/country, rock guitarist
Fenton, Paul "Happy"/b. Rantoul, IL, 1900, r. Wagoner/organist, accordionist,
Ferguson, Charles, E./r. Newkirk, circa 1902/sheet music publisher, composer
Ferguson, Roy/r. Tulsa/country, Western swing singer, guitarist
  co-manages Roy and Candy's Music, Tulsa
Ferrara, William/Oklahoma University music faculty, 2003/opera
Ferris, James/r. Oklahoma City/rock singer, songwriter
Fields, Ernie,b. Texas, r. Tulsa/big band, jazz bandleader
Final Step/f. Lawton
Fireside Bluegrass/f. Oklahoma City/bluegrass group
Fisher, Jerry/b. Oklahoma, 1943/lead singer with Blood, Sweat, and Tears
Fisher, Starr/r. Oklahoma/pop, jazz singer, Miss Black Oklahoma
Fisher, Steve/b. Tulsa, 1954/folk singer
Fixture/f. Yukon/rap group
Flesher, Sandra/University of Central Oklahoma music faculty, 2003/oboist
Flip-Kid Posse/f. Norman/rock and rap group
Flowers, Danny/b. North Carolina/wrote "Tulsa Time"
Flowers, Darren/r. Oklahoma City/singer-songwriter, guitarist, keyboardist
Floy, John/r. Oklahoma City/pop rock guitarist
Floyd, Heather/r. Oklahoma/contemporary Christian singer
Flying L Ranch Quartet/r. Oklahoma/barbershop music group
Flynn, Mike/r. Tulsa/folk music historian
Force 4D/f. Oklahoma/metal group
Ford Brothers Band/f. Oklahoma City/rock and roll group
Ford, Brownie/b. Oklahoma/singing cowboy
Forgiven/f. Ponca City/Southern gospel quartet
  Brooke, Mark/b. Ponca City/tenor vocals
  Green, Mark/b. Ponca City/lead vocals
  Johnson, Stan/b. Enid/bass vocals
For Love Not Lisa/f. Oklahoma City, 1990/hard rock group
  Lewis, Mike/r. Oklahoma City/guitarist, vocalist
  McBay, Clint/r. Oklahoma City/bassist
  Miles/r. Oklahoma City/bassist, background vocalist
  Preston, Aaron/r. Oklahoma City/drummer
Formerly/f. Gore and Tulsa/rock group
Forsyth, Kris/r. Oklahoma/country singer
Fortner, Rick/r. Tulsa/jazz pianist, music director of All Souls Unitarian Church
Fort Oakland Ramblers/f. Tonkawa/southern style powwow group
  Begs-His-Own, Joe/singer
  Flores, J.R./singer
  Patterson, Don/b. near Tonkawa/lead singer
  Patterson, Henry/singer
  Robedeaux, Alde/singer
  Robedeaux, Kyle/singer
  Roy, Chief/singer

Street, Anthony/singer

Fort Sill-Chiricahau-Warm Springs Apache/based in Apache, arrived in I.T., 1894
   Mountain Spirit or Fire Dance, hymns

Fountainhead/f. Norman

Foust, Steve/r. near Ripley/contemporary Christian singer, songwriter

Fox, Jerry/b. Hobart/member of 1980s country group Bandana

Fowler, Michael/Tulsa University music faculty/guitarist

Francis, Riley/r. Tulsa/1050s rock and roll singer, **Tulsa Sound**

Francisco, Andre/University of Central Oklahoma music faculty, 2003/double bassist

Frank, Gerald/Oklahoma State University music faculty, 2003/organist, harpsichordist

Franklin, Bonita/Langston University music faculty, 2003/vocal music director

Franklin, Sam/b. Clearview, 1932/R & B saxophonist

Frazier-Adams, Carleen/r. Tulsa/recorded an album of Scottish fiddle tunes

Freakshow/f. Tulsa/psycho rock

Frejo, Brian/r. Oklahoma City/hip hop producer

The Frequency Bliss/f. Oklahoma/modern rock group

Fried Okra Jones/f. Stillwater, 1999/blues rock group
   Enevoldsen, Adam/bassist
   Enevoldsen, Kyle/drummer
   Isom, "Texas" Ray/b. Ennis, TX/lead guitarist
   Watermelon Slim/b. Boston, MA/vocalist, harp player, slide guitarist

Friends of the Apocalypse/f. Tulsa, disbanded 2002/loud rock group

Friesen, Gordon/b. Weatherford/folk singer, composer, husband of **Agnes Cunningham**

Fresonke, Michael/Oklahoma City University music faculty, 2003/guitarist

Frisco, Rocky/b. Tulsa, 1937/pianist, songwriter, **Tulsa Sound**

From Tomorrow/f. Tulsa/goth rock group

Frost, Cody/r. Afton/flat pick guitarist

Fuchs, Kenneth/OU music faculty, 2003/music theory and composition

Full Flava Kings/f. Tulsa/R&B, rock group
   Fary, Stanley/drummer
   Fite, Travis/guitarist
   Marrow, Rick/keyboardist
   Redd, Charlie/lead singer, bassist, also tours as background singer w/ Jimmie Vaughan

Full Swing/f. Tulsa/R & B group, recorded for Made Records

Fulmer, Fred/Oklahoma City University music faculty, 2003/trombonist

Funkhouser, Joe/b. Hobart/singer, songwriter of songs about rural Oklahoma

Furr, Ronnie/r. Oklahoma/country singer, songwriter, guitarist

Fuzz/f. Tulsa/rock group

G

Gaea Spore/f. Norman

Ganem, I.J./r. Sand Springs/singer in Branson, MO shows

Gant, Dave/b. Ada/**Garth Brooks**'s bandleader, keyboardist, fiddler

Garcia, Lynda/b. Washington, D.C., r. Muskogee/organist at Tuskegee Institute

Garcia, Opalee Randolph/b. Enid, July 7, 1907/Latin musician

Garcia, Skye/ECOU adjunct music faculty, 2003/applied piano, music theory

Garder, Barbara/University of Central Oklahoma music faculty, 2003/pianist

The Gardes/f. Ponca City, 1993/funky folk rock group
  Grover, Lance/guitars
  Horton, Brett/b. Delaware, r. Ponca City/singer, songwriter, guitarist
  Lenhart, Ricky/drummer
Gardner, Chuck/r. Tulsa/jazz pianist
Gardner, Max P./b. Oklahoma City, 1932/country music publisher, broadcaster
Gardner, Sandy/b. Tulsa/jazz singer, bassist
Garner, Dirk/Oklahoma State University music faculty, 2003/choral studies director
Garrison, Leonard/Tulsa University music faculty, 2003/flutist
Gates, Edward/Oklahoma University music faculty, 2003/pianist
Gawhega, Michael/r. Oklahoma/intertribal powwow head singer
Gaylord, Dave/r. Vinita/traditional fiddler
Gaylord, Monte/b. Oolagah/traditional fiddler
Gears of Redemption/f. Oklahoma City/Christian rock group
Geary, Barbara/r. Tulsa/classical pianist
Genevro, Bradley/OSU music faculty, 2003/associate director of bands, music education
Gentzel, Todd/SEOSUadjunct music faculty, 2003/saxophone
George, Scott (Osage)/r. Oklahoma City/intertribal powwow head singer
Getman, Ron/b. Fairfax, 1948/multi-instrumentalist (strings)
  played/recorded with Leonard Cohen, **Steve Ripley,** Tractors
Geyer, Joyce/b. Okmulgee/opera singer
Gibbs, Vince/r. Tulsa/Prince impersonator, appears in Missy Elliot's "Work It" video
Gibson, John, A. (Shawnee)/r. Claremore/stomp dance leader
Gibson, Johnna/r. (Shawnee/Sac & Fox/Seneca-Cayuga) Claremore/shell shaker
Gibson, Terri (Sac & Fox/Seneca-Cayuga)/r. Claremore/shell shaker
Gibson, Tony/r. Claremore/stomp dance leader
Gillette, Betty Barber/r. Tulsa/radio singer on KTUL/KVOO-AM, Tulsa in the 1940s
Gillian, Steve/r. Oklahoma/traditional fiddler
Gilliam, Les/b. Gene Autry, 1934/cowboy singer
Gilliland, Danny/b. Bartlesville, 1958/champion banjo player
Gilliland, Henry, C./ b. MO, r. Altus, OK/ made some of the first fiddle recordings
Gilmore, Gary/r. Tulsa/bassist for Taj Majal, **J.J. Cale**, and others
Gilyard, James/b. Stillwater, 1945/jazz bassist
Gimble, Dick/b. Oklahoma/country bassist
Glare/f. Tulsa, disbanded 2002/rock group
Glaser, Lisa/Tulsa University music faculty/oboist
Glasgow, Robert/b. Shawnee, 1925/classical organist
Glaude, Joesf/b. Virginia, 1966, r. Tulsa/new age guitarist
Glazer, Jon/r. Tulsa/jazz and country keyboardist, performed with The Judds
Glenn, Eddie/r. Tahlequah/"hick hop" singer, songwriter
Glytch/f. Oklahoma City, 1997/rock group
Godding, Antone/OCU music faculty, 2003/theory, composition, piano
Godsey, Glen/r. Tulsa/old time country singer
God's Unwanted Children/f. Tulsa/heavy metal rock group
Goff, Carl, Jr./b. Lexington/country songwriter
Go For Baroque/r. Oklahoma City/Baroque music group
Go With Girls/f. Tahlequah/independent rock
Goldman-Moore, Susan/Tulsa University music faculty/voice and vocal music education

Goldston, Darin/b. Ada, 1967/blues guitarist with Memphis P. Tails
Golliver, April/Oklahoma State University music faculty, 2003/mezzo-soprano, voice
Good, Al/b. Morgantown, WV, r. Oklahoma City 1945-2003, d. 2003/big band leader
Goodfox, Arlen (Pawnee)/r. Shawnee/intertribal powwow head singer
Gordon, Dick, Jr./r. Tulsa/guitar teacher (**Tony Romanello**)
Gorrell, Brian/University of Central Oklahoma music faculty, 2003/saxophonist
Gossell, Karen/2003 TU music student/sings on TU jazz CD, *Sophisticated Ladies*, saxophonist
Gouge, Felix/New Tulsa Ceremonial Grounds/stomp dance leader
Gouge, Thompson/Hullabee Ceremonial Grounds/stomp dance leader
Govich, Marilyn/University of Central Oklahoma music faculty, 2003/voice
Grace, Fanny/r. Oklahoma City/country singer
Graham, Bret/r. Stroud/country singer
Graham, Jeff/b. Joplin, MO, r. Tulsa/singer, songwriter, guitarist
Graham, Phillip/b. Ada/concert pianist
Grant, Earl/b. Oklahoma City, 1933/pianist
Grant, Russell/r. Tulsa/jazz drummer
Grantham, Donald/b. Duncan, 1947/classical composer
Grass, Kenneth/Tulsa University music faculty, 2003/Director of bands, music education
Gravity Propulsion System/f. Norman/rock group
Gray, Sonny/r. Tulsa/jazz pianist, band leader, Rubiot Club owner, TU faculty, 2003
Greenberg, Clay/b. Texas, reared in Oklahoma/folk singer, songwriter
Green, Pamela/University of Central Oklahoma music faculty, 2003/voice
The Green Police/f. Claremore and Verdigris, 2001/punk rock group
Greenawalt, Ross/r. Tulsa circa 2002/anti-folk singer, songwriter
Greenview Circle/f. Sand Springs/pop, rock group
  Deleon, Carlos/bassist
  Deleon, Tony/drummer
  Storm, Dustin/vocalist, guitarist
  Weaver, Cartwright/guitarist
Greg, David/Southeastern Oklahoma State University music faculty, 2003/trombone
Grey/r. Enid/rock and pop singer
Griffin, "Big" Mike/b. Lawton/blues guitarist and singer
Griffith, Lance/r. Oklahoma City/country singer, also with the Long Riders
Grogran, Phil/b. Oklahoma City/classical composer
Groner, Duke/b. Ardmore, 1907/jazz bassist and vocalist
Groove Pilots/f. Tulsa/rock group
Growing Mylow/f. Norman/pop rock group
Gustafson, Karen/Oklahoma City University music staff, 2003/trumpeter
Gut Wrench/f. Broken Arrow/heavy metal rock group
Guyer, Joyce/b. Okmulgee/opera soprano
Guzik, Bernie/Tulsa University, UCO music faculty, 2003/tuba, euphonium
Gyles, Jimmy/r. Tahlequah/flatpick guitarist, mandolinist

H

Habit/f. Ardmore, 2001/rock group
Hadley, John/r. Norman/country songwriter (Dixie Chicks)
Hager, Ty/r. Tulsa/country singer-songwriter

Haggard, Jerry/r. Stillwater/**Red Dirt Sound**, singer-songwriter
Hahn, Chris/Oklahoma City University music faculty, 2003/piano
Half These Girls/f. Norman/rock group
Hall, Charley/r. Oklahoma City/contemporary Christian singer, guitarist
Hall, Gail/Oklahoma University music faculty, 2003/saxophonist
Halsey, Jim/b. Independence, KS, r. Tulsa/artist management
Ham, Jeongwon/Oklahoma University music faculty, 2003/pianist
Ham, Steve/r. Tulsa/trombonist with **Johnnie Lee Wills**, Ray Charles, **Flash Terry**
Hamilton, John (**Kiowa**)/r. Anadarko/intertribal powwow head singer
Hammet, Larry/Oklahoma University music faculty, 2003/guitarist
Hammons, Thomas/b. Shawnee/opera baritone
Hampton, Rhonda/b. Altus/country singer
Haney, Woodrow, Sr./b. Red Mound/American Indian flutist
Hanna, Jack/r. Tulsa/jazz bassist
Hanson, Andrea/r. Tahlequah and Oklahoma City/Miss Oklahoma
Hanson, Dan/USAO music faculty, 2003/instrumental studies director, theory
Hanson, Eric/b. Shawnee/drummer for **Jimmy LaFave** and Mike McClure
Hanson, Jan/USAO music faculty, 2003/choral studies, music history, conducting
Hapless Romantics/f. Tulsa/folk music group leaning toward **Red Dirt Music**
    Cooper, David/drummer, vocalist
    Frisco, Rocky/keyboardist, **Tulsa Sound**
    Gasaway, Wes/fiddler, mandolinist, vocalist
    Skinner, Tom/bassist, vocalist
    Spears, Larry/guitarist, singer, songwriter
    Williams, Gene/electric guitarist
Harbingers/f. Tulsa/gospel group
Hardcastle, Jody/b. Tahlequah, 1950/music educator, piano and keyboard
Hardin, Bud/r. Calumet/country singer
Hardin, Steve/r. Oklahoma/guitarist for 38 Special and Glen Campbell
Hardy, Brad/b. Stillwater/funk, blues, jazz bassist
Hargis, David/University of Central Oklahoma music faculty, 2003/accompanist
Harjo, Joy/b. Tulsa, 1951/**Muscogee** shell shaker, saxophonist, poet
Harjo, Scotty/Tallahassee Wvkokye Ceremonial Grounds/stomp dance leader
Harlow, Dan/r. Oklahoma/bluegrass mandolin player
Harold, Robert/b. Tulsa, 1951/rock guitarist
Harper, Monty/b. Stillwater/children's music songwriter, singer, guitarist
Harper, Thomas/b. Oklahoma/opera tenor with Seattle Opera
Harrington-Hernandez Heather Marie/r. Muskogee/classical organist
Harris, Berry/b. Chockie, 1929/blues guitarist and singer
Harris, Kent/b. Oklahoma City/leads Boogaloo & His Gallant Crew R & B/soul group
Harris, Rodger/b. Duncan, 1945/old-time country and folk music
Harrison, Pete/b. Sallisaw/Western swing guitarist
Harry, Simon/Duck Creek Ceremonial Grounds/stomp dance leader
Harry, Virgle/Duck Creek Ceremonial Grounds/stomp dance leader
Harvest Pickers/f. Spavinaw/bluegrass group
Harvey and the Wallbangers/f. Oklahoma City/classic rock and roll group
Harvey, Lisa/Oklahoma City University music faculty, 2003/oboist, reeds
Hate Furnace/f. Pryor/heavy metal rock group

Hauck, Ross/b. Bartlesville/opera tenor with Wolf Trapp Opera Co.

Hayes, Don/b. Early Mart, CA, 1948/1970s, 80s country singer, father of **Wade Hayes**

Hayes, Chandler/b. Tulsa/singer, songwriter

Headrick, Amos/b. Van Buren, AR, r. Oklahoma/fiddler for **Bob Wills**

Headroom/f. Oklahoma City/rock group

Heap-a-bird, Alfrich/b. Thomas/Cheyenne singer

Heartland Express/f. Oklahoma/bluegrass group

Hefley, Earl/University of Central Oklahoma music faculty, 2003/saxophonist

Hefley, Leon/r. Tulsa/guitarist

Heitzke, Brett/r. Oklahoma City/folksinger, fiddler, storyteller

Helms, Mark/r. Hochatown/songwriter

Hembree, Gene/r. Tulsa/polka multi-instrumentalist

Henderson, Mary Kay/b. Muskogee/gospel singer

Henderson, Bruce/b. Stillwater/country-rock singer, songwriter

Henderson, Marsha/OU music faculty, 1954-2002/voice and musical theater

Henderson, Mike/b. Independence, MO, 1951, r. OK City/country singer, songwriter

Hendricks, Scott/b. Clinton, 1956/country music record producer

Hendricks, Ray/b. Jim Caldwell, r. Stillwater/Louisiana Hayride performer

Hendrickson, Britni/b. Tulsa, 1987/country singer, songwriter

Henley, Jimmy/b. Sayre/banjo player for Roy Clark

Henry, John/r. Tulsa/blues disc jockey (KMOD-FM, Tulsa)
    emcee for 50s rock revival group, Bop Cats

Henry, Shane/r. Oklahoma/blues guitarist, singer

Herbst, Jim/b. Oklahoma City, 1950/country singer

Herendeen, David/Oklahoma City University music faculty, 2003/opera

Herndon, Susan/r. Tulsa/singer, songwriter

Herren, John/b. Elk City/keyboardist for The Electric Prunes

Herrin Burt & The Stringers/f. Edmond/blues group

Hetradox/f. Tulsa/rock group

Hibler, Starla/ECOU music faculty, 2003/music history, piano

Hicks, Benson/Tallahassee Wvkokye Ceremonial Grounds/stomp dance leader

Hicks, Gary/Oklahoma City University music faculty, 2003/voice

Hi-Def Howlers/f. Oklahoma City/pop, rock group

High Eagle, J.C./b. Oklahoma/Cherokee-Osage flutist

Highfill, George/b. Ft. Smith, AR, r. Stigler, OK/country singer, songwriter, harmonica

High Ground/f. Oklahoma City/bluegrass group

Higley, Brewster/r. Shawnee, d. 1911/wrote "Home on the Range"

Hill, Buffalo/Peach Ceremonial Grounds/stomp dance leader

Hill, Jack/Peach Ceremonial Grounds/stomp dance leader

Hill, Sonny/r. Tulsa, 1950s/blues harmonica

Hill, Steve/b. Tulsa/keyboardist and bassist for Bloodrock

Hill-Chief, Roman/Peach Ceremonial Grounds/stomp dance leader

Hills of Home/f. Oklahoma/bluegrass group

HNNC/f. Oklahoma City/rap group

Hoepfner, Gregory/Cameron University music faculty, 2003/music education

Hoffman, Billy/r. Poteau/country singer, songwriter

Hoffman Brothers/f. Muskogee/rock group

Hoke, Jim/b. Oklahoma City/woodwinds for Kenny Loggins

Holder, Kaia/NEOSU adjunct music faculty, 2003/cellist, bassist
Holder, Terrence "T"/b. Texas, r. Muskogee/territory jazz band leader
Holladay, Marvin "Doc"/studied at Phillips University, Enid/baritone saxophonist
Holleman, Brenda/Oklahoma City University music faculty, 2003/voice
Hollingsworth, Mark/ECOU music faculty, 2003/woodwinds, music theory
Hollis/f. Tulsa/independent rock group
Holmberg, Frederich/first director of Oklahoma City Symphony
Holt, Culley/b. McAlester, 1925/singer with the Jordonaires
Holt, John/Southeastern Oklahoma State University adjunct music faculty, 2003/trumpet
The Homesteaders/gospel group/
    Brandt, James/r. Okemah/singer
    Chesser, Lisa/r. Konawa/singer
    Richardson, Wayne/r. Henryetta/singer
    Williamson, Donnie/r. Weleetka/singer
Honea, Sion/University of Central Oklahoma music faculty, 2003/horn, music history
Honeywagon/f. Edmond/rock group
Hooten, David/r. Oklahoma City/trumpeter
Hopkins, Bubba/b. Spavinaw/traditional fiddler
Hopkins, David "Hoppy"/r. Tulsa/guitarist with the Swamptones
   also played w/ Larry Bell, Jim Dowing, and Bill Davis
Hosty Duo/f. Norman/rock, soul, rockabilly, "Hic Hop"
    Hosty, Mike/r. Norman/guitarist
    Tac, Tic/drummer
HotrodboB/f. Claremore, 2002/rockabilly, punk, pop-rock group
    Layton, Bo/drummer
    Layton, Clay/guitarist, vocalist
    Pitts, Jay/bassist, vocalist
Howard, Eddie/Oklahoma Opry house band drummer
Howard, Vernon/Tulsa University music faculty, 2003/trombonist and jazz studies
Howell, Ron/UCO music faculty, 2003/clarinetist, music history
Howlin' 88/f. Norman
Huckaby, Ed/NEOSU-Broken Arrow music professor/contemporary classical composer
Hudson, Richard/b. Seminole, reared Konawa/gospel finger style guitarist
Hudspeth, Charles/OCU graduate/City College of San Francisco music faculty, 2003
Huffer, Jerry/r. Muskogee/music educator
Hughes, Frank Clayton/b. Ada, 1915/classical composer
Hunt, Billy/*/Oklahoma Jazz Hall of Fame inductee
Hunt, William/b. SE Oklahoma/folk music preserver and performer
Hurricane, Jane/f. Oklahoma City/pop rock group
Hurricane Mason/f. Tulsa/blues-rock group
    Flint, Kevin/bassist
    Mason, Matt/guitarist, vocalist
    Montgomery, Shawn/drummer
Hurte, Leroy/b. Muskogee/1940s R & B record company entrepreneur
   notably with Bronze Records in Los Angeles
Hutchison, "Uncle" Dick/b. Disney/old time country fiddler

I

The Ills/f. Norman/progressive jazz group
  Ahmadi, Kasra George/saxophonist
  Jones, Ryan/keyboardist
  Littell, Boyd/drummer
  Nelson, Blaine/guitarist
Infamus/f. Tulsa/rock group
Ingersoll, Clint/r. Pryor/Locust Grove/singer, songwriter
  (songs recorded by Chris Ledoux & John Michael Montgomery)
Ink, Lawrence/Oklahoma State University music faculty, 2003/flutist
Insect Lounge/f. Norman/rock group
Insult to Injury/f. Oklahoma/hardcore punk rock group
Iowa Tribe of Oklahoma/based south of Perkins, moved to I.T., 1880
  Native American Church songs, intertribal powwow
Ira/f. Tulsa/pop rock group
Isco-say/r. Muskogee, Tulsa/rapper
Ivy Mike/f. Norman/rock group
Ivy, Thomas/r. Altus/bluegrass banjoist

J

Jack, Karen & Lucy/f. Skiatook/Americana, roots music group
Jackson, Albert/Langston University music faculty, 2003/instrumental music director
Jacobs, Greg/b. Choctaw/singer, songwriter, **Red Dirt Music**
Jacobson, Garrett "Big G"/b. Oklahoma City, 1983/blues guitarist and singer
Jae, Jana/currently resides in Grove/country fiddler
Jahruba/r. Norman/African percussionist
Jambalaya Jass Band/f. Sapulpa/traditional Dixieland jazz group
  Bennett, Mike/trumpeter
  Chitton, Mike/banjoist
  Crosby, Bill/bassist
  Ham, Steve/trombonist
  Yohe, Tony/drummer
James, Brett/r. Oklahoma City/country songwriter
James, George/b. Beggs, 1906/jazz woodwinds, bandleader
James, Jana/r. Enid/contemporary Christian and Celtic singer
James, Jenny/r. Oklahoma/intertribal powwow singer
James, Patricia/r. Oklahoma/intertribal powwow singer
The James Ray/f. Stillwater, 1995/rock group
  Anderson, Steve/bassist
  Bello, John/guitarist
  Lichtenberger, James/guitarist
  Unruh, Tod/drummer
  Young, Bill/vocalist
James, Tom/b. Oklahoma/country singer, songwriter for Flatt and Scruggs, Rex Allen
  started Klix Records in 1957
Jazzcow/f. Tulsa, 2001/jazz jam band
  Andrews, Airrion/bassist

Combs, Chris/guitarist
Loomis, Mike/drummer
Staub, Michael/saxophonist
Jeffrey, Robert/b. Tulsa, 1915/blues pianist, guitarist, vocalist
Jenkins, Brandon/b. Tulsa, 1969/singer, songwriter, **Red Dirt Music**, OSU graduate
Jenkins, Deborah/Oklahoma City University music faculty, 2003/accompanist
Jennings, Christina/r. Oklahoma/classical flutist/Julliard graduate
Jergensons Shrader, Aija/NWOSU music faculty, 2003/opera singer, vocal pedagogy
Jernigan, Dennis/b. Sapulpa, 1959/contemporary Christian singer
Jesse D/f. Tulsa/classic rock, hard rock, pop rock group
  De La O, Jesse/vocalist, guitarist, bassist, keyboardist
Jewett, Bryan/r. Tulsa/techno folk musician
Jify Trip/f. Tulsa, 1995/rock group
Jimijank/f. Norman/rock group
Jobe, Richard/University of Central Oklahoma music faculty, 2003/accompanist
Joe and Ellen Felzke/f. Tulsa/brother and sister jazz, folk duo
Johnny Reliable/f. Tulsa/1950s-style, contemporary rock group
Johns, Val/b. Shattuck/pianist
Johnson, Brenda/University of Central Oklahoma music faculty, 2003/voice
Johnson, Cecil/b. Shawnee/old time fiddler
Johnson, Christopher/b. Tulsa/classical pipe organist
  at New York City's Riverside Church as of 2003
Johnson, Deborah/USAO music part-time faculty, 2003/choral accompanist
Johnson, Herman/b. Shawnee/old time fiddler
Johnson, Jeff/r. Oklahoma City/jazz bassist
Johnson, Larry/b. Oklahoma City/R & B vocalist, guitarist
Johnson, Lemuel/b. Oklahoma City, 1909/jazz woodwinds, bandleader, vocals
  played with **Oklahoma City Blue Devils**
Johnson, Lewis/enrolled member of the Seminole Nation of OK/American Indian flutist
Johnson, Michael/r. Jones/acoustic guitar champion
Johnson, Scott/University of Central Oklahoma music faculty, 2003/guitarist
Johnson, Seminem/Nuyaka Ceremonial Grounds/stomp dance leader
Jones, Anthony Armstrong/b. Ada, 1949, d. 1996/Top 40 cover singer "Proud Mary,"
  and "Take a Letter From Maria"
Jones, Charles and the Stardusters/f. Oklahoma/1950s rock and roll, Sully Records
Jones, Claude/b. Boley, 1901/jazz trombonist
Jones, Denise/b. Norman/gospel singer with Point of Grace
Jones, Dustin/Oklahoma Opry house band guitarist, sound engineer
Jones, Shawn/b. Lawton, OCU graduate/singer, songwriter
Jones, Stacey/b. Tulsa, but moved away at an early age
  singer for rock group American Hi-Fi
Joose/f. Oklahoma/urban-dance group
  Farmer, Jay
  Lewis, Trell
  McKaufman, Rocky
  Pettis, Leonardo
Joplin, Scott/performed his opera *A Guest of Honor* in Oklahoma City in 1903
  ragtime pianist, composer

Josephson, Kim/b. Ohio, r. Tulsa/opera singer
Just for U/f. Tulsa/contemporary Christian group

K

Karma Syndicate/f. Tulsa/jazz with spoken word
Karstein, Jimmy/b. Tulsa, 1943/drummer for Joe Cocker, Eric Clapton, and **J.J. Cale,
    Tulsa Sound**
Katz, Robert, S./r. Tulsa/educator, classical double bassist
Kaw (Kanza) Nation of Oklahoma/based in Kaw City since 1902/
    powwow, straight dance songs
Kay, Billy/r. Oklahoma/flatpick guitar player
Kayka Momma/r. Tulsa/rapper
Kearney, Jason/r. Tulsa/folk music singer, guitarist
Keeble, Jonathan/Oklahoma State University music faculty, 2003/flutist
Keeton, Scott/r. Del City/blues guitarist, singer
Keith, Jeff/b. Texarkana, r. Idabel/singer for pop metal group Tesla
Keller, Larry/Oklahoma City University music faculty, 2003/voice
Kelley, Pat/r. Tulsa/jazz guitarist, Tulsa Will Rogers High, Tulsa University graduate
Kelly, Clark/Oklahoma University music faculty, 2003/organist
Kelly, David/NEOSU adjunct music faculty, 2003/jazz guitarist
Kelly, Jamie/b. Ada/bassist, guitarist, vocalist for Linville Band
Kelly, Lori Lee/b. Clinton/singer, Miss Oklahoma
Kelly, Sean/b. Cushing/singer, songwriter
Kelly, Vicky/Oklahoma City University music faculty, 2003/voice, music education
Kelly, Walter/b. Stillwater/Berklee School of Music graduate, guitarist
Keltner, Jim/b. Tulsa, 1942/jazz, rock, blues, pop drummer –
    THE session drummer of rock music from 1970s to now
Kemble, John (**Ponca**) (often spelled Kimble)/r. Oklahoma City
    intertribal powwow head singer
Kemble, Kirby/r. Oklahoma/intertribal powwow head singer
Kemp, Julia/r. Oklahoma/opera soprano
Kenner, Clarence/b. Oklahoma/jazz trumpeter
Kentucky Blue/f. Tulsa/bluegrass group
Kern, Michael/r. Lawton/guitarist
Kersting, Kathleen/b. Enid/opera singer
Ketchum, Benny/r. Tulsa/country bandleader, singer
Kettle of Fish/f. Tulsa, 1999/pop rock group
The Kevorkians/f. Tulsa/rock group
KGB/f. Oklahoma City/rock group
Khannanov, Ildar/Oklahoma City University music faculty, 2003/theory, composition
Kickapoo Tribe of Oklahoma/based in McLoud area since 1839
    traditional music, social powwows
Kidd, Travis/r. Tulsa/folk singer
Kidwell, Kent/University of Central Oklahoma music faculty, 2003/jazz trombonist
Kihega, Michael/r. Oklahoma/intertribal powwow head singer
Kilgore, Ben/r. Tulsa/acoustic guitarist, singer, songwriter
Kilgore, Kenneth/r. Oklahoma City/organist, Oklahoma Jazz Hall of Fame inductee

Kilpatrick, Jack F./b. Stilwell/classical composer
Kimera/f. Tulsa/rock group
King, Bug/r. Oklahoma City, OC Douglas graduate/R & B vocalist
King James Verzion/f. Stillwater/rock group
King, Kathy Weinstock/r. Tulsa/educator, classical cellist
Kinky Slinky/f. Oklahoma City/dread rock
Kirkpatrick, Albert J./b. Oklahoma City/classical composer
Kiser, Bob/r. Tulsa/guitarist for John T. **Wills**
Kishketon, Rowe (Kickapoo/Sac & Fox)/r. Shawnee/intertribal powwow head singer
Kizer, Glen/r. Okemah/Broadway musicals
Klages, James/UCO music faculty, 2003/trumpeter, music theory
Kleefeld, Daniel/r. Tulsa/contemporary Christian, jazz, classical multi-instrumentalist
Klipspringer/f. Norman/rock group
Knape, Skip/r. Turley/organist for Bob Seger
Knedler, Mike/NWOSU director of bands, 2003/clarinetist, music education
Knie, Roberta/b. Cordell/opera singer
Knight, Edward/Oklahoma City University music faculty, 2003/theory, composition
Knight, Justin/b. Tulsa/contemporary Christian, new age pianist, composer
Knifechief, John (Pawnee)/r. Pawnee/intertribal powwow head singer
Knifechief, Steve (Pawnee)/r. Pawnee/intertribal powwow head singer
Knifechief, Tom (Pawnee)/r. Pawnee/intertribal powwow head singer
Koenig, Willie/r. Oklahoma City/Latin percussionist
Koomsa, Bill, Jr. (**Kiowa**)/intertribal powwow head singer, gourd dance singer
Kotay, Ralph/r. Oklahoma/intertribal powwow head singer
Kotowich, Bruce/NEOSU music faculty, 2003/conducting, voice
Kottke, Leo/b. Athens, GA, r. Muskogee/solo guitarist
Kubiak, Benny/r. Oklahoma/old time fiddler
Kuehn, Bill/r. Oklahoma/percussionist
Kuleshov, Valery/UCO music faculty, 2003/pianist, artist-in-residence
Kyle, Gari/University of Central Oklahoma music faculty, 2003/pianist

L

Labé, Thomas/Cameron University music faculty, 2003/classical pianist
Labow, Jenny/b. Canada, Stillwater High School graduate, 1991
    pop, rock singer, songwriter, and guitarist
Lacy, Robin H./b. McAlester/country singer, songwriter
    drummer for Johnny Paycheck and Merle Haggard
Lacy, Rudy/b. McAlester, r. Stillwater/country singer, songwriter
Lafort 3/f. Bartlesville/heavy metal group
Lakes, Gary/b. Woodward, 1914/opera tenor
Lamb, Brian/UCO music faculty, 2003/director of bands, wind ensemble, conducting
Lamb, Marvin/Oklahoma University music faculty, 2003/music theory, composition
Lambert, James/Cameron University music faculty, 2003/percussionist
Lancaster, Sound/f. Oklahoma City/modern rock group
    Alsip, Marshall/drummer
    Gulley, Chad/guitarist, keyboardist, vocalist
    Mills, Jennifer/cellist, keyboardist, vocalist

Rosenhamer, Steve/bassist

Stanley, Adam/guitarist, keyboardist, vocalist

Lane, Chris/r. Oklahoma/country music broadcaster

Lang, Kelly/b. Oklahoma City, 1967/country singer

Lang, Terry/r. Oklahoma/gospel singer with Point of Grace

Lanners, Heather/Oklahoma State University music faculty, 2003/pianist

Lanners, Thomas/Oklahoma State University music faculty, 2003/pianist

Laramore, Doug/ECOU music faculty, 2003/assistant director of bands

Larkin/f. Tulsa/Irish music group

Lawrence, David/whistle

Malone, Chad/lead singer

Modglin, Aaron/guitarist

Naifeh, Karen/violinist

Tuttle, Kelly/bassist

Walker, Johnnie/drummer

LaRue, Stoney and the Organic Boogie Band/f. Stillwater/**Red Dirt Music** group

Lasso/f. Norman/rock group

Last Exit/f. T ulsa/rock group

Laughlin, Robert/Oklahoma City University music faculty, 2003/pianist

Laurence, Dave/r. Oklahoma City/folk singer and songwriter

Lawrence, Scott/r. Tahlequah/acousitic blues guitarist

Lay, Rodney/b. Coffeyville, KS, r. Nowata/country singer

Leadingfox, Randal/r. Oklahoma/intertribal powwow head singer

LeBlanc, Gaye/OCU and OU music faculty, 2003/harpist

Lee, Brian/r. Tulsa/pianist

Lee, Mel/University of Central Oklahoma music faculty, 2003/music education

Lee, Michael/Oklahoma University music faculty, 2003/musicologist

Leeper, Jane and Jean/known as "Oklahoma Sweethearts"/recorded for Capitol records

Leffingwell, Dolores/Oklahoma University music faculty, 2003/voice

Leftwich, Brad/b. Stillwater/old time and bluegrass fiddler, Oklahoma Opry manager

Lehman, Lavern/b. Tahlequah, 1944/bass guitarist with Pat Benatar, Joe Cocker,
  Eric Burdon, and Mitch Mitchell

Lehman, Tom/r. Tahlequah/ jazz educator (NEOSU), trombonist

Leonard, Eric/University of Central Oklahoma music faculty, 2003/trombonist

Leseney, Amber/Oklahoma City University music faculty, 2003/voice

The Leveling/f. Tulsa/modern rock group

Leverette, Ken/r. Tulsa/jazz drummer

Levine, Joel/r. Oklahoma City for 27 years/director, OKC Philharmonic

Levy, Marcy/r. Oklahoma/vocalist for Bob Seger and Eric Clapton

Lewis, Curly/b. Stigler/fiddler for **Johnnie Lee Wills** and **Hank Thompson**

Lewis, Landon/USAO part-time music faculty, 2003/brass

Lewis, Sheila/b. Broken Bow/gospel singer

Lewis, William/b. Tulsa, 1935/opera tenor

The Lids/f. Norman/rock group

Liddell/f. Tulsa/soft rock group

Lieb, Kensil or Kinsel/r. Ponca City/intertribal powwow head singer

Lightfoot, Jason/r. Oklahoma/intertribal powwow headsinger

Lincoln, Robert/b. Lawton/intertribal group Thunderhorse

Lindsay, Merl/b. Oklahoma City/country and rockabilly singer, bandleader
Linville, Travis/b. Chickasha/lead singer for Travis Linville and the Burtschi Brothers
Lipinski, Rudy//East Central Oklahoma University adjunct music faculty, 2003/pianist
Litefoot/r. Tulsa, attended Tulsa University/actor, rapper on Red Vinyl Records
Lithium/f. Owasso/rock group
Littleaxe, Dennis (Shawnee/Prarie Band Potawatomi)/r. Oklahoma
    intertribal powwow singer
Littleaxe, Troy, Sr. (Shawnee)/r. Bartlesville/intertribal powwow head singer
    stomp dance leader
Littlebear, Newman/Kelleyville Ceremonial Grounds/stomp dance leader
Littlecreek, Wiley (Shawnee)/r. Oklahoma/intertribal powwow head singer
Little League Hero/f. Oklahoma, 1999/pop rock group
Little Man, Creg/r. Thomas/intertribal powwow head singer
Little Thunder/r. Tahlequah/intertribal powwow singing group
Lobb, Betty Lou/ b. Bennington/*Big D Jamboree* vocalist
Local Hero/f. Tulsa/reggae group
    Bee/drummer
    Cheryl/saxophonist
    Campbell, Kelly/guitarist
    James, Doc/bassist
    Perry, Deborah/keyboardist
    Santanna/percussionist
    U.E./saxophonist
Logan, Charles/r. Oklahoma/intertribal powwow head singer
Logan, Earl/Cameron University music faculty, 2003/voice, concert choir
Logan, Gene/r. Oklahoma/intertribal powwow head singer
Logan, Jan/Cameron University music faculty, 2003/voice, opera
Logan, Stacey/Oklahoma City University graduate/Broadway performer and singer
Logsdon, Guy/b. Ada/Woody Guthrie scholar, Western swing expert, music historian,
    cowboy singer
Loman, Michael (Choctaw)/r. Tulsa/American Indian flutist
Lon, Dave/r. Oklahoma/singer, songwriter, **Red Dirt Music**
Long, Fiddlin' Sam/r. Oklahoma/old time fiddler
Longhorn, Colleen (Shawnee/Sac & Fox/Seneca-Cayuga)/r. Oklahoma/shell shaker
Loose Shoes/r. Oklahoma City/roots music group
Love, Clarence/b. Muskogee, 1908/   territory jazz band leader
Love, Rusti/r. Glenpool/jazz and country rock singer
Low Water Crossing/f. Bowlegs/bluegrass band
Loyal Opposition/f. Stillwater, 1985/pop rock group
Lubin, Howard/Oklahoma University music faculty, 2003/pianist
Ludo/f. Tulsa/modern rock group
Luker, Jack/resides in Oklahoma City/old time fiddler and fiddle judge
Lunsford, Mike/b. Guymon, 1950/country singer and songwriter
Lure/f. Oklahoma City, 1999/rock group
Lushanya, Tessie Mobley/b. near Ardmore/Chickasaw opera singer
Lyons, Robert/r. Lawton/steel beach picnic entertainer (guitars and vocals)
    aboard USS Kitty Hawk, 2003

M

Mabrey, "Shy" Willie/b. Webbers Falls, 1942/blues singer

Madden, Doyle/recorded for Hobart-based Hu-Se-Co label in the 1950s/country singer

Mad Verb/f. Tulsa, 1999, disbanded/melodic hard rock

Maggi, Tanya/r. Tulsa/educator, classical viola player

Magrath, Jane/Oklahoma University music faculty, 2003/pianist

Magrill, Samuel/UCO music faculty, 2003/music theory, composer-in-residence

Magruder Everett, Kyle/b. St. Joseph, MO, r. Oklahoma City/country singer, songwriter,
   recorded with **Jason Boland**

Maguire, Beth/b. Texas, reared in Tulsa/country singer

Mailman, Matthew/Oklahoma City University music faculty, 2003/bands

Maindrayn/f. Tulsa/rock group

Majnun/f. Tulsa/rock group

Malave, Alvaro "Ted"/b. Stillwater, 1960/classical and Spanish guitar

Manifest Destiny/f. Stillwater, 1989/heavy metal rock group
   Allensworth, Trey/b. Stillwater/drummer, vocalist
   Big John/b. Enid/bassist and vocalist
   Filonow, John/b. Lansing, MI, r. Stillwater/lead guitarist
   Hock, Matt/b. Temple, TX, r. Stillwater/lead vocalist
   Moffat, Jake/b. Stillwater/rhythm guitarist and vocalist

Manning, Ron/UCO music faculty, 2003/opera singer, school of music assistant director

Mannafest/f. Tulsa/Christian rock group

Marcotte, Joseph B./b. near Purcell, 1913/cowboy singer and instrumentalist
   performed on KFXR, Oklahoma City, in 1933

Mariachi Orgullo/f. Norman/mariachi music

Mariachi Tulsa/f. Tulsa/mariachi music

Markham, Jimmy "Jr."/b. Tulsa, 1941/singer, songwriter, harmonica player with .38
   Special, A.C. Reed, The Tractorsm, **Tulsa Sound**

Markley, Bob/b. Oklahoma/vocalist and songwriter
   for The West Coast Pop Art Experimental Band

Marks, Marty/UCO music faculty, 2003/marching band, pep band

Marquis, Aldee/b. Tulsa/classical violinist

Marsh, Sharon/b. Broken Bow/gospel singer

Marshallcity/f. Tulsa, 2000 – disbanded 2003/rock group
   Cayton, Jeff/b. California/drummer
   Cook, Colby/b. Joplin, MO, 1973, r. Broken Arrow, 1975/bassist
   Parsons, Jody/b. Mustang, 1976/vocalist, guitarist, mandolinist
   Zoellner, Philip/b. Tulsa/vocalist, guitarist (moved to New York City in 2003)

Martin, Dusty/b. Sallisaw, 1938/country singer for Texas Rose Records

Martini Kings/f. Norman/rock and swing combo

Martin, Rudi/r. Enid/Western swing clarinetist

Martinez, Thomas and Wild Frontier/f. Tulsa/country group

Marvin and Johnny/R & B duo
   Phillips, Marvin/b. Guthrie, 1931/also worked with Jesse Belvin as Jesse & Marvin

Marvin, Rex/b. California, 1947, reared in Oklahoma UCO vocal student/country singer

Mashunkashey, Russell/r. Oklahoma/intertribal powwow head singer

Mason/f. Tulsa, 1970s/hard rock group

Mason, Ashley/2003 TU music student/sings on TU jazz CD, *Sophisticated Ladies*
Masoplast Polka Band/f. Guymon/just like the name says, a polka group
Massey, George/Oklahoma City University music faculty, 2003/voice
Mass Reality/f. Tulsa, 1992/contemporary Christian group
Masters, Denise/b. Norman/gospel singer with Point of Grace
Masters, Sammy/b. Sasakawa, 1930/rockabilly guitarist and singer
Mathews, Lea/b. McAlester, 1925/jazz singer
Matthews, Gilbert/r. Oklahoma/Pawnee Nation drum keeper
Mattingly, Paul/b. Sand Springs, 1921/steel guitarist
Matlick, Eldon/Oklahoma University music faculty, 2003/horn
Matlock, Jarrid/r. Oklahoma City, b. 1974/country singer
Matlock, W.N./r. Cleveland/gospel singer
Mauser, Corey/b. Phoenix, AZ, 1968, moved to Tulsa, 1971/pianist and organist
Mayday Malone/f. Oklahoma City/punk rock group
Mayo, O.W./b. Texas, r. Oklahoma/**Bob Wills**' manager
McAlister, Barbara/b. Muskogee/opera singer
McAuliffe, Leon/b. Houston, TX, r. Tulsa/steel guitarist for **Bob Wills**
McCann, Terry/r. Oklahoma City/blues flutist
McClarty, Matthew/r. Ada/gospel group leader
McClellan, Billy E., Sr./b. Arkansas City, KS, 1954, r. Agra/
    Native American Church singer (has recorded two albums)
McClure, Mike/r. Stillwater/singer, songwriter, guitarist, producer, bandleader, **Red Dirt Music,**
    formerly with **The Great Divide,** now leads the Mike McClure Band with these musicians:
    Clanton, Les Paul/Texan/bassist
    Hanson, Eric/drummer
    Pyeatt, Rodney/Texan/guitarist
McClurg, Mark/b. Claremore/fiddler for Alan Jackson, Stonehorse
    formed country duo McHayes with **Wade Hayes** in 2003
McFarland, T.J./r. Oklahoma/country rock singer, songwriter
McNulty, Larry/r. Tulsa/bassist
McCollum, Jeffrey/r. Oklahoma/baritone with Indianapolis Opera
McCombs, Cody/r. Tulsa/blues singer, guitarist
McConnell, William/Tulsa University music faculty, 2003/TU Chorale
McReynolds, Samuel/b. Oklahoma City/composer, cellist w/ Oklahoma City Symphony
McDaniel, Jan/Oklahoma City University music faculty, 2003/voice
McDonald, "Rusty"/b. Myrl Edwards in Norge/Western swing, rockabilly, singer
McDonald, Tomy/r. Tulsa/rock guitarist
McEntire, Pake/b. Chockie, 1953/country and gospel singer,
    Reba McEntire/Susie Luchsinger's brother
McFadden, Robert/SEOUS music faculty, 2003piano, music history
McFarland, T.J./r. Tulsa/cosmic country singer, songwriter
McGhee, Michelle/University of Central Oklahoma music faculty, 2003/music theory
McGhee, Paul/b. Tulsa/drummer with Texas Playboys
McGinty, Billy/b. MO, parents made land run of 1889/cowboy band leader, **Otto Gray**
McGraw, Clarence/r. Oklahoma/old time fiddler
Mcgrew, Shane/b. Enid/singer, songwriter, fiddler, rhythm guitarist
    (solo, and w/ Fishin' Naked, Hippie the Cowboy)
McIntosh, John/r. Oklahoma/intertribal powwow head singer

McKee, William/Tulsa University music faculty, 2003/French horn

McKerley, David/OCU music faculty, 2003/sound engineering for music and voice

McKinney, Elizabeth/r. Oklahoma/soprano with Santa Fe Chorale

McLinn, Steve/r. Oklahoma City/electro-acoustic world fusion multi-instrumentalist

McQuarters, R.W./b. Tulsa/rapper and founder of Franchise Records, pro football player

McReynolds, Samuel/b. Oklahoma City/classical composer and cellist

Meade, Tyson Todd/b. Bartlesville/singer, /songwriter Chainsaw Kittens

Meazell, Tiger/r. Oklahoma City/jazz alto saxophonist, Selmer artist/clinician

Mecom, Billy/r. Tulsa/1950s country singer, Billy Mecom and the Country Cousins

Mediocre Music Makers/f. Erick, 1999/country, bluegrass duo
  Russell, Annabelle/guitar, vocals
  Russell, Harley/guitar, vocals

MEDU-NETR/comprised of 3 Tulsa rap groups:
  Somatic Souls, HORSEMAN, Black Cosmic Posse

Meehan, Dennis, a.k.a. Clovis Roblaine/b. Oklahoma/bassist with Ray Wylie Hubbard,

Melatonin/f. Tulsa/loud rock group

Mendia, Francis/r. Oaks/intertribal powwow head singer

Men of Made/f. Bixby/R & B and hip hop artists

Mercury 1/f. Weatherford/ rock group

Mericle, Don/r. Wagoner/music educator

Meridian/f. Tulsa/pop rock group
  Brown, Gary/drummer
  Gaylor, Dennis/acoustic guitarist, vocalist, keyboardist
  Hoy, Bill/vocalist, percussionist
  Jarret, Tim/electric guitar
  Mayeux, Ed/bassist

Merrick, Joe/b. Oklahoma City/country songwriter

Merritt, Chris/b. Oklahoma City, 1952/opera tenor

Meyer, Carolyn/b. Nowata, 1952, r. Stillwater/children's music composer,singer,

Meyer, Edgar/b. Tulsa, 1960, moved away at an early age/classical and country bassist

Mezclave Latin Jazz Ensemble/f. Tulsa/the name says it all

Miami Nation/based in Miami, moved to I.T. in 1873/stomp dances and powwow

Michaels, Gus/r. Stillwater/singer, songwriter

Microlight/f. Oklahoma City, 1996/rock group

Midwest Kings/f. Tulsa/rock group, released first CD in 2003
  Briggs, Justin/bassist
  Skibb, Andy/vocalist
  Tiemann, Neal/guitarist, lyricist

Miles, Michael/SEOSU music faculty, 2003/trumpeter, dept. chair

Miles, Stacey/Southeastern Oklahoma State University adjunct music faculty, 2003/horn

Milke/f. Tulsa/singer, songwriter

Miller, Jody/b. AZ, 1941, r. Blanchard/country singer known for "Queen of the House"

Miller, Lula Mae/b. Rentiesville/gospel singer

Milner, Chuck/b. Cheyenne/country songwriter

The Mimsies/f. Norman/glam rock band

Minutes Too Far/f. Oklahoma City/rock group

Missal, Joseph/OSUmusic faculty, 2003/director of bands, trumpeter

Missing Link Band/f. Claremore/blues band

Mr. Nitro/r. Oklahoma City/rapper
Mistress X/f. Tulsa/rock band
Mitchell, Glen/recorded in Tulsa/organist with **Steve Ripley** and The Tractors
Mizelle, Dary John/b. Stillwater, 1940/classical composer
Mockingbird Lane/f. Shawnee/rock group
  Blizzard/drummer, background vocalist
  Christophe/lead vocalist, guitarist
  Elecktra/bassist, background vocalist
Model 2551/f. Oklahoma City/rock group
Modoc Tribe/based in Miami, moved to I.T. in 1873/stomp dance, powwow
Moffat, Jake/r. Stillwater/singer, songwriter
Moguin, Sharon/r. Tulsa/jazz, blues, standards vocalist
Molly's Yes/f. Tulsa, 1998/rock group on Republic/Universal Records
  Goggin, Ed/r. Tulsa/vocalist, keyboardist
  Mitcho, Brad/bassist, vocalist, programming
  Ross, Mac/guitarist, vocalist
  Taylor, Scott/drummer
Monossey, Elrod/r. Oklahoma/intertribal powwow head singer
Monossey, Spencer Ray/r. Oklahoma/intertribal powwow head singer
Montgomery, Melissa/r. Choctaw/country singer
Montgomery, Merle/b. Davidson, 1904/classical composer
Moon, Gene/University of Central Oklahoma music faculty, 2003/pianist
Moore, David, A./r. Tulsa/educator, music composition
Moore, Gary Lee/b. Oklahoma, 1950, r. Seattle/Pacific Northwest old time fiddler
Moore, Melvin/b. Oklahoma City, 1917/jazz singer
Moore, Pat/b. Tulsa, 1948/gospel singer and pianist
Moots, John/Cameron University music faculty, 2003/trumpeter
Moran, David/r. Oklahoma/hammer dulcimer
Moran, Pat/b. Enid, 1934/jazz pianist, bandleader
Moreland, George "Scully"/r. Oklahoma City, OC Douglas graduate
  drummer for Gladys Knight
Moreland, James "Ace"/b. Miami, d. Feb. 8, 2003/**Cherokee** blues guitarist
Morton, Ann/b. Muldrow, 1942/rock singer
Morris, Bobby/b. Tulsa/rhythm guitar for The Champs
Morris, Ralph/UCO music faculty, 2003/music school director, violinist, conductor
Morris, Steve/New Tulsa Ceremonial Grounds/stomp dance leader
Morris, Theodora/University of Central Oklahoma music faculty, 2003/violinist
Morrow, Rick/r. Tulsa/keyboardist
Moseley, Andy/b. Durant, 1933/co-founder of Mosrite guitars used by **Nokie Edwards**
  and The Ventures
Moseley, Semie/b. Durant, 1935/co-founder of Mosrite guitars used by **Nokie Edwards**
  and The Ventures
Mosely, Keith/b. Edmond/bassist for String Cheese Incident
Moses, Ted/r. Tulsa/jazz pianist
Mourning September/f. Tulsa/contemporary Christian group
Mourning Star/f. Shawnee/intertribal powwow singing group
Mourning Three/f. Tulsa/rock group
Moye, Felicia/r. Norman/classical violinist, concertmaster for Oklahoma City

Philharmonic, 2003
Moyer, Laina/ECOU adjunct music faculty, 2003/percussionist
Muddy Chucks/f. Verdigris/Christian punk rock group
Munde, Alan/b. Norman, 1946/country music historian, banjoist
  played with **Byron Berline**
Munds, Ken/r. Okmulgee/gospel singer with Brush Arbor
Mundy, Emily Miller (Smith)/r. Tulsa/vocalist (**Tulsa Sound**)
Mundy, Jim/b. Muldrow, 1934/country singer
Mundy, Marilyn/b. Bokoshe/country singer
Murrow, Rodney/NWOSU music faculty, 2003/pianist, music theory
Myers, Helen/b. Oklahoma City/ethnomusicologist

N

Naifeh, Jerry/b. Tulsa/drummer for **Twilley** and Seymour
Nail, Austin/r. Oklahoma City/blues guitarist, leads Austin Nail Band
Nance, Kregg/r. Ardmore/country singer
Narikawa, Masako/SEOSU adjunct music faculty, 2003/vocal, piano coach
Natural Grass/f. Oklahoma/bluegrass group
  Baker, Pat/bassist, lead vocalist
  Campbell, Pat/guitarist, vocalist
  Campbell, Royce/lead guitarist, vocalist
  Farrar, Ronnie/banjoist, vocalist
  Nuneley, Dick/mandolinist, vocalist
Navel Orange/f. Norman/rock group
Navrath, Joe/b. Ada, r. Stroud/country rock singer, songwriter
Naylor Family/f. Guthrie, 1998/bluegrass group
Negative Nancy/f. Tulsa/rock group
  Brown, J. "Brushdog/b. Tulsa, 1972/drummer,
  Cates, Travis/b. Muskogee, 1975, graduated Oktaha High School/bassist
  Endacott, Steve/b. 1969, attended OSU/singer
  Morris, Steve "Doc"/b. Anaheim, CA, 1968, graduated Pryor High /lead guitarist
Nelson, Jerry/r. Claremore/blues guitarist, vocalist
Nelson, Joy/Oklahoma University music faculty, 2003/music education
Nelson, Willie/r. Perkins/intertribal powwow head singer
Nevaquaya, Sonny (b. Apache, OK) American Indian flutist
  son of **"Doc" Tate Nevequaya**
Neviah Nevi/f. Norman/rock group
New Plainsmen Quartet/f. Chickasha/gospel group
New Science/f. Tulsa, 2002/rock group
  Gilardi, Jason/drummer
  Hosterman, Ben/guitarist
  Jameson, Mike/guitarist, vocalist
  Jones, Scott/bassist
Nichols, Grady/b. Siloam Springs, AR, r. Tulsa/smooth jazz saxophonist
The Nixons/f. Oklahoma City, 1992/rock group
  Brooks, Ricky/guitarist
  Davis, Jesse/bassist

Maloy, Zac/r. Norman/vocalist/solo as of 2002
Robison, Tye/drummer/keyboardist/vocalist
Noe, Candy/r. Tulsa/multi-genre vocalist for **Johnnie Lee Wills**, et al.
co-manager of (Roy and Candy's Music, Tulsa
Noeebo/f. Broken Arrow/electronic dance duo
Hopiard, Chris/keyboardist, synthesizers
Smith, Dough/keyboardist, synthesizers
No Justice/f. Stillwater/blues rock group
Grauberger, Tim/drummer
Payne, Jerry/bassist
Payne, Tony/guitarist
Rice, Steve/vocalist
Norberg, Anna/Tulsa University music faculty, 2003/pianist
Norfleet, Lee/r. Muskogee/trombonist
Norful, Smoke/b. Muskogee/gospel singer on EMI Records
Norton, Spencer Hilton/b. Anadarko, 1909/classical composer
No Small Change/f. Choctaw/Alva/Christian rock group
Nude Furniture/f. Tulsa, OK/pop group
Nuebauer, Sheri/Tulsa University music faculty, 2003/violinist
Null, Annette/b. Quinton, 1929/country singer
Nu World Soul/f. Tulsa/jazz and R & B group
Nymphomercial/f. Bartlesville/modern rock group

O

O'Bannon, Evan/r. Oklahoma/mountain dulcimer
O'Boyle, Maureen/Tulsa University music professor, 2003/violinist
Obrien, Amy/b. Oklahoma City/opera singer
O'Brien, Dwayne/b. Ada, 1963/guitarist and vocalist for Little Texas
Ogden, Dave/b. Stillwater/bassist for Fried Okra Jones
O'Hara, Kelli/r. Oklahoma, OCU Grad/Broadway singer/performer
O'Kelly's Celtic Band/r. Jones/Celtic music
Oklahoma Bass Maniax/f. Tecumseh and Shawnee/rap duo
Oldaker, Jamie/b. Oakland, CA, September 5, 1951/drummer, **Tulsa Sound**
Steve Ripley, The Tractors
Old School/f. Tulsa/rock group
Olive, Marcus/r. Olive Springs/porch guitarist
Olsen, Jennie/r. Oklahoma/soprano with Santa Fe Chorale
O'Mealey, Julie/r. Oklahoma/alto with Santa Fe Chorale
One Accord/f. Stillwater/contemporary Christian group
One Eyed Buffalo/f. Lawton/rock group
1 G.O.P./f. Tulsa/Higher Dimensions Family Church contemporary Christian group
Orange, Richard/r. Tulsa/multi-genre musician
Orloski, Stephanie/2003 TUmusic student/sings on TU jazz CD, *Sophisticated Ladies*
Orphium/f. Tulsa, 1998/rock group
Osage Sweat/recorded at Grayhorse, Osage Nation, 1997/sweat lodge singers
Kaulaity, Herschel (Cheyenne-**Kiowa**)/singer
McAlpine Louis (Osage)/singer

Schonleber, John (Caddo)/singer
Swank, Casey (Osage)/singer
Swank, Chris (Osage)/singer
Osage Tribe/based in Pawhuska, in state for centuries/In-Lon-Shka Ceremonies
  Native American Church, Christian hymns
Osborn, Mark/Oklahoma University music faculty, 2003/bassist
O'Shea. B.J./r. Oklahoma/blues guitarist, singer
Oscillators/f. Tulsa, 1995/blues group
Osterhaus, Carveth/UCO music faculty, 2003/music theatre, opera
The Other Side/f. Oklahoma/rock group
Otoe-Missouria Tribe/based near Red Rock since 1870s
  war dance/powwow/Native American Church
Ottawa Tribe/based in Miami, moved to I.T. in 1867/powwow, Native American Church
Ott, Doy/b. McAlester or Ada/singer with Statesmen Quartet
Oulds, Jerry/r. Bartlesville/R & B, pop singer, songwriter, multi-instrumentalist
Outcast Bluegrass/f. Oklahoma/bluegrass group
The Outlaws/f. Hominy/country group
Overland Bluegrass Express/f. Cushing/bluegrass group
  Blackburn, Fred/guitar, vocals
  Blackburn, Marcella/bass, songwriter
  Hargrove, Jim/guitar, fiddle, vocals
  Hargrove, Wanda/vocals
  Watson, Buddy/banjo, vocals
Owen, Linda/Oklahoma City University music faculty, 2003/pianist
Owens, Buck/recorded his 1960s syndicated TV program, *Buck Owens' Ranch*,
  at WKY in Oklahoma City
Owens, Parthena/Oklahoma City University music faculty, 2003/flutist
Oyebi, Pat (Kiowa)/r. Stilwell/intertribal powwow head singer
OZMA/f. Tulsa/rock group

P

Padgett, Bill/r. Tulsa/drummer with Brian Parton, Brandon McGovern
Page, Walter/b. Gallatin, MS, r. Oklahoma City/leader of **Oklahoma City Blue Devils**
Pagna, Sammy/r. Tulsa/pianist
Pahsetopah, Michael, P. (Osage/Euchee)/r. Oklahoma/intertribal powwow head singer
Pakanli, Princess/b. Ardmore/opera singer
Palmer, Mallory/r. Oklahoma/country singer
Parker, Chris/r. Tulsa/singer, songwriter
Parker, Jeffrey Gray/r. Tahlequah/Coyote Zen, **Red Dirt Music, Cherokee**
Parker, Mark E./Oklahoma City University music faculty, 2003/orchestra
Parton, Brian and the Nashville Rebels/f. Tulsa, 1993/rockabilly group
Parton, Thurman (**Caddo**)/r. Binger/Caddo Turkey Dance head singer
Pascal, Diane/Oklahoma University music faculty, 2003/violinist
Patterson, Donald (Tonkawa)/b. near Tonkawa/Fort Oakland Ramblers
Patterson, Henry (Tonkawa)/r. Tonkawa/intertribal powwow head singer
Paul's Electric Lemonade/r. Tulsa/pop group
Pawnee Nation/based in Pawnee, in state for centuries/hand game songs/Nat. Am

Church/powwow/hymns
Pawnee YellowHorse/f. Pawnee, 1996/Pawnee drum group
  Echo-Hawk, Bunky/singer
  Echo-Hawk, Debbie/back-up singer
  Echo-Hawk, Walter/singer
  Folsom-Minthorn Jennifer/back-up singer
  Gorman, Colleen/back-up singer
  Horsechief, Vance, Jr./lead singer, composer
  Horsechief, Vance III/singer
  Hodshire, Bryan/singer
  Hodshire, Kay/back-up singer
  Howell, Carrie/back-up singer
  Leadingfox, Gary/singer
  Leadingfox, Greg/singer
  Lightfoot, Jason/singer
  Minthorn, Phil/singer
  Moore, C.D./singer
  Muth, Marcie/back-up singer
Pearson, Carlton/r. Tulsa/gospel singer (Warner Alliance Records)
  pastor at Higher Dimensions Family Church in Tulsa
Pearson, Ron/Tulsa University music faculty, 2003/organist
Peck, Hayley/r. Oklahoma/country rock singer
Pederson, Sanna/Oklahoma University music faculty, 2003/musicologist
Pegues, Holly Michelle/b. Tulsa/opera soprano
Pendarvis, Paul/b. Oklahoma/violinist and bandleader
Peoria Tribe/based in Miami, moved to I.T. in 1867/powwow
Pepper, Jim/r. Oklahoma/**Muscogee**/Kansa (Kaw) jazz saxophonist
Peterson, Greg/b. Detroit, MI, 1963/classical, jazz, and studio bassist
Peterson, Quinn/r. Stillwater/country singer, songwriter
Peterson, Susan/Oklahoma City University music faculty, 2003/voice
Peter's Volcano/f. Newscastle/rock group
Petty, Brian/b. Clay Center, KS, r. Stillwater/singer with Dale Warland Singers
Phat Phly/f. Pryor/rock and roll cover band circa 2002
Phelps, Shelly/b. Pauls Valley, 1964/singer, songwriter
Phillips, Eva/r. Tulsa, from 1982/country/gospel songwriter
Pickens, Kel/b. Tulsa, 1949, r. Stillwater/children's music producer
  (Giant Blueberry Music), lyricist
Pierce, Mike/b. Muskogee, 1960, r. Braggs/band road manager, concert merchandising
Pillar/r. Tulsa/Christian hard rock band
Pilot, Jim (a.k.a. Pylant)/r. Oklahoma/country singer
Pinkie & the Snakeshakers/f. Oklahoma City, 1998/blues group
Pinson, Bobby/b. Tulsa/country singer-songwriter
  wrote "Unforgiven" for Tracy Lawrence
Pipestem, Rock/r. Oklahoma/intertribal powwow head singer
Pishney-Floyd, Monte/b. Oklahoma City, 1941/classical composer
Pitcock, Bill IV/b. Tulsa/producer, singer, songwriter, bassist for **Dwight Twilley**
Pitts, Alan/b. Bristow/country singer
Pittsenbarger, Kent/b. Oklahoma City, 1954/drummer w/Memphis P. Tails

Pittsley, Dustin/b. Tulsa, 1983, r. Chandler/blues guitarist/vocalist
Plastic Jack/R & B, rock group
  Enevoldsen, Adam/vocals, guitars
  Enevoldsen, Kyle/drummer
  Isom, Ray/guitars, vocals
  Ogden, Dave/bassist
Platt, Carol/r. Oklahoma/soprano with Santa Fe Chorale
Plumb, Dilla Jean/r. Oklahoma City/singer with Woody Herman in the 1930s and 1940s
The Plumbers/f. Tulsa, late 1990s/rock group
  Mitcho, Brad/guitarist
  Quinn, John/bassist
  Taylor, Scott/drummer
Podank String Band/f. Oklahoma/alternabilly group, released first CD in 2003
Poe, Bobby & the Poe Cats/f. Vinita/rockabilly group included **Big Al Downing**,
  backed **Wanda Jackson**,
Poison Okies/f. Oklahoma City, 1994/rockabilly group
Poor Boys/f. Meeker/southern style intertribal powwow singing group on Arbor Records
  Anquoe, Quinton/singer
  Deer, Michael/singer
  Gawhega, Mike/singer
  Kihega, Mike/singer
  Littlecrow, Amos/singer
  Locust, Knokkovtee/singer
  Logan, Charles/singer
  Tehaund, Rueben/singer
  White, Geoff/b. Tahlequah, r. Claremore, Meeker/head singer
Potter, Kim & Southern Reign/f. Kiefer, 1998/country group
  Green, Clyde/r. Cushing/lead guitar
  Green, Rick/r. Kiefer/keyboards/vocals
  Harris, Jim/r. Tulsa/bassist, mandolinist
  Murphy, Dean/r. Bristow/drummer
  Pierce, Dale/r. Stillwater/dobro, banjo, steel, guitar player, **Red Dirt Music**
  Potter, Doug/r. Kiefer/harmony vocals
  Potter, Kim/r. Kiefer/lead singer
Powell, Doug/b. Stillwater/singer, songwriter
Powell, John, S. /Tulsa University music faculty, 2003/music history, literature
Powell, Susan/b. Elk City/1981 Miss America, classical & opera singer
Powerglide/f. Tulsa, 1999/1960s and 70s rock cover group
  Blue, David/r. Bartlesville/drummer
  Lyon, Wes/graduated Tulsa Will Rogers High School/guitarist
  Ryan, David/graduated Tulsa Will Rogers High School/keyboardist, guitarist
  Shoun, Paul/graduated Tulsa Will Rogers High School/lead singer
  Sullivan, Don/graduated Tulsa Will Rogers High School/bassist
    also played with Roy Clark
Prairie Land String Band/f. Oklahoma City/folk group
The Prairie Twins/b. Oklahoma/cowgirl singers
Prana/f. Tulsa, 2003/loud rock
Predl, Ronald, E./Tulsa University music faculty, 2003/trumpeter

Preslar, Casey/r. Tulsa/singer, Miss Oklahoma 2002
The Rickey Preston Band/f. Tulsa/R & B, blues, soul group
Price, Gary/b. Oklahoma County/banjo and mandolin player, luthier
Price, John Elwood/b. Tulsa, 1935/classical musician
Price, William Roger/Tulsa University music faculty, 2003/pianist, composition
Prill, Julie Baker/r. Terlton/country singer
Prior, Richard/Oklahoma State University music faculty, 2003/composition
Pritchett, Kate/Oklahoma City University music staff, 2003/horn
Proctor, David/Mekko, Tallahassee Wvkokye Ceremonial Grounds/stomp dance leader
Proctor, Michael/Tallahassee Wvkokye Ceremonial Grounds/stomp dance leader
Proctor, Sam/Heles Haya, Tallahassee Wvkokye Ceremonial Grounds
    stomp dance leader, heles hayv (medicine man), **Muscogee (Creek)**
Pryor, Steve/b. Tulsa/blues guitarist, singer, songwriter
Pro Musica Tulsae/f. Tulsa/medieval and Renaissance era music
Pruitt, Bill/r. Oklahoma/champion yodeler
Pugh, Paul/r. Tulsa/pianist
Purple Cow Story/f. Norman

Q

Quapaw Tribe/based in Quapaw, moved to I.T. in 1833/powwow
Quarterless/f. Tulsa/classic and modern rock group
    Harrington, Mel/bassist
    Kay, Matt/vocalist
    Kruse, Ben/lead guitarist
    McCracken, Kelly/percussionist
    Sears, Jeremy/rhythm guitarist
Quetone, Brian/r. Oklahoma/intertribal powwow head singer
Quetone, John (Sac & Fox/**Kiowa**/Otoe)/r. Oklahoma/intertribal powwow head singer
Quinn, Kenny/r. Tulsa/jazz, blues pianist
Quinton, Wade/b. Fairfax, VA, r. Tulsa/country singer

R

R, David/b. Oklahoma/folk singer/songwriter
Rabbit, Jimmy/b. Holdenville/country singer
Radford, Ronald/b. California, moved to Tulsa at four/flamenco guitarist
Radial Angel/f. Norman/contemporary Christian group signed by Warner Brothers'
    Squint Records 2003
    Jones, Eddie/bassist
    Dolezel, Jeremy/guitarist
    Perkins, Tommy/r. Noble/drummer
    Taber, Jared/lead singer
Radial Spangle/f. Oklahoma City, 1991/independent rock group
Radle, Carl/b. Oklahoma City, 1942/drummer for Eric Clapton and Leon Russell,
    Tulsa Sound
Rae, Lana/b. Oklahoma/country singer
Raiber, Michael/Oklahoma University music faculty, 2003/music education
Rains, Peggy/b. Adair County, Chalk Bluff Community/country singer

Rains, Shan/r. Stillwater/country singer

Rainwater, Marvin/b. Wichita, KS, 1925, reared in Oklahoma/country, rockabilly singer

Rambler/f. Oklahoma/21st century honky tonk
   Brown, Dave/bassist, vocalist
   Brown, Tim/lead singer, rhythm guitarist
   Chavez, Troy/guitarist, vocalist
   Emmons, Matt/drummer

RamDogg & Anloc/f. Oklahoma City/hip hop

Ramirez, Debra/b. Buffalo, r. Guymon/contemporary Christian singer

Randall, Lawrence/r. Owasso/gospel singer with The Ambassadors

Raphael/b. Tulsa, 1948/pianist

Rath, Carl/Oklahoma University music faculty, 2003/bassoon

Ratley, Rob/r. Muskogee/blues drummer with **DC Minner** and Shy Willie

Raus, Connor/r. Tulsa/jazz keyboardist

Rausch, Leon/r. Tulsa/Western swing singer, songwriter, bassist (**Bob Wills**)

Raze/f. Tulsa/contemporary Christian group

Record, Donnie/b. Enid, 1952/country singer

Redd, Charlie/r. Tulsa/jazz and blues vocalist, bassist

Redfeather, Tsianina/r. Oklahoma/mezzo soprano

Redins, Trebor/r. Tulsa/rock singer

Redland Singers/f. Tulsa, 1968/intertribal powwow group
   Anquoe, Jack, Jr. (**Kiowa/Cherokee**)/b. Claremore/singer, Grayhorse
   Arkeketa, Anthony (**Ponca**/Otoe)/b. Pawnee/head singer
   Arkeketa, Eddie (**Ponca**/Otoe)/b. Tulsa/singer
   Coser, George (**Muscogee**)/singer
   Coser, Pete, Sr. (**Muscogee**)/singer
   Coser, Pete, Jr. (**Muscogee**/Choctaw)/singer
   Coser, Wayne (**Muscogee**)/singer
   Franklin, Steve (Sac & Fox)/singer
   Mohler, Rod/singer
   Moses, Berwyn (Pawnee/Chiricahua-Warm Springs-Ft. Sill Apache)/singer
   Waters, Joe Don (**Ponca/Kiowa**)/singer
   Welch, Dean (**Cherokee**)/singer

Reed, Larry/Oklahoma City University music faculty, 2003/bassoonist

Reed, Les "The Mess"/r. Owasso/folk singer, children's entertainer

Reed, Luke, H./b. Ringling/cowboy song composer

Reed, Stan/r. Tulsa/rock, blues bassist

Reed, Teresa, L./TU music faculty, 2003/music theory, African-American music

Reeder, Jimmy (Wichita)/r. Anadarko/intertribal powwow head singer

Reiley, Rick/r. Cushing/singer, songwriter, guitarist

Relic/f. Norman

Remede/f. Stillwater/folk rock group

Remy-Schumacher, Tess/University of Central Oklahoma music faculty, 2003/cellist

Renfro, Jessie Mae/r. Oklahoma City/gospel composer and singer

Renter, David/OCU music faculty, 2003/jazz ensembles, saxophonist

Reptable Crew/f. Oklahoma City/hip-hop, rap

ReTroSpecT/f. Stillwater, 2000/rock, country cover band
   Brown, Larry/drummer

Hartley, Bruce/lead and rhythm guitarist
Martin, Augie/lead and rhythm guitarist
Short, Gloria/lead vocalist, keyboardist
Wright, Tony/bassist
The Revolve/f. Norman, Oklahoma City
Rewake/f. Tulsa/gypsy rock band
  Bowlin, Daniel/guitarist until 2002
  Darras, Malan/singer
  Hartley, Eric/drummer as of 2003
  Karleskint, Paul/guitarist as of 2003
  Morrow, Matt/bassist until 2002
  Pickett, Jason/drummer as of 2003
  Snow, Austin/drummer until 2002
Reynolds, Jody/b. Denver, 1938, reared in Oklahoma City/rockabilly singer, guitarist
Reynolds, Mary/r. Oklahoma City/folk singer
Reynolds, Wes/r. Oklahoma City/50s rocker, songwriter, guitarist with The Champs,
  Conway Twitty, Jerry Lee Lewis, et al.
Rhea Tiffany/b. Oklahoma/country, pop singer, songwriter
Rhodes, Violet/b. Oklahoma City/classical viola player
Rhom, Sarah/r. Oklahoma/contemporary Christian folk, rock singer
Ricci T/r. Tulsa/R & B singer, recorded for Made Records
Rice Dance Band/f. Oklahoma City/dance music
Rice, Dave/b. Oklahoma/old time harmonica player
Rice, Frank/b. Bartlesville/barbershop quartet lead singer
Rice, Joni/University of Central Oklahoma music faculty, 2003/percussionist
Richards, Jamie/b. Shawnee/country singer
Richardson, Jeff/r. Tulsa/rapper, a.k.a. Yung Hog
Rich, Charlie/r. Enid at Vance Air Force Base where he organized a jazz band
  country singer
Richie and the Resonators/f. Tulsa/blues rock group w/ country alter-ego, Audio Rodeo
  Buchman, Randy/drummer
  Duncan, Billy/organist
  Gray, Mitch/bassist
  Starks, Mike/harmonica player
  Starks, Richard/guitarist, vocalist
Richman, Pamela/University of Central Oklahoma music faculty, 2003/voice
Richmond, Walter/b. McAlester, OK April 18, 1947/keyboardist with Bonnie Raitt,
  Tractors, **Steve Ripley**
Richter, Brad/b. Enid/classical guitarist
Riddick, Frank/Oklahoma City University music faculty, 2003/theory, composition
Riddick, Leah/University of Central Oklahoma music faculty, 2003/harpist
Riddlin' Kids/f. Tulsa/punk rock group
Riggs, Debbie/b. Ada, r. Stillwater/gospel singer
Riggs, Lynn/b. Claremore/wrote *Green Grow the Lilacs*, basis for musical *Oklahoma!*
Rippinger, Rockwell Ryan/b. Orlando, FL, reared in Tulsa/contemporary Christian
  singer, songwriter
Ritter, Steve/r. Blackgum, graduated Vian High, NSU/country singer, songwriter
Rivers, Jimmy/b. Hockerville/Western swing bandleader, guitarist

Rivers, Joseph, L./TU music faculty, 2003/music theory, music composition

Roark-Strummer, Linda/b. Tulsa/opera singer

Robbins, Everett "Happy"/r. Oklahoma/jazz pianist of the 1920s

Robillard, David/Oklahoma City University music faculty, 2003/accompanist

Rockumentalists/f. Norman/rock group

Rogers, Doug/r. Tulsa/drummer for The Brazos Valley Boys

Rogers, Harlan/r. Oklahoma/keyboardist and pianist with Ricky Skaggs

Rogers, Michael/Oklahoma University music faculty, 2003/music theory

Rodgers, Jesse/b. Claremore, 1913/rockabilly singer

Rohrer, Leah/r. Oklahoma, OCU graduate/Broadway performer/singer

Rollerson, Leon/r. Tulsa/bassist, organized group that became the **GAP Band**,
   played with Al Green, et al.

Romaine, Karl/r. Walters/guitarist

Roark-Strummer, Linda/TU music faculty, 2003/voice, vocal diction, opera workshop

Rosales, Antonio/b. Oklahoma City/country singer,
   president of Oklahoma Country Music Assn.

Rose Hill/southern style powwow group/recorded for Indian House Records in 1995

   Barker, Roland/singer

   Frejo, Brian/singer

   Gwen, Lloyd/singer, leader

   Hamilton, Curtis/singer (**Young Bird**)

   Hamilton, Donnie/singer (**Young Bird**)

   Hamilton, Juaquin/singer (**Young Bird**)

   Harris, R.G., Jr./singer

   Victors, Greg/singer

   Victors, Shude/singer

   Walker, Henry, Jr./singer

   Whitecloud, Hootie/singer

   Whitecloud, J.R./singer

   Whitecloud, Michael/singer

Rose Stone Trio/r. Tulsa/flute, harp, harpsichord chamber group

Rosfeld, Marilyn/oOCU music faculty, 2003/pianist, music education

Ross, Billy/b. Cushing/country songwriter

Ross, Jason/r. Stilwell/intertribal powwow head singer

Ross, J.R.(**Cherokee/Kiowa**)/r. Sapulpa/intertribal powwow head singer

Ross, John Stanley/Cameron University music faculty, 2003/music education

Roubedoux, Jade/r. Oklahoma/intertribal powwow head singer

Roubedoux, Kyle (Ponca/Otoe)/r. Enid/intertribal powwow head singer

Roulain, Cole/r. Stillwater/singer, songwriter, guitarist

Round-Up Boys/f. Tulsa/acoustic traditional country

The Roustabouts/f. Enid, 1997/punk rock group

   Felton, Daniel/b. Enid, r. Waukomis/bassist, guitarist, vocalist

   Smith, Jesse/b. Enid, r. Hennessey/drummer

   Waggoner, Nick/b. Enid, r. Hennessey/guitarist, vocalist

Rowe, Paul/ECOU adjunct music faculty, 2003/applied piano

Rowe, Ray D./r. Tulsa/early GAP band vocalist, fronts Down Home Blues Band in 2003

Rowland, William/b. MO, r. Broken Arrow/ragtime pianist

Royal Crush/f. Tulsa, 1997/modern pop rock group

Roy, George/r. Salina/intertribal powwow head singer
Rucker, Laura/b. Oklahoma/jazz and blues singer
Rucker, Lee/UCO music faculty, 2003/jazz trumpeter (w/ Woody Herman Orchestra)
Rucker, Washington/*/Oklahoma Jazz Hall of Fame inductee, drummer
R.U.I./f. Tulsa/rap group
Rush, Tommy/r. Tulsa/1950s rock and roll singer, **Tulsa Sound**
Rushlow, Tom/r. Midwest City/guitarist, father of **Tim Rushlow**
Russell, David/Oklahoma City University music faculty, 2003/cellist
Russell, Lamon/Oklahoma City University music faculty, 2003/Surrey Singers director
Russell, Pee Wee/b. St. Louis, MO, r. Muskogee/Dixieland clarinetist
Ryan, Donald/r. Tulsa/jazz pianist
Ryan, Frank/r. Tulsa/educator, classical conductor

S

Sac & Fox Nation/based south of Stroud since 1869/Nat. American Church,
  powwow/hymns/War Mothers songs, drum dances
Saied, Jimmy/r. Tulsa/conductor
Salmon, Scottie/r. Red Oak/choreographer w/ Radio City Rockettes,
  Miss American Pageant, and for Barbara Mandrell
Same and the Stylees/f. Tulsa/reggae group
  Frye, Nigel/bassist
  Glendening, Thomas/drummer, guitarist, vocalist
  Jones, Sam/guitarist
  Lokey, Maria/percussionist, vocalist
  Meddler, Brian/vocalist
  Reynolds, Lance/guitarist
  Santana/percussionist
Same Day Service/f. Oklahoma/riot girl punk rock group
Samsarah/f. Tulsa/rock group
Sampson, Phil/b. Chickasha/country singer, songwriter
Samsara/f. Tulsa/independent rock group
Sanctuary/f. Norman/rock group
Sanders, Billy Wade/b. McAlester, 1942/blues guitarist with Delbert McClinton
Sanders, Nathan/b. Oklahoma City/mandolinist, bassist, guitarist
Sanders, Sarah Nicole/b. Muskogee, 1985/gospel singer
San Dimas/f. Tulsa/rock group
Sandkuhl, Ron/r. Broken Arrow/inventor of the G-Stand,
  a guitar stand attached to a guitar's neck plate
Sandman Band/f. Norman/rock group
Sankey, O.T./r. Oklahoma/intertribal powwow head singer
Satepauhoodle, Craig (**Kiowa**/Osage)/b. Hominy/intertribal powwow head singer,
  Gourd Dance singer
Satepauhoodle, Evans Ray (**Kiowa**)/b. Carnegie/intertribal powwow head singer,
  Gourd Dance singer
Satepauhoodle, Silas (**Kiowa**/Osage)/b. Pawhuska/intertribal powwow head singer,
  Gourd Dance singer
Sauer, Amanda/Oklahoma University music faculty, 2003/music theory

Sauer, Gregory/Oklahoma University music faculty, 2003/cellist

Savage, William/Oklahoma University history professor/
  wrote *Singing Cowboys and All That Jazz* (1983)

Scaggs, Boz/b. Ohio, 1944, r. Oklahoma as a child/pop rock singer, songwriter

Schimek, John/Oklahoma City University music faculty, 2003/
  double bassist, music education

Schindler, Angela/SEOSU adjunct music faculty, 2003/oboeist

Schmidt, Scott/r. Bartlesville/national mandolin champion

Schneider, Moe/b. Bessie, 1919/Dixieland trombonist

Schnorrenberg, Nathan/r. Owasso, Norman/singer, songwriter

Scott, Allen/Oklahoma State University music faculty, 2003/historical musicology

Scott, Ernestine/Oklahoma City University music faculty, 2003/pianist

Scott, Shannon/Tulsa University music faculty, 2003/clarinetist

Scotty (b. Concho) and Tommie/traditional country, bluegrass, and gospel duo

Scroggins, Enois/ b. Muskogee/gospel singer

Scroggins, Janice/b. Idabel/blues piano

Seaton, Lynn/b. Tulsa, 1957/jazz double bassist

Second Self/f. Catoosa, Tulsa, and Claremore, 2001/rock group

Seglem, Sara/b. Midwest City/opera soprano

Selby, Mark/b. Oklahoma/guitarist, singer, songwriter (Dixie Chicks, Trisha Yearwood,
  Kenny Wayne Shepherd), also performs solo

Seldom Seen/f. Weleetka/country, bluegrass, and rock group
  Burden, Phillip/fiddler, rhythm guitarist, vocalist
  Burden, Steve/banjoist, guitarist, fiddler, vocalist
  Wisner, Blanche "Toni"/lead and backup vocalist

Seminatore, Gerald/Oklahoma State University music faculty, 2003/tenor, voice, opera

Seminole Nation/based in Wewoka, began moving to I.T. reluctantly, in 1835/
  stomp dance/flute/Christian hymns

Seneca-Cayuga/based in Miami, in I.T. by 1832/
  annual cycle of Longhouse Green Corn Ceremonial songs

Settlemires, Joe/r. Blanchard, USAO part-timemusic faculty, 2003//finger style guitarist

Sever/f. Oklahoma City/heavy metal group

Sewell, Ace/b. Blanchard/old time fiddler

Seymour, Phil/b. Tulsa, 1952/half of original **Dwight Twilley Band**

Shade of the Son/f. Cyril/Christian rock group

Shade Seven/f. Oklahoma City/rock group

Shadid, Margie/r. Oklahoma City/jazz singer

Shadowlake 8/f. Stillwater, circa 1957 and '58/rock and roll band

The Shadows Five/f. Oklahoma/1960s rock and roll band, recorded for Sully Records

Shaffer, Larry/r. Tulsa/concert promoter

Shamblin, Eldon/b. Weatherford, 1916/influential Western swing guitarist for **Bob Wills**

Shamrock/f. Tulsa/rock group

Shanghai Automatic/f. Tulsa/rock group

Shannon, Mike/b. Tulsa, 1953, raised around McAlester, r. Stillwater/songwriter,
  guitarist (**Red Dirt Music**), Daddy O's Music store

Shannon, Tom/r. Tulsa/jazz saxophonist

Shatswell, Danny/b. Oklahoma, 1953/country singer, songwriter

Shaw, Lee/b. Oklahoma/jazz pianist

Shawnee, Mike (Shawnee/Quapaw/Delaware/Muscogee)/r. Owasso/
    intertribal powwow head singer
Shawnee Tribe/based in Miami area since 1871/White Oak Ceremonial Grounds/
    stomp dance/powwow
Sheehan, Megan/r. Broken Arrow/country singer
Sheffield-Charles, Ellen/r. Oklahoma City/jazz and ballet pianist
Sheffield, Leslie/r. Oklahoma City/jazz band leader
Sheff, Spade/b. Tahlequah/country singer, songwriter
Shepard, Brian/Oklahoma University music faculty, 2003/composition, technology
Sherinian, Zoe/Oklahoma University music faculty, 2003/ethnomusicologist
Sherley, Glen/b. Oklahoma, 1936/country giner, songwriter
Shortt Dogg/f. Oklahoma City/blues, R & B group
Shrader, James/NWOSU Music Department Chair, 2003/conductor
Shrock, Dennis/Oklahoma University music faculty, 2003/choral conducting
Sidewinder/r. Tulsa, 2003/rock, Top 40, country cover band
    Davis, Tresa/singer
    Dunlap, Bruce/bassist, vocalist
    Harlan, Joel/lead guitarist
    Huffman/drummer
    Lowther, Chris/rhythm guitarist, vocalist
Sievers, Karl/Oklahoma University music faculty, 2003/trumpeter
Significant Other/f. Tulsa/rock group
Siksigma/f. Tulsa/heavy metal rock group
Silkebakken, Dennis, L./ECOU music faculty, 2003/director of bands, deptartment chair
Silver Creek Bluegrass/f. Oklahoma/bluegrass group
    Bryant, Glenn/banjo player
    Keith, James/fiddler
    Lins, Sue/mandolinist
    Miller, Ken/guitarist
    Rohr, Florence/bassist
Simon, Billy/b. Cleveland/gospel songwriter, vocalist with 4 Runner Quartet
Simpleton/f. Stillwater, 2001/pop rock
    Beier, Matt/drummer
    Hall, James/bassist
    Jones, Chris/guitarist, vocalist
Simpson, John/r. Oklahoma/polka band leader
Singer, Harold "Hal"/b. Tulsa, 1918/jazz clarinetist and tenor saxophonist
Singer, Margaret Ann/r. Oklahoma/classical pianist for the Oklahoma City Symphony
Siren/f. Tahlequah/rock group
Six Foot Landing/f. Tulsa/pop rock group
6point/f. Norman/rock group
Six Foot Six/f. Tulsa/metal group
Skarekrow/f. Tulsa/progressive rock, metal group
Skinner, C.C./*/Oklahoma Jazz Hall of Fame inductee, gospel category
Skinner, Craig/r. Oklahoma/guitarist, **Red Dirt Music**
Skinner, Mike/r. Oklahoma/fiddler, **Red Dirt Music**
Skinner, Tom/b. Bristow, 1954/singer, songwriter, **Red Dirt Music**
Skruface/f. Tulsa/independent rock group

Aaron, Chris/vocalist
Deason, Mike/drummer, vocalist
McCullough, Sean/bassist
Owens, Glen/guitarist
Slash/r. Boynton/lead guitarist for Guns N' Roses
Slaves of the Television/f. Dewey/rock group
Slow Children at Play/f. Norman/rock group
Slow Head Soul/f. Tulsa/improvisational jam band
  Al-Hammami, Zee/drummer, percussionist, vocalist
  Harry, Lelan/bassist, vocalist
  Turner, Isaac/guitarist, vocalist
  Turner, Joshua/guitarist, vocalist
Slowvein/f. Yukon, 1997/rock group
  Berry, Danny/guitarist
  Kruel, Tommy/bassist
  Lea, Susan/backup vocalist
  Leiter, Gary/guitarist
  Ramsey, Mark/drummer
  Turner, Elizabeth/vocalist
Smalley, John Jacob/r. Edmond/*American Idol* performer, 2003
Smarty Pants/f. Oklahoma City, 1997/pop rock group
Smilin' Vic & and the Soul Monkeys/f. 1995, Oklahoma City/blues group
  Feuerborn, Larry/b. Norman/bassist
  Gutierrez, Victor/b. Tulsa/vocalist
  Taylor, Mitch/b. Tulsa/guitarist
  Warren, Cleve/b. Oklahoma City/drummer
Smith, Big Walter/b. Tulsa/blues singer
Smith, Chester/b. Wade, 1930/rockabilly singer
Smith, Fred/b. Tulsa/jazz keyboardist
Smith, Howard/b. Ardmore, 1910/jazz pianist, arranger, composer
Smith, Katie Thomas/r. Coweta/bluegrass guitarist with Umy and the Goodtimers
Smith, Jerry Neil/Oklahoma University music faculty, 2003/clarinetist, saxophonist
Smith, J.T./b. Texas, recorded in OK, 1930s/blues artist
Smith, Jo Ann/r. Oklahoma/autoharp champion
Smith, Orlando/UCO music faculty, 2003/tenor, voice, music theatre
Smith, Roy/Tulsa University music faculty, NEOSUadjunct faculty, 2003/percussionist
Smith, Sam/Tallahassee Wvkokye Ceremonial Grounds/stomp dance leader
Smith, Sammi/b. CA, 1943, r. OK/country singer,
  known for "Help Me Make It Through the Night"
Smith, Steve/r. Oklahoma/ mountain dulcimer champion
Smith, Steve/r. Tulsa/singer, songwriter
Smittle, Betsy/r. Oklahoma/country bassist, vocalist, and **Garth Brooks**' sister
Smoke/f. Tulsa/spoken word, multi-ethnic music
  Glass, Mingo/r. Tulsa/percussionist, flute
  Harris, Nancy/b. Tulsa/poet, spoken word artist
  Henry, Tom/b. near Spring Creek, Cherokee County/guitarist, percussionist
The Smok'n Coyotes/classic country and rock group
  Ecker, Ken/r. on a lake near Edmond/keyboardist

Embrey, Bo/r. Mustang/drummer
Embrey, Mike/r. Mustang/lead guitarist, backup vocalist
Hudson, Larry/r. Norman/bassist, backup vocalist
Keesee, Steve/r. Shawnee/lead vocalist, rhythm guitarist
SnapDragon/f. Tulsa/pop rock group
 Boren, Russell/bassist
 Capps, Matt/drummer
 Gibbons, Kelly/guitarist, keyboardist
 Horn, Robert/guitarist
 Jude, Christine/vocalist
 Sabelo, Tony/percussionist, keyboardist
The SNOTROKITZ/f. Norman/rock group
Snow, Bill/r. Tulsa/singer, songwriter
SOAHC/f. Tulsa/Christian rock group
Sol Mist/f. Oklahoma/contemporary Christian group
Sol Raven/f. Tulsa/heavy metal group
Soul Avengers/f. Tulsa/blues rock group
 Bruce, Mike "Monk"/guitarist, vocalist
 Dragoo, Mike/drummer, vocalist
 Munson, Steve/bassist
Soul Food/f. Tulsa/contemporary Christian group
Sounds Good/f. Tulsa/jazz group
 Bruce, Buddy/guitarist
 Cope, Rick/drummer
 Cummins, Jon/bassist
 Williamson, Gayle/pianist
 Wright, Shelly/vocalist
Sounds of the Southwest/official OK state Western swing band
 via Oklahoma legislature in 1997
 Keith, Becky/r. Oklahoma/lead vocalist, guitarist
 Keith, Matt/r. Oklahoma/vocalist, fiddler
 McLin, Wil/r. Oklahoma/vocalist, guitarist
 Sharp, Richard/r. Oklahoma/vocalist and bassist (also plays with **Byron Berline**)
Southern Boys/r. Oklahoma/southern style powwow group (Arbor Records)
 Cable, Darrell/singer
 Cable, Kelly/singer
 Chasenah, Finton/singer
 Hindsley, Corey/singer
 Mashunkashey, Russell/singer
 Monossey, Althea/back-up singer
 Monossey, Anthony/singer, also intertribal powwow head singer
 Monossey Dobbin/back-up singer
 Monossey, Carl/singer
 Monossey, Larry/singer, also intertribal powwow head singer
 Monossey, Ronald/singer
 Monossey, Sukie/back-up singer
 Redbone, Edgar/singer
 Starr, Marlena/back-up singer

Starr, Ni'vy/backup singer
Southern Steel/f. Collinsville/country metal group
   Casger, Bryan/r. Collinsville/drummer
   Johnson, Richard/r. Collinsville/guitarist
   Overholt, Ryan/r. Collinsville/lead singer
   Rowe, Corbin/r. Collinsville/guitarist
   Thurman, Zak/r. Collinsville/bassist
Southern Thunder/f. Pawnee, 1991/southern style powwow group (Indian House)
   Adson, Aaron/singer
   Adson, Frank M.(Pawnee/Navajo)/head singer
   Adson, Herb/singer
   Adson, Robert/singer
   Beard, Gilbert/singer
   Lightfoot, Crystal Pewo/back-up singer
   Lightfoot, Jason/singer
   Moore, Jordan/singer
   Plumley, Erin/back-up singer
   Rice, Ron, Jr./singer
   Starr, Jimmy/singer
   Starr, Ni'vy/back-up singer
   Tiger, Georgia/back-up singer
   Tiger, Julia/back-up singer
   Tipps, Kyle/singer
   Valliere, George, Jr./singer
South 40 Band/f. southeastern Oklahoma/country rock group
Sovo, Gene/r. Oklahoma/intertribal powwow head singer
Spears, Sheena/r. Oklahoma/country singer
Special Disaster Team/f. Norman/ska, punk rock group
Special Purpose/f. Tulsa/rock group
Spence, Peggy/University of Central Oklahoma music faculty, 2003/pianist
SphereGazer/f. Norman/rock group
Spies, David/SEOSU adjunct music faculty, 2003/low brass
Spiral/f. Tulsa/independent rock group
Spivery, John/r. Oklahoma/keyboardist, recorded for Made Records
Spookie Jar/f. Oklahoma City/hard rock group
Spotted Horse, Brent/r. Edmond/intertribal powwow head singer
Spradlin, Kelly/r. Tulsa/blues vocalist and guitarist
Spraker, Eddie/r. Tulsa/1950s rock and roll singer, **Tulsa Sound**
Springstreet/f. Tulsa/bluegrass group
Squareforce/f. Tulsa/blues rock group
Squirrel, James (Shawnee)/r. Oklahoma/stomp dance leader
Stacy, Clyde/b. Checotah/Briartown vicinity/rockabilly singer, guitarist
Standing on Zero/f. Tulsa/rock group
Starlight Mints/f. Norman, circa 1999/rock group on PIAS Records
   Love Nunez, Marian/bassist
   Nunez, Andy/drummer
   Vest, Allan/singer, guitarist
Starling, Kristy/r. Putnam City/contemporary Christian singer

Starr, Arigon/Kickapoo Tribe of OK tribal member/rock singer
Starr, Jimmy/r. Stroud/intertribal powwow head singer
Starr, Moses/r. Hydro/intertribal powwow head singer
Steffens, David/Oklahoma City University music faculty, 2003/percussionist
The Stellas/f. Emond/rock group on Edmond-based Sonic Blitz Records,
    produced by Trent Bell
    Duncan, Raechel/r. Choctaw/music educator by day/guitarist, vocalist by night
    London, John/drummer, programmer
Stella Luna/f. Norman/experimental music group
    Fitzpatrick, Darin/drummer
    Hanson, Susan/guitarist, vocalist
    Roberts, Rhonda/bassist
    Smith, Devon/guitarist, vocalist
    Sterling, Jennifer/keyboardist, sampler
Stephenson, Kenneth/Oklahoma University music faculty, 2003/music theory
Sterling, Tom/r. Tulsa/jazz saxophonist
Steven Speaks/f. Tulsa/independent pop rock group
Steveson, Kristin/b. Broken Arrow/opera singer
Stewart, Kathryn/b. Bartlesville/opera singer
Still Breathing/f.Oklahoma/Christian metal on Solid State Records, disbanded 2002
Stidham, Jack/r. Chickasha/old time, Western swing fiddler
Stokes, Adam/r. Stillwater (Stillwater High graduate)/folk singer, songwriter
Stomberg, Lawrence/Oklahoma State University music faculty, 2003/cellist
Stonehorse/f. Claremore, 1980/country, Western swing group
    Caple, Roger/bassist, vocalist
    O'Brien, Rich/guitarist
    Passmore, Darlene/drummer
    Self, Mike/guitarist and vocalist
    Stockton, Wade/fiddler, tenor banjo player
    Talbert, Brenda/pianist
    Talbert, Dale/steel guitarist
    Talbert, Donnie /b. Claremore/fiddler, vocalist, bandleader, plays with Alan Jackson
Stone Soup/f. Oklahoma/rock group
Stovall, Vern/b. Altus, 1928/country singer
Strader, Jimmy/b. Tulsa/blues singer, bassist
Straight Shooter/f. Lexington/rock group
Streamline/f. Tulsa/rock group
Streets, Barbara/University of Central Oklahoma music faculty, 2003/voice
Stricklin, Al/b. Texas, r. Tulsa/pianist for **Bob Wills**
Struck, JoAnn/Oklahoma City University music faculty, 2003/music education
The Struggle/f. Norman/rock group
Stubbs, Deni/Oklahoma Opry house band bassist
Studebaker, Donald/NEOSU music faculty, 2003/chorus, orchestra, conducting
Studebaker, Mary/NEOSU music faculty, 2003/violinist, music fundamentals
Studi, Wes/b. No Fire Hollow, 1946/**Cherokee** actor, Firecat of Discord bassist
Sturgeon, Kristi/NEOSU adjunct music faculty, 2003/clarinetist
Subject to Blackout/f. Tulsa/modern rock group
Sub Rosa/f. Oklahoma City and Norman/rock group

Subseven/f. Oklahoma City/contemporary Christian rock group
The Suburbillies/f. Oklahoma City/alternative country group
Sugar Free Allstars/f. Norman/pop rock group
Sullivan Family/r. Boggy Depot, 2002/gospel group
Sullivan, Morey/r. Bartlesville (1975 – 1985)/vocalist, Brazos Valley Boys' leader
Sun Cured Red/f. Stillwater, 1998/improvisational rock group
    Bourland, Chris/saxophonist, flutist, keyboardist, electronics
    Cathey, Josh/bassist
    Loyd, Daniel/vocalist, guitarist
    Seary, Darin/drummer
    Stapp, Jimmy/guitarist, vocalist
SuperChild/f. Miami/rock group
Sutter, Lynn/r. Oklahoma/gospel singer
Sutton, Spencer/b. Wichita, KS, r. Claremore/jazz, pop pianist
Sweatt, Al/recorded on the Tulsa-based KEEN label in the 1950s/rockabilly singer
Sweney, Jim/r. Tulsa/R & B vocalist
Sweeney, Mark/r. Tahlequah/singer, songwriter, guitarist Barton and Sweeney
Sybil's Machine/f. Tulsa/rock group
Syringe/f. Norman/rock group
System X/f. Oklahoma/metal group

T
Tae Meyulks/f. Tulsa/fusion jazz
Tahchawwickah, Victor (Comanche)/r. Oklahoma/intertribal powwow head singer
Tahhawah, Jerome (Comanche)/r. Oklahoma/intertribal powwow head singer
Taming Enos/f. Tulsa/rock group
Tanner, David Case/b. Tulsa, 1951/ blues rock pianist
Tate, Bob, Jr./b. Oklahoma/jazz, R & B saxophonist
Tate, Mary Ann/b. Tulsa/blues singer
Tate, Jerod Sheffer/b. Norman/Chickasaw composer
Taylor, Bobby/r. Tulsa/1950s rock and roll singer, **Tulsa Sound**
Taylor, Jovonia/2003 TU music student/sings on TU jazz CD, *Sophisticated Ladies*
Taylor, Lester/r. Oklahoma City/jazz and R & B percussionist, singer
Taylor, Little Eddy/b. Oklahoma City/blues guitarist, soul singer
Taylor, Ted/b. Okmulgee, 1934/soul and blues singer
Teagarden, Charlie/b. Texas, r. Oklahoma City/jazz trumpeter
Teagarden, Jack/b. Texas, r. Oklahoma City, played in Central High School Band
    jazz trombonist with Louis Armstrong, et. al
Teegarden, David/b. Tulsa/producer, singer, songwriter, singer, drummer, **Tulsa Sound**
Te-Ata/b. December 3, 1895, Emet/Chickasaw singer and storyteller
Terrell, Stephen W./b. Oklahoma City/alternative country artist and journalist
Tex Montana's Fireball 4/f. Tulsa/rock group
Thacker, Ron/b. Duncan/lead guitarist for rock group Aggro
Therogy/f. Norman
13 Stars/f. Oklahoma City/rock group
36 Inches/f. Oklahoma City/rock group
Thai Music/f. Tulsa/the group plays Thai Music at Lanna Thai Restaurant in Tulsa

Thomas, Cherie/NEOSU adjunct music faculty, 2003/flutist
Thomas, Guthrie/ b. Lawton/folksinger
Thomas, Jesse "Babyface"/r. Oklahoma City/blues singer
Thomas, Joe/b. Muskogee, 1908/jazz tenor saxophonist
Thomas, Paul Wesley/b. Oklahoma City/symphony composer
Thomas, Tony/r. Hugo/old time fiddler
Thomas, Walter "Foots"/b. Muskogee, 1907/jazz flutist, saxophonist, bandleader,
Thompson, Chester, D./b. Oklahoma City/pianist, keyboardist with Tower of Power
    and Santana
Thompson, Lee "Trippy"/b. Enid, 1962/rock singer for Dragmules (Atlantic Records)
Thompson, Patti/r. Tulsa, 1965/lead singer for ORU World Action Signers
Thompson, Paulina/b. Saratov, Russia, r. Oklahoma City/singer, songwriter
Thompson, Sandra/UCO music faculty, 2003/choral studies director, music theory
Thompson, Tony/b. Waco, TX, reared in Oklahoma City
    lead singer of Hi-Five, 1990s R & B group
Three Strange Days/f. Tulsa/rock group
351 Windsor/f. Tulsa/jazz jam band
    Jones, Jeffrey/drummer
    Karleskint, Paul/guitarist
    Mayo, Matt/bassist
The Throwbacks/f. Tulsa/Christian rock group
Thunderhorse/f. 2000, Stillwater/northern style intertribal powwow group
    (Arbor Records)
    Allen, Andy/lead singer
    American Horse, Coleman (Northern Cheyenne/Lakota)/singer
    Bear, Jeremy/lead singer
    Coser, Pete, Jr. (**Muscogee**/Choctaw)/b. Tahlequah/singer
    Frank, Seymour (Euchee)/singer
    Gabbard, Wayne/singer
    Larson, Ahsinees/lead singer
    Lincoln, Kyle (Shoshone/Choctaw)/singer
    Lincoln, Robert (Choctaw/Ojibwa)/b. Lawton/lead singer
    Longhorn, Wayne (Navajo/Absentee Shawnee)/singer
    McDaniel, Symphony/back-up singer
    Moyer, Dana (Ojibwa)/back-up singer
    Scott, Gregg (Choctaw)/singer
    Shipman, Paul (Delaware/**Cherokee**)/b. Pittsburgh, KS/singer
    Ware, Bambi (**Kiowa**)/back-up singer
    Washee, Timmy (Cheyenne-Arapaho)/singer
Thurman, Katrina/b. Moore/opera soprano
Thurman, Marty (Comanche/Sac & Fox)/intertribal powwow head singer
Tickle Monsters/f. Tulsa/rock group
Tiddark, Nipper/r. Oklahoma/intertribal powwow head singer
Tidwell, Natalie/b. Oklahoma City/country singer
Tiger, B.J./r. Weleetka/**Muscogee** stomp dance leader (Indian House Records)
Tiger-J/b. Tulsa/rapper
Tiger, Chebon/r. Oklahoma/**Muscogee** blues singer/guitarist
Tiger, Junior/Nuyaka Ceremonial Grounds/stomp dance leader

Tillison, Roger/b. Oklahoma/rock guitarist for **J.J. Cale**, Gary Lewis, and **Jesse Ed Davis**

Tindle, Mark/b. Ft. Monmouth, NJ, r. Tulsa/guitar, banjo, mountain dulcimer player

Tipton, Billy/b. Oklahoma City, 1914/jazz pianist

Tisha/b. Tisha Campbell in Oklahoma City, 1970/R & B, hip hop singer

Tomlin, Truman, "Pinky"/r. Oklahoma/pop composer

Tonkawa Tribe/based in Tonkawa, moved to I.T., 1855/Scalp Dance/ Native American Church songs, powwow

Tonsing, Evan/r. Glencoe/cellist, music professor at OSU, ethnomusicologist

Too Fair for Julie/f. Owasso/raw emo group

Tooisgah, Velma/r. Oklahoma/intertribal powwow singer

Toppah, Cheevers/r. Oklahoma/intertribal powwow head singer

Toppah, Ernest "Iron" (**Kiowa**)/intertribal powwow head singer, traditional Kiowa singer

Toppah, Sidney (**Kiowa**)/r. Wichita, KS/intertribal powwow head singer

Totty, Dennis/r. Tulsa/guitarist, singer, songwriter

Townsend, Glenn R./b. Sulphur, 1948/blues vocalist and guitarist

Traindodge/f. Norman/rock group

Travis, Merle/r. Tahlequah/country guitarist

Trent Malloy/f. Oklahoma City, 2002/independent rock group
  Bell, Mitch/electric guitarist
  Coe, James/bassist, vocalist
  Dani, David/guitarist, vocalist
  Ragland, Dustin/drummer

Tribe of Souls/f. Tulsa/reggae, funk, rock, and ska group
  Butler, Charles/drummer
  Rigney, Mike/bassist, keyboardist
  Simmons, Brian/vocalist, guitarist

Tricinella/f. Tulsa/rock group

Tri-Lads/f. Tulsa 1957-1960/classic rock and roll, doo-wop style group
  Fourneir, Chuck/lead singer
  Miller, Bill/bass singer, 1957-1960
  Ragan, Bill/guitarist, harmony singer
  Webb, James/bass singer, 1957, became Hollywood sound engineer

Trilogy/f. Catoosa, 2002/rock group
  Barnes, Jason/r. Catoosa/lead guitarist
  Poplin, Brandon/r. Coweta/vocalist, guitarist
  Poplin, Shawn/r. Coweta/bassist
  Wise, Josh/r. Tulsa/drummer

Trio Tulsa/r. Tulsa/chamber music

Tripplehorn, Tommy/b. Tulsa, 1944 drummer with Gary Lewis and the Playboys, Bill Davis, **Tulsa Sound**

Troutman, Tory/b. Yukon/ music reviewer

Truckenbrod, Emily/Tulsa University music faculty, 2003/voice

Trudell, John/r. Tulsa/American Indian poet who recorded with **Jesse Ed Davis**

The Truthettes/based in Oklahoma City/gospel group

2treal/f. Oklahoma/hip-hop, rap

Tucker Road/f. Stillwater/pop, rock, country group

Cook, Terry/vocals, lead guitarist, rhythm guitarist
Grauberger, Tim/drummer
Reynolds, Mike/pianist, organist
Rogers, Jason/vocals, rhythm guitarist, mandolin and harmonica player
Rother, Joe/bass guitar
Tulsa Wildcards/f. Tulsa, 1999/pop group driven to save the paddlefish
Freeland, David/saxophone
Lienhart, Edward/lead vocalist, guitarist, keyboardist
Norfleet, Lee/bassist, vocalist
Winkle, John/drummer, vocalist
Turner, Jennifer/SEOSU adjunct music faculty, 2003/flutist
Tweedie, David/b. Stillwater/fiddler with Molasses Creek
Twelve Pearls/f. Stillwater, 1997/rock group
Crabtree, Matt/drummer
Doolen, Jordan/vocalist, guitarist
Jackson, Brad/guitarist
Nowlin, Kit/bassist
20 Minutes to Vegas/f. Oklahoma City/punk rock group
20/20/f. Tulsa, 1970s/pop rock group
Allen, Steve/r. Tulsa/guitarist, vocalist
Flynt, Ron/r. Tulsa/bassist, vocalist
27 Ends/f. Stillwater/"American music" group, a.k.a. a country band
Good, Brad/r. Apache/singer, songwriter, bass guitarist
Lafave, Jesse/r. Cashion/guitarist
McGrew, Shane/r. Enid/fiddler
Woodson, Travis/r. Dewey/drummer
Yarbrough, Josh/r. Purcell, Prosper, Texas/guitarist
Twine, Linda/b. Muskogee, 1947/Broadway conductor, arranger, Tony Award winner
Twitty, Conway/r. Oklahoma City, 1960s-1975/country, rock and roll singer
Tyler, Jared/r. Tulsa/singer, songwriter, guitarist,
    recorded with Malcolm Holcombe, Nora Jones

U

Ultrafix/f. Tulsa/2002 Jim Beam/*Rolling Stone* Rock Band Search "Band of the Year"
Charron, Beau/guitar
DeVore, Angie/singer
Fawcett, Mike/bassist
Green, TJ/drummer
Ultraviolet Seraphic/f. Oklahoma City
Uncle Joey and the Mudpuppies/f. Edmond
Uncle Rumple/f. Tulsa/rock group
Underwood, Kirsten/Cameron University music faculty, 2003/cellist
Unexpected Bliss/f. Oklahoma City and Bethany/rock group
Ungerman, Rebecca/r. Tulsa/blues singer with Blue Combo, Jon Glazer, and solo
United Keetoowah Band of **Cherokees**/based in Tahlequah, in I.T. since 1828/
    Green Corn Ceremonials, powwow
The Unreliables/f. Sapulpa/pop rock group

Upside/f. Tulsa/rock group
The Uptown Horns/f. Tulsa/blues group, formerly **Flash Terry**'s horn section

V

Vagabundus/f. Tulsa/modern rock group
Valliere, George, Jr. (Quapaw/Shawnee)/r. Claremore/intertribal powwow head singer
Van Beek, Casey/b. Leiden, Holland/bassist w/ **Steve Ripley**, Tractors, Linda Ronstadt
Van Dyke, Pam/r. Tulsa/jazz vocalist
Vance, Karen/r. Tulsa/blues vocalist
Vaughn, Countess/b. Idabel, 1978/singer, actress on television program *227*
Vaughn, Danny/University of Central Oklahoma music faculty, 2003/guitarist
The Velveteen Habit/f. Tulsa/rock group
Velvet Leaf/originally from New Orleans, r. Tulsa circa 2002/modern rock group
Verde/f. Tulsa/modern rock group
Vineyard, Randy/r. Tulsa/Barbara Streisand and Cher tribute performer
Vliet, Marcia/ USAO part-time music faculty, 2003/music theatre voice
Von Dreau, Ronald/Oklahoma City University music faculty, 2003/tuba
von Thurn, Reta Ruth/b. Tulsa, 1917/classical composer

W

Wackerly, Gary/r. Oklahoma/old time fiddler
Waffle/f. Oklahoma City. 1995/rock group
  Hart, Brian/guitarist
  Ray, Curtis/guitarist, bassist
  Ray, Travis/drummer
  Wilkinson, Mark/vocalist
Wagner, Carson/r. Tulsa/pianist (classical/ragtime/standards/Christian)
Wagner, Irvin/Oklahoma University music faculty, 2003/trombonist
Wagner, Sarah & the Popadelphics/f. Tulsa/old wave pop
Wahkinney, Rusty/r. Oklahoma/intertribal powwow head singer
Wahpepah, Nick/r. Oklahoma/intertribal powwow head singer
Wakefield, William/Oklahoma University music faculty, 2003/director of bands
Wakeland/f. Stillwater, 1990/pop rock group (Giant Records)
  Heinrichs, Brad/guitarist
  Litsch, Shane/drummer
  Nunez, Andy/bassist
  Sullivan, Chris/vocalist
Walker, Aaron "T-Bone"/b. Linden, TX, 1910, r. Oklahoma City, 1930/blues vocalist,
  guitarist, resided in Oklahoma City for a short time in 1930, taking guitar lessons
Walker, Forrest "Kisko"/r. Shawnee/intertribal powwow head singer
Walker, Harvey/b. Talihina, 1937/banjo player for the Wagonmasters
Walker, Henry, Jr./r. Oklahoma/intertribal powwow head singer
Walker, Mike/University of Central Oklahoma music faculty, 2003/drummer
Walker, Steve/ECOU music faculty, 2003/university chorale director
Walker, Tom/OSUmusic faculty, 2003/trombonist, recorded for Salvationist Records
Wallace, Matt/b. Tulsa, 1960/record producer (Sheryl Crow)
Walters, JD/r. Tulsa/steel-guitarist (Brazos Valley Boys)

Wand, Hart/r. Oklahoma City/wrote first published blues in music history, "Dallas Blues," in 1912, printed three months before W.C. Handy's "St. Louis Blues"

Wanzer, Lloyd/b. Enid/national fiddle champion

Ward, Mike/b. Stillwater/jazz, Western swing guitarist

Ward, Robert/Oklahoma State University music faculty, 2003/choral studies

Ware, Bill/r. Oklahoma/intertribal powwow singer

Ware, Pearl/r. Oklahoma/intertribal powwow singer

Ware, Terry "Buffalo"/b. Shattuck, 1950/solo guitarist, songwriter & guitarist
    for **Ray Wylie Hubbard**

Ware, Tom (**Kiowa**/Comanche)/b. Lawton/intertribal powwow singer, Blues Nation, flutist, "49" singer

Ware, John/b. Tulsa, 1944/rock drummer
    with The West Coast Pop Art Experimental Band

Warford, Tony/r. Collinsville/contemporary Christian acoustic guitarist

Warren, Bobby/b. Norman/guitarist and founder of Shorebird Inpel Records

Warrenpeace/f. Oklahoma City/rock group

  Brann, Steve/guitarist

  King, J.J./vocalist

  McCord, Robbie/drummer

  Scott, Craig/bass

Washington, Wiley/Duck Creek Ceremonial Grounds/stomp dance leader

Wasowski, Andrzej/b. Poland/classical pianist, teacher at ORUfor 16 years

Watts, Valerie/Oklahoma University music faculty, 2003/flutist

Way Out West/f. Okemah/traditional country group

Wayne, Curtis/r. Oklahoma/country songwriter

Weaver, Smiley/b. Ada/vocalist with **Bob Wills**

Webb, Amy/b. Oklahoma/folk singer, songwriter

Webb, Jody/SEOSU adjunct music faculty, 2003/clarinetist

Webb, Toby Lee/r. Tulsa/country singer

Weber, Stephen/USAO music faculty, 2003/piano, dept. coordinator

Webster, Jesse/University of Central Oklahoma music faculty, 2003/voice

Webster, Joe/r. Bartlesville/singer

Weems, Ted/died in Tulsa, May 6, 1963/big band leader

Weger, Stacy/SEOSU music faculty, 2003/choral director

Welch, Herbie/b. Muskogee/R & B guitarist, singer

Weldon, Maxine/*/Oklahoma Jazz Hall of Fame inductee

Wensell, Craig/b. Stillwater/classical double bassist, has recorded for Koch Records

Wesley, George, Jr./b. Oklahoma City/gospel singer

Western Justice/f. Tulsa/country group

  Arnold, Jim/r. Tulsa/drummer

  Bennett, Bruce/r. Rogers, AR/bassist

  Duvall, Brad/r. Tulsa/acoustic guitarist

  Lane, Michael/r. Tulsa/singer, guitarist

West, Speedy/b. Springfield, MO, 1924, r. Tulsa, 1960/steel guitarist

West, Speedy, Jr./r. Tulsa/country and rock guitarist

Whang, Hyunsoon/Cameron University music faculty, 2003/pianist

Wheeler, Ron/r. Tulsa/educator, classical conductor

Wheeler, Ron/b. Alva/folk singer, songwriter

Whisperloud/f. Oklahoma, recording since 1999/contemporary Christian group
  Blumer, Keri/singer
  Carris, Alana/singer
  Gaskill, Tessa/singer
White, Bill/b. Muldrow, 1934/country singer
White, Buck/b. Oklahoma/singer and mandolinist in country group The Whites
WhiteCloud, Gary/r. Oklahoma/head gourd dance singer
White, Craig/Rose State College professor, 2003
  started a music recording option as part of liberal studies program
White, Dionne/Miss Okmulgee, 2003/pop and jazz singer
White, Don/b. Tulsa, 1940/country, rock singer/songwriter, guitarist, **Tulsa Sound**
White, Geoff/r. Tahlequah/intertribal powwow head singer, Gourd Dance singer
White, Greg/UCO music faculty, 2003/music theatre, vocal jazz productions
White, Marc/SEOSU music faculty, 2003/percussionist, asst. bands director
Whitehorse, Mac/r. Oklahoma/intertribal powwow singer
Whitekiller, Johnny/r. Hulbert, Tahlequah area/country and rock singer,
  guitarist, bandleader since early 1970s
Whitesell, Leon/University of Central Oklahoma music faculty, 2003/pianist, organist
Whittle, Elmer/b. Tahlequah, 1927/Western swing guitarist
Wichita & Affiliated Tribes/based in Anadarko, in OK region since "time immemorial"
  traditional music, Christian hymns, powwow
Wig Head/f. Owasso/trippy rock band
Wiggins, Wally/r. Tulsa/**Tulsa Sound** vocalist and bandleader from 1957 to 1960
Wilcox, Harlow/b. Norman/country guitarist known for "Groovy Grubworm"
Wilder, Christian Logan/b. Lawton/opera singer
Wiley, Floyd/Oklahoma Jazz Hall of Fame inductee/gospel category
Wiley-Smith, Grace/University of Central Oklahoma music faculty, 2003/flutist
Wilkerson, Steve/b. Iola, KS, reared in Bartlesville/jazz saxophonist
Wilkerson, Zac/b. Buffalo/pop singer and songwriter
Wilkinson, Jay/Oklahoma University music faculty, 2003/jazz ensembles
Williams, Dennis/r. Oklahoma City/gospel singer w/ The Mighty Wonders
Williams, Gary/b. Pryor, 1971/blues guitarist
Williams, John/b. Tulsa, OK, 1940/50s rock and contemporary jazz saxophonist,
  played with **Leon Russell**
Williams, Mason/b. Abilene, TX, r. Oklahoma City/classical guitarist,
  known for "Classical Gas"
Williamson, Gayle/b. Tulsa/jazz pianist with Sounds Good
Williamson, Josh (Sac & Fox/Choctaw)/intertribal powwow head singer
Williamson, Lulu/Tallahassee Wvkokye Ceremonial Grounds/stomp dance leader
Willis, Aunt Minerva and Uncle Wallace/r. Choctaw Nation/
  first documented singing of "Swing Low, Sweet Chariot"
Willis, Bill/r. Tulsa/jazz and blues organist
Wills, Roger/b. Kiowa/bassist, Alan Jackson's bandleader
Wilson, J. Paul/enrolled Sac & Fox/intertribal powwow head singer
Wilson, Jim/b. Oklahoma City/Choctaw world music producer and musician
Wilson, Jimmie/r. Oklahoma/bandleader, Catfish String Band
Wilson, Mark/r. Oklahoma/opera baritone
Wilson, Reuben/b. Mounds, 1935/soul and jazz organist

Windsor 351/f. Tulsa/modern rock group
Wingers, Warren/r. Owasso/singer, songwriter
Wintle, Betty/SEOSU music faculty, 2003/voice and vocal performance
Wintle, James/SEOSU music faculty, 2003/theory, composition
Wiseman, Craig/b. Lexington/songwriter (Tim McGraw's "Cowboy and Me")
Wolfe, Katherine/Oklahoma State University music faculty, 2003/violinist
Wooden, Lori/University of Central Oklahoma music faculty, 2003/symphonic band
Woods, Betty/ECOU adjunct music faculty, 2003/applied voice, music theory
Wooley, John/b. MN, r. Chelsea/music journalist, Western swing radio host,
    co-wrote "Gone Away" with Steve Ripley, Oklahoma Music Hall of Fame inductee
Wooten, Ruby (Rowan)/b. Fort Gibson/pop, country guitarist, vocalist
    performed with Porter Wagoner
Wooten, Steve/b. Tulsa, 1957/independent country vocalist, guitarist
Word of Mouth/f. Oklahoma/rock group
Wright, Claude, H./b. 1893, Lebanon, KS, moved to Collinsville, I.T. in 1899
    music educator, bandleader
Wright, Dempsey/b. Calumet, 1929/jazz guitarist
Wrightsman, Stan/b. Gotebo or Oklahoma City, 1910/Dixieland pianist
Wyandotte Nation/based in Wyandotte since 1893/powwow

Y

Yancey-Ryan, Lula Maye/b. Red Oak, 1910, r. Owasso, 2002/pianist,
    career music educator at Red Oak public schools
Yarbrough, Tom/r. Oklahoma/country songwriter
Yard, Jocelyn/b. Oklahoma City, 1984/finger style guitarist
Yeagley, David, A./b. Oklahoma City/classical pianist
Yellow Hammer/f. Ponca City and Red Rock, 1995/southern style powwow group
    Botone, Perry Lee, Jr./singer
    Gawhega, Michael, N./singer
    Grant, James, Sr./singer
    Hudson, Wesley/singer
    Kemble, James, Jr./singer, also intertribal powwow head singer
    Kemble, James, Sr./b. Wichita, KS, r. Ponca City/singer
    Kent, Garland, Jr./singer
    Lieb, Kinsel, V./singer
    Little Cook, Oliver, Jr./singer
    Little Cook, Stephen T./singer
    McIntosh, John, Sr./singer
    Moore, Patrick, L./singer
    Morning Star Kemble, Andrea/back-up singer
    Roubedoux, Jade/back-up singer
    Roubedoux, Tesa Dee/back-up singer
Yellow Spotted Horse/f. 1992/southern style powwow group
    Bighorse, Kenny Bob/lead singer
    Bills, K.C./singer
    Blackstar, Linda/singer
    Goodeagle, Guideon/singer

Goodeagle, Laura/singer
Goodeagle, Tesa/singer
Hutchins, Roman/singer
Kimble, Andrea/singer
Kimble, James, Jr./singer
Lazelle, Linda/singer
Littlecook, Littlebear/singer
Littlecook, O.J./singer
Littlecook, Oliver (Ponca)/b. Ponca City/lead singer
Mashunkashey, Russell/singer
Yohe, Tony/r. Tulsa/jazz, blues drummer
York, Paris/b. Indianola/jazz educator
York, Walter Wynn/b. Claremore, 1914/classical composer
Youngbear, J.R./r. Oklahoma/intertribal powwow head singer
Young Hustlas Coalition/f. Tulsa/rap group
  A-Game/rapper
  Anjorin, Femi/rapper
  Brown, Reginald (Dibiasi)/rapper
  CO2/rapper
  Droop Locc/rapper
  Profit/rapper
Young, Ruth Alexander/b. Ardmore/opera singer

Z

Zaremba, Kathryn/b. Broken Arrow/Broadway musical performer, (played Annie on Broadway),
Zeabra/f. Shawnee, 1967 as Sage, renamed Zeabra in Stillwater, 1970s/pop rock group
  Baird, Rusty/r. Shawnee/2nd bassist
  Brown, Donald/r. Shawnee/2nd drummer
  Fuller, Mick/r. Shawnee/original drummer
  Hawkins, Jeff/r. Shawnee/guitarist, vocalist
  Hembree, Mark/r. Shawnee/guitarist, vocalist
  Kelly, Chris/r. Shawnee/keyboards
  McGehee, Tommy/r. Shawnee/original bassist
Zen Hipster/f. Tulsa/alternative rock group
Zero for Conduct/f. Tulsa/space rock group
Zhu, Hong/University of Central Oklahoma music faculty, 2003/violinist
Ziff/f. Tulsa/rock group
Zion Rex/f. Norman/rock group
Zotigh, Dennis (**Kiowa**)/r. Norman/intertribal powwow head singer
Zoux/f. Tulsa/rock group
Zuback, Amy/University of Central Oklahoma music faculty, 2003/flutist, music theory

Please send any new information, suggestions, corrections, additions, biographical material, or music to the *Oklahoma Music Guide* 1018 S. Lewis St., Stillwater, Oklahoma, 74074, or write <u>authors@oklahomamusicguide.com</u>

Photo and Image Credits

The authors of the *Oklahoma Music Guide* wish to thank all of the people, companies, media outlets, and private archivists who have contributed historic images to help illustrate this book. If any information included in these credits is incorrect, or if an image's copyright has been improperly transferred to its current ownership, please contact the authors for a timely resolution and/or correction for the centennial edition of the *Oklahoma Music Guide*. Send comments, concerns, or additional images to authors@oklahomamusicguide.com or New Forums Press, 1018 South Lewis Street, Stillwater, Oklahoma, 74074, U.S.A.

Foreword image of George Carney with Terry "Buffalo" Ware image by Hugh Foley; **Introduction** images by Hugh Foley; **Admiral Twin** photo by C Taylor Crothers courtesy Admiral Twin; **All American Rejects** album cover courtesy Dog House Records; **Tuck Andress** image courtesy www.tuckandpatti.com; **Larry Austin** image courtesy Larry Austin; **Gene Autry** photos from Foley collection; **Hoyt Axton** photo from Foley collection; **Chet Baker** album cover images courtesy of Universal Music and Video Distribution for *Verve Jazz Masters 32* (1994), Entertainers Records (CD 284), and Enja Records with cover photo from *My Favourite Songs: The Last Great Concert* (R179600) by Calle Hesslefors; **Louis Ballard** photo by Abe Eilot courtesy of Louis Ballard; **Carl Belew** photo from Foley collection; **Byron Berline** photo courtesy of Byron Berline; **Elvin Bishop** album covers courtesy of Alligator Records; **Bob Bogle** images courtesy of Bob Bogle; **Jason Boland and the Stragglers** photos courtesy Brandy Reed of RPR Marketing and Public Relations, Nashville; **Johnny Bond** album cover courtesy of Bloodshot Revival and Soundies www.bloodshotrecords.com , design by M Greiner; **Mike Brewer** photo by Jeff Nicholson/courtesy Brewer and Shipley; **Garth Brooks** studio publicity photo by Beverly Parker courtesy Capitol Records, action shot from Foley collection; **Albert Brumley, Sr.** photo courtesy Hartford Music Company and Albert E. Brumley and Sons; **Anita Bryant** album cover photo for *Abide With Me* (WST-8532) by Russ Busby courtesy of WORD Records; **Don Byas** cassette cover of *All the Things You Are* (2673734) courtesy Jazz Life Records, Holland; **Caddo Nation** image courtesy of Thurman Parton; **J.J. Cale album** cover of *Millennium Collection – 20ᵗʰ Century Masters* (2002) courtesy Universal Press and Music Distribution, photo of J.J. Cale with Hugh Foley by Christine Lakeland with Hugh's camera; **Caroline's Spine** photo by Martyn Adkins from *Attention Please* (HR-62133-2) courtesy Hollywood Records; **Kristin Chenoweth** photo courtesy PMK HBH Management; **Cherokee** images of stomp dance, flute workshop, and Mary Kay Henderson by Hugh Foley, image of fiddler Sam O'Field courtesy Cara Cowan, J.B. Dreadfulwater image courtesy of J.B. Dreadfulwater from the album *Guide Me Jehovah* (JB 447), cover image of *Cherokee National Children's Youth Choir* (CNCRC003) by David G. Fitzgerald courtesy Cherokee Nation communications office, Ace Moreland album cover *Give It to Get It* (IHR 9438) photo by Peter J. Everett courtesy ice-house and King Snake Records; **Charlie Christian** images courtesy Columbia Legacy Jazz promotional poster, and Universal Music and Video Distribution for album cover of *Radio Land 1939-1941* (2001); **Roy Clark** publicity photo courtesy William Morris Agency, Inc., Nashville via Michael Varnum of the Poncan Theatre; **Kellie Coffey** photo courtesy of Roseann and Robert Coffey; **Color Me Badd** album cover photos for *Now and Forever* (Giant, 1996) by Jon Ragel, courtesy of Giant and Warner Brothers Records; **Spade Cooley** album cover courtesy of Bloodshot Revival and Soundies www.bloodshotrecords.com , design by M Greiner; **Cross Canadian Ragweed** 1999 publicity photo by Matthew Gambrell courtesy Cross Canadian Ragweed, 2003 image courtesy Brandy Reed of RPR Marketing and Public Relations, Nashville; **Gail Davies** courtesy of Gail Davies; **Jesse Ed Davis** image courtesy Epic records from a limited 7" bonus record that featured a 1973 interview with Jesse Ed Davis; **Yvonne DeVaney** image courtesy of Yvonne DeVaney; **Joe Diffie** photos cour-tesy of Joe Diffie Fan Club; **Big Al Downing** publicity photo courtesy Martha Moore, So Much Moore Media and Marketing; **Jack Dunham** photo courtesy of Jack Dunham; **Ronnie Dunn** photos from Foley collection; **Nokie Edwards** photo courtesy Judy and Nokie Edwards; **Tyler England** album cover for *Two Ways to Fall* (RCA 66930-2) courtesy of RCA Records; **Toni Estes** photo by Anthony Cutajar courtesy of Priority Records and Billy Estes; **Flaming Lips** group photo by J. Michele Martin courtesy Warner Brothers Records, live shot courtesy Hellfire Management, Oklahoma City; **Flash Terry** photo by Mac; **Lowell Fulson** publicity photo by E.K. Waller courtesy of Bullseye and Rounder Records; **Steve and Cassie Gaines** images from Foley collection; **GAP Band** album cover of *Millennium Collection – 20th Century Masters* (2000) courtesy Universal Press and Music Distribution; **Benny Garcia, Sr.** photo courtesy Friends of Oklahoma Music, Inc.; **David Gates** courtesy of Selwyn Miller Management; **Vince Gill** photos courtesy Friends of Oklahoma Music, Inc.; **Otto Gray** and Billy McGinty photos courtesy of Carla and Dale Chlouber at the Washington Irving Trail Museum; **Great Divide** group photo by Jim Herrington courtesy of The Great Divide; **Jack Guthrie** photo from Foley collection; **Woody Guthrie** images courtesy Woody Guthrie Archives; **Merle Haggard** photo from Foley collection; **Hanson** publicity photo courtesy Universal Music and Video Distribution; **Gus Hardin** album cover photo from *Gus Hardin* (RCA, 1983) courtesy RCA Records; **Sam Harris** image courtesy Sam Harris at www.samharris.com; **Wade Hayes** and Mark McClurg photos courtesy of Universal South Records; **Michael Hedges** publicity photo by Ebet Roberts courtesy Windham Hill Records; **Becky Hobbs** photo by Dean Dixon courtesy Beckaroo Productions; **Doyle Holly** album cover photo by Ken Kim from *Just Another Cowboy Song* (BR-15011) courtesy Barnaby Records; **Ray Wylie Hubbard** photo by Maria Camillo courtesy of Ray Wylie Hubbard; **Jacob Fred Jazz Odyssey** images by Hugh Foley; **Wanda Jackson** vintage and modern photos courtesy Wendell Goodman and Wanda Jackson, album cover photo featuring Wanda with guitar from *Rock 'n' Roll Away Your Blues* (VR-025) courtesy Varrick and Rounder Records; **Toby Keith** publicity photo by Richard McLaren courtesy Universal Music and Video Distribution and Dreamworks-Nashville Records; **Barney Kessel** photo by William Gullette courtesy Barney and Phyllis Kessel; **Merle Kilgore** photo by Gordy Collins courtesy Merle Kilgore; **Kiowa** images by Hugh Foley courtesy Kiowa Gourd Clan and the Cozad Family; **Jimmy LaFave** publicity photo by Jim Herrington courtesy Bohemia Beat and Rounder Records; **Don Lamond** image from Slingerland Drums ad from Foley collection; **Susie Luchsinger** image courtesy www.susieluchsinger.com ; **Moon Martin** album cover photo from *Escape from Domination* (Capitol ST-11933) courtesy Moon Martin and Capitol Records; **Tony Matthews** by Hugh Foley; **Mel McDaniel** image from Foley collection; **Reba McEntire** profile publicity photo by McGuire courtesy MCA-Nashville, contemporary image from Foley collection; **Jay McShann** photo courtesy Jay McShann; **Roger Miller** album cover of *All Time Greatest Hits* (Mercury Nashville, 2003) courtesy Universal Music and Video Distribution, photo by Pikow from album cover of *The Return of Roger Miller* (Smash, MGS 27061) courtesy Smash Records; **DC Minner** profile photo from Oklahoma Jazz Hall of Fame Induction by Hugh Foley, publicity photo with Selby courtesy of DC and Selby Minner; **Leona Mitchell** courtesy of Leona Mitchell; **Muscogee (Creek)** images by Hugh Foley courtesy of Tallahassee (Wvkokye) Ceremonial Grounds and Hvtce Cvpv Baptist Church, Joy Harjo photo by Hulleah Tsinhnahjinnie courtesy Joy Harjo, photo of Julian B! courtesy Julian B!; **"Doc" Tate Nevaquaya** publicity photo courtesy Greg Ford of Riversong Soundworks, Ashville, North Carolina; **Norma Jean** album cover image from *Norma Jean Sings a Tribute to Kitty Wells* (LSP-3664) courtesy RCA Records; **Gary P. Nunn** photo by Rick Henson courtesy Ruth Nunn; **Tommy Overstreet** publicity photo from Foley collection; **Bonnie Owens** album cover image from Merle Haggard and Bonnie Owens, *That Makes Two of Us* (JS-6106), courtesy Pickwick and Capitol Records; **Patti Page** photos courtesy of Hot Schatz Public Relations, second photo by Jeff Sedlik; **Billy Parker** photo courtesy of Friends of Oklahoma Music, Inc.; **Sandi Patti** publicity photo from Foley collection; **Tom Paxton** album cover photo by Irene Young from *And Loving You* (FF414) courtesy Flying Fish and Rounder Records; **Oscar Pettiford** album cover image from *The New Oscar Pettiford Sextet* (OJC-112) courtesy Fantasy Records; **Cornel Pewewardy** publicity photo courtesy Cornel Pewewardy; **Ponca** sign by Mac, photo of elder singers by Tony Isaacs courtesy of Tony Isaacs and Indian House Records, images of Tony Arkeketa, Eddie Arkeketa leading the Redland Singers, and Yellowhammer by Hugh Foley; **Red Dirt Music** photo of Garth

Brooks and Santa Fe courtesy *Stillwater News Press*, image of Bob Childers courtesy www.bobchilders.com , Greg Jacobs image by Hugh Foley, Mike McClure image by Hugh Foley, Stoney Larue photo by Todd V. Wolfson courtesy Brandy Reed of RPR Marketing and Public Relations, Nashville; **Red Dirt Rangers** photo courtesy John Cooper; **Jimmie Revard** cover photo from Jimmie Revard and his Oklahoma Playboys, *Oh! Swing It* (Rambler 108) courtesy Mutual Music Corporation, San Francisco; **Ricochet** sign coming in to Vian, Oklahoma by Hugh Foley; **Steve Ripley** photo by Walt Richmond courtesy Charlene and Steve Ripley; **Tony Romanello** publicity photo courtesy of Tony Romanello; **Joe Don Rooney** with guitar from Foley collection, Rascal Flatts from album cover of *Live* (Hollywood, 2003) courtesy Universal Music and Press Distribution; **Mark Rubin** with Danny Barnes in the Bad Livers publicity photo courtesy Sugar Hill Records; **Rushlow** image courtesy www.rushlow.com; **Jimmy Rushing** album cover of *Everyday I Have the Blues/Livin' the Blues* (Verve, 1999) courtesy Universal Music and Press Distribution; **Leon Russell** courtesy Ark 21 Records; **Tom Russell** photo by David Burckhalter courtesy of Hightone Records; **Mike Settle** photo courtesy Mike Settle; **Blake Shelton** photo by Kristin G. Barlowe courtesy Warner Brothers Records; **Cal Smith** album cover photo from *I Just Came Home to Count the Memories* (MCA-2266) courtesy MCA Records; **Kay Starr** photo from sheet music for "Half a Photograph" courtesy Vesta Music Corporation; **James Talley** photo courtesy James Talley; **B.J. Thomas** photo courtesy B.J. Thomas; **Hank Thompson** photo by Lori Eanes courtesy of Hank Thompson Enterprises; **Wayman Tisdale** publicity photo courtesy Warner Brothers Records; **Tulsa Sound** 1959 group photo by Mike Hart courtesy of **Jack Dunham** who also assembled the photos for this entry with the assistance of Janine Stovall, Clyde Stacy photo courtesy of Clyde Stacy, Bobby Taylor photo courtesy of Bobby Taylor, Gene Crose photo courtesy of Gene Crose, Rocky Frisco photo courtesy of Rocky Frisco, Tommy Rush photo courtesy of Tommy Rush, Junior Markham photo courtesy of Junior Markham, Tommy Crook photo courtesy of Tommy Crook, photo of Rockin' Jimmy and the Brothers of the Night from the album cover of 1980's *By the Light of the Moon* (0060-326) courtesy of Pilgrim and Metronome GMBH Records, 2003 photo of Cale, Frisco, and Crose courtesy Jack Dunham; **Dwight Twilley** 7" cover of "Girls" single courtesy EMI-Capitol Records; **Andrew Vasquez** publicity photo copyright 1996 and courtesy Makoché Recording Company; **Billy Wallace** performance still from Foley collection, possibly taken by Jerome Robinson from Bronx, New York in 1939; **Lily Fern Weatherford** photo with the Weatherfords courtesy Bob Duke Talent; **Jimmy Webb** courtesy Jimmy Webb Music; **Bryan White** publicity photo by Pamela Springsteen courtesy Warner Brothers Records Publicity; **Claude "Fiddler" Williams** publicity photo by Russ Dantzler courtesy of Hot Jazz Management and Production; **Wiley and Gene** publicity photo courtesy of Jack Dunham; **Lee Wiley** photo from *Lee*

Wiley: a Bio-Discography courtesy Gus Kuhlman, North Brunswick, New Jersey; **Willis Brothers** publicity photo from Foley Collection; **Kelly Willis** album cover of *One More Time: The MCA Records* (MCA Nashville, 2000) courtesy Universal Music and Video Distribution; **Wills Brothers** group photo courtesy Friends of Oklahoma Music, Inc., Bob Wills headshot from Foley collection, Bob Wills group photo at the Ranch House in Dallas courtesy Jack Dunham, Johnnie Lee Wills *Reunion* album photo courtesy of Berniece Cook and Don Tolle, Don Tolle photo by Berniece Cook, Tommy Perkins photo by Hugh Foley, Pine Valley Cosmonauts cover art by Jon Langford courtesy of Bloodshot Records, www.bloodshotrecords.com; **Sheb Wooley** album cover photo from *The Very Best of Sheb Wooley* (E-4275) courtesy Metro-Goldwyn-Mayer, Inc.; **Young Bird** photo of Curtis Hamilton-Youngbird by Hugh Foley, group photo courtesy Canyon Records. Photo of George Carney and Hugh Foley on **Author Biographies** page by Geri Foley.

Author Biographies

Dr. George O. Carney, Regents Professor of Geography at Oklahoma State University in Stillwater, has authored three books on American music, including *Fast Food, Stock Cars, and Rock 'n' Roll* (1995), *Baseball, Barns, and Bluegrass* (1998), and *The Sounds of People and Places*

Dr. George O. Carney (left) and Dr. Hugh W. Foley, Jr.

(2003), now in its fourth edition. In addition, he has contributed more than 50 scholarly articles and book chapters on American music to such publications as *Popular Music and Society*, *Country Music Annual*, *Journal of Geography*, *Journal of Cultural Geography*, *The Canadian Geographer*, and *GeoJournal*. He has published two major monographs chronicling Oklahoma music—*A Biographical Dictionary of Oklahoma Jazz Artists* (1992) and *Oklahoma Women in American Music* (1999). Carney is also a member of the Friends of Oklahoma Music Board of Directors and the Governor's Oklahoma Music Hall of Fame Board. Dr. Carney resides in Stillwater with his wife, Janie.

An assistant professor of communications and fine arts at Rogers State University in Claremore, Dr. Hugh W. Foley, Jr. has contributed scholarly articles, book chapters, and encyclopedia entries on American Indian music, rock, jazz, blues, and country music to *The Oklahoma Encyclopedia of the Humanities* (2007), *The Sound of People and Places* (2003), *The New York Encyclopedia of the Humanities* (2002), *The Guide to United States Popular Culture* (2001), and *Living Blues* (1998). He is a charter member of the Friends of Oklahoma Music (FOM) Board of Directors, having served as vice-president as well as chair of the Oklahoma Music Hall of Fame induction selection committee. Foley has also been actively involved in radio since 1977 when he started in Muskogee while still in high school. He has worked as a disc-jockey, program director, and announcer at stations in Tulsa, Atlanta, GA, New York City, Berkeley, CA, Frankfurt, Germany, and Osaka, Japan. He currently hosts *Native Air*, an American Indian public affairs and music program on KUSH-AM, Cushing, where he is also the music director and an Americana music format reporter for *Radio and Records*, an industry trade magazine. *Native Air* is also heard on KRSC-FM, the college radio station at Rogers State University where he is a student mentor and the faculty music consultant. Dr. Foley lives in Stillwater with his wife, Geri, and son, Nokose.